Collier Bankruptcy Practice Guide

Local Rules of the Bankruptcy Courts Ninth Circuit (California)

Central District of California

Eastern District of California

Northern District of California

Southern District of California

Bankruptcy Appellate Panel of the Ninth Circuit

The Interim Bankruptcy Rules previously published in this pamphlet have been superseded by the 2008 Amendments to the Federal Rules of Bankruptcy Procedure, effective December 1, 2008. As bankruptcy courts have been advised to repeal or sunset their local rules or orders adopting the Interim Rules, the Interim Rules will no longer be reprinted in this pamphlet. Only the district's new or amended local rules are printed in this Supplement. Rules which were vacated are indicated as such within the Supplement text. Subscribers should disregard the Local Rules Pamphlet version of the amended or vacated rules.

April 2011

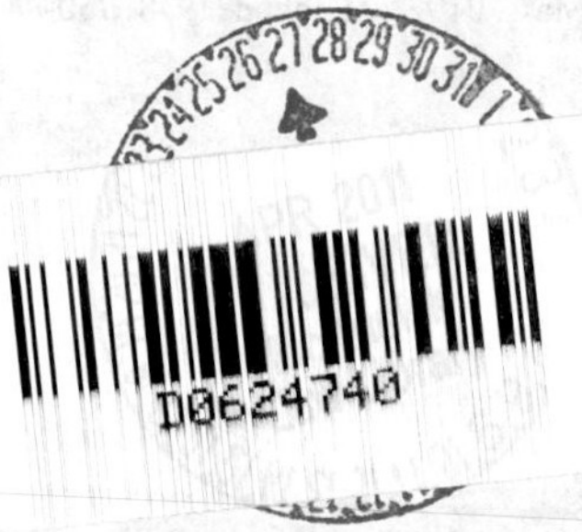

QUESTIONS ABOUT THIS PUBLICATION?

For questions about the **Editorial Content** appearing in these volumes or reprint permission, please call:

James Muh at .... 1-800-306-5230 (ext. 673-3378)
Email: .... james.f.muh@lexisnexis.com
Edward Leung, J.D. at .... 1-800-306-5230 (ext. 673-3369)
Email: .... edward.leung@lexisnexis.com
Outside the United States and Canada please call .... (973) 820-2000

For assistance with replacement pages, shipments, billing or other customer service matters, please call:

Customer Services Department at .... (800) 833-9844
Outside the United States and Canada, please call .... (518) 487-3000
Fax number .... (518) 487-3584
Customer Service Website .... http://www.lexisnexis.com/custserv/

For information on other Matthew Bender Publications, please call
Your account manager or .... (800) 223-1940
Outside the United States and Canada, please call .... (518) 487-3000

Library of Congress Card Number: 81-67269

ISBN 978-0-8205-1200-6

This publication is designed to provide accurate and authoritative information in regard to the subject matter covered. It is sold with the understanding that the publisher is not engaged in rendering legal, accounting, or other professional services. If legal advice or other expert assistance is required, the services of a competent professional should be sought.

Editorial Offices
121 Chanlon Rd., New Providence, NJ 07974 (908) 464-6800
201 Mission St., San Francisco, CA 94105-1831 (415) 908-3200
www.lexisnexis.com

MATTHEW BENDER

(Pub.200)

CENTRAL DISTRICT OF CALIFORNIA

The Central District of California has adopted the following local rules relevant to cases under Title 11, effective January 4, 2010:

GLOSSARY DEFINITIONS

In the Central District Local Bankruptcy Rules (LBR), the terms below are defined as follows:

(a) Appellate Court: The bankruptcy appellate panel or the district court exercising its appellate jurisdiction pursuant to 28 U.S.C. § 158.

(b) Application: Papers should be captioned applications only where the F.R.B.P. rules expressly provide that a request for judicial action shall be made by application. (See *Motion.*)

(c) Attorney or Counsel: Includes attorney, proctor, advocate, solicitor, counsel, or counselor.

(d) Bankruptcy Code: Title 11 of the United States Code.

(e) Brief: Includes briefs, memoranda, points and authorities, and other written argument or compilations of authorities.

(f) Case: A bankruptcy case commenced by the filing of a petition pursuant to 11 U.S.C. §§ 301, 302, 303, or 304.

(g) Clerk: The clerk of the bankruptcy court for the Central District of California and deputy clerks. Different clerks will be specified in the text.

(h) Court: The bankruptcy court of the Central District of California or the district court when exercising its original bankruptcy jurisdiction pursuant to 11 U.S.C. § 1334 including the judge to whom the case or proceeding is assigned.

(i) Court Days: Any day, excluding Saturdays, Sundays, and federal legal holidays.

(j) Courtroom Deputy: A deputy clerk assigned to the courtroom of a judge of the court.

(k) Declaration: Any declaration under penalty of perjury executed in conformance with 28 U.S.C. § 1746 and any properly executed affidavit.

(l) Defendant: Any party against whom a claim for relief is made by complaint, counterclaim, or cross-claim.

(m) District Court: The United States District Court for the Central District of California.

(n) F.R.App.P.: The Federal Rules of Appellate Procedure.

(o) F.R.B.P.: The Federal Rules of Bankruptcy Procedure as adopted by the Supreme Court of the United States.

(p) F.R.Civ.P.: The Federal Rules of Civil Procedure.

(q) F.R.Evid.: The Federal Rules of Evidence.

(r) File: The delivery to and acceptance by the clerk, courtroom deputy, the court, or other person authorized by the court of a document which will be noted in the docket.

(s) Judge: Bankruptcy judge, district court judge, or other judicial officer in a case or proceeding assigned to the court.

(t) Lodge: To deliver to the clerk, courtroom deputy, the court, or other person authorized by the court a document which is tendered to the court but is not approved for filing, such as a proposed form of order.

(u) Motion: All motions, applications, or other requests made for judicial action except by complaint, counterclaim, or cross-claim.

(v) Movant: Any entity requesting an order other than by way of complaint, counterclaim or cross-claim.

(w) Papers: All pleadings, motions, affidavits, declarations, briefs, points and authorities, and all other papers and documents presented for filing or lodging excluding exhibits submitted during a hearing or trial.

(x) Plaintiff: Any party claiming affirmative relief by complaint, counter-claim, or cross-claim.

(y) Proceeding: Motions, adversary proceedings, contested matters and other matters presented to the court. It does not include the case as defined above.

(z) Respondent: Any entity responding to a request for an order other than by way of complaint, counterclaim, or cross-complaint.

(aa) United States Trustee Notices and Guides: The United States Trustee Chapter 11 Notices and Guides and the Notice of Requirements for Debtors In Possession in Chapter 11 Cases.

LBR 1001-1. TITLE, APPLICATION, AND SCOPE OF RULES

(a) TITLE AND CITATION. These are the Local Bankruptcy Rules of the United States Bankruptcy Court for the Central District of California (hereinafter, "Local Bankruptcy Rules" or "rules"). They may be cited as "LBR ____________."

(b) APPLICATION AND CONSTRUCTION.

(1) The Local Bankruptcy Rules are adopted pursuant to 28 U.S.C. § 2075, F.R.Civ.P. 83, and FRBP 9029. They are intended to supplement the FRBP and those portions of the F.R.Civ.P. that are incorporated by the FRBP. The Local Bankruptcy Rules are to be construed consistent with, and subordinate to, the FRBP and F.R.Civ.P. and to promote the just, speedy, and economic determination of every case and proceeding.

(2) The Local Bankruptcy Rules apply to all bankruptcy cases and proceedings (including all cases removed pursuant to 28 U.S.C. § 1452 or 15 U.S.C. § 78eee) pending in the United States Bankruptcy Court for the Central District of California.

(3) The Local Bankruptcy Rules apply in the United States District Court for the Central District of California in lieu of the District Court Rules when the district court is exercising its original bankruptcy jurisdiction pursuant to 28 U.S.C. § 1334.

(c) APPLICATION TO PERSONS APPEARING WITHOUT COUNSEL. A person who appears and is not represented by counsel must comply with the Local Bankruptcy Rules. Each reference in the Local Bankruptcy Rules to "attorney" or "counsel" applies equally to a party who is not represented by counsel, unless the context otherwise requires.

(d) MODIFICATION. The Local Bankruptcy Rules apply uniformly throughout the district, but are not intended to limit the discretion of the court. The court may waive the application of any Local Bankruptcy Rule in any case or proceeding, or make additional orders as it deems appropriate, in the interest of justice.

(e) PROCEDURE IN ABSENCE OF RULE.

(1) A matter not specifically covered by these Local Bankruptcy Rules may be determined, if possible, by parallel or analogy to the F.R.Civ.P., the FRBP, or the District Court Rules.

(2) If no parallel or analogy exists, then the court may proceed in any lawful manner not inconsistent with these Local Bankruptcy Rules and the FRBP.

(f) SANCTIONS FOR NONCOMPLIANCE WITH RULES. The failure of counsel or of a party to comply with these Local Bankruptcy Rules, with the F.R.Civ.P. or the FRBP, or with any order of the court may be grounds for the imposition of sanctions.

(g) EFFECTIVE DATE. These LBRs are effective on January 4, 2010, and will govern all cases and proceedings pending or commenced thereafter. The court in its discretion may order that a case or proceeding pending prior to the effective date be governed by the practice of the court prior to the adoption of these LBRs.

LBR 1001-2. RULES OF CONSTRUCTION

(a) CONSTRUCTION OF TERMS. As used in these rules—

(1) "must" is mandatory.

(2) "must not" is prohibitive, not permissive.

(3) "may" is discretionary.

(4) "or" is not exclusive.

(5) "includes" and "including" are not limiting.

(b) GENDER; PLURALS. Wherever applicable, each gender includes the other gender and the singular includes the plural.

LBR 1002-1. PETITION—GENERAL

(a) DEBTOR'S ADDRESS. In a petition filed under 11 U.S.C. §§ 301, 302, 303, or 1504, the debtor's actual street address must be disclosed in addition to any post office box address.

(b) ATTORNEY INFORMATION.

(1) General. A voluntary petition filed pursuant to 11 U.S.C. §§ 301 and 302 by an attorney on behalf of any party must contain the attorney's state bar identification number, telephone number, fax number, and e-mail address in the attorney name block.

(2) Signature of Counsel. The name of the attorney signing a petition must be printed clearly below the signature line.

(c) NUMBER OF COPIES. For documents that are not electronically filed under the provisions of LBR 5005-4, a list of requirements that specify the minimum number of copies that must be submitted is contained in the Court Manual available from the clerk and on the court's website.

(d) INCOMPLETE PETITIONS.

(1) General. A voluntary petition filed without the complete schedules, statements and other documents required by the FRBP and these rules must include at least the following:

(A) Petition (Official Form 1);

(B) List of Creditors Holding 20 Largest Unsecured Claims (Official Form 4) (chapter 11 cases only);

(C) Master Mailing List (List of Creditors) in format required by LBR 1007-1(a); and

(D) Statement of Social Security Number(s) (Official Form 21) (Required if the debtor is an individual).

A complete list of the papers required to complete the filing is contained in the Court Manual available from the clerk and on the court's website.

(2) Deadline to File Required Documents. Except as provided by FRBP 1019(1)(A), and unless extended by court order, the balance of the papers required by the FRBP and these rules must be filed within 14 days of the petition date, except the Statement of Intention which must be filed not later than 30 days after the filing of the petition.

(3) Motion for Extension of Time to File Documents. A motion for extension of time to file the lists, schedules and other papers required by this rule must comply with LBR 1007-1(e).

(4) Failure to File Required Documents. The case may be dismissed pursuant to LBR 1017-2.

(e) REDACTION OF PERSONAL IDENTIFIERS.

(1) Unless otherwise ordered by the court, a debtor must refrain from including, or must redact where inclusion is necessary, the following personal identifiers from all lists, schedules, statements, payment advices, or other documents filed or required to be filed with the court in accordance with FRBP 9037(a):

(A) SOCIAL SECURITY NUMBERS. If disclosure of a social security number is required, only the last four digits of that number should be used. [This does not apply to Official Form 21, Statement of Social Security Number(s)].

(B) NAMES OF MINOR CHILDREN. If disclosure of the identity of any minor child is required, only the initials of that child should be used.

(C) DATE OF BIRTH. If disclosure of an individual's date of birth is required, only the year should be used.

(D) FINANCIAL ACCOUNT NUMBERS. If disclosure of any financial account number is required, only the last four digits of that number should be used.

(2) The responsibility for redacting these personal identifiers rests solely with the debtor and debtor's counsel. The court will not review documents for compliance with this rule.

(f) EFFECT OF FAILURE TO SPECIFY NECESSARY INFORMATION.

(1) If the petition fails to specify the chapter under which relief is sought, the case will be deemed to have been filed under chapter 7.

(2) If the petition fails to specify whether it is a consumer or business case, it will be presumed to be a consumer case.

(3) If the petition fails to indicate the number of creditors or equity holders, or the amount of assets or debts, it will be presumed that the case falls in the smallest category of each.

(g) JOINT PETITIONS. Individuals filing jointly must present upon request appropriate evidence to support their joint filing status at the 11 U.S.C. § 341(a) meeting, such as a copy of the marriage license.

LBR 1006-1. FILING FEES

(a) PAYMENT OF THE FILING FEE IN INSTALLMENTS.

(1) Eligibility. Only an individual debtor who is unable to pay the full filing fee for a voluntary petition under chapter 7, 11, or 13, may apply for permission to pay the filing fee in installments. A corporation, partnership, limited liability company, unincorporated association, trust, or other artificial entity must pay the filing fee in full at the time the petition is filed.

(2) Application. The debtor must submit a written application for an order permitting payment of the filing fee in installments. The application must be accompanied by a declaration under penalty of perjury establishing that the debtor is unable to pay the filing fee except in installments. The application and declaration must be completed on forms prescribed by the court and presented for filing with the petition. If unrepresented by an attorney, or if required by the court, the debtor must also present evidence of personal identification in the form of a valid government-issued driver's license or identification card, or other similar form of identification satisfactory to the clerk.

(3) Hearing. On the petition date or at a later date and time the designated judge may select for a hearing, the debtor must appear personally before a designated judge to present the application, supporting declaration, and proposed order. The debtor must provide sworn testimony regarding the basis for the application and circumstances of the bankruptcy filing. Unless the court specifically waives the requirement of personal appearance, the debtor's failure to appear and testify at the prescribed time and place will result in denial of the application and dismissal of the bankruptcy case.

(4) Notice. Compliance with the notice and service requirements of LBR 9013-1 is not required, unless otherwise ordered by the designated judge.

(5) Order. An order authorizing payment of filing fee in installments must fix the number of installments and the amount and due date of each installment. The number of installments must not exceed 4. The final installment is payable not later than 120 days after the filing of the petition, unless extended by the court for cause shown to a date not later than 180 days after the petition date. The first payment must be at least $30, unless otherwise ordered by the court.

(6) Dismissal for Nonpayment. The debtor's failure to pay any installment when due may result in dismissal of the case after notice and hearing.

(b) WAIVER OF CHAPTER 7 FILING FEE.

(1) Eligibility. Only an individual debtor may file an application to waive the filing fee in a chapter 7 case.

(2) Application. The debtor must submit a written application for an order waiving payment of the filing fee in a chapter 7 case. The application must be accompanied by a declaration under penalty of perjury establishing that the debtor qualifies for a waiver and is unable to pay the filing fee. The application and declaration must be completed on forms prescribed by the court and presented for filing with the petition. If unrepresented by an attorney, or if required by the court, the debtor must also present evidence of personal identification in the form of a valid government-issued driver's license or identification card, or other similar form of identification satisfactory to the clerk.

(3) Hearing. On the petition date or at a later date and time the designated judge may select for a hearing, the debtor must appear personally before a designated judge to present the application, supporting declaration, and proposed order. The debtor must provide sworn testimony regarding the basis for the application and circumstances of the bankruptcy filing. Unless the court specifically waives the requirement of personal appearance, the debtor's failure to appear and testify at the prescribed time and place will result in denial of the application and dismissal of the bankruptcy case.

(4) Notice. Compliance with the notice and service requirements of LBR 9013-1 is not required, unless otherwise ordered by the designated judge.

(5) Order. An order denying an application to waive the chapter 7 filing fee may provide for payment of the filing fee in installments pursuant to LBR 1006-1(a)(5).

LBR 1007-1. LISTS, SCHEDULES, AND STATEMENTS

(a) MASTER MAILING LIST.

(1) A master mailing list must be filed with the petition in the format specified in the Court Manual available from the clerk and on the court's website.

(2) Unless otherwise ordered, the master mailing list must include the name, mailing address, and zip code of each creditor listed on Schedules D, E, and F.

(b) AMENDMENT OF MASTER MAILING LIST. When an addition or change is required to the master mailing list, a supplemental master mailing list, in the required format, containing only the newly added or changed creditors must be filed. The supplement must not repeat those creditors listed on the original master mailing list.

(c) PARTNERSHIPS, CORPORATIONS, AND LIMITED LIABILITY COMPANIES. If the debtor is a partnership, corporation, or limited liability company, the master mailing list must include the name and address of each general partner, senior corporate officer, or managing member. A list of all limited partners, shareholders, or other equity holders must be provided either as part of the master mailing list or as a separate "Equity Holders' Mailing List." The Equity Holders' Mailing List must comply with the format requirements of subsection (a) of this rule.

(d) VERIFICATION OF COMPLETENESS AND ACCURACY.

(1) The debtor, or such other person as the court may order, is responsible for the accuracy and completeness of the master mailing list, any supplement to the master mailing list, and the Equity Holders'

Mailing List.

(2) The master mailing list and any supplement thereto must be accompanied by a declaration by the debtor or debtor's counsel attesting to the completeness and correctness of the list.

(3) If the master mailing list or any supplement thereto is submitted in a court-approved electronic format and the electronic file is prepared by someone other than the debtor or debtor's counsel, a further declaration must be submitted by the preparer to attest to the accuracy of the electronic file as it relates to the information provided by the debtor or debtor's counsel.

(4) The clerk will not compare the names and addresses of the creditors listed in the schedules with the names and addresses shown on the master mailing list or any supplement thereto.

(e) EXTENSION OF TIME TO FILE SCHEDULES, STATEMENTS, AND OTHER DOCUMENTS.

(1) A motion for an extension of time to file the lists of creditors and equity security holders, or to file the schedules, statements, and other documents must comply with FRBP 1007(c).

(2) The motion must be accompanied by evidence demonstrating cause for the requested extension of time.

LBR 1007-4. DISCLOSURE OF CORPORATE RELATIONSHIPS

(a) MANDATORY STATEMENT. A debtor that is a corporation, other than a governmental unit, must file with the petition a corporate ownership statement that either identifies any corporation, other than a governmental unit, that directly or indirectly owns 10% or more of any class of the debtor corporation's equity interests or states that there are no such entities to report.

(b) SUPPLEMENTAL STATEMENT. The debtor must file a supplemental statement promptly upon any change in circumstances that this rule requires the debtor to identify or disclose.

LBR 1010-1. INVOLUNTARY PETITIONS

The court may dismiss an involuntary petition sua sponte if the petitioner fails to (a) serve the summons and petition within the time allowed by FRBP 7004; (b) file a proof of service of the summons and petition with the court; or (c) appear at the status conference set by the court.

LBR 1015-1. CONSOLIDATION AND JOINT ADMINISTRATION

(a) JOINT CASES. A joint case commenced for spouses by the filing of a single petition under 11 U.S.C. § 302(a) will be deemed substantively consolidated unless the court orders otherwise.

(b) JOINT ADMINISTRATION OF CASES PENDING IN THE SAME COURT.

(1) If 2 or more cases are pending before the same judge, an order of joint administration may be entered, without notice and an opportunity for hearing, upon the filing of a motion for joint administration pursuant to FRBP 1015, supported by a declaration establishing that the joint administration of the cases is warranted, will ease the administrative burden for the court and the parties, and will protect creditors of the different estates against potential conflicts of interest.

(2) An order for joint administration under this rule may be reconsidered upon motion by a party in interest after notice and a hearing.

(3) An order of joint administration under this rule is for procedural purposes only and shall not effect a substantive consolidation of the respective debtors' estates.

(c) JOINT ADMINISTRATION / SUBSTANTIVE CONSOLIDATION. A motion for joint administration or for substantive consolidation must include a motion under LBR 1073-1 to transfer the assignment of the cases to be jointly administered or substantively consolidated if those cases are not all assigned to one judge.

LBR 1015-2. RELATED CASES

(a) DEFINITION OF RELATED CASES. For purposes of this rule, cases are deemed "related cases" if the earlier bankruptcy case was filed or pending at any time before the filing of the new petition, and the debtors in such cases:

(1) Are the same;

(2) Are spouses, former spouses, domestic partners, or former domestic partners;

(3) Are "affiliates," as defined in 11 U.S.C. § 101(2), except that 11 U.S.C. § 101(2)(B) shall not apply;

(4) Are general partners in the same partnership;

(5) Are a partnership and one or more of its general partners;

(6) Are partnerships that share one or more common general partners; or

(7) Have, or within 180 days of the commencement of either of the related cases had, an interest in property that was or is included in the property of another estate under 11 U.S.C. § 541(a), § 1115, § 1207, and/or § 1306.

(b) DISCLOSURE OF RELATED CASES.

(1) A petition commencing a case must be accompanied by court-mandated form F 1015-2.1, Statement of Related Cases.

(2) The petitioner must execute court-mandated form F 1015-2.1 under penalty of perjury disclosing, to the petitioner's best knowledge, information and belief, whether a related case was filed or has been pending at any time and if so, for each such related case:

(A) The name of the debtor in the related case;

(B) The case number of the related case;

(C) The district and division in which the related case is or was pending;

(D) The judge to whom the related case was assigned;

(E) The current status of the related case;

(F) The manner in which the cases are related; and

(G) The real property, if any, listed in the Schedule A that was filed in the related case.

(3) The failure to provide complete and accurate information in court-mandated form F 1015-2.1 may subject the petitioner and its attorney to appropriate sanctions, including the appointment of a trustee or dismissal of the case with prejudice.

LBR 1017-1. CONVERSION

(a) CONVERSION UPON DEBTOR'S REQUEST.

(1) A debtor's notice of conversion under 11 U.S.C. §§ 1208(a) or 1307(a) must be filed and served on the standing trustee and United States trustee. No hearing is required for conversion.

(2) A debtor must request conversion under 11 U.S.C. § 1112(a) by motion filed and served as required by FRBP 9013, but the motion does not require a hearing.

(3) A debtor must request conversion under 11 U.S.C. § 706(a) to a case under chapter 11, 12 or 13 by motion which, unless otherwise ordered by the court, may be granted only after notice of opportunity to request a hearing to the trustee, attorney for the trustee (if any), United States trustee, and parties in interest, as provided in LBR 9013-1(o).

(4) If the case is converted, the clerk will give notice of the order converting the case to another chapter to all creditors and interested parties and to the United States trustee.

(b) ADDITIONAL FEES UPON CONVERSION OF A CASE.

(1) A notice of conversion or motion for conversion, as the case may be, of a case must be accompanied by payment of the filing fee, if any, required for conversion of the case to the chapter for which conversion is sought.

(2) If a conversion to chapter 11 is denied, the filing fee paid when the motion was filed will be refunded to the payor upon written request to the Fiscal Department of the clerk's office. A conformed copy of the order denying the conversion to chapter 11 must be attached to the request for refund.

(3) If a conversion to chapter 7 is denied, the filing fee paid when the motion was filed will not be refunded.

LBR 1017-2. DISMISSAL OF CASE OR SUSPENSION OF PROCEEDINGS

(a) DISMISSAL FOR FAILURE TO FILE DOCUMENTS.

(1) Cause for Dismissal. The failure of the petitioner to file in a timely manner any document required by the Bankruptcy Code, the FRBP, and these rules is cause for dismissal of the case.

(2) Notice of Proposed Dismissal. If a petition is filed without all of the documents required by the Bankruptcy Code, the FRBP, and these rules, the clerk will issue a notice to the petitioner that identifies each of the deficiencies and states that the case will be dismissed without further notice or hearing if the documents listed in the notice, or a request for extension of time within which to file the required documents, are not filed within 14 days from the filing of the petition.

(3) Dismissal Without Further Notice. If the required documents are not filed within 14 days from the filing of the petition or an extension of such 14-day period granted by an order of the court, the case will be dismissed without further notice or hearing.

(b) DISMISSAL OF CHAPTER 7 CASE FOR FAILURE TO ATTEND MEETING OF CREDITORS. The failure of a chapter 7 debtor to appear at the initial meeting of creditors and any continuance thereof is cause for dismissal of the case. The court will dismiss the case upon the trustee's request for dismissal and certification that the debtor has failed to appear at two meetings of creditors.

(c) NOTICE OF DISMISSAL. The clerk will provide notice of an order dismissing a case under this rule to the debtor, debtor's attorney (if any), United States trustee, and parties in interest.

(d) REINSTATEMENT.

(1) A case dismissed for the failure to timely file a required document or for failure to appear at the meeting of creditors may be reinstated on motion of the petitioner pursuant to FBRP 9024, provided that all required documents are filed, or on motion of another party.

(2) In the event a case is reinstated, the court may impose such sanctions as it deems just and reasonable.

(e) REFILING OF DISMISSED CASE. A petitioner who files a petition following the dismissal of a case must disclose the dismissed case pursuant to LBR 1015-2.

(f) MOTION TO DISMISS OR SUSPEND PROCEEDINGS.

(1) A motion by the debtor to dismiss a case filed under 11 U.S.C. §§ 301 or 302, a motion by creditors or the debtor to dismiss an involuntary case filed under 11 U.S.C. § 303, or a motion to suspend all proceedings under 11 U.S.C. § 305 must be supported by a declaration setting forth the reasons for the request for dismissal or suspension.

(2) The declaration in support of the motion must disclose any arrangement or agreement between the debtor and creditors or any other person in connection with the motion for dismissal or suspension.

(3) The court may condition the dismissal upon payment of fees and expenses, including fees due to the United States trustee.

LBR 1071-1. DIVISIONS—PLACE OF FILING

(a) FILING OF PETITION. Unless otherwise ordered by the court, a petition commencing a case under the Bankruptcy Code must be filed with the Clerk of the United States Bankruptcy Court for the Central District of California in the "applicable division."

(1) The "applicable division" is determined by the location of the debtor's residence, principal offices, officers, and books and records, or where the majority of the debtor's assets are located based on a book value determination as set forth on the debtor's most current balance sheet.

(2) Information concerning the "applicable division" for the filing of the petition is contained in the Court Manual available from the clerk and on the court's website.

(b) PETITION FILED IN WRONG DIVISION. If a petition is filed in the wrong division, the court may, on its own, transfer it to the appropriate division or retain the case.

(c) FILING OF PAPERS OTHER THAN A PETITION. Papers other than a petition must be filed only in the divisional office of the clerk to which the relevant case or proceeding has been assigned. However, the clerk may, by special waiver or upon order of the court, accept papers in any office of the clerk irrespective of division.

LBR 1073-1. ASSIGNMENT OF CASES

(a) NEW PETITIONS. Unless otherwise ordered by the court, a new petition commencing a case must be assigned by the clerk according to a random draw so that neither the clerk, the parties, nor their attorneys is able to make a deliberate choice of a particular judge.

(b) ASSIGNMENT OR REASSIGNMENT OF RELATED CASES AND PROCEEDINGS. The court will assign or reassign related cases or proceedings pursuant to the procedures established by the court's General Orders.

(c) MOTION FOR REASSIGNMENT OR CONSOLIDATION OF RELATED CASES.

(1) A motion by a party in interest for reassignment or consolidation of related bankruptcy cases or adversary proceedings must be made to the judge to whom the low-numbered case is assigned.

(2) The motion must be filed and served in accordance with LBR 9013-1(o). Notice must be given to the debtor or debtor in possession, the trustee (if any), the creditors' committee or the 20 largest unsecured creditors if no committee has been appointed, any other committee appointed in the case, counsel for any of the foregoing, the United States trustee, and any other party in interest entitled to notice under FRBP 2002. Notice of a motion seeking the reassignment or consolidation of an adversary proceeding must be given to each party named in the adversary proceeding. A judge's copy of the motion must be served in chambers on the higher-numbered judge.

(3) An order reassigning a related case pursuant to LBR 1015-2 must be titled "Order of Reassignment Pursuant to LBR 1015-2," and must be promptly filed with the clerk and entered by the clerk on the docket. Notice of the order must be given to all parties who are entitled to notice of the order for relief pursuant to FRBP 2002(d)(1) and (f)(1), and to the judge to whom the high-numbered case is assigned.

(d) REASSIGNMENT OF CASES OR PROCEEDINGS DUE TO RECUSAL.

(1) The court will reassign a case or proceeding due to recusal pursuant to the procedures established by the court's General Orders.

(2) Upon recusal of an assigned judge of an entire case, an adversary proceeding, contested matter, or other single matter within a case, the recused case, proceeding or matter will be reassigned by the clerk to another judge by random draw.

(e) ASSIGNMENT OF MISCELLANEOUS MATTERS. Whenever action is required on a miscellaneous matter for which there is no bankruptcy case pending in this district, the clerk will assign the matter by random draw.

(f) NONLIMITATION OF APPLICABILITY. A judge may assign any case or adversary proceeding to another judge.

LBR 2002-1. NOTICE TO AND SERVICE UPON CREDITORS AND OTHER INTERESTED PARTIES

(a) REQUEST FOR SPECIAL NOTICE.

(1) Form. A person or entity filing a request for notices served pursuant to FRBP 2002 must include in the request for special notice: (A) name of the person or entity requesting notice; (B) mailing address, including street address for overnight delivery or personal service; (C) telephone number; (D) facsimile number; (E) e-mail address; (F) name of the person or entity represented, if any; (G) a statement that the requesting party is a creditor and/or equity security holder of the debtor and notice is requested on the basis of the court having limited notice to a committee; and (H) a statement that the request is limited to notices required to be provided under FRBP 2002(a)(2), (a)(3), and (a)(6) and does not include any moving or responsive or reply papers, any evidence, or any proposed orders or entered orders.

(2) Consent to Electronic Service. Subject to the provisions of LBR 9036-1, a creditor or equity security holder of the debtor filing a request for special notice under subsection (a)(1) of this rule is deemed to consent to receive electronic notice and service from the clerk and parties in interest in the case or proceeding.

(b) MAILING LIST IN CHAPTER 9 AND 11 CASES. In chapter 9 and 11 cases only, the debtor in possession or trustee must maintain a current mailing list of entities who have served a request for notice pursuant to FRBP 2002 and must promptly furnish a copy of that list upon the request of any creditor or other interested party.

LBR 2002-2. NOTICE TO AND SERVICE UPON THE UNITED STATES OR FEDERAL AGENCIES

(a) UNITED STATES TRUSTEE.

(1) Duty to Provide Notice to and Service Upon the United States trustee. Pursuant to FRBP 2002(k), FRBP 9034 and these rules, and unless otherwise directed, a copy of any paper filed by a person or entity in a bankruptcy case or adversary proceeding under chapters 7, 9, or 11 must be served upon the United States trustee. Proofs of claim or copies thereof must not be served upon the United States trustee. In chapter 12 or 13 cases, only a notice of conversion or motion to convert the case to another chapter must be served upon the United States trustee.

(2) Consent to Electronic Notice and Service of Papers Filed with the Court. Notwithstanding subsection (a)(1) of this rule, and except as provided in subsection (a)(3) of this rule, the United States trustee consents to electronic notice and service of any paper filed in a bankruptcy case or adversary proceeding.

(A) ELECTRONIC NOTICE. The electronic transmission to the United States trustee of an NEF or a notice through the Bankruptcy Noticing Center constitutes notice to the United States trustee of a paper filed in a bankruptcy case or adversary proceeding, including notice of entry of an order or judgment, whether it is the duty of the clerk or another person or entity to give such notice. A proof of service prepared and filed pursuant to LBR 9013-3 must state that the United States trustee will be served electronically by the court.

(B) ELECTRONIC SERVICE. The electronic transmission to the United States trustee of an NEF regarding a paper filed in a bankruptcy case or adversary proceeding, which is required to be served on the United States trustee pursuant to FRBP 2002(k), FRBP 9022, FRBP 9034 or these rules, constitutes service of the paper on the United States trustee. A proof of service prepared and filed pursuant to LBR 9013-3 must state that the United States trustee will be served electronically by the court.

(3) Exceptions to Electronic Notice and Service. Notwithstanding the foregoing and in addition to the exceptions to electronic notice and service set forth in LBR 9036-1(b), the following papers must be served on the United States trustee non-electronically:

(A) A paper exceeding 50 pages in length, including exhibits;

(B) A matter to be heard as an emergency motion or on shortened time pursuant to LBR 9075-1, and any response thereto;

(C) Any paper filed within 7 days of the date of the hearing;

(D) Proposed orders or judgments if required to be served on the United States trustee under LBR 9021-1(b);

(E) Complaints served upon the United States trustee as a defendant. Persons and entities must comply with FRBP 7004(b)(10) when the United States trustee is named in an adversary proceeding as a party, whether or not the United States trustee is a trustee in the case;

(F) Any paper served upon the United States trustee and/or any of the United States trustee's staff in their capacity as individuals. The service of any such filing must be made in compliance with Rule 4 of the F.R.Civ.P. and with any and all other applicable rules of civil, bankruptcy and/or appellate procedure; and

(G) Any other document specified in the court's CM/ECF Procedures.

(4) Notice of Emergency Motion and Hearing Held on Shortened Notice. Telephonic notice of an emergency motion or hearing set on shortened notice must be given to the United States trustee if the United States trustee would otherwise be entitled to notice of the type of motion or hearing.

(5) Place of Service for Non-electronic Notice or Service. The United States trustee must be included in the master mailing list. For papers for which the United States trustee has not consented to electronic notice and service, the United States trustee must be served non-electronically at the applicable mailing address listed in the Register of Federal and State Governmental Unit Addresses contained in the Court Manual available from the clerk and on the court's website.

(b) UNITED STATES ATTORNEY. The United States attorney for this district has waived notice under FRBP 2002(j). If notice is required in a case or proceeding, the United States attorney must file a request for special notice with the court and serve the debtor, debtor's attorney (if any), the United States trustee, any trustee, and the representatives of any committee appointed in a case.

(c) INTERNAL REVENUE SERVICE.

(1) General Notice Matters. Except with respect to contested matters or adversary proceedings (where service must comply with the requirements of FRBP 7004 and LBR 2002-2(c)(2)), or as otherwise ordered by the court, the United States Internal Revenue Service must be served at the address listed in the Register of Federal and State Governmental Unit Addresses contained in the Court Manual available from the clerk and on the court's website.

(2) Adversary Proceedings and Contested Matters. In all contested matters and adversary proceedings involving the United States Internal Revenue Service, the United States, the Attorney General in Washington, D.C., and the United States attorney in Los Angeles must be served at addresses listed in the Register of Federal and State Governmental Unit Addresses contained in the Court Manual available from the clerk and on the court's website.

LBR 2004-1. MOTIONS FOR EXAMINATION UNDER FRBP 2004

(a) CONFERENCE REQUIRED. Prior to filing a motion for examination or for production of documents under FRBP 2004, the moving party must attempt to confer (in person or telephonically) with the entity to be examined, or its counsel, to arrange for a mutually agreeable date, time, place, and scope of an examination or production.

(b) MOTION. A motion for examination under FRBP 2004 must be filed stating the name, place of residence, and the place of employment of the entity to be examined, if known. The motion must include a certification of counsel stating whether the required conference was held and the efforts made to obtain an agreeable date, time, place, and scope of an examination or production. The motion must also explain why the examination cannot proceed under FRBP 7030 or 9014.

(c) NOTICE AND SERVICE. The motion must be served on the debtor, debtor's attorney (if any), the trustee (if any), the United States trustee, and the entity to be examined. Not less than 21 days notice of the examination must be provided, calculated from the date of service of the motion, unless otherwise ordered by the court.

(d) ORDER. Unless otherwise ordered by the court, an order for examination will be granted without a hearing.

(e) SUBPOENA. If the court approves a Rule 2004 examination of an entity other than the debtor, the attendance of the entity for examination and for the production of documents must be compelled by subpoena issued and served pursuant to FRBP 9016 and F.R.Civ.P. 45.

(f) PROTECTIVE ORDER. The party whose examination is requested may file a motion for protective order if grounds exist under FRBP 7026 and F.R.Civ.P. 26(c). A motion for protective order must be filed and served not less than 14 days before the date of the examination, and set for hearing not less than 2 days before the scheduled examination, unless an order shortening time is granted by the court pursuant to LBR 9075-1. The parties may stipulate, or the court may order, that the examination be postponed so that the motion for protective order can be heard on regular notice under LBR 9013-1.

(g) DISPUTES. The parties must seek to resolve any dispute arising under this rule in accordance with LBR 7026-1(c).

LBR 2010-1. BONDS OR UNDERTAKINGS

(a) BONDS, UNDERTAKINGS, APPROVAL, THIRD-PARTY SURETIES, SECURITY, AND QUALIFICATION.

(1) Approval. The clerk is authorized to approve on behalf of the court all bonds, undertakings, and stipulations of security given in the form and amount prescribed by statute, order of the court, or stipulation of counsel, which comply with the requirements of this rule and contain a certificate by an attorney, as set forth below, except where the approval of a judge is specifically required by law.

(2) Third-party Sureties. No bond or undertaking requiring third-party sureties will be approved unless it bears the names and addresses of sufficient third-party sureties and is accompanied by a declaration by the surety stating that:

(A) The surety is a resident of the State of California;

(B) The surety who intends to deed real property as security owns the real property within the State of California;

(C) The security posted by the surety is worth the amount specified in the bond or undertaking, over and above just debts and liabilities; and

(D) The property, real or personal, which is to be conveyed as security is not exempt from execution and prejudgment attachment.

If specifically approved by the court, real property in any other state of the United States may be part of the surety's undertaking.

(3) Terms and Conditions for Corporate Sureties. Before any corporate surety bond or undertaking is accepted by the clerk, the corporate surety must have on file with the district court clerk or the clerk a duly authenticated copy of a power of attorney appointing the agent executing the bond or undertaking. The appointment must be in a form to permit recording in the State of California.

(4) Ineligible Persons. No clerk, deputy clerk, marshal, magistrate judge, bankruptcy judge, district judge, attorney, or other officer of this court will be accepted as surety upon any bond or undertaking in any action or proceeding in this court.

(5) Cash in Lieu of Bond. Cash may be deposited with the clerk in lieu of any bond or undertaking requiring a personal or corporate surety. A cash deposit in lieu of a bond is subject to all of the provisions of this rule, LBR 7067-1, the FRBP and the F.R.Civ.P. applicable to bonds and undertakings.

(b) CERTIFICATE BY ATTORNEY. A bond or undertaking presented to the clerk for acceptance must be accompanied by a certificate by the attorney for the presenting party in substantially the following form:

"This bond (or undertaking) has been examined pursuant to LBR 2010-1 and is recommended for approval. It (is)(is not) required by law to be approved by a judge."

Date Attorney

The attorney's certificate pursuant to this rule certifies to the court that:

(1) The attorney has carefully examined the bond or undertaking;

(2) The attorney knows the content of the bond or undertaking;

(3) The attorney knows the purpose for which the bond or undertaking is executed;

(4) In the attorney's opinion, the bond or undertaking is in due form;

(5) The attorney believes the declarations of qualification by the surety are true; and

(6) The attorney has determined whether the bond or undertaking is required by law to be approved by a judge.

(c) APPROVAL OF JUDGE. If a bond or undertaking is required by law to be approved by a judge, it must be presented to the judge with the attorney's certificate required by this rule before it is filed by the clerk.

(d) CONSENT TO SUMMARY ADJUDICATION OF OBLIGATION.

(1) A bond or undertaking presented for filing must contain the consent and agreement for the surety that in case of default or contumacy on the part of the principal or surety, the court may upon 14 days notice proceed summarily and render a judgment in accordance with the obligation undertaken and issue a writ of execution upon that judgment.

(2) An indemnitee or party in interest seeking a judgment on a bond or undertaking must proceed by Motion for Summary Adjudication of Obligation and Execution. The motion must be served on a personal surety in the manner provided in F.R.Civ.P. 5(b). A corporate surety must be served in accordance with 31 U.S.C. § 9306.

(e) BONDS OF TRUSTEES. A bond required by a trustee under 11 U.S.C. § 322 is exempt from this rule. The United States trustee must set the amount of such bond and approve the sufficiency of the surety.

LBR 2014-1. EMPLOYMENT OF DEBTOR AND PROFESSIONAL PERSONS

(a) EMPLOYMENT OF DEBTOR'S PRINCIPALS OR INSIDERS IN CHAPTER 11 CASES.

(1) Notice of Setting/Increasing Insider Compensation. No compensation or other remuneration may be paid from the assets of the estate to a debtor's owners, partners, officers, directors, shareholders, or relatives of insiders as defined by 11 U.S.C. § 101(31), from the time of the filing of the petition until the confirmation of a plan nor may approved compensation be increased unless the debtor serves a Notice of Setting/ Increasing Insider Compensation ("Notice") in accordance with procedures adopted by the United States trustee pursuant to this rule.

(2) Service of Notice. The debtor must: (A) serve the Notice on the United States trustee, the creditors' committee or the 20 largest creditors if no committee has been appointed, any other committee appointed in the case, counsel for any of the foregoing, and any secured creditor that claims an interest in cash collateral, and (B) provide proof of service to the United States trustee. As a non-filed document, the Notice does not result in the generation and delivery of an NEF, and therefore consent to electronic service via NEF on the United States trustee and other CM/ECF Users is not applicable to the Notice.

(3) Payment of Insider Compensation. An insider may receive compensation or other remuneration from the estate if no objection is received within 14 days after service of the Notice. An insider may receive an increase in the amount of insider compensation or other remuneration previously approved if no objection is received within 30 days after service of the Notice.

(4) Objection and Notice of Hearing. If an objection is timely received, the debtor must set the matter for hearing. The debtor must file a true and correct copy of the Notice, objection, and the original notice of hearing. The debtor must serve not less than 21 days notice of the date and time of the hearing on the objecting party and the United States trustee.

(b) EMPLOYMENT OF PROFESSIONAL PERSON.

(1) Application for Employment.

(A) An application seeking approval of employment of a professional person pursuant to 11 U.S.C. §§ 327, 328, 1103(a), or 1114 must comply with the requirements of FRBP 2014 and 6003(a) and be filed with the court. The application must specify unambiguously whether the professional seeks compensation pursuant to 11 U.S.C. § 328 or 11 U.S.C. § 330.

(B) The application must be accompanied by a declaration of the person to be employed establishing disinterestedness or disclosing the nature of any interest held by such person.

(C) The United States trustee must be served, in accordance with LBR 2002-2(a), with a copy of the application and supporting declaration not later than the day it is filed with the court. No hearing is required unless requested by the United States trustee or a party in interest, or as otherwise ordered by the court.

(D) A chapter 7 trustee who seeks authorization to act as attorney or accountant for the estate, or to employ the trustee's firm in such capacity, must explain why such employment is in the best interests of the estate.

(E) A timely application for employment is a prerequisite to compensation from the estate. Therefore, an application for the employment of counsel for a debtor in possession should be filed as promptly as possible after the commencement of the case, and an application for employment of any other professional person should be filed as promptly as possible after such person has been engaged.

(F) The substitution of an attorney must also comply with LBR 2091-1(b).

(2) Notice of Application.

(A) Notice of an application by the debtor (if such application is required), debtor in possession, or trustee, to retain a professional person must be filed and served, in accordance with LBR 2002-2(a) and LBR 9036-1, on the United States trustee, the debtor (if a trustee has been appointed), the creditors' committee or the 20 largest unsecured creditors if no committee has been appointed, any other committee appointed in the case, counsel for any of the foregoing, and any other party in interest entitled to notice under FRBP 2002.

(B) Notice of an application by a committee to retain a professional person must be filed and served, in accordance with LBR 2002-2(a) and LBR 9036-1, on the United States trustee, debtor or debtor in possession, the trustee (if appointed), and their counsel.

(C) The notice must be filed and served not later than the day the application is filed with the court.

(3) Content of Notice. The notice must:

(A) State the identity of the professional and the purpose and scope for which it is being employed;

(B) State whether the professional seeks compensation pursuant to 11 U.S.C. § 328 or 11 U.S.C. § 330;

(C) Describe the arrangements for compensation, including the hourly rate of each professional to render services, source of the fees, the source and amount of any retainer, the date on which it was paid, and any provision regarding replenishment thereof;

(D) Provide a name, address, and telephone number of the person who will provide a copy of the application upon request; and

(E) Advise the recipient that any response and request for hearing, in the form required by LBR 9013-1(f)(1), must be filed and served on the applicant (and counsel, if any), and the United States trustee not later than 14 days from the date of service of the notice.

(4) No Response and Request for Hearing. If the response period expires without the filing and service of a response and request for hearing, the applicant must promptly comply with LBR 9013-1(o)(3), except that:

(A) The proposed order and declaration must be served only on the United States trustee; and

(B) The Notice of Entered Order and Service List must limit service by the court to the debtor or debtor in possession, trustee (if any), the creditor's committee, any other committee appointed in the case, counsel for any of the foregoing, and the United States trustee.

(5) Response and Request for Hearing Filed. If a timely response and request for hearing is filed with the court and served upon the applicant and the United States trustee, the applicant must comply with LBR 9013-1(o)(4).

(c) RECONSIDERATION OF EMPLOYMENT TERMS.

(1) If the court approves the terms of a professional's employment, including a fee based on an the hourly rate, fixed or percentage fee, contingency or success fee, or a combination thereof, the court will not reconsider such terms of employment at a subsequent time except as provided in 11 U.S.C. § 328(a).

(2) Notwithstanding the foregoing, the court may exercise its discretion pursuant to 11 U.S.C. § 330(a)(2).

LBR 2015-2. REQUIREMENTS FOR CHAPTER 11 DEBTORS IN POSSESSION OR CHAPTER 11 TRUSTEES

(a) REPORTS BEFORE CONFIRMATION OF PLAN.

(1) The debtor, the debtor in possession, or chapter 11 trustee must provide the United States trustee with financial, management and operational reports, and such other information requested by the United States trustee in writing pursuant to the United States Trustee Notices and Guides as necessary to properly supervise the administration of a chapter

11 case.

(2) The United States trustee may, at any time during the pendency of a case, add or delete requirements where such modifications are necessary or appropriate.

(b) DUTY TO COMPLY WITH REQUIREMENTS OF THE UNITED STATES TRUSTEE NOTICES AND GUIDES. A debtor in possession or chapter 11 trustee must comply with the reasonable requirements of the United States trustee with respect to form, maintenance of records, and reporting requirements as set forth in the United States Trustee Notices and Guides. Timely compliance is mandatory.

(c) INTERIM STATEMENTS AND OPERATING REPORTS.

(1) The debtor in possession or chapter 11 trustee must file with the court a copy of each monthly interim statement and operating report submitted to the United States trustee from the date the chapter 11 case is commenced until the date a plan is confirmed or the case is dismissed or converted to another chapter under title 11.

(2) Each interim statement and operating report must be filed on the date that such documents are submitted to the United States trustee, but not later than the 15th day of the month following expiration of the month which is the subject of the statement or report.

(d) DUTIES UPON CONVERSION TO CHAPTER 7. Upon entry of an order converting a case to one under chapter 7, the debtor in possession or chapter 11 trustee, if any, must, in addition to complying with those duties set forth in FRBP 1019:

(1) Secure, preserve and refrain from disposing of property of the estate;

(2) Contact the chapter 7 trustee and arrange to deliver property of the estate and all books and records to the trustee or the trustee's designated agent; and

(3) Within 7 days after entry of said order, file and serve upon the United States trustee and the chapter 7 trustee, a verified schedule of all property of the estate as of the conversion date.

LBR 2016-1. COMPENSATION OF PROFESSIONAL PERSONS

(a) INTERIM FEE APPLICATIONS.

(1) Form of Fee Application. An application for interim fees incurred or costs advanced by an attorney, accountant or other professional person, and a trustee or examiner must contain the following:

(A) A brief narrative history and report concerning the status of the case, including the following:

(i) CHAPTER 11. Applicant must describe the general operations of the debtor, stating whether the business of the debtor, if any, is being operated at a profit or loss, whether the business has sufficient operating cash flow, whether a plan has been filed, and if not, the prospects for reorganization and the anticipated date for the filing of a plan.

(ii) CHAPTER 7. Applicant must report the status of administration of the estate, discussing the actions taken to liquidate property of the estate, the property remaining to be administered, the reasons the estate is not in a position to be closed, and whether it is feasible to pay an interim dividend to creditors.

(iii) ALL CASES. Applicant must disclose the amount of money on hand in the estate and the estimated amount of other accrued expenses of administration. At the hearing on an application for interim fees, the applicant should be prepared to supplement the application by declaration or by testimony to inform the court of the current financial status of the debtor's estate.

(iv) MULTIPLE FEE APPLICATIONS. If more than 1 application for interim fees in a case is noticed for hearing at the same date and time, the narrative history provided in one of the applications may be incorporated by reference into the other interim fee applications to be heard contemporaneously by the court.

(v) EXCEPTION. A fee application submitted by an auctioneer, real estate broker, or appraiser does not have to comply with subsection (A) of this rule, except that auctioneers, unless otherwise ordered by the court, must file the report required by FRBP 6004(f) prior to receiving final compensation.

(B) The date of entry of the order approving the employment of the individual or firm for whom payment of fees or expenses is sought, and the date of the last fee application for the professional.

(C) A listing of the amount of fees and expenses previously requested, those approved by the court, and how much has been received.

(D) A brief narrative statement of the services rendered and the time expended during the period covered by the application.

(E) Unless employment has been approved on a fixed fee, percentage fee, or contingent fee basis, the application must contain a detailed listing of all time spent by the professional on matters for which compensation is sought, including the following:

(i) Date service was rendered.

(ii) DESCRIPTION OF SERVICE. It is not sufficient to merely state "Research," "Telephone Call," "Court Appearance," etc. Applicant must refer to the particular person, motion, discrete task performed, and other matters related to such service. A summary that lists a number of services under only 1 time period is not satisfactory.

(iii) AMOUNT OF TIME SPENT. A summary is not adequate. Time spent must be accounted for in tenths of an hour and broken down in detail by the specific task performed. Lumping of services is not satisfactory.

(iv) IDENTIFICATION OF PERSON WHO RENDERED SERVICE. If more than 1 person's services are included in the application, applicant must identify the person who performed each item of service.

(F) An application that seeks reimbursement of actual and necessary expenses must include a summary listing of all expenses by category (i.e., long distance telephone, photocopy costs, facsimile charges, travel, messenger and computer research). As to each unusual or costly expense item, the application must state:

(i) The date the expense was incurred;

(ii) A description of the expense;

(iii) The amount of the expense; and

(iv) An explanation of the expense.

(G) Unless employment has been approved on a fixed fee, percentage fee, or contingent fee basis, the application must contain a listing of the hourly rates charged by each person whose services form a basis for the fees requested in the application. The application must contain a summary indicating for each attorney by name:

(i) The hourly rate and the periods each rate was in effect;

(ii) The total hours in the application for which compensation is sought; and

(iii) The total fee requested in the application.

(H) A description of the professional education and experience of each of the individuals rendering services, including identification of the professional school attended, year of graduation, year admitted to practice, publications or other achievements, and explanation of any specialized background or expertise in bankruptcy-related matters.

(I) If the hourly rate has changed during the period covered by the application, the application must specify the rate that applies to the particular hours for which compensation is sought.

(J) A separately filed declaration from the client indicating that the client has reviewed the fee application and has no objection to it. If the client refuses to provide such a declaration, the professional must file a declaration describing the steps that were taken to obtain the client's declaration and the client's response thereto.

(K) A statement that the applicant has reviewed the requirements of this rule and that the application complies with this rule.

(2) Notice of Interim Fee Application and Hearing.

(A) In all cases where the employment of more than one professional person has been authorized by the court, a professional person who files an application for interim fees must give other professional persons employed in the case not less than 45 days notice of the date and time of the hearing.

The notice of hearing must further state:

"Other professional persons retained pursuant to court approval may also seek approval of interim fees at this hearing, provided that they file and serve their applications in a timely manner. Unless otherwise ordered by the court, hearings on interim fee applications will not be scheduled less than 120 days apart."

(B) Applicant must serve not less than 21 days notice of the hearing on the debtor or debtor in possession, the trustee (if any), the creditors' committee or the 20 largest unsecured creditors if no committee has been appointed, any other committee appointed in the case, counsel for any of the foregoing, the United States trustee, and any other party in interest entitled to notice under FRBP 2002. The notice must identify the professional person requesting fees, the period covered by the interim application, the specific amounts requested for fees and reimbursement of expenses, the date, time and place of the hearing, and the deadline for opposition papers.

(C) In addition to the notice, a copy of the application, together with all supporting papers, must be served on the debtor or debtor in possession, the trustee (if any), any committee appointed in the case, counsel for any of the foregoing, and the United States trustee. A copy of the complete application must also be promptly furnished upon specific request to any other party in interest.

(3) Objections. Any opposition or other responsive paper by the United States trustee or other party in interest must be served and filed at least 14 days prior to the hearing in the form required by LBR 9013-1(f).

(b) MOTIONS TO APPROVE COMPENSATION PROCEDURES IN CHAPTER 11 CASES, INCLUDING MONTHLY DRAW-DOWN AND CONTINGENCY OR SUCCESS FEE AGREEMENTS. A professional person employed in a chapter 11 case may request approval for and modifications of draw-down procedures and an order allowing payment of interim compensation more frequently than once every 120 days.

(c) FINAL FEE APPLICATION.

(1) Who Must File. The trustee, if any, and each professional person employed in the case must file a final fee application.

(2) Contents. An application for allowance and payment of final fees and expenses must contain the information required of an interim fee application under LBR 2016-1(a)(1).

(3) When Filed; Notice Required in Chapter 11 Cases.

(A) Unless otherwise ordered by the court, a final fee application by the trustee, if any, and each professional person employed in a chapter 11 case must be filed and set for hearing as promptly as possible after confirmation of a plan.

(B) A final fee application must cover all of the services performed in the case, not just the last period for which fees are sought, and must seek approval of all prior interim fee awards.

(C) Applicant must serve not less than 21 days notice of the hearing on the debtor or debtor in possession, the trustee (if any), any committee appointed in the case, counsel for any of the foregoing, the

United States trustee, and any other party in interest entitled to notice under FRBP 2002. The notice must identify the person or entity requesting a final allowance of fees and expenses, the period covered by the final application, the specific amounts requested for fees and reimbursement of expenses, the date, time and place of the hearing, and the deadline for opposition papers.

(D) In addition to the notice, a copy of the application, together with all supporting papers, must be served on the debtor or debtor in possession, the trustee (if any), any committee appointed in the case, counsel for any of the foregoing, and the United States trustee. A copy of the complete application must also be promptly furnished upon specific request to any other party in interest.

(4) When Filed; Notice Required in Chapter 7 Cases.

(A) A chapter 7 trustee must give at least 30 days written notice of intent to file a final report and account to the attorney for the debtor, the trustee's attorney and accountant, if any, and any other entity entitled to claim payment payable as an administrative expense of the estate.

(B) A professional person seeking compensation must file and serve an application for allowance and payment of final fees and expenses on the trustee within 21 days of the date of the mailing of the trustee's notice. The failure to timely to file an application may be deemed a waiver of compensation.

(C) All final fee applications by professional persons must be set for hearing with the chapter 7 trustee's final application for allowance and payment of fees and expenses. Notice of a final fee application must be given by the chapter 7 trustee as part of the notice of the hearing on the trustee's request for compensation. A separate notice by the applicant is not required.

(5) Objections. Any opposition or other responsive paper by the United States trustee or other party in interest must be served and filed at least 14 days prior to the hearing in the form required by LBR 9013-1(f).

(d) FEE EXAMINER. The court may, either sua sponte or on the motion of a party in interest, exercise its discretion to appoint a fee examiner to review fee applications and make recommendations to the court for approval.

LBR 2016-2. COMPENSATION AND TRUSTEE REIMBURSEMENT PROCEDURES IN CHAPTER 7 ASSET CASES

(a) AUTHORIZATION TO USE ESTATE FUNDS UP TO $1,000 TO PAY CERTAIN EXPENSES. During the course of a chapter 7 case, a trustee may disburse up to $1,000 from estate funds to pay the following actual and necessary expenses of the estate without further authorization from the court (the "Authorized Allocation"):

(1) Actual cost of noticing, postage, copying;

(2) Costs to advertise sale;

(3) Computer charges;

(4) Long distance telephone;

(5) Postage;

(6) Moving or storage of estate assets;

(7) Teletransmission;

(8) Travel charges for trustee (includes lodging, meals, mileage and parking);

(9) Bank charges for research or copies;

(10) Court reporting fees;

(11) Delivery of documents;

(12) Expedited mail;

(13) Filing and process serving;

(14) Notary fees;

(15) Recording fees;

(16) Deposition/transcript fees;

(17) Witness fees;

(18) Locate and move assets;

(19) Prepare litigation support documents;

(20) Insurance;

(21) Locksmith;

(22) Rent;

(23) Security services; and

(24) Utilities.

(b) BOND PREMIUMS AND TAXES. In addition to payments that may be made from the Authorized Allocation, the trustee may pay during the ordinary course of the trustee's administration of an estate:

(1) Bond premiums required by 11 U.S.C. § 322(a); and

(2) Obligations to taxing agencies arising under 11 U.S.C. § 507(a)(2), provided the estate is and is likely to remain administratively solvent.

(c) EXPENSES FOR PREPARATION OF TAX RETURNS. The trustee may, by a single application, seek authorization to employ and pay a tax preparer a flat fee (not to exceed $750 unless the court orders otherwise) for preparation of tax returns for the estate. If the court grants such application, the trustee may pay the flat fee so ordered without further application or order. This amount is in addition to payments that may be made from the Authorized Allocation.

(d) EMERGENCY EXPENSES. The trustee may exceed the Authorized Allocation to pay emergency expenses, without prior court approval, to protect assets of the estate that might otherwise be lost or destroyed. Emergency expenses are limited to:

(1) Charges for storage of the debtor's records to prevent the destruction of those records and related necessary cartage costs;

(2) Insurance premiums to prevent liability to the estate;

(3) Locksmith charges to secure the debtor's real property or business; and

(4) Security services to safeguard the debtor's real or personal property.

If the trustee disburses more than the Authorized Allocation to pay emergency expenses and other expenses for which the Authorized Allocation may be used, the trustee must file and serve a cash disbursement motion, as described in subsection (f) of this rule, within 7 days after such expenses are paid.

(e) PROCEDURES FOR EMPLOYMENT OF PARA-PROFESSIONALS AND PAYMENT OF PARAPROFESSIONAL FEES AND EXPENSES. A trustee must obtain court approval to employ and to pay a paraprofessional.

(1) Definition. The term "paraprofessional" includes all persons or entities other than "professionals" who perform services at the trustee's request and seek payment for services and expenses directly from the bankruptcy estate, including an agent, a field representative, an adjuster, and a tax preparer.

(2) Employment. A trustee may seek court approval to employ a paraprofessional by filing an employment application using court-approved form F 2016-2.1. The court's approval of the employment of any paraprofessional is not a judicial determination as to whether services of the paraprofessional constitute "trustee services." The following is a nonexclusive list of services that the court deems "trustee services" subject to the limitation on compensation contained in 11 U.S.C. § 326(a):

(A) Review schedules;

(B) Acceptance and qualification as a trustee;

(C) Routine investigation regarding location and status of assets;

(D) Initial contact with lessors, secured creditors, assignee for benefit creditors, etc., if same can be accomplished from office;

(E) Turnover or inspection of documents, such as bank documents;

(F) UCC search review;

(G) Recruit and contract appraisers, brokers, and professionals;

(H) Mail forwarding notices;

(I) Routine collection of accounts receivable;

(J) Letters regarding compliance with LBR 2016-1;

(K) Conduct 11 U.S.C. § 341(a) examinations;

(L) Routine objections to exemption;

(M) Routine motions to dismiss;

(N) 11 U.S.C. § 707(b) referral to United States trustee;

(O) Routine documentation of notices of sale, abandonment, compromise, etc.;

(P) Appear at hearings on routine motions;

(Q) Review and execute certificates of sale, deed, or other transfer documents;

(R) Prepare and file notifications of asset case;

(S) Prepare and file cash disbursement motions and necessary attachments;

(T) Prepare exhibits to operating reports;

(U) Prepare quarterly bond reports;

(V) Prepare trustee's interim reports;

(W) Routine claims review and objection;

(X) Prepare and file final reports and accounts and related orders;

(Y) Prepare motions to abandon or destroy books and records;

(Z) Prepare and file FRBP 3011 reports;

(AA) Prepare and file notices and motions to abandon assets and related orders;

(BB) Attend sales;

(CC) Monitor litigation;

(DD) Answer routine creditor correspondence and phone calls;

(EE) Prepare and file applications to employ paraprofessionals;

(FF) Review and comment on professional fee applications;

(GG) Participate in audits;

(HH) Answer United States trustee questions;

(II) Close and open bank accounts;

(JJ) Verify proposed disbursements;

(KK) Post receipts and disbursements;

(LL) Prepare details and calculations for payment of dividend;

(MM) Prepare dividend checks;

(NN) Organize and research bills;

(OO) Prepare checks for the trustee's signature;

(PP) Prepare internal cash summary sheets;

(QQ) Reconcile bank accounts;

(RR) Prepare and make deposits; and

(SS) Additional routine work necessary for administration of the estate.

(3) Reimbursement of Fees and Expenses. A trustee may pay a paraprofessional only upon specific order of the court.

(A) If the paraprofessional or trustee contends that the paraprofessional's services are not "trustee services," the trustee or paraprofessional must present evidence to support that contention. Absent adequate proof, the court may find that the services of the paraprofessional are "trustee services" subject to the limitation on compensation under 11 U.S.C. § 326(a).

(B) If a trustee refuses or neglects to file a fee application for the paraprofessional, the paraprofessional may file a separate fee application pursuant to 11 U.S.C. § 330. In addition to fulfilling the requirements of 11 U.S.C. § 330, FRBP 2014 and these rules, the paraprofessional's fee application must include: (i) a declaration explaining why a separate fee application is necessary; and (ii) evidence establishing which services are "trustee services" and which are not. The paraprofessional must serve any separate fee application on the trustee, debtor, debtor's counsel (if any), the United States trustee, and all professionals and other paraprofessionals employed in the case, and must give notice of the application to all creditors.

(f) CASH DISBURSEMENTS MOTION.

(1) Filing and Service. If the trustee wishes to pay expenses not authorized by this rule from estate funds, the trustee must file a cash disbursements motion to obtain court approval of payments for emergency expenses and all other expenses the trustee deems necessary for effective administration of the case. The cash disbursements motion must be in substantially the same form as court-approved form F 2016-2.2, Trustee's Cash Disbursements Motion. The trustee must serve the cash disbursements motion on the debtor, debtor's counsel (if any), the United States trustee, holders of the 20 largest unsecured claims, and any other party in interest entitled to notice under FRBP 2002. Any objection to the cash disbursements motion must be filed and served on the trustee and trustee's counsel, if any, within 14 days from the date the cash disbursements motion is served. The trustee must file the cash disbursements motion with the court within 21 days after service of the motion. If a timely objection has not been filed, the trustee must include a declaration to that effect. If a timely objection is filed, the trustee must set the matter for hearing and give written notice of the date, time and place of the hearing to the objecting party, debtor, debtor's counsel (if any), and the United States trustee. The trustee may seek an expedited hearing pursuant to LBR 9075-1.

(2) Hearing. The court may set a hearing on a cash disbursements motion regardless of whether an objection is filed. However, if the court does not advise the trustee of a hearing on the motion within 7 days after the motion is filed, the trustee may disburse funds from the estate to pay the expenses referred to in the motion to the extent the trustee deems it necessary, pending an order of the court. If, thereafter, the trustee receives notice that the court has issued an order in which the cash disbursement motion has been disapproved in whole or in part, or that the court has set a hearing, the trustee must stop paying the expenses for which authorization was sought in the motion or otherwise comply with the provisions of the order. The trustee may file a motion for reconsideration pursuant to LBR 9013-4.

(3) Personal Liability and Disclosure. Except as provided in this rule, a trustee who makes a disbursement without prior court approval may be personally liable to the estate for the amount of the disbursement. All disbursements made by the trustee pursuant to this rule must be disclosed in the trustee's final report and in all applications for fees or costs by the trustee and by paraprofessionals employed in the case by the trustee.

(g) NONEXCLUSIVE REMEDY. Nothing in this rule precludes the trustee from seeking court approval to disburse estate funds by way of a noticed motion filed and served pursuant to LBR 9013-1.

LBR 2070-1. CHAPTER 7 OPERATING CASES

(a) PERIODS NOT EXCEEDING 30 DAYS. For a period not exceeding 30 days from the date of the trustee's appointment, a trustee may operate the business of a chapter 7 debtor and pay any actual and necessary expenses from the Authorized Allocation permitted under LBR 2016-2(a) without a court order.

(b) PERIODS EXCEEDING 30 DAYS. To operate the business beyond such 30-day period, the trustee must, prior to expiration of the 30-day period, file and serve a motion for authorization to operate the debtor's business under 11 U.S.C. § 721. The motion must state the approximate length of time the trustee intends to operate the business and be supported by evidence that justifies operation of the business and satisfies the requirements of 11 U.S.C. § 721.

(c) AUTHORIZATION NOT TO EXCEED 1 YEAR. The trustee may seek approval to operate the debtor's business for a period not exceeding 1 year.

(d) DISBURSEMENT OF ESTATE FUNDS PENDING AUTHORIZATION. The court may hold a hearing on the trustee's motion after the expiration of the 30-day period, but the trustee may not disburse estate funds other than the Authorized Allocation after the 30-day period except upon specific order of the court.

(e) EFFECT OF ORDER. An order authorizing the trustee to operate the debtor's business does not excuse the trustee from obtaining appropriate authorization for cash disbursements under LBR 2016-2(f), except to the extent that the operating order expressly approves specific expenditures from the estate.

LBR 2072-1. NOTICE TO OTHER COURTS

(a) NOTICE OF BANKRUPTCY PETITION. Notice of the filing of a bankruptcy petition in this district must be given by the debtor or debtor's counsel, at the earliest possible date, to:

(1) The clerk of any federal or state court in which the debtor is a party to pending litigation or other proceedings; and

(2) The federal or state judge to whom the matter is assigned, all counsel of record in the matter, and to all parties to the action not represented by counsel.

(b) EFFECT OF NOT GIVING NOTICE. The failure to give the notice required by subsection (a) of this rule may constitute cause for annulment of the stay imposed by 11 U.S.C. §§ 362, 922, 1201, or 1301, or may result in the imposition of sanctions or other relief.

LBR 2081-1. CHAPTER 11 CASES

(a) MOTIONS REQUIRING EMERGENCY OR EXPEDITED RELIEF. Subject to FRBP 6003, the following motions may be heard pursuant to LBR 9075-1 either as an emergency motion or on shortened time:

(1) Motion to limit notice;

(2) Motion to extend time to file schedules and statement of financial affairs;

(3) Utility motion pursuant to 11 U.S.C. § 366;

(4) Motion to establish procedures for handling multiple reclamation claims;

(5) Request for regularly scheduled hearing dates. Upon request of a debtor, the court may establish a fixed date and time for hearing all motions and other matters in a chapter 11 case. Once ordered, the dates and time, and exceptions, if any, will be made available through the clerk's office and posted in advance on the court's website;

(6) Motion to pay prepetition payroll and to honor prepetition employment procedures.

The motion must be supported by evidence that establishes:

(A) The employees are still employed;

(B) The necessity for payment;

(C) The benefit of the procedures;

(D) The prospect of reorganization;

(E) Whether the employees are insiders;

(F) Whether the employees' claims are within the limits established by 11 U.S.C. § 507; and that

(G) The payment will not render the estate administratively insolvent;

(7) Motion to honor and comply with customer obligations and deposits. The motion must be supported by evidence that relief is essential to business operations and customer confidence or that the estate may suffer postpetition damages that would prejudice creditors, the reorganization, or the value of property of the estate;

(8) Motion to pay prepetition taxes. The motion must be supported by evidence that establishes:

(A) The necessity for payment;

(B) The prospect of reorganization;

(C) The means to pay;

(D) That the taxes to be paid are entitled to priority pursuant to 11 U.S.C. § 507; and that

(E) The payment will not render the estate administratively insolvent;

(9) Motion for emergency use of cash collateral, debtor in possession financing, or cash management;

(10) Motion for order establishing procedures for sale of estate's assets;

(11) Appointment of a patient care ombudsman under 11 U.S.C. § 333; and

(12) Other motions where special circumstances exist. The motion must be supported by evidence that exigent circumstances exist justifying an expedited hearing.

(b) PREPACKAGED PLANS. A hearing on a motion for order confirming a chapter 11 plan upon which voting was conducted before commencement of the case pursuant to 11 U.S.C. § 1126(b) must be scheduled, if practicable, no more than 30 days after the order for relief.

(c) SEVERANCE COMPENSATION OR EMPLOYEE INCENTIVE MOTIONS.

(1) Notice. A motion for approval of a severance compensation package or employee incentive program must be heard on regular notice, absent exigent circumstances.

(2) Standard. The motion must state whether the employee is an insider. If so, the motion must state whether the insider has a bona fide job offer from another business at the same or greater rate of compensation and establish the elements of 11 U.S.C. § 503(c).

LBR 2085-1. CHAPTER 15 CASES

(a) CHAPTER 15 MOTIONS—FORM AND SERVICE.

(1) A motion under chapter 15 must comply with FRBP 9013.

(2) The motion must be served on the 20 largest unsecured creditors located in the United States, the administrator appointed in any foreign proceeding with respect to the debtor or a member of the same corporate group as the debtor, the 20 largest unsecured creditors in each such foreign proceeding, all United States secured creditors, all secured creditors in foreign countries who are known to the movant, persons requesting special notice under LBR 2002-1(a), and the United States trustee. Furthermore, every such motion other than one which may be considered ex parte must be served by the moving party on the trustee, if the motion arises in a case filed under chapter 7, 9, 11, 12, or 13.

(b) AUTHORIZATION TO ACT IN A FOREIGN COUNTRY.

(1) Every trustee or other entity (including an examiner) appointed in a bankruptcy case pending in the United States (except for a case under chapter 15) must obtain authority under 11 U.S.C. § 1505 before acting in a foreign country.

(2) Authorization to act in a foreign country pursuant to 11 U.S.C. § 1505 must be made on motion of the trustee or other entity seeking such authorization. The motion must be made in compliance with FRBP 9013, and must be served as provided in subsection (a) of this rule.

(3) An order pursuant to this provision may be granted after notice and a hearing.

(c) REQUIREMENT TO OBTAIN ORDER FOR RECOGNITION. Any foreign representative seeking to appear in any United States court or the court of any State in the United States must first obtain an order for recognition under 11 U.S.C. § 1517. No such order is required if the sole purpose of the appearance is to collect accounts receivable on behalf of the foreign debtor.

(d) MOTION FOR COMITY OR COOPERATION. A request for comity or cooperation under 11 U.S.C. § 1509(b)(3) must be made by motion pursuant to subsection (a) of this rule.

(e) ADVICE OF FOREIGN REPRESENTATIVE'S INTENT TO COMMENCE A CASE UNDER 11 U.S.C. § 1511. Any foreign representative who intends to commence a case under 11 U.S.C. § 1511(a) must file a notice of intent to commence a domestic bankruptcy case with the court that has granted a petition for recognition under 11 U.S.C. § 1515. The notice must be served as provided by subsection (a) of this rule.

(f) FILING PROOF OF CLAIM OR EQUITY SECURITY INTEREST BY FOREIGN CREDITOR OR EQUITY SECURITY HOLDER IN CHAPTER 7 LIQUIDATION, CHAPTER 9 MUNICIPALITY, OR CHAPTER 11 REORGANIZATION CASE.

(1) This subsection applies in all chapter 7, 9, and 11 cases to each creditor and equity security holder that does not have an address in the United States.

(2) Every secured creditor described in subsection (f)(1) of this rule must file a proof of claim. This obligation applies to every such creditor claiming rights in rem against property of the debtor (whether moveable or immoveable), or holding a claim based on a registration in a public register or based on intellectual property (such as a patent or trademark).

(3) The filing of a claim or statement of interest under FRBP 3003 by a foreign creditor or security interest holder must be made as provided by that rule.

(4) Notice to a foreign creditor or security interest holder must be given at least 90 days before the deadline for filing a claim or notice of interest, unless otherwise ordered by the court.

(5) Notice of a deadline to file a claim or security interest under FRBP 3003 must be given in the official language of the country to which the notice is directed. In addition, the notice must be delivered by the same means that domestic notices and legal proceedings are delivered in that country, unless the court orders otherwise.

(g) APPLICATION FOR RECOGNITION.

(1) A foreign representative's petition for recognition must be filed with the bankruptcy court in the proper venue as provided by 28 U.S.C. § 1410. In addition, it must be set for hearing pursuant to subsection (a) of this rule upon notice as required by LBR 9013-1 or, if applicable, LBR 9075-1.

(2) A petition for recognition must be served pursuant to subsection (a) of this rule.

(3) If a petition for recognition requests the recognition of a foreign proceeding as a foreign main proceeding, the petition must be accompanied by evidence of the location of the debtor's registered office, or the debtor's residence in the case of an individual. All such documents must be translated into English pursuant to 11 U.S.C. § 1515(d).

(4) A party contending that a foreign proceeding is not a foreign main proceeding must file evidence complying with FRBP 7056 in support of the party's contention.

(5) A party seeking to rebut the presumption of 11 U.S.C. § 1516(c), that the debtor's registered office or habitual residence is the center of the debtor's main interests, must file evidence complying with FRBP 7056 in opposition to such a determination. Should it appear from the affidavits or declarations of such a party that the party cannot for reasons stated present evidence essential to justify the party's opposition, the court may order a continuance to permit evidence to be obtained or discovery to be had or may make such other order as is just. When a motion for recognition of a foreign main proceeding is made and supported as provided in this rule, an adverse party may not rest upon the mere allegations or denials of the adverse party's pleading, but the adverse party's response, supported by admissible evidence, must set forth specific facts showing that there is a genuine issue for trial.

(6) If the court finds that there is a genuine issue for trial on the recognition of a foreign main proceeding, the court will conduct an evidentiary hearing at the earliest practicable time, consistent with 11 U.S.C. § 1517(c).

(h) RELIEF FROM AUTOMATIC STAY; PROHIBITING OR CONDITIONING USE, SALE, OR LEASE OF PROPERTY; USE OF CASH COLLATERAL.

(1) A motion for relief from stay, or prohibiting or conditioning the use, sale, or lease of property must be made pursuant to FRBP 4001(a). A motion for use of cash collateral must be made pursuant to FRBP 4001(b). A motion pursuant to this paragraph must be served pursuant to subsection (a) of this rule.

(2) A motion for relief from the automatic stay of 11 U.S.C. §§ 361 and 362, as provided by 11 U.S.C. § 1520, must be made pursuant to FRBP 4001(a).

(i) ADVERSARY PROCEEDINGS UNDER FRBP 7001.

(1) FRBP 7001 applies to adversary proceedings under chapter 15.

(2) In addition to those proceedings listed in FRBP 7001, the following proceedings in a chapter 15 case are adversary proceedings governed by FRBP 7001, et. seq.:

(A) A proceeding to recover money or property under 11 U.S.C. §§ 549 or 552;

(B) A proceeding to obtain an injunction or other equitable relief under 11 U.S.C. § 1519;

(C) A request for relief under 11 U.S.C. § 1521(a)(1), (2), (3) or (6); and

(D) An action initiated by a foreign representative pursuant to 11 U.S.C. § 1523.

(j) PROTECTION OF CREDITORS AND OTHER INTERESTED PERSONS. Any request for security or bond sought in connection with relief under 11 U.S.C. § 1522(b) or (c) must be made by motion pursuant to subsection (a) of this rule.

(k) INTERVENTION BY A FOREIGN REPRESENTATIVE. Intervention in any proceedings in a state or federal court in the United States by a foreign representative must be pursuant to the rules applicable to that court.

(l) COOPERATION AND DIRECT COMMUNICATION BETWEEN THE TRUSTEE AND FOREIGN COURTS. A trustee or other person, including an examiner, acting on behalf of the debtor must obtain authorization from the court to communicate directly with a foreign judge. Such authorization may be requested by application after notice and a hearing.

(m) PROTOCOLS. A party seeking approval in the form of a protocol of an agreement concerning the coordination of proceedings must seek such approval by motion pursuant to subsection (a) of this rule.

(n) RECOGNITION OF DOMESTIC CASE AS A MAIN OR NON-MAIN PROCEEDING.

(1) A party in interest may request that the court designate a case under chapter 7, 9, 11, 12, or 13 as a main proceeding or a non-main proceeding. Such a request must be made by motion and comply with the requirements of subsection (a) of this rule.

(2) A motion for designation of a case as a main proceeding pursuant to subsection (n)(1) must be supported by evidence that the center of the debtor's main interests is located in the United States.

(3) A motion for designation of a case as a non-main proceeding pursuant to subsection (n)(1) must be supported by evidence that the debtor has an establishment in the United States.

(o) FINAL REPORT BY FOREIGN REPRESENTATIVE. A foreign representative who has been recognized pursuant to 11 U.S.C. § 1517 must file a final report when the purpose of the representative's appearance in a court in the United States is completed. A representative must report completely and accurately on the nature and results of the representative's activities in the court in the United States.

(p) FOREIGN AUTHORITIES. Any paper filed with the court that cites a foreign or international authority in a case under the Bankruptcy Code must attach a copy of the international foreign authority, with a translation into English.

(q) COURT-TO-COURT COMMUNICATION.

(1) A court may communicate with a foreign court in connection with matters relating to proceedings before it for the purposes of coordinating and harmonizing proceedings before it with those in the other State.

(2) A court may communicate with an administrator in a foreign State or an authorized representative of the court in that State in connection with the coordination and harmonization of the proceedings before it with the proceedings in the other State.

(3) A court may permit a duly authorized administrator to communicate with a foreign court directly, subject to the approval of the foreign court, or through an administrator in the other jurisdiction or through an authorized representative of the foreign court on such terms as the court considers appropriate.

(4) A court may receive communications from a foreign court or from an authorized representative of the foreign court or from a foreign administrator. The court may respond directly if the communication is from a foreign court (subject to subsection (q)(6) of this rule) in the case of two-way communications and may respond directly or through an authorized representative of the court or through a duly authorized administrator if the communication is from a foreign administrator.

(5) Communications from a court to a foreign court may take place by or through:

(A) Sending or transmitting copies of formal orders, judgments, opinions, reasons for decision, endorsements, transcripts of proceedings, or other documents directly to the foreign court and providing advance notice to counsel for affected parties in such manner as the court considers appropriate;

(B) Directing counsel, a foreign administrator or a trustee to transmit or deliver copies of documents, pleadings, affidavits, factums, briefs or other documents that are filed or to be filed with the court to the foreign court in such fashion as may be appropriate and providing advance notice to counsel for affected parties in such manner as the court considers appropriate; and

(C) Participating in two-way communications with the foreign court by telephone or video conference call or other electronic means, subject to subsection (q)(6) of this rule.

(6) In the event of communications between the courts in accordance with subsections (q)(1) and (4) by means of telephone or video conference call or other electronic means, unless otherwise directed by either of the two courts:

(A) Counsel for all affected parties may participate in person during the communication. Advance notice of the communication must be given to all parties in accordance with the rules of procedure applicable in each court;

(B) The communication between the courts must be on the record; and

(C) The courts and judges in each court may communicate fully with each other to establish appropriate arrangements for the communication without the necessity for participation by counsel unless otherwise ordered by either of the courts.

(7) In the event of communications between the court and an authorized representative of the foreign court or a foreign administrator in accordance with subsections (q)(2) and (4) by means of telephone or video conference call or other electronic means, unless otherwise directed by the court:

(A) Counsel for all affected parties may participate in person during the communication. Advance notice of the communication must be given to all parties in accordance with the rules of procedure applicable in each court;

(B) The communication must be on the record; and

(C) Judges in each court may communicate fully with the authorized representative of the foreign court or the foreign administrator to establish appropriate arrangements for the communication without necessity for participation by counsel unless otherwise ordered by the court.

(8) A court may conduct a joint hearing with another court. In connection with any such joint hearing, the following provisions apply, unless otherwise ordered or unless otherwise provided in any previously approved protocol applicable to such joint hearing:

(A) Each court must be able to simultaneously hear the proceedings in the other court;

(B) Evidentiary or written materials filed or to be filed in one court must be transmitted to the other court or made available electronically in a publicly accessible system in advance of the hearing. Transmittal of such material to the other court or its public availability in an electronic system must not subject the party filing the material in one court to the jurisdiction of the other court;

(C) Submissions or applications by the representative of any party should be made only to the court in which the representative making the submissions is appearing unless the representative is specifically given permission by the other court to make submissions to it;

(D) Subject to subsection (q)(6)(B), the court may communicate with the foreign court in advance of a joint hearing, with or without counsel being present, to establish guidelines for the orderly making of submissions and rendering of decisions by the courts, and to coordinate and resolve any procedural, administrative or preliminary matters relating to the joint hearing; and

(E) Subject to subsection (q)(6)(B), the court, subsequent to the joint hearing, may communicate with the foreign court, with or without counsel present, for the purpose of determining whether coordinated orders could be made by both courts to coordinate and resolve any procedural or non-substantive matters relating to the joint hearing.

(9) The court may, except upon proper objection on valid grounds and then only to the extent of such objection, recognize and accept as authentic the provisions of statutes, statutory or administrative regulations, and rules of court of general application applicable to the proceedings in the foreign jurisdiction without the need for further proof or exemplification thereof.

(10) The court may, except upon proper objection on valid grounds and then only to the extent of such objection, accept that orders made in the proceedings in the other jurisdiction were duly and properly made or entered on or about their respective dates and accept that such orders require no further proof or exemplification for purposes of the proceedings before it, subject to all such proper reservations as in the opinion of the court are appropriate regarding proceedings by way of appeal or review that are actually pending in respect of any such orders.

(11) The court may coordinate proceedings before it with proceedings in another State by establishing a service list that may include parties that are entitled to receive notice of proceedings before the court in the other State ("non-resident parties").

The court may also order that all notices, applications, motions, and other materials served for purposes of the proceedings before the court be provided to or served on the non-resident parties by making such materials available electronically in a publicly accessible system or by facsimile transmission, certified or registered mail or delivery by courier, or in such other manner as may be directed by the court.

(12) The foreign administrator or a representative of creditors in the proceedings in the other State or an authorized representative of the court in the other State may appear and be heard by the court without thereby becoming subject to the jurisdiction of the court.

(13) The court may direct that any stay of proceedings affecting the parties before it shall, subject to further order of the court, not apply to applications or motions brought by such parties before the other court or that relief be granted to permit such parties to bring such applications or motions before the other court on such terms and conditions as it considers appropriate. Court-to-court communications in accordance with subsections (q)(5) and (6) hereof may take place if an application or motion brought before the court affects or might affect issues or proceedings in the court in the other State.

(14) A court may communicate with a foreign court or with an authorized representative of such court in the manner prescribed by this rule for purposes of coordinating and harmonizing proceedings before it with proceedings in the other jurisdiction regardless of the form of the proceedings before it or before the foreign court wherever there is commonality among the issues and/or the parties in the proceedings.

(15) Directions issued by the court under this rule are subject to such amendments, modifications, and extensions as may be appropriate for the purposes described in this rule and to reflect the changes and developments from time to time in the proceedings before it and before the foreign court. Any directions may be supplemented, modified, and restated from time to time and such modifications, amendments, and restatements should become effective upon being accepted by both courts. If either court intends to supplement, change or abrogate direction issued under this rule in the absence of joint approval by both courts, the court must give the foreign courts involved reasonable notice of its intention to do so.

(16) Arrangements contemplated under this rule do not constitute a compromise or waiver by the court of any powers, responsibilities or authority and do not constitute a substantive determination of any matter in controversy before the court or before the foreign court nor a waiver by any of the parties of any of their substantive rights and claims or a diminution of the effect of any of the orders made by the court or the foreign court.

LBR 2090-1. ATTORNEYS—ADMISSION TO PRACTICE

(a) APPEARANCE BEFORE THE COURT.

(1) Attorney. An attorney admitted to practice before the district court may practice before the bankruptcy court. An attorney who is not admitted to the bar of, or permitted to practice before, the district court may not appear before the court on behalf of a person or entity, except as provided by this rule. Attorneys appearing before the court must have read the FRBP, F.R.Civ.P, F.R.Evid., and these rules in their entirety.

(2) Scope of Appearance.

(A) In a chapter 7 case, an attorney may limit the attorney's appearance to the administration of the case, or one or more proceedings in the case.

(B) In chapter 9, 11, 12, and 13 cases, the attorney for the debtor is presumed to appear for the case and all proceedings in the case, unless otherwise ordered by the court.

(3) Disclosure of Scope of Appearance in Chapter 7 Cases. In a chapter 7 case, the attorney for the debtor must file a statement disclosing the scope of the attorney's appearance on the date of the entry of the order for relief, or, if the attorney has not been employed by such date, then no later than the date of the first appearance made by the attorney. The statement required by this rule must be on a form approved by the court and signed by the debtor.

(b) PRO HAC VICE APPEARANCE.

(1) Permission for Pro Hac Vice Appearance. Any person who is not otherwise eligible for admission to practice before the court, but who is a member in good standing of, and eligible to practice before, the bar of any United States court, or of the highest court of any state, territory, or insular possession of the United States, who is of good moral character, and who has been retained to appear before the court, may, upon written application and at the discretion of the court, be permitted to appear and participate *pro hac vice* in a particular case or in a particular proceeding in a case.

(2) Disqualification from Pro Hac Vice Appearance. Unless authorized by the Constitution of the United States or Act of Congress, an applicant is not eligible for permission to appear pro hac vice if the applicant:

(A) Resides in California; or

(B) Is regularly employed in California; or

(C) Is regularly engaged in business, professional, or other similar activities in California.

(3) Designation of Local Counsel. A person applying to appear pro hac vice must designate an attorney who is a member of the bar of the court and who maintains an office within this district as local counsel with whom the court and opposing counsel may readily communicate regarding the conduct of the case and upon whom papers may be served, unless otherwise ordered by the court.

(4) Designation of Co-counsel. A judge to whom a case is assigned may, in the exercise of discretion, require the designation of an attorney who is a member of the bar of the court and who maintains an office within this district as co-counsel with authority to act as attorney of record for all purposes.

(5) Obtaining Permission for Pro Hac Vice Appearance. An applicant seeking permission to appear pro hac vice must present to the clerk:

(A) Proof of payment of the fee required by the district court; and

(B) A written application on or conforming to court-approved form F 2090-1.2, Application of Non-Resident Attorney to Appear in a Specific Case, disclosing the following:

(i) The applicant's name, and office or residence address;

(ii) The courts to which the applicant has been admitted to practice and the respective dates of admission;

(iii) A statement by the applicant of the good standing to practice before the courts to which the applicant has been admitted;

(iv) Whether the applicant has been disciplined by any court or administrative body, and if disciplinary proceedings are pending, the details of such proceedings, and whether the applicant resigned while disciplinary proceedings were pending;

(v) Whether in the 3 years preceding the application, the applicant has filed for permission to practice pro hac vice before any court within the state of California, together with the court, title and number of each such proceeding, and the disposition of each such application;

(vi) A certificate that the applicant has read the FRBP, the F.R.Civ.P., the F.R.Evid., and these rules in their entirety; and

(vii) The designation required by LBR 2090-1(b)(3) or LBR 2090-1(b)(4) including the office address, telephone number, and written consent of the designee.

(6) Notice and Hearing. An application for permission to appear pro hac vice does not require notice or a hearing.

(c) ATTORNEYS FOR THE UNITED STATES. Any person who is not eligible for admission under LBR 2090-1(b), or Local Civil Rules 83-2.2.1 or 83-2.3 of the district court, who is employed within California and who is a member in good standing of and eligible to practice before the bar of any United States court, or of the highest court of any state, territory or insular possession of the United States, and who is of good moral character, may be granted leave of court to practice in the court in any matter for which such person is employed or retained by the United States or its agencies.

(d) PROFESSIONAL CORPORATIONS, UNINCORPORATED LAW FIRMS, AND IN-HOUSE ATTORNEYS.

(1) Appearance. A professional law corporation or unincorporated law firm (collectively, "law firm") may not make an appearance on behalf of a party nor may pleadings or other documents be signed in the name of the law firm except by an attorney admitted to the bar of or permitted to practice before the court. This rule does not apply to pro se appearances by the attorney individually or on behalf of the attorney's law firm.

(2) Form of Appearance.

(A) A law firm must appear in the following form of designation or its equivalent:

John Smith (state bar number)
Smith and Jones
Address
Telephone Number
Fax Number (if any)
E-Mail Address (if any)
Attorneys for ___________

(B) An in-house attorney must appear in the following form of designation or its equivalent:

John Smith (state bar number)
Name of corporation or business entity
Address
Telephone Number
Fax Number (if any)
E-Mail Address (if any)

Attorney for

(C) Except as provided in LBR 1002-1(b) and LBR 2002-1(a), the disclosure of an e-mail address by an attorney in the form of designation is optional.

(e) LAW STUDENT CERTIFICATION FOR PRACTICE IN BANKRUPTCY COURT. A law student may be certified for practice in the bankruptcy court if the student meets the requirements of Local Civil Rule 83-4 of the district court for appearances in civil cases, except that the student need only complete one-third (rather than one-half) of the legal studies required for graduation. The law student also must have:

(1) Taken or be taking concurrently a course in bankruptcy law; and

(2) Knowledge of and familiarity with the F.R.Civ.P., FRBP, F.R.Evid., the Rules of Professional Conduct of the State Bar of California, and these rules.

LBR 2090-2. ATTORNEYS—DISCIPLINE AND DISBARMENT

(a) STANDARDS OF CONDUCT. An attorney who appears for any purpose in this court is subject to the standards of professional conduct set forth in Local Civil Rule 83-3.1.2 of the district court.

(b) DISCIPLINARY AUTHORITY OF COURT. An attorney appearing in this court submits to the discipline of the court. If a judge has cause to believe that an attorney has engaged in unprofessional conduct, the judge may do one or more of the following:

(1) Initiate proceedings for civil or criminal contempt;

(2) Impose other appropriate sanctions;

(3) Refer the matter to the appropriate disciplinary authority of the state or jurisdiction in which the attorney is licensed to practice; or

(4) Refer the matter pursuant to the procedures set forth in Local Civil Rule 83-3 of the district court or General Order 96-05, Attorney Discipline Procedures in Bankruptcy Court.

LBR 2091-1. ATTORNEYS—WITHDRAWAL, SUBSTITUTION, AND CHANGE OF ADDRESS

(a) MOTION FOR WITHDRAWAL. Except as provided in LBR 2091-1(b) and LBR 3015-1:

(1) An attorney who has appeared on behalf of an entity in any matter concerning the administration of the case, in one or more proceedings, or both, may not withdraw as counsel except by leave of court; and

(2) An entity represented by counsel may not appear without counsel or by a different attorney except by leave of court.

(b) CONSENSUAL SUBSTITUTION OF COUNSEL.

(1) A consensual substitution of attorneys may be filed and served to substitute counsel without leave of court where:

(A) An entity on whose behalf an attorney has appeared in any matter concerning the administration of the case, in one or more proceedings, or both, desires to substitute a different attorney in place of its former attorney; or

(B) A previously unrepresented entity desires to substitute an attorney employed to represent the entity.

(2) A substitution of attorney must be filed in substantially the same form as court-approved form F 2090-1.4, Substitution of Attorney, and served on those persons entitled to notice under LBR 2091-1(c).

(3) An attorney's employment as a "professional person" under 11 U.S.C. §§ 327 or 1103 is not approved merely by the filing of a Substitution of Attorney and service of notice thereof. Approval of employment must be obtained in compliance with the requirements of the Bankruptcy Code, FRBP, and these rules.

(c) NOTICE.

(1) Case. An attorney seeking withdrawal or substitution who has appeared on behalf of an entity in any matter concerning the administration of the case must give notice of the proposed substitution or motion for leave to withdraw to the debtor, the United States trustee, any case trustee, any committee appointed in the case, counsel for any of the foregoing, and parties requesting special notice.

(2) Proceedings. An attorney seeking withdrawal or substitution who has appeared on behalf of an entity only in one or more proceedings must give notice of the proposed substitution or motion for leave to withdraw to the debtor, each party who has been named or who has appeared in such proceeding(s), and the United States trustee.

(3) Cases and Proceedings. An attorney seeking withdrawal or substitution who has appeared on behalf of an entity both in the case and one or more proceedings must give notice of the proposed substitution or motion for leave to withdraw to all entities entitled to notice under subsections (c)(1) and (2) of this rule.

(d) CORPORATION, PARTNERSHIP, UNINCORPORATED ASSOCIATION, OR TRUST. An attorney moving for leave to withdraw from representation of a corporation, a partnership including a limited liability partnership, a limited liability company, or any other unincorporated association, or a trust, concurrently or prior to filing any such motion, must give notice to the client of the consequences of its inability to appear without counsel, including the possibility that a default judgment may be entered against it in pending proceedings; or, if the client is a chapter 11 debtor, that the case may be converted to chapter 7, a trustee may be appointed, or the case may be dismissed.

(e) DELAY BY WITHDRAWAL OR SUBSTITUTION.

(1) A withdrawal or substitution of counsel will not result in a continuance of any matter, absent an order granting a motion for continuance after notice and a hearing pursuant to LBR 9013-1(m).

(2) Unless good cause is shown and the ends of justice require, no substitution or withdrawal will be allowed that will cause unreasonable delay in prosecution of the case or proceeding to completion.

(f) CHANGE OF ADDRESS.

(1) An attorney who changes office address must file and serve a notice of change of address to update the attorney's address in the court's electronic database.

(2) In the absence of a specific request to the contrary, a change of address will update the attorney's address in the court's electronic database and the mailing list in all open cases in which the attorney represents a debtor or other party in interest.

LBR 3001-1. NOTICE OF CLAIMS BAR DATE IN CHAPTER 11 CASES

When the court orders a bar date for the filing of claims in a chapter 11 case, the debtor in possession or the chapter 11 trustee must serve notice of the claims bar date on all creditors and other parties entitled to notice. The following language must be used in the notice:

NOTICE OF CLAIMS DEADLINE

The Bankruptcy Court has set a deadline of ____________, 20______ for creditors and holders of ownership interests in the above-referenced debtor to file proofs of claim against or proofs of interest in the debtor's estate.

The exceptions to this deadline for filing proofs of claim or interest are: (1) claims arising from rejection of executory contracts or unexpired leases; (2) claims of governmental units; and (3) claims arising as the result of transfer avoidance pursuant to chapter 5 of the Bankruptcy Code.

For claims arising from rejection of executory contracts or unexpired leases pursuant to 11 U.S.C. § 365, the last day to file a proof of claim is: (a) 30 days after the date of entry of the order authorizing the rejection, or (b) [repeat the bar date set for all other claims here], whichever is later.

For claims of "governmental units," as that term is defined in 11 U.S.C. § 101(27), proofs of claim are timely filed if filed: (a) before 180 days after the date of the order for relief in this case, or (b) by [repeat the bar date set for all other claims here], whichever is later. 11 U.S.C. § 502(b)(9).

For claims arising from the avoidance of a transfer under chapter 5 of the Bankruptcy Code, the last day to file a proof of claim is: (a) 30 days after the entry of judgment avoiding the transfer, or (b) [repeat the bar date set for all other claims here], whichever is later.

If you are listed on the Schedules of Assets and Liabilities of [debtor] and your claim or interest is not scheduled as disputed, contingent, unliquidated or unknown, your claim or interest is deemed filed in the amount set forth in the schedules, and the filing of a proof of claim or interest is unnecessary if you agree that the amount scheduled is correct and that the category in which your claim or interest is scheduled (secured, unsecured, preferred stock, common stock, etc.) is correct. 11 U.S.C. § 1111(a).

If your claim or interest is not listed on the schedules or is scheduled as disputed, contingent, unliquidated or unknown, or you disagree with the amount or description scheduled for your claim or interest, you must file a proof of claim or interest.

Failure of a creditor or interest holder to file timely a proof of claim or interest on or before the deadline may result in disallowance of the claim or interest or subordination under the terms of a plan of reorganization without further notice or hearing. 11 U.S.C. § 502(b)(9).

Creditors and interest holders may wish to consult an attorney to protect their rights.

LBR 3007-1. OBJECTIONS TO CLAIMS

(a) OBJECTIONS.

(1) An objection to claim is a "contested matter" under FRBP 9014. Except to the extent otherwise provided in this rule, an objection to claim must comply with LBR 9013-1 and be titled "Motion for Order Disallowing Claim" unless the objection is to become an adversary proceeding pursuant to FRBP 3007(b).

(2) A claim objection must include the number, if any, assigned to the disputed claim on the court's claims register.

(3) A separate objection must be filed to each proof of claim unless:

(A) The objection pertains to multiple claims filed by the same creditor;

(B) The objection is an omnibus claim objection; or

(C) The court orders otherwise.

(4) An omnibus claim objection asserts the same type of objection to claims filed by different creditors (e.g., claims improperly filed as priority claims, duplicate claims, claims filed after the bar date, etc., as described in FRBP 3007(d)). In addition to the requirements set forth in FRBP 3007(e), an omnibus claim objection must:

(A) Identify the name of each claimant and the claim number in the caption of the objection; and

(B) Include as exhibits the documents supporting each claim objection organized and indexed by claim number.

(5) If more than 20 objections in a case are noticed for hearing on a single calendar, the objector must comply with the supplemental procedures contained in the Court Manual available from the clerk and on the court's website.

(b) NOTICE AND HEARING.

(1) A claim objection must be set for hearing on notice of not less than 30 days.

(2) The claim objection must be served on the claimant at the address disclosed by the claimant in its proof of claim and at such other addresses and upon such parties as may be required by FRBP 7004 and other applicable rules.

(3) Notice of the objection on or conforming to court-mandated form F 3007-1.3, Notice of Objection to Claim must be served with the claim objection. The notice must advise the claimant of the date, time, and place of hearing, and state:

(A) A response must be filed and served not later than 14 days prior to the date of hearing set forth in the notice; and

(B) If a response is not timely filed and served, the court may grant the relief requested in the objection without further notice or hearing.

(4) The court will conduct a hearing on a claim objection to which there is a timely response.

(5) If the claimant timely files and serves a response, the court, in its discretion, may treat the initial hearing as a status conference if it determines that the claim objection involves disputed fact issues or will require substantial time for presentation of evidence or argument.

(6) If the claimant does not timely file and serve a response, the court may sustain the objection and grant the motion for order disallowing the claim without a hearing.

(A) The objector must file a declaration attesting that no response was served upon the objector. The declaration must identify the docket number and filing date of the objection to claim, notice, and proof of service of the notice and objection to claim, and be served on the claimant.

(B) The objector must also lodge a proposed order prepared and served in accordance with LBR 9021-1 which provides for service of the entered order on the claimant and counsel, if any, and the United States trustee.

(c) EVIDENCE REQUIRED.

(1) An objection to claim must be supported by admissible evidence sufficient to overcome the evidentiary effect of a properly documented proof of claim executed and filed in accordance with FRBP 3001. The evidence must demonstrate that the proof of claim should be disallowed, reduced, subordinated, re-classified, or otherwise modified.

(2) A copy of the complete proof of claim, including attachments or exhibits, must be attached to the objection to claim, together with the objector's declaration stating that the copy of the claim attached is a true and complete copy of the proof of claim on file with the court, or, if applicable, of the informal claim to which objection is made.

(3) If the complete proof of claim is not readily available from the court file, the objector may formally request a copy from the holder of the claim by serving the creditor with a notice in substantially the same form as court-approved form F 3007-1.2, Notice of Request for a Copy of Proof of Claim.

(A) The request must advise the holder of the claim that failure to supply a complete copy of the proof of claim, including all attached documentation, within 30 days of the notice may constitute grounds for objection to the claim based on the claimant's failure to provide requested documentation to support the claim.

(B) If an objection is filed on this basis, it must be accompanied by a declaration providing evidence that the proof of claim was not readily available from the court file or otherwise.

(4) If the basis for the objection is that the proof of claim was filed after the bar date, the objection must include a copy of each of the following:

(A) The bar date order, if any;

(B) The notice of bar date; and

(C) Proof of service of the notice of bar date.

(5) If the basis for the objection is that there are duplicate proofs of claim, the objection must include a complete copy of each proof of claim.

LBR 3011-1. PROCEDURE FOR OBTAINING ORDERS RELEASING UNCLAIMED FUNDS

(a) FORM OF MOTION.

(1) An entity seeking the release of unclaimed funds pursuant to 28 U.S.C. § 2042 must file a motion in compliance with LBR 9013-1 using either court-approved form F 3011-1, Motion for Order Releasing Unclaimed Funds, or a motion containing all of the information and supporting evidence required by the court-approved form.

(2) The failure to comply with this requirement may result in denial of the motion without a hearing under LBR 9013-1.

(b) NOTICE.

(1) A motion for an order releasing unclaimed funds must be served on at least the following parties:

(A) United States attorney for the Central District of California;

(B) United States trustee for the Central District of California;

(C) The trustee appointed in the case and the trustee's counsel (if any);

(D) The debtor, debtor in possession, reorganized debtor, or other fiduciary appointed to supervise the distribution of funds and assets of the estate and its counsel (if any); and

(E) If movant is not the original creditor or an employee thereof, the original creditor, addressed to the attention of the managing officer or person of that creditor, if applicable, and upon the creditor's counsel (if any).

(2) The motion will be denied if not served properly on all parties listed in subsection (b)(1) of this rule.

LBR 3015-1. PROCEDURES REGARDING CHAPTER 13 CASES

(a) APPLICABILITY.

(1) Except as provided herein, this rule relates to chapter 13 cases in all divisions of the bankruptcy court and supersedes any previous orders in conflict with the provisions hereof.

(2) To the extent that this rule conflicts with any other provisions of the Local Bankruptcy Rules, the provisions of this rule prevail. In all other respects, the Local Bankruptcy Rules apply in all chapter 13 cases.

(b) FILING AND SERVICE OF PETITIONS, PLANS, PROOFS OF CLAIM, AND OTHER FORMS.

(1) Filing of Petition. An original and one copy of the petition, schedules and all other documents required to initiate the case must be filed with the court. If the petition is filed electronically, the debtor must provide court copies as required by the CM/ECF Procedures contained in the Court Manual available from the clerk and on the court's website.

Except as provided by FRBP 1019(1)(A), if the chapter 13 schedules, plan, and all other required documents are not filed with the petition, the clerk will issue a notice advising the debtor that, if the missing documents are not filed within 14 days from the date of the filing of the petition, the court may dismiss the case, unless the court grants a motion to extend time filed within the 14 days.

(2) Time Extension. A motion for extension of time must be accompanied by a declaration showing specific cause for an extension of time, the amount of additional time requested, the date the petition was filed, and a proof of service evidencing that the motion and declaration were served on the chapter 13 trustee.

The court may consider the motion without a hearing. If any schedule, the statement, or the plan is not filed within the initial 14 days or within such additional time as the court may allow in response to a timely motion for extension of time, the court may dismiss the case.

(3) Notice and Service. The debtor must serve a notice of the hearing on confirmation of debtor's chapter 13 plan, along with a copy of the chapter 13 plan, on all creditors and the chapter 13 trustee at least 28 days before the date first set for the § 341(a) meeting of creditors, using the court-mandated F 3015-1 form. A proof of service must be filed with the court and served on the chapter 13 trustee at least 14 days prior to the date first set for the meeting of creditors. Chapter 13 papers should not be served on the United States trustee, except as provided in subsection (q) of this rule or when the United States trustee serves as chapter 13 trustee.

(4) Forms. The chapter 13 petition, schedules, statement of financial affairs, and proofs of claim must be prepared on the appropriate Official Form, as required by FRBP 1007(b)(1). All other chapter 13 papers filed by the debtor must be filed using applicable court-mandated forms, if any, or be prepared in the same format.

Any modification to the text of an Official Form or court-mandated form must comply with LBR 9009-1.

If a court-mandated form is not used, the debtor must include a statement under penalty of perjury that either certifies that the document contains all of the language of the court-mandated form or specifies each respect in which the document differs from the court-mandated form.

(5) Proof of Claim. Each proof of claim must be filed in accordance with FRBP 3002 and must be served on the debtor's attorney or the debtor, if not represented by counsel, and on the chapter 13 trustee. Each proof of claim must include a proof of service.

(6) Domestic Support Obligations. In all cases in which there is a domestic support obligation, regardless of the entity holding such claim, the debtor must provide to the chapter 13 trustee within 14 days of the filing of the petition the name, current address, and current telephone number of the holder of the claim along with any applicable case number and account number. Throughout the duration of the case, the debtor must inform the chapter 13 trustee of any new or changed information regarding this requirement. Should a domestic support obligation arise after the filing of the petition, the debtor must provide the required information to the chapter 13 trustee as soon as practicable but no later than 14 days after the duty arises to pay the domestic support obligation.

(c) MEETING OF CREDITORS—§ 341(A).

(1) Notice and Service. Notice of the § 341(a) meeting of creditors and initial confirmation hearing date along with a proof of claim form will be served on all creditors by the court at least 28 days before the date first set for the § 341(a) meeting of creditors.

(2) Attendance Requirement. The debtor and debtor's attorney (if any) must attend the § 341(a) meeting of creditors. If the case is a joint case, both debtors must appear.

(3) Evidence of Income. The debtor must provide evidence of current income (pay stubs, tax returns, or other equivalent documentation) to the chapter 13 trustee at least 7 days before the § 341(a) meeting of creditors. If income from third party contributors will be used to fund the plan, the debtor must also provide evidence (declarations and pay stubs or other appropriate evidence) of the commitment and ability of the third party to make payments.

(4) Required Reports in a Business Case. If the debtor is operating a business or is otherwise self-employed, the debtor must submit to the chapter 13 trustee, at least 7 days before the § 341(a) meeting of creditors, the following reports required to investigate the acts, conduct, assets, liabilities, and financial condition of the debtor, the operation of the debtor's business, and the feasibility of such business:

(A) Projection of average monthly income and expenses for the next 12 months;

(B) Evidence of appropriate business insurance;

(C) Inventory of goods as well as a list of business furnishings and equipment as of the date of the filing of the petition;

(D) Monthly income and expense statements for at least the 6 months preceding the date of the filing of the petition, or for such shorter time if the business has been in operation for less than the requisite 6 months, signed by the debtor under penalty of perjury, including a statement regarding incurred and unpaid expenses;

(E) Tax returns for at least 5 years or since the start of the business, whichever period is shorter; and

(F) Such other evidence requested by the chapter 13 trustee, including bank statements, canceled checks, contracts, or other information relevant to the debtor's ability to fund the proposed plan.

(5) Other Required Documents. The debtor must submit to the chapter 13 trustee, at least 7 days before the § 341(a) meeting of creditors, the Declaration re Payment of Domestic Support Obligation (Pre-confirmation), the Declaration re Tax Returns (Pre-confirmation), and any other required documents.

(6) Failure to Comply. If the debtor fails to comply with any of the requirements of subsection (c) of this rule, such failure may result in:

(A) Disgorgement of attorneys' fees if the failure is attributed to the debtor's attorney;

(B) Continuance of the § 341(a) meeting or confirmation hearing; and/or

(C) Dismissal of the case either (i) without prejudice or (ii) with a 180-day bar to refiling pursuant to 11 U.S.C. § 109(g), if the court finds willful failure of the debtor to abide by orders of the court or to appear before the court in proper prosecution of the case.

(d) CONFIRMATION HEARING. The debtor's attorney or the debtor, if not represented by counsel, must appear at the confirmation hearing unless specifically excused by court order or by the trustee prior to the confirmation hearing in conformance with procedures of the judge to whom the case is assigned.

(1) Varied Calendaring and Appearance Procedures. The judges of this district do not have a uniform policy governing calendaring and appearance at a confirmation hearing. Some judges allow confirmation to take place as early as the date of the § 341(a) meeting of creditors and without court appearance by any party if there are no timely objections to confirmation or all such objections have been resolved.

Some judges require a hearing on all plan confirmations but excuse appearances by the debtor and debtor's attorney (if any) if there are no timely objections to confirmation or all such objections have been resolved. Some judges require a hearing on all plan confirmations and appearance by the debtor and debtor's attorney (if any), regardless of whether there are unresolved objections to confirmation.

Because of this variance in procedure, parties in interest are advised to contact the chapter 13 trustee assigned to the case, consult the chapter 13 trustee's website, or refer to the court's website as it may pertain to the requirements of an individual judge.

(2) Preparation of Order Confirming Plan. Unless otherwise ordered by the court, the chapter 13 trustee will prepare and lodge a proposed Order Confirming Plan ("Order"). The Order will state the amount of the debtor's attorney's fees and costs allowed by the court. If a Rights and Responsibilities Agreement has been signed by the attorney and debtor, filed, and served on the chapter 13 trustee, the order will provide for the amount set forth in that agreement, unless the court orders otherwise.

(e) PERSONAL PROPERTY, INCLUDING VEHICLES.

(1) Postpetition Payments. The plan may provide that postpetition contractual payments on leases of personal property and claims secured by personal property, including vehicles, will be made directly to the creditor. All such direct payments must be made as they come due postpetition. If there are arrearages or the plan changes the amount of payment, duration, or interest rate for any reason, including the fact that a portion of the claim is deemed unsecured, then all payments so provided in the plan must be paid through the chapter 13 trustee. If the plan provides for postpetition contractual payments to be made through the chapter 13 trustee, the debtor must pay the lease and adequate protection payments required by 11 U.S.C. §§ 1326(a)(1)(B) and 1326(a)(1)(C) through the chapter 13 trustee.

(2) Property Surrendered in Confirmed Plan. When the confirmed plan provides for the surrender or abandonment of property, the trustee is relieved from making any payments on the creditor's related secured claim, without prejudice to the creditor's right to file an amended unsecured claim for a deficiency, when appropriate.

(f) DOMESTIC SUPPORT OBLIGATIONS. The plan may provide for current payments of domestic support obligations directly to the creditor. Arrearages must be paid through the chapter 13 trustee unless specific cause is shown, supported by appropriate declaration or other admissible evidence.

(g) OBJECTIONS TO PLAN.

(1) Filing and Service. Objections, if any, to the confirmation of the plan must be in writing, supported by appropriate declarations or other admissible evidence, filed with the court, and served on debtor's attorney, the debtor (if not represented by counsel), and the chapter 13 trustee not less than 7 days before the § 341(a) meeting of creditors.

(2) Form of Objection and Caption.

(A) WRITTEN. A written objection must state in the caption the date, time, and place of the § 341(a) meeting of creditors and the date, time, and place of the confirmation hearing.

(B) ORAL. Notwithstanding subsection (g)(1), an oral objection may be made on the record at the § 341(a) meeting of creditors by any party in interest.

(3) Failure to Object or to Prosecute Objection. The failure either to file a written objection on a timely basis or to appear at the § 341(a) meeting of creditors to prosecute the objection may be deemed a waiver of the objection.

(4) Attendance. Any creditor who objects to confirmation of the plan should attend both the § 341(a) meeting of creditors and the confirmation hearing if the objection is not resolved. If the objecting creditor does not appear at the confirmation hearing, the court may overrule the objection.

(h) AMENDMENTS TO PLAN PRIOR TO CONFIRMATION.

(1) Filing and Service. If a debtor wishes the court to confirm a plan other than the plan originally filed with the court, an amended plan must be received by the chapter 13 trustee and filed with the court at least 7 days before the confirmation hearing. If the amended plan will adversely affect any creditor (for example, if it treats any creditor's claim less favorably than the previously filed plan), the amended plan must also be served on all affected creditors at least 28 days before the confirmation hearing. Failure to comply with these requirements may result in continuance of the confirmation hearing or dismissal of the case.

(2) Form of Amendment and Caption. The caption of an amended plan must identify the pleading as an amended plan (e.g., "First Amended Plan," "Second Amended Plan,") and must state the date, time, and place of the confirmation hearing at which the debtor will seek confirmation.

(3) Amended Plan Payments. If the debtor has filed an amended plan prior to confirmation, the plan payments that come due after the date the amended plan is filed must be made in the amount stated in the amended plan, which may be higher or lower than the amount stated in the original plan. Where successive amended plans are filed, any plan payment that comes due must be made in the amount stated in the most recently filed amended plan.

(i) AMENDMENTS TO PLAN AT THE CONFIRMATION HEARING. An amendment to a plan which does not adversely affect creditors may be made at the confirmation hearing by interlineation in the confirmation order. The proponent should give the chapter 13 trustee an opportunity to review the proposed amendment prior to the confirmation hearing.

(j) OBJECTIONS TO CLAIMS.

(1) Filing and Service. An objection to claim must: (A) be filed with the court and served, subject to subsection (x) of this rule, on the chapter 13 trustee and affected creditor; (B) identify the claim by both the claim number on the court's docket and the claim number on the chapter 13 trustee's docket; (C) give notice of the date, time, and courtroom of hearing on the face of the objection; and (D) comply with LBR 3007-1.

(2) Payments on Claim. Pending resolution, the chapter 13 trustee will make payments on only the uncontroverted portion of the claim subject to an objection, until such time as the court orders otherwise.

(k) PLAN PAYMENTS TO CHAPTER 13 TRUSTEE.

(1) Plan Payment Procedure.

(A) Plan payments are due on the same day of each month beginning not later than 30 days after the petition is filed. If the case was converted from chapter 7, the first plan payment is due 30 days from the date of conversion. However, if the plan payment due date falls on the 29th, 30th, or 31st of the month, then the plan payment is due on the 1st of the following month. Unless otherwise instructed by the assigned chapter 13 trustee, all plan payments that accrue before the § 341(a) meeting of creditors must be tendered, in the form described in subsection (k)(3) of this rule, to the chapter 13 trustee or the trustee's representative at the § 341(a) meeting of creditors.

(B) All plan payments that accrue after the § 341(a) meeting of creditors but prior to confirmation must be tendered on a timely basis to the chapter 13 trustee, as instructed by the chapter 13 trustee at the § 341(a) meeting of creditors.

(C) All plan payments that accrue after confirmation of the plan must be sent to the address provided by the chapter 13 trustee.

(D) To the extent debtor has made plan payments under an original or modified plan prior to confirmation that differ from payments required by the confirmed plan, the confirmation order must account for plan payments made through the date of confirmation and adjust the on-going plan payments accordingly so that the debtor will complete payment of all plan amounts within the term of the confirmed plan.

(2) Adequate Protection Payments. The debtor cannot reduce the amount of the plan payments to the chapter 13 trustee under 11 U.S.C. §§ 1326(a)(1)(B) or 1326(a)(1)(C) without an order of the court.

(A) Pending confirmation of the plan, the chapter 13 trustee will promptly transmit payments received from the debtor as proposed in the debtor's chapter 13 plan to a creditor holding an allowed claim secured by personal property where such security interest is attributable to the purchase of such property.

(B) The chapter 13 trustee may assess an administrative fee for effecting the payments required in subsection (k)(2)(A) of this rule and may collect such fee at the time of making the payment. The allowed expense fee must be no more than the percentage fee established by the Attorney General pursuant to 28 U.S.C. § 586(e)(1)(B) in effect at the time of the disbursement.

(C) Should the case be dismissed or converted prior to or at the hearing on confirmation of the plan, any portion of the balance on hand which has been tendered to the chapter 13 trustee for adequate protection must be disbursed to the creditor to whom those adequate protection payments are owed as soon as practicable.

(3) Form of Payment. Unless and until a payroll deduction order is effective, all plan payments must be in the form of cashier's check, certified funds, or money order made payable to the "Chapter 13 Trustee" and tendered by the debtor as instructed by the chapter 13 trustee. The court may require plan payments through a payroll deduction order. If a payroll deduction order is not issued upon confirmation of a plan or authorized in the confirmation order, whenever a plan payment is more than 20 days late, the chapter 13 trustee may bring a noticed motion requesting the court to issue such an order. The issued order must be served upon the debtor's employer, the debtor, and the debtor's attorney (if any).

(4) Dismissal or Conversion for Non-Payment. If the debtor fails to make a plan payment, the case may be dismissed or converted to a case under chapter 7. If the case is dismissed for willful failure of the debtor to abide by an order of the court, or to appear before the court in proper prosecution of the case, the court may impose a 180-day bar to refiling in accordance with 11 U.S.C. § 109(g).

(l) CHAPTER 13 TRUSTEE'S FEES. The minimum trustee's fee for a chapter 13 in which a plan is not confirmed is $100. The minimum trustee's fee in a case where the plan is confirmed is $200.

(m) PAYMENTS ON MORTGAGES OR TRUST DEEDS.

(1) Scope of Rule. The term "Real Property" as used in this subsection includes both (A) commercial and residential real property and undeveloped land owned by the debtor; and (B) mobile and manufactured homes owned by the debtor and installed on a permanent foundation or used as a dwelling, but does not include any property that the debtor's filed plan specifically states will be surrendered.

(2) Postpetition Payment Procedure. Except for plans in which the debtor elects to make postpetition mortgage payments through the plan, until a plan is confirmed, a debtor must pay in a timely manner directly to each secured creditor all payments that fall due postpetition on debt secured by Real Property, as defined above, and must provide evidence of such payments on court-mandated form F 3015-1.4 in the manner set forth below.

(3) Payment Through Plan. If the debtor elects to pay postpetition mortgage payments through the plan, then the amount of this payment must be included in each monthly plan payment tendered both pre- and postconfirmation to the chapter 13 trustee.

(4) Determination of Due Date. With the exception of the payment due for the month in which the petition is filed (the "Filing Month Payment"), the due date of a payment for the purpose of this subsection is the last day that the payment may be made without a late charge or penalty. The due date of the Filing Month Payment will be the date on which such payment first becomes due under the terms of the applicable promissory note. If that date falls on or before the petition date, the Filing Month Payment will be considered prepetition and need not be paid in order to comply with this subsection.

(5) Form of Payment. The payments required by subsection (m)(2) of this rule must be in the form of money order, cashier's check, wire transfer (including direct payments over the internet or by automatic withdrawals from the debtor's checking account), or other certified funds and must indicate on each item the debtor's name, the bankruptcy case number, and the appropriate loan number or credit account number.

(6) Evidence of Payment. On or before each of the following dates, the debtor must file with the court and serve on the chapter 13 trustee and all secured creditors to whom the debtor is required to make payments under this subsection a declaration executed under penalty of perjury, on court-mandated form F 3015-1.4, evidencing that the debtor has made all of the payments required by subsection (m)(2) or (3) of this rule: (A) the date scheduled for each § 341(a) meeting of creditors; and (B) the date of each hearing to consider confirmation of a chapter 13 plan in the case. Copies of all money orders, cashier's checks or other instruments used to make the payments must be attached to the form.

(7) Submission of Declarations. The debtor must bring a copy of an executed form F 3015-1.4, together with a proof of service reflecting service in accordance with this subsection, to the initial § 341(a) meeting of creditors. The form must reflect all payments made between the date of the petition and the date of the initial § 341(a) meeting of creditors. Thereafter, the debtor must bring an updated form to each continued § 341(a) meeting of creditors and each confirmation hearing, together with proof of service reflecting service of the form in accordance with this subsection. Each updated form must reflect, cumulatively, all payments made between the date of the petition and the date of the form. If the debtor owns more than one Real Property, the debtor must prepare and submit a separate form F 3015-1.4 for each Real Property.

(8) Failure to Make Postpetition Payments. Failure to make all of the payments required by subsection (m)(2) or (3) of this rule in a timely manner will generally result in dismissal of the case. In determining whether a debtor has complied with this subsection at a confirmation hearing, the court will disregard payments as to which a late penalty has not yet accrued or which are due on the date of the confirmation hearing. The failure to submit form F 3015-1.4 at each § 341(a) meeting of creditors and each confirmation hearing, with all required attachments, may result in dismissal of the case, and the court may impose a 180-day bar against refiling pursuant to 11 U.S.C. § 109(g).

(n) MODIFICATION OF CONFIRMED PLAN OR SUSPENSION OF PLAN PAYMENTS. After a chapter 13 plan has been confirmed, its terms can be modified only by court order. A motion to modify a confirmed plan or to suspend plan payments must be made in accordance with subsections (w) and (x) of this rule and must be filed using court-mandated forms.

(o) TAX RETURNS. For each year a case is pending after the confirmation of a plan, the debtor must provide to the chapter 13 trustee within 14 days after the return is filed with the appropriate tax agencies a copy of: (1) the debtor's federal and state tax returns; (2) any request for extension of the deadline for filing a return; and (3) the debtor's forms W-2 and 1099.

(p) SALE OR REFINANCE OF REAL PROPERTY. A sale or refinancing of the debtor's principal residence or other real property must be approved by the court. A motion to approve a sale or refinance of real property may be made by noticed motion in accordance with subsections (w) and (x) of this rule.

(q) DISMISSAL OR CONVERSION.

(1) Voluntary Dismissal.

(A) DEBTOR'S REQUEST FOR DISMISSAL. If the case has not been converted from another chapter, a debtor may seek dismissal of the case by filing with the clerk of the bankruptcy court a request for voluntary dismissal pursuant to 11 U.S.C. § 1307(b) and a proof of service evidencing that the request for dismissal was served upon the chapter 13 trustee and the United States trustee.

(B) MOTION FOR VOLUNTARY DISMISSAL. If the case has been converted from another chapter, a debtor must seek dismissal by motion filed and served in accordance with LBR 9013-1(o). The motion must comply with LBR 1017-2(f). Notice must be given to the chapter 13 trustee, any former trustee, all creditors, and any other party in interest entitled to notice under FRBP 2002.

(C) MANDATORY DISCLOSURE. Whether dismissal is sought by request or motion, debtor must disclose under penalty of perjury whether the present case has been converted from another chapter of the Bankruptcy Code, and whether any motion for relief from, annulment of, or conditioning of the automatic stay has been filed against the debtor in the present case.

(2) Debtor Conversion of Chapter 13 to Chapter 7. Pursuant to FRBP 1017 and LBR 1017-1(a)(1), the conversion of a chapter 13 case to a case under chapter 7 will be effective upon:

(A) The filing by the debtor with the clerk of the bankruptcy court of a notice of conversion pursuant to 11 U.S.C. § 1307(a) and a proof of service evidencing that the notice of conversion was served upon the chapter 13 trustee and the United States trustee, and

(B) Payment of any fee required by 28 U.S.C. § 1930(b); provided however,

(C) Any distributions of estate funds made by the chapter 13 trustee in the ordinary course of business for the benefit of the debtor's estate prior to receipt of notice of dismissal or conversion will not be surcharged to the chapter 13 trustee.

(3) Debtor Conversion of Chapter 13 to Chapter 11. A motion by the debtor to convert a chapter 13 case to a case under chapter 11 must be noticed for hearing.

(4) Interested Party Dismissal or Conversion of Chapter 13 to Chapter 7, 11, or 12. A motion by any other party in interest to either dismiss a chapter 13 case, or alternatively, to convert a chapter 13 case to a case under chapter 7, 11, or 12, must be noticed for hearing by the moving party. This notice must be given to the debtor, debtor's attorney (if any), all creditors, the chapter 13 trustee, any former trustee, and the United States trustee.

(5) Lodging and Service of Order. When an order is required, the moving party must prepare and lodge the proposed order of dismissal or conversion in accordance with LBR 9021-1. Notwithstanding LBR 9021-1(b)(1)(D) and (E), no copies or envelopes are required to be lodged along with the proposed order, as the clerk will prepare a separate notice of dismissal or conversion.

(r) MOTIONS REGARDING STAY OF 11 U.S.C. § 362.

(1) Required Format and Information. A motion regarding the stay of 11 U.S.C. § 362 must comply with LBR 4001-1.

(2) Default Motions.

(A) PRECONFIRMATION DEFAULT. A motion for relief from the automatic stay based solely upon a preconfirmation payment default is premature until a late charge has accrued under the contract on the postpetition obligation that the creditor seeks to enforce. If no late charge is provided, the motion may be brought 14 days after the postpetition payment is due. A motion for relief from stay based on other grounds may be brought at any time.

(B) POSTCONFIRMATION DEFAULT. A motion for relief from the automatic stay based solely on postconfirmation payment default is premature until a late charge has accrued under the contract on the obligation that the creditor seeks to enforce. If no late charge is provided, the motion may be brought 14 days after payment is due.

(3) Stipulations Regarding the Stay of 11 U.S.C. § 362. A stipulation for relief from the automatic stay or to modify the automatic stay, or to impose or continue the stay, does not require the consent or signature of the chapter 13 trustee but must be prepared and lodged in accordance with LBR 4001-1(b)(2)(B).

(4) Payments after Relief from Automatic Stay. If an order for relief from the automatic stay is granted, unless otherwise specified in the order, the chapter 13 trustee is relieved from making any further payments to the secured creditor that obtained such relief. The secured portion of that creditor's claim is deemed withdrawn upon entry of the order for relief, without prejudice to filing an amended unsecured claim for a deficiency when appropriate. The secured creditor that obtains relief from the automatic stay must return to the chapter 13 trustee any payments the creditor receives from the chapter 13 trustee after entry of the order unless the stipulation or order provides otherwise.

(5) Shortened Notice Hearing. A hearing on a motion for relief from the automatic stay on shortened notice may be sought pursuant to LBR 9075-1(b).

(6) No Surcharge of Chapter 13 Trustee. The chapter 13 trustee will not be surcharged for any distribution of funds in the ordinary course of business prior to receiving written notice that the automatic stay is not in effect or a claim should not be paid.

(s) POSTCONFIRMATION ADEQUATE PROTECTION ORDERS.

(1) Filing and Service. After confirmation of a plan, if the debtor and a secured creditor propose to modify the payments by the chapter 13 trustee to the secured creditor by way of an adequate protection/relief from the automatic stay agreement, the debtor or creditor must file and serve a motion for an order approving the modification of the plan by said agreement pursuant to subsections (w) and (x) of this rule.

(2) Payments Pending Plan Modification. Notwithstanding court approval of an adequate protection/relief from the automatic stay agreement, the trustee will continue to make payments and otherwise perform the trustee's duties in accordance with the plan as confirmed unless: (A) the debtor receives a separate court order approving a modification to the plan; or (B) the adequate protection/relief from the automatic stay agreement specifically modifies the treatment of the claim under the confirmed plan.

(t) DISCHARGE PROCEDURES.

(1) General. When the chapter 13 trustee has completed payments under the plan and all other plan provisions have been consummated, the clerk will give to the debtor and the debtor's attorney (if any), a Notice of Requirement to File a Debtor's Certification of Compliance Under 11 U.S.C. § 1328 and Application for Entry of Discharge. Before any discharge may be entered, the debtor must comply with the requirements of the Certification of Compliance and file the certification with the court.

(2) Instructional Course on Personal Financial Management. Debtor must also file a certification that an instructional course concerning personal financial management, as required by 11 U.S.C. § 1328(g)(1), has been completed or that completion of such course is not required under 11 U.S.C. § 1328(g)(2).

(3) Case Closure Without Discharge. If the certifications required by this subsection have not been filed within 60 days of the notice provided under subsection (t)(1) of this rule, then the case may be closed without an entry of discharge.

(u) ATTORNEY REPRESENTATION.

(1) Scope of Employment. LBR 2090-1(a) is modified in chapter 13 cases as follows:

Any attorney who is retained to represent a debtor in a chapter 13 case is responsible for representing the debtor on all matters arising in the case, other than adversary proceedings, subject to the provisions of a "Rights and Responsibilities Agreement Between Chapter 13 Debtors and Their Attorneys," into which the debtor and the attorney have entered and that complies with these rules.

(2) Debtor Unavailable or Unopposed to Request, Application, or Motion Scheduled for Hearing. If an attorney for a debtor is unable to contact the debtor in connection with a request, application or motion (e.g., a motion for relief from the automatic stay) that is scheduled for a hearing, the attorney may file and serve a statement informing the court of this fact. If a debtor does not oppose the request, application or motion, the attorney may file a statement so informing the court and need not appear at the hearing.

(3) Change of Address. An attorney representing a chapter 13 debtor must provide written notice to the chapter 13 trustee and to the court of any change to the attorney's address during the pendency of the case as required by LBR 2090-1(f).

(v) ATTORNEYS' FEES.

(1) Rights and Responsibilities Agreement. The use of court-approved form F 3015-1.7, Rights and Responsibilities Agreement Between Chapter 13 Debtors and Their Attorneys ("RARA") in any case is optional. However, if the debtor's attorney elects to proceed under the RARA, the RARA form is mandatory. If the RARA form is signed by the attorney and the debtor, filed, and served on the chapter 13 trustee, the fees and included costs (excluding the petition filing fee) outlined therein may be approved without further detailed fee application or hearing, subject to the terms of both the RARA and the Guidelines for Allowance of Attorneys' Fees in Chapter 13 Cases ("Guidelines") adopted by the court.

(2) Duties of Debtors and their Attorneys if the RARA is Signed, Filed, and Served. The RARA sets forth the duties and obligations that must be performed by the debtor and debtor's attorney, both before and after the case is filed and before and after confirmation of a plan, if the parties elect to use the RARA. The RARA also specifies the fees that the attorney will charge and the procedures for seeking and objecting to payment of fees. An attorney who elects to use the RARA may not charge more than the maximum fees outlined in subsection (v)(1) of this rule for performing services described in bold face type in the RARA. If the attorney performs tasks on behalf of the debtor not set forth in bold face, the attorney may apply to the court for additional fees and costs, but such applications will be reviewed by both the chapter 13 trustee and the court. Counsel may apply for additional fees if and when justified by the facts of the case.

An application for additional fees and costs must be made by noticed motion subject to subsections (w) and (x) of this rule. The application must be supported by evidence of the nature, necessity, and reasonableness of the additional services rendered and expenses incurred. When additional fees are sought, the court may, in its discretion, require additional supporting information or require a hearing, even though no opposition is filed. In such application, the applicant must disclose to the court any fees paid or costs reimbursed by the debtor and the source of those payments.

If the parties elect to utilize the RARA, the lists of duties and obligations set forth in the RARA may not be modified by the parties. Other portions of the RARA may be modified in the following respects only: (A) the attorneys' fees provided for in the RARA may be reduced; and (B) the agreement may be supplemented to include any additional agreements that may exist between the parties concerning the fees and expenses that the attorney will charge for performing services required by the RARA that are not in bold face type.

(3) Debtor's Signature. The debtor's signature on the RARA certifies that the debtor has read, understands, and agrees to the best of the debtor's ability to carry out the terms of the RARA and has received a signed copy of the RARA.

(4) Attorney's Signature. The attorney's signature on the RARA certifies that before the case was filed the attorney personally met with, counseled, and explained to the debtor all matters set forth in the RARA and verified the number and status of any prior bankruptcy case(s) filed by the debtor or any related entity, as set forth in LBR 1015-2. The RARA does not constitute the written fee agreement contemplated by the California Business and Professions Code.

(5) An Attorney May Elect to be Paid other than Pursuant to the RARA and the Guidelines. At any time, whether or not a RARA is on file in any case, the debtor's attorney may elect to seek an allowance of fees and costs other than pursuant to the RARA and the Guidelines. In that event, the attorney must file and serve an application for fees in accordance with 11 U.S.C. §§ 330 and 331, FRBP 2016 and 2002, and LBR 2016-1 and 3015-1, as well as the "Guide to Applications for Professional Compensation" issued by the United States trustee for the Central District of California.

(6) Court Review of any Attorney's Fee. Upon notice and opportunity for hearing, the court may review any attorney's fee agreement or payment, in accordance with 11 U.S.C. § 329 and FRBP 2017.

(7) Payment of Fees Upon Dismissal. Unless otherwise ordered by the court, the chapter 13 trustee must disburse to the debtor's attorney as soon as practicable after dismissal any portion of the balance on hand which has been tendered to the chapter 13 trustee for payment of the RARA fees, provided:

(A) A RARA was signed by the debtor's attorney and the debtor, filed, and served on the chapter 13 trustee; and

(B) The debtor's case is dismissed prior to or at the hearing on confirmation of the plan.

(w) MOTIONS AND APPLICATIONS FILED ON NOTICE OF OPPORTUNITY TO REQUEST A HEARING.

(1) Motions and Applications. The following motions and applications may be made on notice of opportunity to request a hearing pursuant to LBR 9013-1(o):

(A) Chapter 13 trustee's motion to modify a confirmed plan or dismiss a case;

(B) Motion to modify a confirmed plan or to suspend or extend plan payments, subject to subsections (n) and (x) of this rule, provided that 21 days notice of the motion is given in accordance with FRBP 3015(g);

(C) Motion for approval of sale or refinancing of debtor's residence, subject to subsection (p) of this rule, if the entire equity therein is exempt from the claims of creditors; provided, however, notice is not required if the sale or refinance will pay off the plan and the plan allows 100% to the unsecured claims; and

(D) Application for supplemental attorney's fees, subject to subsections (u), (v) and (x) of this rule.

(2) No Response Filed. If no response has been timely filed and served with respect to a motion or application listed in subsection (w)(1) of this rule, or the chapter 13 trustee's only response is to take no position, the provisions of LBR 9013-1(o)(3) must be complied with, subject to the following modifications:

(A) MOTION TO MODIFY A CONFIRMED PLAN OR TO SUSPEND OR EXTEND PLAN PAYMENTS. The declaration must also attest that the chapter 13 trustee did not timely file and serve a response to the motion, and the declaration and proposed order must be served on the chapter 13 trustee.

(B) APPLICATION FOR SUPPLEMENTAL FEES. The declaration must attest that the chapter 13 trustee did not timely file and serve a response to the application, or took no position, and the declaration and proposed order must be served on the chapter 13 trustee.

(3) Response Filed. If a response is filed with respect to any motion or application listed in subsection (w)(1) of this rule, the provisions of

LBR 9013-1(o)(4) must be complied with, subject to the following modifications:

(A) TRUSTEE'S MOTION TO DISMISS A CASE; TRUSTEE'S MOTION TO MODIFY A CONFIRMED PLAN. The person or entity who timely files and serves a response to a trustee's motion to dismiss a case, or a trustee's motion to modify a confirmed plan, must obtain a hearing date from the court (or use the court'self-calendaring system) and serve notice of the hearing with the response.

(B) DEBTOR'S MOTION TO MODIFY A CONFIRMED PLAN OR SUSPEND OR EXTEND PLAN PAYMENTS. If the chapter 13 trustee timely files and serves any comments regarding the motion, the chapter 13 trustee must promptly lodge a proposed order, electronically via LOU, using court-mandated form F 3015-1.12, and serve the proposed order on the debtor (and debtor's attorney, if any).

(C) APPLICATION FOR SUPPLEMENTAL FEES. If the chapter 13 trustee timely files and serves any comments regarding the application, the chapter 13 trustee must promptly lodge a proposed order, electronically via LOU, using court-mandated form F 3015-1.12, and serve the proposed order on the applicant.

(x) SERVICE OF MOTIONS AND APPLICATIONS. All motions and applications must be served, subject to the electronic service provisions of LBR 9036-1, on the chapter 13 trustee, debtor (and debtor's attorney, if any), and all creditors, with the following exceptions:

(1) A chapter 13 trustee's motion to dismiss a case need be served only on the debtor, debtor's attorney (if any), any prior chapter 7 trustee, and that trustee's attorney (if any);

(2) An objection to a claim need be served only on the chapter 13 trustee, the claimant, and the claimant's attorney (if any). If the claimant is the United States or an officer or agency of the United States, the objection must be served as provided in FRBP 7004(b)(4) and (5) and LBR 2002-2;

(3) A motion for modification, suspension, or extension of the due date of plan payments must be filed using court-mandated forms and must be served on the chapter 13 trustee, but need not be served on creditors if: (A) the proposed modification does not have an adverse effect on the rights of creditors; or (B) the proposed suspension or extension, combined with any prior approved suspensions or extensions, does not exceed 90 days of suspended payments or 90 days of extensions to the plan's term. Any other motion for modification, suspension, or extension must be served on all creditors pursuant to LBR 9013-1(o) in addition to being served on the chapter 13 trustee;

(4) A motion regarding the stay of 11 U.S.C. § 362, which is subject to the notice and service requirements of LBR 4001-1; and

(5) An application by debtor's counsel for additional fees and costs not exceeding $1,000 over and above the limits set forth in the RARA and Guidelines need be served only on the chapter 13 trustee and the debtor.

LBR 3016-1. FORM OF CHAPTER 11 PLAN

Unless otherwise ordered, a plan of reorganization filed with the court may, but need not, conform with court-approved form F 3018-1, Form of Chapter 11 Plan.

LBR 3016-2. FORM OF CHAPTER 11 DISCLOSURE STATEMENT

Unless otherwise ordered, a disclosure statement filed with the court may, but need not, conform with court-approved form F 3017-1, Chapter 11 Disclosure Statement Form.

LBR 3017-1. CHAPTER 11 DISCLOSURE STATEMENT—APPROVAL IN CASE OTHER THAN SMALL BUSINESS CASE

(a) NOTICE OF HEARING ON MOTION FOR APPROVAL OF DISCLOSURE STATEMENT. A hearing on a motion for approval of a disclosure statement must not be set on less than 36 days notice, unless the court, for good cause shown, prescribes a shorter period.

(b) OBJECTIONS TO DISCLOSURE STATEMENT. Objections to a disclosure statement must be filed and served on the proponent not less than 14 days before the hearing, unless otherwise ordered by the court.

LBR 3017-2. CHAPTER 11 DISCLOSURE STATEMENT—APPROVAL IN SMALL BUSINESS CASE

(a) CONDITIONAL APPROVAL OF DISCLOSURE STATEMENT. The court may, on application of the plan proponent or sua sponte, conditionally grant a motion for approval of a disclosure statement filed in accordance with 11 U.S.C. § 1125(f) and FRBP 3016.

(b) PROCEDURE FOR REQUESTING CONDITIONAL APPROVAL OF DISCLOSURE STATEMENT. The plan proponent may file an ex parte motion for conditional approval of the disclosure statement, asking that the hearing on the adequacy of the disclosure statement be combined with the hearing on confirmation. The motion must be supported by a declaration establishing grounds for conditional approval and accompanied by a proposed order consistent with FRBP 2002(b) that conditionally approves the disclosure statement and establishes:

(1) A date by which the holders of claims and interests may accept or reject the plan;

(2) A date for filing objections to the disclosure statement;

(3) A date for the hearing on final approval of the disclosure statement to be held if a timely objection is filed; and

(4) A date for the hearing on confirmation of the plan.

(c) OBJECTIONS AND HEARING ON FINAL APPROVAL.

(1) The debtor must file and serve a notice of the dates set forth above, together with a copy of the disclosure statement and plan, on all creditors and the United States trustee.

(2) Final approval of the disclosure statement is required only when a timely objection is filed and served on the debtor, the trustee (if any), any committee appointed under the Bankruptcy Code, counsel for any of the foregoing, and any other entity as ordered by the court.

LBR 3018-1. BALLOTS—VOTING ON CHAPTER 11 PLAN

(a) BALLOT SUMMARY. The plan proponent must:

(1) Tabulate the ballots of those accepting or rejecting the plan;

(2) File a ballot summary not later than 1 day before the hearing on the motion for order confirming the plan. The ballot summary must be signed by the plan proponent and must certify to the court the amount and number of allowed claims of each class voting to accept or reject the plan and the amount of allowed interests of each class voting to accept or reject the plan; and

(3) Make available at the hearing all of the original ballots for inspection and review by the court and any interested party.

(b) AMENDED BALLOT SUMMARY. In addition to the requirements set forth in subsection (a) of this rule, the court may order an amended ballot summary to be filed with the original ballots attached.

LBR 3020-1. CHAPTER 11 PLAN CONFIRMATION

(a) PAYMENT OF SPECIAL CHARGES. The proposed plan confirmation order must be accompanied by proof of payment of any and all special charges due to the clerk's office.

The amount of the charges to be paid may be obtained from the courtroom deputy of the judge hearing the case.

(b) POSTCONFIRMATION REQUIREMENTS. Unless otherwise provided in the plan, every order confirming a chapter 11 plan must contain the following language:

"Within 120 days of the entry of this order, shall file a status report explaining what progress has been made toward consummation of the confirmed plan of reorganization. The initial report shall be served on the United States trustee, the 20 largest unsecured creditors, and those parties who have requested special notice. Further reports shall be filed every days thereafter and served on the same entities, unless otherwise ordered by the court. [Optional depending on practices of particular judge: A postconfirmation status conference will be held on ___________, 20______ at.m. in Courtroom.]

The status report shall include at least the following information:

(1) A schedule listing for each debt and each class of claims: the total amount required to be paid under the plan; the amount required to be paid as of the date of the report; the amount actually paid as of the date of the report; and the deficiency, if any, in required payments;

(2) A schedule of any and all postconfirmation tax liabilities that have accrued or come due and a detailed explanation of payments thereon;

(3) Debtor's projections as to its continuing ability to comply with the terms of the plan;

(4) An estimate of the date for plan consummation and application for final decree; and

(5) Any other pertinent information needed to explain the progress toward completion of the confirmed plan.

Reporting entities whose equity securities are registered under Section 12(b) of the Securities Exchange Act of 1934 may provide information from their latest 10Q or 10K filing with the S.E.C., if it is responsive to the requirements of this subsection.

Unless otherwise provided in the plan, if the above-referenced case is converted to one under chapter 7, the property of the reorganized debtor shall be revested in the chapter 7 estate, except that, in individual cases, the postpetition income from personal services and proceeds thereof, and postconfirmation gifts or inheritances pursuant to 11 U.S.C. §§ 541(a)(5)(A), 541(a)(6), 1115(a) or 1115(b), shall not automatically revest in the chapter 7 estate."

(c) EFFECT OF FAILURE TO FILE POSTCONFIRMATION REPORTS. The failure to file timely the required reports is cause for dismissal or conversion to a case under chapter 7 pursuant to 11 U.S.C. § 1112(b).

(d) FINAL DECREE IN CHAPTER 11 CASE.

(1) After an estate is fully administered in a chapter 11 reorganization case, a party in interest may file a motion for a final decree in the manner provided in LBR 9013-1(o).

(2) Notice of the motion must be served upon all parties upon whom the plan was served.

LBR 4001-1. STAY OF 11 U.S.C. § 362

(a) GENERAL. Except as provided by this rule, the requirements of LBR 9013-1 through LBR 9013-4 apply to a motion for relief from the automatic stay, extension of the stay, imposition of the stay, or confirmation that the stay is terminated or no longer in effect. If the motion is filed in a chapter 13 case, the moving party must also comply with LBR 3015-1(r).

(b) FORM.

(1) Motions. An entity seeking relief from the automatic stay, extension of the stay, imposition of the stay, or confirmation that the stay is terminated or no longer in effect, must file a motion using the court-mandated F 4001-1 series of form motions. The failure to use the mandatory forms may result in the denial of the motion or the imposition of sanctions.

(2) Orders. In addition to the requirement that all orders on § 362 motions comply with LBR 9021-1:

(A) MANDATORY FORM ORDERS. Any order granting relief from the automatic stay, extension of the stay, imposition of the stay, or confirming that the stay is terminated or no longer in effect, must be lodged using the court-mandated F 4001-1 series of form orders. The failure to use the mandatory form orders may result in the court not signing or entering the order; and

(B) MOTIONS SETTLED BY STIPULATION. Any order granting a motion regarding the stay, as settled by stipulation, must be prepared using the court-mandated F 4001-1 series of form orders and is exempt from the requirements of LBR 9021-1(b)(2). Compliance with the CM/ECF Procedures and Court Manual is required regarding signatures of parties and/or counsel to the stipulated terms.

(c) MOTION FOR RELIEF FROM AUTOMATIC STAY.

(1) Filing and Service. The motion, notice of hearing, and all supporting papers must be served by the moving party in the time and manner prescribed in LBR 9013-1 on the following parties:

(A) RESIDENTIAL UNLAWFUL DETAINER MOTIONS. If the motion seeks relief from the stay to proceed with an unlawful detainer action involving a residential property with a month-to-month tenancy, tenancy at will, or a tenancy terminated by an unlawful detainer judgment, the movant must serve only the debtor and debtor's attorney (if any).

(B) OTHER RELIEF FROM AUTOMATIC STAY MOTIONS. In all other cases, the movant must serve:

(i) The debtor and debtor's attorney (if any);

(ii) The trustee or interim trustee (if any);

(iii) Any applicable codebtor where relief is sought from the codebtor stay under 11 U.S.C. §§ 1201 or 1301;

(iv) If relief is sought as to property of the estate, the holder of a lien or encumbrance against the subject property that is known to the movant, scheduled by the debtor, or appears in the public record; and

(v) Any other party entitled to notice under FRBP 4001.

(2) Hearing. Unless the court orders otherwise at the time of the hearing, the preliminary hearing under 11 U.S.C. § 362(e) is consolidated with the final hearing under 11 U.S.C. § 362(d).

(3) Continuance By Stipulation. A stipulation by the moving party to continue a hearing under 11 U.S.C. § 362(d) to a later date is deemed a waiver of the applicable portions of 11 U.S.C. § 362(e) until the conclusion of the hearing on such later date. Unless otherwise ordered, an order by the court to continue a hearing under 11 U.S.C. § 362 to a later date is deemed to include an order continuing the stay in effect until the conclusion of the hearing on such later date.

(4) Separate Motion. A motion for relief from the automatic stay must be filed separately from, and not combined in the same pleading with, any other request for relief, unless otherwise ordered by the court.

(d) MOTION FOR EXTENSION OR IMPOSITION OF STAY.

(1) An entity seeking an extension of the stay under 11 U.S.C. § 362(c)(3)(B) or imposition of the stay under 11 U.S.C. § 362(c)(4)(B) must file a motion and serve the motion, notice of hearing, and supporting papers as provided in subsection (c)(1) of this rule and upon all other parties in interest against whom extension or imposition of the stay is sought.

(2) The motion must be filed promptly after the petition date to be timely considered and, if necessary, accompanied by a separate motion under LBR 9075-1(b) for a hearing on shortened notice.

(e) MOTION FOR ORDER CONFIRMING TERMINATION OF AUTOMATIC STAY.

(1) An entity requesting an order under 11 U.S.C. § 362(j) confirming termination of the automatic stay must file a motion supported by a declaration containing competent evidence establishing that the stay has terminated or was never in effect under 11 U.S.C. § 362(c).

(2) The motion and supporting declaration must be served as provided in subsection (c)(1) of this rule.

(f) DEPOSIT OF RENT UNDER 11 U.S.C. § 362(L).

(1) Any rent deposited with the clerk of the court pursuant to 11 U.S.C. § 362(l)(1)(B) must be in the form of a certified or cashier's check or money order payable to the lessor or landlord in the amount of any rent that would become due during the 30-day period after the filing of the bankruptcy petition.

(2) The rent must be deposited with the clerk of the court at the time the bankruptcy petition is filed. The rent deposit and the bankruptcy petition must be accompanied by a copy of the judgment for possession.

(3) As the certification to be filed and served pursuant to 11 U.S.C. § 362(l)(2), debtor may use the court-approved form F 4001-1.2, Debtor's Further Certification of Cure of Monetary Default Underlying Judgment for Possession of Residential Property and Proof of Deposit (11 U.S.C. § 362(l)(2)). This certification must be filed and served within 30 days after the filing of the bankruptcy petition in accordance with 11 U.S.C.

§ 362(l)(2).

(4) Pursuant to 11 U.S.C. § 362(l)(5)(D), the clerk will transmit the payment to the lessor at the address listed in the section on page 2 of the bankruptcy petition entitled "Statement by a Debtor Who Resides as a Tenant of Residential Property."

(g) RELIEF FROM AUTOMATIC STAY TO PROCEED IN ANOTHER FORUM. If the court grants a motion to lift the automatic stay and to proceed in another forum, the prevailing party must promptly file a copy of the entered order in that forum.

LBR 4001-2. CASH COLLATERAL AND FINANCING ORDERS

(a) GENERAL. The requirements of LBR 9013-1 through LBR 9013-4 apply to a motion to obtain credit or to approve the use of cash collateral, debtor in possession financing, and/or cash management under 11 U.S.C. §§ 363 or 364 (collectively, "Financing Motion"), except as provided by this rule.

(b) PROVISIONS TO BE IDENTIFIED. To the extent not otherwise required by FRBP 4001(b)(1)(B) and (c)(1)(B), a Financing Motion must identify whether the proposed form of order and/or underlying cash collateral stipulation or loan agreement contains any provision that:

(1) Grants cross-collateralization protection (other than replacement liens or other adequate protection) to the prepetition secured creditors (i.e., clauses that secure prepetition debt by postpetition assets in which the secured creditor would not otherwise have a security interest by virtue of its prepetition security agreement or applicable law);

(2) Binds the estate or all parties in interest with respect to the validity, perfection, or amount of the secured creditor's prepetition lien or debt or the waiver of claims against the secured creditor;

(3) Waives or limits the estate's rights under 11 U.S.C. § 506(c);

(4) Grants to the prepetition secured creditor liens on the debtor's claims and causes of action arising under 11 U.S.C. §§ 544, 545, 547, 548, or 549;

(5) Deems prepetition secured debt to be postpetition debt or that use postpetition loans from a prepetition secured creditor to pay part or all of that secured creditor's prepetition debt, other than as provided in 11 U.S.C. § 552(b);

(6) Provides disparate treatment for the professionals retained by a creditors' committee from that provided for the professionals retained by the debtor with respect to a professional fee carve out; or

(7) Primes any secured lien. If an order is sought to prime a lien, the Financing Motion must:

(A) Identify the location of any such provision in the proposed form of order, cash collateral stipulation, and/or loan agreement; and

(B) Contain specific justification for the priming of the lien.

(c) SUMMARY OF ESSENTIAL TERMS. The Financing Motion must include a summary of the essential terms of the proposed credit, use of cash collateral, or debtor in possession financing (e.g., the interim borrowing limit, the maximum borrowing available on a final basis, borrowing conditions, interest rate, maturity dates, events of default, use of funds limitations, and protections afforded under 11 U.S.C. §§ 363 and 364).

(d) USE OF FORM FOR CASH COLLATERAL AND/OR DEBTOR IN POSSESSION FINANCING STIPULATIONS. Each Financing Motion requesting approval of a stipulation for credit, use of cash collateral, or debtor in possession financing must be accompanied by court-approved form F 4001-2, Statement Pursuant to Local Bankruptcy Rule 4001-2, or a statement consistent with court-approved form F 4001-2.

(e) INTERIM RELIEF. The court may grant interim relief to prevent immediate and irreparable harm to the estate pending a final hearing. In the absence of extraordinary circumstances, the court will not approve an interim order that includes any of the provisions described in subsection (b)(1)–(7) of this rule.

(f) FINAL ORDERS. A final order will be entered only after notice and a hearing pursuant to FRBP 4001(b). Ordinarily, the final hearing will be held at least 14 days after the appointment of the creditors' committee contemplated by 11 U.S.C. § 1102.

LBR 4003-2. LIEN AVOIDANCE

(a) GENERAL. The requirements of LBR 9013-1 through LBR 9013-4 apply to a motion to avoid a lien or other transfer of property pursuant to 11 U.S.C. § 522(f), except as provided by this rule.

(1) A motion to avoid a lien or other transfer of property under 11 U.S.C. § 522(f) may be brought under either LBR 9013-1(a) or LBR 9013-1(o).

(2) A motion to sell property free and clear of liens under 11 U.S.C.

§ 363(h) does not constitute a "proceeding to avoid a lien" within the meaning of this rule.

(b) FORM.

(1) The creditor whose lien is to be avoided must be identified in the title or caption of the notice and motion (*e.g.*, Motion to Avoid Lien of XYZ Co. under 11 U.S.C. § 522(f)). The notice and motion must contain a single caption and be filed in the underlying bankruptcy case. A double caption must not be used nor will a separate reference number be assigned.

(2) If the motion seeks to avoid a lien on real property, the motion and proposed order must include the legal description of the real property.

(c) SERVICE.

(1) The motion, notice, and supporting papers must be served on the holder of the lien to be avoided in the same manner as a summons and complaint under FRBP 7004.

(2) The motion, notice, and supporting papers also must be served on any other holder of a lien or encumbrance against the subject property.

(d) EVIDENCE. The motion must be accompanied by a declaration or other competent evidence establishing:

(1) The balance remaining on the creditor's loan;

(2) The fair market value of the subject property;

(3) The identity of any other holder of a lien encumbering the subject property and the amount due and owing on such lien;

(4) The specific statutory authority for the claimed exemption; and

(5) The value or amount claimed exempt.

LBR 4008-1. REAFFIRMATION AGREEMENTS

(a) FORM. A reaffirmation agreement must conform to Official Form 240A-Reaffirmation Agreement. If the reaffirmation agreement concerns a secured debt, a complete and legible copy of the security agreement, including the front and back of each page, must be attached.

(b) REAFFIRMATION WITHOUT REPRESENTATION OR CERTIFICATION BY DEBTOR'S ATTORNEY. In a case where the debtor is not represented by an attorney, or where the attorney is unwilling or unable to sign Part C: Certification by Debtor's Attorney, the debtor must move for approval of the reaffirmation agreement by the court by completing Part E: Motion for Court Approval of Official Form 240A.

(c) DEADLINE FOR FILING. A reaffirmation agreement and a motion for approval of the reaffirmation agreement under 11 U.S.C. § 524 must be filed by the debtor or creditor within 60 days following the conclusion of the first meeting of creditors under 11 U.S.C. § 341(a), unless otherwise ordered by the court.

(d) HEARING AND APPROVAL BY COURT.

(1) The clerk will set a hearing on the motion for approval of the reaffirmation agreement and give notice to the debtor and creditor of the date, time, and place of such hearing if:

(A) The debtor was not represented by an attorney or the attorney representing the debtor was unwilling or unable to sign Part C: Certification by Debtor's Attorney; or

(B) Where a presumption of undue hardship arising under 11 U.S.C. § 524(m)(1) is not rebutted by the debtor to the satisfaction of the court.

(2) The court will not grant a motion to approve a reaffirmation agreement unless the debtor appears in person at the hearing to respond to questions by the court.

(3) Under all other circumstances, unless otherwise ordered by the court, court approval is not required in a case where the debtor was represented by an attorney during the negotiation of the reaffirmation agreement.

LBR 5003-2. RECORDS AND FILES

(a) RECORDS AND FILES.

(1) When Order Required. No records or objects belonging to the files of the court may be taken from the office or custody of the clerk except upon written order of the court.

(2) Form of Receipt. Any person removing records pursuant to this rule must give the clerk a receipt containing the following information:

(A) The name, address, and telephone number of the person removing the records or objects;

(B) An itemized description of the records or objects removed;

(C) The date of removal;

(D) The place in which records or objects will be used or kept; and

(E) The estimated date of return to the clerk of the records or objects.

(3) Exception for Court Staff. The provisions of this rule do not apply to a judge, members of a judge's staff, magistrate judge, court recorder, clerk, clerk's staff, or courtroom deputy requiring records or objects in the exercise of their official duties. Any court officer removing records or objects must provide the clerk with a receipt in the form required by subsection (a)(2) of this rule.

(b) REMOVAL OF CONTRABAND. Contraband of any kind coming into the possession of the clerk must be turned over to an appropriate governmental agency which will destroy or otherwise dispose of the contraband as provided by law. The agency must give the clerk a receipt for the contraband in the form required by subsection (a)(2) of this rule.

(c) CONFIDENTIAL COURT RECORDS.

(1) Filing under Seal. Subject to 11 U.S.C. § 107, a paper may not be filed under seal without a prior written order of the court. If a filing under seal is requested, a written motion and a proposed order must be presented to the judge along with the paper submitted for filing under seal. The proposed order must authorize the sealing of the paper and, if appropriate, the motion and order as well. The original and judge's copy of the paper must be sealed in separate envelopes with a copy of the title page attached to the front of each envelope. Copies to be conformed need not be placed in sealed envelopes. The motion, paper submitted for filing under seal, and proposed order must not be filed by electronic means. The documents must be filed with the court non-electronically. If the court denies the motion, the paper submitted to be filed under seal will be returned to the movant unless otherwise ordered.

(2) Disclosure of Sealed Papers. No sealed or confidential record of the court maintained by the clerk will be disclosed except upon written order of the court. A party seeking disclosure of sealed or confidential court records must file and serve a motion pursuant to LBR 9013-1. The motion must state with particularity the need for specific information in such records.

LBR 5005-1. FILING PAPERS—REQUIREMENTS

A paper delivered for filing to the clerk will be accepted if accompanied by any required fee and signature, except as provided in LBR 1002-1(d)(1) and LBR 1006-1.

LBR 5005-2. FILING PAPERS—NUMBER OF COPIES

(a) NUMBER OF COPIES. For papers that are not electronically filed under the provisions of LBR 5005-4, a list of requirements that specify the minimum number of copies that must be submitted is contained in the Court Manual available from the clerk and on the court's website.

(b) CONFORMED COPIES. A copy filed with the court must conform to the original, including either a photocopy of a fully executed signature page, or an unsigned signature page that bears a conformed signature or a notation that the original was signed. A conformed copy must be identical to the original in content, pagination, additions, deletions, interlineations, attachments, exhibits, and tabs.

(c) REQUEST FOR COURT CONFORMED COPY. A maximum of 3 copies will be conformed by the clerk's office to show filing or lodging. Copies to be conformed by the clerk's office may consist of either the entire paper or only the first page of the filed paper. The clerk's office is not responsible for verifying that any copy presented for conforming is a true and correct copy of the filed paper. If the party presenting a paper requests the clerk to return a conformed copy by United States mail, an extra copy must be submitted by the party for that purpose, accompanied by a postage-paid, self-addressed envelope.

(d) JUDGE'S COPY. A paper copy of any document filed with the court, either electronically or non-electronically, must be marked "Judge's Copy" and served on the judge in chambers in the manner and not later than the deadline set forth in the Court Manual available from the clerk and on the court's website.

(1) The judge's copy must meet the requirements of LBR 9004-1(a). Exhibits to the judge's copy must be tabbed.

(2) If the document is filed electronically, a judge's copy must be accompanied by a copy of the NEF confirming the filing of the original document.

LBR 5005-4. ELECTRONIC FILING

(a) MANDATORY ELECTRONIC FILING. Except as provided in subsection (c) of this rule, all papers submitted in any case or proceeding must be filed electronically, signed or verified by electronic means in compliance with the court's CM/ECF Procedures contained in the Court Manual available from the clerk and on the court's website.

(b) CM/ECF PROCEDURES CONTROL. In the event of a conflict between these rules and the CM/ECF Procedures, the current version of the CM/ECF Procedures will control.

(c) EXCEPTIONS TO MANDATORY ELECTRONIC FILING REQUIREMENT.

(1) Pro Se Exception. A person who is not represented by an attorney may file and serve papers non-electronically.

(2) Limited Exception for Attorneys.

(A) An attorney who files papers in fewer than 5 bankruptcy cases or adversary proceedings in a single calendar year may file and serve papers non-electronically.

(B) An attorney who files non-electronically papers capable of being filed electronically in 5 or more bankruptcy cases or adversary proceedings in a single calendar year must thereafter file papers electronically through the court's CM/ECF system.

(C) The court reserves the right in its sole discretion to revoke this limited exception at any time upon notice to the attorney.

(3) Paper Filed under Seal. A motion, paper submitted for filing under seal, and proposed order must be filed non-electronically pursuant to LBR 5003-2(c)(1).

LBR 5010-1. REOPENING CASES

(a) MOTION. A motion to reopen a closed bankruptcy case must be supported by a declaration establishing cause therefor. The motion must not contain a request for any other relief.

(b) SEPARATE MOTION OR ADVERSARY PROCEEDING.

(1) A request for any relief other than the reopening of a case, including relief based upon the grounds for reopening the case, must be made in a separate motion or adversary proceeding, which may be filed concurrently with the motion to reopen.

(2) This subsection does not apply to a motion to reopen a case solely for the purpose of seeking an extension of time to file Official Form 23, Debtor's Certification of Completion of Post-petition Instructional Course Concerning Personal Financial Management.

(c) NOTICE. The movant must give notice of the motion to any former trustee in the case and the United States trustee.

(d) FEE. If a fee is required, the movant must pay the fee upon the filing of the motion to reopen, unless otherwise ordered by the court.

(e) EX PARTE CONSIDERATION. A motion to reopen may be considered ex parte. The movant must not calendar a hearing date nor will a hearing be held on the motion, unless otherwise ordered by the court.

(f) ASSIGNMENT. The motion will be assigned to the judge to whom the case was last assigned, if still in office; otherwise, the motion will be assigned at random by the clerk to a judge to hear and rule upon the request.

(g) CLOSING OF CASE. If no motion or adversary proceeding is pending 30 days after the case is reopened and if no trustee has been ordered appointed, the case may be closed without further notice.

LBR 5011-1. WITHDRAWAL OF REFERENCE

(a) GENERAL. Pursuant to 28 U.S.C. § 157(a), the district court refers to the bankruptcy court for this district all cases under title 11 and all proceedings under title 11 or arising in or related to a case under title 11.

(b) PROCEDURE. A motion to withdraw the reference of a case or proceeding under 28 U.S.C. § 157(d) must be filed with the clerk of the district court. The motion must comply with Rule 6.1 of Chapter IV, Local Rules of the District Court Governing Bankruptcy Appeals, Cases and Proceedings.

LBR 5073-1. PHOTOGRAPHY, RECORDING DEVICES, AND BROADCASTING

(a) PROHIBITION OF BROADCASTING, TELEVISION, AND PHOTOGRAPHY. Unless otherwise ordered by the court, between 7:00 a.m. and 7:00 p.m., Monday through Friday, and at all other times when the court is in session, the use of any form, means, or manner of radio or television broadcasting and the taking or making of photographs, motion pictures, video, or sound recordings is prohibited in:

(1) Any and all courtrooms occupied by any judge;

(2) Any and all chambers assigned to any judge;

(3) Any and all areas used by the clerk and court staff;

(4) Any garage or parking facility reserved for the judges or their staff; and

(5) All hallways and public areas adjacent to the above-specified locations.

(b) EXCEPTIONS. This rule does not prohibit:

(1) Recordings made by official court recorders in the performance of their official duties. No other use may be made of an official recording of a court proceeding without an express, written order of the court;

(2) The taking of photographs, when specifically authorized in writing, at ceremonial or non-judicial functions in the chambers of a judge of this court;

(3) The videotaping or other electronic recording of depositions for trial purposes, nor the preparation and perpetuation of testimony taken by, or under the direction of, a judge of this court or a visiting judge. No part of such videotape or other electronic recording may be used without an express, written order of the court; or

(4) The possession of video or sound recording, photographic, radio, or television broadcasting equipment. Any equipment taken into or through the areas enumerated in this rule is subject to such security regulations as may be adopted from time to time by the court.

(c) ENFORCEMENT OF RULE. The United States Marshal, the General Services Administration police, and the security force contracted for service by the court enforce the provisions of this rule. A violation of this rule constitutes contempt of court.

LBR 5075-1. MOTIONS FOR ADMINISTRATIVE ORDERS PURSUANT TO 28 U.S.C. § 156(c)

(a) GENERAL. This rule applies to motions by which a party in interest seeks an order from the bankruptcy court approving employment of persons or entities to perform certain duties of the clerk's office, the debtor, or the debtor in possession such as (1) processing proofs of claim and maintaining the claims register; (2) serving notices; (3) scanning documents; or (4) providing photocopies of documents filed in the case (collectively, "administrative order").

(b) PROCEDURE. A motion for administrative order must include a completed declaration on court-mandated form F 5075-1.1, Declaration to be Filed with Motion Establishing Administrative Procedures Re 28 U.S.C. § 156(c) with the completed Mega Case Procedures Checklist attached thereto. A copy of the motion, including the declaration and checklist, must also be provided to the clerk's office at the time the motion is filed.

Movant's counsel must consult with the clerk's office in completing the checklist to the satisfaction of the clerk's office. Unless the judge to whom the case is assigned orders otherwise, any such motion that is not accompanied by the completed checklist may be denied by the court and any hearing thereon previously scheduled may be vacated.

LBR 5095-1. INVESTMENT OF ESTATE FUNDS

(a) NOTICE.

(1) The trustee or debtor in possession must give not less than 14 days written notice of a proposed investment of bankruptcy estate funds in a Designated Fund to the United States trustee, the debtor (if a trustee has been appointed), the creditors' committee or the 20 largest unsecured creditors if no committee has been appointed, any other committee appointed in the case, counsel for any of the foregoing, and any other party in interest entitled to notice under FRBP 2002, unless the court for cause shown shortens the time or otherwise modifies or limits notice pursuant to a motion under LBR 9075-1.

(2) The notice must state that any objection or request for hearing must be filed and served not more than 14 days after service of the notice, unless the notice specifies a longer period, or unless otherwise ordered by the court.

(3) If an objection and request for hearing is not filed and served within such 14-day period, the trustee or debtor in possession may proceed with the investment. An order is not required nor will an order be entered under this rule.

(b) OBJECTION AND REQUEST FOR HEARING. If a timely objection and request for hearing is filed and served, the trustee or debtor in possession must, within 21 days from the date of service of such objection, obtain and give not less than 14 days notice of the hearing to each objecting party and to the United States trustee.

(c) DESIGNATED FUND. For purposes of this rule, a "Designated Fund" is an open-end management investment company registered under the Investment Company Act of 1940 and regulated as a "money market fund" pursuant to Rule 2a-7 under the Investment Company Act of 1940, that:

(1) Invests exclusively in United States Treasury bills and United States Treasury Notes owned directly or through repurchase agreements;

(2) Has received the highest money market fund rating from a nationally recognized statistical rating organization, such as Standard & Poor's or Moody's;

(3) Has agreed to redeem fund shares in cash, with payment being made no later than the business day following a redemption request by a shareholder, except in the event of an unscheduled closing of Federal Reserve Banks or the New York Stock Exchange; and

(4) Has adopted a policy that it will notify its shareholders 60 days prior to any change in its investment and redemption policies under subsections (c)(1) and (3) of this rule.

LBR 6004-1. SALE, USE, OR LEASE OF ESTATE PROPERTY

(a) GENERAL. The requirements of LBR 9013-1 through LBR 9013-4 apply to a motion for an order establishing procedures for the sale of estate assets and a motion seeking authorization to sell, use or lease estate property, except as provided by this rule.

(b) MOTION FOR ORDER ESTABLISHING PROCEDURES FOR THE SALE OF ESTATE PROPERTY.

(1) Timing of Hearing. A hearing on a Motion to Establish Procedures for the Sale of the Estate's Assets ("Sale Procedure Motion") may be scheduled on not less than 7 days notice to applicable parties, unless an order shortening the time for a hearing is obtained under LBR 9075-1(b).

(2) Contents of Notice. The notice must describe the proposed bidding procedures and include a copy of the proposed purchase agreement. If the purchase agreement is not available, the moving party must describe the terms of the sale proposed, when a copy of the actual agreement will be filed with the court, and from whom it may be obtained. The notice must describe the marketing efforts undertaken and the anticipated marketing plan, or explain why no marketing is required. The notice must provide that opposition is due on or before 1 day prior to the hearing, unless otherwise ordered by the court.

(3) Service of the Notice and Motion. The moving party must serve the motion and notice of the motion and hearing by personal delivery, messenger, telephone, fax, or e-mail to the parties to whom notice of the motion is required to be given by the FRBP or by these rules, any other party that is likely to be adversely affected by the granting of the motion, and the United States trustee. The notice of hearing must state that any response in opposition to the motion must be filed and served at least 1 day prior to the hearing, unless otherwise ordered by the court.

(4) Opposition. Any opposition and accompanying memorandum of points and authorities and declarations must be filed and served at least 1 day prior to the hearing, unless otherwise ordered by the court. Papers filed in opposition to the motion must be served by personal delivery, messenger, fax, or e-mail. A judge's copy of the opposition must be served on the judge in chambers in accordance with LBR 5005-2(d).

(5) Scheduling Hearing on the Sale. A date and time for a hearing on the motion to approve the sale itself may be obtained at or prior to the hearing on the Sale Procedure Motion. The hearing must be scheduled, if practicable, no more than 30 days following the hearing on the Sale Procedure Motion.

(6) Break-up Fees. If a break-up fee or other form of overbid protection is requested in the Sale Procedure Motion, the request must be supported by evidence establishing:

(A) That such a fee is likely to enhance the ultimate sale price; and

(B) The reasonableness of the fee.

(c) MOTION FOR ORDER AUTHORIZING THE SALE OF ESTATE PROPERTY.

(1) General. Unless otherwise ordered by the court and subject to FRBP 6003(b), an order authorizing the sale of estate property other than in the ordinary course of business may be obtained upon motion of the trustee or debtor in possession in a chapter 7, 11, or 12 case after notice and a hearing pursuant to LBR 9013-1(a) or after notice of opportunity for hearing under LBR 9013-1(o)(1), except the following which must be set for hearing pursuant to LBR 9013-1(a):

(A) A sale of all or substantially all of the debtor's assets in a case under chapter 11 or 12; or

(B) A sale of property that is either subject to overbid or concerning which the trustee or debtor in possession has been contacted by potential overbidders.

(2) Motion.

(A) A motion for an order authorizing the sale of estate property, other than in the ordinary course of business, must be supported by a declaration of the movant establishing the value of the property and that the terms and conditions of the proposed sale, including the price and all contingencies, are in the best interest of the estate.

(B) If the proposed sale is not subject to overbid, the declaration must include a certification that the movant has not been contacted by any potential overbidder and that, in the movant's business judgment, there are no viable alternative purchasers.

(C) A memorandum of points and authorities is not required but may be filed in support of the motion.

(3) Notice of Hearing. If the motion is set for hearing pursuant to LBR 9013-1, the notice must state:

(A) The date, time, and place of the hearing on the proposed sale;

(B) The name and address of the proposed buyer;

(C) A description of the property to be sold;

(D) The terms and conditions of the proposed sale, including the price and all contingencies;

(E) Whether the proposed sale is free and clear of liens, claims or interests, or subject to them, and a description of all such liens, claims, or interests;

(F) Whether the proposed sale is subject to higher and better bids;

(G) The consideration to be received by the estate, including estimated commissions, fees, and other costs of sale;

(H) If authorization is sought to pay a commission, the identity of the auctioneer, broker, or sales agent and the amount or percentage of the proposed commission to be paid;

(I) A description of the estimated or possible tax consequences to the estate, if known, and how any tax liability generated by the sale of the property will be paid; and

(J) The date by which an objection must be filed and served.

(4) Notice of Opportunity for Hearing. If authorization is sought pursuant to LBR 9013-1(o)(1), the notice must include the information required by subsection (c)(3)(B) through (I) of this rule and state:

(A) That a written objection to the proposed sale, together with a request for hearing, must be filed and served pursuant to LBR 9013-1(o)(1) not later than 14 days from the date of service of the notice, unless the notice period is shortened by order of the court; and

(B) That in the absence of an objection, an order may be entered authorizing the sale of the property without further notice or hearing.

(d) NOTICE OF INTENT TO USE, SELL, OR LEASE ESTATE PROPERTY (OPTIONAL PROCEDURE).

(1) Scope of Rule. A trustee or debtor in possession may sell, use or lease property of the estate in a chapter 7, 11, or 12 case, other than in the ordinary course of business, under 11 U.S.C. § 363(b)(1) upon notice, except the following which must be brought by motion and set for hearing pursuant to LBR 9013-1(a):

(A) A sale of all or substantially all of the debtor's assets in a case under chapter 11 or 12; or

(B) A sale of property that is either subject to overbid or concerning which the trustee or debtor in possession has been contacted by potential overbidders.

(2) Notice.

(A) The trustee or debtor in possession must give not less than 14 days written notice by mail to creditors and interested parties who are entitled to notice, unless the court for cause shown shortens the time or otherwise modifies or limits notice pursuant to a motion under LBR 9075-1.

(B) The notice must comply with LBR 6004-1(c)(3)(B) through (I) and include a certification that the trustee or debtor in possession has not been contacted by any potential overbidder and that, in the trustee's or debtor in possession's business judgment, there are no viable alternative purchasers.

(C) The notice must state that any objection and request for hearing must be filed and served not more than 14 days after service of the notice, unless the notice specifies a longer period or unless otherwise ordered by the court, and that in the absence of an objection the property may be sold without further notice.

(D) If an objection and request for hearing is not filed and served within such 14-day period, the trustee or debtor in possession may take the proposed action on the date specified in the notice of intent. An order is not required nor will an order be entered under this subsection.

(3) Objection and Request for Hearing. If a timely objection and request for hearing is filed and served, the trustee or debtor in possession must, within 21 days from the date of service of such objection, obtain and give not less than 14 days notice of the hearing to each objecting party and to the United States trustee.

(e) SALE OF PUBLICLY TRADED ASSETS. If the property consists of assets sold in public markets whose prices are published on national or regional exchanges (e.g., securities, bonds, commodities, or precious metals), the trustee or debtor in possession may sell such assets in a market transaction after providing not less than 14 days written notice by mail to such creditors and interested parties who are entitled to notice, unless the court for cause shown shortens the time or otherwise modifies or limits notice pursuant to a motion under LBR 9075-1.

(1) The notice must identify the asset, the market through which the asset is to be sold, and the published price on the date of the notice.

(2) If a commission is to be paid to a sales agent, the notice must disclose the name and address of the sales agent and the amount of the commission to be paid on account of the sale.

(3) The notice must also state that any objection and request for hearing must be filed and served not more than 14 days after service of the notice, unless the notice specifies a longer period or unless otherwise ordered by the court, and that in the absence of an objection the property may be sold without further notice.

(4) If an objection and request for hearing is not filed and served within such 14-day period, the trustee or debtor in possession may proceed with the sale in accordance with the notice. An order is not required nor will an order be entered under this subsection.

(5) If a timely objection and request for hearing is filed and served, the trustee or debtor in possession must, within 21 days from the date of service of such objection, obtain and give not less than 14 days notice of the hearing to each objecting party and to the United States trustee.

(6) The trustee or debtor in possession need not file an employment application on behalf of a sales agent registered with the Security Investors Protection Corporation, but the sales agent must execute a declaration of disinterestedness which must be filed by the trustee or debtor in possession with the notice.

(f) PUBLICATION OF NOTICE OF SALE OF ESTATE PROPERTY. Whenever the trustee or debtor in possession is required to give notice of a sale or of a motion to sell property of the estate pursuant to FRBP 6004 and 2002(c), an additional copy of the notice and court-approved form F 6004-2, Notice of Sale of Estate Property must be submitted to the clerk at the time of filing for purposes of publication by the clerk on the court's website.

(g) REPORT OF SALE. Unless otherwise ordered by the court, the report of sale required by FRBP 6004(f)(1) must be filed and served not later than 21 days after the date of the sale of any property not in the ordinary course of business.

(h) DISBURSEMENT OF SALE PROCEEDS. Unless otherwise ordered by the court, all proceeds of a sale must be paid directly to any appointed trustee or the debtor in possession. A disbursement of proceeds must not be made without a specific order of the court authorizing the disbursement, except for payment to secured creditors, payment to a debtor of exempt proceeds, and payment for expenses of sale. Proceeds may be disbursed to pay auctioneer's fees and brokers' commissions without additional order of the court if payment is consistent with the terms of the order approving the sale or authorizing the employment of the auctioneer or broker.

(i) CHAPTER 13 CASES. A motion to sell or refinance property in a chapter 13 case must be filed pursuant to LBR 3015-1(p).

LBR 6007-1. ABANDONMENT

(a) NOTICE OF INTENT TO ABANDON. A trustee or debtor in possession who desires to abandon property of the estate may seek to do so by a notice of intent to abandon, without the necessity for filing a motion to abandon.

(b) MOTION TO COMPEL ABANDONMENT. An order compelling the case trustee or debtor in possession to abandon property of the estate may be obtained upon motion of a party in interest after notice of opportunity for hearing pursuant to LBR 9013-1(o)(1).

(c) NOTICE.

(1) Content. Notice of either an intent to abandon or motion to compel abandonment must (a) describe the property to be abandoned, including the address of the property, if applicable; (b) state the basis upon which the party seeking abandonment concludes that the property is burdensome to the estate or that it is of inconsequential value or benefit to the estate; and (c) state that any objection and request for hearing must be filed and served not more than 14 days after service of the notice, unless the notice specifies a longer period or unless otherwise ordered by the court.

(2) Parties to Be Served. The notice must be served on those listed in

FRBP 6007(a).

(d) ABSENCE OF OBJECTION AND REQUEST FOR HEARING.

(1) If no timely objection and request for hearing is filed and served, the property is deemed abandoned without further order of the court.

(2) If an entity desires an order of the court authorizing or directing, and confirming, the case trustee's or debtor in possession's abandonment of the property, that entity may lodge a proposed form of order with the court in accordance with the procedure set forth in LBR 9013-1(o)(3).

(e) OBJECTION AND REQUEST FOR HEARING. If a timely objection and request for hearing is filed and served, the party requesting the abandonment must, within 21 days from the date of service of such objection, obtain a hearing date and furnish not less than 14 days notice of the hearing to each objecting party and to the United States trustee.

LBR 7003-1. ADVERSARY PROCEEDING SHEET

A complaint, filed electronically or non-electronically, must be accompanied by an Official Form B104, Adversary Proceeding Sheet, completed and signed by the attorney or party presenting the complaint. The form must contain the name, address, and telephone number of each party to the adversary proceeding, together with the name, address, and telephone number of each party's attorney, if known.

LBR 7004-1. ISSUANCE AND SERVICE OF SUMMONS AND NOTICE OF STATUS CONFERENCE

(a) PRESENTATION FOR ISSUANCE. The attorney or party must prepare a Summons and Notice of Status Conference using court-mandated form F 7004-1 for execution by the clerk. The summons must be presented concurrently with the filing of a complaint or of an involuntary petition pursuant to 11 U.S.C. § 303.

(b) MANNER OF SERVICE. A summons must be served in the manner authorized in FRBP 7004. If a summons or any paper is served by mail, the mailing address must include the zip code. The notice required by FRBP 7026 and LBR 7026-1 must be served with the summons and complaint.

(c) EXCEPTION—STATUTE OF LIMITATIONS. If the statute of limitations applicable to any claim in a complaint will expire before the summons can be prepared and submitted, the complaint will be accepted by the clerk for filing without a summons. The summons must be presented for issuance within 2 days after the complaint is filed under this exception.

LBR 7004-2. LIMITATIONS ON SERVICE BY MARSHAL

(a) GENERAL. Except as otherwise provided by order of the court or when required by the treaties or statutes of the United States, civil process on behalf of a non-governmental party must not be presented to the United States Marshal for service.

(b) EXCEPTION. Upon request by the government, civil process on behalf of the United States government or an officer or agency thereof may be made by the United States Marshal.

LBR 7008-1. CORE/NON-CORE DESIGNATION

In all adversary proceedings, the statements required by FRBP 7008(a) and 7012(b) must be plainly stated in the first numbered paragraph of the paper.

LBR 7015-1. AMENDED AND SUPPLEMENTAL PLEADINGS

(a) FORM.

(1) An original and 1 copy of the proposed amended pleading must be lodged as a separate document and served with any notice of motion or stipulation to amend a pleading.

(2) Every amended pleading filed as a matter of right or allowed by order of the court must be complete, including exhibits. The amended pleading must not incorporate by reference any part of the prior superseded pleading.

(3) Unless otherwise ordered, a pleading will not be deemed amended absent compliance with this rule and FRBP 7015.

(b) SERVICE OF ALLOWED AMENDED PLEADING.

(1) Unless otherwise ordered, an amended pleading allowed by order of the court will be deemed served upon the parties who have previously appeared on the date the motion to amend is granted or the stipulation therefor is approved, provided the proposed amended pleading was lodged and served in accordance with subsection (a)(1). Otherwise, actual service and filing of the amended pleading is required.

(2) A party who has not previously appeared must be served with an amended pleading as provided in LBR 2002-2 and 7004-1.

LBR 7016-1. STATUS CONFERENCE, PRETRIAL, AND TRIAL PROCEDURE

(a) STATUS CONFERENCE. In any adversary proceeding, the clerk will issue a summons and notice of the date and time of the status conference.

(1) Who Must Appear. Each party appearing at any status conference must be represented by either the attorney (or party, if not represented by counsel) who is responsible for trying the case or the attorney who is responsible for preparing the case for trial.

(2) Contents of Joint Status Report. Unless otherwise ordered by the court, at least 14 days before the date set for each status conference the parties are required to file a joint status report discussing the following:

(A) State of discovery, including a description of completed discovery and detailed schedule of all further discovery then contemplated;

(B) A discovery cut-off date;

(C) A schedule of then contemplated law and motion matters;

(D) Prospects for settlement;

(E) A proposed date for the pretrial conference and/or the trial;

(F) Whether counsel have met and conferred in compliance with LBR 7026-1, and if so, the date of the conference;

(G) Any other issues affecting the status or management of the case; and

(H) Whether the parties are interested in alternative dispute resolution.

(3) Unilateral Status Report. If any party fails to cooperate in the preparation of a joint status report and a response has been filed to the complaint, each party must file a unilateral status report not less than 7 days before the date set for each status conference, unless otherwise ordered by the court. The unilateral status report must contain a declaration setting forth the attempts made by plaintiff to contact or obtain the cooperation of the defendant.

(4) Scheduling Order. Unless otherwise ordered by the court, within 7 days after the status conference the plaintiff must lodge, in accordance with LBR 9021-1(b), a proposed scheduling order setting forth the following:

(A) Deadline to join other parties and to amend the pleadings;

(B) Deadline to complete discovery;

(C) Deadline to file any pretrial motions and/or a joint pretrial order;

(D) Any dates set for further status conferences, a final pretrial conference, and the trial;

(E) Any other appropriate matter; and

(F) Proof of service on all opposing counsel (or parties, if not represented by counsel).

(5) Stipulation for Extension of Deadlines in Scheduling Order. A stipulation for extension of the deadlines set forth in a previously entered scheduling order must contain facts establishing cause for the requested extension and be submitted to the court in accordance with LBR 9021-1(b)(2) and LBR 9071-1.

(b) JOINT PRETRIAL ORDER.

(1) When Required.

(A) In any adversary proceeding or contested matter, unless otherwise ordered by the court, attorneys for the parties must prepare and lodge, in accordance with LBR 9021-1(b), a written joint pretrial order approved by counsel for all parties.

(B) Unless otherwise ordered by the court, the joint pretrial order must be lodged and served not less than 14 days before the date set for the trial or pretrial conference, if one is ordered.

(C) The preparation and filing of the pretrial order is the responsibility of the parties' counsel (or parties, if not represented by counsel). All parties must meet and confer at least 28 days before the date set for trial or pretrial conference, if one is ordered, for the purpose of preparing the pretrial order.

(2) Contents of Pretrial Order. Unless the court orders otherwise, a joint pretrial order must include the following statements in the following order:

(A) "The following facts are admitted and require no proof:" (Set forth a concise statement of each.)

(B) "The following issues of fact, and no others, remain to be litigated:" (Set forth a concise statement of each.)

(C) "The following issues of law, and no others, remain to be litigated:" (Set forth a concise statement of each.)

(D) "Attached is a list of exhibits intended to be offered at the trial by each party, other than exhibits to be used for impeachment only. The parties have exchanged copies of all exhibits." (Attach a list of exhibits in the sequence to be offered, with a description of each, sufficient for identification, and as to each state whether or not there is objection to its admissibility in evidence and the nature thereof.) If deposition testimony is to be offered as part of the evidence, the offering party must comply with LBR 7030-1.

(E) "The parties have exchanged a list of witnesses to be called at trial." The parties must exchange a list of names and addresses of witnesses, including expert witnesses, to be called at trial other than those contemplated to be used for impeachment or rebuttal. The lists of witnesses must be attached to the proposed joint pretrial order together with a concise summary of the subject of their proposed testimony. If an expert witness is to be called at trial, the parties must exchange short narrative statements of the qualifications of the expert and the testimony expected to be elicited at trial. If the expert to be called at trial has prepared a report, the report must be exchanged as well.

(F) "Other matters that might affect the trial such as anticipated motions in limine, motions to withdraw reference due to timely jury trial demand pursuant to LBR 9015-2, or other pretrial motions."

(G) "All discovery is complete."

(H) "The parties are ready for trial."

(I) "The estimated length of trial is."

(J) "The foregoing admissions have been made by the parties, and the parties have specified the foregoing issues of fact and law remaining to be litigated. Therefore, this order supersedes the pleadings and governs the course of trial of this cause, unless modified to prevent manifest injustice."

(c) PLAINTIFF'S DUTY.

(1) It is plaintiff's duty to prepare and sign a proposed joint pretrial order that is complete in all respects except for other parties' lists of exhibits and witnesses.

(2) Unless otherwise ordered by the court, plaintiff must serve the proposed joint pretrial order in such manner so that it will actually be received by the office of counsel for all other parties not later than 4:00 p.m. on the 7th day prior to the last day for lodging the proposed pretrial order.

(d) DUTY OF PARTIES OTHER THAN PLAINTIFF. Each other party must, within 3 days following receipt of plaintiff's proposed order, take the following action:

(1) Agreement With Form of Proposed Order. If plaintiff's proposed order is satisfactory, attach that party's list of exhibits and witnesses to the order, indicate approval of the proposed order by signature, file it with the clerk in time to be received within the time prescribed in subsection (b)(1) of this rule, and serve all other parties with a completed copy of the order so filed; or

(2) Disagreement With Form of Proposed Order. If plaintiff's proposed order is unsatisfactory:

(A) Immediately meet with or telephone plaintiff in a good faith effort to achieve a joint proposed order; and

(B) If such effort is unsuccessful, prepare a separate proposed order and file it, together with plaintiff's order and a declaration of that party setting forth the efforts made to comply with subsection (d)(2)(A) of this rule. The separate proposed order and declaration must be filed and served in such a manner that they will actually be received by the clerk and the plaintiff all within the time set forth in subsection (b)(1) of this rule.

(e) NON-RECEIPT OF PROPOSED JOINT PRETRIAL ORDER.

(1) Plaintiff. A plaintiff who has complied with subsection (c) of this rule and does not receive a timely response from the other parties, must file and serve a unilateral pretrial order at least 14 days before the trial or pretrial conference, if one is ordered. At the same time, plaintiff must file and serve a declaration asserting the failure of the other parties to respond.

(2) Other Parties. Any party other than plaintiff who has not received plaintiff's proposed pretrial order within the time limits set forth in subsection (c) of this rule, must prepare, file, and serve at least 14 days prior to the trial or pretrial conference, if one is ordered, a declaration attesting to plaintiff's failure to prepare and serve a proposed pretrial order in a timely manner.

(f) SANCTIONS FOR FAILURE TO COMPLY WITH RULE. In addition to the sanctions authorized by F.R.Civ.P. 16(f), if a status conference statement or a joint proposed pretrial order is not filed within the times set forth in subsections (a) or (e), respectively, of this rule, the court may order one or more of the following:

(1) A continuance of the trial date, if no prejudice is involved to the party who is not at fault;

(2) An award of monetary sanctions including attorneys' fees against the party at fault, payable to the party not at fault; and/or

(3) An award of non-monetary sanctions against the party at fault.

Monetary sanctions will be assessed against the party at fault and/or counsel, in the court's discretion. Non-monetary sanctions may include the entry of a judgment of dismissal or the entry of an order striking the answer and entering a default.

(g) FAILURE TO APPEAR AT HEARING OR PREPARE FOR TRIAL. The failure of a party's counsel (or the party, if not represented by counsel) to appear before the court at the status conference or pretrial conference, or to complete the necessary preparations therefor, or to appear at or to be prepared for trial may be considered an abandonment or failure to prosecute or defend diligently, and judgment may be entered against the defaulting party either with respect to a specific issue or as to the entire proceeding, or the proceeding may be dismissed.

LBR 7026-1. DISCOVERY

(a) GENERAL. Compliance with FRBP 7026 and this rule is required in all adversary proceedings.

(1) Notice. The plaintiff must serve with the summons and complaint a notice that compliance with FRBP 7026 and this rule is required.

(2) Proof of Service. The plaintiff must file a proof of service of this notice together with the proof of service of the summons and complaint.

(b) DISCOVERY CONFERENCE AND DISCLOSURES.

(1) Conference of Parties. Unless all defendants default, the parties must conduct the meeting and exchange the information required by FRBP 7026 within the time limits set forth therein.

(2) Joint Status Report. Within 7 days after such meeting, the parties must prepare a joint status report containing the information set forth in LBR 7016-1(a)(2). The joint status report will serve as the written report of the meeting required by FRBP 7026.

(c) FAILURE TO MAKE DISCLOSURES OR COOPERATE IN DISCOVERY.

(1) General. Unless excused from complying with this rule by order of the court for good cause shown, a party must seek to resolve any dispute arising under FRBP 7026-7037 or FRBP 2004 in accordance with this rule.

(2) Meeting of Counsel. Prior to the filing of any motion relating to discovery, counsel for the parties must meet in person or by telephone in a good faith effort to resolve a discovery dispute. It is the responsibility of counsel for the moving party to arrange the conference. Unless altered by agreement of the parties or by order of the court for cause shown, counsel for the opposing party must meet with counsel for the moving party within 7 days of service upon counsel of a letter requesting such meeting and specifying the terms of the discovery order to be sought.

(3) Moving Papers. If counsel are unable to resolve the dispute, the party seeking discovery must file and serve a notice of motion together with a written stipulation by the parties.

(A) The stipulation must be contained in 1 document and must identify, separately and with particularity, each disputed issue that remains to be determined at the hearing and the contentions and points and authorities of each party as to each issue.

(B) The stipulation must not simply refer the court to the document containing the discovery request forming the basis of the dispute. For example, if the sufficiency of an answer to an interrogatory is in issue, the stipulation must contain, verbatim, both the interrogatory and the allegedly insufficient answer, followed by each party's contentions, separately stated.

(C) In the absence of such stipulation or a declaration of counsel of noncooperation by the opposing party, the court will not consider the discovery motion.

(4) Cooperation of Counsel; Sanctions. The failure of any counsel either to cooperate in this procedure, to attend the meeting of counsel, or to provide the moving party the information necessary to prepare the stipulation required by this rule within 7 days of the meeting of counsel will result in the imposition of sanctions, including the sanctions authorized by FRBP 7037 and LBR 9011-3.

(5) Contempt. LBR 9020-1 governing contempt proceedings applies to a discovery motion to compel a non-party to comply with a deposition subpoena for testimony and/or documents under FRBP 7030 and 7034.

LBR 7026-2. DISCOVERY DOCUMENTS—RETENTION, FILING, AND COPIES

(a) RETENTION BY PROPOUNDING PARTY. The following discovery documents and proof of service thereof must not be filed with the clerk until there is a proceeding in which the document or proof of service is in issue:

(1) Transcripts of depositions upon oral examination;

(2) Transcripts of depositions upon written questions;

(3) Interrogatories;

(4) Answers or objections to interrogatories;

(5) Requests for the production of documents or to inspect tangible things;

(6) Responses or objections to requests for the production of documents or to inspect tangible things;

(7) Requests for admission;

(8) Responses or objections to requests for admission;

(9) Notices of Deposition, unless filing is required in order to obtain issuance of a subpoena in another district; and

(10) Subpoena or Subpoena Duces Tecum.

(b) PERIOD OF RETENTION FOR DISCOVERY DOCUMENTS. Discovery documents must be held by the attorney for the propounding party pending use pursuant to this rule for the period specified in LBR 9070-1(b) for the retention of exhibits, unless otherwise ordered by the court.

(c) FILING OF DISCOVERY DOCUMENTS.

(1) When required in a proceeding, only that part of the document that is in issue must be filed with the court.

(2) When filed, discovery documents must be submitted with a notice of filing that identifies the date, time, and place of the hearing or trial in which it is to be offered.

(3) Original deposition transcripts are treated as trial exhibits and must be delivered to the judge for use at the hearing or trial. The original deposition transcript and a copy must be lodged with the clerk pursuant to LBR 7030-1(b).

(d) COPIES OF DISCOVERY DOCUMENTS.

(1) Unless an applicable protective order otherwise provides, any entity may obtain a copy of any discovery document described in subsection (a) of this rule by making a written request therefor to the clerk and paying duplication costs.

(2) The clerk will give notice of the request to all parties in the case or proceeding, and the party holding the original of the requested discovery document must lodge the original or an authenticated copy with the clerk within 14 days after service of the clerk's notice.

(3) Promptly after duplication, the clerk will return the original to the party who provided it.

LBR 7026-3. INTERROGATORIES AND REQUESTS FOR ADMISSION

(a) FORM.

(1) Interrogatories and requests for admission must comply with the form requirements of LBR 9004-1.

(2) Interrogatories and requests for admissions must be numbered sequentially without repeating the numbers used on any prior set of interrogatories or requests for admission propounded by that party.

(b) NUMBER OF INTERROGATORIES PERMITTED. A party must not, without leave of the court and for good cause shown, serve more than 25 interrogatories on any other party. Each subdivision of an interrogatory is considered a separate interrogatory. A motion for leave to serve additional interrogatories may be made pursuant to LBR 9013-1.

(c) ANSWERS AND OBJECTIONS. The party answering or objecting to interrogatories or requests for admission must quote each interrogatory or request in full immediately preceding the statement of any answer or objection thereto.

(d) RETENTION BY PROPOUNDING PARTY. The original of the interrogatories or requests for admission must be held by the attorney propounding the interrogatories or requests pursuant to LBR 7026-2 pending use or further order of the court.

LBR 7030-1. DEPOSITIONS

(a) CUSTODY OF ORIGINAL TRANSCRIPT.

(1) The original transcript of a deposition must be sent to the attorney noticing the deposition after signing and correction or waiver of the same unless otherwise stipulated to on the record at the deposition.

(2) It is the duty of the attorney noticing the deposition to obtain from the reporter the original transcript thereof in a sealed envelope and to safely retain the same under conditions suitable to protect it from tampering, loss, or destruction.

(3) Upon request of any party intending to offer deposition evidence at a contested hearing or trial, a copy of the transcript must be sent to that party for marking in compliance with subsection (b) of this rule.

(b) USE OF DEPOSITION EVIDENCE IN CONTESTED HEARING OR TRIAL. Unless otherwise ordered by the court, each party intending to offer any evidence by way of deposition testimony pursuant to F.R.Civ.P. 32 and F.R.Evid. 803 or 804 must:

(1) Lodge the original deposition transcript and a copy pursuant to this rule with the clerk at least 7 days before the hearing or trial at which it is to be offered;

(2) Identify on the copy of the transcript the testimony the party intends to offer by bracketing in the margins the questions and answers that the party intends to offer at trial. The opposing party must likewise countermark any testimony that it plans to offer. The parties must agree between themselves on a separate color to be used by each party which must be used consistently by that party for all depositions marked in the case;

(3) Mark objections to the proffered evidence of the other party in the margins of the deposition by briefly stating the ground for the objection; and

(4) Serve and file notice of the portions of the deposition marked or countermarked by stating the pages and lines so marked, objections made, and the grounds indicated therefor. The notice must be served and filed within 7 days after the party has marked, countermarked, or objects to the deposition evidence.

(c) DEPOSITION SUMMARY. In appropriate cases and when ordered by the court, the parties may jointly prepare a deposition summary to be used in lieu of question and answer reading of a deposition at trial.

LBR 7041-1. DISMISSAL OF ADVERSARY PROCEEDING

(a) DISMISSAL FOR WANT OF PROSECUTION. A proceeding that has been pending for an unreasonable period of time without any action having been taken therein may be dismissed for want of prosecution upon notice and opportunity to request a hearing.

(b) DISMISSAL FOR FAILURE TO APPEAR. If a party fails to appear at the noticed hearing of a motion or trial of the proceeding, the court may make such orders in regard to the failure as are just, including dismissal of the matter for want of prosecution. Unless the court provides otherwise, any dismissal pursuant to this rule is without prejudice.

(c) REINSTATEMENT—SANCTIONS. If any proceeding dismissed pursuant to this rule is reinstated, the court may impose such sanctions as it deems just and reasonable.

(d) NOTICE OF DISMISSAL. The clerk will provide to all parties to the proceeding notice of entry of any order dismissing a proceeding under this rule.

LBR 7052-1. FINDINGS OF FACT AND CONCLUSIONS OF LAW

(a) PREPARATION AND LODGING. In all cases where written findings of fact and conclusions of law are required, the prevailing party must within 7 days of the date of the hearing at which oral findings and conclusions were rendered, lodge electronically via LOU proposed findings of fact and conclusions of law, unless otherwise ordered by the court.

(b) FINDINGS OF FACT. The proposed findings of fact must:

(1) Be in separately numbered paragraphs;

(2) Be in chronological order; and

(3) Not make reference to allegations contained in the pleadings.

(c) CONCLUSIONS OF LAW. The proposed conclusions of law must follow the findings of fact, and:

(1) Must be in separately numbered paragraphs; and

(2) May include brief citations of appropriate authority.

LBR 7054-1. TAXATION OF COSTS AND AWARD OF ATTORNEYS' FEES

(a) WHO MAY BE AWARDED COSTS. When costs are allowed by the FRBP or other applicable law, the court may award costs to the prevailing party. No costs will be allowed unless a party qualifies as, or is determined by the court to be, the prevailing party under this rule. Counsel are advised to review 28 U.S.C. § 1927 regarding counsel's liability for excessive costs.

(b) PREVAILING PARTY. For purposes of this rule, the prevailing party is defined as follows:

(1) Recovery on Complaint. The plaintiff is the prevailing party when it recovers on the entire complaint.

(2) Dismissal or Judgment in Favor of Defendant. The defendant is the prevailing party when the proceeding is terminated by court-ordered dismissal or judgment in favor of defendant on the entire complaint.

(3) Partial Recovery. Upon request of one or more of the parties, the court will determine the prevailing party when there is a partial recovery or a recovery by more than one party.

(4) Voluntary Dismissal. Upon request of one or more of the parties, the court will determine the prevailing party when the proceeding is voluntarily dismissed or otherwise voluntarily terminated.

(5) Offer of Judgment. If a party defending against a claim files under seal a written offer of judgment before trial and the judgment finally obtained by the offeree is not more favorable than the offer, the party offering the judgment is the prevailing party.

(c) BILL OF COSTS. The prevailing party who is awarded costs must file and serve a bill of costs not later than 30 days after entry of judgment. Each item claimed must be set forth separately in the bill of costs. The prevailing party, or the party's attorney or agent having knowledge of the facts must file a declaration with the bill of costs certifying that:

(1) The items claimed as costs are correct;

(2) The costs were necessarily incurred in the case;

(3) The services for which fees have been charged were actually and necessarily performed; and

(4) The costs were paid or the obligation for payment was incurred.

(d) ITEMS TAXABLE AS COSTS. A list of the items taxable as costs is contained in the Court Manual available from the clerk and on the court's website.

(e) OBJECTION TO BILL OF COSTS. Not later than 7 days after service of a copy of a bill of costs, a party dissatisfied with the costs claimed may file and serve an objection to taxation of the costs sought. The grounds for objection must be stated specifically. The court may resolve the matter without a hearing or set the matter for hearing.

(f) ENTRY OF COSTS. If a timely objection to a bill of costs is not filed or, in the event of a timely objection, as soon as practicable after an order determining the objection becomes final, the clerk will insert the amount of costs awarded to the prevailing party into the blank left in the judgment for that purpose and enter a similar notation on the docket sheet.

(g) MOTION FOR ATTORNEYS' FEES.

(1) If not previously determined at trial or other hearing, a party seeking an award of attorneys' fees where such fees may be awarded must file and serve a motion not later than 30 days after the entry of judgment or other final order, unless otherwise ordered by the court.

(2) The requirements of LBR 9013-1 through LBR 9013-4 apply to a motion for attorneys' fees under this rule.

(h) EXECUTION. Upon request, the clerk will issue a writ of execution to recover costs and attorneys' fees included in the judgment:

(1) Upon presentation of a certified copy of the final judgment in the bankruptcy court or in the district court; or

(2) Upon presentation of a mandate of the district court, bankruptcy appellate panel, or court of appeals to recover costs taxed by the appellate court.

LBR 7055-1. DEFAULT

(a) ENTRY OF DEFAULT. A request for the clerk to enter default must be supported by a declaration establishing the elements required by F.R.Civ.P. 55(a), as incorporated into FRBP 7055, and a proof of service on the defaulting party.

(b) MOTION FOR DEFAULT JUDGMENT.

(1) Form of Motion. A motion for default judgment must state:

(A) The identity of the party against whom default was entered and the date of entry of default;

(B) Whether the defaulting party is an infant or incompetent person and, if so, whether that person is represented by a general guardian, committee, conservator, or other representative;

(C) Whether the individual defendant in default is currently on active duty in the armed forces of the United States, based upon an appropriate declaration in compliance with the Service-members Civil Relief Act (Pub. L. 108-189) (50 U.S. Code App. §§ 501-594). When the individual defendant is the debtor, the party seeking the default may rely upon the debtor's sworn statements contained in a statement of financial affairs, by following the appropriate procedure for requesting judicial notice of that document pursuant to F.R.Evid. 201; and

(D) That notice of the motion has been served on the defaulting party, if required by F.R.Civ.P. 55(b)(2).

(2) Evidence of Amount of Damages. Unless otherwise ordered, if the amount claimed in a motion for judgment by default is unliquidated, the movant must submit evidence of the amount of damages by declarations in lieu of live testimony. Notice must be given to the defaulting party of the amount requested. Any opposition to the amount of damages by the party against whom the judgment is sought must be in writing and supported by competent evidence.

(3) Other Relief. Other proceedings necessary or appropriate to the entry of a judgment by default may be taken as provided in F.R.Civ.P. 55(b)(2).

(4) Attorneys' Fees.

(A) When a promissory note, contract, or applicable statute provides a basis for the recovery of attorneys' fees, a reasonable attorneys' fee may be allowed in a default judgment. Subject to subsection (b)(4)(B), the reasonableness of the attorneys' fee will be calculated based upon the amount of the judgment, exclusive of costs, according to the following schedule:

Amount of Judgment	Attorneys' Fees Award
$0.01–$1,000	30% with a minimum of $250
$1,000.01–$10,000	$300 plus 10% of the amount over $1,000
$10,000.01–$50,000	$1,200 plus 6% of the amount over $10,000
$50,000.01–$100,000	$3,600 plus 4% of the amount over $50,000
Over $100,000	$5,600 plus 2% of the amount over $100,000

(B) An attorney seeking fees in excess of the schedule may request in the motion for default judgment to have a reasonable attorneys' fee fixed by the court. The court will hear the request and render judgment for such fee as the court may deem reasonable.

LBR 7056-1. SUMMARY JUDGMENT

(a) GENERAL. The requirements of LBR 9013-1 through LBR 9013-4 apply to a motion for summary judgment, except as provided by this rule.

(b) MOTION AND SUPPORTING DOCUMENTS.

(1) Motion. A notice of motion and motion for summary judgment or partial summary adjudication pursuant to FRBP 7056 must be served and filed not later than 36 days before the date of the hearing on the motion.

(2) Statement of Uncontroverted Facts and Conclusions of Law and Proposed Summary Judgment.

(A) The movant must serve, file, and lodge with the motion for summary judgment or partial summary adjudication a proposed statement of uncontroverted facts and conclusions of law and a separate proposed summary judgment.

(B) Unless otherwise ordered by the court, the proposed statement of uncontroverted facts and conclusions of law must be lodged electronically via LOU. The statement must identify each of the specific material facts relied upon in support of the motion and cite the particular portions of any pleading, affidavit, deposition, interrogatory answer, admission, or other document relied upon to establish each such fact.

(3) Evidence. The movant is responsible for filing with the court all evidentiary documents cited in the moving papers in accordance with LBR 9013-1(i).

(c) RESPONSE AND SUPPORTING DOCUMENTS.

(1) Response. Any party who opposes the motion must serve and file a response not later than 21 days before the date of the hearing on the motion.

(2) Statement of Genuine Issues.

(A) The respondent must serve, file, and lodge a separate concise statement of genuine issues with the response.

(B) Unless otherwise ordered by the court, the respondent's statement of genuine issues must be lodged electronically via LOU. The respondent's statement must identify each material fact that is disputed and cite the particular portions of any pleading, affidavit, deposition, interrogatory answer, admission, or other document relied upon to establish the dispute and the existence of a genuine issue precluding summary judgment or adjudication.

(3) Evidence. The respondent is responsible for filing with the court all necessary evidentiary documents cited in the responding papers in accordance with LBR 9013-1(i).

(4) Need for Discovery. If a need for discovery is asserted as a basis for denial of the motion, the respondent must identify the specific facts or issues on which discovery is necessary and justify the request for additional time to pursue such discovery.

(d) REPLY. Movant must serve and file any reply not later than 14 days before the hearing on the motion.

(e) STIPULATED FACTS. The parties may file a stipulation setting forth a statement of stipulated undisputed facts. The parties so stipulating may state that their stipulations are entered into solely for purposes of the motion for summary judgment and are not intended to be binding otherwise.

(f) FACTS DEEMED ADMITTED. In determining any motion for summary judgment or partial summary adjudication, the court may assume that the material facts as claimed and adequately supported by the movant are admitted to exist without controversy, except to the extent that such facts are:

(1) Included in the "statement of genuine issues," and

(2) Adequately controverted by declaration or other evidence filed in opposition to the motion.

LBR 7064-1. SEIZURE OF PERSONS AND PROPERTY

(a) ISSUANCE OF WRIT. A writ or other process issued for the seizure of persons or property pursuant to F.R.Civ.P. 64, 69, or 70 must be issued, attested, signed, and sealed as required for writs issued out of this court.

(b) WRIT OR OTHER PROCESS OF SEIZURE. A writ or other process for seizure in a civil action must be directed to, executed, and returned by the United States Marshal, a state or local law enforcement officer authorized by state law, or a private person specially appointed by the court for that purpose pursuant to an application and order.

(c) PROCESS REQUIRING ENTRY UPON PREMISES.

(1) An order of court requiring entry upon private premises without notice must be executed by the United States Marshal, a state or local law enforcement officer authorized by state law, or a private person specially appointed by the court for that purpose pursuant to an application and order.

(2) If a writ or other process is to be executed by a private person, the private person must be accompanied by a United States Marshal or a state or local law enforcement officer present at the premises during the execution of the order.

(d) EVICTION. Any eviction to be made pursuant to a writ of possession issued by the court pursuant to 11 U.S.C. § 365(d)(4) must be effected by a state or local law enforcement officer authorized by state law to execute such writs issued under state law, unless otherwise ordered by the court.

LBR 7065-1. INJUNCTIONS

(a) ADVERSARY PROCEEDING REQUIRED. A temporary restraining order or preliminary injunction may be sought as a provisional remedy only in a pending adversary proceeding, not in the bankruptcy case itself. An adversary complaint must be filed either prior to, or contemporaneously with, a request for issuance of a temporary restraining order ("TRO") or preliminary injunction.

(b) TEMPORARY RESTRAINING ORDERS AND PRELIMINARY INJUNCTIONS.

(1) When a TRO is not requested, a preliminary injunction must be sought by noticed motion and not by order to show cause.

(2) When a TRO is requested, a preliminary injunction must be sought by order to show cause.

(3) If the TRO is granted without notice, the hearing on the order to show cause must be set within 14 days after the entry of the TRO unless otherwise agreed by the parties.

(4) If the TRO is denied or granted after reasonable notice, the court may set the hearing on the order to show cause re preliminary injunction without regard to the notice of motion requirements set forth in LBR 9013-1(d)(2).

(c) APPROVAL OF BONDS, UNDERTAKINGS, AND STIPULATIONS REGARDING SECURITY. A bond, undertaking, or stipulation regarding security given in conjunction with the issuance of a TRO or preliminary injunction must satisfy the requirements of FRBP 7065(c) and LBR 2010-1.

LBR 7067-1. REGISTRY FUND

(a) DEPOSIT OF REGISTRY FUNDS.

(1) General. Funds must not be sent to the court or the clerk for deposit into the court's registry without a court order.

(2) Form of Order. A party seeking authorization to deposit funds into the court's registry must prepare an order that meets the requirements of LBR 9004-1 and states (A) the exact amount to be deposited; (B) that the funds are to be deposited into an interest bearing account; and (C) that the funds will remain on deposit until further order of the court. The order must also contain the following provision:

"IT IS ORDERED that the clerk is directed to deduct from the income earned on the investment a fee, not exceeding that authorized by the Judicial Conference of the United States and set by the Director of the Administrative Office, whenever such income becomes available for deduction in the investment so held and without further order of the court."

(3) Tender of Funds. The funds must be submitted to the clerk by check or money order made payable to "U. S. Bankruptcy Court" in the exact amount specified in the court order.

(b) NOTICE TO CLERK.

(1) Whenever the court orders that money deposited into court must be deposited by the clerk in an interest bearing account, the party seeking the order must forthwith personally serve a copy of such order upon the clerk or chief deputy clerk along with the deposit.

(2) The failure of the party seeking an order of deposit to an interest bearing account to serve the clerk or chief deputy with a copy of the order releases the clerk from liability for loss of interest upon the money subject to the order of deposit.

(c) AUTHORIZED DEPOSITORIES. Unless otherwise ordered by the court, the clerk must deposit money pursuant to an order of deposit in any institution that the United States trustee has authorized for deposit of funds administered by debtors in possession or appointed trustees, subject to the same terms and conditions as for such funds. The clerk may also invest such money in United States Treasury bills.

(d) TIMING OF DEPOSIT. The clerk must deposit the money pursuant to an order of deposit as soon as practicable following service of a copy of the order by the party authorized to deposit funds.

(e) FEES CHARGED ON REGISTRY FUNDS. All funds deposited on or after December 1, 1990 and invested as registry funds will be assessed a charge of 10% of the income earned. Fees may be deducted periodically without further order and will be subject to any subsequent exceptions or adjustments by directive of the Administrative Office of the United States Courts.

(f) DISBURSEMENTS OF REGISTRY FUNDS.

(1) General. The clerk will disburse funds on deposit in the registry of the court only pursuant to a court order.

(2) Form of Order. The disbursement order must contain a provision relieving the clerk from liability for loss of interest, if any, for early withdrawal of the funds. The order must state the name and taxpayer identification number for each party who is to receive funds and the amount or percentage of the principal each is to receive. The order must also state the percentage of the interest each party is to receive. Funds will be disbursed only after the time for appeal of any related judgment or order has expired, or upon approval by the court of a written stipulation by all parties.

LBR 7069-1. ENFORCEMENT OF JUDGMENT AND PROVISIONAL REMEDIES

(a) USE OF UNITED STATES MARSHAL IS DISCOURAGED. The court encourages the use of state remedies and officers wherever appropriate to enforce judgments or obtain available remedies. The United States Marshals Service is available to enforce federal judgments as necessary.

(b) FORMS.

(1) Unless the court has adopted its own form, the applicable form approved by the Judicial Council of California for use in California courts must be used in this court whenever a provisional remedy is sought or a judgment is enforced in accordance with state law as provided in FRBP 7064 and 7069.

(2) The caption must be revised to specify "United States Bankruptcy Court for the Central District of California," rather than the California courts, and the form must be modified, as necessary, to meet the requirements of LBR 9004-1 and LBR 9009-1.

LBR 7069-2. DISCOVERY IN AID OF ENFORCEMENT OF JUDGMENT

(a) DISCOVERY PERMITTED. With respect to a judgment of the bankruptcy court and as allowed by FRBP 7069, except to the extent that a federal statute applies, a judgment creditor may obtain discovery from any person to aid in enforcing a judgment in the manner provided by F.R.Civ.P. 26-37 or in the manner provided by state law.

(b) RULE 2004 EXAMINATION NOT PERMITTED. A judgment creditor may not use FRBP 2004 to collect information to use to enforce a judgment.

LBR 8000-1. RULES APPLICABLE TO BANKRUPTCY APPEALS

(a) APPEALS TO DISTRICT COURT. A bankruptcy appeal pending before the district court is governed by Chapter IV, Local Rules of the District Court Governing Bankruptcy Appeals, Cases and Proceedings.

(b) APPEALS TO BANKRUPTCY APPELLATE PANEL. A bankruptcy appeal pending before the bankruptcy appellate panel is governed by the Rules of the United States Bankruptcy Appellate Panel of the Ninth Circuit.

(c) DIRECT APPEALS TO NINTH CIRCUIT. In an appeal arising out of a bankruptcy case filed on or after October 17, 2005, a certification of a judgment, order, or decree of the court to the Ninth Circuit, as permitted by 28 U.S.C. § 158(d)(2), must be made in accordance with FRBP 8001(f) and 8003, as well as any applicable interim rules approved by the Committee on Rules of Practice and Procedure of the United States Judicial Conference and the Judicial Conference of the United States.

LBR 8001-1. NOTICE OF APPEAL

A notice of appeal must be filed in accordance with FRBP 8001(a) and Rule 2.2 of Chapter IV, Local Rules of the District Court Governing Bankruptcy Appeals, Cases and Proceedings.

LBR 8001-3. STATEMENT OF ELECTION

A statement of election to have an appeal heard by the district court instead of the bankruptcy appellate panel must be filed in accordance with FRBP 8001(e) and Rules 2.1.1 through 2.1.2.2 of Chapter IV, Local Rules of the District Court Governing Bankruptcy Appeals, Cases and Proceedings.

LBR 8003-1. LEAVE TO APPEAL FROM INTERLOCUTORY ORDERS

(a) APPLICABILITY.

(1) This rule is applicable solely to appeals referred to the bankruptcy appellate panel.

(2) Leave to appeal from an interlocutory order to the district court is governed by Rule 3 of Chapter IV, Local Rules of the District Court Governing Bankruptcy Appeals, Cases and Proceedings.

(b) MOTION FOR LEAVE TO APPEAL. Leave to appeal under 28 U.S.C. § 158(a) must be sought by filing a motion for leave with the clerk within the time provided by FRBP 8002 for filing a notice of appeal, with proof of service by the applicant in accordance with FRBP 8008(b).

(c) CONTENT OF MOTION. A motion for leave to appeal must include all elements required by FRBP 8003(a).

(d) ANSWER. Within 14 days after service of the motion, an adverse party may file with the clerk an answer in opposition.

(e) DISPOSITION.

(1) Unless a party to the appeal has filed with the clerk of the bankruptcy appellate panel a written objection to the disposition of the appeal by the bankruptcy appellate panel, the clerk will transmit the motion for leave to appeal and any answer thereto to the clerk of the bankruptcy appellate panel as soon as all parties have filed answers or the time for filing an answer has expired.

(2) If an objection is duly filed after the motion has been referred to the bankruptcy appellate panel but before it has been determined, then the motion will be transferred to the district court for decision.

(3) The motion and answer will be considered without oral argument, unless otherwise ordered.

(f) DESIGNATION AND TRANSMISSION OF RECORD.

(1) If leave to appeal is granted, the clerk will notify counsel for appellant within 7 days. The record will be designated and transmitted and the appeal will be docketed in accordance with FRBP 8006 and 8007.

(2) The time fixed by FRBP 8006 and 8007 for designating and transmitting the record and docketing the appeal will run from the date of the notice by the clerk of entry of the order granting leave to appeal.

LBR 8004-1. SERVICE OF NOTICE OF APPEAL

(a) SERVICE ON PARTIES TO APPEAL. Within 3 days after the filing of a notice of appeal, the clerk will serve upon all parties to the appeal a copy of the notice of appeal, Notice of Referral of Appeal, Transcript Order Form, Notice of Transcript, and a copy of the below referenced applicable order:

(1) Amended Order Establishing and Continuing the Bankruptcy Appellate Panel of the Ninth Circuit (referencing appeals originating in bankruptcy cases filed on or before October 22, 1994).

(2) Order Continuing Bankruptcy Appellate Panels of the Ninth Circuit (referencing appeals originating in bankruptcy cases filed after October 22, 1994).

(b) TRANSMISSION TO APPELLATE COURT. A copy of the notice of appeal will also be transmitted to the clerk of the bankruptcy appellate panel or clerk of the district court.

LBR 8009-1. BRIEFS IN APPEALS TO DISTRICT COURT

Briefs in an appeal pending before the district court are governed by Rule 5 of Chapter IV, Local Rules of the District Court Governing Bankruptcy Appeals, Cases and Proceedings.

LBR 8011-4. EMERGENCY MOTIONS IN APPEALS TO DISTRICT COURT

An emergency motion in an appeal pending in the district court must be made in accordance with Rule 6.3 of Chapter IV, Local Rules of the District Court Governing Bankruptcy Appeals, Cases and Proceedings.

LBR 8014-1. COSTS ON APPEAL TO DISTRICT COURT

Costs on appeal to the district court are governed by Rule 9 of Chapter IV, Local Rules of the District Court Governing Bankruptcy Appeals, Cases and Proceedings.

LBR 9001-1. DEFINITIONS

(a) DEFINITION OF TERMS. As used in these rules, the following words and phrases are defined as follows:

(1) "Appellate Court" means the bankruptcy appellate panel or the district court exercising its appellate jurisdiction pursuant to 28 U.S.C. § 158.

(2) "Application" means a request for judicial action that must be sought by application rather than motion under the FRBP.

(3) "Attorney" or "Counsel" includes attorney, proctor, advocate, solicitor, counsel, or counselor.

(4) "Bankruptcy Appellate Panel" means the United States Bankruptcy Appellate Panel of the Ninth Circuit.

(5) "Bankruptcy Code" or "Code" means title 11 of the United States Code.

(6) "Brief" includes briefs, memoranda, points and authorities, and other written argument or compilations of authorities.

(7) "Case" means a bankruptcy case commenced by the filing of a petition pursuant to 11 U.S.C. §§ 301, 302, 303, or 1504.

(8) "Clerk" means the clerk of the United States Bankruptcy Court for the Central District of California and deputy clerks. Other clerks may be specified in the text.

(9) "CM/ECF" means the court's Case Management/Electronic Case Files System.

(10) "CM/ECF Procedures" means the Administrative Procedures for Filing, Signing, and Verifying Pleadings and Papers Using the Case Management/Electronic Case Files (CM/ECF) System as authorized and approved by General Order 06-03 on November 7, 2006. The instructions for registration and procedures for use of CM/ECF are posted on the court's website at the CM/ECF home page and contained in the Court Manual available from the clerk and on the court's website.

(11) "CM/ECF User" means a person or entity registered to use the court's Case Management/Electronic Case Files System.

(12) "Court" means the United States Bankruptcy Court of the Central District of California or the district court when exercising its original bankruptcy jurisdiction pursuant to 11 U.S.C. § 1334, including the judge to whom a case or proceeding is assigned.

(13) "Court Manual" means the procedural manual maintained and updated periodically by the clerk that includes: General Court Information; Filing Information and Procedures; CM/ECF Procedures; LOU Procedures; Other Court Technology; and Clerk's Forms. The Court Manual is available from the clerk and on the court's website.

(14) "Courtroom Deputy" means a deputy clerk assigned to the courtroom of a judge of the court.

(15) "Court's Website" means www.cacb.uscourts.gov.

(16) "Declaration" means any declaration under penalty of perjury executed in conformance with 28 U.S.C. § 1746 and any properly executed affidavit.

(17) "Defendant" means a party against whom a claim for relief is made by complaint, counterclaim, or cross-claim.

(18) "District Court" means the United States District Court for the Central District of California.

(19) "District Court Rules" means the Local Civil Rules of the United States District Court for the Central District of California; Chapter IV, Local Rules of the District Court Governing Bankruptcy Appeals, Cases and Proceedings; and such other rules and general orders adopted by the district court concerning cases or proceedings filed or pending in the bankruptcy court.

(20) "F.R.App.P." means the Federal Rules of Appellate Procedure.

(21) "FRBP" means the Federal Rules of Bankruptcy Procedure.

(22) "F.R.Civ.P." means the Federal Rules of Civil Procedure.

(23) "F.R.Evid." means the Federal Rules of Evidence.

(24) "File" means the delivery, including electronically via CM/ECF, to and acceptance by the clerk, courtroom deputy, the court, or other person authorized by the court of a paper that will be noted in the docket.

(25) "Judge" means a bankruptcy judge, district court judge, or other judicial officer in a case or proceeding assigned to the court.

(26) "Lodge" means to deliver, including electronically via LOU, to the clerk, courtroom deputy, the court, or other person authorized by the court a paper that is tendered to the court but is not approved for filing, such as a proposed form of order.

(27) "LOU" means the court's Lodged Order Upload program.

(28) "LOU Procedures" means the procedures for LOU posted on the court's website at the CM/ECF home page and contained in the Court Manual available from the clerk and on the court's website.

(29) "Motion" includes all motions, applications, objections to claims that are not adversary proceedings, or other requests made for judicial action except by complaint, counterclaim, or cross-claim.

(30) “Movant” means an entity requesting an order other than by way of complaint, counterclaim, or cross-claim.

(31) “NEF” means the Notice of Electronic Filing, and hyperlink to the document filed, automatically generated when a paper is electronically or non-electronically added to the docket or a docket event is entered. As set forth in the CM/ECF Procedures, an NEF and hyperlink to the document or docket event is transmitted electronically to parties who have a CM/ECF login and password and who are either a party in a case or adversary proceeding or have otherwise participated in the case or adversary proceeding.

(32) “Ninth Circuit” means the United States Court of Appeals for the Ninth Circuit.

(33) “Notice of Entry”means a document completed by the clerk that provides notice to appropriate persons or entities that an order or judgment has been entered.

(34) “Paper” includes all pleadings, motions, affidavits, declarations, briefs, points and authorities, and all other papers and documents presented for filing or lodging, excluding exhibits submitted during a hearing or trial.

(35) “Plaintiff” means a party claiming affirmative relief by complaint, counterclaim, or cross-claim.

(36) “Proceeding” includes motions, adversary proceedings, contested matters, and other matters presented to the court. It does not include a “case” as defined above.

(37) “Proof of Service” means a document certifying that a person or entity who filed or lodged a paper with the court served other appropriate persons or entities with a copy of the paper filed or lodged.

(38) “Respondent” means an entity responding to a request for an order other than by way of complaint, counterclaim, or cross-complaint.

(39) “United States attorney” means the United States Attorney for the Central District of California, and any assistant United States attorney, employee, or designee of the United States attorney.

(40) “United States trustee” means the United States Trustee for Region 16, and any assistant United States trustee, employee, or designee of the United States trustee.

(41) “United States Trustee Notices and Guides” means the United

States Trustee Chapter 11 Notices and Guides and the Notice of Requirements for Debtors In Possession in Chapter 11 Cases.

(b) TERMS NOT OTHERWISE DEFINED. A term not defined in this rule will have the meaning provided in the Bankruptcy Code or the FRBP.

LBR 9004-1. FORM OF PAPERS FILED OR LODGED WITH COURT

(a) GENERAL.

(1) Unless otherwise expressly provided by these rules, a paper filed or lodged with the court and any exhibit thereto must comply with the form and format requirements contained in the Court Manual available from the clerk and on the court's website.

(2) This rule does not prevent the use of Official Forms or court-approved forms in accordance with LBR 9009-1.

(b) SIGNATURE OF PERSON.

(1) General. The name of the person signing a paper must be printed clearly below the signature line.

(2) Facsimile or Electronically Produced Signature. Unless otherwise provided in a case, the clerk may accept papers for filing that bear a facsimile or electronically produced signature as the equivalent of an original signature, provided the filing party and clerk comply strictly with the court's electronic filing procedures described in LBR 5005-4 for the safeguarding of paper documents with original signatures.

LBR 9009-1. FORMS

(a) OFFICIAL FORMS. Official Forms prescribed by the Judicial Conference of the United States may be used in any case or proceeding filed in this court.

(b) COURT-APPROVED FORMS.

(1) In addition to the Official Forms prescribed by the Judicial Conference of the United States, the court provides additional court-approved forms, copies of which are available from the clerk and on the court's website.

(2) Unless specifically designated as a mandatory form or unless otherwise specifically ordered, a court-approved form provided in these rules is optional and is provided for the convenience of the parties.

(c) COURT-MANDATED FORMS.

(1) A court-mandated form is a court-approved form designated as "mandatory." A court-mandated form must be filed with the exact language provided in the form. If the court-mandated form is an order or judgment, the form order or judgment must be lodged with the exact language provided in the form, except that it may include additional language that has been approved by the court.

(2) No modification of the original text of a court-mandated form is permitted. Any proposed modification must be added as an attachment so that the suggested modification of the standard language of the court-mandated form is obvious.

(d) CERTIFICATE OF SUBSTANTIAL COMPLIANCE. If a modified version of an Official Form or a court-approved form is used, then such paper must include a certificate that the form contains the same substance as the Official Form or court-approved form, as applicable.

LBR 9011-2. PERSONS APPEARING WITHOUT COUNSEL

(a) CORPORATION, PARTNERSHIP, UNINCORPORATED ASSOCIATION, OR TRUST. A corporation, a partnership including a limited liability partnership, a limited liability company, or any other unincorporated association, or a trust may not file a petition or otherwise appear without counsel in any case or proceeding, except that it may file a proof of claim, file or appear in support of an application for professional compensation, or file a reaffirmation agreement, if signed by an authorized representative of the entity.

(b) INDIVIDUALS. Any individual representing himself or herself without an attorney must appear personally for such purpose.

(c) MINORS OR INCOMPETENTS. A non-attorney guardian for a minor or an incompetent person must be represented by counsel. Local Civil Rule 83-5 of the district court is incorporated herein by reference.

(d) COMPLIANCE WITH RULES. Any person appearing without counsel must comply with the F.R.Civ.P., F.R.Evid., F.R.App.P., FRBP, and these rules. The failure to comply may be grounds for dismissal, conversion, appointment of a trustee or an examiner, judgment by default, or other appropriate sanctions.

LBR 9011-3. SANCTIONS

(a) VIOLATION OF RULES. The violation of, or failure to conform to, the FRBP or these rules may subject the offending party or counsel to penalties, including monetary sanctions, the imposition of costs and attorneys' fees payable to opposing counsel, and/or dismissal of the case or proceeding.

(b) FAILURE TO APPEAR OR PREPARE. Unless otherwise ordered by the court, the failure of counsel for any party to take any of the following steps may be deemed an abandonment or failure to prosecute or defend diligently by the defaulting party:

(1) Complete the necessary preparation for pretrial;

(2) Appear at pretrial or status conference;

(3) Be prepared for trial on the date set; or

(4) Appear at any hearing where service of notice of the hearing has been given or waived.

(c) PENALTIES FOR AN UNNECESSARY OR UNWARRANTED MOTION OR OPPOSITION. Pursuant to FRBP 9011, the presentation to the court of an unnecessary motion and the unwarranted opposition to a motion, which unduly delays the course of an action or proceeding, or failure to comply fully with these rules, subjects the offender and attorney at the discretion of the court to appropriate discipline, including the imposition of costs and the award of attorneys' fees to opposing counsel, payment of 1 day's jury fees of the panel, if one has been called for the trial, and such other sanctions, including denial of the motion or dismissal of the proceeding, as may appear proper to the court under the circumstances. This section applies to violations of the LBRs which may otherwise not be subject to sanctions under either FRBP 9011 or F.R.Civ.P. 11.

LBR 9013-1. MOTION PRACTICE AND CONTESTED MATTERS

(a) APPLICABILITY.

(1) Unless otherwise ordered by the court, parties must file, serve, and set for hearing all contested matters, including motions, whether filed in the bankruptcy case or an adversary proceeding, objections, applications, orders to show cause, and other matters for which a hearing is necessary (collectively, "motions"), in accordance with this rule, any other applicable LBR, the FRBP, and the Bankruptcy Code.

(2) This rule applies to objections to claims, except as provided in LBR 3007-1.

(3) This rule applies to motions for summary judgment, except as provided in LBR 7056-1.

(4) This rule does not apply to a motion to reject a collective bargaining agreement which is governed by 11 U.S.C. § 1113.

(b) MOTION CALENDAR.

(1) Each judge of the court maintains a motion calendar and instructions for self-setting hearings that are available from the clerk and posted on the court's website.

(2) A party must self-set a motion for hearing at a date and time permitted on the judge's motion calendar in accordance with the judge's self-set calendaring instructions.

(3) If a judge's calendar does not permit the self-setting of a hearing on a particular type of motion or the judge does not schedule a regular law and motion day, a hearing on the motion must be noticed only with the approval of the judge or courtroom deputy.

(c) FORM AND CONTENT OF MOTION AND NOTICE.

(1) Oral Motions. Unless otherwise provided by rule or order of the court, an oral motion is not permitted except during trial.

(2) Notice of Motion. Every motion must be accompanied by written notice of motion specifying briefly the relief requested in the motion and, if applicable, the date, time, and place of hearing. Except as set forth in LBR 7056-1 with regard to motions for summary judgment or partial summary adjudication, or as otherwise ordered, the notice of motion must advise the opposing party that LBR 9013-1(f) requires a written response to be filed and served at least 14 days before the hearing. If the motion is being heard on shortened notice pursuant to LBR 9075-1, the notice must specify the deadline for responses set by the court in the order approving the shortened notice.

(3) Motion. There must be served and filed with the motion and as a part thereof:

(A) Duly authenticated copies of all photographs and documentary evidence that the moving party intends to submit in support of the motion, in addition to the declarations required or permitted by FRBP 9006(d); and

(B) A written statement of all reasons in support thereof, together with a memorandum of the points and authorities upon which the moving party will rely.

(4) Exception. Unless warranted by special circumstances of the motion, or otherwise ordered by the court, a memorandum of points and authorities is not required for applications to retain or compensate professionals, motions for relief from automatic stay, or motions to sell, use, lease, or abandon estate assets.

(d) TIME LIMITS FOR SERVICE AND FILING OF MOTIONS.

(1) Persons or Entities to be Served with the Notice and Motion. Except for a motion under LBRs 2014-1(b), 2016-1(a)(2), 3015-1(w) and (x), 7026-1(c), and 9075-1, and subject to LBR 2002-2(a) and FRBP 9034, a motion and notice thereof must be served upon the adverse party (by serving the adverse party's attorney of record, if any; or if the adverse party is the debtor, by serving the debtor and the debtor's attorney, if any; or the adverse party, if there is no attorney of record).

(2) Deadline for Filing and Serving of Notice and/or Notice and Motion. The notice of motion and motion must be filed and served not later than 21 days before the hearing date designated in the notice except as set forth in: (A) LBR 7056-1 with regard to motions for summary judgment or partial summary adjudication; (B) LBRs 2014-1(b), 2016-1(a)(2), 3015-1(w) and (x), and 9013-1(o) with regard to motions and matters that may not require a hearing; (C) LBR 3007-1 with regard to motions for orders disallowing claims; and (D) LBR 9075-1 with regard to motions to be heard on an emergency or shortened notice basis. The court, for good cause, may prescribe a different time.

(e) PROOF OF SERVICE. Every paper filed pursuant to this rule must be accompanied by a proof of service in the form specified in LBR 9013-3.

(f) OPPOSITION, JOINDERS, AND RESPONSES TO MOTIONS. Except as set forth in LBR 7056-1 with regard to motions for summary judgment or partial summary adjudication, LBRs 2014-1(b), 2016-1(a)(2), 3015-1(w) and (x), and 9013-1(o) with regard to motions and matters that may not require a hearing, LBR 9075-1 with regard to motions to be heard on an emergency or shortened notice basis or unless otherwise ordered by the court, each interested party opposing, joining, or responding to the motion must file and serve on the moving party and the United States trustee not later than 14 days before the date designated for hearing either:

(1) A complete written statement of all reasons in opposition thereto or in support or joinder thereof, declarations and copies of all photographs and documentary evidence on which the responding party intends to rely, and any responding memorandum of points and authorities. The opposing papers must advise the adverse party that any reply to the opposition must be filed with the court and served on the opposing party not later than 7 days prior to the hearing on the motion; or

(2) A written statement that the motion will not be opposed.

(g) REPLY PAPERS. Except as set forth in LBR 7056-1 with regard to motions for summary judgment or partial summary adjudication, or unless otherwise ordered by the court, the moving party (or the opposing party in instances where a joinder has been filed) may file and serve a reply memorandum not later than 7 days before the date designated for hearing.

(1) The reply memorandum and declarations or other evidence attached, must respond directly to the opposition papers.

(2) Service of reply papers is required only upon the United States trustee subject to FRBP 9034 and LBR 2002-2(a) and on persons or entities (or their attorneys, if any) who filed an opposition to a motion, and must be made by personal service, e-mail, or by overnight mail delivery service. A judge's copy of the reply must be served on the judge in chambers in accordance with LBR 5005-2(d).

(3) Unless the court finds good cause, a reply paper not filed or served in accordance with this rule will not be considered.

(h) FAILURE TO FILE REQUIRED PAPERS. Papers not timely filed and served may be deemed by the court to be consent to the granting or denial of the motion, as the case may be.

(i) EVIDENCE ON MOTIONS, RESPONSES TO MOTIONS, OR REPLY PAPERS. Factual contentions involved in any motion, opposition or other response to a motion, or reply papers, must be presented, heard, and determined upon declarations and other written evidence. The verification of a motion is not sufficient to constitute evidence on a motion, unless otherwise ordered by the court.

(1) The court may, at its discretion, in addition to or in lieu of declaratory evidence, require or allow oral examination of any declarant or any other witness in accordance with FRBP 9017. When the court intends to take such testimony, it will give the parties 2 days notice of its intention, if possible, or may grant such a continuance as it may deem appropriate.

(2) An evidentiary objection may be deemed waived unless it is (A) set forth in a separate document; (B) cites the specific Federal Rule of Evidence upon which the objection is based; and (C) is filed with the responsive or reply papers.

(3) In lieu of oral testimony, a declaration under penalty of perjury will be received into evidence.

(4) Unless the court orders otherwise, a witness need not be present at the first hearing on a motion.

(5) If the court decides to hear oral testimony, the matter may be continued to another date for final hearing.

(j) APPEARANCE AT HEARING.

(1) Appearance is Mandatory. Counsel for the moving and opposing parties, and the moving and opposing parties who are appearing without counsel, must be present at the hearing on the motion and must have such familiarity with the case as to permit informed discussion and argument of the motion. The failure of counsel or an unrepresented party to appear, unless excused by the court in advance, may be deemed consent to a ruling upon the motion adverse to that counsel's or unrepresented party's position.

(2) Waiver of Personal Appearance. With the consent of the court, counsel may waive personal appearance at the hearing. Counsel who have agreed to waive personal appearance must advise the courtroom deputy of such agreement by telephone message or letter which reaches the courtroom deputy by no later than noon on the third day preceding the hearing date. The courtroom deputy will advise the parties by no later than noon on the day preceding the hearing date as to whether the court has consented to the waiver of personal appearance.

(3) Oral Argument. If the court decides in its discretion to dispense with oral argument on any motion, the courtroom deputy will attempt to give counsel and unrepresented parties notice of the court's intention to do so at least 24 hours prior to the hearing date and time. The court may also dispense with oral argument and waive appearance by tentative or final ruling posted on the court's web site the day before the hearing.

(4) Telephonic Appearance at Hearing. A party who wishes to appear telephonically must consult the court's web site to determine whether a telephonic appearance on a particular matter is permissible and to review the judge's procedures for telephonic appearances. See LBR 9074-1.

(k) VOLUNTARY DISMISSAL OF MOTION. A party who seeks to voluntarily dismiss a motion must, not less than 2 days prior to the hearing date: (1) give telephonic notice thereof to opposing counsel and the courtroom deputy of the judge before whom the matter is pending; and (2) file with the court, and serve on the United States trustee and persons or entities who have filed an opposition or other response to the motion, a notice thereof with the court. An order may be required.

(l) MOTION PREVIOUSLY DENIED. Whenever any motion for an order or other relief has been made to the court and has been denied in whole or in part, or has been granted conditionally or on terms, and a subsequent motion is made for the same relief in whole or in part upon the same or any allegedly different state of facts, it is the continuing duty of each party and attorney seeking such relief to present to the judge to whom any subsequent motion is made, a declaration of a party or witness or certified statement of an attorney setting forth the material facts and circumstances surrounding each prior motion including:

(1) The date of the prior motion;

(2) The identity of the judge to whom the prior motion was made;

(3) The ruling, decision or order on the prior motion; and

(4) The new or different facts and circumstances claimed to exist, which either did not exist or were not shown upon the prior motion.

The failure to comply with the foregoing requirement is grounds for the court to set aside any order or ruling made on the subsequent motion, and subjects the offending party or attorney to sanctions.

(m) CONTINUANCE.

(1) Ex Parte Motion for Continuance. Unless otherwise ordered, an ex parte motion for the continuance of a hearing under this rule must be filed with the court and served upon all previously noticed parties by facsimile, e-mail, personal service, or overnight mail at least 3 days before the date set for the hearing.

(A) The motion must set forth in detail the reasons for the continuance, state whether any prior continuance has been granted, and be supported by the declaration of a competent witness attesting to the necessity for the continuance.

(B) A proposed order for continuance must, in accordance with LBR 9021-1(b), be lodged with the court upon the filing of the motion.

(C) Unless the ex parte motion for continuance is granted by the court at least 1 day before the hearing, the parties must appear at the hearing.

(2) Stipulations For Continuances. Parties stipulating to a continuance of a hearing under this rule must notify the courtroom deputy immediately of their agreement for a continuance. The stipulation is subject to approval by the court under subsection (m)(3) of this rule. Unless the continuance is approved by the court at least 1 day before the hearing, the parties must appear at the hearing. A stipulation for continuance must contain facts establishing cause for the requested continuance and be submitted to the court in accordance with LBR 9021-1(b)(2) and LBR 9071-1.

(3) Court Approval. A continuance (whether stipulated to by counsel or not) is not effective unless the continuance is granted in open court, the court approves the continuance in writing, or the clerk or court staff informs the parties that the court has authorized a continuance.

(4) Extension of Time Due to Continuance of Hearing Date. Unless an order for continuance states otherwise, a continuance of the hearing of a motion automatically extends the time for filing and serving opposing papers and reply papers.

(n) DISCOVERY. Unless otherwise ordered by the court, Fed.R.Civ.P. 26(a), (d) and (f), as incorporated into FRBP 7026 and LBR 7026-1, do not apply to contested matters under FRBP 9014 and this rule.

(o) MOTIONS AND MATTERS NOT REQUIRING A HEARING.

(1) Matters That May Be Determined Upon Notice of Opportunity to Request Hearing. Except as to matters specifically noted in subsection (o)(2) below, and as otherwise ordered by the court, any matter that may be set for hearing in accordance with LBR 9013-1 may be determined upon notice of opportunity to request a hearing.

(A) NOTICE. When the notice of opportunity for hearing procedure is used, the notice must:

(i) Succinctly and sufficiently describe the nature of the relief sought and set forth the essential facts necessary for a party in interest to determine whether to file a response and request a hearing;

(ii) State that LBR 9013-1(o)(1) requires that any response and request for hearing must be filed with the court and served on the movant and the United States trustee within 14 days after the date of service of the notice; and

(iii) Be filed with the court and served by the moving party on all creditors and other parties in interest who are entitled to notice of the particular matter.

(B) MOTION. The motion and supporting papers must be filed with the notice, but must be served only on the United States trustee and those parties who are directly affected by the requested relief.

(2) Matters that May Not be Determined Upon Notice of Opportunity to Request Hearing. Unless otherwise ordered by the court, the following matters may not be determined by the procedure set forth in subsection (o)(1) above:

(A) Objections to claims;

(B) Motions regarding the stay of 11 U.S.C. § 362;

(C) Motions for summary judgment and partial summary adjudication;

(D) Motions for approval of cash collateral stipulations;

(E) Motions for approval of postpetition financing;

(F) Motions for continuance;

(G) Adequacy of chapter 11 disclosure statements;

(H) Confirmation of plans in chapter 9, chapter 11, chapter 12, and chapter 13 cases;

(I) Motions for orders establishing procedures for the sale of the estate's assets under LBR 6004-1(b);

(J) Motions for recognition of a foreign proceeding as either a main or a nonmain proceeding;

(K) Motions for the adoption of a chapter 15 administrative order; and

(L) Motions for the adoption of a cross-border protocol.

(3) No Response and Request for Hearing. If the response period expires without the filing and service of any response and request for hearing, the moving party must do all of the following:

(A) FILE DECLARATION OF SERVICE AND NON-RESPONSE. Promptly file a declaration attesting that no timely response and request for hearing was served upon the moving party. A copy of the motion, notice, and proof of service of the notice and motion must be attached as exhibits to the declaration. No service is required prior to filing the declaration.

(B) LODGE PROPOSED ORDER. Lodge a proposed order in accordance with LBR 9021-1, except that: (i) the proposed order need not be served prior to lodging, except as otherwise required in these rules; and (ii) the Notice of Entered Order and Service List must limit service by the court to only the debtor or debtor in possession (and debtor's attorney, if any), and the United States trustee.

(C) DELIVER COPIES TO COURT. Promptly deliver to the court: (i) a copy of the declaration; and (ii) the appropriate proposed order, copies, and envelopes, as specified in LBR 9021-1 and the LOU Procedures.

(4) Response and Request for Hearing Filed. If a timely response and request for hearing is filed and served, within 21 days from the date of service of the response and request for hearing the moving party must schedule and give not less than 14 days notice of a hearing to those responding and to the United States trustee. If movant fails to obtain a hearing date, the court may deny the motion without prejudice, without further notice or hearing.

LBR 9013-2. BRIEFS AND MEMORANDA OF LAW

(a) TRIAL BRIEFS.

(1) Unless otherwise ordered by the court, at least 7 days before trial is scheduled to commence, each counsel may file and serve a trial brief which may contain:

(A) A concise statement of the facts of the case;

(B) All admissions and stipulations;

(C) A short summary of the points of law involved, citing authorities in support thereof; and

(D) Any anticipated evidentiary problems.

(2) In appropriate cases, the court may require submission of trial briefs.

(b) FORM OF BRIEFS.

(1) Length. A brief must not exceed 35 pages in length, unless otherwise ordered by the court.

(2) Appendices. Appendices must not include any matters that properly belong in the body of the brief.

(3) Table of Contents and Table of Authorities. Any brief exceeding 10 pages in length, excluding exhibits, must be accompanied by an indexed table of contents setting forth the headings and subheadings contained in the body thereof and by an indexed table of the cases, statutes, rules, and other authorities cited.

(4) Unpublished Opinions. If a party cites an unpublished judicial opinion, order, judgment, or other written disposition, the party must file and serve a copy of that opinion, order, judgment, or disposition with the brief or other paper in which it is cited.

(c) CITATIONS.

(1) Acts of Congress. A citation to an Act of Congress must include a parallel citation to the United States Code by title and section, if codified.

(2) Regulations. A citation to a federal regulation must include a citation to the Code of Federal Regulations by title and section and the date of promulgation of the regulation.

(3) Cases.

(A) FEDERAL. The initial citation of a United States Supreme Court case must be to the United States Reports. A citation to the Federal Reporter, Federal Supplement, or Federal Rules Decisions must be used where available.

(B) STATE. The initial citation to a state court decision must include both the official report and any regional reporter published by West Publishing Company. California parallel citations may be limited to the official reports and California Reporter.

(C) BANKRUPTCY. A bankruptcy case citation must be to West's Bankruptcy Reporter, where available.

(D) UNREPORTED DECISIONS. Where a citation to the above-named reporters is not available, the party citing the case must provide the court with an unmarked, complete copy of the decision.

(E) CITATION FORM. A case citation must include the name and district or circuit of the issuing court and the year of the decision.

(4) Internal Page Citation. A case citation must include a further citation to the page where the proposition of law is found.

LBR 9013-3. PROOF OF SERVICE

(a) FORM.

(1) Declaration. Proof of service may be made by declaration of the person accomplishing the service. The declaration must include the following information:

(A) The day and manner of service;

(B) The person and/or entity served;

(C) The method of service employed (*e.g.*, electronic, personal, mail, substituted, etc.);

(D) Identification of the papers served;

(E) The exact address (including zip code) at which service was made, or the email address or facsimile number if service is by electronic means; and

(F) The capacity in which the person or entity was served.

(2) Identification of Persons or Entities Served. The following example is illustrative, not exhaustive, of the manner in which persons or entities may be identified in a proof of service required by this rule, if service of a document is required to be made upon such person or entity:

(A) SERVICE ON NON-ATTORNEY. DEBTOR:

Jane Jones
123 Main St.
Any Town, CA 91234

TWENTY LARGEST UNSECURED CREDITORS:

[The full names and addresses must be listed for each person or entity served in this category. If there are less than 20 unsecured creditors of the estate, the proof of service must indicate that all unsecured creditors were served.]

SPECIAL NOTICE LIST:

[The full names and addresses must be listed for each person or entity served in this category.]

(B) SERVICE ON ATTORNEY. ATTORNEY FOR TRUSTEE:

Harold Smith, Esq.
Smith & Smith
234 First St., Suite 100

Any Town, CA 91234

(b) ELECTRONIC VERSUS NON-ELECTRONIC SERVICE. The proof of service must differentiate between electronic and non-electronic service by: (1) stating that service will be accomplished through an NEF for parties and counsel who are registered CM/ECF Users; and (2) describing the manner by which service was accomplished on any other party or counsel who is not a CM/ECF User or is a CM/ECF User who has not consented to electronic service.

(c) SERVICE BY MAIL. Proof of service by mail may be made by the declaration of the person mailing or causing the papers to be mailed.

(d) PERSONAL SERVICE. In addition to any other method authorized by law, proof of personal service may also be shown by declaration in the same manner as for mail that the declarant has caused the papers to be served by hand or shown by acknowledgment of service by the person receiving a copy thereof on the original of the copy served. The declarant must be the attorney for the party, the person in charge of the attorney's office, or the party appearing without counsel.

(e) SERVICE BY MAIL EQUIVALENTS. Proof of service by messenger or overnight courier may be made by the person causing such service.

(f) SERVICE BY FAX MACHINE OR EMAIL. Proof of service by fax machine or email may be made by the person causing the paper to be transmitted. Such proof of service must state the telephone number or email address to which the paper was transmitted and the method of confirmation that the transmission was received. A paper exceeding a total of 15 pages must not be served by fax machine, unless expressly authorized by the party receiving the transmission or by court order.

(g) FILING. Except for matters being heard on notice shortened under LBR 9075-1, proof of service must be filed in the clerk's office no later than 7 days after service and the serving party must bring a conformed copy to the hearing. If the proof or acknowledgment of service is attached to the original document, it must be attached as the last page of the document.

(h) FAILURE TO FILE. The failure to prepare or file the proof of service required by this rule does not affect the validity of the service. The court may at any time allow the proof of service to be amended or supplied unless to do so would be prejudicial to the rights of any party.

LBR 9013-4. NEW TRIAL OR HEARING ON CONTESTED MATTERS

(a) GROUNDS. The grounds for a motion for a new trial, a new hearing in a contested matter, or amendment of judgment pursuant to FRBP 9023 or F.R.Civ.P. 59(a) include, but are not necessarily limited to, the following:

(1) Irregularity in the proceedings of the court, adverse party, or jury;

(2) Any order of the court or abuse of discretion by which the party was prevented from receiving a fair trial;

(3) Misconduct by the jury;

(4) Accident or surprise that could not have been guarded against by the exercise of ordinary prudence;

(5) Newly discovered evidence material to the interest of the party making the application that could not with reasonable diligence have been discovered and produced at trial;

(6) Excessive or inadequate damages appearing to have been determined under the influence of passion or prejudice;

(7) Insufficiency of the evidence to justify the verdict or other decision; and

(8) Errors of law occurring at the trial.

(b) PROCEDURE.

(1) Error of Law. If the ground for the motion is error of law occurring at the trial, the error or errors relied upon must be stated specifically.

(2) Insufficiency of Evidence. If the ground for the motion is the insufficiency of the evidence, the motion must specify with particularity wherein the evidence is claimed to be insufficient.

(3) Newly Discovered Evidence. If the ground for the motion is newly discovered evidence, the motion must be supported by declarations by the party, or the agent of the party having personal knowledge of the facts, showing:

(A) When the evidence was first discovered;

(B) Why it could not with reasonable diligence have been produced at trial or the original hearing on a motion;

(C) What attempts were made to discover and present the evidence at trial or the original hearing on a motion;

(D) If the evidence is oral testimony, the nature of the testimony and the willingness of the witness to so testify; and

(E) If the evidence is documentary, the documents or duly authenticated copies thereof, or satisfactory evidence of their contents where the documents are not then available.

(c) HEARING. The motion will be determined based upon:

(1) The pleadings and papers on file;

(2) The recorder's transcript or digital recording; and

(3) Declarations, if the ground is other than error of law or insufficiency of the evidence and the facts or circumstances relied on do not otherwise appear in the records of the court.

(d) DECLARATIONS—TIME FOR FILING. Declarations in support of a motion for a new trial must be filed concurrently with the motion unless the court fixes a different time.

(e) CALENDARING OF MOTION. The motion for a new trial must be noticed and heard (if required by the court) as provided in LBR 9013-1.

LBR 9015-1. JURY TRIALS

(a) NUMBER OF JURORS. If a trial of the proceeding or matter is to be before a jury, the jury must consist of not less than 6 members. The court may impanel such number of alternate jurors as it determines desirable.

(b) INSTRUCTIONS.

(1) Proposed jury instructions must be in writing, and must be filed and served at least 7 days before trial is scheduled to begin. Each requested jury instruction must:

(A) Be set forth in full on a separate page;

(B) Embrace only one subject or principle of law; and

(C) Not repeat a principle of law contained in any other request.

(2) The identity of the party requesting the jury instructions must be disclosed on a cover page only and must not be disclosed on the proposed instructions.

(3) The authority or source of each proposed instruction must be set forth on a separate page or document and must not be disclosed on the proposed instruction.

(c) OBJECTIONS TO INSTRUCTIONS.

(1) Objections to proposed instructions must be filed and served on or before the first day of trial unless the court permits oral objections.

(2) Written objections must be numbered and must specify distinctly the objectionable matter in the proposed instruction. Each objection must be accompanied by citation of authority.

(3) Where applicable, the objecting party must submit an alternative instruction covering the subject or principle of law. The alternative instruction must be set forth on a separate paper. The identity of the requesting party or the authority or source of the proposed instruction must not be disclosed on the alternative instruction.

(d) SPECIAL VERDICTS AND INTERROGATORIES.

(1) Any request for a special verdict or a general verdict accompanied by answers to interrogatories must be filed and served at least 7 days before trial is scheduled to commence.

(2) Special verdicts and interrogatories must conform to the requirements of F.R.Civ.P. 49, and must not bear any identification of the party presenting the form.Identification must be made only on a separate page appended to the front of the special verdict and interrogatory form.

LBR 9015-2. DEMAND FOR JURY TRIAL

(a) RIGHT TO TRIAL BY JURY.

(1) A party claiming a right to trial by jury must make a demand as specified in subsection (b) of this rule.

(2) Nothing contained in this rule shall be deemed to create or imply a right to a jury trial where no such right exists under applicable law.

(b) DEMAND.

(1) Time and Form of Demand. A party must demand a trial by jury in accordance with Fed. R.Civ.P. 38(b).

(2) Statement of Consent. A demand must include a statement that the party does or does not consent to a jury trial conducted by the bankruptcy court. Within 14 days of the service of the demand and statement of consent or non-consent, all other parties must file and serve a statement of consent or non-consent to a jury trial conducted by the bankruptcy court.

(3) Specification of Issues. In the demand a party may specify the issues which the party wishes so tried; otherwise the party shall be deemed to have demanded trial by jury for all the issues so triable. If a party has demanded trial by jury for only some of the issues, any other party within 14 days after service of the demand or such lesser time as the court may order may serve a demand for trial by jury of any other or all of the issues of fact in the action.

(4) Determination by Court. On motion or on its own initiative the court may determine whether there is a right to trial by jury of the issues for which a jury trial is demanded or whether a demand for trial by jury in a proceeding on a contested petition must be granted.

(5) Cover Sheet Insufficient. Any notation on Official Form B104, Adversary Proceeding Sheet filed under LBR 7003-1 concerning whether a jury trial is, or is not, demanded does not constitute a demand for jury trial sufficient to comply with F.R.Civ.P. 38(b) or this rule.

(c) WITHDRAWAL OF DEMAND. A demand for trial by jury made in accordance with this rule may not be withdrawn without the consent of the parties.

(d) WAIVER.

(1) The failure of a party to file and serve a demand in accordance with this rule, and to file it as required by FRBP 5005, constitutes a waiver of trial by jury.

(2) Notwithstanding the failure of a party to demand a jury when such a demand might have been made of right, the court on its own initiative may order a trial by jury of any or all issues.

(e) TRIAL BY THE COURT.

(1) Subject to the provisions of subsection (d)(2) of this rule, an issue not demanded for trial by jury will be tried by the court.

(2) Where a demand for trial by jury has been made in accordance with this rule, the parties or their attorneys of record, by written stipulation filed with the court or by an oral stipulation made in open court and entered in the record, may consent to trial by the court sitting without a jury.

(f) ADVISORY JURY AND TRIAL BY CONSENT. In all actions not triable of right by jury, the court on motion or on its own initiative may try any issue with an advisory jury or, except in actions against the United States when a statute of the United States provides for trial without a jury, the court, with the consent of both parties, may order a trial with a jury whose verdict has the same effect as if trial by jury had been a matter of right.

(g) PRETRIAL PROCEDURE WHERE JURY TRIAL REQUESTED. Where a jury is demanded, all pretrial proceedings, through approval and entry of the pretrial order, will be conducted by the bankruptcy judge.

(h) MOTION FOR WITHDRAWAL OF REFERENCE.

(1) Within 7 days of the entry of the pretrial order, any party may file and serve a motion to the district court to withdraw reference pursuant to LBR 5011-1.

(2) The failure of any party to file and serve a motion to withdraw reference within the 7-day time period constitutes consent by all parties to the jury trial being presided over by the bankruptcy judge.

(3) Nothing in this rule precludes an earlier motion to withdraw reference on the grounds set forth in 28 U.S.C. § 157(d).

LBR 9019-1. SETTLEMENTS

(a) GENERAL.

(1) Parties must inform the courtroom deputy immediately by telephone or other expeditious means when a matter set for hearing has been settled out of court and that a stipulation will be filed and a proposed order approving the stipulation will be lodged.

(2) If a written stipulation executed in compliance with LBR 9071-1 resolving all issues as to all parties is filed at least 2 days before a scheduled hearing and a judge's copy is delivered to chambers, no appearance at the hearing will be necessary, provided that the stipulation is accompanied by a notice and motion to approve compromise of controversy if required under FRBP 9019.

(b) FAILURE TO COMPLYY—SANCTIONS. The failure to comply with the provisions of this rule may subject counsel to the imposition of sanctions under LBR 9011-3.

LBR 9020-1. ORDER TO SHOW CAUSE RE CONTEMPT

(a) GENERAL. Unless otherwise ordered by the court, contempt proceedings are initiated by filing a motion that conforms with LBR 9013-1 and a proposed order to show cause re contempt.

(b) MOTION. The motion must be served on the responding party which shall have 7 days to object to the issuance of the order to show cause.

(c) PROPOSED ORDER TO SHOW CAUSE RE CONTEMPT.

(1) The proposed order must clearly apprise the party to whom it is to be directed that such party must show cause, if any there is, why that party should not be held in contempt for the allegedly contemptuous conduct.

(2) The allegedly contemptuous conduct must be clearly identified in the proposed order and not just by reference to the content of the motion.

(3) The proposed order must have blank spaces in which the court may fill in the date, time, and location of the hearing and the dates by which a responsive pleading and reply thereto are due.

(d) HEARING ON ISSUANCE OF ORDER TO SHOW CAUSE RE CONTEMPT.

(1) If no responsive pleadings to the motion for the order to show cause are received by the court within the time allowed, the court may conclude that there is no objection to issuance of the order to show cause.

(2) No hearing on the motion for issuance of the order to show cause will be held unless the court so orders.

(3) If the motion for order to show cause is granted without a hearing, the court will issue and forward to the moving party the order to show cause setting the date and time of the contempt hearing.

(e) SERVICE OF ORDER TO SHOW CAUSE RE CONTEMPT.

(1) Unless the court orders otherwise in the order to show cause, the moving party must serve the issued order to show cause on the respondent not later than 21 days before the date set for the hearing.

(2) Personal service of the issued order to show cause is required on any entity not previously subject to the personal jurisdiction of the court.

(3) All other entities may be served either personally or by mail in accordance with FRBP 7004.

(f) HEARING ON MERITS OF ORDER TO SHOW CAUSE RE CONTEMPT. At the hearing, the court may treat as true any uncontroverted facts established by declaration and limit testimony to controverted facts only.

LBR 9021-1. ORDERS AND JUDGMENTS

(a) GENERAL. A proposed order or judgment (collectively, "order") must be submitted either in paper form or electronically via LOU in accordance with the LOU Procedures and these rules. Unless required as a court-mandated form order pursuant to LBR 9009-1 or otherwise ordered by the court, an order must not contain any attached agreement or other exhibit. If an order approves a motion which is based in whole or part upon an agreement or other exhibit, the order must refer to the docket number and/or title of the document in which the agreement or exhibit is found. Nothing in this rule prevents a prevailing party from serving a copy of an entered order along with a copy of an agreement or other exhibit referred to in the order.

(b) PREPARATION, LODGING, AND SIGNING OF ORDERS.

(1) Form of Proposed Order. A proposed order must be set forth in a separately captioned document complying with LBRs 9004-1 and 9009-1, and must include the Notice of Entered Order and Service List prepared in accordance with subsection (b)(1)(E) of this rule. Except for an order submitted at the hearing, a proposed order must be accompanied by a proof of service reflecting service of the proposed order on the parties required by subsection (b)(1)(E) of this rule and as the court directs.

(A) WHO MUST PREPARE. Unless the court otherwise directs, a proposed order must be prepared by the attorney for the prevailing party.

(B) WHEN DUE IF A HEARING WAS SCHEDULED. If not presented at the hearing, a proposed order must be served and lodged with the clerk within 7 days of the granting thereof. Except as provided in LBR 7056-1(b)(2) and LBR 7016-1(b)(1) or if the presiding judge has posted a tentative ruling authorizing the submission of a proposed order, a proposed order must not be lodged prior to the hearing or trial of the underlying matter.

(C) FAILURE TO LODGE TIMELY ORDER. If the prevailing party fails to serve and lodge a proposed order within the allotted time, then any other party present at the hearing may lodge and serve a proposed order. All other parties shall have 7 days within which to file and serve an objection in compliance with subsection (b)(3) of this rule. If no party submits a proposed order, the court may prepare and enter such order as it deems appropriate, including an order to show cause why the motion or proceeding should not be dismissed without prejudice for failure to prosecute.

(D) COPIES AND ENVELOPES. Subject to subsection (b)(1)(E) of this rule, LBR 9036-1, and the LOU Procedures, the original proposed order must be accompanied by: (i) stamped, addressed envelopes for all persons or entities who will be served by the court non-electronically under subsection (b)(1)(E)(i) of this rule, to include only the debtor (and debtor's attorney, if any), movant (or movant's attorney, if any), and all parties (or their attorneys, if any) who filed an opposition or other objection to the relief requested; and (ii) the same number of copies of the proposed order to match the number of envelopes required.

(E) NOTICE OF ENTERED ORDER AND SERVICE LIST.

(i) ENTERED ORDER SERVED BY THE COURT. If an entered order is to be served by the court, the proposed order must be accompanied by court-mandated Form 9021-1.1, Notice of Entered Order and Service List, regardless of whether the proposed order is lodged non-electronically or electronically pursuant to the LOU Procedures.

(ii) ENTERED ORDER SERVED OTHER THAN BY THE COURT. If an entered order is to be served other than by the court, the party responsible for lodging the proposed order must promptly serve a copy of the entered order and file a proof of service of the entered order in the form and manner required by LBR 9013-3.

(2) Order upon Stipulation. Except as provided in LBR 3015-1(r)(3) and LBR 4001-1(b)(2)(B), a proposed order approving a written stipulation must refer to the title of the stipulation and be contained in a separate document prepared and lodged upon the filing of the stipulation with the court. A proposed order lodged electronically must be prepared and uploaded in accordance with the LOU Procedures.

(3) Proposed Order when Opposition to Motion was Filed.

(A) SERVICE OF PROPOSED ORDER ON CONTESTING PARTY. The attorney who has the duty to prepare any order required by this rule must serve a copy of the proposed order on counsel, or party if filed without counsel, who filed an opposition or other objection to the relief requested, either before or on the same day that the order is lodged with the court and must file a proof of service with the order. Alternatively, the attorney preparing the order may present it to opposing counsel for approval as to form before the order is lodged, in which case opposing counsel must immediately approve or disapprove the form of order and return it to counsel who prepared it. Where a proposed order is tendered at the hearing, the order may be lodged without prior service on the opposition.

(B) SEPARATE OBJECTION TO PROPOSED ORDER. Opposing counsel may, within 7 days after service of a copy of a proposed order prepared pursuant to this rule, file and serve an objection to the form of the order, setting forth the grounds therefor. Opposing counsel must attach as exhibits to the objection (i) a copy of the order that is the subject of the objection and (ii) a copy of the proposed alternative form of order. The proposed alternative form of order so labeled, must be lodged with the objection. A judge's copy of the objection and proposed alternative form of order must be served on the judge in chambers in accordance with LBR 5005-2(d). The failure to file and serve a timely objection will constitute a waiver of any defects in the form of the order.

(C) ENDORSEMENT OF COUNSEL. Unless the court otherwise directs, a proposed order will not be signed by the judge unless (i) opposing counsel has endorsed thereon an approval as to form; (ii) opposing counsel has stipulated thereto on the record at the hearing, or (iii) the time for objection to a form of order properly served has expired under subsection (b)(3)(B) of this rule. If it finds the ends of justice so requires, the court may conduct a hearing on the proper form of the order or decide any objection thereto without a hearing.

(4) Proposed Orders on Unopposed Motions. Notwithstanding subsection (b)(3) of this rule, if no opposition was filed or made by a party or counsel at the hearing, no service of the proposed order is required prior to lodging of the proposed order, and the non-opposing party will be deemed to have waived any objection to the form of the order. The court may sign a proposed order on an unopposed motion at the hearing or immediately upon its lodging with the clerk without waiting for the objection period of subsection (b)(3)(B) of this rule to expire.

(5) Signing of Orders for Absent Judges. Except as otherwise provided by F.R.Civ.P. 63, application for any order on a case or proceeding must be made to the judge to whom the case is assigned. If the judge to whom the case or proceeding is assigned is not available and there is an emergency necessitating an order, the judge's courtroom deputy must be consulted to determine whether a judge of this court has been designated to handle matters in the absence of the assigned judge. If a designation has been made, the application must be presented to the designated judge. If no designation has been made, then the matter must be presented to the duty judge, if any, or in his or her absence, to any other judge in accordance with normal divisional practices. If no emergency exists, the application will be held by the assigned judge's courtroom deputy until the assigned judge is available. Any judge may sign an order for another judge.

(6) Obtaining Certified Copies of Order. Payment for a certified copy of an order must be made to the cashier in the clerk's office. No checks will be accepted in the courtroom or by courtroom deputies. If a certified copy of a stipulated or default order is desired, the order may either be presented in the courtroom together with a clerk's receipt showing prepayment of the certification fee, or the certified copy may be requested from the clerk's office after the order has been signed and entered.

(c) ENTRY OF ORDERS.

(1) Timing of Taxation of Costs. Entry of an order must not be delayed pending taxation of costs to be included therein pursuant to LBR 7054-1. A blank space must be left in the form of an order for insertion of costs by the clerk after they have been taxed.

(2) Calculation of Interest. If interest is accruing or will accrue on any order, the party preparing the proposed form of order must indicate by memorandum attached thereto the applicable interest rate as computed under 28 U.S.C. § 1961(a) or 26 U.S.C. § 6621 and the amount of interest to be added for each day the document remains unsigned.

(3) By Stipulation with Entry of Order. The court may withhold entry of an order to permit the parties to submit, either separately or jointly by stipulation, the computation of the amount of money to be awarded in accordance with the court's determination of the issues.

(4) Contested Computation. If the parties do not stipulate to a computation as provided in this rule, any party may file and serve a computation claimed to be in accordance with the determination of the issues by the court. Within 7 days of service of the computation, an opposing party may file and serve an objection accompanied by an alternate computation. If no objection is filed within 7 days, the order may be entered in accordance with the original computation submitted.

(5) Hearing on Contested Computation. If it finds the ends of justice so require, the court may place the matter on calendar for hearing provided there is at least 7 days notice to the parties. After hearing, the court will determine the correct amount on which the order will be entered. The hearing will be limited to a determination of the correct amount to be entered in the order and shall not constitute an opportunity for rehearing or reconsideration of the determination of other issues previously ruled on by the court.

(6) Effect of Stipulation to Amount of Costs. A stipulation by the parties to the amount to be entered pursuant to the determination of the issues by the court will not be deemed to be a waiver of any rights of the parties to appeal or otherwise challenge the determination of such issues by the court.

(7) Delegation of Authority to Sign Designated Orders. The court may delegate authority to the clerk to:

(A) Sign specified form orders involving ministerial matters; and

(B) Facsimile stamp specified orders consistent with oral rulings by the court.

(d) DUTY OF CLERK AS TO AN ORDER DIRECTING AN ACTION BY AN OFFICIAL OF THE UNITED STATES. When an order is entered by the court directing any officer of the United States to perform any act, unless such officer is present in court when the order is made, the clerk must forthwith transmit a copy of the order to the officer ordered to perform the act.

(e) AMENDED OR CORRECTED ORDERS.

(1) If an error or omission in the form of an entered or lodged order is discovered, a party in interest may request amendment or correction of the order by filing and serving a motion under LBR 9013-1(a) or LBR 9013-1(o).

(2) The motion must set forth specifically the changes requested in the form of the order and reasons such changes are necessary and appropriate. A copy of the proposed amended order must be attached as an exhibit to the motion when filed and served.

(3) The amended order must state in its caption the date of entry of the original order and, if applicable, the date, time, and place of the original hearing.

(4) If the motion is filed and served pursuant to LBR 9013-1(o), the proposed amended order itself must be lodged at the same time as the required declaration establishing that no timely objection was served.

LBR 9027-1. REMOVAL AND REMAND

(a) NOTICE OF REMOVAL. A notice of removal must be filed with the clerk of the bankruptcy court.

(b) STATUS CONFERENCE.

(1) Upon the filing of a notice of removal pursuant to FRBP 9027, the clerk will issue a notice of status conference before the judge to whom the case or proceeding has been assigned.

(2) The status conference will be set not later than 45 days after the date that the notice of status conference is mailed, unless otherwise ordered by the court.

(3) Within 7 days of receipt, the removing party must serve the notice of status conference on all other parties to the removed action, including any trustee appointed in the case.

(c) REMAND. A motion for remand must be filed with the clerk of the bankruptcy court not later than 30 days after the date of filing of the notice of removal.

(d) FILING OF PLEADINGS.

(1) Unless otherwise ordered by the court, the party filing the notice of removal must file with the clerk, in chronological order, copies of all process, papers, minute entries, orders, and other documents filed in the litigation prior to removal, together with a copy of the docket of the removed action from the court where the removed litigation was pending.

(2) All such documents must be filed not later than:

(A) 30 days after the date of filing of the notice of removal; or

(B) if a motion to remand is filed prior to expiration of such 30-day period, 14 days after entry of an order denying such motion to remand.

(e) DEMAND FOR JURY TRIAL. Within 14 days after service of the notice of removal, a party must comply with LBR 9015-2 to preserve any right to a trial by jury.

LBR 9036-1. NOTICE AND SERVICE BY ELECTRONIC TRANSMISSION

(a) SERVICE BY ELECTRONIC MEANS.

(1) Upon the addition of any document or item to a CM/ECF docket, whether electronically or non-electronically, an NEF is automatically generated by CM/ECF and sent electronically to all persons or entities that are CM/ECF Users and have consented to electronic service. Regardless of whether it is the duty of the court or of another person or entity to provide notice or service, service of the NEF constitutes notice and service pursuant to the F.R.Civ.P., FRBP, and these rules for all persons and entities that have consented to electronic service.

(2) A person or entity that is entitled to service of a document, but is not a CM/ECF User or is a CM/ECF User who has not consented to electronic service, must be served as otherwise provided by the F.R.Civ.P., FRBP, and these rules.

(b) EXCEPTIONS. Electronic transmission of an NEF does not constitute service or notice of the following documents that must be served non-electronically:

(1) Service of a summons and complaint under FRBP 7004;

(2) Service of a subpoena under FRBP 9016;

(3) Service of a summons and petition under FRBP 1010;

(4) Service upon the United States trustee of papers listed as exceptions under LBR 2002-2(a)(3); and

(5) Where conventional service is otherwise required under the F.R-.Civ.P., FRBP, LBRs, or by court order.

LBR 9070-1. EXHIBITS

(a) TRIAL EXHIBITS.

(1) Identification. Unless otherwise ordered by the court, all exhibits to be offered into evidence at trial of an adversary proceeding or contested matter must be numbered and marked for identification with tags available from the clerk's office.

(2) Numbering. Whenever feasible, exhibits of plaintiffs or movants must be marked with numbers, and exhibits of defendants or respondents must be marked with letters.

(3) Exhibit Register. The parties presenting exhibits must tag the exhibits and prepare an exhibit register on the form available from the clerk's office prior to trial.

(4) Lodging Exhibits. Unless otherwise ordered by the court, the tagged exhibits and completed exhibit register must be delivered in the courtroom to the courtroom deputy or court recorder prior to the beginning of trial.

(5) Copies. Each party must bring sufficient copies of each exhibit for all counsel, the witness, and the judge.

(b) RETENTION AND DISPOSITION OF TRIAL EXHIBITS.

(1) All models, diagrams, documents, or other exhibits lodged with the clerk that are admitted into evidence or marked at trial will be retained by the clerk until expiration of the time for appeal without any appeal having been taken, entry of a stipulation waiving or abandoning the right to appeal, final disposition of any appeal, or order of the court, whichever occurs first.

(2) If any exhibit is not withdrawn from the clerk's office within 30 days after the person or persons to whom it belongs are given written notice to claim it, the clerk may destroy the exhibit or otherwise dispose of it as the court may approve.

LBR 9071-1. STIPULATION

(a) GENERAL.

(1) Oral Stipulation. An oral stipulation will be enforceable by the court if made and approved in open court.

(2) Written Stipulation. A written stipulation entered into pursuant to these rules must be filed with the court, but will not be effective until a separate order thereon is entered.

(3) Order on Stipulation. An order on a stipulation must be prepared and lodged in accordance with LBR 9021-1(b)(2).

(b) STIPULATION REQUIRING NOTICE UNDER FRBP 4001(D) OR 9019.

(1) Unless otherwise ordered by the court, the notice requirement of FRBP 4001(d) or FRBP 9019 may be satisfied by either serving the motion on each of the entities specified in the applicable rule when it is filed or by serving on such entities a motion for approval of the proposed settlement stipulation pursuant to LBR 9013-1(o).

(2) A stipulation requiring notice under either FRBP 4001(d) or FRBP 9019 requires approval by the court.

LBR 9074-1. TELEPHONIC APPEARANCES AT COURT HEARINGS

A party who wishes to appear telephonically at a court hearing must consult the court's web site to determine whether a telephonic appearance on a particular matter is permissible and to obtain the judge's procedure for telephonic appearances.

LBR 9075-1. EMERGENCY MOTIONS AND APPLICATIONS FOR ORDERS SHORTENING TIME

(a) EMERGENCY MOTION.

(1) Scope of Rule. An emergency motion requiring an order on less than 48 hours notice must be obtained in accordance with this rule.

(2) Obtaining Hearing Date and Time. Unless otherwise ordered by the court, a hearing date and time may be obtained by telephoning the chambers of the judge to whom the case is assigned or such member of the judge's staff as may be designated to schedule hearings on emergency motions. The identity of the designated member of the judge's staff is available from the clerk's office and posted on the court's website. Prior to telephoning chambers, the court's website should be consulted to determine whether the judge has additional procedures or instructions for obtaining a hearing on an emergency motion.

(3) Contents of Moving Papers. The motion must: (A) state the relief requested, (B) comply with any other applicable provisions of these rules regarding the relief requested, and (C) be accompanied by the declaration of one or more competent witnesses under penalty of perjury that (i) justifies the setting of a hearing on an emergency basis and (ii) supports the granting of the motion itself on the merits. A separate motion for an expedited hearing is not required under this rule.

(4) Telephonic Notice. Unless otherwise ordered by the court, immediately upon obtaining a hearing date and time, movant must give telephonic notice of the emergency hearing and the substance of the motion to the parties to whom notice of the motion is required to be given under the FRBP and these rules, the United States trustee, and any other party that is likely to be adversely affected by the granting of the motion. Movant must also advise the parties by telephone whether the moving papers will be served by e-mail, fax, or personal service.

(5) Service of Moving Papers. Unless otherwise ordered by the court, movant must serve the moving papers by e-mail, fax, or personal service on the parties set forth in subsection (a)(4) not later than the time the moving papers are filed with the court.

(6) Filing of Moving Papers. Unless otherwise ordered by the court, the moving papers must be filed not later than 2 hours before the time set for the hearing and a judge's copy served on the judge in chambers in accordance with LBR 5005-2(d).

(7) Response to Moving Papers. Any response, written or oral, to the moving papers may be presented at the time of the hearing on the motion.

(8) Proof of Notice to be Presented at the Hearing. At the time of the hearing, movant must present to the court and file (A) a declaration of the efforts made to give telephonic notice of the hearing and substance of the emergency motion to the parties set forth in subsection (a)(4) and (B) a proof of service of the moving papers.

(b) APPLICATION FOR ORDER SHORTENING TIME.

(1) Scope of Rule. A party may request that a non-emergency motion be heard on notice shorter than would otherwise be required by these rules. Such a request must be made by written application consistent with court-approved form F 9075-1.1, Application for Order Shortening Time ("application"). The application may be granted for good cause shown in accordance with this rule.

(2) Contents of Application. Unless otherwise ordered by the court, the application must:

(A) Describe the nature of the relief requested in the underlying motion, identify the parties affected by the relief requested in the motion, and state the reasons necessitating a hearing on shortened time; and

(B) Be supported by the declaration of one or more competent witnesses under penalty of perjury that justifies the setting of a hearing on shortened time and establishes a prima facie basis for the granting of the underlying motion.

(3) Filing of Application. An application must be filed with the clerk concurrently with the moving papers that are to be heard on shortened notice.

(4) Service of Application. Unless otherwise ordered by the court, movant must serve the application and the moving papers on each of the parties to whom notice of the underlying motion is required to be given under the FRBP and these rules, the United States trustee, and any other party that is likely to be adversely affected by the granting of the underlying motion. A separate notice of the application is not required.

(5) Proposed Order Shortening Time. At the time the application and underlying motion are filed, movant must lodge a separate proposed order consistent with court-approved form F 9075-1.2, Order Setting Hearing on Shortened Notice that (A) identifies the parties to whom notice is proposed to be given; (B) states the nature and timing of the proposed shortened notice, which must not be less than 48 hours; (C) states the means of service, *i.e.*, telephone, fax, e-mail, personal service, or as ordered by the court; and (D) contains appropriate blanks for the court to insert the date and time of the hearing and the date for filing and serving the opposition papers.

(6) Court Ruling on Application. The application will be determined ex parte by the court on the basis of the papers submitted with the application, subject to the right of any party to object to the adequacy of notice pursuant to subsection (c) of this rule. The court will promptly notify the movant of its decision on the application and, if granted, the date and time set for the hearing.

(7) Notice of Hearing.

(A) If the application is granted, movant must serve the order setting the hearing on shortened notice on each of the parties to whom notice of the underlying motion is required to be served by the FRBP and these rules, the United States trustee, any other party that is likely to be adversely affected by the granting of the underlying motion, and as otherwise ordered by the court. Notice must be given by telephone, fax, e-mail, personal service, or as ordered by the court.

(B) If the application is denied, movant may, unless otherwise ordered by the court, set the underlying motion for hearing on regular notice and serve notice of the hearing in accordance with LBR 9013-1.

(8) Proof of Service. Proof of service of all required documents must be filed at least 2 days before the hearing, unless otherwise ordered by the court.

(c) OBJECTION TO TIMING OF HEARING. At the hearing on the motion, any party may object to the adequacy of the notice provided and seek a continuance for good cause shown.

APPENDIX I

LOCAL BANKRUPTCY RULES FORMS LIST

FORM NUMBER	FORM TITLE
F 1002-1.2. MOTION	*Motion for Protective Order Pursuant to 11 U.S.C. § 107(c) and FRBP 9037 to Restrict Access to Filed Documents Containing Personal Data Identifiers (Optional)*
F 1002-1.2. ORDER	*Order on Motion for Protective Order Pursuant to 11 U.S.C. § 107(c) and FRBP 9037 to Restrict Access to Filed Documents Containing Personal Data Identifiers (Optional)*
F 1010-1	*Summons and Notice of Status Conference in an Involuntary Bankruptcy Case (Mandatory)*
F 1015-2.1	*Statement of Related Cases (Mandatory)*
F 1017-1.1	*Debtor's Motion to Convert Case Under 11 U.S.C. §§ 706(a), 1112(a) (Mandatory)*
F 1017-1.2	*Order on Debtor's Motion to Convert Case Under 11 U.S.C. §§ 706(a), 1112(a) (Mandatory)*
F 1017-1.3	*Notice of Debtor's Motion to Convert Case Under 11 U.S.C. § 706(a) (Mandatory)*
F 1017-1.4	*Debtor's Notice of Conversion Under 11 U.S.C. §§ 1208(a) or 1307(a) (Mandatory)*
F 2014-1	*Statement of Disinterestedness for Employment of Professional Person Under F.R.B.P. 2014 (File with Application for Employment) (Optional)*
F 2016-1.1	*Notice of Hearing on Application for Payment of Interim or Final Fees and/or Expenses Under 11 U.S.C. § 331 or 330 (Optional)*
F 2016-1.2	*Application for Payment of: Interim Fees and/or Expenses (11 U.S.C. § 331); Final Fees and/or Expenses (11 U.S.C. § 330) (Optional)*
F 2016-1.3	*Order on Application for Payment of: Interim Fees and/or Expenses (11 U.S.C. § 331); Final Fees and/or Expenses (11 U.S.C. § 330) (Optional)*
F 2016-2.1	*Trustee's Notice of Motion and Motion Under Local Bankruptcy Rule 2016-2 For: Authorization to Employ Paraprofessionals, and/or Authorization to Pay Flat Fee To Tax Preparer; Notice of Opportunity to Request Hearing; Declaration of Trustee; and Declaration of Paraprofessional (Optional)*
F 2016-2.1A	*Order on Trustee's Motion Under Local Bankruptcy Rule 2016-2 For Authorization to Employ Paraprofessionals and/or Authorization to Pay Flat Fee to Tax Preparer (Optional)*
F 2016-2.2	*Notice of Motion and Motion No. Under Local Bankruptcy Rule 2016-2 for Approval of Cash Disbursements by the Trustee; Opportunity to Request Hearing; and Declaration of Trustee (Optional)*
F 2016-2.2A	*Order on Trustee's Motion No. ________ Under Local Bankruptcy Rule 2016-2 For Approval of Case Disbursements by the Trustee (Optional)*
F 2085-1.1. SUMMONS	*Summons and Notice of Hearing on Petition Pursuant to 11 U.S.C. Chapter 15 for Recognition of a Foreign Non-main Proceeding*
F 2090-1.1	*Declaration Re: Limited Scope of Appearance Pursuant to Local Bankruptcy Rule 2090-1 (Optional)*
F 2090-1.2. APPLICATION	*Application of Non-Resident Attorney to Appear in a Specific Case [Local Bankruptcy Rule 2090-1(b)] (Optional)*
F 2090-1.3	*Order on Application of Non-Resident Attorney to Appear in a Specific Case [Local Bankruptcy Rule 2090-1(b)] (Optional)*
F 2090-1.4	*Substitution of Attorney (Optional)*
F 3001.1	*Request for Issuance of Notice of Transfer of Claim Under F.R.B.P. 3001(e) (Optional)*

FORM NUMBER	FORM TITLE
F 3001.2	*Notice of Transfer of Claim Pursuant to F.R.B.P. 3001(e) (Optional)*
F 3007-1.1	*Order on Objection to Claims (Optional)*
F 3007-1.2	*Notice of Trustee's/Debtor-in-Possession's Request for a Copy of Proof of Claim (Optional)*
F 3007-1.3	*Notice of Objection to Claim (Mandatory)*
F 3011-1	*Motion for Order Releasing Unclaimed Funds (Optional)*
F 3015-1.1	*Chapter 13 Plan (Mandatory)*
F 3015-1.1. ADDEN-DUM	*Addendum to Chapter 13 Plan Concerning Debtors Who are Repaying Debt Secured by a Mortgage on Real Property or a Lien on Personal Property the Debtor Occupies as the Debtor's Principal Residence (Optional)*
F 3015-1.2	*Notice of Section 341(a) Meeting and Hearing on Confirmation of Chapter 13 Plan with Copy of Chapter 13 Plan (Mandatory)*
F 3015.1.4	*Declaration Setting Forth Postpetition, Preconfirmation Deed of Trust Payments [Local Bankruptcy Rules 3015-1(m)] (Mandatory)*
F 3015-1.5	*Notice of Motion Under Local Bankruptcy Rule 3015-1(n) and (w) to Modify Plan or Suspend Plan Payments (Mandatory)*
F 3015-1.6	*Motion Under Local Bankruptcy Rules 3015-1(n) and (w) to Modify Plan or Suspend Plan Payments (Mandatory)*
F 3015-1.7	*Rights and Responsibilities Agreement Between Chapter 13 Debtors and Their Attorneys (Mandatory)*
F 3015-1.8	*Declaration RE Payment of Domestic Support Obligations (Preconfirmation) (Mandatory)*
F 3015-1.9	*Declaration RE Tax Returns (Preconfirmation) (Mandatory)*
F 3015-1.10	*Declaration Setting Forth Postpetiton, Preconfirmation Payments on: 1. Leases of Personal Property; 2. Purchase Money Security Liens in Personal Property (Mandatory)*
F 3015-1.11	*Trustee's Comments on or Objection to Application for Supplemental Fees*
F 3015-1.12	*Order on Application for Supplemental Fees*
F 3015-1.13	*Trustee's Comments on or Objection To:*
F 3015-1.14	Order On:
F 3015-1.15	*Debtor's Motion for Authority to Refinance Real Property Under LBR 3015-1(p) (Mandatory)*
F 3015-1.16	*Debtor's Motion for Authority to Sell Real Property Under LBR 3015-1(p) (Mandatory)*
F 3015-1.17	*Debtor's Motion for Authority to Incur Debt (Personal Property) (Mandatory)*
F 3015-1.18	*Debtor's Request for Voluntary Dismissal of Chapter 13 Case (Mandatory)*
F 3015-1.20	*Declarations of Current/Post-Petition Income and Expenses (Mandatory)*
F 3017-1	Chapter 11 Disclosure Statement
F 3018-1	*Chapter 11 Plan*
F 3018-2	*Plan Ballot Summary (Optional)*
F 4001-1.DEC	*Declaration of RE: Default Under Adequate Protection Order; Request for Entry of Order Granting Relief From Stay (Mandatory)*
F 4001-1M.CUST	*Notice of Motion and Motion for (A) Relief From the Automatic Stay Under 11 U.S.C. § 362 (Real Property),and (B) Relief from Turnover Under 11 U.S.C. § 543 by Prepetition Receiver or Other Custodian (with supporting declarations) (Mandatory)*
F 4001-1M.ER	*Extraordinary Relief Attachment (Optional to the Judge)*
F 4001-1M.IS	*Notice of Motion in Individual Case for Order Imposing a Stay or Continuing the Automatic Stay as the Court Deems Appropriate (Mandatory)*

FORM NUMBER	FORM TITLE
F 4001-1M.NA	*Notice of Motion and Motion for Relief From the Automatic Stay Under 11 U.S.C. § 362 (with supporting declarations) (Action in Non-Bankruptcy Forum) (Mandatory)*
F 4001-1M.PP	*Notice of Motion and Motion for Relief From the Automatic Stay Under 11 U.S.C. § 362 (with supporting declarations) (Personal Property) (Mandatory)*
F 4001-1M.RP	*Notice of Motion and Motion for Relief From the Automatic Stay Under 11 U.S.C. § 362 (with supporting declarations) (Real Property) (Mandatory)*
F 4001-1M.TCS	*Trustee's Notice of Motion and Motion for Order Continuing the Automatic Stay Under 11 U.S.C. § 362(h)(2), for Adequate Protection and for Delivery of Personal Property in Individual Case (with supporting declarations) (Mandatory)*
F 4001-1M.TS	*Notion of Motion and Motion in Individual Case for Order Confirming Termination of Stay Under 11 U.S.C. § 362(j) or that No Stay is in Effect Under 11 U.S.C. § 362(c)(4)(A)(ii) (with supporting declarations) (Mandatory)*
F 4001-1M.UD	*Notice of Motion and Motion for Relief From the Automatic Stay or for Order Confirming that the Automatic Stay Does Not Apply Under 11 U.S.C. § 362(l) (with supporting declarations) (Mandatory)*
F 4001-1M.13	*Declaration of Agent for Standing Trustee (Chapter 12 and 13 cases only; Attach to Relief From Stay Motion) (Mandatory)*
F 4001-1M.RES	*Response to Motion for Order to Terminate, Annul, Modify, or Condition the Automatic Stay Under 11 U.S.C. § 362 and Declaration(s) in Support (Optional)*
F 4001-1O.CUST	*Order Granting Motion for (1) Relief From the Automatic Stay Under 11 U.S.C. § 362, and (2) Relief from Turnover Under 11 U.S.C. § 543 by Prepetition Receiver or Other Custodian (Mandatory)*
F 4001-1O.DENY	*Order Denying Motion for Relief From the Automatic Stay Under 11 U.S.C. § 362 (Mandatory)*
F 4001-1O.ER	*Extraordinary Relief Attachment (Optional to the Judge)*
F 4001-1O.NA	*Order Granting Motion for Relief From the Automatic Stay Under 11 U.S.C. § 362 (Action in Non-Bankruptcy Forum) (Mandatory)*
F 4001-1O.PP	*Order Granting Motion for Relief From the Automatic Stay Under 11 U.S.C. § 362 (Personal Property) (Mandatory)*
F 4001-1O.RP	*Order Granting Motion for Relief From the Automatic Stay Under 11 U.S.C. § 362 (Real Property) (Mandatory)*
F 4001-1-1O.TCS	*Order Granting Trustee's Motion for Order Continuing the Automatic Stay, for Adequate Protection and for Delivery of Personal Property in Individual Case (Mandatory)*
F 4001-1O.IS	*Order Granting Motion for Order Imposing a Stay or Continuing the Automatic Stay (Mandatory)*
F 4001-1O.UD	*Order Granting Motion for Relief From Stay Under 11 U.S.C. § 362 (Unlawful Detainer) (Mandatory)*
F 4001-1.2	*Debtor's Further Certification of Cure of Monetary Default Underlying Judgment for Possession of Residential Property and Proof of Deposit (11 U.S.C. § 362(l)(2)) (Optional)*
F 4001-1.3	*Lessor's Objection to Debtor's Certification and/or Debtor's Further Certification Concerning Residential Property and Notice of Hearing (11 U.S.C. § 362(l)(3)(A)) (Optional)*
F 4001-1.4	*Lessor's Certification of (1) Prepetition Eviction Action Seeking Possession of Residential Property Based on Debtor's Prepetiton Endangerment of Property or Illegal Use of a Controlled Substance, or (2) Endangerment of the Property or Illegal Use of a Controlled Substance within the Last 30 Days (11 U.S.C. § 362(b)(23)) (Optional)*

FORM NUMBER	FORM TITLE
F 4001-1.5	*Debtor's Objection to Lessor's Certification and Notice of Hearing (11 U.S.C. § 362(m)(2)(A) and (B)) (Optional)*
F 4001-2	*Statement Pursuant to Local Bankruptcy Rule 4001-2 (Cash Collateral Stipulations) (Optional)*
F 4008-1.1	*Replaced by national Form 240A Reaffirmation Agreement (Mandatory)*
F 4008-1.2	*Notice of Hearing Re: Reaffirmation Agreement (Mandatory)*
F 4008-1.3	*Order Disapproving Reaffirmation Agreement with Notice of Entry (Mandatory)*
F 4008-1.4	*Order Approving Reaffirmation Agreement with Notice of Entry (Mandatory)*
F 5010-1.1M	*Debtor's Motion to Reopen Case and For Extension of Time to File Debtor's Certification of Completion of Postpetition Instructional Course Concerning Personal Financial Management (Mandatory)*
F 5010-1.1O	*Order on Debtor's Motion to Reopen Case and For Extension of Time to File Debtor's Certification of Completion of Postpetition Instructional Course Concerning Personal Financial Management (Mandatory)*
F 5075-1.1	*Declaration to be Filed with Motion Establishing Administrative Procedures RE 28 U.S.C. § 156(c) (Mandatory)*
F 6004-2	*Notice of Sale of Estate Property*
F 7004-1	*Summons and Notice of Status Conference (Mandatory)*
F 7016-1.1	*Joint Status Report—Local Bankruptcy Rule 7016-1(a)(2) (Optional)*
F 7016-1.1a	*Joint Status Report—Additional Party Attachment (Optional)*
F 7016-1.2	*Status Conference and Scheduling Order Pursuant to Local Bankruptcy Rule 7016-1(a)(4) (Optional)*
F 7026-2.1	*Request for Disclosure of Discover of Documents Under Local Bankruptcy Rule 7026-2(d) (Optional)*
F 7055-1.1	*Request for Entry of Default Under Local Bankruptcy Rule 7055-1 (Optional)*
F 7055-1.2	*Motion for Default Judgment Under Local Bankruptcy Rule 7055- 1 (Optional)*
F 9013-1.1	*Notice of Motion For (Mandatory)*
F 9013-1.2	*Notice of Motion Under Local Bankruptcy Rule 9013-1(o) for: (Optional)*
F 9013-1.3	*Notice of Opposition and Request for a Hearing (Optional)*
F 9013-1.4	*Notice of Non-Opposition (Optional)*
F 9013-1.5	*Notice of Motion and Motion to Avoid Lien Under 11 U.S.C. § 522(f) (Real Property) (Optional)*
F 9013-1.6	*Order on Motion to Avoid Lien Under 11 U.S.C. § 522(f) (Real Property) (Optional)*
F 9013-1.7	*Notice of Motion and Motion to Avoid Lien Under 11 U.S.C. § 522(f) (Personal Property) (Optional)*
F 9013-1.8	*Order on Motion to Avoid Lien Under 11 U.S.C. § 522(f) (Personal Property) (Optional)*
F 9013-1.9	*Declaration Re: Entry of Order Without Hearing Pursuant to Local Bankruptcy Rule 9013-1(o) (Optional)*
F 9013-3.1	*Proof Of Service of Document (Mandatory)*
F 9021-1.1	*Notice of Entered Order and Service List (Mandatory)*
F 9021-1.4	*Default Judgment (Without Prior Judgment) (Optional)*
F 9021-1.5	*Default Judgment (Based on Prior Judgment) (Optional)*
F 9075-1	*Order Shortening Time [Local Bankruptcy Rule 9075- 1(b)] (Optional)*

Appendix II ATTORNEY DISCIPLINE PROCEDURES IN BANKRUPTCY COURT (General Order No. 96-05)

(a) APPLICABILITY This general order establishes a process for court wide discipline of attorneys in the bankruptcy court. These procedures shall apply when any judge of this court wishes to challenge the right of an attorney to practice before this court or recommends the imposition of attorney discipline intended to apply in all bankruptcy cases in this court. Nothing in this general order is intended to limit or restrict the authority of any judge to impose sanctions on any attorney in any case or cases assigned to that judge.

(1) Initiation of Disciplinary Proceedings. If a bankruptcy judge wishes to initiate disciplinary proceedings under this general order, the judge shall prepare and file with the Clerk of Court a written Statement of Cause setting forth the judge's basis for recommending discipline and a description of the discipline the referring judge believes is appropriate.

The clerk shall open a case file, assign a miscellaneous case number, initiate a docket for the file, select three bankruptcy judges of this district at random (excluding the judge who filed the Statement of Cause) to serve on the Hearing Panel (the "Panel") which will determine whether the attorney shall be disciplined and, if so, the type and extent of discipline. The most senior judge assigned to the Panel shall be the Presiding Judge.

The clerk shall prepare a Designation of Hearing Panel and Presiding Judge which shall include a signature line for each of the designated judges. The signature of each judge shall certify his or her acceptance of assignment to the Panel. Should any judge decline to serve, the clerk shall select another judge to serve on the Panel, give written notice thereof to the other judges on the Panel and issue a Supplemental Designation of Hearing Panel, which shall contain a signature line for the newly appointed judge to accept the assignment.

Once the clerk has obtained the acceptance of three judges to serve on the Panel, the clerk shall prepare a Notice of Assignment of Hearing Panel, which the clerk will serve on the attorney named in the Statement of Cause ("the attorney") and on the local Office of the United States Trustee, along with a copy of the Statement of Cause and a copy of this general order. The attorney may file a motion for recusal as to any of the judges assigned to the Panel within ten days of the service of the Notice of the Assignment of Hearing Panel and serve the motion on the Office of the United States Trustee. That motion may be heard by any judge other than the referring judge, any judge assigned to the Panel, or any judge who has declined to serve on the Panel. The assignment of the recusal motion to a judge shall be made at random by the clerk, who shall give notice of the recusal hearing to the attorney and to the Office of the United States Trustee at least 10 calendar days before the hearing date.

Once the period for bringing a recusal motion has terminated, or after disposition of any recusal motion, the Presiding Judge shall advise the clerk of the date, time, and place for the Disciplinary Hearing, whereupon the clerk shall prepare a Notice of Disciplinary Hearing and mail the notice to the attorney and to the Office of the United States Trustee at least 21 calendar days before the hearing date.

(2) Hearing Procedures. The attorney may appear at the Disciplinary Hearing with legal counsel and may present evidence:

(A) Refuting the statements contained in the Statement of Cause,

(B) Mitigating the discipline (i.e., that notwithstanding the validity of the statements in the Statement of Cause the attorney should not be disciplined), and

(C) Bearing on the type and extent of disciplinary action appropriate under the circumstances.

The Federal Rules of Evidence shall apply to the presentation of evidence at the Disciplinary Hearing, and an official record of the proceedings shall be maintained as though the Disciplinary Hearing were a contested matter as that term is defined in the Federal Rules of Bankruptcy Procedure. The United States Trustee for the district may appear at the hearing in person or by counsel and may participate in the presentation of evidence as though she or he were a party to the proceeding. If the United States Trustee wishes to appear at the hearing, she or he must file a Notice of Intent to Appear, setting forth the purposes for the appearance, and serve that notice on the attorney at least 11 days before the hearing. The Panel may disregard written statements or declarations of innocence or in mitigation of the attorney's conduct unless they are filed with the court with copies delivered promptly thereafter to the chambers of each member of the Panel at least five court days prior to the hearing. Written statements presented to the Panel for consideration as evidence may be disregarded by the Panel if the declarant is unavailable at the hearing for cross-examination and for examination by the Panel.

(3) Ruling. At the conclusion of the Disciplinary Hearing, the judges of the Panel will adjourn to a private session to consider the matter. The ruling of the Panel will be made by majority vote of the judges on the Panel. The Presiding Judge will assign to a judge in the majority the task of drafting the Panel's Memorandum of Decision setting forth the majority's decision and its reasons. Any member of the Panel may issue a concurring or dissenting opinion which will be made a part of the Memorandum of Decision.

If the Panel imposes discipline on an attorney, the Presiding Judge shall issue a Discipline Order based on the Panel's Memorandum of Decision. That order may provide for any appropriate discipline, including but not limited to revocation or suspension of the right to practice before all the judges of this court. The Discipline Order will become final 10 days after entry or, if a motion for rehearing is filed, 10 days after entry of an order denying the attorney's motion for rehearing. The same rule as to finality will apply to a new or revised Discipline Order, if one is issued by the Panel after rehearing.

The Discipline Order shall be sent by the clerk to the Clerk of the District Court. Should the Panel so order, a Discipline Order also may be transmitted by the clerk to the State Bar of California or published in designated periodicals, or both.

If an attorney's practice privileges have been revoked, modified, or suspended by final order of a Panel, the attorney may not appear before any of the judges of this court representing any other persons or entities except in compliance with the terms of the Discipline Order.

(4) Reinstatement. An attorney whose privileges have been revoked, modified, or suspended under this general order may apply to the Chief Judge of this court for reinstatement of privileges on the following schedule:

(A) If privileges were revoked without condition for an unlimited period of time, the attorney may apply for reinstatement after five years from the date the Discipline Order becomes final;

(B) If privileges were revoked or suspended with specified conditions precedent to reinstatement, the attorney may apply for reinstatement upon fulfillment of the conditions set forth in the Discipline Order; and

(C) If privileges were suspended for a specified period of time, the attorney may apply for reinstatement at the conclusion of the period of suspension or five years after the Discipline Order becomes final, whichever first occurs.

An Application for Reinstatement of Privileges must include a copy of the Discipline Order, proof that all conditions justifying reinstatement have been fulfilled, and proof that the applicant is in good standing before the United States District Court for the Central District of California and is a member in good standing of the State Bar of California. If the attorney's privileges were revoked, or if the suspension was for a time in excess of five years and was without any conditions precedent to reinstatement, it shall be within the sole discretion of the Chief Judge whether to issue a reinstatement order. If the Chief Judge determines that the attorney is entitled to reinstatement of practice privileges, he or she may issue a Reinstatement Order. Upon entry of the Reinstatement Order, the attorney affected thereby shall be deemed eligible to practice before all the judges of this court except to the extent any judge of this court has issued an order, other than under this rule, denying that attorney the right to appear before that judge or to appear in a particular case.

Upon entry, the clerk shall transmit a copy to all judges of this court and to the attorney, the clerk of the District Court, and to the United States Trustee. In addition, if the Discipline Order was sent to the State Bar or published, the Clerk shall transmit the Reinstatement Order to the State Bar and publish it in the same publication, if possible.

If the Chief Judge does not grant the Application for Reinstatement of Privileges, he or she shall issue an order denying the application together with a separate written statement of the reasons for his or her decision. That order will become final 10 days after entry.

If an attorney's Application for Reinstatement of Privileges is denied, he or she may reapply for reinstatement after one year from the date of entry of the order denying the previous application or within such other time or upon fulfillment of such conditions as may be set forth in the order denying reinstatement.

(5) Maintenance of Discipline Files. The clerk will place in the court's file for each disciplinary proceeding all documents referred to above and others received or issued by this court relating thereto, and notations thereof shall be entered on the docket for that proceeding. Those files shall be maintained in accordance with applicable law and rules for maintenance of miscellaneous files of this court and shall be available for review and copying by members of the public unless, by order of the Chief Judge or the Presiding Judge of the Panel to which the matter was assigned, access to the file is restricted or prohibited.

The clerk shall close a disciplinary file 30 days after entry of a dispositive order (for example, an Order Re Revocation of Privileges or a Reinstatement Order) in that proceeding unless within that time the clerk receives a Notice of Appeal of any order rendered in the proceeding or other information justifying maintenance of the file in an open status. The clerk shall reopen a disciplinary file upon the request of the attorney, for the convenience of the court, or upon order of any judge of this court, whereupon the clerk shall advise the Chief Judge accordingly. So long as any disciplinary files remain open, the clerk shall provide the Chief Judge a quarterly status report of all such open files to which will be attached copies of their dockets. The Chief Judge may order any such files closed when he or she deems it appropriate, consistent with the provisions hereof and the status of any such matter.

(6) Appeals. All orders issued pursuant to this rule shall be appealable to the extent permitted by applicable law and rules of court.

Appendix III ADOPTION OF MEDIATION PROGRAM FOR BANKRUPTCY CASES AND ADVERSARY PROCEEDINGS (Second Amended General Order No. 95-01)

1.0 PURPOSE AND SCOPE The United States Bankruptcy Court for the Central District of California (the "Court") recognizes that formal litigation of disputes in bankruptcy cases and adversary proceedings frequently imposes significant economic burdens on parties and often delays resolution of those disputes. The procedures established herein are intended primarily to provide litigants with the means to resolve their disputes more quickly, at less cost, and often without the stress and pressure of litigation.

The Court also notes that the volume of cases, contested matters and adversary proceedings filed in this district has placed substantial burdens upon counsel, litigants and the Court, all of which contribute to the delay in the resolution of disputed matters. A Court-authorized mediation program, in which litigants and counsel meet with a mediator, offers an opportunity for parties to settle legal disputes promptly, less expensively, and to their mutual satisfaction. The judges of the Court hereby adopt the Mediation Program for Bankruptcy Cases and Adversary Proceedings (the "Mediation Program") for these purposes.

It is the Court's intention that the Mediation Program shall operate in such a way as to allow the participants to take advantage of and utilize a wide variety of alternative dispute resolution methods. These methods may include, but are not limited to, mediation, negotiation, early neutral evaluation and settlement facilitation. The specific method or methods employed will be those that are appropriate and applicable as determined by the mediators and the parties, and will vary from matter to matter.

Nothing contained herein is intended to preclude other forms of dispute resolution with the consent of the parties.

2.0 CASES ELIGIBLE FOR ASSIGNMENT TO THE MEDIATION PROGRAM Unless otherwise ordered by the judge handling the particular matter (the "Judge"), all controversies arising in an adversary proceeding, contested matter, or other dispute in a bankruptcy case are eligible for referral to the Mediation Program.

3.0 PANEL OF MEDIATORS

3.1 Selection.

a. The Court shall establish and maintain a panel ("Panel") of qualified professionals who have volunteered and been chosen to serve as a mediator ("Mediator") for the possible resolution of matters referred to the Mediation Program. The Panel shall be comprised of both attorneys and non-attorneys.

b. Applicants shall submit an Application (in the form attached) (the "Application") to the judge appointed as the administrator of the Mediation Program (the "Mediation Program Administrator"), setting forth their qualifications as described in Paragraph 3.3 below.

c. The judges of the Court will select the Panel from the applications submitted to the Mediation Program Administrator. The judges will consider each applicant's training and experience in mediation or other alternative dispute resolution, if any, as well as the applicant's professional experience and location. Appointments may be limited to keep the Panel at an appropriate size and to ensure that the Panel is comprised of individuals who have broad based experience, superior skills, and qualifications from a variety of legal specialties and other professions.

3.2 Term. Mediators shall serve as members of the Panel for a term of three years unless the Mediator is advised otherwise by the Court or submits a written request to withdraw from the Panel to the Mediation Program Administrator. Reappointment will occur at the judges' discretion, and an application for reappointment is not required.

3.3 Qualifications.

a. Attorney Applicants. An attorney applicant shall certify to the Court in the application that the applicant:

1. Is, and has been, a member in good standing of the bar of any state or of the District of Columbia for at least five (5) years;

2. Is a member in good standing of the federal courts for the Central District of California;

3. Has served as a principal attorney of record in at least three (3) bankruptcy cases (without regard to the party represented) from case commencement to conclusion or, if the case is still pending, to the date of the Application, or has served as the principal attorney of record for a party in interest in at least three (3) adversary proceedings or contested matters from commencement to conclusion or, if the case is still pending, to the date of the Application; and

4. Is willing to undertake to evaluate or mediate at least one matter each quarter of each year, subject only to unavailability due to conflicts, personal or professional commitments, or other matters which would make such service inappropriate.

b. Non-Attorney Applicants. A non-attorney applicant shall certify to the Court in the Application that the applicant has been a member in good standing of the applicant's particular profession for at least five (5) years, and shall submit a statement of professional qualifications, experience, training and other information demonstrating, in the applicant's opinion, why the applicant should be appointed to the Panel. Non-attorney applicants shall make the same certification required of attorney applicants contained in Paragraph 3.3.a.4.

3.4 Geographic Areas of Service. Applicants shall indicate on the Application all counties within the Central District in which they are willing to serve. Applicants must be willing to travel to all such counties to conduct Mediation Conferences.

4.0 ADMINISTRATION OF THE MEDIATION PROGRAM The Chief Judge will appoint a judge of the Court to serve as the Mediation Program Administrator. The Mediation Program Administrator will be aided by assigned staff members of the Court, who will maintain and collect applications, maintain the roster of the Panel, track and compile results of the Mediation Program, and handle such other administrative duties as are necessary.

5.0 ASSIGNMENT OF MATTERS TO THE MEDIATION PROGRAM

5.1 Assignment by Request of Parties. A contested matter in a case, adversary proceeding, or other dispute (hereinafter collectively referred to as "Matter" or "Matters") may be assigned to the Mediation Program if requested in writing by the parties in the form attached as Official Forms 701 and 702.

5.2 Assignment by Judge. Matters may also be assigned by order of the Judge at a status conference or other hearing. While participation by the parties in the Mediation Program is generally intended to be voluntary, the Judge, acting sua sponte or on the request of a party, may designate specific Matters for inclusion in the Mediation Program. The Judge may do so over the objections of the parties. If a Matter is assigned to the Mediation Program by the Judge at a status conference or other hearing, the parties will be presented with an order assigning the Matter to the Mediation Program, and with a current roster of the Panel. The parties shall normally be given the opportunity to confer and to select a mutually acceptable Mediator and an Alternate Mediator from the Panel. If the parties cannot agree, or if the Judge deems selection by the Judge to be appropriate and necessary, the Judge shall select a Mediator and an Alternate Mediator from the Panel.

5.3 Assignment of Non-Panel Mediators. The Judge may, in his or her sole discretion, appoint individuals who are not members of the Panel as the Mediator and Alternate Mediator at the request of the parties and for good cause shown.

5.4 Use of Official Court Order Assigning Matter to Mediation Program. The order appointing the Mediator and Alternate Mediator and assigning a Matter to the Mediation Program shall be in the form attached as Official Form 702 ("Mediation Order"). The original Mediation Order shall be docketed and retained in the case or adversary proceeding file and copies shall be mailed, by the party so designated by the Judge, to the Mediator, the Alternate Mediator, the Mediation Program Administrator, and to all other parties to the dispute.

5.5 Existing Case Deadlines Not Affected by Assignment to Mediation. Assignment to the Mediation Program shall not alter or affect any time limits, deadlines, scheduling matters or orders in the case, any adversary proceeding, contested matter or other proceeding, unless specifically ordered by the Judge.

5.6 Disclosure of Conflicts of Interest. No Mediator may serve in any Matter in violation of the standards regarding judicial disqualification set forth in 28 U.S.C. § 455.

a. Disclosure by Attorney Mediators. An attorney Mediator shall promptly determine all conflicts or potential conflicts in the manner prescribed by the California Rules of Professional Conduct and disclose same to all parties in writing. If the attorney Mediator's firm has represented one or more of the parties, the Mediator shall promptly disclose that circumstance to all parties in writing.

b. Disclosure by Non-Attorney Mediators. A non-attorney Mediator shall promptly determine all conflicts or potential conflicts in the same manner as a non-attorney would under the applicable rules pertaining to the non-attorney Mediator's profession and disclose same to all parties in writing. If the Mediator's firm has represented one or more of the parties, the Mediator shall promptly disclose that circumstance to all parties in writing.

c. Report of Conflict Issue by Parties. A party who believes that the assigned Mediator and/or the Alternate Mediator has a conflict of interest shall promptly bring the issue to the attention of the Mediator and/or the Alternate Mediator, as applicable, and shall disclose same to all parties in writing.

d. Resolution of Conflict Issue by Judge. If the Mediator and/or the Alternate Mediator does not withdraw from the assignment, the issue shall be brought to the attention of the Judge in writing by the Mediator, the Alternate Mediator, or any of the parties in the form attached as Official Form 704. The notice shall be filed with the Court, and copies of the notice shall be mailed to the Judge, all of the parties to the dispute, their counsel, if any, the Mediator, the Alternate Mediator, and the Mediation Program Administrator.

The Judge will then take whatever action(s) he or she deems necessary and appropriate under the circumstances to resolve the conflict of interest issue.

6.0 CONFIDENTIALITY

6.1 In General. No written or oral communication made, or any document presented, by any party, attorney, Mediator, Alternate Mediator or other participant in connection with or during any Mediation Conference, including the written Mediation Conference statements referred to in Paragraph 7.8 below, may be disclosed to anyone not involved in the Mediation, nor may any such communication be used in any pending or future proceeding in this Court or any other court. All such communications and documents shall be subject to all of the protections afforded by

FED. R. BANKR. P. 7068. Such communication(s) may be disclosed, however, if all participants in the Mediation, including the Mediator, agree in writing to such disclosure. In addition, nothing contained herein shall be construed to prohibit parties from entering into written agreements resolving some or all of the Matter(s), or entering into or filing procedural or factual stipulations based on suggestions or agreements made in connection with a Mediation Program conference ("Mediation Conference").

6.2 Non-Confidentiality of Otherwise Discoverable Evidence. Notwithstanding the foregoing, nothing herein shall require the exclusion of any evidence otherwise discoverable merely because it is presented in the course of a Mediation Conference.

6.3 Written Confidentiality Agreement Required. The parties and the Mediator shall enter into a written confidentiality agreement in the form attached as Official Form 708.

6.4 Effect of Recorded Settlement Agreement on Confidentiality. An oral agreement reached in the course of a Mediation Conference is not made inadmissible or protected from disclosure if all of the following conditions are satisfied:

a. The oral agreement is recorded by a court reporter, tape recorder, or other reliable means of sound recording;

b. The terms of the oral agreement are recited on the record in the presence of the parties and the Mediator, and the parties express on the record that they agree to the terms recited;

c. The parties to the oral agreement expressly state on the record that the agreement is enforceable or binding or words to that effect; and

d. The recording is reduced to writing and the writing is signed by the parties and their counsel, if any, within 72 hours after it is recorded.

6.5 Effect of Written Settlement Agreement on Confidentiality. A written settlement agreement prepared in the course of a Mediation Conference is not made inadmissible or protected from disclosure if the agreement is signed by the settling parties and their counsel, if any, and either of the following conditions are satisfied:

a. The agreement provides that it is admissible or subject to disclosure, or words to that effect; or

b. The agreement provides that it is enforceable or binding or words to that effect.

6.6 Court Evaluation of Mediation Program Not Precluded by Confidentiality Provisions. Nothing contained herein shall be construed to prevent Mediators, parties, and their counsel, if any, from responding in absolute confidentiality to inquiries or surveys by persons authorized by the Court to evaluate the Mediation Program.

6.7 Confidentiality of Suggestions and Recommendations of Mediator. The Mediator shall have no obligation to make any written suggestions or recommendations but may, as a matter of discretion, provide counsel for the parties (or the parties, where proceeding in pro per), with a written settlement recommendation memorandum. No copy of any such memorandum shall be filed with the Court or made available, in whole or in part, directly or indirectly, to the Judge.

7.0 MEDIATION PROCEDURES

7.1 Selection of Mediator. Counsel for the parties (or the parties, where proceeding in pro per), are encouraged to contact the proposed Mediator and Alternate Mediator as soon as practicable (preferably before submitting the Mediation Order to the judge for approval, if possible) to determine the availability of the Mediator and Alternate Mediator to serve in the Matter.

7.2 Availability of Mediator. If the Mediator is not available to serve in the Matter, the Mediator shall notify the parties, the Alternate Mediator, and the Mediation Program Administrator of that unavailability by mail in the form attached as Official Form 703 as soon as possible, but no later than seven (7) calendar days from the date of receipt of notification of appointment. Upon notification of the Mediator's unavailability to serve, the Alternate Mediator shall automatically serve as the Mediator without the necessity for further court order.

7.3 Availability of Alternate Mediator. If the Alternate Mediator is not available to serve in the Matter, the Alternate Mediator shall notify the parties and the Mediation Program Administrator of that unavailability by mail in the form attached as Official Form 703 as soon as possible, but no later than seven (7) calendar days from the receipt of notification by the Mediator, pursuant to Paragraph 7.1 above, of the Mediator's unavailability to serve.

7.4 Selection of Successor Mediator.

a. By Parties. Within seven (7) calendar days of receipt of the

Alternate Mediator's notification of unavailability, the parties shall choose a mutually acceptable Successor Mediator and Successor Alternate Mediator by mail in the form attached as Official Form 702. (This is the same Official Form which is used to appoint the original Mediator and Alternate Mediator, as described in Paragraph 5.4 above. However, the word "Successor" must be inserted in the caption of the Mediation Order in front of the words "Mediator" and "Alternate Mediator"). The parties shall file such form with the Court and provide a courtesy copy to the Judge and the Mediation Program Administrator.

b. By Judge. If the parties are unable to agree on a choice of Successor Mediator and Successor Alternate Mediator, they shall notify the Judge and the Mediation Program Administrator of their inability to do so by mail in the form attached as Official Form 704. In that event, the Judge shall appoint the Successor Mediator and Successor Alternate Mediator.

c. Use of Official Court Order Assigning Successor Mediator. When the Successor Mediator and Successor Alternate Mediator have been chosen by the parties and/or appointed by the Judge, the Judge shall execute an order appointing the Successor Mediator and Successor Alternate Mediator in the form attached as Official Form 702. (This is the same Official Form which is used to appoint the original Mediator and Alternate Mediator, as described in Paragraph 5.4 above. However, the word "Successor" must be inserted in the caption of the Mediation Order in front of the words "Mediator" and "Alternate Mediator").

7.5 Initial Telephonic Conference. Promptly, but no later than fifteen (15) calendar days of receipt of notification of appointment, the Mediator shall conduct a telephonic conference with counsel for the parties (or the parties, where appearing in pro per) to discuss (1) fixing a convenient date and place for the Mediation Conference, (2) the procedures that will be followed during the Mediation Conference, (3) who shall attend the Mediation Conference on behalf of each party, (4) what material or exhibits should be provided to the Mediator before the Mediation Conference, and (5) any issues or maters that it would be especially helpful to have the parties address in their written Mediation Conference Statements.

7.6 Mediation Conference Scheduling. Also within fifteen (15) calendar days of receipt of notification of appointment, the Mediator shall give notice to the parties of the date, time and place for the Mediation Conference. The Mediation Conference shall commence no later than thirty (30) calendar days following the receipt of notification by the Mediator, and shall be held in a suitable neutral setting such as the office of the Mediator, or at a location convenient and agreeable to the parties and the Mediator.

a. Continuance of Mediation Conference. The date for the Mediation Conference may be continued for a period not to exceed thirty (30) calendar days upon written stipulation between the Mediator and the parties. The stipulation need not be filed with the Court but the parties must mail a copy of it to the Judge and the Mediation Program Administrator.

b. Additional Continuance. At the written request of the parties and for good cause shown, the Judge may, in his or her sole discretion, approve an additional continuance of the Mediation Conference beyond the period specified in Paragraph 7.6.a.

7.7 Mandatory Service of Mediation Order Prior to Mediation Conference. Prior to the Mediation Conference, the parties' counsel shall serve a copy of the Mediation Order on the Mediator, Alternate Mediator, Mediation Program Administrator, and all parties to the dispute.

7.8 Mediation Conference Statements. Each party shall submit a written Mediation Conference statement ("Mediation Statement") directly to the Mediator and to the parties to the Mediation Conference no less than five (5) court days prior to the date of the initial Mediation Conference, unless modified by the Mediator.

a. Format. Mediation Statements shall not exceed ten (10) pages, excluding exhibits and attachments. Mediation Statements shall comply with all of the requirements of Local Bankruptcy Rule 1002-1(d)(1), (2), (3) and (7), unless such compliance is excused by the Mediator.

b. Confidentiality. Mediation Statements shall be subject to all of the protections afforded by the confidentiality provisions contained herein and by FED. R. BANKR. P. 7068.

c. Statements Not Filed with Court. The Mediation Statements shall not be filed with the Court, and the Judge shall not have access to them. In addition, the phrase "CONFIDENTIAL—NOT TO BE FILED WITH THE COURT" shall be typed on the first page of the Mediation Statements.

d. Mandatory Contents. Mediation Statements must:

1. Identify the person(s), in addition to counsel, who will attend the Mediation Conference as representative(s) of the party, who have authority to make decisions;

2. Describe briefly the substance of the dispute;

3. Address any legal or factual issue(s) that might appreciably reduce the scope of the dispute or contribute significantly to settlement;

4. Identify the discovery that could contribute most to preparing the parties for meaningful discussions;

5. Set forth the history of past settlement discussions, including disclosure of any prior and any presently outstanding offers and demands;

6. Make an estimate of the cost and time to be expended for further discovery, pretrial motions, expert witnesses and trial;

7. Indicate presently scheduled dates for further status conferences, pretrial conferences, trial, or otherwise; and

8. Attach copies of the document(s) from which the dispute has arisen (e.g., contracts), or the document(s) whose availability would materially advance the purposes of the Mediation Conference.

e. Recommended Additional Contents. Parties may identify in the Mediation Statements the person(s) connected to a party opponent (including a representative of a party opponent's insurance carrier) whose presence at the Mediation Conference would substantially improve the prospects for making the session productive. The fact that a person has been so identified shall not, by itself, result in an order compelling that person to attend the Mediation Conference.

f. Additional Mediation Statements for Mediator Only. Each party may submit directly to the Mediator, for his or her eyes only, a separate confidential Mediation Statement describing any additional interests, considerations, or matters that the party would like the Mediator to understand before the Mediation Conference begins. Such Mediation Statements shall not exceed ten (10) pages, excluding exhibits and attachments, and shall comply with all of the requirements of Local Bankruptcy Rule 1002-1(d)(1), (2), (3), and (7) unless such compliance is excused by the Mediator.

7.9 Mandatory Attendance at Mediation Conference.

a. By Counsel. Counsel for each party who is primarily responsible for the Matter (or the party, where proceeding in pro per) shall personally attend the Mediation Conference and any adjourned session(s) of that conference, unless excused by the Mediator for cause. Counsel for each party shall come prepared to discuss all liability issues, all damage issues, and the position of the party relative to settlement, in detail and in good faith.

b. By Parties. All individual parties, and representatives with authority to negotiate and to settle the Matter on behalf of parties other than individuals, shall personally attend the Mediation Conference and any adjourned session(s) of that conference, unless excused by the Mediator for cause. Each party shall come prepared to discuss all liability issues, all damage issues, and the position of the party relative to settlement, in detail and in good faith.

c. By Governmental Agencies. A unit or an agency of government satisfies this attendance requirement if represented by a person who has, to the greatest extent feasible, authority to settle, and who is knowledgeable about the facts of the case, the governmental unit's position, and the procedures and policies under which the governmental unit decides whether to accept proposed settlements.

d. Telephonic Appearance. Any party or lawyer who is excused by the Mediator from appearing in person at the Mediation Conference may be required by the Mediator to participate by telephone. This decision is within the Mediator's sole discretion.

7.10 Consequences of Failure to Attend Mediation Conference and Other Violations of Mediation Program Procedures. Willful failure to attend the Mediation Conference and/or other violations of the Mediation Program procedures shall be reported to the Judge by the Mediator by written notice in the form attached as Official Form 705, and may result in the imposition of sanctions by the Judge. The Mediator's notice shall be filed with the Court and copies of the notice shall be mailed to the Judge, all of the parties to the dispute, their counsel, if any, and the Mediation Program Administrator.

The Judge will then take whatever action(s) he or she deems necessary and appropriate under the circumstances to resolve the issue of such willful failure to attend the Mediation Conference and/or other violations of the Mediation Program procedures.

7.11 Conduct at the Mediation Conference. The Mediation Conference shall proceed informally. Rules of evidence shall not apply. There shall be no formal examination or cross-examination of witnesses. The Mediator may conduct continued Mediation Conferences after the initial session where necessary. As appropriate, the Mediator may:

a. Permit each party (through counsel or otherwise) to make an oral presentation of its position;

b. Help the parties identify areas of agreement and, where feasible, enter into stipulations;

c. Assess the relative strengths and weaknesses of the parties' contentions and evidence, and explain as carefully as possible the reasoning of the Mediator that supports these assessments;

d. Assist the parties, through separate consultation or otherwise, in settling the dispute;

e. Estimate, where feasible, the likelihood of liability and the dollar range of damages;

f. Help the parties devise a plan for sharing the important information and/or conducting the key discovery that will assist them as expeditiously as possible to participate in meaningful settlement discussions or to posture the case for disposition by other means; and

g. Determine whether some form of follow up to the Mediation Conference would contribute to the case development process or to settlement.

7.12 Suggestions and Recommendations of Mediator. If the Mediator makes any oral or written suggestions as to the advisability of a change in any party's position with respect to settlement, the attorney for that party shall promptly transmit that suggestion to the client. The Mediator shall have no obligation to make an written comments or recommendations, but may, as a matter of discretion, provide the parties with a written settlement recommendation memorandum. No copy of any such memorandum shall be filed with the Court or made available in whole or in part directly or indirectly, to the Judge.

8.0 PROCEDURE UPON COMPLETION OF MEDIATION CONFERENCE

8.1 Upon the conclusion of the Mediation Conference, the following procedures shall be followed:

a. If Matter Settled. If the parties have reached an agreement regarding the disposition of the Matter, the parties, with the advice of the Mediator, shall determine who shall prepare the writing to dispose of the Matter. If necessary, the parties may, with the Mediator's consent, continue the Mediation Conference to a date convenient for all parties and the Mediator. Where required, they shall promptly submit a fully executed settlement stipulation to the Judge for approval, and shall mail a copy to the Mediation Program Administrator. The Judge will accommodate parties who desire to place any resolution of a Matter on the record during or following the Mediation Conference.

b. Mediator's Certificate of Completion of Conference. Within ten (10) calendar days of the Mediation Conference, the Mediator shall file with the Court and serve on the parties and the Mediation Program Administrator a certificate in the form attached as Official Form 706, which shows whether there has been compliance with the Mediation Conference requirements and whether or not a settlement has been reached. Regardless of the outcome of the Mediation Conference, the Mediator will not provide the Judge with any details of the substance of the Mediation Conference.

c. Confidential Evaluation. In order to assist the Mediation Program Administrator in compiling useful data to evaluate the Mediation Program and aid the Court in assessing the efforts of the members of the Panel, the Mediator shall provide a Mediation Conference Report to the Mediation Program Administrator in the form attached as Official Form 709. The Mediation Conference Report shall not be filed with the Court and the Judge shall not have access to it. In addition, the phrase "CONFIDENTIAL—NOT TO BE FILED WITH THE COURT" shall be typed on the first page of the Mediation Conference Report.

9.0 PRO BONO AND COMPENSATED SERVICE OF MEDIATORS

9.1 Mandatory Pro Bono Service. The Mediator shall serve on a pro bono basis and shall not require compensation or reimbursement of expenses for the first full day of at least one Mediation Conference per quarter per year. If, at the conclusion of the first full day of the Mediation Conference, it is determined by the parties that additional time will be both necessary and productive in order to complete the Mediation Conference, then:

a. If the Mediator consents to continue to serve on a pro bono basis, the parties may agree to continue the Mediation Conference; or

b. If the Mediator does not consent to continue to serve on a pro bono basis, the Mediator's compensation shall be on such terms as are satisfactory to the Mediator and the parties, and shall be subject to the prior approval of the Judge if the estate is to be charged with such expense.

9.2 Compensated Service Upon Completion of Mandatory Pro Bono Service. After a Mediator has concluded at least one pro bono mediation for the particular quarter, nothing herein shall prohibit the Mediator and the parties from agreeing that the Mediator may be compensated for services rendered by the Mediator. The amount of such compensation and the terms governing the amount and payment shall be as agreed upon among the parties. If applicable, any party or parties to the mediation may apply to the Judge for authorization to compensate the Mediator from property of the estate. Nothing in this provision, however, shall require any party to compensate a Mediator other than as may be mutually agreed upon among the parties and the Mediator.

10.0 IMPLEMENTATION

10.1 The Mediation Program became effective on July 1, 1995.

10.2 Judge Barry Russell is appointed the Mediation Program Administrator.

Appendix IV GUIDELINES FOR ALLOWANCE OF ATTORNEYS' FEES IN CHAPTER 13 CASES

THESE GUIDELINES GOVERN THE ALLOWANCE OF ATTORNEYS' FEES IN CHAPTER 13 CASES IN THIS DISTRICT.

AN ATTORNEY MAY RECEIVE AN ORDER APPROVING FEES UP TO THE AMOUNTS SET FORTH HEREIN WITHOUT FILING A DETAILED APPLICATION IF:

The attorney has filed with the court and served the chapter 13 trustee with the statement required pursuant to Rule 2016 of the Federal Rules of Bankruptcy Procedure and a fully executed copy of the "Rights and Responsibilities Agreement Between Chapter 13 Debtors and Their Attorneys," copies of which are available in the clerk's office and in the chapter 13 trustees' offices; and

No objection to the requested fees has been raised.

THE MAXIMUM FEE WHICH CAN BE APPROVED THROUGH THE PROCEDURE DESCRIBED HEREIN IS:

$4,500 in a case in which the debtor is engaged in a business; or

$4,000 in all other cases;

IF AN ATTORNEY SEEKS ADDITIONAL FEES OR ELECTS TO BE PAID OTHER THAN PURSUANT TO THESE GUIDELINES:

The attorney shall file and serve an application for fees in accordance with 11 U.S.C. §§ 330 and 331, Rules 2016 and 2002 of the Federal Rules of Bankruptcy Procedure and Local Bankruptcy Rules 2016-1 and 3015-1, as well as the "Guide To Applications For Professional Compensation" issued by the United States Trustee for the Central District of California.

In any event, on its own motion or the motion of any party in interest, the court may order a hearing to review any attorney's fee agreement or payment, in accordance with 11 U.S.C. § 329 and Rule 2017 of the Federal Rules of Bankruptcy Procedure.

General Order 99-02 In re Assignment And Reassignment Of Related Cases And Proceedings And Cases And Proceedings Due To Recusal

To assist in the orderly conduct of the business of this Court, the Judges of the United States Bankruptcy Court for the Central District of California hereby enter General Order 99-02, dated March 31, 1999, regarding assignment and reassignment of related cases and proceedings and cases and proceedings due to recusal.

BACKGROUND

The recently promulgated Local Bankruptcy Rules, which became effective on July 1, 1998, do not contain a provision similar to that of prior Local Bankruptcy Rule 104(4) (c) or 104(4) (d), as the Ninth Circuit Review of Local Rules determined that the procedures concerning assignment and reassignment of related cases were more appropriately implemented in a General Order. This General Order establishes procedures by which related cases and proceedings are assigned and reassigned and by which cases and proceedings are reassigned due to recusal.

PROCEDURE FOR ASSIGNMENT AND REASSIGNMENT OF RELATED CASES AND PROCEEDINGS

Assignment of Related Cases

The following procedure shall be used for the assignment of 13 related cases by the Clerk of the Court.

When a Rule 1015-2 Statement (as defined in Local Bankruptcy Rule 1015-2(2) (b)) discloses a Related Case (as defined in Local Bankruptcy Rule 1015-2(1)) which is or was pending in this District, the newly-filed case shall be assigned by the Clerk in the following manner:

(a) Except as provided in subsection (c), if the Judge to whom such Related Case was most recently assigned is still in office, then to such judge;

(b) If such Judge is no longer in office, then according to the administrative orders of this Court; and

(c) If the new petition was properly filed in a division of this District different from the division in which the Judge to whom the prior case was assigned now sits, the new case will be assigned to a Judge in the division in which it was filed and not to the Judge to whom the prior case was assigned.

Reassignment of Related Cases and Proceedings

The following procedure shall apply to the reassignment of related cases and proceedings by the Court:

(1) The Judge before whom a later-filed case or proceeding is pending may, with or without motion, notice or hearing, order the reassignment of such case or proceeding to the Judge before whom a prior Related Case or proceeding is pending.

(2) The Judge before whom a prior case or proceeding is pending or was pending may, with or without motion, notice or hearing, order the reassignment to his or her docket of a later-filed case or proceeding pending before another Judge. Any reassignment of a case or proceeding pursuant to this paragraph (2) shall require the concurrence of the Judges to whom and from whom such case or proceeding is to be reassigned.

(3) The Judges to whom a Related Case or proceeding have been assigned may, by mutual consent, order the reassignment of a prior Related Case or proceeding to the Judge to whom a later-filed case or proceeding has been assigned for good cause based upon the convenience of the parties or where justice otherwise requires.

Reassignment of Cases or Proceedings Due to Recusal

If a case or proceeding is assigned to a Judge and the assigned Judge discovers grounds to recuse himself or herself pursuant to Federal Rule of Bankruptcy Procedure 5004, the assigned Judge may not cause the case or proceeding to be reassigned unless the assigned Judge first signs an order that specifies the basis for recusal and, hence, reassignment. The form Orders of Recusal are attached as Exhibit "A" to this order.

The preceding paragraph applies no matter how the case or proceeding was assigned to the assigned Judge.

IT IS SO ORDERED.

DATED: March 31, 1999

GERALDINE MUND
Chief Judge, United States Bankruptcy Court

General Order 02-03 Suspension of Provisions Relating to 6 Month Rule in Local Bankruptcy Rules 3015-1(m)(2) and 3015-1(r)(2)(A)

[Vacated.]

GENERAL ORDER 05-01 CLERK'S OFFICE ELECTRONIC SYSTEMS REFUND POLICY

WHEREAS the Judicial Conference of the United States' current policy, JCUSMAR 49, generally prohibits refunds of fees due upon filing, even if a party filed the case or the document in error or the court dismissed the case or proceeding; and

WHEREAS in March 2005, the Judicial Conference of the United States approved guidance for the courts regarding the refund of fees that are paid electronically; and

WHEREAS such guidance provides that courts should develop procedures for addressing refunds of electronic payments; refunds should be requested by motion or application; the decision whether to refund is a judicial determination that may be delegated to the clerk, as long as procedures clearly address the types of refunds clerks may authorize; and refunds should be processed electronically, not through checks;

IT IS HEREBY ORDERED that:

1. The Executive Officer/Clerk of the United States Bankruptcy Court, Central District of California has the authority to approve refunds for fees paid electronically for monies collected by or paid to the Court in error, such as duplicate charges or electronic system errors.

2. In instances where the Court discovers an error, the Executive Officer/Clerk may automatically initiate a refund.

3. Claimants seeking a refund must submit a written application in the form of a letter with the supporting documentation set forth below. The letter must include the name, address, and telephone number of the party requesting the refund. In support of the refund request, the following documentation generated from the Court's electronic case management system must be enclosed: the receipt for payment of fees and the Notice of Electronic Filing.

The letter and supporting documentation should be sent to the following address:

Financial Services Department
United States Bankruptcy Court
255 East Temple Street, Suite 1067
Los Angeles, CA 90012

4. Refunds will be processed through the electronic credit card system. Refund checks will not be issued.

5. If a claimant's refund request is denied, the claimant may seek reconsideration of the request from the judge presiding over the case in which the subject document was filed by filing a motion to that effect.

6. In the event that a particular attorney or law firm continues to make repeated mistakes when submitting fees and repeatedly requests refunds, the Court will consider remedial action and may issue an order to show cause as to why further requests for refunds should be considered.

DATED: September 21, 2005

General Order No. 05-02 ADOPTION OF INTERIM BANKRUPTCY RULES

[Vacated.]

CENTRAL DISTRICT OF CALIFORNIA

GENERAL ORDER 05-03 DEPOSITING RENT WITH COURT PURSUANT TO 11 U.S.C. § 362 (l)

[Vacated.]

AMENDED GENERAL ORDER 06-01 AMENDMENT OF LOCAL BANKRUPTCY RULE 3015-l(u)(l) AND GUIDELINES TO REFLECT CHANGES IN THE MAXIMUM FEE ALLOWABLE UNDER THE RARA AND THE GUIDELINES

Effective as of the date of this Order, Local Bankruptcy Rule 3015-1(u)(1) and the Guidelines for Allowance of Attorney's Fees in Chapter 13 Cases ("Guidelines") are amended, in relevant part, to provide that the maximum fee allowable under the Rights and Responsibilities Agreement Between Chapter 13 Debtors and Their Attorneys ("RARA") and the Guidelines is:

> "$3,500 in a case in which the debtor is self-employed; or $3,000 in all other cases."

In all other respects, Local Bankruptcy Rule 3015-1(u)(1) and the Guidelines are unchanged.

GENERAL ORDER 06-02 AUTHORIZATION FOR CHAPTER 13 TRUSTEES TO DISBURSE ADEQUATE PROTECTION PAYMENTS AND LEASE PAYMENTS ON PERSONAL PROPERTY PRIOR TO CONFIRMATION

[Vacated.]

GENERAL ORDER 06-03 FILING, SIGNING, AND VERIFYING DOCUMENTS BY ELECTRONIC MEANS USING CM/ECF SYSTEM

WHEREAS Federal Rule of Civil Procedure 83 and Federal Rules of Bankruptcy Procedure 5005(a)(2), 7005(e), and 9029 authorize courts to establish practices and procedures for the filing, signing, and verification of documents by electronic means; and

WHEREAS in addition to the Court's eFile system described in Second Amended General Order 02-01, the Court has implemented the Case Management/Electronic Case Files ("CM/ECF") system for the filing, signing, and verification of documents by electronic means; and

WHEREAS the Clerk of Court has established certain Administrative Procedures for Filing, Signing, and Verifying Pleadings and Papers Using the Case Management/Electronic Case Files (CM/ECF) System (along with any subsequent amendments or supplements thereto, the "Administrative Procedures") and has made them available on the Court's CM/ECF home page;

IT IS HEREBY ORDERED that:

1. The Administrative Procedures are adopted for use in all cases and proceedings in the United States Bankruptcy Court, Central District of California.

2. Documents may be filed, signed, and verified by electronic means using the Court's CM/ECF system in accordance with the Administrative Procedures. In regard to the filing, signing, or verification of documents by electronic means, this General Order 06-03 and the Administrative Procedures shall apply to documents filed electronically using the CM/ECF system, and Second Amended General Order 02-01 shall continue to apply to documents filed electronically using the eFile system.

3. All attorneys and trustees practicing in the United States Bankruptcy Court for the Central District of California eventually will be required to file all documents electronically using the CM/ECF system, except for those documents listed in the Administrative Procedures that must be filed conventionally. The Clerk of Court shall give reasonable notice of the requirement to file documents electronically using the CM/ECF system by public notice.

4. The electronic filing of a document, including virtual documents as defined in the Administrative Procedures, in accordance with the Administrative Procedures, together with the transmission by the Court of a Notice of Electronic Filing to the user filing the document, constitutes the filing of the document for all purposes of the Federal Rules of Bankruptcy Procedure and the Court's Local Bankruptcy Rules and constitutes entry of the document on the docket by the clerk under Federal Rule of Bankruptcy Procedure 5003. Nothing contained herein shall alter or eliminate any requirements concerning the physical delivery of chambers and/or courtesy copies to the Court to the extent set forth in the Administrative Procedures.

5. A document filed electronically using the Court's CM/ECF system, including virtual documents, constitutes a written document or written paper for the purpose of applying the Federal Rules of Bankruptcy Procedure, the Federal Rules of Civil Procedure made applicable by the Federal Rules of Bankruptcy Procedure, § 107 of the Bankruptcy Code, and the Court's Local Bankruptcy Rules.

6. When a document has been filed electronically, or filed in paper format and its image electronically recorded by the Court, the official record of the document shall be the electronic recording of the document as stored by the Court.

7. In order to use the Court's CM/ECF system to file documents electronically, users must first register and obtain a login and password and attend the training required by the Court in accordance with the Administrative Procedures. By registering and receiving a login and password, the user agrees to adhere to this General Order and the Administrative Procedures, any supplements and/or amendments thereto, and any Local Bankruptcy Rule, general order, or other directive regarding the filing, signing, or verification of documents by electronic means that may hereafter be issued.

8. It shall be the duty of the registered user to retain control of, and to protect and secure the confidentiality of, his or her login and password, and to prevent their disclosure to any person not authorized to utilize them. No registered user shall knowingly permit or cause to permit his or her login and password to be utilized by anyone other than an authorized individual empowered to act on behalf of the registered user. A registered user shall immediately notify the Court in writing upon learning that the security of his or her login and password has been compromised.

9. No person shall knowingly utilize or cause another person to utilize the login and password of a registered user unless such person is an authorized member or employee of the registered user's law firm or organization.

10. The use of a registered user's login and password to file a document electronically shall constitute the signature of the registered user on the document being electronically filed. The signature of the registered user on electronically filed documents shall be denoted by "Is/," followed by the registered user's name, on the signature lines where such signatures are required or applicable. Failure to denote "Is/," followed by the registered user's name, on applicable signature lines shall constitute a failure to sign the documents on such signature lines. If the registered user is an attorney, the use of the registered attorney's login and password to file a document electronically shall constitute authorization of "/s/," followed by the registered user's name, as the signature of that attorney on that document under Federal Rule of Bankruptcy Procedure 9011 and Local Bankruptcy Rule 1002- 1 (a).

11. The signature of the debtor or other party represented by the registered user on electronically filed documents shall be denoted by "Is/," followed by the debtor's or other party's name, on the signature lines where such signatures are required or applicable. Documents filed electronically using the CM/ECF system shall be accompanied by a scanned copy of an Electronic Filing Declaration signed by the debtor or other party, or an Electronic Filing Declaration of Authorized Signatory if the debtor or other party is a corporation or partnership. Failure to denote "Is/," followed by the debtor's or other party's name, on applicable signature lines shall constitute a failure to sign the documents on such signature lines, and the failure to submit the Declaration shall constitute a failure to sign in the locations indicated by "/s/," followed by the debtor's or other party's name, by the debtor or other party.

The registered user electronically filing the document shall maintain the executed original of the Declaration for a period of five years after the closing of the case or adversary proceeding in which the document is filed, and shall make the executed original of the Declaration available for review upon request of the Court or other parties. Any subsequently filed amended petitions, schedules, statements, or plans must either be filed electronically with the imaged signature of the debtor(s) or accompanied by a Declaration containing the imaged signature of the debtor(s).

12. Regarding documents containing the signature of the filing user in accordance with paragraph 10 above and/or the signature of the debtor or other party represented by the filing user in accordance with paragraph 11 above, the attorney and/or the debtor or other party, as applicable, shall sign a true and correct hard copy of the document before the electronic version of the same has been electronically filed. The registered user electronically filing the document shall maintain the executed original of the document for a period of five years after the closing of the case or adversary proceeding in which the document is filed, and shall make the executed original available for review upon request of the Court or other parties.

13. Documents that require the verified signature of a person other than the registered user who is electronically filing the document or the debtor or other party represented by the registered user shall be electronically imaged using scanning technology and electronically filed in a format specified by the Clerk of Court. The use of the registered user's login and password by the attorney electronically filing the document is the attorney's representation that the document being filed is a true and correct copy of the original document bearing such other individual's signature. The registered user electronically filing the document shall maintain the executed original of the document for a period of five years after the closing of the case or adversary proceeding in which the document is filed, and shall make the executed original available for review upon request of the Court or other parties.

14. Whenever a document is filed electronically in accordance with the Administrative Procedures, the filing party automatically will be sent a Notice of Electronic Filing by electronic means at the time of docketing. A document filed electronically is deemed to have been filed on the date and at the time set forth on the Notice of Electronic Filing. Filing must be completed before midnight, Pacific Standard or Daylight Saving Time, whichever is then in effect, to be considered filed that day. The Notice of Electronic Filing shall also serve as confirmation that the document has been entered on the docket kept by the Clerk under Federal Rule of Bankruptcy Procedure 5003.

15. Registering and obtaining a login and password from the Court shall constitute (i) consent in writing to receive notice electronically and waiver of the right to receive notice by any other means; and (ii) consent in writing to electronic service, except in regard to service of a summons and complaint under Federal Rule of Bankruptcy Procedure 7004, and waiver of any right to service by any other means. The consent and waiver includes, without limitation, notice of the entry of a judgment or order under Federal Rule of Bankruptcy Procedure 9022. The foregoing consents and waivers shall be effective upon the registered user's activation of the login and password in the CM/ECF system.

16. Electronic transmission of the Notice of Electronic Filing through the Court's transmission facilities constitutes service of notice of the filed document to registered users and others who have consented in writing to accept such service of notice. The party filing the document using the Court's CM/ECF system shall serve the document on other parties as required by the Federal Rules of Bankruptcy Procedure and the Local Bankruptcy Rules.

17. Copies of documents that have been filed electronically which the Court is required to transmit to the United States Trustee shall be transmitted to the United States Trustee electronically.

18. A judgment or order filed electronically by the judge presiding over the matter and therefore without the judge's original signature shall have the same force and effect as if the judge had affixed his or her signature to a paper copy of the order and such order had been entered on the docket in a conventional manner. The filing of a judgment or order in accordance with the Administrative Procedures shall constitute entry of the judgment or order pursuant to Federal Rule of Bankruptcy Procedure 9021.

19. The electronic transmission of the Notice of Electronic Filing to registered ECF users and others who have consented to electronic service or notice in the case or proceeding shall constitute the service on such parties of the notice of entry of the judgment or order required by Federal Rule of Bankruptcy Procedure 9022. The Clerk's Office shall give notice of the entry of the judgment or order by mail to parties who have not consented to service or notice by electronic transmission.

20. This General Order 06-03 and the Administrative Procedures shall govern in the event of any conflict with a provision set forth in a Local Bankruptcy Rule or prior general order.

DATED: November 7, 2006

GENERAL ORDER 07-01 CHAPTER 15 PROCEDURES

[Vacated.]

Public Notice 08-007 CONSENT TO ELECTRONIC NOTICE AND SERVICE OF DOCUMENTS ON UNITED STATES TRUSTEE

EFFECTIVE APRIL 1, 2008

The United States Trustee ("U.S. Trustee") has consented to receive electronic notice and service of most documents filed with the United States Bankruptcy Court for the Central District of California. This applies in all bankruptcy cases regardless of petition date, and in all adversary proceedings filed on or after April 1, 2008. The following guidelines apply when providing notice and service of documents on the U.S. Trustee:

1) Documents Filed in Bankruptcy Cases and Adversary Proceedings:

Persons and entities do not need to serve the U.S. Trustee with a paper copy of any document filed unless the document is on the attached Exceptions to Electronic Notice & Service on the United States Trustee ("Exceptions" list). The electronic transmission to the U.S. Trustee of a Notice of Electronic Filing ("NEF") with a hyperlink to a document, or via a similar procedure through the Bankruptcy Noticing Center ("BNC") constitutes notice [per FRBP 2002 and LBR 2002-2(a)(1)] and service [per FRBP 9034 and LBR 2002-2(a)(1)]. When preparing a Proof of Service list, indicate that the U.S. Trustee will be served electronically by the Court.

2) Entered Orders and Judgments

Similarly, the Court does not need to serve the U.S. Trustee with a paper copy of any entered order or judgment in a bankruptcy case or adversary proceeding. The electronic transmission to the U.S. Trustee of an NEF with a hyperlink to a document, or via a similar procedure through the BNC constitutes completion of the Court's duty to serve the entered order or judgment per FRBP 9022. When preparing a Service List for Notice of Entry of Order, indicate that the U.S. Trustee will be served electronically by the Court.

Note: This consent does not apply when a person or entity is serving the U.S. Trustee or any of the U.S. Trustee's staff in their capacity as individuals. Please refer to the attached "Exceptions" list or the Court's CM/ECF Administrative Procedures for those documents exempted from electronic notice and service. The CM/ECF Administrative Procedures can be accessed from the Court's website at www.cacb.uscourts.gov, under Electronic Systems & Status>CM/ECF Home Page.

For questions regarding the U.S. Trustee's consent to electronic notice and service, please contact our ECF Help Desk at (213) 894-2365.

Exceptions to Electronic Notice & Service on United States Trustee

Beginning April 1, 2008, persons or entities filing the following documents must also serve the U.S. Trustee by U.S. mail, overnight mail, Federal Express, or courier on or before the date the document is filed. The proof of service must indicate that the U.S. Trustee was served via one of the foregoing forms of service for:

A) Proposed Orders or Judgments

Persons and entities must continue to comply with the Court's Local Bankruptcy Rules regarding service of proposed orders or judgments, whether or not the proposed order or judgment is electronically lodged via the Court's Electronic Lodged Upload (LOU) program.

B) Complaints Served Upon United States Trustee as a Defendant

Persons and entities must comply with FRBP 7004(b)(10) when the U.S. Trustee is named in an adversary proceeding as a party within the meaning of Part VII of the FRBP, whether or not the U.S. Trustee is a trustee in the case. This requirement is consistent with the Court's CM/ECF Administrative Procedures, paragraph VII.A.

C) Other Documents Specified in the Court's CM/ECF Administrative Procedures or Local Bankruptcy Rules (LBR) relevant to Electronic Notice & Service.

Persons and entities must comply with the Court's other LBR and CM/ECF Administrative Procedures that require non-electronic notice and/or service of specified documents.

D) Special Situations

Persons and entities filing the following documents must serve the U.S. Trustee by U.S. mail, overnight mail, Federal Express, or courier on or before the date that the document is filed. The proof of service must indicate that the U.S. Trustee was served via one of the foregoing forms of service for:

1) Documents exceeding 50 pages in length. When determining page length, all pages, including but not limited to exhibits, declarations and proof of service, are to be counted.

2) All Requests to Hear Matters on Emergency Basis or Shortened Notice, or for Relief Without Hearing. These documents include papers:

a) making the request;

b) responding to the request; and

c) relating to chapter 11 first day motions.

3) Any Document Filed within 10 Days of a Hearing. This includes documents:

a) filed timely or untimely;

b) related to hearings set on regular notice; and

c) related to hearings set on shortened notice or emergency basis.

4) Individual Capacity Matters (e.g., complaints, motions or other filings filed against the United States Trustee and/or any of the United States Trustee's staff in their capacity as individuals). The service of any such filing must be made in compliance with either Rule 4 of the Federal Rules of Civil Procedure and with any and all other applicable rules or civil, bankruptcy and/or appellate procedure.

GENERAL ORDER 09-01 ORDER VACATING GENERAL ORDERS THAT ARE OBSOLETE, SUPERSEDED, OR INCORPORATED INTO THE LOCAL BANKRUPTCY RULES

IT IS HEREBY ORDERED that the following general orders are vacated effective January 5,2009, for the reasons stated below:

05/26/93	93-01 Automatic Dismissal of Cases For Failure of Debtor(s) to Appear at Scheduled 341(a) Meetings	Incorporated into Local Bankruptcy Rules as LBR 10 17-2(b)
08/05/97	97-04 Chapter 7 Joint Petition Income Tax Returns	Superseded by LBR 1015-l(a)
4/17/02	02-02 Chapter 11 Procedures	Incorporated into Local Bankruptcy Rules as LBR 2081-1, et al.
09/26/02	02-03 Suspension of Provisions Relating to 6 Month Rule in Local Bankruptcy Rule 3015-1	Superseded by amendment to LBR3015-l(m), (m)(2) and 3015-l(r)(2)(A) effective July 2007

12/13/05	05-03 Depositing Rent With Court Pursuant to 11 U.S.C. 362(1)	Incorporated into Local Bankruptcy Rules as LBR 4001—1(f)
03/07/06	06-01 Amendment of Local Bankruptcy Rule 301 5-1(u)(l) and Guidelines to Reflect Changes in the Maximum Fee Allowable Under the RARA and the Guidelines	Superseded by Amended General Order 06-01
11/07/06	06-02 Authorization for Chapter 13 Trustees to Disburse Adequate Protection Payments and Lease Payments on Personal Property Prior to Confirmation	Superseded by amendment to LBR 3015-1(k)(2), effective July 2007
06/05/07	07-01 Chapter 15 Procedures	Incorporated into Local Bankruptcy Rules as LBR 2085-1 and;

IT IS FURTHER ORDERED that Interim Rule 1007-1 is adopted effective December 19, 2008; and

IT IS FURTHER ORDERED that General Order 05-02, Adoption of Interim Bankruptcy Rules dated October 3, 2005, is vacated, effective December 1, 2008. Notwithstanding the foregoing, the court will retain Interim Rule 5012 until it is replaced by a permanent national rule.

DATED: January 12, 2009

COURT MANUAL

(Rev. 1/04/10)

Section One General Court Information

LOCATIONS

OFFICE OF THE CLERK
Edward R. Roybal Federal Building and United States Courthouse
255 East Temple Street
Los Angeles, CA 90012

LOS ANGELES DIVISION

Edward R. Roybal Federal Building and United States Courthouse
255 E. Temple Street, Suite 940
Los Angeles, CA 90012

RIVERSIDE DIVISION

3420 Twelfth Street
Riverside, CA 92501

SANTA ANA DIVISION

Ronald Reagan Federal Building and United States Courthouse
411 West Fourth Street
Santa Ana, CA 92701

NORTHERN DIVISION

1415 State Street
Santa Barbara, CA 93101

SAN FERNANDO VALLEY DIVISION

21041 Burbank Boulevard
Woodland Hills, CA 91367-6603

WEB SITE

<*www.cacb.uscourts.gov*>

CM/ECF Support Center

(213) 894-2365
Monday through Friday

TELEPHONE DIRECTORY

LOS ANGELES DIVISION

General Information (213) 894-3118
Emergency Filings (213) 894-4981

RIVERSIDE DIVISION

General Information (951) 774-1000
Emergency Filings (951) 774-1102

SANTA ANA DIVISION

General Information (714) 338-5300
Emergency Filings (714) 338-5330

NORTHERN DIVISION

General Information (805) 884-4800
Emergency Filings (805) 884-4878

SAN FERNANDO VALLEY DIVISION

General Information (818) 587-2900
Emergency Filings (818) 587-2865

AUTOMATED TELEPHONE SYSTEM FOR CASE INFORMATION

For free automated bankruptcy case information for any division of the Central District of California Bankruptcy Court, please call the Voice Case

Information System (VCIS) at (213) 894-4111 or the toll free number at (866) 522-6053. VCIS enables direct access to the court's case management system from a touch-tone telephone, and is available 24 hours a day, 7 days a week.

FEE ACCEPTANCE POLICY

The Bankruptcy Court will accept cash, U.S. Postal Service money orders, cashier's checks from an acceptable financial institution, attorney or law firm checks (payable to the U. S. Bankruptcy Court) and American Express, Diner's Club, Discover, MasterCard, and VISA for payment of fees. Credit card transactions must be made in person by the cardholder; however, this does not apply to electronically filed documents. The court does not accept personal checks or credit cards from debtors to pay fees. All attorney/law firm checks must include a current pre-printed name, street address, telephone number and California attorney bar number.

ABBREVIATED FEE SCHEDULE (EFFECTIVE 1/1/07)

New Petition:	Chapter 7 $ 299.00
	Chapter 9 $1,039.00
	Chapter 11 (not a Railroad) $1,039.00
	Chapter 11 (Railroad) $1,039.00
	Chapter 12 (Family Farmer) $ 239.00
	Chapter 13 $ 274.00
	Chapter 15 (replaces Ancillary (Sec.304)) $1,039.00
Case Reopening:*	Chapter 7 $ 260.00
	Chapter 11 $1,000.00
	Chapter 12 $ 200.00
	Chapter 13 $ 235.00
Case Conversions:	Chapter 7 to 13 No Fee
	Chapter 7 to 11 $ 755.00
	Chapter 13 to 11 $ 765.00
	Chapter 13 to 7 $ 25.00

Amendments: Schedules "D," "E," or "F" $ 26.00

Master Mailing List $ 26.00

---

* The court must collect these fees unless the reopening is to correct an administrative error or for actions related to the debtor's discharge. (See Reopening a Bankruptcy Case, section 2-8(b)).

Motions:	Motion to Terminate, Annul, Modify, or Condition the Automatic Stay $ 150.00
	Motion to Compel Abandonment of Property $ 150.00
	Motion to Withdraw Reference $ 150.00
	Adversary Complaint $ 250.00
Other:	Abstract of Judgment $ 9.00
	Appeal* $ 255.00
	Certification $ 9.00
	Complaint $ 250.00
	Cross-Appeal* $ 255.00
	Exemplification $ 18.00
	Filing or Indexing of Miscellaneous Paper $ 39.00
	Issuance of Out of District Subpoena $ 39.00
	Photocopies made by Court Personnel (per page) $ 0.50
	Registration of Judgment from Another District $ 39.00
	Reproduction of Audio Recording (regardless of the medium) $ 26.00
	Retrieval of a Record from the NARA $ 45.00
	Returned Check Charge $ 45.00
	Search of Court Records (per name/item searched) $ 26.00

*If a trustee or debtor in possession is the appellant, the fee should be payable only from the estate and to the extent that any estate is realized. This exception applies to the $250.00 appellate filing fee required by the fee schedule and not to the $5.00 notice of appeal fee authorized under 28 U.S.C. § 1930(c).

1-2. Federal Holidays

The United States Bankruptcy Court is closed on the following holidays:

(a) New Year's Day

(b) Dr. Martin Luther King Jr. Day

(c) President's Day

(d) Memorial Day

(e) Independence Day

(f) Labor Day

(g) Columbus Day

(h) Veteran's Day

(i) Thanksgiving Day

(j) Christmas Day

1-3. Legal Publications

The following list of publications may be helpful for reference (most are available at law libraries or on the Internet. See Appendix E for law library locations):

(a) Bankruptcy Code

(b) Federal Rules of Bankruptcy Procedure (FRBP)

(c) Federal Rules of Civil Procedure (F.R.Civ.P.)

(d) Local Bankruptcy Rules

(e) Federal Rules of Evidence

(f) California Commercial Code

1-4. Local Bankruptcy Rules and Cross Reference Table

(a) The Court's Local Bankruptcy Rules. The Local Bankruptcy Rules are promulgated under the authority of F.R.Civ.P. 83 and FRBP 9029. Suggestions for improving the Local Bankruptcy Rules may be directed to the Executive Officer/Clerk of Court.

(b) Obtaining the Local Bankruptcy Rules. The Local Bankruptcy Rules, which include the Local Bankruptcy Rules forms, may be downloaded free of charge from the court's web site, < www.cacb.uscourts.gov>, or purchased from the Clerk's Office in the Los Angeles, Riverside, Santa Ana, San Fernando Valley and Northern divisions.

Cross-Reference Index:

Local Bankruptcy Rule References to the Court Manual

Rule Number	Title	Subsection Title	Court Manual Section
LBR 1002-1	Petition - General	(c) Number of Copies	2-1(a);
		(d)(1) Incomplete Petitions	3-5(b);
		(e) Redaction of Personal Identifiers	2-8; 3-6
LBR 1007-1	Lists, Schedules, and Statements	(a) Master Mailing List	2-3
LBR 1071-1	Divisions - Place of Filing	(a)(2) Filing of Petition	2-1(a)(5)
LBR 2002-2	Notice to and Service Upon the United States or Federal Agencies	(a)(3) United States Trustee; Exceptions to Electronic Notice and Service	3-8(e); 4-2(b); Appendix C;

Rule Number	Title	Subsection Title	Court Manual Section
		(a)(5) Place of Service for Non-electronic Notice or Service	Appendix D
		(c) Internal Revenue Service; General Notice Matters and Adversary Proceedings and Contested Matters	
LBR 3007-1	Objections to Claims	(a)(5) More than 20 Objections	2-7
LBR 3015-1	Procedures Regarding Chapter 13 Cases	(b)(1) Filing and Service of Petitions, and Other Case Commencement Documents	2-1(a) 2-1(f)
LBR 4001-1	Automatic Stay	(b)(2)(B) Form; Orders for Relief From the Automatic Stay as Settled by Stipulation	4-2
LBR 5005-2	Filing Papers - Number of Copies	(a) Number of Copies	2-1(a);
		(d) Judge's Copy	2-5(a); 3-5(b); Appendix F
LBR 5005-4	Electronic Filing	(a) Mandatory Electronic Filing	3-1(b); 3-11
		(c) Exceptions to Mandatory Electronic Filing Requirement	
LBR 5010-1	Reopening a Bankruptcy Case	(a) Motion (d) Fee	2-8(b)
LBR 5075-1	Motions for Administrative Orders Pursuant to 28 U.S.C. § 156(c)	(b) Procedure	2-8(c)
LBR 7054-1	Taxation of Costs and Award of Attorneys' Fees	(d) Items Taxable as Costs	2-8(e)
LBR 9004-1	Form of Papers Filed or Lodged with Court	(a)(1) General	2-5
LBR 9013-1	Motion Practice and Contested Matters	(o)(3)(B) Motions and Matters Not Requiring a Hearing; No Response and Request for Hearing; Lodged Proposed Order	4-2
LBR 9021-1	Orders and Judgments	(a) General (b)(1) Preparation, Lodging and Signing of Orders	4-1; 4-2
LBR 9036-1	Notice and Service By Electronic Transmission	(a)(1) Service by Electronic Means	3-8
LBR 9075-1	Emergency Motions and Applications For Orders Shortening Time	(a)(2) Obtaining Hearing Date and Time	3-5(f)

1-5. Case and Adversary Numbers

(a) Format.

A bankruptcy case number consists of a one-digit divisional office code, a two-digit year of filing, a two-character case type, five additional digits, and a two-character judge designation. For example, 2:05-bk-12345-AA is a case filed in the Los Angeles Division in 2005, followed by the two character case type, the five-digit case number; and it is assigned to Judge Alan Ahart. (Example of an Adversary Case, 2:05-ap-12345-AA.)

Division	One-Digit Code
Los Angeles	2
Riverside	6
Santa Ana	8
Northern	9
San Fernando Valley	1

Judge	Code	Judge	Code
Alan M. Ahart	AA	Geraldine Mund	GM
Theodor C. Albert	TA	Richard M. Neiter	RN
Catherine E. Bauer	CB	Richard M. Neiter	RN
Sheri Bluebond	BB	Robin L. Riblet	RR
Samuel L. Bufford	SB Ernest M.	Robles	ER
Ellen Carroll	EC	Barry Russell	BR
Peter H. Carroll	PC	Erithe A. Smith	ES
Thomas B. Donovan	TD	Kathleen Thompson	KT
Meredith A. Jury	MJ	Maureen A. Tighe	MT
Victoria S. Kaufman	VK	Vincent P. Zurzolo	VZ
Robert Kwan	RK		

(b) Finding a Case Number.

There are several ways to find the bankruptcy case number.

(1) VCIS.

See section 5-6 for access to this 24-hour free automated system.

(2) Public Computers.

Located in each division, computers in the public areas are available at no charge to review Court records for a case number and other related information.

(3) General Information.

Call the General Information number listed in the Quick Guide to the

Court, section 1-1, for the division where the case was filed.

(4) PACER.

For a fee, registered PACER users can check court records for a case number and other related information. (See PACER, section 5-3.)

(5) Mail.

Send a letter to the division's Intake Section. (See Quick Guide to the Court, section 1-1 for the address of each division.) Include a $26.00 search fee for each name or item requested and the name of the parties in the case.

1-6. Determining the Assigned Trustee

The trustee is listed on the case docket. Trustee addresses and telephone numbers are listed in Appendix C.

1-7. Case Files

Case files are available for public viewing at each division. PACER and computers in public areas can also be used to view and print electronic images of most case file documents. (See Obtaining Copies of Court Records, section 1-12.)

1-8. Archived Files

(a) National Archives and Records Administration.

The court transfers older closed paper case files to the National Archives and Records Administration (NARA), Office of Regional Records Services, in Perris, California, for storage. Each division has its own schedule for sending case files and dockets to the NARA.

(b) Determining if a File is Stored at the NARA.

(1) Call the General Information number for the division in which the case was filed. (See Quick Guide to the Court, section 1-1.)

(2) Go to the Intake Section of the division in which the case was filed.

(3) There is a $26.00 search fee to obtain this information through the mail from the Clerk's Office.

(4) The Clerk's Office staff will provide you with file location information and the information needed to retrieve case documents from the NARA (e.g., accession and box numbers).

(c) Clerk's Office File Retrieval.

For a $45.00 fee, the Clerk's Office will retrieve the case file from the NARA for the requester. To have an Intake Clerk order the file for you, complete and submit to the Clerk's Office a Request for Court to Retrieve Material from the National Archives and Records Administration. (See Forms, section 6.) Payment must be made before the Clerk's Office will request a file from the NARA.

(d) Viewing Archived Files at the NARA.

Archived files may be reviewed at the NARA in Perris, California. To request an appointment to review an archived file:

(1) Contact the General Information telephone number listed for the division where the case was originally filed to obtain the accession, box and NARA location number. (See Quick Guide to the Court, section 1-1.)

(2) Call (951) 956-2000, Monday through Friday, 9:00 a.m. to 2:30 p.m., and provide the NARA representative with the city in which the court is located, case file name(s), case file number, accession, box and location number. The NARA representative will then schedule an appointment to review the archived file.

(e) Obtaining Copies from the NARA.

To obtain a copy of the case file by mail or fax directly from the NARA, complete a Request by Mail or Fax form.

(1) The NARA will assess a separate charge for photocopies. (See Forms, section 6, for fees and forms.)

(2) The NARA does not accept telephone requests and will not accept mail or facsimile requests without payment. If paying by credit card, requesters may fax requests to the NARA at (951) 956-2029.

(f) Directions to the NARA.

The address for the NARA is:

National Archives and Records Administration
Office of Regional Records Services—Pacific Region (Riverside County)
23123 Cajalco Road
Perris, CA 92570-7298

(1) From Los Angeles, Santa Barbara or San Fernando Valley.

Take U.S. Highway 101 south to State Highway 60 east to Interstate 215 south. Take the Cajalco Expressway exit westbound (toward

Ramona Expressway). Turn on Harvill Avenue. Turn right on Cajalco Road to end of street.

(2) From Riverside.

Take Interstate 215 south. Take the Cajalco Expressway exit westbound (toward Ramona Expressway). Turn left on Harvill Avenue. Turn right on Cajalco Road to end of street.

(3) From Santa Ana.

Take State Highway 91 east to Interstate 215 south. Take the Cajalco Expressway exit westbound (toward Ramona Expressway). Turn left on Harvill Avenue. Turn right on Cajalco Road to end of street.

1-9. Dockets and Claims Registers

(a) The Docket.

A docket contains a chronological summary of all court proceedings and filed documents in each bankruptcy case and adversary proceeding. A claims register (sometimes called a claims docket) is a summary of claims filed in a bankruptcy case.

(b) To View a Case Docket or Claims Register.

(1) Public Area Computers.

You can view dockets and claims registers at computers located in the public areas of each division. There is no fee for this service.

(2) PACER.

See PACER, section 5-3, to register for this Internet access to dockets, claims registers, case information, and images of many case file documents. There is a fee for this service.

(3) Intake Area Public Counter.

If the docket or claims register is not accessible from the public area computer or PACER, check with the Intake staff at the public counter for assistance.

(4) Obtaining Copies.

See Obtaining Copies of Court Records, section 1-12, for information about obtaining a copy of a docket or claims register by mail or fax.

(5) Cases Filed in 1991 or Later.

Dockets and claims registers for cases filed on or after the following dates are available electronically through PACER or public area computers in each division.

Division	PACER Docket and Claims Register Availability for Cases Filed
Los Angeles	1995 or later
Riverside	On or after June 3, 1991
Santa Ana	On or after June 3, 1991
Northern	On or after June 1, 1992
San Fernando Valley	July 1996 or later

1-10. Hearing Information

(a) Obtaining a Hearing Date.

To set a hearing date, first determine if the judge uses self-calendaring for the type of matter that is being scheduled. If self-calendaring does not apply, contact the Courtroom Deputy for the judge who is to hear the matter to obtain a hearing date, time, and location. (See Appendix A.)

(b) Self-Calendaring.

The self-calendaring system is designed to enable counsel and parties to schedule hearing dates for matters heard on regular notice without having to contact the Courtroom Deputy to obtain a hearing date. All bankruptcy judges in all divisions of the court use self-calendaring to some degree. Self-calendaring instructions, types of matters that may be self-calendared, and hearing dates for each judge are posted on the court's web site, < www.cacb.uscourts.gov> Information -> Self-Calendaring.

NOTE: Self-calendaring must be used for electronically filed Motions for Relief from Stay.

(c) Self-calendaring Information.

Self calendaring information can also be accessed at each division by using the following automated telephone systems.

Division	Telephone Number	Quick Access to Automated Telephone Self-Calendaring Information
Los Angeles	(213) 894-3118	Once connected, press 1, then #, then 2.
Riverside	(951) 774-1100	Once connected, choose the appropriate judge.

Santa Ana	(714) 338-5300	Once connected, press 3, then 4.
Northern	(805) 884-4800	Once connected, press 2, then 4.
San Fernando Valley	(818) 587-2900	Once connected, press 4.

(d) Viewing the Court Calendar.

(1) The court calendar and tentative rulings (if issued by the judge) are available to the public on PACER and at computers in the public areas of each courthouse. (See PACER, section 5-3.)

(2) Kiosks are available at the Los Angeles, Riverside, and San Fernando Valley divisions that display each judge's calendar and tentative rulings (when applicable).

(3) Printed calendars for the current hearing date are posted outside of the judge's courtroom.

(e) Making Special Hearing Arrangements.

(1) Telephonic and video conferencing may be available for parties who are not able to appear in the courtroom. Advance approval by the judge hearing the matter is required. (See Teleconferencing, section 5-4, and Videoconferencing, section 5-5.)

(2) For persons with partial hearing loss, courtrooms are equipped with special headphones that are connected to the courtroom sound system. Prior to the hearing, contact the Courtroom Deputy to determine the availability of the equipment. (See Appendix A.)

(3) Language or sign language interpreters may be provided by the court to assist parties in the courtroom. (See Language and Sign Language Interpreters, section 1-11.)

(f) Obtaining a Transcript or Audio Recording of a Hearing.

Upon conclusion of a hearing, the public may request a transcript or audio recording of the hearing for a fee. (See Audio Recordings of Court Proceedings Ordering Information, section 1-14, and Transcript Ordering Instructions, section 1-15.) (Order forms may be found in this manual under section 6, Forms.)

1-11. Language and Sign Language Interpreters

(a) Language Interpreters.

The United States government will pay for language interpreters in a court hearing only if the United States government initiates the hearing.

(b) Sign Language Interpreters.

(1) The United States will pay for sign language interpreters in a judicial proceeding whether or not the proceeding is initiated by the United States.

(2) To request approval for a sign language interpreter, at least one week in advance of the hearing, contact the Deputy-in-Charge at the division where the proceeding will be held. (See Appendix A.)

(c) Interpreters for § 341(a) Meeting of Creditors.

Because the § 341(a) Meeting of Creditors is not a judicial proceeding, requests for a sign language interpreter at these meetings must be made directly to the trustee assigned to the case. All requests should be made at least two weeks prior to the scheduled meeting. (See Appendix C.)

1-12. Obtaining Copies of Court Records

(a) Public Intake Counter.

The Intake Section at each division will provide copies of case file documents for a fee. Only the Intake Section can provide certified copies of case file documents. To request a copy, complete a Document Request Form and present it at the public counter.

(b) PACER.

See PACER, section 5-3, to register for Internet access to dockets, claims registers, case information, and images of many case file documents. There is a fee for this service.

(c) By Mail.

To request copies or certified documents by mail from the Clerk's Office, send a self-addressed, stamped envelope to the Intake/ Correspondence Section at the appropriate divisional office. Include the following information with the request:

(1) Case number;

(2) Document title;

(3) Document number (if available);

(4) Your name, address, and telephone number; and

(5) Applicable fees.

1-13. Obtaining Central District Bankruptcy Forms

(a) Court's Web Site.

Many court forms, including complete petition packages with instructions, are available at no charge from the court's web site at < www.cacb.uscourts.gov> Forms/Rules/General Orders section. Most forms are in fillable format and can be printed from any computer with Internet access and Adobe Portable Document Format (PDF) Reader software. (A link to the Adobe web site is also available on the court's web site.)

(b) Intake Section.

A number of forms are available at no charge in the Public Information and/or Intake Section at each division. See Forms, section 6, for a list of these forms.

1-14. Audio Recordings of Court Proceedings Ordering Information

(a) Digital Technology.

The Bankruptcy Court for the Central District of California has converted the method used to record court hearings from an analog tape system to digital technology. The court has selected the FTR Gold™ digital recording product, as it offers superior sound reproduction capability compared to the former tape process. (Forms are available at < www.cacb.uscourts.gov> Forms/Rules/General Orders ->Court Forms.)

(b) Audio Recordings.

Audio recordings of court proceedings requested for hearings held after an office converted to the new digital system will be provided on a compact disc (CD). Audio recordings of hearings held before implementation of the new system will continue to be provided in a cassette tape format. The cost of either one compact disc (CD) or one cassette tape is $26.00 each.

(c) Audio Requests.

Audio requests provided on compact discs may be ordered in one of three formats, FTR Gold, Windows Audio, or Audio CD (the most generic format).

(1) FTR Gold

This format must be played using FTR Player Plus™ which is

available at no charge on the FTR Gold™ web site at, < www.ftr-gold.com>. (Note the minimum system requirements as listed on the FTR Gold™ web site and the availability of separate downloads for various Windows products.) If audio is played using this software the user will be able to navigate through the recording by using the time references from the actual hearing. One day's hearings may be provided on one CD using this format.

(2) Windows Audio

This format will play using the standard Windows Media Player software installed on most personal computers. One day's hearings may be provided on one compact disc (CD) using this format.

(3) Audio CD

This generic format will play on most CD-R and CD-RW compatible players designed to play music and other audio programs. Select this option if the audio will be played in a vehicle or on a personal CD player. In addition, this is the only format which is compatible with Macintosh or Apple computers. However, this format is not able to contain as much audio as the other two options. Compact discs formatted in this generic format will hold a maximum of 70 minutes of recordings. For example, a 90-minute hearing provided in this format will be provided on two compact discs (CD) at a cost of $52.00.

(d) Offices in the Central District converted to digital recording in 2004.

Should you have questions regarding digital recording, please contact one of the Clerk's Office numbers listed.

Division	Contact Numbers
San Fernando Valley	(818) 587-2860
Riverside	(951) 774-1085
Santa Ana	(714) 338-5361
Northern	(805) 884-4873
Los Angeles Judges	(213) 894-3150

1-15. Transcript Ordering Instructions

(a) Transcript Requests.

A separate form must be completed for each hearing date requested. The court does not accept fax or telephonic requests. Forms are available at < www.cacb.uscourts.gov> Forms/Rules/General Orders ->Court Forms. Two types of transcript orders are:

(1) Ordinary Basis: 30 working days

(2) Expedited Basis: 7 working days

(b) Transcript Processing.

Once a request for a transcript has been received, the required deposit will be calculated; the ordering party will be notified as to this amount by telephone. After the deposit is received, the transcript order will be processed by a court clerk and forwarded to the transcription agency which will then mail the completed transcript directly to the ordering party. Transcripts may not be picked up at the court. Original transcripts will be sent to the ordering party within the number of working days designated above.

(c) Forms of Payment.

Transcription agencies accept cashier's checks, U.S. Postal Service money orders, and law firm checks all made payable to the transcription agency. Checks from attorneys must include a valid State of California Bar identification number. Personal checks are not accepted.

(d) Submission.

Requests for transcripts and payments should be submitted to:

DIVISION ADDRESS

Los Angeles United States Bankruptcy Court
255 E. Temple Street, Suite 940
Los Angeles, CA 90012

Attn: Transcript Orders (Appropriate Court Recorder's Name)

Northern United States Bankruptcy Court
1415 State Street
Santa Barbara, CA 93101

Attn: Transcript Orders (Appropriate Court Recorder's Name)

Riverside United States Bankruptcy Court
3420 Twelfth Street
Riverside, CA 92501

Attn: Transcript Orders (Appropriate Court Recorder's Name)

San Fernando Valley United States Bankruptcy Court
21041 Burbank Boulevard
Woodland Hills, CA 91367

Attn: Transcript Orders (Appropriate Court Recorder's Name)

Santa Ana United States Bankruptcy Court Ronald Reagan Federal Building & US Courthouse
411 West Fourth Street
Santa Ana, CA 92701

Attn: Transcript Orders (Appropriate Court Recorder's Name)

1-16. Mediation Program

(a) Coordination.

The court, in cooperation with local bar associations, coordinates a mediation program to enable parties in a case to settle their dispute without going to court. Through mediation, cases may be resolved more quickly, at a lower cost, and to the parties' mutual satisfaction, often without the stress and pressure of litigation. The program is governed by Second Amended General Order 95-01.

(b) Cases Eligible for Mediation Program.

Almost all controversies arising in an adversary proceeding, contested matter, or other dispute in a bankruptcy case are eligible for referral to the Mediation Program.

(c) How Cases are Assigned to the Mediation Program.

A judge assigns a case to mediation in one of three ways:

(1) At the request of the parties, by filling out a Request for Assignment to Mediation Program form and a related Proposed Order Assigning Matter to Mediation and Appointing Mediator and Alternate Mediator.

(2) By order of the judge during the course of a court hearing.

(3) By order of the judge outside the course of a court hearing.

(d) Who May be Appointed as a Mediator.

(1) Both attorneys and non-attorneys may serve on the Panel of Mediators. Individuals who want to serve on the Panel apply to the Administrator of the Mediation Program in response to a court-established deadline. After receiving Court approval, mediators are appointed to the panel for a three-year term. Mediators must meet certain qualifications before they are appointed and must complete 30 hours of mediation training (unless excused by the court due to a sufficient amount of previous mediation training and experience).

(2) Except in certain limited circumstances, mediators serve without pay (pro bono). If payment is requested, the mediator's compensation shall be on such terms as are satisfactory to the mediator and the parties and is subject to the prior approval of the judge if the estate is to be charged with the expense.

(e) How Cases Proceed in the Mediation Program.

(1) When the judge assigns a matter to the Mediation Program, a mediator and an alternate mediator are appointed. The parties are normally given the opportunity to select a mediator and an alternate mediator from a list (Panel of Mediators) provided by the court. If the parties cannot agree on a mediator, the judge will assign one. However, the judge may select and appoint a mediator and an alternate mediator without the parties' consent.

(2) After selection, the mediator will contact the parties and arrange a time and a place to meet for a mediation conference. The parties must prepare a Mediation Statement five court days prior to the meeting. This statement is confidential and is not filed with the court. No statements made in the Mediation Statement may be used for any purpose outside of the mediation conference. Mediation conferences are informal; the rules of procedure that apply in court are not used.

(3) At the conclusion of the mediation conference, the mediator files Mediator's Certificate Regarding Conclusion of Mediation Conference (Form 706) with the court advising the judge whether the matter settled. If the parties reach a settlement, a document, providing details of the settlement, is prepared and filed with the court. The court must approve all agreements. If the parties cannot reach an agreement, the judge will hear the case in court.

(f) How to Learn More about the Mediation Program.

Mediation Program materials are available at no charge from the court's web site, < www.cacb.uscourts.gov>Forms/Rules/General Orders -> Mediation Forms. They may also be purchased from the Intake Section at each division. (See Obtaining Central District Bankruptcy Forms, section 1-13, and section 6, Forms.) Materials available include:

Mediation Materials Available from the Court's Web Site

Bankruptcy Mediation Program Application

Bankruptcy Mediation Program Materials Addendum

Bankruptcy Mediation Program - Panel of Mediators - Biographical Information

Bankruptcy Mediation Program - Panel of Mediators - Contact Information

Bankruptcy Mediation Program - Panel of Mediators - Counties in Which Mediators are

Authorized to Serve

Bankruptcy Mediation Program - Panel of Mediators - Foreign Languages Spoken

Bankruptcy Mediation Program - Panel of Mediators - Non-Attorney Professions

Bankruptcy Mediation Program - Procedures Manual

Mediation Form Number	Description of Mediation Form
Form 701	Request for Assignment to Mediation Program; [Proposed] Order Thereon
Form 702	Order Assigning Matter to Mediation Program and Appointing Mediator and Alternate Mediator [No Hearing Required]
Form 703	Notice of Mediator's or Alternate Mediator's Unavailability to Serve in Mediation Matter
Form 704	Notice of Request and Request for Appointment of Successor Mediator and/or Alternate Successor Mediator to Mediation Program
Form 705	Notice of Non-Compliance with Second Amended General Order No. 95-01 Governing Mediation Program
Form 706	Mediator's Certificate Regarding Conclusion of Mediation Conference
Form 708	Initial Mediation Confidentiality Agreement [Confidential - Not to be Filed with the Court]
Form 709	Mediator's Report of Mediation Conference [Confidential - Not to be Filed with the Court]
n/a	Notice of Entry of Order Assigning Matter to Mediation Program and Appointing Mediator and Alternate Mediator and Certificate of Mailing

2. FILING REQUIREMENTS AND PROCEDURES

2-1. Case Commencement (Bankruptcy Petition) Documents

(a) General Requirements [LBR 1002-1].

The following requirements must be met in order to file a voluntary petition with the court, either electronically or non-electronically, with the exception of Chapter 9 and 15 (refer to section 2-1(c) regarding Chapter 9 and section 2-1(g) regarding Chapter 15). These are the minimum requirements for filing a Chapter 7, 11, 12 or 13 Bankruptcy Case. A complete list of papers required to complete the filing and their corresponding deadlines are detailed in sections 2-1(a) through 2-1(g).

(1) Incomplete Petitions.

A voluntary petition filed without the complete schedules, statements and other documents required by the FRBP must include at least the following:

(A) Petition (Official Form 1);

(B) List of Creditors Holding 20 Largest Unsecured Claims (Official Form 4)(chapter 11 cases only);

(C) Master Mailing List (List of Creditors) in format required by LBR 1007-1(a);

(D) Statement of Social Security Number(s) (Official Form 21) (required if the debtor is an individual); and

(2) Deadline to File Required Documents.

Unless extended by court order, the balance of the papers required by the FRBP must be filed within 15 days of the petition date, except the Statement of Intention in a Chapter 7 case, which must be filed not later than 30 days after the filing of the petition.

(3) Debtor's Address.

If a petition is filed under 11 U.S.C. §§ 301, 302, 303, or 1504, the debtor's actual street address must be disclosed in addition to any post office box address.

(4) Attorney Information:

(A) General.

A voluntary petition filed pursuant to 11 U.S.C. §§ 301 and 302 by an attorney on behalf of any party must contain the attorney's state bar identification number, telephone number, fax number, and e-mail address in the attorney name block.

(B) Signature of Counsel.

The name of the attorney signing a petition must be typed clearly below the signature line.

(5) Divisions - Place of Filing [LBR 1071-1].

(A) Filing of Petition.

Unless otherwise ordered by the court, a petition must be filed in the "applicable division. The applicable division is determined by the location of the debtor's residence, principal offices, officers, and books and records, or where the majority of the debtor's assets are located based on a book value determination as set forth on the debtor's most current balance sheet. (Refer to Appendix B for the applicable division.)

(B) Filing of Papers Other Than a Petition.

Papers other than a petition must be filed only in the divisional office of the clerk to which the relevant cases or proceeding has been assigned. However, the clerk may, by special waiver or upon order of the court, accept papers in any office of the clerk irrespective of the division.

(6) Petition Forms.

Complete petition packages with instructions are available at no charge from the court's website, < www.cacb.uscourts.gov> Forms/ Rules/General Orders> Petition Forms section.

(7) Number of Copies [LBR 5005-2].

(A) Documents Not Electronically Filed:

(i) Chapter 7, 12, and 13.

An original and 1 copy marked as "Judge's Copy."

(ii) Chapter 9 and 11.

An original and 2 copies, 1 copy marked as "Judge's Copy."

(iii) Chapter 15.

Refer to section 2-1(g).

(B) Documents Filed Electronically.

A paper copy of any document filed electronically must be immediately served on the judge in accordance with LBR 5005-2 and section 3-5(b) of this Manual.

(C) Assembly of papers. All papers must be assembled in complete sets. The first set must be the signed original.

(D) Conformed Copy of Documents Not Electronically Filed.

If you file a document in person at the intake window, please bring an extra set if you wish to take a conformed copy back with you. If you wish to have a conformed copy mailed to you, include a self-addressed stamped envelope with sufficient postage to cover the cost of mailing the conformed copy.

(b) Chapter 7 Case Commencement (Bankruptcy Petition) Documents.

(1) Documents Required to File a Voluntary Chapter 7 Case.

The following documents are required, in the order indicated below:

(A)* Statement of Social Security-Number(s) (or Other Individual Taxpayer-Identification Number (ITIN)) (required for individual debtors only, not corporations or partnerships) (If filing electronically, see section 3-6(b) of this Manual)

(B)* Voluntary Petition (first three pages)

(C)* Electronic Filing Declaration (only for electronically filed petitions)

(D) Exhibit "C" to Voluntary Petition (if Exhibit "C" "yes" box is checked on page two of the Voluntary Petition)

(E) Exhibit D - Individual Debtor's Statement of Compliance with Credit Counseling Requirement (counseling usually MUST be obtained BEFORE filing, even if certificate is filed later)

(F) Corporate Resolution Authorizing Filing of the Petition (if debtor is a corporation)

(G) Corporate ownership statement as specified by LBR 1007-4 (required for partnerships, corporations, or limited liability companies that are not a governmental unit)

(H) Statement of Related Cases [required by LBR 1015-2(b)(2)]

(I) Notice of Available Chapters [required for individuals whose debts are primarily consumer debts (11 U.S.C. § 342(b)]

(J) Summary of Schedules and Statistical Summary of Certain

Liabilities and Related Data (28 U.S.C. § 159) (Official Form B6)

(K) Schedules A through J (for corporations, A, B, and D through H only)

(L) Declaration Concerning Debtor's Schedules (Official Form B6 - Declaration)

(M) Statement of Financial Affairs (Official Form 7)

(N) Chapter 7 Individual Debtor's Statement of Intention (11 U.S.C. § 521(a)(2)(A)) [must be filed within 30 days from filing Petition (not required for corporations)]

(O) Statement Regarding Assistance of Non-Attorney with Respect to the Filing of Bankruptcy Case (for persons not represented by an attorney)

(P) Disclosure of Compensation of Bankruptcy Petition Preparer (for persons not represented by an attorney and where a bankruptcy petition preparer prepared the paperwork)

(Q) Declaration and Signature of Non-Attorney Bankruptcy Petition Preparer, if applicable (Official Form 19, page 1)

(R) Notice to Debtor by Non-Attorney "Bankruptcy Petition Preparer", if applicable (Official Form 19, page 2)

(S) Disclosure of Compensation of Attorney for Debtor (for petitions of persons who are represented by legal counsel or where an attorney has prepared the paperwork)

(T) Declaration Re: Limited Scope of Appearance Pursuant to LBR 2090-1(a) (if applicable)

(U) Copies of all payment advices (pay stubs) or other evidence of payment received by the debtor from any employer within 60 days before the filing of the petition. If the debtor(s) was self-employed or unemployed during the 60 days prior to the filing of the petition, the debtor(s) should certify this fact and use the optional form Debtor's Certification of Employment Income Pursuant to 11 U.S.C. § 521(a)(1)(B)(iv) to do so. This form can also be used to attach payment advices (pay stubs)

(V) Statement of Current Monthly Income and Means Test Calculation (Official Form B22A)

(W) Verification of Creditor Mailing List [LBR 1007-1(d)]

(X)* Master Mailing List (in format required by section 2-3 of this manual)

(2) To be Filed along with the Petition, but as Separate Documents:

(A) Certificate of Credit Counseling or a motion for determination by the court of any election made to Exhibit D to the petition

(B) Debt Repayment Plan, if one is prepared by credit counselor (required if the debtor is an individual)

(C) Computer Readable CD-ROM of Master Mailing List (required for petition with over 100 creditors) [LBR 1007-1(a)]

(3) Required Documents Must Be Filed.

Even if certain of the schedules or statements of Official Forms 6 and 7 do not apply to a debtor's particular situation, the schedules or statements must be filed with either the notation "None" marked thereon or the applicable box checked indicating that there is nothing to report for that particular schedule or statement.

*Required at the time of filing

(c) Chapter 9.

[Under Construction]

(d) Chapter 11 Case Commencement (Bankruptcy Petition) Documents.

(1) Documents Required to File a Voluntary Chapter 11 Case.

The following documents are required, either electronically or non-electronically, in the order indicated below:

(A)* Statement of Social Security-Number(s) (or Other Individual Taxpayer- Identification Number (ITIN)) (required for individual debtors only, not corporations or partnerships) (If filing electronically, see section 3-6(b) of this Manual)

(B)* Voluntary Petition (first three pages)

(C) Electronic Filing Declaration (electronically filed petitions only)

(D) Exhibit "A" to Petition (if debtor is a corporation)

(E) Exhibit "C" to Voluntary Petition (if Exhibit "C" "yes" box is checked on page two of the Voluntary Petition)

(F) Exhibit D - Individual Debtor's Statement of Compliance with Credit Counseling Requirement (counseling usually MUST be obtained BEFORE filing, even if certificate is filed later)

(G) Corporate Resolution Authorizing Filing of the Petition (if debtor is a corporation)

(H) Corporate ownership statement as specified in LBR 1007-4 [required for corporations that are not a governmental unit]

(I)* List of Creditors Holding 20 Largest Unsecured Claims

(J) List of Equity Security Holders (for corporations or partnerships), if not included on Master Mailing List. Must follow the same format as Master Mailing List

(K) Venue Disclosure Form for Corporations Filing Chapter 11 (Official Form VEN-C) (if debtor is a corporation) or Venue Disclosure Form for Partnerships Filing Chapter 11 (Official Form VEN-P) (if debtor is a partnership)

(L) Statement of Related Cases [required by LBR 1015-2(b)]

(M) Notice of Available Chapters [required for individuals whose debts are primarily consumer debts [11 U.S.C. § 342(b)]

(N) Summary of Schedules and Statistical Summary of Certain Liabilities and Related Data (28 U.S.C. § 159) (Official Form B6)

(O) Schedules A through J (for corporations, A, B, D through H only)

(P) Declaration Concerning Debtor's Schedules (included with schedules) (Official Form B6 - Declaration)

(Q) Statement of Financial Affairs (Official Form 7)

(R) Disclosure of Compensation of Attorney for Debtor (for petitions of persons who are represented by legal counsel or where an attorney has prepared the paperwork)

(S) Statement Regarding Assistance of Non-Attorney with Respect to the Filing of Bankruptcy Case (for persons not represented by counsel)

(T) Declaration and Signature of Non-Attorney Bankruptcy

Petition Preparer, if applicable (Official Form 19, page 1)

(U) Notice to Debtor by Non-Attorney "Bankruptcy Petition Preparer," if applicable (Official Form 19, page 2)

(V) Disclosure of Compensation of Bankruptcy Petition Preparer (for persons not represented by counsel and where a bankruptcy petition preparer prepared the paperwork)

(W) Copies of all payment advices (pay stubs) or other evidence of payment received by the debtor from any employer within 60 days before the filing of the petition. If the debtor(s) was self-employed or unemployed during the 60 days prior to the filing of the petition, the debtor(s) should certify this fact and use the optional form Debtor's Certification of Employment Income Pursuant to 11 U.S.C. § 521(a)(1)(B)(iv) to do so. This form can also be used to attach payment advices (pay stubs)

(X) Statement of Current Monthly Income (Official Form B22B) (required if the debtor is an individual)

(Y) Verification of Creditor Mailing List [LBR 1007-1(d)]

(Z) Master Mailing List (in format required by section 2-3 of this manual

(2) To be Filed along with the Petition, but as Separate Documents.

(A) Certificate of Credit Counseling or a motion for determination by the court of any election made to Exhibit D to the petition

(B) Debt Repayment Plan, if one is prepared by credit counselor (required if the debtor is an individual)

(C) Computer Readable CD-ROM of Master Mailing List (required for petition with over 100 creditors) [LBR 1007-1(a)]

(3) Required Documents must be Filed.

Even if certain of the schedules or statements of Official Forms 6 and 7 do not apply to a debtor's particular situation, the schedules or statements must be filed with either the notation "None" marked thereon or the applicable box checked indicating that there is nothing to report for that particular schedule or statement.

*Required at the time of filing

(e) Chapter 12 Case Commencement (Bankruptcy Petition) Documents.

(1) Documents Required to File a Voluntary Chapter 12 Case.

The following documents are required, either electronically or non-electronically, in the order indicated below:

(A)* Statement of Social Security-Number(s) (or Other Individual Taxpayer-Identification Number (ITIN)) (required for individual debtors only, not corporations or partnerships)

(B)* Voluntary Petition (first three pages)

(C) Electronic Filing Declaration (electronically filed petitions only)

(D) Exhibit "C" to Voluntary Petition (if Exhibit "C" "yes" box is checked on page two of the Voluntary Petition)

(E) Exhibit D - Individual Debtor's Statement of Compliance with Credit Counseling Requirement (counseling usually MUST be obtained BEFORE filing, even if certificate is filed later)

(F) Statement of Related Cases [required by LBR 1015-2(b)]

(G) Notice of Available Chapters [required for individuals whose debts are primarily consumer debts (11 U.S.C. § 342(b)]

(H) Summary of Schedules and Statistical Summary of Certain Liabilities and Related Data (28 U.S.C. § 159) (Official Form B6)

(I) Schedules A through J

(J) Declaration Concerning Debtor's Schedules

(K) Statement of Financial Affairs (Official Form 7)

(L) Disclosure of Compensation of Attorney for Debtor (for petitions of persons who are represented by legal counsel or where an attorney has prepared the paperwork)

(M) Statement Regarding Assistance of Non-Attorney with Respect to the Filing of Bankruptcy Case (for persons not represented by counsel)

(N) Disclosure of Compensation of Bankruptcy Petition Preparer (for persons not represented by counsel and where a bankruptcy petition preparer prepared the paperwork)

(O) Declaration and Signature of Non-Attorney Bankruptcy Petition Preparer, if applicable (Official Form 19, page 1)

(P) Notice to Debtor by Non-Attorney "Bankruptcy Petition Preparer", if applicable (Official Form 19, page 2)

(Q) Copies of all payment advices (pay stubs) or other evidence of payment received by the debtor from any employer within 60 days before the filing of the petition. If the debtor(s) was self-employed or unemployed during the 60 days prior to the filing of the petition, the debtor(s) should certify this fact and use the optional form Debtor's Certification of Employment Income Pursuant to 11 U.S.C. § 521(a)(1)(B)(iv) to do so. This form can also be used to attach payment advices (pay stubs)

(R) Verification of Creditor Mailing List [LBR 1007-1(d)]

(S)* Master Mailing List (in format required by LBR 1007-2)

(2) To be Filed along with the Petition, but as Separate Documents.

(A) Chapter 12 Plan (11 U.S.C. § 1221). Must be filed within 90 days from the petition date.

(B) Certificate of Credit Counseling or a motion for determination by the court of any election made to Exhibit D to the petition

(C) Debt Repayment Plan, if one is prepared by credit counselor (required if the debtor is an individual)

(D) Computer Readable CD-ROM of Master Mailing List (required for petition with over 100 creditors) [LBR 1007-1(d)]

(3) Required Documents must be Filed.

Even if certain of the schedules or statements of Official Forms 6 and 7 do not apply to a debtor's particular situation, the schedules or statements must be filed with either the notation "None" marked thereon or the applicable box checked indicating that there is nothing to report for that particular schedule or statement.

(f) Chapter 13 Case Commencement (Bankruptcy Petition) Documents.

(1) Documents Required to File a Voluntary Chapter 13 Case.

The following documents are required, either electronically or non-electronically, in the order indicated below:

(A)* Statement of Social Security-Number(s) (or Other Individual Taxpayer-Identification Number (ITIN)) (required for individual debtors only, not corporations or partnerships)

(B)* Voluntary Petition (first three pages)

(C) Electronic Filing Declaration (electronically filed petitions only)

(D) Exhibit "C" to Voluntary Petition (if Exhibit "C" "yes" box is checked on page two of the Voluntary Petition)

(E) Exhibit D - Individual Debtor's Statement of Compliance with Credit Counseling Requirement (counseling usually MUST be obtained BEFORE filing, even if certificate is filed later)

(F) Statement of Related Cases [required by LBR 1015-2(b)(2)]

(G) Notice of Available Chapters [required for individuals whose debts are primarily consumer debts (11 U.S.C. § 342(b)]

(H) Summary of Schedules and Statistical Summary of Certain Liabilities and Related Data (28 U.S.C. § 159) (Official Form B6)

(I) Schedules A through J

(J) Declaration Concerning Debtor's Schedules (Official Form B6 -Declaration)

(K) Statement of Financial Affairs (Official Form 7)

(L) Disclosure of Compensation of Attorney for Debtor (for petitions of persons who are represented by legal counsel or where an attorney has prepared the paperwork)

(M) Statement Regarding Assistance of Non-Attorney with Respect to the Filing of Bankruptcy Case (for persons not represented by counsel)

(N) Disclosure of Compensation of Bankruptcy Petition Preparer (for persons not represented by counsel and where a bankruptcy petition preparer prepared the paperwork)

(O) Declaration and Signature of Non-Attorney Bankruptcy

Petition Preparer, if applicable (Official Form 19, page 1)

(P) Notice to Debtor by Non-Attorney "Bankruptcy Petition Preparer," if applicable (Official Form 19, page 2)

(Q) Copies of all payment advices (pay stubs) or other evidence of payment received by the debtor from any employer within 60 days before the filing of the petition. If the debtor(s) was self-employed or unemployed during the 60 days prior to the filing of the petition, the debtor(s) should certify this fact and use the optional form Debtor's Certification of Employment Income Pursuant to 11 U.S.C. § 521(a)(1)(B)(iv) to do so. This form can also be used to attach payment advices (pay stubs)

(R) Statement of Current Monthly Income and Calculation of Commitment Period and Disposable Income (Official Form B22C)

(S) Verification of Creditor Mailing List [LBR 1007-1(d)]

(T)* Master Mailing List (in format required by section 2-3 of this manual)

(2) To be Filed along with the Petition, but as Separate Documents.

(A) Chapter 13 Plan (LBR Form F 3015-1.1)

(B) Addendum to Chapter 13 Plan Concerning Debtors Who are Repaying Debt Secured by a Mortgage on Real Property or a Lien on Personal Property the Debtor Occupies as the Debtor's Principal Residence (optional LBR Form F 3015-1.1A)

(C) Certificate of Credit Counseling or a motion for determination by the court of any election made to Exhibit D to the petition

(D) Debt Repayment Plan, if one is prepared by credit counselor (required if the debtor is an individual)

(E) Computer Readable CD-ROM of Master Mailing List (required for petition with over 100 creditors) [LBR 1007-1(d)]

(3) Required Documents must be Filed.

Even if certain of the schedules or statements of Official Forms 6 and 7 do not apply to a debtor's particular situation, the schedules or statements must be filed with either the notation "None" marked thereon or the applicable box checked indicating that there is nothing to report for that particular schedule or statement.

*Required at the time of filing.

(g) Chapter 15.

UNDER CONSTRUCTION

2-2. Incomplete Case Commencement Filings

(a) Deficient Pleadings.

Pleadings are considered deficient if the document:

(1) Does not comply with either the FRBP or the LBRs.

(2) Is submitted with insufficient funds or paid in a method not accepted by the court. (See Fee Acceptance Policy, section 2-4(b).)

(b) Emergency Filings.

(1) Emergency filings, before and after regular business hours, are handled by Clerk's Office staff on a case-by-case basis. Some examples of what the Clerk's Office considers to be legitimate requests for emergency filings include:

(A) Petitioner is involved in a pending sale or foreclosure;

(B) Unlawful detainer order;

(C) Wage garnishment;

(D) Expedited hearings on shortened notice (e.g., Ex Parte Motion); and

(E) Unusually large volume of documents (e.g., mega case pleadings).

(2) Approval for an emergency filing must be coordinated with the Intake Supervisor or other court official. For more information, call:

Division	Telephone Number
Los Angeles	(213) 894-8401
Riverside	(951) 774-1102
Santa Ana	(714) 338-5332
Northern	(805) 884-4875
San Fernando Valley	(818) 587-2860

2-3. Master Mailing List Format and Technical Instructions

[LBR 1007-1]

(a) A Master Mailing List must be Filed with the Petition. The master mailing list must include the name, mailing address, and zip code for each creditor listed on Schedules D, E, and F. Refer to Appendix D of this Manual for federal and state government unit addresses that must be included in the Master Mailing List. Guidelines for filing the master mailing list are set forth below.

(b) Filing a Printed Paper Petition at the Intake Section.

(1) If more than 100 creditors, please see Exhibit 3. If less than 100 creditors, the Master Mailing List for a printed paper petition must be formatted as follows.

(A) Typed on blank, unlined, standard white 8-1/2 × 11 inch bond paper using uppercase and lowercase letter quality characters no smaller than 10 point nor greater than 14 point in either Courier, Times New Roman, Helvetica, or Orator;

(B) Typed in a single column with no letters closer than 1-1/2 inches from any edge of the paper and left justified;

(C) Typed with no more than 8 name/address blocks per page. Each block must consist of no more than 4 lines total for each name/address with at least 2 blank lines in between;

(D) Include a FIRST PAGE reserved only for: Debtor, Joint Debtor, Attorney for Debtor(s), Office of the United States Trustee. (See Exhibit 1.) All subsequent pages contain the remaining creditors from Schedules D, E, and F of the petition;

(E) Each line must be no more than 35 characters in length including spaces.

The attention line, if any, must be included on the second line of the block. DO NOT INCLUDE ACCOUNT NUMBERS. The city, state (2-letter abbreviation in capital letters only, e.g., CA), and zip code must be on the last line. Nine-digit zip codes should be separated by a hyphen. (See Exhibit 2.);

(F) Contains NO PUNCTUATION, except for one comma between city and state (for example, Los Angeles, CA 90012);

(G) Provide page number on the back of each page;

(H) If a separate Equity Holders List is filed, it must comply with the above format requirements; and

(I) For petitions not electronically filed with more than 100 creditors, the printed Master Mailing List and, if applicable, the printed Equity Holders List must be submitted along with a computer-readable CD-ROM of all entities. Technical requirements for the CD-ROM are listed in Exhibit 3.

Exhibit 1 Example of First Page of Master Mailing List

Exhibit 2 Format for List of Creditors

Acme Auto Repair
1234 S Street
Los Angeles, CA 90005

Acme Hair Repair
Attn Herman
1234 S Ave
Los Angeles, CA 90005-0001

Internal Revenue Service
Address*
City, State Zip Code

Acme Talent Agency
421 N Copper Canyon Way
Burbank, CA 91505-0002

Loans By Acme
7485 Chromium Circle
Beverly Hills, CA 90210

Acme And Sons Insurance
Attn D Acme
13363 Hierro Street Suite 25
Van Nuys, CA 91401

Acme Bar and Grill
114 Aluminum Alley
Chatsworth, CA 91313

Exhibit 3 Technical Requirements for Compact Disc (CD-ROM) (100 or more creditors)

For cases with more than 100 creditors that are not electronically

* See Appendix D for Internal Revenue Service addresses required by LBR 2002-2(c).

filed, the printed creditor matrix must be submitted along with a non-returnable computer-compatible data storage media containing the names and addresses of all entities shown in Schedules D, E, and F of the petition. The media must meet the following requirements:

1. PC-compatible virus-free data storage media such as a CD-ROM.

2. Labeled with case name and number.

3. Text in ASCII-readable format. File name must be "Creditor.TXT."

4. No page breaks, miscellaneous characters, or other computer instructions are to be included in text.

5. Names and addresses of Debtor, Joint Debtor, Attorney for Debtor(s), and the Office of the United States Trustee are specifically to be excluded from CD-ROM contents but must still be submitted on the printed copy.

2-4. Filing Fees

(a) Fee Schedule.

For a list of current filing fees, refer to the Quick Guide to the Court in section 1-1.

(b) Fee Acceptance Policy.

The Bankruptcy Court will accept cash, U. S. Postal Service money orders, cashier's checks from an acceptable financial institution, attorney or law firm checks (payable to the U. S. Bankruptcy Court) and American Express, Diner's Club, Discover, MasterCard, and VISA for payment of fees. Credit card transactions must be made in person by the cardholder; however, this does not apply to electronically filed documents. The court does not accept personal checks or credit cards from debtors to pay fees. All attorney/law firm checks must include a current preprinted name, street address, telephone number, and California attorney bar number.

2-5. Subsequent Filings [LBRs 5005-2; 9004-1]

(a) Copies Required.

The following requirements are for papers filed with the court, either electronically or non-electronically:

(1) Documents Not Electronically Filed.

For all pleadings filed subsequent to a petition, file only the original. One copy should be marked as "Judge's Copy" and must comply with sections 2-5 and 3-5(b), and be served according to sections 3-5(b) and Appendix F. If you wish to have a conformed copy mailed to you, you must include an additional copy and a self-addressed stamped envelope with sufficient postage to cover the cost of mailing the conformed copy.

(2) Documents Filed Electronically.

For subsequent pleadings filed by electronic means refer to Judge's Copies, section 3-5(b).

(b) Form and Format of Papers.

(1) General.

Unless otherwise expressly provided by the LBRs or section 3-5 of this Manual, a paper filed or lodged with the court and any exhibit hereto must comply with the following form and format requirements:

(A) Legibility.

A paper submitted for filing must be typewritten, legibly printed if prepared by hand, computer generated, or prepared by a photocopying or other duplicating process that will produce clear and permanent copies equally legible to printing, in black or dark blue ink.

(B) Paper.

The original of a paper must be submitted on white, letter size (8 ½ × 11 inches), opaque, unglazed paper of medium weight not less than 20-pound weight capable of producing a good quality image when scanned using the court's equipment and software. Coated paper, glossy paper, oversized paper (larger than 8 ½ × 11 inches), lightweight paper (less than 20-pound weight), bond paper, card stock, and onion skin may cause paper jams when scanned and must not be used. The paper must be numbered on the left margin with not more than 28 lines per page. The lines on each page must be numbered consecutively.

(C) Typeface.

With the exception of bankruptcy forms, the typeface must not be smaller than 12 point. As an example, this is 12-point type. Required typefaces are Arial, Courier, Times New Roman, Helvetica, Geneva or Letter Gothic. Font sizes smaller than 12 point may not be legible after imaging and must not be used. Line 1 must begin at least 1 inch below the top edge of the paper. All pages of each paper (including exhibits) must be printed on 1 side of the paper only.

(D) Pagination.

All papers must be numbered consecutively at the bottom of each page, including any attached exhibits. A reference to an exhibit in a paper must include the consecutive page numbers of the exhibit.

(E) Originals, Copies, Telecopies, and E-mails.

The original of a paper filed in paper format must be labeled as the original and, except for exhibits, must consist entirely of the original pages, except that a telecopy or e-mail of all or part of a paper (or copy of such telecopy or e-mail) may be filed and served instead of the original of the paper, provided that the telecopy or e-mail meets the legibility requirement set forth in subsection (b)(1) of this rule. The original of any document that is filed, including the original signature of the attorney, party, or declarant, must be maintained by the filing party until the conclusion of the case, including any applicable appeal period, subject to being produced upon reasonable notice. All copies must be marked "COPY."

(F) Interlineation.

No interlineation is allowed on a paper unless the interlineations are noted by the clerk or the judge by marginal initials at the time of the filing.

(G) Assembly of Papers Not Electronically Filed.

Original papers and a Judge's copy must be assembled in compliance with the following guidelines:

(i) Original multi-page documents must not be hole

punched or bound by staples, prong fasteners or standard metal or plastic paper clips that puncture the paper. Original multi-page documents must be bound at the top left corner with binder clips or clamps. A paper presented for filing must be flat and unfolded to facilitate scanning.

(ii) As a general rule, the clerk's office will conform and return one copy of a document to the filing party. If more than one copy of the document is needed, the copies must be fastened together with a binder clip. The copies must not be attached to the original documents.

(iii) A Judge's copy of multi-page documents must be fastened with a single staple in the upper lefthand corner or otherwise bound.

(iv) Documents must not be "blue-backed" or otherwise bound. A transcript must be unbound and fastened with a binder clip prior to filing.

(H) Spacing.

Except as provided herein, the typing or printing on papers must be double-spaced, including citations. Footnotes may be single-spaced but the font must not be less than 12 point. Real property descriptions may be single-spaced. Quotations from cited cases or other authorities must be clearly indented not less than 5 spaces or more than 20 spaces and may be single-spaced if the quotation is 50 or more words.

(I) Exhibits and Other Attached Papers.

(i) Original Document.

Each declaration, exhibit, or other attachment to an original of a paper must be separated by a separator sheet printed on white, letter size (8½ × 11 inches), unglazed, opaque, paper of medium weight.

(ii) Judge's Copy.

Each declaration, exhibit or other attachment to a Judge's copy must be tabbed.

(c) Caption and Format of Title Page.

(1) Adversary Proceedings.

A complaint or other paper filed in an adversary proceeding must bear a "double caption" in substantially the following format:

In re ABC, Debtor. XYZ Co., Plaintiff, COMPLAINT TO DETERMINE NONDISCHARGEABILITY OF DEBT vs. ABC, Defendant. (Hearing date to be set by summons)	Case No. Chapter Adv. No.

(2) Small Business Cases.

A pleading or other paper filed in a case that has been designated a small business case under FRBP 1020 must bear a legend stating that the case is subject to FRBP 1020. The legend must appear to the right of the caption immediately below the case number in substantially the following format:

In re ABC, Debtor.	Case No. Chapter SMALL BUSINESS CASE UNDER FRBP 1020

(3) The First Page of a Paper to be Filed or Lodged Must Include:

(A) Attorney.

The name, state bar identification number, address, telephone number, fax number, and e-mail address, if any, of the attorney presenting the paper for filing must be displayed commencing with line 1 at the left margin. If the party is not represented by counsel, the name, address, telephone number, fax number, and e-mail address, if any, of the party presenting the paper for filing must be displayed commencing with line 1 at the left margin. The actual street address must be disclosed in addition to any post office box address. Immediately beneath, the party on whose behalf the paper is presented must be identified. This information must be single-spaced.

(B) Clerk's Space.

The space between lines 1 and 7 to the right of the center of the page must be left blank for use by the clerk.

(C) Title of Court.

The title of the court, including the division, must be centered on or below line 8.

(D) Names of Parties.

The names of the parties must be placed below the title of the court and to the left of center and single-spaced. If the parties are too numerous, the names may be continued on the second or successive pages in the same space. In all papers after the initial pleadings, only the names of the first-named party on each side need appear; and, if lengthy, those names may be abbreviated.

(E) Bankruptcy Case Number.

The bankruptcy case number must be placed to the right of the center of the page immediately opposite the names of the parties on the first page. Case numbers must be consistent with the following example: 1:05-bk-12345-MT, with the first number being the location of the division in which the case was filed (e.g., San Fernando Valley: 1, Los Angeles: 2, Riverside: 6, Santa Ana: 8, Santa Barbara: 9), the two numbers after the semicolon representing the last two digits of the year in which the case was filed, a two-character case type (bk for bankruptcy case, ap for adversary case) and the third set of numbers following the first dash representing the 5-digit case number followed by the initials of the bankruptcy judge assigned to the case.

(F) Chapter Number.

The chapter number of the case must appear immediately below the case number.

(G) Adversary Number.

The adversary number, if any, must appear immediately below the case number and chapter number (e.g. 2:05-ap-12345-AA).

(H) Title.

On the first page immediately below the adversary or chapter number or the caption, there must be a concise title of the document (e.g., Notice of Motion for Summary Judgment, Complaint To Determine Dischargeability of Debt). When a document contains multiple pleadings (for example, an answer to a complaint and a counterclaim or cross claim), all pleadings contained in the document must be listed in the caption.Where possible, the proponent's name should be included in the title of the document (e.g., Creditor ABC's Motion to Dismiss).

(I) Hearing.

The time, date, and place of the hearing on the matter to which the paper is addressed must appear immediately below the title or, if appropriate, a statement that no hearing is required or that a hearing will be scheduled by the court. All information required in subsections (c)(5) through (9) of this rule must always appear on the first page of the paper.

(d) Exhibits to Papers.

(1) Exhibits Attached to Papers.

Unless the physical nature of the exhibit makes it impracticable, an exhibit must be securely bound to the paper to which it relates with a binder clip or clamp.

(2) Numbering.

An exhibit must be identified at the bottom of each page consecutively to the principal paper. For example, if the pleading contains 5 pages and 3 exhibits of 5 pages each are attached, the pages would be numbered 1 through 20 consecutively. The exhibit identification must be placed immediately above or below the page number on each page of the exhibit.

(3) Identifying Exhibits.

(A) Original to be Filed.

Exhibits must be placed in sequential order and separated by separator sheets marked with the exhibit letter or number. Whenever feasible, exhibits of plaintiffs or movants must be marked with numbers, and exhibits of defendants or respondents must be marked with letters.

(B) Judge's Copy.

Exhibits must be placed in sequential order and tabbed with the exhibit letter or number. Whenever feasible, exhibits of plaintiffs or movants must be marked with numbers, and exhibits of defendants or respondents must be marked with letters.

(4) Size of Paper.

An exhibit must be on standard letter size (8½ × 11 inches) opaque, unglazed paper. The filing party is responsible for reducing larger size documents to the standard letter size and for copying smaller size documents on standard letter size paper. Two-sided exhibits must be photocopied and filed with text printed only on one side of each page.

2-6. Proofs of Claim

(a) Filing a Proof of Claim.

In the event that a distribution of assets in a bankruptcy case is likely, the court will mail to all creditors a Proof of Claim form with the § 341(a) Meeting of Creditors notice.

(1) Proof of Claim Forms are also Available:

(A) At no cost, in all divisions of the court;

(B) In fillable format on the court's web site at < www.cacb.uscourts.gov>Forms/Rules/General Orders ->Court Forms;

(C) By mail.

Send your request in writing to the Intake Section in the appropriate divisional office. The court will mail you a

Proof of Claim form; and

(D) By phone.

Contact the Intake Section in the appropriate divisional office. The court will mail you a Proof of Claim form.

(2) Instructions/Definitions.

Instructions for completing a Proof of Claim and related definitions are located on the back of the Proof of Claim form. To receive a "filed" stamped copy of the Proof of Claim, provide a copy of the claim at the time of filing along with a self-addressed, stamped envelope.

(3) Where to File.

The Proof of Claim should be filed at the division where the bankruptcy case is pending. A completed Proof of Claim can be electronically filed through CM/ECF by registered users, mailed to the division (see Quick Guide to the Court, section 1-1, or Appendix A for division addresses), or filed at the Intake window during Court hours.

(4) Fee.

There is no fee to file a Proof of Claim form.

2-7. Multiple Objections to Claims Calendar [LBR 3007-1]

(a) General Procedure for Filing More than 20 Objections to Claims.

(1) Pursuant to LBR 3007-1(a)(5), if more than 20 objections to claims are noticed for hearing on a single calendar, the objector must submit a Multiple Objections to Claim Calendar.

(2) A Portable Document Format (.pdf) version of the calendar listing (see Exhibit 4 for a list of the requirements) including a cover page (see Exhibit 5) must be electronically filed via the CM/ECF system. The calendar listing (see Exhibit 6) should be organized by type of objection and should specify the following information for each claim in order of claim number or alphabetical order:

(A) The claims docket number;

(B) The claimant's name;

(C) The amount of the claim;

(D) The basis for the objection; and

(E) The portion of the claim subject to the objection (if different from the total amount of the claim).

(b) Exception to General Procedure.

Many judges have their own procedure. Please consult the judge's section of the court's website at < www.cacb.uscourts-.gov> Information for specific requirements (if any) and/or call the Courtroom Deputy for the particular judge.

Telephone contacts are located in Appendix A of the court manual.

Exhibit 4 Calendar Format

The calendar must be submitted in the following format:

1. Typed on a 8-1/2" × 11" page using uppercase and lowercase letter quality characters using Courier 10-point font.

2. The document must contain a header on the first page only as follows:

Claim
Number
Claimant Name Claim Amount Basis for
Objection
(If applicable)

Portion of Claim Subject to Objection*

3. The claimant information must be typed with no more than 10 claims blocks per page. In cases where the claimant name is longer than the allowed 20 characters, the name should be continued on the next line.

4. Each line of the text must contain no more than 75 characters maximum and should not extend within one-half inch of any edge of the page.

5. Each block must consist of no more than 4 lines with at least 1 blank line between each.

6. The document must contain the original amount of the claim and, if different from the total amount of the claim, the portion of the claim subject to the objection.

7. The document must have a cover page containing the Case Name, Case Number, Title of Pleading, Hearing Date, Hearing Time, and Judge. Please see examples in Exhibits 5 and 6.

*If different from the total amount of the claim.

Exhibit 5 Sample Cover Page for Multiple Objections to Claim

Advent Development Corp. LA 98-10000-BB
Hrg RE: Trustee's Motion to Disallow Claim of Andrews Adjustment Service for
Insufficient Documentation
Hearing Date: September 30, 2002
Hearing Time: 2:00 PM
Judge: Hon. Sheri Bluebond

Exhibit 6 Sample Calendar Listing For Multiple Objections to Claims

Claim

Number

Claimant

Name Claim Amount

Basis of Objection

(If applicable)

Portion of Claim

Subject to Objection

2-8. Miscellaneous

(a) Privacy Policy [LBR 1002-1(e)].

The Judicial Conference of the United States approved amendments to the FRBP, which implement the judiciary's privacy policy, effective December 1, 2003. It is the responsibility of the filing party, not the Clerk's Office, to ensure compliance with this policy.

(1) Filers should redact "personal identifiers" from documents filed with the court, including attachments. "Personal identifiers" are considered to be the following:

(A) Social Security Numbers.

If an individual's Social Security number (SSN), or Individual Tax Payer Identification Numbers (ITIN) must be included in the document, only the last four digits of that number should be used.

However, the debtor is required to submit a Statement of Social Security Number(s) containing their full nine-digit SSN or ITIN at the time his/her petition is filed. This form is not part of the public case file. On all other forms and documents, only the last four digits of the SSN or ITIN should be used;

(B) Financial Account Numbers.

If financial account numbers are relevant, only the last four digits of these numbers should be used;

(C) Dates of Birth.

If an individual's date of birth must be included in the document, only the year should be used; and

(D) Names of Minor Children.

If the name of a minor child must be mentioned, only the initials of that child should be used.

(2) The privacy policy applies to all documents filed with the court, whether submitted by electronic means or submitted non-electronically. The policy is not retroactive.

(3) A full copy of the policy can be found on the Judiciary Privacy Policy Page at < www.privacy.uscourts.gov> under "Judiciary Privacy Policy."

(b) Reopening a Bankruptcy Case [LBR 5010-1].

The following table outlines the court's policy for reopening a bankruptcy case. This table may be used to determine if a case must be reopened and whether or not a fee is required. If it is required that a case be reopened, a motion and order must be submitted to the court. The order reopening the case must be entered before the subsequent filing can be filed.

(c) Mega Case Procedures Checklist [LBR 5075-1].

(1) The Mega Case Procedures Checklist was developed by the Clerk's Office to streamline the approval process for administrative orders in large bankruptcy cases. LBR 5075-1 requires that all motions for administrative orders approving employment of persons or entities to perform certain duties of the Clerk's Office include the Mega Case Procedures Checklist form (along with completed LBR form F 5075-1.1, Declaration to be Filed with Motion Establishing Administrative Procedures RE 28 U.S.C. § 156(c)). These duties include:

(A) Processing proofs of claim and maintaining the claims register;

(B) Serving notices;

(C) Scanning documents; and

(D) Providing photocopies of documents filed in the case.

(2) A judge's copy of the motion, including the declaration and Mega Case Procedures Checklist, is to be provided to the Clerk's Office at the time the motion is filed. Movant's counsel must consult with the Clerk's Office in order to complete the checklist to the satisfaction of the Clerk's Office. The most recent version of the Mega Case Procedures Checklist is available on the court's web site, < www.cacb.uscourts.gov>, Forms/Rules/General Orders -> Court Forms. (Also see section 6, Forms.)

(d) Bill of Costs [LBR 7054-1].

A bill of costs filed electronically or non-electronically must comply with LBR 7054-1. The prevailing party who is awarded costs must file and serve a bill of costs not later than 30 days after entry of judgment. Each item claimed must be set forth separately in the bill of costs.

(e) Items Taxable as Costs.

Pursuant to LBR 7054-1, the following items are taxable as costs:

(1) Filing Fees. The clerk's filing fees;

(2) Fees for Service of Process.

Fees for service of process (whether served by the United States Marshal or in any other manner authorized by FRBP 7004);

(3) United States Marshal's Fees.

Fees of the United States Marshal collected and taxed as costs pursuant to 28 U.S.C. § 1921;

(4) Clerk's Fees.

Fees for certification of documents necessary for preparation for a hearing or trial; and

(5) Transcripts and Digital Recordings.

The cost of the original and one copy of all or any part of a trial transcript, daily transcript, or a transcript of matters occurring before or after trial, if requested by the court or prepared pursuant to stipulation. The cost of a digital recording, if requested by the court or obtained pursuant to stipulation.

(6) Depositions.

Costs incurred in connection with taking depositions, including:

(A) The cost of the original and one copy of each deposition taken for any purpose in connection with the case;

(B) The reasonable fees of the deposition reporter, the notary, and any other person required to report, record, or transcribe the deposition;

(C) Reasonable witness fees paid to a deponent, including fees actually paid to an expert witness deponent pursuant to F.R.Civ.P. 26(b)(4)(c);

(D) Reasonable fees paid to an interpreter when necessary to the taking of the deposition; and

(E) The cost of reproducing exhibits used at the deposition and made a part of the deposition transcript.

(7) Witness Fees.

Fees paid to witnesses, including:

(A) Per diem, mileage, subsistence, and attendance fees as provided in 28 U.S.C. § 1821 paid to witnesses subpoenaed or actually attending the proceeding;

(B) Witness fees for a party if required to attend by opposing party; and

(C) Witness fees for officers and employees of a corporation if they are not parties in their individual capacities.

(8) Interpreter's and Translator's Fees.

Fees paid to interpreters and translators, including:

(A) The salaries, fees, expenses and costs of an interpreter as provided by 28 U.S.C. §§ 1827 and 1828; and

(B) Fees for translation of documents received in evidence, used as part of the proceeding, or when otherwise reasonably necessary to the preparation of the case.

(9) Docket Fees.

Docket fees as provided by 28 U.S.C. § 1923.

(10) Certification, Exemplification, and Reproduction of Documents.

Document preparation costs, including:

(A) The cost of copies of an exhibit attached to a document necessarily filed and served;

(B) The cost of copies of a document admitted into evidence when the original is not available or the copy is substituted for the original at the request of an opposing party;

(C) Fees for an official certification of proof respecting the non-existence of a document or record;

(D) Patent Office charges for the patent file wrappers and prior art patents necessary to the prosecution or defense of a proceeding involving a patent;

(E) Notary fees incurred in notarizing a document when the cost of the document is taxable; and

(F) Fees for necessary certification or exemplification of any document.

(11) Premium on Undertakings and Bonds.

Premiums paid on undertakings, bonds, security stipulations, or substitutes therefor where required by law or court order, or where necessary to enable a party to secure a right granted in the proceeding.

(12) Other Costs.

Upon order of the court, additional items, including the following, may be taxed as costs:

(A) Summaries, computations, polls, surveys, statistical comparisons, maps, charts, diagrams, and other visual aids reasonably necessary to assist the court or jury in understanding the issues at the trial;

(B) Photographs, if admitted in evidence or attached to documents necessarily filed and served upon the opposing party; and

(C) The cost of models if ordered by the court in advance of or during trial.

(13) Removed Cases.

Costs incurred in state court prior to removal that are recoverable under state statutes are recoverable by the prevailing party in this court.

(14) Costs on Appeal.

(A) The taxation of costs on a bankruptcy appeal to the bankruptcy appellate panel are governed by FRBP 8014 and Bankruptcy Appellate Panel Rule 8014-1.

(B) The taxation of costs on a bankruptcy appeal to the district court are governed by FRBP 8014 and Local Civil Rules 54-5 and 54-6 of the district court.

3. CM/ECF PROCEDURES

(Case Management/Electronic Case Filing)

3-1. CM/ECF Overview [LBR 5005-4]

(a) What is CM/ECF?

Case Management/Electronic Case Filing (CM/ECF) is a case management system that allows attorneys to electronically file petitions and other documents via the internet. Case information, dockets and documents filed in CM/ECF may be accessed through the internet with a PACER account.

(b) Mandatory Electronic Filing.

Usage of the court's CM/ECF system is mandatory as of April 1, 2007, for all documents, except for those documents listed in section 3-11. The mandatory electronic filing policy provisions are set forth in LBR 5005-4, in Paragraph 19 of Second Amended General Order 02-01 and in General Order 06-03, dated November 7, 2006.

(c) Advantages of Using CM/ECF.

(1) CM/ECF is available 24 hours a day, 7 days a week to registered users and can be accessed from virtually any computer with an Internet connection.

(2) CM/ECF saves time and money as registered users no longer need to travel to the court or send a courier to file the types of documents accepted electronically.

(3) The submission process is fast, and the electronic forms are easy to complete.

(4) The Clerk's Office has taken substantial measures to secure all activity on the CM/ECF site.

(5) Electronically filed documents are immediately entered on the court's docket, and an image of the filed document is simultaneously available for viewing in CM/ECF Pacer.

(6) CM/ECF allows filers to directly pay filing fees through CM/ECF using the U.S. Treasury Internet credit card service. Upon successful submission of a docket entry, the filer is immediately offered the option to pay the filing fee via the Internet. Upon the successful processing of the credit card payment, filer receives a Internet credit card payment receipt. The receipt for payment is automatically entered onto the case docket.

(7) The CM/ECF Support Center is available during business hours (Monday through Friday, 9:00 a.m. to 4:00 p.m., excluding federal holidays) for customer assistance (213) 894-2365.

(8) The submission of a judge's copy is required. A paper copy of all electronically filed documents via the CM/ECF system must be immediately delivered (by courier or mail) to the judge's chambers of the divisional office to which the relevant case or proceeding has been assigned. Please refer to LBR 5005-2 and section 3-5(b) of this Manual.

(d) Hardware/Software Equipment.

Item Requirement

Computer Running Windows 95/98 or higher or Macintosh OS.

Printer Any printer compatible with your computer.

Scanner Any scanner compatible with your computer.

Browser Internet Explorer 4.x and above with SSL enabled or Netscape Navigator.

Exchange Software

The full version of Adobe Acrobat, which contains both Adobe PDF Writer and Adobe Reader. Adobe Versions 4 and above meet the CM/ECF filing requirements.

E-mail Account

An e-mail account that is configured to send and receive attachments.

You should be aware of any mailbox size limitations imposed by the email provider.

(e) Registering for CM/ECF.

(1) Attorneys must first be admitted to practice in the Central District of California. If you are an out-of-state attorney, you are required to have local sponsoring counsel pursuant to LBR 2090-1(b)(3).

(A) To register for CM/ECF, attorneys, trustees, and limited filers must complete an on-line application for training. Upon completion of court-sponsored training and requisite training assignments, registrants will be provided with a login and password for CM/ECF. The attorney's authorized staff may be allowed to use the assigned login and password.

(B) Attorneys cannot knowingly permit a password to be used by anyone who does not have authorized access to the program. Please see section 3-2(d) for more information.

(2) The online registration process takes less than 10 minutes to complete. To register, go to < www.cacb.uscourts.gov> -> Electronic Systems & Status -> CM/ECF home page -> Registration/Training -> ECF Training Registration and complete the required form.

(A) Training is not required for limited filers (those filing proof of claims).

(B) Training is required for all trustees and attorneys, unless they have been trained and issued a Login ID and Password in another bankruptcy court district.

(f) Procedures and Frequently Asked Questions.

For CM/ECF procedures, refer to Terms, Eligibility, Registration, Training, Passwords, section 3-2. The most frequently asked questions and online procedures may be found at the court's web site at <

www.cacb.uscourts.gov> Electronic Systems & Status ->CM/ECF home page - >Procedures and Rules ->ECF Procedures.

(g) CM/ECF Documents.

Most documents can be filed using the CM/ECF system. The exceptions to electronic filing are documents filed under seal; Writs of execution; Abstracts of judgments; Bonds; and Interpleader with attached checks. These documents must be filed at the Intake window (See Exceptions to Mandatory Electronic Filing, section 3-11). Refer to Proposed Orders, section 3-9, for procedures regarding electronically lodged orders.

3-2. Terms, Eligibility, Registration, Training, Passwords

(a) Terms.

(1) "CM/ECF system" refers to the court's Case Management/ Electronic Case Files System that receives documents filed in electronic format.

(2) "ECF User" refers to those who have a Court-issued login and password to file documents electronically.

(3) "Notice of Electronic Filing" refers to the notice automatically generated by the CM/ECF system each time a docket event is entered or a document is filed.

(b) Eligibility.

(1) Full Participants.

Attorneys admitted to practice in the Central District of California, currently in good standing, (including those admitted pro hac vice to the bar of the court and attorneys authorized to represent the United States without being admitted to the bar), United States trustees and their assistants, trustees in bankruptcy and their assistants, attorneys representing the United States of America, and others as the court deems appropriate, may register as full participant ECF Users.

(2) Limited Participants.

The court may designate additional individuals or entities as eligible for registration as limited participant ECF Users. Such ECF Users may be limited to filing electronically certain types of documents, such as proofs of claim, or limited to filing documents in a particular case or proceeding.

(c) Registration for the CM/ECF System.

(1) Registration.

Each attorney desiring to file pleadings or papers through the court's CM/ECF system must complete and sign a Registration Form, attend the training required by the court, and prove competence on the CM/ECF system. Attorneys who have attended training for the CM/ECF system and are registered in another district may be allowed to register with this Court without further training. Limited use passwords may or may not be issued to ECF Users without formal training, depending on their intended use of the CM/ECF system. Persons wishing to register as limited users must follow the same registration procedures.

Registration information is available on the court's web site at < www.cacb.uscourts.gov>.

(2) Certification of Requirements.

Upon certification of the requirements stated in Paragraph (c)(1) above, the Clerk will provide the registering ECF User with a login and password for the CM/ECF system.

(3) Registration as Consent to Receive Notice and Service Electronically.

Registration by an ECF User shall constitute: (1) consent in writing to receive notice electronically and waiver of the right to receive notice by any other means; and (2) consent in writing to electronic service, except in regard to service of a summons and complaint under FRBP 7004, and waiver of any right to service by any other means. The consent and waiver includes, without limitation, notice of the entry of an order or judgment under FRBP 9022. The consent and waiver is effective upon activation of the participating ECF User's login and password in the CM/ECF system live database.

(4) Notification of Change in Registration Information.

Registered ECF Users shall promptly notify the Clerk of Court in writing of any changes in address, telephone number, fax number, or e-mail address. In addition, whenever an attorney changes firm affiliation, there shall be filed in each case in which that attorney has appeared, a notice as to the attorney and law firm that will thereafter represent that party. Registered ECF Users shall notify the ECF Support Center at (213) 894-2365 and an e-mail shall be sent to

ECF_support@cacb.uscourts.gov to provide the court with the notification of change in registration information.

(d) Login and Password.

(1) Use of Login and Password.

It shall be the duty of the registered ECF User to retain control of, and to protect and secure the confidentiality of, his or her login and password, and to prevent their disclosure to any person not authorized to use them. No registered ECF User shall knowingly permit or cause to permit his or her login and password to be utilized by anyone other than an individual empowered (such as a paralegal or legal assistant) to act on behalf of the registered user. A registered ECF User shall immediately notify the ECF Support Center at (213) 894-2365 upon learning that the security of his or her login and password has been compromised. A follow-up e-mail shall also be sent to ECF_support@cacb.uscourts.gov.

(2) Suspension or Cancellation by Court.

The court may suspend or revoke an ECF User's password and, therefore, his or her authority and ability to electronically file documents for: (1) failure to comply with any provision of the agreement contained in the ECF User's Registration Form; (2) failure to adequately protect his or her password; (3) failure to comply with the provisions of the CM/ECF Administrative Procedures; (4) failure to pay fees required for documents filed electronically; (5) other misuse of the CM/ECF system; or (6) a sanction ordered by the court after notice and opportunity for hearing.

3-3. Effective Date of Filing

(a) Effectiveness of Electronically Filed Document.

The electronic filing of a document, together with the transmission by the court of a Notice of Electronic Filing to the user filing the document, constitutes the filing of the document for all purposes of the FRBP and the court's Local Bankruptcy Rules and constitutes entry of the document on the docket by the Clerk under FRBP 5003. The official record of all documents is the electronic recording of the document as stored by the court.

(b) Time of Filing.

Filing of a document electronically does not alter the filing deadline for that document. Filing must be completed before midnight, Pacific

Standard or Daylight Saving Time, whichever is then in effect, to be considered timely filed that day. The date and time of filing is stated on the Notice of Electronic Filing from the court. This time stamp is based on the time of the electronic receipt of the document by the court, and not by the time of transmission by the ECF User.

(c) Virtual Documents.

Virtual documents are certain documents (including some orders) which are frequently used by trustees and the court, and the text of which does not vary from case to case. A virtual document consists entirely of the text contained in the docket entry and is not embodied in any other document or electronic recording. The docket entry for a virtual document shall be fully effective despite the absence of a document or electronic recording apart from the docket entry. Examples of virtual documents are a trustee's report of no distribution, a trustee's initial report in an asset case, and a final decree closing the case.

3-4. Signatures

(a) Registered ECF User

(1) Use of Login and Password.

The use of a registered ECF User's login and password to file a document electronically shall constitute the signature of the registered ECF User on the document being electronically filed. The attorney shall sign a true and correct hard copy of the document before the electronic version of the same has been electronically filed.

(2) Use of "/s/".

The signature of the registered ECF User on electronically filed documents shall be denoted by "/s/," followed by the registered ECF User's name, on the signatures lines where such signatures are required or applicable. Failure to denote "/s/," followed by the registered ECF User's name, on applicable signature lines shall constitute a failure to sign the documents on such signature lines. If the registered ECF User is an attorney, the use of the registered attorney's login and password to file a document electronically shall constitute the signature of that attorney on that document under FRBP 9011and LBR 1002-1(a).

(3) Virtual Documents.

The use of the trustee's ECF User login and password shall constitute the trustee's signature on a virtual document. A virtual document that is a court notice or order entered by the court shall be deemed signed by the individual whose name appears as Judge or Clerk of the Court.

(4) Retention of Original Signatures.

The registered ECF User electronically filing the document shall maintain the executed original of the document for a period of five years after the closing of the case or adversary proceeding in which the document is filed, and shall make the executed original available for review upon request of the court or other parties.

(b) Debtor(s) or Other Parties Represented by Registered ECF User.

(1) Use of "s/."

The signature of the debtor or other party on electronically filed documents shall be denoted by "/s/," followed by the debtor's or other party's name, on the signature lines where such signatures are required or applicable.

Failure to denote "/s/," followed by the debtor's or other party's name, on applicable signature lines shall constitute a failure to sign the documents on such signature lines. The debtor or other party shall sign a true and correct hard copy of the document before the electronic version of the same has been electronically filed. Any subsequently filed amended petitions, schedules, statements, or plans must either be filed electronically with the imaged signature of the debtor(s) or accompanied by a Electronic Filing Declaration or Electronic Filing Declaration of Authorized Signatory containing the imaged signatures of the debtor or the debtor's representatives.

(2) Original Signatures.

Documents filed electronically using the CM/ECF system shall be accompanied by a scanned copy of an Electronic Filing Declaration signed by the debtor(s) or other party, and the attorney, or an Electronic Filing Declaration of Authorized Signatory if the debtor is a corporation or partnership.

Failure to submit the Declaration shall constitute a failure to sign in the locations indicated by "s/," followed by the debtor's or other party's name, by the debtor or other party.

(3) Retention of Original Signatures.

The attorney or other ECF User electronically filing such documents shall maintain the executed original of the Declaration for a period of five years after the closing of the case or adversary proceeding in which the document is filed, and shall make the executed original of the Declaration available for review upon request of the court or other parties.

(c) Party Other Than Registered ECF User, Debtor, or Other Party Represented by Registered ECF User.

(1) Image of Signature.

Documents that require the verified signature of a party other than the registered ECF User who is electronically filing the document, the debtor(s), or other party represented by registered ECF User shall be electronically imaged using scanning technology and electronically filed in portable document format (.pdf) as specified by the Clerk of Court.

(2) Verification of Documents.

The use of the registered ECF User's login and password by the attorney electronically filing the document is the attorney's representation that the document being filed is a true and correct copy of the original document bearing such other individual's signature.

(3) Retention of Original Signatures.

The registered ECF User electronically filing the document shall maintain the executed original of the document for a period of five years after the closing of the case or adversary proceeding in which the document is filed, and shall make the executed original available for review upon request of the court or other parties.

(d) Documents with Multiple Signatures (i.e., Stipulations, etc.).

Documents requiring the signatures of more than one party, such as a stipulation, must be electronically filed as follows:

(1) Verification of Content of Document.

The attorney electronically filing the document shall initially confirm that the content of the document is acceptable to all persons required to sign the document by obtaining their original signatures on the document.

(2) Image of Signatures.

The document containing the original signatures shall be imaged using scanning technology and electronically filed in portable document format (.pdf).

(3) Retention of Original Signatures.

The attorney electronically filing the document shall maintain the executed original for a period of five years after the closing of the case or adversary proceeding in which the document is filed, and shall make the executed original available for review upon request of the court or other parties.

(e) Employee of Registered CM/ECF User.

An employee of a registered ECF User who has a CM/ECF password may submit an electronic signature solely for the purpose of verifying proofs of service of documents. The signature of the employee on the proof of service shall be denoted by "/s/," followed by the employee's name on the signature line where such signatures are required or applicable. The registered ECF User whose password was used to electronically file or lodge the document is responsible for the accuracy of the verification.

3-5. Electronic Filing Protocols

(a) General.

Except as provided by LBR 5005-4(c), all papers submitted in any case or proceeding must be filed electronically, signed or verified by electronic means in compliance with the court's CM/ECF procedures posted on the court's web site and available at the Clerk's Office.

(b) Judge's Copy [LBR 5005-2].

Local Bankruptcy Rule 5005-2(d) requires that a copy of every document filed must be served on the judge who presides over the bankruptcy case or adversary proceeding. A paper copy of any document filed with the court, either electronically or non-electronically must comply with section 2-5, must be marked "Judge's Copy" on the front page, and must be served on the judge in chambers in the manner prescribed below:

(1) The judge's copy must meet the requirements of LBR 9004-1(a). As also required in section 2-5(d)(3), exhibits and other declarations attached to the judge's copy must be tabbed.

(2) If the document is filed electronically, a copy of the Notice of

Electronic Filing (NEF) confirming the filing of the original document must be stapled or otherwise attached to the back of a judge's copy.

(3) The judge's copy must be served no later than 24 hours after the document is filed.

(4) The Proof of Service must be on mandatory Local Bankruptcy Rule form F9013-3.1 and indicate the date and manner in which the judge was served. Refer to Appendix F, Serving Judge's Copy of Documents, to determine the deadline, the method, and the address to serve the judge.

(5) Service by mail on the judge is permissible if one of the following is true:

(A) The document relates to a hearing that is scheduled to occur at least 14 days after the date of service of the document on the judge;

(B) The document relates to a hearing that was held prior to the date of service on the judge; or

(C) There is no hearing currently on calendar to which the document relates.

(6) If the document relates to a hearing that is scheduled to occur less than 14 days after service of the document on the judge, service must be accomplished by overnight courier or hand-delivery so as to ensure that the judge's copy is served no later than 24 hours after the document is filed and arrives at the judge's chambers not later than two court days prior to the date scheduled for the hearing to which it relates, or such later deadline as may be established by the judge for the receipt of papers that relate to an emergency hearing or a hearing held on shortened time.

(c) Document Size.

Document files shall not be larger than 2 megabytes (MB) in size. An ECF User should check the size of the file prior to attempting to upload it in the CM/ECF system. Generally, 40 pages of text converted from a standard word processing format to a PDF image should not exceed 2 MB. However, a PDF file created through scanning a document or by inserting additional pages that have been scanned may result in a file exceeding 2 MB. In particular, scanning a document with graphics or dark areas will significantly affect file size. A file exceeding the 2 MB limit must be broken into smaller sections and uploaded as consecutively numbered attachments to the main document.

(d) Image Size.

Individual pages of documents shall not exceed 8.5 × 11 inches. An ECF User should check the page size prior to attempting to upload the PDF in the CM/ECF system. PDF files with pages exceeding the 8.5 × 11 inch limit must be modified before uploading.

(e) Hyperlinks.

Documents filed using the CM/ECF system may include the following type of hyperlinks:

(1) Hyperlinks to other portions of the same document; and

(2) Hyperlinks to a location on the Internet that contains a source document for a citation or other reference materials.

NOTE: Hyperlinks to cited authority may not replace standard citation format. Complete citations must be included in the text of the filed document. Neither a hyperlink, nor any site to which it refers, shall be considered part of the record. Hyperlinks are simply convenient mechanisms for accessing material cited in a filed document. The court accepts no responsibility for, and does not endorse, any product, organization, or content at any hyperlink site, or at any site to which that site may be linked. The court accepts no responsibility for the availability or functionality of any hyperlink.

(f) Emergency Motions.

ECF Users seeking to file emergency motions or other expedited matters shall immediately advise the assigned judge's courtroom deputy of the filing by phone. Compliance with LBR 9075-1(a) is required. The name and phone number of the courtroom deputy for each judge are posted on the court's web site at < www.cacb.uscourts-.gov>.

(g) Title of Docket Entries.

The ECF User must designate a title for the document using one of the main categories provided in the CM/ECF system (e.g., motion, application, etc.).

(h) Correcting Documents Filed in Error.

(1) When a document has been filed electronically, the official record is the electronic recording of the document as stored by the court. Only the Clerk's Office can make changes to the docket entry.

(2) A document incorrectly filed in a case may be the result of posting the wrong PDF file to a docket entry, selecting the wrong document type from the menu, or entering the wrong case number. If an error is detected after an item is on the docket, DO NOT ATTEMPT TO RE-FILE THE DOCUMENT.

(3) After an error is discovered, contact the ECF Support Center at (213) 894-2365 as soon as possible. Be sure to have the case number and document number for which the correction is being requested. If appropriate, the court will make an entry indicating that the document was filed in error. A follow-up e-mail shall also be sent to ECF_support@cacb.uscourts.gov. You will be advised if you need to re-file the document. The CM/ECF system will not permit you to make changes to a document or docket entry once the transaction has been accepted.

(4) If an error regarding a fee occurs, do not pay the fee until after speaking with someone at the ECF Support Center.

(i) Verification of Document Image.

An ECF User shall verify, by checking the link in the Notice of Electronic Filing or by reviewing the docket within 2 business days after the electronic filing, that the image of the filed document is a correct and complete copy of the document intended to be filed. An ECF User shall immediately notify the ECF Support Center at (213) 894-2365 of the discovery of an incorrect or incomplete image of a document. A follow-up e-mail shall also be sent to ECF_support@cacb.uscourts.gov.

(j) Anti-Virus Software.

Each ECF User shall utilize updated anti-virus software at all locations from which Internet access is made. The filing party must check all electronic files submitted on disk or transmitted by e-mail to the Clerk's Office or a judge's chambers for viruses or worms.

3-6. Privacy [LBR 1002-1]

(a) Redaction of Personal Identifiers.

In compliance with the policy of the Judicial Conference of the United States and the E-government Act of 2002, and in order to promote electronic access to case files while also protecting personal privacy and other legitimate interests, parties shall refrain from including, or shall partially redact where inclusion is necessary, the following personal data identifiers from all documents and pleadings filed with the court, including exhibits thereto, whether filed electronically or in paper format, unless otherwise ordered by the court or required by statute, the FRBP, or the Official Bankruptcy Forms.

(1) Social Security Numbers.

If disclosure of a Social Security number is required, only the last four digits of that number should be used. (This does not apply toOfficial Form 21, Statement of Social Security Number(s)).

(2) Names of Minor Children.

If disclosure of the identity of any minor child is required, only the initials of that child should be used.

(3) Dates of Birth.

If disclosure of an individual's date of birth is required by any statement or schedule, only the year should be used.

(4) Financial Account Numbers.

If disclosure of any financial account number is required, only the last four digits of that number should be used.

NOTE: The responsibility for redacting the personal identifiers listed above rests solely with counsel and the parties. The Clerk's Office will not review each document for compliance with this rule.

(b) Statement of Social Security Number(s) - Official Form B21.

(1) When to Submit to the Court.

Beginning January 1, 2009, attorneys who electronically file petitions using the court's CM/ECF system must electronically submit the Statement of Social Security Number(s) (Official Form B21) to the court on the same day of the filing of the petition pursuant to Public Notice 08-024 (dated 12/11/08).

(2) How to Submit to the Court.

To ensure the privacy of the debtor's Social Security Number, the court requires that the Statement of Social Security Number(s) be printed, signed by the debtor(s), scanned as a separate PDF file, and docketed separately from the Voluntary Petition using the ''private'' event code Statement of Social Security Number (BK - Other). DO NOT file an amended Statement of Social Security Number(s) as ''Amendment'' since this event will cause the document and the Social Security Number to appear on the public docket. Use ''private'' event code Statement of Social Security Number(s) Form B21 (AMENDED STATEMENT) (BK - Other). More detailed instructions on how to submit the Statement of Social Security Number(s) or an Amended Statement of Social Security Number(s) are available on the court's website. From the court's homepage, click on Electronic Systems & Status>CM/ECF Home Page>Procedures and Rules>Statement of Social Security Number(s).

(3) Privacy of the Debtor(s) Social Security Number(s).

Attorneys must use the proper event code to prevent the full social security number(s) from appearing on the public docket, which is a violation of FRBP 9037.

3-7. Payment of Filing Fees

(a) When Fees are Due.

For filings that require a fee, the CM/ECF system will prompt the ECF User to enter credit card information (card number and expiration date) and the payment amount following the transaction. The credit card receipt shall include a reference to the case and docket number. Funds will be automatically charged to the card holder's account by the United States Treasury Department. All applicable filing fees shall be paid at the time in which the transaction requiring a fee occurs.

(b) Consequences of Not Paying Fees Timely.

The CM/ECF system will automatically disable access for registered ECF Users with filing fees outstanding. The registered ECF User whose access to the CM/ECF system has been disabled will be able to login to the system, but will not be able to view or file any documents until he or she pays the outstanding fees. Once the outstanding fees are paid, the registered ECF User's system access to file and view electronic documents will be reinstated upon review and approval by the Clerk of Court.

3-8. Service of Documents by Electronic Means [LBR 9036-1]

(a) Consent to Electronic Service.

ECF Users shall be required to consent to electronic service of all documents, except with regard to LBR 7004-1, service of a summons and complaint, as a condition of participation in the CM/ECF system. The consent is effective upon activation of the ECF User's login and password in the live CM/ECF system. The consent shall apply in all cases in which the consenting entity is a party. The entity may withdraw consent to electronic service by giving notice of not less than 30 days to all parties in matters in which the entity is a party. An entity that is not a party to the case but is a registered ECF User may request to receive a Courtesy Notification of Electronic Filing pursuant to Public Notice 08-015.

(b) Notice of Electronic Filing (NEF).

(1) Whenever a document is filed electronically using the court's CM/ECF system, the filing party automatically will be sent a Notice of Electronic Filing by electronic means at the time of docketing. Electronic transmission of the Notice of Electronic Filing through the court's transmission facilities constitutes service of the notice of the filed document to registered users and others who have consented in writing to accept such service of notice. The party filing the document using the court's CM/ECF system shall serve the document on other parties as required by the FRBP and the Local Bankruptcy Rules.

(2) A certificate of service must be filed pursuant to Local Bankruptcy Rule 7004-1(b) for all documents filed electronically, indicating that service was accomplished through the Notice of Electronic Filing for parties and counsel who are registered ECF Users, and indicating how service was accomplished on any party or counsel who is not an ECF User.

(3) A party entitled to service who is not a registered ECF User in the CM/ECF system is entitled to a paper copy of any electronically filed pleading or paper. The filing party must serve the non-registered party with the pleading or paper according to the FRBP and the Local Bankruptcy Rules.

(4) Copies of documents that have been filed electronically which the court is required to transmit to the United States Trustee shall be transmitted to the United States Trustee electronically.

(c) Courtesy Notification of Electronic Filing (NEF).

(1) Registered CM/ECF users who wish to receive courtesy electronic notification of documents filed in a particular bankruptcy case may submit a request to the court using the form Request for Courtesy Notification of Electronic Filing (NEF). This form is available on the court's website < www.cacb.uscourts.gov>Forms/ Rules/General Orders >Court Forms.

(2) All requests for a courtesy NEF must be filed electronically with the court. The courtesy electronic notification shall be delivered via the court's CM/ECF system as an NEF. Requests for a Courtesy NEF will not be accepted at the Intake window. (See Public Notice 08-015.)

(d) Notice of Claim Filed by Debtor or Trustee.

A debtor's attorney or a trustee electronically filing a proof of claim on behalf of a creditor under FRBP 3004 shall be responsible for giving notice of the filing to the creditor, debtor and trustee as required by that rule.

(e) Electronic Notice & Service on United States Trustee [LBR 2002-2].

Beginning April 1, 2008, persons or entities filing the following documents must also serve the U.S. Trustee by U.S. mail, overnight mail, Federal Express, or courier on or before the date the document is filed. The proof of service must indicate that the U.S. Trustee was served via one of the foregoing forms of service for:

(1) Proposed Orders or Judgments if Required under LBR 9021-1(b)(3).

Persons and entities must continue to comply with the court's Local Bankruptcy Rules regarding service of proposed orders or judgments, whether or not the proposed order or judgment is electronically lodged via the court's Electronic Lodged Upload (LOU) program;

(2) Complaints Served Upon United States Trustee as a Defendant.

Persons and entities must comply with FRBP 7004(b)(10) when the U.S. Trustee is named in an adversary proceeding as a party within the meaning of Part VII of the FRBP, whether or not the U.S. Trustee is a trustee in the case. This requirement is consistent with the court's CM/ECF Administrative Procedures, paragraph VII.A; and

(3) Other Documents Specified in the court's CM/ECF Administrative Procedures or Local Bankruptcy Rules (LBR) relevant to Electronic Notice & Service.

Persons and entities must comply with the court's other LBR and CM/ECF Administrative Procedures that require non-electronic notice and/or service of specified documents.

(4) Special Situations.

Persons and entities filing the following documents must serve the U.S. Trustee by U.S. mail, overnight mail, Federal Express, or courier on or before the date that the document is filed. The proof of service must indicate that the U.S. Trustee was served via one of the foregoing forms of service for:

(A) Documents exceeding 50 pages in length.

When determining page length, all pages, including but not limited to exhibits, declarations, and proof of service, are to be counted.

(B) All Requests to Hear Matters on Emergency Basis or Shortened Notice, or for Relief Without Hearing.

These documents include papers:

(i) making the request;

(ii) responding to the request; and

(iii) relating to chapter 11 first day motions.

(C) Any Document Filed within 10 Days of a Hearing.

This includes documents:

(i) filed timely or untimely;

(ii) related to hearings set on regular notice; and

(iii) related to hearings set on shortened notice or emergency basis.

(D) Individual Capacity Matters. (e.g., complaints, motions, or other filings filed against the United States Trustee and/or any of the United States Trustee's staff in their capacity as individuals).

The service of any such filing must be made in compliance with either Rule 4 of the F.R.Civ.P. and with any and all other applicable rules or civil, bankruptcy, and/or appellate procedure.

3-9.Proposed Orders [LBR 9021-1]

Unless otherwise authorized by the court, proposed orders may be lodged electronically on all cases and adversary proceedings using the court's Lodged Order Upload (LOU) program in CM/ECF. The procedures for using the court's Lodged Order Upload program are located in section 4. Online procedures may be found on the court's web site at < www.cac-b.uscourts.gov> Electronic Systems & Status -> CM/ECF homepage -> Procedures and Rules ->ECF Procedures.

3-10. Entry of Judgments and Orders

(a) Electronic Transmission.

Immediately upon the entry of a judgment or order, the Clerk's Office shall electronically transmit a Notice of Electronic Filing to registered ECF users and others who have consented to electronic service or notice in the case or proceeding through the court's transmission facilities. The electronic transmission of the Notice of Electronic Filling shall constitute the service on such persons ore entities of the notice of entry of the judgment or order required by FRBP 9022.

(b) Notice and Service by Mail.

The Clerk's Office will give notice of the entry of the judgment or order by mail to persons ore entities who have not consented to service or notice by electronic transmission and who are entitled to such service or notice from the court pursuant to FRBP 9022 and LBR 9021-1(b).

3-11. Exceptions to Mandatory Electronic Filing [LBR 5005-4]

(a) Document Exception.

The following documents shall be filed conventionally and not electronically unless specifically authorized by the court:

(1) Documents filed under seal;

(2) Writs of execution;

(3) Abstracts of judgments;

(4) Applications for renewals of judgments;

(5) Bonds; and

(6) Interpleader with attached checks.

(b) Pro Se Exception.

A person who is not represented by an attorney may file and serve papers non-electronically.

(c) Limited Exception for Attorneys.

(1) An attorney who files papers in fewer than 5 bankruptcy cases or adversary proceedings in a single calendar year may file and serve papers nonelectronically.

(2) An attorney who files non-electronically papers capable of being filed electronically in 5 or more bankruptcy cases or adversary proceedings in a single calendar year must thereafter file papers electronically through the court's CM/ECF system.

(3) The court reserves the right in its sole discretion to revoke this limited exception at any time upon notice to the attorney.

3-12. Technical Failures

An ECF User whose filing is made untimely as a result of a technical failure may seek appropriate relief from the court.

3-13. Public Access to the CM/ECF System

(a) Internet Access.

Internet access to the CM/ECF system is not available without a PACER login and password. A PACER login and password can be secured by contacting the PACER Service Center to establish an account. Registration may be made online at http://pacer.psc.uscourts.gov or by calling the PACER Service Center at (800) 676-6856.

Such access to the CM/ECF system will allow the retrieval of the docket sheet and documents. Access to the CM/ECF system will be on a "read only" basis.

(b) Public Access at the Court.

The public will have electronic access at the Clerk's Office during regular business hours for viewing the docket sheet and filed documents in the CM/ECF system.

(c) Conventional Copies and Certified Copies.

Conventional and certified copies of electronically filed documents may be purchased at the Clerk's Office during regular business hours. The fee for copying and certification will be in accordance with the provisions of 28 U.S.C. § 1930.

Section Four [LOU (Lodged Order Upload)]

5. OTHER COURT TECHNOLOGY

5-1. Web Site

The web site for the United States Bankruptcy Court for the Central District of California is < www.cacb.uscourts.gov>. The court provides this site as a public service, offering convenient public access to court reports, court news and information, local bankruptcy rules and forms, general orders, public notices, written opinions, and other information that is of interest to the public.

5-2. Electronic Systems Status

The court posts the status of the electronic systems serving the public on its web site, < www.cacb.uscourts.gov>. Click on Electronic Systems & Status on the homepage.

5-3. PACER (Public Access to Court Electronic Records)

(a) Internet-Based System.

PACER is an Internet-based system that enables registered users to view and print case information and images of the most often requested case file documents for a fee. PACER is user-friendly and has the "look and feel" of an Internet web site.

(b) Retrieving Case Information.

Users can retrieve the following case information:

(1) Case number;

(2) Adversary proceeding number;

(3) Name of debtor and last four digits of the Debtor's Social Security Number or Tax Identification Number (if applicable);

(4) Bankruptcy case and adversary proceeding dockets and claims registers;

(5) Judges' calendars and tentative rulings, if available;

(6) Images of most case file documents including all orders and bankruptcy petitions and other than those items specifically excluded from electronic filing per the court's administrative order; and

(7) Case status and other pertinent information such as § 341(a)

meeting date, complaint bar date, discharge or dismissal date (if applicable), debtor's attorney, assigned trustee, fees paid to professionals, etc.

(c) PACER Registration.

To access PACER information, users may register from the web site, < www.pacer.psc.uscourts.gov>, or by calling the PACER Service Center at (800) 676-6856, Monday through Friday, 8:00 a.m. to 5:00 p.m. (Central Time).

(d) Required Equipment for PACER.

Item Requirement

Computer Any computer system that has an Internet connection.

Printer Any printer compatible with your computer.

Browser Javascript enabled web browser

Internet Service Provider (ISP)

An Internet connection. Examples of ISPs include AOL, MSN, Earthlink, Compuserve, etc.

(e) Accessing CM/ECF PACER.

(1) From the court's web site, < www.cacb.uscourts.gov> Electronic Systems & Status -> CM/ECF PACER ACCESS.

(2) From the CM/ECF PACER page, select Central District of California - Document Filing System.

(f) CM/ECF PACER Fees.

The cost of CM/ECF PACER is $0.08 per page. For billing purposes, a page is defined as 54 lines per page (without HTML formatting). Images will be billed according to the number of pages scanned; therefore, one scanned page equals one billable page.

5-4. Teleconferencing

(a) Availability.

A number of judges at the court accommodate counsel or other parties by making telephonic appearances available, within guidelines, for those unable to appear in the courtroom. To determine if a judge offers telephonic appearances and obtain specific telephonic appearance procedures, contact the appropriate Courtroom Deputy. (See Appendix A.)

(b) Connection.

All remote parties are connected to the courtroom sound system, and their participation is recorded as part of the official court record.

(c) Procedures and Contact Information.

Some of the participating judges provide telephonic appearance procedures and contact information on the court's web site, < www.cacb.uscourts.gov> Information -> Judges' Procedures/ Information.

(d) Fees.

Users of telephonic appearance services are responsible for all expenses charged by vendors.

5-5. Videoconferencing

(a) Availability.

Videoconferencing is provided by the court in every division to accommodate counsel or other parties that are unable to appear in the courtroom. Videoconferencing uses two-way audio and video monitors to connect parties between a courtroom and an off-site location.

(b) Connection.

All remote parties are connected to the courtroom video system, and their participation is recorded as part of the official court record.

(c) Procedures and Contact Information.

(1) Obtain approval for scheduling a videoconference court hearing. Approval to use videoconferencing must be obtained to utilize the system. Contact the judge's Courtroom Deputy or Law Clerk to request approval for scheduling a videoconference hearing. See Appendix A for Courtroom Deputy/Law Clerk contact information.

(2) Test the videoconferencing equipment and connection.

(A) A connection test between the off-site location and the court must be conducted before scheduling a hearing. The test will determine if equipment between the locations is compatible. It also allows the users to gain familiarity with the videoconferencing equipment and process.

(B) Contact the court's Courtroom Technology Specialist at

(213) 894-8264 to schedule a test date or discuss technical issues. System compatibility must be confirmed before a hearing date is scheduled.

(3) Schedule the videoconference hearing.

Contact the judge's Courtroom Deputy to schedule the videoconference hearing. Be sure to inform the Courtroom Deputy that all videoconferencing requirements specified by the court's Courtroom Technology Specialist have been met. The Courtroom Deputy will provide the procedures and time frames for connecting to the hearing.

(d) Fees.

Ordinarily, the court will not charge a fee for the use of videoconferencing. However, if videoconferencing results in the imposition of charges on the judiciary, then the party seeking permission for videoconferencing may be required to pay those costs. Users of videoconference appearance services are responsible for all expenses charged by vendors.

(e) Technical Specifications.

(1) Comply with the telecommunications industry standard H.320 specification for videoconferencing via the ISDN circuits.

(2) Have a minimum of three BRI (Basic Rate Interface) circuits with a total circuit equivalent to 384Kbs bandwidth.

(3) Connect using either of the following methods:

(A) Bonding 0 (using all six telephone numbers); or

(B) Bonding 1 (using one telephone number).

(4) Have the capability of properly viewing all litigants attending and/or participating in the hearing.

(5) Have a microphone system capable of properly picking up the voices of all participants.

5-6. VCIS (Voice Case Information System)

(a) What is VCIS?

(1) The Voice Case Information System (VCIS) enables the public to directly access the court's case management system from a touch-tone telephone. This service is provided free of charge and is available 24 hours a day, 7 days week.

(2) Case information is available approximately 24 hours after the case has been filed. A computer-synthesized voice relays the information to the caller. VCIS provides the following bankruptcy information:

(A) Case number

(B) Names of debtors

(C) Case filing date

(D) Case chapter

(E) Name, address, and telephone number of debtor's attorney

(F) Name of trustee

(G) Name of assigned judge

(H) Discharge and closed dates

(I) Case status

(J) Asset information

(b) Using VCIS.

Using a touch-tone telephone, dial (213) 894-4111 or the toll free number at (866) 522-6053 and follow the computer-synthesized voice prompts.

5-7. Automated Telephone System

(a) Recorded General Information.

The automated telephone system enables callers to access recorded general information about the court and is available in all divisions (see section 5-7(c) of this manual). Callers may obtain:

(1) General information regarding filing, claims, motions, and adversary proceedings;

(2) Court locations;

(3) Information about incomplete and emergency filings;

(4) Court fees and Fee Acceptance Policy;

(5) Records and case status information;

(6) Tape and transcript information; and

(7) Calendar and hearing matter information.

(b) Other Languages.

The Los Angeles and San Fernando Valley Divisions offer some information in Spanish. By pressing menu option zero, the caller will be transferred to a customer service representative during regular business hours (Monday through Friday, 9:00 a.m. to 4:00 p.m., excluding federal holidays).

(c) Automated Telephone System Phone Numbers:

Division	Telephone Number
Los Angeles	(213) 894-3118
Riverside	(951) 774-1000
Santa Ana	(714) 338-5300
Northern	(805) 884-4800
San Fernando Valley	(818) 587-2900

6. FORMS

(Official Bankruptcy Forms, Local Bankruptcy Rules Forms, Court Forms)

6-1. Obtaining Copies of Forms

Official Bankruptcy Forms must be used to file and take action in bankruptcy cases. Local Bankruptcy Rules Forms must be used if mandated by the court in a bankruptcy case or proceeding pending in the Unites States Bankruptcy Court for the Central District of California. Court Forms and Mediation Forms may also be necessary for use during the course of some bankruptcy or adversary proceedings. All of these forms may be downloaded free of charge from the court's website at < www.cacb.uscourts.gov> Forms/Rules/General Orders.

6-2. Index of Official Bankruptcy Forms

FORM DATE	FORM TITLE	LAST REVISION
B1	Voluntary Petition	1/08
B1	Exhibit "A" to Voluntary Petition	3/98
B1	Exhibit "C" to Voluntary Petition	9/01

FORM DATE	FORM TITLE	LAST REVISION
B1	Exhibit "D" - Individual Debtor's Statement of Compliance with Credit Counseling Requirement	12/08
B1, page 3	Declaration under Penalty of Perjury on Behalf of a Corporation or Partnership	6/90
B3A	Application and Order to Pay Filing Fee in Installments	12/07
B3B	Application for Waiver of Chapter 7 Filing Fee	12/07
B4	List of Creditors Holding 20 Largest Unsecured Claims	12/07
B5	Involuntary Petition	12/07
B6	Form 6. Summary of Schedules	12/07
B6	Summary of Schedules and Statistical Summary of Certain Liabilities and Related Data (28 U.S.C. § 159)	12/07
B6A	Schedule A - Real Property	12/07
B6B	Schedule B - Personal Property	12/07
B6C	Schedule C - Property Claimed as Exempt	12/07
B6D	Schedule D - Creditors Holding Secured Claims	12/07
B6E	Schedule E - Creditors Holding Unsecured Priority Claims	12/07
B6F	Schedule F - Creditors Holding Unsecured Nonpriority Claims	12/07
B6G	Scheduled G - Executory Contracts and Unexpired Leases	12/07
B6H	Schedule H - Codebtors	12/07
B6I	Schedule I - Current Income of Individual Debtor(s)	12/07

FORM DATE	FORM TITLE	LAST REVISION
B6J	Schedule J - Current Expenditures of Individual Debtor(s)	12/07
B6	Declaration Concerning Debtor's Schedules	12/07
B7	Statement of Financial Affairs	12/07
B8	Chapter 7 Individual Debtor's Statement of Intention	12/08
B10	Proof of Claim	12/07
B14	Ballot for Accepting or Rejecting Plan (Chapter 11 only)	7/98
B19	Declaration and Signature of Non-Attorney Bankruptcy Petition Preparer (11.U.S.C. § 110)	12/07
B21	Statement of Social Security Number(s) or (Other Individual Taxpayer- Identification Number (ITIN))	12/07
B22A	Statement of Current Monthly Income and Means Test Calculation (For use in Chapter 7)	12/08
B22B	Statement of Current Monthly Income (For use in Chapter 11)	1/08
B22C	Statement of Current Monthly Income and Calculation of Commitment Period and Disposable Income (For use in Chapter 13)	1/08
B23	Debtor's Certification of Completion of Post-Petition Instructional Course Concerning Personal Financial Management	12/08
B24	Certification to Court of Appeals By All Parties	12/07
B25A	Plan of Reorganization for Small Business Case under Chapter 11	12/08

FORM DATE	FORM TITLE	LAST REVISION
B25B	Disclosure Statement in Small Business Case under Chapter 11	12/08
B25C	Small Business Monthly Operating Report	12/08
B26	Periodic Report Regarding Value, Operations and Profitability of Entities in Which the Debtor's Estate Holds a Substantial or Controlling Interest	12/08
B104	Adversary Proceeding Cover Sheet	8/07
B201	Notice of Available Chapters	12/08
B203	Disclosure of Compensation of Attorney	1/88
B254	Subpoena for Rule 2004 Examination	12/06
B255	Subpoena in an Adversary Proceeding	12/06
B256	Subpoena in a Case Under the Bankruptcy Code	12/06
B265	Certification of Judgment for Registration in Another District	3/98

6-3. Index of Local Bankruptcy Rules Forms

Form Date	Form Title Mandatory/Optional	Last Revision
F 1010 -1	Summons and Notice of Status Conference in an Involuntary Case (MANDATORY)	11/07
F1015 - 2.1	Statement of Related Cases (MANDATORY)	5/04
F 1017-1.1	Debtor's Motion to Convert Case under 11 U.S.C. §§ 706(a), 1112(a) (MANDATORY)	1/08
F 1017 - 1.2	Order on Debtor's Motion to Convert Case under 11 U.S.C. §§ 706(a), 1112(a) (MANDATORY)	1/08

Form Date	Form Title Mandatory/Optional	Last Revision
F 1017 - 1.3	Notice of Debtor's Motion to Convert Case Under 11 U.S.C. §§ 706(a) (MANDATORY)	1/08
F 1017 - 1.4	Debtor's Notice of Conversion Under 11 U.S.C. §§ 1208(a) or 1307(a) (MANDATORY)	1/08
F 2014 - 1	Statement of Disinterestedness for Employment of Professional Person Under F.R.B.P. 2014 (File with Application for Employment) (OPTIONAL)	5/98
F 2016 - 1.1	Notice of Hearing on Application for Payment of Interim or Final Fees and/or Expenses under 11 U.S.C. § 331 or 330 (OPTIONAL)	12/98
F 2016 - 1.2	Application for Payment of: Interim Fees and/or Expenses (11 U.S.C. § 331); Final Fees and/or Expenses (11 U.S.C. § 330) (OPTIONAL)	5/98
F 2016 - 1.3	Order on Application for Payment of: Interim Fees and/or Expenses (11 U.S.C. § 331); Final Fees and/or Expenses (11 U.S.C. § 330) (OPTIONAL)	5/98
F 2016 - 2. 1	Trustee's Notice of Motion and Motion Under Local Bankruptcy Rule 2016-2 For: Authorization to Employ Paraprofessionals Last Revision Date (OPTIONAL)	3/08
F 2016 - 2.1A	Order on Trustee's Motion Under Local Bankruptcy Rule 2016-2 For Authorization to Employ Paraprofessionals and/or Authorization to Pay Flat Fee to Tax Preparer (OPTIONAL)	3/08
F 2016 - 2.2	Notice of Motion and Motion No. _______ Under Local Bankruptcy Rule 2016-2 for Approval of Cash Disbursements by the Trustee; Opportunity to Request Hearing; Declaration of Trustee (OPTIONAL)	3/08

Form Date	Form Title Mandatory/Optional	Last Revision
F 2016 - 2.2A	Order on Trustee's Motion No.________ Under Local Bankruptcy Rule 2016-2 For Approval of Cash Disbursements by the Trustee (OPTIONAL)	3/08
F 2090 -1.1	Declaration Re: Limited Scope of Appearance Pursuant to Local Bankruptcy Rule 2090-1 (OPTIONAL)	1/01
F 2090 - 1.2	Application of Non-Resident Attorney to Appear in a Specific Case [Local Bankruptcy Rule 2090-1(b)] (OPTIONAL)	11/06
F 2090- 1.3	Order on Application of Non-Resident Attorney to Appear in a Specific Case [Local Bankruptcy Rule 2090-1(b)] (OPTIONAL)	5/98
F 2090 - 1.4	Substitution of Attorney (OPTIONAL)	5/02
F 3001.1	Request for Issuance of Notice of Transfer of Claim Pursuant to F.R.B.P. 3001(e) (OPTIONAL)	5/98
F 3001.2	Notice of Transfer of Claim Pursuant to F.R.B.P. 3001(e) (OPTIONAL)	5/98
F 3007 - 1.1	Order on Objection to Claims (OPTIONAL)	5/98
F3007-1.2	Notice of Trustee's/Debtor in Possession's Request for Copy of Proof of Claim (OPTIONAL)	5/98
F 3007 - 1.3	Notice of Objection to Claim (MANDATORY)	1/08
F 3011 - 1	Motion for Order Releasing Unclaimed Funds (OPTIONAL)	11/08
F 3015-1.1	Chapter 13 Plan (MANDATORY)	11/06
F 3015 - 1.1A	Addendum to Chapter 13 Plan Concerning Debtors Who are Repaying Debt Secured by a Mortgage on Real Property or a Lien on Personal Property the Debtor Occupies as the Debtor's Principal Residence (OPTIONAL)	3/08
F 3015 -1.2	Notice of Section 341(a) Meeting and Hearing on Confirmation of Chapter 13 Plan with Copy of Chapter 13 Plan (MANDATORY)	7/08

Form Date	Form Title Mandatory/Optional	Last Revision
F 3015 - 1.4	Declaration Setting Forth Postpetition, Preconfirmation Deed of Trust Payments [Local Bankruptcy Rule 3015-1(m)] (MANDATORY)	5/03
F 3015 - 1.5	Notice of Motion Under Local Bankruptcy Rules 3015-1(n) and (w) to Modify Plan or Suspend Plan Payments (MANDATORY)	9/1/08
F 3015 - 1.6	Motion Under Local Bankruptcy Rules 3015-1(n) and (w) to Modify Plan or Suspend Plan Payments (MANDATORY)	9/1/08
F 3015 - 1.7	Rights and Responsibilities Agreement Between Chapter 13 Debtors and Their Attorneys (MANDATORY)	1/09
F 3015 - 1.8	Declaration RE Payment of Domestic Support Obligations (Preconfirmation) (MANDATORY)	10/05
F3015 - 1.9	Declaration RE Tax Returns (Preconfirmation) (MANDATORY)	10/05
F 3015 - 1.10	Declaration Setting Forth Post Petition, Preconfirmation Payments on: 1. Leases of Personal Property; 2. Purchase Money Security Liens in Personal Property (MANDATORY)	10/05
F 3015 - 1.11	Trustee's Comments on or Objection to Application for Supplemental Fees (NEW) (MANDATORY)	9/08
F 3015 - 1.12	Order on Application for Supplemental Fees (NEW)(MANDATORY)	9/08
F 3015 - 1.13	Trustee's Comments on or Objection To: (NEW) (MANDATORY)	9/08
F 3015 - 1.14	Order on: (MANDATORY)	9/08
F 3015 - 1.15	Debtor's Motion for Authority to Refinance Real Property Under LBR 3015-1(p) (MANDATORY)	1/09
F 3015 -1.16	Debtor's Motion for Authority to Refinance Real Property Under LBR 3015-1(p) (MANDATORY)	1/09
F 3015 - 1.17	Debtor's Motion for Authority to Incur Debt [Personal Property] (MANDATORY)	1/09

Form Date	Form Title Mandatory/Optional	Last Revision
F 3015 - 1.18	Debtor's Request for Voluntary Dismissal of Chapter 13 Case (MANDATORY)	1/09
F 3015 - 1.20	Declarations of Current/Post-Petition Income and Expenses (MANDATORY)	1/09
F 3017 - 1	Chapter 11 Disclosure Statement (MANDATORY)	8/05
F 3017 - 2	Plan Ballot Summary (MANDATORY)	6/00
F 3018 - 1	Chapter 11 Plan (MANDATORY)	8/05
F 4001 -1.DEC	Declaration of ______________ RE: Default Under Adequate Protection Order; Request for Entry of Order Granting Relief From Stay (MANDATORY)	5/04
F 4001 -1M.CUST	Notice of Motion and Motion for (A) Relief From the Automatic Stay under 11 U.S.C. § 362 (Real Property): and (B) Relief from Turnover under 11 U.S.C. § 543 by Prepetition Receiver or Other Custodian (with supporting declarations) ([formerly 350 CUST]) (MANDATORY)	5/04
F 4001 - 1M.ER	Extraordinary Relief Attachment (Optional to the Judge) [formerly 350 ER] (MANDATORY)	5/04
F 4001 - 1M.IS	Notice of Motion in Individual Case for Order Imposing a Stay or Continuing the Automatic Stay as the Court Deems Appropriate (MANDATORY)	10/05
F 4001 - 1M.NA	Notice of Motion and Motion for Relief From the Automatic Stay under 11 U.S.C. § 362 (with supporting declarations) (Action in Non-Bankruptcy Forum) [formerly 350 NA] (MANDATORY)	5/04
F 4001 - 1M.PP	Notice of Motion and Motion for Relief From the Automatic Stay under 11 U.S.C. § 362 (with supporting declarations) (Personal Property) (MANDATORY)	5/04
F 4001 - 1M.RP	Notice of Motion and Motion for Relief from the Automatic Stay Under 11 U.S.C. § 362 (Real Property) (MANDATORY)	10/05

Form Date	Form Title Mandatory/Optional	Last Revision
F 4001 - 1M.TCS	Trustee's Notice of Motion and Motion for Order Continuing the Automatic Stay Under 11 § 362 U.S.C.(h)(2), for Adequate Protection and for Delivery of Personal Property in Individual Case (MANDATORY)	10/05
F 4001- 1M.TS	Notice of Motion and Motion in Individual Case for Order Confirming Termination of Stay Under 11 U.S.C. § 362(j) or that No Stay is in Effect Under 11 U.S.C. § 362(c)(4)(A)(ii) (MANDATORY)	10/05
F 4001 - 1M.UD	Notice of Motion and Motion for Relief from the Automatic Stay or for Order Confirming that the Automatic Stay Does Not Apply Under 11 U.S.C. § 362(l) (MANDATORY)	10/05
F 4001 - 1M.13	Declaration of bottom right for Standing Trustee (Chapter 12 and 13 Cases only; Attach to Stay Motion) [formerly 350.13] (MANDATORY)	5/04
F 4001- 1M.RES	Response to Motion for Order to Terminate, Annul, Modify, or Condition the Automatic Stay under 11 U.S.C. § 362 and Declaration(s) in Support [formerly 390] (OPTIONAL)	5/04
F 4001-10.CUST	Order Granting Motion for (1) Relief From the Automatic Stay under 11 U.S.C. § 362, and (2) Relief from Turnover under 11 U.S.C. § 543 by Prepetition Receiver or Other Custodian [formerly 351 CUST] (MANDATORY)	5/04
F 4001-10.DENY	Order Denying Motion for Relief From the Automatic Stay Under 11 U.S.C. § 362 (MANDATORY)	10/05
F 4001-10.ER	Extraordinary Relief Attachment [formerly 351 ER] (OPTIONAL)	5/04
F 4001-10.NA	Order Granting Motion for Relief From the Automatic Stay under 11 U.S.C. § 362 (MANDATORY)	5/04

Form Date	Form Title Mandatory/Optional	Last Revision
F 4001-10.PP	Order Granting Motion for Relief From the Automatic Stay under 11 U.S.C. § 362 (Personal Property) (MANDATORY)	5/04
F 4001.10.RP	Order Granting Motion for Relief From the Automatic Stay Under 11 U.S.C. § 362 (Real Property) (MANDATORY)	7/07
F 4001-10.TCS	Order Granting Trustee's Motion for Order Continuing the Automatic Stay, for Adequate Protection and for Delivery of Personal Property in Individual Case (MANDATORY)	10/05
F 4001-10.IS	Order Granting Motion for Order Imposing a Stay or Continuing the Automatic Stay (MANDATORY)	10/05
F 4001-10.UD	Order Granting Motion for Relief From the Automatic Stay under 11 U.S.C. § 362 (Unlawful Detainer) [formerly 351UD] (MANDATORY)	5/04
F 4001-1.2	Debtor's Further Certification of Cure of Monetary Default Underlying Judgment for Possession of Residential Property and Proof of Deposit (11 U.S.C. 362(l)(2)) (OPTIONAL)	10/05
F 4001-1.3	Lessor's Objection to Debtor's Certification and/or Debtor's Further Certification Concerning Residential Property and Notice of Hearing (11 U.S.C. §§ 362(I)(3)(A) (OPTIONAL)	10/05
F 4001 - 1.4	Lessor's Certification of (1) prepetition Eviction Action Seeking Possession of Residential Property Based on Debtor's Prepetition Endangerment of Property or Illegal Use of a Controlled Substance, or (2) Endangerment of the Property or Illegal Use of Controlled Substance within the last 30 Days (11 U.S.C. § 362(b)(I)(3)(A) (OPTIONAL)	10/05
F 4001 - 1.5	Debtor's Objection to Lessor's Certification and Notice of Hearing (11 U.S.C. § 362(b)(23)) (OPTIONAL)	10/05

Form Date	Form Title Mandatory/Optional	Last Revision
F 4001 - 2	Statement Pursuant to Local Bankruptcy Rule 4001-2 (Cash Collateral Stipulations) (OPTIONAL)	5/98
F 4008 - 1.1	Reaffirmation Agreement (Note: Replaced by Form 240A) Order on Reaffirmation Agreement Form 240B (MANDATORY) Replaced by Official Forms B240A and B240B	
F 4008 1.2	Notice of Hearing RE: Reaffirmation Agreement (MANDATORY)	10/05
F 4008 - 1.3	Order Disapproving Reaffirmation Agreement (OPTIONAL)	12/07
F 4008 - 1.4	Order Approving Reaffirmation Agreement with Notice of Entry (OPTIONAL)	12/07
F 5010 - 1.1M	Debtor's Motion to Reopen Case and For Extension of Time to File Debtor's Certification of Completion of Postpetition Instructional Course Concerning Personal Financial Management (NEW) (MANDATORY)	12/07
F 5010-.10	Order on Debtor's Motion to Reopen Case and For Extension of Time to File Debtor's Certification of Completion of Postpetition Instructional Course Concerning Personal Financial Management (NEW) (MANDATORY)	12/07
F 5075 - 1.1	Declaration to be Filed with Motion Establishing Administrative Procedures RE 28 U.S.C. § 156(c) (MANDATORY)	5/04
F 6004 - 2	Notice of Sale of Estate Property (OPTIONAL)	1/01
F 7004 -1	Summons and Notice of Status Conference (MANDATORY)	12/98
F 7016 - 1.1	Joint Status Report - Local Bankruptcy Rule 7016-1(a)(2) (OPTIONAL)	8/05
F 7016 - 1.1a	Joint Status Report - Additional Party Attachment (OPTIONAL)	8/05
F 7016 - 1.2	Status Conference and Scheduling Order Pursuant to Local Bankruptcy Rule 7016-1(a)(3) (OPTIONAL)	8/05

Form Date	Form Title Mandatory/Optional	Last Revision
F 7027 - 1	Request for Disclosure of Discovery Documents under Local Bankruptcy Rule 7027-1(d) (OPTIONAL)	10/01
F 9013 -1.1	Notice of Motion For: (Hearing Required) (MANDATORY)	9/98
F 9013 - 1.2	Notice of Motion under Local Bankruptcy Rule 9013-1(g)(1)(o) (OPTIONAL)	5/98
F 9013 - 1.3	Notice of Opposition and Request for a Hearing (OPTIONAL)	12/02
F 9013 - 1.4	Notice of Non-Opposition (OPTIONAL)	5/98
F 9013 - 1.5	Notice of Motion and Motion to Avoid Lien under 11 U.S.C. § 522(f) (Real Property) (OPTIONAL)	8/05
F 9013 - 1.6	Order on Motion to Avoid Lien under 11 U.S.C. § 522(f) (Real Property) (OPTIONAL)	1/01
F 9013 - 1.7	Notice of Motion and Motion to Avoid Lien under 11 U.S.C. § 522(f) (Personal Property) (OPTIONAL)	1/01
F 9013 - 1.8	Order on Motion to Avoid Lien under 11 U.S.C. § 522(f) (Personal Property) (OPTIONAL)	5/98
F 9013 - 1.9	Declaration Re: Entry of Order Without Hearing Pursuant to Local Bankruptcy Rule 9013-1(o) (OPTIONAL)	8/05
F9013 - 3.1	Proof of Service of Document (MANDATORY)	1/09
F 9021 - 1.1	Notice of Entered Order and Service List (MANDATORY)	1/09
F 9021 - 1.2	Request for Entry of Default under Local Bankruptcy Rule 9021-1 (OPTIONAL)	5/98
F 9021 - 1.3	Motion for Default Judgment under Local Bankruptcy Rule 9021-1 (OPTIONAL)	12/02
F 9021 - 1.4	Default Judgment (without prior judgment) (OPTIONAL)	11/99
F 9021 - 1.5	Default Judgment (based on prior judgment) (OPTIONAL)	11/99
F 9075 - 1	Order Shortening Time [Local Bankruptcy Rule 9075-1(b)] (Optional) (OPTIONAL)	3/08

6-4. Index of Court Forms

Form Number*	Form Title	Last Revision Date
TBA	Abbreviated Fee Schedule and Order of Documents	12/07
TBA	Abstract of Judgment	7/99
TBA	Affidavit and Request for Issuance of Writ of Execution	8/98
TBA	Amended Schedules(s) and/or Statements	11/03
TBA	Amended Statement of Social Security Number(s) or ITIN Number	12/07
TBA	Audio Recording of Court Proceedings Order Form	12/07
TBA	Change of Address	3/03
TBA	Corporate Ownership Statement Pursuant to FRBP 1007(a)(1) and 7007.1, and LBR 1002-5	4/07
TBA	Debtor's Certification of Compliance Under 11 U.S.C. § 1328(a) and Application for Entry of Discharge (PDF Fillable)	9/07
TBA	Debtor's Certification of Compliance Under 11 U.S.C. § 1328(a) and Application for Entry of Discharge (Interim Case) (PDF Fillable)	9/07
TBA	Debtor's Certification of Employment Income Pursuant to 11 U.S.C. Section 521(a)(1)(B)(iv)	2/06
TBA	Disclosure of Compensation of Bankruptcy Petition Preparer	12/03
TBA	Exhibit Register and Notice Re: Disposition of Exhibits	8/97
TBA	Instructions For Requesting An Order: (1) Authorizing You to Pay the Filing Fee in Installments; or (2) Excusing You From Paying the Filing Fee in a Chapter 7 Case	3/07
TBA	Mediation Forms	7/99
TBA	Mega Case Procedures Checklist	6/03
TBA	National Archive and Records Administration (NARA) Request Forms	9/05

Form Number*	Form Title	Last Revision Date
TBA	Notice of Address to be Used in Specific Case Pursuant to 11 USC § 342(e)	10/04
TBA	Notice of Appeal (PDF Fillable)	5/04
TBA	Notice of Motion and Motion For Approval of Cash Disbursement By the Trustee: Opportunity to Request Hearing: Declaration of Trustee and Order Thereon (Exhibit D)	3/00
TBA	Notice of Transcript(s) (Adversary)	5/02
TBA	Notice of Transcript(s) (Bankruptcy)	12/07
TBA	Petition Package (Chapter 7 - Complete)	12/07
TBA	Petition Package (Chapter 11 - Complete)	12/07
TBA	Petition Package (Chapter 13 - Complete)	12/07
TBA	Request for Courtesy Notification of Electronic Filing (NEF) and Instructions	9/08
TBA	Request for Special Notice	9/08
TBA	Statement Regarding Assistance of Non-Attorney with Respect to the Filing of Bankruptcy Case	12/03
TBA	Self-Help Clinic Transmittal Form	9/07
TBA	Transcript Order Form and Instructions	9/08
TBA	Trustee's Notice of Motion and Motion Under General Order 00-01 (Exhibit C)	3/00
TBA	Trustee's Notice of Motion and Motion Under General Order 00-01 (Exhibit D)	3/00
TBA	Verification fo Creditor Mailing List	10/05
TBA	Venue Disclosure Form for Corporations (VEN-C)	12/99
TBA	Venue Disclosure Form for Partnerships (VEN-P)	12/99

*Form Numbers are to be announced (TBA)

6-5. Mediation Information and Forms

Mediation information and forms may be downloaded free of charge from the court's web site at < www.cacb.uscourts.gov> Forms/Rules/ General Orders -> Mediation Forms or purchased from the Clerk's Office in the Los Angeles, Riverside, Santa Ana, San Fernando Valley, and Northern Divisions.

APPENDIX A Telephone Directory and Court Locations

1.0 United States Bankruptcy Court

Central District of California
Edward R. Roybal Federal Building and Courthouse
255 East Temple Street
Los Angeles, CA 90012

1.1 Clerk's Office Administration

a. Executive Management

Executive Officer/Clerk of Court . . . . (213) 894-6244

Secretary to Executive Officer/Clerk of Court . . . . . . (213) 894-6050

Chief Deputy, Operations . . . . (213) 894-7693

Senior Deputy-In-Charge . . . . (213) 894-7318

b. Administrative Services

Manager . . . . (213) 894-1175

Procurement Manager . . . . (213) 894-3836

c. Analysis & Information

Manager . . . . (213) 894-1296

d.

CM/ECF Help Desk . . . . (213) 894-2365

e. Financial Services

Financial Services Manager . . . . (213) 894-3836

f. Human Resources

Receptionist . . . . (213) 894-0213

24-Hour Job Information Line . . . . (213) 894-3129

g. Information Technology

Network Division Manager . . . . (213) 894-1659

Technology Administration Division Manager . . . . . . (213) 894-1155

Telecommunications Specialist (Videoconferencing) . (213) 894-8264

h. Office Services

Manager . . . . (213) 894-1740

2.0 Los Angeles Division

255 E. Temple Street, Suite 940
Los Angeles, CA 90012

2.1 Clerk's Office

a. General Information

Automated Telephone System; Self-Calendaring . . . . (213) 894-3118

Voice Case Information System (VCIS) 24-Hour Access . . . . . (213) 894-4111 (866) 522-6053

b. Administration

Deputy-in-Charge . . . . (213) 894-1156

c. Courtroom Services

Division Manager . . . . (213) 894-4902

Supervisor (Ahart, Bluebond, E. Carroll, Kaufman, Neiter, and Zurzolo Teams) . . . . (213) 894-2008

Supervisor (Bufford, Donovan, Robles, and Russell Teams) . . . (213) 894-1435

d. Case Initiation (Intake and Records)

Supervisor . . . . (213) 894-6751

Supervisor . . . . (213) 894-3141

2.2 Judges, Chambers, and Courtroom Services Staffs

a. Chief Judge Vincent P. Zurzolo (VZ), Courtroom 1368

Chambers . . . . (213) 894-3755

Law Clerk . . . . (213) 894-3721

Law Clerk . . . . (213) 894-3635

Courtroom Deputy . . . . (213) 894-5855

Court Recorder Contact . . . . (213) 894-3150

b. Judge Alan M. Ahart (AA), Courtroom 1375

Chambers . . . . (213) 894-3745

Law Clerk . . . . (213) 894-1530

Law Clerk .... (213) 894-3592
Courtroom Deputy .... (213) 894-5856
Court Recorder Contact .... (213) 894-6498

c. Judge Sheri Bluebond (BB), Courtroom 1475

Chambers .... (213) 894-8980
Law Clerk .... (213) 894-8981
Law Clerk .... (213) 894-8982
Courtroom Deputy .... (213) 894-3688
Court Recorder Contact .... (213) 894-1480

d. Judge Samuel L. Bufford (SB), Courtroom 1575

Chambers .... (213) 894-0992
Judicial Assistant .... (213) 894-0993
Law Clerk .... (213) 894-0994
Courtroom Deputy .... (213) 894-0995
Court Recorder Contact .... (213) 894-3303

e. Judge Ellen Carroll (EC), Courtroom 1639

Chambers .... (213) 894-4034
Law Clerk .... (213) 894-4033
Law Clerk .... (213) 894-4039
Courtroom Deputy .... (213) 894-4085
Court Recorder Contact .... (213) 894-6498

f. Judge Thomas B. Donovan (TD), Courtroom 1345

Chambers .... (213) 894-3728
Law Clerk .... (213) 894-3746
Law Clerk .... (213) 894-1577
Courtroom Deputy .... (213) 894-6172
Court Recorder Contact .... (213) 894-5011

g. Judge Victoria S. Kaufman (VK), Courtroom 1675

Chambers .... (213) 894-2552
Law Clerk .... (213) 894-2553
Law Clerk .... (213) 894-2494

Courtroom Deputy .... (213) 894-7341

Court Recorder Contact .... (213) 894-3720

h. Judge Richard M. Neiter (RN), Courtroom 1645

Chambers .... (213) 894-4080

Law Clerk .... (213) 894-4082

Law Clerk .... (213) 894-1804

Courtroom Deputy .... (213) 894-5860

Court Recorder Contact .... (213) 894-1485

i. Judge Ernest M. Robles (ER), Courtroom 1568

Chambers .... (213) 894-1522

Law Clerk .... (213) 894-0294

Law Clerk .... (213) 894-0295

Courtroom Deputy .... (213) 894-4843

Court Recorder Contact .... (213) 894-6233

j. Judge Barry Russell (BR), Courtroom 1668

Chambers .... (213) 894-6091

Judicial Assistant .... (213) 894-6092

Law Clerk .... (213) 894-6093

Courtroom Deputy .... (213) 894-3687

Court Recorder Contact .... (213) 894-7202

3.0 Riverside Division

3420 Twelfth Street, Room 125
Riverside, CA 92501-3819

3.1 Clerk's Office

a. General Information

General Information/Automated Telephone System .. (951) 774-1000

Voice Case Information System (VCIS) 24-Hour Access ..... (213) 894-4111 (866) 522-6053

b. Administration

Deputy-in-Charge .... (951) 774-1005

Secretary to Deputy-in-Charge .... (951) 774-1002

Operations Manager .... (951) 774-1003
Automation Systems Specialist .... (951) 774-1015
Case Initiation Supervisor .... (951) 774-1101

3.2 Judges, Chambers, and Courtroom Services Staffs

a. Judge Sheri Bluebond (BB), Courtroom 303

Chambers .... (213) 894-8980
Law Clerk .... (213) 894-8981
Law Clerk .... (213) 894-8982
Courtroom Deputy .... (951) 774-1085
Court Recorder Contact .... (951) 774-1085

b. Judge Peter H. Carroll (PC), Courtroom 304

Chambers .... (951) 774-1031
Judicial Assistant .... (951) 774-1031
Law Clerk .... (951) 774-1032
Courtroom Deputy .... (951) 774-1097
Court Recorder Contact .... (951) 774-1097

c. Judge Thomas B. Donovan (TD), Courtroom 303

Chambers .... (213) 894-3728
Law Clerk .... (213) 894-3746
Law Clerk .... (213) 894-1577
Courtroom Deputy .... (951) 774-1098
Court Recorder Contact .... (951) 774-1098

d. Judge Meredith A. Jury (MJ), Courtroom 302

Chambers .... (951) 774-1043
Judicial Assistant .... (951) 774-1043
Law Clerk .... (951) 774-1045
Courtroom Deputy .... (951) 774-1091
Court Recorder Contact .... (951) 774-1091

e. Judge Richard M. Neiter (RN), Courtroom 301

Chambers .... (213) 894-4080

Law Clerk . . . . (213) 894-4082

Law Clerk . . . . (213) 894-1804

Courtroom Deputy . . . . (951) 774-1075

Court Recorder Contact . . . . (951) 774-1075

4.0 Santa Ana Division

411 West Fourth Street, Suite 2030
Santa Ana, CA 92701-4593

4.1 Clerk's Office

a. General Information

General Information/Telephone Information System . (714) 338-5300

Voice Case Information System (VCIS) 24-Hour Access . . . . . (714) 338-5401 (866) 522-6053

b. Administration

Operations Manager . . . . (714) 338-5341

Secretary to Operations Manager . . . . (714) 338-5350

Automation Systems Specialist . . . . (714) 338-5339

4.2 Judges, Chambers, and Courtroom Services Staffs

a. Judge Theodor C. Albert (TA), Courtroom 5B

Chambers . . . . (714) 338-5430

Judicial Assistant . . . . (714) 338-5430

Law Clerk . . . . (714) 338-5432

Courtroom Deputy . . . . (714) 338-5383

Court Recorder Contact . . . . (714) 338-5381

b. Judge Robert Kwan (RK), Courtroom 5D

Chambers . . . . (714) 338-5450

Courtroom Deputy . . . . (714) 338-5366

Court Recorder Contact . . . . (714) 338-5369

c. Judge Erithe Smith (ES), Courtroom 5A

Chambers . . . . (714) 338-5440

Judicial Assistant . . . . (714) 338-5441

Law Clerk . . . . (714) 338-5443

Courtroom Deputy .... (714) 338-5360

Court Recorder Contact .... (714) 338-5361

5.0 Northern Division

1415 State Street
Santa Barbara, CA 93101-2511

5.1 Clerk's Office

a. General Information

General Information/Automated Telephone System .. (805) 884-4800

Voice Case Information System (VCIS) 24-Hour Access ..... (213) 894-4111 (866) 522-6053

b. Administration

Senior Deputy-in-Charge .... (805) 884-4876

Operations Supervisor .... (805) 884-4885

Information Systems Analyst .... (805) 884-4893

Team Leader .... (805) 884-4878

5.2 Judge, Chambers, and Courtroom Services Staffs

a. Judge Robin L. Riblet (RR), Courtroom 201

Chambers .... (805) 884-4860

Law Clerk .... (805) 884-4861

Law Clerk .... (805) 884-4868

Courtroom Deputy .... (805) 884-4873

Court Recorder Contact .... (805) 884-4873

b. Visiting Judge, Courtroom 202

Chambers .... (805) 884-4850

Judicial Assistant .... (805) 884-4850

Law Clerk .... (805) 884-4851

5.3 Courtroom Services Clerks

Select the last digit of the case number from the following table. The corresponding phone number will connect you to the clerk responsible for the case. For example, if the case number is ND94-10351RR, select the telephone number for digit 51.

Digits 01-50 .... (805) 884-4873

Digits 51-00 .... (805) 884-4881

6.0 San Fernando Valley Division

21041 Burbank Boulevard
Woodland Hills, CA 91367-6603

6.1 Clerk's Office

a. General Information

General Information/Automated Telephone System .. (818) 587-2900

Voice Case Information System (VCIS) 24-Hour Access ..... (213) 894-4111 (866) 522-6053

b. Administration

Senior Deputy-in-Charge .... (818) 587-2811

Secretary to Senior Deputy-in-Charge .... (818) 587-2885

Operations Manager .... (818) 587-2805

Operations Supervisor .... (818) 587-2860

6.2 Judges, Chambers, and Courtroom Services Staffs

a. Judge Geraldine Mund (GM), Courtroom 303

Chambers .... (818) 587-2840

Law Clerk .... (818) 587-2840

Law Clerk .... (818) 587-2843

Courtroom Services Specialist .... (818) 587-2833

Court Recorder Contact .... (818) 587-2853

b. Judge Kathleen Thompson (KT), Courtroom 301

Chambers .... (818) 587-2823

Law Clerk .... (818) 587-2825

Law Clerk .... (818) 587-2826

Courtroom Deputy .... (818) 587-2832

Court Recorder Contact .... (818) 587-2820

c. Judge Maureen A. Tighe (MT), Courtroom 302

Chambers .... (818) 587-2806

Law Clerk .... (818) 587-2808

Law Clerk .... (818) 587-2809

Courtroom Deputy .... (818) 587-2815

Court Recorder Contact .... (818) 587-2816

APPENDIX B Areas Served by the Central District of California

1.0 Areas Served by the Central District of California

1.1 Los Angeles Division.

Los Angeles County, except for the zip codes served by the San Fernando Valley Division.

1.2 Riverside Division.

San Bernardino and Riverside Counties.

1.3 Santa Ana Division.

Orange County.

1.4 Northern Division.

Santa Barbara and San Luis Obispo Counties and portions of Ventura County.

1.5 San Fernando Valley Division.

Portions of Los Angeles and Ventura Counties.

a. The geographic area served is approximately as follows:

1. Ventura/Los Angeles County line to the west;

2. Kern/Los Angeles County line to the north; and

3. San Bernardino/Los Angeles County line to the northeast.

b. Also included are the cities of San Fernando, North Hollywood, Studio City, Sherman Oaks, Encino, and Tarzana.

c. The southern border for this office is the Pacific Ocean at Malibu.

d. The following communities are served by the San Fernando Valley Division:

Acton

Agoura Hills

Calabasas

Canoga Park

Canyon Country

Castaic

Chatsworth

Edwards

Encino

Granada Hills

Lake Hughes

Lancaster

Lebec

Littlerock

Llano

Malibu

Mission Hills

Newbury Park

Newhall

North Hills

North Hollywood

Northridge

Oak Park

Pacoima

Palmdale

Panorama City

Pearblossom

Reseda

San Fernando

Santa Clarita

Sherman Oaks

Simi Valley

Stevenson Ranch

Studio City

e. The San Fernando Valley Division serves communities with the following zip codes:

90263
90265
90290
91301
91302
91303
91304
91305
91306
91307
91308
91309
91310
91311
91312
91313
91316
91319
91320
91321
91322
91324
91325
91326
91327
91328
91329
91330
91331
91333
91334

91335
91337
91340
91341
91342
91343
91344
91345
91346
91350
91351
91352
91353
91354
91355
91356
91357
91358
91359
91360
91361
91362
91363
91364
91365
91367
91371
91372
91376
91377
91380

91381
91382
91383
91384
91385
91386
91387
91388
91390
91392
91394
91395
91396
91399
91401
91402
91403
91404
91405
91406
91407
91408
91409
91410
91411
91412
91413
91416
91423
91426
91436

91470

91482

91495

91496

91497

91499

91601

91602

91603

91604

91605

91606

91607

91608

91609

91610

91611

91612

91614

91615

91616

91617

91618

93062

93063

93065

93093

93094

93510

93532

93534

93535

93536

93539

93543

93544

93550

93551

93552

93553

93563

93584

APPENDIX C United States Trustee Information

1.0 United States Trustee Information

1.1 The Office of the United States Trustee is an Executive Branch agency of the Department of Justice. Its responsibilities include monitoring the administration of bankruptcy cases and detecting bankruptcy fraud.

1.2 It is also responsible for appointing interim trustees (from a previously appointed panel of private individuals) to administer chapter 7 cases, lending support to and overseeing the Debtor in Possession in chapter 11 cases, and appointing standing trustees in chapter 13 cases.

1.3 See Appendix D for U. S. Trustee service addresses as required by FRBP 5003(e) and Local Bankruptcy Rule 2002-2(a)(4).

1.4 The locations and telephone numbers of the Office of the United States Trustee for the Central District of California are:

Division Served	Location	Telephone Number
Los Angeles	725 S. Figueroa Street, 26th Floor, Los Angeles, CA 90017	(213) 894-6811
Riverside	3685 Main Street, Suite 300, Riverside, CA 92501	(951) 276-6990
Santa Ana	411 W. Fourth Street, Suite 9041, Santa Ana, CA 92701	(714) 338-3400
Northern	128 E. Carrillo Street, Suite 126, Santa Barbara, CA 93101	

Division Served	Location	Telephone Number
San Fernando Valley	21051 Warner Center Lane, Suite 115, Woodland Hills, CA 91367	(818) 716-8800

1.5 For additional information regarding either the trustee program or individual trustees, contact the Office of the United States Trustee at:

725 South Figueroa Street
26th Floor
Los Angeles, CA 90017
(213) 894-6811

1.6 The locations of the trustee meeting rooms used for § 341(a) meetings and other trustee matters are:

Division Served	Meeting Room/Location	
Los Angeles	Chapters 7 and 13 725 South Figueroa Street Lobby Level Los Angeles, CA 90017	Chapter 11 725 South Figueroa Street 20th Floor Los Angeles, CA 90017
Riverside	3685 Main Street, First Floor Riverside, CA 92501	
Santa Ana	Chapters 7 and 11 411 West Fourth Street Third Floor Santa Ana, CA 92701	Chapter 13 411 West Fourth Street First Floor Santa Ana, CA 92701
Northern	1415 State Street Santa Barbara, CA 93101	
San Fernando Valley	21051 Warner Center Lane, Suite 115 Woodland Hills, CA 91367	

2.0 Panel of Interim Trustees, Los Angeles Division

James L. Brown
Law Offices of James L. Brown
3660 Wilshire Boulevard
Suite 1118
Los Angeles, CA 90048
Office (213) 251-2330

Richard K. Diamond
Danning, Gill, Diamond & Kollitz

2029 Century Park East
Third Floor
Los Angeles, CA 90067-3005
Office (310) 277-0077

Carolyn A. Dye
3435 Wilshire Blvd.
Suite 1045
Los Angeles, CA 90010
Office (310) 368-5000

Howard M. Ehrenberg
SulmeyerKupetz
333 South Hope Street
35th Floor
Los Angeles, CA 90071-1406
Office (213) 626-2311

Helen Ryan Frazer
Atkinson, Andelson, Loya, Ruud & Romo
17871 Park Plaza Drive
Suite 200
Cerritos, CA 90703
Office (562) 653-3200

David A. Gill
Danning, Gill, Diamond & Kollitz
2029 Century Park East
Third Floor
Los Angeles, CA 90067-3005
Office (310) 277-0077

Jeffrey I. Golden
Weiland, Golden, Smiley, Wang-Ekvall & Strok, LLP
650 Town Center Drive, Suite 950
Costa Mesa, CA 92626
Office (714) 966-1000

Rosendo Gonzalez
Gonzalez & Associates
515 South Figueroa Street
Suite 1970
Los Angeles, CA 90071
Office (213) 452-0071

David L. Hahn
Hahn Fife & Co., LLP

22342 Avenida Empresa
Suite 260
Rancho Santa Margarita, CA 92688
Office (949) 888-1010

Nancy Knupfer
Danning, Gill, Diamond & Kollitz
2029 Century Park East
3rd Floor
Los Angeles, CA 90067-3005
Office (310) 277-0077

Heide C. Kurtz
2515 South Western Avenue
Suite 11
San Pedro, CA 90732
Office (310) 832-3604

Sam S. Leslie
Leslie, Engell & Associates, LLP
6310 San Vicente Boulevard
Suite 320
Los Angeles, CA 90048
Office (323) 549-6900

John J. Menchaca
835 Wilshire Boulevard
Suite 300
Los Angeles, CA 90017
Office (213) 683-3317
Fax (213) 683-1883

Elissa D. Miller
SulmeyerKuptez
333 South Hope Street
35th Floor
Los Angeles, CA 90071
Office (213) 626-2311

R. Todd Neilson
Neilson, Elggren, LLP
10100 Santa Monica Boulevard
Suite 410
Los Angeles, CA 90067
Office (310) 282-9911

John P. Pringle
Roquemore, Pringle & Moore, Inc.

6055 East Washington Boulevard
Suite 608
Los Angeles, CA 90040-2466
Office (323) 724-3117

David L. Ray
Saltzburg, Ray & Bergman
12121 Wilshire Boulevard
Suite 600
Los Angeles, CA 90025
Office (310) 481-6700

Jason M. Rund
840 Apollo Street
Suite 351
El Segundo, CA 90245
Office (310) 640-1200
Fax (310) 640-0200

Alfred H. Siegel
Siegel, Gottlieb, Mangel & Levine, LLP
15233 Ventura Boulevard
9th Floor
Sherman Oaks, CA 91403
Office (818) 325-8441

Alberta P. Stahl
Law Offices of Alberta P. Stahl
221 North Figueroa Street
Suite 1200
Los Angeles, CA 90012
Office (213) 580-7977

Edward M. Wolkowitz
Robinson, Diamant & Wolkowitz
1888 Century Park East
Suite 1500
Los Angeles, CA 90067
Office (310) 277-7400

Timothy Yoo
Robinson, Diamant & Wolkowitz
1888 Century Park East
Suite 1500
Los Angeles, CA 90067
Office (310) 277-7400

3.0 Chapter 13 Standing Trustees, Los Angeles Division

Chapter 13 cases assigned to Judges Ahart, E. Carroll, Donovan, Robles, and Albert are assigned to:

Kathy A. Dockery
700 South Flower Street
Suite 1950
Los Angeles, CA 90017
Office (213) 996-4400

Nancy K. Curry
606 South Olive Street
Suite 1850
Los Angeles, CA 90014
Office (213) 689-3014

4.0 Panel of Interim Trustees, Riverside Division

Karl T. Anderson
Karl T. Anderson & Co.
700 East Tahquitz Canyon Way
Suite H
Palm Springs, CA 92262
Office (760) 778-4889

Christopher R. Barclay
Mack Barclay, Inc.
600 Anton Boulevard
Suite 1350
Costa Mesa, CA 92626
Office (714) 662-0800

Sandra L. Bendon
15411 Redhill Avenue
Suite A
Tustin, CA 92780
Office (714) 258-7992

Arturo M. Cisneros
3403 Tenth Street
Suite 711
Riverside, CA 92501
Office (951) 682-9705

Robert L. Goodrich
3600 Lime Street
Building 2, Suite 221
Riverside, CA 92501
Office (951) 341-9304

Norman L. Hanover
3880 Lemon Street, 5th Floor
Riverside, CA 92502
Office (951) 680-1257

Stephen Speier
3403 Tenth Street
Suite 742
Riverside, CA 92501
Office (951) 778-3071

Robert Whitmore
3600 Lime Street
Suite 611
Riverside, CA 92501
Office (951) 276-9292

Patricia J. Zimmerman
P. J. Zimmerman Trustee Office
31566 Railroad Canyon Road
Suite 306
Canyon Lake, CA 92587
Office (951) 244-8544

5.0 Chapter 13 Standing Trustee, Riverside Division

Rodney A. Danielson
3435 Fourteenth Street
Suite 100
Riverside, CA 92501
Office (951) 826-8000

6.0 Panel of Interim Trustees, Santa Ana Division

Thomas H. Casey
Law Office of Thomas H. Casey
22342 Avenida Empresa
Suite 260
Rancho Santa Margarita, CA 92688
Office (949) 766-8787

Charles W. Daff
2122 North Broadway
Suite 210
Santa Ana, CA 92706
Office (714) 541-0301

James J. Joseph
Danning, Gill, Diamond & Kollitz

2029 Century Park East
3rd Floor
Los Angeles, CA 90067-3005
Office (310) 277-0077

Weneta M. A. Kosmala
P. O. Box 16279
Irvine, CA 92623-9998
Office (714) 708-8190

Richard A. Marshack
Shulman, Hodges & Bastian
26632 Towne Center Drive
Suite 300
Foothill Ranch, CA 92610-2808
Office (949) 340-3400

Karen S. Naylor
P.O. Box 504
Santa Ana, CA 92701
Office (949) 262-1748

John M. Wolfe
5450 Trabuco Road
Irvine, CA 92620
Office (800) 436-4646

7.0 Chapter 13 Standing Trustee, Santa Ana Division

Amrane Cohen
770 The City Drive South
Suite 3300
Orange, CA 92868
Office (714) 621-0200

8.0 Panel of Interim Trustees, Northern Division

Sandra K. McBeth
2450 Professional Parkway
Suite 240
Santa Maria, CA 93455
Office (805) 938-9236

Jerry Namba
625 East Chapel Street
Santa Maria, CA 93454
Office (805) 922-2575

David Y. Farmer
Farmer & Ready

1254 Marsh Street
San Luis Obispo, CA 93401
Office (805) 541-5390

9.0 Chapter 13 Standing Trustee, Northern Division

Elizabeth F. Rojas
15301 Ventura Boulevard
Building B, Suite 400
Sherman Oaks, CA 91403
Office (818) 933-5700

10.0 Panel of Interim Trustees, San Fernando Valley Division

Amy L. Goldman
Lewis, Brisbois, Bisgaard & Smith
221 North Figueroa Street
Suite 1200
Los Angeles, CA 90012
Office (213) 250-1800

David K. Gottlieb
Siegel, Gottlieb, Mangel & Levine, LLP
15233 Ventura Boulevard, 9th Floor
Sherman Oaks, CA 91403-2201
Office (818) 325-8441

David R. Hagen
Merritt & Hagen, PC
6320 Canoga Avenue
Suite 1400
Woodland Hills, CA 91367
Office (818) 992-1940

Brad Krasnoff
Lewis, Brisbois, Bisgaard & Smith
221 North Figueroa Street
Suite 1200
Los Angeles, CA 90012
Office (213) 250-1800

David Seror
Rein, Evans & Sestanovich, LLP
1925 Century Park East, 16th Floor
Los Angeles, CA 90067
Office (310) 551-3100

Diane Weil
Rein, Evans & Sestanovich, LLP

1925 Century Park East, 16th Floor
Los Angeles, CA 90067
Office (310) 551-3100
(310) 551-2096

Nancy H. Zamora
Citibank Center
444 South Flower Street
Suite 1550
Los Angeles, CA 90071
Office (213) 892-0254

11.0 Chapter 13 Standing Trustee, San Fernando Valley Division

Elizabeth F. Rojas
15301 Ventura Boulevard
Building B, Suite 400
Sherman Oaks, CA 91403
Office (818) 933-5700

APPENDIX D Register of Federal and State Government Unit Addresses [FRBP 5003(e)]

1.0 Federal Rules of Bankruptcy Procedure 5003(e)

Pursuant to Federal Rules of Bankruptcy Procedure 5003(e) effective December 1, 2000, federal and state agencies filed a statement with the court designating their mailing addresses. See Local Bankruptcy Rule 2002-2 for related noticing requirements.

2.0 Federal Agencies

2.1 Internal Revenue Service (IRS)

Internal Revenue Service
P.O. Box 21126
Philadelphia, PA 19114

2.2 Securities Exchange Commission

Securities Exchange Commission
5670 Wilshire Boulevard, 11th Floor
Los Angeles, CA 90036

2.3 United States Trustee.

a. Master Mailing List.

The Office of the United States Trustee shall be included in the Master Mailing List.

b. Electronic Notice and Service.

The Office of the United States Trustee consented to electronic notice and service of documents, effective April 1, 2008 (see Public Notice 08-007). Therefore, service of documents by U.S. mail is not necessary in cases a Notice of Electronic Filing is generated upon filing a document with the court electronically in CM/ECF.

c. Notice and Service by U.S. Mail.

When service by U.S. mail is necessary, papers shall be served on the Office of the United States Trustee at the following addresses:

1. Papers in All Cases and Proceedings Assigned to Los Angeles Judges:

United States Trustee
725 South Figueroa Street, 26th Floor
Los Angeles, CA 90017

2. Papers in All Cases and Proceedings Assigned to Santa Ana Division Judges:

United States Trustee
411 West Fourth Street, Suite 9041
Santa Ana, CA 92701-4593

3. Papers in All Cases and Proceedings Assigned to Riverside Division Judges:

United States Trustee
3685 Main Street, Suite 300
Riverside, CA 92501

4. Papers in All Cases and Proceedings Assigned to Northern Division and San Fernando Valley Judges:

United States Trustee
21051 Warner Center Lane, Suite 115
Woodland Hills, CA 91367

2.4 United States Attorney.

In contested matters and adversary proceedings involving the United States (other than those involving the Internal Revenue Service), the United States Attorney and Attorney General shall be served at the following addresses:

a. Civil Process Clerk

United States Attorney's Office

Federal Building, Room 7516
300 North Los Angeles Street
Los Angeles, CA 90012

b. Attorney General

United States Department of Justice
Ben Franklin Station
P. O. Box 683
Washington, DC 20044

3.0 State Agencies

3.1 State of California Employment Development Department

Employment Development Department
Bankruptcy Group MIC 92E
P. O. Box 826880
Sacramento, CA 94280-0001

3.2 State of California Franchise Tax Board

Franchise Tax Board
Attention: Bankruptcy
P. O. Box 2952
Sacramento, CA 95812-2952

APPENDIX E Law Library Locations

1.0 Law Libraries

1.1 Law libraries are located throughout the Central District.

1.2 At the time of publication, the locations and hours of operation are as follows:

County Location and Telephone Number	Hours of Operation
Los Angeles Court of Appeals Law Library 125 South Grand Avenue Pasadena, CA 91105 (626) 229-7192	Monday - Friday, 8:30 a.m. - 5:00 p.m.
Edward R. Roybal Federal Building 255 East Temple Street Street Level, Room 132 Los Angeles, CA 90012 (213) 894-8900	Monday - Friday, 8:30 a.m. - 4:30 p.m.

Los Angeles County Law Library 301 West First Street Los Angeles, CA 90012 (213) 629-3531	Monday - Friday, 8:30 a.m. - 6:00 p.m. Saturday, 9:00 a.m. - 5:00 p.m.
Riverside Riverside County Law Library 3989 Lemon Street Riverside, CA 92501-3674 (951) 275-6390	Monday - Thursday, 8:00 a.m - 7:00 p.m. Friday, 8:00 a.m. - 5:00 p.m. Saturday, 9:00 a.m. - 1:00 p.m.
San Bernardino County Law Library 402 North "D" Street San Bernardino, CA 92401 (909) 885-3020	Monday - Thursday, 8:30 a.m. - 7:00 p.m. Friday, 8:30 a.m. - 5:00 p.m. Saturday, 9:00 a.m. - 3:00 p.m.
San Luis Obispo San Luis Obispo County Law Library County Government Center 1050 Monterey Street, Room 125 San Luis Obispo, CA 93408 (805) 781-5855	Monday and Friday, 8:30 a.m. - 4:30 p.m. Saturday, 10:00 a.m. - 3:00 p.m.
Santa Ana Orange Law Library Civic Center Plaza 515 North Flower Street, Building #32 Santa Ana, CA 92703 (714) 834-3397	Monday - Thursday, 8:00 a.m. - 8:00 p.m. Friday, 8:00 a.m. - 6:00 p.m. Saturday, 9:00 a.m. - 6:00 p.m.
Santa Barbara Santa Barbara County Courthouse 1100 Anacapa Street Santa Barbara, CA 93101 (805) 568-2296	Monday - Friday, 8:00 a.m. - 5:00 p.m. Saturday, 12:00 p.m. - 4:45 p.m.
Ventura Ventura County Law Library Government Center, Hall of Justice 800 South Victoria Avenue First Floor Ventura, CA 93009 (805) 642-8982	Tuesday & Wednesday, 8:00 a.m - 8:00 p.m. Friday, 8:00 a.m. - 5:00 p.m. Saturday, 9:00 a.m. - 4:00 p.m.

APPENDIX F Serving Judge's Copy of Documents

1.0 Serving Judge's Copy of Documents [LBR 5005-2(d)]

1.1 Local Bankruptcy Rule 5005-2(d) requires that a copy of every document filed must be served on the judge who presides over the bankruptcy case or adversary proceeding.

1.2 The Proof of Service of Document must indicate the date and manner in which the judge was served, and must be on Local Bankruptcy Rules (LBR) form F 9013-3.1 unless the Proof of Service of Document has been included in the LBR form being used.

2.0 Deadline, Method, and Address to Serve the Judge

Consult the following charts to determine the deadline, the method, and the address to serve the judge.

2.1 Deadline and Method

What is the Deadline for Serving the Judge's Copy?

What Methods Can I Use to Serve the Judge?

If the document relates to a hearing, and the hearing is 14 days or more after the document is filed: the document must be served on the judge no later than 24 hours after the document is filed, by personal delivery, overnight mail, or U.S. mail.

If the document relates to a hearing, and the hearing is fewer than 14 days after the document is filed: the document must be served on the judge no later than 24 hours after the document is filed, by personal delivery or overnight mail.

In no event shall the document arrive in chambers no later than 2 court days prior to the hearing.

If the document is NOT related to a hearing The document must be served on the judge no later than 24 hours after the document is filed, by personal delivery, overnight mail or U.S. mail.

2.2 Proof of Service

Should I Put the Judge's Name on the Proof of Service?

YES - Use mandatory LBR Form F 9013-3.1 "Proof of Service of Document" unless the "Proof of Service of Document" has been included in the LBR form being filed.

The judge will be in either:

- Category II. "Served by U.S. Mail or Overnight Mail" or
- Category III. "Served by Personal Delivery"

2.3 Judge's Address

At What Address do I Serve the Judge's Copy?

Division & Mailing Address Judge Name Suite # for Regular or Overnight Mail Location for Personal Delivery

NORTHERN DIVISION

U.S. Bankruptcy Court
1415 State Street
Santa Barbara, CA 93101-2511

Robin L. Riblet 103 Bin outside of Suite 103

SFV DIVISION

U.S. Bankruptcy Court
21041 Burbank Blvd.
Woodland Hills, CA 91367-6606

Geraldine Mund 342 Bin outside of Elevators on 3rd Floor

Kathleen Thompson

305 Bin outside of Elevators on 3rd Floor

Maureen A. Tighe 325 Bin outside of Elevators on 3rd Floor

SANTA ANA DIVISION

U.S. Bankruptcy Court,
Ronald Reagan Federal Building
411 W. Fourth Street
Santa Ana, CA 92701-4593

Theodor C. Albert 5085 Bin outside of Room 5097

Robert Kwan 5165 Bin outside of Room 5097

Erithe A. Smith 5041 Bin outside of Room 5097

RIVERSIDE DIVISION

U.S. Bankruptcy Court,
3420 Twelfth Street
Riverside, CA 92501-3819

Sheri Bluebond See L.A. Division

Bin outside of L.A. Suite 1482

Peter H. Carroll 365 Bin outside of R.S. Courtroom 304

Thomas Donovan See L.A. Division

Bin outside of R.S. Courtroom 303,

Ch 11 cases - Bin outside of L.A. Suite 1352

Meredith A. Jury 345 Bin outside of R.S. Courtroom 302

Richard Neiter See L.A. Division

Bin outside of R.S. Courtroom 301

LOS ANGELES DIVISION

U.S. Bankruptcy Court,
Roybal Federal Building
255 E. Temple Street
Los Angeles, CA 90012-3332

Alan M. Ahart 1382 Bin outside of Suite 1382

Sheri Bluebond 1482 Bin outside of Suite 1482

Samuel L. Bufford 1582 Bin outside of Courtroom 1575

Ellen Carroll 1634 Bin outside of Suite 1634

Thomas B. Donovan 1352 Bin outside of Suite 1352

Victoria S. Kaufman 1682 Bin outside of Suite 1682

Richard M. Neiter 1652 Bin outside of Suite 1652

Ernest M. Robles 1560 Bin outside of Suite 1560

Barry Russell 1660 Bin outside of Suite 1660

Vincent P. Zurzolo 1360 Bin outside of Suite 1360

HELPFUL HINTS

2009-001 Pursuant to LBR 1017-1(a) and 3015(q)(2)(A), it is no longer necessary to lodge a proposed order when filing a Debtor's Notice of Conversion under 11 U.S.C. §§ 1208(a) or 1307(a) if there is no previous conversion. Under our new procedure and rules effective January 5, 2009, the Court will give notice of the conversion to all creditors, interested parties, and the United States trustee upon the filing by the debtor of the notice of conversion and a proof of service evidencing that the notice of conversion was served upon the chapter 13 trustee and the United States trustee.

General Order 96-02 Judicial Workload Equalization Pilot Program

The Ninth Circuit has established a Workload Equalization Pilot Program that allows for the hearing and determination of all issues through trial in certain adversary proceedings by designated judges from other districts within the Ninth Circuit.

IT IS HEREBY ORDERED that, effective immediately, the United States Bankruptcy Court for the Central District of California implement the Judicial Workload Equalization Pilot Program.

For adversary complaints which have been selected for this program, the procedure for filing papers with the Court is as follows:

(a) The parties shall continue to file the original and one copy of the adversary complaint with the Clerk of the United States Bankruptcy Court, Central District of California. The Clerk will transmit a copy of the complaint to the designated judge of the other participating court;

(b) Except in those instances where a judge's signature is required, the parties shall continue to file the original and one copy of all subsequent pleadings with the Clerk of the United States Bankruptcy Court, Central District of California. In addition, the parties shall mail a separate copy of all subsequent pleadings directly to the chambers of the judge of the other participating court;

(c) Where a judge's signature is required, such as on a default judgment, summary judgment or pre-trial order, the original and one copy shall be mailed directly to the chambers of the judge of the other participating court and a copy filed with the Central District of California Bankruptcy Court.

Proceedings requiring physical appearances will continue to be held in Los Angeles. It is the intent of the program that issues be resolved via teleconferencing whenever possible; however, it will be at the discretion of the judge hearing the matter whether an in-court appearance will be required or whether teleconferencing will be utilized.

DATED: March 27, 1996

General Order 96-06 Order Grantable As A Matter Of Course By The Clerk Of The Bankruptcy Court

WHEREAS, the Court may issue any order, process, or judgment that is necessary or appropriate to carry out provisions of the Bankruptcy Code pursuant to Section 105(a) of the Bankruptcy Code,

IT IS HEREBY ORDERED that the following orders may be entered by the Clerk of Bankruptcy Court without further direction from the Court as a matter of course:

1. ORDER FIXING TIME TO FILE CLAIMS (FOR POSSIBLE DIVIDENDS)
2. ORDER FIXING TIME TO FILE CLAIMS (FOR SURPLUS OF FUNDS)
3. ORDER FOR CREDITORS TO FILE CLAIMS INCURRED AFTER THE COMMENCEMENT OF THE CHAPTER 11 PROCEEDINGS
4. ORDER TO COMPLY WITH FRBP 1007 AND 3015(b) AND

NOTICE OF INTENT TO DISMISS CASE UNDER 11 U.S.C. SECTION 109(g)(1)

5. ORDER OF DISMISSAL FOR FAILURE TO FILE COMPLETE CASE COMMENCEMENT DOCUMENTATION
6. ORDER OF DISMISSAL FOR FAILURE TO FILE COMPLETE CASE COMMENCEMENT DOCUMENTATION WITH 180-DAYS RESTRICTION
7. ORDER OF DISMISSAL FOR FAILURE TO FILE SCHEDULES, STATEMENTS, OR PLAN WITH 180-DAY RESTRICTION
8. ORDER OF DISMISSAL FOR FAILURE TO FILE SCHEDULES, STATEMENTS, OR PLAN
9. ORDER OF DISMISSAL FOR FAILURE TO APPEAR AT 341(a) MEETING OF CREDITORS WITH 180-DAY RESTRICTION
10. ORDER OF DISMISSAL FOR FAILURE TO APPEAR AT 341(a) MEETING OF CREDITORS (BUSINESS ONLY)
11. ORDER DISMISSING PROCEEDINGS FOR FAILURE TO PAY CLERK'S FILING FEES
12. ORDER OF DISMISSAL FOR FAILURE TO COMPLY WITH INSTALLMENT PAYMENT SCHEDULE
13. ORDER OF DISMISSAL FOR FAILURE TO COMPLY WITH LOCAL RULE 105(6)(c)—FILING OF DISKETTE FOR CASES WITH MORE THAN 100 CREDITORS OR EQUITY HOLDERS
14. ORDER TO SHOW CAUSE RE: DISMISSAL FOR FAILURE TO PAY CONVERSION FEE
15. ORDER OF DISMISSAL FOR FAILURE TO PAY CONVERSION FEE
16. ORDER CLOSING A DISMISSED CASE
17. ORDER DISCHARGING DEBTOR.
18. ORDER DISCHARGING DEBTOR AFTER COMPLETION OF CHAPTER 12 PLAN
19. ORDER DISCHARGING DEBTOR AFTER COMPLETION OF CHAPTER 13 PLAN
20. ORDER TO SHOW CAUSE RE: DISMISSAL FOR FAIL-

URE TO REPAY FILING FEES FOR INSUFFICIENTLY FUNDED CHECK

21. ORDER TO SHOW CAUSE RE: DISMISSAL FOR FAILURE TO COMPLY WITH LOCAL RULE 105(6)(c)—FILING OF DISKETTE FOR CASES WITH MORE THAN 100 CREDITORS OR EQUITY HOLDERS
22. ORDER TO SHOW CAUSE RE: DISMISSAL FOR NONPAYMENT OF FILING FEES PURSUANT TO FRBP 1006(a) OR (b)
23. ORDER VACATING THE ORDER OF CONVERSION (DUE TO CLERICAL ERROR)
24. ORDER VACATING DISCHARGE (DUE TO CLERICAL ERROR)
25. ORDER VACATING ORDER OF DISMISSAL (DUE TO CLERICAL ERROR)
26. ORDER FOR RELIEF AND ORDER TO FILE SCHEDULES, STATEMENTS, AND LISTS
27. ORDER TO FILE FINAL REPORT AND ACCOUNT AND SCHEDULE OF UNPAID DEBTS INCURRED AFTER COMMENCEMENT OF THE CHAPTER 11, 12, OR 13 PETITION PURSUANT TO FRBP 1019(5)
28. ORDER DISCHARGING TRUSTEE AND CLOSING CASE.

DATED: August 12, 1996

AMENDED SCHEDULES

UNITED STATES BANKRUPTCY COURT
CENTRAL DISTRICT OF CALIFORNIA

Filer's Name: ____________ Atty Name (if applicable): ____________

Street Address: ____________ CA Bar No. (if applicable): ____________

____________ Atty Fax No. (if applicable): ____________

Filer's Telephone No.: ____________

In re:	Case No.: ____________
	Chapter 7 ______ 11 ______ 13 ______

AMENDED SCHEDULE(S) AND/OR STATEMENT(S)

A filing fee of $26.00 is required to amend any or all of Schedules "D" through "F." An addendum mailing list is also required as an attachment if creditors are being added to the creditors list. Is/are creditor(s) being added? Yes ________ No ________

Indicate below which schedule(s) and/or statement(s) is(are) being amended.

A ____ B ____ C ____ D ____ E ____ F ____ G ____ H ____ I ____ J ____

Statement of Social Security Number(s) ____ Statement of Financial Affairs ____

Statement of Intention ____ Other ____

NOTE: IT IS THE RESPONSIBILITY OF THE DEBTOR TO MAIL COPIES OF ALL AMENDMENTS TO THE TRUSTEE AND TO NOTICE ALL CREDITORS LISTED IN THE AMENDED SCHEDULE(S) AND TO COMPLETE AND FILE WITH THE COURT THE PROOF OF SERVICE ON THE BACK OF THIS PAGE.

I/We, ________________________, the person(s) who subscribed to the foregoing Amended Schedule(s) and/or Statement(s) do hereby declare under penalty of perjury that the foregoing is true and correct.

DATED: ____________________

____
Debtor Signature

____
Co-Debtor Signature

****FOR COURT USE ONLY****

SEE REVERSE SIDE**

B-1008 *Revised November 2003*

CDCAL-311 C.D. CALIFORNIA

PROOF OF SERVICE

I hereby certify that a copy of the Amendment(s) was(were) mailed to the Trustee and that notice was given to the additional creditors listed.

DATED: ______________________ ______________________________
Print or Type Name

____
Signature

(SEE ATTACHED MAILING LIST.)

Abstract of Judgment

☐ Recording requested by a return to:	FOR COURT USE ONLY
UNITED STATES BANKRUPTCY COURT **CENTRAL DISTRICT OF CALIFORNIA**	
In re:	CASE NUMBER
Debtor	ADVERSARY NUMBER
Plaintiff vs. Defendant	**ABSTRACT OF JUDGMENT**

The Judgment Creditor applies for an abstract of judgment and represents:

1. The Judgment Debtor's:
   a. Name and address ______________________

   ____

   ____

   ☐ Address Unknown

   b. Driver's License No. ______________________ ☐ Unknown

   c. Social Security No. ______________________ ☐ Unknown

2. The Summons was personally served at, or mail to (address):

   ____

3. ☐ Information regarding additional judgment debtors is shown on reverse side.

Dated: ______________________ ______________________
(Signature of Judgment Creditor or Attorney)

(Continued on Reverse Side)

Revised July 1999

CDCAL-313 C.D. CALIFORNIA

Abstract of Judgment - Page Two

In re (SHORT TITLE) Debtor(s).	CHAPTER ______ ADVERSARY NO.: ______

4. I certify that in the above-entitled action and Court, Judgment was entered on ____________________,

in favor of ____________________ and against ____________________

for $ ____________________ Principal,

$ ____________________ Interest,

$ ____________________ Attorney's Fees, and

$ ____________________ Costs.

A lien in favor of a judgment creditor is:

☐ not endorsed on the judgment.

☐ endorsed on the judgment as follows:

1. Amount $ ____________________
2. In favor of (name) ____________________

A stay of execution has:

☐ not been ordered by the Court.

☐ been ordered by the Court effective until (date): ____________________

Attested this ____________________ day of ____________________.

JON D. CERETTO
Clerk of the Bankruptcy Court

By: ____________________
Deputy Clerk

Information regarding additional judgment debtors:

____

____

____

____

Revised July 1999

Addendum to Chapter 13 Plan Concerning Debtors Who are Repaying Debt Secured by a Mortgage on Real Property or a Lien on Personal Property the Debtor Occupies as the Debtor's Principal Residence (F 3015-1.1A)

Attorney or Party Name, Address, Telephone & FAX Numbers, and California State Bar Number ☐ Individual appearing without counsel ☐ Attorney for:	FOR COURT USE ONLY
UNITED STATES BANKRUPTCY COURT CENTRAL DISTRICT OF CALIFORNIA	
In re Debtor(s).	CHAPTER 13 CASE NO.

Addendum to Chapter 13 Plan Concerning Debtors Who are Repaying Debt Secured by a Mortgage on Real Property or a Lien on Personal Property the Debtor Occupies as the Debtor's Principal Residence

(A) **Scope: Consumer Debts Secured by a Mortgage on Real Property, or Secured by Manufactured Housing that the Debtor Occupies as the Debtor's Principal Residence**

(1) For purposes of this Addendum, which is incorporated into the debtor's chapter 13 plan (the "Plan"), the term "Mortgage Creditor" includes all creditors whose claims represent consumer debts secured in whole or in part by a security interest in real property or manufactured housing, which real property or manufactured housing constitutes the debtor's principal residence. The provisions of this Addendum are effective until the earlier of: (a) dismissal of the case; (b) the closing of the case; (c) entry of an order granting the debtor a discharge; and (d) entry of an order terminating the automatic stay under 11 U.S.C. § 362(d) as the stay applies to the Mortgage Creditor.

(2) Except as provided in paragraphs (3) and (4) below, if the Mortgage Creditor provided monthly statements to the debtor pre-petition, the Mortgage Creditor must provide monthly statements to the debtor. The monthly statements must contain at least the following information concerning post-petition mortgage payments to be made outside the Plan:

In re	CHAPTER 13
Debtor(s).	CASE NUMBER

(a) The date of the statement and the date the next payment is due;

(b) The amount of the current monthly payment;

(c) The portion of the payment attributable to escrow, if any;

(d) The post-petition amount past due, if any, and from what date;

(e) Any outstanding post-petition late charges;

(f) The amount and date of receipt of all payments received since the date of the last statement;

(g) A telephone number and contact information that the debtor or the debtor's attorney may use to obtain reasonably prompt information regarding the loan and recent transactions; and

(h) The proper payment address.

(3) No monthly statement will be required in this case where post-petition mortgage payments are to be made to the chapter 13 trustee through the Plan, unless the amount of the monthly payment is scheduled to change (because of adjustable interest rate, charges paid by the Mortgage Creditor for taxes, insurance, attorney's fees or any other expenses or fees charged or incurred by the Mortgage Creditor, such as property inspection fees, servicing fees or appraisal fees). If a Mortgage Creditor does send a monthly statement to the debtor or the chapter 13 trustee and the statement complies with subsection (B)(2) below, the Mortgage Creditor is entitled to the protections set out in such subsection.

(4) If, pre-petition, the Mortgage Creditor provided the debtor with "coupon books" or some other pre-printed, bundled evidence of payments due, the Mortgage Creditor is not required to provide monthly statements under subsection (2) of this section. However, the Mortgage Creditor must supply the debtor with additional coupon books as needed or requested in writing by the debtor. If a Mortgage Creditor does send a monthly statement to the debtor or the chapter 13 trustee and the statement complies with subsection (B)(2) below, the Mortgage Creditor is entitled to the protections set out in such subsection.

(5) The Mortgage Creditor must provide the following information to the debtor upon the reasonable written request of the debtor:

(a) The principal balance of the loan;

(b) The original maturity date;

(c) The current interest rate;

Addendum to Chapter 13 Plan Concerning Debtors Who are Repaying Debt Secured by a Mortgage on Real Property or a Lien on Personal Property the Debtor Occupies as the Debtor's Principal Residence - *Page 3 of 5*

In re	CHAPTER 13
Debtor(s).	CASE NUMBER

(d) The current escrow balance, if any;

(e) The interest paid year to date; and

(f) The property taxes paid year to date, if any.

(6) The Mortgage Creditor must provide the following information to the debtor, the debtor's attorney and, when the debtor is making ongoing mortgage or arrearage payments through the chapter 13 trustee, the chapter 13 trustee, at least quarterly, and upon reasonable written request of the debtor or the chapter 13 trustee: (a) any other amounts due or proposed change in payments arising from an adjustable interest rate, charges paid by the Mortgage Creditor for taxes, insurance, attorney's fees or any other expenses or fees charged or incurred by the Mortgage Creditor, such as property inspection fees, servicing fees or appraisal fees; (b) the nature of the expense or charge; and (c) the date of the payment.

(7) If the secured consumer debt payable to the Mortgage Creditor is not modified by or paid through the Plan and the Mortgage Creditor believes the debtor to be in default, the Mortgage Creditor must send a letter alleging such default to the debtor and the debtor's attorney upon any perceived or actual default by the debtor and before taking any steps to modify the automatic stay.

(B) **Form of Communication; Modification of the Automatic Stay; and Motions for Order to Show Cause**

(1) For the purposes of this Addendum, Mortgage Creditors will be considered to have sent the requisite documents or monthly statements to the debtor or the debtor's attorney, as applicable, when the Mortgage Creditor has placed the required document in any form of communication, which in the usual course would result in the debtor and the debtor's attorney receiving the document, to the address that the debtor and the debtor's attorney last provided to the Court. The form of communication may include, but is not limited to, electronic communication, United States Postal Service or use of a similar commercial communications carrier.

(2) To the extent that the automatic stay arising in this case would otherwise prohibit such conduct, the automatic stay is modified as follows: Mortgage Creditors who provide account information or monthly statements under subsections (A)(1-6) above will not be found to have violated the automatic stay by doing so, and Mortgage Creditors may contact the debtor about the status of insurance coverage on property that is collateral for the Mortgage Creditor's claim, may respond to inquiries and requests for information about the account from the debtor and may send the debtor statements, payment coupons or other correspondence that the Mortgage Creditor sends to its non-debtor customers, without violating the automatic stay. In order for communication to be protected under this provision, the communication must indicate it is provided for information purposes and does not constitute demand for payment.

This form is optional. It has been approved for use by the United States Bankruptcy Court for the Central District of California.

In re	CHAPTER 13
Debtor(s).	CASE NUMBER

(3) As a result of a Mortgage Creditor's alleged non-compliance with this Addendum, the debtor may file a Motion for Order to Show Cause in compliance with Local Bankruptcy Rule 9020-1 no earlier than sixty days after the Mortgage Creditor's failure to comply with sections (A) or (B). Before filing the motion, the debtor must make good faith attempts in writing to contact the Mortgage Creditor and to determine the cause of any non-compliance, and must indicate in the Motion for Order to Show Cause the good faith steps taken, together with a summary description of any response provided by the Mortgage Creditor.

(4) If a Mortgage Creditor's regular billing system can provide a statement to the debtor that substantially complies with this Addendum, but does not fully conform to all of its requirements, the Mortgage Creditor may request that the debtor accept such statement. If the debtor declines to accept the non-conforming statement, a Mortgage Creditor may file a motion, on notice to the debtor, the debtor's attorney and the chapter 13 trustee, seeking a declaration of the Court that cause exists to allow such non-conforming statements to satisfy the Mortgage Creditor's obligations under this Addendum. For good cause shown, the Court may grant a waiver for purposes of this case and for either a limited or unlimited period of time.

In re	CHAPTER 13
Debtor(s).	CASE NUMBER

Instructions for Attaching

Addendum to Chapter 13 Plan Concerning Debtors who are Repaying Debt Secured by a Mortgage on Real Property or a Lien on Personal Property the Debtor Occupies as the Debtor's Principal Residence

This optional addendum concerns chapter 13 debtors who are repaying debt secured by a mortgage on real property or a lien on personal property the debtor occupies as the debtor's principal residence.

A chapter 13 debtor may attach this addendum to his/her chapter 13 plan. This is a court-approved form and may not be altered, except for interlineations clearly marked on the court-approved form which are subject to the Court's review and approval upon consideration of the plan for confirmation. When attaching this form to the chapter 13 plan form (F 3015-1.1), the debtor must indicate in section V.F. (Page 6) of the chapter 13 plan form that the "Addendum to Chapter 13 Plan (F 3015-1.1A) is attached."

CDCAL-319 C.D. CALIFORNIA

Adversary Proceeding Sheet (B-104)

FORM B104 (08/07) 2007 USBC, Central District of California

ADVERSARY PROCEEDING COVER SHEET (Instructions on Page 2)	ADVERSARY PROCEEDING NUMBER (Court Use Only)
PLAINTIFFS	DEFENDANTS
ATTORNEYS (Firm Name, Address, and Telephone No.)	ATTORNEYS (If Known)
PARTY (Check One Box Only) ☐ Debtor ☐ U.S. Trustee/Bankruptcy Admin ☐ Creditor ☐ Other ☐ Trustee	PARTY (Check One Box Only) ☐ Debtor ☐ U.S. Trustee/Bankruptcy Admin ☐ Creditor ☐ Other ☐ Trustee

CAUSE OF ACTION (WRITE A BRIEF STATEMENT OF CAUSE OF ACTION, INCLUDING ALL U.S. STATUTES INVOLVED)

NATURE OF SUIT

(Number up to five (5) boxes starting with lead cause of action as 1, first alternative cause as 2, second alternative cause as 3, etc.)

FRBP 7001(1) – Recovery of Money/Property
- ☐ 11-Recovery of money/property - §542 turnover of property
- ☐ 12-Recovery of money/property - §547 preference
- ☐ 13-Recovery of money/property - §548 fraudulent transfer
- ☐ 14-Recovery of money/property - other

FRBP 7001(2) – Validity, Priority or Extent of Lien
- ☐ 21-Validity, priority or extent of lien or other interest in property

FRBP 7001(3) – Approval of Sale of Property
- ☐ 31-Approval of sale of property of estate and of a co-owner - §363(h)

FRBP 7001(4) – Objection/Revocation of Discharge
- ☐ 41-Objection / revocation of discharge - §727(c),(d),(e)

FRBP 7001(5) – Revocation of Confirmation
- ☐ 51-Revocation of confirmation

FRBP 7001(6) – Dischargeability
- ☐ 66-Dischargeability - §523(a)(1),(14),(14A) priority tax claims
- ☐ 62-Dischargeability - §523(a)(2), false pretenses, false representation, actual fraud
- ☐ 67-Dischargeability - §523(a)(4), fraud as fiduciary, embezzlement, larceny

(continued next column)

FRBP 7001(6) – Dischargeability (continued)
- ☐ 61-Dischargeability - §523(a)(5), domestic support
- ☐ 68-Dischargeability - §523(a)(6), willful and malicious injury
- ☐ 63-Dischargeability - §523(a)(8), student loan
- ☐ 64-Dischargeability - §523(a)(15), divorce or separation obligation (other than domestic support)
- ☐ 65-Dischargeability - other

FRBP 7001(7) – Injunctive Relief
- ☐ 71-Injunctive relief – imposition of stay
- ☐ 72-Injunctive relief – other

FRBP 7001(8) Subordination of Claim or Interest
- ☐ 81-Subordination of claim or interest

FRBP 7001(9) Declaratory Judgment
- ☐ 91-Declaratory judgment

FRBP 7001(10) Determination of Removed Action
- ☐ 01-Determination of removed claim or cause

Other
- ☐ SS-SIPA Case – 15 U.S.C. §§78aaa *et.seq.*
- ☐ 02-Other (e.g. other actions that would have been brought in state court if unrelated to bankruptcy case)

☐ Check if this case involves a substantive issue of state law	☐ Check if this is asserted to be a class action under FRCP 23
☐ Check if a jury trial is demanded in complaint	Demand $

Other Relief Sought

FORM B104 (08/07), page 2 — 2007 USBC, Central District of California

BANKRUPTCY CASE IN WHICH THIS ADVERSARY PROCEEDING ARISES		
NAME OF DEBTOR		BANKRUPTCY CASE NO.
DISTRICT IN WHICH CASE IS PENDING	DIVISIONAL OFFICE	NAME OF JUDGE
RELATED ADVERSARY PROCEEDING (IF ANY)		
PLAINTIFF	DEFENDANT	ADVERSARY PROCEEDING NO.
DISTRICT IN WHICH ADVERSARY IS PENDING	DIVISIONAL OFFICE	NAME OF JUDGE
SIGNATURE OF ATTORNEY (OR PLAINTIFF)		
DATE	PRINT NAME OF ATTORNEY (OR PLAINTIFF)	

INSTRUCTIONS

The filing of a bankruptcy case creates an "estate" under the jurisdiction of the bankruptcy court which consists of all of the property of the debtor, wherever that property is located. Because the bankruptcy estate is so extensive and the jurisdiction of the court so broad, there may be lawsuits over the property or property rights of the estate. There also may be lawsuits concerning the debtor's discharge. If such a lawsuit is filed in a bankruptcy court, it is called an adversary proceeding.

A party filing an adversary proceeding must also must complete and file Form 104, the Adversary Proceeding Cover Sheet, unless the party files the adversary proceeding electronically through the court's Case Management/Electronic Case Filing system (CM/ECF). (CM/ECF captures the information on Form 104 as part of the filing process.) When completed, the cover sheet summarizes basic information on the adversary proceeding. The clerk of court needs the information to process the adversary proceeding and prepare required statistical reports on court activity.

The cover sheet and the information contained on it do not replace or supplement the filing and service of pleadings or other papers as required by law, the Bankruptcy Rules, or the local rules of court. The cover sheet, which is largely self-explanatory, must be completed by the plaintiff's attorney (or by the plaintiff if the plaintiff is not represented by an attorney). A separate cover sheet must be submitted to the clerk for each complaint filed.

Plaintiffs and Defendents. Give the names of the plaintiffs and defendants exactly as they appear on the complaint.

Attorneys. Give the names and addresses of the attorneys, if known.

Party. Check the most appropriate box in the first column for the plaintiffs and the second column for the defendants.

Demand. Enter the dollar amount being demanded in the complaint.

Signature. This cover sheet must be signed by the attorney of record in the box on the second page of the form. If the plaintiff is represented by a law firm, a member of the firm must sign. If the plaintiff is pro se, that is, not presented by an attorney, the plaintiff must sign.

CDCAL-321 C.D. CALIFORNIA

Affidavit and Request for Issuance of Writ of Execution

Form B-1037 (Rev. 8/98) 1998 USBC, Central District of California

Attorney or Party Name, Address, Telephone & FAX Numbers, and California State Bar Number Attorney for: ______________________	FOR COURT USE ONLY
UNITED STATES BANKRUPTCY COURT CENTRAL DISTRICT OF CALIFORNIA	
In re Debtor.	CASE NO.: ADVERSARY NO.:
Plaintiff(s) vs. Defendant(s).	AFFIDAVIT AND REQUEST FOR ISSUANCE OF WRIT OF EXECUTION

STATE OF CALIFORNIA, COUNTY OF ______________________

I, ______________________ hereby state under penalty of perjury that,

1. Judgment for $______________ was entered on ______________ (date)

   in the docket of the above-entitled action in favor of:

   ____

   as Judgment Creditor, and against

   ____

   as Judgment Debtor

   (If registered Judgment, fill in below)

   Said Judgment was registered herein under Title 28, U.S. Code, Section 1963, being a Judgment which was obtained in Case No. ______________ in the United States Bankruptcy Court, Central District of California and which has become FINAL.

2. I am the Judgment Creditor, or the attorney for said Judgement Creditor, and request issuance of a Writ of Execution on the Judgment.

3. ACCRUED since the entry of judgment are the following sums:

   $______________ accrued interest, computed at ______________% (see note)

   $______________ accrued costs

Form B-1037 (Rev. 8/98) 1998 USBC, Central District of California

In re:	CASE NO.:
Debtor.	ADVERSARY NO.:

Credit must be given for payments and partial satisfaction in the amount of $________________________ which is to be credited against the total accrued costs and accrued interest, with any excess credited against the judgment as entered.

I declare under penalty of perjury that the foregoing is true and correct.

Executed at ____, State of California, this ______________

day of __________________________________, __________
(year)

____
Signature

NOTE: Judgments registered under 28 U.S.C. 1963 bear the rate of interest of the District of origin.

Application for Order Setting Hearing on Shortened Notice [LBR 9075-1(b)] (F 9075-1.1)

Attorney or Party Name, Address, Telephone & FAX Nos., State Bar No. & Email Address ☐ *Individual appearing without attorney* ☐ *Attorney for:*	FOR COURT USE ONLY
UNITED STATES BANKRUPTCY COURT **CENTRAL DISTRICT OF CALIFORNIA** ________________ **DIVISION**	
In re: Debtor(s).	CASE NO: CHAPTER: **APPLICATION FOR ORDER SETTING HEARING ON SHORTENED NOTICE [LBR 9075-1(b)]**

1. Movant applies under LBR 9075-1(b) for an order setting a hearing on shortened notice on the following motion:
   a. *Title of motion:* ____________________________
   b. *Date of filing of motion:* ________________
2. Compliance with LBR 9075-1(b)(2)(A): ***(The following three sections must be completed)***
   a. Briefly specify the relief requested in the motion:

b. Identify the parties affected by the relief requested in the motion:

c. State the reasons necessitating a hearing on shortened time:

3. Compliance with LBR 9075-1(b)(2)(B): The attached declaration(s) justifies setting a hearing on shortened notice, and establishes a *prima facie* basis for the granting of the motion.

4. Movant has lodged a proposed Order Setting Hearing on Shortened Notice on mandatory Form 9075-1.2.ORDER

Date:

____
Print Law Firm Name (if applicable)

_______________________________ _______________________________
Print Name of Individual Movant or Attorney for Movant *Signature of Individual Movant or Attorney for Movant*

PROOF OF SERVICE OF DOCUMENT

I am over the age of 18 and not a party to this bankruptcy case or adversary proceeding. My business address is:

A true and correct copy of the foregoing document described as_ **APPLICATION FOR ORDER SETTING HEARING ON SHORTENED NOTICE** will be served or was served **(a)** on the judge in chambers in the form and manner required by LBR 5005-2(d); and **(b)** in the manner indicated below:

I. <u>TO BE SERVED BY THE COURT VIA NOTICE OF ELECTRONIC FILING ("NEF")</u> – Pursuant to controlling General Order(s) and LBR(s), the foregoing document will be served by the court via NEF and hyperlink to the document. On ______________________ I checked the CM/ECF docket for this bankruptcy case or adversary proceeding and determined that the following person(s) are on the Electronic Mail Notice List to receive NEF transmission at the email address(es) indicated below:

☐ Service information continued on attached page

II. <u>SERVED BY UNITED STATES MAIL OR OVERNIGHT MAIL</u><u>(indicate method for each person or entity served):</u>
On ______________________ I served the following person(s) and/or entity(ies) at the last known address(es) in this bankruptcy case or adversary proceeding by placing a true and correct copy thereof in a sealed envelope in the United States mail, first class, postage prepaid, and/or with an overnight mail service addressed as follows. Listing the judge here constitutes a declaration that mailing to the judge <u>will be</u> completed no later than 24 hours after the document is filed.

☐ Service information continued on attached page

III. <u>SERVED BY PERSONAL DELIVERY, FACSIMILE TRANSMISSION OR EMAIL</u> <u>(indicate method for each person or entity served):</u> Pursuant to F.R.Civ.P. 5 and/or controlling LBR, on______________________ I served the following person(s) and/or entity(ies) by personal delivery, or (for those who consented in writing to such service method), by facsimile transmission and/or email as follows. Listing the judge here constitutes a declaration that personal delivery on the judge <u>will be</u> completed no later than 24 hours after the document is filed.

☐ Service information continued on attached page

I declare under penalty of perjury under the laws of the United States of America that the foregoing is true and correct.

Date	*Type Name*	*Signature*

APPLICATION FOR PAYMENT OF INTERIM OR FINAL FEES AND/OR EXPENSES (F 2016-1.2)

Attorney or Party Name, Address, Telephone & FAX Numbers, and California State Bar Number *Attorney for*	FOR COURT USE ONLY
UNITED STATES BANKRUPTCY COURT CENTRAL DISTRICT OF CALIFORNIA	
In re:	CHAPTER ____ CASE NUMBER
Debtor.	DATE: TIME: COURTROOM:

APPLICATION FOR PAYMENT OF:

❑ INTERIM FEES AND/OR EXPENSES (11 U.S.C. § 331)

❑ FINAL FEES AND/OR EXPENSES (11 U.S.C. § 330)

1. Name of Applicant *(specify)*:

2. Type of Services Rendered:
   a. ❑ Attorney for *(specify)*:
   b. ❑ Accountant for *(specify)*:
   c. ❑ Other Professional *(specify)*:

3. Date of Filing of Petition under Chapter of the Bankruptcy Code:

4. Date of Entry of Order Approving Applicant's Employment:

5. Date of Filing of last Fee and/or Expense Application:

6. Total Fees allowed or paid to Applicant to Date (including Retainers and Prior Approved Fee Applications): $

   a. Retainer received: $

   b. Retainer remaining as of the date of this application: $

   c. Total amount requested in all prior applications: $

   d. Total amount actually paid pursuant to prior approved applications: $

   e. Total amount currently due but unpaid pursuant to prior approved applications: $

   f. Total amount allowed but reserved pending final fee application: $

(Continued on next page)

In re	CHAPTER ______
Debtor.	CASE NUMBER

7. **Summary of Requested Fees**: (Attach detailed supporting documentation to this Application)

	Professional Person's Name	Hourly Rate	x	Total Hours this Person	=	Total Fees this Person
a.		$	x		=	$
b.		$	x		=	$
c.		$	x		=	$
d.		$	x		=	$
e.		$	x		=	$
f.		$	x		=	$

g. ❑ Continued on Attached Page

8. The hourly rates above are the same rates charged by the above professionals for non-bankruptcy services except as follows: ❑ See Attached Page

9. Bonus requested (final fee applications only): $
(Attach Declaration and Memorandum of Points and Authorities justifying bonus)

10. **TOTAL FEES REQUESTED THIS APPLICATION**: $

11. Total Expenses paid to Applicant to Date (including Retainers and Prior Approved Expense Applications): $

12. **Summary of Requested Expense Reimbursement**: (Attach detailed supporting documentation to this Application)

	Type of Expense	Reimbursement Requested this Application
a.		$
b.		$
c.		$
d.		$
e.		$
f.		$

g. ❑ Continued on Attached Page

13. **TOTAL EXPENSE REIMBURSEMENT REQUESTED THIS APPLICATION:** $

14. Applicant submits the following in support of the Application herein pursuant to Local Bankruptcy Rule 2016-1 *(specify)*:

15. Total Number of attached pages of supporting documentation: ________

16. Applicant declares under penalty of perjury under the laws of the United States of America that the foregoing Application and all attached supporting documentation are true and correct and accurately reflect services rendered and expenses incurred.

17. Executed on the _____ day of _________________, 20_____, at __________________________, California.

______________________________ ______________________________

Type Name of Applicant *Signature of Applicant*

Application of Non-Resident Attorney to Appear in a Specific Case (F 2090-1.2)

Attorney or Party Name, Address, Telephone & FAX Nos., State Bar No. & Email Address Attorney for	FOR COURT USE ONLY
UNITED STATES BANKRUPTCY COURT CENTRAL DISTRICT OF CALIFORNIA __________ DIVISION	
In re: Debtor(s),	CASE NO: CHAPTER: ADVERSARY NO.:
Plaintiff(s), vs.	**APPLICATION OF NON-RESIDENT ATTORNEY TO APPEAR IN A SPECIFIC CASE [LBR 2090-1(b)]**
Defendant(s),	DATE: TIME: COURTROOM: PLACE:

1. I, ____________________________, hereby apply to the Court under LBR 2090-1(b) for permission to appear and participate in the above-entitled action on behalf of the following named party, by whom I have been retained *(Specify Name of Party)*:

2. I am a lawyer with the following law firm *(Specify Name and Address of Law Firm)*:

3. I am a member in good standing and eligible to practice before the following courts, and admitted to practice on the following dates *(Specify Name of Jurisdiction and Date of Admission to Practice in such Jurisdiction)*:

4. I am not a resident of, nor am I regularly employed, engaged in business, professional or other activities in the state of California. I am not currently suspended or disbarred in any court.

5. I have concurrently or within the past 36 months made *pro hac vice* applications to this court in the following actions:

Court	Case Number	Title of Action	Date of Application	Disposition of Application

(Continued on next page)

6. I ☐ have ☐ have not been disciplined by any court or administrative body ☐ disciplinary proceedings are pending; details are as follows:

____

____

____

____

I ☐ resigned ☐ did not resign while disciplinary proceedings were pending.

7. I certify that I have read the LBRs, the FRBP, the F.R.Civ.P., and the F.R.Evid., in their entirety.

8. I designate the following person of the following law firm who is a member of the bar of this court and maintains an office in this district for the practice of law, as the attorney with whom the court and opposing counsel may readily communicate regarding the conduct of this case, and upon whom papers may be served:

Name of Attorney (Designee):

Name and Address of Law Firm, or residence address:

Telephone number of Law Firm:

9. I declare under penalty of perjury under the laws of the United States of America that the foregoing is true and correct.

Date:

______________________ ______________________

Type Name of Applicant *Signature of Applicant*

CONSENT OF DESIGNEE

I hereby consent to the foregoing designation.

Date:

______________________ ______________________

Type Name of Designee *Signature of Designee*

NOTE: When using this form to indicate service of a proposed order, **DO NOT** list any person or entity in Category I. Proposed orders do not generate an NEF because only orders that have been entered are placed on a CM/ECF docket.

PROOF OF SERVICE OF DOCUMENT

I am over the age of 18 and not a party to this bankruptcy case or adversary proceeding. My business address is:

A true and correct copy of the foregoing document described as ______________________________ will be served or was served **(a)** on the judge in chambers in the form and manner required by LBR 5005-2(d), and **(b)** in the manner indicated below:

I. TO BE SERVED BY THE COURT VIA NOTICE OF ELECTRONIC FILING ("NEF") - Pursuant to controlling General Order(s) and LBR(s), the foregoing document will be served by the court via NEF and hyperlink to the document. On ______________ I checked the CM/ECF docket for this bankruptcy case or adversary proceeding and determined that the following person(s) are on the Electronic Mail Notice List to receive NEF transmission at the email addressed indicated below:

☐ Service information continued on attached page

II. SERVED BY UNITED STATES MAIL OR OVERNIGHT MAIL (indicate method for each person or entity served):
On ______________ I served the following person(s) and/or entity(ies) at the last known address(es) in this bankruptcy case or adversary proceeding by placing a true and correct copy thereof in a sealed envelope in the United States mail, first class, postage prepaid, and/or with an overnight mail service addressed as follow. Listing the judge here constitutes a declaration that mailing to the judge will be completed no later than 24 hours after the document is filed.

☐ Service information continued on attached page

III. SERVED BY PERSONAL DELIVERY, FACSIMILE TRANSMISSION OR EMAIL (indicate method for each person or entity served): Pursuant to F.R.Civ.P. 5 and/or controlling LBR, on ______________ I served the following person(s) and/or entity(ies) by personal delivery, or (for those who consented in writing to such service method) by facsimile transmission and/or email as follows. Listing the judge here constitutes a declaration that mailing to the judge will be completed no later than 24 hours after the document is filed.

☐ Service information continued on attached page

I declare under penalty of perjury under the laws of the United States of America that the foregoing is true and correct.

______________________________ ______________________________

Date *Type Name* *Signature*

Audio Recording of Court Proceedings Order Form

Audio Recordings of Court Proceedings Ordering Information

The Bankruptcy Court for the Central District of California has converted the method used to record court hearings from an analog tape system to digital technology. The Court has selected the *FTR Gold*™ digital recording product, as it offers superior sound reproduction capability compared to the former tape process.

Audio recordings of court proceedings requested for hearings held after an office converted to the new digital system will be provided on a compact disc (CD). Audio recordings of hearings held before implementation of the new system will continue to be provided in a cassette tape format. The cost of either one compact disc (CD) or one cassette tape is $26.00 each.

Audio requests provided on compact discs may be ordered in one of three formats, ***FTR Gold, Windows Audio,*** or ***Audio CD*** *(the most generic format).*

1. ***FTR Gold*** - This format must be played using *FTR Player Plus*™ which is available at no charge on the *FTR Gold*™ web site at, *<www.ftrgold.com>*. (Please note the minimum system requirements as listed on the *FTR Gold*™ web site and the availability of separate downloads for various Windows products.) If audio is played using this software the user will be able to navigate through the recording by using the time references from the actual hearing. One day's hearings may be provided on one CD using this format.

2. ***Windows Audio*** - This format will play using the standard Windows Media Player software installed on most personal computers. One day's hearings may be provided on one compact disc (CD) using this format.

3. ***Audio CD*** - This generic format will play on most CD-R and CD-RW compatible players designed to play music and other audio programs. Select this option if the audio will be played in a vehicle or on a personal CD player. **In addition, this is the <u>only format which is compatible with Macintosh or Apple computers</u>.** ***However, this format is not able to contain as much audio as the other two options. Compact discs formatted in this generic format will hold a maximum of 70 minutes of recordings.*** For example, a 90-minute hearing provided in this format will be provided on two compact discs (CD) at a cost of $52.00.

Offices in the Central District converted to digital recording in stages and each office's implementation date is listed below. Should you have questions regarding digital recording, please contact one of the Clerk's Office staff members listed.

Division	Effective Date	Contact Person
San Fernando Valley	April 4, 2007	Josie Womack (818) 587-2860
Riverside	April 4, 2007	Rita Cargill (951) 774-1085
Santa Ana	April 4, 2007	Rick Reid (714) 338-5361
Northern	June 21, 2004	Kam Rust (805) 884-4873
Los Angeles Judges: Ahart, Bluebond, Bufford, Kaufman, Zurzolo	July 26, 2004	Sandra Peters (213) 894-3150
Los Angeles Judges: Carroll, Donovan, Neiter, Robles, Russell	August 23, 2004	

Revised April 4, 2007

Order # ______________

United States Bankruptcy Court
Central District of California

Audio Recording of Court Proceedings Order Form

Ordering Party: Name, Address, and Telephone Number	**Case/Debtor Name:**
Name ______________	**Case Number: Chapter No.:**
Firm ______________	□ **Bankruptcy** □ **Adversary**
Address ______________	
City, State, Zip ______________	**Presiding Judge** ______________
Phone ______________	

Hearing Information (A separate form must be completed for **each** hearing date requested.)

Date of Hearing: ______________ **Time of Hearing:** ________ **Calendar Matter Number:** ______
(Use one form for each hearing date.)

Do you want a recording of the □ entire hearing □ ruling, or □ part of a hearing. If you want a recording of only part of the hearing, please indicate which part below:

Number of Copies Requested: ________

Digital Formats (If the hearing date requested is prior to implementation of digital recording, please skip this section.)

For audio requests of hearings held ***after an office converted to digital recording***, you have the option to select the format for your CD-ROM. Please make your selection below.
□**CD - FTR Gold format** you must download the free *FTR Player Plus*™ onto your computer from <*www.ftrgold.com*>.
□**CD - Windows Audio format** will play using standard software installed on most computers.
□**CD - PC Audio format** (generic format) can be played on most CD-R and CD-RW compatible players designed to play music. **This is the only format which is compatible with either a Macintosh or Apple computer.**

Cost

The cost for one compact disc (CD) or one cassette tape is $26.00. A deposit of $26.00 is required for each hearing date before an audio request may be processed. Audio requests are ordinarily completed within two business days from receipt of the deposit. The ordering party will be notified by telephone when the audio request is ready. If additional fees are required, the ordering party will be notified. Payment of additional fees is required prior to picking up the completed order.

Signature of Ordering Party: Date: ______			**Pick-up Verification:** Date:	
By signing, I certify that I will pay all charges upon completion of the audio recording request.			# Media Duplicated	Total Cost: $
Order Received	Date	By	Deposit Paid	
Deposit Paid			Total Charges	
Audio Duplicated			Less Deposit	
Party Notified to Pick-up			Total Due	

Cashier Verification: Receipt Number Stamp (Seal) Rev. 2/04

Ballot for Accepting or Rejecting a Plan (Chapter 11 Only)

Form B14 - (Rev. 7/98) 1998 USBC, Central District of California

Attorney or Party Name, Address, Telephone & FAX Numbers, and California State Bar Number ❑ Attorney for Plan Proponent ______ *[insert name and capacity (e.g., Debtor in Possession, Creditors' Committee, Debtor XYZ, etc.)]*	FOR COURT USE ONLY
UNITED STATES BANKRUPTCY COURT CENTRAL DISTRICT OF CALIFORNIA	CHAPTER 11 CASE NO.:
In re: Debtor.	DATE: TIME: CTRM:

BALLOT FOR ACCEPTING OR REJECTING PLAN

1. Proponent of Plan *[specify name]* ______ has filed a Plan of Reorganization ("Plan") on *[date]* ______ for the Debtor in this case. By this ballot you will vote to accept or reject this Plan.

2. The Court has approved a Disclosure Statement with respect to the Plan. The Disclosure Statement provides information to assist you in deciding how to vote your ballot. If you do not have a Disclosure Statement, you may obtain a copy from the proponent or proponent's attorney at the address set forth above. Court approval of the Disclosure Statement does not indicate approval of the Plan by the Court.

3. You should review the Disclosure Statement and the Plan before you vote. You may wish to seek legal advice concerning the Plan and your classification and treatment under the Plan.

   Your *[check one box only]* ❑ **claim** ❑ **equity interest** has been placed in Class *[insert Class]* ___ under the Plan. If you hold claim(s) or equity interest(s) in more than one Class, you will receive a ballot for each Class in which you are entitled to vote.

4. If your ballot is not received by the proponent's attorney or other party *[insert other party's name and address]* ______ on or before ______, and such deadline is not extended, your vote will not count as either an acceptance or rejection of the Plan, unless the Judge otherwise determines that a non-vote will be treated as a rejection of the plan.

5. If the Plan is confirmed by the Bankruptcy Court, it will be binding on you whether or not you vote.

ACCEPTANCE OR REJECTION OF THE PLAN

6. Complete the appropriate line below that describes your claim or equity interest *[select only one]*:

❑ 6.1 The undersigned is the holder of a Class *[insert Class]* ___ *[check one]* ❑ **secured** ❑ **priority** ❑ **unsecured nonpriority** claim against the Debtor in the unpaid amount of $ ______.

❑ 6.2 The undersigned is the holder of a Class *[insert Class]* ___ *[check one]* ❑ **bond** ❑ **debenture** ❑ **debt security** claim against the Debtor, consisting of $______, principal amount of *[describe bond, debenture, or other debt security]* ______ of the Debtor. (For purposes of this Ballot, you should not adjust the principal amount for any accrued or unmatured interest.)

❑ 6.3 The undersigned is the holder of a Class *[insert Class]* ___ equity interest in the Debtor, consisting of *[number of shares]* ___ or other interests *[describe equity interest]* ______ in the Debtor.

Other Classes: ❑ See Attached Continuation Page

Ballot for Accepting or Rejecting Plan - Page Two of Three

In re: (SHORT TITLE)	CHAPTER 11
Debtor.	CASE NO.:

7. **The undersigned** *[check one box only]*:

❑ **ACCEPTS THE PLAN** ❑ **REJECTS THE PLAN**

Dated:__________

Name *[Print or type]*: ____________________

Signature: ____________________

Title *[if corporation or partnership]*: ____________________

Address: ____________________

____

____

Telephone No.: ____________________

Fax No.: ____________________

RETURN THIS BALLOT TO:

[Type in name and address of proponent's attorney or other appropriate party]

In re: (SHORT TITLE)	CHAPTER 11
Debtor.	CASE NO.:

PROOF OF SERVICE

STATE OF CALIFORNIA

COUNTY OF ____________________

1. I am employed in the County of ____________________, State of California. I am over the age of 18 and not a party to the within action. My business address is as follows:

2. Regular Mail Service:

   On *[insert date]* ____________, I served the document described as: **BALLOT FOR ACCEPTING OR REJECTING PLAN** on the interested parties at their last known address in this action by placing a true and correct copy thereof in a sealed envelope with postage thereon fully prepaid in the United States Mail at ____________________, California, addressed as set forth below.

   ☐ Addresses continued on attached page

I declare under penalty of perjury, under the laws of the United States of America, that the foregoing is true and correct.

Dated:

____________________ ____________________

Type Name *Signature*

Certification of Judgment for Registration in Another District (B265)

UNITED STATES BANKRUPTCY COURT
______________________ **District of** ______________________

In re

Bankruptcy Case No.

Debtor

Plaintiff

v. Adversary Proceeding No.

Defendant

CERTIFICATION OF JUDGMENT FOR REGISTRATION IN ANOTHER DISTRICT

I, clerk of the bankruptcy court of this district do certify that the attached judgment is a true and correct copy of the original judgment entered in the above entitled proceeding on ______________________
(date)
as it appears of record in my office, and that:

❒ No notice of appeal from this judgment has been filed, and no motion of the kind set forth in Federal Rule of Civil Procedure 60, as made applicable by Bankruptcy Rule 9024, has been filed.

❒ No notice of appeal from this judgment has been filed, and any motions of the kind set forth in Federal Rule of Civil Procedure 60, as made applicable by Bankruptcy Rule 9024, have been disposed of, the latest order disposing of such motion having been entered on ______________________.
(date)

❒ An appeal was taken from this judgment, and the judgment was affirmed by mandate of the ______________________ issued on ______________________.
(name of court) (date)

❒ An appeal was taken from this judgment, and the appeal was dismissed by order entered on ______________________.
(date)

____
Clerk of the Bankruptcy Court

______________________ By: ______________________
Date Deputy Clerk

[B265 rev 3/98]

CDCAL-337 C.D. CALIFORNIA

Certification to Court of Appeals By All Parties

Form B24 - (Official From 24) (Rev. 12/07) **2007 USBC, Central District of California**

Attorney or Party Name, Address, Telephone & FAX Numbers, and California State Bar Number *Attorney for*	FOR COURT USE ONLY
UNITED STATES BANKRUPTCY COURT CENTRAL DISTRICT OF CALIFORNIA	CASE NO.: ADVERSARY NO.:
In re: Debtor.	**CERTIFICATION TO COURT OF APPEALS BY ALL PARTIES**

A notice of appeal having been filed in the above-styled matter on ____________ *[Date]*, ____________________, ____________________, and ____________________, *[Names of all the appellants and all the appellees, if any]*, who are all the appellants [and all the appellees] hereby certify to the court under 28 U.S.C. § 158(d)(2)(A) that a circumstance specified in 28 U.S.C. § 158(d)(2) exists as stated below.

Leave to appeal in this matter ☐ is ☐ is not required under 28 U.S.C. § 158(a).

[If from a final judgment, order, or decree] This certification arises in an appeal from a final judgment, order, or decree of the United States Bankruptcy Court for the ____________________ District of ____________________ entered on ____________________ *[Date]*.

[If from an interlocutory order or decree] This certification arises in an appeal from an interlocutory order or decree, and the parties hereby request leave to appeal as required by 28 U.S.C. § 158(a).

[The certification shall contain one or more of the following statements, as is appropriate to the circumstances.]

The judgment, order, or decree involves a question of law as to which there is no controlling decision of the court of appeals for this circuit or of the Supreme Court of the United States, or involves a matter of public importance.

Or

The judgment, order, or decree involves a question of law requiring resolution of conflicting decisions.

Or

An immediate appeal from the judgment, order, or decree may materially advance the progress of the case or proceeding in which the appeal is taken.

Form B24 - (Official Form 24) (Rev. 12/07) 2007 USBC, Central District of California

Certification to Court of Appeals By All Parties
Page 2 of 2

In re	CASE NUMBER:
Debtor.	ADVERSARY NUMBER:

[The parties may include or attach the information specified in Rule 8001(f)(3)(C).]

Signed: *[If there are more than two signatories, all must sign and provide the information requested below. Attach additional signed sheets if needed.]*

______________________	______________________
Attorney for Appellant (or Appellant, if not represented by an attorney)	Attorney for Appellee (or Appellee if not represented by an attorney)
______________________	______________________
Printed Name of Signer	Printed Name of Signer
______________________	______________________
______________________	______________________
Address	Address
______________________	______________________
Telephone No.	Telephone No.
______________________	______________________
Date	Date

CDCAL-339 C.D. CALIFORNIA

CHANGE OF ADDRESS

REQUESTOR'S NAME: ______________________

ADDRESS: ______________________

____

TELEPHONE NO.: ______________________

UNITED STATES BANKRUPTCY COURT
CENTRAL DISTRICT OF CALIFORNIA

In re	CASE NO.: Chapter 7 _____ 11 _____ 13 _____
	CHANGE OF ADDRESS _____ DEBTOR _____ CREDITOR **CHECK ONLY ONE**

(Please print or type) **MUST BE FILED IN DUPLICATE**

NAME: ______________________

NEW MAILING ADDRESS: ______________________

____

____

Dated: ______________ ______________________
Signature

____
Title (Corporation officer, partner or agent)

All future notices shall be sent to the above address.

B-1098
Revised 03/03

Chapter 7 Debtor's Certification of Completion of Postpetition Instructional Course Concerning Personal Financial Management

Form B23 (Official Form 23) - (12/08) 2008 USBC, Central District of California

UNITED STATES BANKRUPTCY COURT CENTRAL DISTRICT OF CALIFORNIA	
In re: Debtor(s).	CHAPTER: CASE NO.:

DEBTOR'S CERTIFICATION OF COMPLETION OF POSTPETITION INSTRUCTIONAL COURSE CONCERNING PERSONAL FINANCIAL MANAGEMENT

Every individual debtor in a chapter 7, chapter 11 in which § 1141(d)(3) applies, or chapter 13 case must file this certification. If a joint petition is filed, each spouse must complete and file a separate certification. Complete one of the following statements and file by the deadline stated below:

☐ I, ________________________________ *(Printed Name of Debtor)*, the debtor in the above-styled case, hereby certify that on ______________________ *(Date)*, I completed an instructional course in personal financial management provided by ________________________________ *(Name of Provider)*, an approved personal financial management provider.

Certificate No. *(if any)*: ______________________.

☐ I, ________________________________ *(Printed Name of Debtor)*, the debtor in the above-styled case, hereby certify that no personal financial management course is required because of *[Check the appropriate box.]*:

- ☐ Incapacity or disability, as defined in 11 U.S.C. § 109(h);
- ☐ Active military duty in a military combat zone; or
- ☐ Residence in a district in which the United States trustee *(or bankruptcy administrator)* has determined that the approved instructional courses are not adequate at this time to serve the additional individuals who would otherwise be required to complete such courses.

Date: ______________________ Signature of Debtor: ________________________________

Instructions: Use this form only to certify whether you completed a course in personal financial management. (Fed. R. Bankr. P. 1007(b)(7).) Do NOT use this form to file the certificate given to you by your prepetition credit counseling provider and do NOT include with the petition when filing your case.

Filing Deadlines: In a chapter 7 case, file within 45 days of the first date set for the meeting of creditors under § 341 of the Bankruptcy Code. In a chapter 11 or 13 case, file no later than the last payment made by the debtor as required by the plan or the filing of a motion for a discharge under § 1141(d)(5)(B) or § 1328(b) of the Code. (See Fed. R. Bankr. P. 1007(c).)

CDCAL-341 C.D. CALIFORNIA

Chapter 7 Declaration Re: Limited Scope of Appearance Pursuant to Local Bankruptcy Rule 2090-1

Attorney or Party Name, Address, Telephone & FAX Numbers, and California State Bar Number *Attorney for*	FOR COURT USE ONLY
UNITED STATES BANKRUPTCY COURT CENTRAL DISTRICT OF CALIFORNIA	
In re: Debtor.	CHAPTER ______ CASE NUMBER
	(No Hearing Required)

DECLARATION RE: LIMITED SCOPE OF APPEARANCE PURSUANT TO LOCAL BANKRUPTCY RULE 2090-1

TO THE COURT, THE DEBTOR, THE TRUSTEE (if any), AND THE UNITED STATES TRUSTEE:

1. I am the attorney for the Debtor in the above-captioned bankruptcy case.

2. On *(specify date)* ______________________________, I agreed with the Debtor that for a fee of $__________, I would provide only the following services:

   a. ☐ Prepare and file the Petition and Schedules
   b. ☐ Represent the Debtor at the 341(a) Meeting
   c. ☐ Represent the Debtor in any relief from stay actions
   d. ☐ Represent the Debtor in any proceeding involving an objection to Debtor's discharge pursuant to 11 U.S.C. § 727
   e. ☐ Represent the Debtor in any proceeding to determine whether a specific debt is nondischargeable under 11 U.S.C. § 523
   f. ☐ Other *(specify)*:

3. I declare under penalty of perjury under the laws of the United States of America that the foregoing is true and correct and that this declaration was executed on the following date at the city set forth in the upper left-hand corner of this page.

Dated:

____
Law Firm Name

I HEREBY APPROVE THE ABOVE:

By: ______________________________

____
Signature of Debtor

Name: ______________________________
Attorney for Debtor

Declaration Re: Limited Scope of Appearance - *Page 2* **F 2090-1.1**

In re	CHAPTER ______
Debtor.	CASE NUMBER

PROOF OF SERVICE

STATE OF CALIFORNIA
COUNTY OF ____________________

I am employed in the County of ____________________________, State of California. I am over the age of 18 and not a party to the within action. My business address is as follows:

On ______________________________, I served the foregoing document described as: DECLARATION RE: LIMITED SCOPE OF APPEARANCE PURSUANT TO LOCAL BANKRUPTCY RULE 2090-1 on the interested parties at their last known address in this action by placing a true and correct copy thereof in a sealed envelope with postage thereon fully prepaid in the United States Mail at ______________________, California, addressed as set forth below.

☐ Addresses continued on attached page

I declare under penalty of perjury under the laws of the United States of America that the foregoing is true and correct.

Dated:

________________________________ ________________________________
Type Name *Signature*

Chapter 7 Notice of Available Chapters

B 201 - Notice of Available Chapters (Rev. 12/08) USBC, Central District of California

Name: ______________________________

Address: ______________________________

____

Telephone: ______________ Fax: ______________

☐ Attorney for Debtor
☐ Debtor in Pro Per

UNITED STATES BANKRUPTCY COURT CENTRAL DISTRICT OF CALIFORNIA	
List all names including trade names, used by Debtor(s) within last 8 years:	Case No.:
	NOTICE OF AVAILABLE CHAPTERS (Notice to Individual Consumer Debtor Under § 342(b) of the Bankruptcy Code)

In accordance with § 342(b) of the Bankruptcy Code, this notice to individuals with primarily consumer debts: (1) Describes briefly the services available from credit counseling services; (2) Describes briefly the purposes, benefits and costs of the four types of bankruptcy proceedings you may commence; and (3) Informs you about bankruptcy crimes and notifies you that the Attorney General may examine all information you supply in connection with a bankruptcy case.

You are cautioned that bankruptcy law is complicated and not easily described. Thus, you may wish to seek the advice of an attorney to learn of your rights and responsibilities should you decide to file a petition. Court employees cannot give you legal advice.

Notices from the bankruptcy court are sent to the mailing address you list on your bankruptcy petition. In order to ensure that you receive information about events concerning your case, Bankruptcy Rule 4002 requires that you notify the court of any changes in your address. If you are filing a **joint case** (a single bankruptcy case for two individuals married to each other), and each spouse lists the same mailing address on the bankruptcy petition, you and your spouse will generally receive a single copy of each notice mailed from the bankruptcy court in a jointly-addressed envelope, unless you file a statement with the court requesting that each spouse receive a separate copy of all notices.

1. **Services Available from Credit Counseling Agencies**

   With limited exceptions, § 109(h) of the Bankruptcy Code requires that all individual debtors who file for bankruptcy relief on or after October 17, 2005, receive a briefing that outlines the available opportunities for credit counseling and provides assistance in performing a budget analysis. The briefing must be given within 180 days __before__ the bankruptcy filing. The briefing may be provided individually or in a group (including briefings conducted by telephone or on the Internet) and must be provided by a nonprofit budget and credit counseling agency approved by the United States trustee or bankruptcy administrator. The clerk of the bankruptcy court has a list that you may consult of the approved budget and credit counseling agencies. Each debtor in a joint case must complete the briefing.

   In addition, after filing a bankruptcy case, an individual debtor generally must complete a financial management instructional course before he or she can receive a discharge. The clerk also has a list of approved financial management instructional courses. Each debtor in a joint case must complete the course.

2. **The Four Chapters of the Bankruptcy Code Available to Individual Consumer Debtors**

Chapter 7: Liquidation ($245 filing fee, $39 administrative fee, $15 trustee surcharge: Total fee $299)

1. Chapter 7 is designed for debtors in financial difficulty who do not have the ability to pay their existing debts. Debtors whose debts are primarily consumer debts are subject to a "means test" designed to determine whether the case should be permitted to proceed under chapter 7. If your income is greater than the median income for your state of residence and family size, in some cases, creditors have the right to file a motion requesting that the court dismiss your case under § 707(b) of the Code. It is up to the court to decide whether the case should be dismissed.
2. Under chapter 7, you may claim certain of your property as exempt under governing law. A trustee may have the right to take possession of and sell the remaining property that is not exempt and use the sale proceeds to pay your creditors.
3. The purpose of filing a chapter 7 case is to obtain a discharge of your existing debts. If, however, you are found to have committed certain kinds of improper conduct described in the Bankruptcy Code, the court may deny your discharge and, if it does, the purpose for which you filed the bankruptcy petition will be defeated.
4. Even if you receive a general discharge, some particular debts are not discharged under the law. Therefore, you may still be responsible for most taxes and student loans; debts incurred to pay nondischargeable taxes; domestic support and property settlement obligations; most fines, penalties, forfeitures, and criminal restitution obligations; certain debts which are not properly listed in your bankruptcy papers; and debts for death or personal injury caused by operating a motor vehicle, vessel, or aircraft while intoxicated from alcohol or drugs. Also, if a creditor can prove that a debt arose from fraud, breach of fiduciary duty, or theft, or from a willful and malicious injury, the bankruptcy court may determine that the debt is not discharged.

Chapter 13: Repayment of All or Part of the Debts of an Individual with Regular Income ($235 filing fee, $39 administrative fee: Total fee $274)

1. Chapter 13 is designed for individuals with regular income who would like to pay all or part of their debts in installments over a period of time. You are only eligible for chapter 13 if your debts do not exceed certain dollar amounts set forth in the Bankruptcy Code.
2. Under chapter 13, you must file with the court a plan to repay your creditors all or part of the money that you owe them, using your future earnings. The period allowed by the court to repay your debts may be three years or five years, depending upon your income and other factors. The court must approve your plan before it can take effect.
3. After completing the payments under your plan, your debts are generally discharged except for domestic support obligations; most student loans; certain taxes; most criminal fines and restitution obligations; certain debts which are not properly listed in your bankruptcy papers; certain debts for acts that caused death or personal injury; and certain long term secured obligations.

Chapter 11: Reorganization ($1000 filing fee, $39 administrative fee: Total fee $1039)
Chapter 11 is designed for the reorganization of a business but is also available to consumer debtors. Its provisions are quite complicated, and any decision by an individual to file a chapter 11 petition should be reviewed with an attorney.

Chapter 12: Family Farmer or Fisherman ($200 filing fee, $39 administrative fee: Total fee $239)
Chapter 12 is designed to permit family farmers and fishermen to repay their debts over a period of time from future earnings and is similar to chapter 13. The eligibility requirements are restrictive, limiting its use to those whose income arises primarily from a family-owned farm or commercial fishing operation.

3. **Bankruptcy Crimes and Availability of Bankruptcy Papers to Law Enforcement Officials**

A person who knowingly and fraudulently conceals assets or makes a false oath or statement under penalty of perjury, either orally or in writing, in connection with a bankruptcy case is subject to a fine, imprisonment, or both. All information supplied by a debtor in connection with a bankruptcy case is subject to examination by the Attorney General acting through the Office of the United States Trustee, the Office of the United States Attorney, and other components and employees of the Department of Justice.

WARNING: Section 521(a)(1) of the Bankruptcy Code requires that you promptly file detailed information regarding your creditors, assets, liabilities, income, expenses and general financial condition. Your bankruptcy case may be dismissed if this information is not filed with the court within the time deadlines set by the Bankruptcy Code, the Bankruptcy Rules, and the local rules of the court.

Certificate of [Non-Attorney] Bankruptcy Petition Preparer

I, the [non-attorney] bankruptcy petition preparer signing the debtor's petition, hereby certify that I delivered to the debtor this notice required by § 342(b) of the Bankruptcy Code.

____
Printed name and title, if any, of Bankruptcy Petition Preparer

____
Address:

X______________________________
Signature of Bankruptcy Petition Preparer or officer, principal, responsible person, or partner whose Social Security number is provided above.

____
Social Security number (If the bankruptcy petition preparer is not an individual, state the Social Security number of the officer, principal, responsible person, or partner of the bankruptcy petition preparer.) (Required by 11 U.S.C. § 110.)

Certificate of the Debtor

I (We), the debtor(s), affirm that I (we) have received and read this notice.

____
Printed Name(s) of Debtor(s)

Case No. (if known) ______________

____
Signature of Debtor Date

X______________________________
Signature of Joint Debtor (if any) Date

Chapter 7 Statement of Current Monthly Income and Means Test Calculation

Form B22A (Chapter 7) (12/08) 2008 USBC, Central District of California

In re: Debtor.	Case No.: (If known)

According to the calculations required by this statement:
- ☐ **The presumption arises.**
- ☐ **The presumption does not arise.**
- ☐ **The presumption is temporarily inapplicable.**

(Check the box as directed in Part I, III, and VI of this statement)

STATEMENT OF CURRENT MONTHLY INCOME AND MEANS TEST CALCULATION FOR USE IN CHAPTER 7

In addition to Schedules I and J, this statement must be completed by every individual chapter 7 debtor, whether or not filing jointly. Unless the exclusion in Line 1C applies, joint debtors may complete a single statement. If the exclusion in Line 1C applies, each joint filer must complete a separate statement. Joint debtors may complete one statement only.

Part I. MILITARY AND NON-CONSUMER DEBTORS	
1. A	**Disabled Veterans.** If you are a disabled veteran described in the Declaration in this Part IA, (1) check the box at the beginning of the Declaration, (2) check the box for "The presumption does not arise" at the top of this statement, and (3) complete the verification in Part VIII. Do not complete any of the remaining parts of this statement. ☐ **Declaration of Disabled Veteran.** By checking this box, I declare under penalty of perjury that I am a disabled veteran (as defined in 38 U.S.C. § 3741(1)) whose indebtedness occurred primarily during a period in which I was on active duty (as defined in 10 U.S.C. § 101(d)(1)) or while I was performing a homeland defense activity (as defined in 32 U.S.C. § 901(1)).
1. B	**Non-consumer Debtors.** If your debts are not primarily consumer debts, check the box below and complete the verification in Part VIII. Do not complete any of the remaining parts of this statement. ☐ Declaration of non-consumer debts. By checking this box, I declare that my debts are not primarily consumer debts.
1.C	**Reservists and National Guard Members; active duty or homeland defense activity.** Members of a reserve component of the Armed Forces and members of the National Guard who were called to active duty (as defined in 10 U.S.C. § 101(d)(1)) after September 11, 2001, for a period of at least 90 days, or who have performed homeland defense activity (as defined in 32 U.S.C. § 901(1)) for a period of at least 90 days, are excluded from all forms of means testing during the time of active duty or homeland defense activity and for 540 days thereafter (the "exclusion period"). If you qualify for this temporary exclusion, (1) check the appropriate boxes and complete any required information in the Declaration of Reservists and National Guard Members below, (2) check the box for "The presumption is temporarily inapplicable" at the top of this statement, and (3) complete the verification in Part VIII. **During your exclusion period you are not required to complete the balance of this form, but you must complete the form no later than 14 days after the date on which your exclusion period ends, unless the time for filing a motion raising the means test presumption expires in your case before your exclusion period ends.** ☐ **Declaration of Reservists and National Guard Members.** By checking this box and making the appropriate entries below, I declare that I am eligible for a temporary exclusion from means testing because, as a member of a reserve component of the Armed Forces or the National Guard a. ☐ I was called to active duty after September 11, 2001, for a period of at least 90 days and ☐ I remain on active duty /or/ ☐ I was released from active duty on ______________, which is less than 540 days before this bankruptcy case was filed; OR b. ☐ I am performing homeland defense activity for a period of at least 90 days /or/ ☐ I performed homeland defense activity for a period of at least 90 days, terminating on ______________, which is less than 540 days before this bankruptcy case was filed.

Part II. CALCULATION OF MONTHLY INCOME FOR § 707(b)(7) EXCLUSION	
2	**Marital/filing status.** Check the box that applies and complete the balance of this part of this statement as directed. a. ☐ Unmarried. **Complete only Column A ("Debtor's Income") for Lines 3-11.** b. ☐ Married, not filing jointly, with declaration of separate households. By checking this box, debtor declares under penalty of perjury: "My spouse and I are legally separated under applicable non-bankruptcy law or my spouse and I are living apart other than for the purpose of evading the requirements of § 707(b)(2)(A) of the Bankruptcy Code." **Complete only Column A ("Debtor's Income") for Lines 3-11.** c. ☐ Married, not filing jointly, without the declaration of separate households set out in Line 2.b above. **Complete both Column A ("Debtor's Income") and Column B (Spouse's Income) for Lines 3-11.** d. ☐ Married, filing jointly. **Complete both Column A ("Debtor's Income") and Column B ("Spouse's Income") for Lines 3-11.**

	All figures must reflect average monthly income received from all sources, derived during the six calendar months prior to filing the bankruptcy case, ending on the last day of the month before the filing. If the amount of monthly income varied during the six months, you must divide the six-month total by six, and enter the result on the appropriate line.	**Column A Debtor's Income**	**Column B Spouse's Income**
3.	**Gross wages, salary, tips, bonuses, overtime, commissions.**	$	$
4.	**Income from the operation of a business, profession or farm.** Subtract Line b from Line a and enter the difference in the appropriate column(s) of Line 4. If you operate more than one business, profession or farm, enter aggregate numbers and provide details on an attachment. Do not enter a number less than zero. **Do not include any part of the business expenses entered on Line b as a deduction in Part V.** a. Gross receipts — $ b. Ordinary and necessary operating expenses — $ c. Business income — Subtract Line b from Line a	$	$
5.	**Rent and other real property income.** Subtract Line b from Line a and enter the difference in the appropriate column(s) of Line 5. Do not enter a number less than zero. **Do not include any part of the operating expenses entered on Line b as a deduction in Part V.** a. Gross receipts — $ b. Ordinary and necessary operating expenses — $ c. Rental income — Subtract Line b from Line a	$	$
6.	**Interest, dividends and royalties.**	$	$
7.	**Pension and retirement income.**	$	$
8.	**Any amounts paid by another person or entity, on a regular basis, for the household expenses of the debtor or the debtor's dependents, including child support paid for that purpose.** Do not include alimony or separate maintenance payments or amounts paid by your spouse if Column B is completed.	$	$
9.	**Unemployment compensation.** Enter the amount in the appropriate column(s) of Line 9. However, if you contend that unemployment compensation received by you or your spouse was a benefit under the Social Security Act, do not list the amount of such compensation in Column A or B, but instead state the amount in the space below Unemployment compensation claimed to be a benefit under the Social Security Act — Debtor $ ________ — Spouse $ ________	$	$
10.	**Income from all other sources.** Specify source and amount. If necessary, list additional sources on a separate page. Total and enter on Line 9. **Do not include alimony or separate maintenance payments paid by your spouse if Column B is completed, but include all other payments of alimony or separate maintenance.** Do not include any benefits received under the Social Security Act or payments received as a victim of a war crime, crime against humanity, or as a victim of international or domestic terrorism. a. — $ b. — $ Total and enter on Line 10	$	$
11.	**Subtotal of Current Monthly Income for § 707(b)(7).** Add Lines 3 thru 10 in Column A, and, if Column B is completed, add Lines 3 through 10 in Column B. Enter the total(s).	$	$
12.	**Total Current Monthly Income for § 707(b)(7).** If Column B has been completed, add Line 11, Column A to Line 11, Column B, and enter the total. If Column B has not been completed, enter the amount from Line 11, Column A.	$	

	Part III. APPLICATION OF § 707(b)(7) EXCLUSION	
13.	**Annualized Current Monthly Income for § 707(b)(7).** Multiply the amount from Line 12 by the number 12 and enter the result.	$
14.	**Applicable median family income.** Enter the median family income for the applicable state and household size. (This information is available by family size at www.usdoj.gov/ust/ or from the clerk of the bankruptcy court.) a. Enter debtor's state of residence: ________ b. Enter debtor's household size: ________	$

15.	**Application of Section 707(b)(7).** Check the applicable box and proceed as directed. ☐ The amount on Line 13 is less than or equal to the amount on Line 14. Check the box for "The presumption does not arise" at the top of page 1 of this statement, and complete Part VIII; do not complete Parts IV, V, VI or VII. ☐ The amount on Line 13 is more than the amount on Line 14. Complete the remaining parts of this statement.	$

Complete Parts IV, V, VI, and VII of this statement only if required. (See Line 15.)

	Part IV. CALCULATION OF CURRENT MONTHLY INCOME FOR § 707(b)(2)	
16.	**Enter the amount from Line 12.**	$
17.	**Marital adjustment.** If you checked the box at Line 2.c, enter on Line 17 the total of any income listed in Line 11, Column B that was NOT paid on a regular basis for the household expenses of the debtor or the debtor's dependents. Specify in the lines below the basis for excluding the Column B income (such as payment of the spouse's tax liability or the spouse's support of persons other than the debtor or the debtor's dependents) and the amount of income devoted to each purpose. If necessary, list additional adjustments on a separate page. If you did not check box at Line 2.c, enter zero. a. | | $ b. | | $ c. | | $ Total and enter on Line 17.	$
18.	**Current monthly income for § 707(b)(2).** Subtract Line 17 from Line 16 and enter the result.	$
	Part V. CALCULATION OF DEDUCTIONS FROM INCOME	
	Subpart A: Deductions under Standards of the Internal Revenue Service (IRS)	
19A	**National Standards: food, clothing and other items.** Enter in Line 19A the "Total" amount from IRS National Standards for Food, Clothing and Other Items for the applicable household size. (This information is available at www.usdoj.gov/ust/ or from the clerk of the bankruptcy court.)	$
19B	**National Standards: health care.** Enter in Line a1 below the amount from IRS National Standards for Out-of-Pocket Health Care for persons under 65 years of age, and in Line a2 the IRS National Standards for Out-of-Pocket Health Care for persons 65 years of age or older. (This information is available at www.usdoj.gov/ust/ or from the clerk of the bankruptcy court.) Enter in Line b1 the number of members of your household who are under 65 years of age, and enter in Line b2 the number of members of your household who are 65 years of age or older. (The total number of household members must be the same as the number stated in Line 14b.) Multiply Line a1 by Line b1 to obtain a total amount for household members under 65, and enter the result in Line c1. Multiply Line a2 by Line b2 to obtain a total amount for household members 65 and older, and enter the result in Line c2. Add Lines c1 and c2 to obtain a total health care amount, and enter the result in Line 19B. **Household members under 65 years of age**: a1. Allowance per member; b1. Number of members; c1. Subtotal **Household members 65 years of age or older**: a2. Allowance per member; b2. Number of members; c2. Subtotal	$
20A	**Local Standards: housing and utilities; non-mortgage expenses.** Enter the amount of the IRS Housing and Utilities Standards; non-mortgage expenses for the applicable county and household size. (This information is available at www.usdoj.gov/ust/ or from the clerk of the bankruptcy court).	$
20B	**Local Standards: housing and utilities; mortgage/rent expense.** Enter, in Line a below, the amount of the IRS Housing and Utilities Standards; mortgage/rent expense for your county and household size (this information is available at www.usdoj.gov/ust/ or from the clerk of the bankruptcy court); enter on Line b the total of the Average Monthly Payments for any debts secured by your home, as stated in Line 42; subtract Line b from Line a and enter the result in Line 20B. **Do not enter an amount less than zero.** a. IRS Housing and Utilities Standards; mortgage/rental expense | $ b. Average Monthly Payment for any debts secured by your home, if any, as stated in Line 42 | $ c. Net mortgage/rental expense | Subtract Line b from Line a.	$

21.	**Local Standards: housing and utilities; adjustment.** If you contend that the process set out in Lines 20A and 20B does not accurately compute the allowance to which you are entitled under the IRS Housing and Utilities Standards, enter any additional amount to which you contend you are entitled, and state the basis for your contention in the space below: __________ __________ __________	$
22A.	**Local Standards: transportation; vehicle operation/public transportation expense.** You are entitled to an expense allowance in this category regardless of whether you pay the expenses of operating a vehicle and regardless of whether you use public transportation. Check the number of vehicles for which you pay the operating expenses or for which the operating expenses are included as a contribution to your household expenses in Line 8. ☐ 0 ☐ 1 ☐ 2 or more. If you checked 0, enter on Line 22A the "Public Transportation" amount from IRS Local Standards: Transportation. If you checked 1 or 2 or more, enter on Line 22A the "Operating Costs" amount from IRS Local Standards: Transportation for the applicable number of vehicles in the applicable Metropolitan Statistical Area or Census Region. (These amounts are available at www.usdoj.gov/ust/ or from the clerk of the bankruptcy court.)	$
22B.	**Local Standards: transportation; additional public transportation expense.** If you pay the operating expenses for a vehicle and also use public transportation, and you contend that you are entitled to an additional deduction for your public transportation expenses, enter on Line 22B the "Public Transportation" amount from IRS Local Standards: Transportation. (This amount is available at www.usdoj.gov/ust/ or from the clerk of the bankruptcy court.)	$
23.	**Local Standards: transportation ownership/lease expense; Vehicle 1.** Check the number of vehicles for which you claim an ownership/lease expense. (You may not claim an ownership/lease expense for more than two vehicles.) ☐ 1 ☐ 2 or more. Enter, in Line a below, the "Ownership Costs" for "One Car" from the IRS Local Standards: Transportation (available at www.usdoj.gov/ust/ or from the clerk of the bankruptcy court); enter in Line b the total of the Average Monthly Payments for any debts secured by Vehicle 1, as stated in Line 42; subtract Line b from Line a and enter the result in Line 23. **Do not enter an amount less than zero.** a. | IRS Transportation Standards, Ownership Costs | $ b. | Average Monthly Payment for any debts secured by Vehicle 1, as stated in Line 42 | $ c. | Net ownership/lease expense for Vehicle 1 | Subtract Line b from Line a.	$
24.	**Local Standards: transportation ownership/lease expense; Vehicle 2.** Complete this Line only if you checked the "2 or more" Box in Line 23. Enter, in Line a below, the "Ownership Costs" for "One Car" from the IRS Local Standards: Transportation (available at www.usdoj.gov/ust/ or from the clerk of the bankruptcy court); enter in Line b the total of the Average Monthly Payments for any debts secured by Vehicle 2, as stated in Line 42; subtract Line b from Line a and enter the result in Line 24. **Do not enter an amount less than zero.** a. | IRS Transportation Standards, Ownership Costs | $ b. | Average Monthly Payments for debts secured by Vehicle 2, if any, as stated in Line 42 | $ c. | Net ownership/lease expense for Vehicle 2 | Subtract Line b from Line a.	$
25.	**Other Necessary Expenses: taxes.** Enter the total average monthly expense that you actually incur for all federal, state and local taxes, other than real estate and sales taxes, such as income taxes, self-employment taxes, social-security taxes, and Medicare taxes. **Do not include real estate or sales taxes.**	$
26.	**Other Necessary Expenses: involuntary deductions for employment.** Enter the total average monthly payroll deductions that are required for your employment, such as retirement contributions, union dues, and uniform costs. **Do not include discretionary amounts, such as voluntary 401(k) contributions.**	$
27.	Other Necessary Expenses: life insurance. Enter total average monthly premiums that you actually pay for term life insurance for yourself. **Do not include premiums for insurance on your dependents, for whole life or for any other form of insurance.**	$
28.	**Other Necessary Expenses: court-ordered payments.** Enter the total monthly amount that you are required to pay pursuant to the order of a court or administrative agency, such as spousal or child support payments. Do not include payments on past due obligations included in Line 44.	$

29.	**Other Necessary Expenses: education for employment or for a physically or mentally challenged child.** Enter the total average monthly amount that you actually expend for education that is a condition of employment and for education that is required for a physically or mentally challenged dependent child for whom no public education providing similar services is available.	$
30	**Other Necessary Expenses: childcare.** Enter the total average monthly amount that you actually expend on childcare—such as baby-sitting, day care, nursery and preschool. **Do not include other educational payments.**	$
31.	**Other Necessary Expenses: health care.** Enter the total average monthly amount that you actually expend on health care that is required for the health and welfare of yourself or your dependents, that is not reimbursed by insurance or paid by a health savings account, and that is in excess of the amount entered in Line 19B. **Do not include payments for health insurance or health savings accounts listed in Line 34.**	$
32.	**Other Necessary Expenses: telecommunication services.** Enter the total average monthly amount that you actually pay for telecommunication services other than your basic home telephone and cell phone service—such as pagers, call waiting, caller id, special long distance, or internet service—to the extent necessary for your health and welfare or that of your dependents. **Do not include any amount previously deducted.**	$
33.	**Total Expenses Allowed under IRS Standards.** Enter the total of Lines 19 through 32.	$
	Subpart B: Additional Living Expense Deductions **Note: Do not include any expenses that you have listed in Lines 19-32**	
34.	**Health Insurance, Disability Insurance, and Health Savings Account Expenses.** List the monthly expenses in the categories set out in lines a-c below that are reasonably necessary for yourself, your spouse, or your dependents a. Health Insurance $ b. Disability Insurance $ c. Health Savings Account $ Total and enter on Line 34 If you do not actually expend this total amount, state your actual total average monthly expenditures in the space below: $ ________	$
35.	**Continued contributions to the care of household or family members.** Enter the total average actual monthly expenses that you will continue to pay for the reasonable and necessary care and support of an elderly, chronically ill, or disabled member of your household or member of your immediate family who is unable to pay for such expenses.	$
36.	**Protection against family violence.** Enter the total average reasonably necessary monthly expenses that you actually incurred to maintain the safety of your family under the Family Violence Prevention and Services Act or other applicable federal law. The nature of these expenses is required to be kept confidential by the court.	$
37.	**Home energy costs.** Enter the total average monthly amount, in excess of the allowance specified by IRS Local Standards for Housing and Utilities, that you actually expend for home energy costs. **You must provide your case trustee with documentation of your actual expenses, and you must demonstrate that the additional amount claimed is reasonable and necessary.**	$
38.	**Education expenses for dependent children less than 18.** Enter the total average monthly expenses that you actually incur, not to exceed $137.50 per child, for attendance at a private or public elementary or secondary school by your dependent children less than 18 years of age. **You must provide your case trustee with documentation of your actual expenses, and you must explain why the amount claimed is reasonable and necessary and not already accounted for in the IRS Standards.**	$
39.	**Additional food and clothing expense.** Enter the total average monthly amount by which your food and clothing expenses exceed the combined allowances for food and clothing (apparel and services) in the IRS National Standards, not to exceed 5% of those combined allowances. (This information is available at www.usdoj.gov/ust/ or from the clerk of the bankruptcy court.) **You must demonstrate that the additional amount claimed is reasonable and necessary.**	$
40.	**Continued charitable contributions.** Enter the amount that you will continue to contribute in the form of cash or financial instruments to a charitable organization as defined in 26 U.S.C. § 170(c)(1)-(2).	$
41.	**Total Additional Expense Deductions under § 707(b).** Enter the total of Lines 34 through 40	$

Subpart C: Deductions for Debt Payment

42. **Future payments on secured claims.** For each of your debts that is secured by an interest in property that you own, list the name of the creditor, identify the property securing the debt, state the Average Monthly Payment, and check whether the payment includes taxes or insurance. The Average Monthly Payment is the total of all amounts scheduled as contractually due to each Secured Creditor in the 60 months following the filing of the bankruptcy case, divided by 60. If necessary, list additional entries on a separate page. Enter the total of the Average Monthly Payments on Line 42.

	Name of Creditor	Property Securing the Debt	Average Monthly Payment	Does payment include taxes or insurance?
a.			$	☐ yes ☐ no
b.			$	☐ yes ☐ no
c.			$	☐ yes ☐ no
			Total: Add Lines a, b and c	

$

43. **Other payments on secured claims.** If any of debts listed in Line 42 are secured by your primary residence, a motor vehicle, or other property necessary for your support or the support of your dependents, you may include in your deduction 1/60th of any amount (the "cure amount") that you must pay the creditor in addition to the payments listed in Line 42, in order to maintain possession of the property. The cure amount would include any sums in default that must be paid in order to avoid repossession or foreclosure. List and total any such amounts in the following chart. If necessary, list additional entries on a separate page.

	Name of Creditor	Property Securing the Debt	1/60 of the Cure Amount
a.			$
b.			$
c.			$
			Total: Add Lines a, b and c

$

44. **Payments on prepetition priority claims.** Enter the total amount, divided by 60, of all priority claims, such as priority tax, child support and alimony claims, for which you were liable at the time of your bankruptcy filing. Do not include current obligations, such as those set out in Line 28. $

45. **Chapter 13 administrative expenses.** If you are eligible to file a case under chapter 13, complete the following chart, multiply the amount in line a by the amount in line b, and enter the resulting administrative expense.

a.	Projected average monthly Chapter 13 plan payment.	$
b.	Current multiplier for your district as determined under schedules issued by the Executive Office for United States Trustees. (This information is available at www.usdoj.gov/ust/ or from the clerk of the bankruptcy court.)	x
c.	Average monthly administrative expense of Chapter 13 case	Total: Multiply Lines a and b

$

46.	**Total Deductions for Debt Payment.** Enter the total of Lines 42 through 45.	$

Subpart D: Total Deductions from Income

47.	**Total of all deductions allowed under § 707(b)(2).** Enter the total of Lines 33, 41, and 46.	$

Part VI. DETERMINATION OF § 707(b)(2) PRESUMPTION

48.	**Enter the amount from Line 18 (Current monthly income for § 707(b)(2))**	$
49.	**Enter the amount from Line 47 (Total of all deductions allowed under § 707(b)(2))**	$
50.	**Monthly disposable income under § 707(b)(2).** Subtract Line 49 from Line 48 and enter the result.	$
51.	**60-month disposable income under § 707(b)(2).** Multiply the amount in Line 50 by the number 60 and enter the result.	$

Form B22A (Chapter 7)(12/08) 2008 USBC, Central District of California

52.	**Initial presumption determination.** Check the applicable box and proceed as directed. ☐ **The amount on Line 51 is less than $6,575.** Check the box for "The presumption does not arise" at the top of page 1 of this statement, and complete the verification in Part VIII. Do not complete the remainder of Part VI. ☐ **The amount set forth on Line 51 is more than $10,950.** Check the box for "The presumption arises" at the top of page 1 of this statement, and complete the verification in Part VIII. You may also complete Part VII. Do not complete the remainder of Part VI. ☐ **The amount on Line 51 is at least $6,575, but not more than $10,950.** Complete the remainder of Part VI (Lines 53 through 55).	
53.	**Enter the amount of your total non-priority unsecured debt**	$
54.	**Threshold debt payment amount.** Multiply the amount in Line 53 by the number 0.25 and enter the result.	$
55.	**Secondary presumption determination.** Check the applicable box and proceed as directed. ☐ The amount on Line 51 is less than the amount on Line 54. Check the box for "The presumption does not arise" at the top of page 1 of this statement, and complete the verification in Part VIII. ☐ **The amount on Line 51 is equal to or greater than the amount on Line 54.** Check the box for "The presumption arises" at the top of page 1 of this statement, and complete the verification in Part VIII. You may also complete Part VII.	

Part VII: ADDITIONAL EXPENSE CLAIMS

56. **Other Expenses.** List and describe any monthly expenses, not otherwise stated in this form, that are required for the health and welfare of you and your family and that you contend should be an additional deduction from your current monthly income under § 707(b)(2)(A)(ii)(I). If necessary, list additional sources on a separate page. All figures should reflect your average monthly expense for each item. Total the expenses.

	Expense Description	Monthly Amount
a.		$
b.		$
c.		$
	Total: Add Lines a, b and c	$

Part VIII: VERIFICATION

57. I declare under penalty of perjury that the information provided in this statement is true and correct. *(If this is a joint case, both debtors must sign.)*

Date: ____________ Signature ____________________
(Debtor)

Date: ____________ Signature ____________________
(Joint Debtor, if any)

CDCAL-353 C.D. CALIFORNIA

Chapter 11 Debtor's Certification of Completion of Postpetition Instructional Course Concerning Personal Financial Management

Form B23 (Official Form 23) - (12/08) 2008 USBC, Central District of California

UNITED STATES BANKRUPTCY COURT
CENTRAL DISTRICT OF CALIFORNIA

In re: Debtor(s).	CHAPTER: CASE NO.:

DEBTOR'S CERTIFICATION OF COMPLETION OF POSTPETITION INSTRUCTIONAL COURSE CONCERNING PERSONAL FINANCIAL MANAGEMENT

Every individual debtor in a chapter 7, chapter 11 in which § 1141(d)(3) applies, or chapter 13 case must file this certification. If a joint petition is filed, each spouse must complete and file a separate certification. Complete one of the following statements and file by the deadline stated below:

☐ I, ______________________ *(Printed Name of Debtor)*, the debtor in the above-styled case, hereby certify that on ______________ *(Date)*, I completed an instructional course in personal financial management provided by ______________________ *(Name of Provider)*, an approved personal financial management provider.

Certificate No. *(if any)*: ______________.

☐ I, ______________________ *(Printed Name of Debtor)*, the debtor in the above-styled case, hereby certify that no personal financial management course is required because of *[Check the appropriate box.]*:

☐ Incapacity or disability, as defined in 11 U.S.C. § 109(h);
☐ Active military duty in a military combat zone; or
☐ Residence in a district in which the United States trustee *(or bankruptcy administrator)* has determined that the approved instructional courses are not adequate at this time to serve the additional individuals who would otherwise be required to complete such courses.

Date: ______________ Signature of Debtor: ______________________

Instructions: Use this form only to certify whether you completed a course in personal financial management. (Fed. R. Bankr. P. 1007(b)(7).) Do NOT use this form to file the certificate given to you by your prepetition credit counseling provider and do NOT include with the petition when filing your case.

Filing Deadlines: In a chapter 7 case, file within 45 days of the first date set for the meeting of creditors under § 341 of the Bankruptcy Code. In a chapter 11 or 13 case, file no later than the last payment made by the debtor as required by the plan or the filing of a motion for a discharge under § 1141(d)(5)(B) or § 1328(b) of the Code. (See Fed. R. Bankr. P. 1007(c).)

Chapter 11 Disclosure Statement (F 3017-1)

UNITED STATES BANKRUPTCY COURT
CENTRAL DISTRICT OF CALIFORNIA

CENTRAL DISTRICT OF CALIFORNIA

APPROVED FORM FOR PRODUCING A

CHAPTER 11 DISCLOSURE STATEMENT

WordPerfect Format

NAME OF ATTORNEY - State Bar No. ____________
NAME OF ATTORNEY - State Bar No. ____________
NAME OF LAW FIRM
Address
City, State Zip Code
Telephone ( ) -

Attorneys for ________________

UNITED STATES BANKRUPTCY COURT

CENTRAL DISTRICT OF CALIFORNIA

In re NAME OF DEBTOR, Debtor	Bk. No. __ __-_____-__ In a Case Under Chapter 11 of the Bankruptcy Code (11 U.S.C. § 1101 et seq.) ______[1] DISCLOSURE STATEMENT DESCRIBING ______[2] CHAPTER 11 PLAN **Disclosure Statement Hearing** Date: ________ Time: ________ Ctrm: {Insert Courtroom #} {Insert Full Court Address Here} **Plan Confirmation Hearing** Complete This Section When Applicable Date: ________ Time: ________ Ctrm: {Insert Courtroom #} {Insert Full Court Address Here}

TABLE OF CONTENTS

I. **INTRODUCTION** 1
A. Purpose of This Document 1
B. Deadlines for Voting and Objecting; Date of Plan Confirmation Hearing 2
1. Time and Place of the Confirmation Hearing 3
2. Deadline for Voting For or Against the Plan 3
3. Deadline for Objecting to the Confirmation of the Plan 3
4. Identity of Person to Contact for More Information Regarding the Plan 3
C. Disclaimer 3

II. **BACKGROUND** 4
A. Description and History of the Debtor's Business 4
B. Principals/Affiliates of Debtor's Business 4
C. Management of the Debtor Before and After the Bankruptcy 4
D. Events Leading to Chapter 11 Filing 4
E. Significant Events 4
1. Bankruptcy Proceedings 4
2. Other Legal Proceedings 4
3. Actual and Projected Recovery of Preferential or Fraudulent Transfers 4
4. Procedures Implemented to Resolve Financial Problems 5
5. Current and Historical Financial Conditions 5

III. **SUMMARY OF THE PLAN OF REORGANIZATION** 5
A. What Creditors and Interest Holders Will Receive Under the Proposed Plan 5
B. Unclassified Claims 5
1. Administrative Expenses 6
2. Priority Tax Claims 7
C. Classified Claims and Interests 7
1. Classes of Secured Claims 7
2. Classes of Priority Unsecured Claims 8
3. Classes of General Unsecured Claims 9
4. Class(es) of Interest Holders 10
D. Means of Effectuating the Plan 10
1. Funding for the Plan 10
2. Post-Confirmation Management 10
3. Disbursing Agent 10
E. Risk Factors 10
F. Other Provisions of the Plan 11
1. Executory Contracts and Unexpired Leases . . 11
a. Assumptions 11
b. Rejections 11

Changes in Rates Subject to Regulatory Approval 12
3. Retention of Jurisdiction 12
6. Tax Consequences of Plan 12

IV. **CONFIRMATION REQUIREMENTS AND PROCEDURES** 13
A. Who May Vote or Object 13
1. Who May Object to Confirmation of the Plan 13
2. Who May Vote to Accept/Reject the Plan 13
a. What is an Allowed Claim/Interest 13
b. What Is an Impaired Claim/Interest 14
3. Who is <u>Not</u> Entitled to Vote 15
4. Who Can Vote in More Than One Class 15
5. Votes Necessary to Confirm the Plan 16
6. Votes Necessary for a Class to Accept the Plan 16
7. Treatment of Nonaccepting Classes 16
8. Request for Confirmation Despite Nonacceptance by Impaired Class(es) 17
B. Liquidation Analysis 17
C. Feasibility 20

V. **EFFECTS OF CONFIRMATION OF PLAN** 22
A. Discharge 22
B. Revesting of Property in the Debtor 22
C. Modification of Plan 22
D. Post-Confirmation Status Report 23
E. Quarterly Fees 23
F. Post-Confirmation Conversion/Dismissal 23
G. Final Decree 24

VI. **SUPPORTING DECLARATIONS** 25

EXHIBIT A - LIST OF ALL ASSETS 26
EXHIBIT B - FINANCIAL STATEMENT 27
EXHIBIT C - UNEXPIRED LEASES TO BE ASSUMED 28
EXHIBIT D - EXECUTORY CONTRACTS TO BE ASSUMED 29
EXHIBIT E - LIQUIDATION ANALYSIS 30
EXHIBIT F - LIST OF ADMINISTRATIVE EXPENSE CLAIMS . . . 31
EXHIBIT G - LIST OF PRIORITY UNSECURED CLAIMS 32
EXHIBIT H - LIST OF GENERAL UNSECURED CLAIMS 38
EXHIBIT I - LIST OF EQUITY INTERESTS. 39

I.

INTRODUCTION

________[3] is the Debtor in a Chapter 11 bankruptcy case. On ______[4], ________[5] commenced a bankruptcy case by filing ________[6] Chapter 11 ______[6b] petition under the United States Bankruptcy Code ("Code"), 11 U.S.C. § 101 et seq., Chapter 11 allows the Debtor, and under some circumstances, creditors and others parties in interest, to propose a plan of reorganization ("Plan"). The Plan may provide for the Debtor to reorganize by continuing to operate, to liquidate by selling assets of the estate, or a combination of both. ________[7] is the party proposing the Plan sent to you in the same envelope as this document. THE DOCUMENT YOU ARE READING IS THE DISCLOSURE STATEMENT FOR THE ENCLOSED PLAN.

This is a ______[8] plan. In other words, the Proponent seeks to accomplish payments under the Plan by _____[9]. The Effective Date of the proposed Plan is ________[10].

A. Purpose of This Document

This Disclosure Statement summarizes what is in the Plan, and tells you certain information relating to the Plan and the process the Court follows in determining whether or not to confirm the Plan.

READ THIS DISCLOSURE STATEMENT CAREFULLY IF YOU WANT TO KNOW ABOUT:

(1) WHO CAN VOTE OR OBJECT,

(2) WHAT THE TREATMENT OF YOUR CLAIM IS (i.e., what your claim will receive if the Plan is confirmed), AND HOW

THIS TREATMENT COMPARES TO WHAT YOUR CLAIM WOULD RECEIVE IN LIQUIDATION,

(3) THE HISTORY OF THE DEBTOR AND SIGNIFICANT EVENTS DURING THE BANKRUPTCY,

(4) WHAT THINGS THE COURT WILL LOOK AT TO DECIDE WHETHER OR NOT TO CONFIRM THE PLAN,

(5) WHAT IS THE EFFECT OF CONFIRMATION, AND

(6) WHETHER THIS PLAN IS FEASIBLE.

This Disclosure Statement cannot tell you everything about your rights. You should consider consulting your own lawyer to obtain more specific advice on how this Plan will affect you and what is the best course of action for you.

Be sure to read the Plan as well as the Disclosure Statement. If there are any inconsistencies between the Plan and the Disclosure Statement, the Plan provisions will govern.

The Code requires a Disclosure Statement to contain "adequate information" concerning the Plan. The Bankruptcy Court ("Court") has approved this document as an adequate Disclosure Statement, containing enough information to enable parties affected by the Plan to make an informed judgment about the Plan. Any party can now solicit votes for or against the Plan.

B. Deadlines for Voting and Objecting; Date of Plan Confirmation Hearing

THE COURT HAS NOT YET CONFIRMED THE PLAN DESCRIBED IN THIS DISCLOSURE STATEMENT. IN OTHER WORDS, THE TERMS OF THE PLAN ARE NOT YET BINDING ON ANYONE. HOWEVER, IF THE COURT LATER CONFIRMS THE PLAN, THEN THE PLAN WILL BE BINDING ON THE DEBTOR AND ON ALL CREDITORS

AND INTEREST HOLDERS IN THIS CASE.

1. Time and Place of the Confirmation Hearing

The hearing where the Court will determine whether or not to confirm the Plan will take place on ________[11], at ____ (A.M./ P.M.) in Courtroom ____, (Insert Courthouse Name), (Insert Full Court Address, City, State, Zip Code).

2. Deadline For Voting For or Against the Plan

If you are entitled to vote, it is in your best interest to timely vote on the enclosed ballot and return the ballot in the enclosed envelope to ________[12].

Your ballot must be received by ________[13] or it will not be counted.

3. Deadline For Objecting to the Confirmation of the Plan

Objections to the confirmation of the Plan must be filed with the Court and served upon ________[14] by ________[15].

4. Identity of Person to Contact for More Information Regarding the Plan

Any interested party desiring further information about the Plan should contact ________[16].

C. Disclaimer

The financial data relied upon in formulating the Plan is based on ________[17]. The information contained in this Disclosure Statement is provided by ________[18]. The Plan Proponent represents that everything stated in the Disclosure Statement is true to the Proponent's best knowledge. The Court has not yet determined whether or not the Plan is confirmable and makes no recommendation as to whether or not you should support or oppose the Plan.

II.

BACKGROUND

A. Description and History of the Debtor's Business

The Debtor is a ____________[19].

The Debtor is in the business of ____________[20].

The Debtor has been in this business since ____________[21].

B. Principals/Affiliates of Debtor's Business

____________[22].

C. Management of the Debtor Before and After the Bankruptcy

____________[23].

D. Events Leading to Chapter 11 Filing

Here is a brief summary of the circumstances that led to the filing of this Chapter 11 case: ____________[24].

E. Significant Events During the Bankruptcy

1. Bankruptcy Proceedings

The following is a chronological list of significant events which have occurred during this case: ____________[25]

The Court has approved the employment of the following professionals: ____________[26]

Currently, the following significant adversary proceedings and motions are still pending: ____________[27].

2. Other Legal Proceedings

In addition to the proceedings discussed above, the Debtor is currently involved in the following nonbankruptcy legal proceedings: [28] ________.

3. Actual and Projected Recovery of Preferential or Fraudulent Transfers [29]

____[30]____ is estimated to be realized from the recovery of fraudulent and preferential transfers. The following is a summary of the fraudulent conveyance and preference actions filed or to be filed in this case: ____[31]

D. Procedures Implemented to Resolve Financial Problems

To attempt to fix the problems that led to the bankruptcy filing, Debtor has implemented the following procedures: ____[32]

E. Current and Historical Financial Conditions

____[33]____.

The identity and fair market value of the estate's assets are listed in Exhibit A. See also the Debtor's financial history set forth in Exhibit B.

III.

SUMMARY OF THE PLAN OF REORGANIZATION

A. What Creditors and Interest Holders Will Receive Under The Proposed Plan

As required by the Bankruptcy Code, the Plan classifies claims and interests in various classes according to their right to priority. The Plan states whether each class of claims or interests is impaired or unimpaired. The Plan provides the treatment each class will receive.

B. Unclassified Claims

Certain types of claims are not placed into voting classes; instead they are unclassified. They are not considered impaired and they do not vote on the Plan because they are automatically entitled to specific treatment provided for them in the Bankruptcy Code. As such, the Proponent has <u>not</u> placed the following claims in a class.

1. Administrative Expenses

Administrative expenses are claims for costs or expenses of administering the Debtor's Chapter 11 case which are allowed under Code Section 507(a)(1). The Code requires that all administrative claims be paid on the Effective Date of the Plan, unless a particular claimant agrees to a different treatment.[34]

The following chart lists <u>all</u> of the Debtor's § 507(a)(1) administrative claims and their treatment under the Plan[35] (see Exhibit F for detailed information about each administrative expense claim).

		[36]

<u>Court Approval of Fees Required</u>:

The Court must rule on all fees listed in this chart before the fees will be owed. For all fees except Clerk's Office fees and U.S. Trustee's fees, the professional in question must file and serve a properly noticed fee application and the Court must rule on the application. Only the amount of fees allowed by the Court will be owed and required to be paid under this Plan.

As indicated above, the Debtor will need to pay ______[37] worth of administrative claims on the Effective Date of the Plan unless the claimant has agreed to be paid later or the Court has not yet ruled on the claim. As indicated elsewhere in this

Disclosure Statement, Debtor will have ____[38]____ amount of cash on hand on the Effective Date of the Plan. The source of this cash will be ____[39]____.

6. Priority Tax Claims

Priority tax claims are certain unsecured income, employment and other taxes described by Code Section 507(a)(8)[40]. The Code requires that each holder of such a 507(a)(8) priority tax claim receive the present value of such claim in deferred cash payments, over a period not exceeding six years from the date of the assessment of such tax.

The following chart lists <u>all</u> of the Debtor's Section 507(a)(8)[41] priority tax claims and their treatment under the Plan:

<u>Description</u>	<u>Amount Owed</u>	<u>Treatment</u>[42]
• Name = • Type of tax = • Date tax assessed =		• Pymt interval[43] = • Pymt amt/interval[44] = • Begin date[45] = = • End date[46] = = $ • Interest Rate %[47] • Total Payout Amount[48] __ %
• Name = • Type of tax = • Date tax assessed =		• Pymt interval = • Pymt amt/interval = • Begin date = = • End date = = $ • Interest Rate % • Total Payout Amount %

C. **Classified Claims and Interests**

1. **Classes of Secured Claims**

Secured claims are claims secured by liens on property of the estate. The following chart lists all classes containing Debtor's secured pre-petition claims and their treatment under this Plan[48a]:

CLASS#	DESCRIPTION	INSIDERS (Y/N)	IMPAIRED (Y/N)	TREATMENT
	Secured claim of: ● Name = ● Collateral description = ● Collateral value = ● Priority of security int. = ● Principal owed = ● Pre-pet. arrearage amount = ● Post-pet. arrearage amount = ● Total claim amount =		[49]	● Pymt interval = = ● Pymt amt/interval = ● Balloon pymt[50] = ● Begin date = = ● End date = $ = ● Interest rate %
	Secured claim of: ● Name = ● Collateral description = ● Collateral value = ● Priority of security int. = ● Principal owed = ● Pre-pet. arrearage amount = ● Post-pet. arrearage amount = ● Total claim amount =			● Pymt interval = ● Pymt amt/interval = ● Balloon pymt = ● Begin date = ● End date = ● Interest rate % = ● Total payout % = $ ● Treatment of Lien =

2. Classes of Priority Unsecured Claims

Certain priority claims that are referred to in Code Sections 507(a)(3), (4), (5), (6), and (7)[51] are required to be placed in classes. These types of claims are entitled to priority treatment as follows: the Code requires that each holder of such a claim receive cash on the Effective Date equal to the allowed amount of such claim. However, a class of unsecured priority claim holders may vote to accept deferred cash payments of a value, as of the Effective Date, equal to the allowed amount of such claims.

The following chart lists all classes containing Debtor's 507(a)(3), (a)(4), (a)(5), (a)(6), and (a)(7)[52] priority unsecured claims and their treatment under this Plan (see Exhibit G for more detailed information about each priority unsecured claim)[53]:

CLASS#	DESCRIPTION	IMPAIRED (Y/N)	TREATMENT
	Priority unsecured claim pursuant to ______[54] ● Total amt of claims = ______[55]		● Paid in full in cash on Effective Date[56]
	Priority unsecured claim pursuant to ______[57] ● Total amt of claims = ______[58]		● Paid in full in cash on Effective Date

3. **Class of General Unsecured Claims**

General unsecured claims are unsecured claims not entitled to priority under Code Section 507(a). The following chart identifies this Plan's treatment of the class containing <u>all</u> of Debtor's general unsecured claims (see Exhibit H for detailed information about each general unsecured claim):

CLASS#	DESCRIPTION	IMPAIRED (Y/N)	TREATMENT
	General unsecured claims ● Total amt of claims =	[59]	● Pymt interval = ● Pymt amt/interval = ● Begin date = ● End date = ● Interest rate % = ● Total payout[59a] ___ % = $

59b.
59c.

4. **Class(es) of Interest Holders**

Interest holders are the parties who hold ownership interest (i.e., equity interest) in the Debtor. If the Debtor is a corporation, entities holding preferred or common stock in the Debtor are interest holders. If the Debtor is a partnership, the interest holders include both general and limited partners. If the Debtor is an individual, the Debtor is the interest holder. The following chart identifies the Plan's treatment of the class[60] of interest holders (see Exhibit I for more detailed information about each interest holder):

CLASS #	DESCRIPTION	IMPAIRED (Y/N)	TREATMENT
	Interest holders	61	

D. **Means of Effectuating the Plan**

1. **Funding for the Plan**

The Plan will be funded by the following:___62___.

2. **Post-confirmation Management**

___63___

3. **Disbursing Agent**

___64___ shall act as the disbursing agent for the purpose of making all distributions provided for under the Plan. The Disbursing Agent shall serve ___65___ bond and shall receive ___66___ for distribution services rendered and expenses incurred pursuant to the Plan.

E. **Risk Factors**

The proposed Plan has the following risks: ________[67]

F. **Other Provisions of the Plan**

1. Executory Contracts and Unexpired Leases

a. Assumptions

The following are the unexpired leases and executory contracts to be assumed as obligations of the reorganized Debtor under this Plan (see Exhibit C for more detailed information on unexpired leases to be assumed and Exhibit D for more detailed information on executory contracts to be assumed):

________[68]

On the Effective Date, each of the unexpired leases and executory contracts listed above shall be assumed as obligations of the reorganized Debtor. The Order of the Court confirming the Plan shall constitute an Order approving the assumption of each lease and contract listed above. If you are a party to a lease or contract to be assumed and you object to the assumption of your lease or contract, you must file and serve your objection to the Plan within the deadline for objecting to the confirmation of the Plan. See Section {I.B.3.} of this document for the specific date.

b. Rejections

On the Effective Date, the following executory contracts and unexpired leases will be rejected:

________[69]

The order confirming the Plan shall constitute an Order

approving the rejection of the lease or contract. If you are a party to a contract or lease to be rejected and you object to the rejection of your contract or lease, you must file and serve your objection to the Plan within the deadline for objecting to the confirmation of the Plan. See Section {I.B.3.} of this document for the specific date.

THE BAR DATE FOR FILING A PROOF OF CLAIM BASED ON A CLAIM ARISING FROM THE REJECTION OF A LEASE OR CONTRACT IS ________[70]. Any claim based on the rejection of a contract or lease will be barred if the proof of claim is not timely filed, unless the Court later orders otherwise.

Changes in Rates Subject to Regulatory Commission Approval

This Debtor ________[71] subject to governmental regulatory commission approval of its rates[71a].

Retention of Jurisdiction.

The Court will retain jurisdiction to the extent provided by law[71b].

G. Tax Consequences of Plan

CREDITORS AND INTEREST HOLDERS CONCERNED WITH HOW THE PLAN MAY AFFECT THEIR TAX LIABILITY SHOULD CONSULT WITH THEIR OWN ACCOUNTANTS, ATTORNEYS, AND/OR ADVISORS. The following disclosure of possible tax consequences is intended solely for the purpose of alerting readers about possible tax issues this Plan may present to the Debtor. The Proponent CANNOT and DOES NOT represent that the tax consequences contained below are the only tax consequences of the Plan because the Tax Code embodies many complicated rules which make it difficult to state completely and accurately all the tax implications of any action.

The following are the tax consequences which the Plan will have on the Debtor's tax liability: ________[72]

IV.

CONFIRMATION REQUIREMENTS AND PROCEDURES

PERSONS OR ENTITIES CONCERNED WITH CONFIRMATION OR THIS PLAN SHOULD CONSULT WITH THEIR OWN ATTORNEYS BECAUSE THE LAW ON CONFIRMING A PLAN OF REORGANIZATION IS VERY COMPLEX. The following discussion is intended solely for the purpose of alerting readers about basic confirmation issues, which they may wish to consider, as well as certain deadlines for filing claims. The proponent CANNOT and DOES NOT represent that the discussion contained below is a complete summary of the law on this topic.

Many requirements must be met before the Court can confirm a Plan. Some of the requirements include that the Plan must be proposed in good faith, acceptance of the Plan, whether the Plan pays creditors at least as much as creditors would receive in a Chapter 7 liquidation, and whether the Plan is feasible. These requirements are not the only requirements for confirmation.

A. Who May Vote or Object

Who May Object to Confirmation of the Plan

Any party in interest may object to the confirmation of the Plan, but as explained below not everyone is entitled to vote to accept or reject the Plan.

Who May Vote to Accept/Reject the Plan

A creditor or interest holder has a right to vote for or against the Plan if that creditor or interest holder has a claim which is both (1) allowed or allowed for voting purposes and (2) classified in an impaired class.

a. What Is an Allowed Claim/Interest

As noted above, a creditor or interest holder must first have an allowed claim or interest to have the right to vote. Generally, any proof of claim or interest will be allowed, unless a party in interest brings a motion objecting to the claim. When an objection to a claim or interest is filed, the creditor or interest holder holding the claim or interest cannot vote unless the Court, after notice and hearing, either overrules the objection or allows the claim or interest for voting purposes.

THE BAR DATE FOR FILING A PROOF OF CLAIM IN THIS CASE WAS ________[73]. A creditor or interest holder may have an allowed claim or interest even if a proof of claim or interest was not timely filed. A claim is deemed allowed if (1) it is scheduled on the Debtor's schedules and such claim is not scheduled as disputed, contingent, or unliquidated, and (2) no party in interest has objected to the claim. An interest is deemed allowed if it is scheduled and no party in interest has objected to the interest. Consult Exhibits F through L to see how the Proponent has characterized your claim or interest.

b. What Is an Impaired Claim/Interest

As noted above, an allowed claim or interest only has the right to vote if it is in a class that is impaired under the Plan. A class is impaired if the Plan alters the legal, equitable, or contractual rights of the members of that class. For example, a class comprised of general unsecured claims is impaired if the Plan fails to pay the members of that class 100% of what they are owed.

In this case, the Proponent believes that classes ________[74] are impaired and that holders of claims in each of these classes are therefore entitled to vote to accept or reject the Plan. The

Proponent believes that classes ________[75] are unimpaired and that holders of claims in each of these classes therefore do not have the right to vote to accept or reject the Plan. Parties who dispute the Proponent's characterization of their claim or interest as being impaired or unimpaired may file an objection to the Plan contending that the Proponent has incorrectly characterized the class.

Who is Not Entitled to Vote

The following four types of claims are <u>not</u> entitled to vote: (1) claims that have been disallowed; (2) claims in unimpaired classes; (3) claims entitled to priority pursuant to Code sections 507(a)(1), (a)(2), and (a)(8)[76]; and (4) claims in classes that do not receive or retain any value under the Plan. Claims in unimpaired classes are not entitled to vote because such classes are deemed to have accepted the Plan. Claims entitled to priority pursuant to Code sections 507(a)(1), (a)(2), and (a)(7) are not entitled to vote because such claims are not placed in classes and they are required to receive certain treatment specified by the Code. Claims in classes that do not receive or retain any value under the Plan do not vote because such classes are deemed to have rejected the Plan. EVEN IF YOUR CLAIM IS OF THE TYPE DESCRIBED ABOVE, YOU MAY STILL HAVE A RIGHT TO OBJECT TO THE CONFIRMATION OF THE PLAN.

Who Can Vote in More Than One Class

A creditor whose claim has been allowed in part as a secured claim and in part as an unsecured claim is entitled to accept or reject a Plan in both capacities by casting one ballot for the secured part of the claim and another ballot for the unsecured claim.

5. Votes Necessary to Confirm the Plan

If impaired classes exist, the Court cannot confirm the Plan unless (1) at least one impaired class has accepted the Plan without counting the votes of any insiders within that class, and (2) all impaired classes have voted to accept the Plan, unless the Plan is eligible to be confirmed by "cramdown" on non-accepting classes, as discussed later in Section {IV.A.8.}.

6. Votes Necessary for a Class to Accept the Plan

A class of claims is considered to have accepted the Plan when more than one-half (1/2) in number and at least two-thirds (2/3) in dollar amount of the claims which actually voted, voted in favor of the Plan. A class of interests is considered to have accepted the Plan when at least two-thirds (2/3) in amount of the interest-holders of such class which actually voted, voted to accept the Plan.

7. Treatment of Nonaccepting Classes

As noted above, even if <u>all</u> impaired classes do not accept the proposed Plan, the Court may nonetheless confirm the Plan if the nonaccepting classes are treated in the manner required by the Code. The process by which nonaccepting classes are forced to be bound by the terms of the Plan is commonly referred to as "cramdown." The Code allows the Plan to be "crammed down" on nonaccepting classes of claims or interests if it meets all consensual requirements except the voting requirements of 1129(a)(8) and if the Plan does not "discriminate unfairly" and is "fair and equitable" toward each impaired class that has not voted to accept the Plan as referred to in 11 U.S.C. § 1129(b) and applicable case law.

3. Request for Confirmation Despite Nonacceptance by Impaired Class(es)

The party proposing this Plan ____[77]____ asks the Court to confirm this Plan by cramdown on impaired classes ____[77a]____ if any of these classes do not vote to accept the Plan.

Please note that the proposed Plan treatment described by this Disclosure Statement cannot be crammed down on the following classes : ____[78]____. AS A RESULT, IF ANY OF THESE CLASSES DOES NOT VOTE TO ACCEPT THE PLAN, THE PLAN WILL NOT BE CONFIRMED.[79]

B. Liquidation Analysis

Another confirmation requirement is the "Best Interest Test", which requires a liquidation analysis. Under the Best Interest Test, if a claimant or interest holder is in an impaired class and that claimant or interest holder does not vote to accept the Plan, then that claimant or interest holder must receive or retain under the Plan property of a value not less than the amount that such holder would receive or retain if the Debtor were liquidated under Chapter 7 of the Bankruptcy Code.

In a Chapter 7 case, the Debtor's assets are usually sold by a Chapter 7 trustee. Secured creditors are paid first from the sales proceeds of properties on which the secured creditor has a lien. Administrative claims are paid next. Next, unsecured creditors are paid from any remaining sales proceeds, according to their rights to priority. Unsecured creditors with the same priority share in proportion to the amount of their allowed claim in relationship to the amount of total allowed unsecured claims. Finally, interest holders receive the balance that remains after all creditors are paid, if any.

For the Court to be able to confirm this Plan, the Court must find that all creditors and interest holders who do not accept the Plan will receive at least as much under the Plan as such holders would receive under a Chapter 7 liquidation. The Plan Proponent maintains that this requirement is met here for the following reasons: ________[80].

Below is a demonstration, in balance sheet format, that all creditors and interest holders will receive at least as much under the Plan as such creditor or interest holder would receive under a Chapter 7 liquidation. (See Exhibit E for a detailed explanation of how the following assets are valued. This information is provided by ________[38].)

ASSETS VALUE AT LIQUIDATION VALUES[81]:

CURRENT ASSETS		
a.	Cash on hand	$
b.	Accounts receivable	$
c.	Inventories	$
	TOTAL CURRENT ASSETS	$
FIXED ASSETS		
a.	Office furniture & equipment	$
b.	Machinery & equipment	$
c.	Automobiles	$
d.	Building & Land[82]	$
	TOTAL FIXED ASSETS	$
OTHER ASSETS		
a.	Customer list	$
b.	Other intangibles	$
	TOTAL OTHER ASSETS	$
TOTAL ASSETS AT LIQUIDATION VALUE		**$**
Less: Secured creditor's recovery[1]		$
Less: Chapter 7 trustee fees and expenses		$
Less: Chapter 11 administrative expenses		$
Less: Priority claims, excluding administrative expense claims		$
Less: Debtor's claimed exemptions		$
(1) Balance for unsecured claims		$
(2) Total amt of unsecured claims		$

% OF THEIR CLAIMS WHICH UNSECURED CREDITORS WOULD RECEIVE OR RETAIN IN A CH. 7 LIQUIDATION[2]: = ________[83]

% OF THEIR CLAIMS WHICH UNSECURED CREDITORS WILL RECEIVE OR RETAIN UNDER THIS PLAN: = ________[84]

1/ Note: The deficiency portion of a secured recourse claim must be added to the total amount of unsecured claims.

2/ Note: If this percentage is greater than the amount to be paid to the unsecured creditors on a "present value basis" under the Plan, the Plan is not confirmable unless Proponent obtains acceptance by every creditor in the general unsecured class.

Below is a demonstration, in tabular format, that all creditors and interest holders will receive at least as much under the Plan as such creditor or holder would receive under a Chapter 7 liquidation.

CLAIMS & CLASSES[85]	PAYOUT PERCENTAGE UNDER THE PLAN	PAYOUT PERCENTAGE IN CHAPTER 7 LIQUIDATION
Administrative Claims		
Priority Tax Claims		
Class 1 ____[86]		
Class 2 ____[87]		
Class 3 ____[88]		
Class 4 ____[89]		

C. Feasibility

Another requirement for confirmation involves the feasibility of the Plan, which means that confirmation of the Plan is not likely to be followed by the liquidation, or the need for further financial reorganization, of the Debtor or any successor to the Debtor under the Plan, unless such liquidation or reorganization is proposed in the Plan.

There are at least two important aspects of a feasibility analysis. The first aspect considers whether the Debtor will have enough cash on hand on the Effective Date of the Plan to pay all the claims and expenses which are entitled to be paid on such date. The Plan Proponent maintains that this aspect of feasibility is satisfied as illustrated here:

Cash Debtor will have on hand by Effective Date[90]	$ ________
To Pay: Administrative claims	- ________
To Pay: Statutory costs & charges	- ________
To Pay: Other Plan Payments due on Effective Date	- ________
Balance after paying these amounts...............	$ ________

The sources of the cash Debtor will have on hand by the Effective Date, as shown above are:

$ ________	Cash in DIP Account now
+ ________	Additional cash DIP will accumulate from net earnings between now and Effective Date
+ ________	Borrowing
+ ________	Capital Contributions
+ ________	Other
$ ________	**Total**[91]

Borrowing is from ___[92]___ and will be paid back as follows: ___[93]___.

The second aspect considers whether the Proponent will have enough cash over the life of the Plan to make the required Plan payments.[94]

The Proponent has provided financial statements which include both historical and projected financial information. Please refer to Exhibit B for the relevant financial statements.

YOU ARE ADVISED TO CONSULT WITH YOUR ACCOUNTANT OR FINANCIAL ADVISOR IF YOU HAVE ANY QUESTIONS PERTAINING TO THESE FINANCIAL STATEMENTS.

In summary, the Plan proposes to pay ______[95] each ______[96]. As Debtor's financial projections demonstrate, Debtor will have an average cash flow, after paying operating expenses and post-confirmation taxes, of ________[97] each ________[98] for the life of the Plan. The final Plan payment is expected to be paid on ________[99]. The Plan Proponent contends that Debtor's financial projections are feasible. As shown by Debtor's historical financial statements, Debtor's average ________[100] cash flow, after paying operating expenses and post-confirmation taxes in the three years preceding the filing of this bankruptcy case is ________[101]. Debtor's average ________[102] cash flow, after paying operating expenses and post-confirmation taxes, during the bankruptcy case is ________[103]. Furthermore, as discussed earlier in the Disclosure Statement at Section {II.E.4}, Debtor has implemented procedures to ________[104].

V.

EFFECT OF CONFIRMATION OF PLAN

A. Discharge[105]

This Plan provides that upon ________[106], Debtor shall be discharged of liability for payment of debts incurred before confirmation of the Plan, to the extent specified in 11 U.S.C.§ 1141. However, the discharge will not discharge any liability imposed by the Plan.

B. Revesting of Property in the Debtor

Except as provided in Section {V.E.}, and except as provided elsewhere in the Plan, the confirmation of the Plan revests all of the property of the estate in the Debtor.

C. Modification of Plan

The Proponent of the Plan may modify the Plan at any time before confirmation. However, the Court may require a new disclosure statement and/or revoting on the Plan.

The Proponent of the Plan may also seek to modify the Plan at any time after confirmation only if (1) the Plan has not been substantially consummated <u>and</u> (2) the Court authorizes the proposed modifications after notice and a hearing.

D. Post-Confirmation Status Report

Within 120 days of the entry of the order confirming the Plan, Plan Proponent shall file a status report with the Court explaining what progress has been made toward consummation of the confirmed Plan. The status report shall be served on the United States Trustee, the twenty largest unsecured creditors, and those parties who have requested special notice. Further status reports shall be filed every 120 days and served on the same entities.

E. Quarterly Fees

Quarterly fees accruing under 28 U.S.C. § 1930(a)(6) to date of confirmation shall be paid to the United States Trustee on or before the effective date of the plan. Quarterly fees accruing under 28 U.S.C. § 1930(a)(6) after confirmation shall be paid to the United States Trustee in accordance with 28 U.S.C. § 1930(a)(6) until entry of a final decree, or entry of an order of dismissal or conversion to chapter 7.

F. Post-Confirmation Conversion/Dismissal

A creditor or party in interest may bring a motion to convert or dismiss the case under § 1112(b), after the Plan is confirmed, if there is a default in performing the Plan. If the Court orders, the case converted to Chapter 7 after the Plan is confirmed, then all property that had been property of the Chapter 11 estate, and that has not been disbursed pursuant to the Plan, will revest in the Chapter 7, estate. The automatic

stay will be reimposed upon the revested property, but only to the extent that relief from stay was not previously authorized by the Court during this case.

The order confirming the Plan may also be revoked under very limited circumstances. The Court may revoke the order if the order of confirmation was procured by fraud and if the party in interest brings an adversary proceeding to revoke confirmation within 180 days after the entry of the order of confirmation.

G. Final Decree

Once the estate has been fully administered as referred to in Bankruptcy Rule 3022, the Plan Proponent, or other party as the Court shall designate in the Plan Confirmation Order, shall file a motion with the Court to obtain a final decree to close the case.

Date: ____________________

____
Name and Identity of Plan Proponent

____
Signature of Plan Proponent
(optional unless party is pro se)

____
Signature of Attorney for Plan Proponent

____
Name of Attorney for Plan Proponent

____
Name of Law Firm for Plan Proponent

VI.

SUPPORTING DECLARATIONS[107]

EXHIBIT A - LIST OF ALL ASSETS[108]

EXHIBIT B - FINANCIAL STATEMENTS

As directed by the Court, the historical financial statements for the three years preceding the petition date and projected financial statements for the life of the Plan are attached.[109] This information is supplied by ___[18]___ and is based on the ___[17]___.

EXHIBIT C - UNEXPIRED LEASES TO BE ASSUMED[109a]

LEASES	ARREARS/DMGS	METHODS OF CURE
• Description =[110] • Lessor's name = • Lessee's name = • Expiration date =	• Default amt = • Actual pecuniary loss[111] =	• Method of curing default & loss = • Means of assuring future performance[112] =
• Description = • Lessor's name = • Lessee's name = • Expiration date =	• Default amt = • Actual pecuniary loss =	• Method of curing default & loss = • Means of assuring future performance =
• Description = • Lessor's name = • Lessee's name = • Expiration date =	• Default amt = • Actual pecuniary loss =	• Method of curing default & loss = • Means of assuring future performance =

EXHIBIT D - EXECUTORY CONTRACTS TO BE ASSUMED

CONTRACT	DEFAULT/DMGS	METHODS OF CURE
• Contract description = • Contracting parties = 1. 2.	• Default amt = • Actual pecuniary loss =	• Method of curing default & loss = • Means of assuring performance =
• Contract description = • Contracting parties = 1. 2.	• Default amt = • Actual pecuniary loss =	• Method of curing default & loss = • Means of assuring performance =
• Contract description = • Contracting parties = 1. 2.	• Default amt = • Actual pecuniary loss =	• Method of curing default & loss = • Means of assuring performance =

EXHIBIT E - LIQUIDATION ANALYSIS

SUPPORTING VALUATION

CURRENT ASSETS:

CASH ON HAND[113]
a. Acct Number: $
b. Acct Number: $
c. Total Cash $

ACCOUNTS RECEIVABLE
a. Accounts receivable $
b. **Less:** uncollectible accounts $
c. Net Accounts Receivables $

INVENTORIES[114] $

FIXED ASSETS:

OFFICE FURNITURE, MACHINERY & EQUIPMENT[115] $

TRANSPORTATION EQUIPMENT[116] $

BUILDINGS, LAND & OTHER REAL PROPERTY[117]
a. Real Property at: $
b. Real Property at: $
c. Total $

OTHER ASSETS:[118] $

TOTAL ASSETS AT LIQUIDATION VALUE $
============

EXHIBIT F - LIST OF ADMINISTRATIVE EXPENSE CLAIMS

UNCLASSIFIED CLAIMS: ADMINISTRATIVE CLAIMS						
		Amounts (Allowed + Estimated = Total Amount - Paid = Total Due)				
Name	Code $	Allowed to date	Estimated	Total Amount	Paid	Total Due
==> Insert rows here.						
TOTAL AMOUNTS						

EXHIBIT G - LIST OF PRIORITY UNSECURED CLAIMS

CLASSIFIED CLAIMS: §507(a)(3) PRIORITY CLAIMS							
				SCHEDULED CLAIMS		FILED CLAIMS	
Class	**Name**	**Insider**	**Impaired**	Amount	D/C/U*	Amount	Objection
	<== Insert rows here.						
TOTAL AMOUNT FOR CLASS							

* Disputed/contingent/unliquidated

EXHIBIT G - LIST OF PRIORITY UNSECURED CLAIMS

CLASSIFIED CLAIMS: §507(a)(4) PRIORITY CLAIMS							
				SCHEDULED CLAIMS		FILED CLAIMS	
Class	Name	Insider	Impaired	Amount	D/C/U*	Amount	Objection
	<== Insert rows here.						
TOTAL AMOUNT FOR CLASS							

* Disputed/contingent/unliquidated

EXHIBIT G - LIST OF PRIORITY UNSECURED CLAIMS

CLASSIFIED CLAIMS: §507(a)(5) PRIORITY CLAIMS							
				SCHEDULED CLAIMS		FILED CLAIMS	
Class	**Name**	**Insider**	**Impaired**	Amount	D/C/U*	Amount	Objection
	<== Insert rows here.						
TOTAL AMOUNT FOR CLASS							

* Disputed/contingent/unliquidated

EXHIBIT G - LIST OF PRIORITY UNSECURED CLAIMS

CLASSIFIED CLAIMS: §507(a)(6) PRIORITY CLAIMS							
				SCHEDULED CLAIMS		FILED CLAIMS	
Class	Name	Insider	Impaired	Amount	D/C/U*	Amount	Objection
	<== Insert rows here.						
TOTAL AMOUNT FOR CLASS							

* Disputed/contingent/unliquidated

EXHIBIT G - LIST OF PRIORITY UNSECURED CLAIMS

CLASSIFIED CLAIMS: §507(a)(7) PRIORITY CLAIMS							
				SCHEDULED CLAIMS		FILED CLAIMS	
Class	**Name**	**Insider**	**Impaired**	Amount	D/C/U*	Amount	Objection
<== Insert rows here.							
TOTAL AMOUNT FOR CLASS							

* Disputed/contingent/unliquidated

EXHIBIT G - LIST OF PRIORITY UNSECURED CLAIMS

CLASSIFIED CLAIMS: §507(a)(8) PRIORITY CLAIMS							
				SCHEDULED CLAIMS		FILED CLAIMS	
Class	Name	Insider	Impaired	Amount	D/C/U*	Amount	Objection
	<== Insert rows here.						

TOTAL AMOUNT FOR CLASS		

* Disputed/contingent/unliquidated

EXHIBIT H - LIST OF GENERAL UNSECURED CLAIMS

CLASSIFIED CLAIMS: UNSECURED CLAIMS							
				SCHEDULED CLAIMS		FILED CLAIMS	
Class	Name	Insider	Impaired	Amount	D/C/U*	Amount	Objection
	<== Insert rows here.						
TOTAL AMOUNT FOR CLASS							

* Disputed/contingent/unliquidated

EXHIBIT I - LIST OF EQUITY INTERESTS

CLASSIFIED INTEREST: EQUITY SECURITY INTEREST HOLDERS							
				SCHEDULED INTERESTS		FILED INTERESTS	
Class	Name	Insider	Impaired	Percentage	D/C/U*	Percentage	Objection
	<== Insert rows here.						

CROSS REFERENCE KEY

I. Overview to Cross Reference Key

This Disclosure Statement is a "fill in the blank form."

The user only fills in the blanks. DO NOT CHANGE THE LANGUAGE IN THE REST OF THE FORM, EXCEPT IN THE FEW PLACES WHERE THE INSTRUCTIONS EXPRESSLY TELL YOU THAT YOU MAY OMIT A SENTENCE OR CLASS IF IT IS NOT NEEDED FOR YOUR CASE.

As you read this Form, you will notice blanks with numbers in them, and also numbers at the end of certain sentences or phrases.

* Here is an example of a blank with a number:

  1
  ____

* Here is an example of a sentence with a number:

  This is an example.[2]

These numbers refer to the numbered instructions in this "Cross Reference Key." When you encounter one of these numbers in the form itself, you need to refer to the "Cross Reference Key," and read the applicable numbered instruction. In our example above, instructions number 1 and 2 would be applicable instructions. Follow the instructions to fill in the needed information.

a. Why the Instructions in this Cross Reference Key are in Two Different Types of Print

When you read the numbered instructions in the "Cross Reference Key" you will see that these instructions are printed in two different types of print, Courier New 12 pt. and Helvetica 10 pt.

Instructions in Courier New 12 pt. font (the font you are currently reading), mean that you are to simply provide the information requested in the endnote and insert it in the corresponding blank. For example, if instruction number 1 states "Debtor's name", then you should insert the Debtor's name in blank number 1.

Instructions in Helvetica 10 pt. font may contain explanations on how to use the disclosure statement form, explanations of the law, or examples of what should be inserted in a particular blank. Read and follow these instructions also.

II. **Key Notes 1 through 118**

1. Put which version of Disclosure Statement (Original, First Amended, Second Amended Disclosure Statement). Do not use the term "Modified" when describing any version subsequent to the Original.

2. Put what Plan is being described (Original, First Amended, Second Amended Plan, etc.)

3. Debtor's name.

4. Petition date.

5. Insert the applicable information, depending on who filed the petition:
   (a) Debtor's name
   (b) Names of the petitioning creditors

6. Insert one of the following:
   (a) a voluntary
   (b) an involuntary

6b. If case was commenced in a chapter other than Chapter 11 and later converted to Chapter 11, so state and state date of conversion to Chapter 11.

7. Proponent's name.

8. Insert the applicable phrases:
   (a) liquidating
   (b) reorganizing
   (c) combined liquidating and reorganizing

9. Provide a brief summary of how Proponent proposes to fund the Plan. If applicable, include statement that this plan is a joint plan, or is otherwise related to a plan in another bankruptcy case, or is a consensual plan between one or more parties to this Chapter 11 case.

10. Effective date of the Plan.

11. Date of the confirmation hearing.

12. Name, address, and telephone number of the Plan Proponent or Counsel to the Plan Proponent.

If applicable, the Disclosure Statement should indicate that there are two or more competing plans, and should tell readers to look at their ballots for special instructions on marking them. The ballots should be modified to contain any applicable special instructions.

13. Deadline for receipt of ballots. **(Note: This date will be provided by the Court at the hearing where the Court approves the Disclosure Statement.)**

14. Name and address of the Plan Proponent or Counsel to the Plan Proponent.

15. Deadline for filing and serving any objection to the confirmation of the Plan. **(Note:** This date will be provided to you by the Court at the hearing where the Court approves the Disclosure Statement.)

16. Name, address, and telephone number of Plan Proponent or Counsel to the Plan Proponent. In cases where there is a creditor's committee, include the name, address, and telephone number of counsel for the creditor's committee.

17. Insert documents such as Debtor's books and records, financial statements such as projections, appraisals, and evaluations, as well as who provided these documents.

18. Identify by name and title the party providing the financial information (i.e., corporate officer, managing agent, accountant, accounting firm, bookkeeper, etc.). Accountants who assist clients in the preparation of financial statements should consult Statement of Position 90-7, Financial Reporting by Entities in Reorganization Under the Bankruptcy Code, dated November 19, 1990 and prepared by the AICPA Task Force on Financial Reporting by Entities in Reorganization Under the Bankruptcy Code.

19. Insert the applicable phrase:
    (a) corporation
    (b) partnership
    (c) individual

    (Note: If the Debtor is an entity that is not listed above, provide a description of Debtor's entity and verify that such an entity is eligible to be a debtor.)

20. Type of business conducted by the Debtor (if applicable). **(Note**: See examples on next page.)

Note: For example, if the Debtor is in the business of developing real estate, the following should be listed:
(a) The location of the properties/lots
(b) The size of the lots
(c) The stage of the development for each lot
(d) The type of development, e.g., commercial, industrial or residential

If the Debtor is a manufacturer or service provider, the following should be listed:
(a) The type of products manufactured or services provided
(b) The location of Debtor's business

If the Debtor is in the business of renting real estate, the following should be listed:
(a) Location of the building(s)
(b) Size of the building(s)
(c) Cureent occupancy rate(s)
(d) Type(s) of building, e.g., residential, commercial, industrial
(e) Debtor's interest in the building(s) being leased

If the Debtor is an individual, the following should be listed:
(a) Debtor's employer and description of the employer's type of business
(b) Length of Debtor's employment
(c) Debtor's position, including title, number of hours worked, salaried or hourly
(d) Description of Debtor's duties
(e) Amount of Debtor's compensation

If Debtor is no longer in business, the above information should still be provided with respect to Debtor's business immediately preceding the bankruptcy. The date Debtor ceased to conduct business should also be provided.

21. Approximate date and year debtor's business commenced.

22. Detailed list of the names and identity of Debtor's principals and affiliates. Include the amount of compensation currently paid to principals and affiliates. **(Note:** See examples below.)

For example, if Debtor is a corporation, the following must be listed:
(a) Key members of the board of directors.
(b) Key officers of the corporation.
(c) Key shareholders and their respective percentage interest.

If Debtor is a partnership, the following must be provided:
(a) Identity of all general partners since the inception of the partnership
(b) Identity of all current limited partners.
(c) If the general partner is a corporation, the board members, officers and shareholders must be listed.

23. List key management of the Debtor before the bankruptcy petition was filed; list key management of the Debtor during the course of the bankruptcy; and lastly, list key management of the Debtor after the bankruptcy.

24. Discuss the specific events and dates which led the debtor to file bankruptcy. **(Note:** A statement

to the effect that the recession caused debtor's business to fail is not specific enough.) Proponent must disclose the receipt of any notices from any governmental agency relating in any manner to actual or potential liability on the part of the Debtor for any environment or toxic waste hazards, whether or not occurring on the Debtor's premises.

25. In chronological order, list the significant events and orders that have been entered in this case and the entry dates of the orders. Also, give a brief description of the proceedings that led to the entry of the orders.

26. Detailed list of the professionals who have obtained court approval of their employment, including (1) the professional's name, (2) scope of employment, and (3) date court approved the employment.

27. Brief description of the following: (1) each significant adversary proceeding or motion that is still pending, including objections to claims, (2) the status of each matter, (3) the effects winning or losing the matter will have on the Plan, and (4) the anticipated cost of pursuing or defending the matter.

28. Brief description of the following: (1) each significant matter that is still pending in other courts, (2) status of each matter, (i.e. whether the matter is stayed), (3) effect the outcome of the matter will have on the Plan, and (4) the anticipated cost of pursuing or defending the matter.

29. If no preference or fraudulent conveyance actions exist and none are expected to be filed, then insert an affirmative statement to that effect and delete the rest of the text under this heading.

30. Estimated total recovery in dollar amount from avoiding preferential and fraudulent transfers and anticipated total expense of pursuing those matters.

31. Provide a brief summary of each fraudulent conveyance or preference action. For each action, include the name of the defendant, summary of the underlying facts, status of the action, and the estimated amount of recovery.

32. Describe post-petition efforts made by the Debtor to remedy the problems that led to the filing of bankruptcy. (**Note:** Be specific.) Also describe the goals Debtor had in mind when implementing these procedures (e.g., save costs, increase profits).

33. The Proponent should provide a textual discussion pertaining to the Debtor's current financial condition. This discussion should inform the reader about the Debtor's current income and expenses and whether Debtor's operations, if any, are currently profitable. Each document shall identify (i) the accounting method used (e.g. cash or accrual), (ii) whether the financial statements are prepared in conformity with generally accepted accounting principles, and (iii) if the financial statements have been audited.

34. If professional(s) have agreed to payment over time, state the precise terms and payment schedule (e.g. $______ per months over ______ months).

35. For each chart, add more rows to the tables as necessary.

36. **NOTE:** Pursuant to policy of the Central District Clerk's Office, Court will not sign the order confirming the Plan until the Clerk's Office fees have been paid in full.

37. Total amount of administrative claims to be paid on

Effective Date.

38. Amount of cash on hand on Effective Date.

39. The source(s) of all cash Debtor will have on Effective Date.

(Note: Be specific. If several sources of cash exist, list each source and the amount of cash expected to be generated from that source.)

40. Denominated as Section 507(a)(7) for bankruptcy cases filed before October 22, 1994.

41. Denominated as Section 507(a)(7) for bankruptcy cases filed before October 22, 1994.

42. **Section 507(a)(7) [now renumbered 507(a)(8) for cases filed after October 22, 1994] describing certain priority tax claims. All 507(a)(7) tax claims must be fully paid within 6 years from the date of assessment. Only unsecured tax claims of the kind described by 11 U.S.C. § 507(a)(7)[8] should be inserted here.**

43. Identify the proposed payment interval (e.g., monthly, quarterly, yearly).

44. Amount of payment per payment interval.

45. The date Plan payments will commence.

46. The date Plan payments will end.

47. **The interest rate paid to a Section 507(a)(8) priority tax claimant should be consistent with the rate provided by 26 U.S.C. § 6621.**

48. Total percentage of claim proposed to be paid to claimant over the life of the Plan plus total dollar amount to be paid to the claimant over life of the Plan.

48.a **Each secured claim should be placed in a separate class, unless the secured claims have identical collateral, priority, and terms of indebtedness.**

Begin numbering the classes with the number "1". The subsequent class should be numbered with the number "2". Do not use subclasses, e.g., 1.1, 1.2, etc.

49. If this class is <u>Not Impaired</u>, put the following in the box: "Not Impaired; claims in this class are not entitled to vote on Plan, class is deemed to have accepted Plan."

If this class is <u>Impaired</u>, put the following in the box: "Impaired; claims in this class are entitled to vote on the Plan"; unless this class is <u>not</u> retaining or receiving any value under the Plan. <u>In</u> this latter case only, put "<u>Impaired</u>, and claims in this class are deemed to have rejected Plan."

50. Balloon payment amount, if any.

50a. Total percent of claim proposed to be paid to claimant over the life of the Plan plus total dollar amount to be paid to claimant over the life of Plan.

51. Omit reference to 507(a)(7) (alimony/child support priority) if case was filed before October 22, 1994 because priority would not exist for cases filed before that date.

52. Omit reference to 507(a)(7) (alimony/child support priority) if case was filed before October 22, 1994 because priority would not exist for cases filed before that date.

53. Each of the four categories of priority unsecured claims should be placed in a separate class. A separate class is not necessary for a particular category of priority unsecured claims if no claim exist in that category.

54. Insert one of the following:
(a) 11 U.S.C. § 507(a)(3)
(b) 11 U.S.C. § 507(a)(4)
(c) 11 U.S.C. § 507(a)(5)
(d) 11 U.S.C. § 507(a)(6)

55. Total amount of claims in this class.

56. If the Plan does not provide for cash payment in full on Effective Date, Plan Proponent must be able to prove that this class has accepted deferred payments pursuant to 11 U.S.C § 1129(a)(9) before the Plan can be confirmed.

57. Insert one of the following:
(a) 11 U.S.C. § 507(a)(3)
(b) 11 U.S.C. § 507(a)(4)
(c) 11 U.S.C. § 507(a)(5)
(d) 11 U.S.C. § 507(a)(6)

58. Total amount of claims in this class.

59. If this class is Not Impaired, put the following in the box: "Not Impaired; claims in this class are not entitled to vote on Plan, class is deemed to have accepted Plan."

If this class is Impaired, put the following in the box: "Impaired; claims in this class are entitled to vote on the Plan"; unless this class is not retaining or receiving any value under the Plan. In this latter case only, put "Impaired, and claims in this class are deemed to have rejected Plan."

59a. Total percent of claim proposed to be paid to claimant over the life of the Plan plus total dollar amount to be paid to claimant over the life of Plan.

59b. If you have a convenience class allowed under 1122(b), then add as an additional unsecured class here, and at Page 5, line 17 of the Plan form, ", except general unsecured claims placed in the convenience class described hereafter."

59c. If you have an additional general unsecured class(es), add each here, with a separate class number. The norm is to have a single general unsecured class, or where appropriate, to have a general unsecured class plus a convenience general unsecured class (as described in footnote 59a). However, there are a few limited circumstances where it is permissible to have additional general unsecured classes, primarily where one or more general unsecured creditors are agreeing to receive worse treatment than is being given to the

rest of the general unsecured creditors, then the creditors agreeing to be treated worse can be placed in a separate general unsecured class. Do not use more than one general unsecured class unless you can justify doing so under applicable law.

60. If there is more than one class of equity holders (e.g. preferred stock and common stock), put each in a separate class and change "class" to "classes."

61. If this class is Not Impaired, put the following in the box: "Not Impaired; claims in this class are not entitled to vote on Plan, class is deemed to have accepted Plan."

If this class is Impaired, put the following in the box: "Impaired; claims in this class are entitled to vote on the Plan"; unless this class is not retaining or receiving any value under the Plan. In this latter case only, put "Impaired, and claims in this class are deemed to have rejected Plan."

62. Describe the source of funding for this Plan. Be specific and consistent with the information set forth in Section {IV.C.}

1. If property of the estate is being sold and 11 U.S.C. § 1129(B)(2)(A)(ii) applies, then explain how that section impacts on the rights of a lienholder at a sale of the property.
2. If a buyer of the property has already been identified, then disclose the financial solvency of the proposed buyer.

63. For each entity who will be involved in post-confirmation management, state or explain the following:
(a) Identity
(b) Post-confirmation managerial duties
(c) Amount of compensation paid pre-petition, paid currently, and to be paid post-confirmation
(d) Description of expertise

64. Name and identity of disbursing agent.

65. Select one:
(a) with
(b) without

66. Explain whether Disbursing Agent will be compensated or reimbursed for services and expenses rendered and incurred in connection with making distributions under the Plan. If Disbursing Agent will be compensated or reimbursed, specify the exact amount and the interval of payment.

NOTE: If disbursing agent will be compensated or reimbursed, be sure to account for these additional costs when evaluating feasibility of the Plan.

67. Detailed description of all the risks that may exist which

may prevent the successful consummation of the proposed Plan.

Note: For example, if the Plan will be funded by sale of property, the following risks should be disclosed:

(a) Failure to find a buyer or a buyer willing to pay the listed price by the stated deadline set by the Plan
(b) Inability of proposed buyer to complete sale
(c) Possibility of foreclosure by secured creditor if debtor defaults under the plan
(d) Terms of the sale, if known

For plans which provide for payment over time, the following risks should be discussed:

(a) Possibility of default under terms of the Plan, i.e., possibility of inability to pay Plan payments
(b) Financial projections provided by the Proponent may not be realized, thereby causing inability to pay Plan payments
(c) Business environment
(d) Debtor's competition
(e) Nonbankruptcy law and regulation
(f) Nonbankruptcy litigation

68. List the unexpired leases and executory contracts in sufficient detail to enable the reader to determine which Leases and contracts will be assumed. This list will enable a party to a lease or contract to quickly ascertain whether he or she needs to refer to Exhibit C or D.

Exhibits C and D are intended to provide detailed information on each Lease or contract to be assumed so that the court and any party to a particular Lease or contract can decide whether assumption is proper and desirable.

69. List all executory contracts and unexpired Leases to be rejected in sufficient detail to enable a reader to quickly ascertain whether any particular Lease or contract will be rejected.

70. Deadline for filing proof of claim based on claim arising from rejection of contract or lease. **(Note:** Typically, this date will be 30 days from Effective Date.)

71. Select one:
(a) is
(b) is not

71a. See 11 U.S.C. § 1129(a)(6). This section is only applicable if Debtor's business is regulated by a governmental regulatory commission. Examples include certain transportation companies and public utility companies. If Debtor is not regulated by a governmental commission, insert an affirmative statement to that effect in the Disclosure Statement. If debtor is regulated, state this and Plan must comply with 11 U.S.C. § 1129(a)(6).

71b. Do not change the language in this section unless the judge to whom your case is assigned has different or additional language that judge wishes to use in this section and directs you to insert that judge's specific language.

72. State the expected tax consequences of the Plan. For example, tax ramifications may include such issues as

capital gains on the sale of real property and operating loss-carry forwards.

Note: If the Proponent has <u>no</u> idea of what such consequences might be, then the document must disclose that fact and why it is so.

Few situations exist where the tax liability should not be considered because any tax liability would affect distribution to creditors. Tax considerations might affect the likelihood of continued successful post-confirmation operation of the Debtor and may also affect the feasibility analysis. For these reasons, the Proponent should know the tax consequences of the Plan.

73. Bar date for filing a proof of claim.

Note: In most bankruptcy cases it is necessary that a bar date for filing proof of claims and interests has passed before creditors and interest holders may vote on the plan. Knowing which claims and interests have been allowed will allow the Plan Proponent to easily determine who is entitled to vote. Also, without knowing the amount and nature of the claims against the estate, it is impossible to complete a precise liquidation analysis and difficult to determine whether the Plan is feasible.

If the claims bar date has not yet passed, the motion for order approving the disclosure statement should explain why the disclosure statement and plan are proposed now instead of after the claim bar date.

74. Classes that are impaired.

75. Classes that are unimpaired. (For cases filed after October 22, 1994 please note that the Bankruptcy Reform Act of 1994 deleted § 1124(3). Therefore, creditors who receive cash in full equal to their allowed claim by the effective date would be considered impaired under the Bankruptcy Reform Act of 1994).

76. Denominated as 507(a)(7) for bankruptcy cases filed before October 22, 1994.

77. Select one:
(a) will
(b) will not

77a. List class number of each impaired class which Plan Proponent will seek to cram Plan down on if class does not accept Plan.

78. List classes that are clearly not receiving the type of treatment provided for in section 1129(b)(1). Also, in the "SUMMARY OF THE PLAN OF REORGANIZATION" section (section III.C. of the Disclosure Statement), after each class that is not receiving the type of treatment provided for in Code section 1129(b)(1), insert the following statement: "If this class does not vote to accept the Plan, the Proponent will not be allowed to cram the Plan down on this class and the Plan will not be confirmed".

79. Delete the preceding two sentences if (1) no unimpaired classes exist, or (2) the Plan does not discriminate unfairly and will give fair and equitable treatment to <u>all</u> impaired classes.

80. Insert the following reasons, if applicable:

a. The liquidation value of the "x" is less than its fair market value because ____________________. **(Note:** Be specific when justifying the difference between liquidation value and fair market value. State the basis for your justification.)

b. In a chapter 7 case, a trustee is appointed and entitled to compensation from the bankruptcy estate in an amount not to exceed 25% of the first $5,000 of all moneys disbursed, 10% on any amount over $5,000 but less than $50,000, 5% on any amount over $50,000 but not in excess of $1 million, and 3% on all amounts over $1 million. In this case, the trustee's compensation is estimated to equal "x".

c. A chapter 7 recovery is less because the Debtor is permitted to exempt a certain amount of the sales proceeds before unsecured creditors are paid anything. **(Note:** Be specific when relying on Debtor's claimed exemptions. List each exempt property, the code section which entitles the Debtor to the claimed exemption, and the amount of each exemption.)

Note: If Debtor is a partnership then § 723(a) provides that the general partners of the partnership are liable for any deficiency of property of the estate to pay in full all allowed claims. Therefore, the Proponent must disclose the financial condition of the individual general partners from whom chapter 7 trustee could seek to collect if this was a Chapter 7 case.

81. In appropriate cases, this format may be supplemented, but not reduced.

82. If Debtor owns more than one piece of real property, list each real property and its value <u>separately</u>.

83. Divide "Balance for unsecured claims" by "Total amt of unsecured claims". Insert the result.

84. Divide the total amount proposed to be paid to unsecured claimants under the Plan by the "Total amt of unsecured claims". Insert the result.

85. Add or delete the rows to the table when necessary to provide a row for each class of claims or interest.

86. Description of claims in Class 1.

87. Description of claims in Class 2.

88. Description of claims in Class 3.

89. Description of claims in Class 4. **(Note:** Insert more rows in the table if the Plan contains more than 4 classes.)

90. Explain sources of cash Debtor will have on Effective Date if Debtor does not currently have sufficient cash on hand to pay all claims that must be paid on Effective Date.

91. Total must match figure shown above as "Cash debtor will have on hand by Effective Date".

92. Put person or entity funds are being borrowed from.

93. Put how loan will be paid back (example, lender has agreed it will not be paid until all Plan payments are completed and then will be paid at $____ per month at ___% until paid in full). If gift instead of borrowing, change "Borrowing" to "Gift" and state amount will never be paid back.

94. If the Plan is a liquidating plan or a plan that proposes to pay all claims on Effective Date, this section may not be applicable and may be deleted upon stating why this aspect of feasibility is not applicable to the Plan.

95. Total amount of Plan Payments to be made each payment interval.

96. Plan payment interval (e.g., monthly, yearly, quarterly).

97. Average cash flow per Plan payment interval, after paying operating expenses and post-confirmation taxes.

98. Plan payment interval.

99. The last Plan payment date.

100. Payment interval (e.g., monthly, yearly, quarterly).

101. Amount of <u>actual</u> average cash flow per Plan payment interval, after paying operating expenses and post-confirmation taxes, for the three years preceding the filing of this bankruptcy case.

102. Plan payment interval (e.g., monthly, yearly, quarterly).

103. Debtor's average cash flow per Plan payment interval, after paying operating expenses and post-confirmation taxes, during the bankruptcy case.

104. Select one:
(a) decrease costs
(b) increase costs
(c) decrease costs and increase income

105.

NOTE: If the Debtor is not entitled to a discharge pursuant to 11 U.S.C. 1141(d), change this heading to "NO DISCHARGE," and follow instruction #106.

106. Choose one of the following:
(a) confirmation of the Plan
(b) payment in full of proposed plan payments to the unsecured creditors
(c) upon substantial confirmation of plan
(d) other. You must state what the other condition for or date of discharge is.

Alternatively, if debtor does not meet the test of 11 U.S.C. 1141(d)(3) for getting a discharge, then the debtor is not entitled to any discharge, and the whole paragraph under "Discharge" must be omitted and replaced with:

(e) Debtor will not receive any discharge in this bankruptcy case because debtor does not meet the test for receiving a discharge specified under 11 U.S.C. § 1141(d)(3).

Note: More evidence regarding feasibility of the Plan may be required if the Plan Proponent seeks discharge upon Plan confirmation.

107. Proponent should provide a declaration from someone who has personal knowledge of Debtor's operations and assisted in preparing the Disclosure Statement. The declarant should attest to the truthfulness and accuracy of everything stated in the Disclosure Statement.

108. The exhibit should include the following information for all assets:

1. description of property (e.g., commercial/residential real property)
2. fair market value
3. basis for opinion of value (e.g. income/sales approach)
4. qualifications of person rendering opinion
5. any significant differences between an asset's value as listed in this exhibit and its value as stated in the Debtor's schedules should be explained in a footnote to this exhibit.

TOTAL ASSETS = ___________

Proponent must describe each item of property with particularity and give a value for each item separately. If possible, Proponent should also provide a going concern value for the business as a whole so long as the foundation for that opinion is explained. For accounts receivable, the Proponent must explain the likelihood of collecting the accounts and for what amount. In addition, the debtor's status as a plaintiff in a lawsuit represents potential value to the estate. Although it may be difficult to estimate the exact value of a lawsuit, an effort must be made to present a low and high range of value and the foundation for such belief. The amount of cash on hand must also be disclosed, including, for any real property, any prepaid rent or security deposits paid by tenants and held by the Debtor.

109. List and attach actual financial statements for the three years preceding bankruptcy (e.g., balance sheets, cash flow statements, income and expense statements).

List and attach projected financial statements for the life of the Plan.

(**Note:** Income and expense statements should be organized at the payment interval rate. In other words, if the Plan proposes to make payments on a monthly interval, the historical and projected income and expense statements should be organized on a monthly basis unless the Judge directs otherwise.)

109a. Note that the Court can only confirm a plan which provides for assumption of executory contracts or unexpired leases if the plan proponent proves, as part of plan confirmation, that all elements of 11 U.S.C. § 365 governing assumption of executory contracts and unexpired leases are met --

including curing all defaults, paying all damages caused by defaults and providing that the party assuming the contract has capacity to perform the remainder of the contract/ lease. Each of these elements necessary for assumption must be proved by declarations or other admissible evidence presented to the court by plan proponent as part of the plan confirmation process.

110. Description of leased property or asset, including address of real property, if applicable.

111. Actual pecuniary loss consists of damages other than lease payment default amount, if any.

112. Describe how the Debtor is assuring performance on the remaining obligation under the lease, e.g., addition of guarantor.

113. List cash in <u>all</u> accounts in the manner shown in Exhibit E.

114. Assets in inventory should be valued at the amount they can be sold for in an orderly liquidation. If someone other than a qualified appraiser provides this value, then the basis for the non-appraiser's knowledge <u>must</u> be disclosed. If an appraiser, auctioneer, or other financial advisor is hired to determine this value, a report from the appraiser should be attached as an exhibit. The appraiser, auctioneer, or other financial advisor should be independent of the Debtor and should provide a declaration certifying his/her independence and qualifications as an expert for valuation of this type of asset.

115. Office furniture, equipment and machinery should be valued at the amount they can be sold for in an orderly liquidation. Disclose whether the total liquidation value assumes sales items individually or by lot.

If someone other than a qualified appraiser, auctioneer, or other financial advisor provides this value, the basis for the non-appraiser's knowledge <u>must</u> be disclosed. If an appraiser, auctioneer, or other financial advisor is hired to determine this value, a report should be attached as an exhibit. The appraiser, auctioneer, or other financial advisor should be independent of the Debtor and should provide a declaration certifying his/her independence and qualifications as an expert for valuation of this type of asset.

116. Provide an itemized list of assets and the corresponding value for each asset.

Automobiles should be valued at wholesale value as reported by the most recent "Kelley Blue Book." Unlisted transportation equipment should be valued by an independent appraiser. The appraisal report should be attached as an exhibit and the appraiser should submit a declaration attesting to his/her independence and qualifications as an expert for valuing this type of asset. If someone other than a qualified appraiser provides this value, the basis for the non-appraiser's knowledge <u>must</u> be disclosed.

117. Real property assets should be valued at the amount they can be sold for in an orderly liquidation. Provide an <u>itemized</u> list of real properties and the corresponding liquidation value for <u>each</u> property.

An appraiser or a real estate broker should be utilized to determine this value. A report from the appraiser should be attached as an exhibit. The appraiser should be independent of the Debtor and the appraiser should provide a declaration certifying his/her independence and qualifications as an expert for valuation of this type of asset. If someone other than a qualified appraiser provides this value, the basis for the non-appraiser's knowledge <u>must</u> be disclosed.

118. Other assets should be valued at the amount they can be sold for in an orderly liquidation. Provide an itemized list of assets and the corresponding liquidation value for each. Other assets may include, but are not limited to, assets to which exemptions apply, antiques and collectibles, trademarks, stock, liquor licenses and other assets listed on the Debtor's Schedule

B.

An appraiser, auctioneer, or other financial advisor should be hired to determine the liquidation value. A report from the appraiser, auctioneer, or other financial advisor should be attached as an exhibit. The appraiser, auctioneer, or other financial advisor should be independent of the debtor and should provide a declaration certifying his/her independence and qualifications as an expert for valuation of this type of asset. If someone other than a qualified appraiser provides this value, the basis for the non-appraiser's knowledge must be disclosed. If a Chapter 7 Trustee could realize value from any of the avoidance actions, preference actions or other lawsuits which are assets of the Debtor, the value of such actions likely to be realized by the Chapter 7 Trustee must also be disclosed, as well as the assumptions underlying the value.

Chapter 11 Disclosure Statement in Small Business Case under Chapter 11

Form B25B (Official Form 25B) (12/08) 2008 USBC, Central District of California

UNITED STATES BANKRUPTCY COURT CENTRAL DISTRICT OF CALIFORNIA	
In re: Debtor(s).	CHAPTER 11 CASE NO.:

SMALL BUSINESS CASE UNDER CHAPTER 11

[NAME OF PLAN PROPONENT]'S DISCLOSURE STATEMENT, DATED [INSERT DATE]

Table of Contents

[Insert when text is finalized]

I. INTRODUCTION

This is the disclosure statement (the "Disclosure Statement") in the small business chapter 11 case of_____________________________ (the "Debtor"). This Disclosure Statement contains information about the Debtor and describes the [insert name of plan] (the "Plan") filed by [the Debtor] on [insert date]. A full copy of the Plan is attached to this Disclosure Statement as Exhibit A. ***Your rights may be affected. You should read the Plan and this Disclosure Statement carefully and discuss them with your attorney. If you do not have an attorney, you may wish to consult one.***

The proposed distributions under the Plan are discussed at pages ___-___ of this Disclosure Statement. [General unsecured creditors are classified in Class ____, and will receive a distribution of ___% of their allowed claims, to be distributed as follows __________.]

A. Purpose of This Document

This Disclosure Statement describes:

- The Debtor and significant events during the bankruptcy case,
- How the Plan proposes to treat claims or equity interests of the type you hold (*i.e.*, what you will receive on your claim or equity interest if the plan is confirmed),
- Who can vote on or object to the Plan,
- What factors the Bankruptcy Court (the "Court") will consider when deciding whether to confirm the Plan,
- Why [the Proponent] believes the Plan is feasible, and how the treatment of your claim or equity interest under the Plan compares to what you would receive on your claim or equity interest in liquidation, and
- The effect of confirmation of the Plan.

Be sure to read the Plan as well as the Disclosure Statement. This Disclosure Statement describes the Plan, but it is the Plan itself that will, if confirmed, establish your rights.

B. Deadlines for Voting and Objecting; Date of Plan Confirmation Hearing

The Court has not yet confirmed the Plan described in this Disclosure Statement. This section describes the procedures pursuant to which the Plan will or will not be confirmed.

1. *Time and Place of the Hearing to [Finally Approve This Disclosure Statement and] Confirm the Plan*

The hearing at which the Court will determine whether to [finally approve this Disclosure Statement and] confirm the Plan will take place on [insert date], at [insert time], in Courtroom _____, at the [Insert Courthouse Name, and Full Court Address, City, State, Zip Code].

2. *Deadline For Voting to Accept or Reject the Plan*

If you are entitled to vote to accept or reject the plan, vote on the enclosed ballot and return the ballot in the enclosed envelope to [insert address]. See section IV.A. below for a discussion of voting eligibility requirements.

Your ballot must be received by [insert date] or it will not be counted.

3. *Deadline For Objecting to the [Adequacy of Disclosure and] Confirmation of the Plan*

Objections to [this Disclosure Statement or to] the confirmation of the Plan must be filed with the Court and served upon [insert entities] by [insert date].

4. *Identity of Person to Contact for More Information*

If you want additional information about the Plan, you should contact [insert name and address of representative of plan proponent].

C. Disclaimer

The Court has [conditionally] approved this Disclosure Statement as containing adequate information to enable parties affected by the Plan to make an informed judgment about its terms. The Court has not yet determined whether the Plan meets the legal requirements for confirmation, and the fact that the Court has approved this Disclosure Statement does not constitute an endorsement of the Plan by the Court, or a recommendation that it be accepted. [The Court's approval of this Disclosure Statement is subject to final approval at the hearing on confirmation of the Plan. Objections to the adequacy of this Disclosure Statement may be filed until ______.]

II. BACKGROUND

A. Description and History of the Debtor's Business

The Debtor is a [corporation, partnership, etc.]. Since [insert year operations commenced], the Debtor has been in the business of __________. [Describe the Debtor's business].

B. Insiders of the Debtor

[Insert a detailed list of the names of Debtor's insiders as defined in §101(31) of the United States Bankruptcy Code (the "Code") and their relationship to the Debtor. For each insider, list all compensation paid by the Debtor or its affiliates to that person or entity during the two years prior to the commencement of the Debtor's bankruptcy case, as well as compensation paid during the pendency of this chapter 11 case.]

C. Management of the Debtor Before and During the Bankruptcy

During the two years prior to the date on which the bankruptcy petition was filed, the officers, directors, managers or other persons in control of the Debtor (collectively the "Managers") were [List the Managers of the Debtor prior to the petition date].

The Managers of the Debtor during the Debtor's chapter 11 case have been: [List Managers of the Debtor during the Debtor's chapter 11 case.]

After the effective date of the order confirming the Plan, the directors, officers, and voting trustees of the Debtor, any affiliate of the Debtor participating in a joint Plan with the Debtor, or successor of the Debtor under the Plan (collectively the "Post Confirmation Managers"), will be: [List Post Confirmation Managers of the Debtor.] The responsibilities and compensation of these Post Confirmation Managers are described in section __ of this Disclosure Statement.

D. Events Leading to Chapter 11 Filing

[Describe the events that led to the commencement of the Debtor's bankruptcy case.]

E. Significant Events During the Bankruptcy Case

[Describe significant events during the Debtor's bankruptcy case:

- Describe any asset sales outside the ordinary course of business, debtor in possession financing, or cash collateral orders.
- Identify the professionals approved by the court.
- Describe any adversary proceedings that have been filed or other significant litigation that has occurred (including contested claim disallowance proceedings), and any other significant legal or administrative proceedings that are pending or have been pending during the case in a forum other than the Court.
- Describe any steps taken to improve operations and profitability of the Debtor.
- Describe other events as appropriate.]

F. Projected Recovery of Avoidable Transfers [Choose the option that applies]

[Option 1 – If the Debtor does not intend to pursue avoidance actions]

The Debtor does not intend to pursue preference, fraudulent conveyance, or other avoidance actions.

[Option 2 – If the Debtor intends to pursue avoidance actions]

The Debtor estimates that up to $ ________________ may be realized from the recovery of fraudulent, preferential or other avoidable transfers. While the results of litigation cannot be predicted with certainty and it is possible that other causes of action may be identified, the following is a summary of the preference, fraudulent conveyance and other avoidance actions filed or expected to be filed in this case:

Transaction	Defendant	Amount Claimed

[Option 3 – If the Debtor does not yet know whether it intends to pursue avoidance actions]

The Debtor has not yet completed its investigation with regard to prepetition transactions. If you received a payment or other transfer within 90 days of the bankruptcy, or other transfer avoidable under the Code, the Debtor may seek to avoid such transfer.

G. Claims Objections

Except to the extent that a claim is already allowed pursuant to a final non-appealable order, the Debtor reserves the right to object to claims. Therefore, even if your claim is allowed for voting purposes, you may not be entitled to a distribution if an objection to your claim is later upheld. The procedures for resolving disputed claims are set forth in Article V of the Plan.

H. Current and Historical Financial Conditions

The identity and fair market value of the estate's assets are listed in Exhibit B. [Identify source and basis of valuation.]

The Debtor's most recent financial statements [if any] issued before bankruptcy, each of which was filed with the Court, are set forth in Exhibit C.

[The most recent post-petition operating report filed since the commencement of the Debtor's bankruptcy case are set forth in Exhibit D.] [A summary of the Debtor's periodic operating reports filed since the commencement of the Debtor's bankruptcy case is set forth in Exhibit D.]

III. SUMMARY OF THE PLAN OF REORGANIZATION AND TREATMENT OF CLAIMS AND EQUITY INTERESTS

A. What is the Purpose of the Plan of Reorganization?

As required by the Code, the Plan places claims and equity interests in various classes and describes the treatment each class will receive. The Plan also states whether each class of claims or equity interests is impaired or unimpaired. If the Plan is confirmed, your recovery will be limited to the amount provided by the Plan.

B. Unclassified Claims

Certain types of claims are automatically entitled to specific treatment under the Code. They are not considered impaired, and holders of such claims do not vote on the Plan. They may, however, object if, in their view, their treatment under the Plan does not comply with that required by the Code. As such, the Plan Proponent has *not* placed the following claims in any class:

1. *Administrative Expenses*

Administrative expenses are costs or expenses of administering the Debtor's chapter 11 case which are allowed under § 507(a)(2) of the Code. Administrative expenses also include the value of any goods sold to the Debtor in the ordinary course of business and received within 20 days before the date of the bankruptcy petition. The Code requires that all administrative expenses be paid on the effective date of the Plan, unless a particular claimant agrees to a different treatment.

The following chart lists the Debtor's estimated administrative expenses, and their proposed treatment under the Plan:

Type	Estimated Amount Owed	Proposed Treatment
Expenses Arising in the Ordinary Course of Business After the Petition Date		Paid in full on the effective date of the Plan, or according to terms of obligation if later
The Value of Goods Received in the Ordinary Course of Business Within 20 Days Before the Petition Date		Paid in full on the effective date of the Plan, or according to terms of obligation if later
Professional Fees, as approved by the Court.		Paid in full on the effective date of the Plan, or according to separate written agreement, or according to court order if such fees have not been approved by the Court on the effective date of the Plan
Clerk's Office Fees		Paid in full on the effective date of the Plan
Other administrative expenses		Paid in full on the effective date of the Plan or according to separate written agreement
Office of the U.S. Trustee Fees		Paid in full on the effective date of the Plan
TOTAL		

2. *Priority Tax Claims*

Priority tax claims are unsecured income, employment, and other taxes described by § 507(a)(8) of the Code. Unless the holder of such a § 507(a)(8) priority tax claim agrees otherwise, it must receive the present value of such claim, in regular installments paid over a period not exceeding 5 years from the order of relief.

The following chart lists the Debtor's estimated § 507(a)(8) priority tax claims and their proposed treatment under the Plan:

Description (name and type of tax)	Estimated Amount Owed	Date of Assessment	Treatment
			Pmt interval = [Monthly] payment = Begin date = End date = Interest Rate % = Total Payout Amount = $
			Pmt interval = [Monthly] payment = Begin date = End date = Interest Rate % = Total Payout Amount = $

C. Classes of Claims and Equity Interests

The following are the classes set forth in the Plan, and the proposed treatment that they will receive under the Plan:

1. *Classes of Secured Claims*

Allowed Secured Claims are claims secured by property of the Debtor's bankruptcy estate (or that are subject to setoff) to the extent allowed as secured claims under § 506 of the Code. If the value of the collateral or setoffs securing the creditor's claim is less than the amount of the creditor's allowed claim, the deficiency will [be classified as a general unsecured claim].

The following chart lists all classes containing Debtor's secured prepetition claims and their proposed treatment under the Plan:

Class #	Description	Insider? (Yes or No)	Impairment	Treatment
	Secured claim of: Name = Collateral description = Allowed Secured Amount = $_________ Priority of lien = Principal owed = $_________ Pre-pet. arrearage = $_________ Total claim = $_________		[State whether impaired or unimpaired]	[Monthly] Pmt = Pmts Begin = Pmts End = [Balloon pmt] = Interest rate % = Treatment of Lien = [Additional payment required to cure defaults] =
	Secured claim of: Name = Collateral description = Allowed Secured Amount = $_________ Priority of lien = Principal owed = $_________ Pre-pet. arrearage = $_________ Total claim = $_________		[State whether impaired or unimpaired]	Monthly Pmt = Pmts Begin = Pmts End = [Balloon pmt] = Interest rate % = Treatment of Lien = [Additional payment required to cure defaults]

2. *Classes of Priority Unsecured Claims*

Certain priority claims that are referred to in §§ 507(a)(1), (4), (5), (6), and (7) of the Code are required to be placed in classes. The Code requires that each holder of such a claim receive cash on the effective date of the Plan equal to the allowed amount of such claim. However, a class of holders of such claims may vote to accept different treatment.

The following chart lists all classes containing claims under §§ 507(a)(1), (4), (5), (6), and (a)(7) of the Code and their proposed treatment under the Plan:

Class #	Description	Impairment	Treatment
	Priority unsecured claim pursuant to Section [insert] Total amt of claims = $	[State whether impaired or unimpaired]	
	Priority unsecured claim pursuant to Section [insert] Total amt of claims = $	[State whether impaired or unimpaired]	

3. *Class[es] of General Unsecured Claims*

General unsecured claims are not secured by property of the estate and are not entitled to priority under § 507(a) of the Code. [Insert description of § 1122(b) convenience class if applicable.]

The following chart identifies the Plan's proposed treatment of Class[es] ___ through ___, which contain general unsecured claims against the Debtor:

Class #	Description	Impairment	Treatment
	[1122(b) Convenience Class]	[State whether impaired or unimpaired]	[Insert proposed treatment, such as "Paid in full in cash on effective date of the Plan or when due under contract or applicable nonbankruptcy law"]
	General Unsecured Class	[State whether impaired or unimpaired]	Monthly Pmt = Pmts Begin = Pmts End = [Balloon pmt] = Interest rate % from [date] Estimated percent of claim paid = =

4. *Class[es] of Equity Interest Holders*

Equity interest holders are parties who hold an ownership interest (*i.e.*, equity interest) in the Debtor. In a corporation, entities holding preferred or common stock are equity interest holders. In a partnership, equity interest holders include both general and limited partners. In a limited liability company ("LLC"), the equity interest holders are the members. Finally, with respect to an individual who is a debtor, the Debtor is the equity interest holder.

The following chart sets forth the Plan's proposed treatment of the class[es] of equity interest holders: [There may be more than one class of equity interests in, for example, a partnership case, or a case where the prepetition debtor had issued multiple classes of stock.]

Class #	Description	Impairment	Treatment
	Equity interest holders	[State whether impaired or unimpaired]	

D. Means of Implementing the Plan

1. *Source of Payments*

Payments and distributions under the Plan will be funded by the following:

[Describe the source of funds for payments under the Plan.]

2. *Post-confirmation Management*

The Post-Confirmation Managers of the Debtor, and their compensation, shall be as follows:

Name	Affiliations	Insider (yes or no)?	Position	Compensation

E. Risk Factors

The proposed Plan has the following risks:

[List all risk factors that might affect the Debtor's ability to make payments and other distributions required under the Plan.]

F. Executory Contracts and Unexpired Leases

The Plan, in Exhibit 5.1, lists all executory contracts and unexpired leases that the Debtor will assume under the Plan. Assumption means that the Debtor has elected to continue to perform the obligations under such contracts and unexpired leases, and to cure defaults of the type that must be cured under the Code, if any. Exhibit 5.1 also lists how the Debtor will cure and compensate the other party to such contract or lease for any such defaults.

If you object to the assumption of your unexpired lease or executory contract, the proposed cure of any defaults, or the adequacy of assurance of performance, you must file and serve your objection to the Plan within the deadline for objecting to the confirmation of the Plan, unless the Court has set an earlier time.

All executory contracts and unexpired leases that are not listed in Exhibit 5.1 will be rejected under the Plan. Consult your adviser or attorney for more specific information about particular contracts or leases.

If you object to the rejection of your contract or lease, you must file and serve your objection to the Plan within the deadline for objecting to the confirmation of the Plan.

[*The Deadline for Filing a Proof of Claim Based on a Claim Arising from the Rejection of a Lease or Contract Is* ______. Any claim based on the rejection of a contract or lease will be barred if the proof of claim is not timely filed, unless the Court orders otherwise.]

G. Tax Consequences of Plan

Creditors and Equity Interest Holders Concerned with How the Plan May Affect Their Tax Liability Should Consult with Their Own Accountants, Attorneys, And/Or Advisors.

The following are the anticipated tax consequences of the Plan: [List the following general consequences as a minimum: (1) Tax consequences to the Debtor of the Plan; (2) General tax consequences on creditors of any discharge, and the general tax consequences of receipt of plan consideration after confirmation.]

IV. CONFIRMATION REQUIREMENTS AND PROCEDURES

To be confirmable, the Plan must meet the requirements listed in §§ 1129(a) or (b) of the Code. These include the requirements that: the Plan must be proposed in good faith; at least one impaired class of claims must accept the plan, without counting votes of insiders; the Plan must distribute to each creditor and equity interest holder at least as much as the creditor or equity interest holder would receive in a chapter 7 liquidation case, unless the creditor or equity interest holder votes to accept the Plan; and the Plan must be feasible. These requirements are <u>not</u> the only requirements listed in § 1129, and they are not the only requirements for confirmation.

A. Who May Vote or Object

Any party in interest may object to the confirmation of the Plan if the party believes that the requirements for confirmation are not met.

Many parties in interest, however, are not entitled to vote to accept or reject the Plan. A creditor or equity interest holder has a right to vote for or against the Plan only if that creditor or equity interest holder has a claim or equity interest that is both (1) allowed or allowed for voting purposes and (2) impaired.

In this case, the Plan Proponent believes that classes ______ are impaired and that holders of claims in each of these classes are therefore entitled to vote to accept or reject the Plan. The Plan Proponent believes that classes _______ are unimpaired and that holders of claims in each of these classes, therefore, do not have the right to vote to accept or reject the Plan.

1. *What Is an Allowed Claim or an Allowed Equity Interest?*

Only a creditor or equity interest holder with an allowed claim or an allowed equity interest has the right to vote on the Plan. Generally, a claim or equity interest is allowed if either (1) the Debtor has scheduled the claim on the Debtor's schedules, unless the claim has been scheduled as disputed, contingent, or unliquidated, or (2) the creditor has filed a proof of claim or equity interest, unless an objection has been filed to such proof of claim or equity interest. When a claim or equity interest is not allowed, the creditor or equity interest holder holding the claim or equity interest cannot vote unless the Court, after notice and hearing, either overrules the objection or allows the claim or equity interest for voting purposes pursuant to Rule 3018(a) of the Federal Rules of Bankruptcy Procedure.

The deadline for filing a proof of claim in this case was _____.
[If applicable – The deadline for filing objections to claims is______.]

2. *What Is an Impaired Claim or Impaired Equity Interest?*

As noted above, the holder of an allowed claim or equity interest has the right to vote only if it is in a class that is *impaired* under the Plan. As provided in § 1124 of the Code, a class is considered impaired if the Plan alters the legal, equitable, or contractual rights of the members of that class.

3. *Who is **Not** Entitled to Vote*

The holders of the following five types of claims and equity interests are *not* entitled to vote:

- holders of claims and equity interests that have been disallowed by an order of the Court;
- holders of other claims or equity interests that are not "allowed claims" or "allowed equity interests" (as discussed above), unless they have been "allowed" for voting purposes.

- holders of claims or equity interests in unimpaired classes;
- holders of claims entitled to priority pursuant to §§ 507(a)(2), (a)(3), and (a)(8) of the Code; and
- holders of claims or equity interests in classes that do not receive or retain any value under the Plan;
- administrative expenses.

Even If You Are Not Entitled to Vote on the Plan, You Have a Right to Object to the Confirmation of the Plan [and to the Adequacy of the Disclosure Statement].

4. *Who Can Vote in More Than One Class*

A creditor whose claim has been allowed in part as a secured claim and in part as an unsecured claim, or who otherwise hold claims in multiple classes, is entitled to accept or reject a Plan in each capacity, and should cast one ballot for each claim.

B. Votes Necessary to Confirm the Plan

If impaired classes exist, the Court cannot confirm the Plan unless (1) at least one impaired class of creditors has accepted the Plan without counting the votes of any insiders within that class, and (2) all impaired classes have voted to accept the Plan, unless the Plan is eligible to be confirmed by "cram down" on non-accepting classes, as discussed later in Section [B.2.].

1. *Votes Necessary for a Class to Accept the Plan*

A class of claims accepts the Plan if both of the following occur: (1) the holders of more than one-half (1/2) of the allowed claims in the class, who vote, cast their votes to accept the Plan, and (2) the holders of at least two-thirds (2/3) in dollar amount of the allowed claims in the class, who vote, cast their votes to accept the Plan.

A class of equity interests accepts the Plan if the holders of at least two-thirds (2/3) in amount of the allowed equity interests in the class, who vote, cast their votes to accept the Plan.

2. *Treatment of Nonaccepting Classes*

Even if one or more impaired classes reject the Plan, the Court may nonetheless confirm the Plan if the nonaccepting classes are treated in the manner prescribed by § 1129(b) of the Code. A plan that binds nonaccepting classes is commonly referred to as a "cram down" plan. The Code allows the Plan to bind nonaccepting classes of claims or equity interests if it meets all the requirements for consensual confirmation except the voting requirements of § 1129(a)(8) of the Code, does not "discriminate unfairly," and is "fair and equitable" toward each impaired class that has not voted to accept the Plan.

You should consult your own attorney if a "cramdown" confirmation will affect your claim or equity interest, as the variations on this general rule are numerous and complex.

C. **Liquidation Analysis**

To confirm the Plan, the Court must find that all creditors and equity interest holders who do not accept the Plan will receive at least as much under the Plan as such claim and equity interest holders would receive in a chapter 7 liquidation. A liquidation analysis is attached to this Disclosure Statement as Exhibit E.

D. **Feasibility**

The Court must find that confirmation of the Plan is not likely to be followed by the liquidation, or the need for further financial reorganization, of the Debtor or any successor to the Debtor, unless such liquidation or reorganization is proposed in the Plan.

1. *Ability to Initially Fund Plan*

The Plan Proponent believes that the Debtor will have enough cash on hand on the effective date of the Plan to pay all the claims and expenses that are entitled to be paid on that date. Tables showing the amount of cash on hand on the effective date of the Plan, and the sources of that cash are attached to this disclosure statement as Exhibit F.

2. *Ability to Make Future Plan Payments And Operate Without Further Reorganization*

The Plan Proponent must also show that it will have enough cash over the life of the Plan to make the required Plan payments.

The Plan Proponent has provided projected financial information. Those projections are listed in Exhibit G.

The Plan Proponent's financial projections show that the Debtor will have an aggregate annual average cash flow, after paying operating expenses and post-confirmation taxes, of $___. The final Plan payment is expected to be paid on _____.

[Summarize the numerical projections, and highlight any assumptions that are not in accord with past experience. Explain why such assumptions should now be made.]

You Should Consult with Your Accountant or other Financial Advisor If You Have Any Questions Pertaining to These Projections.

V. **EFFECT OF CONFIRMATION OF PLAN**

A. **DISCHARGE OF DEBTOR** [If the Debtor is not entitled to discharge pursuant to 11 U.S.C. § 1141(d)(3) change this heading to "**NO DISCHARGE OF DEBTOR.**"]

[Option 1 – If Debtor is an individual and § 1141(d)(3) is not applicable]

Discharge. Confirmation of the Plan does not discharge any debt provided for in the Plan until the court grants a discharge on completion of all payments under the Plan, or as otherwise provided in § 1141(d)(5) of the Code. Debtor will not be discharged from any debt excepted from discharge under § 523 of the Code, except as provided in Rule 4007(c) of the Federal Rules of Bankruptcy Procedure.

[Option 2 – If the Debtor is a partnership and § 1141(d)(3) of the Code is not applicable]

Discharge. On the effective date of the Plan, the Debtor shall be discharged from any debt that arose before confirmation of the Plan, subject to the occurrence of the effective date, to the extent specified in § 1141(d)(1)(A) of the Code. However, the Debtor shall not be discharged from any debt imposed by the Plan. After the effective date of the Plan your claims against the Debtor will be limited to the debts imposed by the Plan.

[Option 3 – If the Debtor is a corporation and § 1141(d)(3) is not applicable]

Discharge. On the effective date of the Plan, the Debtor shall be discharged from any debt that arose before confirmation of the Plan, subject to the occurrence of the effective date, to the extent specified in § 1141(d)(1)(A) of the Code, except that the Debtor shall not be discharged of any debt (i) imposed by the Plan, (ii) of a kind specified in § 1141(d)(6)(A) if a timely complaint was filed in accordance with Rule 4007(c) of the Federal Rules of Bankruptcy Procedure, or (iii) of a kind specified in § 1141(d)(6)(B). After the effective date of the Plan your claims against the Debtor will be limited to the debts described in clauses (i) through (iii) of the preceding sentence.

[Option 4 – If § 1141(d)(3) is applicable]

No Discharge. In accordance with § 1141(d)(3) of the Code, the Debtor will not receive any discharge of debt in this bankruptcy case.

B. Modification of Plan

The Plan Proponent may modify the Plan at any time before confirmation of the Plan. However, the Court may require a new disclosure statement and/or revoting on the Plan.

[If the Debtor is not an individual, add the following: "The Plan Proponent may also seek to modify the Plan at any time after confirmation only if (1) the Plan has not been substantially consummated *and* (2) the Court authorizes the proposed modifications after notice and a hearing."]

[If the Debtor is an individual, add the following: "Upon request of the Debtor, the United States trustee, or the holder of an allowed unsecured claim, the Plan may be modified at any time after confirmation of the Plan but before the completion of payments under the Plan, to (1) increase or reduce the amount of payments under the Plan on claims of a particular class, (2) extend or reduce the time period for such payments, or (3) alter the amount of distribution to a creditor whose claim is provided for by the Plan to the extent necessary to take account of any payment of the claim made other than under the Plan."]

C. Final Decree

Once the estate has been fully administered, as provided in Rule 3022 of the Federal Rules of Bankruptcy Procedure, the Plan Proponent, or such other party as the Court shall designate in the Plan Confirmation Order, shall file a motion with the Court to obtain a final decree to close the case. Alternatively, the Court may enter such a final decree on its own motion.

VI. OTHER PLAN PROVISIONS

[Insert other provisions here, as necessary and appropriate.]

____

[Signature of the Plan Proponent]

____

[Signature of the Attorney for the Plan Proponent]

Exhibit B - Identity and Value of Material Assets of Debtor

Exhibit C - Prepetition Financial Statements
(to be taken from those filed with the court)

Exhibit D - [Most Recently Filed Postpetition Operating Report] [Summary of Postpetition Operating Reports]

Exhibit E – Liquidation Analysis

Plan Proponent's Estimated Liquidation Value of Assets

Assets	
a. Cash on hand	$
b. Accounts receivable	$
c. Inventory	$
d. Office furniture & equipment	$
e. Machinery & equipment	$
f. Automobiles	$
g. Building & Land	$
h. Customer list	$
i. Investment property (such as stocks, bonds or other financial assets)	$
j. Lawsuits or other claims against third-parties	$
k. Other intangibles (such as avoiding powers actions)	$
Total Assets at Liquidation Value	$
Less: Secured creditors' recoveries	$
Less: Chapter 7 trustee fees and expenses	$
Less: Chapter 11 administrative expenses	$
Less: Priority claims, excluding administrative expense claims	$
[Less: Debtor's claimed exemptions]	$
(1) Balance for unsecured claims	$
(2) Total dollar amount of unsecured claims	$
Percentage of Claims Which Unsecured Creditors Would Receive Or Retain in a Chapter 7 Liquidation:	$
Percentage of Claims Which Unsecured Creditors Will Receive or Retain under the Plan:	____% [Divide (1) by (2)]
	____%

Exhibit F - Cash on hand on the effective date of the Plan

Cash on hand on effective date of the Plan:	$
Less -	
Amount of administrative expenses payable on effective date of the Plan	-
Amount of statutory costs and charges	-
Amount of cure payments for executory contracts	-
Other Plan Payments due on effective date of the Plan	-
Balance after paying these amounts..............	$

The sources of the cash Debtor will have on hand by the effective date of the Plan are estimated as follows:

$	Cash in Debtor's bank account now
+	Additional cash Debtor will accumulate from net earnings between now and effective date of the Plan [state the basis for such projections]
+	Borrowing [separately state terms of repayment]
+	Capital Contributions
+	Other
$	Total [This number should match "cash on hand" figure noted above]

Exhibit G - Projections of Cash Flow and Earnings for Post-Confirmation Period

Chapter 11 Exhibit "A" to Voluntary Petition

Form B1, Exhibit A - (Rev. 3/98) 1998 USBC, Central District of California

Exhibit "A"

[If debtor is required to file periodic reports (e.g., forms 10K and 10Q) with the Securities and Exchange Commission pursuant to Section 13 or 15(d) of the Securities Exchange Act of 1934 and is requesting relief under chapter 11 of the Bankruptcy Code, this Exhibit "A" shall be completed and attached to the petition.]

[Caption as in Form 16B]

Exhibit "A" to Voluntary Petition

1. If any of the debtor's securities are registered under Section 12 of the Securities Exchange Act of 1934, the SEC file number is ______________________.

2. The following financial data is the latest available information and refers to the debtor's condition on ____________.

   a. Total assets $______________

   b. Total debts (including debts listed in 2.c., below) $______________

				Approximate Number of holders
c. Debt securities held by more than 500 holders.				
❑ secured	❑ unsecured	❑ subordinated	$__________	______
❑ secured	❑ unsecured	❑ subordinated	$__________	______
❑ secured	❑ unsecured	❑ subordinated	$__________	______
❑ secured	❑ unsecured	❑ subordinated	$__________	______
❑ secured	❑ unsecured	❑ subordinated	$__________	______
d. Number of shares of preferred stock			__________	______
e. Number of shares common stock			__________	______

   Comments, if any:

   ____

3. Brief description of debtor's business:

   ____

4. List the names of any person who directly or indirectly owns, controls, or holds, with power to vote, 5% or more of the voting securities of debtor:

   ____

Chapter 11 Form 4 -- List of Creditors Holding 20 Largest Unsecured Claims

Form B4 (Official Form 4) - (12/07)

2007 USBC, Central District of California

UNITED STATES BANKRUPTCY COURT CENTRAL DISTRICT OF CALIFORNIA	
In re	CHAPTER:
Debtor(s).	CASE NO.:

Form 4.
LIST OF CREDITORS HOLDING 20 LARGEST UNSECURED CLAIMS

Following is the list of the debtor's creditors holding the 20 largest unsecured claims. The list is prepared in accordance with Fed. R. Bankr. P. 1007(d) for filing in this chapter 11 [*or* chapter 9] case. The list does not include (1) persons who come within the definition of "insider" set forth in 11 U.S.C. § 101, or (2) secured creditors unless the value of the collateral is such that the unsecured deficiency places the creditor among the holders of the 20 largest unsecured claims. If a minor child is one of the creditors holding the 20 largest unsecured claims, state the child's initials and the name and address of the child's parent or guardian, such as "A.B., a minor child, by John Doe, guardian." Do not disclose the child's name. See, 11 U.S.C. §112 and Fed. R. Bankr. P. 1007(m).

(1)	(2)	(3)	(4)	(5)
Name of creditor and complete mailing address including zip code	Name, telephone number and complete mailing address including zip code, of employee, agent, or department of creditor familiar with claim who may be contacted	Nature of claim (trade debt, bank loan, govern-ment contract, etc.)	Indicate if claim is contingent, unliquidated, disputed or subject to setoff	Amount of claim [if secured also state value of security]

Date: ____________________

____
Debtor

[Declaration as in Form 2]

Form B4 (Official Form 4) - (12/07) 2007 USBC, Central District of California

UNITED STATES BANKRUPTCY COURT
CENTRAL DISTRICT OF CALIFORNIA

In re Debtor(s).	CHAPTER: CASE NO.:

LIST OF CREDITORS HOLDING 20 LARGEST UNSECURED CLAIMS
(Continuation Sheet)

(1) Name of creditor *and complete* mailing address including zip code	(2) Name, telephone number and complete mailing address including zip code, of employee, agent, or department of creditor familiar with claim who may be contacted	(3) Nature of claim (trade debt, bank loan, govern-ment contract, etc.)	(4) Indicate if claim is contingent, unliquidated, disputed or subject to setoff	(5) Amount of claim [if secured also state value of security]

Chapter 11 Notice of Available Chapters (Individual Only)

B 201 - Notice of Available Chapters (Rev. 12/08) USBC, Central District of California

Name: ______________________________

Address: ______________________________

____

Telephone: ______________ Fax: ______________

☐ Attorney for Debtor
☐ Debtor in Pro Per

<table>
<tr><td colspan="2">UNITED STATES BANKRUPTCY COURT
CENTRAL DISTRICT OF CALIFORNIA</td></tr>
<tr><td rowspan="2">List all names including trade names, used by Debtor(s) within last 8 years:</td><td>Case No.:</td></tr>
<tr><td>NOTICE OF AVAILABLE CHAPTERS
(Notice to Individual Consumer Debtor Under § 342(b) of the Bankruptcy Code)</td></tr>
</table>

In accordance with § 342(b) of the Bankruptcy Code, this notice to individuals with primarily consumer debts: (1) Describes briefly the services available from credit counseling services; (2) Describes briefly the purposes, benefits and costs of the four types of bankruptcy proceedings you may commence; and (3) Informs you about bankruptcy crimes and notifies you that the Attorney General may examine all information you supply in connection with a bankruptcy case.

You are cautioned that bankruptcy law is complicated and not easily described. Thus, you may wish to seek the advice of an attorney to learn of your rights and responsibilities should you decide to file a petition. Court employees cannot give you legal advice.

Notices from the bankruptcy court are sent to the mailing address you list on your bankruptcy petition. In order to ensure that you receive information about events concerning your case, Bankruptcy Rule 4002 requires that you notify the court of any changes in your address. If you are filing a **joint case** (a single bankruptcy case for two individuals married to each other), and each spouse lists the same mailing address on the bankruptcy petition, you and your spouse will generally receive a single copy of each notice mailed from the bankruptcy court in a jointly-addressed envelope, unless you file a statement with the court requesting that each spouse receive a separate copy of all notices.

1. **Services Available from Credit Counseling Agencies**

   With limited exceptions, § 109(h) of the Bankruptcy Code requires that all individual debtors who file for bankruptcy relief on or after October 17, 2005, receive a briefing that outlines the available opportunities for credit counseling and provides assistance in performing a budget analysis. The briefing must be given within 180 days **before** the bankruptcy filing. The briefing may be provided individually or in a group (including briefings conducted by telephone or on the Internet) and must be provided by a nonprofit budget and credit counseling agency approved by the United States trustee or bankruptcy administrator. The clerk of the bankruptcy court has a list that you may consult of the approved budget and credit counseling agencies. Each debtor in a joint case must complete the briefing.

   In addition, after filing a bankruptcy case, an individual debtor generally must complete a financial management instructional course before he or she can receive a discharge. The clerk also has a list of approved financial management instructional courses. Each debtor in a joint case must complete the course.

2. **The Four Chapters of the Bankruptcy Code Available to Individual Consumer Debtors**

Chapter 7: Liquidation ($245 filing fee, $39 administrative fee, $15 trustee surcharge: Total fee $299)

1. Chapter 7 is designed for debtors in financial difficulty who do not have the ability to pay their existing debts. Debtors whose debts are primarily consumer debts are subject to a "means test" designed to determine whether the case should be permitted to proceed under chapter 7. If your income is greater than the median income for your state of residence and family size, in some cases, creditors have the right to file a motion requesting that the court dismiss your case under § 707(b) of the Code. It is up to the court to decide whether the case should be dismissed.
2. Under chapter 7, you may claim certain of your property as exempt under governing law. A trustee may have the right to take possession of and sell the remaining property that is not exempt and use the sale proceeds to pay your creditors.
3. The purpose of filing a chapter 7 case is to obtain a discharge of your existing debts. If, however, you are found to have committed certain kinds of improper conduct described in the Bankruptcy Code, the court may deny your discharge and, if it does, the purpose for which you filed the bankruptcy petition will be defeated.
4. Even if you receive a general discharge, some particular debts are not discharged under the law. Therefore, you may still be responsible for most taxes and student loans; debts incurred to pay nondischargeable taxes; domestic support and property settlement obligations; most fines, penalties, forfeitures, and criminal restitution obligations; certain debts which are not properly listed in your bankruptcy papers; and debts for death or personal injury caused by operating a motor vehicle, vessel, or aircraft while intoxicated from alcohol or drugs. Also, if a creditor can prove that a debt arose from fraud, breach of fiduciary duty, or theft, or from a willful and malicious injury, the bankruptcy court may determine that the debt is not discharged.

Chapter 13: Repayment of All or Part of the Debts of an Individual with Regular Income ($235 filing fee, $39 administrative fee: Total fee $274)

1. Chapter 13 is designed for individuals with regular income who would like to pay all or part of their debts in installments over a period of time. You are only eligible for chapter 13 if your debts do not exceed certain dollar amounts set forth in the Bankruptcy Code.
2. Under chapter 13, you must file with the court a plan to repay your creditors all or part of the money that you owe them, using your future earnings. The period allowed by the court to repay your debts may be three years or five years, depending upon your income and other factors. The court must approve your plan before it can take effect.
3. After completing the payments under your plan, your debts are generally discharged except for domestic support obligations; most student loans; certain taxes; most criminal fines and restitution obligations; certain debts which are not properly listed in your bankruptcy papers; certain debts for acts that caused death or personal injury; and certain long term secured obligations.

Chapter 11: Reorganization ($1000 filing fee, $39 administrative fee: Total fee $1039)
Chapter 11 is designed for the reorganization of a business but is also available to consumer debtors. Its provisions are quite complicated, and any decision by an individual to file a chapter 11 petition should be reviewed with an attorney.

Chapter 12: Family Farmer or Fisherman ($200 filing fee, $39 administrative fee: Total fee $239)
Chapter 12 is designed to permit family farmers and fishermen to repay their debts over a period of time from future earnings and is similar to chapter 13. The eligibility requirements are restrictive, limiting its use to those whose income arises primarily from a family-owned farm or commercial fishing operation.

3. **Bankruptcy Crimes and Availability of Bankruptcy Papers to Law Enforcement Officials**

A person who knowingly and fraudulently conceals assets or makes a false oath or statement under penalty of perjury, either orally or in writing, in connection with a bankruptcy case is subject to a fine, imprisonment, or both. All information supplied by a debtor in connection with a bankruptcy case is subject to examination by the Attorney General acting through the Office of the United States Trustee, the Office of the United States Attorney, and other components and employees of the Department of Justice.

WARNING: Section 521(a)(1) of the Bankruptcy Code requires that you promptly file detailed information regarding your creditors, assets, liabilities, income, expenses and general financial condition. Your bankruptcy case may be dismissed if this information is not filed with the court within the time deadlines set by the Bankruptcy Code, the Bankruptcy Rules, and the local rules of the court.

B 201 - Notice of Available Chapters (Rev. 12/08) USBC, Central District of California

Certificate of [Non-Attorney] Bankruptcy Petition Preparer

I, the [non-attorney] bankruptcy petition preparer signing the debtor's petition, hereby certify that I delivered to the debtor this notice required by § 342(b) of the Bankruptcy Code.

____
Printed name and title, if any, of Bankruptcy Petition Preparer

____
Social Security number (If the bankruptcy petition preparer is not an individual, state the Social Security number of the officer, principal, responsible person, or partner of the bankruptcy petition preparer.) (Required by 11 U.S.C. § 110.)

Address:
____

X______________________________
Signature of Bankruptcy Petition Preparer or officer, principal, responsible person, or partner whose Social Security number is provided above.

Certificate of the Debtor

I (We), the debtor(s), affirm that I (we) have received and read this notice.

____
Printed Name(s) of Debtor(s)

X______________________________
Signature of Debtor Date

Case No. (if known) ______________

X______________________________
Signature of Joint Debtor (if any) Date

CDCAL-449 C.D. CALIFORNIA

Chapter 11 Periodic Report Regarding Value, Operations and Profitability of Entities in Which the Debtor's Estate Holds a Substantial or Controlling Interest

Form B26 (Official Form 26) (12/08) 2008 USBC, Central District of California

UNITED STATES BANKRUPTCY COURT CENTRAL DISTRICT OF CALIFORNIA	
In re: Debtor(s).	CHAPTER 11 CASE NO.:

PERIODIC REPORT REGARDING VALUE, OPERATIONS AND PROFITABILITY OF ENTITIES IN WHICH THE ESTATE OF [NAME OF DEBTOR] HOLDS A SUBSTANTIAL OR CONTROLLING INTEREST

This is the report as of __________ on the value, operations and profitability of those entities in which the estate holds a substantial or controlling interest, as required by Bankruptcy Rule 2015.3. The estate of [Name of Debtor] holds a substantial or controlling interest in the following entities:

Name of Entity	Interest of the Estate	Tab #

This periodic report (the "Periodic Report") contains separate reports ("Entity Reports") on the value, operations, and profitability of each entity listed above.

Each Entity Report shall consist of three exhibits. Exhibit A contains a valuation estimate for the entity as of a date not more than two years prior to the date of this report. It also contains a description of the valuation method used. Exhibit B contains a balance sheet, a statement of income (loss), a statement of cash flows, and a statement of changes in shareholders' or partners' equity (deficit) for the period covered by the Entity Report, along with summarized footnotes. Exhibit C contains a description of the entity's business operations.

THIS REPORT MUST BE SIGNED BY A REPRESENTATIVE OF THE TRUSTEE OR DEBTOR IN POSSESSION.

The undersigned, having reviewed the above listing of entities in which the estate of [Debtor] holds a substantial or controlling interest, and being familiar with the Debtor's financial affairs, verifies under the penalty of perjury that the listing is complete, accurate and truthful to the best of his/her knowledge.

Date: ___________

____
Signature of Authorized Individual

____
Name of Authorized Individual

____
Title of Authorized Individual

[If the Debtor is an individual or in a joint case]

Signature(s) of Debtor(s) (Individual/Joint)

____
Signature of Debtor

____
Signature of Joint Debtor

Exhibit A
Valuation Estimate for [Name of Entity]

[Provide a statement of the entity's value and the value of the estate's interest in the entity, including a description of the basis for the valuation, the date of the valuation and the valuation method used. This valuation must be no more than two years old. Indicate the source of this information.]

Exhibit B

Financial Statements for [Insert Name of Entity]

Exhibit B-1
Balance Sheet for [Name of Entity]
As of [date]

[Provide a balance sheet dated as of the end of the most recent six-month period of the current fiscal year and as of the end of the preceding fiscal year. Indicate the source of this information.]

Exhibit B-2
Statement of Income (Loss) for [Name of Entity]
Period ending [date]

[Provide a statement of income (loss) for the following periods:

(i) For the initial report:
 a. the period between the end of the preceding fiscal year and the end of the most recent six-month period of the current fiscal year; and
 b. the prior fiscal year.
(ii) For subsequent reports, since the closing date of the last report.

Indicate the source of this information.]

Exhibit B-3

Statement of Cash Flows for [Name of Entity]

For the period ending [date]

[Provide a statement of changes in cash flows for the following periods:

(i) For the initial report:

a. the period between the end of the preceding fiscal year and the end of the most recent six-month period of the current fiscal year; and

b. the prior fiscal year.

(ii) For subsequent reports, since the closing date of the last report.

Indicate the source of this information.]

Exhibit B-4
Statement of Changes in Shareholders'/Partners' Equity (Deficit) for [Name of Entity]
period ending [date]

[Provide a statement of changes in shareholders'/partners equity (deficit) for the following periods:

(i) For the initial report:
  a. the period between the end of the preceding fiscal year and the end of the most recent six-month period of the current fiscal year; and
  b. the prior fiscal year.

(ii) For subsequent reports, since the closing date of the last report.

Indicate the source of this information.]

Exhibit C
Description of Operations for [name of entity]

[Describe the nature and extent of the estate's interest in the entity.

Describe the business conducted and intended to be conducted by the entity, focusing on the entity's dominant business segment(s). Indicate the source of this information.]

Chapter 11 Plan (F 3018-1)

UNITED STATES BANKRUPTCY COURT
CENTRAL DISTRICT OF CALIFORNIA

CENTRAL DISTRICT OF CALIFORNIA

APPROVED FORM FOR PRODUCING A

CHAPTER 11 PLAN

WordPerfect Format

NAME OF ATTORNEY - State Bar No. ____________
NAME OF ATTORNEY - State Bar No. ____________
NAME OF LAW FIRM
Address
City, State Zip Code
Telephone ( ) -

Attorneys for ______________

UNITED STATES BANKRUPTCY COURT

CENTRAL DISTRICT OF CALIFORNIA

In re NAME OF DEBTOR, Debtor	Bk. No. __ __-_____-__ In a Case Under Chapter 11 of the Bankruptcy Code (11 U.S.C. § 1101 et seq.) _____[1] **CHAPTER 11** _____[2] **PLAN** **Disclosure Statement Hearing**[3] Date: ____________ Time: ____________ Ctrm: {Insert Courtroom #} {Insert Full Court Address Here} **Plan Confirmation Hearing** **See Disclosure Statement for Voting and Objecting Procedures** Date: ____________ Time: ____________ Ctrm: {Insert Courtroom #} {Insert Full Court Address Here}

TABLE OF CONTENTS

I. INTRODUCTION 1

II. CLASSIFICATION AND TREATMENT OF CLAIMS AND INTERESTS . 1
A. General Overview 1
B. Unclassified Claims 1
1. Administrative Expenses 2
2. Priority Tax Claims 2
C. Classified Claims and Interests 3
1. Classes of Secured Claims 3
2. Classes of Priority Unsecured Claims 4
3. Class of General Unsecured Claims 5
4. Class(es) of Interest Holders 5
D. Means of Performing the Plan 6
1. Funding for the Plan 6
2. Post-Confirmation Management 6
3. Disbursing Agent 6

III. TREATMENT OF MISCELLANEOUS ITEMS 6
A. Executory Contracts and Unexpired Leases 6
1. Assumptions 6
2. Rejections 7
B. Changes in Rates Subject to Regulatory Commission Approval 8
C. Retention of Jurisdiction 8

IV. EFFECT OF CONFIRMATION OF PLAN 8
A. Discharge 8
B. Revesting of Property in the Debtor 8
C. Modification of Plan 8
D. Post-Confirmation Status Report 9
E. Quarterly Fees 9
F. Post-Confirmation Conversion/Dismissal 9
G. Final Decree 9

EXHIBIT A - UNEXPIRED LEASES TO BE ASSUMED 11
EXHIBIT B - EXECUTORY CONTRACTS TO BE ASSUMED 12

I.

INTRODUCTION

______[4] is the Debtor in a Chapter 11 bankruptcy case. On ______[5], ______[6] commenced a bankruptcy case by filing ______[7] Chapter 11 petition under the United States Bankruptcy Code ("Bankruptcy Code"), 11 U.S.C. § 101 et seq. This document is the Chapter 11 Plan ("Plan") proposed by ______[8] ("Plan Proponent"). Sent to you in the same envelope as this document is the Disclosure Statement which has been approved by the Court, and which is provided to help you understand the Plan.

This is a ______[9] plan. In other words, the Proponent seeks to accomplish payments under the Plan by ______[10]. The Effective Date of the proposed Plan is ______[11].

II.

CLASSIFICATION AND TREATMENT OF CLAIMS AND INTERESTS

A. General Overview

As required by the Bankruptcy Code, the Plan classifies claims and interests in various classes according to their right to priority of payments as provided in the Bankruptcy Code. The Plan states whether each class of claims or interests is impaired or unimpaired. The Plan provides the treatment each class will receive under the Plan.

B. Unclassified Claims

Certain types of claims are not placed into voting classes; instead they are unclassified. They are not considered impaired and they do not vote on the Plan because they are automatically entitled to specific treatment provided for them in the Bankruptcy Code. As such, the Proponent has <u>not</u> placed the following claims in a class. The treatment of these claims is provided below.

1. Administrative Expenses

Administrative expenses are claims for costs or expenses of administering the Debtor's Chapter 11 case which are allowed under Code Section 507(a)(1). The Code requires that all administrative claims be paid on the Effective Date of the Plan, unless a particular claimant agrees to a different treatment.[12]

The following chart lists <u>all</u> of the Debtor's § 507(a)(1) administrative claims and their treatment under this Plan.[13]

Name	Amount Owed	Treatment
Clerk's Office Fees		Paid in full on Effective Date
Office of the U.S. Trustee Fees		Paid in full on Effective Date
TOTAL		

<u>Court Approval of Fees Required:</u>

The Court must approve all professional fees listed in this chart. For all fees except Clerk's Office fees and U.S. Trustee's fees, the professional in question must file and serve a properly noticed fee application and the Court must rule on the application. Only the amount of fees allowed by the Court will be required to be paid under this Plan.

2. Priority Tax Claims

Priority tax claims are certain unsecured income, employment and other taxes described by Code Section 507(a)(8)[14]. The Code requires that each holder of such a 507(a)(8) priority tax claim receive the present value of such claim in deferred cash payments, over a period not exceeding six years form the date of the assessment of such tax.

The following chart lists <u>all</u> of the Debtor's Section 507(a)(8)[15] priority tax claims and their treatment under this Plan.

Description	Amount Owed	Treatment[16]
• Name = • Type of tax = • Date tax assessed =		• Pymt interval[17] = = • Pymt amt/interval[18] = • Begin date[19] = = • End date[20] = $ • Interest Rate %[21] • Total Payout Amount[22] ___ %
• Name = • Type of tax = • Date tax assessed =		• Pymt interval = = • Pymt amt/interval = • Begin date = = • End date = $ • Interest Rate % • Total Payout Amount %

C. Classified Claims and Interests

1. Classes of Secured Claims

Secured claims are claims secured by liens on property of the estate. The following chart lists all classes containing Debtor's secured pre-petition claims and their treatment under this plan[23]:

CLASS#	DESCRIPTION	INSIDERS (Y/N)	IMPAIRED (Y/N)	TREATMENT
	Secured claim of: ● Name = ● Collateral description = ● Collateral value = ● Priority of security int. = ● Principal owed = ● Pre-pet. arrearage amount = ● Post-pet. arrearage amount = ● Total claim amount =		23a.	● Pymt interval = = ● Pymt amt/interval = ● Balloon pymt[24] = ● Begin date = = ● End date = $ = ● Interest rate % ● Total payout[24a] ___ % ● Treatment of Lien
	Secured claim of:			● Pymt interval =

	• Name = • Collateral description = • Collateral value = • Priority of security int. = • Principal owed = • Pre-pet. arrearage amount = • Post-pet. arrearage amount = • Total claim amount =			• Pymt amt/interval = • Balloon pymt = • Begin date = • End date = • Interest rate % = • Total payout % = $ • Treatment of Lien =

2. Classes of Priority Unsecured Claims

Certain priority claims that are referred to in Code Sections 507(a)(3), (4), (5), (6), and (7)[25] are required to be placed in classes. These types of claims are entitled to priority treatment as follows: the Code requires that each holder of such a claim receive cash on the Effective Date equal to the allowed amount of such claim. However, a class of unsecured priority claim holders may vote to accept deferred cash payments of a value, as of the Effective Date, equal to the allowed amount of such claims.

The following chart lists all classes containing Debtor's 507(a)(3), (4), (5), (6), and (7)[26] priority unsecured claims and their treatment under this Plan[27]:

CLASS#	DESCRIPTION	IMPAIRED (Y/N)	TREATMENT
	Priority unsecured claim pursuant to ____[28] • Total amt of claims = ____[29]		• Paid in full in cash on Effective Date[30]
	Priority unsecured claim pursuant to ____[31] • Total amt of claims =		• Paid in full in cash on Effective Date

3. Class of General Unsecured Claims

General unsecured claims are unsecured claims not entitled to priority under Code Section 507(a). The following chart identifies this Plan's treatment of the class containing <u>all</u> of Debtor's general unsecured claims:

CLASS#	DESCRIPTION	IMPAIRED (Y/N)	TREATMENT
	General unsecured claims ● Total amt of claims =	[33]	● Pymt interval = ● Pymt amt/interval = ● Begin date = ● End date = ● Interest rate % = ● Total payout [33a] ___% = $

[33b]
[33c]

4. Class(es) of Interest Holders

Interest holders are the parties who hold ownership interest (i.e., equity interest) in the Debtor. If the Debtor is a corporation, entities holding preferred or common stock in the Debtor are interest holders. If the Debtor is a partnership, the interest holders include both general and limited partners. If the Debtor is an individual, the Debtor is the interest holder. The following chart identifies this Plan's treatment of the class[34] of interest holders:

CLASS #	DESCRIPTION	IMPAIRED (Y/N)	TREATMENT
	Interest holders	[35]	

D. Means of Performing the Plan

1. Funding for the Plan

The Plan will be funded by the following: ____[36]____.

2. Post-confirmation Management ____[37]____

3. Disbursing Agent ____[38]____ shall act as the disbursing agent for the purpose of making all distributions provided for under the Plan. The Disbursing Agent shall serve ____[39]____ bond and shall receive ____[40]____ for distribution services rendered and expenses incurred pursuant to the Plan.[41]

III.

TREATMENT OF MISCELLANEOUS ITEMS

A. Executory Contracts and Unexpired Leases

Assumptions

The following are the unexpired leases and executory contracts to be assumed as obligations of the reorganized Debtor under this Plan (see Exhibit A for more detailed information on unexpired leases to be assumed and Exhibit B for more detailed information on executory contracts to be assumed): ____[42]____

On the Effective Date, each of the unexpired leases and executory contracts listed above shall be assumed as obligations of the reorganized Debtor. The Order of the Court confirming the Plan shall constitute an Order approving the assumption of each lease and contract listed above. If you are a party to a lease or contract to be assumed and you object to the assumption of your lease or contract, you must file and serve your objection to the Plan within the deadline for objecting to the confirmation of the Plan. See Section {I.B.3.} of the Disclosure Statement describing this Plan for the specific date.

2. Rejections

On the Effective Date, the following executory contracts and unexpired leases will be rejected: ____[43]

The order confirming the Plan shall constitute an order approving the rejection of the lease or contract. If you are a party to a contract or lease to be rejected and you object to the rejection of your contract or lease, you must file and serve your objection to the Plan within the deadline for objecting to the confirmation of the Plan. See Disclosure Statement for the specific date.

THE BAR DATE FOR FILING A PROOF OF CLAIM BASED ON A CLAIM ARISING FROM THE REJECTION OF A LEASE OR CONTRACT IS ____[44]. Any claim based on the rejection of an executory contract or unexpired lease will be barred if the proof of claim is not timely filed, unless the Court later orders otherwise.

B. Changes in Rates Subject to Regulatory Commission Approval

This Debtor ____[45] subject to governmental regulatory commission approval of its rates[45a].

C. Retention of Jurisdiction.

The Court will retain jurisdiction to the extent provided by law.[46]

IV.

EFFECT OF CONFIRMATION OF PLAN

A. Discharge[47]

This Plan provides that upon ___48___, Debtor shall be discharged of liability for payment of debts incurred before confirmation of the Plan, to the extent specified in 11 U.S.C.§ 1141. However, any liability imposed by the Plan will <u>not</u> be discharged.

B. Revesting of Property in the Debtor

Except as provided in Section (IV.E.), and except as provided elsewhere in the Plan, the confirmation of the Plan revests all of the property of the estate in the Debtor.

C. Modification of Plan

The Proponent of the Plan may modify the Plan at any time before confirmation. However, the Court may require a new disclosure statement and/or revoting on the Plan if proponent modifies the plan before confirmation.

The Proponent of the Plan may also seek to modify the Plan at any time after confirmation so long as (1) the Plan has not been substantially consummated <u>and</u> (2) if the Court authorizes the proposed modifications after notice and a hearing.

D. Post-Confirmation Status Report

Within 120 days of the entry of the order confirming the Plan, Plan Proponent shall file a status report with the Court explaining what progress has been made toward consummation of the confirmed Plan. The status report shall be served on the United States Trustee, the twenty largest unsecured creditors, and those parties who have requested special notice. Further status reports shall be filed every 120 days and served on the same entities.

E. Quarterly Fees

Quarterly fees accruing under 28 U.S.C. § 1930(a)(6) to date of confirmation shall be paid to the United States Trustee on or before the effective date of the plan. Quarterly fees accruing under 28 U.S.C. § 1930(a)(6) after confirmation shall be paid to the United States Trustee in accordance with 28 U.S.C. § 1930(a)(6) until entry of a final decree, or entry of an order of dismissal or conversion to chapter 7.

F. Post-Confirmation Conversion/Dismissal

A creditor or party in interest may bring a motion to convert or dismiss the case under § 1112(b), after the Plan is confirmed, if there is a default in performing the Plan. If the Court orders the case converted to Chapter 7 after the Plan is confirmed, then all property that had been property of the Chapter 11 estate, and that has not been disbursed pursuant to the Plan, will revest in the Chapter 7 estate, and the automatic stay will be reimposed upon the revested property only to the extent that relief from stay was not previously granted by the Court during this case.

G. Final Decree

Once the estate has been fully administered as referred to in Bankruptcy Rule 3022, the Plan Proponent, or other party as the Court shall designate in the Plan Confirmation Order, shall file a motion with the Court to obtain a final decree to close the case.

Date: ______________________

____

Signature of Party (optional unless party is pro se)

Name of Plan Proponent

Signature of Attorney for Plan Proponent

Name of Attorney for Plan Proponent

Name of Law Firm for Plan Proponent

EXHIBIT A - UNEXPIRED LEASES TO BE ASSUMED

LEASES	ARREARS/DMGS	METHODS OF CURE
• Description =[1] • Lessor's name = • Lessee's name = • Expiration date =	• Default amt = • Actual pecuniary loss[2] =	• Method of curing default & loss = • Means of assuring future performance[3] =
• Description = • Lessor's name = • Lessee's name = • Expiration date =	• Default amt = • Actual pecuniary loss =	• Method of curing default & loss = • Means of assuring future performance =
• Description = • Lessor's name = • Lessee's name = • Expiration date =	• Default amt = • Actual pecuniary loss =	• Method of curing default & loss = • Means of assuring future performance =

EXHIBIT B - EXECUTORY CONTRACTS TO BE ASSUMED

CONTRACT	DEFAULT/DMGS	METHODS OF CURE
• Contract description = • Contracting parties = 1. 2.	• Default amt = • Actual pecuniary loss =	• Method of curing default & loss = • Means of assuring performance =
• Contract description = • Contracting parties = 1. 2.	• Default amt = • Actual pecuniary loss =	• Method of curing default & loss = • Means of assuring performance =
• Contract description = • Contracting parties = 1. 2.	• Default amt = • Actual pecuniary loss =	• Method of curing default & loss = • Means of assuring performance =

CROSS REFERENCE KEY

I. **Overview to Cross Reference Key**

This Chapter 11 Plan is a "fill in the blank form."

The user only fills in the blanks. DO NOT CHANGE THE LANGUAGE IN THE REST OF THE FORM, EXCEPT IN THE FEW PLACES WHERE THE INSTRUCTIONS EXPRESSLY TELL YOU THAT YOU MAY OMIT A SENTENCE OR CLASS IF IT IS NOT NEEDED FOR YOUR CASE.

As you read this Form, you will notice blanks with numbers in them, and also numbers at the end of certain sentences or phrases.

* Here is an example of a blank with a number:

  ___1___

* Here is an example of a sentence with a number:

  This is an example.[2]

These numbers refer to the numbered instructions in this "Cross Reference Key." When you encounter one of these numbers, in the form itself, you need to refer to the "Cross Reference Key," and read the applicable numbered instruction. In our examples above, instructions number 1 and 2 would be applicable instructions. Follow the instructions to fill in the needed information.

a. Why the Instructions in this Cross Reference Key are in Two Different Types of Print

When you read the numbered instructions in the "Cross Reference Key" you will see that these instructions are printed in two different types of print, Courier New 12 pt. and Helvetica 10 pt.

Instructions in Courier New 12 pt. font (the font you are currently reading), mean that you are to simply provide the information requested in the endnote and insert it in the corresponding blank. For example, if instruction number 1 states "Debtor's name", then you should insert the Debtor's name in blank number 1.

Instructions in Helvetica 10 pt. font may contain explanations on how to use the disclosure statement form, explanations of the law, or examples of what should be inserted in a particular blank. Read and follow these instructions also.

II. Key Notes 1 through 48

1. Name of party proposing the Plan (e.g. Debtor's, Creditor Committee's, etc.)

2. Put which version of the Plan this is, i.e., Original, First Amended, Second Amended, etc. Do not use the term "modified" when describing Plans subsequent to the Original Plan unless the Court directs you to do so.

3. Delete Disclosure Statement Hearing information when the Disclosure Statement has been approved and the upcoming hearing is the Plan Confirmation hearing.

4. Debtor's name.

5. Petition date.

6. Insert the applicable information, depending on who filed the petition:
   (a) Debtor's name
   (b) Names of the petitioning creditors

7. Insert one of the following:
   (a) a voluntary
   (b) an involuntary

8. Plan proponent's name.

9. Insert the applicable phrases:
   (a) liquidating
   (b) reorganizing
   (c) combined liquidating and reorganizing

10. Provide a brief summary of how Proponent proposes to fund the Plan.

11. Effective date of the Plan.

12. Holders of administrative expenses under § 507(b) are paid before other administrative expenses. If any such expenses must be paid, so state.

13. For each chart, add more rows to the tables as necessary.

14. Denominated as Section 507(a)(7) for bankruptcy cases filed before October 22, 1994.

15. Denominated as Section 507(a)(7) for bankruptcy cases filed before October 22, 1994.

16. Section 507(a)(7) priority tax claims must be fully paid within 6 years from the date of assessment.

17. Identify the proposed payment interval (e.g., monthly, quarterly, yearly).

18. Amount of payments per payment interval.

19. The date Plan payments will commence.
20. The date Plan payments will end.

21. The interest rate paid to a Section 507 (a)(7) priority tax claimant should be consistent with the rate provided by 26 U.S.C. § 6621.

22. Total percentage of claim proposed to be paid to claimant over the life of the Plan plus total dollar amount to be paid to the claimant over life of the plan.

23. Each secured claim should be placed in a separate class, unless the secured claims have identical collateral, priority, and terms of indebtedness. Begin numbering the classes with the number "1". The subsequent class should be numbered with the number "2". Do not use subclass, e.g., 1.1, 1.2, etc.

23a. If this class is Not Impaired, put the following in the box: "Not Impaired; claims in this class are not entitled to vote on Plan, class is deemed to have accepted Plan."

If this class is Impaired, put the following in the box: "Impaired; claims in this class are entitled to vote on the Plan"; unless this class is not retaining or receiving any value under the Plan. In this latter case only, put "Impaired, and claims in this class are deemed to have rejected Plan."

24. Balloon payment amount, if any.

24a. Total percentage of claim proposed to be paid to claimant over the life of the plan plus total dollar amount to be paid to claimant over life of plan.

25. Omit reference to 507(a)(7) (alimony/child support priority) if case was filed before October 22, 1994 because priority would not exist for cases filed before that date.

26. Omit reference to 507(a)(7) (alimony/child support priority) if case was filed before October 22, 1994 because priority would not exist for cases filed before that date.

27. Each of the four categories of priority unsecured claims should be placed in a separate class. A separate class is not necessary for a particular category of priority unsecured claims if no claim exist in that category.

28. Insert one of the following:
    (a) 11 U.S.C. § 507(a)(3)
    (b) 11 U.S.C. § 507(a)(4)
    (c) 11 U.S.C. § 507(a)(5)
    (d) 11 U.S.C. § 507(a)(6)

29. Total amount of claims in this class.

30. If the Plan does not provide for cash payment in full on Effective Date, Plan Proponent must be able to prove that this class has accepted deferred payments pursuant to 11 U.S.C § 1129(a)(9) before the Plan can be confirmed.

31. Insert one of the following:
(a) 11 U.S.C. § 507(a)(3)
(b) 11 U.S.C. § 507(a)(4)
(c) 11 U.S.C. § 507(a)(5)
(d) 11 U.S.C. § 507(a)(6)

32. Total amount of claims in this class.

33. If this class is Not Impaired, put the following in the box: "Not Impaired; claims in this class are not entitled to vote on Plan, class is deemed to have accepted Plan."

If this class is Impaired, put the following in the box:"Impaired; claims in this class are entitled to vote on the Plan"; unless this class is not retaining or receiving any value under the Plan. In this latter case only, put "Impaired, and claims in this class are deemed to have rejected Plan."

33a. Total percentage of claim proposed to be paid to claimant over the life of the Plan plus total dollar amount to be paid to claimant over life of the plan.

33b. If you have a convenience class allowed under 1122(b), then add as an additional unsecured class here, and at page 5, line 17 of the Plan form: ", except general unsecured claims placed in the convenience class described hereafter."

33c. If you have an additional general unsecured class(es), add each here, with a separate class number. The norm is to have a single general unsecured class, or where appropriate, to have a general unsecured class plus a convenience general unsecured class (as described in footnote 33a). However, there are a few limited circumstances where it is permissible to have additional general unsecured classes, primarily where one or more general unsecured creditors are agreeing to receive worse treatment than is being given to the rest of the general unsecured creditors, then the creditors agreeing to be treated worse can be placed in a separate general unsecured class. Do not use more than one general unsecured class unless you can justify doing so under applicable law.

34. If there is more than one class of equity holders (e.g., preferred stock and common stock), put each in a separate class and change "class" to "classes."

35. If this class is <u>Not Impaired</u>, put the following in the box: "Not Impaired; claims in this class are not entitled to vote on Plan, class is deemed to have accepted Plan."

    If this class is <u>Impaired</u>, put the following in the box: "Impaired; claims in this class are entitled to vote on the Plan"; unless this class is <u>not</u> retaining or receiving any value under the Plan. In this latter case only, put "<u>Impaired</u>, and claims in this class are deemed to have rejected Plan."

36. Describe the source of funding for this Plan. Be specific.

37. For each entity who will be involved in post-confirmation management, state or explain the following:
    (a) Identity
    (b) Post-confirmation managerial duties
    (c) Amount of compensation paid pre-petition and to be paid post-confirmation
    (d) Description of expertise

38. Name and identity of disbursing agent.

39. Select one:
    (a) with
    (b) without

40. Explain whether Disbursing Agent will be compensated or reimbursed for services and expenses rendered and incurred in connection with making distributions under the Plan. If Disbursing Agent will compensated or reimbursed, specify the exact amount and the interval of payment.

    NOTE: If disbursing agent will be compensated or reimbursed, be sure to account for these additional costs when evaluating feasibility of the Plan.

41. If the Disbursing Agent will be making distributions from a fund created under the Plan, the Plan and Disclosure Statement should provide that the fund will be maintained in a segregated interest- bearing account.

42. List the unexpired leases and executory contracts in sufficient detail to enable the reader to determine which Leases and contracts will be assumed. This list will enable a party to a lease or contract to quickly ascertain whether he or she needs to refer to Exhibit C or D.

    Exhibits C and D are intended to provide detailed information on each Lease or contract to be assumed so that the court and any party to a particular Lease or contract can decide whether assumption is proper and desirable.

43. List all executory contracts and unexpired Leases to be rejected in sufficient detail to enable a reader to quickly ascertain whether any particular Lease or contract will be rejected.

44. Deadline for filing proof of claim based on claim arising from rejection of contract or lease.
    (**Note:** Typically, this date will be 30 days from Effective Date.)

45. Select one:
(a) is
(b) is not

45a. See 11 U.S.C. § 1129(a)(6). This section is only applicable if Debtor's business is regulated by a governmental regulatory commission. Examples include certain transportation companies and public utility companies. If Debtor is not regulated by a governmental commission, insert an affirmative statement to that effect in the Disclosure Statement. If debtor is regulated, state this and Plan must comply with 11 U.S.C. § 1129(a)(6).

46. Do not change the language in this section unless the judge to whom your case is assigned has different or additional language that judge wishes to use in this section and directs you to insert that judge's specific language.

47.

NOTE: If the Debtor is not entitled to a discharge pursuant to 11 U.S.C. 1141(d), change this heading to "NO DISCHARGE." Read and follow instruction #48.

48. **Choose on of the following:**
(a) confirmation of the Plan
(b) payment in full of proposed plan payments to the unsecured creditors
(c) substantial consummation of plan
(d) other. You must state what the other condition for or date of discharge is.

Alternatively, if debtor does not meet the test of 11 U.S.C. 1141(d)(3) for getting a discharge, then the debtor is not entitled to any discharge, and the whole paragraph under "Discharge" must be omitted and replaced with:

(e) Debtor will not receive any discharge in this case because debtor does not meet the test for receiving a discharge specified under 11 U.S.C. § 1141(d)(3).

NOTE: More evidence regarding feasibility of the Plan may be required if the Plan Proponent seeks discharge upon Plan confirmation.

Instructions Relating to Exhibits A & B

1. Description of leased property or asset, including address of real property, if applicable.

2. Actual pecuniary loss consists of damages other than lease payment default, if any.

3. Describe how the Debtor is assuring performance on the remaining obligation under the lease, e.g., addition of guarantor.

Chapter 11 Plan of Reorganization in Small Business Case under Chapter 11

B25A (Official Form 25A) (12/08) 2008 USBC, Central District of California

UNITED STATES BANKRUPTCY COURT CENTRAL DISTRICT OF CALIFORNIA	
In re: Debtor(s).	CHAPTER 11 CASE NO.:

SMALL BUSINESS CASE UNDER CHAPTER 11

[NAME OF PROPONENT]'S PLAN OF REORGANIZATION, DATED [INSERT DATE]

ARTICLE I
SUMMARY

This Plan of Reorganization (the "Plan") under chapter 11 of the Bankruptcy Code (the "Code") proposes to pay creditors of [insert the name of the debtor] (the "Debtor") from [specify sources of payment, such as an infusion of capital, loan proceeds, sale of assets, cash flow from operations, or future income].

This Plan provides for _______________ classes of secured claims; _____________ classes of unsecured claims; and _____________ classes of equity security holders. Unsecured creditors holding allowed claims will receive distributions, which the proponent of this Plan has valued at approximately ____ cents on the dollar. This Plan also provides for the payment of administrative and priority claims [if payment is not in full on the effective date of this Plan with respect to any such claim (to the extent permitted by the Code or the claimant's agreement), identify such claim and briefly summarize the proposed treatment.]

All creditors and equity security holders should refer to Articles III through VI of this Plan for information regarding the precise treatment of their claim. A disclosure statement that provides more detailed information regarding this Plan and the rights of creditors and equity security holders has been circulated with this Plan. **Your rights may be affected. You should read these papers carefully and discuss them with your attorney, if you have one. (If you do not have an attorney, you may wish to consult one.)**

ARTICLE II
CLASSIFICATION OF CLAIMS AND INTERESTS

2.01 Class 1. All allowed claims entitled to priority under § 507 of the Code (except administrative expense claims under § 507(a)(2), ["gap" period claims in an involuntary case under § 507(a)(3),] and priority tax claims under § 507(a)(8)).

2.02 Class 2. The claim of ________________________________, to the extent allowed as a secured claim under § 506 of the Code.

[Add other classes of secured creditors, if any. Note: Section 1129(a)(9)(D) of the Code provides that a secured tax claim which would otherwise meet the description of a priority tax claim under § 507(a)(8) of the Code is to be paid in the same manner and over the same period as prescribed in § 507(a)(8).]

2.03 Class 3. All unsecured claims allowed under § 502 of the Code.

[Add other classes of unsecured claims, if any.]

2.04 Class 4. Equity interests of the Debtor. [If the Debtor is an individual, change this heading to "The interests of the individual Debtor in property of the estate."]

ARTICLE III
TREATMENT OF ADMINISTRATIVE EXPENSE CLAIMS,
U.S. TRUSTEES FEES, AND PRIORITY TAX CLAIMS

3.01 Unclassified Claims. Under section § 1123(a)(1), administrative expense claims, ["gap" period claims in an involuntary case allowed under § 502(f) of the Code,] and priority tax claims are not in classes.

3.02 Administrative Expense Claims. Each holder of an administrative expense claim allowed under § 503 of the Code, [and a "gap" claim in an involuntary case allowed under § 502(f) of the Code,] will be paid in full on the effective date of this Plan (as defined in Article VII), in cash, or upon such other terms as may be agreed upon by the holder of the claim and the Debtor.

3.03 Priority Tax Claims. Each holder of a priority tax claim will be paid [specify terms of treatment consistent with § 1129(a)(9)(C) of the Code].

3.04 United States Trustee Fees. All fees required to be paid by 28 U.S.C. §1930(a)(6) (U.S. Trustee Fees) will accrue and be timely paid until the case is closed, dismissed, or converted to another chapter of the Code. Any U.S. Trustee Fees owed on or before the effective date of this Plan will be paid on the effective date.

ARTICLE IV
TREATMENT OF CLAIMS AND INTERESTS UNDER THE PLAN

4.01 Claims and interests shall be treated as follows under this Plan:

Class	Impairment	Treatment
Class 1 - Priority Claims	[State whether impaired or unimpaired.]	[Insert treatment of priority claims in this Class, including the form, amount and timing of distribution, if any. For example: "Class 1 is unimpaired by this Plan, and each holder of a Class 1 Priority Claim will be paid in full, in cash, upon the later of the effective date of this Plan as defined in Article VII, or the date on which such claim is allowed by a final non-appealable order. Except: ________."]
Class 2 – Secured Claim of [Insert name of secured creditor.]	[State whether impaired or unimpaired.]	[Insert treatment of secured claim in this Class, including the form, amount and timing of distribution, if any.] [Add class[es] of secured claims if applicable]
Class 3 - General Unsecured Creditors	[State whether impaired or unimpaired.]	[Insert treatment of unsecured creditors in this Class, including the form, amount and timing of distribution, if any.] [Add administrative convenience class if applicable]
Class 4 - Equity Security Holders of the Debtor	[State whether impaired or unimpaired.]	[Insert treatment of equity security holders in this Class, including the form, amount and timing of distribution, if any.]

ARTICLE V
ALLOWANCE AND DISALLOWANCE OF CLAIMS

5.01 Disputed Claim. A disputed claim is a claim that has not been allowed or disallowed [by a final non-appealable order], and as to which either: (i) a proof of claim has been filed or deemed filed, and the Debtor or another party in interest has filed an objection; or (ii) no proof of claim has been filed, and the Debtor has scheduled such claim as disputed, contingent, or unliquidated.

5.02 Delay of Distribution on a Disputed Claim. No distribution will be made on account of a disputed claim unless such claim is allowed [by a final non-appealable order].

5.03 Settlement of Disputed Claims. The Debtor will have the power and authority to settle and compromise a disputed claim with court approval and compliance with Rule 9019 of the Federal Rules of Bankruptcy Procedure.

ARTICLE VI
PROVISIONS FOR EXECUTORY CONTRACTS AND UNEXPIRED LEASES

6.01 Assumed Executory Contracts and Unexpired Leases.

(a) The Debtor assumes the following executory contracts and/or unexpired leases effective upon the [Insert "effective date of this Plan as provided in Article VII," "the date of the entry of the order confirming this Plan," or other applicable date]:

[List assumed executory contracts and/or unexpired leases.]

(b) The Debtor will be conclusively deemed to have rejected all executory contracts and/or unexpired leases not expressly assumed under section 6.01(a) above, or before the date of the order confirming this Plan, upon the [Insert "effective date of this Plan," "the date of the entry of the order confirming this Plan," or other applicable date]. A proof of a claim arising from the rejection of an executory contract or unexpired lease under this section must be filed no later than ___________ (___) days after the date of the order confirming this Plan.

ARTICLE VII
MEANS FOR IMPLEMENTATION OF THE PLAN

[Insert here provisions regarding how the plan will be implemented as required under §1123(a)(5) of the Code. For example, provisions may include those that set out how the plan will be funded, as well as who will be serving as directors, officers or voting trustees of the reorganized debtor.]

ARTICLE VIII
GENERAL PROVISIONS

8.01 Definitions and Rules of Construction. The definitions and rules of construction set forth in §§ 101 and 102 of the Code shall apply when terms defined or construed in the Code are used in this Plan, and they are supplemented by the following definitions: [Insert additional definitions if necessary].

8.02 Effective Date of Plan. The effective date of this Plan is the eleventh business day following the date of the entry of the order of confirmation. But if a stay of the confirmation order is in effect on that date, the effective date will be the first business day after that date on which no stay of the confirmation order is in effect, provided that the confirmation order has not been vacated.

8.03 Severability. If any provision in this Plan is determined to be unenforceable, the determination will in no way limit or affect the enforceability and operative effect of any other provision of this Plan.

8.04 Binding Effect. The rights and obligations of any entity named or referred to in this Plan will be binding upon, and will inure to the benefit of the successors or assigns of such entity.

8.05 Captions. The headings contained in this Plan are for convenience of reference only and do not affect the meaning or interpretation of this Plan.

[8.06 Controlling Effect. Unless a rule of law or procedure is supplied by federal law (including the Code or the Federal Rules of Bankruptcy Procedure), the laws of the State of __________ govern this Plan and any agreements, documents, and instruments executed in connection with this Plan, except as otherwise provided in this Plan.]

[8.07 Corporate Governance. [If the Debtor is a corporation include provisions required by § 1123(a)(6) of the Code.]]

ARTICLE IX
DISCHARGE

[If the Debtor is not entitled to discharge under 11 U.S.C. § 1141(d)(3) change this heading to **"NO DISCHARGE OF DEBTOR."**]

9.01. **[Option 1 – If Debtor is an individual and § 1141(d)(3) is not applicable]**

Discharge. Confirmation of this Plan does not discharge any debt provided for in this Plan until the court grants a discharge on completion of all payments under this Plan, or as otherwise provided in § 1141(d)(5) of the Code. The Debtor will not be discharged from any debt excepted from discharge under § 523 of the Code, except as provided in Rule 4007(c) of the Federal Rules of Bankruptcy Procedure.

[Option 2 -- If the Debtor is a partnership and section 1141(d)(3) of the Code is not applicable]

Discharge. On the confirmation date of this Plan, the debtor will be discharged from any debt that arose before confirmation of this Plan, subject to the occurrence of the effective date, to the extent specified in § 1141(d)(1)(A) of the Code. The Debtor will not be discharged from any debt imposed by this Plan.

[Option 3 -- If the Debtor is a corporation and § 1141(d)(3) is not applicable]

Discharge. On the confirmation date of this Plan, the debtor will be discharged from any debt that arose before confirmation of this Plan, subject to the occurrence of the effective date, to the extent specified in § 1141(d)(1)(A) of the Code, except that the Debtor will not be discharged of any debt: (i) imposed by this Plan; (ii) of a kind specified in § 1141(d)(6)(A) if a timely complaint was filed in accordance with Rule 4007(c) of the Federal Rules of Bankruptcy Procedure; or (iii) of a kind specified in § 1141(d)(6)(B).

[Option 4 – If § 1141(d)(3) is applicable]

No Discharge. In accordance with § 1141(d)(3) of the Code, the Debtor will not receive any discharge of debt in this bankruptcy case.

ARTICLE X
OTHER PROVISIONS

[Insert other provisions, as applicable.]

Respectfully submitted,

By: ______________________________
The Plan Proponent

By: ______________________________
Attorney for the Plan Proponent

Chapter 11 Small Business Monthly Operating Report

Form B25C (Official Form 25C) (12/08) **2008 USBC, Central District of California**

UNITED STATES BANKRUPTCY COURT CENTRAL DISTRICT OF CALIFORNIA	
In re: Debtor(s).	CHAPTER 11 CASE NO.:

SMALL BUSINESS MONTHLY OPERATING REPORT

Month: ____________ Date filed: ____________________

Line of Business: ______________________ NAISC Code: ________________

IN ACCORDANCE WITH TITLE 28, SECTION 1746, OF THE UNITED STATES CODE, I DECLARE UNDER PENALTY OF PERJURY THAT I HAVE EXAMINED THE FOLLOWING SMALL BUSINESS MONTHLY OPERATING REPORT AND THE ACCOMPANYING ATTACHMENTS AND, TO THE BEST OF MY KNOWLEDGE, THESE DOCUMENTS ARE TRUE, CORRECT AND COMPLETE.

RESPONSIBLE PARTY:

____
Original Signature of Responsible Party

____
Printed Name of Responsible Party

Questionnaire: *(All questions to be answered on behalf of the debtor.)*	**Yes**	**No**
1. IS THE BUSINESS STILL OPERATING?	❑	❑
2 HAVE YOU PAID ALL YOUR BILLS ON TIME THIS MONTH?	❑	❑
3. DID YOU PAY YOUR EMPLOYEES ON TIME?	❑	❑
4. HAVE YOU DEPOSITED ALL THE RECEIPTS FOR YOUR BUSINESS INTO THE DIP ACCOUNT THIS MONTH?	❑	❑
5. HAVE YOU FILED ALL OF YOUR TAX RETURNS AND PAID ALL OF YOUR TAXES THIS MONTH?	❑	❑
6. HAVE YOU TIMELY FILED ALL OTHER REQUIRED GOVERNMENT FILINGS?	❑	❑
7. HAVE YOU PAID ALL OF YOUR INSURANCE PREMIUMS THIS MONTH?	❑	❑
8. DO YOU PLAN TO CONTINUE TO OPERATE THE BUSINESS NEXT MONTH?	❑	❑
9. ARE YOU CURRENT ON YOUR QUARTERLY FEE PAYMENT TO THE U.S. TRUSTEE?	❑	❑
10. HAVE YOU PAID ANYTHING TO YOUR ATTORNEY OR OTHER PROFESSIONALS THIS MONTH?	❑	❑
11. DID YOU HAVE ANY UNUSUAL OR SIGNIFICANT UNANTICIPATED EXPENSES THIS MONTH?	❑	❑

12. HAS THE BUSINESS SOLD ANY GOODS OR PROVIDED SERVICES OR TRANSFERRED ANY ASSETS TO ANY BUSINESS RELATED TO THE DIP IN ANY WAY? ❑ ❑
13. DO YOU HAVE ANY BANK ACCOUNTS OPEN OTHER THAN THE DIP ACCOUNT? ❑ ❑
14. HAVE YOU SOLD ANY ASSETS OTHER THAN INVENTORY THIS MONTH? ❑ ❑
15. DID ANY INSURANCE COMPANY CANCEL YOUR POLICY THIS MONTH? ❑ ❑
16. HAVE YOU BORROWED MONEY FROM ANYONE THIS MONTH? ❑ ❑
17. HAS ANYONE MADE AN INVESTMENT IN YOUR BUSINESS THIS MONTH? ❑ ❑
18. HAVE YOU PAID ANY BILLS YOU OWED BEFORE YOU FILED BANKRUPTCY? ❑ ❑

TAXES

DO YOU HAVE ANY PAST DUE TAX RETURNS OR PAST DUE POST-PETITION TAX OBLIGATIONS? ❑ ❑

IF YES, PLEASE PROVIDE A WRITTEN EXPLANATION INCLUDING WHEN SUCH RETURNS WILL BE FILED, OR WHEN SUCH PAYMENTS WILL BE MADE AND THE SOURCE OF THE FUNDS FOR THE PAYMENT.

(Exhibit A)

INCOME

PLEASE SEPARATELY LIST ALL OF THE INCOME YOU RECEIVED FOR THE MONTH. THE LIST SHOULD INCLUDE ALL INCOME FROM CASH AND CREDIT TRANSACTIONS. *(THE U.S. TRUSTEE MAY WAIVE THIS REQUIREMENT.)*

TOTAL INCOME $__________

SUMMARY OF CASH ON HAND

Cash on Hand at Start of Month $__________

Cash on Hand at End of Month $__________

PLEASE PROVIDE THE TOTAL AMOUNT OF CASH CURRENTLY AVAILABLE TO YOU TOTAL $__________

(Exhibit B)

EXPENSES

PLEASE SEPARATELY LIST ALL EXPENSES PAID BY CASH OR BY CHECK FROM YOUR BANK ACCOUNTS THIS MONTH. INCLUDE THE DATE PAID, WHO WAS PAID THE MONEY, THE PURPOSE AND THE AMOUNT. *(THE U.S. TRUSTEE MAY WAIVE THIS REQUIREMENT.)*

TOTAL EXPENSES $__________

(Exhibit C)

CASH PROFIT

INCOME FOR THE MONTH *(TOTAL FROM EXHIBIT B)* $__________

EXPENSES FOR THE MONTH *(TOTAL FROM EXHIBIT C)* $__________

(Subtract Line C from Line B) **CASH PROFIT FOR THE MONTH** $__________

UNPAID BILLS

PLEASE ATTACH A LIST OF ALL DEBTS (INCLUDING TAXES) WHICH YOU HAVE INCURRED SINCE THE DATE YOU FILED BANKRUPTCY BUT HAVE NOT PAID. THE LIST MUST INCLUDE THE DATE THE DEBT WAS INCURRED, WHO IS OWED THE MONEY, THE PURPOSE OF THE DEBT AND WHEN THE DEBT IS DUE. *(THE U.S. TRUSTEE MAY WAIVE THIS REQUIREMENT.)*

TOTAL PAYABLES $__________

(Exhibit D)

MONEY OWED TO YOU

PLEASE ATTACH A LIST OF ALL AMOUNTS OWED TO YOU BY YOUR CUSTOMERS FOR WORK YOU HAVE DONE OR THE MERCHANDISE YOU HAVE SOLD. YOU SHOULD INCLUDE WHO OWES YOU MONEY, HOW MUCH IS OWED AND WHEN IS PAYMENT DUE. *(THE U.S. TRUSTEE MAY WAIVE THIS REQUIREMENT.)*

TOTAL RECEIVABLES $__________

(Exhibit E)

BANKING INFORMATION

PLEASE ATTACH A COPY OF YOUR LATEST BANK STATEMENT FOR EVERY ACCOUNT YOU HAVE AS OF THE DATE OF THIS FINANCIAL REPORT OR HAD DURING THE PERIOD COVERED BY THIS REPORT.

(Exhibit F)

EMPLOYEES

NUMBER OF EMPLOYEES WHEN THE CASE WAS FILED? $__________

NUMBER OF EMPLOYEES AS OF THE DATE OF THIS MONTHLY REPORT? $__________

PROFESSIONAL FEES

BANKRUPTCY RELATED:

PROFESSIONAL FEES RELATING TO THE BANKRUPTCY CASE PAID DURING THIS REPORTING PERIOD? $__________

TOTAL PROFESSIONAL FEES RELATING TO THE BANKRUPTCY CASE PAID SINCE THE FILING OF THE CASE? $__________

NON-BANKRUPTCY RELATED:

PROFESSIONAL FEES NOT RELATING TO THE BANKRUPTCY CASE PAID DURING THIS REPORTING PERIOD? $__________

TOTAL PROFESSIONAL FEES NOT RELATING TO THE BANKRUPTCY CASE PAID SINCE THE FILING OF THE CASE? $__________

PROJECTIONS

COMPARE YOUR ACTUAL INCOME AND EXPENSES TO THE PROJECTIONS FOR THE FIRST 180 DAYS OF YOUR CASE PROVIDED AT THE INITIAL DEBTOR INTERVIEW.

	Projected	Actual	Difference
INCOME	$__________	$__________	$__________
EXPENSES	$__________	$__________	$__________
CASH PROFIT	$__________	$__________	$__________

TOTAL PROJECTED INCOME FOR THE NEXT MONTH: $__________

TOTAL PROJECTED EXPENSES FOR THE NEXT MONTH: $__________

TOTAL PROJECTED CASH PROFIT FOR THE NEXT MONTH $__________

ADDITIONAL INFORMATION

PLEASE ATTACH ALL FINANCIAL REPORTS INCLUDING AN INCOME STATEMENT AND BALANCE SHEET WHICH YOU PREPARE INTERNALLY.

Chapter 11 Statement of Current Monthly Income

Form B22B (Chapter11) - (1/08) **2008 USBC, Central District of California**

In re Debtor.	Case No.: (If known)

STATEMENT OF CURRENT MONTHLY INCOME
FOR USE IN CHAPTER 11

In addition to Schedules I and J, this statement must be completed by every individual Chapter 11 debtor, whether or not filing jointly. Joint debtors may complete one statement only.

	Part I. CALCULATION OF CURRENT MONTHLY INCOME		
1.	**Marital/filing status.** Check the box that applies and complete the balance of this part of this statement as directed. a. ☐ Unmarried. **Complete only Column A ("Debtor's Income") for Lines 2-10.** b. ☐ Married, not filing jointly. **Complete only Column A ("Debtor's Income") for Lines 2-10.** c. ☐ Married, filing jointly. **Complete both Column A ("Debtor's Income") and Column B ("Spouse's Income") for Lines 2-10.**		
	All figures must reflect average monthly income received from all sources, derived during the six calendar months prior to filing the bankruptcy case, ending on the last day of the month before the filing. If the amount of monthly income varied during the six months, you must divide the six-month total by six, and enter the result on the appropriate line	**Column A Debtor's Income**	**Column B Spouse's Income**
2.	**Gross wages, salary, tips, bonuses, overtime, commissions.**	$	$
3.	**Net income from the operation of a business, profession, or farm.** Subtract Line b from Line a and enter the difference in the appropriate column(s) of Line 3. If more than one business, profession or farm, enter aggregate numbers and provide details on an attachment. Do not enter a number less than zero. a. Gross receipts — $ b. Ordinary and necessary business expenses — $ c. Business income — Subtract Line b from Line a	$	$
4.	**Net rental and other real property income.** Subtract Line b from Line a and enter the difference in the appropriate column(s) of Line 4. Do not enter a number less than zero. a. Gross receipts — $ b. Ordinary and necessary operating expenses — $ c. Rental and other real property income — Subtract Line b from Line a	$	$
5.	**Interest, dividends, and royalties.**	$	$
6.	**Pension and retirement income.**	$	$
7.	**Any amounts paid by another person or entity, on a regular basis, for the household expenses of the debtor or the debtor's dependents, including child support paid for that purpose.** Do not include alimony or separate maintenance payments or amounts paid by the debtor's spouse if Column B is completed.	$	$
8.	**Unemployment compensation.** Enter the amount in the appropriate column(s) of Line 8. However, if you contend that unemployment compensation received by you or your spouse was a benefit under the Social Security Act, do not list the amount of such compensation in Column A or B, but instead state the amount in the space below: Unemployment compensation claimed to be a benefit under the Social Security Act — Debtor $________ Spouse $________	$	$

9.	**Income from all other sources.** Specify source and amount. If necessary, list additional sources on a separate page. Total and enter on Line 9. **Do not include alimony or separate maintenance payments paid by your spouse if Column B is completed, but include all other payments of alimony or separate maintenance. Do not include** any benefits received under the Social Security Act or payments received as a victim of a war crime, crime against humanity, or as a victim of international or domestic terrorism. a. ___ $ b. ___ $	$	$
10.	**Subtotal of current monthly income.** Add Lines 2 thru 9 in Column A, and, if Column B is completed, add Lines 2 through 9 in Column B. Enter the total(s).	$	$
11.	**Total current monthly income.** If Column B has been completed, add Line 10, Column A to Line 10, Column B, and enter the total. If Column B has not been completed, enter the amount from Line 10, Column A.	$	

Part II: VERIFICATION

12.	I declare under penalty of perjury that the information provided in this statement is true and correct. *(If this a joint case, both debtors must sign.)* Date: ______ Signature: ______ (Debtor) Date: ______ Signature: ______ (Joint Debtor, if any)

Chapter 13 Addendum to Chapter 13 Plan Concerning Debtors Who Are Repaying Debt Secured by a Mortgage on Real Property or a Lien on Personal Property the Debtor Occupies as the Debtor's Principal Residence

Attorney or Party Name, Address, Telephone & FAX Numbers, and California State Bar Number ☐ Individual appearing without counsel ☐ Attorney for:	FOR COURT USE ONLY
UNITED STATES BANKRUPTCY COURT CENTRAL DISTRICT OF CALIFORNIA	
In re Debtor(s).	CHAPTER 13 CASE NO.

Addendum to Chapter 13 Plan Concerning Debtors Who are Repaying Debt Secured by a Mortgage on Real Property or a Lien on Personal Property the Debtor Occupies as the Debtor's Principal Residence

(A) **Scope: Consumer Debts Secured by a Mortgage on Real Property, or Secured by Manufactured Housing that the Debtor Occupies as the Debtor's Principal Residence**

(1) For purposes of this Addendum, which is incorporated into the debtor's chapter 13 plan (the "Plan"), the term "Mortgage Creditor" includes all creditors whose claims represent consumer debts secured in whole or in part by a security interest in real property or manufactured housing, which real property or manufactured housing constitutes the debtor's principal residence. The provisions of this Addendum are effective until the earlier of: (a) dismissal of the case; (b) the closing of the case; (c) entry of an order granting the debtor a discharge; and (d) entry of an order terminating the automatic stay under 11 U.S.C. § 362(d) as the stay applies to the Mortgage Creditor.

(2) Except as provided in paragraphs (3) and (4) below, if the Mortgage Creditor provided monthly statements to the debtor pre-petition, the Mortgage Creditor must provide monthly statements to the debtor. The monthly statements must contain at least the following information concerning post-petition mortgage payments to be made outside the Plan:

In re	CHAPTER 13
Debtor(s).	CASE NUMBER

(a) The date of the statement and the date the next payment is due;

(b) The amount of the current monthly payment;

(c) The portion of the payment attributable to escrow, if any;

(d) The post-petition amount past due, if any, and from what date;

(e) Any outstanding post-petition late charges;

(f) The amount and date of receipt of all payments received since the date of the last statement;

(g) A telephone number and contact information that the debtor or the debtor's attorney may use to obtain reasonably prompt information regarding the loan and recent transactions; and

(h) The proper payment address.

(3) No monthly statement will be required in this case where post-petition mortgage payments are to be made to the chapter 13 trustee through the Plan, unless the amount of the monthly payment is scheduled to change (because of adjustable interest rate, charges paid by the Mortgage Creditor for taxes, insurance, attorney's fees or any other expenses or fees charged or incurred by the Mortgage Creditor, such as property inspection fees, servicing fees or appraisal fees). If a Mortgage Creditor does send a monthly statement to the debtor or the chapter 13 trustee and the statement complies with subsection (B)(2) below, the Mortgage Creditor is entitled to the protections set out in such subsection.

(4) If, pre-petition, the Mortgage Creditor provided the debtor with "coupon books" or some other pre-printed, bundled evidence of payments due, the Mortgage Creditor is not required to provide monthly statements under subsection (2) of this section. However, the Mortgage Creditor must supply the debtor with additional coupon books as needed or requested in writing by the debtor. If a Mortgage Creditor does send a monthly statement to the debtor or the chapter 13 trustee and the statement complies with subsection (B)(2) below, the Mortgage Creditor is entitled to the protections set out in such subsection.

(5) The Mortgage Creditor must provide the following information to the debtor upon the reasonable written request of the debtor:

(a) The principal balance of the loan;

(b) The original maturity date;

(c) The current interest rate;

Addendum to Chapter 13 Plan Concerning Debtors Who are Repaying Debt Secured by a Mortgage on Real Property or a Lien on Personal Property the Debtor Occupies as the Debtor's Principal Residence - *Page 3 of 5*

In re	CHAPTER 13
Debtor(s).	CASE NUMBER

(d) The current escrow balance, if any;

(e) The interest paid year to date; and

(f) The property taxes paid year to date, if any.

(6) The Mortgage Creditor must provide the following information to the debtor, the debtor's attorney and, when the debtor is making ongoing mortgage or arrearage payments through the chapter 13 trustee, the chapter 13 trustee, at least quarterly, and upon reasonable written request of the debtor or the chapter 13 trustee: (a) any other amounts due or proposed change in payments arising from an adjustable interest rate, charges paid by the Mortgage Creditor for taxes, insurance, attorney's fees or any other expenses or fees charged or incurred by the Mortgage Creditor, such as property inspection fees, servicing fees or appraisal fees; (b) the nature of the expense or charge; and (c) the date of the payment.

(7) If the secured consumer debt payable to the Mortgage Creditor is not modified by or paid through the Plan and the Mortgage Creditor believes the debtor to be in default, the Mortgage Creditor must send a letter alleging such default to the debtor and the debtor's attorney upon any perceived or actual default by the debtor and before taking any steps to modify the automatic stay.

(B) **Form of Communication; Modification of the Automatic Stay; and Motions for Order to Show Cause**

(1) For the purposes of this Addendum, Mortgage Creditors will be considered to have sent the requisite documents or monthly statements to the debtor or the debtor's attorney, as applicable, when the Mortgage Creditor has placed the required document in any form of communication, which in the usual course would result in the debtor and the debtor's attorney receiving the document, to the address that the debtor and the debtor's attorney last provided to the Court. The form of communication may include, but is not limited to, electronic communication, United States Postal Service or use of a similar commercial communications carrier.

(2) To the extent that the automatic stay arising in this case would otherwise prohibit such conduct, the automatic stay is modified as follows: Mortgage Creditors who provide account information or monthly statements under subsections (A)(1-6) above will not be found to have violated the automatic stay by doing so, and Mortgage Creditors may contact the debtor about the status of insurance coverage on property that is collateral for the Mortgage Creditor's claim, may respond to inquiries and requests for information about the account from the debtor and may send the debtor statements, payment coupons or other correspondence that the Mortgage Creditor sends to its non-debtor customers, without violating the automatic stay. In order for communication to be protected under this provision, the communication must indicate it is provided for information purposes and does not constitute demand for payment.

In re	CHAPTER 13
Debtor(s).	CASE NUMBER

(3) As a result of a Mortgage Creditor's alleged non-compliance with this Addendum, the debtor may file a Motion for Order to Show Cause in compliance with Local Bankruptcy Rule 9020-1 no earlier than sixty days after the Mortgage Creditor's failure to comply with sections (A) or (B). Before filing the motion, the debtor must make good faith attempts in writing to contact the Mortgage Creditor and to determine the cause of any non-compliance, and must indicate in the Motion for Order to Show Cause the good faith steps taken, together with a summary description of any response provided by the Mortgage Creditor.

(4) If a Mortgage Creditor's regular billing system can provide a statement to the debtor that substantially complies with this Addendum, but does not fully conform to all of its requirements, the Mortgage Creditor may request that the debtor accept such statement. If the debtor declines to accept the non-conforming statement, a Mortgage Creditor may file a motion, on notice to the debtor, the debtor's attorney and the chapter 13 trustee, seeking a declaration of the Court that cause exists to allow such non-conforming statements to satisfy the Mortgage Creditor's obligations under this Addendum. For good cause shown, the Court may grant a waiver for purposes of this case and for either a limited or unlimited period of time.

In re	CHAPTER 13
Debtor(s).	CASE NUMBER

Instructions for Attaching

Addendum to Chapter 13 Plan Concerning Debtors who are Repaying Debt Secured by a Mortgage on Real Property or a Lien on Personal Property the Debtor Occupies as the Debtor's Principal Residence

This optional addendum concerns chapter 13 debtors who are repaying debt secured by a mortgage on real property or a lien on personal property the debtor occupies as the debtor's principal residence.

A chapter 13 debtor may attach this addendum to his/her chapter 13 plan. This is a court-approved form and may not be altered, except for interlineations clearly marked on the court-approved form which are subject to the Court's review and approval upon consideration of the plan for confirmation. When attaching this form to the chapter 13 plan form (F 3015-1.1), the debtor must indicate in section V.F. (Page 6) of the chapter 13 plan form that the "Addendum to Chapter 13 Plan (F 3015-1.1A) is attached."

Chapter 13 Debtor's Certification of Completion of Postpetition Instructional Course Concerning Personal Financial Management

Form B23 (Official Form 23) - (12/08) 2008 USBC, Central District of California

UNITED STATES BANKRUPTCY COURT CENTRAL DISTRICT OF CALIFORNIA	
In re: Debtor(s).	CHAPTER: CASE NO.:

DEBTOR'S CERTIFICATION OF COMPLETION OF POSTPETITION INSTRUCTIONAL COURSE CONCERNING PERSONAL FINANCIAL MANAGEMENT

Every individual debtor in a chapter 7, chapter 11 in which § 1141(d)(3) applies, or chapter 13 case must file this certification. If a joint petition is filed, each spouse must complete and file a separate certification. Complete one of the following statements and file by the deadline stated below:

☐ I, ______________________ *(Printed Name of Debtor)*, the debtor in the above-styled case, hereby certify that on ______________________ *(Date)*, I completed an instructional course in personal financial management provided by ______________________ *(Name of Provider)*, an approved personal financial management provider.

Certificate No. *(if any)*: ______________________.

☐ I, ______________________ *(Printed Name of Debtor)*, the debtor in the above-styled case, hereby certify that no personal financial management course is required because of *[Check the appropriate box.]*:

☐ Incapacity or disability, as defined in 11 U.S.C. § 109(h);
☐ Active military duty in a military combat zone; or
☐ Residence in a district in which the United States trustee *(or bankruptcy administrator)* has determined that the approved instructional courses are not adequate at this time to serve the additional individuals who would otherwise be required to complete such courses.

Date: ______________________ Signature of Debtor: ______________________

Instructions: Use this form only to certify whether you completed a course in personal financial management. (Fed. R. Bankr. P. 1007(b)(7).) Do NOT use this form to file the certificate given to you by your prepetition credit counseling provider and do NOT include with the petition when filing your case.

Filing Deadlines: In a chapter 7 case, file within 45 days of the first date set for the meeting of creditors under § 341 of the Bankruptcy Code. In a chapter 11 or 13 case, file no later than the last payment made by the debtor as required by the plan or the filing of a motion for a discharge under § 1141(d)(5)(B) or § 1328(b) of the Code. (See Fed. R. Bankr. P. 1007(c).)

Chapter 13 Notice of Available Chapters

B 201 - Notice of Available Chapters (Rev. 12/08) USBC, Central District of California

Name: ______________________________

Address: ______________________________

____

Telephone: ________________ Fax: ________________

☐ Attorney for Debtor

☐ Debtor in Pro Per

UNITED STATES BANKRUPTCY COURT CENTRAL DISTRICT OF CALIFORNIA	
List all names including trade names, used by Debtor(s) within last 8 years:	Case No.:
	NOTICE OF AVAILABLE CHAPTERS (Notice to Individual Consumer Debtor Under § 342(b) of the Bankruptcy Code)

In accordance with § 342(b) of the Bankruptcy Code, this notice to individuals with primarily consumer debts: (1) Describes briefly the services available from credit counseling services; (2) Describes briefly the purposes, benefits and costs of the four types of bankruptcy proceedings you may commence; and (3) Informs you about bankruptcy crimes and notifies you that the Attorney General may examine all information you supply in connection with a bankruptcy case.

You are cautioned that bankruptcy law is complicated and not easily described. Thus, you may wish to seek the advice of an attorney to learn of your rights and responsibilities should you decide to file a petition. Court employees cannot give you legal advice.

Notices from the bankruptcy court are sent to the mailing address you list on your bankruptcy petition. In order to ensure that you receive information about events concerning your case, Bankruptcy Rule 4002 requires that you notify the court of any changes in your address. If you are filing a **joint case** (a single bankruptcy case for two individuals married to each other), and each spouse lists the same mailing address on the bankruptcy petition, you and your spouse will generally receive a single copy of each notice mailed from the bankruptcy court in a jointly-addressed envelope, unless you file a statement with the court requesting that each spouse receive a separate copy of all notices.

1. **Services Available from Credit Counseling Agencies**

   With limited exceptions, § 109(h) of the Bankruptcy Code requires that all individual debtors who file for bankruptcy relief on or after October 17, 2005, receive a briefing that outlines the available opportunities for credit counseling and provides assistance in performing a budget analysis. The briefing must be given within 180 days **before** the bankruptcy filing. The briefing may be provided individually or in a group (including briefings conducted by telephone or on the Internet) and must be provided by a nonprofit budget and credit counseling agency approved by the United States trustee or bankruptcy administrator. The clerk of the bankruptcy court has a list that you may consult of the approved budget and credit counseling agencies. Each debtor in a joint case must complete the briefing.

   In addition, after filing a bankruptcy case, an individual debtor generally must complete a financial management instructional course before he or she can receive a discharge. The clerk also has a list of approved financial management instructional courses. Each debtor in a joint case must complete the course.

2. The Four Chapters of the Bankruptcy Code Available to Individual Consumer Debtors

Chapter 7: Liquidation ($245 filing fee, $39 administrative fee, $15 trustee surcharge: Total fee $299)

1. Chapter 7 is designed for debtors in financial difficulty who do not have the ability to pay their existing debts. Debtors whose debts are primarily consumer debts are subject to a "means test" designed to determine whether the case should be permitted to proceed under chapter 7. If your income is greater than the median income for your state of residence and family size, in some cases, creditors have the right to file a motion requesting that the court dismiss your case under § 707(b) of the Code. It is up to the court to decide whether the case should be dismissed.
2. Under chapter 7, you may claim certain of your property as exempt under governing law. A trustee may have the right to take possession of and sell the remaining property that is not exempt and use the sale proceeds to pay your creditors.
3. The purpose of filing a chapter 7 case is to obtain a discharge of your existing debts. If, however, you are found to have committed certain kinds of improper conduct described in the Bankruptcy Code, the court may deny your discharge and, if it does, the purpose for which you filed the bankruptcy petition will be defeated.
4. Even if you receive a general discharge, some particular debts are not discharged under the law. Therefore, you may still be responsible for most taxes and student loans; debts incurred to pay nondischargeable taxes; domestic support and property settlement obligations; most fines, penalties, forfeitures, and criminal restitution obligations; certain debts which are not properly listed in your bankruptcy papers; and debts for death or personal injury caused by operating a motor vehicle, vessel, or aircraft while intoxicated from alcohol or drugs. Also, if a creditor can prove that a debt arose from fraud, breach of fiduciary duty, or theft, or from a willful and malicious injury, the bankruptcy court may determine that the debt is not discharged.

Chapter 13: Repayment of All or Part of the Debts of an Individual with Regular Income ($235 filing fee, $39 administrative fee: Total fee $274)

1. Chapter 13 is designed for individuals with regular income who would like to pay all or part of their debts in installments over a period of time. You are only eligible for chapter 13 if your debts do not exceed certain dollar amounts set forth in the Bankruptcy Code.
2. Under chapter 13, you must file with the court a plan to repay your creditors all or part of the money that you owe them, using your future earnings. The period allowed by the court to repay your debts may be three years or five years, depending upon your income and other factors. The court must approve your plan before it can take effect.
3. After completing the payments under your plan, your debts are generally discharged except for domestic support obligations; most student loans; certain taxes; most criminal fines and restitution obligations; certain debts which are not properly listed in your bankruptcy papers; certain debts for acts that caused death or personal injury; and certain long term secured obligations.

Chapter 11: Reorganization ($1000 filing fee, $39 administrative fee: Total fee $1039)
Chapter 11 is designed for the reorganization of a business but is also available to consumer debtors. Its provisions are quite complicated, and any decision by an individual to file a chapter 11 petition should be reviewed with an attorney.

Chapter 12: Family Farmer or Fisherman ($200 filing fee, $39 administrative fee: Total fee $239)
Chapter 12 is designed to permit family farmers and fishermen to repay their debts over a period of time from future earnings and is similar to chapter 13. The eligibility requirements are restrictive, limiting its use to those whose income arises primarily from a family-owned farm or commercial fishing operation.

3. Bankruptcy Crimes and Availability of Bankruptcy Papers to Law Enforcement Officials

A person who knowingly and fraudulently conceals assets or makes a false oath or statement under penalty of perjury, either orally or in writing, in connection with a bankruptcy case is subject to a fine, imprisonment, or both. All information supplied by a debtor in connection with a bankruptcy case is subject to examination by the Attorney General acting through the Office of the United States Trustee, the Office of the United States Attorney, and other components and employees of the Department of Justice.

WARNING: Section 521(a)(1) of the Bankruptcy Code requires that you promptly file detailed information regarding your creditors, assets, liabilities, income, expenses and general financial condition. Your bankruptcy case may be dismissed if this information is not filed with the court within the time deadlines set by the Bankruptcy Code, the Bankruptcy Rules, and the local rules of the court.

Certificate of [Non-Attorney] Bankruptcy Petition Preparer

I, the [non-attorney] bankruptcy petition preparer signing the debtor's petition, hereby certify that I delivered to the debtor this notice required by § 342(b) of the Bankruptcy Code.

____
Printed name and title, if any, of Bankruptcy Petition Preparer

____
Address:

X______________________________
Signature of Bankruptcy Petition Preparer or officer, principal, responsible person, or partner whose Social Security number is provided above.

____
Social Security number (If the bankruptcy petition preparer is not an individual, state the Social Security number of the officer, principal, responsible person, or partner of the bankruptcy petition preparer.) (Required by 11 U.S.C. § 110.)

Certificate of the Debtor

I (We), the debtor(s), affirm that I (we) have received and read this notice.

____
Printed Name(s) of Debtor(s)

Case No. (if known) ______________

____
Signature of Debtor Date

X______________________________
Signature of Joint Debtor (if any) Date

CDCAL-503 C.D. CALIFORNIA

Chapter 13 Statement of Current Monthly Income and Calculation of Commitment Period and Disposable Income

Form B22C (Chapter13) - (1/08) 2008 USBC, Central District of California

In re	Case No.:
Debtor(s).	(If known)

According to the calculations required by this statement:
- ☐ The applicable commitment period is 3 years
- ☐ The applicable commitment period is 5 years
- ☐ Disposable income determined under § 1325(b)(3)
- ☐ Disposable income not determined under § 1325(b)(3)

(Check the boxes as directed in Lines 17 and 23 of this statement)

STATEMENT OF CURRENT MONTHLY INCOME AND CALCULATION OF COMMITMENT PERIOD AND DISPOSABLE INCOME FOR USE IN CHAPTER 13

In addition to Schedules I and J, this statement must be completed by every individual Chapter 13 debtor, whether or not filing jointly. Joint debtors may complete one statement only.

	Part I. REPORT OF INCOME		
1.	**Marital/filing status.** Check the box that applies and complete the balance of this part of this statement as directed. a. ☐ Unmarried. **Complete only Column A ("Debtor's Income") for Lines 2-10.** b. ☐ Married. **Complete both Column A ("Debtor's Income") and Column B ("Spouse's Income") for Lines 2-10.**		
	All figures must reflect average monthly income received from all sources, derived during the six calendar months prior to filing the bankruptcy case, ending on the last day of the month before the filing. If the amount of monthly income varied during the six months, you must divide the six-month total by six, and enter the result on the appropriate line.	**Column A Debtor's Income**	**Column B Spouse's Income**
2.	**Gross wages, salary, tips, bonuses, overtime, commissions.**	$	$
3.	**Income from the operation of a business, profession, or farm.** Subtract Line b from Line a and enter the difference in the appropriate column(s) of Line 3. If you operate more than one business, profession or farm, enter aggregate numbers and provide details on an attachment. Do not enter a number less than zero. **Do not include any part of the business expenses entered on Line b as a deduction in Part IV.** a. Gross receipts — $ b. Ordinary and necessary business expenses — $ c. Business income — Subtract Line b from Line a	$	$
4.	**Rent and other real property income.** Subtract Line b from Line a and enter the difference in the appropriate column(s) of Line 4. Do not enter a number less than zero. **Do not include any part of the operating expenses entered on Line b as a deduction in Part IV.** a. Gross receipts — $ b. Ordinary and necessary operating expenses — $ c. Rent and other real property income — Subtract Line b from Line a	$	$
5.	**Interest, dividends, and royalties.**	$	$
6.	**Pension and retirement income.**	$	$
7.	**Any amounts paid by another person or entity, on a regular basis, for the household expenses of the debtor or the debtor's dependents, including child support paid for that purpose.** Do not include alimony or separate maintenance payments or amounts paid by the debtor's spouse.	$	$
8.	**Unemployment compensation.** Enter the amount in the appropriate column(s) of Line 8. However, if you contend that unemployment compensation received by you or your spouse was a benefit under the Social Security Act, do not list the amount of such compensation in Column A or B, but instead state the amount in the space below: Unemployment compensation claimed to be a benefit under the Social Security Act — Debtor $_____ Spouse $_____	$	$

9.	**Income from all other sources.** Specify source and amount. If necessary, list additional sources on a separate page. Total and enter on Line 9. **Do not include alimony or separate maintenance payments paid by your spouse, but include all other payments of alimony or separate maintenance. Do not include** any benefits received under the Social Security Act or payments received as a victim of a war crime, crime against humanity, or as a victim of international or domestic terrorism. a. ___ $ b. ___ $	$	$
10.	**Subtotal.** Add Lines 2 thru 9 in Column A, and, if Column B is completed, add Lines 2 through 9 in Column B. Enter the total(s).	$	$
11.	**Total.** If Column B has been completed, add Line 10, Column A to Line 10, Column B, and enter the total. If Column B has not been completed, enter the amount from Line 10, Column A.	$	

	Part II. CALCULATION OF § 1325(b)(4) COMMITMENT PERIOD	
12.	**Enter the amount from Line 11.**	
13.	**Marital adjustment.** If you are married, but are not filing jointly with your spouse, AND if you contend that calculation of the commitment period under § 1325(b)(4) does not require inclusion of the income of your spouse, enter on Line 13 the amount of the income listed in Line 10, Column B that was NOT paid on a regular basis for the household expenses of you or your dependents and specify, in the lines below, the basis for excluding this income (such as payment of the spouse's tax liability or the spouse's support of persons other than the debtor or the debtor's dependents) and the amount of income devoted to each purpose. If necessary, list additional adjustments on a separate page. If the conditions for entering this adjustment do not apply, enter zero. a. ___ $ b. ___ $ c. ___ $ Total and enter on Line 13.	$
14.	**Subtract Line 13 from Line 12 and enter result.**	
15.	**Annualized current monthly income for § 1325(b)(4).** Multiply the amount from Line 14 by the number 12 and enter the result.	$
16.	**Applicable median family income.** Enter the median family income for applicable state and household size. (This information is available by family size at www.usdoj.gov/ust/ or from the clerk of the bankruptcy court.) a. Enter debtor's state of residence: ______ b. Enter debtor's household size: ______	$
17.	**Application of § 1325(b)(4).** Check the applicable box and proceed as directed. ☐ **The amount on Line 15 is less than the amount on Line 16.** Check the box for "The applicable commitment period is 3 years" at the top of page 1 of this statement and continue with this statement. ☐ **The amount on Line 15 is not less than the amount on Line 16.** Check the box for "The applicable commitment period is 5 years" at the top of page 1 of this statement and continue with this statement.	

	Part III. APPLICATION OF § 1325(b)(3) FOR DETERMINING DISPOSABLE INCOME	
18.	**Enter the amount from Line 11.**	$
19.	**Marital adjustment.** If you are married, but are not filing jointly with your spouse, enter on Line 19 the total of any income listed in Line 10, Column B that was NOT paid on a regular basis for the household expenses of the debtor or the debtor's dependents. Specify in the lines below the basis for excluding the Column B income (such as payment of the spouse's tax liability or the spouse's support of persons other than the debtor or the debtor's dependents) and the amount of income devoted to each purpose. If necessary, list additional adjustments on a separate page. If the conditions for entering this adjustment do not apply, enter zero. a. ___ $ b. ___ $ c. ___ $ Total and enter on Line 19.	$
20.	**Current monthly income for § 1325 (b)(3).** Subtract Line 19 from Line 18 and enter the result.	$

Form B22C (Chapter13) - (1/08) 2008 USBC, Central District of California

21.	**Annualized current monthly income for § 1325(b)(3).** Multiply the amount from Line 20 by the number 12 and enter the result.	$
22.	**Applicable median family income.** Enter the amount from line 16.	$
23.	**Application of § 1325(b)(3).** Check the applicable box and proceed as directed. ☐ **The amount on Line 21 is more than the amount on Line 22.** Check the box for "Disposable income is determined under § 1325 (b)(3)" at the top of page 1 of this statement and complete the complete the remaining parts of this statement. ☐ **The amount on Line 21 is not more than the amount on Line 22.** Check the box for "Disposable income is not determined under § 1325 (b)(3)" at the top of page 1 of this statement and complete Part VII of this statement. **Do not complete Part IV, V, or VI.**	
	Part IV. CALCULATION OF DEDUCTIONS FROM INCOME	
	Subpart A: Deductions under Standards of the Internal Revenue Service (IRS)	
24A.	**National Standards: food, apparel and services, housekeeping supplies, personal care, and miscellaneous.** Enter in Line 24A the "Total" amount from IRS National Standards for Allowable Living Expenses for the applicable household size. (This information is available at www.usdoj.gov/ust/ or from the clerk of the bankruptcy court.)	$
24B.	**National Standards: health care.** Enter in Line a1 below the amount from IRS National Standards for Out-of-Pocket Health Care for persons under 65 years of age, and in Line a2 the IRS National Standards for Out-of-Pocket Health Care for persons 65 years of age or older. (This information is available at www.usdoj.gov/ust/ or from the clerk of the bankruptcy court.) Enter in Line b1 the number of members of your household who are under 65 years of age, and enter in Line b2 the number of members of your household who are 65 years of age or older. (The total number of household members must be the same as the number stated in Line 16b.) Multiply Line a1 by Line b1 to obtain a total amount for household members under 65, and enter the result in Line c1. Multiply Line a2 by Line b2 to obtain a total amount for household members 65 and older, and enter the result in Line c2. Add Lines c1 and c2 to obtain a total health care amount, and enter the result in Line 24B.	$

Household members under 65 years of age			Household members 65 years of age or older		
a1.	Allowance per member		a2.	Allowance per member	
b1.	Number of members		b2	Number of members	
c1.	Subtotal		c2	Subtotal	

25A.	**Local Standards: housing and utilities; non-mortgage expenses.** Enter the amount of the IRS Housing and Utilities Standards; non-mortgage expenses for the applicable county and household size. (This information is available at www.usdoj.gov/ust/ or from the clerk of the bankruptcy court).	$
25B.	**Local Standards: housing and utilities; mortgage/rent expense.** Enter, in Line a below, the amount of the IRS Housing and Utilities Standards; mortgage/rent expense for your county and household size (this information is available at www.usdoj.gov/ust/ or from the clerk of the bankruptcy court); enter on Line b the total of the Average Monthly Payments for any debts secured by your home, as stated in Line 47; subtract Line b from Line a and enter the result in Line 25B. **Do not enter an amount less than zero.**	$

a.	IRS Housing and Utilities Standards; mortgage/rent Expense	$
b.	Average Monthly payment for any debts secured by your home, if any, stated in Line 47	$
c.	Net mortgage/rental expense.	Subtract Line b from Line a

26.	**Local Standards: housing and utilities; adjustment.** If you contend that the process set out in Lines 25A and 25 B does not accurately compute the allowance to which you are entitled under the IRS Housing and Utilities Standards, enter any additional amount to which you contend you are entitled, and state the basis for your contention in the space below: ________________ ________________ ________________	$
27A.	**Local Standards: transportation; vehicle operation/public transportation expense.** You are entitled to an expense allowance in this category regardless of whether you pay the expenses of operating a vehicle and regardless of whether you use public transportation. Check the number of vehicles for which you pay the operating expenses or for which the operating expenses are included as a contribution to your household expenses in Line 7. ☐ 0 ☐ 1 ☐ 2 or more. If you checked 0, enter on Line 27A the "Public Transportation" amount from IRS Local Standards: Transportation. If you checked 1 or 2 or more, enter on Line 27A the "Operating Costs" amount from IRS Local Standards: Transportation for the applicable number of vehicles in the applicable Metropolitan Statistical Area or Census Region. (These amounts are available at www.usdoj.gov/ust/ or from the clerk of the bankruptcy court.)	$

27B.	**Local Standards: transportation; additional public transportation expense.** If you pay the operating expenses for a vehicle and also use public transportation, and you contend that you are entitled to an additional deduction for your public transportation expenses, enter on Line 27B the "Public Transportation" amount from IRS Local Standards: Transportation. (This amount is available at www.usdoj.gov/ust/ or from the clerk of the bankruptcy court.)	$
28.	**Local Standards: transportation ownership/lease expense; Vehicle 1.** Check the number of vehicles for which you claim an ownership/lease expense. (You may not claim an ownership/lease expense for more than two vehicles.) ☐ 1 ☐ 2 or more. Enter, in Line a below, the "Ownership Costs" for "One Car" from the IRS Local Standards: Transportation (available at www.usdoj.gov/ust/ or from the clerk of the bankruptcy court); enter in Line b the total of the Average Monthly Payments for any debts secured by Vehicle 1, as stated in Line 47; subtract Line b from Line a and enter the result in Line 28. **Do not enter an amount less than zero.** a. IRS Transportation Standards, Ownership Costs — $ b. Average Monthly Payment for any debts secured by Vehicle 1, as stated in Line 47 — $ c. Net ownership/lease expense for Vehicle 1 — Subtract Line b from Line a.	$
29.	**Local Standards: transportation ownership/lease expense; Vehicle 2.** Complete this Line only if you checked the "2 or more" Box in Line 28. Enter, in Line a below, the "Ownership Costs" for "One Car" from the IRS Local Standards: Transportation (available at www.usdoj.gov/ust/ or from the clerk of the bankruptcy court); enter in Line b the total of the Average Monthly Payments for any debts secured by Vehicle 2, as stated in Line 47; subtract Line b from Line a and enter the result in Line 29. **Do not enter an amount less than zero.** a. IRS Transportation Standards, Ownership Costs, Second — $ b. Average Monthly Payment for any debts secured by Vehicle 2, as stated in Line 47 — $ c. Net ownership/lease expense for Vehicle 2 — Subtract Line b from Line a.	$
30.	**Other Necessary Expenses: taxes.** Enter the total average monthly expense that you actually incur for all federal, state and local taxes, other than real estate and sales taxes, such as income taxes, self employment taxes, social security taxes, and Medicare taxes. **Do not include real estate or sales taxes.**	$
31.	**Other Necessary Expenses: involuntary deductions for employment.** Enter the total average monthly deductions that are required for your employment, such as mandatory retirement contributions, union dues, and uniform costs. **Do not include discretionary amounts, such as voluntary 401(k) contributions.**	$
32.	**Other Necessary Expenses: life insurance.** Enter total average monthly premiums that you actually pay for term life insurance for yourself. **Do not include premiums for insurance on your dependents, for whole life or for any other form of insurance.**	$
33.	**Other Necessary Expenses: court-ordered payments.** Enter the total monthly amount that you are required to pay pursuant to the order of a court or administrative agency, such as spousal or child support payments. **Do not include payments on past due obligations included in Line 49.**	$
34.	**Other Necessary Expenses: education for employment or for a physically or mentally challenged child.** Enter the total average monthly amount that you actually expend for education that is a condition of employment and for education that is required for a physically or mentally challenged dependent child for whom no public education providing similar services is available.	$
35.	**Other Necessary Expenses: childcare.** Enter the total average monthly amount that you actually expend on childcare-such as baby-sitting, day care, nursery and preschool. **Do not include other educational payments.**	$
36.	**Other Necessary Expenses: health care.** Enter the total average monthly amount that you actually expend on health care that is required for the health and welfare of yourself or your dependents, that is not reimbursed by insurance or paid by a health savings account, and that is in excess of the amount entered in Line 24B. **Do not include payments for health insurance or health savings accounts listed in Line 39.**	$
37.	**Other Necessary Expenses: telecommunication services.** Enter the total average monthly amount that you actually pay for telecommunication services other than your basic home telephone and cell phone service-such as pagers, call waiting, caller id, special long distance, or internet service—to the extent necessary for your health and welfare or that of your dependents. **Do not include any amount previously deducted.**	$
38.	**Total Expenses Allowed under IRS Standards.** Enter the total of Lines 24 through 37.	$

	Subpart B: Additional Living Expense Deductions **Note: Do not include any expenses that you have listed in Lines 24-37**	
39	**Health Insurance, Disability Insurance, and Health Savings Account Expenses.** List the monthly expenses in the categories set out in lines a-c below that are reasonably necessary for yourself, your spouse, or your dependents. a. Health Insurance $ b. Disability Insurance $ c. Health Savings Account $ Total and enter on Line 39	$
	If you do not actually expend this total amount, state your actual total average monthly expenditures in the space below: $ ________	
40.	**Continued contributions to the care of household or family members.** Enter the total average actual monthly expenses that you will continue to pay for the reasonable and necessary care and support of an elderly, chronically ill, or disabled member of your household or member of your immediate family who is unable to pay for such expenses. **Do not include payments listed in Line 34.**	$
41.	**Protection against family violence.** Enter the total average reasonably necessary monthly expenses that you actually incur to maintain the safety of your family under the Family Violence Prevention and Services Act or other applicable federal law. The nature of these expenses is required to be kept confidential by the court.	$
42.	**Home energy costs.** Enter the total average monthly amount, in excess of the allowance specified by IRS Local Standards for Housing and Utilities, that you actually expend for home energy costs. **You must provide your case trustee with documentation of your actual expenses, and you must demonstrate that the additional amount claimed is reasonable and necessary.**	$
43.	**Education expenses for dependent children under 18.** Enter the total average monthly expenses that you actually incur, not to exceed $137.50 per child, for attendance at a private or public elementary or secondary school by your dependent children less than 18 years of age. **You must provide your case trustee with documentation of your actual expenses, and you must explain why the amount claimed is reasonable and necessary and not already accounted for in the IRS Standards.**	$
44.	**Additional food and clothing expense.** Enter the total average monthly amount by which your food and clothing expenses exceed the combined allowances for food and clothing (apparel and services) in the IRS National Standards, not to exceed 5% of those combined allowances. (This information is available at www.usdoj.gov/ust/ or from the clerk of the bankruptcy court.) **You must demonstrate that the additional amount claimed is reasonable and necessary.**	$
45.	**Charitable contributions.** Enter the amount reasonably necessary for you to expend each month on charitable contributions in the form of cash or financial instruments to a charitable organization as defined in 26 U.S.C. § 170(c)(1)-(2). **Do not include any amount in excess of 15% of your gross monthly income.**	$
46.	**Total Additional Expense Deductions under § 707(b).** Enter the total of Lines 39 through 45.	$

	Subpart C: Deductions for Debt Payment	
47.	**Future payments on secured claims.** For each of your debts that is secured by an interest in property that you own, list the name of the creditor, identify the property securing the debt, state the Average Monthly Payment, and check whether the payment includes taxes or insurance. The Average Monthly Payment is the total of all amounts scheduled as contractually due to each Secured Creditor in the 60 months following the filing of the bankruptcy case, divided by 60. If necessary, list additional entries on a separate page. Enter the total of the Average Monthly Payments on Line 47.	

	Name of Creditor	Property Securing the Debt	Average Monthly Payment	Does payment include taxes or insurance?
a.			$	☐ yes ☐ no
b.			$	☐ yes ☐ no
c.			$	☐ yes ☐ no
			Total: Add Lines a, b, and c	

$

48.	**Other payments on secured claims.** If any of debts listed in Line 47 are secured by your primary residence, a motor vehicle, or other property necessary for your support or the support of your dependents, you may include in your deduction 1/60th of any amount (the "cure amount") that you must pay the creditor in addition to the payments listed in Line 47, in order to maintain possession of the property. The cure amount would include any sums in default that must be paid in order to avoid repossession or foreclosure. List and total any such amounts in the following chart. If necessary, list additional entries on a separate page.	

	Name of Creditor	Property Securing the Debt in Default	1/60th of the Cure Amount
a.			$
b.			$
c.			$
			Total: Add Lines a, b, and c

49.	**Payments on prepetition priority claims.** Enter the total amount, divided by 60, of all priority claims, such as priority tax, child support and alimony claims, for which you were liable at the time of your bankruptcy filing. **Do not include current obligations, such as those set out in Line 33.**	$
50.	**Chapter 13 administrative expenses.** Multiply the amount in Line a by the amount in Line b, and enter the resulting administrative expense	

a.	Projected average monthly Chapter 13 plan payment.	$
b.	Current multiplier for your district as determined under schedules issued by the Executive Office for United States Trustees. (This information is available at www.usdoj.gov/ust/ or from the clerk of the bankruptcy court.)	X
c.	Average monthly administrative expense of Chapter 13 case	Total: Multiply Lines a and b

		$
51.	**Total Deductions for Debt Payment.** Enter the total of Lines 47 through 50.	$

Subpart D: Total Deductions from Income

52.	**Total of all deductions from income.** Enter the total of Lines 38, 46, and 51.	$

Part V. DETERMINATION OF DISPOSABLE INCOME UNDER § 1325(b)(2)

53.	**Total current monthly income.** Enter the amount from Line 20.	$
54.	**Support income.** Enter the monthly average of any child support payments, foster care payments, or disability payments for a dependent child, reported in Part I, that you received in accordance with applicable nonbankruptcy law, to the extent reasonably necessary to be expended for such child.	$
55.	**Qualified retirement deductions.** Enter the monthly total of (a) all amounts withheld by your employer from wages as contributions for qualified retirement plans, as specified in § 541(b)(7) and (b) all required repayments of loans from retirement plans, as specified in § 362(b)(19).	$
56.	**Total of all deductions allowed under § 707(b)(2).** Enter the amount from Line 52.	$
57.	**Deduction for special circumstances.** If there are special circumstances that justify additional expenses for which there is no reasonable alternative, describe the special circumstances and the resulting expenses in lines a-c below. If necessary, list additional entries on a separate page. Total the expenses and enter the total in Line 57. **You must provide your case trustee with documentation of these expenses and you must provide a detailed explanation of the special circumstances that make such expenses necessary and reasonable.**	

	Nature of special circumstances	Amount of expense
a.		
b.		
c.		

58.	**Total adjustments to determine disposable income.** Add the amounts on Lines 54, 55, 56, and 57 and enter the result.	$
59.	**Monthly Disposable Income Under § 1325(b)(2).** Subtract Line 58 from Line 53 and enter the result.	$

Part VI: ADDITIONAL EXPENSE CLAIMS

60. **Other Expenses.** List and describe any monthly expenses, not otherwise stated in this form, that are required for the health and welfare of you and your family and that you contend should be an additional deduction from your current monthly income under § 707(b)(2)(A)(ii)(I). If necessary, list additional sources on a separate page. All figures should reflect your average monthly expense for each item. Total the expenses.

	Expense Description	Monthly Amount
a.		$
b.		$
c.		$
	Total: Add Lines a, b, and c	$

Part VII: VERIFICATION

61. I declare under penalty of perjury that the information provided in this statement is true and correct. *(If this is a joint case, both debtors must sign.)*

Date:________________ Signature:________________________
(Debtor)

Date:________________ Signature:________________________
(Joint Debtor, if any)

Corporate Ownership Statement Pursuant to FRBP 1007 (a)(1) and 7007.1, and LBR 1007-4 (F 1007-4)

Attorney or Party Name, Address, Telephone & FAX Numbers, and California State Bar Number ☐ Attorney for:	FOR COURT USE ONLY
UNITED STATES BANKRUPTCY COURT **CENTRAL DISTRICT OF CALIFORNIA**	
In re: Debtor(s), Plaintiff(s), Defendant(s).	CASE NO.: ADV. NO.: CHAPTER:

Corporate Ownership Statement Pursuant to FRBP 1007(a)(1) and 7007.1, and LBR 1007-4

Pursuant to FRBP 1007(a)(1) and 7007.1, and LBR 1007-4, any corporation, other than a governmental unit, that is a debtor in a voluntary case or a party to an adversary proceeding or a contested matter shall file this statement identifying all its parent corporations and listing any publicly held company, other than a governmental unit, that directly or indirectly own 10% or more of any class of the corporation's equity interest, or state that there are no entities to report. This Corporate Ownership Statement must be filed with the initial pleading filed by a corporate entity in a case or adversary proceeding. A supplemental statement must promptly be filed upon any change in circumstances that renders this Corporate Ownership Statement inaccurate.

I, ______________________________, the undersigned in the above-captioned case, hereby declare
(*Print Name of Attorney or Declarant*)

under penalty of perjury under the laws of the United States of America that the following is true and correct:

[Check the appropriate boxes and, if applicable, provide the required information.]

1. I have personal knowledge of the matters set forth in this Statement because:

☐ I am the president or other officer or an authorized agent of the debtor corporation
☐ I am a party to an adversary proceeding
☐ I am a party to a contested matter
☐ I am the attorney for the debtor corporation

2. a. ☐ The following entities, other than the debtor or a governmental unit, directly or indirectly own 10% or more of any class of the corporation's(s') equity interests:

[For additional names, attach an addendum to this form.]

b. ☐ There are no entities that directly or indirectly own 10% or more of any class of the corporation's equity interest.

______________________________ ______________________
Signature of Attorney or Declarant Date

____
Printed Name of Attorney or Declarant

This form is optional. It has been approved for use by the United States Bankruptcy Court for the Central District of California.

June 2009 F 1007-4

CDCAL-511 C.D. CALIFORNIA

DEBTOR'S MOTION TO REOPEN CASE AND FOR EXTENSION OF TIME (F5010-1.1M)

Attorney or Party Name, Address, Telephone & FAX Numbers, and California State Bar Number *Attorney for:*	FOR COURT USE ONLY
UNITED STATES BANKRUPTCY COURT **CENTRAL DISTRICT OF CALIFORNIA**	
In re: Debtor(s).	CHAPTER: ____ CASE NO.:

DEBTOR'S MOTION TO REOPEN CASE AND FOR EXTENSION OF TIME TO FILE DEBTOR'S CERTIFICATION OF COMPLETION OF POSTPETITION INSTRUCTIONAL COURSE CONCERNING PERSONAL FINANCIAL MANAGEMENT

(For Case Closed Without Entry of Discharge Due to Noncompliance With 11 U.S.C. §§ 727(a)(11) or 1328(g)(1))

TO THE HONORABLE UNITED STATES BANKRUPTCY JUDGE.

1. **Bankruptcy Case Filing Information:**

   a. A voluntary petition under chapter ☐ 7 ☐ 13 was filed on:

   b. Because the Debtor(s) failed to file Official Form 23, Debtor's Certification of Completion of Postpetition Instructional Course Concerning Personal Financial Management ("OF 23") within the time limit set forth in F.R.B.P. 1007(c), the court closed this case without entering a discharge.

2. I, ______________________________, the Debtor in this case, and ______________________________, (if joint debtors) hereby request that the court enter an order: (a) reopening the case pursuant to 11 U.S.C. § 350(b) and F.R.B.P. 5010; and (b) extending the time for the Debtor(s) to file the OF 23 for a period of 30 days from the date of entry of an order granting this motion.

3. The Debtor(s) failed to file the OF 23 by the original deadline, and therefore need to have the case reopened so that the required OF 23 can be filed and a discharge can be entered because: (Explain circumstances that prevented the Debtor(s) from filing the OF 23 in a timely manner.)

____
____
____
____
____
____,

and I declare this under penalty of perjury.

Debtor's Motion to Reopen Case and for Extension of Time To File Debtor's Certification of of Postpetition Instructional Course Concerning Personal Financial Management - Page 2

In re	CHAPTER:
Debtor(s).	CASE NO.:

WHEREFORE, the Debtor(s) pray(s) that this court issue an order (the form of which is submitted herewith and has been served) reopening this case and extending the time to file the OF 23 so that the Debtor(s) discharge may be entered.

Debtor's Signature Dated City State

Joint Debtor's Signature Dated City State

PROOF OF SERVICE BY MAIL

STATE OF CALIFORNIA
COUNTY OF ____________________

I am employed in the above County, State of California. I am over the age of 18 and not a party to the within action. My business address is as follows:

On ____________________, I served the foregoing document described as : DEBTOR'S MOTION TO REOPEN CASE AND FOR EXTENSION OF TIME TO FILE DEBTOR'S CERTIFICATION OF COMPLETION OF POSTPETITION INSTRUCTIONAL COURSE CONCERNING PERSONAL FINANCIAL MANAGEMENT on the chapter ___ trustee and the United States Trustee at their last known addresses by placing a true and correct copy thereof in a sealed envelope with postage thereon fully prepaid in the United States Mail at ______________________________, California, addressed as follows:

I declare under penalty of perjury under the laws of the United States of America that the foregoing is true and correct.

Dated:

Type Name *Signature*

This form is mandatory by Order of the United States Bankruptcy Court for the Central District of California.

Revised December 7, 2007

F 5010-1.1M

Debtor's Complaint to Avoid Junior Lien on Principal Residence [11 U.S.C. § 506(a),(d); FRBP 3012] (Optional) (F 4003-2.5.COMPLAINT)

Attorney or Party Name, Address, Telephone & FAX Nos., State Bar No. & Email Address ☐ Attorney for Plaintiff(s); ☐ Plaintiff(s) appearing without attorney	FOR COURT USE ONLY
UNITED STATES BANKRUPTCY COURT **CENTRAL DISTRICT OF CALIFORNIA - ________________ DIVISION**	
In re: Debtor(s).	CASE NO.: CHAPTER 13 ADVERSARY NO.:
Plaintiff(s), vs. Defendant.	**DEBTOR'S COMPLAINT TO AVOID JUNIOR LIEN ON PRINCIPAL RESIDENCE [11 U.S.C. § 506(a),(d); FRBP 3012]** TO BE FILED CONCURRENTLY WITH LBR FORM F 7004-1 SUMMONS AND NOTICE OF STATUS CONFERENCE AND FORM B-104 ADVERSARY PROCEEDING COVER SHEET

NAME OF CREDITOR HOLDING JUNIOR LIEN ("Defendant"): ____________________

A. Introduction: This is an adversary proceeding brought by the Plaintiff(s), ____________________, in order to determine the value of a claim secured by a lien on principal residence of Plaintiff(s) which the estate has an interest, and to avoid the junior deed of trust, mortgage or other encumbrance (hereinafter, "Lien") of Defendant, pursuant to 11 U.S.C. § 506.

B. Jurisdiction: This adversary proceeding arises out of and is related to the above-captioned chapter 13 case now pending in United States Bankruptcy Court. The complaint involves a "core" proceeding pursuant to 28 U.S.C. § 157(b)(2). The court has jurisdiction in this adversary proceeding pursuant to 28 U.S.C. §§ 157, 1334; and General Order No. 266 of the United States District Court for the Central District of California.

C. Venue: Venue for this adversary proceeding is proper in this court pursuant to 28 U.S.C. § 1409(a).

D. General Allegations:

1. Property at Issue: Plaintiff(s) owns real property (the "Property"), which is the principal residence of Plaintiff(s), described below, encumbered by a lien held by Defendant:

Street Address: ______________________
Unit Number: __________
City, State, Zip Code: ______________________

Legal description or document recording number (including county of recording):

☐ See attached page

2. Grounds for Avoidance of Junior Lien:

a. As of__________, the Property is subject to the following liens in the amounts specified securing the debt against the Property, which the Plaintiff(s) seeks to have treated as indicated:

i. ______________________in the amount of $ ______________;

ii. ______________________ in the amount of $ ______________ ☐ is ☐ is not to be avoided;

iii. ______________________ in the amount of $ ______________ ☐ is ☐ is not to be avoided;

☐ See attached page for additional lien(s).

b. As of__________, Property is worth no more than $ ______________.

c. As a result, Defendant's claim related to the Lien on the Property is ☐ wholly ☐ partially unsecured.

E. Claim For Relief:

1. Pursuant to 11 U.S.C. § 506(a), Defendant's claim as of the date of filing is unsecured.

2. Pursuant to 11 U.S.C. § 506(d) the Defendant's Lien may be avoided.

F. Wherefore, Plaintiff prays for the following:

1. The Property is valued at no more than $______________.

2. The Defendant's claim related to the Lien shall be allowed as a non-priority general unsecured claim in the amount per the filed Proof of Claim.

3. The avoidance of Defendant's Lien is contingent upon ☐ Debtor's completion of the chapter 13 plan, or ☐ Debtor's receipt of a chapter 13 discharge.

4. The Defendant shall retain its lien in the junior position for the full amount due under the corresponding note and lien in the event of either the dismissal of Debtor's chapter 13 case, the conversion of Debtor's chapter 13 case to any other chapter under the United States Bankruptcy Code, or if the Property is sold or refinanced prior to: ☐ Debtor's completion of the chapter 13 plan, or ☐ Debtor's receipt of a chapter 13 discharge.

5. In the event that the holder of the first position lien or any senior lien on the Property forecloses on its interest and extinguishes Defendant's lien rights prior to: ☐ Debtor's completion of the chapter 13 plan, or ☐ Debtor's receipt of a chapter 13 discharge,

6. ☐ See attached continuation page for additional provisions.

Dated: ____________

Respectfully submitted,

By: ______________________________
Signature of Plaintiff or Attorney for Plaintiff

Name: ______________________________
Type Name of Plaintiff or Attorney for Plaintiff

PROOF OF SERVICE OF DOCUMENT

I am over the age of 18 and not a party to this bankruptcy case or adversary proceeding. My business address is:

A true and correct copy of the foregoing document described as **DEBTOR'S COMPLAINT TO AVOID JUNIOR LIEN ON PRINCIPAL RESIDENCE** will be served or was served **(a)** on the judge in chambers in the form and manner required by LBR 5005-2(d); and **(b)** in the manner indicated below:

I. **TO BE SERVED BY THE COURT VIA NOTICE OF ELECTRONIC FILING ("NEF")** – Pursuant to controlling General Order(s) and Local Bankruptcy Rule(s) ("LBR"), the foregoing document will be served by the court via NEF and hyperlink to the document. On__________________, I checked the CM/ECF docket for this bankruptcy case or adversary proceeding and determined that the following person(s) are on the Electronic Mail Notice List to receive NEF transmission at the email address(es) indicated below:

☐ Service information continued on attached page

II. **SERVED BY U.S. MAIL OR OVERNIGHT MAIL**(indicate method for each person or entity served):
On ____________________, I served the following person(s) and/or entity(ies) at the last known address(es) in this bankruptcy case or adversary proceeding by placing a true and correct copy thereof in a sealed envelope in the United States Mail, first class, postage prepaid, and/or with an overnight mail service addressed as follows. Listing the judge here constitutes a declaration that mailing to the judge will be completed no later than 24 hours after the document is filed.

☐ Service information continued on attached page

III. **SERVED BY PERSONAL DELIVERY, FACSIMILE TRANSMISSION OR EMAIL** (indicate method for each person or entity served): Pursuant to F.R.Civ.P. 5 and/or controlling LBR, on __________________, I served the following person(s) and/or entity(ies) by personal delivery, or (for those who consented in writing to such service method), by facsimile transmission and/or email as follows. Listing the judge here constitutes a declaration that personal delivery on the judge will be completed no later than 24 hours after the document is filed.

☐ Service information continued on attached page

I declare under penalty of perjury under the laws of the United States of America that the foregoing is true and correct.

____ ____________________________
Date *Type Name* *Signature*

II. SERVED BY U.S. MAIL, CERTIFIED MAIL OR OVERNIGHT MAIL (indicate method for each person or entity served):
(Attached page to Proof of Service-please include any additional or alternative addresses and attach additional pages if needed)
(Certified Mail required for service on national bank.)

Name of 1st Name of 1st Lien Holder & Address	Address from: ☐ Proof of claim ☐ Secretary of State ☐ FDIC website ☐ Other: *specify*	Delivery Method ☐ US Mail ☐ Certified mail – Tracking # ___ ☐ Overnight mail – Tracking # ___ Carrier Name: ___
Name of 1st Lien Holder- Agent for Service of Process	Address from: ☐ Proof of claim ☐ Secretary of State ☐ FDIC website ☐ Other: *specify*	Delivery Method ☐ US Mail ☐ Certified mail – Tracking # ___ ☐ Overnight mail – Tracking # ___ Carrier Name: ___
Name of 1st Lien Holder – Servicing Agent	Address from: ☐ Proof of claim ☐ Secretary of State ☐ FDIC website ☐ Other: *specify*	Delivery Method ☐ US Mail ☐ Certified mail – Tracking # ___ ☐ Overnight mail – Tracking # ___ Carrier Name: ___

Name of 2nd Lien Holder & Address	Address from: ☐ Proof of claim ☐ Secretary of State ☐ FDIC website ☐ Other: *specify*	Delivery Method ☐ US Mail ☐ Certified mail – Tracking # ___ ☐ Overnight mail – Tracking # ___ Carrier Name: ___
Name of 2nd Lien Holder- Agent for Service of Process	Address from: ☐ Proof of claim ☐ Secretary of State ☐ FDIC website ☐ Other: *specify*	Delivery Method ☐ US Mail ☐ Certified mail – Tracking # ___ ☐ Overnight mail – Tracking # ___ Carrier Name: ___
Name of 2nd Lien Holder – Servicing Agent	Address from: ☐ Proof of claim ☐ Secretary of State ☐ FDIC website ☐ Other: *specify*	Delivery Method ☐ US Mail ☐ Certified mail – Tracking # ___ ☐ Overnight mail – Tracking # ___ Carrier Name: ___

Name of 3rd Lien Holder & Address	Address from: ☐ Proof of claim ☐ Secretary of State ☐ FDIC website ☐ Other: *specify*	Delivery Method ☐ US Mail ☐ Certified mail – Tracking # _____ ☐ Overnight mail – Tracking #_____ Carrier Name: _____
Name of 3rd Lien Holder- Agent for Service of Process	Address from: ☐ Proof of claim ☐ Secretary of State ☐ FDIC website ☐ Other: *specify*	Delivery Method ☐ US Mail ☐ Certified mail – Tracking # _____ ☐ Overnight mail – Tracking #_____ Carrier Name: _____
Name of 3rd Lien Holder – Servicing Agent	Address from: ☐ Proof of claim ☐ Secretary of State ☐ FDIC website ☐ Other: *specify*	Delivery Method ☐ US Mail ☐ Certified mail – Tracking # _____ ☐ Overnight mail – Tracking #_____ Carrier Name: _____

Alternative/Additional Address	Address from: ☐ Proof of claim ☐ Secretary of State ☐ FDIC website ☐ Other: *specify*	Delivery Method ☐ US Mail ☐ Certified mail – Tracking # _____ ☐ Overnight mail – Tracking #_____ Carrier Name: _____
Alternative/Additional Address	Address from: ☐ Proof of claim ☐ Secretary of State ☐ FDIC website ☐ Other: *specify*	Delivery Method ☐ US Mail ☐ Certified mail – Tracking # _____ ☐ Overnight mail – Tracking #_____ Carrier Name: _____

Debtor's Motion for Default Judgment RE Complaint to Avoid Junior Lien on Real Property [11 U.S.C. § 506(a),(d): FRBP 3012] (Optional) (F 4003-2.5.DEFAULT.MOTION)

Attorney or Party Name, Address, Telephone & FAX Nos., State Bar No. & Email Address ☐ *Attorney for Plaintiff(s)* ☐ Plaintiff(s) *appearing without attorney*	FOR COURT USE ONLY
UNITED STATES BANKRUPTCY COURT **CENTRAL DISTRICT OF CALIFORNIA - __________ DIVISION**	
In re: Debtor(s).	CASE NO.: CHAPTER 13 ADVERSARY NO.:
Plaintiff(s),	**DEBTOR'S MOTION FOR DEFAULT JUDGMENT RE COMPLAINT TO AVOID JUNIOR LIEN ON PRINCIPAL RESIDENCE [11 U.S.C. § 506(a),(d), FRBP 3012]**
vs. Defendant.	DATE: TIME: COURTROOM: PLACE:

NAME OF CREDITOR HOLDING JUNIOR LIEN: ____________________

1. Name of Defendant(s) against whom default judgment is sought: ________________ (hereinafter, "Defendant").

2. Plaintiff(s) filed the Complaint in the above-captioned proceeding on __________.

3. The Summons and Complaint were served on Defendant by ☐ Personal Service ☐ Mail Service on the following date __________.

4. A conformed copy of the completed Return of Summons form is attached hereto.

5. The time for filing an answer or other response expired on ____________.

6. No answer or other response has been filed or served by Defendant.

7. The default of Defendant:

   a. ☐ Has not yet been entered, but is hereby requested.

   b. ☐ Was Entered on ____________________.

8. **A Status Conference:**

   a. ☐ Is scheduled for ____.
   Specify date, time, and place

   b. ☐ Was held on ____.
   Specify date, time, and place

9. ☐ **DECLARATION OF NON-MILITARY STATUS:** No defendant named in Paragraph 1 above is in the military service so as to be entitled to the benefits of the Servicemembers Civil Relief Act (Pub. L. 108-189) (50 U.S. Code App. §§ 501-594). The undersigned declares under penalty of perjury that this statement of defendant's non-military status is true and correct and is made under penalty of perjury under the laws of the United States of America based upon the undersigned's review of said Defendant's Statement of Affairs and Statement of Income and Expenditures filed in this case and is based upon the undersigned's lack of any information or belief that there has been any change of circumstances as to the defendant's non-military status.

10. ☐ Defaulting party is **not** an **infant** or **incompetent** party.

11. **Property at Issue:**

Plaintiff moves to avoid the junior deed of trust, mortgage or other encumbrance (hereinafter, "Junior lien") encumbering the following real property ("Property"), which is principal residence of Plaintiff(s).

Street Address: ____
Unit Number.: ________
City, State, Zip Code: ____

Legal description or document recording number (including county of recording):

☐ See attached page.

12. **Grounds for Determining Unsecured Status and Avoidance of Junior Lien:**

a. As of ____________________, the Property is subject to the following liens in the amounts specified securing the debt against the Property, which the debtor seeks to have treated as indicated:

____________________ in the amount of $____________

i. ____________________ in the amount of $____________ ☐ is ☐ is not to be avoided;

ii. ____________________ in the amount of $____________ ☐ is ☐ is not to be avoided;

☐ See attached page for additional lien(s).

b. As of ____________________, Property is worth no more than $____________.

c. As a result, Defendant's claim related to the Junior lien on the Property is ☐ wholly ☐ partially unsecured.

13. **Evidence in Support of Motion:**

a. ☐ The amount of the 1st lien identified in paragraph 12(a)(i) is based on ____________________, ____________________ attached hereto and identified as Exhibit ____.

b. ☐ The amount of the 2nd lien identified in paragraph 12(a)(ii) is based on ____________________ ____________________ attached hereto and identified as Exhibit ____.

c. ☐ The amount of the 3rd lien identified in paragraph 12(a)(iii) is based on ____________________ ____________________, attached hereto and identified as Exhibit ____.

d. ☐ The relative priority of the liens encumbering the Property is established by evidence attached as Exhibit ____.

e. ☐ The value of the Property from paragraph 3(b) is based on ____________________, ____________________ attached as Exhibit ____;

f. ☐ Plaintiff submits the attached Declaration.

g. ☐ Other evidence *(specify)*: ____________________.

14. **WHEREFORE, Plaintiff prays that this Court issue an Order granting the following relief:**

a. That the Property is valued at no more than $____________.
That Defendant's claim related to the Junior lien shall be allowed as a non-priority general unsecured claim in the amount per the filed Proof of Claim.

b. The avoidance of Defendant's Junior lien is contingent upon ☐ Debtor's completion of the chapter 13 plan, or ☐ Debtor's receipt of a chapter 13 discharge.

c. The Defendant shall retain its lien in the junior position for the full amount due under the corresponding note and lien in the event of either the dismissal of Debtor's chapter 13 case, the conversion of Debtor's chapter 13 case to any other chapter under the United States Bankruptcy Code, or if the Property is sold or refinanced prior to:
☐ Debtor's completion of the chapter 13 plan, or
☐ Debtor's receipt of a chapter 13 discharge.

d. In the event that the holder of the first position lien or any senior lien on the Property forecloses on its interest and extinguishes Defendant's lien rights prior to: ☐ Debtor's completion of the chapter 13 plan, or ☐ Debtor's receipt of a chapter 13 discharge, Defendant's lien shall attach to the proceeds greater than necessary to pay the senior lien, if any, from the foreclosure sale.

e. ☐ See attached continuation page for additional provisions.

Dated: ________________ Respectfully submitted,

By: ________________________________
Signature of Plaintiff or Attorney for Plaintiff

Name: ________________________________
Type Name of Plaintiff or Attorney for Plaintiff

PROOF OF SERVICE OF DOCUMENT

I am over the age of 18 and not a party to this bankruptcy case or adversary proceeding. My business address is:

A true and correct copy of the foregoing document described as **DEBTOR'S MOTION FOR DEFAULT JUDGMENT RE COMPLAINT TO AVOID JUNIOR LIEN ON PRINCIPAL RESIDENCE** will be served or was served **(a)** on the judge in chambers in the form and manner required by LBR 5005-2(d); and **(b)** in the manner indicated below:

I. **TO BE SERVED BY THE COURT VIA NOTICE OF ELECTRONIC FILING ("NEF")** – Pursuant to controlling General Order(s) and Local Bankruptcy Rule(s) ("LBR"), the foregoing document will be served by the court via NEF and hyperlink to the document. On ______________________, I checked the CM/ECF docket for this bankruptcy case or adversary proceeding and determined that the following person(s) are on the Electronic Mail Notice List to receive NEF transmission at the email address(es) indicated below:

☐ Service information continued on attached page

II. **SERVED BY U.S. MAIL OR OVERNIGHT MAIL**(indicate method for each person or entity served):
On ______________________, I served the following person(s) and/or entity(ies) at the last known address(es) in this bankruptcy case or adversary proceeding by placing a true and correct copy thereof in a sealed envelope in the United States Mail, first class, postage prepaid, and/or with an overnight mail service addressed as follows. Listing the judge here constitutes a declaration that mailing to the judge will be completed no later than 24 hours after the document is filed.

☐ Service information continued on attached page

III. **SERVED BY PERSONAL DELIVERY, FACSIMILE TRANSMISSION OR EMAIL** (indicate method for each person or entity served): Pursuant to F.R.Civ.P. 5 and/or controlling LBR, on ______________________, I served the following person(s) and/or entity(ies) by personal delivery, or (for those who consented in writing to such service method), by facsimile transmission and/or email as follows. Listing the judge here constitutes a declaration that personal delivery on the judge will be completed no later than 24 hours after the document is filed.

☐ Service information continued on attached page

I declare under penalty of perjury under the laws of the United States of America that the foregoing is true and correct.

Date	*Type Name*	*Signature*

II. **SERVED BY U.S. MAIL, CERTIFIED MAIL OR OVERNIGHT MAIL** (indicate method for each person or entity served):
(Attached page to Proof of Service-please include any additional or alternative addresses and attach additional pages if needed)
(Certified Mail required for service on a national bank.)

Name of 1st Name of 1st Lien Holder & Address	Address from: ☐ Proof of claim ☐ Secretary of State ☐ FDIC website ☐ Other: *specify*	Delivery Method ☐ US Mail ☐ Certified mail – Tracking # ______ ☐ Overnight mail – Tracking # ______ Carrier Name: ______
Name of 1st Lien Holder- Agent for Service of Process	Address from: ☐ Proof of claim ☐ Secretary of State ☐ FDIC website ☐ Other: *specify*	Delivery Method ☐ US Mail ☐ Certified mail – Tracking # ______ ☐ Overnight mail – Tracking # ______ Carrier Name: ______
Name of 1st Lien Holder – Servicing Agent	Address from: ☐ Proof of claim ☐ Secretary of State ☐ FDIC website ☐ Other: *specify*	Delivery Method ☐ US Mail ☐ Certified mail – Tracking # ______ ☐ Overnight mail – Tracking # ______ Carrier Name: ______

Name of 2nd Lien Holder & Address	Address from: ☐ Proof of claim ☐ Secretary of State ☐ FDIC website ☐ Other: *specify*	Delivery Method ☐ US Mail ☐ Certified mail – Tracking # ______ ☐ Overnight mail – Tracking # ______ Carrier Name: ______
Name of 2nd Lien Holder- Agent for Service of Process	Address from: ☐ Proof of claim ☐ Secretary of State ☐ FDIC website ☐ Other: *specify*	Delivery Method ☐ US Mail ☐ Certified mail – Tracking # ______ ☐ Overnight mail – Tracking # ______ Carrier Name: ______
Name of 2nd Lien Holder – Servicing Agent	Address from: ☐ Proof of claim ☐ Secretary of State ☐ FDIC website ☐ Other: *specify*	Delivery Method ☐ US Mail ☐ Certified mail – Tracking # ______ ☐ Overnight mail – Tracking # ______ Carrier Name: ______

Name of 3rd Lien Holder & Address	Address from: ☐ Proof of claim ☐ Secretary of State ☐ FDIC website ☐ Other: *specify*	Delivery Method ☐ US Mail ☐ Certified mail – Tracking # ______ ☐ Overnight mail – Tracking #______ Carrier Name: ______
Name of 3rd Lien Holder- Agent for Service of Process	Address from: ☐ Proof of claim ☐ Secretary of State ☐ FDIC website ☐ Other: *specify*	Delivery Method ☐ US Mail ☐ Certified mail – Tracking # ______ ☐ Overnight mail – Tracking #______ Carrier Name: ______
Name of 3rd Lien Holder – Servicing Agent	Address from: ☐ Proof of claim ☐ Secretary of State ☐ FDIC website ☐ Other: *specify*	Delivery Method ☐ US Mail ☐ Certified mail – Tracking # ______ ☐ Overnight mail – Tracking #______ Carrier Name: ______

Alternative/Additional Address	Address from: ☐ Proof of claim ☐ Secretary of State ☐ FDIC website ☐ Other: *specify*	Delivery Method ☐ US Mail ☐ Certified mail – Tracking # ______ ☐ Overnight mail – Tracking #______ Carrier Name: ______
Alternative/Additional Address	Address from: ☐ Proof of claim ☐ Secretary of State ☐ FDIC website ☐ Other: *specify*	Delivery Method ☐ US Mail ☐ Certified mail – Tracking # ______ ☐ Overnight mail – Tracking #______ Carrier Name: ______

Debtor's Motion to Avoid Junior Lien on Principal Residence [11 U.S.C. § 506(d)] (Optional) (F 4003-2.4-MOTION)

Attorney or Party Name, Address, Telephone & FAX Nos., State Bar No. & Email Address ☐ Attorney for Debtor(s) ☐ Debtor(s) appearing without an attorney	FOR COURT USE ONLY
UNITED STATES BANKRUPTCY COURT **CENTRAL DISTRICT OF CALIFORNIA - ________________ DIVISION**	
In re: Debtor(s).	CASE NO.: CHAPTER: 13
	DEBTOR'S MOTION TO AVOID JUNIOR LIEN ON PRINCIPAL RESIDENCE [11 U.S.C. § 506(d)]
	DATE: TIME: COURTROOM: PLACE:

NAME OF CREDITOR HOLDING JUNIOR LIEN ("Respondent"): ________________________________

____

A. **Property at Issue:** Debtor moves to avoid the junior deed of trust, mortgage or other encumbrance (hereinafter, "Lien") encumbering the following real property (hereinafter, the "Property"), which is the principal residence of debtor(s).

Street Address: ________________________________
Unit Number: ______________
City, State, Zip Code: ________________________________

Legal description or document recording number (including county of recording):

☐ See attached page.

B. Case History:

1. A voluntary petition under Chapter ☐ 7 ☐ 11 ☐ 12 ☐ 13 was filed on: ____________

2. ☐ An Order of Conversion to Chapter 13 was entered on *(specify date)*:

C. Grounds for Avoidance of Junior Lien:

1. As of__________, the Property is subject to the following liens in the amounts specified securing the debt against the Property, which the debtor seeks to have treated as indicated:

   i. ____________________in the amount of $____________.

   ii. ____________________in the amount of $____________ ☐ is ☐ is not to be avoided;

   iii. ____________________in the amount of $____________ ☐ is ☐ is not to be avoided;

   ☐ See attached page for additional lien(s).

2. As of____________, Property is worth no more than $____________.

   a. As a result, Respondent's Lien encumbering the Property is wholly unsecured.

3. **Evidence in Support of Motion:**

   a. ☐ The amount of the lien identified in paragraph C(1)(i) is based on____________, attached hereto and identified as Exhibit ___ .

   b. ☐ The amount of the lien identified in paragraph C(1)(ii) is based on ____________, attached hereto and identified as Exhibit ___ .

   c. ☐ The amount of the lien identified in paragraph C(1)(iii)) is based on____________, attached hereto and identified as Exhibit ___ .

   d. ☐ The relative priority of the liens encumbering the Property is established by evidence attached as Exhibit ___.

   e. ☐ The value of the Property from paragraph C(2) is based on____________, attached as

   f. ☐ Exhibit_____.

   g. ☐ Debtor submits the attached Declaration(s).

   h. ☐Other evidence *(specify)*: ____________

4. **WHEREFORE, Debtor prays that this Court issue an Order granting the following relief:**

   a. That the Property is valued at no more than $________________.

   b. That no payments are to be made on the secured claim of the Respondent, and regular mortgage maintenance payments are not to be made, before the Debtor's ☐ completion of the chapter 13 plan, or ☐ receipt of a chapter 13 discharge.

   c. That the Respondent's claim on the junior position lien shall be allowed as a non-priority general unsecured claim in the amount per the filed Proof of Claim.

   d. That the avoidance of the Respondent's junior lien is contingent upon: The Debtor's ☐ completion of the chapter 13 plan, or ☐ receipt of a chapter 13 discharge.

   e. That the Respondent shall retain its lien in the junior position for the full amount due under the corresponding note and lien in the event of either the dismissal of the Debtor's chapter 13 case, the conversion of the Debtor's chapter 13 case to any other chapter under the United States Bankruptcy Code, or if the Property is sold or refinanced prior to the Debtor's ☐ completion of the chapter 13 plan, or ☐ receipt of a chapter 13 discharge.

   f. That in the event that the holder of the first position lien or any senior lien on the Property forecloses on its interest and extinguishes the Respondent's lien rights prior to the Debtor's completion of the chapter 13 plan and receipt of a chapter 13 discharge, the Respondent's lien shall attach to the proceeds greater than necessary to pay the senior lien, if any, from the foreclosure sale.

5. ☐See attached continuation page for additional provisions.

Dated: ______________________

Respectfully submitted,

By: ______________________________
Signature of Debtor or Attorney for Debtor

Name: ______________________________
Type Name of Debtor or Attorney for Debtor

PROOF OF SERVICE OF DOCUMENT

I am over the age of 18 and not a party to this bankruptcy case or adversary proceeding. My business address is:

A true and correct copy of the foregoing document described as **MOTION TO AVOID JUNIOR LIEN ON PRINCIPAL RESIDENCE [11 U.S.C. § 506(d)]** will be served or was served **(a)** on the judge in chambers in the form and manner required by LBR 5005-2(d); and **(b)** in the manner indicated below:

I. <u>TO BE SERVED BY THE COURT VIA NOTICE OF ELECTRONIC FILING ("NEF")</u> – Pursuant to controlling General Order(s) and Local Bankruptcy Rule(s) ("LBR"), the foregoing document will be served by the court via NEF and hyperlink to the document. On____________________, I checked the CM/ECF docket for this bankruptcy case or adversary proceeding and determined that the following person(s) are on the Electronic Mail Notice List to receive NEF transmission at the email address(es) indicated below:

☐ Service information continued on attached page

II. <u>SERVED BY U.S. MAIL OR OVERNIGHT MAIL</u><u>(indicate method for each person or entity served):</u>
On____________________, I served the following person(s) and/or entity(ies) at the last known address(es) in this bankruptcy case or adversary proceeding by placing a true and correct copy thereof in a sealed envelope in the United States Mail, first class, postage prepaid, and/or with an overnight mail service addressed as follows. Listing the judge here constitutes a declaration that mailing to the judge <u>will be</u> completed no later than 24 hours after the document is filed.

☐ Service information continued on attached page

III. <u>SERVED BY PERSONAL DELIVERY, FACSIMILE TRANSMISSION OR EMAIL</u> <u>(indicate method for each person or entity served):</u> Pursuant to F.R.Civ.P. 5 and/or controlling LBR, on____________________, I served the following person(s) and/or entity(ies) by personal delivery, or (for those who consented in writing to such service method), by facsimile transmission and/or email as follows. Listing the judge here constitutes a declaration that personal delivery on the judge <u>will be</u> completed no later than 24 hours after the document is filed.

☐ Service information continued on attached page

I declare under penalty of perjury under the laws of the United States of America that the foregoing is true and correct.

____________ ____________________ ____________________
Date *Type Name* *Signature*

II. SERVED BY U.S. MAIL, CERTIFIED MAIL OR OVERNIGHT MAIL (indicate method for each person or entity served):

(Attached page to Proof of Service-please include any additional or alternative addresses and attach additional pages if needed)
(Certified Mail required for service on a national bank.)

Name of 1st Name of 1st Lien Holder & Address	Address from: ☐ Proof of claim ☐ Secretary of State ☐ FDIC website ☐ Other: *specify*	Delivery Method ☐ US Mail ☐ Certified mail – Tracking # ______ ☐ Overnight mail – Tracking #______ Carrier Name: ______
Name of 1st Lien Holder- Agent for Service of Process	Address from: ☐ Proof of claim ☐ Secretary of State ☐ FDIC website ☐ Other: *specify*	Delivery Method ☐ US Mail ☐ Certified mail – Tracking # ______ ☐ Overnight mail – Tracking #______ Carrier Name: ______
Name of 1st Lien Holder – Servicing Agent	Address from: ☐ Proof of claim ☐ Secretary of State ☐ FDIC website ☐ Other: *specify*	Delivery Method ☐ US Mail ☐ Certified mail – Tracking # ______ ☐ Overnight mail – Tracking #______ Carrier Name: ______

Name of 2nd Lien Holder & Address	Address from: ☐ Proof of claim ☐ Secretary of State ☐ FDIC website ☐ Other: *specify*	Delivery Method ☐ US Mail ☐ Certified mail – Tracking # ______ ☐ Overnight mail – Tracking #______ Carrier Name: ______
Name of 2nd Lien Holder- Agent for Service of Process	Address from: ☐ Proof of claim ☐ Secretary of State ☐ FDIC website ☐ Other: *specify*	Delivery Method ☐ US Mail ☐ Certified mail – Tracking # ______ ☐ Overnight mail – Tracking #______ Carrier Name: ______
Name of 2nd Lien Holder – Servicing Agent	Address from: ☐ Proof of claim ☐ Secretary of State ☐ FDIC website ☐ Other: *specify*	Delivery Method ☐ US Mail ☐ Certified mail – Tracking # ______ ☐ Overnight mail – Tracking #______ Carrier Name: ______

Name of 3rd Lien Holder & Address	Address from: ☐ Proof of claim ☐ Secretary of State ☐ FDIC website ☐ Other: *specify*	Delivery Method ☐ US Mail ☐ Certified mail – Tracking # ______ ☐ Overnight mail – Tracking #______ Carrier Name: ______
Name of 3rd Lien Holder- Agent for Service of Process	Address from: ☐ Proof of claim ☐ Secretary of State ☐ FDIC website ☐ Other: *specify*	Delivery Method ☐ US Mail ☐ Certified mail – Tracking # ______ ☐ Overnight mail – Tracking #______ Carrier Name: ______
Name of 3rd Lien Holder – Servicing Agent	Address from: ☐ Proof of claim ☐ Secretary of State ☐ FDIC website ☐ Other: *specify*	Delivery Method ☐ US Mail ☐ Certified mail – Tracking # ______ ☐ Overnight mail – Tracking #______ Carrier Name: ______

Alternative/Additional Address	Address from: ☐ Proof of claim ☐ Secretary of State ☐ FDIC website ☐ Other: *specify*	Delivery Method ☐ US Mail ☐ Certified mail – Tracking # ______ ☐ Overnight mail – Tracking #______ Carrier Name: ______
Alternative/Additional Address	Address from: ☐ Proof of claim ☐ Secretary of State ☐ FDIC website ☐ Other: *specify*	Delivery Method ☐ US Mail ☐ Certified mail – Tracking # ______ ☐ Overnight mail – Tracking #______ Carrier Name: ______

Debtor's Notice of Conversion of Bankruptcy Case From Chapter 12 to Chapter 7 [11 U.S.C. § 1208(a), LBR 1017-1] (Mandatory) (F 1017-1.4.NOTICE. CONVERT.CH12)

Attorney or Party Name, Address, Telephone & FAX Nos., State Bar No. & Email Address ☐ *Attorney for Debtor(s)* ☐ *Debtor(s), appearing without an attorney*	FOR COURT USE ONLY
UNITED STATES BANKRUPTCY COURT **CENTRAL DISTRICT OF CALIFORNIA - ______________ DIVISION**	
In re: Debtor(s).	CASE NO.: CHAPTER: 12 **DEBTOR'S NOTICE OF CONVERSION OF BANKRUPTCY CASE FROM CHAPTER 12 TO CHAPTER 7 [11 U.S.C. § 1208(a), LBR 1017-1]** [No hearing required. No order required.]

PLEASE TAKE NOTICE THAT DEBTOR CONVERTS THIS CHAPTER 12 CASE TO A CASE UNDER CHAPTER 7 ON THE FOLLOWING GROUNDS:

1. A voluntary petition under chapter 12 was filed on (*insert date*): ______________________
2. Name of chapter 12 trustee appointed: ______________________
3. This case has not previously been converted.
4. The additional filing fee is being paid concurrently with the filing of this notice.
5. This notice of conversion is filed in good faith, and Debtor is eligible for relief under chapter 7.

Dated: ____________

Respectfully submitted,

By: ______________________
Signature of Debtor(s) or Attorney for Debtor(s)

Name: ______________________
Type Name of Debtor(s) or Attorney for Debtor(s)

PROOF OF SERVICE OF DOCUMENT

I am over the age of 18 and not a party to this bankruptcy case or adversary proceeding. My business address is:

A true and correct copy of the foregoing document described as **DEBTOR'S NOTICE OF CONVERSION OF BANKRUPTCY CASE FROM CHAPTER 12 TO CHAPTER 7** will be served or was served **(a)** on the judge in chambers in the form and manner required by LBR 5005-2(d); and **(b)** in the manner indicated below:

I. TO BE SERVED BY THE COURT VIA NOTICE OF ELECTRONIC FILING ("NEF") – Pursuant to controlling General Order(s) and Local Bankruptcy Rule(s) ("LBR"), the foregoing document will be served by the court via NEF and hyperlink to the document. On ______________, I checked the CM/ECF docket for this bankruptcy case or adversary proceeding and determined that the following person(s) are on the Electronic Mail Notice List to receive NEF transmission at the email address(es) indicated below:

U. S. Trustee:
Chapter 12 Trustee:

☐ Service information continued on attached page

II. SERVED BY U.S. MAIL OR OVERNIGHT MAIL(indicate method for each person or entity served):
On ______________, I served the following person(s) and/or entity(ies) at the last known address(es) in this bankruptcy case or adversary proceeding by placing a true and correct copy thereof in a sealed envelope in the United States Mail, first class, postage prepaid, and/or with an overnight mail service addressed as follows. Listing the judge here constitutes a declaration that mailing to the judge will be completed no later than 24 hours after the document is filed.

☐ Service information continued on attached page

III. SERVED BY PERSONAL DELIVERY, FACSIMILE TRANSMISSION OR EMAIL (indicate method for each person or entity served): Pursuant to F.R.Civ.P. 5 and/or controlling LBR, on ______________, I served the following person(s) and/or entity(ies) by personal delivery, or (for those who consented in writing to such service method), by facsimile transmission and/or email as follows. Listing the judge here constitutes a declaration that personal delivery on the judge will be completed no later than 24 hours after the document is filed.

☐ Service information continued on attached page

I declare under penalty of perjury under the laws of the United States of America that the foregoing is true and correct.

Date	*Type Name*	*Signature*

Debtor's Notice of Conversion of Bankruptcy Case from Chapter 13 to Chapter 7 [11 U.S.C. § 1307(a), LBR 1017-1, LBR 3015-1(q)(2)] (Mandatory) (F 3015-1.21.1.NOTICE.CONVERT.CH13)

Attorney or Party Name, Address, Telephone & FAX Nos., State Bar No. & Email Address ☐ *Attorney for Debtor(s)* ☐ *Debtor(s), appearing without an attorney*	FOR COURT USE ONLY
UNITED STATES BANKRUPTCY COURT **CENTRAL DISTRICT OF CALIFORNIA - ______________ DIVISION**	
In re: Debtor(s).	CASE NO.: CHAPTER: 13 **DEBTOR'S NOTICE OF CONVERSION OF BANKRUPTCY CASE FROM CHAPTER 13 TO CHAPTER 7 [11 U.S.C. §1307(a), LBR 1017-1, LBR 3015-1(q)(2)]** No hearing required. No order required.

PLEASE TAKE NOTICE THAT DEBTOR CONVERTS THIS CHAPTER 13 CASE TO A CASE UNDER CHAPTER 7 ON THE FOLLOWING GROUNDS:

1. A voluntary petition under chapter 13 was filed on (*insert date*):
2. Name of chapter 13 trustee appointed:
3. This case has not previously been converted.
4. The additional filing fee is being paid concurrently with the filing of this notice.
5. This notice of conversion is filed in good faith, and Debtor is eligible for relief under chapter 7.

Dated: ____________________

Respectfully submitted,

By: ______________________________
Signature of Debtor or Attorney for Debtor(s)

Name: ______________________________
Type Name of Debtor or Attorney for Debtor(s)

PROOF OF SERVICE OF DOCUMENT

I am over the age of 18 and not a party to this bankruptcy case or adversary proceeding. My business address is:

A true and correct copy of the foregoing document described as **DEBTOR'S NOTICE OF CONVERSION OF BANKRUPTCY CASE FROM CHAPTER 13 to CHAPTER 7** will be served or was served **(a)** on the judge in chambers in the form and manner required by LBR 5005-2(d); and **(b)** in the manner indicated below:

I. <u>TO BE SERVED BY THE COURT VIA NOTICE OF ELECTRONIC FILING ("NEF")</u> – Pursuant to controlling General Order(s) and Local Bankruptcy Rule(s) ("LBR"), the foregoing document will be served by the court via NEF and hyperlink to the document. On ____________________, I checked the CM/ECF docket for this bankruptcy case or adversary proceeding and determined that the following person(s) are on the Electronic Mail Notice List to receive NEF transmission at the email address(es) indicated below:

U. S. Trustee:
Chapter 13 Trustee:

☐ Service information continued on attached page

II. <u>SERVED BY U.S. MAIL OR OVERNIGHT MAIL</u><u>(indicate method for each person or entity served):</u>
On ____________________, I served the following person(s) and/or entity(ies) at the last known address(es) in this bankruptcy case or adversary proceeding by placing a true and correct copy thereof in a sealed envelope in the United States Mail, first class, postage prepaid, and/or with an overnight mail service addressed as follows. Listing the judge here constitutes a declaration that mailing to the judge <u>will be</u> completed no later than 24 hours after the document is filed.

☐ Service information continued on attached page

III. <u>SERVED BY PERSONAL DELIVERY, FACSIMILE TRANSMISSION OR EMAIL</u> <u>(indicate method for each person or entity served):</u> Pursuant to F.R.Civ.P. 5 and/or controlling LBR, on ____________________, I served the following person(s) and/or entity(ies) by personal delivery, or (for those who consented in writing to such service method), by facsimile transmission and/or email as follows. Listing the judge here constitutes a declaration that personal delivery on the judge <u>will be</u> completed no later than 24 hours after the document is filed.

☐ Service information continued on attached page

I declare under penalty of perjury under the laws of the United States of America that the foregoing is true and correct.

Date	*Type Name*	*Signature*

This form is mandatory. It has been approved for use in the United States Bankruptcy Court for the Central District of California.

ORDER ON DEBTOR'S MOTION TO REOPEN CASE AND FOR EXTENSION OF TIME (F5010-1.10)

Attorney or Party Name, Address, Telephone & FAX Numbers, and California State Bar Number *Attorney for:*	FOR COURT USE ONLY
UNITED STATES BANKRUPTCY COURT **CENTRAL DISTRICT OF CALIFORNIA**	
In re: Debtor(s).	CHAPTER: CASE NO.:

ORDER ON DEBTOR'S MOTION TO REOPEN CASE AND FOR EXTENSION OF TIME TO FILE DEBTOR'S CERTIFICATION OF COMPLETION OF POSTPETITION INSTRUCTIONAL COURSE CONCERNING PERSONAL FINANCIAL MANAGEMENT

(For Case Closed Without Entry of Discharge Due To Noncompliance With 11 U.S.C. §§ 727(a)(11) or 1328(g)(1))

The above referenced case having been closed without the entry of a discharge due to noncompliance with 11 U.S.C. §§ 727(a)(11) or 1328(g)(1) attributable to the failure to file Official Form 23, Debtor's Certification of Completion of Postpetition Instructional Course Concerning Personal Financial Management ("OF 23"), and the Debtor(s) having moved to reopen the case pursuant to 11 U.S.C. § 350(b) and F.R.B.P 5010 and for an extension of time under F.R.B.P. 1007(c) to file the OF 23 so that a discharge may be entered, and the Court, having reviewed and considered the motion,

1. ☐ The Court finds cause to reopen the case and to extend the time for the Debtor(s) to file the OF 23. Accordingly, IT IS HEREBY ORDERED that:

   a. The above-entitled bankruptcy case be, and the same is hereby reopened pursuant to 11 U.S.C. § 350(b) and F.R.B.P. 5010;
   b. A trustee shall not be appointed in this case absent further order of the Court;
   c. The deadline for the Debtor(s) to file the OF 23 is extended 30 days from the date of entry of this order;
   d. If the Debtor(s) is/are otherwise eligible, upon the filing of the OF 23, the clerk shall enter the discharge of the Debtor(s) and close the case; and
   e. In the event the OF 23 is not filed, the case shall be closed immediately after the expiration of 30 days from the date of entry of this order.

2. ☐ IT IS HEREBY ORDERED that the motion is denied without prejudice on the following grounds (*specify*):
   ☐ See Attached Page

   ____
   ____

3. ☐ This matter is set for hearing as follows:

   Date: *Time:* *Ctrm:*

4. ☐ Notice is required as follows (*specify*): ☐ See Attached Page

   ____
   ____
   ____

This form is mandatory by Order of the United States Bankruptcy Court for the Central District of California.

CDCAL-537 C.D. CALIFORNIA

Order on Debtor's Motion to Reopen Case and for Extension of Time to File Debtor's Certification of Completion of Postpetition Instructional Course Concerning Personal Financial Management - Page 2

In re	CHAPTER:
Debtor(s).	CASE NO.:

5. ☐ The Court Further orders as follows *(specify)*: ☐ See Attached Page

____

____

____

Dated:

____
UNITED STATES BANKRUPTCY JUDGE

PROOF OF SERVICE BY MAIL

STATE OF CALIFORNIA
COUNTY OF ______________________

I am employed in the above County, State of California. I am over the age of 18 and not a party to the within action. My business address is as follows:

On ______________________, I served the foregoing document described as : ORDER ON DEBTOR'S MOTION TO REOPEN CASE AND FOR EXTENSION OF TIME TO FILE DEBTOR'S CERTIFICATION OF COMPLETION OF POSTPETITION INSTRUCTIONAL COURSE CONCERNING PERSONAL FINANCIAL MANAGEMENT on the chapter ___ trustee and the United States Trustee at their last known addresses by placing a true and correct copy thereof in a sealed envelope with postage thereon fully prepaid in the United States Mail at ______________________, California, addressed as follows:

I declare under penalty of perjury under the laws of the United States of America that the foregoing is true and correct.

Dated:

______________________ ______________________
Type Name *Signature*

CHAPTER 13 PLAN (F 3015–1.1)

Name ____________________________

Address ____________________________

____

Telephone ______________ (FAX) ______________

Email Address ______________

☐ Attorney for Debtor
State Bar No. ______________

☐ Debtor in Pro Se (Any reference to the singular shall include the plural in the case of joint debtors.)

UNITED STATES BANKRUPTCY COURT CENTRAL DISTRICT OF CALIFORNIA	
List all names (including trade names) used by the debtor within the last 8 years:	Chapter 13 Case No.: **CHAPTER 13 PLAN** **CREDITOR'S MEETING:** **Date:** **Time:** **Place:** **CONFIRMATION HEARING:** **Date:** **Time:** **Place:**

NOTICE

This Chapter 13 Plan is proposed by the above Debtor. The Debtor attests that the information stated in this Plan is accurate. Creditors cannot vote on this Plan. However, creditors may object to this Plan being confirmed pursuant to 11 U.S.C. §1324. Any objection must be in writing and must be filed with the court and served upon the Debtor, Debtor's attorney (if any), and the Chapter 13 Trustee not less than 8 days before the date set for the meeting of creditors. Unless an objection is filed and served, the court may confirm this Plan. The Plan, if confirmed, modifies the rights and duties of the Debtor and creditors to the treatment provided in the Plan as confirmed, with the following IMPORTANT EXCEPTIONS:

Unless otherwise provided by law, each creditor will retain its lien until the earlier of payment of the underlying debt determined under non-bankruptcy law or discharge under 11 U.S.C.§1328. If the case under this chapter is dismissed or converted without completion of the Plan, such lien shall also be retained by such holder to the extent recognized by applicable non-bankruptcy law.

Defaults will be cured using the interest rate set forth below in the Plan. Any ongoing obligation will be paid according to the terms of the Plan.

HOLDERS OF SECURED CLAIMS AND CLASS 1 CLAIMANTS WILL BE PAID ACCORDING TO THIS PLAN AFTER CONFIRMATION UNLESS THE SECURED CREDITOR OR CLASS 1 CLAIMANT FILES A PROOF OF CLAIM IN A DIFFERENT AMOUNT THAN THAT PROVIDED IN THE PLAN. If a secured creditor or a class 1 creditor files a proof of claim, that creditor will be paid according to that creditor's proof of claim, unless the court orders otherwise.

HOLDERS OF ALL OTHER CLAIMS MUST TIMELY FILE PROOFS OF CLAIMS, IF THE CODE SO REQUIRES, OR THEY WILL NOT BE PAID ANY AMOUNT. A Debtor who confirms a Plan may be eligible thereafter to receive a discharge of debts to the extent specified in 11 U.S.C. § 1328.

The Debtor proposes the following Plan and makes the following declarations:

I. PROPERTY AND FUTURE EARNINGS OR INCOME SUBJECT TO THE SUPERVISION AND CONTROL OF THE CHAPTER 13 TRUSTEE

The Debtor submits the following to the supervision and control of the Chapter 13 Trustee:

A. Payments by Debtor of $____________ per month for _____months. This monthly Plan Payment will begin within 30 days of the date the petition was filed.

B. The base plan amount is $____________ which is estimated to pay ________% of the allowed claims of nonpriority unsecured creditors. If that percentage is less than 100%, the Debtor will pay the Plan Payment stated in this Plan for the full term of the Plan or until the base plan amount is paid in full, and the Chapter 13 Trustee may increase the percentage to be paid to creditors accordingly.

C. Amounts necessary for the payment of post petition claims allowed under 11 U.S.C. §1305.

D. Preconfirmation adequate protection payments for any creditor who holds an allowed claim secured by personal property where such security interest is attributable to the purchase of such property and preconfirmation payments on leases of personal property whose allowed claim is impaired by the terms proposed in the plan. Preconfirmation adequate protection payments and preconfirmation lease payments will be paid to the Chapter 13 Trustee for the following creditor(s) in the following amounts:

Creditor/Lessor Name	Collateral Description	Last 4 Digits of Account #	Amount
			$
			$
			$

Each adequate protection payment or preconfirmation lease payment will commence on or before the 30th day from the date of filing of the case. The Chapter 13 Trustee shall deduct the foregoing adequate protection payment(s) and/or preconfirmation lease payment from the Debtor's Plan Payment and disburse the adequate protection payment or preconfirmation lease payment to the secured(s) creditor(s) at the next available disbursement or as soon as practicable after the payment is received and posted to the Chapter 13 Trustee's account. The Chapter 13 Trustee will take his or her statutory fee on all disbursements made for preconfirmation adequate protection payments or preconfirmation lease payments.

E. Other property: ____
(specify property or indicate none)

II. ORDER OF PAYMENTS; CLASSIFICATION AND TREATMENT OF CLAIMS:

Except as otherwise provided in the Plan or by court order, the Chapter 13 Trustee shall disburse all available funds for the payment of claims as follows:

A. ORDER OF PAYMENTS:

1. If there are Domestic Support Obligations, the order of priority shall be:

   (a) Domestic Support Obligations and the Chapter 13 Trustee's fee not exceeding the amount accrued on payments made to date;

   (b) Administrative expenses (Class 1(a)) in an amount not exceeding _______ % of each Plan Payment until paid in full;

2. If there are no Domestic Support Obligations, the order of priority shall be the Chapter 13 Trustee's fee not exceeding the amount accrued on payments made to date, and administrative expenses (Class 1(a)) in an amount not exceeding _____ % of each Plan Payment until paid in full.

3. Notwithstanding 1 and 2 above, ongoing payments on secured debts that are to be made by the Chapter 13 Trustee from the Plan Payment; such secured debt may be paid by the Chapter 13 Trustee commencing with the inception of Plan Payments.

4. Subject to 1, 2, and 3 above, pro rata to all other claims except as otherwise provided in the Plan.

5. No payment shall be made on nonpriority unsecured claims until all secured and priority claims have been paid in full.

B. CLASSIFICATION AND TREATMENT OF CLAIMS:

CLASS 1

ALLOWED UNSECURED CLAIMS ENTITLED TO PRIORITY UNDER 11 U.S.C. §507

The Debtor will pay Class 1 claims in full; except the debtor may provide for less than full payment of Domestic Support Obligations pursuant to 11 U.S.C. §1322(a)(4).

CATEGORY	AMOUNT OF PRIORITY CLAIM	INTEREST RATE, if any	MONTHLY PAYMENT	NUMBER OF MONTHS	TOTAL PAYMENT
a. Administrative Expenses					
(1) Chapter 13 Trustee's Fee – estimated at 11% of all payments to be made to all classes through this Plan.					
(2) Attorney's Fees	$		$		$
(3) Chapter 7 Trustee's Fees (Specify Trustee Name)	$		$		$
(4) Other	$		$		$
b. Other Priority Claims					
(1) Internal Revenue Service	$	%	$		$
(2) Franchise Tax Board	$	%	$		$
(3) Domestic Support Obligation	$	%	$		$
(4) Other	$	%	$		$
c. Domestic Support Obligations that are not to be paid in full in the Plan (Specify Creditor Name):					
	$	%	$		$

CLASS 2

CLAIMS SECURED SOLELY BY PROPERTY THAT IS THE DEBTOR'S PRINCIPAL RESIDENCE ON WHICH OBLIGATION MATURES AFTER THE FINAL PLAN PAYMENT IS DUE

1. ☐ The post-confirmation monthly mortgage payment will be made by the Chapter 13 Trustee from the Plan Payment to:
2. ☐ The post-confirmation monthly mortgage payment will be made by the Debtor directly to:

_______________ (name of creditor) _______________ (last 4 digits of account number)

_______________ (name of creditor) _______________ (last 4 digits of account number)

The Debtor will cure all prepetition arrearages for the primary residence through the Plan Payment as set forth below.

Name of Creditor	Last Four Digits of Account Number	Cure of Default				
		AMOUNT OF ARREARAGE	INTEREST RATE	MONTHLY PAYMENT	NUMBER OF MONTHS	TOTAL PAYMENT
		$	%	$		$
		$	%	$		$

CLASS 3

CLAIMS SECURED BY REAL OR PERSONAL PROPERTY WHICH ARE PAID IN FULL DURING THE TERM OF THE PLAN

Name of Creditor	Last Four Digits of Account No.	CLAIM TOTAL	SECURED CLAIM AMOUNT	INTEREST RATE	Equal Monthly Payment	NUMBER OF MONTHS	TOTAL PAYMENT
		$	$	%	$		$
		$	$	%	$		$

CLASS 4

OTHER SECURED CLAIMS ON WHICH THE LAST PAYMENT IS DUE AFTER THE DATE ON WHICH THE FINAL PAYMENT UNDER THE PLAN IS DUE

1. ☐ The post-confirmation monthly payment pursuant to the promissory note will be made by the Chapter 13 Trustee from the Plan Payment to:
2. ☐ The post-confirmation monthly payment pursuant to the promissory note will be made by the Debtor directly to:

____________________ (name of creditor) ________________ (last 4 digits of account number)

____________________ (name of creditor) ________________ (last 4 digits of account number)

The Debtor will cure all prepetition arrearages on these claims through the Plan Payment as set forth below.

Name of Creditor	Last Four Digits of Account Number	Cure of Default				
		AMOUNT OF ARREARAGE	INTEREST RATE	MONTHLY PAYMENT	NUMBER OF MONTHS	TOTAL PAYMENT
		$	%	$		$
		$	%	$		$

CLASS 5

NON-PRIORITY UNSECURED CLAIMS

The Debtor estimates that non-priority unsecured claims total the sum of $____________.

Class 5 claims will be paid as follows:

(Check one box only.)

☐ Class 5 claims (including allowed unsecured amounts from Class 3) are of one class and will be paid pro rata.

OR

☐ Class 5 claims will be divided into subclasses as shown on the attached exhibit (which also shows the justification for the differentiation among the subclasses) and the creditors in each subclass will be paid pro rata.

III. COMPARISON WITH CHAPTER 7

The value as of the effective date of the Plan of property to be distributed under the Plan on account of each allowed claim is not less than the amount that would be paid on such claim if the estate of the Debtor were liquidated under chapter 7 of the Bankruptcy Code on such date. The amount distributed to nonpriority unsecured creditors in chapter 7 would be $_________ which is estimated to pay ________% of the scheduled nonpriority unsecured debt.

IV. PLAN ANALYSIS

CLASS 1a	$
CLASS 1b	$
CLASS 1c	$
CLASS 2	$
CLASS 3	$
CLASS 4	$
CLASS 5	$
SUB-TOTAL	$
CHAPTER 13 TRUSTEE'S FEE (Estimated 11% unless advised otherwise)	$
TOTAL PAYMENT	$

V. OTHER PROVISIONS

A. The Debtor rejects the following executory contracts and unexpired leases.

___

B. The Debtor assumes the executory contracts or unexpired leases set forth in this section. As to each contract or lease assumed, any defaults therein and Debtor's proposal for cure of said default(s) is described in Class 4 of this Plan. The Debtor has a leasehold interest in personal property and will make all post-petition payments directly to the lessor(s):

___

C. In addition to the payments specified in Class 2 and Class 4, the Debtor will make regular payments, including any preconfirmation payments, directly to the following:

___

D. The Debtor hereby surrenders the following personal or real property. (Identify property and creditor to which it is surrendered.)

___

E. The Debtor shall incur no debt greater than $500.00 without prior court approval unless the debt is incurred in the ordinary course of business pursuant to 11 U.S.C. §1304(b) or for medical emergencies.

F. Miscellaneous provisions: (Use Attachment, if necessary)

___

G. The Chapter 13 Trustee is authorized to disburse funds after the date confirmation is announced in open court.

H. The Debtor will pay timely all post-confirmation tax liabilities directly to the appropriate taxing authorities as they come due.

I. The Debtor will pay all amounts required to be paid under a Domestic Support Obligation that first became payable after the date of the filing of the petition.

VI. REVESTING OF PROPERTY

Property of the estate shall not revest in the Debtor until such time as a discharge is granted or the case is dismissed or closed without discharge. Revestment shall be subject to all liens and encumbrances in existence when the case was filed, except those liens avoided by court order or extinguished by operation of law. In the event the case is converted to a case under chapter 7, 11, or 12 of the Bankruptcy Code, the property of the estate shall vest in accordance with applicable law. After confirmation of the Plan, the Chapter 13 Trustee shall have no further authority or fiduciary duty regarding use, sale, or refinance of property of the estate except to respond to any motion for proposed use, sale, or refinance as required by the Local Bankruptcy Rules. Prior to any discharge or dismissal, the Debtor must seek approval of the court to purchase, sell, or refinance real property.

Dated: ______________________

____
Attorney for Debtor

____
Debtor

____
Joint debtor

ADDENDUM TO CHAPTER 13 PLAN (F3015-1.1A)

Attorney or Party Name, Address, Telephone & FAX Numbers, and California State Bar Number ☐ Individual appearing without counsel ☐ Attorney for:	FOR COURT USE ONLY
UNITED STATES BANKRUPTCY COURT **CENTRAL DISTRICT OF CALIFORNIA**	
In re Debtor(s).	CHAPTER 13 CASE NO.

Addendum to Chapter 13 Plan Concerning Debtors Who are Repaying Debt Secured by a Mortgage on Real Property or a Lien on Personal Property the Debtor Occupies as the Debtor's Principal Residence

(A) **Scope: Consumer Debts Secured by a Mortgage on Real Property, or Secured by Manufactured Housing that the Debtor Occupies as the Debtor's Principal Residence**

(1) For purposes of this Addendum, which is incorporated into the debtor's chapter 13 plan (the "Plan"), the term "Mortgage Creditor" includes all creditors whose claims represent consumer debts secured in whole or in part by a security interest in real property or manufactured housing, which real property or manufactured housing constitutes the debtor's principal residence. The provisions of this Addendum are effective until the earlier of: (a) dismissal of the case; (b) the closing of the case; (c) entry of an order granting the debtor a discharge; and (d) entry of an order terminating the automatic stay under 11 U.S.C. § 362(d) as the stay applies to the Mortgage Creditor.

(2) Except as provided in paragraphs (3) and (4) below, if the Mortgage Creditor provided monthly statements to the debtor pre-petition, the Mortgage Creditor must provide monthly statements to the debtor. The monthly statements must contain at least the following information concerning post-petition mortgage payments to be made outside the Plan:

In re	CHAPTER 13
Debtor(s).	CASE NUMBER

(a) The date of the statement and the date the next payment is due;

(b) The amount of the current monthly payment;

(c) The portion of the payment attributable to escrow, if any;

(d) The post-petition amount past due, if any, and from what date;

(e) Any outstanding post-petition late charges;

(f) The amount and date of receipt of all payments received since the date of the last statement;

(g) A telephone number and contact information that the debtor or the debtor's attorney may use to obtain reasonably prompt information regarding the loan and recent transactions; and

(h) The proper payment address.

(3) No monthly statement will be required in this case where post-petition mortgage payments are to be made to the chapter 13 trustee through the Plan, unless the amount of the monthly payment is scheduled to change (because of adjustable interest rate, charges paid by the Mortgage Creditor for taxes, insurance, attorney's fees or any other expenses or fees charged or incurred by the Mortgage Creditor, such as property inspection fees, servicing fees or appraisal fees). If a Mortgage Creditor does send a monthly statement to the debtor or the chapter 13 trustee and the statement complies with subsection (B)(2) below, the Mortgage Creditor is entitled to the protections set out in such subsection.

(4) If, pre-petition, the Mortgage Creditor provided the debtor with "coupon books" or some other pre-printed, bundled evidence of payments due, the Mortgage Creditor is not required to provide monthly statements under subsection (2) of this section. However, the Mortgage Creditor must supply the debtor with additional coupon books as needed or requested in writing by the debtor. If a Mortgage Creditor does send a monthly statement to the debtor or the chapter 13 trustee and the statement complies with subsection (B)(2) below, the Mortgage Creditor is entitled to the protections set out in such subsection.

(5) The Mortgage Creditor must provide the following information to the debtor upon the reasonable written request of the debtor:

(a) The principal balance of the loan;

(b) The original maturity date;

(c) The current interest rate;

In re	CHAPTER 13
Debtor(s).	CASE NUMBER

(d) The current escrow balance, if any;

(e) The interest paid year to date; and

(f) The property taxes paid year to date, if any.

(6) The Mortgage Creditor must provide the following information to the debtor, the debtor's attorney and, when the debtor is making ongoing mortgage or arrearage payments through the chapter 13 trustee, the chapter 13 trustee, at least quarterly, and upon reasonable written request of the debtor or the chapter 13 trustee: (a) any other amounts due or proposed change in payments arising from an adjustable interest rate, charges paid by the Mortgage Creditor for taxes, insurance, attorney's fees or any other expenses or fees charged or incurred by the Mortgage Creditor, such as property inspection fees, servicing fees or appraisal fees; (b) the nature of the expense or charge; and (c) the date of the payment.

(7) If the secured consumer debt payable to the Mortgage Creditor is not modified by or paid through the Plan and the Mortgage Creditor believes the debtor to be in default, the Mortgage Creditor must send a letter alleging such default to the debtor and the debtor's attorney upon any perceived or actual default by the debtor and before taking any steps to modify the automatic stay.

(B) **Form of Communication; Modification of the Automatic Stay; and Motions for Order to Show Cause**

(1) For the purposes of this Addendum, Mortgage Creditors will be considered to have sent the requisite documents or monthly statements to the debtor or the debtor's attorney, as applicable, when the Mortgage Creditor has placed the required document in any form of communication, which in the usual course would result in the debtor and the debtor's attorney receiving the document, to the address that the debtor and the debtor's attorney last provided to the Court. The form of communication may include, but is not limited to, electronic communication, United States Postal Service or use of a similar commercial communications carrier.

(2) To the extent that the automatic stay arising in this case would otherwise prohibit such conduct, the automatic stay is modified as follows: Mortgage Creditors who provide account information or monthly statements under subsections (A)(1-6) above will not be found to have violated the automatic stay by doing so, and Mortgage Creditors may contact the debtor about the status of insurance coverage on property that is collateral for the Mortgage Creditor's claim, may respond to inquiries and requests for information about the account from the debtor and may send the debtor statements, payment coupons or other correspondence that the Mortgage Creditor sends to its non-debtor customers, without violating the automatic stay. <u>In order for communication to be protected under this provision, the communication must indicate it is provided for information purposes and does not constitute demand for payment</u>.

In re	CHAPTER 13
Debtor(s).	CASE NUMBER

(3) As a result of a Mortgage Creditor's alleged non-compliance with this Addendum, the debtor may file a Motion for Order to Show Cause in compliance with Local Bankruptcy Rule 9020-1 no earlier than sixty days after the Mortgage Creditor's failure to comply with sections (A) or (B). Before filing the motion, the debtor must make good faith attempts in writing to contact the Mortgage Creditor and to determine the cause of any non-compliance, and must indicate in the Motion for Order to Show Cause the good faith steps taken, together with a summary description of any response provided by the Mortgage Creditor.

(4) If a Mortgage Creditor's regular billing system can provide a statement to the debtor that substantially complies with this Addendum, but does not fully conform to all of its requirements, the Mortgage Creditor may request that the debtor accept such statement. If the debtor declines to accept the non-conforming statement, a Mortgage Creditor may file a motion, on notice to the debtor, the debtor's attorney and the chapter 13 trustee, seeking a declaration of the Court that cause exists to allow such non-conforming statements to satisfy the Mortgage Creditor's obligations under this Addendum. For good cause shown, the Court may grant a waiver for purposes of this case and for either a limited or unlimited period of time.

In re	CHAPTER 13
Debtor(s).	CASE NUMBER

Instructions for Attaching

Addendum to Chapter 13 Plan Concerning Debtors who are Repaying Debt Secured by a Mortgage on Real Property or a Lien on Personal Property the Debtor Occupies as the Debtor's Principal Residence

This optional addendum concerns chapter 13 debtors who are repaying debt secured by a mortgage on real property or a lien on personal property the debtor occupies as the debtor's principal residence.

A chapter 13 debtor may attach this addendum to his/her chapter 13 plan. This is a court-approved form and may not be altered, except for interlineations clearly marked on the court-approved form which are subject to the Court's review and approval upon consideration of the plan for confirmation. When attaching this form to the chapter 13 plan form (F 3015-1.1), the debtor must indicate in section V.F. (Page 6) of the chapter 13 plan form that the "Addendum to Chapter 13 Plan (F 3015-1.1A) is attached."

DEBTOR'S CERTIFICATION OF COMPLIANCE UNDER 11 U.S.C. § 1328(A) AND APPLICATION FOR ENTRY OF DISCHARGE

Attorney or Party Name, Address, Telephone & FAX Numbers, and California State Bar Number ☐ Individual appearing without counsel ☐ Attorney for:	FOR COURT USE ONLY
UNITED STATES BANKRUPTCY COURT **CENTRAL DISTRICT OF CALIFORNIA**	
In re: Debtor	CHAPTER 13 CASE NO.:

DEBTORS CERTIFICATION OF COMPLIANCE UNDER 11 U.S.C. § 1328(a) AND APPLICATION FOR ENTRY OF DISCHARGE

(In a joint bankruptcy case, each co-debtor must file a separate Certificate of Compliance and Application for Entry of Discharge.)

The debtor in the above-captioned bankruptcy case certifies:

1. ☐ I have completed all payments required by my confirmed plan, including all domestic support obligations, if any.

2. ☐ I have made all domestic support payments required by a judicial or administrative order, or by statute which have come due since the filing of this case.

3. ☐ My address is: ____.

4. ☐ My most recent employer's name and address are:
____
____

5. ☐ The following creditors hold debts which have been determined to be nondischargeable under 11 U.S.C. §523(a)(2) or (a)(4):
____
____

6. ☐ The following creditors hold debts which have I have reaffirmed in writing:
____
____

7. ☐ I have not executed a written waiver of discharge in this case.

8. ☐ I have not received a discharge in a case filed under chapter 7, 11, or 12 during the 4-year period preceding the date of the order for relief under chapter 13 in the present case.

9. ☐ I have not received a discharge in a case filed under chapter 13 during the 2-year period preceding the date of the order for relief under chapter 13 in the present case.

CDCAL-551 C.D. CALIFORNIA

Debtors Certification of Compliance Under 11 U.S.C. § 1328(a) and Application for Entry of Discharge   2006 USBC Central District of California

In re (SHORT TITLE)	CHAPTER 13
Debtor	CASE NO.:

10. ☐ Since the filing of this case:

☐ I have completed an instructional course concerning personal financial management approved by the United States Trustee.
A copy of the certificate of completion is attached hereto.

☐ I have been excused from compliance with the requirement to complete an instructional course concerning financial management approved by the United States Trustee.

11. ☐ I have not exempted more than $125,000 in any of the following:
(a) real or personal property used as a residence by me or any of my dependents, OR
(b) in a cooperative that owns property used as a residence by me or any of my dependents, OR
(c) in a burial plot for me or any of my dependents, OR
(d) in any real or personal property in which I or any of my dependents has claimed as a homestead.

12. You must answer the following inquiries ONLY if you have exempted more than $125,000 in property described in Question 11 above

A. The property is reasonably necessary for my support and the support of my dependents.

B. ☐ I was not convicted of a felony before the filing of this case.
☐ I was convicted of a felony before the filing of this case.
☐ I have been convicted of a felony during the pendency of this case.
☐ I am not aware of any pending proceeding in which I may be found guilty of a felony.

Please describe the circumstances: ______________________________

____
(additional sheet may be attached if necessary)

C. I owe a debt arising from one or more of the following:
☐ a violation of federal or state securities laws or regulations or orders issued under federal or state securities laws;
☐ fraud, deceit or manipulation in connection with the sale or purchase of any registered security;
☐ a civil remedy under section 1964 of title 18; or
☐ a criminal act, intentional tort, or willful or reckless misconduct that caused serious physical injury or death to another individual in the preceding 5 years.
☐ none of the above.

D. I am not aware of any pending proceeding in which I may be found liable for a debt of the kind described in Statement No. 12(C) above.

I declare under penalty of perjury that the foregoing is true and correct.

Date:________________ Debtor's Signature ______________________________

Debtors Certification of Compliance Under 11 U.S.C. § 1328 (a) and Application for Entry Discharge (Interim Case)

Attorney or Party Name, Address, Telephone & FAX Numbers, and California State Bar Number ☐ *Individual appearing without counsel* ☐ *Attorney for:*	FOR COURT USE ONLY
UNITED STATES BANKRUPTCY COURT CENTRAL DISTRICT OF CALIFORNIA	
In re: Debtor	CHAPTER 13 CASE NO.:

DEBTOR'S CERTIFICATION OF COMPLIANCE UNDER 11 U.S.C. § 1328(a) AND APPLICATION FOR ENTRY OF DISCHARGE (INTERIM CASE)[1]

(In a joint bankruptcy case, each co-debtor must file a separate Certificate of Compliance and Application for Entry of Discharge (Interim Case).)

The debtor in the above-captioned bankruptcy case certifies:

1. ☐ I have completed all payments required by my confirmed plan.

2. ☐ My address is: ______________________.

3. ☐ My most recent employer's name and address are:
____
____

4. ☐ I have not executed a written waiver of discharge in this case.

5. ☐ I have not exempted more than $125,000 in any of the following:
   (a) real or personal property used as a residence by me or any of my dependents, OR
   (b) in a cooperative that owns property used as a residence by me or any of my dependents, OR
   (c) in a burial plot for me or any of my dependents, OR
   (d) in any real or personal property which I or any of my dependents has claimed as a homestead.

6. You must answer the following inquiries ONLY if you have exempted more than $125,000 in property described in Question 5 above.

   A. The property is reasonably necessary for my support and the support of my dependents.

[1]An "interim case" is a case commenced on or after April 20, 2005 but before October 17, 2005.

In re (SHORT TITLE)	CHAPTER 13
Debtor	CASE NO.:

B. ☐ I was not convicted of a felony before the filing of this case.
☐ I was convicted of a felony before the filing of this case.
☐ I have been convicted of a felony during the pendency of this case.
☐ I am not aware of any pending proceeding in which I may be found guilty of a felony.

Please describe the circumstances:
____
____
(additional sheet may be attached if necessary)

C. I owe a debt arising from one or more of the following:
☐ a violation of federal or state securities laws or regulations or orders issued under federal or state securities laws;
☐ fraud, deceit or manipulation in connection with the sale or purchase of any registered security;
☐ a civil remedy under section 1964 of title 18; or
☐ a criminal act, intentional tort, or willful or reckless misconduct that caused serious physical injury or death to another individual in the preceding 5 years.
☐ none of the above.

D. I am not aware of any pending proceeding in which I may be found liable for a debt of the kind described in Statement No. 6(C) above.

I declare under penalty of perjury that the foregoing is true and correct.

Date:________________ Debtor's Signature____________________________________

DEBTOR'S CERTIFICATION OF EMPLOYMENT INCOME PURSUANT TO 11 USC § 521(A)(1)(B)(IV)

February 2006 | 2006 USBC Central District of California

UNITED STATES BANKRUPTCY COURT CENTRAL DISTRICT OF CALIFORNIA	
In re Debtor(s).	CHAPTER: CASE NO.:

DEBTOR'S CERTIFICATION OF EMPLOYMENT INCOME PURSUANT TO 11 U.S.C. § 521(a)(1)(B)(iv)

Please fill out the following blank(s) and check the box next to one of the following statements:

I, ______________________________, the debtor in this case, declare under penalty
(Print Name of Debtor)

of perjury under the laws of the United States of America that:

☐ I have attached to this certificate copies of my pay stubs, pay advices and/or other proof of employment income for the 60-day period prior to the date of the filing of my bankruptcy petition.
(*NOTE: the filer is responsible for blacking out the Social Security number on pay stubs prior to filing them.*)

☐ I was self-employed for the entire 60-day period prior to the date of the filing of my bankruptcy petition, and received no payment from any other employer.

☐ I was unemployed for the entire 60-day period prior to the date of the filing of my bankruptcy petition.

I, ______________________________, the debtor in this case, declare under penalty of
(Print Name of Joint Debtor, if any)

perjury under the laws of the United States of America that:

☐ I have attached to this certificate copies of my pay stubs, pay advices and/or other proof of employment income for the 60-day period prior to the date of the filing of my bankruptcy petition.
(*NOTE: the filer is responsible for blacking out the Social Security number on pay stubs prior to filing them.*)

☐ I was self-employed for the entire 60-day period prior to the date of the filing of my bankruptcy petition, and received no payment from any other employer.

☐ I was unemployed for the entire 60-day period prior to the date of the filing of my bankruptcy petition.

Date ____________________ Signature ______________________________
Debtor

Date ____________________ Signature ______________________________
Joint Debtor (if any)

Debtor's Further Certification of Cure of Monetary Default Underlying Judgment for Possession of Residential Property and Proof of Deposit (11 U.S.C. § 362(l)(2)) (F 4001-1.2)

Attorney or Party Name, Address, Telephone & FAX Numbers, and California State Bar Number ☐ *Attorney for:* ☐ *Individual debtor appearing without counsel* (Pro Se Debtor)	FOR COURT USE ONLY
UNITED STATES BANKRUPTCY COURT CENTRAL DISTRICT OF CALIFORNIA	
In re: Debtor(s).	CHAPTER: CASE NO.: **DEBTOR'S FURTHER CERTIFICATION OF CURE OF MONETARY DEFAULT UNDERLYING JUDGMENT FOR POSSESSION OF RESIDENTIAL PROPERTY AND PROOF OF DEPOSIT (11 U.S.C. § 362(l)(2))**

NOTE: THIS FURTHER CERTIFICATION MUST BE FILED WITHIN 30 DAYS OF THE FILING OF DEBTOR'S PETITION.

Concerning the residential property commonly known as:________________________________("Property")
(Complete Address)

Debtor(s) certifies: *(Check all that apply)*

1. ☐ Debtor(s) has filed and served the "Debtor's Certification that Circumstances Exist Which Would Allow Cure of Monetary Default Underlying Judgment for Possession of Residential Property and Proof of Deposit" ("Original Certification") on__________(date Original Certification was filed and served) together with Debtor(s)' petition. A copy of the Original Certification is attached as Exhibit____.

2. ☐ Debtor(s), or an adult dependent of Debtor, on the date of the petition, deposited the sum of $ 50,000.00 representing total rent which would have become due under the lease of the property for the 30-day period beginning on the date the petition in this bankruptcy was filed.

3. To Debtor's knowledge, Lessor ☐ has ☐ has not filed an Objection to the Original Certification.

4. ☐ Debtor(s) has cured, under nonbankruptcy law, the entire monetary default that gave rise to the judgment under which possession is sought by the lessor.

5. ☐ Debtor(s) is entitled to relief from the judgment for possession of the property by reason of the following facts and nonbankrutpcy law: *(Check all that apply)*
   - ☐ California Civil Code § 3275
   - ☐ California Code of Civil Procedure § 1174(c)
   - ☐ California Code of Civil Procedure § 1179
   - ☐ Other: ________________________________

   ☐ supporting memorandum of points and authorities attached

(Continued on next page)

In re (SHORT TITLE)	CHAPTER:
Debtor(s).	CASE NO.:

6. Debtor is entitled to relief from the judgment for possession of the property by reason of the following facts:____ ☐ continuation page attached.

7. Debtor ☐ has ☐ has not filed and served herewith further supporting declarations.

8. Debtor ☐ has ☐ has not filed and served herewith a supporting memorandum of points and authorities.

Declaration of Debtor

I, ______________________, am the debtor in these proceedings. I declare under penalty of perjury that I have read the foregoing, including all continuation pages, and that all statements therein are true and correct.

Executed this __________ day of ______________ (Month), __________ (Year) at ____________________.

____
Signature of Debtor

____
Print Name of Debtor

____
Print the Name of the Law Firm Representing the Debtor (if applicable)

____
Signature of the Attorney Representing the Debtor (if applicable)

____
Print the Name of the Attorney Representing the Debtor (if applicable)

In re (SHORT TITLE)	CHAPTER:
Debtor(s).	CASE NO.:

NOTE: When using this form to indicate service of a proposed order, **DO NOT** list any person or entity in Category I. Proposed orders do not generate an NEF because only orders that have been entered are placed on a CM/ECF docket.

PROOF OF SERVICE OF DOCUMENT

I am over the age of 18 and not a party to this bankruptcy case or adversary proceeding. My business address is:

A true and correct copy of the foregoing document described as ______________________________ ______________________________ will be served or was served **(a)** on the judge in chambers in the form and manner required by LBR 5005-2(d), and **(b)** in the manner indicated below:

I. <u>TO BE SERVED BY THE COURT VIA NOTICE OF ELECTRONIC FILING ("NEF")</u> - Pursuant to controlling General Order(s) and Local Bankruptcy Rule(s) ("LBR"), the foregoing document will be served by the court via NEF and hyperlink to the document. On ____________________ I checked the CM/ECF docket for this bankruptcy case or adversary proceeding and determined that the following person(s) are on the Electronic Mail Notice List to receive NEF transmission at the email addressed indicated below:

☐ Service information continued on attached page

II. <u>SERVED BY U.S. MAIL OR OVERNIGHT MAIL</u> <u>(indicate method for each person or entity served)</u>:
On ____________________ I served the following person(s) and/or entity(ies) at the last known address(es) in this bankruptcy case or adversary proceeding by placing a true and correct copy thereof in a sealed envelope in the United States Mail, first class, postage prepaid, and/or with an overnight mail service addressed as follow. Listing the judge here constitutes a declaration that mailing to the judge <u>will be</u> completed no later than 24 hours after the document is filed.

☐ Service information continued on attached page

III. <u>SERVED BY PERSONAL DELIVERY, FACSIMILE TRANSMISSION OR EMAIL</u> <u>(indicate method for each person or entity served)</u>: Pursuant to F.R.Civ.P. 5 and/or controlling LBR, on ____________________ I served the following person(s) and/or entity(ies) by personal delivery, or (for those who consented in writing to such service method) by facsimile transmission and/or email as follows. Listing the judge here constitutes a declaration that mailing to the judge <u>will be</u> completed no later than 24 hours after the document is filed.

☐ Service information continued on attached page

I declare under penalty of perjury under the laws of the United States of America that the foregoing is true and correct.

Date	*Type Name*	*Signature*

This form is optional. It has been approved by the United States Bankruptcy Court for the Central District of California.

In re (SHORT TITLE)	CHAPTER:
Debtor(s).	CASE NO.:

ADDITIONAL SERVICE INFORMATION (if needed):

CDCAL-559 C.D. CALIFORNIA

Debtor's Motion for Authority to Incur Debt (Personal Property) (F 3015-1.17)

Attorney or Party Name, Address, Telephone & FAX Numbers, and California State Bar Number ☐ Attorney for ☐ Pro Se Debtor	FOR COURT USE ONLY
UNITED STATES BANKRUPTCY COURT CENTRAL DISTRICT OF CALIFORNIA	CHAPTER 13 CASE NUMBER
In re: Debtor(s).	**DEBTOR'S MOTION FOR AUTHORITY TO INCUR DEBT [PERSONAL PROPERTY]** (No Hearing Required)

Debtor moves this Court for an order authorizing the debtor to incur debt pursuant to the terms and conditions described herein.

1. Debtor's Chapter 13 Plan (the "Plan"), providing for a payment in the amount of $________ per month for ________ months, was confirmed on: ____________________.

2. Debtor desires to purchase:____________________________
____
Copies of the proposed purchase and loan agreements are attached as Exhibit "A."

3. The purchase price of the ____________________ is $__________ from
Dealership/Store name: ____________________
Address: ____________________
____________________.

4. After the loan is made and any down payment is credited, there will remain owing on the loan the sum of $____________, to be paid over ______ months at $________ per month.

5. Debtor desires to acquire the property to be financed for the following reasons:
____
____
____
____
____
(Please attach additional pages if needed.)

Debtor's Motion For Authority to Incur Debt - *Page 2* **F 3015-1.17**

In re:	CHAPTER 13
Debtor(s).	CASE NUMBER

6. Debtor's monthly income at this time (take home pay plus any other income received) is $_______________.
   Debtor's monthly expenses at this time (**excluding** the Plan payment and the contemplated monthly finance payment) total $ _______________.

   The attached *Declaration of Current/Post-Petition Income* and *Declaration of Current/Post-Petition Expenses* accurately reflect Debtor's monthly income and expenses at this time.

Dated:____________________________ ____
Attorney for Debtor(s)

I declare under penalty of perjury that the foregoing is true and correct.

Dated:____________________________ ____
Debtor

Dated:____________________________ ____
Joint Debtor

In re:	CHAPTER 13
Debtor(s).	CASE NUMBER

NOTE: When using this form to indicate service of a proposed order, **DO NOT** list any person or entity in Category I. Proposed orders do not generate an NEF because only orders that have been entered are placed on a CM/ECF docket.

PROOF OF SERVICE OF DOCUMENT

I am over the age of 18 and not a party to this bankruptcy case or adversary proceeding. My business address is:

A true and correct copy of the foregoing document described as ______________________________ ______________________________ will be served or was served **(a)** on the judge in chambers in the form and manner required by LBR 5005-2(d), and **(b)** in the manner indicated below:
QWRERWER

I. <u>TO BE SERVED BY THE COURT VIA NOTICE OF ELECTRONIC FILING ("NEF")</u> - Pursuant to controlling General Order(s) and Local Bankruptcy Rule(s) ("LBR"), the foregoing document will be served by the court via NEF and hyperlink to the document. On ________________ I checked the CM/ECF docket for this bankruptcy case or adversary proceeding and determined that the following person(s) are on the Electronic Mail Notice List to receive NEF transmission at the email addressed indicated below:

☐ Service information continued on attached page

II. <u>SERVED BY U.S. MAIL OR OVERNIGHT MAIL</u> <u>(indicate method for each person or entity served)</u>:
On ________________ I served the following person(s) and/or entity(ies) at the last known address(es) in this bankruptcy case or adversary proceeding by placing a true and correct copy thereof in a sealed envelope in the United States Mail, first class, postage prepaid, and/or with an overnight mail service addressed as follow. Listing the judge here constitutes a declaration that mailing to the judge <u>will be</u> completed no later than 24 hours after the document is filed.

☐ Service information continued on attached page

III. <u>SERVED BY PERSONAL DELIVERY, FACSIMILE TRANSMISSION OR EMAIL</u> <u>(indicate method for each person or entity served)</u>: Pursuant to F.R.Civ.P. 5 and/or controlling LBR, on ________________ I served the following person(s) and/or entity(ies) by personal delivery, or (for those who consented in writing to such service method) by facsimile transmission and/or email as follows. Listing the judge here constitutes a declaration that mailing to the judge <u>will be</u> completed no later than 24 hours after the document is filed.

☐ Service information continued on attached page

I declare under penalty of perjury under the laws of the United States of America that the foregoing is true and correct.

________________ ________________ ________________
Date *Type Name* *Signature*

Debtor's Motion For Authority to Incur Debt - *Page 4* **F 3015-1.17**

In re: Debtor(s).	CHAPTER 13 CASE NUMBER

ADDITIONAL SERVICE INFORMATION (if needed):

Debtor's Motion for Authority to Refinance Real Property Under LBR 3015-1(p) (F 3015-1.15)

Attorney or Party Name, Address, Telephone & FAX Numbers, and California State Bar Number ☐ Attorney for ☐ Pro Se Debtor	FOR COURT USE ONLY
UNITED STATES BANKRUPTCY COURT CENTRAL DISTRICT OF CALIFORNIA	CHAPTER 13 CASE NUMBER
In re Debtor(s).	DEBTOR'S MOTION FOR AUTHORITY TO REFINANCE REAL PROPERTY UNDER LBR 3015-1 (p) (No Hearing Required)

Debtor moves this Court for an order authorizing the debtor to refinance the real property, described below, pursuant to the terms and conditions described herein.

1. Debtor's Chapter 13 Plan (the "Plan") was confirmed on: ____________________.

2. Debtor wishes to refinance the real property (the "Property") located at:
   ____
   ____

   The Property is more particularly described in Exhibit "A" attached hereto.

   ☐ Debtor wishes to modify the Plan for early payment of the Plan as described in the *Motion to Modify Plan* submitted by Debtor concurrently with this Motion.

3. Debtor requests authority to borrow the sum of $______________ from
   Lender name: ____________________________
   Address: ____________________________
   ____________________________.

   Debtor also requests authority to execute a promissory note secured by a _____ deed of trust on the Property.

4. From the proceeds of this loan, the following encumbrances of record against the Property will be paid through escrow:
   a) ____
   b) ____
   c) ____

Debtor's Motion For Authority to Refinance Real Property – *Page 2* **F 3015-1.15**

In re: Debtor(s).	CHAPTER 13
	CASE NUMBER

5. After payment of the foregoing encumbrances and all costs of sale:
   - ☐ there will remain the approximate sum of $________________; OR
   - ☐ no proceeds will remain.

6. ☐ (a) The Chapter 13 Trustee is hereby authorized to make demand upon escrow for sufficient funds to pay off the Plan with a:
   - ☐ 100% dividend to unsecured creditors; OR
   - ☐ ____% dividend as indicated in the confirmed plan.

   After escrow's payment of the encumbrances listed above, any remaining funds shall be paid directly to debtor.

   OR

   ☐ (b) The Chapter 13 Trustee is hereby authorized to make demand upon escrow for the balance remaining after escrow's payment of the encumbrances listed above even though the amount is insufficient to pay off the Plan. The refinance is in the best interest of the creditors.

7. The escrow is being processed by:
   - Escrow company name: ______________________________
   - Address: ______________________________
     ____
   - Telephone: ______________________________
   - Facsimile: ______________________________
   - Escrow officer: ______________________________
   - Escrow number: ______________________________

8. Supporting documents attached to this Motion are:
   a) Exhibit "A" – Legal Description with street address
   b) Exhibit "B" – Escrow Instructions and Documents
   c) Exhibit "C" – Estimated Closing Statement
   d) Exhibit "D" – Schedules I and J of the bankruptcy petition
   (Note – Debtor must provide to Chapter 13 Trustee a certified copy of the escrow closing statement within 14 days of the close of escrow.)

Dated:______________________________ ______________________________
Attorney for Debtor(s)

I declare under penalty of perjury that the foregoing is true and correct.

Dated:______________________________ ______________________________
Debtor

Dated:______________________________ ______________________________
Joint Debtor

In re:	CHAPTER 13
Debtor(s).	CASE NUMBER

NOTE: When using this form to indicate service of a proposed order, **DO NOT** list any person or entity in Category I. Proposed orders do not generate an NEF because only orders that have been entered are placed on a CM/ECF docket.

PROOF OF SERVICE OF DOCUMENT

I am over the age of 18 and not a party to this bankruptcy case or adversary proceeding. My business address is:

A true and correct copy of the foregoing document described as ______________________________ ______________________________ will be served or was served **(a)** on the judge in chambers in the form and manner required by LBR 5005-2(d), and **(b)** in the manner indicated below:

I. TO BE SERVED BY THE COURT VIA NOTICE OF ELECTRONIC FILING ("NEF") - Pursuant to controlling General Order(s) and Local Bankruptcy Rule(s) ("LBR"), the foregoing document will be served by the court via NEF and hyperlink to the document. On ______________ I checked the CM/ECF docket for this bankruptcy case or adversary proceeding and determined that the following person(s) are on the Electronic Mail Notice List to receive NEF transmission at the email addressed indicated below:

☐ Service information continued on attached page

II. SERVED BY U.S. MAIL OR OVERNIGHT MAIL (indicate method for each person or entity served):
On ______________ I served the following person(s) and/or entity(ies) at the last known address(es) in this bankruptcy case or adversary proceeding by placing a true and correct copy thereof in a sealed envelope in the United States Mail, first class, postage prepaid, and/or with an overnight mail service addressed as follow. Listing the judge here constitutes a declaration that mailing to the judge will be completed no later than 24 hours after the document is filed.

☐ Service information continued on attached page

III. SERVED BY PERSONAL DELIVERY, FACSIMILE TRANSMISSION OR EMAIL (indicate method for each person or entity served): Pursuant to F.R.Civ.P. 5 and/or controlling LBR, on ______________ I served the following person(s) and/or entity(ies) by personal delivery, or (for those who consented in writing to such service method) by facsimile transmission and/or email as follows. Listing the judge here constitutes a declaration that mailing to the judge will be completed no later than 24 hours after the document is filed.

☐ Service information continued on attached page

I declare under penalty of perjury under the laws of the United States of America that the foregoing is true and correct.

Date	*Type Name*	*Signature*

This form is mandatory. It has been approved for use by the United States Bankruptcy Court for the Central District of California.

Debtor's Motion for Authority to Sell Real Property Under LBR 3015-1(p) (F 3015-1.16)

Attorney or Party Name, Address, Telephone & FAX Numbers, and California State Bar Number ☐ Attorney for ☐ Pro Se Debtor	FOR COURT USE ONLY
UNITED STATES BANKRUPTCY COURT **CENTRAL DISTRICT OF CALIFORNIA**	CHAPTER 13 CASE NUMBER
In re Debtor(s).	**DEBTOR'S MOTION FOR AUTHORITY TO SELL REAL PROPERTY UNDER LBR 3015-1 (p)** (No Hearing Required)

Debtor moves this Court for an order authorizing the debtor to sell the real property, described below, pursuant to the terms and conditions described herein.

1. Debtor's Chapter 13 Plan (the "Plan") was confirmed on: ______________________.

2. Debtor wishes to sell the real property (the "Property") located at:

   ____

   ____

   The Property is more particularly described in Exhibit "A" attached hereto.

   ☐ Debtor wishes to modify the Plan for early payment of the Plan as described in the *Motion to Modify Plan* submitted by Debtor concurrently with this Motion.

3. The sale price of the Property is $_______________. The following are all of the encumbrances of record against the Property:

   a) ______________________________________
   b) ______________________________________
   c) ______________________________________
   d) ______________________________________
   e) ______________________________________

(Add additional page if necessary)

This form is mandatory. It has been approved for use by the United States Bankruptcy Court for the Central District of California.

In re:	CHAPTER 13
Debtor(s).	CASE NUMBER

4. After payment of the foregoing encumbrances and all costs of sale:
   ☐ there will remain the approximate sum of $__________; OR
   ☐ no proceeds will remain.

5. ☐ (a) The Chapter 13 Trustee is hereby authorized to make demand upon escrow for sufficient funds to pay off the Plan with a:
   ☐ 100% dividend to unsecured creditors; OR
   ☐ ____% dividend as indicated in the confirmed plan.

   After escrow's payment of the encumbrances listed above, any remaining funds shall be paid directly to debtor.

   OR

   ☐ (b) The Chapter 13 Trustee is hereby authorized to make demand upon escrow for the balance remaining after escrow's payment of the encumbrances listed above even though the amount is insufficient to pay off the Plan. The sale is for the fair market value of the Property.

6. The escrow is being processed by:
   Escrow company name: ____________________
   Address: ____________________
   ____
   Telephone: ____________________
   Facsimile: ____________________
   Escrow officer: ____________________
   Escrow number: ____________________

7. Supporting documents attached to this Motion are:
   a) Exhibit "A" – Legal Description with street address
   b) Exhibit "B" – Escrow Instructions and Documents
   c) Exhibit "C" – Estimated Closing Statement
   d) Exhibit "D" – Schedules I and J of the bankruptcy petition
   (Note – Debtor must provide a certified copy of the escrow closing statement within 14 days of the close of escrow.)

Dated:____________________ ____________________
Attorney for Debtor(s)

I declare under penalty of perjury that the foregoing is true and correct.

Dated:____________________ ____________________
Debtor

Dated:____________________ ____________________
Joint Debtor

Motion to Modify Plan or Suspend Plan Payments – *Page 3* **F 3015-1.16**

In re: Debtor(s).	CHAPTER 13
	CASE NUMBER

NOTE: When using this form to indicate service of a proposed order, **DO NOT** list any person or entity in Category I. Proposed orders do not generate an NEF because only orders that have been entered are placed on a CM/ECF docket.

PROOF OF SERVICE OF DOCUMENT

I am over the age of 18 and not a party to this bankruptcy case or adversary proceeding. My business address is:

A true and correct copy of the foregoing document described as ______________________________ ______________________________ will be served or was served **(a)** on the judge in chambers in the form and manner required by LBR 5005-2(d), and **(b)** in the manner indicated below:

I. **TO BE SERVED BY THE COURT VIA NOTICE OF ELECTRONIC FILING ("NEF")** - Pursuant to controlling General Order(s) and Local Bankruptcy Rule(s) ("LBR"), the foregoing document will be served by the court via NEF and hyperlink to the document. On ______________ I checked the CM/ECF docket for this bankruptcy case or adversary proceeding and determined that the following person(s) are on the Electronic Mail Notice List to receive NEF transmission at the email addressed indicated below:

_ Service information continued on attached page

II. **SERVED BY U.S. MAIL OR OVERNIGHT MAIL** (indicate method for each person or entity served):
On ______________ I served the following person(s) and/or entity(ies) at the last known address(es) in this bankruptcy case or adversary proceeding by placing a true and correct copy thereof in a sealed envelope in the United States Mail, first class, postage prepaid, and/or with an overnight mail service addressed as follow. Listing the judge here constitutes a declaration that mailing to the judge will be completed no later than 24 hours after the document is filed.

☐ Service information continued on attached page

III. **SERVED BY PERSONAL DELIVERY, FACSIMILE TRANSMISSION OR EMAIL** (indicate method for each person or entity served): Pursuant to F.R.Civ.P. 5 and/or controlling LBR, on ______________ I served the following person(s) and/or entity(ies) by personal delivery, or (for those who consented in writing to such service method) by facsimile transmission and/or email as follows. Listing the judge here constitutes a declaration that mailing to the judge will be completed no later than 24 hours after the document is filed.

☐ Service information continued on attached page

I declare under penalty of perjury under the laws of the United States of America that the foregoing is true and correct.

Date	Type Name	Signature

This form is mandatory. It has been approved for use by the United States Bankruptcy Court for the Central District of California.

DEBTOR 'S MOTION TO CONVERT CASE UNDER 11 U.S.C §§ 706(A) OR 1112(A) (F 1017-1.1)

Attorney or Party Name, Address, Telephone & FAX Numbers, and California State Bar Number Attorney for **UNITED STATES BANKRUPTCY COURT** **CENTRAL DISTRICT OF CALIFORNIA**	FOR COURT USE ONLY
In re: Debtor.	CHAPTER ________ CASE NUMBER

DEBTOR'S MOTION TO CONVERT CASE
UNDER 11 U.S.C. §§ 706(a) OR 1112(a)

TO THE HONORABLE UNITED STATES BANKRUPTCY JUDGE:

1. Debtor hereby moves this Court for an Order converting the above chapter _____ case to a case under chapter _____ on the grounds set forth below:

2. **Filing Information:**

   a. ☐ A Voluntary Petition under chapter ☐ 7 ☐ 11 ☐ 12 ☐ 13 was filed on:

   b. ☐ An Involuntary Petition under chapter ☐ 7 ☐ 11 was filed on:
   ☐ An Order of Relief under chapter ☐ 7 ☐ 11 was entered on:

   c. ☐ An Order of Conversion to chapter ☐ 7 ☐ 11 ☐ 12 ☐ 13 was entered on:

   d. ☐ Other *(specify)*:

3. **Procedural Status**:

   a. Name of trustee appointed *(if any)*:

   b. Name of Attorney of Record for trustee *(if any)*:

4. Debtor alleges that this case has not been previously converted.

(Continued on next page)

Debtor's Motion to Convert Case - *Page 2* **F 1017-1.1**

In re	CHAPTER ______
Debtor.	CASE NUMBER

5. Debtor alleges that the motion is filed in good faith, and that Debtor is eligible for relief under the chapter for which conversion is requested.

WHEREFORE, Debtor prays that this Court issue an Order (the form of which is submitted herewith and has been served) converting this case from one under chapter ______ to a case under chapter ______.

Dated: Respectfully submitted,

____
Firm Name

By: ______________________________

Name: ______________________________
Attorney for Debtor/Trustee

PROOF OF SERVICE BY MAIL

STATE OF CALIFORNIA
COUNTY OF ____________________

I am employed in the above County, State of California. I am over the age of 18 and not a party to the within action. My business address is as follows:

On ______________________________, I served the foregoing document described as: DEBTOR'S MOTION TO CONVERT CASE UNDER 11 U.S.C. §§ 706(a) OR 1112(a) on the United States trustee, and if conversion is sought under § 706(a), on the chapter 7 trustee, attorney for the chapter 7 trustee (if any), and parties in interest at their last known addresses by placing a true and correct copy thereof in a sealed envelope with postage thereon fully prepaid in the United States Mail at ______________________, California, addressed as follows:

☐ Addresses continued on attached page

I declare under penalty of perjury under the laws of the United States of America that the foregoing is true and correct.

Dated:

______________________________ ______________________________
Type Name *Signature*

DEBTOR'S NOTICE OF CONVERSION UNDER 11 U.S.C § 1208(A) OR 1307(A) (F1017-1.4)

Attorney or Party Name, Address, Telephone & FAX Numbers, and California State Bar Number *Attorney for*	FOR COURT USE ONLY
UNITED STATES BANKRUPTCY COURT **CENTRAL DISTRICT OF CALIFORNIA**	
In re: Debtor.	CHAPTER ______ CASE NUMBER (No Hearing Required)

DEBTOR'S NOTICE OF CONVERSION
UNDER 11 U.S.C. §§ 1208(a) OR 1307(a)

TO THE HONORABLE UNITED STATES BANKRUPTCY JUDGE:

1. Debtor hereby gives notice that Debtor converts the above chapter ______ case to a case under chapter 7 on the grounds set forth below:
2. A Voluntary Petition under chapter ☐ 12 ☐ 13 was filed on:
3. Name of trustee appointed:
4. Debtor alleges that this case has not been previously converted.
5. Debtor alleges that this notice is filed in good faith, and that Debtor is eligible for relief under chapter 7.

Dated: Respectfully submitted,

____
Firm Name

By: ________________________

Name: ________________________
Attorney for Debtor/Trustee

(Continued on next page)

Debtor's Notice of Conversion - *Page 2* **F 1017-1.4**

In re	CHAPTER ______
Debtor.	CASE NUMBER

PROOF OF SERVICE BY MAIL

STATE OF CALIFORNIA
COUNTY OF ____________________

I am employed in the above County, State of California. I am over the age of 18 and not a party to the within action. My business address is as follows:

On ____________________________________, I served the foregoing document described as: DEBTOR'S NOTICE OF CONVERSION UNDER 11 U.S.C. §§ 1208(a) OR 1307(a) on the chapter _____ trustee and the United States trustee at their last known addresses by placing a true and correct copy thereof in a sealed envelope with postage thereon fully prepaid in the United States Mail at ________________________, California, addressed as follows:

☐ Addresses continued on attached page

I declare under penalty of perjury under the laws of the United States of America that the foregoing is true and correct.

Dated:

________________________________ ________________________________
Type Name *Signature*

CDCAL-573 C.D. CALIFORNIA

Debtor's Motion to Reopen Case and For Extension of Time to File Debtor's Certification of Completion of Postpetition Instructional Course Concerning Personal Financial Management (F 5010-1.1M)

Attorney or Party Name, Address, Telephone & FAX Numbers, and California State Bar Number Attorney for:	FOR COURT USE ONLY
UNITED STATES BANKRUPTCY COURT CENTRAL DISTRICT OF CALIFORNIA	
In re: Debtor(s).	CHAPTER: ____ CASE NO.:

DEBTOR'S MOTION TO REOPEN CASE AND FOR EXTENSION OF TIME TO FILE DEBTOR'S CERTIFICATION OF COMPLETION OF POSTPETITION INSTRUCTIONAL COURSE CONCERNING PERSONAL FINANCIAL MANAGEMENT

(For Case Closed Without Entry of Discharge Due to Noncompliance With 11 U.S.C. §§ 727(a)(11) or 1328(g)(1))

TO THE HONORABLE UNITED STATES BANKRUPTCY JUDGE:

1. **Bankruptcy Case Filing Information:**

   a. A voluntary petition under chapter ☐ 7 ☐ 13 was filed on:

   b. Because the Debtor(s) failed to file Official Form 23, Debtor's Certification of Completion of Postpetition Instructional Course Concerning Personal Financial Management ("OF 23") within the time limit set forth in F.R.B.P. 1007(c), the court closed this case without entering a discharge.

2. I, ______________________________, the Debtor in this case, and ______________________________, (if joint debtors) hereby request that the court enter an order: (a) reopening the case pursuant to 11 U.S.C. § 350(b) and F.R.B.P. 5010; and (b) extending the time for the Debtor(s) to file the OF 23 for a period of 30 days from the date of entry of an order granting this motion.

3. The Debtor(s) failed to file the OF 23 by the original deadline, and therefore need to have the case reopened so that the required OF 23 can be filed and a discharge can be entered because: (Explain circumstances that prevented the Debtor(s) from filing the OF 23 in a timely manner.)

____

____

____

____

____

____,

and I declare this under penalty of perjury.

This form is mandatory by Order of the United States Bankruptcy Court for the Central District of California.

Debtor's Motion to Reopen Case and for Extension of Time To File Debtor's Certification of of Postpetition Instructional Course Concerning Personal Financial Management - Page 2

In re Debtor(s).	CHAPTER: CASE NO.:

WHEREFORE, the Debtor(s) pray(s) that this court issue an order (the form of which is submitted herewith and has been served) reopening this case and extending the time to file the OF 23 so that the Debtor(s) discharge may be entered.

Debtor's Signature	Dated	City	State
Joint Debtor's Signature	Dated	City	State

Debtor's Motion to Reopen Case and for Extension of Time To File Debtor's Certification of of Postpetition Instructional Course Concerning Personal Financial Management - Page 3

In re	CHAPTER:
Debtor(s).	CASE NO.:

NOTE: When using this form to indicate service of a proposed order, **DO NOT** list any person or entity in Category I. Proposed orders do not generate an NEF because only orders that have been entered are placed on a CM/ECF docket.

PROOF OF SERVICE OF DOCUMENT

I am over the age of 18 and not a party to this bankruptcy case or adversary proceeding. My business address is:

A true and correct copy of the foregoing document described as ______________________________ ______________________________ will be served or was served **(a)** on the judge in chambers in the form and manner required by LBR 5005-2(d), and **(b)** in the manner indicated below:

I. TO BE SERVED BY THE COURT VIA NOTICE OF ELECTRONIC FILING ("NEF") - Pursuant to controlling General Order(s) and Local Bankruptcy Rule(s) ("LBR"), the foregoing document will be served by the court via NEF and hyperlink to the document. On ____________________ I checked the CM/ECF docket for this bankruptcy case or adversary proceeding and determined that the following person(s) are on the Electronic Mail Notice List to receive NEF transmission at the email addressed indicated below:

☐ Service information continued on attached page

II. SERVED BY U.S. MAIL OR OVERNIGHT MAIL (indicate method for each person or entity served):
On ____________________ I served the following person(s) and/or entity(ies) at the last known address(es) in this bankruptcy case or adversary proceeding by placing a true and correct copy thereof in a sealed envelope in the United States Mail, first class, postage prepaid, and/or with an overnight mail service addressed as follow. Listing the judge here constitutes a declaration that mailing to the judge will be completed no later than 24 hours after the document is filed.

☐ Service information continued on attached page

III. SERVED BY PERSONAL DELIVERY, FACSIMILE TRANSMISSION OR EMAIL (indicate method for each person or entity served): Pursuant to F.R.Civ.P. 5 and/or controlling LBR, on ____________________ I served the following person(s) and/or entity(ies) by personal delivery, or (for those who consented in writing to such service method) by facsimile transmission and/or email as follows. Listing the judge here constitutes a declaration that mailing to the judge will be completed no later than 24 hours after the document is filed.

☐ Service information continued on attached page

I declare under penalty of perjury under the laws of the United States of America that the foregoing is true and correct.

Date *Type Name* *Signature*

Debtor's Motion to Reopen Case and for Extension of Time To File Debtor's Certification of of Postpetition Instructional Course Concerning Personal Financial Management - Page 4

In re	CHAPTER:
Debtor(s).	CASE NO.:

ADDITIONAL SERVICE INFORMATION (if needed):

Debtor's Objection to Lessor's Certification and Notice of Hearing (11 U.S.C. § 362(m)(2)(A) and (B)) (F 4001-1.5)

Attorney or Party Name, Address, Telephone & FAX Numbers, and California State Bar Number ☐ Attorney for: ☐ Individual debtor appearing without counsel (Pro Se Debtor)	FOR COURT USE ONLY
UNITED STATES BANKRUPTCY COURT CENTRAL DISTRICT OF CALIFORNIA	
In re: Debtor(s).	CHAPTER: CASE NO.:
	DEBTOR'S OBJECTION TO LESSOR'S CERTIFICATION AND NOTICE OF HEARING (11 U.S.C. § 362(m)(2)(A) and (B)) DATE: TIME: CTRM: FLOOR:

NOTE: THIS OBJECTION MUST BE FILED WITHIN 15 DAYS OF LESSOR'S CERTIFICATION.

1. In response to "Lessor's Certification of (1) Prepetition Eviction Action Seeking Possession of Residential Property Based on Debtor's Prepetition Endangerment of Property or Illegal Use of a Controlled Substance or (2) Endangerment of the Property or Illegal Use of a Controlled Substance within the Last 30 Days" filed herein on__________ ("Lessor's Certification"), concerning the residential property commonly known as ____________________ (Complete Address), the Debtor objects and declares: *(Check all that apply)*

   a. ☐ The Lessor's Certification is false in the following respects: ____________________ ☐ continuation page(s) attached.

   b. ☐ The Lessor's Certification lacks legal sufficiency in the following respects: ____________________ ☐ continuation page(s) attached.

   c. ☐ The conditions described in the Lessor's Certification have been remedied, as follows: ____________________ ☐ continuation (s) page attached.

2. Supporting declaration(s) ☐ are ☐ are not attached hereto and incorporated herein.

3. A memorandum of points and authorities supporting this Objection ☐ is ☐ is not attached hereto and incorporated herein.

(Continued on next page)

In re (SHORT TITLE)	CHAPTER:
Debtor(s).	CASE NO.:

4. Debtor requests that the truth or falsity of the Lessor's certification, and/or the sufficiency of the remedial action by Debtor described above within the meaning of 11 U.S.C. § 362 (m)(2)(C), be determined within 10 days of the filing of this Objection, and Debtor has obtained from the Court through the assigned judge's calendar clerk, or where applicable, the assigned judge's self-calendering system the date of ________________ at __________ (am / pm) which is within that 10 day period.

   Hearing Location:
   - ☐ **255 East Temple Street, Los Angeles**
   - ☐ **411 West Fourth Street, Santa Ana**
   - ☐ **21041 Burbank Boulevard, Woodland Hills**
   - ☐ **1415 State Street, Santa Barbara**
   - ☐ **3420 Twelfth Street, Riverside**

Declaration of Debtor

I, ____________________________, am the debtor in these proceedings. I declare under penalty of perjury that I have read the foregoing, including all continuation pages, and that all statements therein are true and correct.

Executed this ______________ day of ________________, ____________ at _________________________.
(Month) (Year)

____
Signature of Debtor

____
Print Name of Debtor

____
Print the Name of the Law Firm Representing the Debtor (if applicable)

____
Signature of the Attorney Representing the Debtor (if applicable)

____
Print the Name of the Attorney Representing the Debtor (if applicable)

In re (SHORT TITLE)	CHAPTER:
Debtor(s).	CASE NO.:

NOTE: When using this form to indicate service of a proposed order, **DO NOT** list any person or entity in Category I. Proposed orders do not generate an NEF because only orders that have been entered are placed on a CM/ECF docket.

PROOF OF SERVICE OF DOCUMENT

I am over the age of 18 and not a party to this bankruptcy case or adversary proceeding. My business address is:

A true and correct copy of the foregoing document described as ____ will be served or was served **(a)** on the judge in chambers in the form and manner required by LBR 5005-2(d), and **(b)** in the manner indicated below:

I. __TO BE SERVED BY THE COURT VIA NOTICE OF ELECTRONIC FILING ("NEF")__ - Pursuant to controlling General Order(s) and Local Bankruptcy Rule(s) ("LBR"), the foregoing document will be served by the court via NEF and hyperlink to the document. On ______________________ I checked the CM/ECF docket for this bankruptcy case or adversary proceeding and determined that the following person(s) are on the Electronic Mail Notice List to receive NEF transmission at the email addressed indicated below:

☐ Service information continued on attached page

II. __SERVED BY U.S. MAIL OR OVERNIGHT MAIL (indicate method for each person or entity served)__:
On ______________________ I served the following person(s) and/or entity(ies) at the last known address(es) in this bankruptcy case or adversary proceeding by placing a true and correct copy thereof in a sealed envelope in the United States Mail, first class, postage prepaid, and/or with an overnight mail service addressed as follow. Listing the judge here constitutes a declaration that mailing to the judge __will be__ completed no later than 24 hours after the document is filed.

☐ Service information continued on attached page

III. __SERVED BY PERSONAL DELIVERY, FACSIMILE TRANSMISSION OR EMAIL (indicate method for each person or entity served)__: Pursuant to F.R.Civ.P. 5 and/or controlling LBR, on ______________________ I served the following person(s) and/or entity(ies) by personal delivery, or (for those who consented in writing to such service method) by facsimile transmission and/or email as follows. Listing the judge here constitutes a declaration that mailing to the judge __will be__ completed no later than 24 hours after the document is filed.

☐ Service information continued on attached page

I declare under penalty of perjury under the laws of the United States of America that the foregoing is true and correct.

Date	*Type Name*	*Signature*

Debtor's Request for Voluntary Dismissal of Chapter 13 Case (F 3015-1.18)

Attorney or Party Name, Address, Telephone & FAX Numbers, and California State Bar Number ☐ Attorney for ☐ Pro Se Debtor	FOR COURT USE ONLY
UNITED STATES BANKRUPTCY COURT **CENTRAL DISTRICT OF CALIFORNIA**	CHAPTER 13 CASE NUMBER
In re: Debtor(s).	**DEBTOR'S REQUEST FOR VOLUNTARY DISMISSAL OF CHAPTER 13 CASE** (No Hearing Required)

Debtor moves this Court for an order dismissing the above-entitled bankruptcy case pursuant to 11 U.S.C. § 1307(b), and Local Bankruptcy Rule 3015-1(q)(1):

1. ☐ (a) The above-entitled case was commenced by the filing of a voluntary petition under Chapter 13 and has not been converted under 11 U.S.C. §§ 706, 1112, or 1208;

   OR

   ☐ (b) The above-entitled case was commenced by the filing of a voluntary petition under Chapter ______ and was converted to a case under Chapter 13 on __________________.

2. ☐ (a) There is no motion for relief from, annulment of, or conditioning of the automatic stay pending in this case and no such motions have been filed in this case.

   OR

   ☐ (b) The following motion for relief from, annulment of, or conditioning of the automatic stay is currently pending in this case OR was filed and resolved OR has been withdrawn or denied:

Filing Date: ______________________________

Movant: ______________________________

Personal or Real Property: ______________________________

____

Status: ☐ Pending ☐ Resolved ☐ Withdrawn/Denied

(Please attach additional pages if needed.)

In re:	CHAPTER 13
Debtor(s).	CASE NUMBER

4. ☐ (a) Debtor has made no arrangements or agreements with any creditor or other person in connection with this request for dismissal.

OR

☐ (b) Debtor has made the following arrangements or agreements with the creditor(s) or other person(s) identified below in connection with this request for dismissal:

____

____

____

(Please attach additional pages if needed.)

5. Debtor seeks dismissal of this case for the following reasons:

____

____

____

____

____

(Please attach additional pages if needed.)

Dated:____________________ ____________________
Attorney for Debtor(s)

I declare under penalty of perjury that the foregoing is true and correct.

Dated:____________________ ____________________
Debtor

Dated:____________________ ____________________
Joint Debtor

Debtor's Request For Voluntary Dismissal of Chapter 13 - *Page 3* **F 3015-1.18**

In re:	CHAPTER 13
Debtor(s).	CASE NUMBER

NOTE: When using this form to indicate service of a proposed order, **DO NOT** list any person or entity in Category I. Proposed orders do not generate an NEF because only orders that have been entered are placed on a CM/ECF docket.

PROOF OF SERVICE OF DOCUMENT

I am over the age of 18 and not a party to this bankruptcy case or adversary proceeding. My business address is:

A true and correct copy of the foregoing document described as ______________________________ ______________________________ will be served or was served **(a)** on the judge in chambers in the form and manner required by LBR 5005-2(d), and **(b)** in the manner indicated below:

I. <u>TO BE SERVED BY THE COURT VIA NOTICE OF ELECTRONIC FILING ("NEF")</u> - Pursuant to controlling General Order(s) and Local Bankruptcy Rule(s) ("LBR"), the foregoing document will be served by the court via NEF and hyperlink to the document. On ______________ I checked the CM/ECF docket for this bankruptcy case or adversary proceeding and determined that the following person(s) are on the Electronic Mail Notice List to receive NEF transmission at the email addressed indicated below:

☐ Service information continued on attached page

II. <u>SERVED BY U.S. MAIL OR OVERNIGHT MAIL</u> <u>(indicate method for each person or entity served)</u>:
On ______________ I served the following person(s) and/or entity(ies) at the last known address(es) in this bankruptcy case or adversary proceeding by placing a true and correct copy thereof in a sealed envelope in the United States Mail, first class, postage prepaid, and/or with an overnight mail service addressed as follow. Listing the judge here constitutes a declaration that mailing to the judge <u>will be</u> completed no later than 24 hours after the document is filed.

☐ Service information continued on attached page

III. <u>SERVED BY PERSONAL DELIVERY, FACSIMILE TRANSMISSION OR EMAIL</u> <u>(indicate method for each person or entity served)</u>: Pursuant to F.R.Civ.P. 5 and/or controlling LBR, on ______________ I served the following person(s) and/or entity(ies) by personal delivery, or (for those who consented in writing to such service method) by facsimile transmission and/or email as follows. Listing the judge here constitutes a declaration that mailing to the judge <u>will be</u> completed no later than 24 hours after the document is filed.

☐ Service information continued on attached page

I declare under penalty of perjury under the laws of the United States of America that the foregoing is true and correct.

Date	*Type Name*	*Signature*

This form is mandatory. It has been approved for use by the United States Bankruptcy Court for the Central District of California.

January 2009 **F 3015-1.18**

In re:	CHAPTER 13
Debtor(s).	CASE NUMBER

ADDITIONAL SERVICE INFORMATION (if needed):

DEBTOR'S REQUEST TO CONVERT CHAPTER 13 CASE (F 3015–1.3)

Attorney or Party Name, Address, Telephone & FAX Numbers, and California State Bar Number *Attorney for*	FOR COURT USE ONLY
UNITED STATES BANKRUPTCY COURT CENTRAL DISTRICT OF CALIFORNIA	
In re: Debtor.	CHAPTER ______ CASE NUMBER
	(No Hearing Required)

DEBTOR'S REQUEST TO CONVERT CHAPTER 13 CASE TO ONE UNDER CHAPTER 7 PURSUANT TO 11 U.S.C. § 1307(a)

TO THE HONORABLE UNITED STATES BANKRUPTCY JUDGE:

Debtor hereby requests that this Court enter an Order converting the above Chapter 13 case to a case under Chapter 7 on the grounds set forth below:

1. A Voluntary Petition under Chapter 13 was filed on:

2. This case has not been previously converted.

Dated:

Respectfully submitted,

____

Firm Name

By: ______________________________

Name: ______________________________

Attorney for Debtor/Trustee

Rev. 1/01 This form is optional. It has been approved for use by the United States Bankruptcy Court for the Central District of California. **F 3015-1.3**

CDCAL-585 C.D. CALIFORNIA

Declaration and Signature of Non-Attorney "Bankruptcy Petition Preparer" (If applicable)

Form 19 - Page 1 (Rev. 12/07) 2007 USBC, Central District of California

UNITED STATES BANKRUPTCY COURT
Central District of California

In re	Case No.:
Debtor.	(If known)

DECLARATION AND SIGNATURE OF NON-ATTORNEY BANKRUPTCY PETITION PREPARER (11 U.S.C. § 110)

I declare under penalty of perjury that:
(1) I am a bankruptcy petition preparer as defined in 11 U.S.C. § 110;
(2) I prepared the accompanying document(s) listed below for compensation and have provided the debtor with a copy of the document(s) and the attached notice as required by 11 U.S.C. §§ 110(b), 110(h), and 342(b); and
(3) if rules or guidelines have been promulgated pursuant to 11 U.S.C. § 110(h) setting a maximum fee for services chargeable by bankruptcy petition preparers, I have given the debtor notice of the maximum amount before preparing any document for filing for a debtor or accepting any fee from the debtor, as required by that section.

Accompanying documents:

____

Printed or Typed Name and Title, if any, of Bankruptcy Petition Preparer

____

Social Security No. of Bankruptcy Petition Preparer (Required by 11 U.S.C. § 110)

If the bankruptcy petition preparer is not an individual, state the name, title (if any), address, and social security number of the officer, principal, responsible person or partner who signs this document.

____

Address

X ______________________
Signature of Bankruptcy Petition Preparer

____
Date

Names and social-security numbers of all other individuals who prepared or assisted in preparing this document, unless the bankruptcy petition preparer is not an individual:

If more than one person prepared this document, attach additional signed sheets conforming to the appropriate Official Form for each person.

A bankruptcy petition preparer's failure to comply with the provisions of title 11 and the Federal Rules of Bankruptcy Procedure may result in fines or imprisonment or both. 11 U.S.C. § 110; 18 U.S.C. § 156.

Form 19 - Page 2 (Rev. 12/07) 2007 USBC, Central District of California

In re	Case No.:
Debtor.	(If known)

NOTICE TO DEBTOR BY NON-ATTORNEY BANKRUPTCY PETITION PREPARER

[Must be filed with any document(s) prepared by a bankruptcy petition preparer.]

I am a bankruptcy petition preparer. I am not an attorney and may not practice law or give legal advice. Before preparing any document for filing as defined in § 110(a)(2) of the Bankruptcy Code or accepting any fees, I am required by law to provide you with this notice concerning bankruptcy petition preparers. Under the law, § 110 of the Bankruptcy Code (11 U.S.C. § 110), I am forbidden to offer you any legal advice, including advice about any of the following:

- whether to file a petition under the Bankruptcy Code (11 U.S.C. § 101 et seq.);
- whether commencing a case under chapter 7, 11, 12, or 13 is appropriate;
- whether your debts will be eliminated or discharged in a case under the Bankruptcy Code;
- whether you will be able to retain your home, car, or other property after commencing a case under the Bankruptcy Code;
- the tax consequences of a case brought under the Bankruptcy Code;
- the dischargeability of tax claims;
- whether you may or should promise to repay debts to a creditor or enter into a reaffirmation agreement with a creditor to reaffirm a debt;
- how to characterize the nature of your interests in property or your debts; or
- bankruptcy procedures and rights.

[The notice may provide additional examples of legal advice that a bankruptcy petition preparer is not authorized to give.]

In addition, under 11 U.S.C. § 110(h), the Supreme Court or the Judicial Conference of the United States may promulgate rules or guidelines setting a maximum allowable fee chargeable by a bankruptcy petition preparer. As required by law, I have notified you of this maximum allowable fee, if any, before preparing any document for filing or accepting any fee from you.

______________________________ ______________________________

Signature of Debtor Date Joint Debtor (if any) Date

[In a joint case, both spouses must sign.]

CDCAL-587 C.D. CALIFORNIA

Declaration Concerning Debtor's Schedules

Form B6 - Declaration (Rev. 12/07) **2007 USBC, Central District of California**

In re Debtor.	Case No.: (If known)

DECLARATION CONCERNING DEBTOR'S SCHEDULES

DECLARATION UNDER PENALTY OF PERJURY BY INDIVIDUAL DEBTOR

I declare under penalty of perjury that I have read the foregoing summary and schedules, consisting of ____________ sheets, and that they are true and correct to the best of my knowledge, information, and belief.

Date ____________ Signature: ____________
Debtor

Date ____________ Signature: ____________
(Joint Debtor, if any)
[If joint case, both spouses must sign.]

DECLARATION AND SIGNATURE OF NON-ATTORNEY BANKRUPTCY PETITION PREPARER (See 11 U.S.C. § 110)

I declare under penalty of perjury that: (1) I am a bankruptcy petition preparer as defined in 11 U.S.C. § 110; (2) I prepared this document for compensation and have provided the debtor with a copy of this document and the notices and information required under 11 U.S.C. §§ 110(b), 110(h) and 342(b); and, (3) if rules or guidelines have been promulgated pursuant to 11 U.S.C. § 110(h) setting a maximum fee for services chargeable by bankruptcy petition preparers, I have given the debtor notice of the maximum amount before preparing any document for filing for a debtor or accepting any fee from the debtor, as required by that section.

____
Printed or Typed Name and Title, if any, of Bankruptcy Petition Preparer

____
Social Security No.
(Required by 11 U.S.C. § 110.)

If the bankruptcy petition preparer is not an individual, state the name, title (if any), address, and social security number of the officer, principal, responsible person, or partner who signs this document.

____
____
____
Address

X ____________
Signature of Bankruptcy Petition Preparer

____
Date

Names and Social Security numbers of all other individuals who prepared or assisted in preparing this document, unless the bankruptcy petition preparer is not an individual:

If more than one person prepared this document, attach additional signed sheets conforming to the appropriate Official Form for each person.

A bankruptcy petition preparer's failure to comply with the provisions of title 11 and the Federal Rules of Bankruptcy Procedure may result in fines or imprisonment or both. 11 U.S.C. § 110; 18 U.S.C. § 156.

DECLARATION UNDER PENALTY OF PERJURY ON BEHALF OF A CORPORATION OR PARTNERSHIP

I, the ____________ [the president or other officer or an authorized agent of the corporation or a member or an authorized agent of the partnership] of the ____________ [corporation or partnership] named as debtor in this case, declare under penalty of perjury that I have read the foregoing summary and schedules, consisting of ____________ sheets, and that they are true and correct to the best of my knowledge, information, and belief. *(Total shown on summary page plus 1.)*

Date ____________ Signature: ____________

____
[Print or type name of individual signing on behalf of debtor.]

[An individual signing on behalf of a partnership or corporation must indicate position or relationship to debtor.]

Penalty for making a false statement or concealing property: Fine of up to $500,000 or imprisonment for up to 5 years or both. 18 U.S.C. §§ 152 and 3571.

Declaration of Agent for Standing Trustee (Chapter 12 and 13 Cases only; Attach to Stay Motion) (F 4001-1M.13)

Motion for Relief from Stay - *Page* ____ of ____ **F 4001-1M.13**

In re (SHORT TITLE) Debtor(s)	CHAPTER: CASE NO.:

DECLARATION OF AGENT FOR STANDING TRUSTEE
(MOVANT: ____________________)
(Chapter 12 and 13 cases only; Attach to the Relief From Stay Motion)

I, ________________________________, declare and state as follows:

1. ____________________ is the standing ☐ Chapter 13 ☐ Chapter 12 Trustee ("Trustee") in the above-captioned case.

2. I am employed by the Trustee as a ____________________. I am one of the custodians of, and have personally worked on, the books, records, and files of the Trustee concerning this case. One of my job responsibilities is the recording or verification of mortgage, car, and plan payments delivered to the Trustee's office by debtors in connection with their plans. It is the regular business practice of the Trustee's office to record in the Trustee's books and records all such payments promptly upon receipt, and promptly to transmit any payments due to the secured creditors. These entries are made by a person with personal knowledge of the event being recorded in the ordinary course of business.

3. The Debtor(s)'s plan in this case provides for plan payments of $____________ per month for a period of _______ months, which is expected to result in payment of _____% of unsecured creditors' claims.

4. The plan
   - ☐ was confirmed at a confirmation hearing held on ____________________.
   - ☐ is set for confirmation hearing on ____________________.
   - ☐ was denied confirmation at a confirmation hearing held on ____________________.

5. The last plan payment received by the Trustee's office from the Debtor(s) was:

   Amount: $____________________
   Date received: ____________________

6. As of the date of this Declaration, the Debtor(s) is/are delinquent __________ plan payments.

7. The last mortgage payment received by the Trustee's office from the Debtor(s) was:

   Amount: $____________________
   Date received: ____________________

8. As of the date of this Declaration, the Debtor(s) is/are delinquent __________ postpetition mortgage payments.

9. A true and correct history of all payments received from Debtor(s) in this case is attached as Exhibit A.

10. ☐ The Standing Trustee has filed a motion to dismiss this case because of the delinquent plan payments. It was served on the Debtor(s) on *(specify date)* ____________________. A true and correct copy of this motion to dismiss this case is attached as Exhibit B.

I declare under penalty of perjury under the laws of the United States of America that the foregoing is true and correct and that this declaration was executed on ______________, ______, at ____________________ *(city, state).*

____________________ ____________________
Typed Name of Declarant *Signature of Declarant*

Declaration of _____ RE: Default Under Adequate Protection Order; Request for Entry of Order Granting Relief From Stay (F 4001-1.DEC)

Attorney or Party Name, Address, Telephone & FAX Numbers, and California State Bar Number ☐ *Individual appearing without counsel* ☐ *Attorney for:*	FOR COURT USE ONLY
UNITED STATES BANKRUPTCY COURT CENTRAL DISTRICT OF CALIFORNIA	
In re: Debtor(s).	CHAPTER: CASE NO.: DATE: TIME: CTRM: FLOOR:

DECLARATION OF ______________________________
RE: DEFAULT UNDER ADEQUATE PROTECTION ORDER;
REQUEST FOR ENTRY OF ORDER GRANTING RELIEF FROM STAY

I, ____, declare as follows:
(print name of declarant)

1. I have personal knowledge of the matters set forth in this declaration and, if called upon to testify, I could and would testify competently hereto. I am over 18 years of age.

2. On ______________________, the Court entered an order conditioning continuation of the automatic stay in the above-entitled bankruptcy case on the performance by the debtor of certain obligations for the benefit of __________ ____________________ *(name of Movant)* (the "Adequate Protection Order"). A true and correct copy of the Adequate Protection Order is attached hereto as Exhibit "A."

3. I have knowledge regarding the debtor's performance (or lack of performance) under the terms of the Adequate Protection Order because *(specify)*:

   ☐ I am the party for whose benefit the Adequate Protection Order was entered (the "Movant"), and the Adequate Protection Order required the debtor to make payments directly to me.

   ☐ I am counsel for the Movant and the Adequate Protection Order required the debtor to make payments directly to me.

   ☐ I am employed as ____________________________ for the Movant and, as such, am one of the custodians of the books, records and files of Movant that relate to payments received from the debtor. I have personally worked on those books, records and files, and as to the following facts, I know them to be true of my own knowledge or I have gained knowledge of them from the business records of Movant on behalf of Movant, which were made at or about the time of the events recorded, and which are maintained in the ordinary course of Movant's business at or near the time of the acts, conditions or events to which they relate. Any such document was prepared in the ordinary course of business of Movant by a person who had personal knowledge of the event being recorded and had or has a business duty to record accurately such event. The business records are available for inspection and copies can be submitted to the Court if required.

Declaration of ______________________ RE: Default Under **F 4001-1.DEC**
Adequate Protection Order; Request for Entry of Order Granting Relief From Stay - *Page 2*

In re (SHORT TITLE) Debtor(s).	CHAPTER:
	CASE NO.:

☐ Other *(specify)*:

4. The debtor defaulted upon his/her/its obligations under the Adequate Protection Order by *(specify)*:

☐ Failing to make the payment(s) due ______________________ *(date(s))* under the terms of the Adequate Protection Order.

☐ Failing to provide evidence of the existence of insurance coverage required under the terms of the Adequate Protection Order in a timely manner.

☐ Other *(specify)*:

5. ☐ a. Movant caused a notice of default (the "Notice") identifying the default(s) referenced in paragraph 4 above to be served on the debtor on ____________________ *(date)*. A true and correct copy of the Notice is attached hereto as Exhibit "B."

☐ b. Movant was not required to serve a notice of the default specified in paragraph 4, because the Adequate Protection Order only required Movant to serve a maximum of _______ *(number)* notices of default and Movant had already served the required number of notices of default (collectively the "Notices") at the time the default specified in paragraph 4 occurred. Copies of all of the Notices are attached hereto as Exhibit "B."

6. Debtor failed to cure the defaults identified in the Notice within the cure period established by the Adequate Protection Order.

7. In light of the foregoing, under the terms of the Adequate Protection Order, Movant is entitled to relief from the automatic stay. Concurrently herewith, Movant is lodging a proposed form of order granting Movant relief from the automatic stay.

I declare under penalty of perjury under the laws of the United States of America that the foregoing is true and correct and that this Declaration was executed on ______________________, ______, at ______________________ *(city, state)*.

______________________ ______________________
Print Declarant's Name *Signature of Declarant*

Declaration of ______________________ RE: Default Under **F 4001-1.DEC**
Adequate Protection Order; Request for Entry of Order Granting Relief From Stay - *Page 3*

In re (SHORT TITLE)	CHAPTER:
Debtor(s).	CASE NO.:

NOTE: When using this form to indicate service of a proposed order, **DO NOT** list any person or entity in Category I. Proposed orders do not generate an NEF because only orders that have been entered are placed on a CM/ECF docket.

PROOF OF SERVICE OF DOCUMENT

I am over the age of 18 and not a party to this bankruptcy case or adversary proceeding. My business address is:

A true and correct copy of the foregoing document described as ______________________ ______________________ will be served or was served **(a)** on the judge in chambers in the form and manner required by LBR 5005-2(d), and **(b)** in the manner indicated below:

I. TO BE SERVED BY THE COURT VIA NOTICE OF ELECTRONIC FILING ("NEF") - Pursuant to controlling General Order(s) and Local Bankruptcy Rule(s) ("LBR"), the foregoing document will be served by the court via NEF and hyperlink to the document. On ______________ I checked the CM/ECF docket for this bankruptcy case or adversary proceeding and determined that the following person(s) are on the Electronic Mail Notice List to receive NEF transmission at the email addressed indicated below:

☐ Service information continued on attached page

II. SERVED BY U.S. MAIL OR OVERNIGHT MAIL (indicate method for each person or entity served):
On ______________ I served the following person(s) and/or entity(ies) at the last known address(es) in this bankruptcy case or adversary proceeding by placing a true and correct copy thereof in a sealed envelope in the United States Mail, first class, postage prepaid, and/or with an overnight mail service addressed as follow. Listing the judge here constitutes a declaration that mailing to the judge will be completed no later than 24 hours after the document is filed.

☐ Service information continued on attached page

III. SERVED BY PERSONAL DELIVERY, FACSIMILE TRANSMISSION OR EMAIL (indicate method for each person or entity served): Pursuant to F.R.Civ.P. 5 and/or controlling LBR, on ______________ I served the following person(s) and/or entity(ies) by personal delivery, or (for those who consented in writing to such service method) by facsimile transmission and/or email as follows. Listing the judge here constitutes a declaration that mailing to the judge will be completed no later than 24 hours after the document is filed.

☐ Service information continued on attached page

I declare under penalty of perjury under the laws of the United States of America that the foregoing is true and correct.

______________________________ ______________________
Date *Type Name* *Signature*

Declaration of ____________________________ RE: Default Under **F 4001-1.DEC**
Adequate Protection Order; Request for Entry of Order Granting Relief From Stay - *Page 4*

In re (SHORT TITLE) Debtor(s).	CHAPTER:
	CASE NO.:

ADDITIONAL SERVICE INFORMATION (if needed):

DECLARATION RE: ENTRY OF ORDER WITHOUT HEARING (F 9013–1.9)

Attorney or Party Name, Address, Telephone & FAX Numbers, and California State Bar Number *Attorney for*	FOR COURT USE ONLY
UNITED STATES BANKRUPTCY COURT CENTRAL DISTRICT OF CALIFORNIA In re: Debtor(s).	CHAPTER: CASE NO.: (No Hearing Required)

DECLARATION RE: ENTRY OF ORDER WITHOUT HEARING PURSUANT TO LOCAL BANKRUPTCY RULE 9013-1(g)

1. I am the ☐ Movant ☐ Movant's Attorney in this matter and hereby declare as follows:
2. On *(specify date)*: ______________________, Movant filed a motion entitled *(specify)*:
3. A copy of the motion and notice of motion is attached hereto.
4. Pursuant to Local Bankruptcy Rule 9013-1(g), the motion was served by mail on *(specify date)*: _______________, together with a notice stating that any party objecting to the motion has 15 days within which to file and serve any written objection and request a hearing on the above motion.
5. More than _______ days have passed since the service of the notice of motion.
6. No objection has been timely served on Movant at the address specified in the notice. Therefore, no hearing is required.
7. The proposed Order is submitted herewith. *(Submit original and appropriate copies of Order with envelopes and Notice of Entry)*

WHEREFORE, Movant requests that the Order granting the relief requested in the motion be signed and entered forthwith.

I declare under penalty of perjury under the laws of the United States of America that the foregoing is true and correct and that this declaration was executed on the following date at ___________________________________, California.

Dated:

_______________________________ _______________________________
Typed Name of Declarant *Signature of Declarant*

Declaration Re: Entry of Order without Hearing Pursuant to Local Bankruptcy Rule 9013-1(g) - *Page 2*

F 9013-1.9

In re	CHAPTER:
Debtor(s).	CASE NO.:

PROOF OF SERVICE BY MAIL

STATE OF CALIFORNIA COUNTY OF ______________________________

I am employed in the above County, State of California. I am over the age of 18 and not a party to the within action. My business address is as follows:

On ______________________________, I served the foregoing document described as: DECLARATION RE: ENTRY OF ORDER WITHOUT HEARING PURSUANT TO LOCAL BANKRUPTCY RULE 9013-1(g) on the interested parties at their last known address in this action by placing a true and correct copy thereof in a sealed envelope with postage thereon fully prepaid in the United States Mail at ______________________________, California, addressed as follows:

☐ Addresses continued on attached page

I declare under penalty of perjury under the laws of the United States of America that the foregoing is true and correct.

Dated:

______________________________ ______________________________

Typed Name *Signature*

CDCAL-595 C.D. CALIFORNIA

DECLARATION RE: LIMITED SCOPE OF APPEARANCE (F 2090–1.1)

Attorney or Party Name, Address, Telephone & FAX Numbers, and California State Bar Number Attorney for	FOR COURT USE ONLY
UNITED STATES BANKRUPTCY COURT **CENTRAL DISTRICT OF CALIFORNIA**	
In re: Debtor.	CHAPTER ______ CASE NUMBER
	(No Hearing Required)

DECLARATION RE: LIMITED SCOPE OF APPEARANCE
PURSUANT TO LOCAL BANKRUPTCY RULE 2090-1

TO THE COURT, THE DEBTOR, THE TRUSTEE (if any), AND THE UNITED STATES TRUSTEE:

1. I am the attorney for the Debtor in the above-captioned bankruptcy case.

2. On *(specify date)* , I agreed with the Debtor that for a fee of $, I would provide only the following services:

   a. ❑ Prepare and file the Petition and Schedules
   b. ❑ Represent the Debtor at the 341(a) Meeting
   c. ❑ Represent the Debtor in any relief from stay actions
   d. ❑ Represent the Debtor in any proceeding involving an objection to Debtor's discharge pursuant to 11 U.S.C. § 727
   e. ❑ Represent the Debtor in any proceeding to determine whether a specific debt is nondischargeable under 11 U.S.C. § 523
   f. ❑ Other *(specify)*:

3. I declare under penalty of perjury under the laws of the United States of America that the foregoing s true and correct and that this declaration was executed on the following date at the city set forth in the upper left-hand corner of this page.

Dated: ______________________________

Law Firm Name

I HEREBY APPROVE THE ABOVE:

By:

______________________________ Name: ______________________________

Signature of Debtor *Attorney for Debtor*

Declaration Re: Limited Scope of Appearance - *Page 2* **F 2090-1.1**

In re	CHAPTER ______
Debtor.	CASE NUMBER

PROOF OF SERVICE

STATE OF CALIFORNIA
COUNTY OF ________________

I am employed in the County of ________________________, State of California. I am over the age of 18 and not a party to the within action. My business address is as follows:

On ________________________, I served the foregoing document described as: DECLARATION RE: LIMITED SCOPE OF APPEARANCE PURSUANT TO LOCAL BANKRUPTCY RULE 2090-1 on the interested parties at their last known address in this action by placing a true and correct copy thereof in a sealed envelope with postage thereon fully prepaid in the United States Mail at ____________________, California, addressed as set forth below.

☐ Addresses continued on attached page

I declare under penalty of perjury under the laws of the United States of America that the foregoing is true and correct.

Dated:

______________________________ ______________________________

Type Name *Signature*

CDCAL-597 C.D. CALIFORNIA

DECLARATION RE: PAYMENT OF DOMESTIC SUPPORT OBLIGATIONS (F 3015–1.8)

Attorney or Party Name, Address, Telephone & FAX Numbers, and California State Bar Number ☐ Attorney for ☐ Pro Se Debtor	FOR COURT USE ONLY
UNITED STATES BANKRUPTCY COURT CENTRAL DISTRICT OF CALIFORNIA In re Debtor(s).	CHAPTER 13 CASE NUMBER **DECLARATION RE PAYMENT OF DOMESTIC SUPPORT OBLIGATIONS[1] (PRECONFIRMATION)** **Confirmation Hearing set for:**

In a joint case, each debtor must file a separate form. This declaration must be filed with the court and served on the Chapter 13 trustee not later than 10 days before the meeting of creditors pursuant to 11 U.S.C. § 341(a). Further declarations on the status of the Debtor's domestic support obligations must be filed on or before the date of each hearing on confirmation of the Debtor's plan. Check the appropriate boxes.

I, ______________________________ *(Debtor's name)*, hereby declare:

☐ As of the date of this declaration, I have paid all amounts that are required to be paid under a domestic support obligation that first became payable after the date of the filing of the petition.

☐ No domestic support obligations will come due between the date of this declaration and the date set for hearing on confirmation of my plan set forth above.

☐ As of the date of this declaration, I have NOT paid all amounts that are required to be paid under a domestic support obligation that first became payable after the date of the filing of the petition.

☐ I do not owe any domestic support obligations.

I declare under penalty of perjury that the foregoing is true and correct.

Dated: ______________________ ______________________________
Debtor

[1] The term "domestic support obligation" is defined in 11 U.S.C. § 101(14A).

DECLARATION RE: TAX RETURNS (F 3015–1.9)

Attorney or Party Name, Address, Telephone & FAX Numbers, and California State Bar Number ☐ Attorney for ☐ Pro Se Debtor	FOR COURT USE ONLY
UNITED STATES BANKRUPTCY COURT CENTRAL DISTRICT OF CALIFORNIA In re Debtor(s).	CHAPTER 13 CASE NUMBER **DECLARATION RE TAX RETURNS (PRECONFIRMATION)** **Confirmation Hearing set for:**

In a joint case, each debtor must file a separate form. This declaration must be filed with the court and served on the Chapter 13 trustee not later than 10 days before the date on which the meeting of creditors pursuant to 11 U.S.C. § 341(a) is first scheduled. Check the appropriate boxes.

I, ______________________________ *(Debtor's name)*, hereby declare:

☐ I have filed all tax returns required to be filed with federal, state, or local taxing authorities for all taxable periods ending during the 4 year period ending on the date of the filing of the petition, as required by 11 U.S.C. § 1308.

☐ I have NOT filed all tax returns required to be filed with federal, state, or local taxing authorities for all taxable periods ending during the 4 year period ending on the date of the filing of the petition, as required by 11 U.S.C. § 1308. I have not filed the following return(s) for the following years:[1]

Year	Taxing Authority (federal, state, or local)	Proposed Date for Filing Return
______	______________________	______________________
______	______________________	______________________

☐ I am not required to file federal, state, or local tax returns because: ______________________
____

I declare under penalty of perjury that the foregoing is true and correct:

Dated:______________________ ______________________________
Debtor

[1] Attach additional pages as necessary.

This form is mandatory. It has been approved for use by the United States Bankruptcy Court for the Central District of California.

DECLARATION SETTING FORTH POSTPETITION, PRECONFIRMATION DEED OF TRUST PAYMENTS (F 3015–1.4)

Attorney or Party Name, Address, Telephone & FAX Numbers, and California State Bar Number ☐ Attorney for ☐ Pro Se Debtor	FOR COURT USE ONLY
UNITED STATES BANKRUPTCY COURT **CENTRAL DISTRICT OF CALIFORNIA** In re Debtor(s).	CHAPTER 13 CASE NUMBER **DECLARATION SETTING FORTH POSTPETITION, PRECONFIRMATION DEED OF TRUST PAYMENTS** **LOCAL BANKRUPTCY RULE 3015-1(m)**

I, ______________________________ *(Debtor's name)*, hereby declare:

1. I am the debtor in this chapter 13 bankruptcy case that was filed on ____________________.

2. I am the owner of real property[1] at the following street address:

   ____

   ______________________________ (the "Property").

3. The Property is encumbered by the following deeds of trust:

   a. First deed of trust in favor of ______________________________.

   b. Second deed of trust in favor of ______________________________ *(if applicable)*.

   c. Third deed of trust in favor of ______________________________ *(if applicable)*.

(Continued on next page)

[1]A separate declaration shall be filed and served for each parcel of real property owned by the Debtor(s).

Declaration Setting Forth Postpetition, Preconfirmation Deed of Trust Payments **F 3015-1.4**
Local Bankruptcy Rule 3015-1(m) - *Page 2 of 3*

In re	CHAPTER 13
Debtor(s).	CASE NUMBER

4. The following are the postpetition deed of trust payments[2] up to the date of plan confirmation (the "Payments") that I have caused to be mailed/delivered[3] to the appropriate deed of trust holder (the "Creditor")[4]:

Creditor	Payment Amount	Due Date[5]	Date Mailed/Delivered
Creditor			
Creditor			

5. The Payments were in the form of money order, cashier's check, wire transfer, or other certified funds payable to the appropriate Creditor and had written on each item my name, the bankruptcy case number and the appropriate loan number.

(Continued on next page)

[2]Postpetition deed of trust payments are payments that first become due after the bankruptcy filing date.

[3]A U. S. Postal Service Certificate of Mailing, stamped by a Postal Service employee, must be obtained for each mailed Payment and copies of the Certificates of Mailing must be attached. If Payments are not mailed, Debtor must state how the Payments were delivered to the deed of trust holder and must provide documents that prove that the Payments have been delivered. For example, a copy of a statement, signed by the deed of trust holder's representative, acknowledging receipt of the Payment(s), would provide such proof.

[4]Attach additional pages if necessary.

[5] "Due Date" refers to the last day the Payment can be paid without a late charge penalty.

In re	CHAPTER 13
Debtor(s).	CASE NUMBER

6. Attached to this declaration are copies of the:

   ☐ cashier's checks, ☐ money orders, ☐ certified funds, or

   ☐ other proof of the Payments described in Paragraph 4 above.

7. Also attached to this declaration are copies of the:

   ☐ U. S. Post Office Certificate(s) of Mailing, stamped by a U. S. Postal Service employee,

   ☐ acknowledgment(s) signed by the Creditor's representative, or

   ☐ other documents that prove delivery of the Payments described in Paragraph 4 above.

   I declare under penalty of perjury that the foregoing is true and correct.

Dated: ______________________ ______________________________
Debtor

DECLARATION SETTING FORTH POST PETITION, PRECONFIRMATION PAYMENTS ON LEASES OF PERSONAL PROPERTY AND PURCHASE MONEY SECURITY LIENS IN PERSONAL PROPERTY (F 3015-1.10)

Attorney or Party Name, Address, Telephone & FAX Numbers, and California State Bar Number ☐ Attorney for ☐ Pro Se Debtor	FOR COURT USE ONLY
UNITED STATES BANKRUPTCY COURT CENTRAL DISTRICT OF CALIFORNIA	CHAPTER 13 CASE NUMBER
In re Debtor(s).	**DECLARATION SETTING FORTH POST PETITION, PRECONFIRMATION PAYMENTS ON:** **1. LEASES OF PERSONAL PROPERTY;** **2. PURCHASE MONEY SECURITY LIENS IN PERSONAL PROPERTY**

I, ______________________________ *(Debtor's name)*, hereby declare:

1. I am the debtor in this chapter 13 bankruptcy case that was filed on ____________________.

2. PERSONAL PROPERTY LEASES[1]

   A. I am the obligor (Lessee) on lease(s) of personal property as set forth below.

Property Description[2]	Lessor's Name	Acct. No. (last 4 digits)	Due Date[3]	Date Late	Payment Amount

[1] Attach additional pages as necessary.

[2] Include make, model, and year as applicable.

[3] "Due Date" refers to the last day the Payment can be paid without a late charge penalty.

This form is mandatory. It has been approved for use by the United States Bankruptcy Court for the Central District of California.

Declaration Setting Forth Post Petition, Preconfirmation Payments On: Leases of Personal Property; Purchase Money Security Liens in Personal Property **F 3015-1.10**

In re	CHAPTER 13
Debtor(s).	CASE NUMBER

B. The following are the post-petition payments[4] up to the date of plan confirmation (the "Payments") that I have caused to be mailed/delivered[5] to the appropriate Lessor as required pursuant to 11 U.S.C. § 1326(a)(1)(B).

Lessor	Payment Amount	Due Date	Date Tendered	Method of Delivery

3. PURCHASE MONEY SECURITY CONTRACTS FOR PERSONAL PROPERTY

A. I am the obligor on a contract for the sale of personal property subject to a purchase money security interest as set forth below.

Property Description	Creditor's Name	Acct. No. (last 4 digits)	Due Date	Date Late	Payment Amount

[4] Post petition payments are payments that first become due after the bankruptcy filing date.

[5] A U. S. Postal Service Certificate of Mailing, stamped by a Postal Service employee, must be obtained for each mailed Payment and copies of the Certificates of Mailing must be attached. If Payments were not mailed, Debtor must state how the Payments were delivered to the Lessor/Creditor and must provide documents that prove that the Payments have been delivered. For example, a copy of a statement, signed by the Lessor/Creditor's representative, acknowledging receipt of the Payment(s), would provide such proof.

Declaration Setting Forth Post Petition, Preconfirmation Payments On: Leases of Personal Property; Purchase Money Security Liens in Personal Property **F 3015-1.10**

Page 3 of 3

In re	CHAPTER 13
Debtor(s).	CASE NUMBER

B. The following are the post-petition Payments up to the date of plan confirmation that I have caused to be mailed/delivered to the appropriate Creditor pursuant to 11 U.S.C. § 1326(a)(1)(C).

Creditor	Payment Amount	Due Date	Date Tendered	Method of Delivery

4. The Payments set forth above were in the form of money order, cashier's check, wire transfer, or other certified funds payable to the appropriate Creditor and had written on each item my name, the bankruptcy case number and the appropriate loan number.

5. Attached to this declaration are copies of the:

__ cashier's checks __ money orders __ certified funds, or

__ other proof of the Payments described in Paragraphs 2B and 3B above.

6. Also attached to this declaration are copies of the:

__ U. S. Post Office Certificate(s) of Mailing, stamped by a U. S. Postal Service employee.

__ acknowledgment(s) signed by the Lessor/Creditor's representative, or

__ other documents that prove delivery of the Payments described in Paragraphs 2B and 3B above.

I declare under penalty of perjury that the foregoing is true and correct.

Dated: ____________________ ____________________
Debtor

This form is mandatory. It has been approved for use by the United States Bankruptcy Court for the Central District of California.

Declaration to be Filed with Motion Establishing Administrative Procedures RE 28 U.S.C. § 156(c) (F 5075-1.1)

Attorney or Party Name, Address, Telephone & FAX Numbers, and California State Bar Number	FOR COURT USE ONLY
UNITED STATES BANKRUPTCY COURT CENTRAL DISTRICT OF CALIFORNIA	CHAPTER: CASE NO.:
In re: Debtor(s).	**DECLARATION TO BE FILED WITH MOTION ESTABLISHING ADMINISTRATIVE PROCEDURES RE 28 U.S.C. § 156(c)**

I have obtained the most recent and applicable version of the Mega Case Procedures Checklist from the Clerk of Court and have consulted with the Clerk or designee. The completed checklist is attached.

I declare under penalty of perjury under the laws of the United States of America that the attached Mega Case Procedures Checklist is true and correct and that this Declaration was executed on ____________________, _____, at ______________________________ *(city, state).*

____________________________ ____________________________

Print Declarant's Name *Signature of Declarant*

This form is mandatory by Order of the United States Bankruptcy Court for the Central District of California.

DEFAULT JUDGMENT (F 9021–1.4)

Attorney or Party Name, Address, Telephone & FAX Numbers, and California State Bar Number Attorney for	FOR COURT USE ONLY
UNITED STATES BANKRUPTCY COURT CENTRAL DISTRICT OF CALIFORNIA	
In re: Debtor.	
Plaintiff(s),	CHAPTER ______ CASE NUMBER
vs.	ADVERSARY NUMBER
Defendant(s).	DATE: TIME: COURTROOM:

DEFAULT JUDGMENT
(WITHOUT PRIOR JUDGMENT)

Based on the Defendant's failure to respond to the Complaint, the Court renders its judgment, as follows:

1. Judgment shall be entered in favor of Plaintiff *(specify name)*:
   and against Defendant *(specify name)*:

2. a. ☐ Plaintiff is awarded damages in the following amount: $
   b. ☐ Plaintiff is awarded costs in the following amount: $
   c. ☐ Plaintiff is awarded attorney fees in the following amount: $
   d. ☐ Plaintiff is awarded interest at the rate of ________% per year from the following date to the date of entry of this Judgment *(Specify date from which interest shall begin to run)*:
   e. ☐ Plaintiff is granted the following relief *(specify)*: ☐ See Attached Page

3. ☐ This Judgment or claim is determined to be non-dischargeable under: ☐ Bankruptcy Code § 523(a) ________ ☐ Other *(specify)*:

4. ☐ The Court further adjudges as follows: ☐ See Attached Page

Dated: ______________________________

____
JUDGE OF THE UNITED STATES BANKRUPTCY COURT
CENTRAL DISTRICT OF CALIFORNIA

This form is optional. It has been approved for use by the United States Bankruptcy Court for the Central District of California.

Revised November 1999

F 9021-1.4

In re Debtor.	CHAPTER ______ CASE NUMBER

PROOF OF SERVICE BY MAIL

STATE OF CALIFORNIA COUNTY OF ______________________________

I am employed in the above County, State of California. I am over the age of 18 and not a party to the within action. My business address is as follows:

On ___________________________________, I served the foregoing document described as: DEFAULT JUDGMENT on the interested parties at their last known address in this action by placing a true and correct copy thereof in a sealed envelope with postage thereon fully prepaid in the United States Mail at ________________________, California, addressed as follows:

☐ Addresses continued on attached page

I declare under penalty of perjury under the laws of the United States of America that the foregoing is true and correct.

Dated:

_________________________________ *Type Name*

_________________________________ *Signature*

This form is optional. It has been approved for use by the United States Bankruptcy Court for the Central District of California.

Default Judgment (based on prior judgment) (F 9021-1.5)

Attorney or Party Name, Address, Telephone & FAX Numbers, and California State Bar Number Attorney for	FOR COURT USE ONLY
UNITED STATES BANKRUPTCY COURT CENTRAL DISTRICT OF CALIFORNIA	
In re: Debtor.	
Plaintiff(s), vs.	CHAPTER ________ CASE NUMBER ADVERSARY NUMBER
Defendant(s).	DATE: TIME: COURTROOM:

DEFAULT JUDGMENT
(BASED ON PRIOR JUDGMENT)

Based on the Defendant's failure to respond to the Complaint, the Court renders its judgment, as follows:

1. Judgment shall be entered in favor of Plaintiff *(specify name)*:
   and against Defendant *(specify name)*:

2. ☐ The liability resulting from the judgment previously entered in favor of the Plaintiff as described below is hereby determined to be non-dischargeable under: ☐ Bankruptcy Code § 523(a) ______
   ☐ Other *(specify)*:

   Case: ______________________
   Court: ______________________

   A copy of the underlying judgment is attached.

3. a. ☐ Plaintiff is awarded costs in the following amount: $
   b. ☐ Plaintiff is awarded attorney fees in the following amount: $
   c. ☐ Plaintiff is granted the following relief *(specify)*: ☐ See Attached Page

4. ☐ The Court further adjudges as follows: ☐ See Attached Page

Dated: ______________________

JUDGE OF THE UNITED STATES BANKRUPTCY COURT
CENTRAL DISTRICT OF CALIFORNIA

This form is optional. It has been approved for use by the United States Bankruptcy Court for the Central District of California.

January 2009 **F 9021-1.5**

In re	CHAPTER:
Debtor.	CASE NO.:

NOTE: When using this form to indicate service of a proposed order, **DO NOT** list any person or entity in Category I. Proposed orders do not generate an NEF because only orders that have been entered are placed on a CM/ECF docket.

PROOF OF SERVICE OF DOCUMENT

I am over the age of 18 and not a party to this bankruptcy case or adversary proceeding. My business address is:

A true and correct copy of the foregoing document described as ______________________________ ______________________________ will be served or was served **(a)** on the judge in chambers in the form and manner required by LBR 5005-2(d), and **(b)** in the manner indicated below:

I. TO BE SERVED BY THE COURT VIA NOTICE OF ELECTRONIC FILING ("NEF") - Pursuant to controlling General Order(s) and Local Bankruptcy Rule(s) ("LBR"), the foregoing document will be served by the court via NEF and hyperlink to the document. On ______________ I checked the CM/ECF docket for this bankruptcy case or adversary proceeding and determined that the following person(s) are on the Electronic Mail Notice List to receive NEF transmission at the email addressed indicated below:

☐ Service information continued on attached page

II. SERVED BY U.S. MAIL OR OVERNIGHT MAIL (indicate method for each person or entity served):
On ______________ I served the following person(s) and/or entity(ies) at the last known address(es) in this bankruptcy case or adversary proceeding by placing a true and correct copy thereof in a sealed envelope in the United States Mail, first class, postage prepaid, and/or with an overnight mail service addressed as follow. Listing the judge here constitutes a declaration that mailing to the judge will be completed no later than 24 hours after the document is filed.

☐ Service information continued on attached page

III. SERVED BY PERSONAL DELIVERY, FACSIMILE TRANSMISSION OR EMAIL (indicate method for each person or entity served): Pursuant to F.R.Civ.P. 5 and/or controlling LBR, on ______________ I served the following person(s) and/or entity(ies) by personal delivery, or (for those who consented in writing to such service method) by facsimile transmission and/or email as follows. Listing the judge here constitutes a declaration that mailing to the judge will be completed no later than 24 hours after the document is filed.

☐ Service information continued on attached page

I declare under penalty of perjury under the laws of the United States of America that the foregoing is true and correct.

______________ ______________ ______________
Date *Type Name* *Signature*

In re	CHAPTER:
Debtor.	CASE NO.:

ADDITIONAL SERVICE INFORMATION (if needed):

In re	CHAPTER:
Debtor.	CASE NO.:

NOTE TO USERS OF THIS FORM:

1) Attach this form to the last page of a proposed Order or Judgment. Do not file as a separate document.
2) The title of the judgment or order and all service information must be filled in by the party lodging the order.
3) Category I. below: The United States trustee and case trustee (if any) will always be in this category.
4) Category II. below: List ONLY addresses for debtor (and attorney), movant (or attorney) and person/entity (or attorney) who filed an opposition to the requested relief. DO NOT list an address if person/entity is listed in category I.

NOTICE OF ENTERED ORDER AND SERVICE LIST

Notice is given by the court that a judgment or order entitled (*specify*) ______________________________ ______________________________ was entered on the date indicated as "Entered" on the first page of this judgment or order and will be served in the manner indicated below:

I. SERVED BY THE COURT VIA NOTICE OF ELECTRONIC FILING ("NEF") - Pursuant to controlling General Order(s) and Local Bankruptcy Rule(s), the foregoing document was served on the following person(s) by the court via NEF and hyperlink to the judgment or order. As of______________________, the following person(s) are currently on the Electronic Mail Notice List for this bankruptcy case or adversary proceeding to receive NEF transmission at the email address(es) indicated below.

☐ Service information continued on attached page

II. SERVED BY THE COURT VIA U.S. MAIL: A copy of this notice and a true copy of this judgment or order was sent by United States Mail, first class, postage prepaid, to the following person(s) and/or entity(ies) at the address(es) indicated below:

☐ Service information continued on attached page

III. TO BE SERVED BY THE LODGING PARTY: Within 72 hours after receipt of a copy of this judgment or order which bears an "Entered" stamp, the party lodging the judgment or order will serve a complete copy bearing an "Entered" stamp by U.S. Mail, overnight mail, facsimile transmission or email and file a proof of service of the entered order on the following person(s) and/or entity(ies) at the address(es), facsimile transmission number(s), and/or email address(es) indicated below:

☐ Service information continued on attached page

In re	CHAPTER:
Debtor.	CASE NO.:

ADDITIONAL SERVICE INFORMATION (if needed):

Disclosure of Compensation of Attorney for Debtor

Form B203 - Disclosure of Compensation of Attorney for Debtor - (1/88) 1998 USBC, Central District of California

<table>
<tr><td colspan="2">UNITED STATES BANKRUPTCY COURT
CENTRAL DISTRICT OF CALIFORNIA</td></tr>
<tr><td rowspan="2">In re

Debtor.</td><td>Case No.:</td></tr>
<tr><td>DISCLOSURE OF COMPENSATION
OF ATTORNEY FOR DEBTOR</td></tr>
</table>

1. Pursuant to 11 U.S.C. § 329(a) and Bankruptcy Rule 2016(b), I certify that I am the attorney for the above-named debtor(s) and that compensation paid to me within one year before the filing of the petition in bankruptcy, or agreed to be paid to me, for services rendered or to be rendered on behalf of the debtor(s) in contemplation of or in connection with the bankruptcy case is as follow:

   For legal services, I have agreed to accept .... $________

   Prior to the filing of this statement I have received.................................. $________

   Balance Due.. $________

2. The source of the compensation paid to me was:

   ❑ Debtor ❑ Other *(specify)*

3. The source of compensation to be paid to me is:

   ❑ Debtor ❑ Other *(specify)*

4. ❑ I have not agreed to share the above-disclosed compensation with any other person unless they are members and associates of my law firm.

   ❑ I have agreed to share the above-disclosed compensation with a person or persons who are not members or associates of my law firm. A copy of the agreement, together with a list of the names of the people sharing in the compensation, is attached.

5. In return for the above-disclosed fee, I have agreed to render legal service for all aspects of the bankruptcy case, including:

   a. Analysis of the debtor's financial situation, and rendering advice to the debtor in determining whether to file a petition in bankruptcy;

   b. Preparation and filing of any petition, schedules, statement of affairs and plan which may be required;

   c. Representation of the debtor at the meeting of creditors and confirmation hearing, and any adjourned hearings thereof;

   d. Representation of the debtor in adversary proceedings and other contested bankruptcy matters;

   e. [Other provisions as needed].

Form B203 Page Two - Disclosure of Compensation of Attorney for Debtor (1/88) 1998 USBC, Central District of California

6. By agreement with the debtor(s), the above-disclosed fee does not include the following services

CERTIFICATION

I certify that the foregoing is a complete statement of any agreement or arrangement for payment to me for representation of the debtor(s) in this bankruptcy proceeding.

_________________________ _________________________
Date *Signature of Attorney*

____
Name of Law Firm

Disclosure of Compensation of Bankruptcy Petition Preparer

Disclosure of Compensation - (Rev. 12/03) 2003 USBC, Central District of California

UNITED STATES BANKRUPTCY COURT
CENTRAL DISTRICT OF CALIFORNIA

Attorney or Party Name, Address, and Telephone Number	FOR COURT USE ONLY
In re Debtor.	CASE NO.: CHAPTER: Debtor Address:

DISCLOSURE OF COMPENSATION OF BANKRUPTCY PETITION PREPARER

1. Under 11 U.S.C. § 110(h), I declare under penalty of perjury that I am not an attorney or employee of an attorney, that I prepared or caused to be prepared one or more documents for filing by the above-named debtor(s) in connection with this bankruptcy case, and that compensation paid to me within one year before the filing of the bankruptcy petition, or agreed to be paid to me, for services rendered on behalf of the debtor(s) in contemplation of or in connection with the bankruptcy case is as follows:

   For document preparations services, I have agreed to accept .... $______

   Prior to the filing of this statement I have received .... $______

   Balance Due .... $______

2. I have prepared or caused to be prepared the following documents *(itemize)*:

   and provided the following services *(itemize)*:

3. The source of the compensation paid to me was:

   ☐ debtor ☐ Other *(specify)*:

4. The source of compensation to be paid to me is:

   ☐ debtor ☐ Other *(specify)*:

5. The foregoing is a complete statement of any agreement or arrangement for payment to me for preparation of the petition filed by the debtor(s) in this bankruptcy case.

6. To my knowledge no other person has prepared for compensation a document for filing in connection with this bankruptcy case except as listed below:

________________ ________________
Name Complete Social Security Number

Disclosure of Compensation - Page 2 - (Rev. 12/03) 2003 USBC, Central District of California

In re Debtor.	Case No.: (If known)

DECLARATION OF BANKRUPTCY PETITION PREPARER

I declare under penalty of perjury that the foregoing is true and correct to the best of my knowledge, information, and belief.

_______________ _______________ _______________

Signature Complete Social Security Number Date

Name (Print): _______________

Address: _______________

____

A bankruptcy petition preparer's failure to comply with the provisions of title 11 and the Federal Rules of Bankruptcy Procedure may result in fines or imprisonment or both. 11 U.S.C. § 110; 18 U.S.C. § 156.

Default Judgment RE Complaint to Avoid Junior Lien on Principal Residence [11 U.S.C. § 506(a),(d); FRBP 3012] (Optional) (F 4003-2.5.DEFAULT.JUDGMENT)

Attorney or Party Name, Address, Telephone & FAX Nos., State Bar No. & Email Address ☐ *Attorney for Plaintiff(s)* ☐ Plaintiff(s) *appearing without attorney*	FOR COURT USE ONLY
UNITED STATES BANKRUPTCY COURT **CENTRAL DISTRICT OF CALIFORNIA - ________________ DIVISION**	
In re: Debtor(s).	CASE NO.: CHAPTER 13 ADVERSARY NO.:
Plaintiff(s), vs. Defendant.	**DEBTOR'S MOTION FOR DEFAULT JUDGMENT RE COMPLAINT TO AVOID JUNIOR LIEN ON PRINCIPAL RESIDENCE [11 U.S.C. § 506(a),(d), FRBP 3012]** DATE: TIME: COURTROOM: PLACE:

NAME OF CREDITOR HOLDING JUNIOR LIEN: ____

1. Name of Defendant(s) against whom default judgment is sought: ________________________ *(hereinafter,* "Defendant").
2. Plaintiff(s) filed the Complaint in the above-captioned proceeding on ______________.
3. The Summons and Complaint were served on Defendant by ☐ Personal Service ☐ Mail Service on the following date _______________.

4. A conformed copy of the completed Return of Summons form is attached hereto.

5. The time for filing an answer or other response expired on ______________.

6. No answer or other response has been filed or served by Defendant.

7. The default of Defendant:

a. ☐ Has not yet been entered, but is hereby requested.

b. ☐ Was Entered on ______________________.

8. **A Status Conference:**

a. ☐ Is scheduled for ____.
Specify date, time, and place

b. ☐ Was held on ____.
Specify date, time, and place

9. ☐ **DECLARATION OF NON-MILITARY STATUS:** No defendant named in Paragraph 1 above is in the military service so as to be entitled to the benefits of the Servicemembers Civil Relief Act (Pub. L. 108-189) (50 U.S. Code App. §§ 501-594). The undersigned declares under penalty of perjury that this statement of defendant's non-military status is true and correct and is made under penalty of perjury under the laws of the United States of America based upon the undersigned's review of said Defendant's Statement of Affairs and Statement of Income and Expenditures filed in this case and is based upon the undersigned's lack of any information or belief that there has been any change of circumstances as to the defendant's non-military status.

10. ☐ Defaulting party is **not** an **infant** or **incompetent** party.

11. **Property at Issue:**

Plaintiff moves to avoid the junior deed of trust, mortgage or other encumbrance (hereinafter, "Junior lien") encumbering the following real property ("Property"), which is principal residence of Plaintiff(s).

Street Address: ____
Unit Number.: __________
City, State, Zip Code: ____

Legal description or document recording number (including county of recording):

☐ See attached page.

12. **Grounds for Determining Unsecured Status and Avoidance of Junior Lien:**

a. As of ________________________, the Property is subject to the following liens in the amounts specified securing the debt against the Property, which the debtor seeks to have treated as indicated:

________________________ in the amount of $________________

i. ________________________ in the amount of $________________ ☐ is ☐ is not to be avoided;

ii. ________________________ in the amount of $________________ ☐ is ☐ is not to be avoided;

☐ See attached page for additional lien(s).

b. As of ________________________, Property is worth no more than $________________.

c. As a result, Defendant's claim related to the Junior lien on the Property is ☐ wholly ☐ partially unsecured.

13. **Evidence in Support of Motion:**

a. ☐ The amount of the 1st lien identified in paragraph 12(a)(i) is based on ________________________, ________________________ attached hereto and identified as Exhibit ____.

b. ☐ The amount of the 2nd lien identified in paragraph 12(a)(ii) is based on ________________________ ________________________ attached hereto and identified as Exhibit ____.

c. ☐ The amount of the 3rd lien identified in paragraph 12(a)(iii) is based on ________________________ ________________________, attached hereto and identified as Exhibit ____.

d. ☐ The relative priority of the liens encumbering the Property is established by evidence attached as Exhibit ____.

e. ☐ The value of the Property from paragraph 3(b) is based on ________________________, ________________________attached as Exhibit ____:

f. ☐ Plaintiff submits the attached Declaration.

g. ☐ Other evidence *(specify)*: ________________________.

14. **WHEREFORE, Plaintiff prays that this Court issue an Order granting the following relief:**

a. That the Property is valued at no more than $________________.
That Defendant's claim related to the Junior lien shall be allowed as a non-priority general unsecured claim in the amount per the filed Proof of Claim.

b. The avoidance of Defendant's Junior lien is contingent upon ☐ Debtor's completion of the chapter 13 plan, or ☐ Debtor's receipt of a chapter 13 discharge.

c. The Defendant shall retain its lien in the junior position for the full amount due under the corresponding note and lien in the event of either the dismissal of Debtor's chapter 13 case, the conversion of Debtor's chapter 13 case to any other chapter under the United States Bankruptcy Code, or if the Property is sold or refinanced prior to:
☐ Debtor's completion of the chapter 13 plan, or
☐ Debtor's receipt of a chapter 13 discharge.

d. In the event that the holder of the first position lien or any senior lien on the Property forecloses on its interest and extinguishes Defendant's lien rights prior to: ☐ Debtor's completion of the chapter 13 plan, or ☐ Debtor's receipt of a chapter 13 discharge, Defendant's lien shall attach to the proceeds greater than necessary to pay the senior lien, if any, from the foreclosure sale.

e. ☐ See attached continuation page for additional provisions.

Dated: ____________________

Respectfully submitted,

By: ______________________________
Signature of Plaintiff or Attorney for Plaintiff

Name: ______________________________
Type Name of Plaintiff or Attorney for Plaintiff

CDCAL-621 C.D. CALIFORNIA

PROOF OF SERVICE OF DOCUMENT

I am over the age of 18 and not a party to this bankruptcy case or adversary proceeding. My business address is:

A true and correct copy of the foregoing document described as **DEBTOR'S MOTION FOR DEFAULT JUDGMENT RE COMPLAINT TO AVOID JUNIOR LIEN ON PRINCIPAL RESIDENCE** will be served or was served **(a)** on the judge in chambers in the form and manner required by LBR 5005-2(d); and **(b)** in the manner indicated below:

I. **TO BE SERVED BY THE COURT VIA NOTICE OF ELECTRONIC FILING ("NEF")** – Pursuant to controlling General Order(s) and Local Bankruptcy Rule(s) ("LBR"), the foregoing document will be served by the court via NEF and hyperlink to the document. On ____________________, I checked the CM/ECF docket for this bankruptcy case or adversary proceeding and determined that the following person(s) are on the Electronic Mail Notice List to receive NEF transmission at the email address(es) indicated below:

☐ Service information continued on attached page

II. **SERVED BY U.S. MAIL OR OVERNIGHT MAIL** (indicate method for each person or entity served):
On ____________________, I served the following person(s) and/or entity(ies) at the last known address(es) in this bankruptcy case or adversary proceeding by placing a true and correct copy thereof in a sealed envelope in the United States Mail, first class, postage prepaid, and/or with an overnight mail service addressed as follows. Listing the judge here constitutes a declaration that mailing to the judge will be completed no later than 24 hours after the document is filed.

☐ Service information continued on attached page

III. **SERVED BY PERSONAL DELIVERY, FACSIMILE TRANSMISSION OR EMAIL** (indicate method for each person or entity served): Pursuant to F.R.Civ.P. 5 and/or controlling LBR, on ____________________, I served the following person(s) and/or entity(ies) by personal delivery, or (for those who consented in writing to such service method), by facsimile transmission and/or email as follows. Listing the judge here constitutes a declaration that personal delivery on the judge will be completed no later than 24 hours after the document is filed.

☐ Service information continued on attached page

I declare under penalty of perjury under the laws of the United States of America that the foregoing is true and correct.

Date *Type Name* *Signature*

II. **SERVED BY U.S. MAIL, CERTIFIED MAIL OR OVERNIGHT MAIL** (indicate method for each person or entity served):
(Attached page to Proof of Service-please include any additional or alternative addresses and attach additional pages if needed)
(Certified Mail required for service on a national bank.)

Name of 1st Name of 1st Lien Holder & Address	Address from: ☐ Proof of claim ☐ Secretary of State ☐ FDIC website ☐ Other: *specify*	Delivery Method ☐ US Mail ☐ Certified mail – Tracking # ______ ☐ Overnight mail – Tracking # ______ Carrier Name: ______
Name of 1st Lien Holder- Agent for Service of Process	Address from: ☐ Proof of claim ☐ Secretary of State ☐ FDIC website ☐ Other: *specify*	Delivery Method ☐ US Mail ☐ Certified mail – Tracking # ______ ☐ Overnight mail – Tracking # ______ Carrier Name: ______
Name of 1st Lien Holder – Servicing Agent	Address from: ☐ Proof of claim ☐ Secretary of State ☐ FDIC website ☐ Other: *specify*	Delivery Method ☐ US Mail ☐ Certified mail – Tracking # ______ ☐ Overnight mail – Tracking # ______ Carrier Name: ______

Name of 2nd Lien Holder & Address	Address from: ☐ Proof of claim ☐ Secretary of State ☐ FDIC website ☐ Other: *specify*	Delivery Method ☐ US Mail ☐ Certified mail – Tracking # ______ ☐ Overnight mail – Tracking # ______ Carrier Name: ______
Name of 2nd Lien Holder- Agent for Service of Process	Address from: ☐ Proof of claim ☐ Secretary of State ☐ FDIC website ☐ Other: *specify*	Delivery Method ☐ US Mail ☐ Certified mail – Tracking # ______ ☐ Overnight mail – Tracking # ______ Carrier Name: ______
Name of 2nd Lien Holder – Servicing Agent	Address from: ☐ Proof of claim ☐ Secretary of State ☐ FDIC website ☐ Other: *specify*	Delivery Method ☐ US Mail ☐ Certified mail – Tracking # ______ ☐ Overnight mail – Tracking # ______ Carrier Name: ______

Name of 3rd Lien Holder & Address	Address from: ☐ Proof of claim ☐ Secretary of State ☐ FDIC website ☐ Other: *specify*	Delivery Method ☐ US Mail ☐ Certified mail – Tracking # ☐ Overnight mail – Tracking # Carrier Name:
Name of 3rd Lien Holder- Agent for Service of Process	Address from: ☐ Proof of claim ☐ Secretary of State ☐ FDIC website ☐ Other: *specify*	Delivery Method ☐ US Mail ☐ Certified mail – Tracking # ☐ Overnight mail – Tracking # Carrier Name:
Name of 3rd Lien Holder – Servicing Agent	Address from: ☐ Proof of claim ☐ Secretary of State ☐ FDIC website ☐ Other: *specify*	Delivery Method ☐ US Mail ☐ Certified mail – Tracking # ☐ Overnight mail – Tracking # Carrier Name:

Alternative/Additional Address	Address from: ☐ Proof of claim ☐ Secretary of State ☐ FDIC website ☐ Other: *specify*	Delivery Method ☐ US Mail ☐ Certified mail – Tracking # ☐ Overnight mail – Tracking # Carrier Name:
Alternative/Additional Address	Address from: ☐ Proof of claim ☐ Secretary of State ☐ FDIC website ☐ Other: *specify*	Delivery Method ☐ US Mail ☐ Certified mail – Tracking # ☐ Overnight mail – Tracking # Carrier Name:

ELECTRONIC FILING DECLARATION OF AUTHORIZED SIGNATORY OF DEBTOR (CAC)

Attorney or Party Name, Address, Telephone & FAX Numbers, and California State Bar Number ☐ Attorney for:	FOR COURT USE ONLY
UNITED STATES BANKRUPTCY COURT CENTRAL DISTRICT OF CALIFORNIA	
In re: Debtor(s).	CASE NO.: CHAPTER: ADV. NO.:

ELECTRONIC FILING DECLARATION
(CORPORATION/PARTNERSHIP)

☐ Petition, statement of affairs, schedules or lists — Date Filed: ______________
☐ Amendments to the petition, statement of affairs, schedules or lists — Date Filed: ______________
☐ Other: ______________________________ — Date Filed: ______________

PART I - DECLARATION OF AUTHORIZED SIGNATORY OF DEBTOR OR OTHER PARTY

I, the undersigned, hereby declare under penalty of perjury that: (1) I have been authorized by the Debtor or other party on whose behalf the above-referenced document is being filed (Filing Party) to sign and to file, on behalf of the Filing Party, the above-referenced document being filed electronically (Filed Document); (2) I have read and understand the Filed Document; (3) the information provided in the Filed Document is true, correct and complete; (4) the "/s/," followed by my name, on the signature lines for the Filing Party in the Filed Document serves as my signature on behalf of the Filing Party and denotes the making of such declarations, requests, statements, verifications and certifications by me and by the Filing Party to the same extent and effect as my actual signature on such signature lines; (5) I have actually signed a true and correct hard copy of the Filed Document in such places on behalf of the Filing Party and provided the executed hard copy of the Filed Document to the Filing Party's attorney; and (6) I, on behalf of the Filing Party, have authorized the Filing Party's attorney to file the electronic version of the Filed Document and this *Declaration* with the United States Bankruptcy Court for the Central District of California.

_______________________________________ _______________________
Signature of Authorized Signatory of Filing Party Date

____
Printed Name of Authorized Signatory of Filing Party

____
Title of Authorized Signatory of Filing Party

PART II - DECLARATION OF ATTORNEY FOR FILING PARTY

I, the undersigned Attorney for the Filing Party, hereby declare under penalty of perjury that: (1) the "/s/," followed by my name, on the signature lines for the Attorney for the Filing Party in the Filed Document serves as my signature and denotes the making of such declarations, requests, statements, verifications and certifications to the same extent and effect as my actual signature on such signature lines; (2) an authorized signatory of the Filing Party signed the *Declaration of Authorized Signatory of Debtor or Other Party* before I electronically submitted the Filed Document for filing with the United States Bankruptcy Court for the Central District of California; (3) I have actually signed a true and correct hard copy of the Filed Document in the locations that are indicated by "/s/," followed by my name, and have obtained the signature of the authorized signatory of the Filing Party in the locations that are indicated by "/s/," followed by the name of the Filing Party's authorized signatory, on the true and correct hard copy of the Filed Document; (4) I shall maintain the executed originals of this *Declaration*, the *Declaration of Authorized Signatory of Debtor or Other Party*, and the Filed Document for a period of five years after the closing of the case in which they are filed; and (5) I shall make the executed originals of this *Declaration*, the *Declaration of Authorized Signatory of Debtor or Other Party*, and the Filed Document available for review upon request of the Court or other parties.

_______________________________________ _______________________
Signature of Attorney for Filing Party Date

____
Printed Name of Attorney for Filing Party

This form is mandatory by Order of the United States Bankruptcy Court for the Central District of California.

November 2006

CDCAL-625 C.D. CALIFORNIA

ELECTRONIC FILING DECLARATION OF DEBTOR(S) - INDIVIDUAL (CAC)

Attorney or Party Name, Address, Telephone & FAX Numbers, and California State Bar Number ☐ Attorney for:	FOR COURT USE ONLY
UNITED STATES BANKRUPTCY COURT **CENTRAL DISTRICT OF CALIFORNIA**	
In re: Debtor(s).	CASE NO.: CHAPTER: ADV. NO.:

ELECTRONIC FILING DECLARATION
(INDIVIDUAL)

☐ Petition, statement of affairs, schedules or lists — Date Filed: ____________
☐ Amendments to the petition, statement of affairs, schedules or lists — Date Filed: ____________
☐ Other: ______________________________ — Date Filed: ____________

PART I - DECLARATION OF DEBTOR(S) OR OTHER PARTY

I (We), the undersigned Debtor(s) or other party on whose behalf the above-referenced document is being filed (Signing Party), hereby declare under penalty of perjury that: (1) I have read and understand the above-referenced document being filed electronically (Filed Document); (2) the information provided in the Filed Document is true, correct and complete; (3) the "/s/," followed by my name, on the signature line(s) for the Signing Party in the Filed Document serves as my signature and denotes the making of such declarations, requests, statements, verifications and certifications to the same extent and effect as my actual signature on such signature line(s); (4) I have actually signed a true and correct hard copy of the Filed Document in such places and provided the executed hard copy of the Filed Document to my attorney; and (5) I have authorized my attorney to file the electronic version of the Filed Document and this *Declaration* with the United States Bankruptcy Court for the Central District of California. If the Filed Document is a petition, I further declare under penalty of perjury that I have completed and signed a *Statement of Social Security Number(s)* (Form B21) and provided the executed original to my attorney.

______________________________ ______________________________
Signature of Signing Party Date

____
Printed Name of Signing Party

______________________________ ______________________________
Signature of Joint Debtor (if applicable) Date

____
Printed Name of Joint Debtor (if applicable)

PART II - DECLARATION OF ATTORNEY FOR SIGNING PARTY

I, the undersigned Attorney for the Signing Party, hereby declare under penalty of perjury that: (1) the "/s/," followed by my name, on the signature lines for the Attorney for the Signing Party in the Filed Document serves as my signature and denotes the making of such declarations, requests, statements, verifications and certifications to the same extent and effect as my actual signature on such signature lines; (2) the Signing Party signed the *Declaration of Debtor(s) or Other Party* before I electronically submitted the Filed Document for filing with the United States Bankruptcy Court for the Central District of California; (3) I have actually signed a true and correct hard copy of the Filed Document in the locations that are indicated by "/s/," followed by my name, and have obtained the signature(s) of the Signing Party in the locations that are indicated by "/s/," followed by the Signing Party's name, on the true and correct hard copy of the Filed Document; (4) I shall maintain the executed originals of this *Declaration*, the *Declaration of Debtor(s) or Other Party*, and the Filed Document for a period of five years after the closing of the case in which they are filed; and (5) I shall make the executed originals of this *Declaration*, the *Declaration of Debtor(s) or Other Party*, and the Filed Document available for review upon request of the Court or other parties. If the Filed Document is a petition, I further declare under penalty of perjury that: (1) the Signing Party completed and signed the *Statement of Social Security Number(s)* (Form B21) before I electronically submitted the Filed Document for filing with the United States Bankruptcy Court for the Central District of California; (2) I shall maintain the executed original of the *Statement of Social Security Number(s)* (Form B21) for a period of five years after the closing of the case in which they are filed; and (3) I shall make the executed original of the *Statement of Social Security Number(s)* (Form B21) available for review upon request of the Court.

______________________________ ______________________________
Signature of Attorney for Signing Party Date

____
Printed Name of Attorney for Signing Party

This form is mandatory by Order of the United States Bankruptcy Court for the Central District of California.

Exhibit "C" to Voluntary Petition

Form B1, Exhibit C - (9/98) 2001 USBC, Central District of California

Exhibit "C"

[If, to the best of the debtor's knowledge, the debtor owns or has possession of property that poses or is alleged to pose a threat of imminent and identifiable harm to the public health or safety, attach this Exhibit "C" to the petition.]

[Caption as in Form 16B]

Exhibit "C" to Voluntary Petition

1. Identify and briefly describe all real or personal property owned by or in possession of the debtor that, to the best of the debtor's knowledge, poses or is alleged to pose a threat of imminent and identifiable harm to the public health or safety (attach additional sheets if necessary):

____

____

____

____

____

2. With respect to each parcel of real property or item of personal property identified in question 1, describe the nature and location of the dangerous condition, whether environmental or otherwise, that poses or is alleged to pose a threat of imminent and identifiable harm to the public health or safety (attach additional sheets if necessary):

____

____

____

____

Exhibit "D" - Individual Debtor's Statement of Compliance with Credit Counseling

Official Form 1- Exhibit D (Rev 12/08) Page 1 2008 USBC, Central District of California

UNITED STATES BANKRUPTCY COURT CENTRAL DISTRICT OF CALIFORNIA	
In re: Debtor(s).	CHAPTER: CASE NO.:

EXHIBIT D - INDIVIDUAL DEBTOR'S STATEMENT OF COMPLIANCE WITH CREDIT COUNSELING REQUIREMENT

Warning: You must be able to check truthfully one of the five statements regarding credit counseling listed below. If you cannot do so, you are not eligible to file a bankruptcy case, and the court can dismiss any case you do file. If that happens, you will lose whatever filing fee you paid, and your creditors will be able to resume collection activities against you. If your case is dismissed and you file another bankruptcy case later, you may be required to pay a second filing fee and you may have to take extra steps to stop creditors' collection activities.

Every individual debtor must file this Exhibit D. If a joint petition is filed, each spouse must complete and file a separate Exhibit D. Check one of the five statements below and attach any documents as directed.

□ 1. Within the 180 days **before the filing of my bankruptcy case**, I received a briefing from a credit counseling agency approved by the United States trustee or bankruptcy administrator that outlined the opportunities for available credit counseling and assisted me in performing a related budget analysis, and I have a certificate from the agency describing the services provided to me. *Attach a copy of the certificate and a copy of any debt repayment plan developed through the agency.*

□ 2. Within the 180 days **before the filing of my bankruptcy case**, I received a briefing from a credit counseling agency approved by the United States trustee or bankruptcy administrator that outlined the opportunities for available credit counseling and assisted me in performing a related budget analysis, but I do not have a certificate from the agency describing the services provided to me. *You must file a copy of a certificate from the agency describing the services provided to you and a copy of any debt repayment plan developed through the agency no later than 15 days after your bankruptcy case is filed.*

□ 3. I certify that I requested credit counseling services from an approved agency but was unable to obtain the services during the five days from the time I made my request, and the following exigent circumstances merit a temporary waiver of the credit counseling requirement so I can file my bankruptcy case now. *[Summarize exigent circumstances here.]* ____________________

____

____

____

If your certification is satisfactory to the court, you must still obtain the credit counseling briefing within the first 30 days after you file your bankruptcy petition and promptly file a certificate from the agency that provided the counseling, together with a copy of any debt management plan developed through the agency. Failure to fulfill these requirements may result in dismissal of your case. Any extension of the 30-day deadline can be granted only for cause and is limited to a maximum of 15 days. Your case may also be dismissed if the court is not satisfied with your reasons for filing your bankruptcy case without first receiving a credit counseling briefing.

□ 4. I am not required to receive a credit counseling briefing because of: *[Check the applicable statement.] [Must be accompanied by a motion for determination by the court.]*

□ Incapacity. (Defined in 11 U.S.C. § 109(h)(4) as impaired by reason of mental illness or mental deficiency so as to be incapable of realizing and making rational decisions with respect to financial responsibilities.);

□ Disability. (Defined in 11 U.S.C. § 109(h)(4) as physically impaired to the extent of being unable, after reasonable effort, to participate in a credit counseling briefing in person, by telephone, or through the Internet.);

□ Active military duty in a military combat zone.

□ 5. The United States trustee or bankruptcy administrator has determined that the credit counseling requirement of 11 U.S.C. § 109(h) does not apply in this district.

I certify under penalty of perjury that the information provided above is true and correct.

Signature of Debtor: ______________________________

Date: ______________________________

Exhibit Register and Notice Re Disposition of Exhibits

Attorney for Plaintiff/Movant(s): ❐ or Defendant/Respondent(s): ❐

UNITED STATES BANKRUPTCY COURT
CENTRAL DISTRICT OF CALIFORNIA

In re:	Case No.: ______
	Adversary No.: ______
	Chapter 7 ❐ 11 ❐ 13 ❐
Debtor(s)	**EXHIBIT REGISTER AND NOTICE RE DISPOSITION OF EXHIBITS**
Plaintiff/Movant(s)	Hearing Date: ______
vs.	Hearing Time: ______
Defendant/Respondent(s)	Hearing Place: ______

LIST OF EXHIBITS (*NUMBERED, TAGGED AND A BRIEF DESCRIPTION OF EXHIBIT)

1. ______
2. ______
3. ______
4. ______
5. ______
6. ______
7. ______
8. ______
9. ______
10. ______
11. ______
12. ______
13. ______
14. ______
15. ______

B-3024 * **EXHIBITS OF PLAINTIFF/MOVANT(S) SHALL BE MARKED WITH NUMBERS.**
EXHIBITS OF DEFENDANT/RESPONDENT(S) SHALL BE MARKED WITH LETTERS.

Revised 8/97

NOTICE RE DISPOSITION OF EXHIBITS

NOTICE IS HEREBY GIVEN THAT EXHIBITS PRESENTED TO THE COURT MUST BE WITHDRAWN FROM THE CLERK'S OFFICE AFTER THE EXPIRATION OF THE TIME FOR APPEAL, OR WHERE NO APPEAL IS TAKEN, ENTRY OF A STIPULATION WAIVING OR ABANDONING THE RIGHT TO APPEAL, FINAL DISPOSITION OF THE APPEAL, OR BY ORDER OF THE COURT (LOCAL RULE 5003-2). EXHIBITS MUST BE WITHDRAWN WITHIN THIRTY (30) DAYS OF THIS NOTICE. EXHIBITS WHICH ARE NOT WITHDRAWN SHALL BE DESTROYED.

____
Date

JON D. CERETTO
U. S. Bankruptcy Court

By: ____________________________
Deputy Clerk

Disposed of on ____________________ Deputy Clerk ____________________

Withdrawn on ____________________ By: ____________________

Extraordinary Relief Attachment (F 4001-1M.ER)

Motion for Relief from Stay - *Page* ____ *a of* ____ **F 4001-1M.ER**

In re (SHORT TITLE)	CHAPTER:
Debtor(s).	CASE NO.:

(OPTIONAL)
EXTRAORDINARY RELIEF ATTACHMENT
(MOVANT: ______________________)
(This Attachment is the continuation page for Paragraph ____ of the Relief From Stay Motion)

Based upon evidence of efforts by Debtor(s) or others acting in concert with Debtor(s) to delay, hinder or defraud Movant by abusive bankruptcy filings or otherwise, Movant also asks that the Order include the following provisions:

1. ☐ That the Order be binding and effective in any bankruptcy case commenced by or against the above-named Debtor(s) for a period of 180 days, so that no further automatic stay shall arise in that case as to the Property.

2. ☐ That the Order be binding and effective in any bankruptcy case commenced by or against any successors, transferees, or assignees of the above-named Debtor(s) for a period of 180 days from the hearing of this Motion
   - ☐ without further notice.
   - ☐ upon recording of a copy of this Order or giving appropriate notice of its entry in compliance with applicable non-bankruptcy law.

3. ☐ That the Order be binding and effective in any bankruptcy case commenced by or against any Debtor(s) who claim(s) any interest in the Property for a period of 180 days from the hearing of this Motion
   - ☐ without further notice.
   - ☐ upon recording of a copy of this Order or giving appropriate notice of its entry in compliance with applicable non-bankruptcy law.

4. ☐ That the Order be binding and effective in any future bankruptcy case, no matter who the Debtor(s) may be
   - ☐ without further notice.
   - ☐ upon recording of a copy of this Order or giving appropriate notice of its entry in compliance with applicable non-bankruptcy law.

5. ☐ That the Debtor(s) be enjoined from transferring all or any portion of the Property for a period of 180 days from the hearing of this Motion, and any transfer in violation of this Order be deemed void.

6. ☐ That the Sheriff or Marshal may evict the Debtor(s) and any other occupant from the subject Property regardless of any future bankruptcy filing concerning the Property for a period of 180 days from the hearing of this Motion
   - ☐ without further notice.
   - ☐ upon recording of a copy of this Order or giving appropriate notice of its entry in compliance with applicable non-bankruptcy law.

7. ☐ Other *(specify)*:

This form is OPTIONAL TO THE JUDGE and may only be used if the judge to whom the case has been assigned allows such extraordinary relief to be requested by motion. Many judges require the filing of an adversary proceeding to obtain some or all of these forms of relief.

Extraordinary Relief Attachment (Optional to the Judge) (F 4001-1O.ER)

Order Granting Motion for Relief from Stay – Page ___ of ___ **F4001-1O.ER**

In re (SHORT TITLE) Debtor(s).	CHAPTER: CASE NO.:

(*OPTIONAL*)
EXTRAORDINARY RELIEF ATTACHMENT
(MOVANT: ______________________)

(This Attachment is the continuation page for Paragraph ____ of the foregoing Order.)

Based upon evidence of efforts by Debtor(s) or others acting in concert with Debtor(s) to delay, hinder or defraud Movant by abusive bankruptcy filings, this court further orders as follows:

1. ☐ This Order is binding and effective in any bankruptcy case commenced by or against the Debtor(s) for a period of 180 days from the hearing of the Motion.

2. ☐ This Order is binding and effective in any bankruptcy case commenced by or against any successors, transferees, or assignees of the above-named Debtor(s) for a period of 180 days from the hearing of the Motion.
   ☐ without further notice.
   ☐ upon recording of a copy of this Order or giving appropriate notice of its entry in compliance with applicable non-bankruptcy law.

3. ☐ This Order is binding and effective in any bankruptcy case commenced by or against any debtor(s) who claim(s) any interest in the Property for a period of 180 days from the hearing of the Motion.
   ☐ without further notice.
   ☐ upon recording of a copy of this Order or giving appropriate notice of its entry in compliance with applicable non-bankruptcy law.

4. ☐ This Order is binding and effective in any future bankruptcy case, no matter who the debtor(s) may be
   ☐ without further notice.
   ☐ upon recording of a copy of this Order or giving appropriate notice of its entry in compliance with applicable non-bankruptcy law.

5. ☐ The Debtor(s) is/are hereby enjoined from transferring all or any portion of the Property for a period of 180 days from the hearing of the Motion except as may be authorized by further order of this Court, and any transfer in violation of this Order is void.

6. ☐ The Sheriff or Marshal may evict the Debtor(s) and any other occupant from the subject Property regardless of any future bankruptcy filing concerning the Property for a period of 180 days from the hearing of the Motion.
   ☐ without further notice.
   ☐ upon recording of a copy of this Order or giving appropriate notice of its entry in compliance with applicable non-bankruptcy law.

7. ☐ Other (*specify*):

Judge's Initials

This form is OPTIONAL TO THE JUDGE and may only be used if the judge to whom the case has been assigned allows such extraordinary relief to be requested by motion. Many judges require the filing of an adversary proceeding to obtain some or all of these forms of relief.

Revised May 2004 **F4001-1O.ER**

CDCAL-633 C.D. CALIFORNIA

Fee Installments and Waiver Application

UNITED STATES BANKRUPTCY COURT
CENTRAL DISTRICT OF CALIFORNIA

INSTRUCTIONS

HOW TO REQUEST AN ORDER:
(1) AUTHORIZING YOU TO PAY THE FILING FEE IN INSTALLMENTS; OR
(2) EXCUSING YOU FROM PAYING THE FILING FEE IN A CHAPTER 7 CASE

If you cannot afford to pay the full fee at the time of filing, you may apply to pay the fee in installments. A form, which is available from the Clerk of the Court, must be completed to make that application. If your application to pay in installments is approved, you will be permitted to file your petition, completing payment of the fee within six months.

Permission to do so is only given when the judge is persuaded by testimony given under oath that usually you cannot afford to pay the entire filing fee, and are not filing bankruptcy to forestall eviction from residential premises occupied on a month-to-month tenancy or on a tenancy at will, or for any improper purpose.

The procedure for requesting permission to pay fees in installments is as follows:

1. Tell the clerk that you wish to request permission from the Court to pay the filing fee in installments.
2. Complete the "Application to Pay Filing Fee in Installments."
3. Return the application form and your filing papers, i.e., petition, to the filing window where you obtained the installment payment information.
4. Be prepared to show the clerk a California driver's license, California identification card, or other similar form of identification.
5. Ask the clerk for the name of the judge who will rule on your motion, the time and location of a hearing, if a hearing is required.

IF YOU ARE REQUIRED TO APPEAR AT A HEARING AND FAIL TO APPEAR, THE MOTION WILL BE DENIED. YOU MAY NOT BE PERMITTED TO FILE ANY BANKRUPTCY CASE FOR 180 DAYS FROM THE DATE OF THE HEARING, AND YOU AND YOUR PROPERTY MAY NOT BE PROTECTED FROM THE ACTIONS OF YOUR CREDITORS IF YOU DO FILE A BANKRUPTCY CASE DURING THOSE 180 DAYS OR LATER.

The hearing on your application will take place in a courtroom and will be conducted by a United States Bankruptcy Judge.

If your application is denied, you must pay the fees in full within the time ordered by the judge or your bankruptcy case will be dismissed; and if the judge orders, you may not file another bankruptcy case for 180 days from the date of the hearing. **IF (1) YOUR CASE IS DISMISSED AND (2) YOU FILE BANKRUPTCY AGAIN WITHIN THE NEXT YEAR, IT IS LIKELY THAT YOU WILL BE TREATED AS HAVING FILED MORE THAN ONE BANKRUPTCY CASE WITHIN A 12-MONTH PERIOD. IF THIS OCCURS, IT MAY SIGNIFICANTLY REDUCE THE PROTECTION YOU WILL RECEIVE FROM THE AUTOMATIC STAY IN THE LATER BANKRUPTCY CASE.**

If your application is granted, it will almost always be necessary for you to make a first installment payment immediately after the hearing. The number of installments permitted shall not exceed four, and the final installment shall be payable not later than 120 days after the filing of the petition, unless extended by the Court for cause shown to a date not later than 180 days after the date of the filing of the petition. Failure to pay any installment when due may be grounds for dismissal of the case upon notice and hearing.

In a chapter 7 case, if you cannot afford to pay the fee either in full at the time of filing or in installments, then you may request an order excusing you from paying the filing fee by completing an "Application for Waiver of the Chapter 7 Filing Fee for Individuals Who Cannot Pay the Filing Fee in Full or In Installments" and filing it with the Clerk of the Court along with your petition. Permission to do so is only given when the judge is persuaded by testimony given under oath that usually you cannot afford to pay the entire filing fee, and are not filing bankruptcy to forestall eviction from residential premises occupied on a month-to-month tenancy or on a tenancy at will, or for any improper purpose. A judge will decide whether you have to pay the fee.

By law, you may be excused from paying the fee only if your income is less than 150 percent of the official poverty line applicable to your family size and you are unable to pay the fee in installments. See the attached U.S. Department of Health and Human Services (DHHS) table to determine if you are eligible.

Required information. Complete all items in the application, and attach requested schedules. Then sign the application on the last page. If you and your spouse are filing a joint bankruptcy petition, you both must provide information as requested and sign the application.

The procedure for requesting an order for excusing you from paying the filing fee in a chapter 7 case is as follow:

1. Tell the clerk that you wish to request permission from the Court to be excused from paying the filing fee installments.
2. Complete an "Application for Waiver of the Chapter 7 Filing Fee for Individuals Who Cannot Pay the Filing Fee in Full or In Installments."
3. Return the application form and your filing papers, i.e., petition, to the filing window where you obtained the installment payment information.
4. Be prepared to show the clerk a California driver's license, California identification card, or other similar form of identification.
5. Ask the clerk for the name of the judge who will rule on your motion, the time and location of a hearing, if a hearing is required.

You may submit both applications only if you believe you are eligible for both: (1) being excused from paying the filing fee in full, and (2) if the judge disagrees, paying the filing fee in installments.

If your income is greater than the amount set forth in the attached U.S. Department of Health and Human Services (DHSS) table and you can swear truthfully under oath that you cannot pay the full filing fee today, then only submit the Application to Pay Filing Fee in Installments.

150% of the HHS Poverty Guidelines for 2009* Monthly Basis			
Persons in family unit	48 Contiguous States and D.C.	Alaska	Hawaii
1	$1,353.75	$1,691.25	$1,557.50
2	$1,821.25	$2,276.25	$2,095.00
3	$2,288.75	$2,861.25	$2,632.50
4	$2,756.25	$3,446.25	$3,170.00
5	$3,223.75	$4,031.25	$3,707.50
6	$3,691.25	$4,616.25	$4,245.00
7	$4,158.75	$5,201.25	$4,782.50
8	$4,626.25	$5,786.25	$5,320.00
For each additional person add	$467.50	$585.00	$537.50

* As required by section 673(2) of the Omnibus Budget Reconciliation Act of 1981 (Pub. L. 97-35 - reauthorized by Pub. L. 105-285, Section 201 (1988)).

Form B3 (Official Form 3A) - (Rev. 12/07) 2007 USBC, Central District of California

UNITED STATES BANKRUPTCY COURT CENTRAL DISTRICT OF CALIFORNIA	
In re Debtor(s).	CHAPTER: CASE NO.:

APPLICATION TO PAY FILING FEE IN INSTALLMENTS

1. In accordance with F.R.B.P. 1006, I apply for permission to pay the filing fee amounting to $_______________ in installments.

2. I certify that I am unable to pay the filing fee except in installments.

3. Until the filing fee is paid in full, I will not make any additional payment or transfer any additional property to an attorney or any other person for services in connection with this case.

4. I propose the following terms for the payment of the filing fee.*

   $____________________ Check one ☐ With the filing of the petition, or
   ☐ On or before ____________________

   $____________________ on or before ____________________
   $____________________ on or before ____________________
   $____________________ on or before ____________________

   * The number of installments proposed shall not exceed four (4), and the final installment shall be payable not later than 120 days after filing the petition. For cause shown, the court may extend the time of any installment, provided the last installment is paid not later than 180 days after filing the petition. F.R.B.P. 1006(b)(2).

5. I am requesting permission to pay the filing fee in installments because:

   ____

6. I need to file my bankruptcy petition today instead of waiting until I have the full amount of the fee because:

   ____

7. Check all the following that apply:

   ☐ My landlord has filed an unlawful detainer complaint and I need to stop the eviction.

   ☐ My home is about to be foreclosed upon and I need to file bankruptcy to stop the foreclosure. The name of the foreclosing creditor is _______________ and the date of the foreclosure is _______________.

   ☐ My wages are being garnished by ____________________.

   ☐ My utilities are scheduled to be turned off. Name of utility company(s):____________________
   Turn off date: ____________________.

   ☐ None of this applies to me.

8. I understand that if I fail to pay any installment when due, my bankruptcy case may be dismissed, and I may not receive a discharge of my debts.

Signature of Attorney *Date*	*Signature of Debtor* *Date* (In a joint case, both spouses must sign.)
Name of Attorney	*Signature of Joint Debtor (if any)* *Date*

Form B3 (Official Form 3A) - (Rev 12/07) 2007 USBC, Central District of California

UNITED STATES BANKRUPTCY COURT CENTRAL DISTRICT OF CALIFORNIA	
In re Debtor(s).	CHAPTER: CASE NO.:

DECLARATION AND SIGNATURE OF NON-ATTORNEY BANKRUPTCY PETITION PREPARER (See 11 U.S.C. § 110)

I declare under penalty of perjury that: (1) I am a bankruptcy petition preparer as defined in 11 U.S.C. § 110; (2) I prepared this document for compensation and have provided the debtor with a copy of this document and the notices and information required under 11 U.S.C. §§ 110(b), 110(h), and 342(b); (3) if rules or guidelines have been promulgated pursuant to 11 U.S.C. § 110(h) setting a maximum fee for services chargeable by bankruptcy petition preparers, I have given the debtor notice of the maximum amount before preparing any document for filing for a debtor or accepting any fee from the debtor, as required under that section; and (4) I will not accept any additional money or other property from the debtor before the filing fee is paid in full.

Printed or Typed Name and Title, if any, of Bankruptcy Petition Preparer   Social-Security No. (Required by 11 U.S.C. § 110.)

If the bankruptcy petition preparer is not an individual, state the name, title (if any), address, and social-security number of the officer, principal, responsible person, or partner who signs the document.

Address

x____________________

Signature of Bankruptcy Petition Preparer   Date

Names and Social-Security numbers of all other individuals who prepared or assisted in preparing this document, unless the bankruptcy petition preparer is not an individual:

If more than one person prepared this document, attach additional signed sheets conforming to the appropriate Official Form for each person.

A bankruptcy petition preparer's failure to comply with the provisions of title 11 and the Federal Rules of Bankruptcy Procedure may result in fines or imprisonment or both. 11 U.S.C. § 110; 18 U.S.C. § 156. Bankruptcy Procedure may result in fines or imprisonment or both. 11 U.S.C. § 110; 18 U.S.C. § 156.

Form B3B (Official Form 3) - (Rev. 12/07) 2007 USBC, Central District of California

UNITED STATES BANKRUPTCY COURT CENTRAL DISTRICT OF CALIFORNIA	
In re Debtor(s).	CHAPTER: 7 CASE NO.:

APPLICATION FOR WAIVER OF THE CHAPTER 7 FILING FEE FOR INDIVIDUALS WHO CANNOT PAY THE FILING FEE IN FULL OR IN INSTALLMENTS

Part A. Family Size and Income

1. Including yourself, your spouse, and dependents you have listed or will list on Schedule I (Current Income of Individual Debtors(s)), how many people are in your family? (Do not include your spouse if you are separated AND are not filing a joint petition.) ______________

2. Restate the following information that you provided, or will provide, on Line 16 of Schedule I. Attach a completed copy of Schedule I, if it is available.

   Total Combined Monthly Income (Line 16 of Schedule I): $__________

3. State the monthly net income, if any, of dependents included in Question 1 above. Do not include any income already reported in Item 2. If none, enter $0.

   $__________

4. Add the "Total Combined Monthly Income" reported in Question 2 to your dependents' monthly net income from Question 3.

   $__________

5. Do you expect the amount in Question 4 to increase or decrease by more than 10% during the next 6 months? Yes____ No____

   If yes, explain.

Part B: Monthly Expenses

6. EITHER (a) attach a completed copy of Schedule J (Schedule of Monthly Expenses), and state your total monthly expenses reported on Line 18 of that Schedule, OR (b) if you have not yet completed Schedule J, provide an estimate of your total monthly expenses.

   $__________

7. Do you expect the amount in Question 6 to increase or decrease by more than 10% during the next 6 months? Yes____ No____

   If yes, explain.

Form B3B (Official Form 3) - (Rev. 12/07) 2007 USBC, Central District of California

UNITED STATES BANKRUPTCY COURT CENTRAL DISTRICT OF CALIFORNIA	
In re Debtor(s).	CHAPTER: 7 CASE NO.:

Part C. Real and Personal Property

EITHER (1) attach completed copies of Schedules A (Real Property) and Schedule B (Personal Property), OR (2) if you have not yet completed those schedules, answer the following questions.

8. State the amount of cash you have on hand: $ ________

9. State below any money you have in savings, checking, or other accounts in a bank or other financial institution.

Bank or Other Financial Institution:	Type of Account such as savings, checking, CD:	Amount:
________	________	$ ________
________	________	$ ________

10. State below the assets owned by you. **Do not list ordinary household furnishings and clothing.**

Home	Address: ________	Value: $ ________
	________	Amount owed on mortgages and liens: $ ________
Other real estate	Address: ________	Value: $ ________
	________	Amount owed on mortgages and liens: $ ________
Motor vehicle	Model/Year: ________	Value: $ ________
	________	Amount owed: $ ________
Motor vehicle	Model/Year: ________	Value: $ ________
	________	Amount owed: $ ________
Other	Description ________	Value: $ ________
	________	Amount owed: $ ________

11. State below any person, business, organization, or governmental unit that owes you money and the amount that is owed.

Name of Person, Business, or Organization that Owes You Money	Amount Owed
________	$ ________
________	$ ________

Form B3B (Official Form 3) - (Rev. 12/07) 2007 USBC, Central District of California

UNITED STATES BANKRUPTCY COURT CENTRAL DISTRICT OF CALIFORNIA	
In re Debtor(s).	CHAPTER: 7 CASE NO.:

Part D. Additional Information.

12. Have you paid an **attorney** any money for services in connection with this case, including the completion of this form, the bankruptcy petition, or schedules? Yes ____ No ____

    If yes, how much have you paid? $ ____________________

13. Have you promised to pay or do you anticipate paying an **attorney** in connection with your bankruptcy case? Yes ____ No ____

    If yes, how much have you promised to pay or do you anticipate paying? $ ________________

14. Have you paid **anyone other than an attorney** (such as a bankruptcy petition preparer, paralegal, typing service, or another person) any money for services in connection with this case, including the completion of this form, the bankruptcy petition, or schedules? Yes ____ No ____

    If yes, how much have you paid? $ ____________________

15. Have you promised to pay or do you anticipate paying **anyone other than an attorney** (such as a bankruptcy petition preparer, paralegal, typing service, or another person) any money for services in connection with this case, including the completion of this form, the bankruptcy petition, or schedules? Yes ____ No ____

    If yes, how much have you promised to pay or do you anticipate paying? $

16. Has anyone paid an attorney or other person or service in connection with this case, on your behalf? Yes ____ No ____

    If yes, explain.

17. Have you previously filed for bankruptcy relief during the past eight years? Yes ___ No ___

Case Number (if known)	Year filed	Location of filing	Did you obtain a discharge? (if known)
________________	_______	______________	Yes __ No ___ Don't know ____
________________	_______	______________	Yes __ No ___ Don't know ____

18. Please provide any other information that helps to explain why you are unable to pay the filing fee in installments.

19. I (we) declare under penalty of perjury that I (we) cannot currently afford to pay the filing fee in full or in installments and that the foregoing information is true and correct.

Executed on: ______________ ________________________________
Date Signature of Debtor

______________ ________________________________
Date Signature of Co-debtor

Form B3B (Official Form 3) - (Rev. 12/07) 2007 USBC, Central District of California

UNITED STATES BANKRUPTCY COURT CENTRAL DISTRICT OF CALIFORNIA	
In re	CHAPTER: 7
Debtor(s).	CASE NO.:

DECLARATION AND SIGNATURE OF BANKRUPTCY PETITION PREPARER (See 11 U.S.C. § 110)

I declare under penalty of perjury that: (1) I am a bankruptcy petition preparer as defined in 11 U.S.C. § 110; (2) I prepared this document for compensation and have provided the debtor with a copy of this document and the notices and information required under 11 U.S.C. §§ 110(b), 110(h), and 342(b); and (3) if rules or guidelines have been promulgated pursuant to 11 U.S.C. § 110(h) setting a maximum fee for services chargeable by bankruptcy petition preparers, I have given the debtor notice of the maximum amount before preparing any document for filing for a debtor or accepting any fee from the debtor, as required under that section.

Printed or Typed Name and Title, if any, of Bankruptcy Petition Preparer

Social Security No. (Required by 11 U.S.C. §110.)

If the bankruptcy petition preparer is not an individual, state the name, title (if any), address, and social security number of the officer, principal, responsible person, or partner who signs the document.

Address

x

Signature of Bankruptcy Petition Preparer

Date

Names and Social Security numbers of all other individuals who prepared or assisted in preparing this document, unless the bankruptcy petition preparer is not an individual:

If more than one person prepared this document, attach additional signed sheets conforming to the appropriate Official Form for each person.

A bankruptcy petition preparer's failure to comply with the provisions of title 11 and the Federal Rules of Bankruptcy Procedure may result in fines or imprisonment or both. 11 U.S.C. § 110; 18 U.S.C. § 156.

Form B3B (Official Form 3) - (Rev. 12/07) 2007 USBC, Central District of California

UNITED STATES BANKRUPTCY COURT CENTRAL DISTRICT OF CALIFORNIA	
In re Debtor(s).	CHAPTER: 7 CASE NO.:

ORDER ON DEBTOR'S APPLICATION FOR WAIVER OF THE CHAPTER 7 FILING FEE

Upon consideration of the debtor's "Application for Waiver of the Chapter 7 Filing Fee," the court orders that the application be

[ ] GRANTED.

This order is subject to being vacated at a later time if developments in the administration of the bankruptcy case demonstrate that the waiver was unwarranted.

[ ] DENIED.

The debtor shall pay the chapter 7 filing fee according to the following terms:

$__________ on or before __________

$__________ on or before __________

$__________ on or before __________

$__________ on or before __________

Until the filing fee is paid in full, the debtor shall not make any additional payment or transfer any additional property to an attorney or any other person for services in connection with this case.

IF THE DEBTOR FAILS TO TIMELY PAY THE FILING FEE IN FULL OR TO TIMELY MAKE INSTALLMENT PAYMENTS, THE COURT MAY DISMISS THE DEBTOR'S CHAPTER 7 CASE.

[ ] SCHEDULED FOR HEARING.

A hearing to consider the debtor's "Application for Waiver of the Chapter 7 Filing Fee" shall be held on __________ at ________ am/pm at ______________________________.
(address of courthouse)

IF THE DEBTOR FAILS TO APPEAR AT THE SCHEDULED HEARING, THE COURT MAY DEEM SUCH FAILURE TO BE THE DEBTOR'S CONSENT TO THE ENTRY OF AN ORDER DENYING THE FEE WAIVER APPLICATION BY DEFAULT.

BY THE COURT:

DATE: ______________

____
United States Bankruptcy Judge

FORM 1 - VOLUNTARY PETITION (CAC)

Form B1 (Official Form 1) - (Rev. 04/07) 2007 USBC, Central District of California

UNITED STATES BANKRUPTCY COURT
CENTRAL DISTRICT OF CALIFORNIA

Voluntary Petition

Name of Debtor (if individual, enter Last, First, Middle):	Name of Joint Debtor (Spouse) (Last, First, Middle):
All Other Names used by the Debtor in the last 8 years (include married, maiden, and trade names):	All Other Names used by the Joint Debtor in the last 8 years (include married, maiden, and trade names):
Last four digits of Soc. Sec. No./Complete EIN or other Tax I.D. No. (if more than one, state all):	Last four digits of Soc. Sec. No./Complete EIN or other Tax I.D. No. (if more than one, state all):
Street Address of Debtor (No. & Street, City, and State): ZIP CODE	Street Address of Joint Debtor (No. & Street, City, and State): ZIP CODE
County of Residence or of the Principal Place of Business:	County of Residence or of the Principal Place of Business:
Mailing Address of Debtor (if different from street address): ZIP CODE	Mailing Address of Joint Debtor (if different from street address): ZIP CODE

Location of Principal Assets of Business Debtor (if different from street address above):
ZIP CODE

Type of Debtor (Form of Organization) (Check **one** box.)

- ☐ Individual (includes Joint Debtors) *See Exhibit D on page 2 of this form*
- ☐ Corporation (includes LLC and LLP)
- ☐ Partnership
- ☐ Other (If debtor is not one of the above entities, check this box and state type of entity below)

Nature of Business (Check **one** box.)

- ☐ Health Care Business
- ☐ Single Asset Real Estate as defined in 11 U.S.C. § 101 (51B)
- ☐ Railroad
- ☐ Stockbroker
- ☐ Commodity Broker
- ☐ Clearing Bank
- ☐ other

Tax-Exempt Entity (Check one box, if applicable)

- ☐ Debtor is a tax-exempt organization under Title 26 of the United States Code (the Internal Revenue Code.)

Chapter of Bankruptcy Code Under Which the Petition is Filed (Check one box)

- ☐ Chapter 7
- ☐ Chapter 9
- ☐ Chapter 11
- ☐ Chapter 12
- ☐ Chapter 13
- ☐ Chapter 15 Petition for Recognition of a Foreign Main Proceeding
- ☐ Chapter 15 Petition for Recognition of a Foreign Nonmain Proceeding

Nature of Debts (Check one box.)

- ☐ Debts are primarily consumer debts, defined in 11 U.S.C. § 101(8) as "incurred by an individual primarily for a personal, family, or house hold purpose."
- ☐ Debts are primarily business debts.

Filing Fee (Check one box)

- ☐ Full Filing Fee attached
- ☐ Filing Fee to be paid in installments (Applicable to individuals only). Must attach signed application for the court's consideration certifying that the debtor is unable to pay fee except in installments. Rule 1006(b). See Official Form 3A.
- ☐ Filing Fee waiver requested (Applicable to chapter 7 individuals only). Must attach signed application for the court's consideration. See Official Form 3B.

Chapter 11 Debtors:

Check one box:
- ☐ Debtor is a small business debtor as defined in 11 U.S.C. § 101(51D).
- ☐ Debtor is not a small business debtor as defined in 11 U.S.C. § 101 (51D).

Check if:
- ☐ Debtor's aggregate noncontingent liquidated debts (excluding debts owed to insiders or affiliates) are less than $2,190,000.

Check all applicable boxes:
- ☐ A plan is being filed with this petition
- ☐ Acceptances of the plan were solicited prepetition from one or more classes of creditors, in accordance with 11 U.S.C. § 1126(b)

Statistical/Administrative Information

- ☐ Debtor estimates that funds will be available for distribution to unsecured creditors.
- ☐ Debtor estimates that, after any exempt property is excluded and administrative expenses paid, there will be no funds available for distribution to unsecured creditors.

THIS SPACE FOR COURT USE ONLY

Estimated Number of Creditors

1-49	50-99	100-199	200-999	1,000-5,000	5,001-10,000	10,001 25,000	25,001-50,000	50,001-100,000	OVER 100,000
☐	☐	☐	☐	☐	☐	☐	☐	☐	☐

Estimated Assets

$0 to $10,000	$10,001 to $100,000	$100,001 to $1 million	$1,000,001 to $100 million	More than $100 million
☐	☐	☐	☐	☐

Estimated Liabilities

$0 to $50,000	$50,001 to $100,000	$100,001 to $1 million	$1,000,001 to $100 million	More than $100 million
☐	☐	☐	☐	☐

Form B1 (Official Form 1) (Rev. 04/07) 2007 USBC, Central District of California

FORM B1, Page 2

Voluntary Petition

(This page must be completed and filed in every case.)

Name of Debtor(s):

Prior Bankruptcy Case Filed Within Last 8 Years (If more than two, attach additional sheet)

Location Where Filed:	Case Number:	Date Filed:
Location Where Filed:	Case Number:	Date Filed:

Pending Bankruptcy Case Filed by any Spouse, Partner or Affiliate of this Debtor (If more than one, attach additional sheet)

Name of Debtor:	Case Number:	Date Filed:
District:	Relationship:	Judge:

Exhibit A

(To be completed if debtor is required to file periodic reports (e.g., forms 10K and 10Q) with the Securities and Exchange Commission pursuant to Section 13 or 15(d) of the Securities Exchange Act of 1934 and is requesting relief under chapter 11.)

☐ Exhibit A is attached and made a part of this petition.

Exhibit B

(To be completed if debtor is an individual whose debts are primarily consumer debts.)

I, the attorney for the petitioner named in the foregoing petition, declare that I have informed the petitioner that [he or she] may proceed under chapter 7, 11, 12, or 13 of title 11, United States Code, and have explained the relief available under each such chapter. I further certify that I have delivered to the debtor the notice required by 11 U.S.C. § 342(b).

X ______________________________

Signature of Attorney for Debtor(s) Date

Exhibit C

Does the debtor own or have possession of any property that poses or is alleged to pose a threat of imminent and identifiable harm to public health or safety?

☐ Yes, and Exhibit C is attached and made a part of this petition.

☐ No

Exhibit D

(To be completed by every individual debtor. If a joint petition is filed, each spouse must complete and attach a separate Exhibit D.)

☐ Exhibit D completed and signed by the debtor is attached and made a part of this petition.

If this is a joint petition:

☐ Exhibit D also completed and signed by the joint debtor is attached and made a part of this petition.

Information Regarding the Debtor - Venue

(Check any applicable box)

☐ Debtor has been domiciled or has had a residence, principal place of business, or principal assets in this District for 180 days immediately preceding the date of this petition or for a longer part of such 180 days than in any other District.

☐ There is a bankruptcy case concerning debtor's affiliate, general partner, or partnership pending in this District.

☐ Debtor is a debtor in a foreign proceeding and has its principal place of business or principal assets in the United States in this District, or has no principal place of business or assets in the United States but is a defendant in an action or proceeding [in a federal or state court] in this District, or the interests of the parties will be served in regard to the relief sought in this District.

Statement by a Debtor Who Resides as a Tenant of Residential Property

Check all applicable boxes.

☐ Landlord has a judgment against the debtor for possession of debtor's residence. (If box checked, complete the following.)

____

(Name of landlord that obtained judgment)

____

(Address of landlord)

☐ Debtor claims that under applicable nonbankruptcy law, there are circumstances under which the debtor would be permitted to cure the entire monetary default that gave rise to the judgment for possession, after the judgment for possession was entered, and

☐ Debtor has included in this petition the deposit with the court of any rent that would become due during the 30-day period after the filing of the petition.

Form B1 (Official Form 1) (Rev. 04/07) 2007 USBC, Central District of California

Voluntary Petition
(This page must be completed and filed in every case)

Name of Debtor(s): FORM B1, Page 3

Signatures

Signature(s) of Debtor(s) (Individual/Joint)

I declare under penalty of perjury that the information provided in this petition is true and correct. [If petitioner is an individual whose debts are primarily consumer debts and has chosen to file under chapter 7] I am aware that I may proceed under chapter 7, 11, 12 or 13 of title 11, United States Code, understand the relief available under each such chapter, and choose to proceed under chapter 7. [If no attorney represents me and no bankruptcy petition preparer signs the petition] I have obtained and read the notice required by 11 U.S.C. § 342(b).

I request relief in accordance with the chapter of title 11, United States Code, specified in this petition.

X ______________________
Signature of Debtor

X ______________________
Signature of Joint Debtor

____
Telephone Number (If not represented by attorney)

____
Date

Signature of a Foreign Representative

I declare under penalty of perjury that the information provided in this petition is true and correct, that I am the foreign representative of a debtor in a foreign main proceeding, and that I am authorized to file this petition.

(Check only **one** box.)

☐ I request relief in accordance with chapter 15 of title 11, United States Code. Certified copies of the documents required by 11 U.S.C. § 1515 are attached.

☐ Pursuant to 11 U.S.C. § 1511, I request relief in accordance with the chapter of title 11 specified in this petition. A certified copy of the order granting recognition of the foreign main proceeding is attached.

X ______________________
(Signature of Foreign Representative)

____
(Printed Name of Foreign Representative)

____
Date

Signature of Attorney

X ______________________
Signature of Attorney for Debtor(s)

____
Printed Name of Attorney for Debtor(s)

____
Firm Name

____
Address

____
Telephone Number

____
Date Bar Number

Signature of Debtor (Corporation/Partnership)

I declare under penalty of perjury that the information provided in this petition is true and correct, and that I have been authorized to file this petition on behalf of the debtor.

The debtor requests relief in accordance with the chapter of title 11, United States Code, specified in this petition.

X ______________________
Signature of Authorized Individual

____
Printed Name of Authorized Individual

____
Title of Authorized Individual

____
Date

Signature of Non-Attorney Bankruptcy Petition Preparer

I declare under penalty of perjury that: (1) I am a bankruptcy petition preparer as defined in 11 U.S.C. § 110; (2) I prepared this document for compensation and have provided the debtor with a copy of this document and the notices and information required under 11 U.S.C. §§ 110(b), 110(h), and 342(b); and, (3) if rules or guidelines have been promulgated pursuant to 11 U.S.C. § 110(h) setting a maximum fee for services chargeable by bankruptcy petition preparers, I have given the debtor notice of the maximum amount before preparing any document for filing for a debtor or accepting any fee from the debtor, as required in that section. Official Form 19B is attached.

____
Printed Name and title, if any, of Bankruptcy Petition Preparer

____
Social Security number (If the bankruptcy petition preparer is not an individual, state the Social Security number of the officer, principal, responsible person or partner of the bankruptcy petition preparer.) (Required by 11 U.S.C. § 110.)

____
Address

____

X ______________________
Date

Signature of bankruptcy petition preparer or officer, principal, responsible person, or partner whose Social Security number is provided above.

Names and Social Security numbers of all other individuals who prepared or assisted in preparing this document unless the bankruptcy petition preparer is not an individual.

If more than one person prepared this document, attach additional sheets conforming to the appropriate official form for each person.

A bankruptcy petition preparer's failure to comply with the provisions of title 11 and the Federal Rules of Bankruptcy Procedure may result in fines or imprisonment or both. 11 U.S.C. § 110; 18 U.S.C. § 156.

FORM 3 - APPLICATION TO PAY FILING FEE IN INSTALLMENTS (CAC)

Form B3 (Official Form 3A) - (Rev. 10/05) 2005 USBC, Central District of California

UNITED STATES BANKRUPTCY COURT CENTRAL DISTRICT OF CALIFORNIA	
In re Debtor(s).	CHAPTER: CASE NO.:

APPLICATION TO PAY FILING FEE IN INSTALLMENTS

1. In accordance with F.R.B.P. 1006, I apply for permission to pay the filing fee amounting to $________________ in installments.

2. I certify that I am unable to pay the filing fee except in installments.

3. I propose the following terms for the payment of the filing fee.*

   $________________ Check one ☐ With the filing of the petition, or
   ☐ On or before ________________

   $________________ on or before ________________
   $________________ on or before ________________
   $________________ on or before ________________

   * The number of installments proposed shall not exceed four (4), and the final installment shall be payable not later than 120 days after filing the petition. For cause shown, the court may extend the time of any installment, provided the last installment is paid not later than 180 days after filing the petition. F.R.B.P. 1006(b)(2).

4. I am requesting permission to pay the filing fee in installments because:

   ____

5. I need to file my bankruptcy petition today instead of waiting until I have the full amount of the fee because:

   ____

6. Check all the following that apply:

   ☐ My landlord has filed an unlawful detainer complaint and I need to stop the eviction.

   ☐ My home is about to be foreclosed upon and I need to file bankruptcy to stop the foreclosure. The name of the foreclosing creditor is ________________ and the date of the foreclosure is ________________.

   ☐ My wages are being garnished by ________________.

   ☐ My utilities are scheduled to be turned off. Name of utility company(s): ________________
   Turn off date: ________________.

   ☐ None of this applies to me.

7. I understand that if I fail to pay any installment when due, my bankruptcy case may be dismissed, and I may not receive a discharge of my debts.

Signature of Attorney	*Date*	*Signature of Debtor* (In a joint case, both spouses must sign.)	*Date*
Name of Attorney		*Signature of Joint Debtor (if any)*	*Date*

Form B3 (Official Form 3A) - (Rev 10/05) 2005 USBC, Central District of California

UNITED STATES BANKRUPTCY COURT
CENTRAL DISTRICT OF CALIFORNIA

In re	CHAPTER:
Debtor(s).	CASE NO.:

CERTIFICATION AND SIGNATURE OF NON-ATTORNEY BANKRUPTCY PETITION PREPARER (See 11 U.S.C. § 110)

I certify that I am a bankruptcy petition preparer as defined in 11 U.S.C. § 110, that I prepared this document for compensation and that I have provided the Debtor with a copy of this document. I also certify that I will not accept money or any other property from the Debtor before the filing fee is paid in full.

Printed or Typed Name of Bankruptcy Petition Preparer

Complete Social Security Number
(Required by 11 U S C § 110)

Address

Names and complete Social Security numbers of all other individuals who prepared or assisted in preparing this document:

If more than one person prepared this document, attach additional sheets conforming to the appropriate Official Form for each person.

Signature of Bankruptcy Petition Preparer

Date

A bankruptcy petition preparer's failure to comply with the provisions of title 11 and the Federal Rules of Bankruptcy Procedure may result in fines or imprisonment or both. 11 U.S.C. § 110; 18 U.S.C. § 156.

FORM 3 - ORDER ON APPLICATION TO PAY FILING FEES IN INSTALLMENTS (CAC)

UNITED STATES BANKRUPTCY COURT CENTRAL DISTRICT OF CALIFORNIA	
In re Debtor(s).	CHAPTER: CASE NO.:

ORDER ON APPLICATION TO PAY FILING FEE IN INSTALLMENTS

Having considered the *Application to Pay Filing Fee in Installments* ("Application") filed by the Debtor; *[check any that apply]*

☐ the testimony in support of the Application submitted by Debtor in the Application;
☐ the testimony in support of the Application submitted by Debtor at the hearing on the Application;
☐ Debtor's failure to appear at the hearing;
☐ any argument made in support of or in opposition to the Application;

IT IS ORDERED THAT:

☐ The Debtor may pay the filing fee in installments on the terms proposed in the foregoing application.

☐ The Debtor may pay the filing fee in installments on the terms as outlined below:

$__________ Check one ☐ On the day the petition is filed
☐ On or before __________

$__________ on or before __________
$__________ on or before __________
$__________ on or before __________

☐ The Court shall conduct a hearing on the Application at ___:___ _.m. on __________, in Courtroom _____ of the above-entitled Court.

☐ A copy of the Application and written notice of the hearing thereon and the deadline for opposing the Application shall be served as follows:

a. ☐ Personal Delivery or Facsimile ☐ Overnight Mail ☐ First Class Mail

b. Deadline for Service: Date:__________ Time:__________

c. Parties to be Served:__________

☐ Any oppositions to the Motion must be filed with the Court, a file-stamped copy delivered to the Judge's chambers, and served upon Debtor as follows:

a. ☐ Personal Delivery or Facsimile ☐ Overnight Mail ☐ First Class Mail

b. Deadline for Service: Date:__________ Time:__________

☐ The Application is denied and the Debtor shall pay the filing fee in full on this day. If the filing fee is not paid in full on this day, the case shall be dismissed.

Rev. 9/05 This form is mandatory. It has been approved for use by the United States Bankruptcy Court for the Central District of California.

<table>
<tr><td colspan="2">UNITED STATES BANKRUPTCY COURT
CENTRAL DISTRICT OF CALIFORNIA</td></tr>
<tr><td rowspan="2">In re

Debtor(s).</td><td>CHAPTER:</td></tr>
<tr><td>CASE NO.:</td></tr>
</table>

☐ The Application is denied and the Debtor shall pay the filing fee in full not later than ________________. If the filing fee is not paid in full by this date, the case shall be dismissed.

☐ The Application is denied and the Debtor's Voluntary Petition ("Petition") is dismissed, **AND IT IS FURTHER ORDERED THAT:**

☐ The stay of 11 U.S.C. § 362(a) created by the filing of the Petition is annulled and terminated as if the Petition were never filed.

☐ Because the Debtor has willfully failed to appear before the Court in proper prosecution of this bankruptcy case, unless leave of the Court is first obtained,

1. Any refiling of another bankruptcy petition by or against the Debtor is prohibited for 180 days from the date this Order is entered;

2. If the Debtor does file another bankruptcy petition within 180 days from the date this Order is entered, the Debtor will not be protected by the stay of 11 U.S.C. § 362(a). Notwithstanding the filing of a subsequent petition, creditors may evict the Debtor or foreclose and sell the Debtor's property.

☐ OTHER ____

Dated:

____
United States Bankruptcy Judge

UNITED STATES BANKRUPTCY COURT CENTRAL DISTRICT OF CALIFORNIA	
In re Debtor(s).	CHAPTER: CASE NO.:

NOTICE OF ENTRY OF JUDGMENT OR ORDER AND CERTIFICATE OF MAILING

TO ALL PARTIES IN INTEREST ON THE ATTACHED SERVICE LIST:

1. You are hereby notified that an ORDER ON APPLICATION TO PAY FILING FEE IN INSTALLMENTS was entered on *(specify date)*:

2. I hereby certify that I mailed a copy of this Notice and a true copy of the Order or Judgment to the persons and entities on the attached service list on *(specify date)*:

Dated:

JON D. CERETTO
Clerk of the Bankruptcy Court

By: ______________________________
Deputy Clerk

Rev. 9/05 This form is mandatory. It has been approved for use by the United States Bankruptcy Court for the Central District of California.

FORM 3B - APPLICATION FOR WAIVER OF CHAPTER 7 FILING FEE (CAC)

Form B3B (Official Form 3) - (Rev. 10/05) 2005 USBC, Central District of California

UNITED STATES BANKRUPTCY COURT CENTRAL DISTRICT OF CALIFORNIA	
In re Debtor(s).	CHAPTER: 7 CASE NO.:

ORDER ON DEBTOR'S APPLICATION FOR WAIVER OF THE CHAPTER 7 FILING FEE

Upon consideration of the debtor's "Application for Waiver of the Chapter 7 Filing Fee," the court orders that the application be:

[ ] GRANTED.

This order is subject to being vacated at a later time if developments in the administration of the bankruptcy case demonstrate that the waiver was unwarranted.

[ ] DENIED.

The debtor shall pay the chapter 7 filing fee according to the following terms:

$ __________ on or before ____________

$ __________ on or before ____________

$ __________ on or before ____________

$ __________ on or before ____________

Until the filing fee is paid in full, the debtor shall not make any additional payment or transfer any additional property to an attorney or any other person for services in connection with this case.

IF THE DEBTOR FAILS TO TIMELY PAY THE FILING FEE IN FULL OR TO TIMELY MAKE INSTALLMENT PAYMENTS, THE COURT MAY DISMISS THE DEBTOR'S CHAPTER 7 CASE.

[ ] SCHEDULED FOR HEARING.

A hearing to consider the debtor's "Application for Waiver of the Chapter 7 Filing Fee" shall be held on ____ ______________ at ________ am/pm at ____.
(address of courthouse)

IF THE DEBTOR FAILS TO APPEAR AT THE SCHEDULED HEARING, THE COURT MAY DEEM SUCH FAILURE TO BE THE DEBTOR'S CONSENT TO THE ENTRY OF AN ORDER DENYING THE FEE WAIVER APPLICATION BY DEFAULT.

BY THE COURT:

DATE: ______________

____
United States Bankruptcy Judge

FORM 3B - ORDER ON DEBTOR'S APPLICATION FOR WAIVER OF THE CHAPTER 7 FILING FEE (CAC)

Form B3B (Official Form 3) - (Rev. 04/09/06) 2005 USBC, Central District of California

UNITED STATES BANKRUPTCY COURT CENTRAL DISTRICT OF CALIFORNIA	
In re Debtor(s).	CHAPTER: 7 CASE NO.:

APPLICATION FOR WAIVER OF THE CHAPTER 7 FILING FEE
FOR INDIVIDUALS WHO CANNOT PAY THE FILING FEE IN FULL OR IN INSTALLMENTS

Part A.Family Size and Income

1. Including yourself, your spouse, and dependents you have listed or will list on Schedule I (Current Income of Individual Debtors(s)), how many people are in your family? (Do not include your spouse if you are separated AND are not filing a joint petition.) ____________

2. Restate the following information that you provided, or will provide, on Line 16 of Schedule I. Attach a completed copy of Schedule I, if it is available.

   Total Combined Monthly Income (Line 16 of Schedule I): $__________

3. State the monthly net income, if any, of dependents included in Question 1 above. Do not include any income already reported in Item 2. If none, enter $0.

   $__________

4. Add the "Total Combined Monthly Income" reported in Question 2 to your dependents' monthly net income from Question 3.

   $__________

5. Do you expect the amount in Question 4 to increase or decrease by more than 10% during the next 6 months? Yes ____ No____

   If yes, explain.

Part B: Monthly Expenses

6. EITHER (a) attach a completed copy of Schedule J (Schedule of Monthly Expenses), and state your total monthly expenses reported on Line 18 of that Schedule, OR (b) if you have not yet completed Schedule J, provide an estimate of your total monthly expenses.

   $__________

7. Do you expect the amount in Question 6 to increase or decrease by more than 10% during the next 6 months? Yes ____ No ____

   If yes, explain.

Form B3B (Official Form 3) - (Rev. 04/09/06) 2005 USBC, Central District of California

UNITED STATES BANKRUPTCY COURT
CENTRAL DISTRICT OF CALIFORNIA

In re	CHAPTER: 7
Debtor(s).	CASE NO.:

Part C. Real and Personal Property

EITHER (1) attach completed copies of Schedules A (Real Property) and Schedule B (Personal Property), OR (2) if you have not yet completed those schedules, answer the following questions.

8. State the amount of cash you have on hand: $ ________

9. State below any money you have in savings, checking, or other accounts in a bank or other financial institution.

Bank or Other Financial Institution:	Type of Account such as savings, checking, CD:	Amount:
________	________	$ ________
________	________	$ ________

10. State below the assets owned by you. **Do not list ordinary household furnishings and clothing.**

Home Address: ________ Value: $ ________
________ Amount owed on mortgages and liens: $ ________

Other real estate Address: ________ Value: $ ________
________ Amount owed on mortgages and liens: $ ________

Motor vehicle Model/Year: ________ Value: $ ________
________ Amount owed: $ ________

Motor vehicle Model/Year: ________ Value: $ ________
________ Amount owed: $ ________

Other Description ________ Value: $ ________
________ Amount owed: $ ________

11. State below any person, business, organization, or governmental unit that owes you money and the amount that is owed.

Name of Person, Business, or Organization that Owes You Money	Amount Owed
________	$ ________
________	$ ________

Form B3B (Official Form 3) - (Rev. 04/09/06) 2005 USBC, Central District of California

UNITED STATES BANKRUPTCY COURT CENTRAL DISTRICT OF CALIFORNIA	
In re Debtor(s).	CHAPTER: 7 CASE NO.:

Part D. Additional Information.

12. Have you paid an **attorney** any money for services in connection with this case, including the completion of this form, the bankruptcy petition, or schedules? Yes ____ No ____

If yes, how much have you paid? $ ________________

13. Have you promised to pay or do you anticipate paying an **attorney** in connection with your bankruptcy case? Yes ____ No ____

If yes, how much have you promised to pay or do you anticipate paying? $ ______________

14. Have you paid **anyone other than an attorney** (such as a bankruptcy petition preparer, paralegal, typing service, or another person) any money for services in connection with this case, including the completion of this form, the bankruptcy petition, or schedules? Yes ____ No ____

If yes, how much have you paid? $ ________________

15. Have you promised to pay or do you anticipate paying **anyone other than an attorney** (such as a bankruptcy petition preparer, paralegal, typing service, or another person) any money for services in connection with this case, including the completion of this form, the bankruptcy petition, or schedules? Yes ____ No ____

If yes, how much have you promised to pay or do you anticipate paying? $ ____________________

16. Has anyone paid an attorney or other person or service in connection with this case, on your behalf? Yes ____ No ____

If yes, explain.

17. Have you previously filed for bankruptcy relief during the past eight years? Yes ___ No ___

Case Number (if known)	Year filed	Location of filing	Did you obtain a discharge? (if known)
________________	______	____________	Yes __ No __ Don't know ____
________________	______	____________	Yes __ No ___ Don't know ____

18. Please provide any other information that helps to explain why you are unable to pay the filing fee in installments.

19. I (we) declare under penalty of perjury that I (we) cannot currently afford to pay the filing fee in full or in installments and that the foregoing information is true and correct.

Executed on: ____________ ______________________________
Date Signature of Debtor

____________ ______________________________
Date Signature of Co-debtor

Form B3B (Official Form 3) - (Rev. 04/09/06) 2005 USBC, Central District of California

UNITED STATES BANKRUPTCY COURT CENTRAL DISTRICT OF CALIFORNIA	
In re Debtor(s).	**CHAPTER: 7** CASE NO.:

DECLARATION AND SIGNATURE OF BANKRUPTCY PETITION PREPARER (See 11 U.S.C. § 110)

I declare under penalty of perjury that: (1) I am a bankruptcy petition preparer as defined in 11 U.S.C. § 110; (2) I prepared this document for compensation and have provided the debtor with a copy of this document and the notices and information required under 11 U.S.C. §§ 110(b), 110(h), and 342(b); and (3) if rules or guidelines have been promulgated pursuant to 11 U.S.C. § 110(h) setting a maximum fee for services chargeable by bankruptcy petition preparers, I have given the debtor notice of the maximum amount before preparing any document for filing for a debtor or accepting any fee from the debtor, as required under that section.

____ ______________________

Printed or Typed Name and Title, if any, of Bankruptcy Petition Preparer — Social Security No. (Required by 11 U.S.C. §110.)

If the bankruptcy petition preparer is not an individual, state the name, title (if any), address, and social security number of the officer, principal, responsible person, or partner who signs the document.

____

____

Address

x____ ______________________

Signature of Bankruptcy Petition Preparer — Date

Names and Social Security numbers of all other individuals who prepared or assisted in preparing this document, unless the bankruptcy petition preparer is not an individual:

If more than one person prepared this document, attach additional signed sheets conforming to the appropriate Official Form for each person.

A bankruptcy petition preparer's failure to comply with the provisions of title 11 and the Federal Rules of Bankruptcy Procedure may result in fines or imprisonment or both. 11 U.S.C. § 110; 18 U.S.C. § 156.

FORM 6 - DEBTOR'S DECLARATION OF SCHEDULES

Form B6 - Declaration(Rev. 10/06) 2006 USBC, Central District of California

In re	Case No.:
Debtor.	(If known)

DECLARATION CONCERNING DEBTOR'S SCHEDULES

DECLARATION UNDER PENALTY OF PERJURY BY INDIVIDUAL DEBTOR

I declare under penalty of perjury that I have read the foregoing summary and schedules, consisting of ______ sheets, and that they are true and correct to the best of my knowledge, information, and belief. (Total shown on summary page plus 2)

Date ______ Signature: ______
Debtor

Date ______ Signature: ______
(Joint Debtor, if any)
[If joint case, both spouses must sign.]

DECLARATION AND SIGNATURE OF NON-ATTORNEY BANKRUPTCY PETITION PREPARER (See 11 U.S.C. § 110)

I declare under penalty of perjury that: (1) I am a bankruptcy petition preparer as defined in 11 U.S.C. § 110; (2) I prepared this document for compensation and have provided the debtor with a copy of this document and the notices and information required under 11 U.S.C. §§ 110(b), 110(h) and 342(b); and, (3) if rules or guidelines have been promulgated pursuant to 11 U.S.C. § 110(h) setting a maximum fee for services chargeable by bankruptcy petition preparers, I have given the debtor notice of the maximum amount before preparing any document for filing for a debtor or accepting any fee from the debtor, as required by that section.

______
Printed or Typed Name and Title, if any, of Bankruptcy Petition Preparer

______
Social Security No.
(Required by 11 U.S.C. § 110.)

If the bankruptcy petition preparer is not an individual, state the name, title (if any), address, and social security number of the officer, principal, responsible person, or partner who signs this document.

______
______
______
Address

X ______
Signature of Bankruptcy Petition Preparer

______
Date

Names and Social Security numbers of all other individuals who prepared or assisted in preparing this document, unless the bankruptcy petition preparer is not an individual:

If more than one person prepared this document, attach additional signed sheets conforming to the appropriate Official Form for each person.

A bankruptcy petition preparer's failure to comply with the provisions of title 11 and the Federal Rules of Bankruptcy Procedure may result in fines or imprisonment or both. 11 U.S.C. § 110; 18 U.S.C. § 156.

DECLARATION UNDER PENALTY OF PERJURY ON BEHALF OF A CORPORATION OR PARTNERSHIP

I, the ______ [the president or other officer or an authorized agent of the corporation or a member or an authorized agent of the partnership] of the ______ [corporation or partnership] named as debtor in this case, declare under penalty of perjury that I have read the foregoing summary and schedules, consisting of ______ sheets, and that they are true and correct to the best of my knowledge, information, and belief. (Total shown on summary page plus 1.)

Date ______ Signature: ______

______
[Print or type name of individual signing on behalf of debtor.]

[An individual signing on behalf of a partnership or corporation must indicate position or relationship to debtor.]

Penalty for making a false statement or concealing property: Fine of up to $500,000 or imprisonment for up to 5 years or both. 18 U.S.C. §§ 152 and 3571.

Form 6. Summary of Schedules (Official Form B6)

FORM 6. SCHEDULES

Summary of Schedules

Summary of Schedules
Statistical Summary of Certain Liabilities and Related Data (28 U.S.C. § 159)

Schedule A - Real Property

Schedule B - Personal Property

Schedule C - Property Claimed as Exempt

Schedule D - Creditors Holding Secured Claims

Schedule E - Creditors Holding Unsecured Priority Claims

Schedule F - Creditors Holding Unsecured Nonpriority Claims

Schedule G - Executory Contracts and Unexpired Leases

Schedule H - Codebtors

Schedule I - Current Income of Individual Debtor(s)

Schedule J - Current Expenditures of Individual Debtor(s)

Unsworn Declaration under Penalty of Perjury

GENERAL INSTRUCTIONS: The first page of the debtor's schedules and the first page of any amendments thereto must contain a caption as in Form 16B. Subsequent pages should be identified with the debtor's name and case number. If the schedules are filed with the petition, the case number should be left blank.

Schedules D, E, and F have been designed for the listing of each claim only once. Even when a claim is secured only in part or entitled to priority only in part, it still should be listed only once. A claim which is secured in whole or in part should be listed on Schedule D only, and a claim which is entitled to priority in whole or in part should be listed on Schedule E only. Do not list the same claim twice. If a creditor has more than one claim, such as claims arising from separate transactions, each claim should be scheduled separately.

Review the specific instructions for each schedule before completing the schedule.

Form B6 - Summary (12/07) 2007 USBC, Central District of California

UNITED STATES BANKRUPTCY COURT
Central District of California

In re	Case No.:
Debtor.	(If known)

SUMMARY OF SCHEDULES

Indicate as to each schedule whether that schedule is attached and state the number of pages in each. Report the totals from Schedules A, B, D, E, F, I, and J in the boxes provided. Add the amounts from Schedules A and B to determine the total amount of the debtor's assets. Add the amounts of all claims from Schedules D, E, and F to determine the total amount of the debtor's liabilities. Individual debtors also must complete the "Statistical Summary of Certain Liabilities and Related Data" if they file a case under chapter 7, 11, or 13.

	NAME OF SCHEDULE	ATTACHED (YES/NO)	NO. OF SHEETS	ASSETS	LIABILITIES	OTHER
A -	Real Property			$		
B-	Personal Property			$		
C-	Property Claimed as Exempt					
D-	Creditors Holding Secured Claims				$	
E-	Creditors Holding Unsecured Priority Claims (Total of Claims on Schedule E)				$	
F-	Creditors Holding Unsecured Nonpriority Claims				$	
G-	Executory Contracts and Unexpired Leases					
H-	Codebtors					
I-	Current Income of Individual Debtor(s)					$
J-	Current Expenditures of Individual Debtors(s)					$
			TOTAL	$	$	

Official Form B6 - Statistical Summary (12/07) 2007 USBC, Central District of California

UNITED STATES BANKRUPTCY COURT CENTRAL DISTRICT OF CALIFORNIA	
In re Debtor(s).	CHAPTER: CASE NO.:

STATISTICAL SUMMARY OF CERTAIN LIABILITIES AND RELATED DATA (28 U.S.C. § 159)

If you are an individual debtor whose debts are primarily consumer debts, as defined in § 101(8) of the Bankruptcy Code (11 U.S.C. § 101(8)), filing a case under chapter 7, 11 or 13, you must report all information requested below.

☐ Check this box if you are an individual debtor whose debts are NOT primarily consumer debts. You are not required to report any information here.

This information is for statistical purposes only under 28 U.S.C. § 159.

Summarize the following types of liabilities, as reported in the Schedules, and total them.

Type of Liability	Amount
Domestic Support Obligations (from Schedule E)	$
Taxes and Certain Other Debts Owed to Governmental Units (from Schedule E)	$
Claims for Death or Personal Injury While Debtor Was Intoxicated (from Schedule E) (whether disputed or undisputed)	$
Student Loan Obligations (from Schedule F)	$
Domestic Support, Separation Agreement, and Divorce Decree Obligations Not Reported on Schedule E	$
Obligations to Pension or Profit-Sharing, and Other Similar Obligations (from Schedule F)	$
TOTAL	$

State the following:

Average Income (from Schedule I, Line 16)	$
Average Expenses (from Schedule J, Line 18)	$
Current Monthly Income (from Form 22A Line 12; **OR**, Form 22B Line 11; **OR**, Form 22C Line 20)	$

State the following:

1. Total from Schedule D, "UNSECURED PORTION, IF ANY" column		$
2. Total from Schedule E, "AMOUNT ENTITLED TO PRIORITY" column.	$	
3. Total from Schedule E, "AMOUNT NOT ENTITLED TO PRIORITY, IF ANY" column		$
4. Total from Schedule F		$
5. Total of non-priority unsecured debt (sum of 1, 3, and 4)		$

FORM 8 - CHAPTER 7 INDIVIDUAL DEBTOR'S STATEMENT OF INTENTION

Form B8 (Official Form 8) - (Rev. 10/05) 2005 USBC, Central District of California

UNITED STATES BANKRUPTCY COURT
Central District of California

In re

Debtor

Case No.:

Chapter:

CHAPTER 7 INDIVIDUAL DEBTOR'S STATEMENT OF INTENTION

- ☐ I have filed a schedule of assets and liabilities which includes consumer debts secured by property of the estate.
- ☐ I have filed a schedule of executory contracts and unexpired leases which includes personal property subject to an unexpired lease.
- ☐ I intend to do the following with respect to the property of the estate which secures those debts or is subject to a lease:

Description of Secured Property	Creditor's Name	Property will be Surrendered	Property is claimed as exempt	Property will be redeemed pursuant to 11 U.S.C. § 722	Debt will be reaffirmed pursuant to 11 U.S.C. § 524(c)

Description of Leased Property	Lessor's Name	Lease will be assumed pursuant to 11 U.S.C. § 362(h)(1)(A)

Date:________________

____
Signature of Debtor

DECLARATION OF NON-ATTORNEY BANKRUPTCY PETITION PREPARER (See 11 U.S.C. § 110)

I declare under penalty of perjury that: (1) I am a bankruptcy petition preparer as defined in 11 U.S.C. § 110; (2) I prepared this document for compensation and have provided the debtor with a copy of this document and the notices and information required under 11 U.S.C. §§ 110(b), 110(h), and 342(b); and, (3) if rules or guidelines have been promulgated pursuant to 11 U.S.C. § 110(h) setting a maximum fee for services chargeable by bankruptcy petition preparers, I have given the debtor notice of the maximum amount before preparing any document for filing for a debtor or accepting any fee from the debtor, as required in that section.

____
Printed or Typed Name of Bankruptcy Petition Preparer

____
Complete Social Security Number (Required under 11 U.S.C. § 110.)

If the bankruptcy petition preparer is not an individual, state the name, title (if any), address, and social security number of the officer, principal, responsible person or partner who signs this document.

____

____
Address

____
Signature of Bankruptcy Petition Preparer

____
Date

Names and Social Security Numbers of all other individuals who prepared or assisted in preparing this document unless the bankruptcy petition preparer is not an individual:

If more than one person prepared this document, attach additional signed sheets conforming to the appropriate Official Form for each person.

A bankruptcy petition preparer's failure to comply with the provisions of title 11 and the Federal Rules of Bankruptcy Procedure may result in fines or imprisonment or both. 11 U.S.C. § 110; 18 U.S.C. § 156.

FORM 21 - STATEMENT OF SOCIAL-SECURITY NUMBER OR INDIVIDUAL TAXPAYER-IDENTIFICATION NUMBER (ITIN) (CAC)

Form B21 (Official Form 21) - (10/06) 2006 USBC, Central District of California

UNITED STATES BANKRUPTCY COURT CENTRAL DISTRICT OF CALIFORNIA	
In re *(set forth here all names including married, maiden, and trade names used by the debtor within last 8 years):* Debtor.	FOR COURT USE ONLY
Address:	Case No.: Chapter:
Last four digits of Social Security Number(s): Complete Employer's Tax Identification Number(s) *(if any)*:	**STATEMENT OF SOCIAL SECURITY NUMBER(S)***

1. Name of Debtor *(enter Last, First, Middle)*: ______________________
   (Check the appropriate box and, if applicable, provide the required information.)

   ☐ Debtor has a Social Security Number and it is: ___ ___ ___-___ ___-___ ___ ___ ___
   (If more than one, state all.)

   ☐ Debtor does not have a Social Security Number.

2. Name of Joint Debtor *(enter Last, First, Middle)*: ______________________
   (Check the appropriate box and, if applicable, provide the required information.)

   ☐ Joint Debtor has a Social Security Number and it is: ___ ___ ___-___ ___-___ ___ ___ ___
   (If more than one, state all.)

   ☐ Joint Debtor does not have a Social Security Number.

I declare under penalty of perjury that the foregoing is true and correct.

______________________ ______________________
Signature of Debtor Date

______________________ ______________________
Signature of Joint Debtor Date

***Joint debtors must provide information for both spouses.**

Penalty for making a false statement: **Fine of up to $250,000 or up to 5 years imprisonment or both. 18 U.S.C. §§ 152 and 3571.**

FORM 21A - AMENDED STATEMENT OF SOCIAL-SECURITY NUMBER(S) (OR OTHER INDIVIDUAL TAXPAYER-IDENTIFICATION NUMBER (ITIN))(CAC)

Form B21A - (12/03) 2003 USBC, Central District of California

UNITED STATES BANKRUPTCY COURT CENTRAL DISTRICT OF CALIFORNIA	
In re *(set forth here all names including married, maiden, and trade names used by the debtor within last 6 years)*: Debtor.	FOR COURT USE ONLY
Address:	Case No.: Chapter:
Last four digits of Social Security Number(s): Complete Employer's Tax Identification Number(s) *(if any)*:	**AMENDED STATEMENT OF SOCIAL SECURITY NUMBER(S)***

1. Name of Debtor *(enter Last, First, Middle)*: ______________________
   (Check the appropriate box and, if applicable, provide the required information.)

   a. ☐ Debtor's incorrect Social Security Number as originally provided: ___ ___ ___-___ ___-___ ___ ___ ___

   Debtor's amended Social Security Number: ___ ___ ___-___ ___-___ ___ ___ ___

   b. ☐ Correct as originally provided.

2. Name of Joint Debtor *(enter Last, First, Middle)*: ______________________
   (Check the appropriate box and, if applicable, provide the required information.)

   a. ☐ Joint Debtor's incorrect Social Security Number as originally provided: ___ ___ ___-___ ___-___ ___ ___ ___

   Joint Debtor's amended Social Security Number: ___ ___ ___-___ ___-___ ___ ___ ___

   b. ☐ Correct as originally provided.

I declare under penalty of perjury that the foregoing is true and correct.

______________________ ______________________
Signature of Debtor Date

______________________ ______________________
Signature of Joint Debtor Date

***Joint debtors must provide information for both spouses.**

Penalty for making a false statement: **Fine of up to $250,000 or up to 5 years imprisonment or both. 18 U.S.C. §§ 152 and 3571.**

REAFFIRMATION AGREEMENT (CAC)

Form 240A - Reaffirmation Agreement (1/07)

UNITED STATES BANKRUPTCY COURT CENTRAL DISTRICT OF CALIFORNIA	FOR COURT USE ONLY
In re: Debtor(s). ❑ Presumption of Undue Hardship ❑ No Presumption of Undue Hardship (Check box as directed in Part D: Debtor's Statement in Support of Reaffirmation Agreement.)	
Creditor's Name and Address: ❑ *[Check this box if]* Creditor is a Credit Union as defined in §19(b)(1)(a)(iv) of the Federal Reserve Act	CHAPTER: CASE NO.: **REAFFIRMATION AGREEMENT**

REAFFIRMATION AGREEMENT

[Indicate all documents included in this filing by checking each applicable box.]

- ☐ Part A: Disclosures, Instructions, and Notice to Debtor (pages 1 - 5)
- ☐ Part B: Reaffirmation Agreement
- ☐ Part C: Certification by Debtor's Attorney
- ☐ Part D: Debtor's Statement in Support of Reaffirmation Agreement
- ☐ Part E: Motion for Court Approva

*[**Note:** Complete Part E only if debtor was not represented by an attorney during the course of negotiating this agreement. **Note also:** If you complete Part E, you must prepare and file Form 240B - Order on Reaffirmation Agreement.]*

PART A: DISCLOSURE STATEMENT, INSTRUCTIONS AND NOTICE TO DEBTOR

1. DISCLOSURE STATEMENT

Before Agreeing to Reaffirm a Debt, Review These Important Disclosures:

SUMMARY OF REAFFIRMATION AGREEMENT

This Summary is made pursuant to the requirements of the Bankruptcy Code.

AMOUNT REAFFIRMED

The amount of debt you have agreed to reaffirm: $______________

The amount of debt you have agreed to reaffirm includes all fees and costs (if any) that have accrued as of the date of this disclosure. Your credit agreement may obligate you to pay additional amounts which may come due after the date of this disclosure. Consult your credit agreement.

In re (SHORT TITLE) Debtor(s).	CASE NO.:

ANNUAL PERCENTAGE RATE

[The annual percentage rate can be disclosed in different ways, depending on the type of debt.]

a. If the debt is an extension of "credit" under an "open end credit plan," as those terms are defined in § 103 of the Truth in Lending Act, such as a credit card, the creditor may disclose the annual percentage rate shown in (i) below or, to the extent this rate is not readily available or not applicable, the simple interest rate shown in (ii) below, or both.

(i) The Annual Percentage Rate disclosed, or that would have been disclosed, to the debtor in the most recent periodic statement prior to entering into the reaffirmation agreement described in Part B below or, if no such periodic statement was given to the debtor during the prior six months, the annual percentage rate as it would have been so disclosed at the time of the disclosure statement: ________%.

--- And/Or ---

(ii) The simple interest rate applicable to the amount reaffirmed as of the date this disclosure statement is given to the debtor: __________%. If different simple interest rates apply to different balances included in the amount reaffirmed, the amount of each balance and the rate applicable to it are:

$____________ @ ____________%;
$____________ @ ____________%;
$____________ @ ____________%.

b. If the debt is an extension of credit other than under than an open end credit plan, the creditor may disclose the annual percentage rate shown in (I) below, or, to the extent this rate is not readily available or not applicable, the simple interest rate shown in (ii) below, or both.

(i) The Annual Percentage Rate under §128(a)(4) of the Truth in Lending Act, as disclosed to the debtor in the most recent disclosure statement given to the debtor prior to entering into the reaffirmation agreement with respect to the debt or, if no such disclosure statement was given to the debtor, the annual percentage rate as it would have been so disclosed: ________%.

--- And/Or ---

(ii) The simple interest rate applicable to the amount reaffirmed as of the date this disclosure statement is given to the debtor: ____________%. If different simple interest rates apply to different balances included in the amount reaffirmed,

the amount of each balance and the rate applicable to it are:

$____________ @ ____________%;
$____________ @ ____________%;
$____________ @ ____________%.

c. If the underlying debt transaction was disclosed as a variable rate transaction on the most recent disclosure given under the Truth in Lending Act:

The interest rate on your loan may be a variable interest rate which changes from time to time, so that the annual percentage rate disclosed here may be higher or lower.

d. If the reaffirmed debt is secured by a security interest or lien, which has not been waived or determined to be void by a final order of the court, the following items or types of items of the debtor's goods or property remain subject to such security interest or lien in connection with the debt or debts being reaffirmed in the reaffirmation agreement described in Part B.

In re (SHORT TITLE) Debtor(s).	CASE NO.:

Item or Type of Item Original Purchase Price or Original Amount of Loan

Optional---At the election of the creditor, a repayment schedule using one or a combination of the following may be provided:

Repayment Schedule:

Your first payment in the amount of $____________ is due on _________ (date), but the future payment amount may be different. Consult your reaffirmation agreement or credit agreement, as applicable.

— Or —

Your payment schedule will be: ________ (number) payments in the amount of $____________ each, payable (monthly, annually, weekly, etc.) on the __________ (day) of each ____________ (week, month, etc.), unless altered later by mutual agreement in writing.

— Or —

A reasonably specific description of the debtor's repayment obligations to the extent known by the creditor or creditor's representative.

2. INSTRUCTIONS AND NOTICE TO DEBTOR

Reaffirming a debt is a serious financial decision. The law requires you to take certain steps to make sure the decision is in your best interest. If these steps are not completed, the reaffirmation agreement is not effective, even though you have signed it.

1. Read the disclosures in this Part A carefully. Consider the decision to reaffirm carefully. Then, if you want to reaffirm, sign the reaffirmation agreement in Part B (or you may use a separate agreement you and your creditor agree on).

2. Complete and sign Part D and be sure you can afford to make the payments you are agreeing to make and have received a copy of the disclosure statement and a completed and signed reaffirmation agreement.

3. If you were represented by an attorney during the negotiation of your reaffirmation agreement, the attorney must have signed the certification in Part C.

4. If you were not represented by an attorney during the negotiation of your reaffirmation agreement, you must have completed and signed Part E.

5. The original of this disclosure must be filed with the court by you or your creditor. If a separate reaffirmation agreement (other than the one in Part B) has been signed, it must be attached.

6. If the creditor is not a Credit Union and you were represented by an attorney during the negotiation of your reaffirmation agreement, your reaffirmation agreement becomes effective upon filing with the court unless the reaffirmation is presumed to be an undue hardship as explained in Part D. If the creditor is a Credit Union and you were represented by an attorney during the negotiation of your reaffirmation agreement, your reaffirmation agreement becomes effective upon filing with the court.

In re (SHORT TITLE) Debtor(s).	CASE NO.:

7. If you were not represented by an attorney during the negotiation of your reaffirmation agreement, it will not be effective unless the court approves it. The court will notify you and the creditor of the hearing on your reaffirmation agreement. You must attend this hearing in bankruptcy court where the judge will review your reaffirmation agreement. The bankruptcy court must approve your reaffirmation agreement as consistent with your best interests, except that no court approval is required if your reaffirmation agreement is for a consumer debt secured by a mortgage, deed of trust, security deed, or other lien on your real property, like your home.

YOUR RIGHT TO RESCIND (CANCEL) YOUR REAFFIRMATION AGREEMENT

You may rescind (cancel) your reaffirmation agreement at any time before the bankruptcy court enters a discharge order, or before the expiration of the 60-day period that begins on the date your reaffirmation agreement is filed with the court, whichever occurs later. To rescind (cancel) your reaffirmation agreement, you must notify the creditor that your reaffirmation agreement is rescinded (or canceled).

Frequently Asked Questions:

What are your obligations if you reaffirm the debt? A reaffirmed debt remains your personal legal obligation. It is not discharged in your bankruptcy case. That means that if you default on your reaffirmed debt after your bankruptcy case is over, your creditor may be able to take your property or your wages. Otherwise, your obligations will be determined by the reaffirmation agreement which may have changed the terms of the original agreement. For example, if you are reaffirming an open end credit agreement, the creditor may be permitted by that agreement or applicable law to change the terms of that agreement in the future under certain conditions.

Are you required to enter into a reaffirmation agreement by any law? No, you are not required to reaffirm a debt by any law. Only agree to reaffirm a debt if it is in your best interest. Be sure you can afford the payments you agree to make.

What if your creditor has a security interest or lien? Your bankruptcy discharge does not eliminate any lien on your property. A "lien" is often referred to as a security interest, deed of trust, mortgage or security deed. Even if you do not reaffirm and your personal liability on the debt is discharged, because of the lien your creditor may still have the right to take the security property if you do not pay the debt or default on it. If the lien is on an item of personal property that is exempt under your State's law or that the trustee has abandoned, you may be able to redeem the item rather than reaffirm the debt. To redeem, you make a single payment to the creditor equal to the current value of the security property, as agreed by the parties or determined by the court.

NOTE: When this disclosure refers to what a creditor "may" do, it does not use the word "may" to give the creditor specific permission. The word "may" is used to tell you what might occur if the law permits the creditor to take the action. If you have questions about your reaffirming a debt or what the law requires, consult with the attorney who helped you negotiate this agreement reaffirming a debt. If you don't have an attorney helping you, the judge will explain the effect of your reaffirming a debt when the hearing on the reaffirmation agreement is held.

In re (SHORT TITLE) Debtor(s).	CASE NO.:

PART B: REAFFIRMATION AGREEMENT.

I (we) agree to reaffirm the debts arising under the credit agreement described below.

1. Brief description of credit agreement:

2. Description of any changes to the credit agreement made as part of this reaffirmation agreement:

SIGNATURE(S):

Borrower:

____
(Print Name)

____
(Signature)

Date: __________

Co-borrower, if also reaffirming these debts:

____
(Print Name)

____
(Signature)

Date: __________

Accepted by creditor:

____
(Printed Name of Creditor)

____
(Address of Creditor)

____
(Signature)

____
(Printed Name and Title of Individual Signing for Creditor)

Date of creditor acceptance:

____

In re (SHORT TITLE) Debtor(s).	CASE NO.:

PART C: CERTIFICATION BY DEBTOR'S ATTORNEY (IF ANY).

[To be filed only if the attorney represented the debtor during the course of negotiating this agreement.]

I hereby certify that (1) this agreement represents a fully informed and voluntary agreement by the debtor; (2) this agreement does not impose an undue hardship on the debtor or any dependent of the debtor; and (3) I have fully advised the debtor of the legal effect and consequences of this agreement and any default under this agreement.

☐ *[Check box, if applicable and the creditor is not a Credit Union.]* A presumption of undue hardship has been established with respect to this agreement. In my opinion, however, the debtor is able to make the required payment.

Printed Name of Debtor's Attorney: ______________________________

Signature of Debtor's Attorney: : ______________________________

Date: ____________________

In re (SHORT TITLE) Debtor(s).	CASE NO.:

PART D: DEBTOR'S STATEMENT IN SUPPORT OF REAFFIRMATION AGREEMENT

*[Read and complete sections 1 and 2, **OR**, if the creditor is a Credit Union and the debtor is represented by an attorney, read section 3. Sign the appropriate signature line(s) and date your signature. If you complete sections 1 and 2 **and** your income less monthly expenses does not leave enough to make the payments under this reaffirmation agreement, check the box at the top of page 1 indicating "Presumption of Undue Hardship." Otherwise, check the box at the top of page 1 indicating "No Presumption of Undue Hardship"]*

1. I believe this reaffirmation agreement will not impose an undue hardship on my dependents or me. I can afford to make the payments on the reaffirmed debt because my monthly income (take home pay plus any other income received) is $____________, and my actual current monthly expenses including monthly payments on post-bankruptcy debt and other reaffirmation agreements total $____________, leaving $____________ to make the required payments on this reaffirmed debt.

I understand that if my income less my monthly expenses does not leave enough to make the payments, this reaffirmation agreement is presumed to be an undue hardship on me and must be reviewed by the court. However, this presumption may be overcome if I explain to the satisfaction of the court how I can afford to make the payments here:

____

____

____

(Use an additional page if needed for a full explanation.)

2. I received a copy of the Reaffirmation Disclosure Statement in Part A and a completed and signed reaffirmation agreement.

Signed: ________________________
(Debtor)

____
(Joint Debtor, if any)

Date: ________________________

— Or —

[If the creditor is a Credit Union and the debtor is represented by an attorney]

3. I believe this reaffirmation agreement is in my financial interest. I can afford to make the payments on the reaffirmed debt. I received a copy of the Reaffirmation Disclosure Statement in Part A and a completed and signed reaffirmation agreement.

Signed: ________________________
(Debtor)

____
(Joint Debtor, if any)

Date: ________________________

In re (SHORT TITLE) Debtor(s).	CASE NO.:

PART E: MOTION FOR COURT APPROVAL
[To be completed and filed only if the debtor is not represented by an attorney during the course of negotiating this agreement.]

MOTION FOR COURT APPROVAL OF REAFFIRMATION AGREEMENT

I (we), the debtor(s), affirm the following to be true and correct:

I am not represented by an attorney in connection with this reaffirmation agreement.

I believe this reaffirmation agreement is in my best interest based on the income and expenses I have disclosed in my Statement in Support of this reaffirmation agreement, and because (provide any additional relevant reasons the court should consider):

Therefore, I ask the court for an order approving this reaffirmation agreement under the following provisions (*check all applicable boxes)*:

☐ 11 U.S.C. § 524(c)(6) (debtor is not represented by an attorney during the course of the negotiation of the reaffirmation agreement)

☐ 11 U.S.C. § 524(m) (presumption of undue hardship has arisen because monthly expenses exceed monthly income)

Signed: ____________________
(Debtor)

____
(Joint Debtor, if any)

Date: ____________________

This form is mandatory. It has been approved by the United States Bankruptcy Court for the Central District of California.

Revised January 2007

FORM 240B - ORDER APPROVING REAFFIRMATION AGREEMENT(CAC)

Form 240B - Order on Reaffirmation Agreement (1/07)

UNITED STATES BANKRUPTCY COURT CENTRAL DISTRICT OF CALIFORNIA	FOR COURT USE ONLY
In re: Debtor(s).	CHAPTER: CASE NO.:

ORDER ON REAFFIRMATION AGREEMENT

The debtor(s) ________________________ has (have) filed a motion for approval of the reaffirmation agreement
(Name(s) of debtor(s))

dated ____________________ made between the debtor(s) and ________________________.
(Date of agreement) (Name of creditor)

The court held the hearing required by 11 U.S.C. § 524(d) on notice to the debtor(s) and the creditor on ____________.
(Date)

COURT ORDER:

- ☐ The court grants the debtor's motion under 11 U.S.C. § 524(c)(6)(A) and approves the reaffirmation agreement described above as not imposing an undue hardship on the debtor(s) or a dependent of the debtor(s) and as being in the best interest of the debtor(s).
- ☐ The court grants the debtor's motion under 11 U.S.C. § 524(k)(8) and approves the reaffirmation agreement described above.
- ☐ The court does not disapprove the reaffirmation agreement under11 U.S.C. § 524(m).
- ☐ The court disapproves the reaffirmation agreement under 11 U.S.C. § 524(m).
- ☐ The court does not approve the reaffirmation agreement.

BY THE COURT

Dated: ____________________

____
United States Bankruptcy Judge

This form is mandatory. It has been approved by the United States Bankruptcy Court for the Central District of California.

Revised January 2007

Initial Mediation Confidentiality Agreement Confidential - Not To Be Filed With the Court

UNITED STATES BANKRUPTCY COURT

FOR THE CENTRAL DISTRICT OF CALIFORNIA

In re Debtor(s).	Bk. No. [Chapter]
Plaintiff(s)/Movant(s), v. Defendant(s)/Respondent(s).	Adv. No. INITIAL MEDIATION CONFIDENTIALITY AGREEMENT **CONFIDENTIAL -- NOT TO BE FILED WITH THE COURT**

This is an Agreement between the parties and the Mediator to enter into confidential discussions about the mediation of the following issues: ____________

____

____

____

[Attach additional page(s) if necessary.]

The undersigned understand and agree to the strict confidentiality of their mediation. Mediation discussions, any draft resolutions and any unsigned mediated agreements shall not be disclosed to anyone not involved in the Mediation Program and shall not be admissible in any court or administrative proceeding. Only an agreement signed by all parties may be so admissible.

The parties further agree not to call the Mediator to testify concerning the mediation nor to provide any materials from the Mediation Program in any court or administrative proceeding between the parties, except as to matters governed by FED. R. BANKR. P. 7068.

In addition, the Mediator shall not be compelled to divulge any materials from the Mediation Program or to testify in regard to the mediation in any judicial or other proceeding.

DATED: ____________________ ______________________________
(Name of Party)

____
(Signature of Party)

DATED: ____________________ ______________________________
(Name of Party's Counsel)

____
(Signature of Party's Counsel)

DATED: ____________________ ______________________________
(Name of Party)

____
(Signature of Party)

DATED: ____________________ ______________________________
(Name of Party's Counsel)

____
(Signature of Party's Counsel)

DATED: ____________________

____
(Name of Mediator)

____
(Signature of Mediator)

[Attach additional page(s) if necessary.]

Instructions Regarding Amendments to Social Security Number

UNITED STATES BANKRUPTCY COURT
Central District of California

Instructions Regarding Amendments to Social Security Number

The United States Bankruptcy Court for the Central District of California has revised its procedures for amending a debtor's Social Security Number in order to conform with the Judicial Conference Privacy Policy that went into effect December 1, 2003. Please note that the Judicial Conference Privacy Policy does not alter any requirements to provide a full Social Security Number.

Beginning December 1, 2003, the following are required to amend the debtor's Social Security Number:

1. *Amended Statement of Social Security Number(s)* (Form B21A):

   Submit an original *Amended Statement of Social Security Number(s)* (Form B21A) setting forth the debtor's incorrect and amended Social Security Number and signed by debtor(s) under penalty of perjury. Please note that Form B21A is not part of the public record and will not be included in the case file.

2. *Amendment Cover Sheet* (Form B-1008):

   Clearly specify on the *Amendment Cover Sheet* (Form B-1008) that the *Statement of Social Security Number(s)* and Voluntary Petition pages are being amended.

   The debtor is required by F.R.B.P. 1009(a) to give notice of the amendment to the creditors, the trustee, and the U. S. Trustee. The notice must include the debtor's full Social Security Number as required by 11 U.S.C. § 342(c). **These requirements are not affected by the Judicial Conference Privacy Policy and remain in effect after December 1, 2003.**

   Attach the following to the original *Amendment Cover Sheet*:

   a. **The redacted original page one and signed page two of the amended Voluntary petition; and**

   b. **A redacted copy of the notice that was mailed to the creditors, the trustee, and the U. S. Trustee. The Court's copy of the notice should be redacted to show only the last four digits of the Social Security Number. Please note that the Clerk's Office will not redact the full Social Security Number if listed in the notice.**

   File the original and three complete copies for chapter 7 and 13 cases or original and six complete copies for chapter 11 cases of the *Amendment Cover Sheet* and attachments along with the completed *Proof of Service* and service list.

3. **If the case is closed, a motion and order to reopen must be filed and accompanied by the filing fee. Upon entry of the order reopening the case, the process for amending the Social Security Number, as detailed above, may begin.**

Revised November 15, 2004

Involuntary Petition Official Form

Form B5 (Official Form 5) - (Rev. 12/07) 2007 USBC, Central District of California

UNITED STATES BANKRUPTCY COURT CENTRAL DISTRICT OF CALIFORNIA — **Involuntary Petition**

IN RE (Name of Debtor - If Individual: Last, First, Middle)	ALL OTHER NAMES used by the debtor in the last 8 years (Include married, maiden, and trade names.)
Last four digits of Soc. Sec. No./Complete EIN or other Tax I.D. No. (If more than one, state all.):	
STREET ADDRESS OF DEBTOR (No. and street, city, state, and zip code)	MAILING ADDRESS OF DEBTOR (If different from street address)
County of Residence or Principal Place of Business / ZIP CODE	ZIP CODE

LOCATION OF PRINCIPAL ASSETS OF BUSINESS DEBTOR (If different from previously listed addresses)

CHAPTER OF BANKRUPTCY CODE UNDER WHICH PETITION IS FILED

☐ Chapter 7 ☐ Chapter 11

INFORMATION REGARDING DEBTOR (Check applicable boxes)

Name of Debts (Check one box.)	Type of Debtor (Form of Organization)	Nature of Business (Check one box.)
Petitioners believe: ☐ Debts are primarily consumer debts ☐ Debts are primarily business debts	☐ Individual (Includes Joint Debtor) ☐ Corporation (Includes LLC and LLP) ☐ Partnership ☐ Other (If debtor is not one of the above entities, check this box and state type of entity below.) ____________	☐ Health Care Business ☐ Single Asset Real Estate as defined in 11 U.S.C. § 101(51)(B) ☐ Railroad ☐ Stockbroker ☐ Commodity Broker ☐ Clearing Bank ☐ Other

VENUE	FILING FEE (Check one box)
☐ Debtor has been domiciled or has had a residence, principal place of business or principal assets in the District for 180 days immediately preceding the date of this petition or for a longer part of such 180 days than in any other District. ☐ A bankruptcy case concerning debtor's affiliate, general partner, or partnership is pending in this District.	☐ Full Filing Fee attached ☐ Petitioner is a child support creditor or its representative, and the form specified in § 304(g) of the Bankruptcy Reform Act of 1994 is attached. *[If a child support creditor or its representative is a petitioner, and if the petitioner files the form specified in § 304(g) of the Bankruptcy Reform Act of 1994, no fee is required.]*

PENDING BANKRUPTCY CASE FILED BY OR AGAINST ANY PARTNER OR AFFILIATE OF THIS DEBTOR (Report information for any additional cases on attached sheets.)

Name of Debtor	Case Number	Date
Relationship	District	Judge

ALLEGATIONS
(Check applicable boxes)

1. ☐ Petitioner(s) are eligible to file this petition pursuant to 11 U.S.C. § 303(b).
2. ☐ The debtor is a person against whom an order for relief may be entered under title 11 of the United States Code.

3.a. ☐ The debtor is generally not paying such debtor's debts as they become due, unless such debts are the subject of a bona fide dispute as to liability or amount;

or

b. ☐ Within 120 days preceding the filing of this petition, a custodian, other than a trustee receiver, or agent appointed or authorized to take charge of less than substantially all of the property of the debtor for the purpose of enforcing a lien against such property, was appointed or took possession.

THIS SPACE FOR COURT USE ONLY

Form B5 (Official Form 5) - Page 2 (Rev. 12/07) 2007 USBC, Central District of California

Involuntary Petition	Name of Debtor

TRANSFER OF CLAIM

☐ Check this box if there has been a transfer of any claim against the debtor by or to any petitioner. Attach all documents that evidence the transfer and any statements that are required under Bankruptcy Rule 1003(a).

REQUEST FOR RELIEF

Petitioner(s) request that an order for relief be entered against the debtor under the chapter of title 11, United States Code, specified in this petition. If any petitioner is a foreign representative appointed in a foreign proceeding, a certified copy of the order of the court granting recognition is attached.

Petitioner(s) declare under penalty of perjury that the foregoing is true and correct according to the best of their knowledge, information, and belief.

X ______ Signature of Petitioner or Representative (State Title)	X ______ Signature of Attorney ______ Date
Name of Petitioner ______ Date Signed	Name of Attorney Firm (If any)
Name & Mailing Address of Individual Signing in Representative Capacity	Address
	Telephone No.
X ______ Signature of Petitioner or Representative (State Title)	X ______ Signature of Attorney ______ Date
Name of Petitioner ______ Date Signed	Name of Attorney Firm (If any)
Name & Mailing Address of Individual Signing in Representative Capacity	Address
	Telephone No.
X ______ Signature of Petitioner or Representative (State Title)	X ______ Signature of Attorney ______ Date
Name of Petitioner ______ Date Signed	Name of Attorney Firm (If any)
Name & Mailing Address of Individual Signing in Representative Capacity	Address
	Telephone No.

PETITIONING CREDITORS

Name and Address of Petitioner	Nature of Claim	Amount of Claim
Name and Address of Petitioner	Nature of Claim	Amount of Claim
Name and Address of Petitioner	Nature of Claim	Amount of Claim
Note: If there are more than three petitioners, attach additional sheets with the statement under penalty of perjury, each petitioner's signature under the statement and the name of attorney and petitioning creditor information in the format above.		Total Amount of Petitioners' Claims

______ Continuation Sheets attached

Joint Status Report - Additional Party Attachment (F 7016-1.1a)

In re	CHAPTER:
	CASE NO.:
Debtor(s).	ADVERSARY NO.:

Additional Party Name: ____________________

Plaintiff _____ Defendant _____ Other *(specify)*: ____________________

B. READINESS FOR TRIAL:

1. When will you be ready for trial in this case?

2. If your answer to the above is more than four (4) months after the summons issued in this case, give reasons for further delay.

3. When do you expect to complete your discovery efforts?

4. What additional discovery do you require to prepare for trial?

C. TRIAL TIME:

1. What is your estimate of the time required to present your side of the case at trial (including rebuttal stage if applicable)?

2. How many witnesses do you intend to call at trial (including opposing parties)?

3. How many exhibits do you anticipate using at trial?

D. PRE-TRIAL CONFERENCE:

A pre-trial conference is usually conducted between a week to a month before trial, at which time a pre-trial order will be signed by the court. [See Local Bankruptcy Rule 7016-1.] If you believe that a pre-trial conference is not necessary or appropriate in this case, please so note below, stating your reasons:

Pre-trial conference ___ (is)/ ___ (is not) requested.

Reasons: ____________________

____

Pre-trial conference should be set after (date): ____________________

(Continued on next page)

Joint Status Report - Additional Party Attachment - *Page 2 of 2* **F 7016-1.1a**

In re	CHAPTER:
	CASE NO.:
Debtor(s).	ADVERSARY NO.:

E. SETTLEMENT:

1. What is the status of settlement efforts?

2. Has this dispute been formally mediated? ☐ Yes ☐ No
If so, when?

3. Do you want this matter sent to mediation at this time? ☐ Yes ☐ No

F. ADDITIONAL COMMENTS/RECOMMENDATIONS RE TRIAL: *(Use additional page if necessary.)*

Respectfully submitted,

Dated: ______________________ ______________________
Firm Name

By: ______________________

This form is optional. It has been approved for use by the United States Bankruptcy Court for the Central District of California.

Joint Status Report - Local Bankruptcy Rule 7016-1(a)(2) (F 7016-1.1)

Attorney or Party Name, Address, Telephone & FAX Numbers and California State Bar Number Attorney for	FOR COURT USE ONLY
UNITED STATES BANKRUPTCY COURT CENTRAL DISTRICT OF CALIFORNIA	
In re: Debtor(s).	
Plaintiff(s).	CHAPTER: CASE NO.:
vs.	ADVERSARY NO.:
Defendant(s).	DATE: TIME: PLACE:

JOINT STATUS REPORT
LOCAL BANKRUPTCY RULE 7016-1(a)(2)

TO THE HONORABLE UNITED STATES BANKRUPTCY JUDGE:

The parties submit the following JOINT STATUS REPORT in accordance with Local Bankruptcy Rule 7016-1(a)(2):

A. **PLEADINGS/SERVICE:**

1. Have all parties been served? ☐ Yes ☐ No
2. Have all parties filed and served answers to the complaint/counter-complaints/etc.? ☐ Yes ☐ No
3. Have all motions addressed to the pleadings been resolved? ☐ Yes ☐ No
4. Have counsel met and conferred in compliance with Local Bankruptcy Rule 7026-1? ☐ Yes ☐ No
5. If your answer to any of the four preceding questions is anything other than an unqualified "YES," then please explain below *(or on attached page)*:

(Continued on next page)

In re	CHAPTER:
	CASE NO.:
Debtor(s).	ADVERSARY NO.:

B. READINESS FOR TRIAL:

1. When will you be ready for trial in this case?
   Plaintiff Defendant

2. If your answer to the above is more than four (4) months after the summons issued in this case, give reasons for further delay.
   Plaintiff Defendant

3. When do you expect to complete your discovery efforts?
   Plaintiff Defendant

4. What additional discovery do you require to prepare for trial?
   Plaintiff Defendant

C. TRIAL TIME:

1. What is your estimate of the time required to present your side of the case at trial (including rebuttal stage if applicable)?
   Plaintiff Defendant

2. How many witnesses do you intend to call at trial (including opposing parties)?
   Plaintiff Defendant

3. How many exhibits do you anticipate using at trial?
   Plaintiff Defendant

(Continued on next page)

In re	CHAPTER:
	CASE NO.:
Debtor(s).	ADVERSARY NO.:

D. **PRE-TRIAL CONFERENCE:**

A pre-trial conference is usually conducted between a week to a month before trial, at which time a pre-trial order will be signed by the court. [See Local Bankruptcy Rule 7016-1.] If you believe that a pre-trial conference is not necessary or appropriate in this case, please so note below, stating your reasons:

Plaintiff	Defendant
Pre-trial conference __ (is)/ __ (is not) requested.	Pre-trial conference __ (is)/ __ (is not) requested.
Reasons: ________________	Reasons: ________________

Plaintiff	Defendant
Pre-trial conference should be set after:	Pre-trial conference should be set after:
(date) ________________	(date) ________________

E. **SETTLEMENT:**

1. What is the status of settlement efforts?

2. Has this dispute been formally mediated? ☐ Yes ☐ No
   If so, when?

3. Do you want this matter sent to mediation at this time?

Plaintiff	Defendant
☐ Yes ☐ No	☐ Yes ☐ No

(Continued on next page)

In re	CHAPTER:
	CASE NO.:
Debtor(s).	ADVERSARY NO.:

F. **ADDITIONAL COMMENTS/RECOMMENDATIONS RE TRIAL:** *(Use additional page if necessary.)*

Respectfully submitted,

Dated: ____________________	Dated: ____________________
____________________ *Firm Name*	____________________ *Firm Name*
By: ____________________	By: ____________________
Name: ____________________	Name: ____________________
Attorney for: ____________________	Attorney for: ____________________

In re	CHAPTER:
	CASE NO.:
Debtor(s).	ADVERSARY NO.:

NOTE: When using this form to indicate service of a proposed order, **DO NOT** list any person or entity in Category I. Proposed orders do not generate an NEF because only orders that have been entered are placed on a CM/ECF docket.

PROOF OF SERVICE OF DOCUMENT

I am over the age of 18 and not a party to this bankruptcy case or adversary proceeding. My business address is:

A true and correct copy of the foregoing document described as ______________________________ ______________________________ will be served or was served **(a)** on the judge in chambers in the form and manner required by LBR 5005-2(d), and **(b)** in the manner indicated below:

I. TO BE SERVED BY THE COURT VIA NOTICE OF ELECTRONIC FILING ("NEF") - Pursuant to controlling General Order(s) and Local Bankruptcy Rule(s) ("LBR"), the foregoing document will be served by the court via NEF and hyperlink to the document. On ____________________ I checked the CM/ECF docket for this bankruptcy case or adversary proceeding and determined that the following person(s) are on the Electronic Mail Notice List to receive NEF transmission at the email addressed indicated below:

☐ Service information continued on attached page

II. SERVED BY U.S. MAIL OR OVERNIGHT MAIL (indicate method for each person or entity served):
On ____________________ I served the following person(s) and/or entity(ies) at the last known address(es) in this bankruptcy case or adversary proceeding by placing a true and correct copy thereof in a sealed envelope in the United States Mail, first class, postage prepaid, and/or with an overnight mail service addressed as follow. Listing the judge here constitutes a declaration that mailing to the judge will be completed no later than 24 hours after the document is filed.

☐ Service information continued on attached page

III. SERVED BY PERSONAL DELIVERY, FACSIMILE TRANSMISSION OR EMAIL (indicate method for each person or entity served): Pursuant to F.R.Civ.P. 5 and/or controlling LBR, on ____________________ I served the following person(s) and/or entity(ies) by personal delivery, or (for those who consented in writing to such service method) by facsimile transmission and/or email as follows. Listing the judge here constitutes a declaration that mailing to the judge will be completed no later than 24 hours after the document is filed.

☐ Service information continued on attached page

I declare under penalty of perjury under the laws of the United States of America that the foregoing is true and correct.

______________________________ ______________________________
Date *Type Name* *Signature*

Joint Status Report - *Page 6* **F 7016-1.1**

In re	CHAPTER:
	CASE NO.:
Debtor(s).	ADVERSARY NO.:

ADDITIONAL SERVICE INFORMATION (if needed):

Lessor's Certification of (1) Prepetition Eviction Action, or (2) Endangerment of the Property or Illegal Use of a Controlled Substance within the Last 30 Days (11 U.S.C. § 362(b)(23)) (F 4001-1.4)

Attorney or Party Name, Address, Telephone & FAX Numbers, and California State Bar Number ☐ *Attorney for:* Debtor ☐ *Individual lessor appearing without counsel* (Pro Se Lessor)	FOR COURT USE ONLY
UNITED STATES BANKRUPTCY COURT CENTRAL DISTRICT OF CALIFORNIA	
In re: Debtor(s).	CHAPTER: CASE NO.:
	LESSOR'S CERTIFICATION OF (1) PREPETITION EVICTION ACTION SEEKING POSSESSION OF RESIDENTIAL PROPERTY BASED ON DEBTOR'S PREPETITION ENDANGERMENT OF PROPERTY OR ILLEGAL USE OF A CONTROLLED SUBSTANCE, OR (2) ENDANGERMENT OF THE PROPERTY OR ILLEGAL USE OF A CONTROLLED SUBSTANCE WITHIN THE LAST 30 DAYS (11 U.S.C. § 362 (b)(23))

1. ______________________ ("Lessor") hereby certifies the following regarding that residential property commonly known as ______________________________ ("Property"): *(Check all that apply)*
(Complete Address)

   a. ☐ The Property is the subject of an eviction action in which possession is sought, filed by the Lessor before the petition was filed in this case. The eviction action was filed on __________ in ______________________ (Describe Court and Case No.) (the "Eviction Action"). A copy of the complaint filed in the Eviction Action is attached as Exhibit ____.

   b. ☐ Debtor has endangered the property, or used or allowed illegal use of controlled substances on the property, as shown by the following facts: ______________________________ ☐ continuation page(s) attached.

   c. ☐ The conduct described in paragraph (b):
      ☐ Is described in the eviction action referred to in paragraph (a); or
      ☐ Occurred during the 30-day period preceding the date this certification was filed and served.

2. Lessor ☐ has ☐ has not filed and served on Debtor and parties in interest a declaration(s) supporting this certification, and ☐ has ☐ has not filed and served on Debtor and parties in interest a memorandum of points and authorities supporting Lessor's rights under 11 U.S.C. § 362, subsections (m)(1), (m)(2)(D), and (b)(23).

(Continued on next page)

In re (SHORT TITLE)	CHAPTER:
Debtor(s).	CASE NO.:

Declaration of Lessor

I, ______________________, am the ☐ lessor, ☐ an officer or authorized agent of the lessor of the property described herein. I declare under the penalty of perjury that I have read the foregoing, including all continuation pages, and that all statements therein are true and correct.

Executed this ____________ day of ______________ (Month), __________ (Year) at ______________.

____
Signature of the Lessor or Agent of the Lessor

____
Print Name of the Lessor or Agent of the Lessor

____
Print the Name of the Law Firm Representing the Lessor (if applicable)

____
Signature of the Attorney Representing the Lessor (if applicable)

____
Print the Name of the Attorney Representing the Lessor (if applicable)

Lessor's Certification (Endangerment of Property by Debtor) - *Page 3 of* ____ **F 4001-1.4**

In re (SHORT TITLE) Debtor(s).	CHAPTER: CASE NO.:

NOTE: When using this form to indicate service of a proposed order, **DO NOT** list any person or entity in Category I. Proposed orders do not generate an NEF because only orders that have been entered are placed on a CM/ECF docket.

PROOF OF SERVICE OF DOCUMENT

I am over the age of 18 and not a party to this bankruptcy case or adversary proceeding. My business address is:

A true and correct copy of the foregoing document described as ________________ will be served or was served **(a)** on the judge in chambers in the form and manner required by LBR 5005-2(d), and **(b)** in the manner indicated below:

I. <u>TO BE SERVED BY THE COURT VIA NOTICE OF ELECTRONIC FILING ("NEF")</u> - Pursuant to controlling General Order(s) and Local Bankruptcy Rule(s) ("LBR"), the foregoing document will be served by the court via NEF and hyperlink to the document. On ____________ I checked the CM/ECF docket for this bankruptcy case or adversary proceeding and determined that the following person(s) are on the Electronic Mail Notice List to receive NEF transmission at the email addressed indicated below:

☐ Service information continued on attached page

II. <u>SERVED BY U.S. MAIL OR OVERNIGHT MAIL</u> <u>(indicate method for each person or entity served)</u>:
On ____________ I served the following person(s) and/or entity(ies) at the last known address(es) in this bankruptcy case or adversary proceeding by placing a true and correct copy thereof in a sealed envelope in the United States Mail, first class, postage prepaid, and/or with an overnight mail service addressed as follow. Listing the judge here constitutes a declaration that mailing to the judge <u>will be</u> completed no later than 24 hours after the document is filed.

☐ Service information continued on attached page

III. <u>SERVED BY PERSONAL DELIVERY, FACSIMILE TRANSMISSION OR EMAIL</u> <u>(indicate method for each person or entity served)</u>: Pursuant to F.R.Civ.P. 5 and/or controlling LBR, on ____________ I served the following person(s) and/or entity(ies) by personal delivery, or (for those who consented in writing to such service method) by facsimile transmission and/or email as follows. Listing the judge here constitutes a declaration that mailing to the judge <u>will be</u> completed no later than 24 hours after the document is filed.

☐ Service information continued on attached page

I declare under penalty of perjury under the laws of the United States of America that the foregoing is true and correct.

Date	*Type Name*	*Signature*

This form is optional. It has been approved by the United States Bankruptcy Court for the Central District of California.

In re (SHORT TITLE)	CHAPTER:
Debtor(s).	CASE NO.:

ADDITIONAL SERVICE INFORMATION (if needed):

Lessor's Objection to Debtor's Certification and/or Debtor's Further Certification Concerning Residential Property and Notice of Hearing (11 U.S.C. § 362(l)(3)(A)) (F 4001-1.3)

Attorney or Party Name, Address, Telephone & FAX Numbers, and California State Bar Number ☐ *Attorney for:* ☐ *Individual lessor appearing without counsel* (Pro Se Lessor)	FOR COURT USE ONLY
UNITED STATES BANKRUPTCY COURT **CENTRAL DISTRICT OF CALIFORNIA**	
In re: Debtor(s).	CHAPTER: CASE NO.: **LESSOR'S OBJECTION TO DEBTOR'S CERTIFICATION AND/OR DEBTOR'S FURTHER CERTIFICATION CONCERNING RESIDENTIAL PROPERTY AND NOTICE OF HEARING (11 U.S.C. § 362 (l)(3)(A))** DATE: TIME: CTRM: FLOOR:

________________________("Lessor") is the lessor of the residential property commonly known as ________________________
____("Property").
(Give Full Address of Subject Property)

1. Lessor objects to the following: *(Check all that apply)*

   a. ☐ "Debtor's Certification That Circumstances Exist Which Would Allow Cure of Monetary Default Underlying Judgment For Possession of Residential Property and Proof of Deposit" ("Certification") filed with the petition; 11 U.S.C. § 362 (l)(1)(A)&(B)

   b. ☐ "Further Certification of Cure of Monetary Default Underlying Judgment For Possession of Residential Property And Proof of Deposit" ("Further Certification") filed herein on________________; 11 U.S.C. § 362 (l)(2)

2. Lessor alleges that the ☐ Certification ☐ Further Certification is incorrect, improper, or ineffective for the following reasons:
____
____
____
____ ☐ continuation page attached.

3. Lessor ☐ has ☐ has not filed and served herewith a declaration(s) contesting the facts asserted in the Certification or the Further Certification.

4. Lessor ☐ has ☐ has not filed and served herewith a memorandum of points and authorities supporting this Objection.

(Continued on next page)

In re (SHORT TITLE)	CHAPTER:
Debtor(s).	CASE NO.:

5. Lessor further notifies Debtor and parties in interest that the Lessor has scheduled through the assigned judge's calendar clerk or, where applicable, the assigned judge's self-calendaring system, a hearing (within 10 days of the filing and service of this Objection) on Lessor's objection and the truth of Debtor's Certification and/or Further Certification, which hearing will be held on ____________ at ______(am / pm) in courtroom ______ at:

Hearing Location: ☐ **255 East Temple Street, Los Angeles** ☐ **411 West Fourth Street, Santa Ana** ☐ **21041 Burbank Boulevard, Woodland Hills** ☐ **1415 State Street, Santa Barbara** ☐ **3420 Twelfth Street, Riverside**

Declaration of Lessor

I, __________________________, am the ☐ lessor, or ☐ an officer, partner, or authorized agent of the lessor. I declare under penalty of perjury that I have read the foregoing, including all continuation pages, and that all statements therein are true and correct.

Executed this ____________ day of ________________ (Month), ____________ (Year) at ______________________.

____
Signature of the Lessor or Agent of the Lessor

____
Print Name of the Lessor or Agent of the Lessor

____
Print the Name of the Law Firm Representing the Lessor (if applicable)

____
Signature of the Attorney Representing the Lessor (if applicable)

____
Print the Name of the Attorney Representing the Lessor (if applicable)

Lessor's Objection to Debtor's Certification - *Page 3 of* ____ **F 4001-1.3**

In re (SHORT TITLE) Debtor(s).	CHAPTER: CASE NO.:

NOTE: When using this form to indicate service of a proposed order, **DO NOT** list any person or entity in Category I. Proposed orders do not generate an NEF because only orders that have been entered are placed on a CM/ECF docket.

PROOF OF SERVICE OF DOCUMENT

I am over the age of 18 and not a party to this bankruptcy case or adversary proceeding. My business address is:

A true and correct copy of the foregoing document described as ____________________ will be served or was served **(a)** on the judge in chambers in the form and manner required by LBR 5005-2(d), and **(b)** in the manner indicated below:

I. <u>TO BE SERVED BY THE COURT VIA NOTICE OF ELECTRONIC FILING ("NEF")</u> - Pursuant to controlling General Order(s) and Local Bankruptcy Rule(s) ("LBR"), the foregoing document will be served by the court via NEF and hyperlink to the document. On ____________ I checked the CM/ECF docket for this bankruptcy case or adversary proceeding and determined that the following person(s) are on the Electronic Mail Notice List to receive NEF transmission at the email addressed indicated below:

☐ Service information continued on attached page

II. <u>SERVED BY U.S. MAIL OR OVERNIGHT MAIL</u> <u>(indicate method for each person or entity served)</u>:
On ____________ I served the following person(s) and/or entity(ies) at the last known address(es) in this bankruptcy case or adversary proceeding by placing a true and correct copy thereof in a sealed envelope in the United States Mail, first class, postage prepaid, and/or with an overnight mail service addressed as follow. Listing the judge here constitutes a declaration that mailing to the judge <u>will be</u> completed no later than 24 hours after the document is filed.

☐ Service information continued on attached page

III. <u>SERVED BY PERSONAL DELIVERY, FACSIMILE TRANSMISSION OR EMAIL</u> <u>(indicate method for each person or entity served)</u>: Pursuant to F.R.Civ.P. 5 and/or controlling LBR, on ____________ I served the following person(s) and/or entity(ies) by personal delivery, or (for those who consented in writing to such service method) by facsimile transmission and/or email as follows. Listing the judge here constitutes a declaration that mailing to the judge <u>will be</u> completed no later than 24 hours after the document is filed.

☐ Service information continued on attached page

I declare under penalty of perjury under the laws of the United States of America that the foregoing is true and correct.

Date *Type Name* *Signature*

In re (SHORT TITLE)	CHAPTER:
Debtor(s).	CASE NO.:

ADDITIONAL SERVICE INFORMATION (if needed):

Mediator's Certificate Regarding Conclusion of Mediation Conference

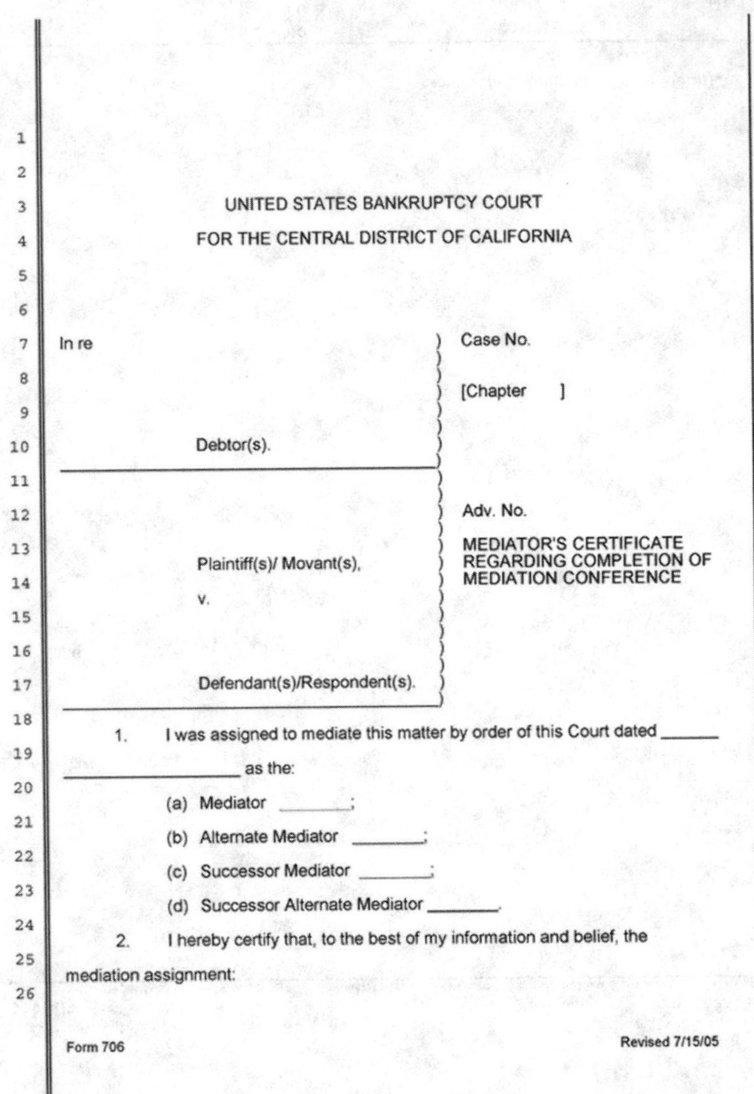

UNITED STATES BANKRUPTCY COURT

FOR THE CENTRAL DISTRICT OF CALIFORNIA

In re Debtor(s).	Case No. [Chapter]
Plaintiff(s)/ Movant(s), v. Defendant(s)/Respondent(s).	Adv. No. MEDIATOR'S CERTIFICATE REGARDING COMPLETION OF MEDIATION CONFERENCE

1. I was assigned to mediate this matter by order of this Court dated ______ __________________ as the:

(a) Mediator ________;

(b) Alternate Mediator ________;

(c) Successor Mediator ________;

(d) Successor Alternate Mediator ________.

2. I hereby certify that, to the best of my information and belief, the mediation assignment:

Form 706 Revised 7/15/05

(a) Settled _______;

(b) Did NOT settle _______.

3. If the matter SETTLED:

(a) Did the matter settle prior to the mediation conference without a mediation conference being held? ______________________________

(b) If you conducted a mediation conference that settled, on what date(s) did the conference occur? ______________________________

(c) If you conducted a mediation conference that settled, who did you designate to prepare the settlement documentation? ____________________.

4. If the matter DID NOT settle:

(a) Was the matter dismissed by the Court prior to the mediation conference? ______________________________

(b) Did you conduct a mediation conference? __________

(c) If you conducted a mediation conference, on what date(s) did the conference occur? ______________________________

______________________________.

DATED: ____________________

____
(Name of Mediator)

____
(Signature of Mediator)

cc: Hon. Barry Russell
Mediation Program Administrator
United States Bankruptcy Court
255 East Temple Street, Suite 1660
Los Angeles, California 90012

Mediator's Report of Mediation Conference Confidential - Not To Be Filed With the Court

UNITED STATES BANKRUPTCY COURT

FOR THE CENTRAL DISTRICT OF CALIFORNIA

In re Debtor(s).	Bk. No. [Chapter]
Plaintiff(s)/Movant(s), v. Defendant(s)/Respondent(s).	Adv. No. MEDIATOR'S **CONFIDENTIAL** REPORT OF MEDIATION CONFERENCE **CONFIDENTIAL -- NOT TO BE FILED WITH THE COURT**

I hereby certify that the following information is true and correct to the best of my information and belief:

1. How did you learn of your mediation assignment? (PLEASE CHECK ALL THAT APPLY)

   (a) Received Court order _____; (b) Phone call _____;

   (c) Fax from Mediation Program staff _____;

   (d) Other ____.

2. In what capacity did you serve?

   (a) Mediator _____; (b) Alternate Mediator _____;

   (c) Successor Mediator _____; (d) Successor Alternate Mediator _____.

3. How did the mediation assignment conclude?

(a) Settled _____; (b) Did NOT settle _____.

4. How many hours did you spend scheduling and preparing for the mediation conference? _______

5. How many hours did you spend attending the conference? _____

6. Which dispute resolution procedure(s) did you use? (IF MORE THAN ONE METHOD USED, PLEASE ESTIMATE PERCENTAGE OF TIME SPENT ON EACH)

(a) Early neutral evaluation: _____ (_____%)

(b) Settlement negotiation: _____ (_____%)

(c) Mediation: _____ (_____%)

(d) Other: _____ (_____%)

(Describe): ____

____

7. Were you compensated for your mediation services? __________

8. Have you filed Form 706 (Mediator's Certificate Regarding Completion of Mediation Conference) with the Court, and mailed courtesy copies to the judge assigned to the matter and to Judge Russell (the Mediation Program Administrator)? _______

9. Comments/suggestions: ____

____

____

____

____

DATED: ____________________ ____________________
(Name of Mediator)

____
(Signature of Mediator)

MEDIATION CONFERENCE ATTENDANCE FORM

Case Name: ____________________

Case No.: ____________________

Adversary Proceeding Name: ____________________

Adversary Proceeding No.: ____________________

Date(s) of Conference(s): ____________________

Mediator: ____________________

Instructions: All attorneys and client representatives who attend the conference shall provide the following information to the Mediator. **PLEASE WRITE OR PRINT CLEARLY.**

ATTORNEYS

Name: ____________________
Firm: ____________________
Address: ____________________
____
Phone: ____________________
E-mail: ____________________
Attorney for: ____________________
____

Name: ____________________
Firm: ____________________
Address: ____________________
____
Phone: ____________________
E-mail: ____________________
Attorney for: ____________________
____

Name: ____________________
Firm: ____________________
Address: ____________________
____
Phone: ____________________
E-mail: ____________________
Attorney for: ____________________
____

Name: ____________________
Firm: ____________________
Address: ____________________
____
Phone: ____________________
E-mail: ____________________
Attorney for: ____________________
____

[Attach additional page(s) if necessary.]

CLIENT AND/OR CLIENT REPRESENTATIVES

Name: ______________________
Title: ______________________
Organization: ______________________
____
Address: ______________________
____
____
Phone: ______________________
Party Representing: ______________________
____

Name: ______________________
Title: ______________________
Organization: ______________________
____
Address: ______________________
____
____
Phone: ______________________
Party Representing: ______________________
____

Name: ______________________
Title: ______________________
Organization: ______________________
____
Address: ______________________
____
____
Phone: ______________________
Party Representing: ______________________
____

Name: ______________________
Title: ______________________
Organization: ______________________
____
Address: ______________________
____
____
Phone: ______________________
Party Representing: ______________________
____

[Attach additional page(s) if necessary.]

Mail to: Hon. Barry Russell
Mediation Program Administrator
United States Bankruptcy Court
255 East Temple Street, Suite 1660
Los Angeles, California 90012

Mega Case Procedures Checklist

Attorney or Party Name, Address, Telephone & FAX Numbers, and California State Bar Number	CHAPTER: CASE NO.:
UNITED STATES BANKRUPTCY COURT CENTRAL DISTRICT OF CALIFORNIA	CASE NAME:

MEGA CASE PROCEDURES CHECKLIST

Estimate of:
Number of Creditors ______ Assets ______
Number of Claims to be filed ______
Number of Pleadings to be filed ______
Number of Adversary Proceedings to be filed ______

It is proposed the following will be employed by the estate *(check all that apply)*:

Noticing Agent/Claims Processor ______ Estate Clerk ______ Independent Printer ______ Other ______

Instructions: Mark either the "YES" or "NO" box for each question listed in this declaration. For each question that a "NO" box is marked (other than question 1, 20 or 30), an explanation must be provided on the "COMMENTS" page.

I. Noticing Agent/Claims Processor

Delegation of Noticing/Claims Service Functions - The noticing/claims agent ("Agent") maintains the claims docket for the Court and performs all claims functions required by statute. The noticing/claims agent also maintains a database of all creditors in the case and sends notices to these creditors, as requested by the Court.

YES NO

☐ ☐ 1. Are you proposing the estate hire a Noticing Agent/Claims Processor? ***(If no, skip to Section II.)***

☐ ☐ 2. Is the price list attached to the motion and are the service charges fair and reasonable?

☐ ☐ 3. Does the motion state the Debtor has surveyed or solicited bids from different claims processing and noticing agents before designating a proposed agent?

3a. If no, what criteria was used to select the agent? ______

☐ ☐ 4. Does the motion state the Agent is not a creditor in the case?

☐ ☐ 5. Does the motion state the Agent shall be subject to the consent and approval of the Clerk of Court?

☐ ☐ 6. Does the motion state the Agent shall be at the expense of the estate and be paid directly by the Debtor?

YES NO

☐ ☐ 7. Does the motion state the Agent shall be under the supervision and control of the Clerk of Court but not be an employee of the United States government?

☐ ☐ 8. Does the motion state the Agent shall waive any rights to receive compensation from the United States government in its capacity as Agent in this case?

☐ ☐ 9. Does the motion state the Agent shall not employ any past or present employees of the Debtor in connection with its work as the Agent in this case unless otherwise approved by the Clerk of Court?

☐ ☐ 10. Does the motion state the Agent shall maintain copies of all proofs of claim or interest at a location other than where the originals are maintained?

☐ ☐ 11. Does the motion state the Agent shall implement security measures to ensure the completeness and integrity of the claims registers as approved by the Clerk of Court?

☐ ☐ 12. Does the motion state the Agent shall transmit to the Clerk of Court a copy of the claims registers every week or as frequently as requested by the Clerk of Court?

☐ ☐ 13. Does the motion state the Agent shall provide a proof of claim viewing area **without charge** during normal business hours (9:00 a.m.-4:00 p.m. Pacific Time)?

13a. In what city is the viewing area located? *(provide address)* ______________________

☐ ☐ 14. Does the motion state the Clerk of Court shall be entitled to inspect the Agent's premises at anytime?

☐ ☐ 15. Does the motion state the Agent shall audit the claims information periodically to satisfy the Clerk of Court that the claims information is being appropriately and accurately recorded in the Court's claims register?

☐ ☐ 16. Does the motion state the Clerk of Court shall be able to independently audit the claims information at anytime?

II. Motions and Other Pleadings

☐ ☐ 17. Does the motion state the party submitting a particular pleading or other document with the Court shall be responsible for all noticing and service functions relevant to the particular matter as may be required under applicable rules and shall file with the Clerk of Court a declaration of service regarding such noticing and service?

III. Notice of Entry of Order or Judgment

☐ ☐ 18. Does the motion state the attorney for the party submitting the proposed order or judgment shall serve copies upon all parties entitled to receive notice of the entry of the order or judgment as soon as practicable?

☐ ☐ 19. Does the motion state the attorney shall be responsible for photocopying the conformed copies in order to relieve the Clerk's Office from the large burden of photocopying these orders?

IV. Employment of Special Employees of the Estate (Estate Clerk)

YES NO

☐ ☐ 20. Does the motion state the Debtor shall furnish one or more employees to assist the Clerk's Office in the administration of this case as the Clerk of Court deems necessary. ***(If no, skip to Section V.)***

☐ ☐ 21. The employee shall not be designated as a part-time employee in the motion or order?

☐ ☐ 22. Does the motion state the employee of the Estate shall be subject to the consent and approval of the Clerk of Court?

☐ ☐ 23. Does the motion state the employee of the Estate shall be at the expense of the estate and be paid directly by the Debtor?

☐ ☐ 24. Does the motion state the employee of the Estate shall be under the supervision and control of the Clerk of Court but not be an employee of the United States government?

☐ ☐ 25. Does the motion state an employee of the Estate shall waive any rights to receive compensation from the United States government in its capacity as an employee in this case?

☐ ☐ 26. Does the motion state an employee of the Estate shall not be a past or present employee of the Debtor unless otherwise approved by the Clerk of Court?

☐ ☐ 27. Does the motion state an employee of the Estate may perform non-estate functions as the Clerk of Court deems necessary in exchange for Clerk's Office employees performing court-related docketing functions for the Estate?

V. Additional Space and Equipment

☐ ☐ 28. Does the motion state the Debtor shall be directly responsible for the cost of any additional space or equipment such as designated telephone lines and automation equipment, etc., if necessary?

☐ ☐ 29. Does the motion state the Debtor shall be responsible for payment for the designated post office boxes retained for receiving filings in this case?

VI. Independent Printer

Delegation of Printer Functions - At an offsite location near the Court, the independent printer ("Printer") maintains copies of all orders, pleadings and other documents filed in the case for inspection by the public during business hours. The printer also provides copies of these documents and case dockets to the public for a fee.

☐ ☐ 30. Are you proposing the estate hire a Printer? ***(If no, skip to the signature section VII.)***

☐ ☐ 31. Is the Printer located off the Court's premises but in close proximity to the appropriate divisional office of the Court?

☐ ☐ 32. Is the price list attached to the motion and are the service charges fair and reasonable?

☐ ☐ 33. Does the motion state the service charges cannot be changed without prior approval from the Clerk of Court?

YES	NO		
☐	☐	34.	Does the motion state the Debtor has surveyed or solicited bids from different printing services before designating a proposed printer?
		34a.	If no, what criteria was used to select the proposed Printer? ________________
☐	☐	35.	Does the motion state the Printer shall not be a creditor in the case?
☐	☐	36.	Does the motion state the Printer shall be subject to the consent and approval of the Clerk of Court?
☐	☐	37.	Does the motion state the Printer shall be at the expense of the estate and be paid directly by the Debtor?
☐	☐	38.	Does the motion state the Printer shall be under the supervision and control of the Clerk of Court but not be an employee of the United States government?
☐	☐	39.	Does the motion state the Printer shall waive any rights to receive compensation from the United States government in its capacity as Printer in this case?
☐	☐	40.	Does the motion state the Printer shall not employ any past or present employees of the Debtor in connection with its work as the Printer in this case unless otherwise approved by the Clerk of Court?
☐	☐	41.	Does the motion state the Printer shall provide a proof of claim viewing area **without charge** during normal business hours (9:00 a.m.-4:00 p.m. Pacific Time)?
		41a.	In what city is the viewing area located? *(provide address)* ________________
☐	☐	42.	Does the motion state the Printer shall provide the Clerk of Court copies of any document filed in this case without charge?
☐	☐	43.	Does the motion state the Printer shall implement security measures to ensure the completeness and integrity of the set of pleadings as approved by the Clerk of Court?
☐	☐	44.	Does the motion state the Clerk of Court shall be entitled to inspect the Printer's premises at anytime?

COMMENTS: If you need additional space, please attach an additional piece of paper.	
Item # ____	Comment: ____
Item # ____	Comment: ____
Item # ____	Comment: ____
Item # ____	Comment: ____
Item # ____	Comment: ____

COMMENTS OF THE CLERK'S OFFICE

☐ The Clerk's Office has no objection.

☐ The Clerk's Office objects as set forth below.

☐ Other:

Dated: ____________________ By: ____________________
Signature

____
Print Name and Title

Motion for Protective Order Pursuant to 11 U.S.C. § 107(c) and FRBP 9037 to Restrict Access to Filed Documents Containing Personal Data Identifiers (F 1002-1.2.MOTION)

Attorney or Party Name, Address, Telephone & FAX Nos., State Bar No. & Email Address ☐ Individual appearing without attorney ☐ Attorney for:	FOR COURT USE ONLY
UNITED STATES BANKRUPTCY COURT **CENTRAL DISTRICT OF CALIFORNIA** ________________ **DIVISION**	
In re: Debtor	CASE NO.: CHAPTER:
	MOTION FOR PROTECTIVE ORDER PURSUANT TO 11 U.S.C. § 107(c) AND FRBP 9037 TO RESTRICT ACCESS TO FILED DOCUMENTS CONTAINING PERSONAL DATA IDENTIFIERS
	(No hearing Required)

Movant ______________________________ hereby moves this court, pursuant to 11 U.S.C. § 107(c) and FRBP 9037 for a protective order to restrict public access to filed documents containing personal data identifiers for an individual (including but not limited to, an individual's social security number or tax identification number, financial account numbers, birth dates and/or names of minor children). See also LBR 1002-1(e). Movant further moves that the court authorize the redaction of personal data identifiers from these documents and direct the clerk of the court to restrict public access to these documents as originally filed, whether electronically or manually, so that the personal data identifiers are not available to public access.

Movant hereby certifies that the documents on the attached list containing personal data identifiers were filed on the dates indicated below and that public disclosure of personal data identifiers would create undue risk of identity theft or other unlawful injury to the individual or his/her property. (List each document separately and provide the date(s) of filing of the document and its assigned docket entry or claim number(s). You may attach as many continuation pages as necessary.)

I declare under penalty of perjury that the foregoing is true and correct.

Date	Type Movant's Name	Movant's Signature
Date	Attorney's Name	Attorney for Movant

ATTACHMENT TO MOTION FOR PROTECTIVE ORDER PURSUANT TO 11 U.S.C. § 107(c) AND FRBP 9037 TO RESTRICT ACCESS TO FILED DOCUMENTS CONTAINING PERSONAL DATA IDENTIFIERS

LIST OF DOCUMENTS IDENTIFIED IN MOTION TO BE REDACTED AND PUBLIC ACCESS TO BE RESTRICTED.

Docket or Claim No.	Date Filed	Name of Document

PROOF OF SERVICE OF DOCUMENT

I am over the age of 18 and not a party to this bankruptcy case or adversary proceeding. My business address is:

A true and correct copy of the foregoing document described as ______________________________ will be served or was served **(a)** on the judge in chambers in the form and manner required by LBR 5005-2(d); and **(b)** in the manner indicated below:

I. TO BE SERVED BY THE COURT VIA NOTICE OF ELECTRONIC FILING ("NEF") – Pursuant to controlling General Order(s) and Local Bankruptcy Rule(s) ("LBR"), the foregoing document will be served by the court via NEF and hyperlink to the document. On ______________ I checked the CM/ECF docket for this bankruptcy case or adversary proceeding and determined that the following person(s) are on the Electronic Mail Notice List to receive NEF transmission at the email address(es) indicated below:

☐ Service information continued on attached page

II. SERVED BY U.S. MAIL OR OVERNIGHT MAIL (indicate method for each person or entity served):
On ______________ I served the following person(s) and/or entity(ies) at the last known address(es) in this bankruptcy case or adversary proceeding by placing a true and correct copy thereof in a sealed envelope in the United States Mail, first class, postage prepaid, and/or with an overnight mail service addressed as follows. Listing the judge here constitutes a declaration that mailing to the judge will be completed no later than 24 hours after the document is filed.

☐ Service information continued on attached page

III. SERVED BY PERSONAL DELIVERY, FACSIMILE TRANSMISSION OR EMAIL (indicate method for each person or entity served): Pursuant to F.R.Civ.P. 5 and/or controlling LBR, on ______________ I served the following person(s) and/or entity(ies) by personal delivery, or (for those who consented in writing to such service method), by facsimile transmission and/or email as follows. Listing the judge here constitutes a declaration that personal delivery on the judge will be completed no later than 24 hours after the document is filed.

☐ Service information continued on attached page

I declare under penalty of perjury under the laws of the United States of America that the foregoing is true and correct.

Date	*Type Name*	*Signature*

CDCAL-709 C.D. CALIFORNIA

MOTION FOR DEFAULT JUDGMENT (F 9021–1.3)

Attorney or Party Name, Address, Telephone & FAX Numbers, and California State Bar Number *Attorney for*	FOR COURT USE ONLY
UNITED STATES BANKRUPTCY COURT CENTRAL DISTRICT OF CALIFORNIA In re: Debtor(s).	
Plaintiff(s), vs. Defendant(s).	CHAPTER: CASE NO.: ADVERSARY NO.: (No Hearing Required)

MOTION FOR DEFAULT JUDGMENT UNDER LOCAL BANKRUPTCY RULE 9021-1

TO THE DEFENDANT, DEFENDANT'S ATTORNEY AND OTHER INTERESTED PARTIES:

1. Name of Defendant(s) against whom default judgment is sought *(Name)*:
2. Plaintiff filed the Complaint in the above-captioned proceeding on *(specify date)*:
3. The Summons and Complaint were served on Defendant by ☐ Personal Service ☐ Mail Service on the following date *(specify date)*:
4. A conformed copy of the completed Return of Summons form is attached hereto.
5. The time for filing an Answer or other response expired on *(specify date)*:
6. No Answer or other response has been filed or served by Defendant.
7. The default of Defendant:
   a. ☐ Has not yet been entered, but is hereby requested
   b. ☐ Was entered on *(specify date)*:
8. **A Status Conference:**
   a. ☐ Is scheduled for *(specify date, time, and place)*:
   b. ☐ Was held on *(specify date, time, and place)*:

(Continued on next page)

Motion for Default Judgment under Local Bankruptcy Rule 9021-1 - *Page 2* **F 9021-1.3**

In re	CHAPTER:
Debtor(s).	CASE NO.:

9. As proof that Plaintiff is entitled to the relief requested in the Complaint, Plaintiff:
   a. ☐ Relies on the Complaint and documents attached thereto.
   b. ☐ Attaches the following documents to establish a prima facie case:
      (1) ☐ Declaration of *(specify)*:

      (2) ☐ Declaration of *(specify)*:

      (3) ☐ Other *(specify)*:

10. As further support for entry of a Default Judgment, Plaintiff submits a Memorandum of Points and Authorities *(Optional)*.

11. **DECLARATION OF NON-MILITARY STATUS:** No defendant named in Paragraph 1 above is in the military service so as to be entitled to the benefits of the Servicemembers Civil Relief Act (Pub. L. 108-189) (50 U.S. Code App. §§ 501-594). The undersigned declares under penalty of perjury that this statement of defendant's non-military status is true and correct and is made under penalty of perjury under the laws of the United States of America based upon the undersigned's review of said Defendant's Statement of Affairs and Statement of Income and Expenditures filed in this case and is based upon the undersigned's lack of any information or belief that there has been any change of circumstances as to defendant's non-military status.

12. Defaulting party is not an infant or incompetent party.

WHEREFORE, Plaintiff prays that this Court enter a Default Judgment in favor of Plaintiff. A Copy of the proposed Default Judgment is submitted herewith and has been served.

Dated: Respectfully submitted,

____
Firm Name

By: ____________________________

Name: ____________________________
Attorney for Plaintiff or Plaintiff

In re	CHAPTER:
Debtor(s).	CASE NO.:

PROOF OF SERVICE BY MAIL

STATE OF CALIFORNIA COUNTY OF ______________________________

I am employed in the above County, State of California. I am over the age of 18 and not a party to the within action. My business address is as follows:

On ____________________, I served the foregoing document described as: MOTION FOR DEFAULT JUDGMENT UNDER LOCAL BANKRUPTCY RULE 9021-1 on the interested parties at their last known address in this action by placing a true and correct copy thereof in a sealed envelope with postage thereon fully prepaid in the United States Mail at ____________________, California, addressed as follows:

☐ Addresses continued on attached page

I declare under penalty of perjury under the laws of the United States of America that the foregoing is true and correct.

Dated:

______________________________ ______________________________

Typed Name *Signature*

NOTICE OF DEBTOR'S MOTION TO CONVERT CASE UNDER 11 U.S.C § 706(A) (F1017-1.3)

Attorney or Party Name, Address, Telephone & FAX Numbers, and California State Bar Number *Attorney for*	FOR COURT USE ONLY
UNITED STATES BANKRUPTCY COURT **CENTRAL DISTRICT OF CALIFORNIA**	
In re: Debtor.	CHAPTER ______ CASE NUMBER

NOTICE OF DEBTOR'S MOTION TO CONVERT CASE UNDER 11 U.S.C. § 706(a)

1. TO *(specify name)*:

2. NOTICE IS HEREBY GIVEN that Debtor will move this Court for an Order granting the relief sought in Debtor's Motion to Convert Case Under 11 U.S.C. § 706(a) ("Motion"), a copy of which is attached hereto and served herewith. Debtor seeks a conversion of this case under 11 U.S.C. § 706(a) based upon the grounds set forth in the said Motion. Debtor's Motion is made pursuant to Local Bankruptcy Rule 9013-1(g)(1), which provides for granting of motions without a hearing.

3. **Deadline for Opposition Papers and Request for a Hearing**: Pursuant to Local Bankruptcy Rule 9013-1(g)(1), any party objecting to the accompanying Motion may file and serve a written objection and request a hearing of this Motion. If you fail to file a written response within fifteen (15) days of the date of service of this Notice, the Court may treat such failure as a waiver of your right to oppose this Motion and may grant the requested relief.

Dated: ____________________
Law Firm Name

By: ____________________

Date Notice Mailed: Name: ____________________
Attorney for Movant

In re

CHAPTER ______

Debtor. CASE NUMBER

PROOF OF SERVICE

STATE OF CALIFORNIA COUNTY OF ________________________

1. I am employed in the County of ____________________________, State of California. I am over the age of 18 and not a party to the within action. My business address is as follows:

2. **Regular Mail Service**: On ____________________________________, pursuant to Local Bankruptcy Rules 1017-1 and 9013-1, I served the documents described as: NOTICE OF DEBTOR'S MOTION TO CONVERT CASE UNDER 11 U.S.C. § 706(a) on the chapter 7 trustee, attorney for chapter 7 trustee (if any), United States trustee, and parties in interest at their last known addresses by placing a true and correct copy thereof in a sealed envelope with postage thereon fully prepaid in the United States Mail at ______________________, California, addressed as set forth below:

☐ Addresses continued on attached page

I declare under penalty of perjury under the laws of the United States of America that the foregoing is true and correct.

Dated:

______________________	______________________
Type Name	*Signature*

Motion for Default Judgment under Local Bankruptcy Rule 7055-1 (F 7055-1.2)

Attorney or Party Name, Address, Telephone & FAX Numbers, and California State Bar Number Attorney for	FOR COURT USE ONLY
UNITED STATES BANKRUPTCY COURT CENTRAL DISTRICT OF CALIFORNIA	
In re: Debtor(s).	
Plaintiff(s),	CHAPTER: CASE NO.:
vs.	ADVERSARY NO.:
Defendant(s).	(No Hearing Required)

MOTION FOR DEFAULT JUDGMENT UNDER LOCAL BANKRUPTCY RULE 7055-1

TO THE DEFENDANT, DEFENDANT'S ATTORNEY AND OTHER INTERESTED PARTIES:

1. Name of Defendant(s) against whom default judgment is sought *(Name)*:
2. Plaintiff filed the Complaint in the above-captioned proceeding on *(specify date)*:
3. The Summons and Complaint were served on Defendant by ☐ Personal Service ☐ Mail Service on the following date *(specify date)*:
4. A conformed copy of the completed Return of Summons form is attached hereto.
5. The time for filing an Answer or other response expired on *(specify date)*:
6. No Answer or other response has been filed or served by Defendant.
7. The default of Defendant:
   a. ☐ Has not yet been entered, but is hereby requested
   b. ☐ Was entered on *(specify date)*:
8. **A Status Conference:**
   a. ☐ Is scheduled for *(specify date, time, and place)*:
   b. ☐ Was held on *(specify date, time, and place)*:

(Continued on next page)

In re	CHAPTER:
Debtor(s).	CASE NO.:

9. As proof that Plaintiff is entitled to the relief requested in the Complaint, Plaintiff:
   a. ☐ Relies on the Complaint and documents attached thereto.
   b. ☐ Attaches the following documents to establish a prima facie case:
      (1) ☐ Declaration of *(specify)*:
      (2) ☐ Declaration of *(specify)*:
      (3) ☐ Other *(specify)*:

10. As further support for entry of a Default Judgment, Plaintiff submits a Memorandum of Points and Authorities *(Optional)*.

11. **DECLARATION OF NON-MILITARY STATUS:** No defendant named in Paragraph 1 above is in the military service so as to be entitled to the benefits of the Servicemembers Civil Relief Act (Pub. L. 108-189) (50 U.S. Code App. §§ 501-594). The undersigned declares under penalty of perjury that this statement of defendant's non-military status is true and correct and is made under penalty of perjury under the laws of the United States of America based upon the undersigned's review of said Defendant's Statement of Affairs and Statement of Income and Expenditures filed in this case and is based upon the undersigned's lack of any information or belief that there has been any change of circumstances as to defendant's non-military status.

12. Defaulting party is not an infant or incompetent party.

WHEREFORE, Plaintiff prays that this Court enter a Default Judgment in favor of Plaintiff. A Copy of the proposed Default Judgment is submitted herewith and has been served.

Dated:

Respectfully submitted,

____
Firm Name

By: ______________________________

Name: ______________________________
Attorney for Plaintiff or Plaintiff

Motion for Default Judgment under Local Bankruptcy Rule 7055-1 - *Page 3* **F 7055-1.2**

In re	CHAPTER:
Debtor(s).	CASE NO.:

NOTE: When using this form to indicate service of a proposed order, **DO NOT** list any person or entity in Category I. Proposed orders do not generate an NEF because only orders that have been entered are placed on a CM/ECF docket.

PROOF OF SERVICE OF DOCUMENT

I am over the age of 18 and not a party to this bankruptcy case or adversary proceeding. My business address is:

A true and correct copy of the foregoing document described as ______________________________ ______________________________ will be served or was served **(a)** on the judge in chambers in the form and manner required by LBR 5005-2(d), and **(b)** in the manner indicated below:

I. <u>TO BE SERVED BY THE COURT VIA NOTICE OF ELECTRONIC FILING ("NEF")</u> - Pursuant to controlling General Order(s) and Local Bankruptcy Rule(s) ("LBR"), the foregoing document will be served by the court via NEF and hyperlink to the document. On ____________________ I checked the CM/ECF docket for this bankruptcy case or adversary proceeding and determined that the following person(s) are on the Electronic Mail Notice List to receive NEF transmission at the email addressed indicated below:

☐ Service information continued on attached page

II. <u>SERVED BY U.S. MAIL OR OVERNIGHT MAIL</u> <u>(indicate method for each person or entity served)</u>:
On ____________________ I served the following person(s) and/or entity(ies) at the last known address(es) in this bankruptcy case or adversary proceeding by placing a true and correct copy thereof in a sealed envelope in the United States Mail, first class, postage prepaid, and/or with an overnight mail service addressed as follow. Listing the judge here constitutes a declaration that mailing to the judge <u>will be</u> completed no later than 24 hours after the document is filed.

☐ Service information continued on attached page

III. <u>SERVED BY PERSONAL DELIVERY, FACSIMILE TRANSMISSION OR EMAIL</u> <u>(indicate method for each person or entity served)</u>: Pursuant to F.R.Civ.P. 5 and/or controlling LBR, on ____________________ I served the following person(s) and/or entity(ies) by personal delivery, or (for those who consented in writing to such service method) by facsimile transmission and/or email as follows. Listing the judge here constitutes a declaration that mailing to the judge <u>will be</u> completed no later than 24 hours after the document is filed.

☐ Service information continued on attached page

I declare under penalty of perjury under the laws of the United States of America that the foregoing is true and correct.

______________ ______________ ______________
Date *Type Name* *Signature*

This form is optional. It has been approved for use by the United States Bankruptcy Court for the Central District of California.

In re Debtor(s).	CHAPTER: CASE NO.:

ADDITIONAL SERVICE INFORMATION (if needed):

Motion for Order Releasing Unclaimed Funds (F 3011-1)

Attorney or Party Name, Address, Telephone & FAX Numbers, and California State Bar Number	FOR COURT USE ONLY
UNITED STATES BANKRUPTCY COURT CENTRAL DISTRICT OF CALIFORNIA	
In re:	CASE NUMBER
Debtor.	HEARING DATE: TIME: PLACE:

MOTION FOR ORDER RELEASING UNCLAIMED FUNDS

I, under penalty of perjury under the laws of the United States of America declare (or certify, verify, or state) that the following statements and information are true and correct:

1. I request an order releasing the total amount of $__________________ which is the sum of all monies deposited with the court on the following date(s)____ on behalf of the creditor____ on claim number(s) ____

2. Please check and complete the applicable subparagraph(s) below:

☐ a. I am the creditor named in paragraph 1.

☐ b. I am an employee of the creditor named in paragraph 1 and my title is ____________________. The creditor is still legally entitled to the monies and I am authorized by the creditor to this petition. Submit evidence establishing authority to act on behalf of creditor.

☐ c. I am the creditor and have appointed ____ as my lawful attorney-in-fact who is duly authorized by the attached original power of attorney to file this motion.

☐ d. Subparagraphs a, b, and c above do not apply, but I am entitled to payment of such monies because (submit evidence establishing basis for right to obtain payment).

____

____

____

____

(Continued on next page)

In re	CHAPTER ______
Debtor.	CASE NUMBER

3. Please complete each of the following subparagraphs:

   a. The following is the creditor's address and phone number:

   ____

   ____

   ____

   ____

   b. A brief history of the creditor (from the filing of the claim to the present) which includes, if applicable, identification of any sale of the company and the new and prior owner(s). Submit evidence establishing the sale of the company from the prior to the new owner(s):

   ____

   ____

   ____

   ____

   ____

   ____

4. I understand that, pursuant to 18 U.S.C. § 152, I may be fined or imprisoned, or both, if I have knowingly and fraudulently made any false statements in this document.

Motion for Order Releasing Unclaimed Funds - *Page 3* **F 3011-1**

In re	CHAPTER ______
Debtor.	CASE NUMBER

____
Signature of Creditor/Successor

(Corporate Seal

____
Type or Print Creditor's/Successor's Name

if applicable)

____
Creditor's/Successor's Address

____

____

STATE OF CALIFORNIA, COUNTY OF _______________________________

On _______________________________ before me, personally appeared *(insert name and title of the signer)*

____

____

personally known to me (or proved to me on the basis of satisfactory evidence) to be the person(s) whose name(s) is/are subscribed to the within instrument and acknowledged to me that he/she/they executed the same in his/her/their authorized capacity(ies), and that by his/her/their signature(s) on the instrument the person(s), or the entity upon behalf of which the person(s) acted, executed the instrument. WITNESS my hand and official seal.

____
Notary Public

(SEAL)

My commission expires on ____________________

In re	CHAPTER ______
Debtor.	CASE NUMBER

____
Signature of Attorney/Attorney-in-Fact (if appointed)

____
Type or Print Name

____
Address

____

____

STATE OF CALIFORNIA, COUNTY OF ______________________________

On ______________________________ before me, personally appeared *(insert name and title of the signer)*

____

____

personally known to me (or proved to me on the basis of satisfactory evidence) to be the person(s) whose name(s) is/are subscribed to the within instrument and acknowledged to me that he/she/they executed the same in his/her/their authorized capacity(ies), and that by his/her/their signature(s) on the instrument the person(s), or the entity upon behalf of which the person(s) acted, executed the instrument. WITNESS my hand and official seal.

____
Notary Public

(SEAL)

My commission expires on ______________________

Presented by:

____

____

____

Motion for Order Releasing Unclaimed Funds - *Page 5* **F 3011-1**

In re	CHAPTER ______
Debtor.	CASE NUMBER

PROOF OF SERVICE

I hereby certify under penalty of perjury under the laws of the United States of America that on ________________, I mailed in a sealed envelope, with postage thereon fully prepaid, a fully completed true and correct copy of the document described as "Motion for Order Releasing Unclaimed Funds" to the United States Attorney, United States Trustee, and other persons and entities required to be served by Local Bankruptcy Rule 3011-1(b) and addressed as follows:

Please insert the name and address of the trustee appointed in the case and the trustee's counsel, if any:

Please insert the name and address of the Debtor, Debtor in Possession, reorganized Debtor, or other fiduciary appointed to supervise the distribution of funds and assets of the estate (if not the claimant) and their counsel, if any:

If Movant is not the original creditor or an employee thereof, please insert the name and address of the original creditor and the creditor's counsel, if any:

Date

Signature

Type or Print Name

CDCAL-723 C.D. CALIFORNIA

National Archives and Records Administration (NARA) Request Forms

Request for Court to Retrieve Material from the National Archives and Records Administration

Date ______________

NAME ____

ADDRESS ____

TELEPHONE NUMBER ____

Please list all materials that will be needed. Provide a complete description, including the full bankruptcy number and debtor's name.

Is this file needed as a rush? YES ☐ NO ☐

Case Number: ____

Name of Debtor: ____

Please indicate the material you need:

Files ☐ Adversary ☐ Claim ☐

You will be notified of the arrival of items requested. The material will be returned to the National Archives and Records Administration after it has been held in this office 15 days from the date of notification. The 15-day period may be extended if a telephonic or written request for extension is received. If requested material is not viewed within the specified time period, it will not be reordered.

You must pay a $45.00 fee for this service.

COURT USE ONLY			
Record Group (21)	Accession #	Box #	Location

Frequently asked questions about court case files in NARA's Riverside County Record Center

1. **Why are court case files in NARA's Records Center?** NARA provides safe, secure, and economical records storage services for the courts. The regional Records Center in Riverside County stores about 700,000 cubic feet of records from Federal agencies and courts combined. Among these files are closed court case files from Federal courts in Phoenix, Tucson; Los Angeles, San Bernardino, San Diego, Santa Ana, and Santa Barbara, CA; and Las Vegas, NV.

2. **Why must I get case file, accession, and location numbers from the courts before I contact NARA?** NARA cannot provide you with information about the existence or location of a file, because the files belong to the courts. Only the courts maintain lists of case file names, which are then indexed to file numbers and locations. In cooperation with the courts, NARA offers public access services to provide faster retrieval. Without this service, you would have to request a case from the court and then wait for the court to retrieve the file from our Records Center.

3. **What causes delays in servicing my order?** Delays are caused by: lack of complete case identifying information (obtained from the court); errors in the case identifying information; failure to include a phone number where we can contact you; lack of payment; credit card disapproval; illegible handwriting; and failure to include a fax number for faxed orders.

4. **How does NARA retrieve case files for public use?** After you get ALL OF THE REQUIRED INFORMATION from the court, NARA staff knows where to find the file among the miles of record storage shelving in our warehouse. If any case information is missing or erroneous, we will probably not locate the file. If necessary, two different people will search for a file. Sometimes we also may call the court for assistance.

5. **What happens if you can't find my file?** If we cannot find your file, we will call you and <u>you</u> must re-check all of the information with the court.

6. **How long does it take to retrieve, copy, and send a file?** After we receive a request, NARA staff will log it in, verify payment, retrieve the file, copy the file, and either mail or fax it to you. **Your photocopies will be sent to you as soon as workload permits.** <u>Please request your copies well in advance of any deadlines you are facing.</u>

7. **What is the fastest way to get a copy?** The fastest way to obtain a file is for you to fax your request and for NARA to fax the file back to you. However, this service is not available for all requests, and you must pay by credit card, and we must first verify payment.

8. **Can I call NARA to check on my order?** Please do <u>NOT</u> call us to confirm that we received your fax request. Your fax machine can provide you with that information. NARA does not offer any expedite service, and operates on a first-come first-serve basis. <u>Your request will be handled in the order it was received.</u>

9. **Should I order a package or a complete file?** You need to discuss your options with your attorney or the party who asked you for the case file information. NARA provides packages of selected documents that suffice for some reasons, but we cannot make the decision for you.

10. **What hours are you open?** We are open 9:00 a.m to 3:30 p.m., Monday through Friday except federal holidays. To request an appointment to review your file <u>at our facility</u>, call (951)956-2000 between 9:00 a.m. and 3:30 p.m.. We do not offer walk-in appointments, or expedite services for walk-ins. No copies will be made after 3:30 p.m.

11. **How do I get to the Records Center and where can I park?** We are located in South Riverside County, near Perris, CA. Take I 215 to the Ramona Expressway exit. Head west one block and turn left at Harvill. Go south one block and turn right on Cajalco Road. Go to the end of the road- we are on the left. Call us or visit our website <<u>http://www.nara.gov/regional/laguna.html</u>> for directions. Parking is free.

12. **What can I expect when I visit the Records Center for my appointment?** Upon arrival you will check in with the front desk receptionist. You may bring only paper and pencil and laptop computers. All other items must be placed in a locker or left in your car. Copies will be provided at $0.50 per page up to a maximum of 50 pages. Arrangements must be made for more then 50 pages. We accept payment by cash, check or credit card. No copies will be made after 3:30 pm. Eating, drinking, and smoking are not permitted in the research room or lobby. There is a soda machine located in the lunch room.

National Archives and Records Administration

700 Pennsylvania Avenue, NW
Washington, DC 20408-0001

Washington, DC...Effective October 1, 2007, the National Archives will amend the fees it charges to reproduce public court documents in National Archives facilities nationwide. The fees are being changed to reflect current costs of providing the reproductions. This is the first fee increase in more than a decade.

As of October 1, 2007, fixed-fee packages for reproductions of commonly-requested court records using the National Archives order forms will be as follows:

Type of Record	Order Form	Fee
SMALL PACKAGES:		
Bankruptcy – Preselected Documents: o Discharge of Debtor (or Order of Dismissal or Final Decree) o Voluntary Petition o Summary of Debts and Property o Schedules D, E and F	NATF Form 90	$25.00
Bankruptcy – Docket Sheet	NATF Form 90	$25.00
Civil – Docket Sheet	NATF Form 91	$25.00
Criminal – Preseleted Documents: o Judgement o Commitment or Probation/Commitment Order or Sentence o Indictment	NATF Form 92	$25.00
Criminal – Docket Sheet	NATF Form 92	$25.00
Court of Appeals – Docket Sheet	NATF Form 93	$25.00
LARGE PACKAGES:		
Bankruptcy – Entire Case File	NATF Form 90	$70.00
Civil – Entire Case File	NATF Form 91	$70.00
Criminal – Entire Case File	NATF Form 92	$70.00
Court of Appeals – Entire Case File	NATF Form 93	$70.00

Entire Case Files that exceed 150 pages will be billed as a large package ($70.00) plus a labor charge billed in 15-minute increments ($13.23 per 15 minutes). Large packages that exceed one box will also incur a $10.00 handling fee for each additional box. The price of certification $15.00.

Appointments only may request case files at National Archives facilities, flag documents within the case file, and request individual copies of these documents. This service will cost $0.90 per page with a $10.00 minimum handling fee for each box retrieved. This option is not available to off-site customers.

For fastest service, off-site requestors are encouraged to use NARA's Order Online! at http://www.archives.gov/research/order/orderonline.html. Requests can also be made via US Mail or fax by submitting the appropriate forms found at http://www.archives.gov/research/court-records/bankruptcy.html along with the correct payment. Additional information about Court copies can be found at http://www.archives.gov/frc/court-records.html or by emailing frc@nara.gov.

National Archives Trust Fund Board NATF Form 90 (09-2005) OMB Control No. 3095-0063 Expires 11-30-2008

NATIONAL ARCHIVES AND RECORDS ADMINISTRATION (NARA)
ORDER FOR COPIES OF
BANKRUPTCY CASES

Copy Packages Available

Pre-Selected Documents (Individual only): Includes the following documents, to the extent that they are contained in the case file: **Discharge of Debtor** (or Order of Dismissal or Final Decree), **Voluntary Petition, Summary of Debts and Property, Schedules D, E** and **F** (Note in some jurisdictions Schedules may be listed as A1, A2 and A3). No substitutions will be made for these documents.

Entire Case File: Includes all documents in a Business and Individual case file.

Docket Sheet: A list of documents filed in a Bankruptcy case; an outline of the case.

* **Certification:** A seal certifying copies to be a valid reproduction of the file. This is available for an additional charge for all packages delivered by mail or express shipping. Certification for fax copies is not available.

If you **do not** want the **Pre-Selected Documents or Entire Case File copied**, please make an appointment to review the file at our facility to select the documents needed, or you may contact the court where the case was closed or filed to make arrangements to review the case at the court location.	**To make an appointment** *to review the file, call us at:* 951-*956-2000*, Monday–Friday (excluding Federal holidays), 9:00 a.m. to 3:30 p.m. Appointments should be made 72 hours in advance.

General Information

- Use a separate NATF Form 90 for each file you request. Blocks 3-7 must be completed on the order form to perform a search for the file. Please discard this instruction sheet. Allow up to 14 days from receipt of payment for processing your order.
- When paying by check or money order for mailed or fax request, a separate payment is required for each individual request. If paying by credit card, you may fax your request form to the fax number provided in Block 1.
- Orders can be sent by overnight delivery (FedEx) at an additional charge.
- Orders can be faxed if the page count is 25 pages or less. All orders exceeding 25 pages will need to be mailed.
- Request may be returned if the necessary information is not supplied or if the credit card is declined. Case information must be obtained from the Court in which the case was filed.
- Please note that contents of recent cases may be in both electronic and paper form. If NARA cannot provide you with documents you requested, we will refer you to the Court that adjudicated the case.

Questions? Concerns? Contact our Research Room staff at the number shown above or visit us at ***www.archives.gov***.

PRIVACY ACT STATEMENT
Collection of this information is authorized by 44 U.S.C. 2108. Disclosure of the information is voluntary; however, we will be unable to respond to your request if you do not furnish your name and address and the minimum required information about the records. The information is used by NARA employees to search for the record; to respond to you; to maintain control over information requests received and answered; and to facilitate preparation of internal statistical reports. If you provide credit card information, that information is used to bill you for copies.

PAPERWORK REDUCTION ACT PUBLIC BURDEN STATEMENT
A Federal agency may not conduct or sponsor, and a person is not required to respond to a collection of information unless it displays a current valid OMB control number. The OMB Control No. for this information collection is 3095-0063. Public burden reporting for this collection of information is estimated to be 10 minutes per response. Send comments regarding the burden estimate or any other aspect of the information collection, including suggestions for reducing this burden, to National Archives and Records Administration (NHP), 8601 Adelphi Road, College Park MD 20740. **DO NOT SEND COMPLETED FORMS TO THIS ADDRESS. SEND COMPLETED FORMS TO THE ADDRESS INDICATED ON THE FORM ITSELF.**

National Archives Trust Fund Board NATF Form 90 (09-2005) OMB Control No. 3095-0083 Expires 11-30-2008

NATIONAL ARCHIVES AND RECORDS ADMINISTRATION
ORDER FOR COPIES OF
BANKRUPTCY CASES

1. LOCATION	**2. AREAS SERVED**
NARA, Pacific Region — Riverside, Trust Fund Unit, Caller Service 8305, Perris, CA 92572-7298 Fax: (951) 956-2029	Southern California, **Arizona, Clark County**, Nevada

3. SELECT COPY PACKAGE (*select only one*)

Copy Package Not Certified	***Copy Package Certified***
☐ Pre-Selected Documents — **$25.00** ☐ Entire Case File — **$70.00** (150 page maximum) ☐ Docket Sheet — **$25.00**	(Certification for fax copies is not available) ☐ Pre-Selected Documents Certified — **$40.00** ☐ Entire Case File Certified — **$85.00** ☐ Docket Sheet — **$40.00**

4. CASE INFORMATION (obtain from the court in which the case was filed)

COURT LOCATION (city & state)	DEBTOR NAME(S)	CASE NUMBER
TRANSFER NUMBER	BOX NUMBER	LOCATION NUMBER

5. DELIVERY METHOD (select only one)

☐ Fax - 25 page limit ☐ Mail ☐ FedEx (additional $25.00) ☐ Charge Fed Ex Account -# ____________

6. YOUR DELIVERY INFORMATION

MAIL COPIES TO:		***FAX COPIES TO:***
NAME		FAX NUMBER
ADDRESS	APT. # / SUITE #	
CITY		ATTENTION
STATE AND ZIP		
DAYTIME TELEPHONE NUMBER		DAYTIME TELEPHONE NUMBER

7. YOUR PAYMENT INFORMATION

Credit Card		***Check or Money Order***
CARD TYPE ☐ VISA ☐ MasterCard ☐ American Express ☐ Discover		Make your check or money order payable to: ***National Archives Trust Fund (NATF)*** Mail your request **with payment** to the address shown in **block 1** at the top of this page.
ACCOUNT NUMBER	EXPIRATION DATE	
NAME ON CARD		
SIGNATURE or THREE DIGIT SECURITY CODE (on back of charge card). Order can not be processed if one of these two items is not provided.		

NARA USE ONLY

SEARCHER	DATE	PAYMENT: ☐ Paid Check # ________
REMARKS	☐ Review – Date: Time:	

Notice of Address to be Used in Specific Case Pursuant to 11 U.S.C. § 342(e)

REQUESTOR'S NAME: ____________________

ADDRESS: ____________________

____

TELEPHONE NO.: ____________________

UNITED STATES BANKRUPTCY COURT
CENTRAL DISTRICT OF CALIFORNIA

In re	CASE NO.: Chapter 7 ______ 13 ______
	NOTICE OF ADDRESS TO BE USED IN SPECIFIC CASE PURSUANT TO 11 U.S.C. § 342(e)

I am a creditor in the above-referenced case. Pursuant to 11 U.S.C. § 342(e), I hereby give notice that the address set forth below is to be used to provide notice to me in this case:

NAME OF CREDITOR: ____________________

ADDRESS FOR NOTICE: ____________________

____

____

I have served a copy of this *Notice of Address to be Used in Specific Case Pursuant to 11 U.S.C. § 342(e)* on the debtor in the above-referenced case.

Dated: ______________ ____________________
Signature

____
Title (Corporation officer, partner or agent)

Notice of Appeal

Attorney or Appellant, Address, Telephone & FAX Numbers, and California State Bar Number *Attorney for Appellant*	FOR COURT USE ONLY
UNITED STATES BANKRUPTCY COURT CENTRAL DISTRICT OF CALIFORNIA	
In re: Debtor(s).	
Last four digits of Social Security Number(s):	CHAPTER: CASE NUMBER:
Employer's Tax Identification No(s) [if any]:	ADVERSARY NUMBER:

NOTICE OF APPEAL

1. NOTICE IS HEREBY GIVEN that the *(check only one box)* ☐ plaintiff ☐ defendant or ☐ other party *(specify name of party)* ______________________, appeals under 28 U.S.C. § 158(a) or (b) from the judgment, order, or decree of the bankruptcy judge *(describe judgment, order, or decree)* ______________________ entered in this adversary proceeding or other proceeding *(describe other proceeding)* ______________________ on the ________ day of ______________, *(year)* ________.

2. The names of all parties to the judgment, order, or decree appealed from and the names, addresses, telephone, and fax numbers of their respective attorneys are as follows *(print or type names, addresses, telephone, and fax numbers)*:

(Continued on next page)

Notice of Appeal - *Page 2* **FORM 17**

In re	CHAPTER:
Debtor(s).	CASE NUMBER:

Dated:

____
Signature (Attorney for Appellant or Appellant if not represented by an Attorney)

____
Attorney Name

____
Address

____
Telephone Number

If a Bankruptcy Appellate Panel Service is authorized to hear this appeal, each party has a right to have the appeal heard by the district court. The appellant may exercise this right only by filing a separate statement of election at the time of the filing of this Notice of Appeal. Any other party may elect, within the time provided in 28 U.S.C. § 158(c), to have the appeal heard by the district court.

If a child support creditor or its representative is the appellant, and if the child support creditor or its representative files the form specified in § 304(g) of the Bankruptcy Reform Act of 1994, no fee is required.

In re	CHAPTER:
Debtor(s).	CASE NUMBER:

PROOF OF SERVICE

STATE OF CALIFORNIA COUNTY OF ______________________

1. I am employed in the County of ______________________, State of California. I am over the age of 18 and not a party to the within action. My business address is as follows:

2. **Regular Mail Service:** On ______________________, I served the documents described as: NOTICE OF APPEAL on the interested parties at their last known address in this action by placing a true and correct copy thereof in a sealed envelope with postage thereon fully prepaid in the United States Mail at ______________________, California, addressed as set forth below.

☐ Addresses continued on attached page

I declare under penalty of perjury under the laws of the United States of America that the foregoing is true and correct.

Dated:

______________________ ______________________
Typed Name *Signature*

Notice of Attorney Change of Address or Law Firm

Attorney or Party Name, Address, Telephone & FAX Numbers, and California State Bar Number ☐ *Attorney for*	FOR COURT USE ONLY
UNITED STATES BANKRUPTCY COURT **CENTRAL DISTRICT OF CALIFORNIA**	
In re Debtor(s), Plaintiff(s), vs. Debtor(s).	CHAPTER CASE NUMBER ☐ ADVERSARY NUMBER (if applicable) ☐ See attached list for multiple cases that require an update to the attorneys information

NOTICE OF ATTORNEY CHANGE OF ADDRESS OR LAW FIRM
(See page 2 for additional requirements)

The following information must be provided:

I, ______________________, ______________, ______________________
Name *Bar ID Number* *E-Mail Address*

❑ am **counsel of record** or
❑ **out-of-state attorney** in the above-entitled cause of action for the following party(s) *(single case)*

____

____

❑ am **counsel of record** or
❑ **out of state attorney** on all cases listed as an attachment to this form *(multiple cases)*

and am requesting the following change(s):

PROVIDE ONLY THE INFORMATION THAT HAS CHANGED

Attorney Name changed to________________________
New Firm/Government Agency Name________________________
New Address________________________
New Telephone Number______________New Facsimile Number______________
New E-Mail Address________________________

SELECT THE CATEGORY AND COMPLETE THE INFORMATION REQUESTED:

❑ **TO UPDATE NAME, ADDRESS OR FIRM INFORMATION:**
- ❑ I am providing the new information above pursuant to Local Rule 2091-1 to be updated on the above-entitled cause of action and/or all cases listed on the attachment.

❑ **TO BE TERMINATED FROM THE CASE:****
- ❑ I am, or
  - ❑ the aforementioned attorney from my firm is no longer counsel of record in the above-entitled cause of action and/or all cases listed on the attachment.

Note: Attorneys for parties are **never** deleted from a case in order to maintain historical data.

CHECK ONE BOX
- ❑ The order relieving me/the aforementioned attorney from my firm was entered on:____________
- ❑ There is/are other attorney(s) from the undersigned attorney's law firm/government agency who is/are counsel of record in this case.
- ❑ I am, or
  - ❑ the aforementioned attorney is no longer with the firm/government agency representing the above-named party in this action. There is/are attorney(s) from my former firm/government agency who are currently counsel of record in this/these case(s).

****This form *cannot* be used as a substitution of attorney form. For substitution of attorney procedures please refer to Local Bankruptcy Rule 2091-1 and form F2090-1.4, *Substitution of Attorney*. At least one member of the firm/government agency MUST continue to represent and receive service for the parties indicated in this action.**

Dated:____________________________ ____________________________

Signature of Present Attorney

IF YOUR FIRM IS **NOT** ALREADY PART OF THIS ACTION AND ARE ASSOCIATING IN AS COUNSEL OF RECORD A **NOTICE OF APPEARANCE** PURSUANT TO F.R.B.P. 9010(b) SHOULD BE FILED. IF YOU ARE GOING TO APPEAR PRO HAC VICE, A SEPARATE **APPLICATION OF NON-RESIDENT ATTORNEY TO APPEAR IN A SPECIFIC CASE** MUST BE FILED PURSUANT TO LBR 2090-1(b).

PLEASE NOTE: CM/ECF users must file this *Notice of Change of Address or Law Firm* separately and electronically for every pending case pursuant to Local Bankruptcy Rule 2091-1. Please refer to the procedures posted on the Court's website on how to file this notice for single or multiple cases. The court will update the case information once filed.

NOTICE OF ENTRY OF JUDGMENT OR ORDER (F 9021–1.1)

NOTE TO USERS OF THIS FORM:
Physically attach this form as the last page of the proposed Order or Judgment.
*Do **not** file this form as a separate document.*

In re Debtor.	CHAPTER ______ CASE NUMBER

NOTICE OF ENTRY OF JUDGMENT OR ORDER
AND CERTIFICATE OF MAILING

TO ALL PARTIES IN INTEREST ON THE ATTACHED SERVICE LIST:

1. You are hereby notified, pursuant to Local Bankruptcy Rule 9021-1(a)(1)(E), that a judgment or order entitled *(specify)*:

   was entered on *(specify date)*:

2. I hereby certify that I mailed a copy of this notice and a true copy of the order or judgment to the persons and entities on the attached service list on *(specify date)*:

Dated:

JON D. CERETTO
Clerk of the Bankruptcy Court

By: ________________________________
Deputy Clerk

CDCAL-735 C.D. CALIFORNIA

NOTICE OF ENTRY OF JUDGMENT OR ORDER AND CERTIFICATE OF MAILING (CAC)

Order on Reaffirmation Agreement - *Page 2*

In re (SHORT TITLE) Debtor(s).	CASE NO.:

NOTICE OF ENTRY OF JUDGMENT OR ORDER AND CERTIFICATE OF MAILING

TO ALL PARTIES ON THE ATTACHED SERVICE LIST:

1. You are hereby notified that a judgment or order entitled Order Approving Reaffirmation Agreement was entered on *(specify date)*:

2. I hereby certify that I mailed a copy of this notice and a true copy of the order or judgment to the persons and entities on the attached service list on *(specify date)*:

Dated: ______________________

Jon D. Ceretto
Clerk of the Bankruptcy Court

By: ______________________
Deputy Clerk

EASTERN DISTRICT OF CALIFORNIA

The Eastern District of California has adopted the following Local Rules relevant to cases under title 11:

LOCAL RULE 1001-1 Scope of Rules; Short Title

(a) Title. These are the Local Rules of Practice for the United Bankruptcy Court, Eastern District of California. They may be cited as "LBR."

(b) Construction. These Local Rules are adopted pursuant to 28 U.S.C. § 2075, FRCivP 83 and FRBP 9029. They are intended to supplement and shall be construed consistently with and subordinate to the FRBP and those portions of the FRCivP that are incorporated by the FRBP.

(c) Applicability of Local Bankruptcy and District Court Rules. The FRBP and these Local Rules govern procedure in all bankruptcy cases and bankruptcy proceedings in the Eastern District of California. Except for Rules 173 (Photographing, Recording or Broadcasting of Judicial Proceedings), 180 (Attorneys), 181 (Certified Student Attorneys), 182 (Attorneys-Appearance and Withdrawal), 183 (Persons Appearing in Propria Persona), 184 (Disciplinary Proceedings Against Attorneys), and 292 (Costs), which are hereby specifically incorporated into these Local Rules, and those Local Rules of Practice of the United States District Court for the Eastern District of California that are restated (renumbered and modified, as appropriate) in these Local Rules, no other Local Rules of Practice of the United States District Court for the Eastern District of California apply.

(d) General and Special Orders, Guidelines, and Policy Statements. Outside the scope of these Rules are matters relating to internal court administration that, in the discretion of the Court en banc, may be accomplished through the use of General Orders. The Clerk shall maintain copies of general and special orders, guidelines, and policy statements that relate to practice before this Court and shall make copies available upon request and payment of a nominal charge.

(e) Availability of Local Rules. The Clerk shall maintain in suitable form updated copies of these Rules and shall promptly notify thc Supreme Court, the Administrative Office of the United States Courts, the Circuit Council of the Ninth Circuit Court of Appeals, the District Court of the Eastern District of California and local law libraries of any changes in these Rules. The Clerk shall make copies of these Rules available on request upon payment of a nominal charge, if set by General Order. Upon admission to practice in the

Eastern District of California, each admittee shall be given a copy of the LBR then in effect.

(f) Procedures Outside the Rules. The Court may make such orders supplementary or contrary to the provisions of these Rules as it may deem appropriate and in the interests of justice in any particular proceeding.

(g) Sanctions for Noncompliance with Rules. Failure of counsel or of a party to comply with these Rules, with the FRCivP or the FRBP, or with any order of the Court may be grounds for imposition of any and all sanctions authorized by statute or Rule or within the inherent power of the Court, including, without limitation, dismissal of any action, entry of default, finding of contempt, imposition of monetary sanctions or attorney's fees and costs, and other lesser sanctions.

AMENDED LOCAL RULE 1002-1 Intra-District Venue

Petitions for relief under Title 11, United States Code, shall be filed in one of the three divisions of the Eastern District as determined by the following:

(a) Fresno Division. Petitions from the Counties of Fresno, Inyo, Kern, Kings, Madera, Mariposa, Merced, and Tulare shall be filed with the Office of the Clerk, United States Bankruptcy Court, 2500 Tulare Street, Suite 2501, Fresno, CA 93721-1318.

(b) Modesto Division. Petitions from the Counties of Calaveras, Stanislaus, and Tuolumne shall be filed with the Office of the Clerk at 1130 12th Street, Suite C, Modesto, California 95354.

(c) Sacramento Division. Petitions from the Counties of Alpine, Amador, Butte, Colusa, El Dorado, Glenn, Lassen, Modoc, Mono, Nevada, Placer, Plumas, Sacramento, San Joaquin, Shasta, Sierra, Siskiyou, Solano, Sutter, Tehama, Trinity, Yolo, and Yuba shall be filed with the Office of the Clerk, United States Bankruptcy Court, 501 I Street, Suite 3-200, Sacramento, CA 95814-2322.

(d) Transfer of Incorrectly Filed Petitions. If the debtor's address on a petition indicates that it should be filed in a division other than the division to which it is presented for filing, the Clerk shall nevertheless accept it, and any other pleadings presented with the petition, for filing on behalf of the proper division. The Clerk shall obtain and place the proper division's case number on the petition and accompanying pleadings and transmit them to the proper division.

(e) Request for Different Venue. If the debtor believes that venue should be in a division other than the division designated for the debtor's address, the debtor may file a motion to transfer the case to another division. The Clerk shall promptly present the motion to any available judge.

Comment: Technical change to Sections (a) and (b) of this Rule; bankruptcy court address update.

AMENDED LOCAL RULE 1007-1 List of Creditors and Master Address List

(a) Listing of Creditors. Creditors shall be listed on the appropriate schedule in alphabetical order by name and complete address (if an address is unknown, it should be so indicated). Addresses of governmental agencies shall be listed in conformance with the requirements specified in LBR 2002-1.

(b) Master Address List. With every petition for relief under the Bankruptcy Code presented for filing, there shall be submitted concurrently a Master Address List which includes the name, address, and zip code of all of the debtor's known creditors. To accommodate modern technology, the Master Address List shall be prepared in strict compliance with instructions of the Clerk in a format approved by the Court.

Comment: Revised rule; renamed to better reflect content of rule. Judicial Conference policy requires local rules to conform as closely as possible to the numbering and subject matter organizational scheme of the FRBP.

LOCAL RULE 1015-1 Related Cases

(a) Notice of Related Cases. When a case on file or about to be filed is related to another case that is pending or that was pending within the last six years, the debtor shall, and a party in interest may, file a Notice of Related Cases, setting forth the title, number and filing date of each related case, together with a brief statement of the relationship.

(b) Cases Deemed Related. Cases deemed to be related within the meaning of this Rule include the following fact situations:

(1) The debtors in both cases are the same entity;

(2) The debtors in both cases are husband and wife;

(3) The debtors in both cases are partners;

(4) The debtor in one case is a general partner or major shareholder of the debtor in the other case;

(5) The debtors in both cases have the same partners or substan-

tially the same shareholders; and

(6) The cases are otherwise so related as to warrant being treated as related.

AMENDED LOCAL RULE 2002-1 Notice Requirements

(a) Listing the United States as a Creditor; Notice to the United States. When listing an indebtedness to the United States for other than taxes and when giving notice, as required by FRBP 2002(j)(4), the debtor shall list both the U.S. Attorney and the federal agency through which the debtor became indebted. The address of the notice to the U.S. Attorney shall include, in parenthesis, the name of the federal agency as follows:

(1) For Cases filed in the Sacramento Division
United States Attorney
(For [insert name of agency])
501 I Street, Suite 10-100
Sacramento, CA 95814

(2) For Cases filed in the Modesto and Fresno Divisions
United States Attorney
(For [insert name of agency])
2500 Tulane St., Suite 4401
Fresno, CA 93721-1318

For example, a notice to the Department of Education for a case filed in the Modesto division would be addressed as follows:

United States Attorney
(For Department of Education)
2500 Tulane St., Suite 4401
Fresno, CA 93721-1318

(b) Notice to Other Governmental Agencies. Certain federal and state agencies specify particular addresses to which notice of bankruptcy proceedings shall be directed. The Clerk shall maintain a roster of such agencies and their addresses and shall make such roster available to the Bar and the public to enable compliance with this Rule and the provisions of FRBP 2002(j). When listing an indebtedness to an agency included on this roster, the debtor and the debtor's attorney shall complete the Master Address List (if required) and the schedule of creditors using the address as shown on the agency roster. When listing an indebtedness to an agency not on the roster, the debtor and the debtor's attorney shall use such address as will effect proper notice to the agency.

(c) Notice to the Internal Revenue Service. In addition to addresses specified on the roster of governmental agencies maintained by the Clerk, notices in adversary proceedings and contested makers relating to the Internal Revenue Service shall be sent to all of the following addresses:

(1) United States Department of Justice
Civil Trial Section, Western Region
Box 683, Ben Franklin Station
Washington, D.C. 20044

(2) To the United States Attorney as specified in LBR 2002-1(a) above.

(3) To the Internal Revenue Service at the addresses specified on the roster of governmental agencies maintained by the Clerk.

Comment: Technical change to Section (a) of this Rule; bankruptcy court and U.S. Attorney's Office address update. Section (d) of this Rule is abrogated. The Court may provide for notice limitations, if appropriate, on a case-by-case basis pursuant to FRBP 2002(h).

LOCAL RULE 2015-1 Monthly Operating and Tax Reports

(a) Cases in Which Required. Monthly operating and tax reports are required from a trustee or debtor in the following cases:

(1) all cases under Chapter 11;
(2) chapter 7 cases where a business is being operated by a trustee;
(3) chapter 12 cases if the court so orders; and
(4) chapter 13 cases where a business is being operated by a debtor, if the court so orders upon motion by the trustee or any party in interest.

(b) Cut off of Books and Records for Reporting Purposes. The books and records of the Debtor shall be closed (cut off) at the close of business on the day immediately preceding the filing of the petition, whether or not a separate estate is created for tax purposes. Pre-petition liabilities shall be segregated and reported separately from post-petition liabilities.

(c) Due Dates and Duration. Monthly reports shall be filed with the Clerk not later than the 15th day of the month following the month of the reported period. Reports shall be filed for the portion of a calendar month from the date of filing, and monthly thereafter through the month in which an order of confirmation, conversion or dismissal is entered. If the portion of a calendar month from the date of filing is seven (7) days or less, the report for such period may be combined with the report due for the following calendar month.

(d) Service of Reports. Not later than five (5) days from the date upon which it is filed with the court, a copy of each monthly report shall be served upon the United States Trustee, the case trustee, the chairperson and counsel of any committee of creditors or equity security holders, and any other entity ordered by the Court.

(e) Format of Reports. Monthly operating reports and monthly tax reports shall be made according to the format established by the United States Trustee as approved by the Court.

(f) Modification of Requirements. The Court, may, for cause, modify the provisions of this Rule to accommodate the needs of a particular case as provided in LBR 1001-1 (f). Any application to modify shall be served on all parties upon whom the monthly report is required to be served.

LOCAL RULE 2016-1 Compensation of Debtor-in-Possession (DIP), Officers and Insiders

[Abrogated.]

LOCAL RULE 3003-1 Filing Proofs of Claim in Chapter 11 Cases

Unless otherwise ordered by the Court, and except as provided in FRBP 3003(c)(3), a proof of claim in a Chapter 11 case shall be filed within 90 days after the date first set for the meeting of creditors called pursuant to 11 U.S.C. § 341(a), unless the claimant is a governmental unit, in which case a proof of claim shall be filed before 180 days after the date of the order for relief or such later time as the Federal Rules of Bankruptcy Procedure may provide.

LOCAL RULE 3007-1 Objections to Proofs of Claim

(a) Where necessary to the proper and timely administration of the bankruptcy estate, the debtor, debtor-in-possession, or trustee, as appropriate, shall, and other parties in interest may, examine proofs of claim filed in the case and file objections to those proofs of claim. Except to the extent provided otherwise in this Local Rule, objections shall comply with LBR 9014-1 and any other applicable Local Rule.

(b) Each objection shall include the name of the claimant, the date the proof of claim was filed with the court, the amount of the claim, and the number of the claim as it appears on the claims register maintained by the court. Unless the basis for the objection appears on the face of the proof of claim, the objection shall be accompanied by evidence establishing its factual allegations and demonstrating that the proof of claim should be disallowed. A mere assertion that the proof of claim is not valid or that the debt is not owed is not sufficient to overcome the presumptive validity of the proof of claim.

(c) Amount of Notice on Objections.

(1) Objections set on 44 days' notice. Unless the objecting party elects to give the notice permitted by LBR 3007-1(c)(2), the objecting party shall file and serve the objection at least forty-four (44) days prior to the hearing date.

(i) Opposition. Opposition, if any, to the sustaining of the objection shall be in writing and shall be served and filed with the court by the responding party at least fourteen (14) days preceding the date or continued date of the hearing. Without good cause, no party shall be heard in opposition to an objection at oral argument if written opposition to the objection has not been timely filed. Failure of the responding party to timely file written opposition may be deemed a waiver of any opposition to the sustaining of the objection or may result in the imposition of sanctions. The opposition shall specify whether the responding party consents to the Court's resolution of disputed material factual issues pursuant to FRCivP 43(e) as made applicable by FRBP 9017. If the responding party does not so consent, the opposition shall include a separate statement identifying each disputed material factual issue. The separate statement shall enumerate discretely each of the disputed material factual issues and cite the particular portions of the record demonstrating that a factual issue is both material and in dispute.

Failure to file the separate statement shall be construed as consent to resolution of the objection and all disputed material factual issues pursuant to FRCivP 43(e).

(ii) Reply. The objecting party may, at least seven (7) days prior to the date of the hearing, serve and file with the court a reply to any written opposition filed by a responding party.If the objecting party does not consent to the Court's resolution of disputed material factual issues pursuant to FRCivP 43(e), the objecting party shall file and serve, within the time required for a reply, a separate statement identifying each disputed material factual issue. The separate statement shall enumerate discretely each of the disputed material factual issues and cite the particular portions of the record demonstrating that a factual issue is both material and in dispute. Failure to file the separate statement shall be construed as consent to resolution of the objection and all disputed material factual issues pursuant to FRCivP 43(e).

Unless the Court determines that an evidentiary hearing is necessary, the evidentiary record closes upon expiration of the time for the filing of the reply.

(iii) Prior to the noticed hearing date, counsel may bring to the Court's attention relevant judicial opinions published after the date the opposition or reply was filed by filing and serving a Statement of Recent Development, containing a citation to and providing a copy of the new opinion without argument. No memoranda, declarations or documents other than those specified in this Local Rule shall be filed without prior Court approval.

(2) Objection set on 30 days' notice. Alternatively, the objecting party may file and serve the objection at least thirty (30) days prior to the hearing date. When fewer than forty-four (44) days' notice of a hearing is given, no party in interest shall be required to file written opposition to the objection. Opposition, if any, shall be presented at the hearing on the objection. If opposition is presented, or if there is other good cause, the Court may continue the hearing to permit the filing of evidence and briefs.

(d) An objection to a proof of claim shall be served on the claimant at the address on the proof of claim, not the address listed in the schedules, if different from the claimant's address noted on the proof of claim.

General Order 08-01 Amendment to Local Rule 3007-1

LOCAL RULE 3015-1 Duties of Chapter 13 Debtors and Chapter 13 Trustees

Part I Duties of Chapter 13 Debtors

(a) Dismissal for Failure to File Schedules, Statement of Affairs or Plan. Failure to file any schedule, Statement of Financial Affairs or a Chapter 13 Plan within fourteen (14) days of the date of filing the petition or obtain a court approved extension as provided for in FRBP 1007 shall be cause for dismissal. The Clerk shall notify each debtor filing a petition for relief without a schedule, Statement or plan of this provision.

(b) Commencement of Payments. Each debtor shall begin making payments to the Trustee in the amount and on the payment dates proposed in the debtor's plan, commencing with the first plan payment due date that occurs after the petition filing date. The first due date may not be more than thirty (30) days after the petition filing date. Should a payment become due prior to the filing of a plan, said payment may be deferred until after the plan is filed. Any deferred payments shall be paid in full prior to confirmation of the debtor's plan. All plan payments shall be timely and must be made payable to the Trustee by cashier's check, money order, business check of the debtor, payroll deduction, or such other method as approved by the Trustee.

(c) Debtor May Not Sell, Transfer or Encumber Property of the Estate. No debtor shall sell, transfer or encumber any property of the estate without first obtaining the permission of the Trustee. If the equity in a nonexempt asset which is not inventory of a business debtor exceeds $2,500, the debtor must also obtain the permission of the Court.

(d) Reporting "Windfalls". Each debtor shall report to the Trustee any windfall received or expected, including but not limited to, injury settlements, income tax refunds, bonuses, inheritance and lottery winnings.

(e) Termination of Employment. Each debtor shall notify the Trustee within seven (7) days of any termination of employment and shall notify the Court and the Trustee of any change in residence address.

Part II Chapter 13 Trustee's Duties

(f) Administration of Debts. The Trustee shall administer all debts except the following:

(1) ongoing real property mortgage payments, provided, however, the Court may order that such payments be made through the plan if, at the time of filing the petition, the debtor had any arrearages related to the mortgage;

(2) an ongoing lease payment;

(3) a debt paid by a third party; and

(4) a long-term debt with a contractual life which exceeds the proposed life of the plan.

(g) Trustee's Submission of Order Confirming Plan. Should a debtor fail to submit a proposed Order Confirming Debtor's Plan, the Trustee may submit such an order.

(h) Trustee's Fees Before Confirmation. The Trustee shall be allowed a fee of up to $250 from available funds in a case that is closed prior to confirmation due to conversion or dismissal. The fee is based on an average of the actual and necessary costs of administration of all Chapter 13 cases.

LOCAL RULE 4001-1 Motions for Relief from Stay

(a) Motions for relief from the automatic stay of 11 U.S.C. § 362(a) shall be set for hearing in accordance with LBR 9014-1. However, if a movant wishes to invoke the time constraints of 11 U.S.C. § 362(e), the motion shall be set for hearing pursuant to paragraph (f)(1) of LBR 9014-1.

(b) Relief from the automatic stay will not be granted if the movant utilizes the notice and opportunity for hearing procedure defined in 11 U.S.C. § 102(1). A hearing must be set on every motion for relief from the automatic stay. See LBR 9014-1.

(c) Relief from Stay Information Sheet. The movant shall file and serve as a separate document a completed Relief from Stay Information Sheet (EDC Approved Form 3-468) with each motion for relief from the automatic stay.

(d) Motions In Chapter 12 and 13 Cases. If relief from the automatic stay is sought in a chapter 12 or 13 case, the motion shall include the following:

(1) When the motion alleges that the debtor or the trustee has failed to maintain postpetition payments on an obligation secured by real or personal property, including, but not limited to, installment payments and lease payments, (i) the motion shall include a verified statement showing all postpetition payments and other obligations that have accrued and all payments received postpetition, the dates of the postpetition payments, and the obligation(s) to which each of the postpetition payments was applied; and (ii) the motion shall state whether a contract or applicable nonbankruptcy law requires that the debtor be given a statement, payment coupon, invoice, or other comparable document and whether such document was sent to the debtor or the trustee as to any postpetition payment(s) allegedly not made by the debtor or the trustee; and (iii) if a document of the kind described in the preceding subparagraph was not sent, or if a contract or applicable nonbankruptcy law does not require one to be sent, the motion shall state whether the debtor or the trustee was advised prior to the filing of the motion of the alleged delinquency and given an opportunity to cure it.

(2) If the motion asserts that the automatic stay should be modified or terminated because the debtor has failed to make plan payments to the chapter 12 or 13 trustee, the movant shall include in the motion a certification that the movant or its counsel conferred with the chapter 12 or 13 trustee before the motion was filed and confirmed that the alleged delinquency under the plan was outstanding within fourteen (14) days of the filing of the motion. This requirement may be satisfied by downloading from the trustee's Internet site, and attaching to the motion, a report indicating that the alleged delinquency was outstanding within fourteen (14) days prior to the filing of the motion. If the movant does not confer with the trustee, the motion shall detail the attempts made to confer with the trustee or explain why no such attempt was made.

LOCAL RULE 5005-1 Electronic Record is the Official Record; Filing of Documents

(a) Electronic Record is the Official Record. Except for documents filed prior to March 1, 1999, the electronic record maintained by the Clerk in the Court's Electronic Case File (ECF) System is the official court record for all cases and proceedings.

(b) Electronic Filing Mandatory. Except as provided in (c), below, all documents shall be submitted for filing in electronic form in strict compliance with instructions of the Clerk in a format approved by the Court.

(c) Exceptions to and Waivers of Requirement to File Documents in Electronic Form.

(1) Pro Se Exception. All unrepresented persons, sometimes referenced as pro se litigants or as persons appearing in propria persona, shall file and serve paper documents.

(2) Attorney and Trustee Waivers. Attorneys who regularly practice and trustees assigned cases in the Eastern District of California shall register as users of the court's electronic filing system and file documents in electronic form, provided, however, that on a case-by-case basis, an attorney or trustee may apply for a waiver of this requirement. A request for waiver shall be submitted as an ex-parte application supported by a declaration demonstrating cause for relief from the requirement to file in electronic form. The decision to permit the filing of paper documents is in the sole discretion of the Court and may be cancelled at any time upon notice to the attorney.

(3) Sealed Document Exception. Unless otherwise ordered by the Court, requests to file documents under seal pursuant to 11 U.S.C. § 107 (b) and (c) and FRBP 9018 shall be filed as paper documents. A paper copy of the order sealing documents shall be attached to the documents under seal and be delivered to the Clerk's Office. The Clerk shall maintain sealed documents in paper form.

(d) Scanning and Disposition of Paper Documents. Paper documents filed pursuant to (c)(1) or (c)(2) of this Rule shall promptly be scanned by the Clerk into electronic form. Once scanned and made part of the ECF system, the paper documents may be discarded.

(e) Violations. The Clerk shall not refuse to file any proffered paper document submitted in violation of this Rule, but following scanning into electronic form, shall bring such paper document to the attention of the Court. Any attorney or trustee who files a document in violation of this Rule may be subject to monetary or non-monetary sanctions.

(f) Time of Filing.

(1) Documents Submitted on Paper. A document submitted on paper shall be deemed filed when the Clerk takes physical possession of such document.

(2) Documents Submitted in Electronic Form. Documents submitted in electronic form shall be deemed filed as of the date and time stated on the Notice of Electronic Filing issued by the Clerk.

(3) Technical Failures Affecting Filing of Documents in Electronic Form. Technical failure shall not alter the registered user's responsibility to comply with all applicable filing deadlines, provided, however, that a registered user whose electronic filing is made untimely as the result of a documented, technical failure of the court's electronic filing system may seek appropriate relief from the Court.

Comment: Part (f)(2) of this rule is amended to provide that documents submitted in electronic form via the Court's Electronic Case Files System shall be deemed filed as of the date and time stated on the Notice of Electronic Filing issued by the Clerk, without regard to whether such documents are filed on a court day or a non-court day. This is a change from the Court's previous practice of deeming documents submitted on non-court days to be filed as of beginning of business on the next court day.

LOCAL RULE 5005.5-1 Eligibility and Registration for Electronic Filing; Use of Passwords

(a) Eligible Persons. Attorneys admitted to practice in this court (including those admitted pro hac vice), attorneys exempt from admission to the bar of this court (including attorneys authorized to represent the United States and attorneys representing child support creditors as authorized by P.L. 103-394, Section 304(g)), U.S. Trustees and their assistants, trustees, claims agents, and others as the Clerk deems appropriate, shall be eligible to apply for registered user status and be issued a username and password authorizing them to access the court's electronic filing system and submit documents in electronic form.

Support staff of registered users are not eligible for a separate username and password, although such staff may attend any electronic filing system training provided by the court and may, with the permission and in the name of a registered user, use the username and password of that registered user to submit documents in electronic form.

(b) Application to be a Registered User. All eligible persons shall complete and submit the online Electronic Filing System Registration Form and User Agreement available on the Court's Internet web site (www.caeb.uscourts.gov). All registered users shall also maintain an account in good standing with the PACER Service Center (http:/ pacer.psc.uscourts.gov).

(c) Training. Prior to receiving an electronic filing system username and password, registered users, or a person authorized to act on behalf of a registered user, must complete minimum required electronic filing system training provided by the court or obtain a waiver of the training requirement from the Clerk.

(d) Unauthorized Use of Password Prohibited.

(1) A registered user shall not use his/her username and password to file pleadings or other documents on behalf of someone who is not a registered user.

(2) No person may use a username and password without the permission of the registered user to whom they were issued. Registered users shall protect the security and confidentiality of their username and password and prevent their disclosure to any person other than the registered user's authorized agent.

(e) Duty to Maintain an e-Mail Account; Update e-Mail Address Changes. Each registered user shall maintain an e-mail account and shall.

Comment: New rule. Defines those eligible to be registered users of electronic filing system; provides procedures for obtaining a username and password; defines and limits use of passwords.

LOCAL RULE 5008-1 Funds of Chapter 11 Estates

(a) New Bank Accounts. Immediately upon filing a Chapter 11 petition, the debtor shall close all bank accounts. The debtor shall open and maintain a new general bank account in a federally insured depository. If the debtor has an ongoing business with employees, the debtor shall similarly open and maintain a tax account, unless the Court deems it unnecessary. If the debtor maintained a separate payroll account immediately prior to filing, the debtor shall similarly open and maintain a payroll account, unless the Court deems it unnecessary. The signature cards for the new accounts shall clearly indicate that the debtor is a "debtor in possession."

(b) Sales of Assets. Unless the Court orders otherwise, the net cash proceeds from the sales of assets pursuant to 11 U.S.C. § 363 shall be deposited in separate, interest-bearing blocked accounts at a federally insured depository. All such accounts shall bear the inscription "not to be disbursed or withdrawn except upon further order of the Bankruptcy Court."

(c) Insured Funds. "Federally insured depository" means a financial institution that is insured by the Federal Deposit Insurance Corporation or other federal agency providing deposit protection. Except with respect to funds that are held on deposit with an entity that is included in the U.S. Trustee's list of cooperating depositories, no account shall be maintained with a balance in excess of $100,000, except as provided in 11 U.S.C. § 345(b). If necessary, additional insured accounts shall be opened in different depositories so that any deposit shall not exceed the insured limits of the account.

LOCAL RULE 5010-1 Motions to Reopen Cases

(a) Contents of a Motion. A motion to reopen a case shall contain a statement of the grounds for reopening the case, but shall contain a request for any other relief.

(b) Separate Motions/Adversary Proceedings. Requests for any relief other than reopening, including relief based upon the grounds for reopening the case, shall be made in separate motions or adversary proceedings, which may be filed concurrently with the motion to reopen. If no motion or adversary proceeding is pending 30 days after the case is reopened and if no trustee has been ordered appointed, the case may be closed without further notice.

(c) Ex Parte Consideration. Motions to reopen may be considered ex parte. The movant shall not calendar a hearing date. A hearing will only be held if the court so orders.

LOCAL RULE 5013-1 Standing of Clerk and Deputy Clerks

The Clerk and Deputy Clerks of this Court are authorized to issue Orders to Show Cause or Notices of Intent to dismiss, convert, or appoint a trustee for failure to prosecute or comply with the Bankruptcy Code, FRBP, these Local Rules and any order of this Court.

LOCAL RULE 7003-1 Cover Sheet and Summons in Adversary Proceedings

At the time of filing a complaint commencing an adversary proceeding, the plaintiff shall present to the Clerk a completed Adversary Proceeding Cover Sheet on Form B 104 unless otherwise ordered by the Court. The attorney for the plaintiff shall prepare the appropriate form of summons for execution by the Clerk.

LOCAL RULE 7005-1 Service by Electronic Means

(a) Consent to Service by Electronic Means. A registered user of the court's electronic filing system may consent to receive service by electronic means pursuant to FRCivP 5(b)(2)(D), as made applicable to bankruptcy cases and proceedings by FRBP 7005.

(b) Opting Out of Service by Electronic Means. A registered user of the court's electronic filing system may opt out of receiving service by electronic means by so indicating on his/her (Electronic Filing System Registration Form and User Agreement online,.

(c) Roster of Those Consenting to Service by Electronic Means. The Clerk shall maintain a roster containing the names and e-mail addresses of registered users who have consented to service by electronic means. The roster shall only be accessible by registered users of the court's electronic filing system and shall be password protected to prevent access by unauthorized persons or entities.

(d) Method of Service.

(1) Upon Those Parties Consenting to Service by Electronic Means. Service by electronic means pursuant to FRCivP 5(b)(2)(D) shall be accomplished by transmitting an e-mail which includes as a PDF attachment the document(s) served. The subject line of the e-mail shall include the words "Service Pursuant to FRCivP 5", along with the case or proceeding number and the title(s) of the document(s) served.

(2) Upon All Other Parties. Service on parties who are not registered users of the court's electronic filing system or who are registered users, but have opted out as provided for in (b) above, must be made in the conventional manner as provided for in FRCivP 5(b)(2).

(3) Certificate of Service. The certificate of service shall include all parties served, whether by electronic or conventional means. Where service was accomplished by electronic means, the certificate of service shall include the e-mail addresses to which the document(s) were transmitted, and the party, if any, whom the recipient represents.

Comment: New rule; establishes procedures for service by electronic means as permitted by FRCivP 5, made applicable to bankruptcy cases and proceedings by FRBP 7005; provides opt out; requires Clerk to maintain a roster of persons consenting to service by electronic means. The roster will permit persons listed to specify one or more e-mail addresses to which service is made and will be accessible only by registered users of the court's electronic filing system or their authorized agents using their assigned username and password.

LOCAL RULE 7026-1 Discovery Limitations

(a) Pursuant to the provisions of FRCivP 26(a)(l), and unless otherwise ordered by the Court in the specific adversary proceeding, contested petition, or contested matter, the automatic disclosure procedures described therein shall not be required in any action pending in this Court, nor shall any automatic disclosures of any type be required in any action pending in this Court.

(b) Pursuant to the provisions of FRCivP 26(a)(2)(B), and unless otherwise ordered by the Court in the specific adversary proceeding, contested petition, or contested matter, the expert witness disclosure requirements described therein shall not be required in any action pending in this Court, and all disclosure of matters pertaining to expert witnesses shall be performed in accordance with the provisions of a scheduling or other order entered in the specific adversary proceeding, contested petition, or contested matter, or pursuant to the provisions of FRCivP 30, 33 and 34, as applicable.

(c) Pursuant to the provisions of FRCivP 26(a)(3), and unless otherwise ordered by the Court in the specific adversary proceeding, contested petition, or contested matter, the pretrial disclosure requirements described therein shall not be required in any action pending in this Court, and all disclosure of matter of the type described therein shall be performed in accordance with the provisions of LBR 9017-1 and any pretrial, scheduling or status order.

(d) Pursuant to the provisions of FRCivP 26(b)(2), and unless otherwise ordered by the Court in the specific adversary proceeding, contested petition, or contested matter, there shall be no presumptive limitations upon the number of oral or written depositions taken (*See* FRCivP 30(a)(2)(A) and 31 (a)(2)(A)) or upon the number of interrogatories to parties served (*See* FRCivP 33(a)) in any action pending in this Court. If any party believes that any such proposed discovery is burdensome, oppressive or otherwise improper, that party shall have the burden of seeking a protective order against such proposed discovery in accordance with the provisions of FRCivP 26(c) and, if applicable, FRCivP 45.

(e) Pursuant to the provisions of FRCivP 26(d) and 26(f), and unless otherwise ordered by the Court in the specific adversary proceeding, contested petition, or contested matter, there is no requirement that parties or counsel engage in any meet-and-confer procedure prior to any scheduling conference or prior to seeking discovery in the first instance.

LOCAL RULE 7030-1 Deposition Transcripts

It shall be the duty of the party requesting a deposition to obtain from the reporter the original transcript thereof in a sealed envelope and to safely retain the same under conditions suitable to protect it from loss, destruction, or tampering until such time as the Court shall order its production.

LOCAL RULE 7038-1 Jury Trial of Right

(a) Right Preserved. FRCivP 38 shall apply in adversary proceedings where there is a right to trial by jury.

(b) Demand. Where demand is made for a jury trial, it shall appear immediately following the title of the complaint or answer containing the demand, or in such other document as may be permitted by FRCivP 38(b). Any notation on the Adversary Proceeding Cover Sheet (Form B 104) concerning whether a jury trial is or is not demanded shall not constitute a demand for a jury trial under these Local Rules.

LOCAL RULE 7039-1 Trial by Jury or the Court

FRCivP 39 applies in adversary proceedings. This Rule shall not be interpreted to suggest that a Bankruptcy Judge will or may preside over a jury trial.

LOCAL RULE 7041-1 Notification to Calendar Clerk of Matters to be Dismissed

For all matters or proceedings that have been calendared for trial, hearing or conference, it is the duty of the plaintiff or moving party to promptly notify the calendar clerk of:

(1) Matters or proceedings that have been settled by stipulation of

the parties;

(2) Motions that are to be dropped at the request of the moving party; and

(3) Matters that have been or are being dismissed.

LOCAL RULE 7056-1 Motions for Summary Judgment or Summary Adjudication

(a) Motions for Summary Judgment or Summary Adjudication. Each motion for summary judgment or summary adjudication shall be accompanied by a "Statement of Undisputed Facts" which shall enumerate discretely each of the specific material facts relied upon in support of the motion and cite the particular portions of any pleading, affidavit, deposition, interrogatory answer, admission or other document relied upon to establish that fact. The moving party shall be responsible for the filing with the Court of all evidentiary documents cited in the moving papers.

(b) Opposition. Any party opposing a motion for summary judgment or summary adjudication shall reproduce the itemized facts in the Statement of Undisputed Facts and admit those facts which are undisputed and deny those which are disputed, including with each denial a citation to the particular portions of any pleading, affidavit, deposition, interrogatory answer, admission or other document relied upon in support of that denial. The opposing party may also file a concise "Statement of Disputed Facts," and the source thereof in the record, of all additional material facts as to which there is a genuine issue precluding summary judgment or adjudication. The opposing party shall be responsible for the filing with the Court of all evidentiary documents cited in the opposing papers. If a need for discovery is asserted as a basis for denial of the motion, the party opposing the motion shall provide a specification of the particular facts on which discovery is to be had or the issues on which discovery is necessary.

(c) Stipulated Facts. All parties-in-interest may jointly file a stipulation setting forth a statement of stipulated facts to which all parties-in-interest agree. As to any stipulated facts, the parties so stipulating may state that their stipulations are entered into only for the purposes of the motion for summary judgment and are not intended to be otherwise binding.

(d) Summary Adjudication. This Rule shall apply to motions for orders specifying material facts that appear without substantial controversy pursuant to FRCivP 56(d), except that the proposed "Statement of Undisputed Facts" and the "Statement of Disputed Facts" shall be limited to the facts which the moving party asserts are without substantial controversy and the facts the opposing party contends are in dispute.

LOCAL RULE 7065-1 Temporary Restraining Orders

(a) Notice to Affected Parties. Any party seeking a temporary restraining order in the absence of actual notice to the affected parties and/or counsel shall comply with the requirements of FRCivP 65(b). Appropriate notice would inform the affected parties and/or counsel of the intention to seek a temporary restraining order, the date and time for hearing to be requested of the Court, whether the judge will permit a counsel to appear by telephone, and the nature of the relief requested. Once a specific time and location has been set by the Court, additional notice of the time and location of the hearing shall be given.

(b) Documents to be Filed. No hearing on a temporary restraining order will normally be set unless the following documents are filed with the Clerk and, unless impossible under the circumstances, served on the affected parties and/or their counsel:

(1) an adversary complaint;

(2) a motion for temporary restraining order;

(3) a brief on all relevant legal issues presented by the motion;

(4) a declaration in support of the existence of an irreparable injury;

(5) a declaration detailing the notice or efforts to effect notice to the affected parties and/or counsel or showing good cause why notice should not be given; and

(6) a proof of service.

(c) Contents and Service of Proposed Order. The party seeking the order shall deliver to the Court and, unless impossible under the circumstances, serve the affected parties and/or counsel with a proposed temporary restraining order with, if applicable under *FRBP* 7065, a provision for a bond. In all circumstances in which a temporary restraining order is requested ex parte, the proposed order shall further notify the affected parties and/or counsel that they may apply to the Court for modification or dissolution on two (2) days notice by personal service or such other notice as the Court may allow.

(d) Modification or Dissolution. When a preliminary injunction or temporary restraining order has been issued, the affected parties may apply to the Court for modification or dissolution of the injunction or order. Such motion shall normally be accompanied by a brief on all relevant legal issues to be presented in support and declarations supporting modification or dissolution and detailing the notice or efforts to notify the other parties and/or counsel.

LOCAL RULE 7090-1 Disposition of Unclaimed Exhibits

If exhibits are not withdrawn within sixty (60) days after notice to the parties to claim the same, the Clerk may dispose of them as the Clerk may deem fit.

LOCAL RULE 8020-1 Procedures Following Remand by an Appellate Court

Whenever a case, proceeding or matter is remanded by an Appellate Court to the Bankruptcy Court for further proceedings, any party to the appeal may move to set the matter for further proceedings by filing a motion pursuant to LBR 9014-1. The Court will not set the matter for further proceedings as a matter of course.

LOCAL RULE 9001-1 Definitions

These definitions supplement the definitions set forth in FRBP 9001 and 9002. For purposes of these Rules, unless the context otherwise requires, the terms below are defined as follows:

(1) "Briefs" include memoranda, points and authorities, and other written arguments, or compilations of authorities.

(2) "Case" means the bankruptcy case initiated by the filing of a petition for relief.

(3) "Courtroom Deputy" means the deputy clerk assigned to the particular judge to whom a case or proceeding has been assigned or the judge before whom a matter or a part thereof is being conducted.

(4) "Declaration" includes an affidavit prepared in accordance with federal law. *See* 28 U.S.C. § 1746.

(5) "DIP" means debtor in possession.

(6) "Ex Parte" means without prior notice.

(7) "FRBP" means the Federal Rules of Bankruptcy Procedure.

(8) "FRCivP" means the Federal Rules of Civil Procedure.

(9) "Filed" means delivered into the custody of the Clerk and accepted by the Clerk for inclusion in the official records of the case or proceeding.

(10) "Motion" includes all motions, applications, objections, or other requests made to the Court for orders or other judicial activity.

(11) "Order" means any directive by the Court other than a judgment, including oral or telephonic as well as written directives.

(12) "Proceeding" includes adversary proceeding, any hearing conducted by the Court, and any other continuing matter before the Court arising in the bankruptcy case.

AMENDED LOCAL RULE 9004-1 General Requirements of Form

(a) General Format of Documents.

(1) Paper Documents. All documents in paper form presented for filing with the court, other than those on Official Bankruptcy Forms and other forms approved by the court, shall be on white paper, with numbered lines in the left margin, 8½' × 11' in size, and shall otherwise comply with all other applicable provisions of these Rules. Matter contained thereon shall be typewritten or presented by some other clearly legible process, without erasures or interlining which materially defaces the document, and shall appear on one side of each sheet only. Documents shall be double-spaced except for the identification of counsel, titles, headings, footnotes, quotations, exhibits, and descriptions of real property. Each page shall be numbered consecutively at the bottom.

(2) Electronic Documents. All documents in electronic form presented for filing with the court shall be submitted as a PDF file using the court's electronic filing system and when opened for viewing on the electronic case file system shall conform in all respects to the general appearance of traditional paper documents, prepared in the manner and form described in (1), above.

(b) Counsel Identification and Signature. The name, address, (including e-mail address, if the document is to be submitted in electronic form), telephone number, and the California State Bar membership number (not applicable to counsel for the United States) of all counsel (or, if in propria persona, of the party) and the specific identification of each party represented by name and interest in the proceeding (e.g., Debtor Smith, Creditor Bank, Plaintiff Roe, Defendant Doe) shall appear in the upper left-hand corner of the first page of each document presented for filing, except that in the instance of multiparty representation reference may be made to the signature page for the complete list of parties represented.

(c) Signatures Generally. All pleadings and non-evidentiary documents shall be signed by the individual attorney for the party representing them, or by the party involved if that party is appearing in proporia persona. Affidiavits and certificates shall be signed by the person offering the evidentiary material contained in the document. The name of the person signing the document shall be typed underneath the signature.

(1) Signatures on Documents Submitted Electronically.

(a) Signature of the Registered User. The username and password required to access the electronic filing system shall serve as the registered user's signature on all electronic documents filed with the court. They shall also serve as a signature, with the same force and effect as a written signature, for purposes of the Federal Rules of Bankruptcy Procedure and the Local Bankruptcy Rules of this court, including FRBP 9011-1 and LBR 9004-1(c), and for any other purpose for which a signature is required in connection with proceedings before the Court. Unless the electronically filed document has been scanned and shows the registered user's original signature or bears a software-generated electronic signature thereof, an "/s/" and the registered user's name shall be typed in the space where the signature would otherwise appear.

(b) Signatures of Other Persons. Signatures of persons other than the registered user may be indicated by either:

(i) Submitting a scanned copy of the originally signed document;

(ii) Attaching a scanned copy of the signature page(s) to the electronic document, or;

(iii) Through the use of "/s/ Name" or a software-generated electronic signature in the signature block where signatures would otherwise appear. Electronically filed documents on which "/s/ Name" or a software-generated electronic signature is used to indicate the signatures of persons other than the registered user shall be subject to the requirements set forth in (c) and (d), below.

(c) The use of "/s/ Name" or a Software Generated-Electronic Signature. The use of "/s/Name" or a software-generated electronic signature on documents constitutes the registered user's representation that an originally signed copy of the document exists and is in the registered user's possession at the time of filing.

(d) Retention Requirements. When "/s/Name" or a Software-Generated Electronic Signature is Used. When "/s/Name" or a software-generated electronic signature is used in an electronically filed document to indicate the required signature(s) of persons other than that of the registered user, the registered user shall retain the originally signed document in paper form for no less than three (3) years following the closing of the case. On request of the Court, the registered user shall produce the originally signed document(s) for review. The failure to do so may result in the imposition of sanctions on the Court's own motion, or upon motion of the case trustee, U.S. Trustee, U.S. Attorney, or other party.

(2) Signatures on Facsimile Documents. For the purposes of this Rule, the image of the original manual signature appearing on a facsimile (fax) copy filed pursuant to this Rule shall constitute an original signature for all court purposes. The document, which itself may be in whole or in part a fax copy, must be marked "original" prior to submission to the Clerk's Office for filing. The originator of the document, or in the case of an affidavit or certification, the presenting attorney or party, is required to maintain the document containing the original manual signature until the conclusion of the case or proceeding, including any appeal and remand after appeal. In the event there are multiple signatories to a document, the filing party or attorney shall retain the originally signed document(s). The Court may require that the document containing the original manual signature be filed. This Rule does not provide for documents to be transmitted via fax directly to the Clerk's Office. Documents directly faxed to the Clerk or to a chambers of the Court will not be filed, lodged, received, returned, or acknowledged.

Comment: Revised rule; recognizes advent of electronic documents; provides procedures for signatures on electronic documents.

LOCAL RULE 9014-1 Motion Calendar and Procedure

(a) Applicability. Parties shall file, serve, and set for hearing all contested matters, including motions, whether filed in the bankruptcy case or in an adversary proceeding, objections, applications, and other matters for which a hearing is necessary (hereafter referred to collectively as motions), in accordance with this Local Rule, any other applicable Local Rules, and the applicable provisions of Title 11 of the United States Code and the Federal Rules of Bankruptcy Procedure. Except as otherwise provided in LBR 3007-1, this Local Rule shall apply to objections to proofs of claim.

(b) Motion Calendar.

(1) Each judge of the Court shall maintain his or her department's individual motion calendar. All hearings shall be set on the motion calendar of the department to which the case is assigned. A party shall self-set a motion for hearing on the dates and times specified on each department's motion calendar.

(2) Each judge's motion calendar and instructions for self-setting hearings are posted on the Court's Internet site, www.caeb.uscourts.gov, and are also available from the Clerk's Office at the public counters.

(c) Docket Control Number.

(1) In motions filed in the bankruptcy case, a Docket Control Number (designated as DC No.) shall be included by all parties immediately below the case number on all pleadings and other documents, including proofs of service, filed in support of or opposition to motions.

(2) In motions filed in adversary proceedings, the Docket Control Number shall be placed immediately below the adversary number.

(3) The Docket Control Number shall consist of not more than three letters, which may be the initials of the attorney for the moving party (e.g., first, middle, and last name) or the first three initials of the law firm for the moving party, and the number that is one number higher than the number of motions previously filed by said attorney or law firm in connection with that specific bankruptcy case.

Example: The first Docket Control Number assigned to attorney John D. Doe would be DC No. JDD-1, the second DC No. JDD-2, the third DC No. JDD-3, and so on. This sequence would be repeated for each specific bankruptcy case and adversary proceeding in which said attorney or law firm filed motions.

(4) Once a Docket Control Number is assigned, all related papers filed by any party, including motions for orders shortening the amount of notice, shall include the same number. However, motions for reconsideration and countermotions shall be treated as separate motions with a new Docket Control Number assigned in the manner provided for above.

(d) Format and Content of Motions and Notices.

(1) Format. All pleadings and documents filed in support and in opposition to a motion shall contain in the caption the date and time of the hearing and the courtroom [1] in which the hearing will be held. All pleadings and documents filed in support and in opposition to a motion

---

[1] See Form EDC 2-071, Courtroom Locations and Nomenclature, Appendix I.

shall conform with the Court's Guidelines for the Preparation of Documents, effective December 1, 1999, or as thereafter amended.

(2) Separate Notice. Every motion shall be accompanied by a separate notice of hearing stating the docket control number, the date and time of the hearing, the location of the courthouse, the name of the judge hearing the motion, and the courtroom in which the hearing will be held.

(3) Contents of Notice. The notice of hearing shall advise potential respondents whether and when written opposition must be filed, the deadline for filing and serving it, and the names and addresses of the persons who must be served with any opposition. If written opposition is required, the notice of hearing shall advise potential respondents that the failure to file timely written opposition may result in the motion being resolved without oral argument and the striking of untimely written opposition.

(4) Service of Notice Only. When notice of a motion is served without the motion or supporting papers, the notice of hearing shall also succinctly and sufficiently describe the nature of the relief being requested and set forth the essential facts necessary for a party to determine whether to oppose the motion. However, the motion and supporting papers shall be served on those parties who have requested special notice and those who are directly affected by the requested relief.

(5) Legal Authority. Each motion, opposition, and reply shall cite the legal authority relied upon by the filing party.

(6) Evidence. Every motion shall be accompanied by evidence establishing its factual allegations and demonstrating that the movant is entitled to the relief requested. Affidavits and declarations shall comply with FRCivP 56(e).

(e) Service and Proof of Service.

(1) Service of all pleadings and documents filed in support of, or in opposition to, a motion shall be made on or before the date they are filed with the Court.

(2) A proof of service, in the form of a certificate of service, shall be filed with the Clerk concurrently with the pleadings or documents served, or not more than three (3) days after they are filed.

(3) The proof of service for all pleadings and documents filed in support or opposition to a motion shall be filed as a separate document and shall bear the Docket Control Number. Copies of the pleadings and documents served shall not be attached to the proof of service. Instead, the proof of service shall identify the title of the pleadings and documents served.

(f) Amount of Notice.

(1) Motions set on 28 days' notice. Unless additional notice is required by the Federal Rules of Bankruptcy Procedure or these Local Rules, or the moving party elects to give the notice permitted by LBR 9014-1(f)(2), the moving party shall file and serve the motion at least twenty-eight (28) days prior to the hearing date.

(i) If the motion is a motion for relief from the automatic stay, it shall be the duty of the moving party to set a hearing within thirty (30) days of the filing of the motion. The failure of the moving party to set the hearing within thirty (30) days shall be deemed a waiver of the time constraints of 11 U.S.C. § 362(e).

(ii) Opposition. Opposition, if any, to the granting of the motion shall be in writing and shall be served and filed with the Court by the responding party at least fourteen (14) days preceding the date or continued date of the hearing. Opposition shall be accompanied by evidence establishing its factual allegations.

Without good cause, no party shall be heard in opposition to a motion at oral argument if written opposition to the motion has not been timely filed. Failure of the responding party to timely file written opposition may be deemed a waiver of any opposition to the granting of the motion or may result in the imposition of sanctions.

The opposition shall specify whether the responding party consents to the Court's resolution of disputed material factual issues pursuant to FRCivP 43(e) as made applicable by FRBP 9017. If the responding party does not so consent, the opposition shall include a separate statement identifying each disputed material factual issue.

The separate statement shall enumerate discretely each of the disputed material factual issues and cite the particular portions of the record demonstrating that a factual issue is both material and in dispute. Failure to file the separate statement shall be construed as consent to resolution of the motion and all disputed material factual issues pursuant to FRCivP 43(e).

(iii) Reply. The moving party may, at least seven (7) days prior to the date of the hearing, serve and file with the Court a written reply to any written opposition filed by a responding party. If the moving party does not consent to the Court's resolution of disputed material factual issues pursuant to FRCivP 43(e), the moving party shall file and serve, within the time required for a reply, a separate statement identifying each disputed material factual issue. The separate statement shall enumerate discretely each of the disputed material factual issues and cite the particular portions of the record demonstrating that a factual issue is both material and in dispute. Failure to file the separate statement shall be construed as consent to resolution of the motion and all disputed material factual issues pursuant to FRCivP 43(e).

Unless the Court determines that an evidentiary hearing is necessary, the evidentiary record closes upon expiration of the time for the filing of the reply.

(iv) Prior to the noticed hearing date, counsel may bring to the Court's attention relevant judicial opinions published after the date the opposition or reply was filed by filing and serving a Statement of Recent Development, containing a citation to and providing a copy of the new opinion without argument. No memoranda, declarations or documents other than those specified in this Local Rule shall be filed without prior Court approval.

(2) Motions set on 14 days' notice. Alternatively, unless additional notice is required by the Federal Rules of Bankruptcy Procedure or these Local Rules, the moving party may file and serve the motion at least fourteen (14) calendar days prior to the hearing date.

(i) This alternative procedure shall not be used for a motion filed in connection with an adversary proceeding.

(ii) The use of this alternative procedure in connection with a motion for relief from the automatic stay shall be deemed a waiver of the time limitations contained in 11 U.S.C. § 362(e).

(iii) When fewer than twenty-eight (28) days' notice of a hearing is given, no party in interest shall be required to file written opposition to the motion. Opposition, if any, shall be presented at the hearing on the motion. If opposition is presented, or if there is other good cause, the Court may continue the hearing to permit the filing of evidence and briefs.

(3) Orders Shortening Time. In appropriate circumstances and for good cause shown, the Court may order that the amount of notice of a hearing on a motion be shortened to fewer than fourteen (14) days. Unless otherwise ordered, when the time for service is shortened to fewer than fourteen (14) days, no written opposition is required.

If the motion for which notice is to be shortened has not been filed, a copy of it or a summary shall be filed with the application as a separate exhibit document. If the motion or a summary cannot be filed as an exhibit, the application shall describe the motion with particularity and explain why the moving party is unable either to file the motion or file it as an exhibit to the application.

(4) "First Day Orders." In chapter 11, 12, and 13 cases, preliminary hearings on motions for "first day orders," including, but not limited to, motions to use cash collateral, borrow money, and pay employees, shall generally be heard by the Court within two (2) days of the filing of the petition. Counsel for the debtor or the trustee shall contact the chambers of the assigned judge immediately upon the filing of the petition to ascertain what notice will be required and the date and time of the hearing.

(g) Evidentiary Hearings.

(1) If the Court determines that there is a disputed material factual issue that must be resolved before the relief requested in the motion can be granted or denied, testimony shall be taken in accordance with FRCivP 43(a) unless the parties waive such right or consent to proceeding under FRCivP 43(e).

(2) The Court's procedures for scheduling an evidentiary hearing will be set forth in a General Order. The current General Order is 02-01. It, and any General Order supplanting it, are available from the Clerk's Office at the public counters or on the Court's Internet site, www.cae-b.uscourts.gov.

(h) Oral Argument; Removal from Calendar; Tentative Rulings. Unless the assigned judge determines that the resolution of the motion does not require oral argument, he or she may hear appropriate and reasonable oral argument. Alternatively, the motion may be submitted upon the record and briefs on file if the parties stipulate thereto, or the judge so orders, subject to the power of the judge to reopen the matter for further briefs, oral argument or both.

Parties can ascertain which matters are resolved without oral argument and can view tentative rulings by checking the Court's Internet site at www.caeb.uscourts.gov after 4:00 p.m. the day before the hearing. Parties appearing telephonically shall view the tentative ruling prior to the hearing.

(i) Related and Countermotions. Any countermotion or other motion related to the general subject matter of the original motion set for hearing pursuant to this Local Rule may be filed and served no later than the time opposition to the original motion is required to be filed. In the event a counter or related motion is filed by the responding party, the judge may continue the hearing on the original and all related motions so as to give the responding and moving parties reasonable opportunity to serve and file oppositions and replies to all pending motions. No written opposition need be filed to any related matter unless the matter is continued by the Court. Nothing herein shall be construed to require the filing of a counter or related motion.

(j) Continuances. Continuances of hearings must be approved by the Court. A request for a continuance may be made orally at the scheduled hearing or in advance of it if made by written application. A written application shall disclose whether all other parties in interest oppose or support the request for a continuance.

(k) Opportunity for Hearing.

(a) The notice of opportunity for hearing procedure, as defined in 11 U.S.C. § 102(1), may only be used as permitted in the Court's General Order dealing with chapter 13 practice. In all other matters, if an order is necessary or is desired by the moving party, the motion should be set for hearing pursuant to this Local Rule.

(b) When the notice of opportunity for hearing procedure is used, the notice shall:

(i) Succinctly describe the action to be taken;

(ii) State that unless written objections and/or a request for a hearing are served on the moving party and filed with the Clerk on or before the date specified in the notice, the action shall be taken;

(iii) Provide a minimum of fourteen (14) days after service (or the longer periods required by, e.g., FRBP 2002 or 3007) for the filing of the request for hearing or objections by a party-in-interest; and

(iv) Be filed with the Clerk and served by the moving party on all creditors, the debtor, the trustee or other persons as appropriate or required.

(c) No hearing date shall be set by the moving party unless an objection or a request for hearing is made by a party-in-interest, in which event, the moving party shall promptly set the matter for hearing by filing a notice of hearing with the Clerk and serving the notice in accordance with this Local Rule.

(d) If no objection or request for hearing is timely filed, the moving party may proceed to take any proposed action that does not require Court approval.

(l) Sanctions. Failure to comply with the requirements of this Local Rule or the provisions of other Local Rules applicable to motion practice shall constitute grounds, without limitation, to deny the motion, strike late-filed pleadings and documents, continue the hearing on the motion, deem the moving party to have waived the time limitations of 11 U.S.C. § 362(e), deny the offending party the ability to appear by telephone, or assess other appropriate sanctions.

LOCAL RULE 9017-1 Alternate Direct Testimony, Exhibits at Trial, and Qualification of Expert Witnesses

If ordered by the Court, the following procedures shall apply:

(a) Alternate Direct Testimony Procedure.

(1) Purpose. The purpose of this procedure is to facilitate pretrial preparation and to streamline the adducement of direct testimony in trial and contested hearings so as to reduce trial time without sacrificing due process and a fair trial. This procedure shall be known as the Alternate Direct Testimony Procedure.

(2) Applicability. Unless otherwise ordered, the Alternate Direct Testimony Procedure shall be used in all trials and contested hearings not scheduled for the law and motion calendar. The failure of any party to any such trial or contested hearing to object in writing at or before the pretrial conference, if one is held, or if not, on or before the date of the trial setting hearing, shall be deemed as consent to the use of this alternate testimony procedure for such trial or contested hearing.

(3) Content and Preparation. For each witness (excluding hostile or adverse witnesses) that an attorney calls on behalf of his/her client's case, there shall be prepared in triplicate a succinct written declaration, executed under penalty of perjury, of the direct testimony which that witness would be prepared to give as though questions were propounded in the usual fashion. Each statement of fact or opinion shall be separate, sequentially numbered and shall contain only matters that are admissible under the Federal Rules of Evidence (e.g., avoiding redundancies, hearsay, and other obvious objectionable statements).

(b) Submission of Testimony Declarations, Exhibits and Objections. Unless otherwise ordered by the Court, copies of all direct testimony declarations by witnesses and exhibits that are intended to be presented at trial or hearing shall be furnished to opposing counsel as follows:

(1) Plaintiff's Declarations and Exhibits. The plaintiff shall submit to opposing counsel all such declarations and exhibits comprising the plaintiff's case in chief fourteen (14) days before trial.

(2) Defendant's Declarations and Exhibits. The defendant shall submit to opposing counsel all such declarations and exhibits comprising the defendant's case seven (7) days before trial.

(3) Objections to Declarations and Exhibits. Two (2) days before trial or hearing, all such declarations and exhibits, together with any written objections to the admission of any of the exhibits or to any of the declarations or any portion thereof, shall be lodged with the courtroom deputy of the department to which the trial or hearing is assigned. No objections to testimony presented by written declaration or exhibits need be entertained unless in writing and presented as herein specified. The exhibits (no originals) lodged with the courtroom deputy clerk as herein required shall be premarked by counsel (e.g., Plaintiff's Exhibit 1, etc., Defendant's Exhibit A, etc.) and if three (3) or more, shall be accompanied by a cover sheet index containing a brief description of each exhibit.

(c) Utilization of Live Testimony. All cross-examination, rebuttal, surrebuttal and appropriate impeachment evidence shall be given by live testimony. Notwithstanding provisions of this Rule, the Court, in its discretion, may allow live direct testimony.

Comment. This procedure is not used in Department B in Fresno; however, it may be permitted upon request. A modified procedure is used in Department A in Fresno.

(d) Qualifications of Expert Witnesses. Whenever an expert witness is called to testify, it shall be the duty of the party calling such witness to furnish the Court and the opposing party with a declaration of the expert's qualifications. After the expert is sworn and upon verifying the qualification statement, it shall be admitted into evidence. Thereafter, opposing counsel and/or the Court may examine the witness on voir dire.

LOCAL RULE 9019-1 Stipulations

Except stipulations entered into during the course of a deposition and set forth in the transcript thereof, stipulations shall be:

(a) in writing, signed by all counsel or parties in propria persona who have appeared in the proceeding and are affected by the stipulation;

(b) made in open court and noted by the courtroom deputy clerk upon the minutes or by the court reporter in the notes, or

(c) recited in a pretrial order or other court order. Stipulations not in conformity with these requirements will not be recognized unless necessary to prevent manifest injustice.

LOCAL RULE 9022-1 Notice of Entry of Judgment Pursuant to FRBP 9022

(a) On Whom Notice Must Be Served. Unless otherwise ordered by the Court, the requirements of FRBP 9022 shall be satisfied by service of the notice of entry of judgment or of order on only those parties who appeared in connection with the judgment or order.

Appearances are defined in the Local Rules of Practice of the United States District Court for the Eastern District of California, Rules 83-182 and 83-183, which are made applicable to these rules pursuant to LBR 1001-1(c). Contested matters are governed by FRBP 9014.

(b) Procedure

(1) When Proposed Judgment or Order is Submitted By Prevailing Party. Except in those circumstances where the Clerk is required to provide notice by FRBP 2002(f) and except as provided in subsection (2) below, in all matters heard by the Court, the party lodging the judgment or order shall submit with it a Request for Clerk's Notice of Entry (EDC 3-965 for bankruptcy cases and EDC 3-966 for adversary proceedings) containing the names and mailing addresses of all parties to be served.

(2) When Judgment or Order is Prepared By the Court. In those instances where the Court has prepared the judgment or order, the clerk shall serve notice of entry on the parties who appeared in connection with the judgment or order pursuant to subsection (c) below, unless the Court otherwise directs.

(c) Method of Service. The clerk shall serve notice of entry as follows:

(1) By sending the appropriate Bankruptcy Noticing Center (BNC) notice for service on parties who appeared in connection with the judgment or order.

(2) Unless the case is a chapter 9 municipality case, the clerk shall forthwith transmit to the United States Trustee a copy of the judgment or order.

APPENDIX I (Updated 1/15/08) ADMINISTRATIVE INFORMATION

EDC 2-034 Bankruptcy Court Miscellaneous Fee Schedule

EDC 2-035 Required Documents and Fees

EDC 2-036 Electronic Public Access Fee Schedule

EDC 2-070 United States Bankruptcy Courts Within California

EDC 2-071 Courtroom Locations and Nomenclature

EDC 2-190 Revised Guidelines for Preparation of Master Address Lists

EDC 2-195 Revised Diskette Master Address List Specifications

EDC 2-785 Roster of Public Agencies

EDC 5-100 Notice of Electronic Availability of Bankruptcy Case File Information

APPENDIX II GUIDELINES AND POLICY STATEMENTS

Guidelines for Payment of Attorneys' Fees in Chapter 13 Cases

Procedures for Disclosure Statement and Confirmation Hearings

Fresno Division, Department A

Notice to Attorneys and Trustees Concerning Use of the "Opportunity for Hearing"

Procedure; All Divisions

Revised Guidelines for the Preparation of Documents

Guidelines for Inter-Division Filings

Guidelines Pertaining to Bankruptcy Petition Preparers in Eastern District of California Cases

Guidelines for Cash Collateral and Financing Stipulations

Policy Statement Re Applications to Employ Professionals

APPENDIX III LOCAL RULES FORMS

B104 Adversary Proceeding Cover Sheet

B254 Subpoena for Rule 2004 Examination

B255 Subpoena in an Adversary Proceeding

B256 Subpoena in a Case under the Bankruptcy Code

EDC 2-100 Verification of Master Address List

EDC 3-080-05 Chapter 13 Plan and Attachments

EDC 3-081-03 Order Confirming Plan, Valuing Collateral and Avoiding Liens

EDC 3-083-03 Wage Order

EDC 3-085 Declaration Requesting Entry of Order Confirming Chapter 13 Plan
Without Chapter 13 Trustee's Approval of Form of Order

EDC 3-086 Class I Checklist

EDC 3-087 Authorization to Release Information to the Trustee Regarding Secured
Claims Being Paid by the Trustee

EDC 3-095 Application and Declaration Re: Additional Fees and Expenses in Chapter
13 Cases

EDC 3-096 Rights and Responsibilities of Chapter 13 Debtors
and Their Attorneys

EDC 3-468-INST Instructions for Completing Relief From Stay Information Sheet, Form

EDC 3-468

EDC 3-468 Relief from Stay Information Sheet

EDC 3-965 Request for Clerk's Notice of Entry

EDC 3-966 Request for Clerk's Notice of Entry in Adversary Proceedings

EDC 6-970A Order Granting Application For Order of Examination Under Federal Rule
of Bankruptcy Procedure 2004(a) [No Document Production]

EDC 6-970B Order Granting Application For Order of Examination Under Federal Rule
of Bankruptcy Procedure 2004(a)

APPENDIX IV
(Updated 1/29/10)
SELECTED GENERAL ORDERS AND SPECIAL ORDERS

General Order 10-01 Technical Amendment to Local Bankruptcy Rule 1001-1(c)

Special Order 10-01 Delegation of Authority to the Clerk of the Bankruptcy Court and his Deputies

General Order 09-03 Order Adopting Revision to Interim Rule 1007-1

General Order 09-02 Order Adopting Revisions to Local Bankruptcy Rules

General Order 09-01 Electronic Filing of Documents—Time of Filing Per Local Bankruptcy Rule 5005-1(f)(2)

General Order 08-05 Electronic Availability and Redaction of Electronically Filed Transcripts

General Order 08-04 Order Adopting Interim Rule 1007-1

General Order 08-03 Order Vacating General Order 05-04 (Except with Respect to Interim Rule 5012) and Vacating General Order 06-04

General Order 08-02 Amendment to General Order 05-03, Chapter 13 Cases

General Order 08-01 Amendment to Local Rule 3007-1

General Order 07-04 Technical Amendment to Local Rule 9014-1 (d)(1) & (2)

General Order 07-03 Abrogation of General Order 99-1, Order Concerning Filing of Papers

General Order 07-02 Technical Amendment to Local Rule 7005-1(d)(1)

General Order 07-01 Technical Amendments to Local Rules 5005.5-1 (b) & (e) and 7005-1 (a) & (b)

General Order 06-03 Amendment of Local Bankruptcy Rul 9014-1(f)(3)

General Order 06-02 Amendment of Local Bankruptcy Rules 1007-1, 2002-1 and 9004-1 and Adoption of New Local Bankruptcy Rules 5005-1, 5005.5-1 and 7005-1; Technical Amendment of Local Bankruptcy Rules 1002-1 and 1007-1

General Order 06-01 Amendment to General Order 05-03, Chapter 13 Cases

General Order 05-05 Filing of Employer Payment Advices Pursuant to 11 U.S.C. § 521(a)(1)(B)(iv)

General Order 05-03 Order Concerning Chapter 13 Cases (Applies to chapter 13 cases filed on or after 10/17/05, and cases converted to chapter 13 on or after 10/17/05. For cases filed or converted to chapter 13 prior to 10/17/05, see General Order 97-02, 00-02, 01-02, or 03-03.) As Amended by GO 06-01 and GO 08-02.

General Order 05-01 Technical Amendment to Local Bankruptcy Rules 2002-1(d)

General Order 04-04 Deposits of Registry Funds

General Order 04-03 Revision to Local Bankruptcy Rule 1002-1

General Order 04-02 Abrogation of Local Bankruptcy Rule 2016-1 and Revision to Local Bankruptcy Rule 9022-1

General Order 04-01 Amended and Restated Order Concerning Filing, Signing, and Verifying Documents by Electronic Means [Amends, Restates and Supercedes General Order 03-04]

General Order 03-02 Issuance of Orders to Show Cause for Failure to Timely File Documents; For Failure to Attend Meeting of Creditors; and/or for Failure to Pay Filing or Installment Fees

General Order 02-02 New Local Bankruptcy Rule 3007-1 and Revisions to Local Bankruptcy Rules 4001-1 and 9014-1

General Order 02-01 Order Adopting Procedure Under Federal Rule of Bankruptcy Procedure 9014(d) and Local Bankruptcy Rule 9014-1

General Order 01-03 New Local Rule 7056-1 and Revisions to Local Rules 9004-1 and 9014-1

General Order 00-3 Modification of Dispute Resolution Procedures for Bankruptcy Cases and Adversary Proceedings

General Order 98-5 Complaints Against Pro Se Debtors Pursuant to 11 U.S.C. §§ 523 and 727

General Order 95-1 Adoption of Dispute Resolution Procedures for Bankruptcy Cases and Adversary Proceedings

Special Order 05-01 Acceptance and Filing of Documents on October 15 and 16, 2005

GENERAL ORDER 08-05 Electronic Availability and Redaction of Electronically Filed Transcripts

WHEREAS, at its September 2007 session, the Judicial Conference adopted a policy regarding electronic availability of transcripts of court proceedings, and

WHEREAS, the Policy on Privacy and Public Access to Electronic Case Files approved by the Judicial Conference at its March 2008 session contains procedures for redacting personal information from court filings that are electronically available to the public,

IT IS ORDERED that the following procedures regarding the availability and redaction of electronically filed transcripts are adopted and shall apply to transcripts of events taking place in the court's courtrooms:

1. A transcript provided to the court by a court reporter will be available at the Clerk's Office for inspection only, for a period of ninety (90) days after it is filed. No portion of the transcript will be copied or printed at the Clerk's Office during the 90-day restriction period.

2. During the 90-day restriction period, a copy of the transcript may be obtained from the court reporter at the rate established by the Judicial Conference. The transcript will be available within the court for internal use, available at the public terminals at the courthouse, and remotely electronically available to attorneys who have purchased a copy from the court reporter. The name(s) of the purchasing attorney(s) shall be provided to the Clerk of Court (Clerk) by the court reporter via electronic mail sent to an e-mail address designated for this purpose by the Clerk. Members of the general public including unrepresented parties who purchase the transcript will not be given remote electronic access to the transcript or any redacted version filed with the court during the 90-day restriction period.

3. After the 90-day restriction period has ended, the transcript (or redacted version if one has been filed) will be available for viewing and copying at the Clerk's Office public terminals and remotely available for viewing, downloading, and printing through the Judiciary's PACER system.

4. Each party's attorney is required to review a transcript for information that should be redacted under the Judicial Conference's privacy policy and as more particularly described in Fed. R. Bankr. P. 9037. References to social security numbers, individual taxpayer identification numbers and financial account numbers shall include only the last four digits of such numbers. Birth dates shall include the year of birth only. The names of individuals, other than debtors, known to be and identified as minors shall include the minor's initials only.

5. With the exception of transcripts, redaction of the information described in Fed. R. Bankr. P. 9037(a) is the responsibility of the person filing the document. When a transcript is filed, the attorneys and unrepresented parties who entered an appearance at the hearing are solely responsible for redaction of the information described in Fed. R. Bankr. P. 9037(a). Court reporters are not responsible for identifying a need for redaction or for redacting transcripts absent a request by an attorney or an unrepresented party. The court's responsibility is to follow Judicial Conference guidelines for providing public access to the transcript and for restricting access in accordance with the privacy policy. The Clerk is not required to review documents filed with the court for compliance with Rule 9037.

6. The date the transcript is filed is the starting date for all deadlines related

to restriction and redaction of the transcript.

7. Notice of the filing of a transcript (including notice of the deadlines related to restriction and redaction of the transcript) shall be provided by the Clerk to the attorneys and unrepresented parties who entered an appearance at the hearing.

8. Within seven (7) calendar days of a court reporter's filing of the transcript, an attorney or unrepresented party must file a Notice of Intent to Request Redaction that substantially complies with form EDC 3-300 (attached to this General Order as Exhibit 2) with the Clerk if he or she intends to request redaction of information from the transcript, and serve copies on the court reporter and the other attorneys and unrepresented parties who entered an appearance at the hearing. An attorney or unrepresented party is responsible for reviewing the opening and closing statements made on behalf of the party he or she represents, any statements made by the party, and the testimony of any witness called by the party. If no Notice of Intent to Request Redaction is filed during this seven-day period, the court will conclude that redaction of personal data is not necessary, and will make the transcript remotely electronically available to the public through PACER after the 90-day restriction period.

9. Once an attorney or unrepresented party has filed a Notice of Intent to Request Redaction, he or she has twenty-one (21) calendar days from the date of filing of the transcript to review the transcript and file a Redaction Request and List of Items to be Redacted that substantially complies with form EDC 3-301 (attached to this General Order as Exhibit 3) with the Clerk and serve copies on the court reporter and the other attorneys and unrepresented parties who entered an appearance at the hearing that indicates the type of personal data identifier to be redacted, where it appears in the transcript by page and line, and how it is to be redacted. The Court may order this time extended, for good cause shown. If an attorney or unrepresented party files a Notice of Intent to Request Redaction but fails to timely file a Redaction Request and List of Items to be Redacted or a motion to extend time, no redactions will be made and the original transcript will be remotely publicly available after the 90-day restriction period.

10. The court reporter must redact the identifiers, as directed by the attorney or unrepresented party, and then re-file the redacted transcript within thirty-one (31) calendar days of the filing of the original transcript. Also during this time period, an attorney or unrepresented party may, by motion for a protective order, request that additional information be redacted. No remote electronic access to the transcript will be allowed (other than to

attorneys who paid for the original transcript) until the Court has ruled on any such motion.

11. If a redacted transcript is filed with the Clerk, the Clerk shall permanently restrict access to the original transcript and the redacted transcript will be remotely electronically available through PACER after 90 calendar days from the date of filing of the original transcript. If the original transcript is filed without redaction, the original transcript will be remotely electronically available through PACER after 90 calendar days.

12. Charges for access through PACER apply during and after the 90-day restriction period. Charges are not capped at 30 pages. The user will incur PACER charges each time the transcript is accessed even though he or she may have purchased it from the court reporter and obtained remote access. A free copy of the transcript is not available via remote access.

13. This General Order shall apply to all transcripts of court proceedings ordered from the court reporter on or after January 20, 2009, regardless of when the proceedings took place.

DATED: JAN 12, 2009

GENERAL ORDER 98-5 Complaints Against Pro Se Debtors Pursuant to 11 U.S.C. §§ 523 and 727

It is hereby ordered that in all adversary proceedings under Chapter 7 cases in this district filed pursuant to either or both 11 U.S.C. § 523 and 11 U.S.C. § 727 where the debtor or debtors are not represented by counsel, the plaintiff shall serve with the summons and complaint a copy of NOTICE TO PRO SE DEBTOR(S), in the form attached hereto as Exhibit 1, together with a sufficient number of copies for service, filing and conforming of the ANSWER in the form attached hereto as Exhibit 2 with the caption information completed. The "Exhibit" designations shall be deleted from the copies served. When service of Exhibits 1 and 2 is required, the plaintiff shall file with the clerk a declaration that copies of the NOTICE TO PRO SE DEBTOR(S) and the ANSWER, in the required number of copies, were served together with the summons and complaint.

It is further ordered that the clerk shall include a copy of this order and copies of Exhibits 1 and 2 with each summons issued with respect to complaints filed in Chapter 7 cases pursuant to 11 U.S.C. §§ 523 and 727 where the court records do not indicate that the debtor or debtors are represented by counsel.

This General Order supercedes General Order 98-01.

Dated: November 2, 1998

Special Order 06-01 Delegation of Authority to the Clerk of the Bankruptcy Court and his Deputies

IT IS ORDERED that Special Order 93-1, dated September 17, 1993, is hereby abrogated.

IT IS FURTHER ORDERED that Richard G. Heltzel, the duly appointed Clerk of the U.S. Bankruptcy Court for the Eastern District of California and his deputies shall have the same rights and powers, shall perform the same functions and duties, and shall be subject to the same provisions of Title 28, United States Code, as a clerk and other employees appointed under 28 U.S.C. § 751. Pursuant to the provisions of 28 U.S.C. § 956, 11 U.S.C. § 105, and the Federal Rules of Bankruptcy Procedure, the clerk and such deputies as he may designate are authorized to sign and enter without further direction the following orders which are deemed to be of a ministerial, nondiscretionary, nonjudicial, and/or administrative nature:

1. Orders pursuant to Federal Rule of Bankruptcy Procedure 2004, presented on EDC Form 6-970A, authorizing the examination of a person but not compelling the production of documentary evidence;

2. Orders fixing the last dates for the filing of objections to confirmation of chapter 12 and chapter 13 plans, complaints objecting to discharge, complaints to determine the dischargeability of debts, proofs of claim, and amendments thereto;

3. Orders granting applications to pay the filing fee in installments as provided by the Federal Rules of Bankruptcy Procedure;

4. Orders granting discharge of debtors in chapter 7, 12 and 13 cases in which no objection to discharge is pending, and where the debtor has not executed a waiver of discharge or been otherwise denied a discharge;

5. Orders reopening cases pursuant to 11 U.S.C. § 350(b) to administer assets, to permit the debtor's filing of a motion to avoid lien, or to file an adversary proceeding as provided in Federal Rule of Bankruptcy Procedure 4007(b);

6. After Court approval of all amounts awarded therein, orders awarding compensation and expense reimbursements to trustees and other professionals in chapter 7 cases;

7. Final decrees, and orders closing cases and discharging trustees after notice affording opportunity to be heard and no request for hearing or objection having been filed;

8. Except with respect to priority claims, orders substituting the transferee for the original claimant on a proof of claim pursuant to the Federal Rules of Bankruptcy Procedure;

9. Orders presented by the Chapter 13 Standing Trustee ordering or releasing the debtor or any entity from whom the debtor receives income to pay all or part of such income to the trustee;

10. Orders dismissing adversary proceedings for lack of prosecution after notice to the parties affording opportunity to be heard and no request for a hearing having been filed.

IT IS FURTHER ORDERED that, in the interest of justice, a judge may suspend or withdraw the Clerk's and deputy clerks' authority to sign the foregoing orders at any time, on the judge's own motion, and regulate practice in accordance with the judge's direction.

DATED: March 2, 2006

GENERAL ORDER 09-01 [Abrogated]

Application To Pay Filing Fee In Installments (EDC.002-020)

UNITED STATES BANKRUPTCY COURT
EASTERN DISTRICT OF CALIFORNIA

In re)
)
) **Case No.**
)
Debtor(s).) **AMENDMENT COVER SHEET**

Attached hereto are the following amended documents. (Check all that apply.) **DO NOT** use this cover sheet when filing AMENDED PLANS or AMENDMENTS TO PLANS.

- ☐ Petition
- ☐ Creditor Matrix
- ☐ Schedules (check appropriate boxes)
  ☐ A ☐ B ☐ C ☐ D ☐ E ☐ F ☐ G ☐ H ☐ I ☐ J
- ☐ Summary of Schedules
- ☐ Statement of Financial Affairs
- ☐ Statement of Intention
- ☐ List of 20 Largest Unsecured Creditors
- ☐ List of Equity Security Holders
- ☐ Other: ______

Purpose of amendment (check all that apply):

- ☐ For amendments to a debtor's schedules of creditors or list of creditors, **$26 for each amendment**, provided the bankruptcy judge may, for good cause, waive the charge in any case. NOTE: Lists, schedules and statements amended for this purpose should be accompanied by an amended matrix, listing only the names and addresses added and/or corrected.
- ☐ To add or correct information other than creditor names and addresses (please specify): ______
- ☐ Other: ______

Dated: Attorney's Signature: ______
Attorney's Name: ______
Address: ______

DECLARATION BY DEBTOR

I(We), the undersigned debtor(s), hereby declare under penalty of perjury that the information set forth in the amendment(s) attached hereto, consisting of __ pages, is true and correct to the best of my(our) information and belief.

Dated:

______ Debtor's Signature

______ Joint Debtor's Signature

FOR INSTRUCTIONS, SEE FORM EDC 2-015 - INST

EDC 2-015 (Rev. 02/07)

EDCAL-43 E.D. CALIFORNIA

180 DAY BAR NOTIFICATION LETTER

Print Form

Clear Form

APPEALS CHECKLIST

Bankruptcy Case Number:______________________

Adversary Proceeding:________________________

Debtor(s) Name:____

Case Title:____

BAP or DC case number:_____________________________________

Deputy Clerk handling appeal:_________________________________

1. NOTICE OF APPEAL [FRBP 8001]:

   Appeal filed _________________________

2. ELECTION OF APPELLATE FORUM [FRBP 8001(e)]:

   Did Appellant file a Statement of Election to have the appeal heard in District Court when appeal was filed?

   ________ Yes ________ No

   Did Appellee or other party file a Statement of Election to have the appeal heard in District Court within 30 days after service of notice of appeal which was served on the parties (date) ____________?

   ________ Yes ________ No

3. MOTIONS [FRBP 8001(b); 8003; 8005]:

   Did the Appellant file a Motion for Leave to Appeal for an Interlocutory Order?

   ________ Yes ________ No

   NOTE: Motions for Leave to Appeal are to be heard by the Appellate Court, not the Bankruptcy Court.

Did the Appellant file a Motion for Stay Pending Appeal?

_________ Yes _________ No

NOTE: Motions for Stay Pending Appeal are to be heard by the Bankruptcy Judge assigned. A Hearing has been set in Department _________ on _______________, at ___________.

4. RECORD AND ISSUES ON APPEAL [FRBP 8006]:

Appellant's designation of record due 10 days after Notice of Appeal or Order Granting Leave to Appeal - Date due:_______________; Date Filed:________________

Appellant's statement of issues - (same as designation of record) Date due:_______________;Date Filed:____________

NOTE: Ten days after Appellant files the above, Appellee may file a Designation Of Additional Items To Be Included In The Record For Appeal. Date due:_________________; Date Filed:____________________________.

5. COMPLETION OF RECORD:

Request for transcript or a written statement indicating no transcript is needed filed ________________ [FRBP 8006].

Transcript due within 30 days of receipt of the request - Date due:_________________________.

If no request for extension of time to produce the transcript is made by the court reporter and no transcript has been produced by the court reporter, notify bankruptcy judge. Judge _________________ notified of non-completion on ________________________.

6. TRANSMITTAL TO APPELLATE COURT [FRBP 8007(b)]:

Certificate of Record served _______________________.
Notice of Delayed or Incomplete Record served ____________.

7. FINAL DECISIONS OF THE APPELLATE COURT:

   Order/Opinion received from BAP/DC ____________________
   Mandate from BAP received ____________________ NOTE: District Court does not send a mandate, only BAP. BAP sends Mandates 17 days after Memorandum Decision or Opinion is entered.

8. PROCEDURES FOLLOWING REMAND BY APPELLATE COURT [LBR 8020-1]:

   Local Bankruptcy Rule 8020-1 states: Whenever a case, proceeding or matter is remanded by an Appellate Court to the Bankruptcy Court for further proceedings, any party to the appeal may move to set the matter for further proceedings by filing a motion pursuant to LBR 9014-1. The Court will not set the matter for further proceedings as a matter of course.

9. APPEALS TO THE NINTH CIRCUIT COURT OF APPEALS:

   An appeal to the Ninth Circuit will be filed with BAP or DC depending where the original appeal was heard. The appeal must be filed within 30 days after the decision has been made (60 days for U.S.A.)

   Either BAP or DC will forward the Ninth Circuit mandate to us once they receive it.

COMMENTS:____

____

____

____

____

____

____

Print Form

Clear Form

ADVERSARY SUMMONS – FRESNO

UNITED STATES BANKRUPTCY COURT
EASTERN DISTRICT OF CALIFORNIA
FRESNO DIVISION

In re Debtor(s).	Bankruptcy Case No.
Plaintiff(s). v. Defendant(s).	Adversary Proceeding No. **SUMMONS AND NOTICE OF STATUS CONFERENCE IN AN ADVERSARY PROCEEDING**

YOU ARE SUMMONED and required to file a written motion or answer to the complaint which is attached to this summons with the Clerk of the Bankruptcy Court within 30 days after the date of issuance of this summons except that the United States and its officers and agencies shall file a motion or answer to the complaint within 35 days. All stipulations for extensions of time shall: (1) be in writing; (2) be filed with the Court; and (3) be for a period not greater than 30 days.

Address of the Clerk:	Clerk, U.S. Bankruptcy Court United States Courthouse 2500 Tulare Street, Suite 2501 Fresno, CA 93721-1318

At the same time, you must also serve a copy of the motion or answer upon the plaintiff's attorney (or if the plaintiff is not represented by an attorney, upon the plaintiff) whose name and address is:

Name and Address of Plaintiff's Attorney:

If you file a motion, your time to answer is governed by Rule 7012 of the Federal Rules of Bankruptcy Procedure.

YOU ARE NOTIFIED that a status conference at which the Court may make appropriate orders regarding matters including, but not limited to, discovery and date of trial, will be held at the following time and place:

Address:	Room: Date & Time:

Attorneys of record in the adversary proceeding and unrepresented parties must attend the status conference.

IF YOU FAIL TO RESPOND TO THIS SUMMONS BY WRITTEN MOTION OR ANSWER FILED AND SERVED AS SET FORTH ABOVE, YOUR DEFAULT MAY BE ENTERED AND JUDGMENT BY DEFAULT MAY BE TAKEN AGAINST YOU FOR THE RELIEF DEMANDED IN THE COMPLAINT.

R.G. HELTZEL, CLERK OF BANKRUPTCY COURT

______________________ Date

By:______________________ Deputy Clerk

EDC 2-830(f) (Rev. 1/30/2006)

EDCAL-47 E.D. CALIFORNIA

CERTIFICATE OF SERVICE

I,____, certify that I am, and at all times during the service of process was, not less than 18 years of age and not a party to the matter concerning which service of process was made. I further certify that service of this summons and a copy of the complaint was made on ____________________ (date), by:

___ MAIL SERVICE: Regular, first class United States mail, postage fully pre-paid, addressed to:

___ PERSONAL SERVICE: By leaving the process with defendant or with an officer or agent of defendant at:

___ RESIDENCE SERVICE: By leaving the process with the following adult at:

___ PUBLICATION: The defendant was served as follows *[describe briefly]*:

___ STATE LAW: The defendant was served pursuant to the laws of the State of ____________________, as follows *[describe briefly]*:

Under penalty of perjury, I declare that the foregoing is true and correct.

Date: ____________________ Signature: ______________________________

Print Name
Business Address
City, State, Zip

EDC 2-830(f) (Rev. 1/30/06)

APPEALS CHECKLIST

Print Form

Clear Form

APPEALS CHECKLIST

Bankruptcy Case Number:______________________

Adversary Proceeding:________________________

Debtor(s) Name:____

Case Title:____

BAP or DC case number:_______________________________________

Deputy Clerk handling appeal:________________________________

1. NOTICE OF APPEAL [FRBP 8001]:

   Appeal filed _________________________

2. ELECTION OF APPELLATE FORUM [FRBP 8001(e)]:

   Did Appellant file a Statement of Election to have the appeal heard in District Court when appeal was filed?

   ________ Yes ________ No

   Did Appellee or other party file a Statement of Election to have the appeal heard in District Court within 30 days after service of notice of appeal which was served on the parties (date) ____________?

   ________ Yes ________ No

3. MOTIONS [FRBP 8001(b); 8003; 8005]:

   Did the Appellant file a Motion for Leave to Appeal for an Interlocutory Order?

   ________ Yes ________ No

   NOTE: Motions for Leave to Appeal are to be heard by the Appellate Court, not the Bankruptcy Court.

Did the Appellant file a Motion for Stay Pending Appeal?

_______ Yes _______ No

NOTE: Motions for Stay Pending Appeal are to be heard by the Bankruptcy Judge assigned. A Hearing has been set in Department _______ on ____________, at _________.

4. RECORD AND ISSUES ON APPEAL [FRBP 8006]:

Appellant's designation of record due 10 days after Notice of Appeal or Order Granting Leave to Appeal - Date due:___________; Date Filed:___________

Appellant's statement of issues - (same as designation of record) Date due:___________;Date Filed:___________

NOTE: Ten days after Appellant files the above, Appellee may file a Designation Of Additional Items To Be Included In The Record For Appeal. Date due:___________; Date Filed:___________.

5. COMPLETION OF RECORD:

Request for transcript or a written statement indicating no transcript is needed filed ___________ [FRBP 8006].

Transcript due within 30 days of receipt of the request - Date due:___________.

If no request for extension of time to produce the transcript is made by the court reporter and no transcript has been produced by the court reporter, notify bankruptcy judge. Judge ___________ notified of non-completion on ___________.

6. TRANSMITTAL TO APPELLATE COURT [FRBP 8007(b)]:

Certificate of Record served ___________.
Notice of Delayed or Incomplete Record served ___________.

7. FINAL DECISIONS OF THE APPELLATE COURT:

   Order/Opinion received from BAP/DC ______________________
   Mandate from BAP received ______________________ NOTE:
   District Court does not send a mandate, only BAP. BAP sends Mandates 17 days after Memorandum Decision or Opinion is entered.

8. PROCEDURES FOLLOWING REMAND BY APPELLATE COURT [LBR 8020-1]:

   Local Bankruptcy Rule 8020-1 states: Whenever a case, proceeding or matter is remanded by an Appellate Court to the Bankruptcy Court for further proceedings, any party to the appeal may move to set the matter for further proceedings by filing a motion pursuant to LBR 9014-1. The Court will not set the matter for further proceedings as a matter of course.

9. APPEALS TO THE NINTH CIRCUIT COURT OF APPEALS:

   An appeal to the Ninth Circuit will be filed with BAP or DC depending where the original appeal was heard. The appeal must be filed within 30 days after the decision has been made (60 days for U.S.A.)

   Either BAP or DC will forward the Ninth Circuit mandate to us once they receive it.

COMMENTS:____

____

____

____

____

____

____

Print Form

Clear Form

EDCAL-51 E.D. CALIFORNIA

Certification of Notice to Consumer Debtor(s) under § 342(b) of the Bankruptcy Code

________________________ *[Name; Bar ID No.]*
________________________ *[Address]*
____
________________________ *[Telephone]*

Attorney for Debtor(s)

UNITED STATES BANKRUPTCY COURT
EASTERN DISTRICT OF CALIFORNIA

In re	)	**Case No.**
	)	
	)	
	)	
	)	
Debtor.	)	

APPLICATION AND DECLARATION RE: ADDITIONAL FEES AND EXPENSES IN CHAPTER 13 CASES

[For Use Only in Cases Where an Executed Copy of "Rights and Responsibilities" has been Filed]

Pursuant to Bankruptcy Code Section 330 and Bankruptcy Rule 2016(a), the undersigned hereby applies for $____________ in additional fees and $__________ in additional expenses in this Chapter 13 case. In support of this application, the applicant hereby declares under penalty of perjury as follows:

The applicant has served as attorney for the debtor since ___ __________. On ______________ applicant received a retainer of $__________. An executed copy of this Court's "Rights and Responsibilities of Chapter 13 Debtors and Their Attorneys" was filed on ______________. As reflected in that document and in the Bankruptcy Rule 2016(b) disclosure statement, applicant and the debtor agreed that the initial fee for legal services and expenses in connection with this Chapter 13 case would be $___________. Additional fees have been allowed by order(s) of this Court on the following dates and in the following amounts: ________________ ____________________________________. To date, fees in the amount of $___________ have been paid by the Chapter 13 Trustee through the debtor's Chapter 13 plan.

The initial agreed-upon fee, as well as additional fees previously allowed, are not sufficient to fully compensate the attorney for the legal services rendered. The time sheets attached hereto as Exhibit A cover all services rendered to the debtor in connection with this Chapter 13 case since the date the applicant commenced rendering services. [Include a brief description of the specific work for which compensation is sought and a narrative explaining why the fees previously allowed pursuant to the Chapter 13 Fee Guidelines were not sufficient to fairly compensate the applicant for this work in light of the amount or complexity of the work undertaken for the debtor.] ______________________________

____

____

____

____

____.

After exercising reasonable billing judgment, the total number of hours expended in this case for which applicant seeks compensation is _________. The applicant's customary hourly rate for services of this nature is $_______. A reasonable fee for the services rendered would be $_______ (multiply hours times hourly rate to arrive at the lodestar amount). Attached hereto as Exhibit B is an itemization of all out-of-pocket expenses incurred in connection with this Chapter 13 case.

Accordingly, applicant respectfully requests that the Court allow additional fees of $____________ (lodestar amount less initial agreed-upon fee plus any additional fees previously allowed) and $_________ in additional expenses to be paid through the Chapter 13 plan.

I declare under the penalty of perjury under the laws of the State of California that the foregoing is true and correct.

DATED: ____________ __________________________________
Applicant and Attorney for Debtor

If the debtor agrees that the requested compensation is reasonable and should be paid, the debtor should sign below.

If the debtor does not agree that the additional compensation requested in this application is reasonable or is due and owing, the debtor should not sign below and instead should file a brief written explanation of any objection the debtor may have to the requested compensation.

DATED: ____________ __________________________________
Debtor

DATED: ____________ __________________________________
Debtor

APPLICATION BY TRUSTEE OR DEBTOR IN POSSESSION TO DEFER PAYMENT OF FEE FOR FILING COMPLAINT

UNITED STATES BANKRUPTCY COURT
EASTERN DISTRICT OF CALIFORNIA

	)	Bankruptcy Case No.
Debtor(s).	)	
	)	
Plaintiff(s),	)	
vs.	)	Adversary Proceeding No.
	)	
Defendant(s).	)	

APPLICATION BY TRUSTEE OR DEBTOR-IN-POSSESSION TO DEFER PAYMENT OF FEE FOR FILING COMPLAINT AND ORDER

The undersigned applicant, trustee or debtor-in-possession for the estate of the above-named debtor, hereby declares under penalty of perjury that:

1. Applicant is filing herewith a complaint commencing an adversary proceeding under Part VII of the Federal Rules of Bankruptcy Procedure.
2. The amount of money on deposit for the debtor's estate is presently less than the requisite filing fee of $250.00.
3. The filing of this complaint is in the best interest of the estate.
4. For chapter 11 trustees and debtors-in-possession - the chapter 11 plan has not yet been confirmed.

WHEREFORE, Chapter 7 trustee requests permission to file the above-entitled complaint without prepayment of the filing fee, and that said filing fee be deferred until funds become available to pay the filing fee in full.

OR

WHEREFORE, Chapter 11 trustee or debtor-in-possession requests permission to file the above-entitled complaint without prepayment of the filing fee, and that said filing fee be deferred until funds are available to pay the filing fee in full or until 10 days after the order confirming chapter 11 plan is entered, whichever occurs first.

DATED:

Trustee or Debtor-in-Possession

ORDER

IT IS ORDERED that the above-entitled complaint be accepted without prepayment of the requisite filing fee; and

IT IS FURTHER ORDERED that:

____ The Chapter 7 Trustee pay the deferred filing fee from assets of the estate, if any are realized, as soon as the funds become available unless otherwise directed by the court.

____ The Chapter 11 trustee or debtor-in-possession pay the deferred filing fee from assets of the estate as soon as funds are available to pay the fee in full or within 10 days after the order confirming chapter 11 plan is entered, whichever occurs first.

DATED:

FOR THE COURT
RICHARD G. HELTZEL
CLERK, U.S. BANKRUPTCY COURT

By: ____________________
Deputy Clerk

Chapter 7 Individual Debtor's Statement of Intention

UNITED STATES BANKRUPTCY COURT
EASTERN DISTRICT OF CALIFORNIA

In Re:

Name: ______________________________) IN PROCEEDING UNDER
) CHAPTER 13 OF U.S.
) BANKRUPTCY CODE
Name: ______________________________) Case No. ____________________

APPLICATION FOR CONFIRMATION OF PLAN AND
PETITION FOR ALLOWANCE OF ATTORNEY'S FEES

Your Petitioner, ______________________________, being the attorney for the debtor(s), respectfully represents:

That a meeting of creditors has been held after appropriate notice there of being duly given to all creditors and other interested parties, and the debtor appeared at such meeting and submitted to examination under oath, as required by Section 343 of the Code. Notice of Hearing of Confirmation has been duly given. The debtor's Plan of Arrangement, a copy of which is on file herein and is herein incorporated by reference is in compliance with the provisions of Chapter 13 of the Bankruptcy Code and other applicable provisions of such Title; that all fees and charges required to be paid before confirmation have been paid; that the Plan has been proposed in good faith and not by any means forbidden by law; that the value as of the effective date of the Plan of property to be distributed under the Plan on account of cash allowed under unsecured claims is not less than the amount that would be paid on such claim if the estate of the debtor were liquidated under Chapter 7 of the Bankruptcy Code on such date; that with respect to each allowed secured claim provided for by the Plan either (1) the holder of such claim has accepted the Plan, or (2) the Plan provides that the holder of such claim retain the lien securing such claim and the value as of the effective date of the Plan of property to be distributed under the Plan on account of such claim is not less than the allowed amount of such claim or (3) the debtor agrees to surrender the property securing such claim to such holder; that the debtor will be able to make all payments under the Plan and to comply with the Plan; that to the extent the Plan provides for payments over a period longer than three (3) years, the court specifically finds that such additional longer period is reasonably necessary by reason of projected income and expenses of the debtor(s) and his projected ability to pay under the Plan and that such Plan would not be feasible without such extended pay period.

That the reasonable value of services and costs rendered by ______________________________ is the sum of ____________. Your petitioner has neither demanded nor received from the debtor(s) any payment for such services except payment of ____________ and the agreement that the amount prayed for is reasonable compensation and no previous allowance by the Court on account of such services has been made.

WHEREFORE, your petitioner prays that the Plan submitted by the debtor be confirmed by the Court and that an allowance be made for the attorney's fees for professional services rendered by your petitioner in this proceeding and that the Court make such additional and further orders as are necessary or desirable to effectuate the provisions of the Plan.

I, ______________________________, the attorney for the debtor(s) herein, certify under penalty of perjury that the foregoing is true and correct.

Executed on:
FILING FEES PAID IN ADVANCE
TOTAL ATTORNEY FEES AND COSTS
TOTAL ATTORNEY FEES RECEIVED
BALANCE DUE THROUGH PLAN ______________________________

EDCAL-57 E.D. CALIFORNIA

APPLICATION FOR PAYMENT OF UNCLAIMED FUNDS

UNITED STATES BANKRUPTCY COURT EASTERN DISTRICT OF CALIFORNIA	
In Re: Debtor(s).	Case Number: **APPLICATION FOR PAYMENT OF UNCLAIMED FUNDS**

1. On ____________________ [dates], a check in the amount of $____________ belonging to ____________________ ____________________ [name of original creditor/claimant]] was tendered to the Clerk of the above-entitled Court by the case trustee as unclaimed funds for claim(s) numbered: ____________________

2. The funds so tendered were deposited with the United States Treasury by the Clerk and remain unclaimed.

3. Applicant alleges that the following person or entity is the owner of the funds described in paragraph 1 *[provide name, address and telephone number]*: ____________________
____
____
____
(   ) ____________________

4. The original disbursement was not presented for payment because *[specifically state the reason and include a brief history of the creditor/claimant from the filing of the claim to the present. Attach supporting documentation]*: ____________________
____
____
____
____
____

5. Applicant represents that the alleged owner is entitled to receive the requested funds, has made sufficient inquiry and has no knowledge that any other party may be entitled to, and is not aware of any dispute regarding, the funds at issue based upon the following *[check the statement(s) that apply]*:

   - ☐ a. The alleged owner is the creditor/claimant named in paragraph 1 and the owner of the funds appearing on the records of this Court, as evidenced by the attached documents.
   - ☐ b. The alleged owner is the assignee of the creditor/claimant named in paragraph 1, or the assignee's representative, as evidenced by the attached documents.
   - ☐ c. The alleged owner is the successor-in-interest of the creditor/claimant named in paragraph 1, or the successor-in-interest's representative, as evidenced by the attached documents establishing chain of ownership.
   - ☐ d. The alleged owner is the estate of the deceased creditor/claimant named in paragraph 1, as evidenced by the attached certified copies of death certificate and other appropriate probate documents.
   - ☐ e. Subparagraphs (a) through (d) above do not apply. As evidenced by the attached documents, the alleged owner is: ____________________
____

In Re:	CASE NUMBER:

6. Applicant is *[check the statement that applies]:*

☐ a. The alleged owner of the funds. Attach the appropriate *Identification Form for Unclaimed Funds.*

☐ b. A duly authorized corporate officer (if a corporation) or a general partner (if a partnership) and is the representative of the alleged owner of the funds. Attach the appropriate *Identification Form for Unclaimed Funds.*

☐ c. The representative of the estate of a deceased alleged owner of the funds. Attached certified copies of probate documents which substantiates applicant's right to act on behalf of the decedent's estate.

☐ d. The attorney in fact for the alleged owner of the funds authorized by the attached notarized, original Power of Attorney to file this application on behalf of the alleged owner.

☐ e. An attorney representing the interests of the owner of the funds with authority to receive such funds, as evidenced by the attached notarized original Power of Attorney.

7. I understand that, pursuant to 18 U.S.C. § 152, I shall be fined not more than $5,000, or imprisoned not more than five years, or both, if I have knowingly and fraudulently made any false statements in this document or accompanying supporting documents. I further understand that any indications of fraud detected by the Court will be turned over to the U. S. Attorney for possible prosecution.

8. A copy of this completed application (with all supporting documentation) was mailed to the following on *(date):* ______________

(US Attorney)	*(Owner of the funds)*	*(Other)*
United States Attorney	______________________	______________________
501 I Street, 9th Floor	______________________	______________________
Sacramento, CA 95814	______________________	______________________

WHEREFORE, applicant prays for an order directing the Clerk of the above-entitled Court to pay said tendered money to the applicant.

I declare (or certify, or verify, or state) under penalty of perjury under the laws of the United States of America, that the foregoing statements and information are true and correct:

Dated:

____
Applicant's Signature

____
Applicant's Name Typed or Printed

____
Applicant's Address

____

____

(   ) ______________________
Applicant's Telephone Number

In Re:	CASE NUMBER:

STATE OF ____________________, COUNTY OF ____________________

On ____________________ before me, personally appeared (insert name and title of signer) ____________________ personally known to me (or proved to me on the basis of satisfactory evidence) to be the person(s) whose name(s) is/are subscribed to the written instrument and acknowledged to me that he/she/they executed the same in his/her/their authorized capacity(ies), and that by his/her/their signature(s) on the instrument the person(s), or the entity upon behalf of which the person(s) acted, executed the instrument. WITNESS my hand and official seal.

____
Notary Public

(SEAL)

My commission expires on __________

FOR COURT USE ONLY

File and documents reviewed by ____________________ on ____________________

I have carefully reviewed this application and all supporting documents and recommend to the Court that this application be approved.

____________________ ____________________
Financial Administrator, U.S. Bankruptcy Court Date

APPLICATION FOR RELEASE OF UNCLAIMED FUNDS

THIS FORM IS INTERACTIVE!!

Print Form

Clear Form

UNITED STATES BANKRUPTCY COURT
EASTERN DISTRICT OF CALIFORNIA

MEMORANDUM

DATE:

REPLY TO
ATTN OF: Karen Ceriani

SUBJECT: Application for Release of Unclaimed Funds

TO:

We have received an application requesting the release of undistributed funds for:

Case Number:
Debtor:
Creditor:

☐ 1. A request for an order must be made by written application incompliance with Local Bankruptcy Rule 9014-1. Contact the Financial Administrator at (916) 930-4472 to obtain the appropriate form.

☐ 2. Part(s) # ______ of the application has (have) not been completed.

☐ 3. It appears that a copy of the application was not sent to the alleged owner of the funds.

☐ 4. An original power of attorney with a notarized signature was not submitted.

☐ 5. The name of the original creditor/claimant listed on the trustee's report is not the same as the name of alleged owner of the funds stated in the application. No explanation of the difference is provided.

☐ 6. The address of the original creditor/claimant listed on the trustee's report is not the same as the address of alleged owner of the funds stated in the application. No explanation of the difference is provided.

☐ 7. There are no supporting documents showing the alleged owner of the funds to be the successor-in-interest to the funds claimed.

- ☐ 8. The corporate seal is not stamped on the power of attorney.
- ☐ 9. The name on the corporate seal does not match the name listed on the claim.
- ☐ 10. There is no resolution or other document under corporate seal that verifies the person signing the power of attorney is authorized to sign on behalf of the alleged owner of the funds.
- ☐ 11. Supporting documents are not certified copies. (See part 4 of the guidelines)
- ☐ 12. The applicant is not the alleged owner of funds or the owner's duly authorized agent or representative.
- ☐ 13. Signatures are not notarized.
- ☐ 14. The appropriate Identification Form for Unclaimed Funds is not attached to the application.
- ☐ 15. Copies of the application were not mailed to the U. S. Attorney.
- ☐ 16. The fee for search or retrieval of archive file was not included with the application.
- ☐ 17. Other: ______________________________

EDC 4-950 (New 7/01)

APPLICATION FOR SEARCH OF BANKRUPTCY RECORDS

THIS FORM IS INTERACTIVE!!

United States Bankruptcy Court
Eastern District of California

Print Form
Clear Form

APPLICATION FOR SEARCH OF BANKRUPTCY RECORDS

Name of individual or business that is the subject of the search:	Social Security No. or Employer Tax I.D. No. of Subject:

Please search your records for the following information regarding the individual or business named above:
☐ pending or closed bankruptcy cases in this district;
☐ pending or closed adversary proceedings;
☐ judgments/evidence of satisfaction of judgments; and
☐ other [describe briefly]

Please search for the period from ____________________ to ____________________.
A fee of $26.00 is charged for each name or item searched. Payment by check or money order must be enclosed.
Please do not send cash through the mail.

Name, address, and phone number of the person requesting the search:

CERTIFICATE OF SEARCH

The undersigned clerk hereby certifies the following results of a diligent search of the records of the court:
[Check only the items for which a search was requested and a fee paid.]

A. Bankruptcy Cases:
1. ☐ None found.
2. ☐ Case filed on ____________________.
(date)
☐ Voluntary ☐ Involuntary
☐ Pending ☐ Closed on ____________________.
(date)
☐ Discharge granted on ____________________.
(date)

B. Adversary Proceedings:
1. ☐ None found.
2. ☐ Subject is a party to the following proceeding:

____________________ v. ____________________
(Plaintiff) *(Defendant)*

Adversary Proceeding Number ____________________, filed on ____________________.
(date)

Pending Closed on ____________________.
(date)

Disposition: Dismissed on ____________________
(date)

Final Judgment entered on ____________________
(date)

Case Number of Related Bankruptcy Case ____________________.

____
Clerk of the Bankruptcy Court

____________________ By: ____________________
Date Deputy Clerk

EDC.003-100 (New 09/21/03)

APPLICATION FOR WAIVER OF REQUIREMENT TO FILE DOCUMENTS IN ELECTRONIC FORM

UNITED STATES BANKRUPTCY COURT

EASTERN DISTRICT OF CALIFORNIA

In re)
)
)
) Bankruptcy Case No.
)
)
Debtor(s).)

APPLICATION FOR WAIVER OF REQUIREMENT TO FILE DOCUMENTS IN ELECTRONIC FORM

1. In accordance with Local Bankruptcy Rule 5005-1(c)(2), I apply for a waiver of the requirement to file documents in this case in electronic form

2. I am an attorney who regularly practices in the U.S. Bankruptcy Court for the Eastern District of California.

3. My name, state bar ID number, licensing state, firm name, address, and telephone number are as follows:

Name: ______________________________

State Bar ID #: ______________ Licensing State: ______________

Firm Name: ______________________________

Address: ______________________________

____

____

Phone #: ( ) ______________________________

4. I *[please check one]* ☐ am *or* ☐ am not a current user of the Public Access to Court Electronic Records (PACER) system.

5. The basis for this application is as follows: ______________________________

____

____

____

____

____

____

6. A declaration demonstrating cause for relief from the requirement to file documents in electronic form was submitted for filing with this application.

WHEREFORE, I request an order waiving the requirement to file documents in electronic form in this case for the following period: ________________________.

I declare (or certify, or verify, or state) under penalty of perjury under the laws of the United States of America, that the foregoing statements and information are true and correct to the best of my knowledge, information, and belief.

Dated:

____

Applicant's Signature

APPLICATION TO PAY FILING FEE IN INSTALLMENTS

UNITED STATES BANKRUPTCY COURT
Eastern District of California

In re)
)
) Case No.
)
Debtor(s).)
_______________)

APPLICATION TO PAY FILING FEE IN INSTALLMENTS

1. In accordance with Bankruptcy Rule 1006, I (we) apply for permission to pay the filing fee amounting to $ __________ in installments.
2. I am (we are) unable to pay the filing fee except in installments.
3. Until the filing fee is paid in full, I (we) will not make any additional payment or transfer any additional property to an attorney or other person for services in connection with this case.
4. I (we) propose the following terms for the payment of the filing fee:

$__________ (*check one*): ☐ with the filing of the petition **OR**
☐ on or before __________

$__________ on or before __________

$__________ on or before __________

$__________ on or before __________

NOTE: The number of installments proposed shall not exceed four (4), and the final installment shall be payable not later than 120 days after filing the petition. For cause shown, the court may extend the time of any installment, provided the last installment is paid not later than 180 days after filing the petition. Fed. R. Bankr. P. 1006(b)(2).

5. I (we) understand that if I (we) fail to pay any installment when due, my (our) bankruptcy case may be dismissed, and I (we) may not receive a discharge of my (our) debts.
6. I (we) further understand that my (our) discharge, or confirmation of any plan, will be delayed until the filing fee is paid in full.

____
Signature of Attorney (if any) Date

____
Signature of Debtor Date
(In a joint case, both spouses must sign.)

____
Name of Attorney Bar ID Number

____
Signature of Joint Debtor (if any) Date

DECLARATION OF NON-ATTORNEY BANKRUPTCY PETITION PREPARER (See 11 U.S.C. § 110)

I declare under penalty of perjury that: (1) I am a bankruptcy petition preparer as defined in 11 U.S.C. § 110; (2) I prepared this document for compensation and have provided the debtor with a copy of this document and the notices and information required under 11 U.S.C. §§ 110(b), 110(h), and 342(b); and, (3) if rules or guidelines have been promulgated pursuant to 11 U.S.C. § 110(h) setting a maximum fee for services chargeable by bankruptcy petition preparers, I have given the debtor notice of the maximum amount before preparing any document for filing for a debtor or accepting any fee from the debtor, as required in that section.

____
Printed or Typed Name of Bankruptcy Petition Preparer

____
Social Security No. (Required under 11 U.S.C. § 110.)

If the bankruptcy petition preparer is not an individual, state the name, title (if any), address, and social security number of the officer, principal, responsible person or partner who signs this document.

____
____
Address

X_______________________
Signature of Bankruptcy Petition Preparer

____
Date

Names and Social Security Numbers of all other individuals who prepared or assisted in preparing this document unless the bankruptcy petition preparer is not an individual:

If more than one person prepared this document, attach additional signed sheets conforming to the appropriate Official Form for each person. A bankruptcy petition preparer's failure to comply with the provisions of title 11 and the Federal Rules of Bankruptcy Procedure may result in fines or imprisonment or both. 11 U.S.C. § 110; 18 U.S.C. § 156.

EDC 2-020 (Rev. 12/07)

APPOINTMENT OF INTERIM TRUSTEE AND NOTICE OF SELECTION (FRESNO AND MODESTO DIVISIONS)

FILED
06/30/10
UNITED STATES BANKRUPTCY COURT
EASTERN DISTRICT OF CALIFORNIA

UNITED STATES BANKRUPTCY COURT
EASTERN DISTRICT OF CALIFORNIA
FRESNO DIVISION

In re	)	
	)	
	)	
	)	Case No.
	)	
Debtor(s).	)	

APPOINTMENT OF INTERIM TRUSTEE AND NOTICE OF SELECTION

Patrick Kavanagh is hereby appointed Interim Trustee of the above-named Debtor's(s') estate and Trustee if creditors fail to elect a Trustee as provided by the Bankruptcy Code. The Interim Trustee has filed a blanket bond pursuant to Federal Rule of Bankruptcy Procedure 2010(a).

If the Interim Trustee does not notify the Office of the United States Trustee and the Court in writing of rejection of the office within five days after receipt of notice of selection, the Interim Trustee shall be deemed to have accepted the office.

Dated: **06/30/10**

Print Form
Clear Form

Office of the United States Trustee
Region 17 -- Fresno Office

Sara L. Kistler
United States Trustee

EDC-UST 100-FM

EDCAL-67 E.D. CALIFORNIA

APPOINTMENT OF INTERIM TRUSTEE AND NOTICE OF SELECTION (SACRAMENTO DIVISION)

UNITED STATES BANKRUPTCY COURT
EASTERN DISTRICT OF CALIFORNIA

In re)
)
)
) Case No.
)
________________ Debtor(s).)

APPOINTMENT OF INTERIM TRUSTEE AND NOTICE OF SELECTION

Thomas A. Aceituno is hereby appointed Interim Trustee of the above-named Debtor's(s') estate and Trustee if creditors fail to elect a Trustee as provided by the Bankruptcy Code. The Interim Trustee has filed a blanket bond pursuant to Federal Rule of Bankruptcy Procedure 2010(a).

If the Interim Trustee does not notify the Office of the United States Trustee and the Court in writing of rejection of the office within five days after receipt of notice of selection, the Interim Trustee shall be deemed to have accepted the office.

Dated: **06/30/10**

Print Form
Clear Form

Office of the United States Trustee
Region 17 -- Sacramento Office

Sara L. Kistler
United States Trustee

Antonia Darling
Assistant United States Trustee

EDC-UST 100-SM

AUTHORIZATION FOR COMPENSATORY TIME

Print Form
Clear Form

AUTHORIZATION FOR COMPENSATORY TIME

THIS FORM IS INTERACTIVE!!

TO: ______________________________

I. OVERTIME AUTHORIZATION

You are hereby authorized to work overtime as follows:

DATE	OVERTIME HOURS SCHEDULED	ACTUAL OVERTIME HOURS	REASON FOR OVERTIME WORKED

Approved: ______________________________

II. CERTIFICATION OF OVERTIME WORKED

I certify that I worked overtime as shown above.

______________________________ **Signature**

____
Date

EDC 1-085 (11/92)

EDCAL-69 E.D. CALIFORNIA

AUTHORIZATION TO RELEASE INFORMATION TO THE TRUSTEE REGARDING SECURED CLAIMS BEING PAID BY THE TRUSTEE

AUTHORIZATION TO RELEASE INFORMATION TO THE TRUSTEE REGARDING SECURED CLAIMS BEING PAID BY THE TRUSTEE

FILE WITH TRUSTEE ONLY
DO NOT FILE WITH THE COURT

Debtor Name(s): ______________________ Bk Case #: ______________

The debtor(s) in the above captioned bankruptcy case do hereby authorize any and all lien holder(s) on real and personal property of the bankruptcy estate to release information to the standing Trustee (as indicated below) in this bankruptcy filing.

The information to be released includes but is not limited to the amount of the post-petition monthly installment, the annual interest rate and its type, the loan balance, impound accounts, amount of the contractual late charge and the mailing address for payments. This information will only be used by the Trustee and his staff in the administration of the bankruptcy estate and may be included in motions before the Court.

Date: ______________________
Debtor's Signature

Date: ______________________
Joint Debtor's Signature

Standing Trustee (check one):

☐ Jan Johnson
☐ Larry Loheit
☐ Russell Greer
☐ Nelson Enmark
☐ Michael Meyer

EDC.003-087 (Rev. 12/08)

AWARD RECOGNITION

RECOMMENDATION FOR AWARD RECOGNITION

1. Name of nominee: ______________________________

2. Nominee's current title: ______________________________

   Grade/step: ____________ Length of time in position: ____________

3. Date of last award received: ______________________________

   Description of last award: ☐ Special act or service ☐ Suggestion award

   Briefly describe justification for last award recognition:

   ____

   ____

   ____

   ____

   ____

   ____

4. Period of service for which this award is based: ______________________________

5. Attach a description of the service or adopted suggestion and a statement of the resulting benefits derived by the Judiciary.

6. For cash awards, indicate the recommended award dollar amount: ______________

   NOTE: *If this recommendation is for a group award, items 1 through 4 and item 6 must be completed for each nominee.*

7. ______________________________ ____________

   Signature and title of recommending Supervisor Date

8. ______________________________ ____________

   Signature and recommendation ☐ concur ☐ nonconcur of Division Manager Date

   Review committee recommendation: ☐ Concur ☐ Nonconcur Vote ____________

   ______________________________ ____________

   Signature of Chief Deputy Clerk Date

EDC 1-770 (11/92)

EDCAL-71 E.D. CALIFORNIA

BANKRUPTCY APPEAL TRANSMITTAL FORM – TO BAP

THIS FORM IS INTERACTIVE!!

BANKRUPTCY APPEAL TRANSMITTAL FORM

FILED
06/30/10
UNITED STATES BANKRUPTCY COURT
EASTERN DISTRICT OF CALIFORNIA

TO: Bankruptcy Appellate Panel of the Ninth Circuit
125 S. Grand Avenue
Pasadena, CA 91105

FROM: U.S. Bankruptcy Court
Eastern District of California
District Office No. 0972

DATE: 06/30/10

Print Form

Clear Form

Case Name: ______

Bankruptcy No. ______

Adversary No. ______

Reference No. ______

Bankruptcy Judge: ______

Date Notice of Appeal Filed: ______

Date of Entry of Order Appealed From: ______

Date Bankruptcy Filed: ______

Date Notice of Appeal and Notice of Referral of Appeal Mailed to Parties: ______

Filing Fee Paid? (Check One) [ ] Yes [ ] No ______

Please select a division.

- (•) Sacramento
- ( ) Fresno Division
- ( ) Modesto Division

______
Deputy Clerk
U.S. Bankruptcy Court
501 I Street, Suite 3-200
Sacramento, CA 95814-2322
(916) 930-4400

EDC 2-850 (Rev. 1/30/06)

BANKRUPTCY APPEAL TRANSMITTAL FORM – TO DISTRICT COURT

THIS FORM IS INTERACTIVE!!

Is this Certificate addressed to Sacramento or Fresno District Court? Please select one ...

(●) To Sacramento DC

( ) To Fresno DC

BANKRUPTCY APPEAL TRANSMITTAL FORM

TO: U.S. District Court
501 I Street, Suite 4-200
Sacramento, CA 95814
(916) 930-4000

FROM: U.S. Bankruptcy Court
Eastern District of California
District Office No. 0972

FILED
06/30/10
UNITED STATES BANKRUPTCY COURT
EASTERN DISTRICT OF CALIFORNIA

DATE: 06/30/10

Print Form

Clear Form

Case Name: ______________________

Bankruptcy No. ______________________

Adversary No. ______________________

Reference No. ______________________

Bankruptcy Judge: ______________________

Date Notice of Appeal Filed: ______________________

Date of Entry of Order Appealed From: ______________________

Date Bankruptcy Filed: ______________________

Date Notice of Appeal and Notice of Referral of Appeal Mailed to Parties: ______________________

Filing Fee Paid? (Check One) [ ] Yes [ ] No ______________________

Please select a division.

(●) Sacramento

( ) Fresno Division

( ) Modesto Division

____
Deputy Clerk
U.S. Bankruptcy Court
501 I Street, Suite 3-200
Sacramento, CA 95814-2322
(916) 930-4400

EDC 2-851 (Rev. 2/26/09)

BANKRUPTCY COURT MISCELLANEOUS FEE SCHEDULE

BANKRUPTCY COURT MISCELLANEOUS FEE SCHEDULE (28 U.S.C. § 1930)
Effective January 1, 2010

The fees included in the Bankruptcy Court Miscellaneous Fee Schedule are to be charged for services provided by the bankruptcy courts.

- The United States should not be charged fees under this schedule, with the exception of those specifically prescribed in Items 1, 3 and 5 when the information requested is available through remote electronic access.

- Federal agencies or programs that are funded from judiciary appropriations (agencies, organizations, and individuals providing services authorized by the Criminal Justice Act, 18 U.S.C. § 3006A, and bankruptcy administrators) should not be charged any fees under this schedule.

(1) For reproducing any document, $.50 per page. This fee applies to services rendered on behalf of the United States if the document requested is available through electronic access.

(2) For certification of any document, $9. For exemplification of any document, $18.

(3) For reproduction of an audio recording of a court proceeding, $26. This fee applies to services rendered on behalf of the United States if the recording is available electronically

(4) For filing an amendment to the debtor's schedules of creditors, lists of creditors, or mailing list, $26, except:

- The bankruptcy judge may, for good cause, waive the charge in any case.

- This fee must not be charged if -

  - the amendment is to change the address of a creditor or an attorney for a creditor listed on the schedules; or
  - the amendment is to add the name and address of an attorney for a creditor listed on the schedules.

(5) For conducting a search of the bankruptcy court records, $26 per name or item searched. This fee applies to services rendered on behalf of the United States if the information requested is available through electronic access.

(6) For filing a complaint, $250, except:

- If the trustee or debtor-in-possession files the complaint, the fee must be paid only by the estate, to the extent there is an estate.

- This fee must not be charged if -

  - the debtor is the plaintiff; or
  - a child support creditor or representative files the complaint and submits the form required by § 304(g) of the Bankruptcy Reform Act of 1994.

(7) For filing any document that is not related to a pending case or proceeding, $39.

(8) Administrative fee for filing a case under Title 11 or when a motion to divide a joint case under Title 11 is filed, $39.

(9) For payment to trustees pursuant to 11 U.S.C. § 330(b)(2), a $15 fee applies in the following circumstances:

- For filing a petition under Chapter 7.
- For filing a motion to reopen a Chapter 7 case.
- For filing a motion to divide a joint Chapter 7 case.
- For filing a motion to convert a case to a Chapter 7 case.
- For filing a notice of conversion to a Chapter 7.

(10) In addition to any fees imposed under Item 9, above, the following fees must be collected:

- For filing a motion to convert a Chapter 12 case to a Chapter 7 case or a notice of conversion pursuant to 11 U.S.C. § 1208(a), $45.
- For filing a motion to convert a Chapter 13 case to a Chapter 7 case or a notice of conversion pursuant to 11 U.S.C. § 1307(a), $10.

The fee amounts in this item are derived from the fees prescribed in 28 U.S.C. § 1930(a).

If the trustee files the motion to convert, the fee is payable only from the estate that exists prior to conversion.

If the filing fee for the chapter to which the case is requested to be converted is less than the fee paid at the commencement of the case, no refund may be provided.

(11) For filing a motion to reopen, the following fees apply:

- For filing a motion to reopen a Chapter 7 case, $245.
- For filing a motion to reopen a Chapter 9 case, $1000.
- For filing a motion to reopen a Chapter 11 case, $1000.
- For filing a motion to reopen a Chapter 12 case, $200.
- For filing a motion to reopen a Chapter 13 case, $235.
- For filing a motion to reopen a Chapter 15 case, $1000.

The fee amounts in this item are derived from the fees prescribed in 28 U.S.C. § 1930(a).

The reopening fee must be charged when a case has been closed without a discharge being entered.

The court may waive this fee under appropriate circumstances or may defer payment of the fee from trustees pending discovery of additional assets. If payment is deferred, the fee should be waived if no additional assets are discovered.

The reopening fee must not be charged in the following situations:

- to permit a party to file a complaint to obtain a determination under Rule 4007(b); or
- when a debtor files a motion to reopen a case based upon an alleged violation of the terms of the discharge under 11 U.S.C. § 524; or
- when the reopening is to correct an administrative error.

(12) For retrieval of a record from a Federal Records Center, National Archives, or other storage location removed from the place of business of the court, $45.

(13) For a check paid into the court which is returned for lack of funds, $45.

(14) For filing an appeal or cross appeal from a judgment, order or decree, $250.

This fee is collected in addition to the statutory fee of $5 that is collected under 28 U.S.C. § 1930(c) when a notice of appeal is filed.

Parties filing a joint notice of appeal should pay only one fee.

If a trustee or debtor-in-possession is the appellant, the fee must be paid only by the estate, to the extent there is an estate.

Upon notice from the court of appeals that a direct appeal or direct cross appeal has been authorized, an additional fee of $200 must be collected.

(15) For filing a case under Chapter 15 of the Bankruptcy Code, $1000.

This fee is derived from and equal to the fee prescribed in 28 U.S.C. § 1930(a)(3) for filing a case commenced under Chapter 11 of Title 11.

(16) The court may charge and collect fees commensurate with the cost of providing copies of the local rules of court. The court may also distribute copies of the local rules without charge.

(17) The clerk shall assess a charge for the handling of registry funds deposited with the court, to be assessed from interest earnings and in accordance with the detailed fee schedule issued by the Director of the Administrative Office of the United States Courts.

(18) For a motion filed by the debtor to divide a joint case filed under 11 U.S.C. § 302, the following fees apply:

- For filing a motion to divide a joint Chapter 7 case, $245.
- For filing a motion to divide a joint Chapter 11 case, $1000.
- For filing a motion to divide a joint Chapter 12 case, $200.
- For filing a motion to divide a joint Chapter 13 case, $235.

These fees are derived from and equal to the filing fees prescribed in 28 U.S.C. § 1930(a).

(19) For filing the following motions, $150:

- To terminate, annul, modify or condition the automatic stay;
- To compel abandonment of property of the estate pursuant to Rule 6007(b) of the Federal Rules of Bankruptcy Procedure; or
- To withdraw the reference of a case or proceeding under 28 U.S.C. § 157(d).

This fee must not be collected in the following situations:

- For a motion for relief from the co-debtor stay;
- For a stipulation for court approval of an agreement for relief from a stay; or
- For a motion filed by a child support creditor or its representative, if the form required by § 304(g) of the Bankruptcy Reform Act of 1994 is filed.

BATCHING OF CHAPTER 7 CASES FOR ASSIGNMENT TO THE SAME INTERIM TRUSTEE (FRESNO DIVISION) (EFFECTIVE 8/1/05)

UNITED STATES BANKRUPTCY COURT
EASTERN DISTRICT OF CALIFORNIA
FRESNO DIVISION

BATCHING PROCEDURE FOR TRUSTEE ASSIGNMENT BY REGISTERED E-FILERS ONLY

The Fresno Division randomly assigns interim trustees in chapter 7 cases using one of two trustee assignment "pools." The pool used to assign the interim trustee in a particular case is determined by the county of the debtor's residence or principal place of business. The counties falling within each trustee assignment pool are as follows:

Fresno Pool: Fresno, Kings, Madera, Mariposa, Merced, and Tulare counties

Bakersfield Pool: Kern and Inyo counties

Attorneys who are registered e-Filers may request that up to five (5) chapter 7 cases from a given assignment pool be "batched" (assigned to the same trustee). The guidelines applicable to this procedure are as follows:

1. The petitions for all cases in a particular batch must be submitted in a single ".zip" file using the Batch Upload selection for Electronic Case Filing.

2. To avoid potential "trustee shopping" or the appearance of "trustee shopping," an interim trustee must be randomly assigned to the first case entered in the court's automated case intake/financial transaction processing system. The same trustee must then be manually assigned by the cashier to all remaining cases in the batch. For each remaining case, the cashier must indicate that "batching" required manual selection of a trustee, and reference the number of the case in the batch to which the trustee was randomly assigned.

3. The same (or consecutive) 341(a) meeting dates and times will be assigned to batched chapter 7 cases by the automated system whenever possible.

4. Payment for each case in a set of batched cases must be made by credit card.

5. For any case(s) presented for batching where the trustee has previously notified the court in writing of a conflict of interest with certain parties (e.g., family relationships) and that conflict arises on any case(s) appearing on the batch list, that case(s) will be assigned to a non-conflicted trustee and may not be processed as part of the batch.

6. All questions concerning the batching procedure for trustee assignment should be directed to Fresno Division Operations Coordinator Mary Wellington at (559) 499-5856.

EDC 2-051n (Rev. 1/30/06)

BATCHING OF CHAPTER 7 CASES FOR ASSIGNMENT TO THE SAME INTERIM TRUSTEE (SACRAMENTO DIVISION)

UNITED STATES BANKRUPTCY COURT
EASTERN DISTRICT OF CALIFORNIA

BATCHING OF CHAPTER 7 CASES FOR ASSIGNMENT TO THE SAME INTERIM TRUSTEE

The Eastern District of California randomly assigns interim trustees in chapter 7 cases using various trustee assignment "pools." The pool used to assign the interim trustee in a particular case is determined by the county of the debtor's residence or principal place of business. The counties falling within each chapter 7 trustee assignment pool are as follows:

Pool	Counties
East Pool	Alpine, Amador, El Dorado, Mono, Nevada, Placer, Plumas, Sacramento, Sierra, and Yuba
West Pool	Colusa, Sacramento, Solano, Sutter, and Yolo
North Pool	Butte, Glenn, Lassen, Modoc, Shasta, Siskiyou, Tehama, and Trinity
South Pool	San Joaquin
Modesto Pool	Calaveras, Stanislaus, and Tuolumne
Fresno Pool	Fresno, Kings, Madera, Mariposa, Merced, and Tulare
Bakersfield Pool	Kern and Inyo

Attorneys who are registered e-Filers may request that up to five (5) new chapter 7 cases from the same trustee assignment pool be "batched" for assignment to the same interim trustee. The guidelines applicable to this procedure are as follows:

1. The petitions and related documents for all cases in a batch shall be submitted electronically in a single ".zip" file created and uploaded according to the Electronic Filing System's *Chapter 7 Petitions Batched for Trustee Assignment Batch Upload* instructions.

2. To avoid potential "trustee shopping" or the appearance of "trustee shopping," an interim trustee shall be randomly assigned to the first case entered in the court's automated case intake/financial transaction processing system. The same interim trustee shall then be manually assigned by the cashier to all remaining cases in the batch. For each remaining case, the cashier shall indicate that "batching" required manual selection of a trustee, and reference the number of the case in the batch to which the trustee was randomly assigned.

3. The same (or consecutive) 341(a) meeting and time will be assigned by the automated system to batched chapter 7 cases *when possible*, but is **not** guaranteed.

4. Payment for all cases in a batch shall be made by credit card.

5. If the trustee has previously notified the court in writing of a conflict of interest with certain parties (e.g., family relationships) and that conflict arises in any case in the batch, that case will be assigned to a non-conflicted trustee and not processed as part of the batch.

6. The batch limit of five cases **will be strictly enforced**. Batches submitted for filing containing more than five new chapter 7 cases will have each case therein assigned randomly, on an individual case basis.

7. Effective August 2008, cases filed during the last five (5) court days of each month will **not** be eligible for batching for purposes of assignment to the same interim trustee and 341(a) meeting date. Batches of new chapter 7 cases submitted for filing on the last five court days of the month will have each case therein assigned on an individual case-by-case, random basis.

8. Questions concerning the batching of chapter 7 cases for assignment to the same interim trustee shall be directed as follows to the appropriate Operations Coordinator:

Sacramento Division	Modesto Division	Fresno Division
Beverly Door (916) 930-4446	Debby Martin (209) 521-8607	Mary Wellington (559) 499-5856

EDC 2-050 (Rev. 08/11/08)

BDRP PANEL APPLICATION

APPLICATION
UNITED STATES BANKRUPTCY COURT
EASTERN DISTRICT OF CALIFORNIA
BANKRUPTCY DISPUTE RESOLUTION PROGRAM PANEL

Name: ______________________________

Office Address: ______________________________

____
City State Zip

Office Phone: ______________ Office Fax: ______________

ATTORNEY APPLICANTS:

Dates of Admission:
California Bar: __________ (State Bar No. ________)
Eastern District of California: ______________
Other Bars: ______________

List three bankruptcy matters in which you have either:

a. Served as the principal attorney of record (without regard to the party represented) from commencement to conclusion, or date of this application, whichever is earlier; or

b. Served as attorney of record for a party-in-interest in an adversary proceeding or contested matter from commencement through completion (i.e., judgment, order or stipulation).

	Case Title	Case Number	Dates	Representation
1.				
2.				
3.				

OTHER APPLICANTS:

List any professional organization of which you are a member, and the length of your membership.

EDC 3-010 **(General Order 95-1 -- Exhibit A)** (New 5/95) (Front Page)

List any professional licenses you hold. Dates of admission.

List any bankruptcy experience reflecting the requirement that thirty percent (30%) of your practice is devoted to bankruptcy law or debtor/creditor rights during each of the five (5) years immediately preceeding this application your resume may be attached.

FOR ALL APPLICANTS:

List any alternative dispute resolution training, which has qualified for continuing professional education credit or has been approved by a court of competent jurisdiction, that you have completed.

List any state of federal alternative dispute resolution programs in which you have participated and in what capacity.

List other relevant experience, skills, or other information you would like considered in connection with this application:

Cities in which you are willing and available to conduct resolution conferences:

____ Redding ____ Bakersfield
____ Fresno ____ Sacramento
____ Modesto ____ Other (Please specify)
____

I hereby certify that I meet the qualifications set forth in Section 3.4 of General Order No. 95-1, for membership to the Bankruptcy Dispute Resolution Program Panel. I am a member in good standing in the state and federal bar(s) listed above and that the foregoing is true and correct. I consent to disclosure of information contained in this application to parties and their representatives whose matters have been referred to the BDRP and to court personnel.

Dated: ____________ ____________
Signature

BDRP QUESTIONNAIRE

Please select a division.

- ○ Sacramento Division
- ○ Fresno Division
- ⦿ Modesto Division

UNITED STATES BANKRUPTCY COURT
EASTERN DISTRICT OF CALIFORNIA

BANKRUPTCY DISPUTE RESOLUTION PROGRAM QUESTIONNAIRE

Our records indicate that you recently represented a client or yourself in a case that was referred to the Bankruptcy Dispute Resolution Program (BDRP). This is a new program in this District and we need your help to evaluate its effectiveness. Please complete this questionnaire and return it to:

Carlene Walker, Program Coordinator, United States Bankruptcy Court,
United States Courthouse, P.O. Box 5276, Modesto, California 95352.

This information is confidential, will be used solely to evaluate the program, and will not be known to the court, other attorneys, the Resolution Advocate, or the parties. Only aggregate information will be reported.

Case Name:

Case No.: **Chapter No.:**

Proceeding:

Adversary No.:

Resolution Advocate:

A. Evaluating the BDRP Conference OUTCOME

1. As a result of referral to the BDRP, the disputed matter was: ***(Please check all that apply.)***

___ Resolved before the BDRP conference. ***(If so, why?*** **________________________)**
___ Resolved at the BDRP conference.
___ Resolved within approximately one month after the BDRP conference.
___ Not resolved by the BDRP, but it helped us get closer to a resolution of the matter.
___ Not resolved by the BDRP conference and it had little impact on the matter.
___ Not resolved by the BDRP conference and it was detrimental to a resolution of the matter. ***(If so, why?*** **________________________)**

For each statement below, please indicate whether you agree or disagree by circling a number using the following scale.

	Strongly Agree	Agree	Neither	Disagree	Strongly Disagree	N/A
2. A fair settlement was reached as a result of the BDRP conference.	1	2	3	4	5	6
3. I believe the parties will comply with the terms of the settlement reached as a result of the BDRP conference.	1	2	3	4	5	6
4. There was no settlement, but the BDRP conference was helpful; for example, it narrowed or clarified the issues.	1	2	3	4	5	6

5. *Please check any of the following statements below which describe the impact the BDRP conference had on this matter.*

- ___ Enabled the clients to actively participate in the dispute resolution process.
- ___ Enabled the attorneys to actively participate in the dispute resolution process.
- ___ Narrowed the issues in dispute.
- ___ Generated creative settlement options not otherwise considered.
- ___ Hardened positions, making a negotiated outcome more difficult.
- ___ Made me more realistic about the strengths and/or weaknesses of my case.

B. Evaluating the BDRP PROCESS	**Strongly Agree**	**Agree**	**Neither**	**Disagree**	**Strongly Disagree**	**N/A**
6. When this matter was assigned to the BDRP, I was pessimistic about the benefits of mediating this matter.	1	2	3	4	5	6
7. At least one attorney was not adequately prepared for the BDRP conference.	1	2	3	4	5	6
8. At least one party did not participate in good faith in the BDRP conference.	1	2	3	4	5	6
9. At least one attorney did not participate in good faith in the BDRP conference.	1	2	3	4	5	6
10. At least one party did not have sufficient settlement authority.	1	2	3	4	5	6
11. At least one attorney did not have sufficient settlement authority.	1	2	3	4	5	6
12. Additional discovery was needed prior to the BDRP conference.	1	2	3	4	5	6
13. The BDRP conference was too brief to permit a a meaningful discussion of the matter.	1	2	3	4	5	6
14. The BDRP conference helped the parties better express their personal interests, concerns and emotions.	1	2	3	4	5	6
15. The BDRP helped expedite a resolution of the matter.	1	2	3	4	5	6
16. The BDRP helped reduce the cost to litigate the matter.	1	2	3	4	5	6
17. The attempt to resolve this matter through the BDRP (as compared to litigation) helped the parties maintain a continuing relationship	1	2	3	4	5	6
18. I was satisfied with the BDRP.	1	2	3	4	5	6

	1	2	3	4	5	6
19. I would use the BDRP again.	1	2	3	4	5	6

20. Please enter the following dates, using month and year:

   a. Date the issue(s) in dispute originally arose between the parties: __________*(mo/yr)*
   b. Date the bankruptcy case was filed: __________*(mo/yr)*
   c. Date the matter assigned to the BDRP (e.g., the adversary proceeding, motion, etc.) was filed: __________*(mo/yr)*

21. After the matter was assigned to the BDRP, what was the time span (in weeks):

   a. From assignment of the matter to the BDRP to the actual conference: ______*wks*
   b. From the date of the BDRP conference to the settlement, if any, of the matter: ______*wks*
   c. From the date of the conclusion of the BDRP conference to the next court hearing on the matter, if any: ______*wks*

C. **Evaluating the RESOLUTION ADVOCATE**	Strongly **Agree**	Agree	Neither	Disagree	**Strongly Disagree**	**N/A**
22. The Resolution Advocate was adequately prepared to discuss the matter.	1	2	3	4	5	6
23. The Resolution Advocate was effective in getting the clients to engage in meaningful discussion of the matter.	1	2	3	4	5	6
24. The Resolution Advocate was effective in getting the attorneys to engage in meaningful discussion of the matter.	1	2	3	4	5	6
25. The Resolution Advocate was fair and impartial.	1	2	3	4	5	6
26. The Resolution Advocate adequately informed me about the purpose of the BDRP conference and my responsibilities.	1	2	3	4	5	6
27. When the Resolution Advocate was selected, I was confident in the Resolution Advocate's abilities.	1	2	3	4	5	6
28. I would use this Resolution Advocate again.	1	2	3	4	5	6
29. I was satisfied with the process used to select the Resolution Advocate.	1	2	3	4	5	6

30. Who selected the Resolution Advocate?
   ____ Judge appointed ____ Parties stipulated ____ Other *(Selected by whom?* __________)

D. Information about YOU

31. If you **represented yourself**, what was your role?:

___Debtor
___Creditor
___Secured
___Unsecured
___Trustee
___Other (Specify: ____________________)

32. If you were the **attorney** for a party, whom did you represent?

___Debtor
___Creditor
___Secured
___Unsecured
___Trustee
___Other (Specify: ____________________)

33. Prior to the BDRP conference of this matter, had you participated in an alternate dispute program for any dispute other than this one? (Answer is not limited to the Bankruptcy Dispute Resolution Program.)
___Never ___ 1-3 times ___ 4-10 times ___ More than 10 times

E. Additional COMMENTS

34. Your comments about your Resolution Advocate and suggestions for improvements to the Bankruptcy Resolution Dispute Program will be appreciated. *(Please write your comments below or attach a separate page).*

Please return your completed questionnaire to:

Carlene Walker, Program Coordinator, United States Bankruptcy Court, United States Courthouse, P.O. Box 5276, Modesto, California 95352.

THANK YOU!

BILL FOR NOTICE FEES

UNITED STATES BANKRUPTCY COURT
EASTERN DISTRICT OF CALIFORNIA

FILED
06/30/10
UNITED STATES BANKRUPTCY COURT
EASTERN DISTRICT OF CALIFORNIA

In re	)	Case No.
	)	
Debtor(s).	)	

BILL FOR NOTICE FEES

Date of Notice	Type of Notice	No. of Notices	Amount Due

TO: DEBTOR AND DEBTOR'S ATTORNEY

Pursuant to 28 U.S.C. section 1930(b) and the Judicial Conference Schedule of Fees, the above indicated amount is owed to the Clerk, U.S.Bankruptcy Court.

This bill is due within twenty (20) days of the date indicated below. Payment should be directed to the attention of the Financial Administrator and mailed to the Office of the Clerk, U.S. Bankruptcy Court, 501 I Street, Suite 3-200, Sacramento, CA 95814-2322. Payment may also be made by presenting a copy of this bill at the Clerk's Office public counter at the address indicated above.

Please note that **THIS IS THE ONLY BILL YOU WILL RECEIVE**. Failure to remit the amount due or seek an extension of time for payment within the time required will result in the Court's issuing a Notice of Intent to Dismiss Case for failure to pay notice fees, copies of which will be sent to creditors and other interested parties.

For your own protection, do not send cash through the mail. Kindly provide your payment by check or money order attached to a copy of this bill. Checks must be either a cashier's check, certified check or a preprinted check drawn on an attorney trust account. PERSONAL CHECKS WILL NOT BE ACCEPTED. Checks and money orders are to be made payable to "Clerk, U.S. Bankruptcy Court" and to insure proper credit to your account, should contain the case number indicated above.

Questions concerning this bill should be directed to the Financial Administrator at (916) 930-4472.

DATED: **06/30/10**

FOR THE COURT

RICHARD G. HELTZEL
CLERK, U.S. BANKRUPTCY COURT

By: ______________________________
Deputy Clerk

Original has Certificate of Mailing attached (EDC 3-070)

Print Form

Clear Form

Copy Distribution:

_____ **DEBTOR**

_____ **DEBTOR'S ATTORNEY**

_____ **APPOINTED TRUSTEE**

_____ **FINANCIAL ADMINISTRATOR**

EDC.004-040 (Rev. 5/8/00)

EDCAL-85 E.D. CALIFORNIA

CERTIFICATE OF RECORD TO BAP RE: BANKRUPTCY CASES

FILED

UNITED STATES BANKRUPTCY COURT
EASTERN DISTRICT OF CALIFORNIA

UNITED STATES BANKRUPTCY COURT
EASTERN DISTRICT OF CALIFORNIA

In re	)	Bankruptcy Appellate Panel No.
	)	
	)	
	)	Bankruptcy Court Case No.
	)	
	)	
Debtor(s).	)	Docket Control No.

CERTIFICATE OF RECORD

The undersigned Deputy Clerk of the U.S. Bankruptcy Court for the Eastern District of California, certifies pursuant to Rule 4(a) of the Rules of the U.S. Bankruptcy Appellate Panel for the Ninth Circuit, that the record with respect to the above-captioned matter is complete for purposes of appeal. Pursuant to Fed.R.Bankr.P. 8007(b), the original record will be retained by this court. Excerpts of the record, including transcripts, shall be filed and served with briefs as an appendix, pursuant to Fed.R. Bankr.P. 8009(d).

Dated:

FOR THE COURT
RICHARD G. HELTZEL, CLERK

Please select a division.

- ○ Sacramento Division
- ○ Fresno Division
- ⊙ Modesto Division

U.S. Bankruptcy Court
1200 I Street, Suite 4
P.O. Box 5276
Modesto, CA 95352-5276
(209) 521-5160

By:________________________
Deputy Clerk

Print Form

Clear Form

EDC 2-077 (New 02/29/00)

CERTIFICATE OF RECORD TO BAP/DISTRICT COURT RE: ADVERSARY PROCEEDINGS

THIS FORM IS INTERACTIVE!!

Is this Certificate addressed to BAP or District Court? Please select one ...

○ To BAP

⦿ To District Court

UNITED STATES BANKRUPTCY COURT
EASTERN DISTRICT OF CALIFORNIA

FILED
06/30/10
UNITED STATES BANKRUPTCY COURT
EASTERN DISTRICT OF CALIFORNIA

In re	District Court Case No.
Debtor(s).	Bankruptcy Court Case No.
	Adversary Proceeding No.
Plaintiff(s),	
v.	Docket Control No.
Defendant(s).	

CERTIFICATE OF RECORD TO DISTRICT COURT RE: ADVERSARY PROCEEDINGS

The undersigned Deputy Clerk of the U.S. Bankruptcy Court for the Eastern District of California, certifies that the record with respect to the above-captioned matter is complete for purposes of appeal. Pursuant to Fed.R.Bankr.P. 8007(b), the original record will be retained by this court. Excerpts of the record, including transcripts, shall be filed and served with briefs as an appendix, pursuant to Fed.R. Bankr.P. 8009(b).

Dated: 06/30/10

FOR THE COURT
RICHARD G. HELTZEL, CLERK

Please select a division.

○ Sacramento Division

○ Fresno Division

⦿ Modesto Division

U.S. Bankruptcy Court
1200 I Street, Suite 4
P.O. Box 5276
Modesto, CA 95352-5276
(209) 521-5160

By:______________________
Deputy Clerk

Print Form

Clear Form

EDC 2-075 (New 01/30/06)

CERTIFICATE OF RECORD TO DISTRICT COURT RE: BANKRUPTCY CASES

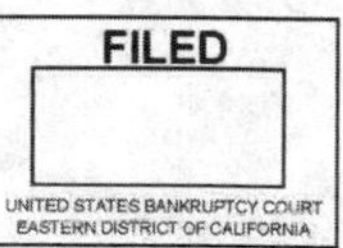

UNITED STATES BANKRUPTCY COURT
EASTERN DISTRICT OF CALIFORNIA

In re	)	District Court Case No.
	)	
	)	
	)	Bankruptcy Court Case No.
	)	
	)	Docket Control No.
Debtor(s).	)	

CERTIFICATE OF RECORD TO DISTRICT COURT RE: BANKRUPTCY CASES

The undersigned Deputy Clerk of the U.S. Bankruptcy Court for the Eastern District of California, certifies that the record with respect to the above-captioned matter is complete for purposes of appeal. Pursuant to Fed.R.Bankr.P. 8007(b), the original record will be retained by this court. Excerpts of the record, including transcripts, shall be filed and served with briefs as an appendix, pursuant to Fed.R. Bankr.P. 8009(d).

Dated:

Please select a division.

- (•) Sacramento Division
- ( ) Fresno Division
- ( ) Modesto Division

FOR THE COURT
RICHARD G. HELTZEL, CLERK

U.S. Bankruptcy Court
501 I Street, Suite 3-200
Sacramento, CA 95814-2322
(916) 930-4400

By:__________________________
Deputy Clerk

Print Form

Clear Form

EDC 2-078 (New 03/23/00)

CERTIFICATE RE: BDRP

UNITED STATES BANKRUPTCY COURT
EASTERN DISTRICT OF CALIFORNIA

In re:	)	
	)	Bankruptcy Case No.
Debtor(s).	)	
Plaintiff(s),	)	
vs.	)	Adversary Proceeding No.
Defendant(s).	)	

CERTIFICATE RE: BDRP CONFERENCE

1. I hereby certify that pursuant to an order of assignment by this Court to the Bankruptcy Dispute Resolution Program dated ______________________, a BDRP Conference was ____/was not____ held.

(If Applicable)

Date:____________________________

Continued Dated: ___________________

2. A settlement of this matter was ____/was not ____ reached.

Dated: ____________

____
Resolution Advocate

____
(Type or Print Name)

EDCAL-89

E.D. CALIFORNIA

CERTIFICATION OF SERVICE OF SUMMONS AND NOTICE OF STATUS CONFERENCE AND COMPLAINT

UNITED STATES BANKRUPTCY COURT
EASTERN DISTRICT OF CALIFORNIA
SACRAMENTO DIVISION

In re	)	
	)	*Bankruptcy Case No.*
	)	
____________ *Debtor(s).*	)	
	)	
	)	
Plaintiff(s),	)	
v.	)	*Adversary Proceeding No.*
	)	
	)	
____________ *Defendant(s).*	)	

CERTIFICATION OF SERVICE OF SUMMONS AND NOTICE OF STATUS CONFERENCE AND COMPLAINT

I, the undersigned, certify that I am, and at all times hereinafter mentioned was, not less than 18 years of age and not a party to the above-captioned matter. I further certify that I served the attached Summons and Notice Status Conference in an Adversary Proceeding, together with a copy of the complaint, as follows:

Service was made on ______________, 19____, by:

___ *MAIL SERVICE:* Regular, first class United States mail, postage fully pre-paid, addressed to:

___ *PERSONAL SERVICE:* By leaving the process with defendant or with an officer or agent of defendant at:

___ *RESIDENCE SERVICE:* By leaving the process with the following adult at:

___ *PUBLICATION:* The defendant was served as follows *[describe briefly]*:

___ STATE LAW: The defendant was served pursuant to the laws of __________, as follows *[describe briefly]*:

Under penalty of perjury, I declare that the foregoing is true and correct.

Dated:

Signature: ____________________

Print Name: ____________________

Address: ____________________

____

EDC 2-080 (New 2/98)

Chapter 7 Statement of Current Monthly Income and Means Test Calculation

UNITED STATES BANKRUPTCY COURT
EASTERN DISTRICT OF CALIFORNIA

Name of Debtor: Case No.

Last four digits of Soc. Sec. No.:
Last four digits of Soc. Sec. No.:

CHAPTER 13 PLAN
☐ MOTION(S) TO VALUE COLLATERAL AND ☐ MOTION(S) TO AVOID LIENS
[check if motion(s) appended]

THIS PLAN AND THESE MOTIONS WILL BE CONSIDERED FOR CONFIRMATION AND APPROVAL AT A COURT HEARING. YOU WILL BE NOTIFIED OF THE HEARING DATE, TIME, LOCATION, AND THE DEADLINE FOR FILING AND SERVING WRITTEN OBJECTIONS. IN THE ABSENCE OF A TIMELY OBJECTION, THE COURT MAY DISPENSE WITH THE HEARING.

Debtor proposes the following Chapter 13 Plan effective from the date it is confirmed:

Section I. Summary of Relevant Financial Information

1.01. Annualized current monthly income under section 1325(b)(4), Line 15, Statement of Current Monthly Income and Calculation of Commitment Period and Disposable Income ("Statement of CMI").	$
1.02. Annualized current monthly income under section 1325(b)(3), Line 21, Statement of CMI.	$
1.03. Applicable median family income, Line 16, Statement of CMI.	$
1.04. Monthly net income from Line 20c of Schedule J.	$
1.05. ***check applicable box and insert appropriate dollar amount*** ☐ If annualized current monthly income is greater than applicable median family income, projected monthly disposable income from Line 58 Statement of CMI. *- or -* ☐ If annualized current monthly income is equal to or less than applicable median family income, projected monthly disposable income calculated without reference to section 707(b)(2)(A) & (B).	$
1.06. The amount entered at section 1.05 multiplied by the commitment period (section 2.03).	$
1.07. The total amount that would be paid to unsecured, nonpriority claims if the estate of Debtor were liquidated under chapter 7 of the Bankruptcy Code.	$

Section II. Plan Payments and Commitment Period
[If sections 2.01, 2.02, or 2.03 are blank, refer to the "Additional Provisions" below.]

2.01. Payments from earnings. To complete this plan, Debtor shall submit to the supervision and control of Trustee on a monthly basis a portion of Debtor's future earnings. Debtor shall pay to Trustee the sum of $__________ each month. The monthly plan payment is subject to adjustment pursuant to section 3.10(d) below. Monthly plan payments must be received by Trustee not later than the 25th day of each month beginning the month after the petition is filed. The monthly plan payment includes all monthly contract installments due on Class 1 secured claims and adequate protection payments due on certain Class 2 secured claims, if any.

2.02. Other payments. In addition to the submission of future earnings, Debtor will make monthly payment(s) derived from property of the bankruptcy estate, property of Debtor, or from other sources, as follows: ________________
____.

2.03. Commitment period. The monthly plan payments will continue for ____ months, the commitment period of the plan. Monthly plan payments must continue for the entire commitment period unless all allowed unsecured claims are paid in full over a shorter period of time. If necessary to complete this plan, Debtor may make monthly payments for up to 6 months beyond the commitment period, but in no event shall monthly payments continue for more than 60 months.

Section III. Claims and Expenses

A. Proofs of Claim

3.01. A timely proof of claim must be filed by or on behalf of a creditor, including a secured creditor, before a claim may be paid pursuant to this plan.

3.02. Notwithstanding section 3.01, monthly contract installments falling due after the filing of the petition shall be paid to holders of Class 1 and Class 4 claims whether or not they have filed proofs of claim or the plan is confirmed.

3.03. Post-petition amounts due on account of domestic support obligations, loans from retirement or thrift savings plans of the types described in section 362(b)(19), and executory contracts and unexpired leases to be assumed shall be paid by Debtor directly to the person or entity entitled to receive such payments whether or not a proof of claim is filed or the plan is confirmed.

3.04. The proof of claim, not this plan or the schedules, shall determine the amount and classification of a claim. If a claim is provided for by this plan and a proof of claim is filed, dividends shall be paid based upon the proof of claim unless the granting of a valuation or a lien avoidance motion, or the sustaining of a claim objection, affects the amount or classification of the claim.

B. Administrative Expenses

3.05. Trustee's fees. Pursuant to 28 U.S.C. § 586(e), Trustee shall receive up to 10% of plan payments, whether made before or after confirmation but excluding direct payments on Class 4 claims.

3.06. Fees of former chapter 7 trustee. Payment of compensation of the type described in section 1326(b)(3) shall be limited to the greater of $25, or 5% of the amount payable to nonpriority unsecured creditors divided by the commitment period, each month for the duration of the plan.

3.07. Administrative expenses. Except to the extent the court approves, and the claimant agrees to, a different treatment, and unless section 1326(b)(3)(B) is applicable, approved administrative expenses shall be paid in full through the plan.

3.08. Debtor's attorney's fees. Debtor paid an attorney $____________ prior to the filing of the petition. Any additional fees the court may approve shall be paid in full through this plan. Debtor estimates that a further $__________ in attorney's fees will be incurred throughout this case.

C. Secured Claims

3.09. Class 1. Long-term secured claims that were delinquent when the petition was filed and mature after the last payment under the plan. This plan will cure all pre-petition arrears but not otherwise modify Class 1 claims. Each claimant will retain its existing lien and receive no less than the equal monthly amount specified below as its plan dividend. Trustee also shall pay all post-petition monthly contract installments falling due on each Class 1 claim.

Class 1 Creditor's Name/ Collateral Description	Monthly Contract Installment	Monthly Late charge	Pre-petition Arrears	Interest Rate	Monthly Dividend
1.					
2.					
3.					

3.10. Monthly contract installments paid by Trustee on Class 1 claims. (a) If Debtor makes a partial plan payment that is insufficient to pay all monthly contract installments due on Class 1 claims, these installments will be paid in the order Debtor has listed Class 1 claims above. **(b)** Trustee will not make a partial payment on account of a monthly contract installment. **(c)** If Debtor makes a partial plan payment, or if it is not paid on time, and Trustee is unable to pay timely a monthly contract installment due on a Class 1 claim, Debtor's cure of this default must be accompanied by the applicable late charge(s). **(d)** Upon their receipt, Debtor shall mail or deliver to Trustee all notices from Class 1 creditors including, without limitation, statements, payment coupons, impound and escrow notices, default notifications, and notices concerning changes of the interest rate on variable interest rate loans. The automatic stay is modified to permit the sending of such notices. Prior to mailing or delivering any such notice to Trustee, Debtor shall affix the chapter 13 case number to it. If any such notice advises Debtor that the amount of the contract installment payment has increased or decreased, the plan payment shall be adjusted accordingly.

3.11. Class 2. Secured claims that are modified by this plan, or that have matured or will mature before the plan is completed. Each Class 2 claim will be paid in full, retain its existing lien, and receive no less than the equal monthly amount specified below as its plan dividend. The amount of a Class 2 claim shall be the amount due under any contract between Debtor and the claimant or under applicable nonbankruptcy law, or, if section 506(a) is applicable, the value of the collateral securing the claim, whichever is less. Section 506(a) is not applicable if the claim is secured by a purchase money security interest and **(a)** was incurred within 910 days of the filing of the petition and is secured by a motor vehicle acquired for the personal use of Debtor, or **(b)** the claim was incurred within 1-year of the filing of the petition and is secured by any other thing of value.

Class 2 Creditor's Name/ Collateral Description	Purchase Money Security Interest? Y/N	Is Claim Subject to § 506(a)? Y/N	Claim Amount	Interest Rate	Monthly Dividend
1.					
2.					
3.					

3.12. Adequate protection payments. Prior to confirmation, Trustee shall pay on account of each allowed Class 2 claim secured by a purchase money security interest in personal property an adequate protection payment as required by section 1326(a)(1)(C). This adequate protection payment shall be the equal monthly amount proposed by this plan as the dividend for each Class 2 claim. Adequate protection payments shall be disbursed by Trustee in connection with his customary month end disbursement cycle beginning the month after the petition is filed. If a Class 2 claimant is paid a monthly adequate protection payment, that claimant shall not be paid a monthly dividend after confirmation for the same month.

3.13. Post-petition interest shall accrue on Class 1 and 2 claims at the above rates. If the plan specifies a "0%" rate, no interest will accrue. However, if the provision for interest is left blank, interest at the rate of 10% per year will accrue.

3.14. Class 3. Secured claims satisfied by the surrender of collateral. Entry of the confirmation order shall constitute an order modifying the automatic stay to allow the holder of a Class 3 secured claim to repossess, receive, take possession of, foreclose upon, and exercise its rights and judicial and nonjudicial remedies against its collateral.

Class 3 Creditor's Name/Collateral Description	Estimated Deficiency	Is Deficiency a Priority Claim? Y/N
1.		
2.		

3.15. Class 4. Secured claims paid directly by Debtor or third party. Class 4 claims mature after the completion of this plan, are not in default, and are not modified by this plan. These claims shall be paid by Debtor or a third person whether or not the plan is confirmed. Entry of the confirmation order shall constitute an order modifying the automatic stay to allow the holder of a Class 4 secured claim to exercise its rights against its collateral in the event of a default under the terms of its loan or security documentation provided this case is then pending under chapter 13.

Class 4 Creditor's Name	Monthly Contract Installment	Maturity Date
1.		
2.		

3.16. Secured claims not listed as Class 1, 2, 3, or 4 claims are not provided for by this plan. The failure to provide for a secured claim in one of these classes may be cause to terminate the automatic stay.

<u>D. Unsecured Claims</u>

3.17. Class 5. Unsecured claims entitled to priority pursuant to section 507 shall be paid in full except as provided in section 3.18.

Class 5 Creditor's Name	Type of Priority	Claim Amount
1.		
2.		
3.		

3.18. If the holder of a priority claim has agreed to accept less than payment in full, or if this plan will not pay a priority claim of the type described in section 1322(a)(4) in full, the identity of the claim holder and the treatment proposed shall be included in the Additional Provisions below. The failure to provide a treatment for a priority claim that complies with sections 1322(a)(2) or 1322(a)(4) is a breach of this plan.

3.19. Class 6. Special unsecured claims. This class includes unsecured claims, such as co-signed unsecured debts, that will be paid in full even though all other unsecured claims may not be paid in full.

Class 6 Creditor's Name	Reason for Special Treatment	Claim Amount
1.		
2.		

3.20. Class 7. General unsecured claims. Claims not listed as Class 5 or 6 claims, and that are not secured by property belonging to Debtor, will receive no less than a __________% dividend pursuant to this plan. Debtor estimates that general unsecured claims, including the under-collateralized portion of secured claims not entitled to priority, total $__________.

Section IV. Executory Contracts And Unexpired Leases

4.01. Debtor assumes the executory contracts and unexpired leases listed below. Debtor shall pay directly to the other party to the executory contract or unexpired lease, before and after confirmation, all post-petition payments. Unless a different treatment is required by section 365(b)(1) (which such treatment shall be set out in the Additional Provisions) any pre-petition arrears shall be paid in full either as a Class 1 or a Class 6 claim.

4.02. Any executory contract or unexpired lease not listed in the table below is rejected. Entry of the confirmation order modifies the automatic stay to allow the nondebtor party to a rejected unexpired lease to obtain possession of leased property.

Name of Other Party to Executory Contract or Unexpired Lease	Pre-petition Arrears	Regular Payment	Will Arrears Be Paid as a Class 1 or 6 Claim?
1.			
2.			

Section V. Payment of Claims and Order of Payment

5.01. After confirmation of this plan, funds available for distribution will be paid monthly by Trustee to holders of allowed claims and approved expenses.

5.02. Distribution of plan payment. Each month, the plan payments (see sections 2.01 and 2.02) must equal at least the aggregate of: **(a)** Trustee's fees; **(b)** any monthly contract installments due on Class 1 claims; **(c) $** __________for administrative expenses described in section 3.06, 3.07, and 3.08, distributed between administrative claimants as specified in section 5.03; and **(d)** the monthly dividends specified above for Class 1 arrearage claims and Class 2 secured claims. To the extent the plan payments are not needed to pay contract installments on Class 1 claims, approved administrative expenses, Class 1 arrearage claims, or Class 2 secured claims, they shall be distributed on a pro rata basis first to Class 5 priority claims, second to holders of Class 6 unsecured claims, and third to Class 7 unsecured claims.

5.03. Priority of payment among administrative expenses. The portion of the monthly plan payment allocated in section 5.02 for administrative expenses of the types described in section 3.06, 3.07, and 3.08 shall be distributed first on account of the monthly dividend due to a former chapter 7 trustee pursuant to section 3.06, then to holders of administrative expenses described in sections 3.07 and 3.08 on a pro rata basis.

5.04. Distributions on account of a Class 1, 2, 5, 6, or 7 allowed claim will be based upon the claim as demanded in the proof of claim rather than as estimated and characterized by this plan except to the extent the disposition of a claim objection, motion to value collateral, or lien avoidance motion requires otherwise.

Section VI. Miscellaneous Provisions

6.01. Vesting of property. Any property of the estate scheduled under section 521 shall [*choose one*] [ ] revest in Debtor on confirmation or [ ] not revest in Debtor until such time as a discharge is granted. In the event the case is converted to a case under Chapter 7, 11, or 12 of the Bankruptcy Code or is dismissed, the property of the estate shall be determined in accordance with applicable law.

6.02. Debtor's duties. In addition to the duties imposed upon Debtor by the Bankruptcy Code and Rules, the Local Bankruptcy Rules, and General Order 05-03, this plan imposes the following additional requirements on Debtor: **(a) Transfers of property and new debt.** Debtor is prohibited from transferring, encumbering, selling, or otherwise disposing of any personal or real property with a value of $1,000 or more other than in the regular course of Debtor's financial or business affairs without first obtaining court authorization. Except as provided in sections 364 and 1304, Debtor shall not incur aggregate new debt exceeding $1,000 without first obtaining court authorization. If Trustee approves a proposed transfer or new debt, court approval may be obtainable without a hearing. To determine the appropriate procedure, Debtor should consult the General Order. A new consumer debt of less than $1,000 shall not be paid through this plan absent compliance with sections 1305(c). **(b) Insurance.** Debtor shall maintain insurance as required by any law or contract and Debtor shall provide evidence of that insurance as required by section 1326(a)(4). **(c) Compliance with applicable non-bankruptcy law.** Debtor's financial and business affairs shall be conducted in accordance with applicable non-bankruptcy law including the timely filing of tax returns and payment of taxes. **(d) Periodic reports.** Upon Trustee's request, Debtor shall provide Trustee with a copy of any tax return, W-2 form, and 1099 form filed or received while the case is pending, and furnish Trustee with quarterly financial information regarding Debtor's business or financial affairs. **(e) Documents required by Trustee.** Debtor shall provide to Trustee not later than the 15 days after the filing of the petition with written notice of the name and address of each person to whom Debtor owes a domestic support obligation together with the name and address of the relevant State child support enforcement agency [see 42 U.S.C. §§ 464 & 466], and a Class 1 Worksheet and Authorization to Release Information for each Class 1 claim.

6.03. Remedies on default. If Debtor defaults under this plan, or if the plan will not be completed within six months of its stated term, not to exceed 60 months, Trustee or any other party in interest may request appropriate relief by filing a motion and setting it for hearing pursuant to Local Bankruptcy Rule 9014-1. This relief may consist of, without limitation, dismissal of the case, conversion of the case to chapter 7, or relief from the automatic stay to pursue rights against collateral. If, on motion of a creditor, the court terminates the automatic stay to permit a creditor holding a Class 1 or 2 secured claim to proceed against its collateral, unless the court orders otherwise, Trustee shall make no further plan payments on account of such secured claim, any portion of the secured claim not previously satisfied under this plan shall be satisfied as a Class 3 claim, and any deficiency remaining after the disposition of the collateral shall be satisfied as a Class 7 unsecured claim provided a timely proof of claim or amended proof of claim is filed and served on Debtor and Trustee.

Section VII. Additional Provisions

7.01. Other than to insert text into the designated spaces, to expand the tables to include additional claims, or to change the title to indicate the plan is a modified plan, the preprinted language of this form shall not be altered. This does not mean that Debtor is prohibited from proposing additional or different plan provisions. As long as consistent with the Bankruptcy Code, Debtor may propose additional or different plan provisions or specify that any of the above provisions will not be applicable. Each such provision or deletion shall be set out on a separate page and shall be identified by a section number (7.02, 7.03, etc.).

Dated: ______________________

Debtor

____

Joint Debtor

ATTACHMENT M-1

Optional – Discard if not used

MOTIONS TO AVOID JUDICIAL LIENS ON DEBTOR'S RESIDENCE (OR OTHER QUALIFIED EXEMPT PROPERTY)

(Pursuant to 11 U.S.C. § 522(f)(1)(A))

(A separate motion must be used to avoid each lien)
NUMBER OF MOTIONS TO AVOID JUDICIAL LIENS IN THIS PLAN: __

NOTICE IS HEREBY GIVEN that Debtor moves to avoid the following judicial lien on Debtor's residence (or other exempt property) pursuant to 11 U.S.C. § 522(f)(1)(A) and to treat the claim secured by such lien as a general unsecured claim. If granted, the claim of the creditor named below will be treated as a general unsecured claim (Class 7).

Name of the creditor holding the judicial lien that is the subject of this motion:

Address of residence or description of other qualified exempt property:

Debtor's opinion of the exempt property's "replacement value"
[as defined and limited by section 506(a)(2)]: $

Amount of the exemption claimed by Debtor: $
Amount of the creditor's judgment: $
The amount owed to and the name of all creditors holding liens or security interests that cannot be avoided pursuant to section 522(f)(1)(A):

Name of Creditor	Amount of Claim

This judicial lien does not secure a domestic support obligation.

Other information relevant to the resolution of this motion:

I (we) declare under penalty of perjury under the laws of the State of California that the foregoing is true and correct.

Dated:

____
Debtor

____
Joint Debtor

CHANGE OF ADDRESS (CAE)

Change of Address

Re: Case No. ______________________________

Name: ______________________________

- ☐ Debtor(s)
- ☐ Husband Only
- ☐ Wife Only
- ☐ Attorney
- ☐ Creditor

NEW ADDRESS:

PHONE NUMBER: ______________________

OLD ADDRESS:

SIGNATURE: ______________________________

____

EDC 2-085 (Rev. 3/29/99)

CHAPTER 12 – DESIGNATION OF TRUSTEE AND NOTICE OF SELECTION (FRESNO AND MODESTO DIVISIONS)

FILED
06/30/10
UNITED STATES BANKRUPTCY COURT
EASTERN DISTRICT OF CALIFORNIA

THIS FORM IS INTERACTIVE!!

UNITED STATES BANKRUPTCY COURT
EASTERN DISTRICT OF CALIFORNIA
FRESNO DIVISION

In re) Case No.

Debtor(s).

DESIGNATION OF TRUSTEE AND NOTICE OF SELECTION

Standing Chapter 12 Trustee **M. Nelson Enmark** is hereby designated Trustee of the above-named Debtor's(s') estate. The Standing Chapter 12 Trustee has filed a blanket bond pursuant to Federal Federal Rule of Bankruptcy Procedure 2010(a).

If the Standing Chapter 12 Trustee does not notify the Office of the United States Trustee and the Court in writing of rejection of the office within five days after receipt of notice of selection, the Standing Chapter 12 Trustee shall be deemed to have accepted the office.

Dated: **06/30/10**

Print Form
Clear Form

Office of the United States Trustee
Region 17 -- Fresno Office

Sara L. Kistler
United States Trustee

EDC-UST 102-F

CHAPTER 12 – DESIGNATION OF TRUSTEE AND NOTICE

UNITED STATES BANKRUPTCY COURT
EASTERN DISTRICT OF CALIFORNIA

FILED
06/30/10
UNITED STATES BANKRUPTCY COURT
EASTERN DISTRICT OF CALIFORNIA

THIS FORM IS INTERACTIVE!!

In re)
)
) Case No.
)
)
Debtor(s).)

DESIGNATION OF TRUSTEE AND NOTICE OF SELECTION

Standing Chapter 12 Trustee Lawrence J. Loheit is hereby designated Trustee of the above-named Debtor's(s') estate. The Standing Chapter 12 Trustee has filed a blanket bond pursuant to Federal Rule of Bankruptcy Procedure 2010(a).

If the Standing Chapter 12 Trustee does not notify the Office of the United States Trustee and the Court in writing of rejection of the office within five days after receipt of notice of selection, the Standing Chapter 12 Trustee shall be deemed to have accepted the office.

Dated: **06/30/10**

Print Form

Clear Form

Office of the United States Trustee
Region 17 -- Sacramento Office

Sara L. Kistler
United States Trustee

Antonia G. Darling
Assistant United States Trustee

EDC-UST 102-SM

CHAPTER 13 DEBTOR'S PLAN AND ATTACHMENTS (FOR USE IN CHAPTER 13 CASES FILED ON OR AFTER 7/1/03 OR CONVERTED TO CHAPTER 13 ON OR AFTER 7/1/03)

UNITED STATES BANKRUPTCY COURT
EASTERN DISTRICT OF CALIFORNIA

In re:) Case No.
)
) DC No.
)
Debtor.)
_______________________________)

CHAPTER 13 PLAN
[ ] MOTION(S) TO VALUE COLLATERAL AND
[ ] MOTION(S) TO AVOID LIENS
[check if motion(s) included]

THIS PLAN AND ANY MOTIONS INCLUDED WITH IT MAY BE APPROVED BY THE COURT WITHOUT A HEARING UNLESS AN OBJECTION IS FILED, SERVED, AND SET FOR HEARING BY A CREDITOR OR THE TRUSTEE. ANY OBJECTION MUST BE FILED AND SERVED UPON DEBTOR, DEBTOR'S ATTORNEY, AND TRUSTEE NOT LATER THAN 14 DAYS AFTER THE CONCLUSION OF THE MEETING HELD PURSUANT TO 11 U.S.C. § 341(a). A HEARING ON ANY OBJECTION MUST BE SET BY THE OBJECTOR ON THE EARLIEST AVAILABLE COURT DATE CONSISTENT WITH GIVING NOTICE PURSUANT TO LOCAL BANKRUPTCY RULE 9014-1(f)(1). THE COURT'S SELF-SET HEARING RULES AND PROCEDURES ARE AVAILABLE ON THE COURT'S INTERNET SITE, WWW.CAEB.USCOURTS.GOV, AND AT ITS PUBLIC COUNTERS.

CHAPTER 13 PLAN

Debtor proposes the following Chapter 13 Plan effective from the date of the petition:

I. Plan Payments and Term

In order to complete this plan, the future projected disposable income of Debtor shall be submitted to the supervision and control of the Chapter 13 Trustee on a monthly basis. Debtor shall pay to Trustee the sum of $_________ each month which includes an amount equal to all monthly contract installments due to Class 1 secured claim holders, if any. This plan will continue for ________ months. Unless all allowed unsecured claims are paid in full, the plan shall not terminate earlier than the stated term or 36 months, whichever is longer. If necessary to complete this plan, the term shall be extended up to 6 months, but the plan may not exceed 60 months in length. [*If any of the foregoing is left blank, refer to the "Additional Provisions" below.*]

II. Classification and Treatment of Claims and Expenses

Claims and expenses owed by Debtor are classified and provided for below. A timely proof of claim must be filed by or on behalf of a creditor, including a secured creditor, before a claim may be paid pursuant to this plan. However, monthly contract installments falling due after the filing of the petition shall be paid to each holder of a Class 1 and Class 4 secured claim whether or not a proof of claim is filed or the plan is confirmed.

The proof of claim, not the plan or the schedules, shall determine the amount and classification of a claim. If a claim is provided for by this plan and a proof of claim is filed, dividends shall be paid based upon the proof of claim unless the granting of a valuation or a lien avoidance motion, or the sustaining of a claim objection, affects the amount or classification of the claim. Secured claims not listed within Classes 1, 2, 3, or 4, and priority claims not listed within Class 5 are not provided for by the plan.

A. Administrative Expenses

1. Chapter 13 Trustee's fees shall be allowed and paid as determined by statute. Trustee may receive up to 10% of payments made under this plan, whether made before or after confirmation, excluding direct payments on account of Class 4 claims.

2. Administrative Expenses: Unless otherwise ordered or the administrative claimant agrees to a different treatment, court approved administrative expenses, including Debtor's attorney's fees, shall be paid after Trustee's administrative fees and monthly contract installments due on Class 1 secured claims but before further payment of Class 1, 2, 5, 6, and 7 pre-petition claims. If there is more than one administrative expense, all such expenses shall be paid on a pro rata basis.

Debtor paid an attorney $__________ prior to the filing of the petition.

[ ] Debtor's attorney opts to have his or her remaining fees approved and paid in accordance with the Court's Guidelines for Payment of Attorneys' Fees in Chapter 13 Cases. Debtor has agreed to pay the attorney an additional $__________.

[ ] Debtor's attorney opts out of the Guidelines for Payment of Attorneys' Fees in Chapter 13 Cases and instead will disclose and seek approval of further fees in accordance with applicable authority including 11 U.S.C. §§ 329 and 330, Fed.R.Bankr.P. 2002, 2016, and 2017. The attorney estimates that additional fees and costs of $ __________ will be incurred by Debtor in confirming this plan.

B. Secured Claims

Class 1. Long-term secured claims that were delinquent when the petition was filed and that mature after the last payment under the plan, including home loans and car loans. Creditors holding Class 1 claims will retain their liens. Pre-petition arrears, together with interest as specified below, will be cured by this plan. Trustee shall pay to Class 1 claim holders all monthly contract installment payments falling due after the filing of the petition. See section III(E). Class 1 claims are not modified by this plan.

CLASS 1 CREDITOR'S NAME/ COLLATERAL DESCRIPTION	REGULAR PAYMENT	MONTHLY LATE CHARGE	PRE-PETITION ARREARS	INTEREST RATE
1.				
2.				
3.				

In the column "Regular Payment" indicate the amount of the monthly contract installment including any impounds. However, whatever Debtor lists as the regular payment, the amount due is the amount required by the contract. In the column "Late Charge" indicate the amount charged for late payment of a monthly contract installment. In the column "Pre-Petition Arrears" include the accrued but unpaid interest and principal through the date of bankruptcy as well as other accrued and unpaid charges such as attorneys' fees and foreclosure costs. In the column "Interest Rate" specify the rate at which pre-petition arrears will accrue interest. If no interest rate is specified, 10% per annum will be imputed.

Class 2. Secured claims that are modified by this plan or that will not extend beyond its length. This class includes any secured claim that has matured or will mature prior to the completion of the plan. It also includes any secured claim, regardless of its original maturity date, that is modified by this plan. Each secured claim will continue to be secured by its existing lien and will be paid its full amount or the market value of its collateral, whichever is less if permitted by § 1322(b)(2), with interest.

CLASS 2 CREDITOR'S NAME/COLLATERAL DESCRIPTION	CLAIM AMOUNT	MARKET VALUE of COLLATERAL	INTEREST RATE
1.			
2.			
3.			

In the column "Claim Amount" include the unmatured principal, the accrued but unpaid principal and interest through the date of bankruptcy, as well as other accrued and unpaid charges such as attorneys' fees and foreclosure costs. If the market value of the creditor's collateral is less than the amount of the claim amount, the market value will be paid provided a Motion to Value Collateral (see Attachment M-3) is granted. Any deficiency will be treated as a Class 7 general unsecured claim unless it is classified as a Class 5 priority claim. If such a motion is not granted, the secured claim will be paid as demanded in the proof of claim. In the column "Interest Rate" specify the rate at which the claim will accrue interest. If no interest rate is specified, 10% per annum will be imputed.

Class 3. Secured claims satisfied by the surrender of collateral. As to personal property secured claims, Debtor shall tender the collateral to the creditor not later than 5 days after confirmation of this plan. As to real property secured claims, the creditor may conduct a foreclosure of the real property. Upon sale, Debtor shall give up possession. Entry of the confirmation order shall constitute an order modifying the automatic stay of 11 U.S.C. § 362 to allow the holder of a Class 3 secured claim to receive, take possession of, foreclose upon, and to exercise its rights and judicial and nonjudicial remedies against its collateral.

CLASS 3 CREDITOR'S NAME/COLLATERAL DESCRIPTION	ESTIMATED DEFICIENCY	IS DEFICIENCY A PRIORITY CLAIM? Y/N
1.		
2.		

Class 4. Secured claims paid directly by Debtor or third party. This class includes secured claims with due dates extending beyond the length of the plan that were not in default when the bankruptcy was filed and are not modified by this plan. Holders of Class 4 claims shall retain their liens. Monthly contract installments shall be made by Debtor or a third party as they fall due whether or not this plan has been confirmed.

CLASS 4 CREDITOR'S NAME	REGULAR PAYMENT	MATURITY DATE
1.		
2.		

C. Unsecured Claims

Class 5. Priority unsecured claims pursuant to 11 U.S.C. § 507 shall be paid in full. Include in the "Claim Amount" column the under-collateralized portion of any secured claim if it is entitled to priority treatment.

CLASS 5 CREDITOR'S NAME	TYPE OF PRIORITY	CLAIM AMOUNT
1.		
2.		
3.		

Class 6. Special unsecured claims. This class includes unsecured claims, such as co-signed unsecured debts, that will be paid in full even though all other unsecured claims may not be paid in full.

CLASS 6 CREDITOR'S NAME	REASON FOR SPECIAL TREATMENT	CLAIM AMOUNT
1.		
2.		

Class 7. Holders of general unsecured claims not entitled to priority or "special treatment" in Class 6, and not secured by a lien on property belonging to Debtor, will receive no less than a ___________% dividend pursuant to this plan. Debtor estimates that general unsecured claims, including the under-collateralized portion of secured claims not entitled to priority, total $_____________.

D. Executory Contracts And Unexpired Leases

Debtor assumes the executory contracts and unexpired leases listed below. Debtor shall pay directly to the other party to the executory contract or unexpired lease, before and after confirmation, all post-petition payments. Any pre-petition arrears shall be paid in full either as a Class 1 or a Class 6 claim, or be paid a specific monthly payment as stated in the Additional Provisions below. Any executory contract or unexpired lease not listed in the table below is rejected. Entry of the confirmation order modifies the automatic stay of 11 U.S.C. § 362 to allow the nondebtor party to a rejected unexpired lease to obtain possession of leased property.

NAME OF OTHER PARTY TO EXECUTORY CONTRACT OR UNEXPIRED LEASE	PRE-PETITION ARREARS	REGULAR PAYMENT	WILL ARREARS BE PAID AS A CLASS 1 OR 6 CLAIM, OR AS STATED IN THE ADDITIONAL PROVISIONS?
1.			
2.			

E. Order of Distribution Between and Among Classes

After confirmation of this plan, funds available for distribution will be paid by Trustee in the following order: **(1)** Trustee's administrative fees; then **(2)** monthly contract installments due on Class 1 claims; then **(3)** approved administrative expenses; then **(4)** the monthly payments set out in the Additional Provisions to be paid on account of arrears on assumed executory contracts and unexpired leases and any other claims specified in the Additional Provisions; then **(5)** Class 1 pre-petition arrearage claims and Class 2 claims; then **(6)** Class 5 priority unsecured claims; then **(7)** Class 6 special unsecured claims and Class 7 general unsecured claims. Within each distribution level except the second level [see III(E)(1) & (2) below], allowed claims shall be paid on a pro rata basis. Unless a claim objection is sustained, or a motion to value collateral or a lien avoidance motion is granted, distributions on account of Class 1, 2, 5, 6, and 7 pre-petition claims and arrears on executory contracts and unexpired leases will be based upon the amount stated in each claim holder's proof of claim rather than the amount estimated by Debtor in this plan.

III. Miscellaneous Provisions

A. Vesting of Property. Any property of the estate scheduled under 11 U.S.C. § 521 shall [*choose one*] [ ] revest in Debtor on confirmation or [ ] not revest in Debtor until such time as a discharge is granted. In the event the case is converted to a case under Chapter 7, 11, or 12 of the Bankruptcy Code or is dismissed, the property of the estate shall be determined in accordance with applicable law.

B. General Order. General Order 03-03 is applicable to all Chapter 13 cases filed or converted to Chapter 13 on or after July 1, 2003. That order mandates the use of this plan and contains mandatory provisions regarding the administration of Chapter 13 cases. Copies of this General Order and the forms required by it may be obtained from the Court's Internet site, www.caeb.uscourts.gov or at the Court's public counters.

C. Debtor's Duties. In addition to the duties and obligations imposed upon Debtor by the Bankruptcy Code and Rules, the Local Bankruptcy Rules, and the General Order, this plan imposes the following additional requirements on Debtor: **(1) Transfers of Property and New Debt.** Debtor is prohibited from transferring, encumbering, selling, or otherwise disposing of any personal or real property with a value of $1,000 or more other than in the regular course of Debtor's financial or business affairs without first obtaining court authorization. Except as provided in 11 U.S.C. §§ 364 and 1304, Debtor shall not incur aggregate new debt exceeding $1,000 without first obtaining court authorization. If Trustee approves a proposed transfer or new debt, court approval may be obtainable without a hearing. To determine the appropriate procedure, Debtor should consult the General Order. A new consumer debt of $1,000 or less shall not be paid through this plan absent compliance with 11 U.S.C. § 1305(c). **(2) Insurance.** Debtor shall maintain insurance as required by any law or contract. **(3) Support Payments.** Debtor shall maintain ongoing child or spousal support payments directly to the court-ordered recipient. **(4) Compliance with Applicable Non-Bankruptcy Law.** Debtor's financial and business affairs shall be conducted in accordance with applicable non-bankruptcy law including the timely filing of tax returns and payment of taxes. **(5) Periodic Reports.** Upon Trustee's request, Debtor shall provide Trustee with a copy of any tax return, W-2 form, and 1099 form filed or received while the case is pending, and furnish Trustee with quarterly financial information regarding Debtor's business.

D. Remedies on Default. If Debtor defaults in the performance of this plan, or if the plan will not be completed within six months of its stated term, not to exceed 60 months, Trustee or any other party in interest may request, appropriate relief by filing a motion and setting it for hearing pursuant to Local Bankruptcy Rule 9014-1.

This relief may consist of, without limitation, the following: **(1) Dismissal** of the case. When Trustee requests dismissal, in addition to setting a motion for hearing pursuant to Local Bankruptcy Rule 9014-1, Trustee may seek dismissal pursuant to Paragraph 7 of the General Order. **(2) Conversion** of the case to chapter 7 of the Bankruptcy Code. **(3) Relief from the automatic stay** to pursue rights against collateral. If the Court, in lieu of terminating or modifying the automatic stay, orders Debtor to make adequate protection payments, those payments, absent an order to the contrary, shall be made to Trustee who shall thereafter distribute them pursuant to the terms of this plan. If the Court terminates the automatic stay to permit a creditor holding a Class 1 or 2 secured claim to proceed against its collateral, unless the Court orders otherwise, Trustee shall make no further plan payments on account of such secured claim. Any portion of the secured claim not previously satisfied under this plan shall be satisfied as a Class 3 claim. Unless the court orders otherwise, any deficiency remaining after the disposition of the collateral shall be satisfied as a Class 7 unsecured claim provided a timely proof of claim or amended proof of claim is filed and served on Debtor and Trustee.

E. Monthly Contract Installments Paid by Trustee on Class 1 Claims. **(1)** If Debtor makes a partial plan payment which is insufficient to pay all monthly contract installments due on Class 1 claims, these installments will be paid in the order Debtor has listed Class 1 claims in the plan. **(2)** Trustee will not make a partial payment on account of a monthly contract installment. **(3)** If Debtor makes a partial plan payment, or if it is not paid on time, and Trustee is unable to pay timely a monthly contract installment due on a Class 1 claim, Debtor shall pay to Trustee with the next plan payment an additional amount sufficient to pay any late charge. Additional amounts for late charges shall be given to Trustee with a writing specifying the amount of each late charge and the Class 1 claim entitled to receive it. **(4)** Upon receipt from any Class 1 creditor, Debtor shall mail or deliver to the Trustee all notices including, without limitation, statements, payment coupons, impound and escrow notices, default notifications, and notices concerning changes of interest rate on variable interest rate loans. The automatic stay is modified to permit the sending of such notices to Debtor and Trustee. Prior to mailing or delivering any such notice to Trustee, Debtor shall affix the chapter 13 case number to it. If any such notice advises Debtor that the amount of the contract installment payment has increased or decreased, Debtor shall increase or decrease, as necessary, the plan payment made to Trustee.

IV. Additional Provisions

Other than expanding tables for listing claims and changing the caption to indicate the plan is an amended or modified plan, the preprinted language of this plan or its attachments shall not be altered. If you wish to change or supplement the preprinted language, insert these provisions in the space below or on an additional page.

Attorney's Name, Address, Phone and Fax Numbers, Email Address:

____

____

____

____

____

Dated:

____

Debtor's Signature

____

Joint Debtor's Signature

CHAPTER 13 PLAN CONTINUATION SHEET

If additional space is needed to list all creditors in Classes 1 through 6, insert them on this page. Use additional pages, if necessary.

CLASS 1 CREDITOR'S NAME/ COLLATERAL DESCRIPTION	REGULAR PAYMENT	MONTHLY LATE CHARGE	PRE-PETITION ARREARS	INTEREST RATE
4.				
5.				
6.				
7.				
8.				

CLASS 2 CREDITOR'S NAME/COLLATERAL DESCRIPTION	CLAIM AMOUNT	MARKET VALUE of COLLATERAL	INTEREST RATE
4.			
5.			
6.			
7.			
8.			

CLASS 3 CREDITOR'S NAME/COLLATERAL DESCRIPTION	ESTIMATED DEFICIENCY	IS DEFICIENCY A PRIORITY CLAIM? Y/N
3.		
4.		
5.		

CLASS 5 CREDITOR'S NAME	TYPE OF PRIORITY	CLAIM AMOUNT
4.		
5.		
6.		

CLASS 6 CREDITOR'S NAME	REASON FOR SPECIAL TREATMENT	CLAIM AMOUNT
3.		
4.		
5.		

ATTACHMENT M-1

Optional – Discard if not used

MOTIONS TO AVOID JUDICIAL LIENS ON DEBTOR'S RESIDENCE (OR OTHER QUALIFIED EXEMPT PROPERTY) (Pursuant to 11 U.S.C. § 522(f)(1)(A))

(A separate motion must be used to avoid each lien)
NUMBER OF MOTIONS TO AVOID JUDICIAL LIENS IN THIS PLAN: __

NOTICE IS HEREBY GIVEN that Debtor moves to avoid the following lien on Debtor's residence (or other exempt property) pursuant to 11 U.S.C. § 522(f)(1)(A) and to treat the claim secured by such lien as a general unsecured claim. If granted, the claim of the creditor named below will be treated as a general unsecured claim (Class 7).

Name of the creditor holding the judicial lien that is the subject of this motion:

Address of residence or description of other qualified exempt property:

Debtor's opinion of the exempt property's replacement value: $
Amount of the exemption claimed by Debtor: $
Amount of the creditor's judgment: $
The amount owed to and the name of all creditors holding liens or security interests that cannot be avoided pursuant to section 522(f)(1)(A):

Name of Creditor	Amount of Claim

Other information relevant to the resolution of this motion:

I (we) declare under penalty of perjury under the laws of the State of California that the foregoing is true and correct.

Dated:

____
Debtor

____
Joint Debtor

ATTACHMENT M-2

Optional – Discard if not used

MOTIONS TO AVOID NONPOSSESSORY NONPURCHASE MONEY LIENS

(Pursuant to 11 U.S.C. § 522(f)(1)(B))

A Separate Motion Must Be Used to Avoid Each Lien

NUMBER OF MOTIONS TO AVOID NONPOSSESSORY LIENS IN THIS PLAN ___

NOTICE IS HEREBY GIVEN that Debtor moves to avoid the lien on Debtor's exempt property (consisting of household goods, tools of the trade, or professionally prescribed health aids) held by the creditor identified below. If granted, the claim of the creditor named below will be treated as a general unsecured claim (Class 7).

Name of the creditor whose nonpossessory, nonpurchase money security interest or lien on the below-described property is being avoided:

Detailed description of exempt property:

Debtor's opinion of the exempt property's replacement value: $
Amount of the creditor's claim: $

Other information relevant to the resolution of this motion:

I (we) declare under penalty of perjury under the laws of the State of California that the foregoing is true and correct.
Dated:

____
Debtor

____
Joint Debtor

EDCAL-107 E.D. CALIFORNIA

ATTACHMENT M-3

Optional – Discard if not used

MOTIONS TO VALUE COLLATERAL
(Pursuant to subsections (a) and (d) of 11 U.S.C. § 506
and Federal Rule of Bankruptcy Procedure 3012)

(A separate motion must be filed as to each creditor)
NUMBER OF MOTIONS TO VALUE COLLATERAL IN THIS PLAN ____

NOTICE IS HEREBY GIVEN that Debtor requests the court to value the property described below. This property secures the claim of the creditor named below. Debtor also requests that the amount of the creditor's secured claim not exceed the value of its security, less the claims of creditors holding senior liens or security interests. This determination will supercede any greater secured claim demanded in a proof of claim. Any objections to the creditor's claim are reserved and will be filed after the creditor has filed a proof of claim. In the opinion of the debtor, the collateral has the replacement value indicated below.

Name of the creditor whose collateral is being valued by this motion:

Total amount of this creditor's claim: $

Description of collateral [*For vehicles include the mileage on the date of the petition and a list of optional equipment. For real property, state the street address and a brief description of it such as "single family residence" or "ten-acre undeveloped lot"*]:

The amount owed to and the name of all creditors holding liens or security interests senior to the lien or security interest of the above-named creditor:

Debtor's opinion of the collateral's replacement value: $

Other information relevant to the resolution of this motion:

I (we) declare under penalty of perjury under the laws of the State of California that the foregoing is true and correct.
Dated:

____
Debtor

____
Joint Debtor

CHAPTER 13 PLAN AND ATTACHMENTS (FOR USE IN CASES FILED FROM 3/1/01 TO 6/30/03)

UNITED STATES BANKRUPTCY COURT
EASTERN DISTRICT OF CALIFORNIA

In re:) Case No.
)
)
)
"Debtor.")
)

CHAPTER 13 PLAN
[ ] MOTION(S) TO VALUE COLLATERAL AND
[ ] MOTION(S) TO AVOID LIENS
[check box if motion(s) included]

CREDITORS MAY NOT VOTE ON THIS PLAN BUT THEY MAY OBJECT TO ITS CONFIRMATION AND TO THE GRANTING OF ANY MOTIONS INCLUDED IN THE PLAN. AN OBJECTION MUST BE FILED AND SERVED UPON DEBTOR, DEBTOR'S ATTORNEY, AND THE CHAPTER 13 TRUSTEE WITHIN 14 DAYS AFTER THE CONCLUSION OF THE CREDITORS' MEETING HELD PURSUANT TO 11 U.S.C. § 341(a) . A HEARING ON THE OBJECTION MUST BE SET BY THE CREDITOR ON A MINIMUM OF 22 DAYS' NOTICE AND MUST TAKE PLACE WITHIN 45 DAYS AFTER THE CONCLUSION OF THE CREDITORS' MEETING. THE COURT'S SELF-SET HEARING RULES AND PROCEDURE ARE AVAILABLE ON THE COURT'S WEBSITE, WWW.CAEB.USCOURTS.GOV, OR AT THE COURT'S PUBLIC COUNTERS. ABSENT A TIMELY OBJECTION AND HEARING, THE COURT MAY CONFIRM THIS PLAN AND GRANT THE MOTIONS WITHOUT A HEARING.

CHAPTER 13 PLAN

Debtor hereby proposes the following Chapter 13 Plan effective from the date of the petition:

I. Plan Payments and Term

In order to complete this plan, the future income of Debtor will be submitted to the supervision and control of the Chapter 13 Trustee ("Trustee"). Debtor shall pay to the Trustee the sum of $__________ each month for _________ months [*if the foregoing is left blank, refer to the "Additional Provisions" portion of this plan*]. The plan payments consist of all Debtor's projected disposable income. Unless all allowed unsecured claims are paid in full, the plan shall not terminate earlier than the stated term or 36 months, whichever is longer. If necessary to complete this plan, the term will be extended up to 6 months, but in no event will the plan exceed 60 months in length.

II. Classification and Treatment of Claims and Expenses

The claims and expenses owed by Debtor are classified and provided for below. To be paid, creditors, including secured creditors, must file proofs of claim. The proof of claim filed by or on behalf of a creditor, not the plan or the schedules, will determine the amount and character of the creditor's claim. If a creditor's claim is provided for by this plan and a proof of claim is filed, dividends will be paid based upon the proof of claim unless the granting of a valuation or a lien avoidance motion, or the sustaining of a claim objection, affects the amount or classification of the claim. Secured claims not listed within Classes 1, 2, 3, or 4, and priority claims not listed within Class 5 are not provided for by the plan. Whether or not a proof of claim is filed, Debtor shall make ongoing post-petition installment payments on Class 1 and 4 claims.

A. Administrative Expenses

1. Chapter 13 Trustee's fees will be allowed and paid as determined by statute. The Trustee may receive up to 10% of the money distributed each month, excluding direct payments by Debtor to Class 1 and Class 4 creditors and refunds from the Trustee to Debtor.

2. Administrative Expenses: In most cases the only additional administrative expenses will be Debtor's attorneys' fees. Attorneys' fees and other administrative expenses must be approved by the bankruptcy court before they can be paid. Once approved, an administrative expense will be paid in full before further payment of Class 1, 2, 5, 6, and 7 claims unless the administrative claimant agrees to a different treatment. After deducting the $__________ pre-petition retainer, $__________ remains to be paid to Debtor's attorney.

[ ] Debtor's attorney opts to have his or her fees approved and paid in accordance with the court's Guidelines for Payment of Attorneys' Fees in Chapter 13 Cases, or

[ ] Debtor's attorney opts out of the Guidelines for Payment of Attorneys' Fees in Chapter 13 Cases and instead will disclose and seek approval of fees in accordance with applicable authority including 11 U.S.C. §§ 329 and 330, Fed.R.Bankr.P. 2002, 2016, and 2017, and the court's general Guidelines for Compensation and Expense Reimbursement of Professionals.

B. Secured Claims

Class 1. Long-term secured claims that were delinquent when the petition was filed and that mature after the last payment under the plan. Home loans and car loans maturing after the term of this plan are typical Class 1 claims. Creditors holding Class 1 claims will retain their liens and security interests. Pre-petition arrears will be paid through the plan together with interest if required by 11 U.S.C. § 1322(e). If no interest rate is specified, 10% per annum will be imputed and paid on Class 1 claims. Other than to cure the pre-petition arrears, Class 1 claims are not modified by this plan.

CLASS 1 CREDITOR'S NAME/COLLATERAL DESCRIPTION	REGULAR PAYMENT	PRE-PETITION ARREARS	INTEREST RATE
1.			
2.			
3.			

[In the column "Regular Payment" state the ongoing post-petition installment payment including any impound amounts. The "regular payment" shall be paid by Debtor directly to the secured creditor. The "regular payment" shall be paid by Debtor whether or not the plan has been confirmed by the court. Do not also include Class 1 claims in Class 4. In the column "Pre-Petition Arrears" include the accrued but unpaid interest and principal through the date of bankruptcy as well as other accrued and unpaid charges such as attorneys' fees and foreclosure costs. Pre-petition arrears owed under an assumed executory contract or unexpired lease (see paragraph II(D) below) may be provided for as a Class 1 secured claim.]

Class 2. Secured claims that are modified by this plan or that will not extend beyond its length. This class includes any secured claim that has matured or will mature prior to the completion of the plan. It also includes any secured claim, regardless of its maturity date, that is modified as permitted by 11 U.S.C. § 1322 (b)(2) or (c)(2). Each secured claim will continue to be secured by its existing lien or security interest and will be paid its full amount or the market value of its collateral, whichever is less if permitted by § 1322(b)(2), together with interest. If no interest rate is specified, 10% per annum will be imputed and paid on all Class 2 claims.

CLASS 2 CREDITOR'S NAME/COLLATERAL DESCRIPTION	CLAIM AMOUNT	MARKET VALUE of COLLATERAL	INTEREST RATE
1.			
2.			
3.			

[In the column "Claim Amount" include the unmatured principal, the accrued but unpaid principal and interest through the date of bankruptcy, as well as other accrued and unpaid charges such as attorneys' fees and foreclosure costs. If the market value of the creditor's collateral is less than the amount of the claim amount, the market value will be paid provided a Motion to Value Collateral (see Attachment M-3) is granted. Any deficiency will be treated as a Class 7 general unsecured claim unless it is a priority claim classified within Class 5. If a motion is not granted, the amount in the proof of claim will be paid.]

Class 3. Secured claims satisfied by the surrender of collateral. Identify in the table below secured creditors whose claims will be satisfied by the surrender of their collateral. As to personal property, Debtor shall offer to surrender the property not later than 5 days after entry of the order of confirmation. As to real property, Debtor consents to termination of the automatic stay to permit a non-judicial foreclosure of the real property and Debtor shall give up possession immediately after the foreclosure sale. Entry of the confirmation order shall constitute an order modifying the automatic stay of 11 U.S.C. § 362 to allow any secured creditor whose collateral is being surrendered to receive or foreclose upon that collateral and to exercise its rights and remedies against its collateral.

CLASS 3 CREDITOR'S NAME/COLLATERAL DESCRIPTION	ESTIMATED DEFICIENCY	IS DEFICIENCY A PRIORITY CLAIM? Y/N
1.		
2.		
3.		

Class 4. Claims to be paid directly by Debtor or third party. This class includes secured claims with due dates extending beyond the length of the plan, that were not delinquent when the bankruptcy was filed, are not modified by this plan, and will be paid directly by Debtor or by a third party with money or property that does not belong to Debtor or to the bankruptcy estate. Holders of Class 4 claims shall retain their liens and security interests. Because Class 4 claims are not modified, payments shall continue to be paid as they become due under the terms of the existing contract. Class 1 claims shall not also be included in Class 4.

CLASS 4 CREDITOR'S NAME	REGULAR PAYMENT	MATURITY DATE
1.		
2.		
3.		

C. Unsecured Claims

Class 5. Priority unsecured claims. Claims entitled to priority pursuant to 11 U.S.C. § 507 shall be paid in full. Include in the "Claim Amount" column the under-collateralized portion of any secured claim if it is entitled to priority.

CLASS 5 CREDITOR'S NAME	TYPE OF PRIORITY	CLAIM AMOUNT
1.		
2.		
3.		

Class 6. Special unsecured claims. Unsecured claims, such as co-signed unsecured claims, that the plan will pay in full even though all other unsecured claims may not be paid in full.

CLASS 6 CREDITOR'S NAME	REASON FOR SPECIAL TREATMENT	CLAIM AMOUNT
1.		
2.		
3.		

Class 7. General unsecured claims. General unsecured claims, that is, claims not entitled to priority nor "special treatment" in Class 6, and not secured with a lien or security interest on property belonging to Debtor will be paid no less than ___________% of their claim. Debtor estimates that general unsecured claims, including the under-collateralized portion of secured claims not entitled to priority, total $____________.

D. Executory Contracts And Unexpired Leases

Debtor assumes the executory contracts and unexpired leases listed in the table below. Debtor shall pay directly to the other party to the executory contract or unexpired lease all on-going post-petition payments. Any pre-bankruptcy arrears shall be paid in full either as a Class 1 claim or as a Class 6 claim, or be paid a specific monthly payment as stated in the Additional Provisions below, as designated by Debtor. Any executory contracts or unexpired leases not listed in the table below are rejected.

NAME OF OTHER PARTY TO EXECUTORY CONTRACT OR UNEXPIRED LEASE	PRE-PETITION ARREARS	REGULAR PAYMENT	WILL ARREARS BE PAID AS A CLASS 1 OR 6 CLAIM, OR AS STATED IN THE ADDITIONAL PROVISIONS?
1.			
2.			
3.			

E. Order of Distribution Between and Among Classes

After confirmation of this plan, funds available for distribution will be paid by the Trustee each month in the following order: (1) the Trustee's monthly administrative fees; then (2) approved administrative expenses; then (3) the monthly payments set out in the Additional Provisions below to be paid on account of pre-bankruptcy arrears on assumed executory contracts and unexpired leases or on other claims; then (4) Class 1 pre-bankruptcy arrearage claims and Class 2 claims; then (5) Class 5 priority unsecured claims; then (6) Class 6 special unsecured claims and Class 7 general unsecured claims. Within each distribution level, allowed claims shall be paid on a pro rata basis. Unless a claim objection is sustained or a motion to value collateral or a lien avoidance motion is granted, distributions on account of Class 1, 2, 5, 6, and 7 claims will be based upon the amount stated in each claim holder's proof of claim rather than the amount estimated by Debtor in this plan.

III. Miscellaneous Provisions

A. Vesting and Possession of Property. Any property of the estate scheduled under 11 U.S.C. § 521 shall [choose one]

[ ] revest in Debtor on confirmation.
[ ] not revest in Debtor until such time as a discharge is granted.

In the event the case is converted to a case under Chapter 7, 11, or 12 of the Bankruptcy Code or is dismissed, the property of the estate shall be determined in accordance with applicable law.

B. General Order. General Order 01-02 is applicable to all Chapter 13 cases filed on or after March 1, 2001. That order mandates the use of this plan and contains mandatory provisions regarding the administration of Chapter 13 cases. Copies of this General Order and the forms required by it may be obtained from the Court's website, www.caeb.uscourts.gov or at the Court's public counters.

C. Debtor's Duties. In addition to the duties and obligations imposed upon Debtor by the Bankruptcy Code and Rules, the Local Bankruptcy Rules, and the General Order, this plan imposes the following additional requirements on Debtor: (a) **Transfers of Property and New Debt.** Debtor is prohibited from transferring, encumbering, selling, or otherwise disposing of any personal or real property with a value of $1,000 or more other than in the regular course of Debtor's financial or business affairs without first obtaining court authorization. Except as provided in 11 U.S.C. §§ 364 and 1304, Debtor shall not incur aggregate new debt exceeding $1,000 without first obtaining court authorization. If the Trustee approves a proposed transfer or new debt, court approval may be obtainable without a hearing. To determine the appropriate procedure, Debtor should consult the General Order. Without compliance with 11 U.S.C. § 1305(c), a new debt of $1,000 or less that is a consumer debt shall not be paid through this plan. (b) **Insurance.** Debtor shall maintain insurance as required by any law, contract, or security agreement. (c) **Support Payments.** Debtor shall maintain ongoing child or spousal support payments directly to the court-ordered recipient. (d) **Compliance with Applicable Non-Bankruptcy Law.** While operating under Chapter 13, Debtor's financial and business affairs shall be conducted in accordance with applicable non-bankruptcy law. This duty includes the timely filing of tax returns and payment of taxes. (e) **Periodic Reports.** Upon the Trustee's request, Debtor shall provide the Trustee with a copy of any tax return, W-2 form, and 1099 form filed or received while the case is pending. The Trustee may require Debtor to furnish quarterly financial information regarding Debtor's business.

D. Dismissal. If Debtor defaults in the performance of this plan or if it will not be completed within six months of its stated term, not to exceed 60 months, the Trustee or any other party in interest may move to dismiss the bankruptcy case. When the Trustee requests dismissal, he may use either of the procedures authorized by Paragraphs 7 or 8 of the General Order.

IV. Additional Provisions

Additional provisions or alterations to this plan shall be set out below. If necessary, use another page. Changes to the preprinted language of this standard Chapter 13 plan or to its attachments will not be given any force or effect.

Attorney's Name, Address, and Phone Number:

____

____

____

____

Dated:

____
Debtor's Signature

____
Joint Debtor's Signature

CHAPTER 13 PLAN CONTINUATION SHEET

If additional space is needed to list all creditors in Classes 1 through 6, insert them on this page. Use additional pages, if necessary.

CLASS 1 CREDITOR'S NAME/COLLATERAL DESCRIPTION	REGULAR PAYMENT	PRE-PETITION ARREARS	INTEREST RATE
4.			
5.			
6.			
7.			
8.			

CLASS 2 CREDITOR'S NAME/COLLATERAL DESCRIPTION	CLAIM AMOUNT	MARKET VALUE of COLLATERAL	INTEREST RATE
4.			
5.			
6.			
7.			
8.			

CLASS 3 CREDITOR'S NAME/COLLATERAL DESCRIPTION	ESTIMATED DEFICIENCY	IS DEFICIENCY A PRIORITY CLAIM? Y/N
4.		
5.		
6.		

CLASS 5 CREDITOR'S NAME	TYPE OF PRIORITY	CLAIM AMOUNT
4.		
5.		
6.		

CLASS 6 CREDITOR'S NAME	REASON FOR SPECIAL TREATMENT	CLAIM AMOUNT
4.		
5.		
6.		

ATTACHMENT M-1

Optional – Discard if not used

MOTIONS TO AVOID JUDICIAL LIENS ON DEBTOR'S RESIDENCE (OR OTHER QUALIFIED EXEMPT PROPERTY) (Pursuant to 11 U.S.C. § 522(f)(1)(A))

(A separate motion must be used to avoid each lien)
NUMBER OF MOTIONS TO AVOID JUDICIAL LIENS IN THIS PLAN: __

NOTICE IS HEREBY GIVEN that Debtor moves to avoid the following lien on Debtor's residence (or other exempt property) pursuant to 11 U.S.C. § 522(f)(1)(A) and to treat the claim secured by such lien as a general unsecured claim. If granted, the claim of the creditor named below will be treated as a general unsecured claim (Class 7).

Name of the creditor holding the judicial lien that is the subject of this motion:

Address of residence or description of other qualified exempt property:

Debtor's opinion of the exempt property's replacement value: $
Amount of the exemption claimed by Debtor: $
Amount of the creditor's judgment: $
The amount owed to and the name of all creditors holding liens or security interests that cannot be avoided pursuant to section 522(f)(1)(A):

Name of Creditor	Amount of Claim

Other information relevant to the resolution of this motion:

I (we) declare under penalty of perjury under the laws of the State of California that the foregoing is true and correct.

Dated: ____________________
Debtor

____
Joint Debtor

ATTACHMENT M-2
Optional – Discard if not used
MOTIONS TO AVOID NONPOSSESSORY NONPURCHASE MONEY LIENS
(Pursuant to 11 U.S.C. § 522(f)(1)(B))

A Separate Motion Must Be Used to Avoid Each Lien
NUMBER OF MOTIONS TO AVOID NONPOSSESSORY LIENS IN THIS PLAN ___

NOTICE IS HEREBY GIVEN that Debtor moves to avoid the lien on Debtor's exempt property (consisting of household goods, tools of the trade, or professionally prescribed health aids) held by the creditor identified below. If granted, the claim of the creditor named below will be treated as a general unsecured claim (Class 7).

Name of the creditor whose nonpossessory, nonpurchase money security interest or lien on the below-described property is being avoided:

Detailed description of exempt property:

Debtor's opinion of the exempt property's replacement value: $
Amount of the creditor's claim: $

Other information relevant to the resolution of this motion:

I (we) declare under penalty of perjury under the laws of the State of California that the foregoing is true and correct.
Dated:

____
Debtor

____
Joint Debtor

ATTACHMENT M-3
Optional – Discard if not used
MOTIONS TO VALUE COLLATERAL
(Pursuant to subsections (a) and (d) of 11 U.S.C. § 506 and Federal Rule of Bankruptcy Procedure 3012)

(A separate motion must be filed as to each creditor)
NUMBER OF MOTIONS TO VALUE COLLATERAL IN THIS PLAN ____

NOTICE IS HEREBY GIVEN that Debtor requests the court to value the property described below. This property secures the claim of the creditor named below. Debtor also requests that the amount of the creditor's secured claim not exceed the value of its security, less the claims of creditors holding senior liens or security interests. This determination will supercede any greater secured claim demanded in a proof of claim. Any objections to the creditor's claim are reserved and will be filed after the creditor has filed a proof of claim. In the opinion of the debtor, the collateral has the replacement value indicated below.

Name of the creditor whose collateral is being valued by this motion:

Total amount of this creditor's claim: $

Description of collateral [*For vehicles include the mileage on the date of the petition and a list of optional equipment. For real property, state the street address and a brief description of it such as "single family residence" or "ten-acre undeveloped lot"*]:

The amount owed to and the name of all creditors holding liens or security interests senior to the lien or security interest of the above-named creditor:

Debtor's opinion of the collateral's replacement value: $

Other information relevant to the resolution of this motion:

I (we) declare under penalty of perjury under the laws of the State of California that the foregoing is true and correct.
Dated:

____
Debtor

____
Joint Debtor

CHAPTER 13 PLAN AND ATTACHMENTS (FOR USE IN CHAPTER 13 CASES FILED 4/15/00 – 2/28/01) (SACRAMENTO AND MODESTO DIVISIONS)

UNITED STATES BANKRUPTCY COURT
EASTERN DISTRICT OF CALIFORNIA
SACRAMENTO AND MODESTO DIVISIONS

In re:	)	Case No.
	)	
	)	Social Security No.
	)	Social Security No.
	)	Employer I.D. No.
______________ Debtor(s).	)	

CHAPTER 13 PLAN
[ ] MOTION(S) TO VALUE COLLATERAL AND
[ ] MOTION(S) TO AVOID LIENS
[check box(es) if motion(s) included]

CREDITORS MAY NOT VOTE ON THIS PLAN BUT THEY MAY OBJECT TO ITS CONFIRMATION AND TO THE GRANTING OF ANY MOTIONS INCLUDED IN THE PLAN. AN OBJECTION MUST BE FILED AND SERVED UPON DEBTOR, DEBTOR'S ATTORNEY, AND THE CHAPTER 13 TRUSTEE WITHIN 14 DAYS AFTER THE CONCLUSION OF THE CREDITORS' MEETING HELD PURSUANT TO 11 U.S.C. § 341(a). A HEARING ON THE OBJECTION MUST BE SET BY THE CREDITOR ON A MINIMUM OF 22 DAYS NOTICE AND MUST TAKE PLACE WITHIN 45 DAYS AFTER THE CONCLUSION OF THE CREDITORS' MEETING. THE COURT'S SELF-SET HEARING RULES AND PROCEDURE ARE AVAILABLE ON THE COURT'S WEBSITE, WWW.CAEB.USCOURTS.GOV, OR AT THE COURT'S PUBLIC COUNTERS. ABSENT A TIMELY OBJECTION AND HEARING, THE COURT MAY CONFIRM THIS PLAN AND GRANT THE MOTIONS WITHOUT A HEARING.

CHAPTER 13 PLAN

Debtor hereby proposes the following Chapter 13 Plan effective from the date of the petition:

I. Plan Payments and Term

In order to complete this plan, the future income of Debtor will be submitted to the supervision and control of the Chapter 13 Trustee ("Trustee"). Debtor shall pay to the Trustee the sum of $__________ each month for ________ months [*if the foregoing is left blank, refer to the "Additional Provisions" portion of this plan*]. The plan payments consist of all Debtor's projected disposable income. Unless all allowed unsecured claims are paid in full, the plan shall not terminate earlier than the stated term or 36 months, whichever is longer. If necessary to complete this plan, the term will be extended up to 6 months, but in no event will the plan exceed 60 months in length.

II. Classification and Treatment of Claims and Expenses

The claims and expenses owed by Debtor are classified and provided for below. To be paid, creditors, including secured creditors, must file proofs of claim. The proof of claim filed by or on behalf of a creditor, not the plan or the schedules, will determine the amount and character of the creditor's claim. If a creditor's claim is provided for by this plan and a proof of claim is filed, dividends will be paid based upon the proof of claim unless the granting of a valuation or a lien avoidance motion, or the sustaining of a claim objection, affects the amount or classification of the claim. Secured claims not listed within Classes 1, 2, 3, or 4, and priority claims not listed within Class 5 are not provided for by the plan. Whether or not a proof of claim is filed, Debtor shall make ongoing post-petition installment payments on Class 1 and 4 claims.

A. Administrative Expenses

1. Chapter 13 Trustee's fees will be allowed and paid as determined by statute. The Trustee may receive up to 10% of the money distributed each month, excluding direct payments by Debtor to Class 1 and Class 4 creditors and refunds from the Trustee to Debtor.

2. Administrative Expenses: In most cases the only additional administrative expenses will be Debtor's attorneys' fees. Attorneys' fees and other administrative expenses must be approved by the bankruptcy court before they can be paid. Once approved, an administrative expense will be paid in full before further payment of Class 1, 2, 5, 6, and 7 claims unless the administrative claimant agrees to a different treatment. After deducting the $____________ pre-petition retainer, $____________ remains to be paid to Debtor's attorney.

[ ] Debtor's attorney opts to have his or her fees approved and paid in accordance with the court's Guidelines for Payment of Attorneys' Fees in Chapter 13 Cases; or

[ ] Debtor's attorney opts out of the Guidelines for Payment of Attorneys' Fees in Chapter 13 Cases and instead will disclose and seek approval of fees in accordance with applicable authority including 11 U.S.C. §§ 329 and 330, Fed.R.Bankr.P. 2002, 2016, and 2017, and the court's general Guidelines for Compensation and Expense Reimbursement of Professionals.

B. Secured Claims

Class 1. Long-term secured claims that were delinquent when the petition was filed and that mature after the last payment under the plan. Home loans and car loans maturing after the term of this plan are typical Class 1 claims. Creditors holding Class 1 claims will retain their liens and security interests. Pre-petition arrears will be paid through the plan together with interest if required by 11 U.S.C. § 1322(e). If no interest rate is specified, 10% per annum will be imputed and paid on Class 1 claims. Other than to cure the pre-petition arrears, Class 1 claims are not modified by this plan.

CLASS 1 CREDITOR'S NAME/COLLATERAL DESCRIPTION	REGULAR PAYMENT	PRE-PETITION ARREARS	INTEREST RATE
1.			
2.			
3.			

[In the column "Regular Payment" state the ongoing post-petition installment payment including any impound amounts. The "regular payment" will be made by Debtor directly to the secured creditor. In the column "Pre-Petition Arrears" include the accrued but unpaid interest and principal through the date of bankruptcy as well as other accrued and unpaid charges such as attorneys' fees and foreclosure costs. Pre-petition arrears owed under an assumed executory contract or unexpired lease (see paragraph II(D) below) may be provided for as a Class 1 secured claim. If additional space is needed to list all Class 1 creditors, use the Chapter 13 Plan Continuation Sheet provided.]

Class 2. Secured claims that are modified by this plan or that will not extend beyond its length. This class includes any secured claim that has matured or will mature prior to the completion of the plan. It also includes any secured claim, regardless of its maturity date, that is modified as permitted by 11 U.S.C. § 1322 (b)(2) or (c)(2). Each secured claim will continue to be secured by its existing lien or security interest and will be paid its full amount or the market value of its collateral, whichever is less if permitted by § 1322(b)(2), together with interest. If no interest rate is specified, 10% per annum will be imputed and paid on all Class 2 claims.

CLASS 2 CREDITOR'S NAME/COLLATERAL DESCRIPTION	CLAIM AMOUNT	MARKET VALUE of COLLATERAL	INTEREST RATE
1.			
2.			
3.			

[In the column "Claim Amount" include the unmatured principal, the accrued but unpaid principal and interest through the date of bankruptcy, as well as other accrued and unpaid charges such as attorneys' fees and foreclosure costs. If the market value of the creditor's collateral is less than the amount of the claim amount, the market value will be paid provided a Motion to Value Collateral (see Attachment M-3) is granted. Any deficiency will be treated as a Class 7 general unsecured claim unless it is a priority claim classified within Class 5. If a motion is not granted, the amount in the proof of claim will be paid. If additional space is needed to list all Class 2 creditors, use the Chapter 13 Plan Continuation Sheet provided.]

Class 3. Secured claims satisfied by the surrender of collateral. Identify in the table below secured creditors whose claims will be satisfied by the surrender of their collateral. As to personal property, Debtor shall offer to surrender the property not later than 5 days after entry of the order of confirmation. As to real property, Debtor consents to termination of the automatic stay to permit a non-judicial foreclosure of the real property and Debtor shall give up possession immediately after the foreclosure sale. Entry of the confirmation order shall constitute an order modifying the automatic stay of 11 U.S.C. § 362 to allow any secured creditor whose collateral is being surrendered to receive or foreclose upon that collateral and to exercise its rights and remedies against its collateral.

CLASS 3 CREDITOR'S NAME/COLLATERAL DESCRIPTION	ESTIMATED DEFICIENCY	IS DEFICIENCY A PRIORITY CLAIM? Y/N
1.		
2.		
3.		

[If additional space is needed to list all Class 3 creditors, use the Chapter 13 Plan Continuation Sheet provided.]

Class 4. Claims to be paid directly by Debtor or third party. This class includes: (a) secured claims with due dates extending beyond the length of the plan, that were not delinquent when the bankruptcy was filed, and are not modified by this plan; and (b) secured and unsecured claims that will be paid with money or property that does not belong to Debtor or to the bankruptcy estate. Holders of Class 4 claims shall retain their liens and security interests. Class 4 claims are not modified in any respect.

CLASS 4 CREDITOR'S NAME	REGULAR PAYMENT	MATURITY DATE
1.		
2.		
3.		

[If additional space is needed to list all Class 4 creditors, use the Chapter 13 Plan Continuation Sheet provided.]

C. Unsecured Claims

Class 5. Priority unsecured claims. Claims entitled to priority pursuant to 11 U.S.C. § 507 shall be paid in full. Include in the "Claim Amount" column the under-collateralized portion of any secured claim if it is entitled to priority.

CLASS 5 CREDITOR'S NAME	TYPE OF PRIORITY	CLAIM AMOUNT
1.		
2.		
3.		

[If additional space is needed to list all Class 5 creditors, use the Chapter 13 Plan Continuation Sheet provided.]

Class 6. Special unsecured claims. Unsecured claims, such as co-signed unsecured claims, that the plan will pay in full even though all other unsecured claims may not be paid in full.

CLASS 6 CREDITOR'S NAME	REASON FOR SPECIAL TREATMENT	CLAIM AMOUNT
1.		
2.		
3.		

[If additional space is needed to list all Class 6 creditors, use the Chapter 13 Plan Continuation Sheet provided.]

Class 7. General unsecured claims. General unsecured claims, that is, claims not entitled to priority nor "special treatment" in Class 6, and not secured with a lien or security interest on property belonging to Debtor will be paid no less than __________% of their claim. Debtor estimates that general unsecured claims, including the under-collateralized portion of secured claims not entitled to priority, total $__________.

D. Executory Contracts And Unexpired Leases

Debtor assumes the executory contracts and unexpired leases listed in the table below. Debtor shall pay directly to the other party to the executory contract or unexpired lease all on-going post-petition payments. Any pre-bankruptcy arrears shall be paid in full either as a Class 1 claim or as a Class 6 claim, or be paid a specific monthly payment as stated in the Additional Provisions below, as designated by Debtor. Any executory contracts or unexpired leases not listed in the table below are rejected.

NAME OF OTHER PARTY TO EXECUTORY CONTRACT OR UNEXPIRED LEASE	PRE-PETITION ARREARS	REGULAR PAYMENT	WILL ARREARS BE PAID AS A CLASS 1 OR 6 CLAIM, OR AS STATED IN THE ADDITIONAL PROVISIONS?
1.			
2.			
3.			

E. Order of Distribution Between and Among Classes

After confirmation of this plan, funds available for distribution will be paid by the Trustee each month in the following order: (1) the Trustee's monthly administrative fees; then (2) approved administrative expenses; then (3) the monthly payments set out in the Additional Provisions below to be paid on account of pre-bankruptcy arrears on assumed executory contracts and unexpired leases or on other claims; then (4) Class 1 pre-bankruptcy arrearage claims and Class 2 claims; then (5) Class 5 priority unsecured claims; then (6) Class 6 special unsecured claims and Class 7 general unsecured claims. Within each distribution level, allowed claims shall be paid on a pro rata basis. Unless a claim objection is sustained or a motion to value collateral or a lien avoidance motion is granted, distributions on account of Class 1, 2, 5, 6, and 7 claims will be based upon the amount stated in each claim holder's proof of claim rather than the amount estimated by Debtor in this plan.

III. Miscellaneous Provisions

A. Vesting and Possession of Property. Any property of the estate scheduled under 11 U.S.C. § 521 shall [choose one]:

[ ] revest in Debtor on confirmation.
[ ] not revest in Debtor until such time as a discharge is granted.

In the event the case is converted to a case under Chapter 7, 11, or 12 of the Bankruptcy Code or is dismissed, the property of the estate shall be determined in accordance with applicable law.

B. General Order. General Order 00-2 is applicable to all Chapter 13 cases filed on or after April 15, 2000. That order mandates the use of this plan and contains mandatory provisions regarding the administration of Chapter 13 cases. Copies of this General Order and the forms required by it may be obtained from the Court's website, www.caeb.uscourts.gov or at the Court's public counters.

C. Debtor's Duties. In addition to the duties and obligations imposed upon Debtor by the Bankruptcy Code and Rules, the Local Bankruptcy Rules, and the General Order, this plan imposes the following additional requirements on Debtor: (a) **Transfers of Property.** Debtor is prohibited from transferring, encumbering, selling, or otherwise disposing of any personal or real property with a value of $1,000 or more other than in the regular course of Debtor's financial or business affairs without first obtaining court authorization. (b) **New Debt.** Except as provided in 11 U.S.C. § 364, Debtor shall not incur aggregate new debt exceeding $1,000 without first obtaining court authorization. Without compliance with 11 U.S.C. § 1305(c), a new debt of $1,000 or less that is a consumer debt shall not be paid through this plan. (c) **Insurance.** Debtor shall maintain insurance as required by any law, contract, or security agreement. (d) **Support Payments.** Debtor shall maintain ongoing child or spousal support payments directly to the court-ordered recipient. (e) **Tax Returns and Periodic Reports.** After confirmation of this plan, Debtor shall timely file all tax returns and, upon the Trustee's request, provide the Trustee with a copy of each tax return, W-2 form, and 1099 form filed or received while the case is pending. The Trustee may require Debtor to furnish quarterly financial information regarding Debtor's business.

D. Dismissal. If Debtor defaults in the performance of this plan or if it will not be completed within six months of its stated term, not to exceed 60 months, the Trustee or any other party in interest may move to dismiss the bankruptcy case. When the Trustee requests dismissal, he may use either of the procedures authorized by Paragraphs 7 or 8 of the General Order.

IV. Additional Provisions

Additional provisions or alterations to this plan shall be set out below. If necessary, use another page. Changes to the preprinted language of this standard Chapter 13 plan or to its attachments will not be given any force or effect.

Attorney's Name, Address, and Phone Number:

____

____

____

____

Dated:

____
Debtor's Signature

____
Joint Debtor's Signature

ATTACHMENT M-1
Optional – Discard if not used

MOTIONS TO AVOID JUDICIAL LIENS ON DEBTORS RESIDENCE (OR OTHER QUALIFIED EXEMPT PROPERTY)
(Pursuant to 11 U.S.C. § 522(f)(1)(A))
(A separate motion must be used to avoid each lien)
NUMBER OF MOTIONS TO AVOID JUDICIAL LIENS IN THIS PLAN: __

NOTICE IS HEREBY GIVEN that Debtor moves to avoid the following lien on Debtor's residence (or other exempt property) pursuant to 11 U.S.C. § 522(f)(1)(A) and to treat the claim secured by such lien as a general unsecured claim. If granted, the claim of the creditor named below will be treated as a general unsecured claim (Class 7).

Name of the creditor holding the judicial lien that is the subject of this motion:

Address of residence or description of other qualified exempt property:

Debtor's opinion of the exempt property's replacement value: $
Amount of the exemption claimed by Debtor: $
Amount of the creditor's judgment: $

The amount(s) owed to and the name(s) of all creditors holding liens or security interests that cannot be avoided pursuant to section 522(f)(1)(A):

Name of Creditor	Amount of Claim

Other information relevant to the resolution of this motion:

I (we) declare under penalty of perjury under the laws of the State of California that the facts stated herein are true and correct.

Dated: ____________ ____________________
Debtor

Dated: ____________ ____________________
Debtor

All motions (Attachments M-1, M-2, and M-3) shall be appended to the Chapter 13 Plan.

EDCAL-123 E.D. CALIFORNIA

ATTACHMENT M-2

Optional – Discard if not used

MOTIONS TO AVOID NONPOSSESSORY. NONPURCHASE MONEY LIENS

(Pursuant to 11 U.S.C. § 522(f)(1)(B))

(A separate motion must be used to avoid each lien)

NUMBER OF MOTIONS TO AVOID NONPOSSESSORY LIENS IN THIS PLAN____

NOTICE IS HEREBY GIVEN that Debtor moves to avoid the lien on Debtor's exempt property (consisting of household goods, tools of the trade, or professionally prescribed health aids) held by the creditor identified below. If granted, the claim of the creditor named below will be treated as a general unsecured claim (Class 7).

Name of the creditor whose nonpossessory, nonpurchase money security interest or lien on the below-described property is being avoided:

Detailed description of exempt property:

Debtor's opinion of the exempt property's replacement value: $

Amount of the creditor's claim: $

Other information relevant to the resolution of this motion:

I (we) declare under penalty of perjury under the laws of the State of California that the facts stated herein are true and correct.

Dated: ________________ ______________________________
Debtor

Dated: ________________ ______________________________
Debtor

All motions (Attachments M-1, M-2, and M-3) shall be appended to the Chapter 13 Plan.

ATTACHMENT M-3

Optional – Discard if not used

MOTIONS TO VALUE COLLATERAL

(Pursuant to subsections (a) and (d) of 11 U.S.C. § 506 and Federal Rule of Bankruptcy Procedure 3012)

(A separate motion must be filed as to each creditor)

NUMBER OF MOTIONS TO VALUE COLLATERAL IN THIS PLAN ______

NOTICE IS HEREBY GIVEN that Debtor requests the court to value the property described below. This property secures the claim of the creditor named below. Debtor also requests that the amount of the creditor's secured claim not exceed the value of its security, less the claims of creditors holding senior liens or security interests. This determination will supercede any greater secured claim demanded in a proof of claim. Any objections to the creditor's claim are reserved and will be filed after the creditor has filed a proof of claim. In the opinion of the debtor, the collateral has the replacement value indicated below.

Name of the creditor whose collateral is being valued by this motion:

Total amount of this creditor's claim: $

Description of collateral *[For vehicles, include the mileage on the date of the petition and a list of optional equipment. For real property, state the street address and a brief description of it such as "single family residence" or "ten-acre undeveloped lot"]:*

The amount owed to and the name of all creditors holding liens or security interests senior to the lien or security interest of the above-named creditor:

Debtor's opinion of the collateral's replacement value: $

Other information relevant to the resolution of this motion:

I (we) declare under penalty of perjury under the laws of the State of California that the facts stated herein are true and correct.

Dated: ________________ ______________________________
Debtor

Dated: ________________ ______________________________
Debtor

All motions (Attachments M-1, M-2, and M-3) shall be appended to the Chapter 13 Plan.

CHAPTER 13 PLAN CONTINUATION SHEET

If additional space is needed to list all creditors in Classes 1 through 6, insert them on this page. Use additional pages, if necessary.

CLASS 1 CREDITORS NAME/COLLATERAL DESCRIPTION	REGULAR PAYMENT	PRE-PETITION ARREARS	INTEREST RATE
4.			
5.			
6.			
7.			
8.			

CLASS 2 CREDITORS NAME/COLLATERAL DESCRIPTION	CLAIM AMOUNT	MARKET VALUE of COLLATERAL	INTEREST RATE
4.			
5.			
6.			
7.			
8.			

CLASS 3 CREDITORS NAME/COLLATERAL DESCRIPTION	ESTIMATED DEFICIENCY	IS DEFICIENCY A PRIORITY CLAIM? Y/N
4.		
5.		
6.		

CLASS 5 CREDITORS NAME	TYPE OF PRIORITY	CLAIM AMOUNT
4.		
5.		
6.		

CLASS 6 CREDITORS NAME	REASON FOR SPECIAL TREATMENT	CLAIM AMOUNT
4.		
5.		
6.		

Chapter 11 Statement of Current Monthly Income

CLASS 1 CHECKLIST

FILE WITH TRUSTEE ONLY
DO NOT FILE WITH THE COURT

Debtor Name(s): ______________________ Bk Case #: ____________

Property Address: ______________________

❑ Residence
❑ Rental
❑ Other Describe: ______________________

Daytime Phone: ______________ Evening: ______________

Attorney name: (if any) ______________________

THE FOLLOWING INFORMATION MUST BE COMPLETED ON ALL CLAIMS LISTED IN CLASS 1. PLEASE BE SURE TO COMPLETE THIS FORM TO THE BEST OF YOUR ABILITY AND ATTACH THE PAYMENT COUPON OR STATEMENT THAT WAS SUPPLIED TO YOU FROM EACH CREDITOR.

Creditor Name: ______________________

Account #: ______________________

Payment Address: ______________________
Street Address

____
City State Zip

Creditor Phone Number: (if known) ______________
Regular Monthly Payment Amount: $ ________ Current Interest Rate: ________ %
Monthly Payment Due Date: ________
Date Payment Late: ________ Monthly Late Charge Amount: $ ________

Is this a variable interest rate loan? ❑ Yes ❑ No
If yes, when is the next anticipated adjustment date? ________

Are property taxes included in the monthly payment? ❑ Yes ❑ No

Is insurance included in the monthly payment? ❑ Yes ❑ No

Is the loan due in full and payable in less than 5 years? ❑ Yes ❑ No
If yes, date due: ________

EDCAL-127 E.D. CALIFORNIA

CORPORATION/BUSINESS IDENTIFICATION FORM FOR UNCLAIMED FUNDS

UNITED STATES BANKRUPTCY COURT
EASTERN DISTRICT OF CALIFORNIA

IN RE:)
)
) **CASE NO:**
)
) **CORPORATION/BUSINESS IDENTIFICATION**
) **FORM FOR UNCLAIMED FUNDS**
)
________________________ **DEBTOR(S).**)

I, ______________________________, hereby state that I am the __________________(Title) of ______________________________ (Business Name), and I am authorized to request payment of unclaimed funds.

Current Telephone No. (   ) ________________
Tax Identification No. ________________
Previous Mailing Address ________________
____
____
Current Mailing Address ________________
____

Dated:

(SEAL*) ________________________
Signature

* Affix seal, if available, and attach appropriate documentation which indicates that the person signing is authorized to do so. This documentation should be a corporate power of attorney signed by the CEO of the company (or other corporate officer) and a statement of the signing officer's authority, or similar documentation, as well as documents establishing the chain of ownership of the original corporate/business claimant, if appropriate.

STATE OF ______________________, COUNTY OF ______________________
On ______________________________ before me, personally appeared (insert name and title of signer) ____
____ personally known to me (or proved to me on the basis of satisfactory evidence) to be the person(s) whose name(s) is/are subscribed to the written instrument and acknowledged to me that he/she/they executed the same in his/her/their authorized capacity(ies), and that by his/her/their signature(s) on the instrument the person(s), or the entity upon behalf of which the person(s) acted, executed the instrument. WITNESS my hand and official seal.

____
Notary Public

(SEAL)

My commission expires on ________________

To ensure payment to the proper party, please fill out the identification portion of this form and submit together with an Application for Payment of Unclaimed Funds (EDC 3-950) and supporting documentation to:

Financial Administrator
United States Bankruptcy Court
Eastern District of California
501 I Street, Suite 3-200
Sacramento, CA 95814

EDC 3-952 (New 11/01)

DEBTOR'S APPLICATION FOR WAIVER OF THE CHAPTER 7 FILING FEE OR OTHER FEE

Official Form 3B 12/2007

DEBTOR'S APPLICATION FOR WAIVER OF THE CHAPTER 7 FILING FEE OR OTHER FEE

The court fee for filing a case under chapter 7 of the Bankruptcy Code is $299.

If you cannot afford to pay the full fee at the time of filing, you may apply to pay the fee in installments. A form, which is available from the bankruptcy clerk's office, must be completed to make that application. If your application to pay in installments is approved, you will be permitted to file your petition, completing payment of the fee over the course of four to six months.

If you cannot afford to pay the fee either in full at the time of filing or in installments, then you may request a waiver of the filing fee by completing this application and filing it with the Clerk of Court. A judge will decide whether you have to pay the fee. By law, the judge may waive the fee only if your income is less than 150 percent of the official poverty line applicable to your family size and you are unable to pay the fee in installments. You may obtain information about the poverty guidelines at www.uscourts.gov or in the bankruptcy clerk's office.

Required information. Complete all items in the application, and attach requested schedules. Then sign the application on the last page. If you and your spouse are filing a joint bankruptcy petition, you both must provide information as requested and sign the application.

Name of Debtor(s):	Case No. (If known):

DEBTOR'S APPLICATION FOR WAIVER OF THE CHAPTER 7 FILING FEE OR OTHER FEE

I / We hereby apply for waiver of:

☐ the Chapter 7 filing fee
or
☐ other fee (specify) ____________________

Part A. Family Size and Income

1. Including yourself, your spouse, and dependents you have listed or will list on Schedule I, Current Income of Individual Debtor(s), how many people are in your family? (Do not include your spouse if you are separated AND are not filing a joint petition.)	
2. Restate the following information that you provided, or will provide, on Line 16 of Schedule I. Attach a completed copy of Schedule I, if it is available. Total Combined Monthly Income (Line 16 of Schedule I)	$
3. State the monthly net income, if any, of dependents included in Question 1 above. Do not include any income already reported in Question 2. If none, enter $ 0.	$
4. Add the "Total Combined Monthlyincome" reported in Question 2 to your dependents' monthly net income from Question 3.	$
5. Do you expect the amount in Question 4 to increase or decrease by more than 10% during the next 6 months? If yes, explain.	☐ No ☐ Yes

Part B. Monthly Expenses

6. EITHER (a) attach a completed copy of Schedule J, Schedule of Monthly Expenses, and state your total monthly expenses reported on Line 18 of that Schedule, OR (b) if you have not yet completed Schedule J, provide an estimate of your total monthly expenses.	$
7. Do you expect the amount in Question 6 to increase or decrease by more than 10% during the next 6 months? If yes, explain.	☐ No ☐ Yes

Part C. Real and Personal Property

EITHER (I) attach completed copies of Schedules A, Real Property, and Schedule B, Personal Property, OR (2) if you have not yet completed those schedules, answer the following questions.

8. State the amount of cash you have on hand.	$

9. State below any money you have in savings, checking, or other accounts in a bank or other financial institution.

Bank or Other Financial Institution	Type of Account (savings, checking, CD)	Amount
		$
		$
		$
		$

10. State below the assets owned by you. **Do not list ordinary household furnishings and clothing.**			
Home	Address:	Value: $	Amount owed in mortgages and liens: $
Other real estate	Address:	Value: $	Amount owed in mortgages and liens: $
Motor vehicle	Model/Year:	Value: $	Amount owed: $
Motor vehicle	Model/Year:	Value: $	Amount owed: $
Other	Description	Value: $	Amount owed: $

11. State below any person, business, organization, or governmental unit that owes you money and the amount that is owed.

Name of Person, Business, or Organization that Owes You Money	Amount Owed
	$
	$
	$

Part D. Additional Information

12. Have you paid, promised to pay, or do you anticipate paying an attorney or anyone other than an attorney (such as a bankruptcy petition preparer, paralegal, typing service, or another person) any money for services in connection with this case, including the completion of this form, the bankruptcy petition, or schedules?

☐ No

☐ Yes. State below the name, address, and amount(s) you have paid, promised to pay, and/or anticipate paying each attorney or other person or entity for services in connection with this case. Attach additional sheets if more than two.

Name and Address	Title (if other than attorney)	Amount Paid	Amount you have promised to pay or anticipate paying
		$	$
		$	$

13. Has anyone paid an attorney or other person or service in connection with this case, on your behalf? ☐ No ☐ Yes
If yes, explain.

EDCAL-131 E.D. CALIFORNIA

14. Have you previously filed for bankruptcy relief during the past eight years? ☐ No ☐ Yes

Case Number (if known)	Year filed	Location of filing	Did you obtain a discharge? (If known)
			☐ Yes ☐ No ☐ Don't know
			☐ Yes ☐ No ☐ Don't know

15. Please provide any other information that helps to explain why you are unable to pay the filing fee in installments.

16. I(we) declare under penalty of perjury that I(we) cannot currently afford to pay the filing fee in full or in installments and that the foregoing information is true and correct.

Executed on: ______________________ ______________________
Date Signature of Debtor

______________________ ______________________
Date Signature of Joint Debtor (if any)

DECLARATION AND SIGNATURE OF NON-ATTORNEY BANKRUPTCY PETITION PREPARER (See 11 U.S.C. § 110)

I declare under penalty of perjury that: (1) I am a bankruptcy petition preparer as defined in 11 U.S.C. § 110; (2) I prepared this document for compensation and have provided the debtor with a copy of this document and the notices and information required under 11 U.S.C. §§ 110(b), 110(h), and 342(b); and, (3) if rules or guidelines have been promulgated pursuant to 11 U.S.C. § 110(h) setting a maximum fee for services chargeable by bankruptcy petition preparers, I have given the debtor notice of the maximum amount before preparing any document for filing for a debtor or accepting any fee from the debtor, as required in that section.

______________________ ______________________
Printed or Typed Name of Bankruptcy Petition Preparer Social Security No. (Required under 11 U.S.C. § 110.)

If the bankruptcy petition preparer is not an individual, state the name, title (if any), address, and social security number of the officer, principal, responsible person or partner who signs this document.

____

____
Address

X______________________ ______________________
Signature of Bankruptcy Petition Preparer Date

Names and Social Security Numbers of all other individuals who prepared or assisted in preparing this document unless the bankruptcy petition preparer is not an individual:

If more than one person prepared this document, attach additional signed sheets conforming to the appropriate Official Form for each person.

A bankruptcy petition preparer's failure to comply with the provisions of title 11 and the Federal Rules of Bankruptcy Procedure may result in fines or imprisonment or both. 11 U.S.C. § 110; 18 U.S.C. § 156.

DEBTOR'S CERTIFICATION CONCERNING PREPARATION OF MASTER ADDRESS LISTS

UNITED STATES BANKRUPTCY COURT
EASTERN DISTRICT OF CALIFORNIA

In re) Case No.
)
)
)
Debtor(s).)
______________________________)

Debtor's Certification Concerning Preparation of Master Address List

I (We), the undersigned Debtor(s), declare under penalty of perjury that I (we) prepared my (our) voluntary petition myself (ourself), am (are) proceeding without representation by counsel or assistance of a typing service, and lack the office equipment necessary to produce the Master Address List required by General Order 90-2.

DATED: ______________________________
Signature of Debtor

____
Signature of Joint Debtor

EDC 2-110 (Rev. 12/92)

DEBTOR'S TABULATION OF BALLOTS

UNITED STATES BANKRUPTCY COURT
EASTERN DISTRICT OF CALIFORNIA

In re) Case No.
)
)
)
Debtor(s))
______________________)

DEBTOR'S TABULATION OF BALLOTS

1. The following Acceptances and Rejections have been field or are attached hereto: Impaired Classes are encircled.

CLASS 1:	Accepts $______	#______
	Rejects $______	#______
CLASS 2:	Accepts $______	#______
	Rejects $______	#______
CLASS 3:	Accepts $______	#______
	Rejects $______	#______
CLASS 4:	Accepts $______	#______
	Rejects $______	#______
CLASS 5:	Accepts $______	#______
	Rejects $______	#______
CLASS 6:	Accepts $______	#______
	Rejects $______	#______
CLASS 7:	Accepts $______	#______
	Rejects $______	#______
CLASS 8:	Accepts $______	#______
	Rejects $______	#______

2. The debtor, by counsel, submits that pursuant to the foregoing, sufficient acceptances (have/have not) been received to confirm the (Plan/Amended Plan) filed ______________________.

Dated:

____
Signed (Attorney for Debtor)

EDC APPROVED FORM 3-836 (REV. 1/93)

DECLARATION REQUESTING ENTRY OF ORDER CONFIRMING CHAPTER 13 PLAN WITHOUT CHAPTER 13 TRUSTEE'S APPROVAL OF FORMS OF ORDER

______________________ [Name; State Bar ID No.]
______________________ [Address]
____
______________________ [Telephone]

Attorney for Debtor(s)

UNITED STATES BANKRUPTCY COURT
EASTERN DISTRICT OF CALIFORNIA

In re) Case No.
)
)
)
)
)
)
Debtor(s).)

DECLARATION REQUESTING ENTRY OF ORDER CONFIRMING CHAPTER 13 PLAN WITHOUT CHAPTER 13 TRUSTEE'S APPROVAL OF FORM OF ORDER

The attorney for the debtor declares:

1. The time for filing objections to confirmation of the plan and to the granting of the valuation and lien avoidance motions included with the plan has expired.

2. All timely objections, if any, have been overruled or the proposed form of order modifies the plan as directed by the court in its ruling on the objection(s).

3. Allowing three calendar days for mailing, the proposed confirmation order lodged with this declaration has been in the chapter 13 trustee's possession for at least ten (10) calendar days. The chapter 13 trustee has neither approved the form of the order nor made any objection to its form.

4. If any valuation motions and/or valuation motions are included with the plan, those motions were served by my office in accordance with paragraph 3 of the General Order on chapter 13

EDC 3-085 (01/03/03) Page 1 of 2

practice as well as the applicable Local Bankruptcy Rules, the Federal Rules of Bankruptcy Procedure, and the bankruptcy code.

5. If the plan provides for the payment of attorneys' fees pursuant to the Guidelines for Payment of Attorneys' Fees in Chapter 13 Cases, a "Rights And Responsibilities of Chapter 13 Debtors and Their Attorneys" form has been filed and no objection has been raised to the attorneys' fees requested in that form by the chapter 13 trustee or any other party interest.

I declare under penalty of perjury that the foregoing is true and correct. Executed on ______, ____, at __________, California.

____
Attorney for Debtor(s)

[Proof of service on the Chapter 13 Trustee is appended.]

DESIGNATION OF TRUSTEE AND NOTICE OF SELECTION (SACRAMENTO AND MODESTO DIVISIONS)

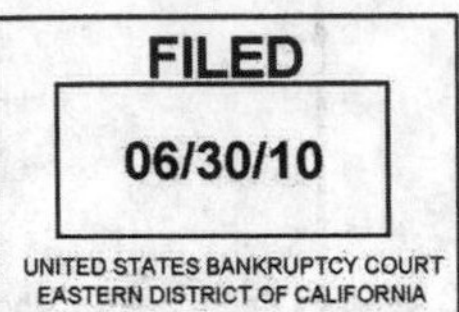
FILED
06/30/10
UNITED STATES BANKRUPTCY COURT
EASTERN DISTRICT OF CALIFORNIA

UNITED STATES BANKRUPTCY COURT
EASTERN DISTRICT OF CALIFORNIA
SACRAMENTO DIVISION

In re)
)
) Case No.
)
)
Debtor(s).)

DESIGNATION OF TRUSTEE AND NOTICE OF SELECTION

Standing Chapter 13 Trustee **Lawrence J. Loheit** is hereby designated Trustee of the above-named Debtor's(s') estate. The Standing Chapter 13 Trustee has filed a blanket bond pursuant to Federal Rule of Bankruptcy Procedure 2010(a).

If the Standing Chapter 13 Trustee does not notify the Office of the United States Trustee and the Court in writing of rejection of the office within five days after receipt of notice of selection, the Standing Chapter 13 Trustee shall be deemed to have accepted the office.

Dated: **06/30/10**

Print Form

Clear Form

Office of the United States Trustee
Region 17 -- Sacramento Office

Sara L. Kistler
United States Trustee

Antonia G. Darling
Assistant United States Trustee

EDC-UST 101-S

EDCAL-137 E.D. CALIFORNIA

DESIGNATION OF TRUSTEE AND NOTICE OF SELECTION (FRESNO DIVISION)

UNITED STATES BANKRUPTCY COURT
EASTERN DISTRICT OF CALIFORNIA
FRESNO DIVISION

FILED
06/30/10
UNITED STATES BANKRUPTCY COURT
EASTERN DISTRICT OF CALIFORNIA

In re) Case No.

Debtor(s).)

DESIGNATION OF TRUSTEE AND NOTICE OF SELECTION

Standing Chapter 13 Trustee Michael H. Meyer is hereby designated Trustee of the above-named Debtor's(s') estate. The Standing Chapter 13 Trustee has filed a blanket bond pursuant to Federal Federal Rule of Bankruptcy Procedure 2010(a).

If the Standing Chapter 13 Trustee does not notify the Office of the United States Trustee and the Court in writing of rejection of the office within five days after receipt of notice of selection, the Standing Chapter 13 Trustee shall be deemed to have accepted the office.

Dated: **06/30/10**

Print Form

Clear Form

Office of the United States Trustee
Region 17 -- Fresno Office

Sara L. Kistler
United States Trustee

EDC-UST 101-FM

DOCUMENT FILED WITHOUT REQUIRED FILING FEE

THIS FORM IS INTERACTIVE!!

FILED

06/30/10

UNITED STATES BANKRUPTCY COURT
EASTERN DISTRICT OF CALIFORNIA

UNITED STATES BANKRUPTCY COURT
EASTERN DISTRICT OF CALIFORNIA

Document Filed Without Required Filing Fee

The following document was filed without the required filing fee on ____________.

[ ] Petition [ ] Adversary [ ] Motion

[ ] Amendment [ ] Conversion [ ] Reopen

[ ] Other________________________

Case Number: ____________________

Debtor Name: ____________________

Filing Party: ____________________

[ ] The e-filing party has been sent an automated email notification.

[ ] The filing party has been contacted and has agreed to send the filing fee

Name of filing party contacted: ____________________

Date contacted: ____________________

[ ] Filing party was not contacted, case manager to follow-up

Date: 03/28/08

Deputy Clerk ____________________

EDC 2-055 (New 3/28/08)

Print Form

Clear Form

EDCAL-139 E.D. CALIFORNIA

DOCUMENT REQUEST

THIS FORM IS INTERACTIVE!!

UNITED STATES BANKRUPTCY COURT
EASTERN DISTRICT OF CALIFORNIA

FILED
06/30/10
UNITED STATES BANKRUPTCY COURT
EASTERN DISTRICT OF CALIFORNIA

TO: ____________________

CASE NO: ____________________

IN RE: ____________________

DOCUMENT REQUEST

The case record indicates that the following document has not been filed with the court. Please provide the court with the document or a letter stating why the document will not be filed at this time.

For the Chapter 7 Trustee:

[ ] Report of trustee at 341 meeting
[ ] Report of no distribution in a no asset case
[ ] Status of asset case (Fresno/Modesto divisions)

For the Office of the U.S. Trustee:

[ ] Status of asset case (Sacramento/Fresno divisions)

For the Chapter 13 Trustee:

[ ] Final report (case dismissed)

Other:

[ ] Regarding: ____________________

Request mailed to: ____________________

DATED: 06/30/10

FOR THE COURT
RICHARD G. HELTZEL, CLERK
U.S. BANKRUPTCY COURT

BY: ____________________
Deputy Clerk

cc: [ ] File
[ ] U.S. Trustee

Print Form
Clear Form

EDC 004 - 866

DOCUMENT REQUEST BY TELEPHONE

UNITED STATES BANKRUPTCY COURT
EASTERN DISTRICT OF CALIFORNIA
OFFICE OF THE CLERK

FILED
03/10/11
UNITED STATES BANKRUPTCY COURT
EASTERN DISTRICT OF CALIFORNIA

CASE NO: ____________________

IN RE: ____________________

DOCUMENT REQUEST BY TELEPHONE

TO WHOM IT MAY CONCERN:

[ ] Contacted Chapter 7 Trustee to request the following:

- [ ] Report of trustee at 341 meeting
- [ ] Report of no distribution in a no asset case
- [ ] Status of asset case (Fresno/Modesto divisions)

[ ] Contacted Office of the U.S. Trustee to request the following:

- [ ] Status of asset case (Sacramento/Fresno divisions)

[ ] Contacted Chapter 13 Trustee to request the following:

- [ ] Final report

[ ] Contacted ____________________ to request an order re:

____

DATED: 03/10/11

FOR THE COURT
RICHARD G. HELTZEL, CLERK
U.S. BANKRUPTCY COURT

BY:____________________
Deputy Clerk

Print Form
Clear Form

cc: [X] File
[ ] U.S. Trustee

EDC 004 - 865

DOCUMENTS REQUIRED FOR PROCESSING AN APPLICATION FOR PAYMENT OF UNCLAIMED FUNDS

UNITED STATES BANKRUPTCY COURT
EASTERN DISTRICT OF CALIFORNIA

DOCUMENTS REQUIRED FOR PROCESSING AN APPLICATION FOR PAYMENT OF UNCLAIMED FUNDS

Applications for payment of unclaimed funds ***will not be processed*** unless accompanied by the following documents:

IF THE OWNER OF THE FUNDS IS AN INDIVIDUAL, submit <u>all</u> of the following:

- ☐ Completed *APPLICATION FOR PAYMENT OF UNCLAIMED FUNDS* (EDC 3-950);
- ☐ Completed *INDIVIDUAL IDENTIFICATION FORM FOR UNCLAIMED FUNDS* (EDC 3-951);
- ☐ Photocopy of current driver's license (attach to *IDENTIFICATION FORM*). If you do not have a current driver's license, other identification containing a photograph and current address is required; and
- ☐ Proposed *ORDER FOR PAYMENT OF UNCLAIMED FUNDS* (EDC 6-950).

IF THE OWNER OF THE FUNDS IS A BUSINESS OR CORPORATION, submit <u>all</u> of the following:

- ☐ Completed *APPLICATION FOR PAYMENT OF UNCLAIMED FUNDS* (EDC 3-950);
- ☐ Completed *CORPORATION/BUSINESS IDENTIFICATION FORM FOR UNCLAIMED FUNDS* (EDC 3-952);
- ☐ Certified copy of Certificate/Articles of Incorporation, certified copy of Certificate/Articles of Merger or Successor Corporation, meeting minutes or other documents (i.e. Affidavit of the Chief Executive Officer or other corporate officer) identifying the representative and establishing that they are a duly authorized representative of the corporation (attach to *IDENTIFICATION FORM*);
- ☐ Photocopy of representative's identification credentials (attach *to IDENTIFICATION FORM*); and
- ☐ Proposed *ORDER FOR PAYMENT OF UNCLAIMED FUNDS* (EDC 6-950).

IF THE OWNER OF THE FUNDS IS REPRESENTED BY A FUNDS LOCATOR, submit <u>all</u> of the following:

- ☐ Completed *APPLICATION FOR PAYMENT OF UNCLAIMED FUNDS* (EDC 3-950);
- ☐ Completed *INDIVIDUAL IDENTIFICATION FORM FOR UNCLAIMED DIVIDENDS* (EDC 3-951) <u>**or**</u> *CORPORATION/BUSINESS IDENTIFICATION FORM FOR UNCLAIMED FUNDS* (EDC 3-952) and supporting documentation;
- ☐ Original Power of Attorney that includes the claimant's notarized signature (attach to *APPLICATION*);
- ☐ Photocopy of the claimant's current driver's license or representative's identification credentials (attach to *IDENTIFICATION FORM*); and
- ☐ Proposed *ORDER FOR PAYMENT OF UNCLAIMED FUNDS* (EDC 6-950).

DOMESTIC SUPPORT OBLIGATION CHECKLIST

DOMESTIC SUPPORT OBLIGATION CHECKLIST

FILE WITH TRUSTEE ONLY
DO NOT FILE WITH THE COURT

COMPLETE 1 FORM FOR EACH SUPPORT OBLIGATION

Debtor Name(s): ____________ Bk Case#: ____________

Debtor Daytime Phone: ( ) ____________ Evening: ( ) ____________

Attorney Name: ____________

Name of Claim Holder: ____________

Address of Claim Holder:

____
Mailing Address City/State Zip

Support Type:
Spousal Support ______
Child Support ______
Both ______

THE FOLLOWING INFORMATION MUST BE COMPLETED ON EACH SUPPORT OBLIGATION. PLEASE BE SURE TO COMPLETE THIS FORM TO THE BEST OF YOUR ABILITY.

Name of Applicable State Agency Where Claim Holder Resides:

____

Payment Address:

____
Mailing Address City/State Zip

Account #: ____________ Agency Phone #: ____________
Monthly Payment Amount: $______ Monthly Due Date: ____________
Date Payment Late: ____________ Years Remaining: ______

Are ongoing payments being made to the claim holder by Wage Order? YES ____ NO ____

Is the Debtor currently employed: YES ____ NO ____
If yes, Employer Information:

____
Name Mailing Address City/State Zip

ELECTRONIC FILING SYSTEM HARDWARE AND SOFTWARE REQUIREMENTS

U.S. Bankruptcy Court
Eastern District of California

Electronic Filing System Hardware and Software Requirements

To file cases and documents electronically, a user must have certain computer hardware and software, as well as access to the Internet.

1. Computer

A computer allows the user to create, save, view, print, and file electronic documents.

Hardware and operating system specifications for electronic filing are provided below. Required minimum specifications should be used to predict whether or not your existing hardware will perform adequately. Recommended optimum specifications should be used as a guide for those purchasing new equipment and services.

Required minimum and recommended optimum specifications are subject to change and it is likely that faster, greater capacity equipment will be needed in the future. Therefore, users are encouraged to purchase the fastest computers and connections they can within budget constraints, even beyond what is recommended. Updated required minimum and recommended optimum specifications will be posted on the court's Internet web site at www.caeb.uscourts.gov.

HARDWARE AND OPERATING SYSTEM SPECIFICATIONS FOR ELECTRONIC FILING	
	Recommended Minimum
CPU	Pentium IV 1.0 Ghz or faster
Random Access Memory (RAM)	256 MB or higher
Display Capability	1024 x 768 x 256
Operating System	Windows 2000 or XP

Additionally, the computer should have adequate hard disk storage; 1 GB of free disk space or more is recommended.

Although not required, law firms may wish to consider acquiring a large capacity storage unit or large capacity removable media drive, as well as an electronic file management system, to address portability and storage requirements. Likewise, to minimize storage, system administration, and file accessibility overheads, law firms with more than 10 computers should consider implementing some level of device and/or file sharing across a local or wide area network. To ascertain whether a change to your current network infrastructure would prove beneficial, please consult your computer professional.

2. Internet Connection

The Electronic Filing System is accessible through an Internet site; therefore, Internet access is essential. To access the Internet, you will need the services and software of an Internet Service Provider (ISP).

Connection to the Internet for the purpose of electronic filing should be faster than a standard dial-up connection.[1] Consequently, use of a dial-up modem to access the Internet for electronic filing purposes *is not* recommended.

The faster the Internet connection, the easier the electronic filing system will be to use. Electronic filers should, therefore, use DSL connections, cable modems, ISDN, or T1 lines to access the Internet.

3. Web Browser

The Electronic Filing System is a web application that operates on the Internet using a Web browser. Use of Internet Explorer 6.0 or higher is highly recommended. However, other browsers, such as Netscape 7.0 or higher, may also be functional. Browsers running on other operating systems, including Macintosh, have not been tested and may not be compatible.

4. Document Preparation Software

a. A word processing application (such as Corel WordPerfect or Microsoft Word) or a forms generation software package will be needed to create documents.

b. Portable Document Format (PDF) writer software (such as Adobe Acrobat PDF Writer) is required to convert electronic documents from a word processing format to PDF.

Adobe Acrobat Version 6.0 (or higher) offers two packages for converting documents to PDF – Acrobat Distiller and Acrobat Writer. Version 6.0's standard installation automatically installs the Distiller package. We recommend, however, that e-filers using Adobe Acrobat 6.0's software opt for 'custom' installation and install Adobe Acrobat Writer 6.0 because it converts files to PDF considerably faster, and produces significantly smaller PDF files, than Adobe Acrobat Distiller. Subsequent versions of Adobe Acrobat install Adobe Writer by default.

c. Zip file creation software (such as WinZip) is required to electronically file batches of documents. Zip files are "archives" used for distributing and storing files. Zip files contain one or more files. Usually the files "archived" in a Zip file are compressed to save space. Zip files make it easy to group files and make transporting and copying these files faster.

[1] Use of a dial-up connection to electronically file documents is extremely slow and would prove unsatisfactory to anyone who makes more than occasional use of the system.

5. Scanner and Scanning Software

Documents that are not in a user's computer in the form of word processing files (for example, a deed to secure a debt or a promissory note) will have to be scanned in order to file them electronically. Scanners range in price from $50 to tens of thousands of dollars. A flat bed scanner may be adequate for most users. If you anticipate imaging many documents, you may wish to consider a scanner with a sheet feeder attachment.

The resolution of documents scanned for subsequent electronic filing must be 300 dpi (dots per inch). Because scanning at higher resolutions produces unnecessarily large image files, and scanning at lower resolutions produces poor quality images, scanning software must be capable of creating images in PDF format at exactly 300 dpi (dots per inch) resolution. Otherwise, software capable of converting the scanned document's image file format to PDF is required.

6. Imaged Document Viewing Software

PDF Reader software is required to view all electronic court documents vis the Public Access to Court Electronic Records (PACER) system..

7. E-mail Account

An e-mail account is needed for receipt of electronic notification.

8. Printer

Notwithstanding the benefits of electronic filing, paper will not be disappearing in the near future. Therefore, you will need a printer adequate to handle your printing needs. Laser printers initially cost more but may prove less expensive in the long run because the cost per page for toner cartridges is much less than the cost per page for ink cartridges.

DUE TO LIMITED RESOURCES, THE COURT IS NOT ABLE TO PROVIDE EXTENSIVE TECHNICAL ASSISTANCE. USERS SHOULD CONTACT THEIR EQUIPMENT VENDOR OR LOCAL SYSTEMS TECHNICIAN FOR PROPER SYSTEM CONFIGURATIONS AND/OR FOR ASSISTANCE WITH IN-OFFICE EQUIPMENT PROBLEMS.

ELECTRONIC PUBLIC ACCESS FEE SCHEDULE

ELECTRONIC PUBLIC ACCESS FEE SCHEDULE

(Issued in accordance with 28 U.S.C. § 1913, 1914, 1926, 1930, 1932)

Effective March 11, 2008

As directed by Congress, the Judicial Conference has determined that the following fees are necessary to reimburse expenses incurred by the judiciary in providing electronic public access to court records. These fees shall apply to the United States unless otherwise stated. No fees under this schedule shall be charged to federal agencies or programs which are funded from judiciary appropriations, including, but not limited to, agencies, organizations, and individuals providing services authorized by the Criminal Justice Act, 18 U.S.C. § 3006A, and bankruptcy administrator programs.

I. For electronic access to court data via a federal judiciary Internet site: eight cents per page, with the total for any document, docket sheet, or case specific report not to exceed the fee for thirty pages – provided, however, that transcripts of federal court proceedings shall not be subject to the thirty-page fee limit. Attorneys of record and parties in a case (including *pro se* litigants) receive one free electronic copy of all documents filed electronically, if receipt is required by law or directed by the filer. No fee is owed under this provision until an account holder accrues charges of more than $10 in a calendar year. Consistent with Judicial Conference policy, courts may, upon a showing of cause, exempt indigents, bankruptcy case trustees, individual researchers associated with educational institutions, courts, section 501(c)(3) not-for-profit organizations, court appointed *pro bono* attorneys, and *pro bono* ADR neutrals from payment of these fees. Courts must find that parties from the classes of persons or entities listed above seeking exemption have demonstrated that an exemption is necessary in order to avoid unreasonable burdens and to promote public access to information. Any user granted an exemption agrees not to sell for profit the data obtained as a result. Any transfer of data obtained as the result of a fee exemption is prohibited unless expressly authorized by the court. Exemptions may be granted for a definite period of time and may be revoked at the discretion of the court granting the exemption.

II. For printing copies of any record or document accessed electronically at a public terminal in the courthouse: ten cents per page. This fee shall apply to services rendered on behalf of the United States if the record requested is remotely available through electronic access.

III. For every search of court records conducted by the PACER Service Center, $26 per name or item searched.

IV. For the PACER Service Center to reproduce on paper any record pertaining to a PACER account, if this information is remotely available through electronic access, 50 cents per page.

V. For a check paid to the PACER Service Center which is returned for lack of funds, $45.

JUDICIAL CONFERENCE POLICY NOTES

Courts should not exempt local, state or federal government agencies, members of the media, attorneys or others not members of one of the groups listed above. Exemptions should be granted as the exception, not the rule. A court may not use this exemption language to exempt all users. An exemption applies only to access related to the case or purpose for which it was given. The prohibition on transfer of information received without fee is not intended to bar a quote or reference to information received as a result of a fee exemption in a scholarly or other similar work.

The electronic public access fee applies to electronic court data viewed remotely from the public records of individual cases in the court, including filed documents and the docket sheet. Electronic court data may be viewed free at public terminals at the courthouse and courts may provide other local court information at no cost. Examples of information that can be provided at no cost include: local rules, court forms, news items, court calendars, opinions, and other information – such as court hours, court location, telephone listings – determined locally to benefit the public and the court.

ENTRY OF DEFAULT AND ORDER RE: DEFAULT JUDGMENT PROCEDURES

UNITED STATES BANKRUPTCY COURT
EASTERN DISTRICT OF CALIFORNIA

In re:	Case No.
Debtor(s).	
Plaintiff(s),	Adversary No.
vs.	
Defendant(s).	

ENTRY OF DEFAULT AND ORDER RE: DEFAULT JUDGMENT PROCEDURES

(This form is to be used for a single defendant only. If you have multiple defendants, please submit a separate form for each.)

It appears from the record that defendant ______________ ______________________________ failed to plead or otherwise defend in this proceeding as required by law.

Therefore, default is entered against defendant ______________________________ as authorized by Federal Rule of Civil Procedure 55 as incorporated by Federal Rule of Bankruptcy Procedure 7055.

( ) Plaintiff(s) shall apply for a default judgment within 30 days of the date of this order. A "prove-up" hearing shall be scheduled on the court's regular law and motion calendar on notice to the defendant pursuant to Local Rule 9014-1. The request for default judgment may be supported by affidavit in lieu of live testimony. Failure to comply with this order may result in the imposition of sanctions pursuant to Fed.R.Civ.P. 16(f), including, without limitation, dismissal of this adversary proceeding without further notice or hearing.

( ) Plaintiff(s) shall apply for a default judgment within 30 days of the date of this order. The motion need not be set for hearing but shall be filed and served on the defendant. The motion shall be supported by declarations or affidavits or other admissible evidence establishing liability and a right to the relief requested. A proposed "Default Judgment" for the court's signature shall be lodged with the motion. <u>See</u> Bankruptcy Rule 7055(b). Failure to comply with this order may result in the imposition of sanctions pursuant to Federal Rule of Civil Procedure 16(f) and 41(b), including, without limitation, dismissal of this adversary proceeding without further notice or hearing.

( ) Plaintiff(s) shall file supplemental declaration(s) documenting the source of the address(es) used for service of defendant.

Dated:

Richard Heltzel, Clerk
United States Bankruptcy Court

By: ______________________________
Deputy Clerk

EXHIBIT LIST/WITNESS MEMORANDUM

Trial Date: ______________

Continued to: ______________

EXHIBITS

Case No. ______________________ Debtor ______________________

Adv. No. ______________________

______________________ vs. ______________________

Plaintiff(s) Defendant(s)

ATTORNEY FOR PLAINTIFF(S)

ATTORNEY FOR DEFENDANT(S)

______________________ ______________________

______________________ ______________________

(Name, Address & Telephone No.) (Name, Address & Telephone No.)

Exhibits

NO.	PLAINTIFF(S) DEFENDANT(S)	NO.	
1		A	
2		B	
3		C	
4		D	
5		E	
6		F	
7		G	
8		H	
9		I	
10		J	

Witnesses

No.	PLAINTIFF(S)	NO.	DEFENDANT(S)
1		1	
2		2	
3		3	
4		4	
5		5	
6		6	
7		7	
8		8	
9		9	
10		10	

EDC 4-163 (Rev. 3/18/94) **EXHIBITS LIST/WITNESS MEMORANDUM**

FEES COMMONLY CHARGED BY THE BANKRUPTCY COURT

FEES COMMONLY CHARGED BY THE BANKRUPTCY COURT
Effective October 1, 2008

New Petitions	Chapter 7 *($245 chapter 7 filing fee, $39 administrative fee, plus $15 chapter 7 trustee fee)*	$ 299.00
	Chapter 9 *($1,000 chapter 9 filing fee plus $39 administrative fee)*	$1,039.00
	Chapter 11 (non-railroad) *($1,000 chapter 11 filing fee plus $39 administrative fee)*	$1,039.00
	Chapter 11 (railroad) *($1,000 chapter 11 filing fee plus $39 administrative fee)*	$1,039.00
	Chapter 12 *($200 chapter 12 filing fee plus $39 administrative fee)*	$ 239.00
	Chapter 13 *($235 chapter 13 filing fee plus $39 administrative fee)*	$ 274.00
	Chapter 15 *($1,000 chapter 15 filing fee plus $39 administrative fee)*	$1,039.00
Reopening Cases (See *Note 1.)*	Chapter 7 *(Includes $15 chapter 7 trustee fee)*	$ 260.00
	Chapter 9	$1,000.00
	Chapter 11 (non-railroad)	$1,000.00
	Chapter 11 (railroad)	$1,000.00
	Chapter 12	$ 200.00
	Chapter 13	$ 235.00
	Chapter 15	$1,000.00
Case Conversions	Chapter 11 to Chapter 7 *($15 chapter 7 trustee fee)*	$ 15.00
	Chapter 12 to Chapter 7 *(Includes $15 chapter 7 trustee fee)*	$ 60.00
	Chapter 13 to Chapter 7 *(Includes $15 chapter 7 trustee fee)*	$ 25.00
	Chapter 7 to Chapter 11	$ 755.00
	Chapter 12 to Chapter 11	$ 800.00
	Chapter 13 to Chapter 11	$ 765.00
	Any Chapter to Chapter 12	None
	Chapter 7 to Chapter 13	None
	Chapter 11 to Chapter 13	None
	Chapter 12 to Chapter 13	$ 35.00
Dividing Joint Cases	Chapter 7 *(Includes $39 administrative fee and $15 chapter 7 trustee fee)*	$ 299.00
	Chapter 11 *(Includes $39 administrative fee)*	$1,039.00
	Chapter 12 *(Includes $39 administrative fee)*	$ 239.00
	Chapter 13 *(Includes $39 administrative fee)*	$ 274.00
Motions	Motion to Compel Abandonment of Property	$ 150.00
	Motion to Terminate, Annul, Modify, or Condition the Automatic Stay	$ 150.00
	Motion to Withdraw Reference	$ 150.00
	Other Motions	None
Amendments	Schedule D, E, or F	$ 26.00
	Master Address List (See *Note 2.)*	$ 26.00
Other Documents and Services	Appeal (See *Note 3.)*	$ 255.00
	Authorization of Direct Appeal (or Cross Appeal) from Bankruptcy Court to Court of Appeals (See *Note 4.)*	$ 200.00
	Certification of Document	$ 9.00
	Complaint (See *Note 5.)*	$ 250.00
	Cross-Appeal (See *Note 6.)*	$ 255.00
	Exemplification of Document	$ 18.00
	Filing Any Document Not Related to a Pending Case or Proceeding	$ 39.00
	Photocopies Made by Court Personnel (per page)	$ .50
	Printing Documents From Public Terminal in Courthouse (per page)	$ .10
	Removal of an Action Pending in Another Court to Bankruptcy Court (See *Note 7.)*	$ 250.00
	Registration of Judgment from Another District	$ 39.00
	Retrieval of Record from Federal Records Center	$ 45.00
	Returned Check	$ 45.00
	Search of Court Records by Court Personnel (per name or item)	$ 26.00

EDC 2-033 (Rev. 03/06/09) (Front)

Office of the Clerk
United States Bankruptcy Court
Eastern District of California

FEES COMMONLY CHARGED BY THE BANKRUPTCY COURT [1]

The Bankruptcy Court will accept cash (exact change only), and money orders, cashier's checks, attorney or law firm checks, and traveler's checks payable to ***Clerk, U.S. Bankruptcy Court*** for payment of fees. The Court does not accept personal checks (other than attorney checks), checks drawn on a debtor's account while the case is open prior to discharge, second or third party checks, and checks or money orders for more than the amount due. ***Please do not send cash through the mail.***

NOTES

1. The reopening fee should be charged when a case is closed without a discharge being entered. The reopening fee will not be charged if the reopening is necessary: (1) to permit a party to file a complaint to obtain a determination under Rule 4007(b); or (2) when a creditor is violating the terms of the discharge under 11 U.S.C. § 524. The court may waive this fee under appropriate circumstances or may defer payment of the fee from trustees pending discovery of additional assets. If payment is deferred, the fee shall be waived if no additional assets are discovered. See *Bankruptcy Court Miscellaneous Fee Schedule (Effective October 1, 2008)* item 11.

2. No fee is required when the nature of the amendment is to change the address of a creditor or an attorney for a creditor listed on the schedules or to add the name and address of an attorney for a listed creditor. See *Bankruptcy Court Miscellaneous Fee Schedule (Effective October 1, 2008)* item 4.

3. The clerk must collect both a notice of appeal fee of $5, and an appeal docketing fee of $250 when a party files an appeal in a bankruptcy case or proceeding. If a trustee or debtor in possession is the appellant, the $250 appeal docketing fee is payable only from the estate and to the extent there is any estate realized. See *Bankruptcy Court Miscellaneous Fee Schedule (Effective October 1, 2008)* item 14. This exception does not apply to the $5.00 notice of appeal fee authorized by 28 U.S.C.§ 1930(c).

4. This fee is in addition to the $255 due upon the filing of an appeal or cross appeal, and shall be payable to the Bankruptcy Court when the Court of Appeals authorizes a direct appeal or a direct cross appeal.

5. If a debtor is the plaintiff, the fee must not be charged. If a child support creditor or its representative files the complaint and submits the form required by § 304(g) of the Bankruptcy Reform Act of 1994, the fee must not be charged. If a trustee or debtor-in-possession is the plaintiff, the fee should be payed by the estate if there is an estate. See *Bankruptcy Court Miscellaneous Fee Schedule (Effective October 1, 2008)* item 6.

6. For cross appeals, the clerk must collect both a notice of appeal fee of $5, and an appeal docketing fee of $250. If a trustee or debtor in possession is the appellant, the $250 appeal docketing fee is payable only from the estate and to the extent there is any estate realized. See *Bankruptcy Court Miscellaneous Fee Schedule (Effective October 1, 2008)* item 14. This exception does not apply to the $5.00 notice of appeal fee authorized by 28 U.S.C.§ 1930(c).

7. The fee for filing an adversary proceeding is due whether a party files the action in bankruptcy court originally or a party removes the action to bankruptcy court from another forum. Thus, when a party files a notice of removal, the clerk must collect the prescribed fee for filing an adversary proceeding, and the exceptions to payment accorded a plaintiff shall apply to a removing party. Consequently, if a debtor files the notice of removal, the fee must not be charged. If a child support creditor or its representative files the notice of removal and submits the form required by § 304(g) of the Bankruptcy Reform Act of 1994, the fee must not be charged. If a trustee or debtor-in-possession files the notice of removal, the fee should be payed by the estate if there is an estate. See *Bankruptcy Court Miscellaneous Fee Schedule (Effective October 1, 2008)* item 6.

[1] Includes fees prescribed by 28 U.S.C. § 1930 and the fee schedules issued by the Judicial Conference of the United States in accordance with 28 U.S.C. §1930(b). For additional fees, see EDC 2-034, *Bankruptcy Court Miscellaneous Fee Schedule*, and EDC 2-036, *Electronic Public Access Fee Schedule*.

EDC 2-033 (Rev. 03/06/09) (Reverse)

EDCAL-153 E.D. CALIFORNIA

FILE REQUEST CARD

U.S. Bankruptcy Court
Eastern District of California

Print Form

Clear Form

FILE REQUEST CARD

INSTRUCTIONS: **A separate form must be completed for each case you want to review.**

1. Type the information requested in Part I below and print the form. [Note: The information you enter in Part I will also appear in Part II on the printed form.]
2. Bring the entire completed form with you to the file window in the lobby of the appropriate divisional Clerk's Office.

DO NOT use a single form to request files in more than one case.

PART I – FILE WINDOW COPY

Date: 03/10/11 Case Number: ____________ Case Name: ____________

Files Requested:

[ ] Parent Case [ ] Current Volume [ ] All Volumes

[ ] Claims [ ] Other (specify) ____________

[ ] Adversary Proceeding Number ____________

[ ] Motion Number ____________

Requestor's Name ____________ Daytime Phone Number____________

- -

PART II – OUT CARD COPY

Date: 03/10/11 Case Number: ____________ Case Name: ____________

Files Requested:

[ ] Parent Case [ ] Current Volume [ ] All Volumes

[ ] Claims [ ] Other (specify) .

[ ] Adversary Proceeding Number ____________

[ ] Motion Number .

Requestor's Name ____________ Daytime Phone Number____________

EDC 207 (Rev. 7/14/00)

FINAL DECREE

FILED

UNITED STATES BANKRUPTCY COURT
EASTERN DISTRICT OF CALIFORNIA

UNITED STATES BANKRUPTCY COURT
EASTERN DISTRICT OF CALIFORNIA

Bankruptcy Case No.

Debtor(s).

FINAL DECREE

It appearing to the Court that the trustee in the above-captioned case, has completed administration of this estate,

IT IS ORDERED that the case is hereby closed, that the trustee is hereby discharged, that the bond of the trustee is hereby canceled, and that the surety of the trustee's bond is hereby released from further liability thereunder, except any liability which may have accrued during the time such bond was in effect.

DATED:

FOR THE COURT
RICHARD G. HELTZEL, CLERK

Please select a division.

- (•) Sacramento Division
- ( ) Fresno Division
- ( ) Modesto Division

U.S. Bankruptcy Court
501 I Street, Suite 3-200
Sacramento, CA 95814-2322
(916) 930-4400

CERTIFICATE OF MAILING

The deputy clerk whose signature appears below certifies that:

☐ A copy of this final decree was mailed today to the case Trustee whose name and address appear below.

OR

☐ The case Trustee whose name and address appear below has waived service of this order.

DATED:

BY: ______________________
Deputy Clerk

EDC 7-170 (Rev. 12/3/99)

Print Form Clear Form

EDCAL-155 E.D. CALIFORNIA

Chapter 13 Debtor's Plan and Attachments (For use in Chapter 13 cases filed on or after 10/17/05 OR converted to Chapter 13 on or after 10/17/05)

UNITED STATES BANKRUPTCY COURT
Eastern District of California

In re)
)
) Case No.
)
Debtor(s).)
____________________________________)

APPLICATION TO PAY FILING FEE IN INSTALLMENTS

1. In accordance with Bankruptcy Rule 1006, I (we) apply for permission to pay the filing fee amounting to $__________ in installments.
2. I am (we are) unable to pay the filing fee except in installments.
3. Until the filing fee is paid in full, I (we) will not make any additional payment or transfer any additional property to an attorney or other person for services in connection with this case.
4. I (we) propose the following terms for the payment of the filing fee:

$__________ *(check one)*: ☐ with the filing of the petition **OR**
☐ on or before __________

$__________ on or before __________

$__________ on or before __________

$__________ on or before __________

NOTE: The number of installments proposed shall not exceed four (4), and the final installment shall be payable not later than 120 days after filing the petition. For cause shown, the court may extend the time of any installment, provided the last installment is paid not later than 180 days after filing the petition. Fed. R. Bankr. P. 1006(b)(2).

5. I (we) understand that if I (we) fail to pay any installment when due, my (our) bankruptcy case may be dismissed, and I (we) may not receive a discharge of my (our) debts.
6. I (we) further understand that my (our) discharge, or confirmation of any plan, will be delayed until the filing fee is paid in full.

______________________________ ______________________________
Signature of Attorney (if any) Date Signature of Debtor Date
(In a joint case, both spouses must sign.)

______________________________ ______________________________
Name of Attorney Bar ID Number Signature of Joint Debtor (if any) Date

---

DECLARATION OF NON-ATTORNEY BANKRUPTCY PETITION PREPARER (See 11 U.S.C. § 110)

I declare under penalty of perjury that: (1) I am a bankruptcy petition preparer as defined in 11 U.S.C. § 110; (2) I prepared this document for compensation and have provided the debtor with a copy of this document and the notices and information required under 11 U.S.C. §§ 110(b), 110(h), and 342(b); and, (3) if rules or guidelines have been promulgated pursuant to 11 U.S.C. § 110(h) setting a maximum fee for services chargeable by bankruptcy petition preparers, I have given the debtor notice of the maximum amount before preparing any document for filing for a debtor or accepting any fee from the debtor, as required in that section.

______________________________ ______________________________
Printed or Typed Name of Bankruptcy Petition Preparer Social Security No. (Required under 11 U.S.C. § 110.)

If the bankruptcy petition preparer is not an individual, state the name, title (if any), address, and social security number of the officer, principal, responsible person or partner who signs this document.

____

____
Address

X______________________________ ______________________________
Signature of Bankruptcy Petition Preparer Date

Names and Social Security Numbers of all other individuals who prepared or assisted in preparing this document unless the bankruptcy petition preparer is not an individual:

If more than one person prepared this document, attach additional signed sheets conforming to the appropriate Official Form for each person. A bankruptcy petition preparer's failure to comply with the provisions of title 11 and the Federal Rules of Bankruptcy Procedure may result in fines or imprisonment or both. 11 U.S.C. § 110; 18 U.S.C. § 156.

Chapter 13 Statement of Current Monthly Income and Calculation of Commitment Period and Disposable Income

Form B21 Official Form (12/03) USBC, EDCA

UNITED STATES BANKRUPTCY COURT
EASTERN DISTRICT OF CALIFORNIA

In re	Case No.:
Debtor(s).	STATEMENT OF SOCIAL SECURITY NUMBER(S)

1. Name of Debtor (enter Last, First, Middle): ______________________

Check the appropriate box and, if applicable, provide the required information.

☐ Debtor has a Social Security Number and it is : ______ - _____ - ______ *(if more than one, state all.)*

☐ Debtor does not have a Social Security Number.

2. Name of Joint Debtor (enter Last, First, Middle): ______________________

Check the appropriate box and, if applicable, provide the required information.

☐ Joint Debtor has a Social Security Number and it is : ______ - _____ - ______ (if more than one, state all.)

☐ Joint Debtor does not have a Social Security Number.

I declare under penalty of perjury that the foregoing is true and correct.

X ______________________________
Signature of Debtor Date

Joint debtors must provide information for both spouses.

Penalty for making a false statement: Fine of up to $250,000 or up to 5 years imprisonment or both. 18 U.S.C. §§ 152 and 3571.

GUIDELINES PERTAINING TO BANKRUPTCY PETITION PREPARERS (CAE)

UNITED STATES BANKRUPTCY COURT
EASTERN DISTRICT OF CALIFORNIA

GUIDELINES PERTAINING TO BANKRUPTCY PETITION PREPARERS IN EASTERN DISTRICT OF CALIFORNIA CASES

The following guidelines are issued pursuant to Local Bankruptcy Rule 1001(d) and concern the compensation and conduct of bankruptcy petition preparers[1] in Eastern District of California bankruptcy cases. They reflect rebuttable presumptions which the court may, upon motion, noticed to the debtor, case trustee and U.S. Trustee, modify in a particular case or class of cases.

1. Bankruptcy petition preparers are authorized to provide typing and document filing services and may type bankruptcy petitions, forms and other documents and submit them for filing with the Clerk's Office. They are not authorized to practice law and are prohibited from giving legal advice, which includes, but is not limited to, the following advice:

   a. Whether to file bankruptcy;

   b. The Bankruptcy Code chapter under which to file a petition;

   c. How the debtor should respond to a question, or questions, set forth in bankruptcy forms and/or the information to be provided in other documents filed in connection with a bankruptcy case;

   d. The exemptions available to the debtor and/or which the debtor should claim;

   e. Whether particular debts are dischargeable or nondischargeable;

   f. The effect that filing bankruptcy will have on a foreclosure action and/or whether the debtor will keep their home;

   g. Whether the debtor may avoid or eliminate any lien or recover any property as a result of bankruptcy;

   h. Whether the debtor may and/or should redeem property;

   i. Whether the debtor may and/or should reaffirm a debt;

   j. Whether the debtor is entitled to a discharge under the Bankruptcy Code, and/or what defenses the debtor may have to an objection to discharge; and

   k. The tax consequences of any aspect of the bankruptcy case.

[1] Section 110(a) of the Bankruptcy Code (11 U.S.C. § 110(a)) defines "bankruptcy petition preparer" as a person, other than an attorney or an employee of an attorney, who prepares for compensation a petition or other document for filing by a debtor in a U.S. bankruptcy court or a U.S. district court in connection with a bankruptcy case.

2. The fee paid by the debtor to a bankruptcy petition preparer for typing and filing a bankruptcy petition may not exceed $125.00, including expenses (such as photocopies, postage,

telephone charges, and courier services).

3. According to section 110(g) of the Bankruptcy Code (11 U.S.C. § 110(g)), the fee for filing a bankruptcy petition must be paid by the debtor directly to the Clerk of the U.S. Bankruptcy Court. No part of the filing fee may be collected or received by the bankruptcy petition preparer from the debtor or on behalf of the debtor for payment to the Clerk by the bankruptcy petition preparer.

4. Leave to pay the filing fee in installments will not be granted to individuals, who within one year prior to filing the petition, paid any money, or transferred any property to, a bankruptcy petition preparer for services in connection with filing the petition. In these cases, the full amount of the fee must be paid at the time the petition is submitted for filing.

5. Upon motion of the debtor, the trustee, a creditor, the United States Trustee, or upon its own motion, the court may disallow and order the turnover of all, or a portion, of the fee paid to a bankruptcy petition preparer. The entire fee may be ordered forfeited where the bankruptcy petition preparer has acted incompetently or illegally, has violated any provision of section 110 of the Bankruptcy Code (11 U.S.C. § 110), or has failed to comply with the provisions of these Guidelines.

6. Before preparing a bankruptcy petition or first document for filing, or accepting any money from or on behalf of the debtor, a bankruptcy petition preparer shall provide a copy of these Guidelines to the debtor, together with a copy of the *Notice to Debtor Concerning Bankruptcy Petition Preparers.* The debtor shall read and sign the notice, and a copy of the signed notice will be provided to the debtor by the bankruptcy petition preparer. The original plus four copies of the Notice must be filed with the court along with the petition or the first document prepared by the bankruptcy petition preparer.

7. Debtors, trustees and others who believe a bankruptcy petition preparer has violated any provision of section 110 of the Bankruptcy Code (11 U.S.C. § 110) should so advise the Office of the United States Trustee.

Dated: October 20, 1997

DAVID E. RUSSELL, CHIEF JUDGE   RICHARD T. FORD, JUDGE

CHRISTOPHER M. KLEIN, JUDGE   BRETT DORIAN, JUDGE

MICHAEL S. MCMANUS, JUDGE   JANE DICKSON MCKEAG, JUDGE

Exhibit "D" to Voluntary Petition, Individual Debtor's Statement of Compliance with Credit Counseling Requirement

ATTACHMENT M-1
Optional – Discard if not used
MOTIONS TO AVOID JUDICIAL LIENS ON DEBTOR'S RESIDENCE (OR OTHER QUALIFIED EXEMPT PROPERTY)
(Pursuant to 11 U.S.C. § 522(f)(1)(A))

(A separate motion must be used to avoid each lien)
NUMBER OF MOTIONS TO AVOID JUDICIAL LIENS IN THIS PLAN: __

NOTICE IS HEREBY GIVEN that Debtor moves to avoid the following judicial lien on Debtor's residence (or other exempt property) pursuant to 11 U.S.C. § 522(f)(1)(A) and to treat the claim secured by such lien as a general unsecured claim. If granted, the claim of the creditor named below will be treated as a general unsecured claim (Class 7).

Name of the creditor holding the judicial lien that is the subject of this motion:

Address of residence or description of other qualified exempt property:

Debtor's opinion of the exempt property's "replacement value"
[as defined and limited by section 506(a)(2)]: $

Amount of the exemption claimed by Debtor: $
Amount of the creditor's judgment: $
The amount owed to and the name of all creditors holding liens or security interests that cannot be avoided pursuant to section 522(f)(1)(A):

Name of Creditor	Amount of Claim

This judicial lien does not secure a domestic support obligation.

Other information relevant to the resolution of this motion:

I (we) declare under penalty of perjury under the laws of the State of California that the foregoing is true and correct.

Dated:

____
Debtor

____
Joint Debtor

Debtor's Application for Waiver of the Chapter 7 Filing Fee or Other Fee

ATTACHMENT M-2
Optional – Discard if not used
MOTIONS TO AVOID NONPOSSESSORY NONPURCHASE MONEY LIENS
(Pursuant to 11 U.S.C. § 522(f)(1)(B))

A Separate Motion Must Be Used to Avoid Each Lien
NUMBER OF MOTIONS TO AVOID NONPOSSESSORY LIENS IN THIS PLAN ___

NOTICE IS HEREBY GIVEN that Debtor moves to avoid the lien on Debtor's exempt property (consisting of household furnishing, household goods [as defined at section 522(f)(4)(A)], wearing apparel, appliances, books, animals, crops, musical instruments, or jewelry held primarily for the personal, family, or household use of Debtor or a dependent of Debtor; implements, professional books, or tools of the trade of Debtor or a dependent of Debtor; or professionally prescribed health aids for Debtor or a dependent of Debtor, held by the creditor identified below. If this motion is granted, the claim of the creditor named below will be treated as a general unsecured claim (Class 7).

Name of the creditor whose nonpossessory, nonpurchase money security interest or lien on the below-described property is being avoided:

Detailed description of exempt property:

Debtor's opinion of the exempt property's "replacement value" [as defined and limited by section 506(a)(2)]: $

Amount of the creditor's claim: $

Other information relevant to the resolution of this motion:

I (we) declare under penalty of perjury under the laws of the State of California that the foregoing is true and correct.
Dated:

____
Debtor

____
Joint Debtor

Declaration Concerning Debtor's Schedules

ATTACHMENT M-3
Optional – Discard if not used
MOTIONS TO VALUE COLLATERAL
(Pursuant to subsections (a) and (d) of 11 U.S.C. § 506 and Federal Rule of Bankruptcy Procedure 3012)

(A separate motion must be filed as to each creditor)
NUMBER OF MOTIONS TO VALUE COLLATERAL IN THIS PLAN ____

NOTICE IS HEREBY GIVEN that Debtor requests the court to value the property described below. This property secures the claim of the creditor named below. Debtor also requests that the amount of the creditor's secured claim not exceed the value of its security, less the claims of creditors holding senior liens or security interests. This determination will supercede any greater secured claim demanded in a proof of claim. Any objections to the creditor's claim are reserved and will be filed after the creditor has filed a proof of claim. In the opinion of the debtor, the collateral has the replacement value indicated below.

Name of the creditor whose collateral is being valued by this motion:

Total amount of this creditor's claim: $

Description of collateral [*For vehicles include the mileage on the date of the petition and a list of optional equipment. For real property, state the street address and a brief description of it such as "single family residence" or "ten-acre undeveloped lot"*]:

The amount owed to and the name of all creditors holding liens or security interests senior to the lien or security interest of the above-named creditor:

Debtor's opinion of the collateral's "replacement value" [as defined and limited by section 506(a)(2)]: $

Other information relevant to the resolution of this motion:

I (we) declare under penalty of perjury under the laws of the State of California that the foregoing is true and correct.
Dated:

____
Debtor

____
Joint Debtor

Disclosure of Compensation of Attorney For Debtor

UNITED STATES BANKRUPTCY COURT
EASTERN DISTRICT OF CALIFORNIA

In re	)	
	)	Bankruptcy Case No.
	)	
	)	
Debtor(s).	)	

NOTICE TO DEBTOR CONCERNING BANKRUPTCY PETITION PREPARERS

Bankruptcy petition preparers are non-attorneys who are not authorized to practice law or give legal advice.

NOTICE IS HEREBY GIVEN that the Court has issued the attached *Bankruptcy Petition Preparer Guidelines* governing the work performed and fees charged by bankruptcy petition preparers in Eastern District of California cases.

Under the *Guidelines*, a bankruptcy petition preparer must give the debtor a copy of this notice before taking any money or property from the debtor or on behalf of the debtor for payment and before preparing any papers for filing in the bankruptcy court. The debtor and the bankruptcy petition preparer must sign a copy of this Notice in the spaces provided below. A copy must be furnished to the debtor by the bankruptcy petition preparer, and the original plus four copies must be filed with the Bankruptcy Court.

California law prohibits any non-attorney from rendering legal advice. Legal advice includes, but is not limited to, advice concerning the following:

- Whether the debtor should file bankruptcy and the chapter under which the petition should be filed;
- Whether debts will be eliminated, or "discharged," in a bankruptcy case;
- Whether the debtor will be able to keep their home after filing a bankruptcy case;
- The tax consequences of filing a bankruptcy case;
- Whether the debtor should promise to repay, or "reaffirm," a debt; and
- The exemptions available in bankruptcy, and what property can be claimed as exempt.

Unless approved by the court, a bankruptcy petition preparer may not charge the debtor more than $125 for preparing a bankruptcy petition, including expenses (such as photocopies, postage, telephone charges, and courier services). This fee does not include the petition filing fee. The filing fee must be paid directly to the Clerk of Court by the debtor.

EDC 3-350 (Rev. 3/5/99)

The attached *Guidelines* contain additional restrictions. The debtor shall read the *Guidelines* in order to know what the Court requires of bankruptcy petition preparers.

Debtors with questions concerning bankruptcy petition preparers or who believe that the *Guidelines* have been violated, should contact the appropriate Office of the U.S. Trustee (Sacramento: (916) 930-2100; Fresno/Modesto: (559) 498-7400).

FOR THE COURT
RICHARD G. HELTZEL, CLERK
U.S. BANKRUPTCY COURT

DEBTOR'S CERTIFICATION

I, , the debtor in the above-captioned case, have read and understand the foregoing information and attached *Guidelines*.

Dated: ______________________ ______________________________

(Debtor's Signature)

BANKRUPTCY PETITION PREPARER'S CERTIFICATION

I, , hereby certify under penalty of perjury that I am the bankruptcy petition preparer who has assisted the debtor(s) in filing the above-captioned case. I have not charged fees in excess of the amount allowed in Guideline 2, nor have I advised the debtor concerning any of the matters referred to in Guideline 1.

Dated: ______________________ ______________________________

(Bankruptcy Petition Preparer's Signature)

____

(Preparer's Social Security/Tax I.D. No.)

____

(Preparer's Printed or Typed Name)

____

____

(Preparer's Address)

Disclosure of Compensation of Bankruptcy Petition Preparer

United States Bankruptcy Court
For the Northern District of California
Oakland Division

Rights and Responsibilities of Chapter 13 Debtors And Their Attorneys

It is important for debtors who file a bankruptcy case under Chapter 13 to understand their rights and responsibilities. It is also important that the debtors know what their attorneys' responsibilities are, and understand the importance of communicating with their attorney to make the case successful. Debtors should know that they may expect certain services to be performed by their attorney. In order to assure that debtors and their attorneys understand their rights and responsibilities in the bankruptcy process, the following guidelines provided by the court are hereby agreed to by the debtors and their attorneys. Unless the Court orders otherwise:

BEFORE THE CASE IS FILED

The debtor agrees to:

1. Provide the attorney with accurate financial information.

2. Discuss with the attorney the debtor's objectives in filing the case.

The attorney agrees to:

1. Meet with the debtor to review the debtor's debts, assets, liabilities, income and expenses.

2. Counsel the debtor regarding the advisability of filing either a Chapter 7 or Chapter 13 case, discuss both procedures with the debtor, and answer the debtor's questions.

3. Explain what payments will be made directly by the debtor and what payments will be made through the debtor's Chapter 13 Plan, with particular attention to mortgage and vehicle loan payments, as well as any other claims which accrue interest.

4. Explain to the debtor how, when and where to make the Chapter 13 plan payment.

5. Explain to the debtor how the attorney fees and trustee fees are paid and provide an executed copy of this document to the debtor.

Rev. October 14, 2005

6. Explain to the debtor that the first plan payment must be made to the Trustee within 30 days after the date of the filing of the plan or order for relief, whichever is earlier.

7. Advise the debtor of the requirement to attend the 341 Meeting of Creditors, and instruct the debtor as to the date, time and place of the meeting.

8. Advise the debtor of the necessity of maintaining liability, collision and comprehensive insurance on vehicles securing loans or lease.

9. Timely prepare and file the debtor's petition, plan, statements and schedules.

10. Accept a retainer of no more than $2,000 for business cases, unless the attorney makes a special application to the court for approval of a larger retainer.

AFTER THE CASE IS FILED

The debtor agrees to:

1. Keep the Trustee and attorney informed of the debtor's address and telephone number.

2. Inform the attorney of any wage garnishments or attachment of assets which occur or continue after the filing of the case.

3. Contact the attorney promptly if the debtor loses his/her job or has other financial problems.

4. Let the attorney know if the debtor is sued during the case.

5. Inform the attorney if any tax refunds the debtor is entitled to are seized or not returned to the debtor by the IRS or Franchise Tax Board.

6. Contact the attorney before buying, refinancing, or selling real property or before entering into any long-term loan agreements to find out what approvals are required.

7. Pay any filing fees and expenses that may be incurred directly to the attorney.

The attorney agrees to provide the following legal services:

1. Appear at the 341 Meeting of Creditors with the debtor.

2. Respond to objections to plan confirmation, and where necessary, prepare an amended plan.

3. Prepare, file and serve necessary modifications to the plan which may include suspending, lowering or increasing plan payments.

4. Prepare, file and serve necessary amended statements and schedules, in accordance with information provided by the debtor.

5. Prepare, file and serve necessary motions to buy, sell or refinance real property when appropriate.

6. Object to improper or invalid claims, if necessary, based upon documentation provided by the debtor.

7. Represent the debtor in motions for relief from stay.

8. Where appropriate, prepare, file and serve necessary motions to avoid liens on real or personal property.

9. Provide such other legal services as are necessary for the administration of the present case before the Bankruptcy Court.

The "Guidelines for Payment of Attorneys fees in Chapter 13 Cases for the Oakland Division" provide for maximum initial fees in the following amounts: $3,500 in non-business cases and $5,000 in business cases. Retainers more than $2,000 in business cases will be closely scrutinized by both the Chapter 13 Trustee and the Court.

Initial fees charged in this case are $________________.
If the initial fees ordered by the court are not sufficient to compensate the attorney for the legal services rendered in the case, the attorney further agrees to apply to the court for any additional fees. Fees shall be paid through the plan unless otherwise ordered. The attorney may not receive fees directly from the debtor other than the initial retainer.

EDCAL-167 E.D. CALIFORNIA

Declaration and Signature of Non-Attorney Bankruptcy Petition Preparer (See U.S.C. §110)

UNITED STATES BANKRUPTCY COURT
Eastern District of California

In re) **Case Number:**
)
) **ORDER CONFIRMING CHAPTER 13 PLAN**
) **AND APPROVING ATTORNEY FEES**
Debtor(s).)
________________________________)

The Chapter 13 plan filed herein, as modified by any amendments filed thereto, came on regularly for hearing on confirmation upon proper notice on ______________________. The plan, or a summary thereof, together with notice of any amendments thereto, was transmitted to creditors as required by Federal Rule of Bankruptcy Procedure 3015. The court having found that the requirements of 11 U.S.C. section 1325 for confirmation have been met.

IT IS ORDERED that the Chapter 13 plan is confirmed subject to the following conditions and/modifications: ____

____

____

____

____

____

IT IS FURTHER ORDERED that for the benefit of general unsecured creditors, payments shall be made for _______ months.

IT IS FURTHER ORDERED that relief from the automatic stay is granted to

____

____

IT IS FURTHER ORDERED that unless otherwise provided in this order, confirmation of the plan: (1) does not constitute a finding as to the amount or nature of any creditor's claim or the nature of any creditor's interest in property of the debtor; (2) does not constitute the cure of any default until the amount required to cure such default has been paid; and (3) constitutes the waiver of the fixing of exemptions claimed by the debtor(s).

IT IS FURTHER ORDERED that attorney fees in the full amount of $__________ for [name] ______________________________ are approved, of which $__________ was paid prior to the filing of the petition. The balance of $__________ shall be paid by the trustee from plan payments at the rate of $100.00 per month or twenty-five percent (25%) of the plan payment, whichever is less, during the first year of the plan.

Dated:

____
United States Bankruptcy Judge

Approved as to form and content:

____
Trustee/Attorney for Trustee

EDC Form 3-181 (Revised 07-31-00)

Exhibit "A" to Voluntary Petition (Required in Chapter 11 cases only)

_______________ *[Name; State Bar ID No.]*
_______________ *[Address]*
____
_______________ *[Telephone]*

Attorney for Debtor/Debtor *In Propria Persona*

UNITED STATES BANKRUPTCY COURT
EASTERN DISTRICT OF CALIFORNIA

In re:) Case No.
)
)
)
)
)
Debtor.)

ORDER CONFIRMING PLAN, VALUING COLLATERAL AND AVOIDING LIENS

The Chapter 13 plan of the above-named debtor(s) has been transmitted to all creditors, and it has been determined after notice and opportunity for a hearing that the debtor(s) plan satisfies the requirements of 11 U.S.C. § 1325.

Therefore, **IT IS ORDERED** that the plan is confirmed.

IT IS FURTHER ORDERED that:

1. The debtor shall immediately notify, in writing, the Clerk of the United States Bankruptcy Court and the trustee of any change in the debtor's address;
2. The debtor shall immediately notify the trustee in writing of any termination, reduction of, or other change in the employment of the debtor; and
3. The debtor shall appear in court whenever notified to do so by the court.

[***The remaining paragraphs are optional and should be used as needed. If a paragraph is not applicable, please delete it. Delete the underlining once the appropriate information is inserted. If additional provisions are necessary, including provisions requested by a title company in connection with a section 522(f)(1)(A) motion, you may insert those provisions.***]

IT IS FURTHER ORDERED that the attorney's fees for the debtor's attorney in the full amount of $__________ are approved, $__________ of which was paid prior to the filing of the petition. The balance of $__________, provided that the attorney and debtor have executed and filed a Rights and Responsibilities of Chapter 13 Debtors and Their Attorneys, shall be paid by the trustee from plan payments at the rate specified in the Guidelines for Payment of Attorneys' Fees in Chapter 13 Cases.

IT IS FURTHER ORDERED that, pursuant to 11 U.S.C. § 1323, the plan is amended as follows:

IT IS FURTHER ORDERED that the motion to avoid the lien of __________________________ is granted. Such lien is a non-possessory, nonpurchase money lien that impairs the exemption of the debtor in property of the debtor described as: ____. Unless the debtor's bankruptcy case is dismissed, the lien of the such creditor is hereby extinguished and the lien shall not survive bankruptcy or affix to or remain enforceable against the aforementioned property of the debtor.

IT IS FURTHER ORDERED that the motion to avoid the lien of __________________________ is granted. Such lien is a judicial lien that impairs the exemption of the debtor in property of the debtor described as: ____. Unless the debtor's bankruptcy case is dismissed, the lien of the such creditor is hereby extinguished and the lien shall not survive bankruptcy or affix to or remain enforceable against the aforementioned property of the debtor.

IT IS FURTHER ORDERED that the motion to value the collateral of ______________________ is granted. The replacement value of the collateral and the secured claim of such creditor is determined to be $_______ and the deficiency shall be allowed as a general unsecured claim provided that a timely proof of claim is filed.

DATED:

BY THE COURT

____
United States Bankruptcy Judge

____
Approved by the Chapter 13 Trustee as to form.

Exhibit "C" to Voluntary Petition

______________________________ [Name; State Bar ID No.]
______________________________ [Address]

______________________________ [Telephone]
Attorney for Debtor(s)

UNITED STATES BANKRUPTCY COURT
EASTERN DISTRICT OF CALIFORNIA

In re	)	
	)	
	)	**Case No.**
	)	
____________________ **Debtor(s).**	)	

RIGHTS AND RESPONSIBILITIES OF CHAPTER 13 DEBTORS AND THEIR ATTORNEYS

It is important for debtors who file a bankruptcy case under Chapter 13 to understand their rights and responsibilities. It is also important that the debtors know what their attorney's responsibilities are, and understand the importance of communicating with their attorney to make the case successful. Debtors should also know that they may expect certain services to be performed by their attorney. In order to assure that debtors and their attorneys understand their rights and responsibilities in the bankruptcy process, absent a contrary court order, debtors and their attorneys agree as follows:

BEFORE THE CASE IS FILED

The debtor agrees to:

1. Provide the attorney with accurate financial information.
2. Discuss with the attorney the debtor's objectives in filing the case.

The attorney agrees to:

1. Meet with the debtor to review the debtor's debts, assets, liabilities, income, and expenses.
2. Counsel the debtor regarding the advisability of filing either a Chapter 7 or Chapter 13 case, discuss both procedures with the debtor, and answer the debtor's questions.
3. Explain what payments will be made directly by the debtor and what payments will be made through the debtor's Chapter 13 plan, with particular attention to mortgage and vehicle loan payments, as well as any other claims which accrue interest.
4. Explain to the debtor how, when, and where to make the Chapter 13 plan payments.
5. Explain to the debtor how the attorney's fees and Trustee's fees are paid and provide an executed copy of this document to the debtor.
6. Explain to the debtor that the plan payment must be made to the Trustee on the twenty-fifth day of each month beginning the month after the petition is filed.

7. Advise the debtor of the requirement to attend the 341 Meeting of the Creditors, and instruct the debtor as to the date, time and place of the meeting.
8. Advise the debtor of the necessity of maintaining liability, collision and comprehensive insurance on vehicles securing loans or leases.
9. Timely prepare and file the debtor's petition, plan, motions to value collateral, motions to avoid liens, statements, and schedules.

AFTER THE CASE IS FILED

The debtor agrees to:

1. Keep the Trustee and attorney informed of the debtor's address and telephone number.
2. Inform the attorney of any wage garnishments or attachments of assets which occur or continue after the filing of the case.
3. Contact the attorney promptly if the debtor loses his/her job or has other financial problems.
4. Let the attorney know if the debtor is sued during the case.
5. Inform the attorney if any tax refunds are seized or not returned to the debtor by the IRS or Franchise Tax Board.
6. Contact the attorney before buying, refinancing, or selling real or personal property with a value of $1,000 or more, before incurring new debt exceeding $1,000.
7. Pay any filing fees and expenses that may be incurred directly to the attorney.

The attorney agrees to provide the following legal services:

1. Timely serve the debtor's petition, plan, statements, and schedules on the chapter 13 trustee.
2. Timely serve the debtor's plan and motions to value collateral and motions to avoid liens together with the notice of hearing required by paragraph 3(b) of General Order 05-03.
3. Appear at the 341 Meeting of Creditors with the debtor.
4. Respond to objections to plan confirmation, and where necessary, prepare an amended plan.
5. Prepare, file, and serve necessary modifications to the plan which may include suspending, lowering, or increasing plan payments.
6. Prepare, file and serve necessary amended statements and schedules, in accordance with information provided by the debtor.
7. Prepare, file, and serve necessary motions to buy, sell, or refinance property when appropriate.
8. Object to improper or invalid claims, if necessary, based upon documentation provided by the debtor.
9. Represent the debtor in motions for relief from stay.
10. Where appropriate, prepare, file, and serve necessary motions to avoid liens on real or personal property and to value the collateral of secured creditors.
11. Provide such other legal services as are necessary for the administration of the present case before the Bankruptcy Court.

The fee charged for a chapter 13 bankruptcy is a matter for negotiation between the attorney and the debtor. While the court's "Guidelines for Payment of Attorneys Fees in Chapter 13 Cases" permit an initial fee of up to $3,500.00 in nonbusiness cases, and $5,000.00 in business cases, lesser fees may be negotiated. These initial fees may be paid, in whole or in part, directly by the debtor prior to the filing of the petition. To the extent not paid by the debtor before the filing of the petition, the fees must be paid through the plan by the Trustee.

Initial fees charged in this case are $_________, and of this amount, $_________ was paid by the debtor before the filing of the petition. While this initial fee should be sufficient to fairly compensate counsel for all preconfirmation services and most post-confirmation services, where substantial and unanticipated post-confirmation work is necessary, the attorney may request the court to approve additional fees. If additional fees are approved, they shall be paid through the plan unless otherwise ordered. The attorney may not receive fees directly from the debtor.

DATED: ____________ ______________________________
Debtor

DATED: ____________ ______________________________
Joint Debtor

DATED: ____________ ______________________________
Attorney for Debtor(s)

EDCAL-173 E.D. CALIFORNIA

List of Creditors Holding 20 Largest Unsecured Claims

UNITED STATES BANKRUPTCY COURT
EASTERN DISTRICT OF CALIFORNIA

In re)
)
)
) Case No.
)
)
________________________ Debtor(s).)

VERIFICATION OF MASTER ADDRESS LIST

I (we) declare under penalty of perjury that the Master Address List submitted for filing in this case *(please check and complete one)*:

[ ] on computer diskette as "pure text" (not delimited) in a file named CREDITOR.SCN, listing a total of _______ creditors, ***[required with conventionally filed petitions prepared by an attorney or bankruptcy petition preparer]***

OR

[ ] typed in scannable format on paper, consisting of ______ pages and listing a total of ______ creditors, ***[only acceptable with conventionally filed petitions not prepared by an attorney or bankruptcy petition preparer]***

OR

[ ] electronically as "pure text" (not delimited) in a file with a .txt extension, listing a total of ______ creditors, ***[required with electronically filed petitions]***

is a true, correct, and complete listing to the best of my (our) knowledge and belief.

I (we) acknowledge that the accuracy and completeness of the Master Address List is the shared responsibility of the debtor(s) and the debtor's(s') attorney or bankruptcy petition preparer, if any.

I (we) further acknowledge that the Court will rely on the Master Address List for all mailings, and that the various schedules and statements required by the Bankruptcy Code and the Federal Rules of Bankruptcy Procedure will not be used for mailing purposes.

DATED:

____________________________ ____________________________
Debtor's Signature Joint Debtor's (if any) Signature

EDC 2-100 (Rev. 9/2004)

Voucher for Attendance Fees for Contract Court Reporter

* AO 336 (Rev. 9/96)	VOUCHER FOR ATTENDANCE FEES FOR CONTRACT COURT REPORTER		VOUCHER NO.
DISTRICT		COURT (Check One): ☐ District Court ☐ Bankruptcy Court	CONTRACT NO.
CONTRACTOR'S NAME		CONTRACTOR TAXPAYER ID NUMBER	ATTENDING REPORTER
STREET ADDRESS		FULL-DAY RATE / HALF-DAY RATE	OVERTIME RATE
CITY AND STATE	ZIP CODE	JUDGE/COURT DESIGNEE (Optional) Signature	Date

Date 1	Last Name of Presiding Judicial Officer 2	Statistical Code No. 3	Loc. Code No. 4	Actual Time of Reporting: Morning Session 5	Actual Time of Reporting: Afternoon Session 6	Actual Time of Reporting: Overtime Session 7	Attending Rptrs (Several Court Reporters Used) 8	Claimed Compensation 9

OTHER COMPENSATION (Travel outside contract geographical

1. TRAVEL—TOTAL ________ x RATE ________
2. TOLLS
3. OTHER (Explain)

TOTAL

CONTRACTOR CERTIFICATION

I hereby certify that the above is a correct statement of the services performed, of expenses incurred, and of the amount due under the above contract.

SIGNATURE OF CONTRACTOR (or authorized agent)	DATE

COURT CERTIFICATION

I hereby certify the above as correct and proper for payment.

SIGNATURE OF COURT REPRESENTATIVE	DATE

BFY	FUND	BUDGET ORG.	COST ORG.	BOC	CHECK NUMBER
PAID BY/D.O./DATE OF PAYMENT					

DISTRIBUTION: DISBURSING OFFICER AO ACCOUNTING COURT REPORTING SUPERVISOR COURT CERTIFIER CONTRACTOR

EDCAL-175 E.D. CALIFORNIA

AO 336
(Rev. 9/96)

INSTRUCTIONS

Use this form for compensation and to report hours claimed by contract court reporters. This form is designed to support payments made to contract court reporters and to collect data on their utilization.

General:

This form is to be completed by the contract court reporter with the assistance of the clerk of court's office to support a request for payment to the contract court reporter. Bankruptcy courts and district courts are given an allocation of funds by the Administrative Office at the beginning of each fiscal year to pay contract court reporters. The allotment is communicated to the clerks of court with fund codes which are to be listed by the disbursing officer in the accounting classification block. The computation of the court reporter's compensation shall be in accordance with the contract cited on this voucher which should be governed by the prevailing rate paid in that district. Please note that payment for court reporter services provided senior judges, bankruptcy judges, magistrate judges, and land commissioners should be made on separate vouchers.

Payee Information:

Provide the complete name and address of the contractor submitting the claim. If the contractor employs a reporter, insert the name of the reporter in the block designated for Attending Reporter. If several reporters are used, insert an asterisk (*) in the Attending Reporter block and enter each reporter's name under Column 8 on the line which indicates the date the services were performed and the presiding judicial officer who was serviced. A taxpayer identifying number must be supplied unless payment will be made to a corporation. The laws of the United States require the court reporter to furnish his or her taxpayer identifying number to the Director of the Administrative Office IRC § 6109, 26 CFR § 301. 6109-1(c) (1978).

Presiding Judicial Officer:

Insert the last name of the presiding judicial officer, his or her statistical code number, and the location code number of the court where the hearings were held.

Hours and Amounts Claimed:

In Columns 5 and 6, enter the actual time in court for each day court reporting services were provided, for example 8:30 to 11:30 a.m.; 1:45 to 5:30 p.m. On any day that a court is unable to cancel the Reporting Service Order (RSO) on or before the preceding working day (as stated in the contract) and compensation is claimed, insert "U/C" in Column 5 and/or 6. The maximum compensation allowed for a cancelled Reporting Service Order is a half-day rate.

In Column 9, provide the amount of compensation which is claimed. Attendance by the reporter at both the morning and afternoon court sessions, regardless of time spent, shall constitute a full day and the reporter shall be entitled to a full-day attendance fee. Attendance by the reporter at any morning or afternoon court session, regardless of time spent, shall constitute a half day to which the reporter will be entitled to a half-day attendance fee. When the court is unable to cancel a Reporting Service Order (RSO), the reporter is entitled to a half-day attendance fee, maximum (morning and/or afternoon sessions). To support the claim for compensation, the contractor's invoice should be attached to the voucher.

Other Compensation (Including Travel Expenses):

This space is provided for recording the different adjustments, including travel expenses, which would affect the total payment to the reporter, and overtime claims in addition to the daily rate. Other adjustments may include any or all of the following items: Payment for reporting services outside the principal period of service; disallowance in reporting fees for failure to appear; and prompt payment discount, if any. Explanation of the amount to be paid or to be deducted should be provided in the space or on an attached sheet, if additional space is necessary.

Relative to payment of overtime, the contractor should provide the *date* and *time* for which overtime services were provided in Column 7.

Relative to travel expenses, the contractor should file a Standard Form 1012, Travel Voucher, completed by the court reporter and certified by the clerk of court or his designee, for reimbursement of travel expenses. Both the travel allowance and subsistence allowance will be allowed in the same manner as for employees of the Judicial Branch. The amount claimed for reimbursement should be set forth on the front of the form on Line 3 of "other compensation (travel outside contract geographical area)," Column 9. Be sure to identify the expenditure as travel and attach the Standard Form 1012 to the completed form AO 336, Voucher for Attendance Fees for Contract Court Reporters.

Court Certification:

A district judge, bankruptcy judge, magistrate judge, clerk, deputy clerk of court, or a designated member of the staff of a full-time magistrate judge who is a certifying officer should sign to certify that the reporter attended the court proceedings for which payment is claimed, and if the services were provided to a magistrate judge, that the proceedings were of the type authorized for use of a court reporter by law or established judiciary policy. This certification will be the authorization for the clerk to make payment.

Schedule A - Real Property

[Name; State Bar ID No.]
[Address]

[Telephone]

Attorney for Debtor(s)

UNITED STATES BANKRUPTCY COURT
EASTERN DISTRICT OF CALIFORNIA

In re	)	Case No.
	)	
	)	
	)	**WAGE ORDER**
	)	
	)	
Debtor(s).	)	

GOOD CAUSE APPEARING, IT IS HEREBY ORDERED THAT

the employer of the above-named debtor, is directed until further court order to deduct from the debtor's wages and to promptly forward to the Chapter 13 Standing Trustee,

____

the sum of $ ___________ each month. Payroll deductions made in accordance with the applicable law for current income tax withholding, federal social security, state disability, insurance premiums, union dues, employee welfare fund contributions, mandatory retirement contributions, and employer sustenance contributions are not affected by this order and may be continued.

This is a voluntary wage order and may include money for living expenses, such as mortgage and vehicle payments.
Therefore, the salary percentage deduction limitations set forth in California Code of Civil Procedure § 706.050 and 15 U.S.C. § 1673(a) do not apply.

A copy of this order shall be served by mail on the present and subsequent employers of the debtor. Monies transmitted to the Trustee must be identified by the debtor's name and case number as they appear above.

DATED:

For the Court
Richard G. Heltzel
Clerk, U.S. Bankruptcy Court

By:
Deputy Clerk

EDC 3-083-03 (Rev.7/1/03)

Schedule B - Personal Property

B 6B (Official Form 6B) (12/07)

In re ______________________________ Case No. ____________________
Debtor (If known)

SCHEDULE B - PERSONAL PROPERTY

Except as directed below, list all personal property of the debtor of whatever kind. If the debtor has no property in one or more of the categories, place an "x" in the appropriate position in the column labeled "None." If additional space is needed in any category, attach a separate sheet properly identified with the case name, case number, and the number of the category. If the debtor is married, state whether the husband, wife, both, or the marital community own the property by placing an "H," "W," "J," or "C" in the column labeled "Husband, Wife, Joint, or Community." If the debtor is an individual or a joint petition is filed, state the amount of any exemptions claimed only in Schedule C - Property Claimed as Exempt.

Do not list interests in executory contracts and unexpired leases on this schedule. List them in Schedule G - Executory Contracts and Unexpired Leases.

If the property is being held for the debtor by someone else, state that person's name and address under "Description and Location of Property." If the property is being held for a minor child, simply state the child's initials and the name and address of the child's parent or guardian, such as "A.B., a minor child, by John Doe, guardian." Do not disclose the child's name. See, 11 U.S.C. §112 and Fed. R. Bankr. P. 1007(m).

TYPE OF PROPERTY	NONE	DESCRIPTION AND LOCATION OF PROPERTY	HUSBAND, WIFE, JOINT, OR COMMUNITY	CURRENT VALUE OF DEBTOR'S INTEREST IN PROPERTY, WITH-OUT DEDUCTING ANY SECURED CLAIM OR EXEMPTION
1. Cash on hand.				
2. Checking, savings or other financial accounts, certificates of deposit or shares in banks, savings and loan, thrift, building and loan, and homestead associations, or credit unions, brokerage houses, or cooperatives.				
3. Security deposits with public utilities, telephone companies, landlords, and others.				
4. Household goods and furnishings, including audio, video, and computer equipment.				
5. Books; pictures and other art objects; antiques; stamp, coin, record, tape, compact disc, and other collections or collectibles.				
6. Wearing apparel.				
7. Furs and jewelry.				
8. Firearms and sports, photographic, and other hobby equipment.				
9. Interests in insurance policies. Name insurance company of each policy and itemize surrender or refund value of each.				
10. Annuities. Itemize and name each issuer.				
11. Interests in an education IRA as defined in 26 U.S.C. § 530(b)(1) or under a qualified State tuition plan as defined in 26 U.S.C. § 529(b)(1). Give particulars. (File separately the record(s) of any such interest(s). 11 U.S.C. § 521(c).)				

B 6B (Official Form 6B) (12/07) -- Cont.

In re ______________________ Case No. ______________
Debtor (If known)

SCHEDULE B - PERSONAL PROPERTY
(Continuation Sheet)

TYPE OF PROPERTY	NONE	DESCRIPTION AND LOCATION OF PROPERTY	HUSBAND, WIFE, JOINT, OR COMMUNITY	CURRENT VALUE OF DEBTOR'S INTEREST IN PROPERTY, WITH-OUT DEDUCTING ANY SECURED CLAIM OR EXEMPTION
12. Interests in IRA, ERISA, Keogh, or other pension or profit sharing plans. Give particulars.				
13. Stock and interests in incorporated and unincorporated businesses. Itemize.				
14. Interests in partnerships or joint ventures. Itemize.				
15. Government and corporate bonds and other negotiable and non-negotiable instruments.				
16. Accounts receivable.				
17. Alimony, maintenance, support, and property settlements to which the debtor is or may be entitled. Give particulars.				
18. Other liquidated debts owed to debtor including tax refunds. Give particulars.				
19. Equitable or future interests, life estates, and rights or powers exercisable for the benefit of the debtor other than those listed in Schedule A – Real Property.				
20. Contingent and noncontingent interests in estate of a decedent, death benefit plan, life insurance policy, or trust.				
21. Other contingent and unliquidated claims of every nature, including tax refunds, counterclaims of the debtor, and rights to setoff claims. Give estimated value of each.				

EDCAL-179 E.D. CALIFORNIA

B 6B (Official Form 6B) (12/07) -- Cont.

In re ______________________ Case No. ______________
Debtor (If known)

SCHEDULE B - PERSONAL PROPERTY

(Continuation Sheet)

TYPE OF PROPERTY	N O N E	DESCRIPTION AND LOCATION OF PROPERTY	HUSBAND, WIFE, JOINT, OR COMMUNITY	CURRENT VALUE OF DEBTOR'S INTEREST IN PROPERTY, WITH-OUT DEDUCTING ANY SECURED CLAIM OR EXEMPTION
22. Patents, copyrights, and other intellectual property. Give particulars.				
23. Licenses, franchises, and other general intangibles. Give particulars.				
24. Customer lists or other compilations containing personally identifiable information (as defined in 11 U.S.C. § 101(41A)) provided to the debtor by individuals in connection with obtaining a product or service from the debtor primarily for personal, family, or household purposes.				
25. Automobiles, trucks, trailers, and other vehicles and accessories.				
26. Boats, motors, and accessories.				
27. Aircraft and accessories.				
28. Office equipment, furnishings, and supplies.				
29. Machinery, fixtures, equipment, and supplies used in business.				
30. Inventory.				
31. Animals.				
32. Crops - growing or harvested. Give particulars.				
33. Farming equipment and implements.				
34. Farm supplies, chemicals, and feed.				
35. Other personal property of any kind not already listed. Itemize.				

_______ continuation sheets attached Total➤ $

(Include amounts from any continuation sheets attached. Report total also on Summary of Schedules.)

Reset Save As... Print

Schedule C - Property Claimed As Exempt

B 6C (Official Form 6C) (04/10)

In re ________________________________ **Case No.** ____________________
Debtor **(If known)**

SCHEDULE C - PROPERTY CLAIMED AS EXEMPT

Debtor claims the exemptions to which debtor is entitled under:
(Check one box)
☐ 11 U.S.C. § 522(b)(2)
☐ 11 U.S.C. § 522(b)(3)

☐ Check if debtor claims a homestead exemption that exceeds $146,450.*

DESCRIPTION OF PROPERTY	SPECIFY LAW PROVIDING EACH EXEMPTION	VALUE OF CLAIMED EXEMPTION	CURRENT VALUE OF PROPERTY WITHOUT DEDUCTING EXEMPTION

* *Amount subject to adjustment on 4/1/13, and every three years thereafter with respect to cases commenced on or after the date of adjustment.*

Reset Save As... Print

EDCAL-181 E.D. CALIFORNIA

Schedule D - Creditors Holding Secured Claims

B 6D (Official Form 6D) (12/07)

In re ______________________________ **Case No.** ______________________________
Debtor **(If known)**

SCHEDULE D - CREDITORS HOLDING SECURED CLAIMS

State the name, mailing address, including zip code, and last four digits of any account number of all entities holding claims secured by property of the debtor as of the date of filing of the petition. The complete account number of any account the debtor has with the creditor is useful to the trustee and the creditor and may be provided if the debtor chooses to do so. List creditors holding all types of secured interests such as judgment liens, garnishments, statutory liens, mortgages, deeds of trust, and other security interests.

List creditors in alphabetical order to the extent practicable. If a minor child is the creditor, state the child's initials and the name and address of the child's parent or guardian, such as "A.B., a minor child, by John Doe, guardian." Do not disclose the child's name. See, 11 U.S.C. §112 and Fed. R. Bankr. P. 1007(m). If all secured creditors will not fit on this page, use the continuation sheet provided.

If any entity other than a spouse in a joint case may be jointly liable on a claim, place an "X" in the column labeled "Codebtor," include the entity on the appropriate schedule of creditors, and complete Schedule H – Codebtors. If a joint petition is filed, state whether the husband, wife, both of them, or the marital community may be liable on each claim by placing an "H," "W," "J," or "C" in the column labeled "Husband, Wife, Joint, or Community."

If the claim is contingent, place an "X" in the column labeled "Contingent." If the claim is unliquidated, place an "X" in the column labeled "Unliquidated." If the claim is disputed, place an "X" in the column labeled "Disputed." (You may need to place an "X" in more than one of these three columns.)

Total the columns labeled "Amount of Claim Without Deducting Value of Collateral" and "Unsecured Portion, if Any" in the boxes labeled "Total(s)" on the last sheet of the completed schedule. Report the total from the column labeled "Amount of Claim Without Deducting Value of Collateral" also on the Summary of Schedules and, if the debtor is an individual with primarily consumer debts, report the total from the column labeled "Unsecured Portion, if Any" on the Statistical Summary of Certain Liabilities and Related Data.

☐ Check this box if debtor has no creditors holding secured claims to report on this Schedule D.

CREDITOR'S NAME AND MAILING ADDRESS INCLUDING ZIP CODE AND AN ACCOUNT NUMBER (*See Instructions Above.*)	CODEBTOR	HUSBAND, WIFE, JOINT, OR COMMUNITY	DATE CLAIM WAS INCURRED, NATURE OF LIEN , AND DESCRIPTION AND VALUE OF PROPERTY SUBJECT TO LIEN	CONTINGENT	UNLIQUIDATED	DISPUTED	AMOUNT OF CLAIM WITHOUT DEDUCTING VALUE OF COLLATERAL	UNSECURED PORTION, IF ANY
ACCOUNT NO.			VALUE $					
ACCOUNT NO.			VALUE $					
ACCOUNT NO.			VALUE $					
____ continuation sheets attached			Subtotal ► (Total of this page)				$	$
			Total ► (Use only on last page)				$	$
							(Report also on Summary of Schedules.)	(If applicable, report also on Statistical Summary of Certain Liabilities and Related Data.)

B 6D (Official Form 6D) (12/07) – Cont.

In re ______________________________ Case No. ______________________________
Debtor (If known)

SCHEDULE D - CREDITORS HOLDING SECURED CLAIMS

(Continuation Sheet)

CREDITOR'S NAME AND MAILING ADDRESS INCLUDING ZIP CODE AND AN ACCOUNT NUMBER (*See Instructions Above.*)	CODEBTOR	HUSBAND, WIFE, JOINT, OR COMMUNITY	DATE CLAIM WAS INCURRED, NATURE OF LIEN , AND DESCRIPTION AND VALUE OF PROPERTY SUBJECT TO LIEN	CONTINGENT	UNLIQUIDATED	DISPUTED	AMOUNT OF CLAIM WITHOUT DEDUCTING VALUE OF COLLATERAL	UNSECURED PORTION, IF ANY
ACCOUNT NO.			VALUE $					
ACCOUNT NO.			VALUE $					
ACCOUNT NO.			VALUE $					
ACCOUNT NO.			VALUE $					
ACCOUNT NO.			VALUE $					
Sheet no. _____ of _____ continuation sheets attached to Schedule of Creditors Holding Secured Claims			Subtotal (s)► (Total(s) of this page)				$	$
			Total(s) ► (Use only on last page)				$	$
							(Report also on Summary of Schedules.)	(If applicable, report also on Statistical Summary of Certain Liabilities and Related Data.)

Reset Save As... Print

EDCAL-183 E.D. CALIFORNIA

Schedule E - Creditors Holding Unsecured Priority Claims

B 6E (Official Form 6E) (04/10)

In re________________________ **Case No.** ____________________
Debtor (If known)

SCHEDULE E - CREDITORS HOLDING UNSECURED PRIORITY CLAIMS

A complete list of claims entitled to priority, listed separately by type of priority, is to be set forth on the sheets provided. Only holders of unsecured claims entitled to priority should be listed in this schedule. In the boxes provided on the attached sheets, state the name, mailing address, including zip code, and last four digits of the account number, if any, of all entities holding priority claims against the debtor or the property of the debtor, as of the date of the filing of the petition. Use a separate continuation sheet for each type of priority and label each with the type of priority.

The complete account number of any account the debtor has with the creditor is useful to the trustee and the creditor and may be provided if the debtor chooses to do so. If a minor child is a creditor, state the child's initials and the name and address of the child's parent or guardian, such as "A.B., a minor child, by John Doe, guardian." Do not disclose the child's name. See, 11 U.S.C. §112 and Fed. R. Bankr. P. 1007(m).

If any entity other than a spouse in a joint case may be jointly liable on a claim, place an "X" in the column labeled "Codebtor," include the entity on the appropriate schedule of creditors, and complete Schedule H-Codebtors. If a joint petition is filed, state whether the husband, wife, both of them, or the marital community may be liable on each claim by placing an "H," "W," "J," or "C" in the column labeled "Husband, Wife, Joint, or Community." If the claim is contingent, place an "X" in the column labeled "Contingent." If the claim is unliquidated, place an "X" in the column labeled "Unliquidated." If the claim is disputed, place an "X" in the column labeled "Disputed." (You may need to place an "X" in more than one of these three columns.)

Report the total of claims listed on each sheet in the box labeled "Subtotals" on each sheet. Report the total of all claims listed on this Schedule E in the box labeled "Total" on the last sheet of the completed schedule. Report this total also on the Summary of Schedules.

Report the total of amounts entitled to priority listed on each sheet in the box labeled "Subtotals" on each sheet. Report the total of all amounts entitled to priority listed on this Schedule E in the box labeled "Totals" on the last sheet of the completed schedule. Individual debtors with primarily consumer debts report this total also on the Statistical Summary of Certain Liabilities and Related Data.

Report the total of amounts not entitled to priority listed on each sheet in the box labeled "Subtotals" on each sheet. Report the total of all amounts not entitled to priority listed on this Schedule E in the box labeled "Totals" on the last sheet of the completed schedule. Individual debtors with primarily consumer debts report this total also on the Statistical Summary of Certain Liabilities and Related Data.

☐ Check this box if debtor has no creditors holding unsecured priority claims to report on this Schedule E.

TYPES OF PRIORITY CLAIMS (Check the appropriate box(es) below if claims in that category are listed on the attached sheets.)

☐ **Domestic Support Obligations**

Claims for domestic support that are owed to or recoverable by a spouse, former spouse, or child of the debtor, or the parent, legal guardian, or responsible relative of such a child, or a governmental unit to whom such a domestic support claim has been assigned to the extent provided in 11 U.S.C. § 507(a)(1).

☐ **Extensions of credit in an involuntary case**

Claims arising in the ordinary course of the debtor's business or financial affairs after the commencement of the case but before the earlier of the appointment of a trustee or the order for relief. 11 U.S.C. § 507(a)(3).

☐ **Wages, salaries, and commissions**

Wages, salaries, and commissions, including vacation, severance, and sick leave pay owing to employees and commissions owing to qualifying independent sales representatives up to $11,725* per person earned within 180 days immediately preceding the filing of the original petition, or the cessation of business, whichever occurred first, to the extent provided in 11 U.S.C. § 507(a)(4).

☐ **Contributions to employee benefit plans**

Money owed to employee benefit plans for services rendered within 180 days immediately preceding the filing of the original petition, or the cessation of business, whichever occurred first, to the extent provided in 11 U.S.C. § 507(a)(5).

* *Amounts are subject to adjustment on 4/01/13, and every three years thereafter with respect to cases commenced on or after the date of adjustment.*

B 6E (Official Form 6E) (04/10) – Cont.

In re ______________________________ **Case No.** ____________________
Debtor **(If known)**

☐ **Certain farmers and fishermen**

Claims of certain farmers and fishermen, up to $5,775* per farmer or fisherman, against the debtor, as provided in 11 U.S.C. § 507(a)(6).

☐ **Deposits by individuals**

Claims of individuals up to $2,600* for deposits for the purchase, lease, or rental of property or services for personal, family, or household use, that were not delivered or provided. 11 U.S.C. § 507(a)(7).

☐ **Taxes and Certain Other Debts Owed to Governmental Units**

Taxes, customs duties, and penalties owing to federal, state, and local governmental units as set forth in 11 U.S.C. § 507(a)(8).

☐ **Commitments to Maintain the Capital of an Insured Depository Institution**

Claims based on commitments to the FDIC, RTC, Director of the Office of Thrift Supervision, Comptroller of the Currency, or Board of Governors of the Federal Reserve System, or their predecessors or successors, to maintain the capital of an insured depository institution. 11 U.S.C. § 507 (a)(9).

☐ **Claims for Death or Personal Injury While Debtor Was Intoxicated**

Claims for death or personal injury resulting from the operation of a motor vehicle or vessel while the debtor was intoxicated from using alcohol, a drug, or another substance. 11 U.S.C. § 507(a)(10).

** Amounts are subject to adjustment on 4/01/13, and every three years thereafter with respect to cases commenced on or after the date of adjustment.*

____ *continuation* sheets attached

EDCAL-185 E.D. CALIFORNIA

B 6E (Official Form 6E) (04/10) – Cont.

In re ________________________________ **Case No.** ____________________
Debtor **(If known)**

SCHEDULE E - CREDITORS HOLDING UNSECURED PRIORITY CLAIMS

(Continuation Sheet)

Type of Priority for Claims Listed on This Sheet

CREDITOR'S NAME, MAILING ADDRESS INCLUDING ZIP CODE, AND ACCOUNT NUMBER *(See instructions above.)*	CODEBTOR	HUSBAND, WIFE, JOINT, OR COMMUNITY	DATE CLAIM WAS INCURRED AND CONSIDERATION FOR CLAIM	CONTINGENT	UNLIQUIDATED	DISPUTED	AMOUNT OF CLAIM	AMOUNT ENTITLED TO PRIORITY	AMOUNT NOT ENTITLED TO PRIORITY, IF ANY
Account No.									
Account No.									
Account No.									
Account No.									

Sheet no. ____ of ____ continuation sheets attached to Schedule of Creditors Holding Priority Claims

	AMOUNT OF CLAIM	AMOUNT ENTITLED TO PRIORITY	AMOUNT NOT ENTITLED TO PRIORITY
Subtotals➤ (Totals of this page)	$	$	
Total➤ (Use only on last page of the completed Schedule E. Report also on the Summary of Schedules.)	$		
Totals➤ (Use only on last page of the completed Schedule E. If applicable, report also on the Statistical Summary of Certain Liabilities and Related Data.)		$	$

Reset Save As... Print

Schedule F - Creditors Holding Unsecured Nonpriority Claims

B 6F (Official Form 6F) (12/07)

In re ______________________________ **Case No.** ____________________
Debtor **(If known)**

SCHEDULE F - CREDITORS HOLDING UNSECURED NONPRIORITY CLAIMS

State the name, mailing address, including zip code, and last four digits of any account number, of all entities holding unsecured claims without priority against the debtor or the property of the debtor, as of the date of filing of the petition. The complete account number of any account the debtor has with the creditor is useful to the trustee and the creditor and may be provided if the debtor chooses to do so. If a minor child is a creditor, state the child's initials and the name and address of the child's parent or guardian, such as "A.B., a minor child, by John Doe, guardian." Do not disclose the child's name. See, 11 U.S.C. §112 and Fed. R. Bankr. P. 1007(m). Do not include claims listed in Schedules D and E. If all creditors will not fit on this page, use the continuation sheet provided.

If any entity other than a spouse in a joint case may be jointly liable on a claim, place an "X" in the column labeled "Codebtor," include the entity on the appropriate schedule of creditors, and complete Schedule H - Codebtors. If a joint petition is filed, state whether the husband, wife, both of them, or the marital community may be liable on each claim by placing an "H," "W," "J," or "C" in the column labeled "Husband, Wife, Joint, or Community."

If the claim is contingent, place an "X" in the column labeled "Contingent." If the claim is unliquidated, place an "X" in the column labeled "Unliquidated." If the claim is disputed, place an "X" in the column labeled "Disputed." (You may need to place an "X" in more than one of these three columns.)

Report the total of all claims listed on this schedule in the box labeled "Total" on the last sheet of the completed schedule. Report this total also on the Summary of Schedules and, if the debtor is an individual with primarily consumer debts, report this total also on the Statistical Summary of Certain Liabilities and Related Data..

☐ Check this box if debtor has no creditors holding unsecured claims to report on this Schedule F.

CREDITOR'S NAME, MAILING ADDRESS INCLUDING ZIP CODE, AND ACCOUNT NUMBER *(See instructions above.)*	CODEBTOR	HUSBAND, WIFE, JOINT, OR COMMUNITY	DATE CLAIM WAS INCURRED AND CONSIDERATION FOR CLAIM. IF CLAIM IS SUBJECT TO SETOFF, SO STATE.	CONTINGENT	UNLIQUIDATED	DISPUTED	AMOUNT OF CLAIM
ACCOUNT NO.							
ACCOUNT NO.							
ACCOUNT NO.							
ACCOUNT NO.							
						Subtotal➤	$
						Total➤ (Use only on last page of the completed Schedule F.) (Report also on Summary of Schedules and, if applicable, on the Statistical Summary of Certain Liabilities and Related Data.)	$

____continuation sheets attached

EDCAL-187 E.D. CALIFORNIA

B 6F (Official Form 6F) (12/07) - Cont.

In re ______________________________ Case No. ____________________
Debtor (If known)

SCHEDULE F - CREDITORS HOLDING UNSECURED NONPRIORITY CLAIMS

(Continuation Sheet)

CREDITOR'S NAME, MAILING ADDRESS INCLUDING ZIP CODE, AND ACCOUNT NUMBER (See instructions above.)	CODEBTOR	HUSBAND, WIFE, JOINT, OR COMMUNITY	DATE CLAIM WAS INCURRED AND CONSIDERATION FOR CLAIM. IF CLAIM IS SUBJECT TO SETOFF, SO STATE.	CONTINGENT	UNLIQUIDATED	DISPUTED	AMOUNT OF CLAIM
ACCOUNT NO.							
ACCOUNT NO.							
ACCOUNT NO.							
ACCOUNT NO.							
ACCOUNT NO.							

Sheet no.____ of____ continuation sheets attached to Schedule of Creditors Holding Unsecured Nonpriority Claims

Subtotal➤ $

Total➤ $
(Use only on last page of the completed Schedule F.)
(Report also on Summary of Schedules and, if applicable on the Statistical Summary of Certain Liabilities and Related Data.)

Reset Save As... Print

Schedule G - Executory Contracts and Unexpired Leases

B 6F (Official Form 6F) (12/07)

In re ______________________ Case No. ______________________
Debtor (If known)

SCHEDULE F - CREDITORS HOLDING UNSECURED NONPRIORITY CLAIMS

State the name, mailing address, including zip code, and last four digits of any account number, of all entities holding unsecured claims without priority against the debtor or the property of the debtor, as of the date of filing of the petition. The complete account number of any account the debtor has with the creditor is useful to the trustee and the creditor and may be provided if the debtor chooses to do so. If a minor child is a creditor, state the child's initials and the name and address of the child's parent or guardian, such as "A.B., a minor child, by John Doe, guardian." Do not disclose the child's name. See, 11 U.S.C. §112 and Fed. R. Bankr. P. 1007(m). Do not include claims listed in Schedules D and E. If all creditors will not fit on this page, use the continuation sheet provided.

If any entity other than a spouse in a joint case may be jointly liable on a claim, place an "X" in the column labeled "Codebtor," include the entity on the appropriate schedule of creditors, and complete Schedule H - Codebtors. If a joint petition is filed, state whether the husband, wife, both of them, or the marital community may be liable on each claim by placing an "H," "W," "J," or "C" in the column labeled "Husband, Wife, Joint, or Community."

If the claim is contingent, place an "X" in the column labeled "Contingent." If the claim is unliquidated, place an "X" in the column labeled "Unliquidated." If the claim is disputed, place an "X" in the column labeled "Disputed." (You may need to place an "X" in more than one of these three columns.)

Report the total of all claims listed on this schedule in the box labeled "Total" on the last sheet of the completed schedule. Report this total also on the Summary of Schedules and, if the debtor is an individual with primarily consumer debts, report this total also on the Statistical Summary of Certain Liabilities and Related Data..

☐ Check this box if debtor has no creditors holding unsecured claims to report on this Schedule F.

CREDITOR'S NAME, MAILING ADDRESS INCLUDING ZIP CODE, AND ACCOUNT NUMBER *(See instructions above.)*	CODEBTOR	HUSBAND, WIFE, JOINT, OR COMMUNITY	DATE CLAIM WAS INCURRED AND CONSIDERATION FOR CLAIM. IF CLAIM IS SUBJECT TO SETOFF, SO STATE.	CONTINGENT	UNLIQUIDATED	DISPUTED	AMOUNT OF CLAIM
ACCOUNT NO.							
ACCOUNT NO.							
ACCOUNT NO.							
ACCOUNT NO.							
						Subtotal➤	$
						Total➤ (Use only on last page of the completed Schedule F.) (Report also on Summary of Schedules and, if applicable, on the Statistical Summary of Certain Liabilities and Related Data.)	$

_____ continuation sheets attached

EDCAL-189

E.D. CALIFORNIA

B 6F (Official Form 6F) (12/07) - Cont.

In re ______________________ **Case No.** ______________________
Debtor **(If known)**

SCHEDULE F - CREDITORS HOLDING UNSECURED NONPRIORITY CLAIMS

(Continuation Sheet)

CREDITOR'S NAME, MAILING ADDRESS INCLUDING ZIP CODE, AND ACCOUNT NUMBER (See instructions above.)	CODEBTOR	HUSBAND, WIFE, JOINT, OR COMMUNITY	DATE CLAIM WAS INCURRED AND CONSIDERATION FOR CLAIM. IF CLAIM IS SUBJECT TO SETOFF, SO STATE.	CONTINGENT	UNLIQUIDATED	DISPUTED	AMOUNT OF CLAIM
ACCOUNT NO.							
ACCOUNT NO.							
ACCOUNT NO.							
ACCOUNT NO.							
ACCOUNT NO.							

Sheet no. _____ of _____ continuation sheets attached to Schedule of Creditors Holding Unsecured Nonpriority Claims

Subtotal➤ $

Total➤ $
(Use only on last page of the completed Schedule F.)
(Report also on Summary of Schedules and, if applicable on the Statistical Summary of Certain Liabilities and Related Data.)

Reset

Save As...

Print

Schedule H - Codebtors

B 6H (Official Form 6H) (12/07)

In re ______________________ **Case No.** ______________________
Debtor **(If known)**

SCHEDULE H - CODEBTORS

Provide the information requested concerning any person or entity, other than a spouse in a joint case, that is also liable on any debts listed by the debtor in the schedules of creditors. Include all guarantors and co-signers. If the debtor resides or resided in a community property state, commonwealth, or territory (including Alaska, Arizona, California, Idaho, Louisiana, Nevada, New Mexico, Puerto Rico, Texas, Washington, or Wisconsin) within the eight-year period immediately preceding the commencement of the case, identify the name of the debtor's spouse and of any former spouse who resides or resided with the debtor in the community property state, commonwealth, or territory. Include all names used by the nondebtor spouse during the eight years immediately preceding the commencement of this case. If a minor child is a codebtor or a creditor, state the child's initials and the name and address of the child's parent or guardian, such as "A.B., a minor child, by John Doe, guardian." Do not disclose the child's name. See, 11 U.S.C. §112 and Fed. R. Bankr. P. 1007(m).

☐ Check this box if debtor has no codebtors.

NAME AND ADDRESS OF CODEBTOR	NAME AND ADDRESS OF CREDITOR

Reset Save As... Print

NORTHERN DISTRICT OF CALIFORNIA

The Northern District of California has adopted the following local rules relevant to cases under title 11, effective August 1, 2010:

TITLE AND APPLICABILITY OF RULES

Local Rule 1001-1. Scope of Rules; Short Title; Construction.

(a) Scope of Rules. The Federal Rules of Bankruptcy Procedure (throughout these Bankruptcy Local Rules referred to as "Bankruptcy Rule(s)") and Official Bankruptcy Forms promulgated under 28 U.S.C. § 2075, together with these Bankruptcy Local Rules govern practice and procedure in all bankruptcy cases and adversary proceedings in this District. These rules supersede all previous Bankruptcy Local Rules for the United States District Court for the Northern District of California.

(b) Relationship to District Court Rules. These Bankruptcy Local Rules are promulgated with other Local Rules of the District and should be cited as "B.L.R. _-_."

(c) Relationship to Bankruptcy Rules. These rules are divided into nine parts to be consistent in format with the Bankruptcy Rules. These rules supplement the Bankruptcy Rules and they shall be construed so as to be consistent with the rules and to promote the just, efficient and economical determination of every bankruptcy case and proceeding. Where there is a substantive relationship between a Bankruptcy Local Rule and a particular Bankruptcy Rule a corresponding rule number is utilized and a reference to the Bankruptcy Rule is included at the end of the Bankruptcy Local Rule.

(d) Relationship to Federal Rules of Civil Procedure. Whenever a Federal Rule of Civil Procedure is incorporated, it shall be incorporated as modified by the Bankruptcy Rules.

(e) Effective Date. These rules take effect on December 1, 2009, and shall apply to all cases and adversary proceedings pending on that date except to the extent the Court determines that such application would materially prejudice the rights of a party (in which event the prior version of these rules shall continue to apply).

(f) Amendment. Civil Local Rules incorporated herein shall be the rules in effect on the effective date of these rules and as thereafter amended, unless otherwise provided by such amendment or by these rules or by such amendment.

Local Rules 1001-2. Applicability of Civil Local Rules.

(a) Incorporation of Civil Local Rules. Except as hereinafter set forth or otherwise ordered by the Court, the following Civil Local Rules shall apply in all bankruptcy cases and adversary proceedings:

(1) 1-5(a) Clerk;

(2) 1-5(b) Court (except that, where appropriate, District Court shall instead refer to Bankruptcy Court);

(3) 1-5(c) Day (except that FRCivP 6(a) shall instead refer to Bankruptcy Rule 9006(a));

(4) 1-5(d) Ex parte;

(5) 1-5(e) File;

(6) 1-5(f) FRCivP.;

(7) 1-5(i) Federal Rule;

(8) 1-5(j) General Orders;

(9) 1-5(k) General Duty Judge;

(10) 1-5(l) Judge;

(11) 1-5(m) Lodge;

(12) 1-5(n) Meet and Confer;

(13) 1-5(o) Standing Orders of Individual Judges;

(14) 1-5(p) Unavailability (except that Civil L.R. 77-1 shall instead refer to B.L.R. 1001-3);

(15) 3-1 Regular Session (with the addition of the Santa Rosa Division);

(16) 3-4 Papers Presented For Filing (except that in subparagraph (a)(3)(C), District Judge and Magistrate Judge shall instead refer to Bankruptcy Judge); in subparagraph (b), FRCivP 42 shall instead refer to Bankruptcy Rule 7042; the second sentence of subparagraph (c)(3) and subparagraph (e) shall not apply;

(17) 3-5(a) Jurisdictional Statement;

(18) 3-6 Jury Demand (except that FRCivP 38(b) shall instead refer to Bankruptcy Rule 9015);

(19) 3-8 Claim of Unconstitutionality;

(20) 3-9(a) Natural Persons Appearing Pro Se; (c) Government and Governmental Agency;

(21) 3-11 Failure to Notify of Address Change (except that the reference to an action in subparagraph (a) shall also refer to a bankruptcy case);

(22) 5-2 Facsimile Filings (except for the references to Civil L.R.s 3-3(a) and 5-1(a) and only when ECF filing is not required);

(23) 5-6 Certificate of Service (except where service has been effected via ECF);

(24) 7-6 Oral Testimony Concerning Motion;

(25) 7-12 Stipulation (except that orders submitted by ECF must be a separate document);

(26) 7-13 Notice Regarding Submitted Matters (except for references to Civil L.R. 5-1);

(27) 10-1 Amended Pleadings;

(28) 11-1 The Bar of this Court;

(29) 11-2 Attorneys for the United States;

(30) 11-3 Pro Hac Vice;

(31) 11-4 (a)&(b) Standards of Professional Conduct;

(32) 11-5 Withdrawal from Case (except that the reference to an action in subparagraph (a) shall also refer to a bankruptcy case);

(33) 11-6 Discipline;

(34) 11-7 Reciprocal Discipline and Discipline Following Felony Conviction;

(35) 11-8 Sanctions for Unauthorized Practice;

(36) 11-9 Student Practice;

(37) 26-1 Custodian of Discovery Documents;

(38) 30-1 Required Consultation Regarding Scheduling;

(39) 30-2 Numbering of Deposition Pages and Exhibits;

(40) 33-1 Form of Answers and Objections;

(41) 33-2 Demands that a Party Set Forth the Basis for a Demand of a

Requested Admission;

(42) 33-3 Motions for Leave to Propound More Interrogatories Than Permitted by FRCivP 33;

(43) 34-1 Form of Responses to Requests for Production;

(44) 36-1 Form of Responses to Requests for Admission;

(45) 36-2 Demands that a Party Set Forth the Basis for a Denial of a Requested Admission;

(46) 37-1 Procedures for Resolving Disputes (except that District Judge or Magistrate Judge shall instead refer to Bankruptcy Judge);

(47) 37-2 Form of Motions to Compel (except for references to Civil L.R. 7);

(48) 37-3 Discovery Cut-Off; Deadline to File Motions to Compel;

(49) 37-4 Motions for Sanctions under FRCivP 37 (except for references to Civil L.R. 7-2 and Civil L.R. 7-8);

(50) 40-1 Continuance of Trial Date; Sanctions for Failure to Proceed (except for the reference to Civil L.R. 7, which shall refer to only the incorporated provisions of that rule);

(51) 54-1 through 54-4 Matters Regarding Costs (except for the last sentence of 54-4(b));

(52) 54-5 Motion for Attorney's Fees (except for references to Civil L.R.s 6-2 and 6-3);

(53) 54-6 Motion for Attorney's Fees (except for references to Civil L.R.s 6-2 and 6-3);

(54) 56-1 Time and Content of Motion for Summary Judgment (except that references to Civil L.R.s 7-2, 7-3 and 7-7 shall instead refer to B.L.R. 7007-1);

(55) 56-2 Separate or Joint Statement of Undisputed Facts;

(56) 56-3 Issues Deemed Established;

(57) 65-1 Temporary Restraining Orders;

(58) 65.1-1 Security;

(59) 77-3 Photography and Public Broadcasting;

(60) 77-4 Official Notices (except in subparagraph (b), the Bankruptcy

Court's website is located at http://www.canb.uscourts.gov);

(61) 77-5 Security of the Court;

(62) 77-6 Weapons in the Courthouse and Courtroom;

(63) 77-8 Complaints Against Judges;

(64) 79-3 Files; Custody and Withdrawal;

(65) 79-4 Custody and Disposition of Exhibits and Transcripts;

(66) 79-5 Filing Documents Under Seal (except for references to Civil L.R. 7-11);

(67) 83-1 Method of Amendment. Civil L.R. 83-1 shall apply such that amendments for form, style, grammar, consistency or other nonsubstantive modifications may be made to the Bankruptcy Local Rules by a majority vote of the active Bankruptcy Judges of the Court;

(b) Modification. Any Judge may, in any case or adversary proceeding, direct that additional Local Rules from other Chapters apply.

PART I. INTRA-DISTRICT VENUE; COMMENCEMENT OF CASES; FILING OF PETITIONS AND PLEADINGS

Local Rule 1001-3. Designation of Bankruptcy Divisions.

The United States Bankruptcy Court for the Northern District of California consists of the divisions shown in subparagraphs (a)-(d). The regular hours of the Offices of the Clerk are from 9:00 a.m. to 4:30 p.m. each day except Saturdays, Sundays, and Court holidays.

(a) Santa Rosa. Division 1 shall consist of the counties of Del Norte, Mendocino, Humboldt, Napa, Sonoma, Marin and Lake. The division office is located at the United States Courthouse, 99 South "E" Street, Santa Rosa, California 95404.

(b) San Francisco. Division 3 shall consist of the counties of San Francisco and San Mateo. The division office is located at 235 Pine Street, 19th Floor, San Francisco, California 94104 (mailing address: P. O. Box 7341, San Francisco, California 94120).

(c) Oakland. Division 4 shall consist of the counties of Alameda and Contra Costa. The division office is located at 1300 Clay Street, Room 300, Oakland, California 94612 (mailing address: P. O. Box 2070, Oakland, California 94604).

(d) San Jose. Division 5 shall consist of the counties of Santa Clara,

Santa Cruz, Monterey and San Benito. The division office is located at the United States Courthouse, 280 South First Street, Room 3035, San Jose, California 95113.

Local Rule 1002-1. Filing of Petition and Other Pleadings.

(a) Intradistrict Venue. All petitions, other than those filed by ECF, shall initially be filed with the Clerk of the Bankruptcy Court in the division of proper intradistrict venue as determined consistent with the venue rules of 28 U.S.C. §§ 1408 and 1410.

(b) Where Papers Filed. Except as provided in B.L.R. 1002-1(d), in bankruptcy cases not withdrawn to the District Court, all papers other than those filed by ECF shall be filed with the Clerk in the division where the case is pending.

(c) Change of Intradistrict Venue. If the petitioner believes that venue should be in a division other than the division of proper intradistrict venue as determined in accordance with subparagraph (a), the petitioner may file an ex parte application for transfer of the case to another division. The Clerk shall promptly present the application to any available Judge of the division where the petition is filed.

(d) Emergency Filings. In the event of a bona fide emergency a petition, other than one filed by ECF, may be presented for filing in a division other than the division of proper intradistrict venue as determined in accordance with subparagraph (a). The Clerk shall accept the petition and any other pleadings presented with the petition on behalf of the proper division, shall obtain the proper division's case number, shall place that number on the petition and other pleadings and shall promptly transmit the petition and other pleadings to the proper division.

(e) Removed Actions. All claims or causes of action removed pursuant to 28 U.S.C. § 1452, other than those removed by ECF filing, shall be removed to the division where the removed claims or causes of action are pending.

Local Rule 1002-2. Copies.

(a) Initial Documents and Other Papers. Except for ECF filings and as provided in subparagraphs (b) and (c) of this rule, petitions, statements, schedules, and lists and all other pleadings and papers shall be filed in the original only, without copies.

(b) Return copies. Parties desiring conformed copies of petitions, schedules, lists and other pleadings and papers, other than those filed by

ECF, should provide copies to the Clerk.

(c) Chambers copies. Parties must provide chambers copies of petitions, schedules, lists and other pleadings and papers, including those filed by ECF, in accordance with the posted chambers copies requirements of the assigned judge.

Local Rule 1005-1. Caption and Title of Papers Filed.

In addition to the information generally required by these rules, the caption of each paper filed in a bankruptcy case or adversary proceeding shall contain all of the following information:

(a) The file number of the bankruptcy case in which the proceeding arises and, where applicable, the adversary proceeding;

(b) The chapter of the Bankruptcy Code under which the case is currently pending; and

(c) The date, time, and location of the hearing or trial, where applicable.

Local Rule 1007-1. Use of Practice Forms.

The Court may approve and require the use of pre-printed practice forms. The Court may also approve practice forms which are not pre-printed but the format of which is required to be followed. Practice forms may be adopted on a district-wide or division-wide basis. Required forms will be available in the Clerk's office, on the Court's website (http://www.canb.uscourts.gov) and, with respect to Chapter 13 practice, in the office of the Chapter 13 Trustee or on the Chapter 13 Trustee's website.

Local Rule 1015-1. Related Cases.

(a) Defined. Related cases are cases where assignment to a single Judge would promote efficient administration of the estates or avoid conflicting or inconsistent rulings. Related cases may include: husband and wife; a partnership and one or more of its general partners; two or more general partners; two or more debtors having an interest in the same asset; or a debtor and an affiliate.

(b) Notice of Related Cases. In the event there are related bankruptcy cases, the debtor shall file a Notice of Related Case(s) at the time of filing of a petition for relief, and shall serve a copy of the notice upon the United States Trustee, other than when filed by ECF. The notice shall list the name, filing date, and case number of any related cases.

(c) Transfer. The Court may, on its own motion or upon the motion of a party in interest, order a case transferred to another Bankruptcy Judge based on the Court's determination as to whether a case is related and whether the transfer will promote the efficient administration of the estates or avoid inconsistent or conflicting rulings.

(d) Procedure. A motion by a party in interest to transfer a case or cases shall be addressed to the Judge presiding in the earliest filed case and served on the debtors and all trustees appointed in the cases.

Local Rule 1017-1. Conversion from Chapter 7 to 13.

(a) Unless moving for conversion to chapter 13 in response to a motion to dismiss filed by the U.S. Trustee under 11 U.S.C. § 707(b), a debtor who wishes to convert to chapter 13 a pending chapter 7 case that has not previously been converted shall serve a motion to convert on the chapter 7 trustee, the U.S. Trustee, and all parties in interest.

(b) When serving a motion to convert to chapter 13, the debtor should utilize the "Notice and Opportunity For Hearing" procedures of B.L.R. 9014-1(b)(3). For purposes of motions made under this rule, the 21 day notice provision of B.L.R. 9014-1(b)(3)(A)(i)(time to object and request a hearing) shall be 14 days. If an objection is filed or served, the 14 day notice provisions of B.L.R. 9014-1(b)(3)(A)(iv) (time for initiating party to give notice of a hearing) shall be 7 days; the notice of hearing should be served on the objecting party, the chapter 7 trustee and the U.S. Trustee. If no party in interest has filed an objection within 14 days following service of the motion to convert, the debtor may file a declaration of no response and upload or lodge an order granting the motion.

(c) The court will not take testimony at the hearing, and may at that time rule on the objection if there is no genuine issue of material fact.

(d) The above-mentioned time periods are subject to modification in accordance with the applicable rules. Nothing contained herein shall be construed to preclude requests for relief of any nature by or against any party in interest during the period between the filing of a motion to convert and the court's disposition thereof.

Local Rule 1017-2. Voluntary Dismissal of Chapter 13 Cases.

(a) Unless otherwise ordered, a debtor who wishes to dismiss a pending chapter 13 case which has not previously been converted shall serve a motion to dismiss on the chapter 13 Standing Trustee, the U.S. Trustee and any creditor who has appeared. The motion to dismiss shall be supported by a declaration stating whether there are pending motions to convert the case to chapter 7 or pending motions to dismiss with prejudice.

(b) When serving the motion to dismiss, the debtor should utilize the "Notice and Opportunity For Hearing" procedures of B.L.R. 9014-1(b)(3). For purposes of motions made under this rule, the 21 day notice provision of B.L.R. 9014-1(b)(3)(A)(i) (time to object and request a hearing) shall be 7 days. If an objection is filed or served, the 14 day notice provisions of B.L.R. 9014-1(b)(3)(A)(iv) (time for initiating party to give notice of a hearing) shall be 7 days; the notice of hearing should be served on the objecting party, the chapter 13 Standing Trustee and the U.S. Trustee. If no objection is filed or served within 7 days following service of the motion to dismiss, the debtor may file a declaration of no response and upload or lodge an order granting the motion.

(c) The court will not take testimony at the hearing, and may at that time rule on the objection if there is no genuine issue of material fact.

(d) The time periods provided in subsection (b) are subject to modification in accordance with applicable rules. Nothing contained in this rule shall be construed to preclude requests for relief of any nature by or against any party-in-interest during the period between the filing of the motion to dismiss and the court's disposition thereof.

PART II. ADMINISTRATION; PROFESSIONAL FEES

Local Rule 2001-1. Mail Redirection.

(a) Consent of Debtor. The filing of a petition under Title 11 by a debtor engaged in business is deemed to be the debtor's consent to mail redirection by the interim trustee and the trustee.

(b) Objection by Debtor. If the debtor does not consent to mail redirection, the debtor shall file a written objection with the Clerk. Upon the filing of the debtor's objection, the Court shall promptly set a hearing on notice to the debtor, trustee and United States Trustee. After the filing of the objection, and pending order of Court, the redirection shall continue, but the trustee shall hold, and not open, the debtor's mail.

Local Rule 2002-1. Notices.

(a) Who Shall Give Notice. Unless otherwise ordered, the initiating party shall give the notices required by Bankruptcy Rules 2002(a)(2)[sale or lease of property]; (a)(3)[compromise or settlement]; (a)(4)[dismissal or conversion]; (a)(5)[modification of plan]; (a)(6)[applications for compensation], except for final applications; and 2002(b)[disclosure statement and plan].

(b) Content of Notice. The notices given pursuant to paragraph (a) shall fully comply with Bankruptcy Rule 2002(c).

(c) Address List. Unless otherwise ordered, all notices shall be served on the persons entitled to notice under Bankruptcy Rule 2002(g). In order to comply with this rule, the initiating party must use a current mailing list.

Commentary: Attorneys should obtain current mailing list by logging onto CM/ECF, clicking on "Reports" and then "Mailing Matrix by Case." This generates the same list the Court would use for notice and permits compliance with this local rule.

(d) Service on Committee. Service on a committee appointed by the United States Trustee shall be made on the committee's counsel. If the committee has no counsel of record, service shall be made upon all members of the committee.

Local Rule 2004-1. Examination.

(a) Issuance of Order. The Clerk may issue on behalf of the Court, ex parte and without notice, orders granting applications for examination of an entity pursuant to Bankruptcy Rule 2004(a).

(b) Disputes. Any dispute or request for relief with respect to any such orders shall be treated as a discovery dispute in accordance with B.L.R. 1001-2(a) which incorporates Civ.L.R. 37-1.

Local Rule 2015-1. Funds of the Estate.

(a) Account Identification. The signature card (or if there is none, the depository agreement) for any account containing funds which are the property of a bankruptcy estate must clearly indicate that the depositor or investor is a "debtor-in-possession" or a trustee in bankruptcy. This rule does not apply to accounts maintained by Chapter 13 debtors.

(b) Compliance with 11 U.S.C. § 345. There shall be a rebuttable presumption that funds which are deposited with an entity which is included on the United States Trustee's most recent list of "cooperating depositories" have been deposited in accordance with 11 U.S.C. § 345(b).

(c) Investment of Bankruptcy Estate Assets In U.S. Treasury Instruments.

(1) Unless otherwise directed by the court, the trustee or debtor in possession may give notice of a proposed investment of bankruptcy estate assets in a Designated Fund to the United States trustee, all creditors, indenture trustees, and committees elected pursuant to § 705 or appointed pursuant to § 1102 of the Code, and shall file such notice with the court, together with a copy of the Designated Fund's prospectus. A party in interest may file and serve an objection within 14 days of the mailing of the notice, or within the time fixed by the court. If a timely objection is made, the court shall set a hearing on notice to the United States trustee and to other entities as the court may direct. If no objection is made, the trustee or debtor in possession may proceed with the investment.

(2) For purposes of this rule, a "Designated Fund" is an open-end management investment company that is registered under the Investment Company Act of 1940, regulated as a "money market fund" pursuant to Rule 2a-7 under the Investment Company Act of 1940, invests exclusively in United States Treasury bills and United States Treasury Notes owned directly or through repurchase agreements, has received the highest money market fund rating from a nationally recognized statistical rating organization, such as Standard & Poor's or Moody's, has agreed to redeem funds shares in cash, with payment being made no later than the business day following a redemption request by a shareholder (except in the event of an unscheduled closing of Federal Reserve Banks or the New York Stock Exchange), and has adopted a policy that it will notify its shareholder 60 days prior to any change in its policy to invest exclusively in Treasury securities as described above or to redeem fund shares in cash no later than the business day following a redemption request by the shareholder (with limited exceptions for unscheduled closings of Federal Reserve Banks or the New York Stock Exchange).

Local Rule 2015-2. Monthly Operating Reports.

(a) Cases in Which Reports Are Required. Monthly operating and tax reports ("monthly reports") are required from a trustee or debtor-inpossession in the following cases:

(1) All cases under Chapter 11 until confirmation of a plan, and Chapter 12;

(2) Chapter 7 cases where a business is being operated by a trustee;

(3) Chapter 13 business cases, if the Court so orders, upon application by the trustee or any party in interest.

(b) Filing Deadline. A monthly report shall be filed by the trustee or debtor-in-possession or a Chapter 13 debtor filing in accordance with this rule no later than the 21st day of the month following the month to which the report pertains. A separate report must be filed for each calendar month, or portion thereof, during which the case is pending and is a case for which a report is required pursuant to B.L.R. 2015-2(a), up to and including the month in which an order of confirmation, conversion, or dismissal is entered.

(c) Service of Reports. A copy of each monthly report shall be served, no later than the day upon which it is filed with the Court, upon the United States Trustee, the chairperson and counsel of record (if any) of each committee of creditors and each committee of equity security holders appointed by the United States Trustee, and such other persons or entities as may be ordered by the Court. In a Chapter 12 or Chapter 13 case, service of a copy of each monthly report also must be made on the trustee.

(d) Form and Content of Reports. Monthly reports shall be prepared on forms and supporting schedules approved by the Judges of the Court, copies of which shall be available in the Office of the Clerk.

(e) Modification of Reporting Requirements. The Court may, on application and for cause, modify the provisions of this rule. Any application to modify shall be served upon all parties upon whom the monthly report is required to be served.

Local Rule 2015-3. Debtor's Books and Records.

(a) Voluntary Cases. In a case filed pursuant to 11 U.S.C. § 301 or § 302, the books and records of the debtor shall be closed on the day immediately preceding the day on which the petition is filed, whether or not a separate estate is created for tax purposes. Pre-petition liabilities shall be segregated and reported separately from post-petition liabilities.

(b) Involuntary Cases. In a case filed pursuant to 11 U.S.C. § 303, the books and records of the debtor shall be closed on the day on which relief is ordered or an interim trustee is appointed, whichever occurs first. Notwithstanding the foregoing, liabilities incurred before the commencement of the case shall be segregated and, in the event relief is granted, reported separately from liabilities incurred after the commencement of the case.

PART III. CLAIMS; DISCLOSURE STATEMENTS AND PLANS; DISCHARGE HEARINGS

Local Rule 3003-1. Filing Proof of Claim or Interest Under Chapters 9 and 11.

Unless otherwise ordered by the Court, proofs of claim or interest shall be filed pursuant to Bankruptcy Rule 3003 and shall be filed within 90 days after the first date set for the meeting of creditors called pursuant to 11 U.S.C. § 341(a).

Local Rule 3007-1. Objections to Claim.

(a) Copy of Claim. Unless the Court orders otherwise, on an objection to claim, a copy of the claim, absent any attachments or exhibits, shall be included.

(b) Factual Dispute. Where a factual dispute is involved, the initial hearing on an objection shall be deemed a status conference at which the Court will not receive evidence. Where the objection involves only a matter of law, the matter may be argued at the initial hearing. Any notice of hearing on a claim objection shall so state.

Local Rule 3015-1. Chapter 12 and 13 Plans.

(a) Chapter 12 Plans.

(1) Hearing on Plan and Objections Thereto. Unless otherwise ordered, notice of the hearing on confirmation of the plan shall be served not less than 35 days prior to the hearing. Objections to confirmation of the plan shall be filed and served on the debtor, the United States Trustee, the Chapter 12 trustee, and on any other entity designated by the Court, not less than 7 days before the hearing.

(2) Confirmation of Plan. The order of confirmation shall be similar to the Official Form for confirmation of plans in Chapter 11 cases, with appropriate changes made for Chapter 12.

(b) Chapter 13 Plans.

(1) Notice by Clerk of the Court. At least 28 days before the first date set for the 11 U.S.C. § 341 meeting of creditors, copies or an adequate summary of the Chapter 13 plan shall be served by the Clerk of the Court on all creditors with the notice of commencement of the case. The Clerk shall certify to the Court that service has been made in accordance with this rule and pursuant to Bankruptcy Rule 2002(b). If the plan is not filed in time for the Clerk to serve it with the notice, the debtor shall serve the plan and provide certification as specified above.

(2) Notice by the Debtor. Prior to confirmation the debtor shall serve all amended plans, together with at least 21 days notice of the date and time of the hearing on confirmation of the amended plan, on the trustee and all adversely affected creditors. Notwithstanding the foregoing, when plans are amended in response to trustee objections, and no creditors are adversely affected, the trustee may schedule confirmation of such amended plan on the next available confirmation calendar without further notice to creditors.

(3) Objections. At or before the 11 U.S.C. § 341 meeting of creditors, a creditor objecting to confirmation shall file with the Court and serve upon the debtor, the debtor's counsel, and the trustee a written objection to confirmation stating the basis for the objection. Objections to amended plans shall be filed and served within 14 days of service of the amended plan. Objections to confirmation need not be considered by the Court unless service has been made in accordance with this rule. Once timely filed, an objection to a plan will be considered an objection to all subsequent versions and amendments until the objection is withdrawn or the objecting party fails to appear at a hearing on confirmation.

(4) Late Objections. Notwithstanding the previous paragraph, late objections will be considered if the objection is raised before the plan is confirmed and the objecting party shows that it acted diligently.

Local Rule 3016-1. Delayed Discharges of Individuals in Chapter 11, 12 and 13 Cases.

(a) All Chapter 11, Chapter 12 or Chapter 13 debtors who have claimed exemptions in excess of the adjusted amount set forth in 11 U.S.C. § 522(q)(1) must file a statement pursuant to Rule 1007(b)(8), not earlier than the date of the last payment under the plan or the date of filing a motion for a discharge under 11 U.S.C. §§ 1141(d)(5)(B), 1228(b), or 1328(b).

(b) Unless otherwise ordered, upon plan completion:

(1) All Chapter 13 debtors must file a certification in support of discharge stating whether or not the debtor:

(A) has completed an instructional course concerning personal financial management described in 11 U.S.C. § 111 and has filed a certificate of completion of that course;

(B) has been required to pay, and has paid, a domestic support obligation as that term is defined in 11 U.S.C. § 101(14A);

(C) has received a discharge in a Chapter 7, 11, 12 bankruptcy case filed within four years prior to filing the present Chapter 13 case, or in a Chapter 13 case filed within two years prior to filing the present Chapter 13 case.

(2) All Chapter 12 debtors must file the certification required in Subparagraph (b)(1)(B).

(3) If a Chapter 12 or Chapter 13 debtor has been required to pay a domestic support obligation as that term is defined in 11 U.S.C. § 101(14A), the debtor shall file a certification of domestic support obligation payees, setting forth the names and last known addresses of those payees. That certification shall be served by the debtor on the case trustee and all of the named domestic support obligation payees.

(c) A debtor required to file the statement required by Subparagraph (a) may combine it with the certification required by Subparagraph (b)(1) or (2).

(d) (1) The Clerk shall serve the statements and certifications required in Subparagraphs (a) and (b)(1) and (2) by mail on all parties in interest.

(2) Any party requesting a delay in the entry of the discharge must file a written response no later than 21 days from the date of service of the debtor's statement and certification and the response must be served by mail on the Chapter 11 Trustee, if any, the Chapter 12 Trustee or the Chapter 13 Trustee, the debtor and the debtor's attorney at the addresses noted on the debtor's statement and certification.

(3) If the delay request is timely filed, the debtor must schedule a hearing on the request and advise the Chapter 11 Trustee, if any, the Chapter 12 Trustee or the Chapter 13 Trustee, and the party requesting the delay, of the date and time of the hearing. The hearing must be held not more than ten (10) days before the date of the entry of the discharge order.

(4) If either no delay request is filed or if the delay request is not timely filed, the Court may enter a discharge order in the case, but not earlier than 30 days after the filing of the statement.

(e) Debtors shall make the statements and certifications required by this rule on forms approved by court in accordance with B.L.R. 1007-1. Those forms shall be available on the court's website and at the offices and on the websites of the district's Chapter 13 trustees.

Local Rule 3017-1. Chapter 11 Disclosure Statement Hearing.
Except as to small business cases subject to the provisions of 11 U.S.C. § 1125 (f), unless otherwise ordered, the plan proponent shall comply with the following procedures:

(a) The plan proponent may calendar and notice the disclosure statement hearing without necessity of a Court order, notwithstanding Official Form No. 12. Notice of the hearing shall be served on the debtor, creditors, equity security holders, United States Trustee, Securities and Exchange Commission, and other parties in interest not less than 35 days prior to the hearing. The notice shall contain the information required by Official Form No. 12 and, unless the Court orders otherwise, shall state that the deadline for the filing of objections is 7 days prior to the hearing.

The proposed plan and proposed disclosure statement shall be served, with the notice, only on the United States Trustee and the persons mentioned in the second sentence of Bankruptcy Rule 3017(a). A certificate of service of the foregoing documents must be filed at least 7 days prior to the hearing.

(b) At least 3 days prior to the hearing (and any continued hearing), the plan proponent shall advise the Judge's chambers by telephone whether the proponent intends to go forward with the hearing.

(c) The plan proponent may establish that the disclosure statement meets the applicable requirements of 11 U.S.C. §§ 1125(a) and (b) by offer of proof, declaration or, if the Court so permits or requires, live testimony. In all cases, a competent witness must be present. Briefs are not required.

(d) At the conclusion of the disclosure statement hearing, the plan proponent shall be prepared to advise the Court of the amount of Court time the confirmation hearing will require. If a contested confirmation hearing is anticipated, the Court will entertain requests that scheduling procedures be established concerning the filing of briefs, exchange and marking of exhibits, disclosure of witnesses, and discovery.

(e) In the event the plan proponent receives an objection to the disclosure statement, the proponent must make a good faith effort to confer with the objecting party to discuss the disclosure statement and to resolve the objection on a consensual basis.

(f) A plan proponent desiring a continuance of the hearing on a disclosure statement shall appear at the scheduled hearing to request a continuance.

(g) Upon approval of the disclosure statement, the plan proponent shall submit to the Court a proposed Order Approving Disclosure Statement and Fixing Time conforming to Official Form No. 13.

Local Rule 3020-1. Chapter 11 Confirmation Hearing.
Unless otherwise ordered, the plan proponent shall comply with the following procedures:

(a) All ballots and a ballot tabulation showing the percentages of acceptances and rejections for each impaired class, in number and dollar amount, must be filed at least 3 days prior to the confirmation hearing. The tabulation should also identify any unimpaired class(es) and state the reason that such class is unimpaired under 11 U.S.C. § 1124. A copy of the ballot tabulation should be served on the United States Trustee and counsel for the Official Creditors' Committee, or if no such committee has been appointed, the creditors included on the list filed pursuant to Bankruptcy Rule 1007(d), and any parties objecting to confirmation.

(b) A certificate of service of the plan, disclosure statement and Order Approving Disclosure Statement (unless 11 U.S.C. § 1125(f) applies), and official ballot, must be filed at least 3 days prior to the confirmation hearing.

Local Rule 3022-1. Chapter 11 Final Decree.

(a) At the confirmation hearing, the proponent of the plan shall advise the Court when all postconfirmation Court proceedings can be completed. The Court may set deadlines for filing reports and an application for a final decree.

(b) Unless the Court orders otherwise, an application for final decree shall be served on the United States Trustee and on counsel for the Creditors' Committee, or, if there is no Committee, on the 20 largest unsecured creditors. Such application shall be considered by the Court without a hearing, unless within 14 days after the date of service of the notice, a party in interest files and serves a request for hearing.

PART IV. AUTOMATIC STAY; DEBTOR'S DUTIES AND BENEFITS

Local Rule 4001-1. Motions For Relief From Stay.

(a) Procedure and Supporting Documents. A motion for relief from stay shall be so titled and shall be accompanied by the declaration of an individual competent to testify which sets forth the factual basis for the motion. The motion shall describe the relief sought and shall advise the respondent to appear personally or by counsel at the preliminary hearing.

(b) Cover Sheet. Every motion for relief from stay shall be filed with a completed Relief From Stay Cover Sheet. Relief From Stay Cover Sheets shall be available in the Office of the Clerk and on the Bankruptcy Court's website.

(c) Preliminary Hearings. Unless otherwise ordered, motions shall be set for preliminary hearing not less than 14 days after service. Motions shall be served the same day they are filed or sent for filing.

(d) Hearing Dates. The Clerk shall make available a list of available hearing dates. It is the responsibility of the moving party to select a hearing date which satisfies the notice requirements of this rule.

(e) Oral Testimony. Unless otherwise ordered, no oral testimony will be received by the Court at any hearing on a motion for relief from stay.

(f) Response. A respondent will not be required to, but may, file responsive pleadings, points and authorities, and declarations for any preliminary hearing.

(g) Inclusion of an Account Statement.

(1) As to motions for relief from the automatic stay wherein the movant alleges that the debtor has failed to maintain post-petition payments on an obligation, the motion shall include a postpetition account statement and a declaration attesting to the statement's accuracy. Both documents shall be written in language comprehensible to a lay person, and shall include the following information:

a. a description of the post-petition obligations that have accrued and are unpaid;

b. all payments received post-petition;

c. the date each post-petition payment was received;

d. the date each post-petition payment was posted to the subject account, if different from the date received.

If, for any reason, the timing or amount of the last payment which fell due pre-petition is different from any payments which have accrued post-petition, the moving party must briefly state the reason for the change and whether the debtor was given written notice of the changed amount.

As to defaults in post-petition payments to a Chapter 13 trustee, a printout from the Chapter 13 trustee's on-line information system itemizing post-petition payments will suffice.

(2) If the motion for relief from the automatic stay is based upon a failure to make pre-petition payments, then the requirements for an account statement referenced in paragraph (g)(1)(a) through (d) shall extend to all pre-petition obligations that have accrued and are unpaid.

(3) If a moving party fails to comply with paragraphs (g)(1) or (2) of this rule, the Court may, in its discretion, impose such monetary or nonmonetary remedies as it deems appropriate.

Local Rule 4001-2. Motions to Extend or Impose the Automatic Stay.

(a) Motion Required. Any party in interest seeking to extend the automatic stay pursuant to 11 U.S.C. § 362(c)(3)(B) or to impose the stay pursuant to 11 U.S.C. § 362(c)(4)(B) must file a motion in accordance with Bankruptcy Rule 9013, thus initiating a contested matter under Bankruptcy Rule 9014.

(b) Contents. The moving party must state whether continuation or imposition of the automatic stay is sought with respect to all creditors or only specified creditors, who must be identified by name. The moving party must also set forth facts in support of the motion, established by declarations as appropriate, showing that the filing of the present case is in good faith as to the creditors to be stayed and describing the circumstances that led to the dismissal of any prior case(s) concerning the debtor.

(c) Service. Service shall be on all creditors to be stayed, the United States Trustee, any trustee appointed in the case, and the debtor (if the debtor is not the moving party). Service shall be in accordance with Bankruptcy Rule 7004, except as to parties who have appeared in the case (in which event Bankruptcy Rule 7005 applies) or unless the court orders otherwise.

(d) Timing.

(1) Hearings should be scheduled on 14 days notice on the assigned judge's regular relief from stay calendar, but if no hearing date which will permit 14 days notice is available within 30 days of the petition date the moving party should comply with the assigned judge's procedures for scheduling a special setting. For hearings on shortened time, the moving party must comply with B.L.R. 9006-1.

(2) Alternatively, the moving party may utilize the "Notice and Opportunity For Hearing" procedures of B.L.R. 9014-1(b)(3). For purposes of motions made under this rule, the 21 day notice provision of B.L.R. 9014-1(b)(3)(A)(i)(time to object and request a hearing) shall be 14 days; the 14 day notice provisions of B.L.R. 9014-1(b)(3)(A)(iv) (time for initiating party to give notice to objecting party) and B.L.R. 9014-1(b)(3)(B) (tentative hearing date) shall be 7 days; and the 7 day provision of B.L.R. 9014-1(c)(3)(time for initiating party to reply) shall be 3 days.

(e) Opposition and Hearing. When a moving party proceeds under ¶ (d)(2) of this rule, a respondent will not be required to, but may, file responsive pleadings, points and authorities, and declarations for any hearing. Any such response shall be filed and served at least 3 days prior to the hearing. Oral opposition may be presented at the hearing. The hearing on a motion to continue the automatic stay must be concluded no later than 30 days after the petition date. See11 U.S.C. § 362(c)(3)(B).

(f) Applicability. This rule shall apply only to cases filed on or after October 17, 2005.

Local Rule 4001-3. Motions for Orders Confirming That No Stay Is In Effect.

(a) Motion Required. Any party in interest seeking an order confirming under 11 U.S.C. § 362(c)(4)(A)(ii) that no stay is in effect must file a motion in accordance with Bankruptcy Rule 9013, thus initiating a contested matter under Bankruptcy Rule 9014.

(b) Service. Service shall be on the debtor, debtor's counsel, the United States Trustee, any trustee appointed in the case, any party who has requested notice pursuant to Bankruptcy Rule 2002(i), and in Chapter 11, the non-insider creditors that hold the 20 largest unsecured claims or the creditors' committee, if one has been appointed.

(c) Procedure. A motion under this rule shall be governed by B.L.R. 9014-1.

(d) Applicability. This rule shall apply only to cases filed on or after October 17, 2005.

Local Rule 4001-4. Conversion from Chapter 7 to 13.

(a) A debtor who wishes to convert a pending chapter 7 case that has not previously been converted under Bankruptcy Code § 1112, 1208, or 1307 to chapter 13 shall serve a motion to convert on the chapter 7 trustee, the U.S. Trustee, and all parties in interest.

(b) If the court finds that the debtor is eligible for relief under chapter 13, then the court may issue its order converting the case to chapter 13 after the passage of 14 days following service of such motion, if no party in interest has filed an objection to such conversion.

(c) Any objections to conversion must be filed within 14 days from service of the motion to convert, and shall be served on the debtor, the chapter 7 trustee, and the U.S. Trustee. If an objection is timely filed and served, the debtor must schedule a hearing on the motion and the objection, to be held on not less than 7 nor more than 14 days notice to the objecting party, the chapter 7 trustee and the U.S. Trustee.

(d) The court will not take testimony at the hearing, and may at that time rule on the objection if there is no genuine issue of material fact.

(e) The above-mentioned time periods are subject to modification in accordance with the applicable rules. Nothing contained herein shall be construed to preclude requests for relief of any nature by or against any party in interest during the period between the filing of a motion to convert and the court's disposition thereof.

Local Rule 4002-1. Designation of Responsible Individual.

(a) Every debtor or debtor-in-possession which is not an individual shall file with the Court an application and proposed order appointing a natural person to be responsible for the duties and obligations of the debtor or debtor-in-possession. The order shall identify such person by name and include the person's address, telephone number, and position within the organization. If the duties are to be divided among two or more individuals, the responsibilities of each shall be specified. The application and order shall be filed with the petition, or promptly thereafter.

(b) If any natural person designated under subparagraph (a) of this rule ceases to perform the designated duties of the debtor or debtor-in-possession, either because such person has ceased to be affiliated with the debtor or debtor-in-possession or for any other reason, the debtor or debtorin- possession shall promptly file a statement to that effect, accompanied by either (i) an application and proposed order appointing a successor natural person to perform such duties, or (ii) a statement that there is no natural person willing and able to serve in that capacity. Any notice or application filed under this subparagraph (b) shall be served on any trustee appointed in the case, on counsel for (or if there is no counsel, the members of) any committee appointed in the case, on the United States Trustee, and on any party who has requested notice pursuant to Bankruptcy Rule 2002(i). Upon the filing of a notice or application under this subparagraph, the Court may, on the request of any party or on its own motion, take such action as it deems appropriate in the circumstances. Neither this subparagraph nor the filing of any application or notice under this subparagraph shall have any effect on the duties, obligations or responsibilities of the person previously designated under subparagraph (a) of this rule unless the Court orders otherwise.

Local Rule 4003-1. Exempt Property.

(a) Orders Setting Apart Exemptions. If no objection to a claim of exemption has been made in a Chapter 7 case within the time provided in Bankruptcy Rule 4003(b), the Court may, at any time, without a hearing and without reopening the case, enter an order approving the exemptions as claimed.

(b) Spousal Exemption Waiver. In a case where the spouse of the debtor is a nondebtor and the debtor wishes to elect the exemptions provided by California Code of Civil Procedure § 703.140(b), the debtor shall file the waiver referred to in California Code of Civil Procedure § 703.140(a)(2) by the deadline for filing the schedules and statements required by Bankruptcy Rule 1007 unless the Court extends the deadline for cause shown.

Local Rule 4004-1. Delayed Discharges of Individuals in Chapter 11, 12 and 13 Cases.

(a) All chapter 11, chapter 12 or chapter 13 debtors who have claimed exemptions in excess of the adjusted amount set forth in 11 U.S.C. § 522(q)(1) must file a statement pursuant to Rule 1007(b)(8), not earlier than the date of the last payment under the plan or the date of filing a motion for a discharge under 11 U.S.C. §§ 1141(d)(5)(B), 1228(b), or 1328(b).

(b) Unless otherwise ordered, upon plan completion:

(1) All chapter 13 debtors must file a certification in support of discharge stating whether or not the debtor:

(A) has completed an instructional course concerning personal financial management described in 11 U.S.C. § 111 and has filed a certificate of completion of that course;

(B) has been required to pay, and has paid, a domestic support obligation as that term is defined in 11 U.S.C. § 101(14A);

(C) has received a discharge in a chapter 7, 11, 12 bankruptcy case filed within four years prior to filing the present Chapter 13 case, or in a Chapter 13 case filed within two years prior to filing the present Chapter 13 case.

(2) All chapter 12 debtors must file the certification required in subparagraph (b)(1)(B).

(3) If a chapter 12 or chapter 13 debtor has been required to pay a domestic support obligation as that term is defined in 11 U.S.C. § 101(14A), the debtor shall file a certification of domestic support obligation payees, setting forth the names and last known addresses of those payees. That certification shall be served by the debtor on the case trustee and all of the named domestic support obligation payees.

(c) A debtor required to file the statement required by Subparagraph (a) may combine it with the certification required by subparagraph (b)(1) or (2).

(d) **(1)** The Clerk shall serve the statements and certifications required in subparagraphs (a) and (b)(1) and (2) by mail on all parties in interest.

(2) Any party requesting a delay in the entry of the discharge must file a written response no later than 21 days from the date of service of the debtor's statement and certification and the response must be served by mail on the chapter 11 Trustee, if any, the chapter 12 Trustee or the chapter 13 Standing Trustee, the debtor and the debtor's attorney at the addresses noted on the debtor's statement and certification.

(3) If the delay request is timely filed, the debtor must schedule a hearing on the request and advise the chapter 11 Trustee, if any, the chapter 12 Trustee or the chapter 13 Standing Trustee, and the party requesting the delay, of the date and time of the hearing. The hearing must be held not more than 10 days before the date of the entry of the discharge order.

(4) If either no delay request is filed or if the delay request is not timely filed, the Court may enter a discharge order in the case, but not earlier than 30 days after the filing of the statement.

(e) Debtors shall make the statements and certifications required by this rule on forms approved by court in accordance with B.L.R. 1007-1. Those forms shall be available on the court's website and at the offices and on the websites of the district's chapter 13 Standing Trustees.

PART V. COURTS AND CLERKS

Local Rule 5005-1. Electronic Case Filing (ECF).

(a) Establishment of Electronic Case Filing Procedures. The Clerk is hereby authorized to establish and promulgate Electronic Case Filing Procedures (the "ECF Procedures"), including the procedure for registration of ECF participants ("Registered Participants") and for distribution of passwords to permit electronic filing by Registered Participants and notice of pleadings and other papers. The Clerk may modify the ECF Procedures from time to time, after conferring with the Chief Bankruptcy Judge and such others judges as he or she shall designate. The ECF Procedures shall be made available to the public in paper form in the clerk's office of each division and by posting on the Court's web site.

(b) Electronic Filing of Documents. The electronic transmission of a document to the Court in a manner consistent with the ECF Procedures, together with the Court's return transmission of a "Notification of Electronic Filing," shall constitute the filing of the document and its entry on the Court's docket for purposes of Bankruptcy Rule 5003. Electronically filed documents must comply with these Bankruptcy Local Rules with respect to form and length.

(c) Mandatory Requirement for Attorneys to File Electronically Via ECF. Unless exempted by the Clerk, all attorneys practicing in the Court, including attorneys admitted pro hac vice, are required to file all documents (excluding documents to be placed under seal) electronically via ECF.

(d) Scanned Documents. The official file in all divisions shall be the electronic file. All documents filed in paper form will be scanned into ECF and will only be accessible electronically.

Local Rule 5005-2. ECF Signatures and Verified Pleadings.

(a) The ECF Procedures shall describe the procedure for designating that a document filed electronically with the Court has been signed. Each such document shall bear the typed name of the person purporting to have signed the document.

(b) The electronic filing of a document purportedly signed by the Registered Participant shall be deemed signed by the Registered Participant for purposes of Bankruptcy Rule 9011 as well as any other applicable rules or statutes.

(c) The electronic filing of a document purportedly signed by someone other than the Registered Participant, including but not limited to the petition, statement of financial affairs, and schedules of assets and liabilities, shall be deemed a certification by the Registered Participant that he or she has the document in question, bearing the person's original signature, in his or her physical possession. The Registered Participant must produce the original signed document on request by the Court and the Registered Participant shall retain the document bearing the original signature until five years after the case or adversary proceeding in which the document was filed is closed.

Local Rule 5011-1. General Reference.

(a) General Referral. Pursuant to 28 U.S.C. § 157(a), all cases under Title 11 and all civil proceedings arising under Title 11 or arising in or related to a case under Title 11 are referred to the Bankruptcy Judges of this District, except as provided in B.L.R. 5011-1(b).

(b) Pending District Court Proceedings. Any civil proceeding arising in or related to a case under Title 11 that is pending in the District Court on the date the Title 11 case is filed shall be referred to a Bankruptcy Judge only upon order of the District Judge before whom the proceeding is pending. Such an order may be entered upon the motion of a party, the District Judge's own motion, or upon the recommendation of a Bankruptcy Judge.

(c) Automatic Stay. Nothing in this rule shall modify any automatic stay imposed by 11 U.S.C. §§ 362(a), 922, 1201(a), or 1301(a).

Local Rule 5011-2. Motions for Withdrawal of Reference.

(a) Motion by Party. A motion to withdraw a case or proceeding under 28 U.S.C. § 157(d) shall be filed with the Clerk of the Bankruptcy Court. The Clerk of the Bankruptcy Court shall transmit the motion forthwith to the District Court, with a copy forwarded to the assigned Bankruptcy Judge.

(b) Recommendation of Bankruptcy Judge. A Bankruptcy Judge may, on the Judge's own motion, upon the filing of a motion under subparagraph (a) of this rule, recommend to the District Court whether the case or proceeding should be withdrawn under 28 U.S.C. § 157(d). Such a recommendation shall be served on the parties to the case or proceeding and forwarded to the Clerk of the District Court.

(c) Assignment of Motion to Judge; Notification to Parties; Filing of Papers. A motion or recommendation made under this rule for withdrawal of the bankruptcy reference shall be assigned by the Clerk of the District Court to a District Judge pursuant to the District Court's Assignment Plan. The Clerk of the District Court shall promptly notify the parties of the name of the assigned District Judge and the District Court case number assigned to the motion, and thereafter any papers filed with respect to the motion or recommendation for withdrawal of the reference (other than a request for stay of proceedings in the Bankruptcy Court) shall be filed with the Clerk of the District Court and shall bear both the District Court civil case number (which shall be stated first) and the Bankruptcy Court case or adversary proceeding number.

(d) Scheduling and Briefing. Unless the assigned District Judge orders otherwise: within 14 days after receiving notice of the assignment to a District Judge under subsection (c) of this rule, any party objecting to withdrawal of the reference shall file in the District Court its opposition brief of not more than ten pages; 14 days thereafter, any party supporting withdrawal of the reference may file a reply brief of not more than ten pages; no hearing will be held unless the assigned District Judge orders otherwise.

(e) Assignment After Withdrawal. A withdrawn case or proceeding shall be assigned to the District Judge who ordered the withdrawal of reference.

PART VI. COLLECTION AND LIQUIDATION OF ESTATE

Local Rule 6004-1. Motions to Sell Free and Clear of Liens and Other Interests.

(a) Procedure. A motion to sell free and clear of liens under 11 U.S.C. § 363(f) shall identify by name, immediately below the caption, the lienholders and other interest holders whose property rights are affected by the motion. The affected lienholders and other interest holders shall be served with a complete set of moving papers pursuant to Bankruptcy Rule 7004(b).

(b) Supporting Papers. The motion shall be supported by the declaration of an individual competent to testify which sets forth the factual basis demonstrating that the moving party comes within 11 U.S.C. § 363(f)(1)-(5). The motion shall identify which subsection of 11 U.S.C. § 363(f) the moving party comes within.

(c) Motions to Sell Property. A motion to sell the subject property may be combined with a motion to sell free and clear of liens. Notice of a motion to sell property shall be given to those specified in Bankruptcy Rule 2002(a).

(d) Form of Order. The order granting a motion to sell free and clear of liens shall specify each lienholder whose interest is to be affected by the order.

Local Rule 6006-1. Motions for Relief Relating to Executory Contracts and Leases.

(a) Notice of Motions. Unless the Court orders otherwise, any motion for relief under 11 U.S.C.§ 365 shall be on notice to: (1) the other contracting parties and to those entities entitled to receive notice under the terms of the contract or lease; (2) the non-insider creditors that hold the 20 largest unsecured claims or to the creditors committee, if one has been appointed; and (3) any party who has requested notice pursuant to Bankruptcy Rule 2002.

(b) Expedited Rejection. Notwithstanding subparagraph (a), a Chapter 7 Trustee may move to reject an unexpired lease of nonresidential real property where the debtor is the tenant on 24 hours notice given only to the other party to the lease, and such motions will normally be considered by the Court without a hearing.

PART VII. ADVERSARY PROCEEDINGS

Local Rule 7003-1. Cover Sheet.

Every complaint initiating an adversary proceeding and every notice of removal pursuant to Bankruptcy Rule 9027 shall be accompanied by a completed Adversary Proceeding Cover Sheet in a form prescribed by the Clerk. Adversary Proceeding Cover Sheets shall be available in the Office of the Bankruptcy Clerk and on the Court's website at www.canb.uscourts.gov.

Local Rule 7007-1. Motions In Adversary Proceeding.

(a) Time. Except as otherwise ordered, and except for motions made during the course of trial, all motions shall be filed and served at least 28 days before the hearing date.

(b) Opposition. Any opposition to a motion shall be filed and served at least 14 days before the hearing date.

(c) Statement of No Opposition. If the party against which the motion is directed does not oppose the motion, that party shall file a Statement of No Opposition within the time for filing and serving any opposition.

(d) Counter-Motions. Together with an opposition, a party responding to a motion may file a counter-motion related to the subject matter of the original motion. Such counter-motion shall be noticed for hearing on the same date as the original motion.

(e) Reply. Any reply to an opposition, or opposition to a counter-motion, shall be filed and served by the moving party at least 7 days before the hearing.

(f) Motion Papers. B.L.R.s 9013-1, 9013-2 and 9013-3 shall apply to motions filed in adversary proceedings.

Local Rule 7016-1. Scheduling Order.

Except as otherwise ordered, that portion of FRCivP 16(b) that fixes a deadline for entry of a scheduling order shall not apply in any adversary proceeding.

Local Rule 7042-1. Related Adversary Proceedings.

(a) Related Adversary Proceedings. Any adversary proceeding is related to another when both concern:

(1) Some of the same parties and is based on the same or similar claims; or

(2) Some of the same property, transactions or events; or

(3) The same facts and the same questions of law; or

(4) When both adversary proceedings appear likely to involve duplication of labor or might create conflicts and unnecessary expenses if heard by different Judges.

(b) Notice of Related Adversary Proceedings. Whenever a party knows or learns that an adversary proceeding, filed in or removed to this Court, is (or the party believes that the action may be) related to another adversary proceeding which is or was pending in this Court, the party shall promptly file a Notice of Related Adversary Proceeding. The Notice shall be filed in the later-filed adversary proceeding in which the party is appearing and shall be served on all known parties to each related case.

(c) Contents of Notice. A Notice of Related Adversary Proceeding shall include:

(1) The date the related adversary proceeding was filed and the current status of that proceeding; and

(2) The title and case number; and

(3) A brief statement of the relationship of the actions according to the criteria set forth in section (a) above.

(d) Transfer. The Court may, on its own motion or upon the motion of a party in interest, order an adversary proceeding transferred to another Bankruptcy Judge based on the Court's determination that the proceeding is related and that the transfer will promote efficient adjudication of the actions or avoid inconsistent or conflicting rulings.

(e) Procedure. A motion by a party in interest to transfer an adversary proceeding or proceedings shall be addressed to the Judge presiding in the earlier filed adversary proceeding and served on all known parties in each of the related adversary proceedings.

PART VIII. BANKRUPTCY APPEALS TO DISTRICT COURT

Local Rule 8001-1. Manner of Taking Appeal.

Upon the filing of a notice of appeal and a statement of election to have the appeal heard by the District court, the Clerk of the Bankruptcy Court shall forward to the Clerk of the District Court the notice of appeal, the statement of election and the docket sheet. If a statement of election is filed by an appellee, the notice of appeal and the statement of election will be received from the Bankruptcy Appellate Panel. In either case, the Clerk of the District Court shall immediately open a file, docket these documents and give notice to the parties of the name of the assigned District Judge and the District Court case number.

Local Rule 8007-1. Procedure in Bankruptcy Appeals.

(a) Record on Appeal. The record on appeal shall include a transcript of the hearing or a summary thereof agreed upon by all parties.

(b) Docketing and Notice. Upon receipt of the record on appeal from the Clerk of the Bankruptcy Court, the Clerk of the District Court shall immediately docket it in the case in which the notice of appeal was filed and give notice to all parties to the appeal of the briefing schedule.

(c) Dismissal For Failure To Perfect Appeal. If the appellant fails to perfect the appeal in the manner prescribed by Bankruptcy Rule 8006:

(1) Motion by Appellee. Any appellee may file a motion in the District Court to dismiss the appeal. The motion shall be supported by an affidavit or declaration of counsel for the moving party, setting forth the date and substance of the judgment or order from which the appeal is taken, the date upon which notice of appeal was filed, and the facts showing appellant's failure to perfect the appeal in the manner prescribed by Bankruptcy Rule 8006.

(2) Recommendation by Bankruptcy Court. The Bankruptcy Court may, on its own motion, transmit the notice of appeal to the District Court with a recommendation that the appeal be dismissed. The transmittal shall be accompanied by a certificate of the Bankruptcy Judge indicating the reasons for the recommendation. The Clerk of the Bankruptcy Court shall serve copies of the transmittal and the certificate on all parties.

(3) Procedure. Upon receipt of a motion under subsection (1) or a recommendation under subsection (2) of this subsection (c), the Clerk of the District Court shall docket the motion in the case previously assigned to the appeal. Unless the assigned District Judge orders otherwise: within 14 days after receiving notice of the assignment to a District Judge, appellant shall file in the District Court a brief of not more than five pages in opposition to dismissal of the appeal; 14 days thereafter, appellee(s) may file a reply brief of not more than five pages; no hearing will be held unless the assigned District Judge orders otherwise.

(d) Other Rules. When the Bankruptcy Rules, the FRCivP and the Civil L.R. are silent as to a particular matter of practice on an appeal to the District Court from the Bankruptcy Court, the assigned District Judge may apply the Rules of the United States Court of Appeals for the Ninth Circuit, the FRAppP, and the Rules of the United States Bankruptcy Appellate Panel of the Ninth Circuit.

Local Rule 8010-1. Briefs.

Unless the assigned District Judge orders otherwise for good cause shown:

(a) The appellant shall serve and file a brief within 28 days after entry of the appeal on the District Court's docket pursuant to Bankruptcy Rule 8007.

(b) The appellee shall serve and file a brief within 21 days after service of appellant's brief. If the appellee has filed a cross-appeal, the brief of appellee shall contain the issues and arguments pertinent to the cross-appeal, denominated as such, and the response to the brief of the appellant.

(c) The appellant may serve and file a reply brief within 14 days after service of appellee's brief, and if the appellee has filed a cross-appeal, the appellee may file and serve a reply brief to the response of the appellant to the issues presented in the cross-appeal within 14 days after service of the reply brief of the appellant.

(d) Briefs shall comply with Bankruptcy Rule 8010; provided however, 50-page and 25-page limits for principal briefs and reply briefs in Bankruptcy Rule 8010(c), respectively, are reduced to 25 pages and 15 pages.

Local Rule 8012-1. Oral argument.

Upon completion of the briefing, the assigned District Judge will set a date for oral argument, if needed; otherwise the matter will be deemed submitted for decision.

PART IX. GENERAL PROVISIONS

Local Rule 9006-1. Enlargement or Shortening of Time.

(a) Requirements for Changing Time. Except as provided in paragraph (b), approval of the Court is required to enlarge or to shorten time to perform any act or to file any paper pursuant to the Federal Rules of Civil Procedure, the Bankruptcy Rules, or these Bankruptcy Local Rules.

(b) Stipulation for Changing Time. Parties may stipulate in writing, without a Court order, to extend the time within which to answer or otherwise respond to the complaint or to enlarge or shorten the time in matters not required to be filed with the Court, provided the change will not alter the date of any hearing or conference set by the Court. Such stipulations shall be promptly filed pursuant to B.L.R. 1002-1.

(c) Requests for Changing time. Any request to enlarge or shorten time may be made by stipulation or motion. Absent exigent circumstances, any motion shall be heard on at least 72 hours notice to the respondent. Any request, whether made by stipulation or motion, shall be accompanied by a declaration stating:

(1) The reason for the particular enlargement or shortening of time requested;

(2) Previous time modifications related to the subject of the request, whether by stipulation or Court order;

(3) The effect of the requested time modification on the schedule for the case or proceeding; and

(4) Where the request is not made by stipulation, the efforts made to speak with the respondent and, if the movant has spoken with the respondent, the reasons given for any refusal to agree to the request.

Local Rule 9010-1. Appearance of Corporation or Partnership Through Counsel.

(a) Appearance and Filing of Papers. A corporation, partnership, or any entity other than a natural person may not appear as a party in an adversary proceeding or a contested matter or as a debtor in a bankruptcy case except through counsel admitted to practice in this District. Petitions and pleadings from parties who are not individuals must bear the signature of an attorney.

(b) Chapter 11 Cases. A corporation, partnership, or any entity other than a natural person may not serve as a debtor-inpossession in a Chapter 11 case unless represented by counsel. If a corporation or partnership does not obtain Court approval of counsel promptly, the Court, after notice as prescribed by Bankruptcy Rule 2002(a), may dismiss the case, order it converted to Chapter 7, or order the appointment of a trustee.

(c) Excepted Matters. Nothing herein shall preclude a corporation, partnership, or any entity other than a natural person from filing a proof of claim, an application for compensation, a reaffirmation agreement, or from appearing at a meeting of creditors through an officer or other authorized agent.

Local Rule 9011-1. Sanctions and Penalties for Non-compliance.

Any petition, schedule, statement, declaration, claim or other document filed and signed or subscribed under any method (digital, electronic, scanned) adopted under the rules of this Court shall be treated for all purposes (both civil and criminal, including penalties for perjury) in the same manner as though manually signed or subscribed.

Failure of counsel or of a party to comply with any provision of these rules or the Bankruptcy Rules shall be grounds for imposition by the Court of appropriate sanctions.

Local Rule 9013-1. Motion Papers.

(a) Matters Covered by Rule. This rule shall apply to initial papers, response papers, and reply papers in any case or adversary proceeding.

(b) Form. Initial papers shall include the following separate documents:

(1) The first document, Notice of Hearing, shall state the date, time, and location of hearing (if any);

(2) The second document, the Motion, shall provide a concise statement of what relief or Court action the movant seeks; and

(3) The third document, the memorandum of points and authorities, shall provide a statement of the issues to be decided, a succinct statement of the relevant facts, and argument of the party, citing supporting authorities.

(c) Length. Unless the Court expressly orders otherwise, the initial memoranda of points and authorities shall not exceed 25 pages of text, and reply memoranda shall not exceed 15 pages of text. Any memorandum exceeding 10 pages of text shall also include a table of contents and a table of authorities.

(d) Affidavits or Declarations.

(1) Factual contentions made in support of or in opposition to any motion, application or objection should be supported by affidavits or declarations and appropriate references to the record. Extracts from depositions, interrogatory answers, requests for admission and other evidentiary matter must be appropriately authenticated by affidavit or declaration.

(2) Affidavits and declarations shall contain only facts, shall conform as far as possible to the requirements of Fed. R. Civ. P. 56(e), and shall avoid conclusions and argument. Any statement made upon information or belief shall specify the basis therefor. Affidavits and declarations not in compliance with this rule may be stricken in whole or in part.

(3) Each affidavit or declaration shall be filed as a separate document.

(e) Supplementary Materials. Prior to the noticed hearing date, counsel may bring to the Court's attention relevant judicial opinions published after the date the opposition or reply was filed by filing and serving a Statement of Recent Development, containing a citation to and providing a copy of the new opinion without argument. Otherwise, once a reply is filed, no additional memoranda, papers or letters shall be filed without prior Court approval.

Local Rule 9013-2. Motions; To Whom Made.

(a) Assigned Case. Motions, applications and objections will be determined by the Judge to whom the case or proceeding is assigned, except as may be otherwise ordered by the assigned Judge. In the Judge's discretion, or upon request by counsel and with the Judge's approval, a motion may be determined without oral argument, or by conference telephone call.

(b) Unassigned Case or Judge Unavailable. A motion, application, or objection may be presented to any other Bankruptcy Judge of the same division as the assigned Judge or, if no such Judge is available, to the Chief Bankruptcy Judge or Acting Chief Bankruptcy Judge when:

(1) The assigned Judge is unavailable and an emergency requires prompt action; or

(2) An order is necessary before an action or proceeding can be filed.

(c) Unavailable. For purposes of this rule, a Judge is unavailable if the Judge has filed a certificate of unavailability or such unavailability is certified by the Judge's courtroom deputy, law clerk, judicial assistant or secretary.

Local Rule 9013-3. Service—Calculating Time; Certifying Service; Electronic Service.

(a) Additional Time after Service. The time limits established in these Bankruptcy Local Rules have been calculated to include the "additional time after service" provided by Bankruptcy Rule 9006(f).

(b) Certificate of Service. A certificate of service shall identify the capacity in which the person or entity was served. Capacity to be identified includes: Debtor(s); Attorney for Debtor(s); Trustee; Attorney for Trustee; Twenty Largest Unsecured Creditors; and Special Notice List. If notice to the 20 largest unsecured creditors is required, and there are less than 20 unsecured creditors of the estate, the certificate of service shall also indicate that all unsecured creditors were served. This subparagraph (b) shall not apply to motions and applications served on all creditors, or to motions served in adversary proceedings.

(c) Service by Electronic Filing. Notwithstanding subparagraph (a) of this rule, transmission of the Notification of Electronic Filing by the Clerk to a Registered Participant who has consented to electronic service shall constitute effective service on that Registered Participant of all papers governed by FRCivP 5(b), as that rule is incorporated by Bankruptcy Rule 7005 and Bankruptcy Rule 9014(b), and of notices of judgment or order governed by Bankruptcy Rule 9022.

Commentary Service of papers that initiate an adversary proceeding under Bankruptcy Rules 7001–7087, i.e., the summons and complaint under Bankruptcy Rule 7004, or that commence a contested matter under Bankruptcy Rule 9014, e.g., a motion for stay relief or objection to claim, are not governed by FRCivP 5, and must still be made by paper. Likewise, general notices to creditors pursuant to Bankruptcy Rule 2002 must still be served by conventional means and are not governed by this rule. Of course, a party may always stipulate to the effectiveness of service by means other than conventional "paper service", including accepting the Notification of Electronic Filing as effective service.

In contrast to initiating papers, service of papers governed by FRCivP 5 or Bankruptcy Rule 9022, including answers to complaints, motions in adversary proceedings, responses to motions, and notices of entry of judgment or order, are governed by subparagraph (c) of this rule. Each ECF Registered Participant who has not refused consent to electronic service and who has appeared in the case or adversary proceeding receives an email from the Court containing a link to the paper. The rule of subparagraph (c) makes service by electronic mail "Notification of Electronic Filing" effective service of these matters. As to matters governed by subparagraph (c), filing parties need only serve persons who either are not ECF Registered Participants or are ECF Registered Participants who have refused consent to electronic service. A list of such "manual notice" parties may be determined by reviewing the Notification of Electronic Filing (which reprints the list) or from the Utilities menu of ECF under "Mailing Information."

Local Rule 9014-1. Case Motions and Objections.

(a) Matters Covered By Rule. This rule shall apply to any motion, application or objection with respect to which the Bankruptcy Code provides that relief may be obtained after "notice and a hearing" or similar phrase, but does not apply to: (1) motions for relief from the automatic stay; (2) proceedings that must be initiated by complaint under Bankruptcy Rule 7001 (adversary proceedings) or motions therein; (3) hearings on approval of disclosure statements and confirmation of Chapter 11, 12 and 13 plans; and (4) matters that may properly be presented to a Judge ex parte.

(b) Procedures For Hearings and Disposition.

(1) Hearing Required. Unless otherwise ordered, the following shall be set for an actual hearing:

(A) Motions governed by Bankruptcy Rule 4001 (b), (c), and (d) other than motions to approve agreements to modify or terminate the automatic stay;

(B) Hearings on applications for compensation or reimbursement of expenses, totaling in excess of $1,000, other than applications for compensation for appraisers, auctioneers, and real estate brokers;

(C) Motions to dismiss a case, other than a debtor's request for dismissal under 11 U.S.C. §§ 1208(b) or 1307(b), or a Chapter 13 trustee's request for dismissal under 11 U.S.C. § 1307(c);

(D) Motions to appoint a trustee or an examiner; and

(E) Objections to a debtor's claim of exemption.

(2) Hearing Permitted. In addition to the required hearings described in B.L.R. 9014-1(b)(1), any matter within the scope of this rule may be set for a hearing.

(3) Notice and Opportunity for Hearing. Unless otherwise ordered, a party in interest may initiate a request for relief, without setting a hearing, regarding any matter within the scope of this rule, other than those matters described in B.L.R. 9014-1(b)(1).

(A) Notice. A request for relief governed by B.L.R. 9014-1(b)(3) shall be accompanied by a Notice and Opportunity for Hearing and shall state conspicuously:

(i) That Bankruptcy Local Rule 9014-1 of the United States Bankruptcy Court for the Northern District of California prescribes the procedures to be followed and that any objection to the requested relief, or a request for hearing on the matter, must be filed and served upon the initiating party within 21 days of mailing of the notice;

(ii) That a request for hearing or objection must be accompanied by any declarations or memoranda of law the party objecting or requesting wishes to present in support of its position;

(iii) That if there is not a timely objection to the requested relief or a request for hearing, the Court may enter an order granting the relief by default; and

(iv) Either:

(a) That the initiating party will give at least 7 days written notice of hearing to the objecting or requesting party, and to any trustee or committee appointed in the case, in the event an objection or request for hearing is timely made; or

(b) The tentative hearing date.

(B) Procedure for Tentative Hearing Dates. A tentative hearing shall be set at least 14 days after the last date for parties to file objections or requests for hearings in accordance with B.L.R. 9014-1(b)(3)(A)(i). The tentative hearing will not go forward unless an objection or request for hearing is timely filed and served, in which case the party initiating the proceedings under B.L.R. 9014-1(b)(3) shall file and serve not less than 7 days before the hearing, notice that the tentative hearing will be conducted as an actual hearing. Such Notice of Hearing is to be in writing, and is to be given to the objecting or requesting party, any trustee and any committee appointed in the case, and the Court. The Court will not schedule the matter on the judges calendar unless the Notice of Hearing has been filed and served timely. The initiating party shall also give 7 days telephonic notice to the Judge's Calendar Clerk/Courtroom Deputy that the tentative hearing will be an actual hearing.

(C) Conduct of Hearing. At the hearing the Court will proceed in accordance with B.L.R. 3007-1 on objections to claims. On other matters in which the Court determines that there is a genuine issue of material fact, the Court may treat the hearing as a status conference and schedule further hearings as appropriate.

(4) Relief Upon Default. When no objection or request for a hearing has been filed or served within the time provided in B.L.R. 9014-1(b)(3)(A)(i), the initiating party may request relief by default by submitting a request for entry of an order by default and a proposed order. A copy of the original motion, application, or objection shall be attached to the request. The request shall be accompanied by a certificate of service of the papers initiating the request, and a declaration confirming that no response has been received.

(A) In the case of an objection to a claim, a motion to avoid a lien pursuant to 11 U.S.C. § 522(f), or other request for relief as against an identified, named entity, the request for entry of order by default shall be served upon the entity against whom relief is sought. If relief is sought against any entity that has filed a claim, all papers shall be mailed to the address shown on the proof of claim.

(B) In cases seeking relief generally, and not against an identified, named entity, the request for entry of order by default and related papers shall be served upon the debtor, any trustee, and any committee of unsecured creditors that has been appointed in the case.

(C) Upon filing of an appropriate request for entry of an order by default, with service in accordance with B.L.R. 9014-1(b)(4), the Court may grant the requested relief.

(c) Schedule For Filing of Papers.

(1) Where the matter is governed by B.L.R. 9014-1(b)(1), or the initiating party desires a hearing under B.L.R. 9014-1(b)(2), and relief is sought against an identified, named entity, the motion, notice of the hearing, supporting declarations, memoranda, and all other papers shall be filed and served at least 28 days before the actual scheduled hearing date. Any opposition shall be filed and served on the initiating party at least 14 days prior to the actual scheduled hearing date. Any reply shall be filed and served at least 7 days prior to the actual scheduled hearing date. Notwithstanding the foregoing, no responsive pleading to an objection to a claim of exemption shall be required.

(2) Where the matter is governed by B.L.R. 9014-1(b)(1) or (b)(2) and relief is sought generally, and not against an identified, named entity, the motion or application, notice of the hearing, supporting declarations, memoranda, and all other papers shall be filed and served at least 21 days before the actual scheduled hearing date. Any opposition to the requested relief shall be filed and served on the initiating party no less than 7 days before the actual scheduled hearing date.

(3) Where the matter is governed by B.L.R. 9014-1(b)(3), the initiating party may file and serve any reply to the objecting party's opposition no less than 7 days before the hearing.

(d) Notice For Sale of Certain Personal Property. A Chapter 7 Trustee may, without the necessity of an order shortening time:

(1) Set for hearing on 7 days notice any motion to sell property of the estate free and clear of, or subject to liens, if the subject property is situated on leased premises for which the estate is accruing periodic administrative rent; and

(2) Move to assume and assign (but not just to assume) or to reject an unexpired lease of nonresidential real property where the debtor is the tenant as provided in B.L.R. 6006-1(a).

(3) Opposition to motions made pursuant to this subparagraph may be presented at or before the hearing.

Local Rule 9015-1. Jury Trial of Right.

FRCivP 38(a)-(d) applies in adversary proceedings.

Local Rule 9015-2. Jury Trials and Personal Injury and Wrongful Death Claims.

(a) Determination of Right. In any proceeding in which a demand for jury trial is made, the Bankruptcy Judge shall, upon the motion of one of the parties, or upon the Bankruptcy Judge's own motion, determine whether the demand was timely made and whether the demanding party has a right to a jury trial. The Bankruptcy Judge may, on the Judge's own motion, determine that there is no right to a jury trial in a proceeding even if all of the parties have consented to a jury trial.

(b) Motion and Certification to District Court. If the Bankruptcy Judge determines that the demand for a jury trial was timely made and the party has a right to a jury trial, and if all parties have not filed written consent to a jury trial before the Bankruptcy Judge, the Bankruptcy Judge shall, after having resolved all pre-trial matters, including dispositive motions, certify to the District Court that the proceeding is to be tried by a jury and that the parties have not consented to a jury trial in the Bankruptcy Court, and shall include in such certification, a report of the status of the proceeding and a recommendation on when the matter would be suitable for withdrawal from the Bankruptcy Court. Upon such certification, the party who has demanded a jury trial shall promptly file a motion in accordance with B.L.R. 5011-2(a) for withdrawal of the reference of the proceeding to be tried to a jury. The motion and the certification shall thereafter be handled in the District Court in accordance with B.L.R. 5011-2(c), (d) and (e).

(c) Jury Trial in Bankruptcy Court. The Bankruptcy Judges of this District are hereby specially designated to conduct jury trials pursuant to 28 U.S.C. § 157(e). If the Bankruptcy Judge determines that a jury demand was timely made and the demanding party has a right to jury trial, and if all parties expressly consent to a jury trial before the Bankruptcy Judge, the Bankruptcy Judge shall try the proceeding by jury and shall enter judgment at the conclusion of the trial.

(d) Personal Injury and Wrongful Death Claims. Upon timely motion of a party or upon the Bankruptcy Judge's own motion, the Bankruptcy Judge may determine that a claim is a personal injury tort or wrongful death claim requiring trial by a District Judge. Upon making such a determination, the Bankruptcy Judge shall, after having resolved all pre-trial matters, including dispositive motions, certify to the District Court that the claim is one which requires trial in the District Court under 28 U.S.C. § 157(b)(5) and shall include in such certification, a report of the status of the proceeding and a recommendation on when the matter would be suitable for withdrawal from the Bankruptcy Court. Upon such certification, the party who has demanded a jury trial shall promptly file a motion in accordance with B.L.R. 5011-2(a) for withdrawal of the reference of the proceeding to be tried to a jury. The motion and the certification shall thereafter shall be handled in the District Court in accordance with B.L.R. 5011-2(c), (d) and (e).

(e) Procedure. In any proceeding within the jurisdiction created by 28 U.S.C. § 1334, FRCivP 38(a)–(d), 39, 47–51, and 81(c) shall govern the demand for and conduct of jury trials.

(f) Remand and Abstention. Nothing contained in this rule shall be construed to preclude the entry of any order of remand or abstention.

Local Rule 9021-1. Submission of Orders.

(a) Prior to Hearings. Unless authorized by the judge or in the assigned judge's posted policies for submission of proposed orders through ECF, no proposed forms of orders granting or denying motions shall be submitted with the moving or opposition papers prior to hearing. A copy of a proposed form of order may be attached as an exhibit to a notice or memorandum.

(b) At Hearings. If authorized by the judge, the prevailing party may submit a proposed order to the Judge hearing the matter at the conclusion of the hearing after permitting all other counsel appearing at the hearing to review the proposed order.

(c) After Hearings. If a form of order is not approved by the Judge at the conclusion of the hearing, the prevailing party, or such other party ordered to do so by the Judge hearing the motion, shall submit a proposed order to the Judge promptly thereafter. The order shall contain the signatures of any other counsel who appeared at the hearing, approving it as to form, or shall be accompanied by a certificate of service evidencing service of the proposed order on all such counsel. Orders not approved as to form will ordinarily be lodged for 7 days after service.

Local Rule 9022-1. Notice of Entry of Order and Judgment.

(a) Service List. Each order or judgment submitted to the Court, including those submitted through ECF, shall be accompanied by a Court Service List identifying, in alphabetical order, all parties required to be served with the order under applicable federal and local rules together with their counsel of record (if any). The Court Service List should not include those parties who have appeared in the case or adversary proceeding by counsel who are ECF Registered Participants and who have consented to electronic service through the Court's ECF Procedures.

(b) Notice of Entry of Order. Upon the entry of each order or judgment on the Court docket, the Notice of Electronic Filing shall constitute notice of entry of judgments and orders by the Court upon all Registered Participants who have consented to electronic service through the Court's ECF Procedures. A paper copy of the order or judgment will be served by the Court on all parties on the Court Service List submitted pursuant to subparagraph (a) above. The date the order of judgment was entered will be reflected on the copy served, which will constitute notice of entry of the order or judgment on non-registered or non-consenting parties.

Local Rule 9029-1. Guidelines.

The Judges of the Bankruptcy Court or any division thereof may adopt, and as needed revise, guidelines concerning the allowance and disallowance of professional fees and expense reimbursement and the contents and format of applications therefor filed pursuant to 11 U.S.C. §§ 330(a) and 331 and Bankruptcy Rule 2016(a), the contents of applications for approval of cash collateral and financing stipulations pursuant to 11 U.S.C. §§ 363(c)(2) or 364(c) and Bankruptcy Rule 4001(b), (c), or (d), and such other matters as the Judges or divisions may deem appropriate. Copies of any guidelines so adopted shall be available in the Office of the Clerk of any division in which they are effective. Although referenced herein, such guidelines are not intended to be local rules, and shall not have the force and effect thereof.

Local Rule 9033-1. Procedure on Bankruptcy Court's Proposed Findings of Fact and Conclusions of Law.

(a) Objections. Any objection to the proposed findings of fact and conclusions of law or proposed order or judgment made by a Bankruptcy Judge in a non-core proceeding pursuant to 28 U.S.C. § 157(c)(1) shall be filed with the Clerk of the Bankruptcy Court and shall state:

(1) The issues raised by the objections;

(2) The specific portion of the proposed findings of fact and conclusions of law or proposed judgment or order to which objection is made; and

(3) Whether the objecting party requests that oral testimony be heard by the District Court, the reason for requesting oral testimony, and the issues on which oral testimony is requested. At the time the objection is filed, the objecting party shall file in the Bankruptcy Court a designation of the record for review, which shall include a transcript of the trial or hearing in the Bankruptcy Court.

(b) Response to Objections. Any response to the objection referred to in subparagraph (a) shall be filed with the Clerk of the Bankruptcy Court and shall state:

(1) Whether oral testimony should be heard by the District Court; and

(2) The issues on which oral testimony should be heard. At the time the response is filed, the responding party shall file any additional designations of the record for review.

(c) Procedure on Objection. If an objection is filed, the Clerk of the Bankruptcy Court shall, within 28 days after the time for filing a response has expired, transmit the proposed findings of fact and conclusions of law and proposed order or judgment, together with the objections, response, transcript and record, to the Clerk of the District Court, who shall assign the matter to a District Judge pursuant to the District Court's Assignment Plan. The Clerk of the District Court shall promptly notify the parties of the name of the assigned District Judge and the District Court case number assigned to the matter. No hearing will be held unless the assigned District Judge orders otherwise,[sic]

(d) Procedure Absent Objection. If no objection is filed within the time specified, unless otherwise ordered by the Bankruptcy Court, the Clerk of the Bankruptcy Court shall transmit the proposed findings of fact and conclusions of law and proposed order or judgment to the Clerk of the District Court, with a certificate that no objection has been filed and a request that the proposed findings of fact, conclusions of law, and order or judgment be assigned to the General Duty Judge, who may take such action on the proposed findings of fact and conclusions of law and proposed order and judgment as the General Duty Judge deems appropriate, including disposition as a default matter without further notice or hearing.

(e) Incomplete or Defective Objections. If an objection is filed within the time specified which does not comply substantially with this rule, the Bankruptcy Judge who issued the proposed findings, conclusions, order or judgment may issue a recommendation that the matter be treated as if no objection had been filed as described in the preceding paragraph. The Clerk of the Bankruptcy Court shall transmit this recommendation to the Clerk of the District Court together with the proposed findings of fact and conclusions of law and proposed order or judgment, and a request that the matter be assigned to the General Duty Judge. The Clerk of the Bankruptcy Court shall serve a copy of the recommendation on all parties to the proceeding at the time of the transmittal. The General Duty Judge may either act on the recommendation and the proposed findings, conclusion and order or judgment after such further notice and proceedings as the General Duty Judge determines to be appropriate, or may direct the Clerk of the District Court to assign the matter to a District Judge pursuant to the District Court's Assignment Plan for such further proceedings as the assigned District Judge determines to be appropriate.

BANKRUPTCY DISPUTE RESOLUTION PROGRAM

Local Rule 9040-1. Bankruptcy Dispute Resolution Program.

The following Local Rules govern the Bankruptcy Dispute Resolution Program ("BDRP") in the United States Bankruptcy Court for the Northern District of California.

Local Rule 9040-2. Purpose and Scope.

(a) Purpose. The Court recognizes that formal litigation of disputes in bankruptcy cases and adversary proceedings frequently imposes significant economic burdens on parties and often delays resolution of those disputes. The procedures established by these Local Rules are intended primarily to provide litigants with the means to resolve their disputes more quickly, at less cost, and often without the stress and pressure of litigation.

The Court also notes that the volume of cases, contested matters and adversary proceedings filed in this District has placed substantial burdens upon counsel, litigants and the Court, all of which contribute to the delay in the resolution of disputed matters. A Court authorized dispute resolution program, in which litigants and counsel meet with a Resolution Advocate, offers an opportunity to parties to settle legal disputes promptly and less expensively, to their mutual satisfaction. By these Local Rules the BDRP is adopted for the United States Bankruptcy Court for the Northern District of California.

It is the Court's intention that the BDRP shall operate in such a way as to allow the participants to take advantage of and utilize a wide variety of alternative dispute resolution methods. These methods may include but are not limited to: mediation, negotiation, early neutral evaluation and settlement facilitation. The specific method or methods employed will be those that are appropriate and applicable as determined by the Resolution Advocate and the parties, and will vary from matter to matter.

(b) Scope. These Local Rules apply to all matters referred to the BDRP. All of the other Bankruptcy Local Rules apply, except to the extent that they are inconsistent with these Bankruptcy Local Rules 9040-1 through 9050-1.

Local Rule 9040-3. Certification.

Unless otherwise ordered, no later than 28 days after the initial status conference set in an Adversary Proceeding and whenever ordered by the Court in other matters, counsel and client shall sign, serve and file a certification of discussion and consideration of ADR options. The certification shall be filed on a form established for that purpose by the Court and in conformity with the instructions approved by the Court. If the client is a government or governmental agency, the certificate shall be signed by a person who meets the requirements of Civil L.R. 3-9(c). Counsel and client shall certify that both have:

(1) Read the information sheet entitled Bankruptcy Dispute Resolution Program Instructions for Parties;

(2) Discussed the available dispute resolution options provided by the Court and private entities; and

(3) Considered whether their case might benefit from any of the available dispute resolution options.

Local Rule 9041-1. Eligible Cases.

Unless otherwise ordered by the Judge handling the particular matter, all controversies arising in an adversary proceeding, contested matter, or other dispute in a bankruptcy case, will be eligible for referral to the BDRP except:

(a) Employment and compensation of professionals;

(b) Compensation of trustees and examiners;

(c) Objections to discharge under 11 U.S.C. § 727, except where such objections are joined with disputes over dischargeability of debts under 11 U.S.C. § §523; and

(d) Matters involving contempt or other types of sanctions.

Local Rule 9042-1. Panel of Resolution Advocates.

(a) The Bankruptcy Court shall establish and maintain a panel of qualified professionals (the "Panel") who have volunteered and have been chosen to serve as Resolution Advocates for the possible resolution of matters referred to the BDRP.

(b) Resolution Advocates shall serve as members of the Panel for a one year term.

(c) Applications to serve as a member of the Panel shall be submitted to the BDRP Administrator by the deadlines established by the Court each year, shall set forth the qualifications described below, and should conform to forms promulgated by the Court.

Local Rule 9042-2. Qualifications of Resolution Advocates.

(a) Attorneys. In order to qualify for service as a Resolution Advocate, each attorney applicant shall certify to the Court that the applicant:

(1) Is, and has been, a member in good standing of the bar of any state or of the District of Columbia for at least 5 years;

(2) Is a member in good standing of the federal courts for the Northern District of California;

(3) Has served as the principal attorney of record in active matters in at least 3 bankruptcy cases (without regard to the party represented) from case commencement to the earlier of the date of the application or conclusion of the case, or has served as the principal attorney of record for a party in interest in at least 3 adversary proceedings or contested matters from commencement through conclusion; and

(4) Is willing to serve as a Resolution Advocate for the next one year term of appointment, and to undertake to evaluate, mediate or facilitate settlement of matters no more often than once each quarter of that year, subject only to unavailability due to conflicts, personal or professional commitments, or other matters which would make such service inappropriate.

(5) Attorneys who do not have the bankruptcy experience described in B.L.R. 9042-2(a)(3), but who do have adequate alternative dispute resolution training and experience to qualify them for appointment as Resolution Advocates, shall be considered qualified for purposes of this rule provided they satisfy the requirements of B.L.R. 9042-2(a)(1) and (4).

(b) Non-attorney Resolution Advocates. Each non-attorney applicant shall submit a statement of professional qualifications, experience, training and other information demonstrating, in the applicant's opinion, why the applicant should be appointed to the Panel. In addition, such applicants shall also make the same certification required of attorney applicants as set forth in B.L.R. 9042-2(a)(4).

Local Rule 9042-3. Annual Selection of Resolution Advocates.

Each appointment year the Bankruptcy Judges of the Court will select the Panel from the applications submitted, giving due regard to alternative dispute resolution training and experience and such matters as professional experience and location so as to make the Panel appropriately representative of the public being served by the BDRP. Appointments will be limited to keep the panel at an appropriate size and to ensure that the panel is comprised of individuals who have broad-based experience, superior skills and qualifications from a variety of legal specialties and other professions.

Local Rule 9042-4. Geographic Areas of Service.

The Resolution Advocates on the Panel will indicate to the Court the city or cities within the District in which they are willing to act or serve.

Local Rule 9042-5. Training.

Before first serving as a Resolution Advocate on any assigned Matters, each person selected pursuant to B.L.R. 9042-3 shall have completed requisite alternative dispute resolution training provided by the Court or approved by the BDRP Administrator.

Local Rule 9043-1. Administration of the BDRP.

A Judge of this Court will be appointed by the Chief Bankruptcy Judge to serve as the BDRP Administrator. The BDRP Administrator will be aided by a staff member of the Court, who will maintain and collect applications, maintain the roster of the Panel, track and compile results of the BDRP, and handle such other administrative duties as are necessary.

Local Rule 9044-1. Assignment to the BDRP.

(a) A contested matter in a case, adversary proceeding, or other dispute (hereinafter collectively referred to as "Matter" or "Matters") may be assigned to the BDRP by order of the Judge at a status conference or other hearing, or if requested by the parties by submission of a stipulated order. While participation in the BDRP is intended to be voluntary, any Judge, acting sua sponte or on the request of a party, may designate specific Matters for inclusion in the program. If a Matter is to be assigned to the BDRP, the parties will be presented with the order assigning the Matter to the BDRP, and with a current roster of the Panel. The parties shall normally be given the opportunity to confer and designate a mutually acceptable Resolution

Advocate as well as an alternate Resolution Advocate. If the parties cannot agree, or if the Judge deems selection by the Court to be appropriate and necessary, the Judge shall select a Resolution Advocate. Nothing contained in these Local Rules is intended to preclude other forms of dispute resolution with consent of the parties and, where required, approval of the Court.

(b) The original of the order assigning a Matter to the BDRP shall be docketed and retained in the case or adversary proceeding file and copies shall be mailed promptly by the party so designated by the Judge to the assigned Resolution Advocate, the alternate Resolution Advocate, the BDRP Administrator's staff assistant and to all other parties to the dispute. Assignment to the BDRP shall not alter or affect any time limits, deadlines, scheduling matters or orders in any adversary proceeding, contested matter or other proceeding, unless specifically ordered by the Court.

Local Rule 9044-2. Service of Resolution Advocate.

No Resolution Advocate may serve in any Matter in violation of the standards set forth in 28 U.S.C. § 455. An attorney Resolution Advocate shall also promptly determine all conflicts or potential conflicts in the same manner as an attorney would under the California Rules of Professional Conduct if any party to the dispute were a client. A non-attorney Resolution Advocate shall promptly determine all conflicts or potential conflicts in the same manner as under the applicable rules pertaining to the Resolution Advocate's profession. If the Resolution Advocate's firm has represented one or more of the parties, the Resolution Advocate shall promptly disclose that circumstance to all parties in writing. A party who believes that the assigned Resolution Advocate has a conflict of interest shall promptly bring the matter to the attention of the Resolution Advocate. If the Resolution Advocate does not withdraw from the assignment, the matter shall be brought to the attention of the Court by the Resolution Advocate or any of the parties.

Local Rule 9045-1. Dispute Resolution Procedures.

(a) Availability of Resolution Advocate. Promptly after appointment, a Resolution Advocate not available to serve in the Matter shall notify the parties, the alternate Resolution Advocate, and the BDRP Administrator's staff assistant of that unavailability. The alternate Resolution Advocate shall thereafter serve as the Resolution Advocate.

(b) Initial Telephonic Conference. As soon as practicable after notification of appointment, the Resolution Advocate shall conduct a telephonic conference with counsel for the parties to provide preliminary information to the Resolution Advocate concerning the nature of the Matter, the expectations of the parties, and anything else which will facilitate the process.

(c) BDRP Conference Scheduling. Within 7 days of the telephonic conference, the Resolution Advocate shall give notice to the parties of the time and place for the BDRP conference, which conference shall commence not later than 28 days following the date of appointment of the Resolution Advocate, and which shall be held in a suitable neutral setting, such as the office of the Resolution Advocate, at a location convenient to the parties. Upon written stipulation between the Resolution Advocate and the parties, the BDRP conference may be continued for a period not to exceed 28 days.

(d) BDRP Statements. Unless modified by the Resolution Advocate, no later than 14 days after the date of the order assigning the Matter to the BDRP, each party shall submit directly to the Resolution Advocate, and shall serve on all other parties, a written BDRP statement. Such statements shall not exceed 15 pages (not counting exhibits and attachments). While such statements may include any information that would be useful, they must:

(1) Identify the person(s), in addition to counsel, who will attend the session as representative of the party with decision making authority;

(2) Describe briefly the substance of the dispute;

(3) Address whether there are legal or factual issues whose early resolution might appreciably reduce the scope of the dispute or contribute significantly to settlement;

(4) Identify the discovery that could contribute most to equipping the parties for meaningful discussions;

(5) Set forth the history of past settlement discussions, including disclosure of prior and any presently outstanding offers and demands;

(6) Make an estimate of the cost and time to be expended for further discovery, pretrial motions, expert witnesses and trial; and

(7) Indicate presently scheduled dates for further status conferences, pretrial conferences, trial or otherwise.

(e) Statements Not To Be Filed. The written BDRP statements shall not be filed with the Court and the Court shall not have access to them.

(f) Identification of Participants. Parties may identify in the BDRP statements persons connected to a party opponent (including a representative of a party opponent's insurance carrier) whose presence at the BDRP conference would improve substantially the prospects for making the session productive; the fact that a person has been so identified, shall not, by itself, result in an order compelling that person to attend the BDRP conference.

(g) Documents. Parties shall attach to their written BDRP statements copies of documents out of which the dispute has arisen, e.g., contracts, or those whose availability would materially advance the purposes of the BDRP conference.

Local Rule 9045-2. Attendance at BDRP Conference.

(a) Counsel. Counsel for each party who is primarily responsible for the Matter (or the party, where proceeding in pro se) shall personally attend the BDRP conference and any adjourned sessions of that conference. Counsel for each party shall come prepared to discuss all liability issues, all damage issues, and the position of the party relative to settlement, in detail and in good faith.

(b) Parties. All individual parties, and representatives with authority to negotiate and to settle the Matter on behalf of parties other than individuals, shall personally attend the BDRP conference unless excused by the Resolution Advocate for cause.

(c) Telephonic Appearance. A party or lawyer who is excused from appearing in person at the BDRP conference may be required to participate by telephone.

Local Rule 9045-3. Failure to Attend BDRP Conference.
Willful failure to attend the BDRP conference and other violations of this order shall be reported to the Court by the Resolution Advocate and may result in the imposition of sanctions by the Court.

Local Rule 9046-1. Conduct of the BDRP Conference.
The BDRP conference shall proceed informally. Rules of evidence shall not apply. There shall be no formal examination or cross-examination of witnesses. Where necessary, the Resolution Advocate may conduct continued BDRP conferences after the initial session. As appropriate, the Resolution Advocate may:

(a) Permit each party, through counsel or otherwise, to make an oral presentation of its position;

(b) Help the parties identify areas of agreement and, where feasible, formulate stipulations;

(c) Assess the relative strengths and weaknesses of the parties' contentions and evidence, and explain as carefully as possible the reasoning of the Resolution Advocate that supports these assessments;

(d) Assist the parties in settling the dispute;

(e) Estimate, where feasible, the likelihood of liability and the dollar range of damages;

(f) Help the parties devise a plan for sharing the important information and/or conducting the key discovery that will equip them as expeditiously as possible to participate in meaningful settlement discussions or to posture the case for disposition by other means; and

(g) Determine whether some form of follow-up to the conference would contribute to the case development process or to settlement.

Local Rule 9047-1. Confidentiality.

(a) All written and oral communications made in connection with or during any BDRP conference, including the BDRP statement referred to in B.L.R. 9045-1(d), shall be subject to all the protections afforded by Fed. R. Evid. 408 and by Bankruptcy Rule 7068. The Resolution Advocate may ask the parties to sign a confidentiality agreement provided by the Court.

(b) No written or oral communication made by any party, attorney, Resolution Advocate or other participant in connection with or during any BDRP conference may be disclosed to anyone not involved in the Matter. Nor may such communication be used in any pending or future proceeding in this Court to prove liability for or invalidity of a claim or its amount. Such communication may be disclosed, however, if all participants in the BDRP, including the Resolution Advocate, so agree. Notwithstanding the foregoing, this B.L.R. 9047-1 does not require the exclusion of any evidence:

(1) Otherwise discoverable merely because it is presented in the course of a BDRP conference; or

(2) Offered for another purpose, such as proving bias or prejudice of a witness, negativing a contention of undue delay, or proving an effort to obstruct a criminal investigation or prosecution.

(c) Nothing in this B.L.R. 9047-1 shall be construed to prevent parties, counsel or Resolution Advocates from responding in absolute confidentiality, to inquiries or surveys by persons authorized by this Court to evaluate the BDRP. Nor shall anything in this section be construed to prohibit parties from entering into written agreements resolving some or all of the Matter or entering or filing procedural or factual stipulations based on suggestions or agreements made in connection with a BDRP conference.

Local Rule 9048-1. Suggestions and Recommendations of Resolution Advocate.

If the Resolution Advocate makes any oral or written suggestions to a party's attorney as to the advisability of a change in that party's position with respect to settlement, the attorney for that party shall promptly transmit that suggestion to the party. The Resolution Advocate shall have no obligation to make any written comments or recommendations, but may, as a matter of discretion, provide the parties with a written settlement recommendation memorandum. No copy of any such memorandum shall be filed with the Clerk or made available in whole or in part, directly or indirectly, to the Court.

Local Rule 9049-1. Procedures Upon Completion of BDRP Conference.

Upon the conclusion of the BDRP conference, the following procedure shall be followed:

(a) If the parties have reached an agreement regarding the disposition of the Matter, the parties shall determine who shall prepare the writing to dispose of the Matter, and they may continue the BDRP conference to a date convenient to all parties and the Resolution Advocate if necessary. The Court will accommodate parties who desire to place any resolution of a Matter on the record during or following the BDRP conference. Where required, they shall promptly submit the fully executed stipulation to the Court for approval;

(b) The Resolution Advocate shall file with the Court and serve on the parties and the BDRP Administrator's staff assistant, within 14 days, a certificate in the form provided by the Court, showing whether there has been compliance with the BDRP conference requirements of these Local Rules, and whether or not a settlement has been reached. Regardless of the outcome of the BDRP conference, the Resolution Advocate will not provide the Court with any details of the substance of the conference.

Local Rule 9049-2. Evaluation.

In order to assist the BDRP Administrator in compiling useful data to evaluate the BDRP, and to aid the Court in assessing the efforts of the members of the Panel, the Resolution Advocate shall report to the BDRP Administrator's staff assistant providing an estimate of the number of hours spent in the BDRP conference and statistical and evaluative information, which report shall be on a form provided by the Court.

Local Rule 9050-1. Fee for Service of Resolution Advocates.

The Resolution Advocates are authorized to charge each side, whether or not represented by counsel, up to $100 for their services. This fee, which is waiveable in whole or in part in the discretion of the Resolution Advocate, is applicable for all matters assigned to the BDRP by Court order dated on or after January 2, 1999.

BANKRUPTCY DISPUTE RESOLUTION PROGRAM ADMINISTRATIVE PROCEDURES FOR ELECTRONIC CASE FILING (Rev. May 1, 2008)

1. Establishment of Electronic Case Filing Procedures:

As authorized by this Court's Bankruptcy Local Rule 5005-1(a), these "Electronic Case Filing Procedures" (ECF Procedures) have been established by the Clerk of Court for the United States Bankruptcy Court, Northern District of California.Advance notice of all modifications to these ECF Procedures will be given via the Court's website at: www.canb.uscourts.gov.

2. Scope of Electronic Filing

Mandatory Requirement for Attorneys to File Electronically via CM/ECF: All cases and adversary proceedings filed or pending in the Court shall be, and hereby are, assigned to the Electronic Case Filing System (the "ECF System"). Unless the filer is exempted, all documents are required to be filed electronically in accordance with Bankruptcy Local Rule 5005-1(c). More detailed information may be obtained from the Court's web site at: www.canb.uscourts.gov ≫ ECF ≫ Reference Desk ≫ Revised ECF Exemption Procedures. In the event that the Court denies the exemption, the Court may also, at its discretion, order the document stricken, or impose such other conditions on the filing as the Court deems proper to preclude future violations.

Any attorney who files a document in violation of BLR 5005-1 (c), including documents that are not accompanied by an application that alleges an extreme hardship that is colorable and reasonable or a previous order granting an exemption that is still in effect, may be subject to monetary or non-monetary sanctions pursuant to BLR 9011-1.

Documents previously filed in paper form prior to January 1, 2005, are not available on the Court's CM/ECF system, and the official file with respect to those documents shall remain the paper file. After January 1, 2005, all documents not filed electronically will be scanned and entered by Clerk's Office staff to the CM/ECF system. The documents scanned by Clerk's

Office staff will be held for a period of five days at the divisional office where the case is pending. Parties and attorneys who wish to retrieve the original paper documents they filed may visit or send a representative to the respective divisional office to locate the documents for retrieval.

3. Electronic Filing of Documents:

Registered Participants shall use a court-issued login and password to access the CM/ECF system. Their use of this login and password will allow them to make entries to the official court docket and to file documents electronically with the Court. When a Registered Participant makes an entry to the docket and files documents electronically, the CM/ECF system will automatically generate and send a return e-mail message of the "Notification of Electronic Filing." This Notification of Electronic Filing is equivalent to the conformed copy traditionally stamped "Filed" or "Original Filed." All Registered Participants are highly encouraged to retain the "Notification of Electronic Filing" as proof of electronic filing.

4. Logins and Passwords:

Each attorney in good standing with the Court (and such others as the Court deems appropriate) is eligible to become a Registered Participant which will entitle the Registered Participant to receive an ECF System login and password. To become a Registered Participant, the person must receive training by the Court unless the Clerk is satisfied that the person has already received adequate training in another district. Pro se parties and bankruptcy petition preparers may not be Registered Participants unless permitted by the Court.

The Clerk's Office will post on the Court's web site a CM/ECF training class schedule. Attorneys in good standing with the Court and trustees are encouraged to access the schedule and sign up to attend this training as soon as possible. This court sponsored CM/ECF training will be held on specified dates and locations as announced on the Court's web site > ECF > Training. Attorneys and trustees who practice in multiple locations may attend training at the location of their preference.

Attorneys and trustees who practice primarily or exclusively in one location are encouraged, but not required, to attend training at that location. Attorneys and trustees are encouraged to enroll all employees who will be making entries to the system to attend the court sponsored CM/ECF training. It is recommended that employees attend the training session with the attorney or trustee with whom they work.

To become a Registered Participant, attorneys and trustees shall complete and submit a registration form (available from the Court's web site). A training login and password will be provided to the Registered Participant at the training session. Once the Registered Participant has completed the assigned training homework (successfully filing to this Court's CM/ECF training data base), they will be issued a new password for the "live CM/ECF" database to begin filing with this court electronically.

Attorneys and trustees must attend a court-sponsored training class to become a CM/ECF Registered Participant in this Court. Attorneys who can demonstrate that they have successfully filed electronically in the past six months with another U.S. Bankruptcy Court may apply to become Registered Participants in this district without having to attend the court-sponsored training. All requests must be made by submitting a completed registration form (available from the Court's web site). The request must identify the name and location of the court(s) where the electronic filings were made and must include copies of the system-generated "Notification of Electronic Filings" reflecting the successful filings. The completed request "package" shall be sent via e-mail to the CM/ECF Help Desk at: helpdesk@canb.uscourts.gov ("Request Training Waiver" in the e-mail subject line). All such requests to obtain a CM/ECF system login and password and to waive court sponsored CM/ECF training are subject to review and approval by the Clerk of Court.

Only the Registered Participant, another attorney in the Registered Participant's office, an employee of the Registered Participant or their law office staff may use the Registered Participant's login and password to file on behalf of the Registered Participant. The Registered Participant shall be responsible for any filings made using his or her login and password. Misuse of the ECF System's login and password may result in the revocation of the Registered Participant's login and password privileges and/or the imposition of sanctions. No Registered Participant shall knowingly permit a password to be used by anyone who is not authorized to use the password and no person shall knowingly use the password of a Registered Participant unless such person is so authorized. If an employee of a Registered Participant is no longer permitted such access or if the Registered Participant has reason to believe that the security of his or her password has been compromised, the Registered Participant shall forthwith contact the CM/ECF Help Desk at the Court's Information Technology Section, (415) 268-2350 to obtain a new password.

A Registered Participant may withdraw for cause or be required to withdraw from participation in the electronic filing component of CM/ECF on order of the Court. The Registered Participant shall provide a written notice of withdrawal for cause to the CM/ECF Help Desk, at the address shown above and provide at least ten days notice to all Registered Participants who are or who represent parties in interest in cases assigned to the ECF System in which the withdrawing Registered Participant has entered an appearance. A court order to withdraw a Registered Participant will be sent by the judicial officer to the CM/ECF Help Desk. Upon receipt of the written request or court order, the Help Desk staff will follow internal procedures to cause the Registered Participant's login and password to be cancelled, and the Registered Participant will be removed from the Notification of Electronic Filing service list(s).

5. Orders:

The Court's electronic filing of orders, decrees, memoranda, opinions and judgments shall constitute entry on the Court's docket for purposes of FRBP 5003 and 9021. Any order filed electronically by the Court has the same force and effect as it would if the judge had affixed the judge's signature to a paper copy of the order, and it had been entered on the docket in a conventional manner.

Each judge shall determine how he or she wishes proposed forms of orders to be submitted. Judges may sign orders manually or by any electronic means permitted by FRBP 5005(a)(2) or may use docket text orders. Registered Participants are directed to the Court's web site > ECF > Reference Desk > E-Orders Submission Procedures, for specific directions regarding the submission of proposed forms of orders (submitted orders) for each Judge.

6. Exhibits and Attachments:

An exhibit or attachment longer than 25 pages may be filed if created from a word processing (text) file. Transmission time for filing documents created by scanning that are more than 25 pages and/or three megabytes in size will frequently time out and fail to file due to system security features. Electronic exhibits and attachments created by scanning (imaging) that are more than 25 pages or more than three megabytes in size must be segmented and filed as multiple attachments (the system will allow multiple attachments to any pleading/document to be filed electronically). All pleadings/documents and attachments/exhibits which are created by scanning (imaging) shall be black and white (without color), in PDF format and the resolution should not exceed 200 DPI.

7. Documents Filed Under Seal:

A motion to file a document(s) under seal shall be filed electronically (unless prohibited by applicable non-bankruptcy law); however the actual document(s) to be sealed shall be filed conventionally, on paper, in accordance with Civil LR 79-5, incorporated by reference by BLR 1001-2 (63). If the motion itself contains confidential information, the movant shall electronically file and serve a redacted version of the motion to file under seal. The movant shall deliver paper copies of the document(s) to be sealed to the Clerk's Office at the divisional office of the assigned judge for in camera review. The order of the court authorizing the filing of such document(s) under seal shall be entered by the Court or the Clerk's Office staff and shall indicate that the motion to file document(s) under seal has been so granted. A paper copy of the order authorizing the filing under seal must be delivered to the Clerk with the documents that the Registered Participant wishes to be filed under seal. The conventionally filed paper version of the sealed document(s) will be maintained by the Clerk's Office in a manner consistent with the Civil LR 79-5, as cited above.

8. Signature and Verified Pleadings:

A Registered Participant who electronically files a document with the Court shall be deemed to have certified under penalty of perjury that he or she has personally reviewed the document, is in good standing with the State Bar of all states in which the attorney is authorized to practice, and is authorized to appear in this Court.

Each electronically filed document shall bear the typed name of the person purporting to have signed the document. Pleadings, including but not limited to petitions, lists, schedules and amendments that are required to be verified under FRBP 1008 or to contain an unsworn declaration as provided in 28 U.S.C. 1746, and all affidavits or other pleadings in which a person verifies, certifies, affirms or swears under oath or penalty of perjury concerning the truth of matters set forth in that pleading or document ('Verified Pleading') may be filed electronically. A Registered Participant filing a Verified Pleading electronically shall insure that the electronic version conforms to the original, signed pleading/document. Each signature on the original, signed pleading/document shall be indicated on the electronically filed Verified Pleading with the typed name of the person purported to have signed the pleading/document. The electronic filing of a Verified Pleading constitutes a representation by the Registered Participant who files it that the Registered Participant has in his or her possession at the time of filing the fully executed original, signed pleading/document.

9. Retention Requirements:

All originally executed pleadings/documents signed by someone other than the Registered Participant (e.g., Verified Pleadings), which are subsequently electronically filed with the Court, must be retained by the Registered Participant for five years after the case or adversary proceeding has been closed. The CM/ECF system provides notice of all case closings to Registered Participants. Upon request of the Court, the Registered Participant filer must provide to the Court the original, signed pleadings/documents for review.

10. Notice of Electronic Filing and Service:

Whenever a pleading, document or court order is filed electronically in accordance with these ECF Procedures, the system will automatically generate the Notification of Electronic Filing, which will be emailed to all Registered Participants who have consented to electronic service and have appeared in the case or adversary proceeding in which the document is filed. This transmission of the Notification of Electronic Filing to a Registered Participant shall constitute effective service in accordance with BLR 9013-3(c) and 9022-1(b).

Beginning May 1, 2008 all new CM/ECF Registered Participants will be given the option to consent in writing to receive service electronically by checking the appropriate box on the Clerk's Office CM/ECF Registration form. CM/ECF Registered Participants who registered prior to April 30, 2008 will be required to reaffirm their consent to receive electronic service. The Clerk's Office shall solicit written consents, consistent with FRCP 5(b)(2)(E), from all those Registered Participants via an electronic consent process.

Registered Participants who DO NOT consent to electronic service WILL NOT receive a Notification of Electronic Filing and their name and mailing address will appear at the bottom of the Notification of Electronic Filing (as an alert that this party will only accept service by regular first class mail).

All Registered Participants who consent to electronic service shall maintain a current and active e-mail address with the court to receive Notification of Electronic Filing. To enable proper service via the transmission of the Notice of Electronic Filing, in pending cases, Registered Participants shall not withdraw their e-mail address from any case or de-activate their e-mail account while involved in any adversary proceeding or contested matter without prior notification to the Clerk's Office of their new e-mail address or the filing of a proper withdrawal from case, consistent with Civil LR 11-5, incorporated by reference by BLR 1001-2(31).

11. Technical Failure:

If the Court's CM/ECF site is unable to accept filings continuously or intermittently over the course of any period of time greater than two hours after 9:00 a.m. on any given day, a party whose filing is made untimely as the result of a technical failure may seek appropriate relief from the Court. The Court shall determine whether a technical failure has occurred on a case by case basis. Problems occurring on the filer's end, including those related to phone lines, Internet Service Providers (ISP) or hardware and software, will not constitute a technical failure under these procedures nor excuse an untimely filing. A filer who cannot file a pleading/document electronically because of a problem on the filer's end must file the pleading/document conventionally or by facsimile pursuant to Civil LR 5-2, incorporated by reference by BLR 1001-2(20).

12. Fees:

For filings that require a fee, the CM/ECF system will prompt the filer (Registered Participant) to enter credit card information (card number, and expiration date and security code) and the payment amount following the transaction. "Credit Card Authorization Forms" are no longer required by the Court for CM/ECF credit card transactions. The credit card receipt shall include a reference to the case and docket number. Funds will be automatically charged to the card holder's account by the United States Treasury Department. All credit card filing fee payments are subject to audit and review by Clerk's Office staff. Any identified discrepancy will be brought to the attention of the filer (Registered Participant). The CM/ECF system will automatically disable access for Registered Participants with filing fees outstanding at midnight of the filing date. The Registered Participant whose access to CM/ECF has been disabled will be able to login to CM/ECF but will not be able to view or file any documents until he or she clicks on the "Utilities" then "Internet Payments Due" and pays the outstanding fees. Once the outstanding fees are paid, the Registered Participant's system's access to file and view electronic documents will be immediately reinstated. Payments must be made within 24-hours or the case/matter is subject to dismissal/being stricken.

13. Summons in an Adversary Proceeding:

To file an adversary proceeding, a Registered Participant shall electronically prepare the standard form 250B, "Summons and Notice of Scheduling Conference in an Adversary Proceeding" (Summons) or for the San Jose division, "Summons and Notice of Telephonic Status Conference or Summons and Notice of Status Conference" (Summons) and electronically file it as an attachment to the electronically filed Complaint. The Court shall continue to issue these Summons in the conventional, paper (hard copy) form. The deputy clerks will print a hard copy of the submitted Summons from the CM/ECF system and will issue and sign the Summons. This completed hard copy of the Summons, with a blank Certificate of Service on the reverse side, will be returned via first class mail to the filer (to be served in the conventional manner). In the event an Alias Summons is required, the original hard copy unexecuted Summons (Summons issued but not served) shall be returned to the Clerk's Office, along with a hard copy proposed form of Alias Summons. The deputy clerk will issue and sign the hard copy Alias Summons and will send it via first class mail to the submitting party.

14. Policy for Chambers Copies of ECF Filed Documents:

The judge(s) at each divisional office (with the exception of the Santa Rosa division) have identified policies and procedures for lodging Chambers copies of ECF Filed documents. Registered Participants are directed to the Court's web site at www.canb.uscourts.gov ≫ ECF ≫ Reference Desk section for specific information regarding the lodging of Chamber's copies.

15. Corrections:

Once a Pleading or document is electronically filed and becomes part of the electronic record, corrections to the docket entry may be made only by the Clerk's Office staff. A pleading or document may be incorrectly filed as the result of e.g., posting the incorrect PDF file to a docket entry, selecting the incorrect document type from the menu selection, or entering the incorrect case number, etc. The CM/ECF system will not permit a Registered Participant to remove or reattach an incorrectly filed pdf document or to change the form of an incorrect docket entry once the transaction has been accepted. In the event an electronic filing error is discovered, the Registered Participant should contact the Clerk's Office as soon as possible at the location where the case is pending and ask the Clerk's Office staff to make the correction. The Registered Participant should be prepared with the case number and document number for which the correction is being requested. If appropriate, the Clerk's Office staff will make an entry indicating that the pleading/document was filed in error. The Registered Participant will be advised if the pleading/document will need to be re-filed and instructed on the proper procedure.

16. CM/ECF System Unavailability:

During 2:00 a.m. to 3:00 a.m. every day and for 24 hours on the third Saturday of every month, the Court's CM/ECF system will be unavailable to Registered Participants for filing due to regular system maintenance and back-up operations. Any other downtime will be posted on both the CM/ECF home page and the Court's internet site. Registered Participants are instructed not to attempt to access this site during these periods of unavailability.

17. Access to CM/ECF via the Clerk's Office Lobby Terminals and PACER:

Electronic access to CM/ECF dockets and documents electronically filed in the system is available to the public for viewing at no charge in each of the divisional offices during regular business hours. A fee for a paper copy of an electronic document is required in accordance with 28 U.S.C. Section 1930. In accordance with the ruling of the Judicial Conference of the United States, a user fee will be charged for access to dockets and documents electronically filed in the system through the Public Access to Court Electronic Records System (PACER).

18. Pro se Filing:

For pro se litigants filing with this Court, all petitions, pleadings and other documents shall be prepared and filed on paper. Pro se litigants shall not have access to electronic filing (except for Limited Access Accounts for filing Proofs of Claim, Transfer of Claims, etc). For more information see the Court's web site at www.canb.uscourts.gov.ecf. All pro se paper filings shall be scanned by Clerk's Office staff to enable an electronic record to be created.

[Memorandum on New Chapter 13 Guidelines] NEW GUIDELINES FOR PAYMENT OF ATTORNEY'S FEES IN CHAPTER 13 CASES AND RIGHTS AND RESPONSIBILITIES OF CHAPTER 13 DEBTORS AND THEIR ATTORNEYS

New *Guidelines for Payment of Attorney's Fees in Chapter 13 Cases* and *Rights and Responsibilities of Chapter 13 Debtors and Their Attorneys* are in effect in the San Francisco and San Jose divisions as of June 1, 1994. For the month of June, 1994, either the prior procedures or the new procedures may be followed by Chapter 13 debtors. Beginning July 1, 1994, the new procedure will govern compensation of attorneys in Chapter 13.

[Chapter 13 Attorney's Fees Guidelines]

GUIDELINES FOR PAYMENT OF ATTORNEY'S FEES IN CHAPTER 13 CASES

Oakland Division

The following are guidelines for the circumstances under which a detailed fee application need not be filed in Chapter 13 cases and the manner in which the Chapter 13 Trustee will disburse fees which are approved.

A. FEE APPLICATIONS.

1. Counsel may receive an order approving fees up to the amounts set forth in Paragraph 2 without filing a detailed application if:

a) Counsel has filed an executed copy of the "Rights and Responsibilities of Chapter 13 Debtors and Their Attorneys," copies of which are available in the Clerk's Office and in the Office of the Chapter 13 Trustee; and

b) No objection to the requested fees has been raised.

2. The maximum fee which can be approved through the procedure described in Paragraph 1 is: $1500 in nonbusiness cases and $2800 in business cases.

Retainers of more than $500 in nonbusiness cases and $1000 in business cases will be closely scrutinized by both the Chapter 13 Trustee and the Court.

3. If an executed copy of the "Rights and Responsibilities of Chapter 13 Debtors and Their Attorneys" is not filed, or there is an objection, an order will not be entered automatically pursuant to these Guidelines. In such cases, counsel must apply for all fees, and shall comply with Bankruptcy Rules 2002 and 2016 as well as the "Guidelines for Compensation and Expense Reimbursement of Professionals" adopted by the Bankruptcy Judges of the Northern District of California.

4. If counsel has filed an executed copy of the "Rights and Responsibilities of Chapter 13 Debtors and Their Attorneys," but the initial fee is not sufficient to fully compensate counsel for the legal services rendered in the case, the attorney may apply for additional fees. The form application attached hereto may be used in place of the procedures set forth in the "Guidelines for Compensation and Expense Reimbursement for Professionals." The necessity for a hearing on the application shall be governed by Bankruptcy Rule 2002(a)(7) and Local Bankruptcy Rule 7-914(b)(1)(B).

5. All fees shall be paid through the plan unless otherwise ordered. The attorney may not receive fees directly from the debtor other than the initial retainer. The Chapter 13 Trustee shall pay 20% of each plan payment to the attorney until the fee is paid in full.

6. On its own motion or the motion of any party in interest, the Court may order a hearing to review any fee paid.

San Francisco and San Jose Divisions

The following are guidelines for the circumstances under which a detailed fee application need not be filed in Chapter 13 cases and the manner in which the Chapter 13 Trustee will disburse fees which are approved.

A. Fee Applications.

1. Counsel may receive an order approving fees up to the amounts set forth in Paragraph 2 without filing a detailed application if:

(a) Counsel has filed and served the Chapter 13 Trustee with an executed copy of the "Rights and Responsibilities of Chapter 13 Debtors and Their Attorneys," copies of which are available in the Clerk's Office and in the Office of the Chapter 13 Trustee;

(b) Counsel has accepted no more than $500 as a retainer in the case, unless counsel thereafter applies for and receives court approval of a larger advance retainer; and

(c) No objection to the requested fees has been raised.

2. The maximum fee which can be approved through the procedure described in Paragraph 1 is:

$1200	for the basic case; and an additional
$500	if the case involves real property claims;
$300	if the case involves state or federal tax claims;
$200	if the case involves vehicle loans or leases; and
$1000	if the case involves an operating business.

3. If an executed copy of the "Rights and Responsibilities of Chapter 13 Debtors and Their Attorneys" is not filed, counsel has accepted more than $500 without court approval, or there is an objection, an order will not be entered automatically pursuant to these Guidelines.

4. If counsel elects to be paid other than pursuant to these Guidelines, all fees including the retainer shall be approved by the court whether or not the fees are payable through the Chapter 13 Trustee's Office and whether or not fees are paid for services in connection with the Chapter 13 case.

5. If counsel applies for fees, counsel shall comply with Rules 2002 and 2016 of the Federal Rules of Bankruptcy Procedure as well as the "Guidelines for Compensation and Expense Reimbursement of Professionals" adopted by the Bankruptcy Judges of the Northern District of California.

6. On its own motion or the motion of any party in interest, the court may order a hearing to review any fee paid or unpaid.

B. Distribution of Funds in Chapter 13 Cases.

Payments shall be disbursed in the following order:

1. $500 towards attorney's fees, less any amount received pre-filing as a retainer;

2. To secured creditors and the balance of attorney's fees. Those secured creditors which are specified in the plan to receive fixed monthly payments will be paid the amount specified. If fixed monthly payments are specified in the plan for all secured creditors, the balance of the plan payment will be disbursed toward attorney's fees. If fixed monthly payments are not specified in the plan for all secured creditors, secured claims without fixed monthly payments and the balance of attorneys fees will be pro-rated;

3. To priority creditors in the order prescribed by the Bankruptcy Code;

4. To unsecured creditors.

Santa Rosa/Eureka Division

In this division, the court does not enforce any maximum or minimum fee structure, nor does it limit the size of counsel's prepetition retainer. Unusually large fees will trigger scrutiny by the court as well as the trustee. No payments should be taken from the debtor after the case is filed (except through the trustee) without order of the court obtained after noticed hearing.

The court agrees with the rights and responsibilities enforced by other divisions. The court further expects that debtors with counsel of record will NEVER appear in court without representation. However, while the court expects compliance with the rights and responsibilities it does not require the filing of a formal statement.

[Chapter 13 Debtor and Attorney Guidelines]

RIGHTS AND RESPONSIBILITIES OF CHAPTER 13 DEBTORS AND THEIR ATTORNEYS (Oakland Division)

RIGHTS AND RESPONSIBILITIES OF CHAPTER 13 DEBTORS AND THEIR ATTORNEYS (San Francisco Division)

RIGHTS AND RESPONSIBILITIES OF CHAPTER 13 DEBTORS AND THEIR ATTORNEYS (San Jose Division)

[Professional Compensation and Expense Reimbursement Guidelines] GUIDELINES FOR COMPENSATION AND EXPENSE REIMBURSEMENT OF PROFESSIONALS AND TRUSTEES (Rev. 7/8/04)

The following guidelines are promulgated pursuant to B.L.R. 9029-1 and govern the most significant issues related to applications for compensation and expense reimbursement. The guidelines cover the narrative portion of an application, time records and expenses. They apply in their entirety to professionals seeking compensation under 11 U.S.C. § 330 and, where indicated, to Chapter 7 and Chapter 11 trustees. The guidelines are not intended to cover every situation. The court is advised that compliance with these guidelines will satisfy the requirements of the United States Trustee.

I. Guidelines Applicable To Attorneys And Other Professionals

The Narrative

1. Employment and Prior Compensation— The application should disclose the date of the order approving applicant's employment and contain a clear statement itemizing the date of each prior request for compensation, the amount requested, the amount approved, and the amount paid.

2. Case Status— With respect to interim requests, the application should briefly explain the history and the present posture of the case.

In chapter 11 cases, the information furnished should describe the general operations of the debtor; whether the business of the debtor, if any, is being operated at a profit or loss; the debtor's cash flow; whether a plan has been filed, and if not, what the prospects are for reorganization and when it is anticipated that a plan will be filed and a hearing set on the disclosure statement.

In Chapter 7 cases, the application should contain a report of the administration of the case including the disposition of property of the estate; what property remains to be disposed of; why the estate is not in a position to be closed; and whether it is feasible to pay an interim dividend to creditors.

In both Chapter 7 and Chapter 11 cases, the application should state the amount of money on hand in the estate and the estimated amount of other accrued expenses of administration. On applications for interim fees, the applicant should orally supplement the application at the hearing to inform the Court of any changes in the current financial status of the debtor's estate since the filing of the application.

With respect to final requests, applications should meet the same criteria except, where a Chapter 7 Trustee's final account is being heard at the same time, the financial information in the final account need not be repeated.

Fee applications submitted by special counsel seeking compensation from a fund generated directly by their efforts, auctioneers, real estate brokers, or appraisers do not have to comply with the above. For all other applications, when more than one application is noticed for the same hearing, they may, to the extent appropriate, incorporate by reference the narrative history furnished in a contemporaneous application.

3. Project Billing— In any application exceeding $10,000, or when the professional's anticipated services for the case will exceed $20,000, the narrative should categorize by subject matter and separately discuss each professional project or task. All work for which compensation is requested should be in a category.

The professional may use reasonable discretion in defining projects for this purpose, provided that the application provides meaningful guidance to the Court as to the complexity and difficulty of the task, the professional's efficiency and the results achieved. (A separate category should generally be created for a project when the fees attributable to that project exceed $5,000.) With respect to each project or task, the number of hours spent and the amount of compensation and expenses requested should be set forth at the conclusion of the discussion of that project or task. Please also note requirements in Guideline 11 relating to time records by project.

4. Billing Summary— Hours and total compensation requested in each application should be aggregated and itemized as to each professional and paraprofessional who provided compensable services.

5. Paraprofessionals— Fees may be sought for paralegals, professional assistants and law clerks only if identified as such and if the following requirements are met:

(a) The services for which compensation is sought would have had to be done by the professional if not done by the paraprofessional, and would have been compensable under these guidelines;

(b) The person who performed the services is specially trained or is a law school student, and is not primarily a secretary or clerical worker; and

(c) The application includes a resume or summary of the paraprofessional's qualifications.

6. Preparation of Application— Reasonable fees for preparation of a fee application may be requested. The aggregate number of hours spent, the amount requested, and the percentage of the total request which the amount represents must be disclosed. If the actual time spent will be reflected and charged in a future fee application this fact should be stated but an estimate nevertheless provided.

7. Client Review of Billing Statement— A debtor in possession, trustee or official committee shall exercise reasonable business judgment in monitoring the fees and expenses of the estate's professionals. Billing statements should be sent to the employing entity (debtor in possession, trustee or official committee) on a monthly basis. A fee application shall be sent to the employing entity at least 20 days prior to the scheduled hearing date. The application shall be transmitted with a cover letter that contains the following statement: "The court's Guidelines for Compensation and Expense Reimbursement of Professionals and Trustees provide that a debtor in possession, a trustee or an official committee must exercise reasonable business judgment in monitoring the fees and expenses of the estate's professionals. We invite you to discuss any objections, concerns or questions you may have with us. The Office of the United States Trustee will also accept your comments. The court will also consider timely filed objections by any party in interest at the time of the hearing."

8. Certification— Each application for compensation and expense reimbursement must contain a certification by the professional designated by the applicant with the responsibility in the particular case for compliance with these guidelines ("Certifying Professional") that (a) the Certifying Professional has read the application; (b) to the best of the Certifying Professional's knowledge, information and belief, formed after reasonable inquiry, the compensation and expense reimbursement sought is in conformity with these guidelines, except as specifically noted in the certification application; and (c) the compensation and expense reimbursement requested are billed at rates, in accordance with practices, no less favorable than those customarily employed by the applicant and generally accepted by the applicant's clients.

9. Short Form Applications— Where the professional is filing only a final request for compensation in a Chapter 7 case and the request, exclusive of costs, does not exceed $15,000 for the case, the professional has the option of utilizing the approved Chapter 7 form application.

In a Chapter 13 case, where the professional has utilized and filed the *RIGHTS AND RESPONSIBILITIES OF CHAPTER 13 DEBTORS AND THEIR ATTORNEYS*, the professional has the option of utilizing the approved Chapter 13 form application when seeking compensation in excess of that approved at the time of confirmation.

Copies of the approved form applications are available in the Clerk's Office.

Time Records

10. Time Records Required— All professionals, except auctioneers, real estate brokers, appraisers and those employed on a contingency fee basis, must keep accurate contemporaneous time records. The Court may, however, specifically direct that time records be kept on a contingent fee matter.

11. Time Records By Project— In any application exceeding $10,000, or where the professional's anticipated services for the case will exceed $20,000, time records should be kept by categories as described in Paragraph 3 relating to Project Billing above. Time records should be sorted, assembled and attached to the application by category corresponding to the discussion in the narrative.

12. Increments— Professionals are required to keep time records in minimum increments no greater than 6 minutes. Professionals who utilize a minimum billing increment greater than.1 hour are subject to a substantial reduction of their requests.

13. Descriptions— At a minimum, the time entries should identify the person preforming the services, the date performed, what was done, and the subject involved. Mere notations of telephone calls, conferences, research, drafting, etc., without identifying the matter involved, may result in disallowance of the time covered by the entries.

14. Clumping— If a number of separate tasks are performed on a single day, the fee application should disclose the time spent for each such task (*i.e.,* no "grouping" or "clumping").

15. Conferences— Professionals should be prepared to explain time spent in conferences with other professionals or paraprofessionals in the same firm. Failure to justify this time may result in disallowance of all fees related to such conferences.

16. Multiple Professionals— Professionals should be prepared to explain the need for more than one professional or paraprofessional from the same firm at the same court hearing, deposition or meeting. Failure to justify this time may be result in compensation for only the person with the lowest billing rate.

17. Airplane Travel Time— Airplane travel time is not compensable, but work actually done during a flight is compensable. If significant airplane travel time is expected in a case, specific guidelines should be obtained for that case.

18. Administrative Tasks— Time spent in addressing, stamping and stuffing envelopes, filing, photocopying or "supervising" any of the foregoing is not compensable, whether performed by a professional, paraprofessional or secretary.

Expenses

19. Firm Practice— All expenses for which reimbursement is sought must be of the kind, and at the least expensive rate, the applicant customarily charges nonbankruptcy/insolvency clients.

20. Actual Cost— Is defined as the amount paid to a third party provider of goods or services without enhancement for handling or other administrative charge.

21. Documentation— Must be retained and made available upon request for all expenditures in excess of $50.00. Where possible, receipts should be obtained for all expenditures.

22. Office Overhead— Not reimbursable. Overhead includes: secretarial time, secretarial overtime, word processing time, charges for after-hour and weekend air conditioning and other utilities, and cost of meals or transportation provided to professionals and staff who work late or on weekends.

23. Word Processing— Not reimbursable.

24. Computerized Research— Actual cost.

25. Paraprofessional Services— May be compensated as a paraprofessional under § 330 but not charged or reimbursed as an expense.

26. Professional Services— A professional employed under § 327 may not employ, and charge as an expense, another professional (e.g., special litigation counsel employing an expert witness) unless the employment of the second professional is approved by the Court prior to the rendering of services.

27. Photocopies (Internal)— Charges must be disclosed on an aggregate and per page basis. If the per page cost exceeds 20¢, the professional must demonstrate to the satisfaction of the Court, with data, that the per page cost represents a good faith estimate of the actual cost of the copies, based upon the purchase or lease cost of the copy machine and supplies therefor including the space occupied by the machine, but not including time spent in operating the machine.

28. Photocopies (Outside)— Actual cost.

29. Postage— Actual cost.

30. Overnight Delivery— Actual cost where shown to be necessary.

31. Messenger Service— Actual cost where shown to be necessary. An in-house messenger service is reimbursable but the estate cannot be charged more than the cost of comparable services available outside the firm.

32. Facsimile Transmission— Actual cost of telephone charges for outgoing transmissions are reimbursable. Transmissions received are reimbursable on a per page basis. If the per page cost exceeds 20¢, the professional must demonstrate to the satisfaction of the Court, with data, that the per page cost represents a good faith estimate of the actual cost of the copies, based upon the purchase or lease cost of the facsimile machine and supplies therefor including the space occupied by the machine, but not including time spent in operating the machine.

33. Long Distance Telephone— Actual cost.

34. Automotive Transportation— Travel of one hour or less round-trip is not reimbursable. Travel expense for trips in excess of one hour round-trip is reimbursable in accordance with the amount allowed by the Internal Revenue Service. (IRC § 274(d) and the current applicable I.R.B. Announcement. At this date the amount is .31¢ per mile.) Travel by a professional, paraprofessional or other staff member between his or her residence and principal place of business is not reimbursable regardless of the day of the week or time of the day.

35. Parking— Actual cost, provided that parking for professionals, paraprofessionals or other staff member at their principal place of business is not reimbursable regardless of the day of the week or time of the day.

36. Air Transportation— Air travel is expected to be at regular coach fare for all flights.

37. Hotels— Due to wide variation in hotel costs in various cities, it is not possible to establish a single guideline for this type of expense. All persons will be required to exercise discretion and prudence in connection with hotel expenditures.

38. Meals—Travel— The cost of lunches while a party is away from the Bay Area, or in the Bay Area from another city, is not reimbursable. Reimbursement may be sought for the reasonable cost of breakfast and dinner while traveling.

39. Meals—Working— Working meals at restaurants or private clubs are not reimbursable. Reimbursement may be sought for working meals only where food is catered to the professional's office in the course of a meeting with clients, such as a Creditors Committee, for the purpose of allowing the meeting to continue through a normal meal period.

40. Amenities— Charges for entertainment, alcoholic beverages, newspapers, dry cleaning, shoe shines, etc. are not reimbursable.

41. Filing Fees— Actual cost.

42. Court Reporter Fees— Actual cost.

43. Witness Fees— Actual cost.

44. Process Service— Actual cost.

45. UCC Searches— Actual cost.

II. Guidelines Applicable to Trustees

Chapter 7 and Chapter 11 trustees must maintain contemporaneous time records in every case. Time records must be maintained by project categories. At a minimum, project categories should include: (1) Assets Recap (asset analysis and recovery/asset disposition); (2) Investigation of Financial Affairs of the Debtor; (3) Claims Administration and Objections; and (4) Fee Applications. Trustees may add additional categories at their discretion. Trustees are also subject to Guidelines 4, 5 (subject to § 326), 10, 12, 13 and 19–45 dealing with expenses.

In cases in which the trustee's compensation request is anticipated to be $5,000 or less, the trustee may submit a brief narrative description of the services performed and a statement of the amount of time spent. In cases in which the final compensation exceeds $5,000, or where an interim request is made and it is anticipated that the total compensation requested will exceed $5,000, the trustee's application must include time records as well as a narrative description of the services performed and comply with the guidelines referenced above.

The guidelines regarding trustee time records shall apply only to cases filed on or after January 1, 1997.

CHAPTER 7 FINAL APPLICATION FOR COMPENSATION

____
____
____
____
____________ For Chapter 7 Trustee

UNITED STATES BANKRUPTCY COURT
NORTHERN DISTRICT OF CALIFORNIA

In re:	Case No. ____________
Debtor(s)	Chapter 7

CHAPTER 7 FINAL APPLICATION FOR COMPENSATION BY

____

This application is submitted pursuant to Guideline 9 of the Guidelines for Compensation and Expense Reimbursement of Professionals and Trustees adopted by the United States Bankruptcy Court for the Northern District of California.

1. Date of Filing of Case: ____________
2. Name of Trustee: ____________
3. Total Receipts of Trustee: $____________
4. Present Balance on Hand: $____________
5. Date of Appointment of Applicant: $____________
6. Time Period of Application: From ___ To ____________
7. Hourly Rate of Professional: $____________
8. Total Hours in this Application: ____________
9. Total Fees Requested: $__________ x . . . hrs. = $____________
10. Amount Included for Anticipated Appearance at Hearing on Application: $____________
11. Total Costs Requested this Application: $____________
12. Total Fees and Costs Requested: $____________

13. Brief Description of Services: ______________________________
____
____
____
____
____
____
____
____

A detailed billing statement including costs is attached hereto as Exhibit A.

Dated: ______________________ ______________________

______________________ For Chapter 7 Trustee

CERTIFICATION

I, ____________, declare as follows:

1. That I am a____________of ____________.

2. That I am familiar with and have read the above application and the facts therein are true to my knowledge and belief. The copies of the billing statements are true and correct copies of ____________'s billing statements for this case.

3. That the firm of____________has not been paid or promised any compensation from any other source for services rendered in connection with this case.

4. That____________has not entered into any agreement or understanding with any other entity for the sharing of compensation received or to be received for services rendered and/or to be rendered in connection with this case.

5. That to the best of my knowledge, information and belief, the compensation and expense reimbursement sought herein is in conformity with the Guidelines for Compensation and Expense Reimbursement of Professionals and Trustees for the United States Bankruptcy Court for the Northern District of California, except to the extent set forth in the application.

6. That this application is submitted in accordance with Guideline No. 9 of the Guidelines for Compensation and Expense Reimbursement of Professionals and Trustees for the United States Bankruptcy Court for the Northern District of California.

7. That the compensation and expenses sought herein were billed at rates no less favorable than those customarily billed by applicant and generally accepted by the applicant's clients.

I declare under penalty of perjury that the foregoing is true and correct and that this certification was executed this____________day of____________at ____________, California.

____

GUIDELINES FOR CASH COLLATERAL AND FINANCING STIPULATIONS

(Oakland, San Francisco and San Jose Divisions)

The judges are often requested to provide guidance to Chapter 11 debtors (or Chapter 11 trustees) and secured parties concerning the provisions in cash collateral stipulations (see Bankruptcy Code § 363(c)(2)) or financing stipulations (see § 364(c)) that the court will not normally approve. In response, the judges offer the following guidelines.

All applications for court approval of a cash collateral or financing stipulation must recite whether the stipulation contains any provision that the court will not normally approve, identify any such provision and explain the justification for the provision.

A. Provisions that will not normally be approved.

1. Cross-collateralization clauses, *i.e.,* clauses that secure prepetition debt by postpetition assets in which the secured party would not otherwise have a security interest by virtue of its prepetition security agreement. *See* Bankruptcy Code § 552.

2. Provisions or findings of fact that bind the estate or all parties in interest with respect to the validity, perfection or amount of the secured party's lien or debt.

3. Provisions or findings of fact that bind the estate or all parties in interest with respect to the relative priorities of the secured party's lien and liens held by persons who are not party to the stipulation. (This would include, for example, an order approving stipulation providing that the secured party's lien is a "first priority" lien.)

4. Waivers of Bankruptcy Code § 506(c), unless the waiver is effective only during the period in which the debtor is authorized to use cash collateral or borrow funds. (Otherwise a future trustee might be faced with a duty to care for and preserve collateral in the trustee's possession and no financial means for discharging that duty.)

5. Provisions that operate, as a practical matter, to divest the debtor in possession of any discretion in the formulation of a plan or administration of the estate or limit access to the court to seek any relief under other applicable provisions of law.

6. Releases of liability for the creditor's alleged prepetition torts or breaches of contract.

7. Waivers of avoidance actions arising under the Bankruptcy Code.

8. Automatic relief from the automatic stay upon default, conversion to Chapter 7, or appointment of a trustee.

9. Waivers of the procedural requirements for foreclosure mandated under applicable non-bankruptcy law.

10. Adequate protection provisions that create liens on claims for relief arising under the Bankruptcy Code (see §§ 506(c), 544, 545, 547, 548, and 549).

11. Waivers, effective on default or expiration, of the debtor's right to move for a court order pursuant to Bankruptcy Code § 363(c)(2)(B) authorizing the use of cash collateral in the absence of the secured party's consent.

12. Findings of fact on matters extraneous to the approval process. (For example, in connection with an application to borrow on a secured basis, a finding that the debtor cannot obtain unsecured credit would be acceptable, whereas a "finding" that the lender acted in good faith in declaring the prepetition loan in default would not be acceptable.)

B. Provisions that will normally be approved.

1. Withdrawal of consent to use cash collateral or termination of further financing, upon occurrence of a default or conversion to Chapter 7.

2. Securing any postpetition diminution in the value of the secured party's collateral with a lien on postpetition collateral of the same type as the secured party had prepetition, if such lien is subordinated to the compensation and expense reimbursement (excluding professional fees) allowed to any trustee thereafter appointed in the case.

3. Securing new advances or value diminution with a lien on other assets of the estate, but only if the lien is subordinated to all the expenses of administration (including professional fees) of a superseding Chapter 7 case.

4. Reservations of rights under Bankruptcy Code § 507(b), unless the stipulation calls for modification of the Code's priorities in the event of a conversion to Chapter 7. *See* Bankruptcy Code § 726(b).

5. Reasonable reporting requirements.

6. Reasonable budgets and use restrictions.

7. Expiration date for the stipulation.

BANKRUPTCY PETITION PREPARER GUIDELINES

The following are guidelines concerning the conduct and compensation of bankruptcy petition preparers (as defined in section 110 of the Bankruptcy Code (11 U.S.C. § 110)) who are not attorneys and who assist debtors in filing voluntary bankruptcy petitions (under Chapter 7, 11, 12 or 13), or in preparing any papers filed in connection with such cases in this court. These guidelines are issued pursuant to B.L.R. 9029-1.

1. The maximum allowable charge for a bankruptcy petition preparer's services is $125, including any and all expenses such as photocopying, messenger or courier charges, postage, telephone, etc. This fee does not include the filing fee that must be paid to the clerk of the bankruptcy court; the debtor(s) is to make that payment directly to the court.

2. If any money has been paid or any property transferred by the debtor to the bankruptcy petition preparer within one year of the filing of the bankruptcy petition, the court's filing fees may not be paid in installments.

3. The bankruptcy petition preparer is not an attorney and is not authorized to practice law. Specifically, the bankruptcy petition preparer may not instruct or advise the debtor(s):

(i) Whether to file a bankruptcy petition;

(ii) Under which chapter of the Bankruptcy Code to file the voluntary petition;

(iii) How to respond to the bankruptcy forms required in connection with the filing of the bankruptcy case;

(iv) What exemptions should be claimed;

(v) Whether any particular debts are dischargeable or nondischargeable;

(vi) The effect of a bankruptcy filing upon a foreclosure and whether the debtor(s) may keep a home;

(vii) Whether the debtor(s) may avoid or eliminate any liens or recover any assets in connection with the bankruptcy case;

(viii) Whether the debtor(s) may redeem property;

(ix) Whether the debtor(s) may or should reaffirm any debts;

(x) Whether the debtor(s) is entitled to a discharge under the Bankruptcy Code, and what defenses the debtor may have to an objection to discharge; and

(xi) Concerning the tax consequences of any aspect of the bankruptcy case.

4. The bankruptcy petition preparer may type forms and file documents.

5. Upon application of the debtor(s), a creditor or any party-in-interest, including the United States Trustee, or on the court's own motion, fees of a bankruptcy petition preparer may be reduced below the amount allowed by these Guidelines. All fees may be forfeited where the bankruptcy petition preparer has acted incompetently or illegally, or has failed to comply with these Guidelines. In addition to liability for criminal penalties, all fees are subject to forfeiture, in any case where the bankruptcy petition preparer has violated any provision of Bankruptcy Code § 110.

6. Before preparing a bankruptcy petition, schedules and statements (or the first of any other paper if the bankruptcy petition preparer has not prepared the petition), and before accepting any money from the debtor(s), the bankruptcy petition preparer must allow the debtor(s) to read and sign a Notice To Debtors About Bankruptcy Petition Preparers (in the form accompanying these Guidelines) and provide a copy thereof and a copy of these Guidelines to the debtor(s). The original and six copies of the Notice must be filed with the court along with the petition or the first paper prepared by the Bankruptcy Petition Preparer.

7. The court encourages debtors, trustees and others who believe a bankruptcy petition preparer has violated section 110 of the Bankruptcy Code (11 U.S.C. § 110) to advise the United States Trustee of the violation.

NOTICE TO DEBTORS ABOUT BANKRUPTCY PETITION PREPARERS

UNITED STATES BANKRUPTCY COURT
NORTHERN DISTRICT OF CALIFORNIA

In re: ____________________ ________________________ __________ Debtor(s)	Bankruptcy Case No. __________________ Chapter __________________

NOTICE TO DEBTORS ABOUT BANKRUPTCY PETITION PREPARERS

PLEASE BE AWARE THAT SPECIAL RULES APPLY TO BANKRUPTCY PETITION PREPARERS IN THIS COURT.

Bankruptcy petition preparers are **non-attorneys who are not authorized to practice law or give legal advice.** The U.S. Bankruptcy Court has issued the *Bankruptcy Petition Preparer Guidelines* (the "Guidelines") to govern the work performed by bankruptcy petition preparers and the fees they may charge.

Under the *Guidelines,* **a bankruptcy petition preparer must give you a copy of this notice before taking any money or property from you for payment and before preparing any papers for filing in the bankruptcy court.** You and the bankruptcy petition preparer must sign a copy of this Notice in the space below, a copy must be given to you, and the original and six copies must be filed with the Bankruptcy Court.

According to the Court's *Guidelines,* a bankruptcy petition preparer **MAY NOT:**

◇ Advise you whether to file bankruptcy or whether chapter 7, 11, 12 or 13 is more appropriate for you;

◇ Advise you whether your debts will be eliminated, or "discharged," in a bankruptcy case;

◇ Advise you whether you will be able to keep your home after filing a bankruptcy case;

◇ Advise you as to the tax consequences of filing a bankruptcy case;

◇ Advise you whether you should promise to repay, or "reaffirm," debts to creditors; or

◇ Charge you more than **$125** for preparing, photocopying and forwarding your bankruptcy papers to the bankruptcy court.

The *Guidelines* contain additional restrictions. A complete copy of the *Guidelines* is attached to this form. YOU SHOULD READ THE *GUIDELINES* TO UNDERSTAND WHAT THE U.S. BANKRUPTCY COURT REQUIRES OF BANKRUPTCY PETITION PREPARERS.

If you have any questions about bankruptcy petition preparers or believe that the *Guidelines* have been violated, please call the **UNITED STATES TRUSTEE** at the following numbers:

SAN FRANCISCO/SANTA ROSA OFFICE	415-705-3333
OAKLAND OFFICE	510-637-3200
SAN JOSE/SALINAS OFFICE	408-535-5525

DEBTOR(S)' CERTIFICATION

I, ____________, and ____________, the debtor(s) in the above-captioned case, have read and understand the foregoing, and have received a copy of the *Guidelines.*

Dated: ____________ ____________________
(signature)

____
(signature)

BANKRUPTCY PETITION PREPARER'S CERTIFICATION

I, ____________, hereby certify under penalty of perjury that I am the bankruptcy petition preparer who has assisted the debtor(s) in filing the above-captioned case. I have not charged fees in excess of the amount allowed in Guideline 1 of the *Guidelines,* attached hereto. I have not advised the debtor(s) concerning any of the matters referred to in Guideline 3.

Dated: ____________ ____________________
(signature)

(Original and 6 copies to be filed with the original petition;
duplicate copy to be given to the debtor(s) by bankruptcy
Petition preparer.)

Public Notice

Change in Local Rules—Compensation of BDRP Resolution Advocates

Bankruptcy Local Rule 9050-1, Voluntary Service of Resolution Advocates, has been amended to permit Resolution Advocates serving in the

Bankruptcy Dispute Resolution Program to receive some compensation for their services. The rule, as amended, now reads as follows:

9050-1. Fee for Service of Resolution Advocates.

The Resolution Advocates are authorized to charge each side, whether or not represented by counsel, up to $100 for their services. This fee, which is waivable in whole or in part in the discretion of the Resolution Advocate, is applicable for all matters assigned to the BDRP by court order dated on or after January, 2, 1999.

Dated: March 23, 1999

REFERENCE MANUAL

Application and Order for Custody of Claims

UNITED STATES BANKRUPTCY COURT
NORTHERN DISTRICT OF CALIFORNIA

In re: Case No.: __________

Debtor(s) Chapter: __________

APPLICATION AND ORDER FOR CUSTODY OF CLAIMS

The undersigned hereby certifies that he/she is the duly appointed trustee in this case, or counsel for the trustee or debtor in possession, and that removal of the claims from the custody of the Clerk is necessary for the administration of the case. The undersigned certifies that he/she shall be personally responsible for the return of the claims by __________, and understands that he/she shall be subject to sanction if the claims numbered __________ through __________ are not returned by that date.

Dated: __________

____
Name

____
Title

____
Address

____

____
Telephone

Upon the above application, IT IS ORDERED that the Clerk may surrender custody of the claims to the applicant, who shall return them by the date specified above.

Date: __________

____
United States Bankruptcy Judge

Stipulation For Continuance Of Confirmation Hearing; And Order Continuing Confirmation Hearing

Name: ____________

Telephone: ____________

Attorney For: ____________

UNITED STATES BANKRUPTCY COURT
NORTHERN DISTRICT OF CALIFORNIA-DIVISION 5

In re: Debtor(s).	Chapter 13 Case No. Stipulation For Continuance Of Confirmation Hearing; And ORDER CONTINUING CONFIRMATION HEARING Currently Set Pre-Hearing Date: Time: Judge: Place: U.S. Bankruptcy Court

Devin Derham-Burk, Standing Chapter 13 Trustee, the debtor(s) by counsel, and (if any) the below named objecting parties, hereby stipulate to continue the contested confirmation hearing as provided in the order below.

Dated: ____
Devin Derham-Burk, Standing Chapter 13 Trustee,

Dated: ____________________ ____________________
Attorney For Debtors

Dated: ____________________ ____________________
Attorney For Objecting Creditor _____

Dated: ____________________ ____________________
Attorney For Objecting Creditor _____

ORDER

Upon the agreement of the parties, the hearing on contested confirmation scheduled for ____________shall be continued to ____________.

Dated: ____________

____
United States Bankruptcy Judge

Statement of Resolution, Consent to Move Confirmation Hearing to Uncontested Calendar and Order Thereon

UNITED STATES BANKRUPTCY COURT
NORTHERN DISTRICT OF CALIFORNIA

In re: Debtor(s)	Case No. Chapter 13 Statement of Resolution, Consent to Move Confirmation Hearing to Uncontested Calendar and Order Thereon

STATEMENT OF RESOLUTION

Dated: ____________________ ____________________
Attorney for Debtor (s)

Dated: ____________________ ____________________
Objecting Party or Counsel

All objections to confirmation having been resolved, the Trustee agrees to move the confirmation hearing originally set for to the calendar set for

Dated: ____________________ ____________________
Devin Derham-Burk, Trustee

Good Cause appearing, IT IS SO ORDERED.

Dated: ____________________ ____________________
United States Bankruptcy Judge

Guidelines for Payment of Attorney's Fees in Chapter 13 Cases

United States Bankruptcy Court
Northern District of California
San Francisco and San Jose Divisions

GUIDELINES FOR PAYMENT OF ATTORNEY'S FEES IN CHAPTER 13 CASES

The following are guidelines for the circumstances under which a detailed fee application need not be flied [*sic*] in Chapter 13 cases and the manner in which the Chapter 13 Trustee will disburse fees which are approved.

A. FEE APPLICATIONS.

1. Counsel may receive an order approving fees up to the amounts set forth in Paragraph 2 without filing a detailed application if:

a) Counsel has flied [*sic*] and served the Chapter 13 Trustee with an executed copy of the "Rights and Responsibilities of Chapter 13 Debtors and Their Attorneys," copies of which are available in the Clerk's Office and in the Office of the Chapter 13 Trustee;

b) Counsel has accepted no more than $500 as a retainer in the case, unless counsel thereafter applies for and receives court approval of a larger advance retainer; and

c) No objection to the requested fees has been raised.

2. The maximum fee which can be approved through the procedure described in Paragraph 1 is:

$1400 for the basic case; and an additional;
$750 if the case involves real property claims;
$400 if the case involves state or federal tax claims;
$200 if the case involves vehicle loans or leases;
$1200 if the case involves an operating business;
$300 if the case involves support arrears claims;
$300 if the case involves student loans.

3. If an executed copy of the "Rights and Responsibilities of Chapter 13 Debtors and Their Attorneys" is not filed, counsel has accepted more than $500 without court approval, or there is an objection, an order will not be entered automatically pursuant to these Guidelines.

4. If counsel elects to be paid other than pursuant to these Guidelines, all fees including the retainer shall be approved by the court whether or not the fees are payable through the Chapter 13 Trustee's Office and whether or not fees are paid for services in connection with the Chapter 13 case.

5. If counsel applies for fees, counsel shall comply with Rules 2002 and 2016 of the Federal Rules of Bankruptcy Procedure as well as the "Guidelines for Compensation and Expense Reimbursement of Professionals" adopted by the Bankruptcy Judges of the Northern District of California.

6. On its own motion or the motion of any party in interest, the court may order a hearing to review any fee paid or unpaid.

B. DISTRIBUTION OF FUNDS IN CHAPTER 13 CASES.

Payments shall be disbursed in the following order:

1. $500 towards attorney's fees, less any amount received pre-filing as a retainer;

2. To secured creditors and the balance of attorney's fees. Those secured creditors which are specified in the plan to receive fixed monthly payments will be paid the amount specified. If fixed monthly payments are specified in the plan for all secured creditors, the balance of the plan payment will be disbursed toward attorney's fees. If fixed monthly payments are not specified in the plan for all secured creditors, secured claims without fixed monthly payments and the balance of attorneys fees will be pro-rated;

3. To priority creditors in the order prescribed by the Bankruptcy Code;

4. To unsecured creditors.

Application for Approval of Attorneys Fees

UNITED STATES BANKRUPTCY COURT
NORTHERN DISTRICT OF CALIFORNIA

In re:

Debtor(s)

Chapter 13
Case No.

APPLICATION FOR APPROVAL OF ATTORNEYS FEES

1. Debtor(s)' attorney, ________, requests the approval of attorneys fees in the sum of $__________ pursuant to the attorneys fee disclosure statement filed with the Court and the Guidelines for Payment of Attorney's Fees in Chapter 13 Cases (San Francisco and San Jose Divisions). Of the sum requested, the amount of $__________ has been previously paid to debtor(s)' attorney. If more than $500 has been previously paid to debtor(s)' attorney, an order approving that payment is attached hereto.
2. In addition to the basic case, the debtor(s)' case involves:

   __________ Real property claims
   __________ State or federal tax claims
   __________ Vehicle loans or leases
   __________ An operating business
3. A copy of the RIGHTS AND RESPONSIBILITIES OF CHAPTER 13 DEBTORS AND THEIR ATTORNEYS, executed by the debtor(s) and debtor(s)' attorney, is attached hereto.
4. All fees are subject to Court approval, whether paid in advance or through the plan.

Dated: ______________________ ______________________
Attorney for Debtor(s)

Notice of Application to Modify Chapter 13 Plan and of Opportunity to Request Hearing

UNITED STATES BANKRUPTCY COURT
NORTHERN DISTRICT OF CALIFORNIA

In re: SS # Debtor(s)	Chapter 13 Case No.

NOTICE OF APPLICATION TO MODIFY CHAPTER 13 PLAN AND OF OPPORTUNITY TO REQUEST HEARING

NOTICE IS HEREBY GIVEN that the debtor(s) have filed an Application to Modify Chapter 13 Plan, a copy of which is attached. Pursuant to Bankruptcy Rule 2002, and the procedures prescribed by Local Rule 9014-1(b)(3)(A); 1) Any objection to the requested relief, or a request for hearing on the matter must be filed with the Clerk of the U.S. Bankruptcy Court at the address listed below, and served on the debtor's attorney and the Chapter 13 Trustee as listed below, within twenty (20) days of mailing of the notice; 2) A request for hearing or objection must be accompanied by any declarations or memoranda of law the party objecting or requesting wishes to present in support of its position; 3) If there is not a timely objection to the requested relief or a request for hearing, the court may enter an order granting the relief by default; and 4) The debtor's attorney will give at least ten (10) days written notice of hearing to the objecting or requesting party, and to the Chapter 13 Trustee in the case, in the event an objection or request for hearing is timely made.

Dated: ____________

____
Attorney for the Debtor(s)

____
____
____
( ) ______________________

Clerk, United States Bankruptcy Court
280 S. First St., Room 3035
San Jose, CA 95113

Chapter 13 Trustee
Devin Derham-Burk
PO Box 50013

San Jose CA 95150

Debtor's Address

*

*

*

PROOF OF SERVICE

I am not less than 18 years of age and not a party to the within case. My business address is: __________. I served this Notice and the attached APPLICATION TO MODIFY CHAPTER 13 PLAN by first class United States mail, postage pre-paid, at __________, California on the date noted below and addressed to those listed in Exhibit A if attached hereto, and on those listed below. I declare under penalty of perjury that the foregoing is true and correct.

Dated: __________, 20______ at __________, California.

____

* Chapter 13 Trustee	*	*
*	*	*
*	*	*
*	*	*

Debtor's Declaration Concerning Application to Modify Chapter 13 Plan And Amended Schedules I & J

UNITED STATES BANKRUPTCY COURT
NORTHERN DISTRICT OF CALIFORNIA

In re: Debtor(s)	Chapter Case No.

DEBTOR'S DECLARATION CONCERNING APPLICATION TO MODIFY CHAPTER 13 PLAN AND AMENDED SCHEDULES I & J

I/we, the debtor(s) in this case, declare that it is not financially possible to continue with the Chapter 13 plan payments currently in effect. The changed circumstances are:

I/we declare under penalty of perjury that I/we have read the above description of my changed circumstances and the attached amended Schedules I and J, consisting of____________pages, and that they are true and correct to the best of my/our knowledge, information, and belief.

Dated: ____________________ ____________________
Debtor

Dated: ____________________ ____________________
Debtor

PROOF OF SERVICE

I am not less than 18 years of age and not a party to the within case. My business address is ____________. I served this DEBTOR'S DECLARATION CONCERNING APPLICATION TO MODIFY CHAPTER 13 PLAN AND AMENDED SCHEDULES I & J by first class United States mail, postage pre-paid, at ____________, California on the date noted below and addressed to the Trustee listed below.

I declare under penalty of perjury that the foregoing is true and correct.

Dated: ____________, 20______.

____
*

* Chapter 13 Trustee*

Declaration of Debtor(s)' Attorney re Application to Modify Chapter 13 Plan and Request for Order

UNITED STATES BANKRUPTCY COURT
NORTHERN DISTRICT OF CALIFORNIA

In re:	
Debtor(s)	Chapter 13 Case No.

DECLARATION OF DEBTOR(S)' ATTORNEY RE APPLICATION TO MODIFY CHAPTER 13 PLAN AND REQUEST FOR ORDER

The undersigned declares:

1. I am the attorney for the debtor(s) in the above action.

2. An Application to Modify Chapter 13 Plan, a copy of which is attached, was filed on ____________.

3. Copies of the Application to Modify Chapter 13 Plan and the Notice of Application and Opportunity to Request Hearing have been served on all creditors, in addition to the Chapter 13 Trustee.

4. If the proposed modification will reduce prospective plan payments. amended Schedules I and J, and a declaration by the debtor explaining the changed circumstances, attached hereto, were served on the Chapter 13 Trustee on ____________.

5. Debtor requests that an Order Modifying the Chapter 13 Plan as proposed in the attached Application be granted. The undersigned declares that my office has not received a request for a hearing within the time provided.

I declare under penalty of perjury that the foregoing is true and correct.

Dated: ____________

____
Attorney for the Debtor(s)

Order Confirming Modified Chapter 13 Plan

UNITED STATES BANKRUPTCY COURT
NORTHERN DISTRICT OF CALIFORNIA

In re: Debtor(s)	Chapter 13 Case No.

ORDER CONFIRMING MODIFIED CHAPTER 13 PLAN

Upon consideration of Debtor(s)' APPLICATION TO MODIFY CHAPTER 13 PLAN filed with the Court on ___________, and good cause appearing therefore;

IT IS ORDERED THAT the modified plan filed on ___________ is confirmed.

Dated: ___________

____
UNITED STATES BANKRUPTCY JUDGE

The Chapter 13 Trustee has reviewed the attached Application to Modify Chapter 13 Plan and amended Schedules I and J, if applicable, and has no objection thereto.

Dated: ___________

____
DEVIN DERHAM-BURK, TRUSTEE

Attachment to Schedule of Property (For Principal Residence Only)

In re:

Debtor(s)

Chapter 13
Case No.

ATTACHMENT TO SCHEDULE OF PROPERTY (FOR PRINCIPAL RESIDENCE ONLY)

DESCRIPTION OF PROPERTY

Address:

Fractional interest (explain):

BASIS

Did the Debtor(s) purchase this property by reinvesting funds from another principal residence and deferring gain (carrying over basis) on that sale? Yes No

If yes, enter the total gain deferred (accumulated from all previous reinvestments) by the purchase of this property? If no, enter zero. ____ [a]

Enter total value of all improvements made to this property (zero if none): ____ [b]

Enter total amount of all tax losses taken on this property (zero if none): ____ [c]

Describe any improvements made to or tax losses taken on, this property:

Purchase price of this property:		________	
Less Deferred gain:	-	________	[a]
Plus Improvements:	+	________	[b]
Less Tax losses:	-	________	[c]
Equals ADJUSTED BASIS:	=	________	[d]

VALUE

Expected sale price:		________	[e]
Less Expense of sale:	-	________	[f]
Equals AMOUNT REALIZED:	=	________	[g]

CAPITAL GAINS TAX

Are the Debtor(s) entitled to take any business losses (after applicable carry-back) which would be carried forward and acquired by a Chapter 7 trustee?
________________ Yes ________________ No

If yes, describe (and reduce the capital gains taxes calculated below by such amounts):

Amount realized:		________	[g]
Less Adjusted basis:	-	________	[d]
Equals GAIN ON SALE:	=	________	[h]
Federal tax on [h]:		________	[Federal form 1041]

Plus State tax on [h]:	+	________	[California form 541]
Equals TOTAL TAX:	=	________	[k]

CHAPTER 7 TRUSTEE'S FEES

Expected sale price:		________	[e]
Less Exemption claimed:	-	________	[j]
Equals CHAPTER 7 ESTATE:	=	________	[m]
Chapter 7 trustee's fees on [m]:		________	[n] [11 U.S.C. 326]

SUMMARY

Expected sale price:		________	[e]
Less Expense of sale:	-	________	[f]
Less Total tax	-	________	[k]
Less Chapter 7 trustee's fees:	-	________	[n]
Equals GROSS VALUE:	=	________	
Less Total liens:	-	________	
Equals NET VALUE:	=	________	
Minus Exemption claimed:	-	________	[j]
Equals NET AMOUNT AVAILABLE FOR PRIORITY & UNSECURED CREDITORS:	=	________	

Application for Order Waiving Requirement for Business Evaluation; and Declaration of Debtor(s)

*
*
*
*

Telephone:
Facsimile:

UNITED STATES BANKRUPTCY COURT NORTHERN DISTRICT OF CALIFORNIA

In re: Debtor(s)	Chapter 13 Case No. APPLICATION FOR ORDER WAIVING REQUIREMENT FOR BUSINESS EVALUATION; AND DECLARATION OF DEBTOR(S) BUSINESS NAME:

Debtor(s) herein requests an order waiving the requirement pursuant to 11 U.S.C. 1302(c) for an evaluation of the debtor(s)' business for the following reason(s) [check all applicable):

____________ The proposed chapter 13 plan provides for 100% repayment on unsecured claims.

____________ The debtor(s)' business is of a *de minimis* nature. The Income derived from the business is nominal and does not comprise the majority of the debtor(s)' net income.

____________ The debtor is an independent contractor.

____________ The debtor either operates the business out of his/her home or does not lease commercial real property for the business.

____________ The debtor is not incurring post-petition trade debt and is current on post-petition taxes.

____________ The debtor is current on post-petition trade debt payments end post-petition taxes.

____________ The debtor either has no employees or employs only members of his/her immediate family.

_____________ Other:

In addition, the proposed plan provide. [*sic*] for payment to the trustee of all projected disposable Income of the debtor(s).

Dated: _____________

____
Debtor(s)' Attorney

DECLARATION OF DEBTOR(S)

I/We, the undersigned debtor(s) herein, declare under penalty of perjury that the foregoing description of the nature of my/our business is true and correct to the best of my/our knowledge.

Dated: ___________________________ ______________________________
Debtor,

Dated: ___________________________ ______________________________
Debtor,

Order Waiving Requirement for Business Evaluation

*
*
*
*
Telephone:
Facsimile:

UNITED STATES BANKRUPTCY COURT
NORTHERN DISTRICT OF CALIFORNIA

In re: Debtor(s)	Chapter 13 Case No. ORDER WAIVING REQUIREMENT FOR BUSINESS EVALUATION BUSINESS NAME:

Upon consideration of Debtor(s)' APPLICATION FOR ORDER WAIVING REQUIREMENT FOR BUSINESS EVALUATION; AND DECLARATION OF DEBTOR(S) in support thereof filed with the Court on ____________, and good cause appearing therefor;

IT IS ORDERED THAT the requirement that the Chapter 13 Trustee conduct an evaluation of the Debtor(s)' business pursuant to 11 U.S.C. § 1302(c) is hereby waived.

Dated: ____________

____
UNITED STATES BANKRUPTCY JUDGE

The Chapter 13 Trustee has reviewed the attached APPLICATION FOR ORDER WAIVING REQUIREMENT FOR BUSINESS EVALUATION: AND DECLARATION OF DEBTOR(S) and has no objection thereto.

Dated: ____________

____
DEVIN DERHAM-BURK, TRUSTEE

Request for Dismissal of Case

UNITED STATES BANKRUPTCY COURT
NORTHERN DISTRICT OF CALIFORNIA

In re:	Chapter 13
Debtor(s)	Case No.

REQUEST FOR DISMISSAL OF CASE

Pursuant to 11 U.S.C. 1307(b), the Debtor(s) herein request the dismissal of this Chapter 13 case forthwith.

Dated: ______________________ ____________________________
Debtor

Dated: ______________________ ____________________________
Debtor

Dated: ______________________ ____________________________
Attorneys for Debtor(s)

PROOF OF SERVICE

I am not less than 18 years of age and not a party to the within case. My business address is: ____________. I served this Request for Dismissal of Case by first class United States mail, postage pre-paid, at ____________, California on the date noted below and addressed to those listed in the attached Exhibit A, and on those listed below. I declare under penalty of perjury that the foregoing is true and correct.

Dated: ____________, 20______ at ____________, California.

____

* * * * * *

Order Dismissing Case

UNITED STATES BANKRUPTCY COURT
NORTHERN DISTRICT OF CALIFORNIA

In re:	Chapter 13
Debtor(s)	Case No.

ORDER DISMISSING CASE

Upon consideration of Debtor's REQUEST FOR DISMISSAL OF CASE, the Debtor's case is dismissed.

Dated: __________

____
UNITED STATES BANKRUPTCY JUDGE

AMENDED GENERAL ORDER 13 ORDER CONCERNING CREDITOR LIST

This General Order sets forth amended requirements regarding the list of creditors to be provided with bankruptcy petitions pursuant to FRBP 1007(a). The amended requirements shall become effective on February 1, 1996.

(1) Unless the debtor appears in propria persona, the debtor, or some other person as the court may direct, shall provide the clerk with a PC computer-readable diskette containing a file with a list of the name and address of each creditor ("diskette") and a scannable creditor list containing the same list of names and addresses ("scannable creditor list").

(2) In cases in which the debtor appears *in propria persona* with **fifty** [sic] more entities that hold either claims or interests, the debtor, or some other person as the court may direct, shall provide the clerk with a diskette and a scannable creditor list.

(3) In cases where the diskette is not required, the debtor, or some other person as the court may direct, shall provide the clerk with a scannable creditor list.

(4) The diskette and scannable creditor list shall be prepared in accordance with instructions and specifications as required by the clerk and shall be provided at the time the petition is filed. Failure to provide the diskette or the scannable creditor list in a timely manner may subject the case to dismissal.

Dated: December 5, 1995
Chief Judge
United States Bankruptcy Court

Pursuant to Amended General Order No. 13

Instructions and Requirements for Diskettes.

All bankruptcy petitions submitted by an attorney for filing must be accompanied by a creditor diskette. For all cases submitted in propria persona with fifty (50) or more entities that hold either claims or interests, a diskette is required. For filing purposes, a scannable creditor list is also required. It is the responsibility of the filing party that the diskette of creditor names and addresses contains the same creditor names and addresses as on the scannable creditor matrix. Creditor matrix diskette can be created using any popular word processing software (e.g. WordPerfect, Word) or bankruptcy software (e.g. Matthew Bender). **Please adhere to the following requirements in preparing diskettes:**

Diskette format, file format and name and diskette label:

The diskette must be 3.5" and formatted in MS-DOS or PC-DOS format.

The creditor matrix file must be in **ASCII (DOS text)** format and must be named FILE.TXT. For instructions on how to save a document in **ASCII format**, refer to the software user manual.

Place a label on the diskette with the debtor name, case number (if known), law firm name and contact person or debtor name if without an attorney, and phone number.

Format of creditor names and addresses:

The text of the ASCII file must conform, as applicable, to the requirements of the scannable creditor matrix. Do not include matrix cover page or signature page, if any.

Creditor names should be first name [space] last name.

Creditor names and address should be in upper and lower case, not all upper case.

Type creditor names and addresses in a single column.

Have **no more than five lines** for each creditor name and address. Maximum of **40 characters** per line.

Put **3 blank lines** between each creditor. See sample sheet attached.

The attention line, account number, or social security number, if any, **should not be the last line,** but may be included on the second line of the address.

The last line of each name and address block must include the city, state, and ZIP code. Use a comma between city and state. **Use the two-letter abbreviations *without periods or other punctuation* for state names.** (See the list at the right.) Nine digit ZIP codes should be typed with a hyphen separating the fifth and sixth digits.

Do not include names and addresses of the debtor(s) or the United States Trustee.

Do not use these symbols * "+ & % #. Do not use the lower case "l" in place of the numeric "1." Do not use the upper or lower case letter "o" in place of the numeric "0."

James Albert
123 Main Street
San Francisco, CA 94104

Anderson Company
4567 Maple Drive
Downers Grove, IL 60515

Bank of Sea Court
Account # 4123 4567 8901 2345
1610 Visa Avenue
San Mateo, CA 94020

Ann Barbara Brown
Ivers, Brown and Wong, Accountants
7890 Peachtree Industrial Blvd.
Atlanta, GA 30322

Coral Designs, Inc.
Attn: Amy Aubergine
Suite 1255
1010 Windsor Drive
Hartford, CT 06003

Barry Cressida
56 Broadway
Hicksville, NY 11802

Dupont Systems
Account number: H 7890 12 345
678 A Street
San Mateo, CA 94111

Instructions and Requirements for Scannable Creditor Matrix.

All bankruptcy petitions submitted for filing must be accompanied by a creditor matrix cover sheet and a properly prepared creditor matrix. A scannable creditor list is required for all cases even when a diskette is required. It is the responsibility of the filing party that the list of creditor names and addresses contains the same creditor names and addresses as on the diskette. **In order for the matrix to be scanned, it must adhere to the following requirements:**

Paper and typeface quality:

Use blank, unlined, standard white 8½ X 11 inch bond paper. The copy should be clean without smudges, smears or stray marks.

Print must be letter quality. Dot matrix print is not acceptable. Use only one of the following typefaces: **Courier 10 pitch, Prestige Elite or Letter Gothic.**

Page format:

The pages should be numbered on the back of each page, not on the front.

All type must be at least one and one-half inches 1½" from any edge of the paper.

Format of creditor names and addresses:

Creditor names should be first name [space] last name.

Creditor names and address should be in upper and lower case, not all upper case.

Have only one column of names and addresses on each page. **Do not use a 3 column format contained in some commercial bankruptcy forms packages.** Do not place more than 8 name and address sets per page. See sample sheet attached.

Have **no more than five lines** for each creditor name and address. Maximum of **40 characters** per line.

Put **3 blank lines** between each creditor.

The attention line, account number, or social security number, if any, **should not be the last line,** but may be included on the second line of the address.

The last line of each name and address must include the city, state, and ZIP code. Use a comma between city and state. **Use the two-letter abbreviations *without periods or other punctuation* for state names**. (See the list at the right.) Nine digit ZIP codes should be typed with a hyphen separating the fifth and sixth digits.

Do not include the names and addresses of the debtor(s) or the United States Trustee.

Do not use these symbols * "+ & % #. Do not use the lower case "l" in place of the numeric "1." Do not use the upper or lower case letter "o" in place of the numeric "0."

James Albert
123 Main Street
San Francisco, CA 94104

Anderson Company
4567 Maple Drive
Downers Grove, IL 60515

Bank of Sea Court
Account # 41234 5678 9012 3456
1610 Visa Avenue
San Mateo, CA 94020

Ann Barbara Brown
Ivers, Brown and Wong, Accountants
7890 Peachtree Industrial Blvd.
Atlanta, GA 30322

Coral Designs, Inc.
Attn: Amy Aubergine
Suite 1255
1010 Windsor Drive
Hartford, CT 06003

Barry Cressida
56 Broadway
Hicksville, NY 11802

Dupont Systems
Account number: H 7890 12 345
678 A Street
San Mateo, CA 94111

[APPENDIX TO LOCAL RULES] SUMMARY OF NOTICE REQUIREMENTS [1]

Bankruptcy Local Rules Northern District of California

Bankruptcy Local Rule Number	Type of Proceeding	Notice Requirement
3015-1(a)	Chapter 12 Confirmation Hearing	Notice of the hearing shall be filed and served by mail at least 32 days before the hearing.
3015-1(b)	Chapter 13 Confirmation Hearing	Plan or summary shall be filed and served by mail to all creditors at least 25 days before the first date set for the 11 U.S.C. § 341 meeting of creditors.
3017-1	Chapter 11 Disclosure Statement Hearing	Notice of the hearing shall be filed and served by mail at least 32 days before the hearing
3018-1	Chapter 11 Confirmation Hearing	Proof of service of the plan, disclosure statement, official ballot and Order Approving Disclosure Statement; all ballots; and a ballot tabulation must be filed at least 3 business days before the confirmation hearing.
4001-1	Motions for Relief from Stay	Motions shall be filed and served by mail at least 15 days before the preliminary hearing.
6006-1(a)	Chapter 7 Trustee's Motions to Reject Nonresidential Real Property Leases	Notice to landlord at least 24 hours before hearing.

[1] This chart is intended only as a summary of the notice provisions of the bankruptcy local rules. It is not a rule and is not to be cited. This chart only covers notice requirements in proceedings before the bankruptcy court, and does not cover time deadlines governing review by the district court or Bankruptcy Appellate Panel of actions of the bankruptcy court.

Bankruptcy Local Rule Number	Type of Proceeding	Notice Requirement
7007-1	Motions in Adversary Proceedings	Moving papers shall be filed and served at least 28 days before the hearing. Opposition shall be filed and served at least 14 days before the hearing. Any reply shall be filed and served at least 7 days before the hearing.
9014-1(b)	Notice and Opportunity for Hearing in a Contested Matter	Notice shall state that objections must be filed and served within 20 days after mailing of the notice.
9014-1(c)(1)	Noticed Hearing in Contested Matter with an Identified Opposing Party	Moving papers shall be filed and served at least 28 days before the hearing. Opposition shall be filed and served at least 14 days before the hearing. Any reply shall be filed and served at least 7 days before the hearing.
9014-1(c)(2)	Noticed Hearing in Contested Matter with No Identified Opposing Party	Moving papers shall be filed and served at least 20 days before the hearing. Opposition shall be filed and served at least 5 days before the hearing.
9014-1(c)(3)	Noticed Hearing After Request for Hearing Filed (See B.L.R. 9014-1(b))	Notice of the hearing shall be filed and served at least 10 days before the hearing. Initiating party's reply to opposition shall be filed and served at least 5 days before the hearing.

GENERAL ORDER NO. 16 ADOPTION OF INTERIM BANKRUPTCY RULES

[Abrogated.]

GENERAL ORDER NO. 18 REQUESTS TO EXTEND OR IMPOSE THE AUTOMATIC STAY IN BAPCPA CASES

[Abrogated.]

GENERAL ORDER NO. 19

[Abrogated.]

GENERAL ORDER NO. 20 Delayed Discharges in Chapter 13 Cases

[Abrogated.]

GENERAL ORDER NO. 21 ABROGATION OF GENERAL ORDERS 16, 17, 18, 19 AND 20

Whereas General Orders 16, 17, 18, 19 and 20 of this Court have been superceded by amendments to the Federal Rules of Bankruptcy Procedure and the Bankruptcy Local Rules of the Northern District of California,

IT IS HEREBY ORDERED that such General Orders are hereby abrogated.

Dated: May 1, 2008

GENERAL ORDER NO. 22 ADOPTION OF INTERIM BANKRUPTCY RULE 1007-1,

Whereas, on October 20,2008 the National Guard and Reservists Debt Relief Act (the Act) was enacted into law; and

Whereas, the provisions ofthe Act are effective on December 19, 2008; and

Whereas, the Advisory Committee on Bankruptcy Rules has prepared Interim Rule 1007-1 designed to implement the substantive and procedural changes mandated by the Act; and

Whereas, the Committee on Rules ofPractice and Procedures ofthe United States Judicial Conference and the Judicial Conference ofthe United States have approved this Interim Rule and recommended the adoption ofthe Interim Rule to provide uniform procedures for implementing the Act; and

Whereas, the general effective date ofthe Act has not provided sufficient time to promulgate rules after appropriate public notice and an opportunity for comment;

NOW THEREFORE, pursuant to 28 U.S.c. section 2071, Rule 83 ofthe Federal Rules of Civil Procedure, and Rule 9029 ofthe Federal Rules ofBankruptcy Procedure, the attached Interim Rule is adopted, effective December 19, 2008.

APPLICATION TO MODIFY CHAPTER 13 PLAN (CAN)

UNITED STATES BANKRUPTCY COURT
NORTHERN DISTRICT OF CALIFORNIA

In re:

SS#

Debtor(s) /

Chapter 13
Case No.

APPLICATION TO MODIFY CHAPTER 13 PLAN

The debtor(s) respectfully requests that the Court modify the Chapter 13 plan as follows:

❑ 1. With regard to the monthly plan payments of $________, those payments shall:

❑ be suspended for the months of ________

❑ be increased to: $________, effective ________

❑ be decreased to: $________, effective ________

❑ Other:

❑ 2. With regard to secured claims:

❑ to treat the claim(s) of ADDITIONAL creditor(s) as secured, as follows:

CREDITOR NAME	VALUE OF COLLATERAL	MONTHLY PAYMENT (if fixed)	INTEREST RATE (must be specified)

❑ to CHANGE the treatment of certain secured claim(s), as follows:

CREDITOR NAME	VALUE OF COLLATERAL	MONTHLY PAYMENT (if fixed)	INTEREST RATE (must be specified)

❑ To treat as UNSECURED the claim(s) of the following creditor(s) which were previously treated as secured.

❑ 3. With regard to unsecured and priority claims not listed in the Motion to Allow Claims, to allow them as filed:

CREDITOR NAME	DATE CLAIM FILED	STATUS	AMOUNT

❑ 4. With regard to unsecured claims, to CHANGE THE PERCENTAGE PAID from ____% to ____%.

❑ 5. Other modifications:

6. Debtor(s)' reason(s) for requesting the above modification are:

7. The plan, if modified, would be completed within sixty (60) months from commencement of the case.
WHEREFORE, the debtor(s) requests that the Court modify the Chapter 13 plan as set forth above.

Dated: ________ ________________

Attorney for Debtor(s)

APPLICATION FOR COMPENSATION DECLARATION (CAN)

UNITED STATES BANKRUPTCY COURT
NORTHERN DISTRICT OF CALIFORNIA

In re:

Chapter 13
Case No.

APPLICATION FOR COMPENSATION;
DECLARATION

Debtor(s) ________________________/

1. Debtor(s') attorney, ________________________________, requests the approval of attorney's fees in the sum of $_____________ pursuant to the attorney's fee disclosure statement filed with the Court and the Guidelines for Payment of Attorney's Fees in Chapter 13 Cases (San Jose Division). Of the sum requested, the amount of $____________ has been previously paid to Debtor(s') attorney.

2. In addition to the basic case, the Debtor(s') case involves:

___ Real property claims
___ Compromise plan use
___ Certain additional real property: ____ piece(s)
___ State or federal tax claims
___ Vehicle loans or leases
___ An operating business
___ Support arrears
___ Student loans
___ 25 or more creditors
___ Motion to commence or extend the automatic stay

3. A copy of the RIGHTS AND RESPONSIBILITIES OF CHAPTER 13 DEBTORS AND THEIR ATTORNEYS, executed by the Debtor(s) and Debtor(s') attorney, has been filed with the Court.

4. All fees are subject to Court approval, whether paid in advance or through the plan.

I, the undersigned, declare, under penalty of perjury, that the foregoing is true and correct to the best of my knowledge.

Dated: ______________________ ________________________________
Attorney for Debtor(s)

Rev. 6/06

NDCAL-107 N.D. CALIFORNIA

CERTIFICATION OF DOMESTIC SUPPORT OBLIGATION PAYEES (CAN)

UNITED STATES BANKRUPTCY COURT
for the
NORTHERN DISTRICT OF CALIFORNIA
OAKLAND, SAN FRANCISCO & SANTA ROSA DIVISIONS

IN RE:	CHAPTER 13 CASE:
	CERTIFICATION OF DOMESTIC SUPPORT OBLIGATION PAYEES
Debtor(s)	

To Trustee:

I have been required by a judicial or administrative order, or by statue to pay a domestic support obligation, as defined in 11 U.S.C. §101(14A), whether prior to or after I filed this case. I certify that prior to the date of this certification, I have paid all amounts due under any Court ordered domestic support obligation, as defined in 11 U.S.C. §101(14A). All Court ordered domestic support obligation payees are as follows:

Name:

Address:

Date: ____________________

____
Debtor

Rev. July 2007

DEBTOR'S CERTIFICATION IN SUPPORT OF DISCHARGE (SAN JOSE DIVISION)

UNITED STATES BANKRUPTCY COURT
for the
NORTHERN DISTRICT OF CALIFORNIA

IN RE:	**CHAPTER 13 CASE:**
	DEBTOR'S CERTIFICATION IN SUPPORT OF DISCHARGE
Debtor(s)	

I, (________________________) certify (mark one choice for each numbered section):

1. ☐ I HAVE completed an instructional course concerning personal financial management described in 11 U.S.C. §111 and have filed a Certification of Completion of Instructional Course Concerning Financial Management.

☐ I HAVE NOT completed an instructional course concerning personal financial management described in 11 U.S.C. §111 pursuant to ☐ §11 U.S.C. 1328 (g)(2) or ☐ court order.

2. ☐ I HAVE NOT been required to pay a domestic support obligation as that term is defined in 11 U.S.C. §101(14A) by any order of a court or administrative agency or by any statute.

☐ I HAVE paid all domestic support obligations as that term is defined in 11 U.S.C. §101(14A) that have become due on or before the date of this certification (including amounts due before the petition was filed, but only to the extent provided for by the plan) under any order of a court or administrative agency or under any statute.

3. ☐ I DID NOT claim an exemption in excess of the adjusted amount set forth in 11 U.S.C. §522(q)(1), therefore 11 U.S.C. §1328(h) is inapplicable.

☐ I DID claim exemptions in excess of the adjusted amount set forth in 11 U.S.C. §522(q)(1). All creditors and other interested parties requesting special notice in this case have or are being served by the court with a statement as to whether there is pending a proceeding in which I may be found guilty of a felony of a kind described in §522(q)(1)(A) or found liable for a debt of the kind described in §522(q)(1)(B).

4. ____ I HAVE NOT received a discharge in a Chapter 7, 11 or 12 bankruptcy case filed within four (4) years prior to filing this Chapter 13 case and I HAVE NOT received a discharge in another Chapter 13 bankruptcy case filed within two (2) years prior to filing this Chapter 13 case.

Declaration Under Penalty of Perjury

I declare under penalty of perjury that the foregoing is true and correct.

Date:______________ ________________________

Debtor

CHAPTER 13 PLAN (OAKLAND DIVISION)

UNITED STATES BANKRUPTCY COURT
NORTHERN DISTRICT OF CALIFORNIA

In re: | Case No.

Chapter 13 Plan

____
Debtor(s).

1. The future earnings of the debtor(s) are submitted to the supervision and control of the trustee, and the debtor(s) will pay to the Trustee the sum of $ ________ each month for ________ months.
Debtor(s) elect a voluntary wage order. ______.

2. From the payments received, the Trustee will make disbursements in accordance with the Distribution Guidelines as follows:
   (a) On allowed claims for expenses of administration required by 11 USC §507 .
   (b) On allowed secured claims, which shall be treated and valued as follows:

§506	Non §506	Name	Value of Collateral	Claim Amount	Pre confirmation Adequate Protection	Post confirmation Payments	Estimated Mortgage Arrears	Interest rate (if specified)
☐	☐							

With respect to secured claims per §506, valuation stated shall bind unless a timely objection to confirmation is filed. With respect to non §506 secured claims as referenced in §1325, the claim, to the extent allowed, shall control.. If an interest rate is not specified, 5/6% per month (10% per annum) will be paid. A secured creditor shall retain its lien until the earlier of the payment of the underlying debt determined under non-bankruptcy law or discharge under section §1328.

   (c) On allowed priority unsecured claims in the order prescribed by 11 USC § 507. Priority claims shall be paid in full except to the extent allowed otherwise under 11 U.S.C. § 1322(a)(4)
   (d) On allowed general unsecured claims the debtor(s) estimate(s) the general unsecured claims will be paid ______%.

3. The following executory contracts are rejected. The debtor(s) waive the protections of the automatic stay provided in 11 U.S.C. § 362 to enable the affected creditor to obtain possession and dispose of its collateral without further order of the court. Any allowed unsecured claim for damages resulting from rejection will be paid under paragraph 2(d).

4. The debtor(s) will pay directly the following fully secured creditors and lessors:

Name	Monthly Payment	Name	Monthly Payment

5. The date this case was confirmed will be the effective date of the plan

6. The debtor(s) elect to have property of the estate revest in the debtor(s) upon plan confirmation. Once the property revests, the debtor(s) may sell or refinance real or personal property without further order of the court, upon approval of the Chapter 13 Trustee.

7. The debtor(s) further propose pursuant to 11 USC § 1322(b):

Dated: ________________ ______________________ ______________________
(Debtor) (Debtor)

I/We ____ am/are legal counsel for the above named debtors(s) and hereby certify that the foregoing Chapter 13 Plan is a verbatim replica of this N.D. Cal., San Francisco and Oakland Divisions, Model Chapter 13 Plan (October 2001), promulgated pursuant to B.L.R. 1007-1.

____
Attorney for Debtor(s)

CHAPTER 13 PLAN (SAN FRANCISCO DIVISION)

UNITED STATES BANKRUPTCY COURT
NORTHERN DISTRICT OF CALIFORNIA
SAN FRANCISCO/SANTA ROSA DIVISIONS

IN RE:) Case No:
)
)
DEBTOR(S))

CHAPTER 13 PLAN

1. **PAYMENTS**
The Debtor or Debtors (hereinafter called "Debtor") submit to the Chapter 13 Trustee all projected disposable income to be received within the applicable commitment period of the Chapter 13 Plan (hereinafter called "Plan"). The total number of payments shall be ______, and in the amount of $ ________. The pre-confirmation Plan payments to the Trustee must begin 30 days from the date of the filing of the Plan or the Order of Relief, whichever is earlier. The post-confirmation Plan payments to the Trustee will commence on the 20th of the first month after the Plan is confirmed. Upon post-confirmation dismissal of this Plan, all funds held by the Trustee shall be disbursed to Administrative Costs and Creditors.

Debtor elects a voluntary wage order ___________

2. **PRE-CONFIRMATION ADEQUATE PROTECTION PAYMENTS**
The following pre-confirmation adequate protection payments on claims secured by personal property shall be paid by the Trustee to the below listed creditors. The Debtor proposing pre-confirmation payments will commence these payments to the Trustee within 30 days of the date this Plan was filed or the Order of Relief, whichever is earlier. Creditors must file a proof of claim to receive payment from the Trustee. Payments by the Trustee should commence to these Creditors within 30 days of the filing of the proof of claim. Upon a pre-confirmation dismissal, all adequate protection order payments held by the Trustee shall be disbursed to Creditors.

Name of Creditor	Collateral Description	Monthly Payment
1.		$
2.		$
3.		$

3. **ADMINISTRATIVE COSTS**
Trustee shall receive a percentage of each plan payment, whether made before or after confirmation, as established by the United States Trustee.

Chapter 13 Attorney fees may be included in a Chapter 13 Plan. Fees and costs requested for allowance are as follows:

Total Fees & Costs Requested	Fees & Costs Received	Balance of Fees & Costs Due	Monthly Payment
$	$	$	$

Fees and costs allowed shall be paid at a monthly rate not to exceed 10% of the balance of the above fees and costs remaining to be paid and will accrue concurrently with pre-confirmation adequate protection payments listed in Section 2 above and will be paid with Secured Debt as listed in Section 4A below. Upon a pre-confirmation dismissal, all accrued pre-confirmation attorney fees and costs payments held by the Trustee shall be disbursed to the attorney.

4. **SECURED CLAIMS**
Interest shall accrue on all secured claims from the date the petition is filed. Interest will be calculated at 10% per annum unless the Debtor specifies otherwise in this Plan. Secured Creditors will retain their liens until their allowed secured claims have been paid.

A) **Post-Confirmation Payments to Creditors Secured by Personal Property**
The Debtor seeks a determination that the value of the collateral is as set forth below. Failure to object to this listed amount shown may result in the Creditor's secured claim being limited to the collateral value amount listed.

With respect to a debt for which Debtor has written "Yes" in the column "Surrender" and where the Creditor files a written objection to the treatment provided such debt, Debtor surrenders all interest in the collateral, and the debt shall be treated under Section 4B below.

Name of Creditor	Collateral Description	Collateral Value	Secured Debt Amount	Interest Rate	Monthly Payment	Surrender Yes/No
1.		$	$	%	$	
2.		$	$	%	$	
3.		$	$	%	$	
4.		$	$	%	$	
5.		$	$	%	$	

B) **Surrender of Property**
The Debtor surrenders any interest in the following collateral. The Debtor waives the protection of the automatic stay and allows the affected Creditor to obtain possession and dispose of its collateral, without further Order of the Court. Any secured claim filed by the below Creditors will be deemed satisfied in full through surrender of the collateral. Any unsecured deficiency claim must be filed by the bar date for unsecured debts.

Name of Creditor	Collateral to be surrendered
1.	
2.	

C) **Post Petition Payments on Real Property Debt Paid by Debtor**

Name of Creditor	Property Address	Monthly Payment Amount
1.		$
2.		$

D) **Pre-Petition Debt on Real Property**
The Trustee shall pay defaulted real property debt. This prorata payment for defaulted real property debts will begin after payment in full of the Attorney fees and costs listed in section 3 above.

Name of Creditor	Property Address	Defaulted Debt	Interest Rate
1.		$	%
2.		$	%

5. **EXECUTORY CONTRACTS/LEASES**

A) The Debtor assumes the executory contract(s)/lease(s) referenced below and provides for the regular contract/lease payment(s), both pre-confirmation and post- confirmation, to be paid directly by the Debtor. Any pre-petition lease arrearage will be paid through this Plan after payment of arrearages listed in 4D above.

Name of Creditor/Lessor	Property Address	Lease Arrearages as of Date of Filing	Arrearage Payment by Trustee	Regular # of Lease Payments Remaining as of Date of Filing	Lease Payment By Debtor
1.		$	$		$

B) The Debtor rejects the following executory contract/lease and surrenders any interest in property securing these executory contracts/leases. The Debtor waives the protection of the automatic stay and allows the affected Creditor to obtain possession and dispose of its collateral, without further Order of the Court. Any unsecured claim resulting from the rejection must be filed by the bar date for unsecured debts:

Name of Creditor/Lessor	Identity of Executory Contract/Lease	Property Subject to Executory Contract/Lease
1.		
2.		

6. **PRIORITY CLAIMS**
Trustee shall pay all unsecured priority claims listed in 6B below, prior to paying those unsecured priority claims listed in sections 6C, 6D, and 6E below, which will be paid prorata . The amount paid on these priority claims will be the amounts of the Creditors' allowed claims.

A) **Post Petition Domestic Support Obligations:**

1) _____ None.

2) The name(s), and address(es) of the holder of ANY domestic support obligation.

Name	Address
1.	
2.	

3) The Debtor will pay all post-petition domestic support obligations directly to the holder of the claim and not through the Chapter 13 Plan.

B) **Pre-Petition Arrearages owed to Domestic Support Obligation Creditors:**

1) _____ None.

2) Name of holder of Domestic Support Obligation Arrearage Claim, arrears and monthly payment.

Name of Holder	Arrearage Claim	Monthly Payment on Arrearage
1.	$	$
2.	$	$

C) **Pre-Petition Domestic Support Obligations assigned to or owed to a governmental unit**:

1) _____ None.

2) Name of Creditor, arrearage claim and payment provisions:

Name of Creditor	Arrearage Claim	Provision for Payment
1.	$	
2.	$	

D) **Priority Tax Claims**:

Name of Creditor	Address	Amount Due
1.		$
2.		$

E) **Other Priority Claims:**

Name of Creditor	Address	Amount Due
1.		$

7. **UNSECURED DEBTS TO BE PAID WITH INTEREST**

A) The following debts shall be paid in full with interest from petition date.

Name of Creditor	Address	Amount Due	Interest Rate
1.		$	%
2.		$	%

8. **OTHER UNSECURED DEBTS**
Allowed unsecured claims in Sections 7 and this Section 8 shall be paid prorata all remaining funds, after payment of the debts described above in Sections 2 through 6 above. The amounts paid in Section 7 and this Section 8 are estimated to be ____% percent of unsecured non-priority debts.

9. Trustee is to be provided, thru the commitment period of the Plan, with Debtor's future Federal Tax Returns, beginning with the ______ tax year, by May 15th of the year following the year of the return. Trustee may request and Debtor must supply current income and expense information, on required Trustee forms, for each of the years that the tax returns are provided.

10. The Debtor elects to have property of the estate revest in the Debtor upon Plan confirmation. Once the property revests, the Debtor may sell or refinance real or personal property, without further order of the Court, upon approval of the Chapter 13 Trustee.

11. The Debtor further proposes pursuant to 11 USC § 1322(b):

Dated: ____________ ______________________ ______________________
(Debtor) (Debtor)

I/We ____ am/are legal counsel for the above named Debtor and hereby certify that the foregoing Chapter 13 Plan is a verbatim replica of this N.D. Cal., San Francisco/Santa Rosa Division, Model Chapter 13 Plan (April 1, 2008), promulgated pursuant to B.L.R. 1007-1.

____
Attorney for Debtor

CHAPTER 13 PLAN (SAN JOSE DIVISION-SHORT VERSION)

UNITED STATES BANKRUPTCY COURT
NORTHERN DISTRICT OF CALIFORNIA

In re: Case No.

______________________________/ CHAPTER 13 PLAN
Debtor(s)

1. The future earnings of the Debtor(s) are submitted to the supervision and control of the Trustee, and the Debtor(s) will pay to the Trustee the sum of $____ each month. Initial attorneys fees are requested in the amount of $______________.
___ Debtor(s) elect a voluntary wage order

2. From the payments received, the Trustee will make disbursements as follows:
(a) On allowed claims for expenses of administration required by 11 U.S.C. § 507(a)(2) in deferred payments.
(b) On allowed secured claims, which shall be treated and valued as follows:

Name	Value of Collateral	Estimated Mortgage/ Lease Arrears	Adequate Protection Payments (If specified)	Interest Rate (If specified)

[The valuations shown above will be binding unless a timely objection to confirmation is filed. Secured claims will be allowed for the value of the collateral or the amount of the claim, whichever is less, and will be paid the adequate protection payments and the interest rates shown above. If an interest rate is not specified, 7% per annum will be paid. The remainder of the amount owing, if any, will be allowed as a general unsecured claim paid under the provisions of ¶ 2(d).]

(c) On allowed priority unsecured claims in the order prescribed by 11 U.S.C. § 507.
(d) On allowed general unsecured claims as follows:
___ at a rate of ____________ cents on the dollar. The estimated term of the plan is ______ months. (Percentage Plan)
___ the sum of ______________ payable over ______ months, distributed pro rata, in amounts determined after allowed administrative, secured and priority unsecured claims are paid. The plan payments will continue at the highest monthly payment provided in ¶ 1 as necessary to pay all allowed administrative, secured and priority unsecured claims within sixty months of confirmation. (Pot Plan)

3. The debtor(s) elect to reject the following executory contracts of leases and surrender to the named creditor(s) the personal or real property that serves as collateral for a claim. The debtor(s) waive the protections of the automatic stay and consent to allow the named creditor(s) to obtain possession and dispose of the following identified property or collateral without further order of the court. Any allowed unsecured claim for damages resulting from the rejection will be paid under paragraph 2(d).

4. The Debtor(s) will pay directly the following fully secured creditors and lessors or creditors holding long-term debt:

Name	Monthly Payment	Name	Monthly Payment

5. The date this case was filed will be the effective date of the plan as well as the date when interest ceases accruing on unsecured claims against the estate.

6. The Debtor(s) elect to have property of the estate:
___ revest in the debtor(s) at such time as a discharge is granted or the case is dismissed.
___ revest in the debtor(s) upon plan confirmation. Once property revests, the Debtor(s) may sell or refinance real or personal property without further order of the court, upon approval of the Chapter 13 Trustee.

Dated: __________________ ______________________________ ______________________________
Debtor Debtor

I, the undersigned, am the attorney for the above-named debtor(s) and hereby certify that the foregoing chapter 13 plan is a verbatim replica of pre-approved chapter 13 plan promulgated pursuant to B.L.R. 1007-1 for use in the San Jose Division.

Dated:__________________ ______________________________
Attorney for Debtor(s)

Rev. 04/06 (This certification must be signed for any Model Chapter 13 Plan generated by WordPerfect, Word, or other word processing program.)

CHAPTER 13 PLAN (SAN JOSE DIVISION-LONG VERSION)

United States Bankruptcy Court

for the *Northern District of California, San Jose Division*

In re

Debtor(s) Case No.
____________________________________/ Chapter 13 Plan

1. **Plan Payments by Debtor**. The future earnings of the debtor(s) are submitted to the supervision and control of the trustee. The debtor(s) will pay to the trustee [☐ pay order ☐ direct pay] the sum of $____ each month.

2. **Disbursements by Trustee**. From the payments received, the trustee will make disbursements as follows:

(a) On allowed claims for expenses of administration required by 11 U.S.C. § 507(a)(2). Initial attorneys fees are requested in the amount of $__________.

(b) On allowed secured claims, which will be treated and valued, as follows:

Creditor	Collateral	Compromise of Claim for Personal Property Described in §1325(a)(9)	Value of Collateral	Estimated Arrears	Adequate Protection	Time Value of Money (Interest)

(c) On allowed priority unsecured claims specified in 11 U.S.C. § 507:
☐ The debtor(s) elect to pay less than the full amount of the assigned support claim listed below and instead will pay the amount listed or the amount of the claim, whichever is less, pursuant to 11 U.S.C. § 1322(a)(4). The debtor(s) acknowledge that this provision does not result in a discharge of the remaining balance of the claim or interest on the claim.

Holder of Claim	Amount to be Paid Through Plan

(d) On allowed general unsecured claims, as follows:

☐ A percentage plan at the rate of_____ cents on the dollar. The estimated term of the plan is__ months.

☐ A pot plan, paying the sum of $______________payable over_______months, distributed pro rata, in amounts determined after allowed administrative, secured and priority unsecured claims are paid. The plan payments will continue at the highest monthly payment amount provided in paragraph 1 as necessary to complete the plan within 60 months of confirmation.

The anticipated distribution of funds is attached as Exhibit 1.

3. **Compromise of Claims Secured By Personal Property Described in § 1325(a)(9)**. The debtor(s) propose the following compromise modifying the amounts payable on secured claims provided in paragraph 2(b). The debtor(s) acknowledge that this plan provision does not alter the other rights provided to holders of secured claims pursuant to 11 U.S.C. §§ 506 and 1325(a)(5)(b) or in the event of conversion.

Creditor	Collateral	Value

4. **Rejection of Executory Contracts and Leases and Surrender of Secured Collateral**. The debtor(s) elect to reject the following executory contracts or leases and surrender to the named creditor(s) the personal or real property that serves as collateral for a claim. The debtor(s) waive the protections of the automatic stay and consent to allow the named creditor(s) to obtain possession and dispose of the following identified property or collateral without further order of the court. Any allowed unsecured claim for damages resulting from rejection will be paid in accordance with paragraph 2(d).

Creditor	Collateral/Executory contracts or leases

5. **Direct Payments by Debtor**. The debtor(s) will pay directly the following secured creditors, lessors, or creditors holding long-term debt:

Creditor	Monthly Payment

6. **Effective Date of Plan**. The date this case was filed will be the effective date of the plan as well as the date when interest ceases accruing on unsecured claims against the estate.

7. **Vesting of Estate Property**. The debtor(s) elect to have property of the estate revest in the debtor(s):

☐ at such time as a discharge is granted or the case is dismissed.
☐ upon plan confirmation.

Once property revests, the debtor may sell or refinance real or personal property without further order of the court, upon approval of the chapter 13 trustee.

8. **Additional Provisions**. The debtor(s) further propose, pursuant to 11 U.S.C. §1322(b):

I certify that this Chapter 13 Plan is a verbatim replica of the Chapter 13 Plan (Rev. 11/15/06), promulgated pursuant to B.L.R. 1007-1 and approved for use in the San Jose Division of the Northern District of California.

Respectfully submitted,

Dated ______________ ______________________________
(debtor)

Dated ______________ ______________________________
(debtor)

Dated ______________ ______________________________
(attorney for debtor(s))

Notice to Creditors Regarding Plan Provisions

Binding Effect of the Plan: The plan will be binding upon creditors if approved at a confirmation hearing. You should review the plan carefully as your legal rights may be affected. You may wish to seek legal advice to understand its terms and to protect your rights.

Written Objection to Confirmation: If you disagree with the terms of this plan, you must file a written objection with the U.S. Bankruptcy Court by the date of the Meeting of Creditors and serve it upon the trustee and debtor's attorney or, if not represented by an attorney, the debtor. If you fail to file a timely written objection to confirmation of this plan and the plan is confirmed by the court, you will be bound by its terms.

Plan Payment: The debtor must make the first payment proposed by the plan within 30 days after the plan is filed or the order for relief is entered, whichever is earlier, or the case may be dismissed without further notice.

Proof of Claim: To receive payments, you must file a proof of claim. You may file the proof of claim electronically if you are a registered participant for electronic filing. If not, a blank claim form is enclosed for your use. The form must be fully executed, legible and you must attach any required documentation. It must be filed with the court and served upon the debtor's attorney or, if not represented by an attorney, the debtor.

Distribution of Funds: Payments will be disbursed by the chapter 13 trustee consistent with 11 U.S.C. § 1326(b)(1) and according to the plan. Creditors secured by personal property will receive adequate protection payments as shown on the anticipated distribution of funds, attached as Exhibit 1, contemporaneous with other administrative claims. Non-administrative priority and unsecured claims under 11 U.S.C. § 507 will be made in their order of priority, except that allowed claims under § 507(a)(1)(B) which are listed in section 2(c) of the plan will be paid after other priority claims. Payments must be credited in accordance with the terms of the plan and § 524(i).

Treatment of Secured Claims: The valuations shown will be binding unless a timely objection to confirmation is filed. Secured claims will be allowed for the value of the collateral or the amount of the claim, whichever is less. The remaining balance of any partially-secured claim will be treated as a general unsecured claim. If the time value of money (interest rate) is not specified, it will be paid at an annual rate of seven percent (7%).

Adequate Protection Payments: Subject to the trustee's monthly disbursement cycle, the trustee will disburse adequate protection payments commencing within 30 days after a proof of claim is properly filed, documenting the nature and extent of a claimed lien. Adequate protection payments may be no less than the monthly depreciation of the collateral.

Proposed Compromise: If the debtor has proposed a compromise affecting your collateral, you may either accept, reject or renegotiate the proposed compromise. If you reach an agreement, the resulting claim will be treated as a secured claim under § 506 and the plan may be confirmed. If you do not affirmatively agree, you must file an objection to confirmation (see above), and the confirmation hearing will be continued for consideration of a modified plan.

Order Establishing Procedures for Objection to Confirmation

Hearing Date, Time and Place: *If an objection to confirmation is filed, a PREHEARING CONFERENCE will be held at the date and time announced at the initial confirmation hearing. Parties may confirm the date by checking the minute order on the court's docket, which indicates "Hearing Continued" in reference to the confirmation hearing. Individuals not represented by counsel may also contact the trustee to learn the continued date.*

Procedures for Early Resolution: *As soon as the objection is resolved, counsel for the debtor is to prepare and forward to the trustee a statement of resolution, which the trustee will set on the court's earliest available calendar.*

Procedures for Prehearing Conference: *Each party objecting to confirmation and counsel for the debtor are ordered to confer regarding resolution of the objection. Debtor's counsel, or the debtor if unrepresented, must contact the objecting party within ten days of receipt of the objection in a good faith effort to resolve the objection. At least 14 calendar days prior to the prehearing conference and each continued hearing, counsel for the debtor must file and serve a prehearing statement with the court indicating:*

a. The date the objection was filed, the date of the initial conference between counsel to resolve the objection and the dates of all subsequent contacts regarding resolution of the objection;
b. A precise and separate statement of each factual and legal issue that must be determined to resolve the objection;
c. Proposed discovery and/or briefing schedules and proposals for alternative dispute resolution;
d. For continued hearings, developments since the last hearing and the current status.

Procedures for Objections to Proposed Compromises: *If a secured creditor affirmatively assents to the proposed compromise or an alternative compromise at or prior to the time of the initial confirmation hearing and no further objections are pending, the plan will be confirmed. If the parties cannot reach a compromise at or prior to that hearing, the court will deny confirmation and will continue the hearing for consideration of a modified plan. If a secured creditor does not affirmatively state its position regarding its collateral at or before the confirmation hearing, the court will continue the hearing for approximately 30 days to allow the debtor additional time to obtain a response.*

Sanctions: *Failure of a party to comply timely with this order may result in the exclusion of evidence, the imposition of monetary or non-monetary sanctions, possible dismissal of the case, or striking of the objection to confirmation.*

IT IS SO ORDERED:

/s/ Marilyn Morgan
UNITED STATES BANKRUPTCY JUDGE

/s/ Arthur S. Weissbrodt
UNITED STATES BANKRUPTCY JUDGE

/s/ Roger L. Efremsky
UNITED STATES BANKRUPTCY JUDGE

CREDITOR MATRIX COVER SHEET

UNITED STATES BANKRUPTCY COURT
NORTHERN DISTRICT OF CALIFORNIA

In re: Case No.:

____________________Debtor(s)______/

CREDITOR MATRIX COVER SHEET

I declare that the attached Creditor Mailing Matrix, consisting of ____ sheets, contains the correct, complete and current names and addresses of all priority, secured and unsecured creditors listed in debtor's filing and that this matrix conforms with the Clerk's promulgated requirements.

DATED:

Signature of Debtor's Attorney or Pro Per Debtor

NDCAL-123 N.D. CALIFORNIA

DECLARATION OF DEBTOR REGARDING INTENTION TO INCUR POST PETITION DEBT (LEASE) (CAN)

UNITED STATES BANKRUPTCY COURT
NORTHERN DISTRICT OF CALIFORNIA

In re:

Debtor(s)
______________________________/

Chapter 13
Case No.:

DECLARATION OF DEBTOR REGARDING INTENTION TO INCUR POST PETITION DEBT (LEASE)

The undersigned declares:

1. I am the debtor in the above action.
2. I am requesting that the Trustee provide a letter of non-opposition to the acquisition of a vehicle lease.
3. The terms of the lease include monthly payments of $ __________ for __________ months.
4. The acquisition of a lease will not impair my ability to perform under the terms of the plan.
5. The acquisition of a lease will not cause me to modify my plan to decrease the dividend to unsecured creditors, nor to decrease my plan payments.
6. I am current in my payments to the Trustee.
7. The plan will be completed within 60 months of confirmation.

I DECLARE UNDER PENALTY OF PERJURY THAT THE FOREGOING IS TRUE AND CORRECT.

Dated: ______________________________
Debtor

Dated: ______________________________
Debtor

6/04

DECLARATION OF DEBTOR REGARDING INTENTION TO INCUR POST PETITION DEBT (PURCHASE) (CAN)

UNITED STATES BANKRUPTCY COURT
NORTHERN DISTRICT OF CALIFORNIA

In re: Debtor(s) _______________________________/	Chapter 13 Case No.: **DECLARATION OF DEBTOR REGARDING INTENTION TO INCUR POST PETITION DEBT (PURCHASE)**

The undersigned declares:

1. I am the debtor in the above action.
2. I am requesting that the Trustee provide a letter of non-opposition to the extension of credit for ______________________.
3. The amount of the loan will not exceed $18,000.00.
4. The acquisition of a loan will not impair my ability to perform under the terms of the plan.
5. The acquisition of a loan will not cause me to modify my plan to decrease the dividend to unsecured creditors, nor to decrease my plan payments.
6. I am current in my payments to the Trustee.
7. The plan will be completed within 60 months of confirmation.

I DECLARE UNDER PENALTY OF PERJURY THAT THE FOREGOING IS TRUE AND CORRECT.

Dated: ______________________________
Debtor

Dated: ______________________________
Debtor

6/04

NDCAL-125 N.D. CALIFORNIA

ORDER CONFIRMING PLAN AND APPROVING ATTORNEYS FEES (CAN)

UNITED STATES BANKRUPTCY COURT
NORTHERN DISTRICT OF CALIFORNIA

In re:

Debtor. /

Chapter 13

Case No.:

ORDER CONFIRMING PLAN AND APPROVING ATTORNEY FEES

The debtor(s) filed a Plan under Chapter 13 of the Bankruptcy Code on ____________, a copy of which was served on creditors (and, if applicable, an amended Plan on ____________).
After hearing on notice on ____________ (date plan confirmed) the Court finds that:

1. The Plan complies with 11 U.S.C. 1325(a), and other applicable bankruptcy laws, rules and procedures.

THEREFORE, IT IS ORDERED THAT:
1. The debtor(s)' Plan (or amended Plan, if applicable) filed on ____________, is confirmed.

2. The future income of the debtor(s) shall be submitted to the supervision and control of Devin Derham-Burk, Trustee herein, as is necessary for the execution of the Plan.

3. Any creditor whose claim is entirely disallowed by final non-appealable order, and any creditor listed in the debtor(s)' original Schedules that has not filed a proof of claim by the claims bar date need not be served with notice of any subsequent action in this case by the debtor(s) or the Trustee unless such creditor files a request for special notice with the Court and serves such request upon the Trustee and the debtor(s)' attorney. Notwithstanding the above, if the proposed action would adversely affect a creditor, that creditor must be served notice.

4. Until the Plan is completed, dismissed, or converted to a case under a different chapter of the Bankruptcy Code, the debtor(s) shall, pursuant to the terms of the Plan, pay to the Trustee the sum of $____________ no later than the last day of each month, at P.O. BOX 50013, San Jose, California 95150.

5. If the debtor(s) fail(s) to timely tender a payment as set forth above, the Plan shall be considered in default. Upon written notice of default by the Trustee, the debtor(s) shall, within Twenty (20) days of said notice, either: 1) cure the Plan default; or 2) meet and confer with the Trustee and enter into a stipulation resolving the default in a manner acceptable to the Trustee; or 3) file and serve an Application to Modify Plan within twenty (20) days of the date of the Trustee's notice, which shall propose terms under which the Plan is not in default and which shall provide for Plan completion within sixty 60 months of the original date the Chapter 13 petition was filed. The foregoing shall be accomplished no later than twenty 20 days after the date of said notice. If the debtor(s) fail(s) to comply with the foregoing within the time prescribed, the case shall be dismissed forthwith without further notice or hearing.

6. Except as otherwise provided in the Plan or in the Order Confirming the Plan, the Trustee shall make payments to creditors under the Plan.

7. Pursuant to the Application for Approval of Attorneys Fees filed by , attorney for debtor(s), attorneys fees in the sum of $____________, are approved, of which $____________, has been previously paid.

Dated: ____________

____
UNITED STATES BANKRUPTCY JUDGE

Approved as to form and content
Dated: ____________

____
DEVIN DERHAM-BURK, Chapter 13 Trustee

(rev. 11/96)

RIGHTS AND RESPONSIBILITIES OF CHAPTER 13 DEBTORS AND THEIR ATTORNEYS (SAN FRANCISCO DIVISION)

United States Bankruptcy Court
for the Northern District of California
San Francisco and San Jose Divisions

RIGHTS AND RESPONSIBILITIES OF CHAPTER 13 DEBTORS AND THEIR ATTORNEYS

It is important for debtors who file a bankruptcy case under Chapter 13 to understand their rights and responsibilities. It is also important that the debtors know what their attorney's responsibilities are, and understand the importance of communicating with their attorney to make the case successful. Debtors should also know that they may expect certain services to be performed by their attorney. In order to assure that debtors and their attorney understand their rights and responsibilities in the bankruptcy process, the following guidelines provided by the court are hereby agreed to by the debtors and their attorneys. Unless the Court orders otherwise,

BEFORE THE CASE IS FILED

The debtor agrees to:

1. Provide the attorney with accurate financial information.
2. Discuss with the attorney the debtor's objectives in filing the case.

The attorney agrees to:

1. Meet with the debtor to review the debtor's debts assets, liabilities, income, and expenses.
2. Counsel the debtor regarding the advisability of filing either a Chapter 7 or Chapter 13 case, discuss both procedures with the debtor, and answer the debtor's questions.
3. Explain what payments will be made directly by the debtor and what payments will be made through the debtor's Chapter 13 plan, with particular attention to mortgage and vehicle loan payments, as well as any other claims which accrue interest.
4. Explain to the debtor how, when, and where to make the Chapter 13 plan payments.
5. Explain to the debtor how the attorney's fees and trustee's fees are paid and provide an executed copy of this document to the debtor.
6. Explain to the debtor that the first plan payment must be made to the

Trustee within 30 days of the date the plan is filed.

7. Advise the debtor of the requirement to attend the 341 Meeting of Creditors, and instruct the debtor as to the date, time and place of the meeting.

8. Advise the debtor of the necessity of maintaining liability, collision and comprehensive insurance on vehicles securing loans or leases.

9. Timely prepare and file the debtor's petition, plan, statements and schedules.

After The Case Is Filed

The debtor agrees to:

1. Keep the trustee and attorney informed of the debtor's address and telephone number.
2. Inform the attorney of any wage garnishments or attachments of assets which occur or continue after the filing of the case.
3. Contact the attorney promptly if the debtor loses his/her job or has other financial problems.
4. Let the attorney know if the debtor is sued during the case.
5. Inform the attorney if any tax refunds the debtor is entitled to are seized or not returned to the debtor by the IRS or Franchise Tax Board.
6. Contact the attorney before buying, refinancing, or selling real property or before entering into any long-term loan agreements to find out what approvals are required.
7. Pay any filing fees and expenses that may be incurred directly to the attorney.

The attorney agrees to provide the following legal services:

1. Appear at the 341 Meeting of Creditors with the debtor.
2. Respond to objections to plan confirmation, and where necessary, prepare an amended plan.
3. Prepare, file, and serve necessary modifications to the plan which may include suspending, lowering, or increasing plan payments.
4. Prepare, file, and serve necessary amended statements and schedules, in accordance with information provided by the debtor.

5. Prepare, file, and serve necessary motions to buy, sell, or refinance real property when appropriate.
6. Object to improper or invalid claims, if necessary, based upon documentation provided by the debtor.
7. Represent the debtor in motions for relief from stay.
8. Where appropriate, prepare, file, and serve necessary motions to avoid liens on real or personal property.
9. Provide such other legal services as are necessary for the administration of the present case before the Bankruptcy Court.

The "Guidelines for Payment of Attorneys Fees in Chapter 13 Cases for the San Francisco and San Jose Divisions" provide for maximum initial fees in the following amounts:

$1400 for the basic case; and an additional
$750 if the case involves real property claims;
$400 if the case involves state or federal tax claims;
$200 if the case involves vehicle loans or leases;
$1200 if the case involves an operating business;
$300 if the case involves support arrears claims;
$300 if the case involves student loans.

Initial fees charged in this case are $________

If the initial fees ordered by the court are not sufficient to compensate the attorney for the legal services rendered in the case, the attorney further agrees to apply to the court for any additional fees. Fees shall be paid through the plan unless otherwise ordered, The attorney may not receive fees directly from the debtor other than the initial retainer.

If the debtor disputes the legal services provided or the fees charged by the attorney, an objection may be filed with the court and the matter set for hearing. The attorney may move to withdraw or the client may discharge the attorney at any time.

Dated: ______________
Debtor

Dated: ______________
Debtor

Dated: ______________
Attorney for Debtor(s)

NDCAL-129 N.D. CALIFORNIA

RIGHTS AND RESPONSIBILITIES OF CHAPTER 13 DEBTORS AND ATTORNEYS (SAN JOSE DIVISION)

UNITED STATES BANKRUPTCY COURT
NORTHERN DISTRICT OF CALIFORNIA

No.:

______________________________ Debtor(s)/

STATEMENT PURSUANT TO RULE 2016(B)

The undersigned, pursuant to Rule 2016(b), Bankruptcy Rules, states that:

1. The undersigned is the attorney for the debtor(s) in this case.

2. The compensation paid or agreed to be paid by the debtor(s), to the undersigned is:
   a) For legal services rendered or to be rendered in contemplation of and in connection with this case..$
   b) Prior to the filing of this statement, debtor(s) have paid................................$____________
   c) The unpaid balance due and payable is...$

3. $________________ of the filing fee in this case has been paid.

4. The Services rendered or to be rendered include the following:
   a) Analysis of the financial situation, and rendering advice and assistance to the debtor(s) in determining whether to file a petition under title 11 of the United States Code.
   b) Preparation and filing of the petition, schedules, statement of affairs and other documents required by the court.
   c) Representation of the debtor(s) at the meeting of creditors.

5. The source of payments made by the debtor(s) to the undersigned was from earnings, wages and compensation for services performed, and

6. The source of payments to be made by the debtor(s) to the undersigned for the unpaid balance remaining, if any, will be from earnings, wages and compensation for services performed, and

7. The undersigned has received no transfer, assignment or pledge of property from debtor(s) except the following for the value stated:

8. The undersigned has not shared or agreed to share with any other entity, other than with members of undersigned's law firm, any compensation paid or to be paid except as follows:

Dated: Respectfully submitted,

Attorney for Debtor:

STATEMENT PURSUANT TO RULE 2016(B) (CAN)

UNITED STATES BANKRUPTCY COURT
NORTHERN DISTRICT OF CALIFORNIA

No.:

______________________ Debtor(s)/

STATEMENT PURSUANT TO RULE 2016(B)

The undersigned, pursuant to Rule 2016(b), Bankruptcy Rules, states that:

1. The undersigned is the attorney for the debtor(s) in this case.

2. The compensation paid or agreed to be paid by the debtor(s), to the undersigned is:
   a) For legal services rendered or to be rendered in contemplation of and in connection with this case...$
   b) Prior to the filing of this statement, debtor(s) have paid.................................$______________
   c) The unpaid balance due and payable is...$

3. $__________________ of the filing fee in this case has been paid.

4. The Services rendered or to be rendered include the following:
   a) Analysis of the financial situation, and rendering advice and assistance to the debtor(s) in determining whether to file a petition under title 11 of the United States Code.
   b) Preparation and filing of the petition, schedules, statement of affairs and other documents required by the court.
   c) Representation of the debtor(s) at the meeting of creditors.

5. The source of payments made by the debtor(s) to the undersigned was from earnings, wages and compensation for services performed, and

6. The source of payments to be made by the debtor(s) to the undersigned for the unpaid balance remaining, if any, will be from earnings, wages and compensation for services performed, and

7. The undersigned has received no transfer, assignment or pledge of property from debtor(s) except the following for the value stated:

8. The undersigned has not shared or agreed to share with any other entity, other than with members of undersigned's law firm, any compensation paid or to be paid except as follows:

Dated: Respectfully submitted,

Attorney for Debtor:

NDCAL-131 N.D. CALIFORNIA

STATEMENT RE PAYMENT ADVICES (CAN)

UNITED STATES BANKRUPTCY COURT
NORTHERN DISTRICT OF CALIFORNIA

In Re:) Bankruptcy Case
) No.
)
Debtor(s))

STATEMENT RE PAYMENT ADVICES

□ Attached are copies of all payment advices or other evidence of payment that I/we received from my/our employer(s) within the 60 days before the filing of this bankruptcy case. I/we have blocked out all but the last four digits of my/our social security number(s) wherever they appear on the attached copies.

□ I/We received no payment advices or other evidence of payment from my/our employer(s) within the 60 days before the filing of this bankruptcy case.

I/we declare under penalty of perjury that the above statement is true and correct to the best of my/our knowledge, information, and belief.

Date:______ ______________________________
Signature of Debtor

Date:______ ______________________________
Signature of Joint Debtor

Date:______ ______________________________
Signature of Attorney

DECLARATION AND SIGNATURE OF NON-ATTORNEY BANKRUPTCY PETITION PREPARER (See 11 U.S.C. § 110)

I declare under penalty of perjury that: (1) I am a bankruptcy petition preparer as defined in 11 U.S.C. § 110; (2) I prepared this document for compensation and have provided the debtor with a copy of this document and the notices and information required under 11 U.S.C. §§ 110(b), 110(h) and 342(b); and (3) if rules or guidelines have been promulgated pursuant to 11 U.S.C. § 110(h) setting a maximum fee for services chargeable by bankruptcy petition preparers, I have given the debtor notice of the maximum amount before preparing any document for filing for a debtor or accepting any fee from the debtor, as required by that section.

______________________________ ______________
Printed or Typed Name of Bankruptcy Petition Preparer Social Security No.
(Required by 11 U.S.C. § 110)

If the bankruptcy petition preparer is not an individual, state the name, title (if any), address, and social security number of the officer, principal, responsible person, or partner who signs this document.

____

____
Address

x______________________________ ______________
Signature of Bankruptcy Petition Preparer Date

Names and Social Security numbers of all other individuals who prepared or assisted in preparing this document, unless the bankruptcy petition preparer is not an individual:

If more than one person prepared this document, attach additional signed sheets conforming to the appropriate Official Form for each person.

A bankruptcy petition preparer's failure to comply with the provisions of title 11 and the Federal Rules of Bankruptcy Procedure may result in fines or imprisonment or both. 11 U.S.C. § 110; 18 U.S.C. § 156.

SOUTHERN DISTRICT OF CALIFORNIA

The Southern District of California has adopted the following rules relevant to cases under title 11:

RULE 1001. TITLE; SCOPE OF RULES; DEFINITIONS

1001-1. TITLE AND CITATION.

The following rules are adopted as Local Bankruptcy Rules to govern the practice before the court until further order and shall be cited as "Local Bankruptcy Rules" or "LBR" to distinguish them from the "Local District Court Rules" which should be cited as "LDR."

1001-2. SCOPE AND EFFECTIVE DATE OF RULES.

(a) These rules supplement the Federal Rules of Bankruptcy Procedure [cited as *Fed. R. Bankr. P.*] and the Federal Rules of Civil Procedure [cited as *Fed. R. Civ. P.*].

(b) These rules become effective April 28, 1996, and shall govern all actions and proceedings pending or commenced on or after that date.

(c) These rules may be amended subsequent to their effective date by "General Order" of the court. Such General Orders will be captioned "General Order No. . . . . Amending Local Bankruptcy Rule . . ." and shall be posted at the court and may be obtained from the clerk.

(d) COMPLIANCE WITH Rules. Unrepresented parties are bound by these rules and any reference in these rules to "attorney" or "counsel" applies to those parties unless the context otherwise provides.

1001-3. ADOPTION OF CERTAIN LOCAL RULES OF THE UNITED STATES DISTRICT COURT.

The provisions of the Local United States District Court Rules are applicable to proceedings in the United States Bankruptcy Court to the extent they are consistent with these Local Bankruptcy Rules, the Fed. R. Bankr. P., and Title 11 of the United States Code. A cross-reference table to the Local Rules of the United States District Court is set forth in Appendix B.

1001-4. DEFINITIONS.

The definitions set forth in 11 U.S.C. §§ 101 and 102 and Fed. R. Bankr. P. 9001 and 9002 shall apply to these Local Rules. Except when a matter is pending before the district court, the references in the Local United States

District Court Rules to "court," "judge" and "clerk" shall be read as the "United States Bankruptcy Court," "bankruptcy judge" and "clerk of the United States Bankruptcy Court," respectively.

1001-5. SANCTIONS FOR NON-COMPLIANCE.

Failure of counsel to comply with these rules, or with any order of the court, may be grounds for imposition by the court of any and all sanctions authorized by statute or rule or within the inherent power of the court, including, without limitation, dismissal of any actions, entry of default, findings of contempt, imposition of monetary sanctions or attorneys' fees and costs, and other sanctions.

RULE 1002. COMMENCEMENT OF CASE

1002-1. PERSONS APPEARING WITHOUT AN ATTORNEY.

(a) CORPORATIONS AND UINCORPORATED ASSOCIATIONS. Corporations, unincorporated associations and partnerships may not file a petition or otherwise appear except through an attorney in any case or proceeding, except for filing a proof of claim or a reaffirmation agreement. Such a proof of claim or reaffirmation agreement must be signed by an officer of the corporation, partner of the partnership, or member of the unincorporated association.

(b) INDIVIDUALS. Any person representing himself or herself without an attorney must appear personally for such purpose. The representation may not be delegated to any other person, including a spouse or relative, nor to any other party.

[The Next Rule is 1006]

RULE 1006. FILING FEE AND SPECIAL CHARGES

1006-1. METHOD OF PAYMENT.

The filing fee tendered by or on behalf of the debtor shall be in the form of a cashier's check, money order, or check of the attorney for the debtor, or may be in cash, if the petition is presented in person. Personal checks of the debtor shall not be accepted. The clerk's office shall not be responsible for cash sent through the mail.

RULE 1006-2. WAIVER OF FILING FEE.

An application to waive the Chapter 7 filing fee shall be accompanied by a proposed order. The application and order shall substantially conform to Local Form CSD 1020, APPLICATION FOR WAIVER OF THE CHAPTER 7 FILING FEE FOR INDIVIDUALS WHO CANNOT PAY THE

FILING FEE IN FULL OR IN INSTALLMENTS, and Local Form CSD 1021, ORDER ON DEBTOR'S APPLICATION FOR WAIVER OF THE CHAPTER 7 FILING FEE.

1006-3. APPROVAL OF INSTALLMENT FEES.

The clerk shall have authority to grant an individual debtor's application to pay the filing fee in installments for a period not to exceed 120 days after the filing of the petition. Any application to extend the time for paying the fee beyond the 120-day period shall be granted only by the court.

1006-4. DISHONORED CHECKS.

(a) All cashier's checks, money orders, drafts, and personal checks tendered in payment of filing fees and special charges shall be accepted by the clerk subject to collection and full credit only when the check or draft has been accepted by the financial institution on which it is drawn. A service charge will be collected for any checks or drafts returned for lack of funds.

(b) If more than one check or draft issued by the same entity is returned by the depository upon which drawn for insufficient funds, the clerk shall accept only cash, a cashier's check or money order from that entity, except for good cause shown.

1006-5. SCHEDULE OF FEES AND SPECIAL CHARGES.

A schedule of fees and special charges collectible by the clerk is attached as Appendix A.

RULE 1007. SPECIAL REQUIREMENTS FOR LISTS AND SCHEDULES OF LIABILITIES AND EQUITY SECURITY HOLDERS

1007-1. SPECIAL REQUIREMENTS FOR MAILING ADDRESSES.

The court's automated noticing system has special requirements for the submission of names and addresses for creditors and other parties in interest. The debtor is required to obtain from the clerk (and fully comply with the specifications set forth in) the most current version of the court document entitled *SPECIAL REQUIREMENTS FOR MAILING ADDRESSES,* Local Form CSD 1007.

1007-2. ASSEMBLY OF PAPERS FOR FILING; NUMBER OF COPIES.

(a) ASSEMBLY OF PAPERS. The original papers and copies thereof required by subsection (b) of this Rule shall be assembled into separate sets. All papers submitted to the court shall be flat and unfolded, except as necessary for presentation of exhibits. Assembly sequence for papers is from top to bottom:

(2) Local Form CSD 1006 entitled "Application to Pay Filing Fees in Installments and Order" (not required if filing fee paid in full when filing petition);

(3) Petition;

(4) Exhibit "A": Corporate Statement (Corporate Filings Only—see Official Bankruptcy Form B1XA);

(5) List containing names and addresses of creditors (not required if Schedules filed with Petition);

(6) Summary of Schedules;

(7) Schedules A-J;

(8) Statement of Financial Affairs;

(9) List of equity security holders (chapter 11 cases only);

(10) List of 20 largest unsecured creditors, exclusive of insiders (chapter 11 cases only);

(11) Chapter 13 Plan, if filed with petition;

(12) Attorney Fee Disclosure Statement required by Fed. R. Bankr. P. 2016(b), if filed with petition;

(13) Statement of Intention required by Fed. R. Bankr. P. 1007(b)(2) [see Official Bankruptcy Form 8], if filed with petition (only in chapter 7 cases for individual debtors);

(14) Notice to Debtor by Non-Attorney Bankruptcy Petition Preparer, [See Official Bankruptcy Form B 19B] (only in cases for unrepresented debtors);

(15) One of the following in cases for individual debtors only:

(A) Certificate of Credit Counseling; or

(B) CERTIFICATE OF EXIGENT CIRCUMSTANCES AND MOTION FOR EXTENSION

OF TIME TO FILE CERTIFICATE OF CREDIT COUNSELING and ORDER in accordance with Local Bankruptcy Rule 9013-6(a)(1)(J) [See Local Forms CSD 1025 and CSD 1026]; or

(C) MOTION FOR EXEMPTION FROM CREDIT COUNSELING AND NOTICE OF OPPORTUNITY FOR HEARING in accordance with Local Bankruptcy Rule 9013-2(b)(4) [See Local Form CSD 1027].

(16) One of the following in cases for individual debtors only:

(A) Chapter 7 Statement of Current Monthly Income and Means Test Calculation [See Official Bankruptcy Form B 22A]; or

(B) Chapter 11 Statement of Current Monthly Income [See Official Bankruptcy Form B 22B]; or

(C) Chapter 13 Statement of Current Monthly Income and Calculation of Commitment Period and Disposable Income [See Official Bankruptcy Form B 22C].

(17) Chapter 11 small business debtors must file either:

(A) the most recent balance sheet, statement of operations, cash-flow statement, and Federal income tax return required by 11 U.S.C. § 1116(1)(A); or

(B) a statement indicating that the documents listed in subsection (A) above have not been prepared or filed as required by 11 U.S.C. § 1116(1)(B).

The diskette shall be accompanied by one (1) paper original Local Form CSD 1004, *DECLARATION RE: FILING OF PETITION, SCHEDULES & STATEMENTS ON DISKETTE*. If financial constraints and/or the inability to access the equipment necessary to produce the diskette would cause an undue hardship on the debtor, a scannable petition and all attachments along with a creditor matrix must be submitted accompanied by an executed *REQUEST FOR WAIVER OF DISKETTE REQUIREMENT*, Local Form CSD 1010.

(b) NUMBER OF COPIES. The court requires that the pdf petition and all attachments be accompanied by two (2) paper copies. The number of required copies includes a copy to be conformed with the clerk's filing stamp and returned to the person presenting it for filing, as provided in Local Bankruptcy Rule 9004-3(n).

(c) DEFERRED FILING OF STATEMENTS, LISTS AND SCHEDULES. Upon the filing of any statements, schedules and/or chapter 13 plan not previously filed with the petition, the court requires two (2) copies. The original and required copies of the papers shall be filed with the clerk, together with proof of service showing compliance with Local Bankruptcy Rule 1007-4. One copy of the same will be returned to the person presenting it for filing, as provided in Local Bankruptcy Rule 9004-3(n).

1007-3. EXTENSION OF TIME; REQUIRED NOTICE.

Service on the United States Trustee of a motion for extension of time for filing schedules and statements in chapter 7, 11, and 12 cases is governed by Local Bankruptcy Rule 9034-1 and, in chapter 13 cases, by Local Rule 9034-2. In addition, a copy of the motion shall be served on the trustee, if any, in chapter 7, 11, and 12 cases.

1007-4. REQUIRED NOTICE WHEN SCHEDULES ARE FILED AFTER THE DATE THE PETITION IS FILED.

Before filing with the clerk any lists, statements and/or schedules that were not filed at the time the petition was filed, the debtor shall:

(a) serve a copy of these papers on the United States Trustee, any interim trustee, trustee and each member of any committee appointed in the case; and

(b) give notice of the date of filing the petition to any entity who was not named in the original lists, schedules and statements filed at the commencement of the case. If applicable, the notice shall be accompanied by:

(1) a copy of the "Order for and Notice of Section 341(a) Meeting"; and

(2) any "Discharge of Debt" or "Notice of Order Confirming Plan"; and

(3) in a chapter 13 case, a claim form and the date, time and location of any pending Section 341(a) meeting or confirmation hearing currently scheduled; and

(c) attach to the papers filed with the court a proof of service showing compliance with this rule; and

(d) in a chapter 7, 11, or 12 case, when noticing any entity not previously named in the original mailing matrix, comply with Local Bankruptcy Rule 1007-1.

1007-5. COMPLETION OF PERSONAL FINANCIAL MANAGEMENT COURSE.

The debtor shall file Official Bankruptcy Form B 23, "Certification of Completion of Instructional Course Concerning Personal Financial Management," together with the certificate obtained from a personal financial management instruction provider (a) no later than forty-five (45) days after the first date set for the meeting of creditors under 11 U.S.C. § 341 in a chapter 7 case; or (b) no later than the last payment made by the debtor as required by the chapter 13 plan or the filing of a motion for entry of a discharge under 11 U.S.C. § 1328(b) in a chapter 13 case.

1007-6. PAYMENT ADVICES.

All payment advices or other evidence of payment received by the debtor from all employers within sixty (60) days before the filing of a petition and required by Fed. R. Bankr. P. 1007(b)(1)(E) shall be submitted to the chapter 7 or 13 trustee assigned to the debtor's case and shall not be filed with the court.

1007-7. CONSUMER DEBTS SECURED BY PROPERTY OF THE ESTATE.

If the trustee claims no interest in property listed in the Statement of Intention filed by an individual debtor, it shall not be the responsibility of the trustee to effect compliance of the debtor with 11 U.S.C. § 521(2)(B).

[The Next Rule is 1009]

RULE 1009. AMENDMENT OF LISTS AND SCHEDULES; FILING FEES; NOTICE; PROOF OF SERVICE

1009-1. APPLICABILITY OF RULE.

This rule applies to all cases in which the lists, schedules and statements required by Fed. R. Bankr. P. 1007 are amended post petition.

1009-2. AMENDMENT; NOTICE.

Any amendment filed shall substantially conform to Local Form CSD 1100, *AMENDMENT*. Service shall be made in the manner required by Local Bankruptcy Rule 1007-4 and shall substantially conform to Local Form CSD

1101, *NOTICE TO CREDITORS OF THE ABOVE-NAMED DEBTOR ADDED BY AMENDMENT.*

1009-3. NUMBER OF COPIES.

The original and two (2) copies of the amendments shall be filed with the clerk, together with proof of service showing compliance with Local Bankruptcy Rule 1007-4. One copy will be returned to the person presenting it for filing, as provided in Local Bankruptcy Rule 9004-3(n).

1009-4. SPECIAL REQUIREMENTS FOR MAILING ADDRESSES.

The debtor must comply with Local Bankruptcy Rule 1007-1 when filing amendments to the schedules of liabilities.

[The Next Rule is 1014]

RULE 1014. MOTION TO CHANGE VENUE

A motion to change venue under 28 U.S.C. § 1412 is filed with the bankruptcy court clerk. The motion is governed by Local Bankruptcy Rule 9014 and is to be calendared for hearing before the bankruptcy judge.

RULE 1015. JOINT ADMINISTRATION OF CASES

1015-1. JOINT PETITIONS.

The estates of debtors filing a joint petition shall be jointly administered without further court order.

1015-2. RELATED CASES.

(a) NOTICE OF RELATED CASES. If a case, other than a chapter 13 case, is related to a case that is pending or was pending within three (3) years of the filing of the later petition, the petitioner shall file a Notice of Related Case(s) setting forth the title, number and filing date of the related case, together with a brief statement of the manner in which the cases are related. The Notice of Related Case(s) shall also be served upon the United States Trustee.

(b) CASES DEEMED RELATED. A case is deemed related to another case if:

(1) the debtors in both cases are the same entity as that term is defined at 11 U.S.C. § 101(15);

(2) the debtors in both cases are spouses or former spouses;

(3) the debtors in both cases are partners;

(4) the debtor in one case is a general partner of the debtor

in the other case;

(5) the debtor in one case is an "affiliate," as that term is defined at 11 U.S.C. § 101(2), of the debtor in the other case;

(6) the debtors are corporations and have one or more common shareholder which owns twenty percent (20%) or more of each corporation;

(7) the debtors are partnerships and have one or more common general partner;

(8) the debtor in one case has, or within 180 days of the commencement of either of the related cases had, an interest in property that as [sic] or is included in the property of the other estate under 11 U.S.C. § 540(a); or

(9) the cases are otherwise so related as to warrant being treated as related to promote efficient administration of the estates.

(c) ASSIGNMENT TO JUDGES. The clerk, whenever apprised of related cases, shall cause the subsequent case to be assigned or reassigned to the judge to whom the prior case was assigned, unless the court orders otherwise. Related cases filed simultaneously shall be assigned to one judge.

[The Next Rule is 1017]

RULE 1017. MOTION FOR DISMISSAL OR CONVERSION OF CASE

1017-1. REQUIRED NOTICE.

(a) A motion by the United States Trustee or a trustee to dismiss a case shall be noticed in accordance with Local Bankruptcy Rule 2002-2.

(b) A motion to dismiss or convert a case, which is filed by a party in interest other than the debtor, United States Trustee or trustee, shall be noticed by the moving party in accordance with Local Bankruptcy Rule 2002-3.

(c) A motion by the debtor to dismiss or convert a case is controlled by Local Bankruptcy Rule 1017-2.

1017-2. MOTION BY DEBTOR TO DISMISS OR CONVERT CASE; NOTICE TO UNITED STATES TRUSTEE AND TRUSTEE.

(a) CHAPTER 7 OR 11 CASE.

(1) MOTION TO CONVERT. A motion by the debtor to convert a chapter 7 or 11 case to another chapter shall be accompanied by the appropriate filing fee and a proposed order using the applicable Local Form: *ORDER CONVERTING CASE UNDER CHAPTER 7 TO CASE UNDER CHAPTER 11* [CSD 1105]; *ORDER CONVERTING CASE UNDER CHAPTER 7 TO CASE UNDER CHAPTER 12* [CSD 1106]; *ORDER CONVERTING CASE UNDER CHAPTER 7 TO CASE UNDER CHAPTER 13* [CSD 1107]; *ORDER CONVERTING CASE UNDER CHAPTER 11 TO CASE UNDER CHAPTER 7* [CSD 1108]; or *ORDER CONVERTING CASE UNDER CHAPTER 11 TO CASE UNDER CHAPTER 12* [CSD 1109].

(2) SERVICE ON CHAPTER 7 OR 11 TRUSTEE. A copy of the motion to convert and proposed order shall be served on any chapter 7 or 11 trustee appointed in the case.

(b) CHAPTER 13 CASE.

(1) REQUESTS FOR DISMISSAL. A request by the debtor to dismiss a chapter 13 case under 11 U.S.C. § 1307(b) shall be accompanied by a proposed order. The request and order shall substantially conform to Local Form CSD 1174, *REQUEST BY DEBTOR FOR DISMISSAL OF CHAPTER 13 AND ORDER.*

(2) NOTICE OF CONVERSION. A notice by the debtor of the conversion of a chapter 13 case to a case under chapter 7 shall be presented on Local Form CSD 1129, *NOTICE OF CONVERSION OF CASE UNDER CHAPTER 13 TO A CASE UNDER CHAPTER 7 BY DEBTOR* together with the appropriate filing fee.

(3) SPECIAL REQUIREMENTS. A chapter 13 debtor seeking conversion shall file with the notice of conversion:

(A) the schedules and statements listed in Fed. R. Bankr. P. 1007(b)(1); and

(B) a separate schedule listing the names and addresses of any creditors who are entitled to assert claims against the debtor or the estate under Fed. R. Bankr. P. 1019(5) and 11 U.S.C. § 348(d).

(4) NUMBER OF COPIES. The original and additional copies of the notice of conversion or request to dismiss and all attachments shall be filed with the clerk, together with proof of service showing compliance with subsection (6) below. One copy will be returned to the person presenting it for filing, as provided in Local Bankruptcy Rule

9004-3(n). Number of copies required:

(A) request to dismiss and proposed order—the original and two (2) copies.

(B) notice of conversion together with the additional papers required by subsection (b)(3) above—the original and three (3) copies.

(5) SERVICE ON CHAPTER 13 TRUSTEE. The notice of conversion or request to dismiss and any additional documents shall be served on the chapter 13 trustee.

(6) PROOF OF SERVICE. Proof of service showing compliance with this rule and Local Bankruptcy Rule 9006-3 shall be attached to the original documents.

[The Next Rule is 1019]

RULE 1019. DUTY OF DEBTOR-IN-POSSESSION OR TRUSTEE TO FILE REPORTS IN CHAPTER 11 OR 12 CASE CONVERTED TO CHAPTER 7

1019-1. REQUIRED REPORTS.

Upon entry of an order converting a case to chapter 7, the debtor or chapter 11 or 12 trustee shall:

(a) secure, preserve, and refrain from disposing of property of the estate;

(b) contact the chapter 7 trustee and arrange to deliver property of the estate and all books and records to the trustee or the trustee's designated agent; and

(c) within seven (7) days after entry of the order for relief, file with the clerk and serve upon the United States Trustee and trustee, if appointed, a verified schedule of all property of the estate as of the date of conversion.

1019-2. PROOF OF SERVICE.

Proof of service showing compliance with this rule and Local Bankruptcy Rule 9006-3 shall be attached to the original documents.

[The Next Rule is 2002]

RULE 2002. NOTICES TO CREDITORS, EQUITY SECURITY HOLDERS, AND THE UNITED STATES

2002-1. APPLICABILITY OF RULE; NOTICES TO ALL CREDI-

TORS AND PARTIES IN INTEREST.

(a) APPLICABILITY OF RULE. This rule clarifies when and how a notice of intended action or a notice of hearing shall be used.

(b) 7-DAY NOTICE (MOTION TO EXTEND AUTOMATIC STAY). The notice required under 11 U.S.C. § 362(c)(3)(B) to extend the automatic stay shall be served not later than seven (7) days after the order for relief.

(c) 30-DAY NOTICE (MOTION TO IMPOSE AUTOMATIC STAY). The notice required under 11 U.S.C. § 362(c)(4)(B) to impose the automatic stay shall be served not later than thirty (30) days after the order for relief.

(d) 28-DAY NOTICE. The notices required by Fed. R. Bankr. P. 2002(a)(2), (3), (5), (6), (7) and (8), and (b)(2) and (d) (1–4) and (7) and Local Bankruptcy Rule 2002-2(a), including notice of the opportunity to object to confirmation of a chapter 13 plan, shall be given at least twenty-eight (28) days before the occurrence of the intended action or hearing, unless the court directs otherwise.

(e) 39-DAY NOTICE (DISCLOSURE STATEMENTS AND PLAN CONFIRMATIONS). The notice to all creditors, parties in interest and equity security holders of a hearing to consider approval of a disclosure statement, confirmation of a plan in other than chapter 13 cases, or the post-confirmation modification of a chapter 13 plan, required by Fed. R. Bankr. P. 2002(a)(6), Fed. R. Bankr. P. 2002(b) and (d) (5–7), shall be given by the proponent at least thirty-nine (39) days before the hearing, unless the court directs otherwise.

(f) NOTICE BY CHAPTER 7 TRUSTEE. In cases where the estate has less than $1,000 in cash, and unless the court directs otherwise, the clerk shall mail any notices required to be mailed to all creditors by the chapter 7 trustee.

(g) NOTICE OF § 341(A) MEETING BY CHAPTER 11 OR 12 DEBTOR.

(1) NOTICE TO CREDITORS. When there are 1,000 or more creditors in a chapter 11 or 12 case, the debtor shall mail the notice of § 341(a) meeting required by Fed. R. Bankr. P. 2002(a)(1). The notice shall be in the format provided by the clerk.

(2) NOTICE TO EQUITY SECURITY HOLDERS. The debtor

shall mail notice of the order for relief and any other notices required by Fed. R. Bankr. P. 2002(d).

(h) FILING OF PAPERS WITH CLERK. The motion and notice together with proof of service showing compliance with this rule, must be filed with the clerk no later than the next business day following the date of service.

2002-2. NOTICES OF INTENDED ACTION.

(a) Notices of intended action shall be used in the following circumstances unless otherwise permitted in subsection (g):

(1) A motion by United States Trustee or trustee for dismissal of a chapter 7, 11, 12, or 13 case based on the failure of the debtor to file the schedules and statements required by Fed. R. Bankr. P. 1007 or to attend the § 341(a) meeting of creditors. The noticing requirements of Fed. R. Bankr. P. 2002 and this subsection are satisfied by including the notice of intended action within the § 341(a) meeting notice;

(2) intended use, sale or lease of property other than in the ordinary course of business as governed by Fed. R. Bankr. P. 6004 and Local Bankruptcy Rule 6004, but excluding motions for sale or lease of personally identifiable information as provided for in Local Bankruptcy Rule 6004-4;

(3) intended abandonment of property by the debtor or trustee as governed by Fed. R. Bankr. P. 6007 and Local Bankruptcy Rule 6007;

(4) intended compromise or settlement of controversy by the debtor or trustee as governed by Fed. R. Bankr. P. 9019 and Local Bankruptcy Rule 9019;

(5) allowance of compensation or other remuneration to the debtor or insiders as provided by Local Bankruptcy Rule 4002-2;

(6) applications for compensation, commissions or expenses of auctioneers, appraisers or brokers to the extent the aggregate compensation and expenses exceed $1000 as governed by Fed. R. Bankr. P. 2002(a)(6);

(7) application for compensation or reimbursement of expenses from the estate when the application is that of the trustee only;

(8) all other matters where the court or Fed. R. Bankr. P. so direct.

(b) Notices of intended action may not be used for motions to dismiss, motions to convert, motions for compensation of professionals other than auctioneers, appraisers, or real estate brokers, or motions to extend time within which to object to the discharge under § 727 or object to the dischargeability of a debt under § 523 and any other actions described in Local Bankruptcy Rule 2002-3.

(c) Any notice of intent given under this section shall be prepared and served by the entity proposing the action and must substantially conform to Local Form CSD 1180, *NOTICE OF INTENDED ACTION AND OPPORTUNITY FOR HEARING.*

(d) Each party opposing an intended action shall serve that opposition and Local Form CSD 1184, *REQUEST AND NOTICE FOR HEARING,* not less than twenty-eight (28) days after service of the notice of intended action, if personally served. If served by mail, the party opposing shall have thirty-one (31) days to serve such opposition as provided by Fed. R. Bankr. P. 9006(f).

(e) If the response period expires without the service of any response and a request for hearing, the moving party shall promptly file a proposed order and comply with Local Bankruptcy Rule 9013-7.

(f) Unless otherwise ordered by the court for cause, the filing of a timely objection to a proposed action shall automatically stay the proposed action until after the hearing.

(g) Upon the affirmative representation of counsel for the movant that substantive opposition is reasonably anticipated, a hearing date may be obtained from the courtroom deputy and the movant may proceed pursuant to Local Bankruptcy Rule 9014.

2002-3. NOTICES OF HEARING.

(a) Except as provided in Local Bankruptcy Rule 2002-2(a), notices of hearing in accordance with Fed. R. Bankr. P. 9014 must be given to all creditors and parties in interest in the following circumstances together with such additional information as noted herein:

(1) motion for conversion of chapter 7, 11, or 12 case, by other than the debtor, as provided by Fed. R. Bankr. P. 1017 and Local Bankruptcy Rule 1017;

(2) motion for dismissal of a case, except as otherwise provided in Local Bankruptcy Rule 2002-2(a)(1);

(3) motion for approval of chapter 11 disclosure statement, together with such papers as required by Fed. R. Bankr. P. 3017(a);

(4) motion for confirmation of chapter 11 plan, together with such papers as required by Fed. R. Bankr. P. 3017(d);

(5) motion for modification of chapter 9 or 11 plan, together with such papers as required by Fed. R. Bankr. P. 3019;

(6) motion for modification of chapter 12 or 13 plan, together with such papers as required by Fed. R. Bankr. P. 3015. Creditors who are not adversely affected are not required to be given notice unless the court orders otherwise;

(7) application for allowance of compensation or reimbursement of expenses in excess of $1000 as provided by Fed. R. Bankr. P. 2002(a)(6) and 2016 and Local Bankruptcy Rule 2016, except as otherwise provided in Local Bankruptcy Rule 2014-2(b);

(8) motion to appoint a trustee or examiner in a chapter 11 case;

(9) motion by the debtor or other party in interest to extend automatic stay under 11 U.S.C. § 362(c)(3)(B);

(10) motion for order imposing automatic stay under 11 U.S.C. § 362(c)(4)(B); and

(11) all other matters where the court or Fed. R. Bankr. P. so direct.

(b) Prior to giving notice of a hearing, the moving party shall obtain a hearing date from the courtroom deputy. Any notice of hearing given under this section shall substantially conform to:

(1) Local Form CSD 1181, *NOTICE OF MOTION AND HEARING;* or

(2) if the notice relates to a hearing on a chapter 11 plan or disclosure statement or modification of a chapter 13 plan after confirmation, Local Form CSD 1149, *NOTICE OF HEARING AND MOTION FOR APPROVAL OF DISCLOSURE STATEMENT, PLAN, OR MODIFIED PLAN*; or

(3) if the notice relates to a hearing to extend or impose the automatic stay under 11 U.S.C. § 362(c)(3)(B) or (c)(4)(B), Local Form CSD 1158, NOTICE OF HEARING AND MOTION TO EXTEND OR IMPOSE THE AUTOMATIC STAY.

2002-4. NOTICING PROCEDURE; MAILING LISTS.

(a) SERVICE OF MOTION AND NOTICE. The moving party shall serve a copy of the moving papers, if required by Local Bankruptcy Rule 9013 or 9014, and the form of notice required by Local Bankruptcy Rule 2002-2 or 2002-3 on the debtor, the debtor's attorney of record, any trustee and/or committee and their attorney, all creditors, and parties requesting special notice. A copy of any required moving papers and all notices shall also be mailed to:

United States Trustee
United States Department of Justice
402 West Broadway, Suite 600
San Diego, CA 92101

(b) SERVICE OF NOTICE. The person responsible for giving notice under Local Bankruptcy Rule 2002-1 shall mail a copy of the notice required by Local Bankruptcy Rule 2002-2 or 2002-3 without the moving papers to all creditors and indenture trustees and, if applicable, equity security creditors whose names and addresses appear in the case records. In a chapter 11 case, a copy of the notice shall also be mailed to:

Chief, Special Procedures
Section—Insolvency
Internal Revenue Service
P. O. Box 30213
Laguna Niguel, CA 92607-0213

and, if the chapter 11 debtor is a corporation, also to:

United States Securities and Exchange Commission
5670 Wilshire Blvd., 11th Floor
Los Angeles, California 90036

(c) LISTING THE UNITED STATES AS A CREDITOR; NOTICE TO THE UNITED STATES. When listing an indebtedness to the United States for other than taxes and when giving notice, as required by Fed. R. Bankr. P. 2002(j)(4), the debtor shall list and notice BOTH the United States Attorney for this district and the federal agency or other federal component through which the debtor became indebted. The address of the notice to the United States Attorney shall include, in parenthesis, the name of the federal agency or other component. For example:

United States Attorney
for the Southern District of California
(For the Department of Energy)
940 Front Street, Room 5152
San Diego, CA 92101-8800

The notice shall also be sent directly to the component agency. For example:

Department of Energy
Street Address
City, State ZIP

(d) MAILING LIST. To facilitate giving the notices required by this rule, upon advance request of not less than seven (7) business days and payment of the requisite cost, the clerk shall furnish a mailing list, provided the clerk has the information readily available to produce such a list.

[The Next Rule is 2004]

RULE 2004. EXAMINATION OF AN ENTITY

2004-1. NOTICE.

(a) ATTORNEY'S DUTY TO STIPULATE. Attorneys will make every reasonable effort to stipulate to the exact times and places for the commencement and resumption of all examinations under Fed. R. Bankr. P. 2004.

(b) FORM. The party requesting an examination under Fed. R. Bankr. P. 2004 shall utilize Local Form CSD 1050, *SUBPOENA FOR RULE 2004 EXAMINATION.*

(c) ORDER FOR EXAMINATION. An order for examination under Fed. R. Bankr. P. 2004 shall require a minimum of twenty-eight (28) days' notice from the date of service of the court's order, unless otherwise agreed by the parties or ordered by the court.

(d) EMERGENCY MOTION. The party whose examination is required or other interested party may file an emergency motion for a protective order if grounds exist under Fed. R. Bankr. P. 26(c).

[The Next Rule is 2014]

RULE 2014. EMPLOYMENT OF PROFESSIONALS

2014-1. APPLICATION TO EMPLOY PROFESSIONAL.

(a) COUNSEL FOR CHAPTER 11 AND 12 DEBTORS. Debtors in chapter 11 or 12 cases who are to be represented by counsel shall submit an application to retain such counsel or to substitute counsel in accordance with Fed. R. Bankr. P. 2014(a), together with a declaration of the attorney and the proposed order.

(b) OTHER PROFESSIONALS. The application for employment of other professionals, including employment of an agent or broker for the sale or lease of estate property or a professional manager or management corporation, shall conform to Fed. R. Bankr. P. 2014(a).

(c) DISCLOSURE STATEMENT. Any applications to employ professionals shall include a copy of the Fed. R. Bankr. P. 2016(b) disclosure statement, if applicable, and a copy of any retainer agreement, guarantee, or security agreement.

(d) NOTICE TO AND STATEMENT OF UNITED STATES TRUSTEE. Service on the United States Trustee of the application to employ counsel or other professionals including appraisers, auctioneers, agents, and brokers by a debtor-in-possession or trustee is governed by Local Bankruptcy Rule 9034-1.

2014-2. CONTRACT FOR EMPLOYMENT OF AGENTS AND BROKERS.

(a) All applications for employment of an agent or broker for the sale or lease of estate property must be accompanied by a copy of the signed written contract employing the agent or broker. All contracts for employment shall provide that they are effective only upon court approval. All contracts for employment shall be for a term not to exceed one hundred eighty (180) days unless otherwise ordered by the court.

(b) To the extent the aggregate compensation and expenses of the agent or broker exceed $1000, a trustee or debtor-in -possession shall give the notice required by Local Bankruptcy Rule 2002-2. Otherwise, the compensation and expenses may be paid without further notice, subject to final review pursuant to 11 U.S.C. § 330.

RULE 2015. DUTY TO KEEP RECORDS AND MAKE REPORTS

2015-1. DUTY TO MAKE REPORTS.

A debtor's responsibility to prepare, file or serve reports shall be the obligation of the following person(s):

(a) if the debtor is a corporation, both the chief executive officer of the debtor and the chief financial officer of the debtor;

(b) if the debtor is a partnership, each general partner;

(c) the person who executed the chapter 11 petition on behalf of the debtor; and

(d) the person who executed the last operating report submitted at or prior to the hearing at which the court ruled that a chapter 11 trustee should be appointed.

2015-2. PAYMENT OF ROUTINE EXPENSES.

The trustee or debtor-in-possession is authorized, without notice or order of the court, to pay appropriate routine administrative expenses up to an aggregate of $1000. These expenses include but are not limited to expenses for adjuster services, insuring property and changing locks. Any such payments are subject to final review pursuant to 11 U.S.C. § 330.

RULE 2016. COMPENSATION FOR SERVICES RENDERED AND REIMBURSEMENT OF EXPENSES

2016-1. CASE WITH MULTIPLE PROFESSIONALS.

In a case with multiple professionals, the debtor or the debtor's counsel, if the debtor is in possession, or the trustee or the trustee's counsel shall coordinate the mailing of one notice of hearing regarding interim and final applications or compensation for all professionals employed by the estate. Local Bankruptcy Rule 2002-3 governs the form of notice.

2016-2. APPLICATION FOR ALLOWANCE OF COMPENSATION AND EXPENSES FOR PROFESSIONAL PERSONS.

(a) Applications for allowance of compensation and expenses for professional persons shall conform with Fed. R. Bankr. P. 2016. Reference should also be made to the most current guidelines of the Office of the United States Trustee for Region XV.

(b) Unless otherwise ordered by the court and except as otherwise set forth in subsection (d) below, all applications for professional fees shall comply with the United States Trustee *Guidelines for Reviewing Applications for Compensation and Reimbursement of Expenses* filed under 11 U.S.C. § 330 with categorized listings of services rendered attached as an exhibit to the application. In addition, all fee applications shall be accompanied by an analysis that substantially conforms to Local Form CSD 1143, *FEE APPLICATION SUMMARY (EXHIBIT "A").*

(c) The initial fee application must include the date of entry of the order authorizing employment and the effective date of the order.

(d) Local Bankruptcy Rule 2016-2(b) shall not apply to applications for professional fees in a chapter 13 case unless the amount of fees sought is in excess of fees set forth in the most current guidelines governing chapter 13 attorney fees issued by the Office of the United States Trustee for

Region XV in effect at the time of the application.

2016-3. FINAL FEE APPLICATIONS.

(a) All professional persons must file final fee applications.

(b) Motions for final fee awards shall contain the following:

(1) all information required of interim fee applications under Local Bankruptcy Rule 2016-2;

(2) a request for approval of all prior interim fee awards; and

(3) a request for payment of all amounts previously allowed but unpaid pursuant to Local Bankruptcy Rule 2016-2.

2016-4. ORDERS FOR COMPENSATION.

All orders for interim or final compensation of professionals shall substantially conform to Local Form CSD 1144, *ORDER APPROVING [INTERIM] [FINAL] APPLICATION OF [APPLICANT] FOR COMPENSATION AND REIMBURSEMENT OF EXPENSES* and shall include the following language:

"All fees and costs allowed by this order may be subject to disgorgement."

[The Next Rule is 3002]

RULE 3002. CLAIMS BAR DATE IN CHAPTER 7 CASES; DUTY OF CHAPTER 7 TRUSTEE; SERVICE OF CHAPTER 13 CLAIM

3002-1. DUTY OF CHAPTER 7 TRUSTEE.

As soon as it becomes apparent to a chapter 7 trustee that the liquidation of an estate will provide funds for a distribution to some class of creditors, the trustee shall immediately notify the clerk that filing proofs of claim by creditors will be required.

3002-2. SERVICE OF CHAPTER 13 CLAIM.

Proofs of claims filed in a chapter 13 case shall be served on the chapter 13 trustee, debtor and debtor's counsel.

RULE 3003. CLAIMS BAR DATE IN CHAPTER 11 CASES

3003-1. CLAIMS BAR DATE.

In a chapter 11 case, the claims bar date is fixed pursuant to Fed. R. Bankr. P. 3003 by the debtor-in-possession or other plan proponent on ex parte motion to the court in accordance with Fed. R. Bankr. P. 3003(c)(3) and Local Bankruptcy Rule 9013-6(a).

3003-2. NOTICE.

All ex parte motions to fix claims bar dates in a chapter 11 case shall contain, as an exhibit, the form of notice proposed to be given to creditors and parties in interest.

3003-3. ORDER.

All orders approving the fixing of a claims bar date in a chapter 11 case must provide that creditors will be given not less than twenty-eight (28) days notice of the last date to file proofs of claim.

[The next Rule is 3007]

RULE 3007. OBJECTION TO CLAIM

3007-1. DUTIES OF CHAPTER 13 DEBTOR.

The chapter 13 debtor shall:

(a) examine proofs of claim filed in the case or the Notice of Filed Claims prepared by the chapter 13 trustee and file objections to the allowance of any improper claim;

(b) file objections to the allowance of any late-filed claim that the debtor does not intend to pay; and

(c) appear and submit to examination at a hearing upon an objection to a claim. If the debtor fails to appear at the hearing, the court may allow the claim as filed.

3007-2. OBJECTION TO ALLOWANCE OF CLAIM.

(a) CONTENT OF OBJECTION. Unless an objection to a claim is joined with a demand for relief of the kind specified in Fed. R. Bankr. P. 7001, thus requiring the institution of an adversary proceeding, the objection shall be filed by motion in the format prescribed by Local Form CSD 2015, *OBJECTION TO CLAIM AND NOTICE THEREOF.*

(b) SERVICE. The party objecting to a claim shall give no less than thirty (30) days notice to the claimant, the debtor, and chapter 13 trustee, if applicable.

(c) PROVIDING COPY OF CLAIM. The objecting party in a chapter 13 case shall attach a copy of the claim to the objection filed with the court.

[The Next Rule is 3013]

RULE 3013. CLASSIFICATION OF CLAIMS IN CHAPTER 13 CASES

3013-1. OBJECTION TO CLASSIFICATION BY CREDITOR.

If a creditor in a chapter 13 case objects to the trustee's classification of the creditor's claim, the creditor shall file with the clerk and serve on the chapter 13 trustee an objection to the classification not later than thirty (30) days following service of the notice of classification.

[The Next Rule is 3015]

RULE 3015. CHAPTER 13 PLAN; EXTENSIONS; MODIFICATION OF OR OBJECTIONS TO CONFIRMATION OF CHAPTER 13 PLANS

3015-1. APPLICABILITY OF RULE.

This rule governs the granting of extensions of time for filing the chapter 13 plan and for filing objections to confirmation of the plan.

3015-2. DISMISSAL BY CHAPTER 12 OR 13 TRUSTEE.

(a) A motion by the chapter 12 or 13 trustee for dismissal based upon the failure of the debtor to file the plan required by Fed. R. Bankr. P. 3015 shall be noticed in accordance with Fed. R. Bankr. P. 2002 and Local Bankruptcy Rule 2002-2(a). These requirements are satisfied by including the notice of intended action within the § 341(a) meeting notice.

(b) A motion by the chapter 12 or 13 trustee to dismiss after plan confirmation may be made on notice only to the debtor and the debtor's attorney, if any.

3015-3. EXTENSION OF TIME FOR FILING.

Service on the chapter 13 trustee of a motion for extension of time to file a chapter 13 plan is governed by Local Bankruptcy Rule 9034-2.

3015-4. FORM OF OBJECTION TO CHAPTER 13 PLAN.

All objections to confirmation of any original or modified chapter 13 plan, including, but not limited to, objections of the chapter 13 trustee, shall be in writing and shall set forth with specificity all provisions of the Bankruptcy Code or Fed. R. Bankr. P. relied upon in support of the objection. Local Form CSD 1172, *OBJECTION TO CONFIRMATION OF CHAPTER 13 PLAN,* may be used to comply with this rule.

3015-5. TIME FOR FILING OBJECTION TO CHAPTER 13 PLAN.

The objecting party must obtain a hearing date from the chapter 13 trustee no later than the date the § 341(a) meeting is concluded. The objecting party must file the original and two (2) copies of its objection to confirmation, together with the notice of hearing required by Local Bankruptcy Rule

3015-8(b) and proof of service, with the clerk on the next court day following the date the § 341(a) meeting is concluded.

3015-6. DUTY TO CONFER.

The plan proponent and objecting party shall confer promptly after the § 341(a) meeting to attempt to resolve plan objections. If objections cannot be resolved, then not later than seven (7) days before the confirmation hearing, the attorneys shall file declarations stating with specificity the nature and extent of the problem, why the court's assistance is required for its resolution, and the date on which the parties conferred. No declaration is required by a chapter 13 trustee when the basis for the objection is only a failure of the debtor to make plan payments.

3015-7. MODIFICATION OF CHAPTER 13 PLAN.

(a) When modification of plan is required prior to confirmation of plan in accordance with § 1323, Local Form CSD 1170, *NOTICE OF MODIFIED CHAPTER 13 PLAN* ***PRIOR*** *TO CONFIRMATION,* may be used to comply with this rule and a copy of the modified plan shall be attached to the notice.

(b) When modification of plan is required after confirmation of plan in accordance with § 1329, Local Form CSD 1149, *NOTICE OF HEARING AND MOTION FOR APPROVAL OF DISCLOSURE STATEMENT, PLAN, OR MODIFIED PLAN,* may be used to comply with this rule and shall be filed with the original modified plan.

3015-8. CONFIRMATION HEARING.

(a) HEARING ON CONFIRMATION OF PLAN. Unless an objection to confirmation is filed in accordance with this rule, a confirmation hearing upon a chapter 13 plan will not be required.

(b) NOTICE OF HEARING.

(1) The party objecting to the confirmation of an original chapter 13 plan or a plan modified prior to confirmation must serve its objection, together with any additional documents required to be served by Local Bankruptcy Rule 9014-2 and a notice substantially conforming to Local Forms CSD 1173, *NOTICE OF HEARING ON OBJECTION TO CONFIRMATION OF CHAPTER 13 PLAN* or CSD 1170, *NOTICE OF MODIFIED CHAPTER 13 PLAN* ***PRIOR*** *TO CONFIRMATION,* on the debtor, the debtor's attorney, the chapter 13 trustee and the United States Trustee.

(2) The party objecting to the confirmation of an original chapter 13 plan or plan modified prior to confirmation must serve the objection and notice not less than twenty-eight (28) days prior to the date set for the hearing, unless the court, for good cause shown, shortens the time for notice or the trustee and debtor waive notice so that an objection can be set on the same calendar as an existing, fully noticed, objection previously set on the court's calendar.

(c) NOTIFICATION OF COURTROOM DEPUTY OF MATTERS TO BE DISMISSED. For all matters or proceedings that have been calendared for hearing, it is the duty of the attorney for the objecting party to promptly advise the parties in interest, including the chapter 13 trustee, and the chapter 13 courtroom deputy by telephone if:

(1) the objection has been settled by stipulation of the parties; or

(2) the objection is to be withdrawn; and

(3) submit for filing the proper pleading disposing of the matter within seven (7) days.

3015-9. REPLY TO OBJECTIONS.

The debtor may file a reply to an objection to confirmation of the chapter 13 plan. Any reply must be filed and received by the objecting party and chapter 13 trustee the earlier of seven (7) days after service of the opposition or three (3) *court* days prior to the date of the confirmation hearing. Service may be by facsimile upon prior agreement of the parties or upon court order. Service of a copy of the pleadings on the United States Trustee is not required. No response to a reply is permitted without court order.

3015-10. ORDER CONFIRMING PLAN; DUTY OF DEBTOR'S ATTORNEY.

The attorney for the debtor shall prepare and deliver to the chapter 13 trustee at the conclusion of the § 341(a) meeting the original and one (1) copy of an order confirming the chapter 13 plan. If a hearing on objections to confirmation results in the plan being confirmed, debtor's attorney shall deliver a confirmation order with one (1) copy to the chapter 13 trustee at the conclusion of the hearing. Any other orders resulting from the hearing shall be delivered with one (1) copy to the chapter 13 trustee at the conclusion of the hearing. Any other orders resulting from the hearing shall be delivered with one (1) copy to the chapter 13 trustee within seven (7) days of the conclusion of the hearing, unless otherwise ordered by the court.

[The Next Rule is 3017]

RULE 3017. MODIFICATION OF OR OBJECTIONS TO DISCLOSURE STATEMENT AND CHAPTER 11 OR 12 PLAN

3017-1. DOCUMENTATION OF MODIFICATIONS; DUTY OF PROPONENT.

Whenever the proponent of a plan amends either the chapter 11 disclosure statement or chapter 11 or 12 plan, the proponent shall clearly indicate on a separate copy, the added, deleted, and/or substituted language. This separate copy must be presented at the time the unmarked original of the amended document is submitted for filing. A copy with the changes indicated shall likewise be attached to the copy served on the United States Trustee and objecting parties.

RULE 3018. ACCEPTANCE OR REJECTION OF CHAPTER 11 PLAN

3018-1. RETURN OF ACCEPTANCES AND REJECTIONS.

(a) The notice of a chapter 11 confirmation hearing shall contain a statement advising creditors to return their ballots to the plan proponent, or as otherwise directed by the court.

(b) The clerk shall prepare a claims register with appropriate claim numbers and make the same available for review at least fourteen (14) days prior to the scheduled confirmation hearing only if the claims bar date has been noticed in accordance with Local Bankruptcy Rule 3003.

(c) The plan proponent shall assemble the ballots, arranged by class, keeping acceptances and rejections separate, and shall note on the lower right corner of the ballots the appropriate claim numbers to the extent that such numbers are available from the clerk. A cover page shall be added showing the case caption and titled "ACCEPTANCES TO PLAN" or "REJECTIONS TO PLAN." The ballots shall be pre-punched and securely bound at the top with a two-hole fastener.

3018-2. SUMMARY OF CLAIMS AND ACCEPTANCES AND REJECTIONS.

(a) The proponent of a chapter 11 plan shall file with the clerk all completed ballots not less than seven (7) days prior to the confirmation hearing. The proponent shall simultaneously file with the clerk and serve on the United States Trustee a summary in the form prescribed by Local Form CSD 1151, *SUMMARY OF BALLOTING ON CHAPTER 11 PLAN,* showing:

(1) the total number and amount of claims allowed by class;

(2) the total number and amount of acceptances on allowed claims by class;

(3) the total number and amount of rejections on allowed claims by class; and,

(4) if applicable, a summary of the number of acceptances and rejections filed by equity security holders whose interests have not been disallowed.

(b) The original and two (2) copies of the summary of balloting shall be filed with the clerk. One copy will be returned to the person presenting it for filing, as provided in Local Bankruptcy Rule 9004-3(n).

[The Next Rule is 3020]

RULE 3020. ESTIMATING DEPOSIT IN CHAPTER 11 CASE

3020-1. ADMINISTRATIVE EXPENSES PAYABLE TO COURT.

No less than twenty-one (21) days before the confirmation hearing, the plan proponent shall request the appropriate case administrator to provide a statement of any unpaid assessments to be collected from the debtor pursuant to Local Bankruptcy Rule 4002-3 using Local Form CSD 1148, *REQUEST FOR SPECIAL CHARGES BY CHAPTER 11 PLAN PROPONENT.*

3020-2. SCHEDULE OF ESTIMATED EXPENSES.

No less than seven (7) days before the date fixed for the confirmation hearing, the plan proponent shall file with the clerk and serve on the United States Trustee a schedule of the estimated costs of administration and any other monies required to be distributed upon the effective date of the plan, together with the documents required by Local Bankruptcy Rule 3018.

[The Next Rule is 4001]

RULE 4001. RELIEF FROM AUTOMATIC STAY; JOINDER OF PARTIES IN INTEREST; USE OF CASH COLLATERAL

4001-1. APPLICABILITY OF RULE AND ASSIGNMENT OF IDENTIFICATION NUMBER TO RELIEF FROM STAY MOTIONS.

(a) APPLICABILITY OF RULE. This rule read in conjunction with Fed. R. Bankr. P. 4001 prescribes procedures for filing motions for relief from the automatic stay pursuant to 11 U.S.C. § 362. This rule does not govern motions for use of cash collateral or to obtain credit. Such motions are governed by Fed. R. Bankr. P. 4001(b), (c) and (d) and Local Bankruptcy Rule 9014.

(b) ASSIGNMENT OF IDENTIFICATION NUMBER TO MOTIONS FOR RELIEF FROM STAY. Prior to serving the motion and the notice of motion required by this rule, the moving party shall assign an identification number to the action, inserted two lines below the case number. This number shall appear on all copies of the motion and notice of motion which are served on any party and on all subsequent pleadings relating to the motion.

(1) The Relief from Stay Number [designated as "RS No."] shall consist of not more than three initials of the attorney for moving party and the number which is one number higher than the number of relief from stay motions previously filed by said attorney in conjunction with that *specific* bankruptcy case. [*Example: the first R.S. Motion Control Number assigned by Attorney John D. Doe in the "Smith" bankruptcy case would be JDD1, the second JDD2, the third JDD3, and so on.]*

(2) This numbering sequence would be repeated for each specific bankruptcy case in which said attorney files a relief from stay motion.

4001-2. CONTENT OF MOTION FOR RELIEF FROM STAY; SERVICE.

(a) A motion for stay relief shall substantially conform to Local Forms CSD 1160, *MOTION FOR RELIEF FROM AUTOMATIC STAY (REAL PROPERTY OR PERSONAL PROPERTY),* or CSD 1163, *MOTION FOR RELIEF FROM AUTOMATIC STAY (UNLAWFUL DETAINER)* and shall:

(1) name, as respondents, the debtor, the trustee, and other entities entitled to receive notice of default or notice of sale under applicable non-bankruptcy law governing foreclosure of real or personal property which is the subject of the motion, or the agents for such parties;

(2) state with particularity the relief or order sought, and the grounds for such relief or order;

(3) state the status of any pending foreclosure or repossession;

(4) if the basis of the motion is lack of equity or adequate protection, and value is relevant, state by declaration the provable value of the subject property and the amount of any known encumbrances. The declaration shall also contain a statement as to the competency of the declarant and the foundation for any opinion therein; and

(5) if the motion is brought for cause, state by declaration or other verified pleading the specific facts that constitute such cause.

(b) Failure to set forth the information required by this rule may be grounds for denial of the relief requested.

(c) The moving party shall serve the motion, together with Local Form CSD 1185, *NOTICE OF FILING OF A MOTION FOR RELIEF FROM AUTOMATIC STAY,* on the parties named in Local Bankruptcy Rule 4001-2(a)(1) above. In a chapter 11 or 12 case, a copy of the motion shall also be served on the United States Trustee.

4001-3. TIME FOR FILING OBJECTIONS TO MOTION; DUTY OF OBJECTING PARTY TO GIVE NOTICE.

(a) Objections to a motion for relief from stay, together with Local Form CSD 1186, *REQUEST FOR HEARING ON MOTION FOR RELIEF FROM AUTOMATIC STAY AND NOTICE OF HEARING,* shall be served upon the movant, named respondents and the United States Trustee within eleven (11) days from the date of service of the motion for relief from stay and notice. The original and two (2) copies of the pleadings shall be filed with the clerk within the same 11-day period. If served by mail, opposing party shall have fourteen (14) days to serve and file such opposition as provided by Fed. R. Bankr. P. 9006(f). If the objection relates to real or personal property, the objection shall substantially conform to Local Form CSD 1161, *OPPOSITION TO MOTION FOR RELIEF FROM AUTOMATIC STAY (REAL PROPERTY OR PERSONAL PROPERTY).*

(b) Prior to serving the objection, it shall be the duty of the objecting party to obtain from the court a date and time for a hearing on the objections. Such information shall be listed on Local Form CSD 1186, *REQUEST FOR HEARING ON MOTION FOR RELIEF FROM AUTOMATIC STAY AND NOTICE OF HEARING,* and in the caption of the objection.

4001-4. CONTENT OF DECLARATION IN OPPOSITION TO MOTION.

Any declaration filed in opposition to a motion for relief from stay shall be signed and verified in the manner prescribed by Fed. R. Bankr. P. 9011 and shall:

(a) identify the interest of the opposing party in the property;

(b) state with particularity the grounds for the opposition;

(c) state the provable value of the property specified in the motion and the amount of equity which would be realized by the debtor after deduction of all encumbrances; and

(d) contain a statement as to competence of the declarant and the foundation for any opinion therein.

4001-5. CONTENT OF ORDER.

(a) NONCONTESTED MOTION. If no objection to the motion for stay relief is timely filed and served, the moving party may submit to the court an appropriate order which substantially conforms to Local Forms CSD 1162, *ORDER ON NONCONTESTED MOTION FOR RELIEF FROM AUTOMATIC STAY (REAL PROPERTY OR PERSONAL PROPERTY)*, or CSD 1165, *ORDER ON NONCONTESTED MOTION FOR RELIEF FROM AUTOMATIC STAY (UNLAWFUL DETAINER)*. The order shall have attached thereto as Exhibit "A" a file-stamped copy of the notice and proof of service required by Local Bankruptcy Rule 4001-2(c) and shall state:

(1) the date the motion was filed;

(2) the particularity of the relief to be granted; and,

(3) if pertaining to real property, provide a full legal description and any street address for the property.

(b) CONTESTED MOTION. At the conclusion of the hearing on a contested motion for stay relief, the prevailing party shall submit an order in accordance with Local Bankruptcy Rule 7054-3.

(c) STIPULATED MOTION. An order approving a motion for approval of a stipulation for relief from stay shall comply with Local Bankruptcy Rule 4001-5(a) and, in chapter 11 cases, provide evidence of compliance with Fed. R. Bankr. P. 4001(d)(1) and (2).

4001-6. SERVICE OF ORDER.

Upon receipt of the entered order and in addition to serving the parties listed in Local Bankruptcy Rule 7054-3(b)(2), the party obtaining stay relief shall mail a conformed copy of the entered order to any persons affected by the order and shall file proof of service with the court no later than the next business day following the date of service.

4001-7. POINTS AND AUTHORITIES.

A motion for relief from the automatic stay, or opposition to the same, need not be accompanied by points and authorities. If points and authorities are filed, they may be incorporated, if so desired, into one captioned pleading containing the supporting or opposing papers.

4001-8. CONTENT OF NOTICE; EX PARTE RELIEF.

Service of Form CSD 1185 is excused when an ex parte motion for relief from stay is otherwise in compliance with the provisions of Fed. R. Bankr. P. 4001(a)(2).

4001-9. DUTY TO CONFER.

The moving and objecting parties shall confer, at least three (3) business days prior to the hearing, to discuss the potential for resolving the matter.

RULE 4002. DUTIES AND COMPENSATION OF DEBTOR

4002-1. SAFEKEEPING OF BOOKS AND RECORDS.

(a) SAFEKEEPING OF BOOKS AND RECORDS. The debtor shall maintain, preserve and keep in safe storage all of the debtor's books and records during the time the case remains open.

(b) TURNOVER OF BOOKS AND RECORDS. Upon request, the debtor shall make the debtor's books and records immediately available to the trustee, the United States Trustee or their designated agents.

(c) LIMITATION OF DISPOSITION.

(1) After the books and records of the debtor are no longer necessary for the administration of the case, the trustee may give thirty (30) days notice to the debtor and debtor's attorney, if any, that said books and records may be disposed of if not claimed within that thirty (30) day period.

(2) Upon notice to the debtor, trustee and United States Trustee, regulatory or governmental entities may apply to the court for permission to take possession and provide for the maintenance and safekeeping of books and records at the expense of the agency.

(3) Upon written notification that an investigation is contemplated or pending by a regulatory or governmental entity, the trustee shall retain any books and records except upon sixty (60) days notice to such entity.

4002-2. COMPENSATION OF DEBTOR AND INSIDERS.

(a) COMPENSATION. Except in chapter 13 cases, no compensation or other remuneration shall be paid to the debtor or any insider unless approved by the court, after notice of intended action to all creditors. See

Local Bankruptcy Rule 2002-2.

(b) EX PARTE INTERIM ORDERS. For cause shown, the court may approve compensation to the debtor or insider from a corporation, partnership, sole proprietorship or other entity owned or controlled by the debtor on an interim basis pending the expiration of the notice period prescribed under subsection (a) of this rule, provided that such compensation may be subject to disgorgement. The ex parte motion for interim compensation shall:

(1) state the date the notice required by subsection (a) was given;

(2) include a personal income and expense declaration for the applicant, where such applicant is an individual, partner, or insider of the debtor;

(3) state the nature and extent of the duties to be performed by the person to be compensated;

(4) state the compensation received from the debtor by the person to be compensated during the one year preceding the date the chapter 11 or 12 petition was filed;

(5) state whether operating reports are due or current;

(6) be accompanied by a proposed order.

(c) STATEMENT OF UNITED STATES TRUSTEE. Service on the United States Trustee of the motion for interim compensation is governed by Local Bankruptcy Rule 9034-1.

4002-3. PAYMENT OF SPECIAL ASSESSMENTS FOR NOTICES MAILED AND PROOFS OF CLAIM PROCESSED BY CLERK.

The clerk shall collect from each debtor-in-possession and each chapter 11 or 12 trustee the cost incurred by the clerk in mailing notices and processing proofs of claim in the amount prescribed by the Judicial Conference of the United States. Failure to pay the required assessment may result in the denial of an order allowing compensation, or the conversion or dismissal of the case.

4002-4. DEPOSIT OF FUNDS WITH CHAPTER 12 TRUSTEE.

The debtor shall deposit with the chapter 12 trustee the sum of $200 within thirty (30) days following the date of filing a petition under chapter 12. The funds are to be used to defray the cost of the bond premium and other expenses of the trustee, subject to final review pursuant to 11 U.S.C.

§ 330.

RULE 4003. OBJECTIONS TO CLAIM OF EXEMPTION

4003-1. PROCEDURE.

Objections to any claim of exemption, as provided in Fed. R. Bankr. P. 4003(b), shall be governed by Local Bankruptcy Rule 9014.

[The Next Rule is 4007]

RULE 4007. MOTION FOR EXTENSION OF TIME FOR FILING COMPLAINT FOR DETERMINATION OF DISCHARGEABILITY OF A DEBT

4007-1. PROCEDURE.

A motion to extend the time to file a complaint to determine the dischargeability of any debt pursuant to 11 U.S.C. § 523(c) shall be filed pursuant to Local Bankruptcy Rule 9013 and shall be served on the debtor, counsel for the debtor, and the trustee.

RULE 4008. REAFFIRMATION AGREEMENTS

4008-1. PROCEDURE.

The presiding officer at a chapter 7 § 341(a) meeting shall provide a copy of Local Form CSD 1230, *INSTRUCTIONS TO UNREPRESENTED DEBTORS REGARDING THE REAFFIRMATION OF A DEBT,* to each debtor appearing without an attorney and a copy of Local Form CSD 1227, INSTRUCTIONS TO DEBTORS REPRESENTED BY AN ATTORNEY REGARDING THE REAFFIRMATION OF A DEBT, to all other debtors.

RULE 5005. FACSIMILE FILINGS

5005-1. METHOD OF FILING.

A fax filing agency will file all fax transmitted pleadings on behalf of the parties or their counsel. NO DOCUMENTS MAY BE TRANSMITTED DIRECTLY TO THE CLERK BY FAX FOR FILING. ANY DOCUMENTS SO TRANSMITTED SHALL BE REJECTED AND NOT FILED.

(a) The fax filing agency acts as the agent of the filing party and not as agent of the court. A document shall be deemed to be filed when it is submitted by the fax filing agency, received in the Clerk's office, and filed by the Clerk. Mere transmission to or receipt by the fax filing agency will not be construed as filing.

(b) The fax filing agency must meet all technical requirements under Local Bankruptcy Rule 9004.

(c) Counsel or parties utilizing a fax filing agency will ensure that additional copies necessary for filing shall be reproduced by the fax filing agency and any applicable filing fees are submitted at the time of filing.

5005-2. WHEN FILED.

Electronic transmission of a document via facsimile machine does not constitute filing. Filing is complete when the document is filed with the Clerk.

5005-3. FORM, PAPER, LEGIBILITY.

Only plain paper (no thermal paper) facsimile machines may be used. All documents shall be on size 8-1/2" x 11" bond. All copies shall be clear, clean and legible, and comply with Local Bankruptcy Rule 9004.

5005-4. ORIGINAL SIGNATURE.

The image of the original manual signature on the fax copy will constitute an original signature for all court purposes. The original signed document shall not be substituted except by court order. The original signed document shall be maintained by the attorney of record or the party originating the document for a period not less than the maximum allowable time to complete the appellate process. Upon request, the original document must be provided to other parties or the court for review.

5005-5. TRANSMISSION RECORD.

The sending party is required to maintain a transmission record in the event fax filing later becomes an issue. A transmission record means the document printed by the sending facsimile machine stating the telephone number of the receiving machine, the number of pages sent, the transmission time, and an indication of errors in transmission.

[The Next Rule is 5010]

RULE 5010. MOTION TO REOPEN A CASE

5010-1. MOTION; NOTICE.

A motion to reopen a closed bankruptcy case shall be accompanied by appropriate declarations required by Local Bankruptcy Rule 9013-2 and Local Form CSD 1182, *NOTICE OF MOTION,* together with proof of service on all parties affected by the proposed action.

5010-2. ORDER; FEE.

After expiration of the last day for serving and filing objections or after hearing, the moving party shall submit Local Form CSD 1490, *ORDER REOPENING ESTATE,* together with the appropriate filing fee. The order shall be submitted in accordance with Local Bankruptcy Rule 7054-3, if contested, or Local Bankruptcy Rule 9013-7, if noncontested.

RULE 5011. WITHDRAWAL OF REFERENCE; ABSTENTION

5011-1. WITHDRAWAL OF REFERENCE.

(a) A motion to withdraw reference of a case or proceeding referred to the bankruptcy court in accordance with 28 U.S.C. § 157(a) must be filed initially with the bankruptcy court clerk.

(b) All responses to a motion to withdraw reference shall be filed within fourteen (14) days from service of motion with the bankruptcy court clerk. After the fourteen (14) day period has expired, the motion and any responses shall be forwarded to the district court clerk for issuance of a case number and assignment to a judge. All further pleadings regarding the matter shall be filed with the district court clerk.

(c) The district court judge has general discretionary authority to withdraw any petition or proceeding from a bankruptcy judge, provided:

(1) The motion for withdrawal is timely made; and

(2) the movant shows good cause for withdrawal.

(d) The motion to withdraw and the response thereto, shall list all motions, adversary proceedings and related cases pending in the bankruptcy court and their assigned number, and shall state:

(1) whether the request is to withdraw reference of the entire case or proceeding, or only a part thereof;

(2) whether the matter to be withdrawn involves similar issues previously determined or presently pending by the bankruptcy court in the same or related case;

(3) whether substantial discovery has been completed in the action;

(4) whether the presentation of evidence has begun before the bankruptcy court;

(5) whether movant is a creditor and is listed in the debtor's schedules; and

(6) when the movant first became aware of the bankruptcy case or proceeding and its interest therein.

5011-2. ABSTENTION.

Motions for abstention under 28 U.S.C. § 1334(c) are to be filed in the bankruptcy court clerk's office. Such motions are governed by Local Bankruptcy Rule 9014 and calendared for hearing before the bankruptcy court.

[The Next Rule is 6004]

RULE 6004. USE, SALE OR LEASE OF PROPERTY NOT IN THE ORDINARY COURSE OF BUSINESS

6004-1. REQUIRED NOTICE.

Notices required by Fed. R. Bankr. P. 6004 shall be provided pursuant to Local Bankruptcy Rule 2002-2.

6004-2. PUBLICATION OF NOTICE.

(a) If an advertisement of sale is required by the court, any such advertisements of sale shall be published in publications most likely to reach interested purchasers; provided, however, that when the anticipated costs of publication will exceed five (5) percent of the estimated sales proceeds, an ex parte motion and proposed order shall be submitted to the court.

(b) *The San Diego Daily Transcript,* of San Diego, California and *The Post-Press,* of El Centro, California are designated as official newspapers for publication of all notices required to be published in bankruptcy matters and of all other notices required to be published by law or order of this court, unless otherwise ordered by this court.

6004-3. REPORT OF SALE.

A court order is not required to consummate a noncontested sale, but the trustee or debtor-in-possession shall file a report of sale as required by Fed. R. Bankr. P. 6004(f) within a reasonable amount of time.

(a) SALE OF REAL PROPERTY.

(1) The person selling real property shall include a full legal description and any street address for the property in the report required by Fed. R. Bankr. P. 6004(f) (see Local Form CSD 2024, *REPORT OF SALE*); and

(2) The trustee or debtor-in-possession shall attach a copy of the escrow statement or other documentation to the final report and accounting showing distribution of the total proceeds of sale.

(b) SERVICE OF REPORT. A copy of the report of sale shall be served on the debtor, United States Trustee, and any official creditors' committee.

6004-4. APPOINTMENT OF A CONSUMER PRIVACY OMBUDSMAN.

(a) Any motion to sell or lease personally identifiable information shall be accompanied by a separate motion and order directing the United States Trustee to appoint a consumer privacy ombudsman. The movant shall provide telephonic notice of the filing of the motion within twenty-four (24) hours to the United States Trustee.

(b) The United States Trustee shall file a notice of the appointment of a privacy ombudsman not less than fourteen (14) days prior to the hearing on the motion to sell or lease personally identifiable information unless otherwise directed by the court.

(c) Not later than seven (7) days before the hearing, the ombudsman shall file a report unless otherwise ordered by the court.

RULE 6005. APPOINTMENT OF AUCTIONEERS

6005-1. CONTENT OF APPLICATION AND ORDER.

(a) AUCTIONEER. An application and order for the appointment of an auctioneer shall comply with Fed. R. Bankr. P. 6005 and conform to Local Forms CSD 2044, *APPLICATION TO EMPLOY AUCTIONEER,* and CSD 2045, *ORDER APPOINTING AUCTIONEER.*

(b) ADDITIONAL REQUIREMENTS. The trustee or debtor-in-possession shall attach to the application required by subsection (a) of this rule:

(1) a detailed explanation of anticipated expenses;

(2) a verified statement of the proposed auctioneer as required by Fed. R. Bankr. P. 2014(a) and 2016(a); and

(3) statement of the maximum amount of compensation to be paid for services.

6005-2. STATEMENT OF UNITED STATES TRUSTEE.

Service on the United States Trustee of the application for the appointment of an auctioneer is governed by Local Bankruptcy Rule 9034-1.

6005-3. DUTY OF AUCTIONEER.

Immediately after completing the auction, and before receiving any compensation or reimbursement of expenses, the auctioneer shall serve on the trustee or debtor-in-possession and file with the clerk:

(a) the auctioneer's report required by Fed. R. Bankr. P. 6004(f); and

(b) a detailed itemization of compensation and actual expenses.

6005-4. PAYMENT OF COMPENSATION.

To the extent the aggregate compensation and expenses of the auctioneer exceed $1000, a trustee or debtor-in-possession shall give the notice required by Local Bankruptcy Rule 2002-2. Otherwise, the compensation and expenses may be paid without further notice, subject to final review pursuant to 11 U.S.C. § 330.

[The Next Rule is 6007]

RULE 6007. ABANDONMENT OR DISPOSITION OF PROPERTY

6007-1. APPLICABILITY OF RULE.

This rule is to be read in conjunction with Fed. R. Bankr. P. 6007 and applies to all cases under chapters 7, 11, 12, and 13.

6007-2. NOTICE REQUIREMENTS.

(a) VOLUNTARY ABANDONMENT.

(1) PROPERTY WITH TOTAL VALUE OF LESS THAN $2,500. When the property to be abandoned has a total value of less than $2,500, the trustee or debtor-in-possession shall give notice of the proposed abandonment to the following: the debtor; the debtor's attorney; the United States Trustee; any other entity entitled to receive notice of default or notice of sale under applicable non-bankruptcy laws governing foreclosure of the real or personal property which is the subject of the motion, or the agents for such parties; and to any committees appointed or elected pursuant to the Bankruptcy Code.

(2) PROPERTY WITH TOTAL VALUE OF $2,500 OR MORE. When the property to be abandoned has a total value of $2,500 or more, the trustee or debtor-in-possession shall give notice of the proposed abandonment pursuant to Local Bankruptcy Rule 2002-2.

(b) MOTION BY PARTY IN INTEREST. A party in interest may file and serve a motion requiring the trustee or debtor-in-possession to abandon property of the estate. The motion and notice shall comply with Local Bankruptcy Rule 9013.

6007-3. PROCEDURE FOLLOWING NOTICE OF ABANDONMENT.

(a) VOLUNTARY ABANDONMENT.

(1) PERSONAL PROPERTY. Where a voluntary abandonment of personal property is not contested in a timely manner, the trustee or debtor-in-possession need only file the notice required by Local Bankruptcy Rule 2002-2(c) and proof of service; no further report need be filed.

(2) REAL PROPERTY. Where a voluntary abandonment or real property is not contested in a timely manner, the trustee or debtor-in-possession shall file Local Form CSD 2018, *REPORT OF ABANDONMENT OF REAL PROPERTY.*

(3) PROOF OF SERVICE. Proof of service required by this subsection shall be attached to the original showing service on the debtor and United States Trustee.

(b) CONTESTED ABANDONMENT. Local Bankruptcy Rule 9014 governs when a proposed abandonment, whether voluntary or on motion, is contested.

[The Next Rule is 7003]

RULE 7003. COMMENCEMENT OF ADVERSARY PROCEEDING; ADDITIONAL REQUIREMENTS

7003-1. COMMENCEMENT OF ADVERSARY PROCEEDINGS.

(a) DOCUMENTS REQUIRED TO COMMENCE AN ADVERSARY PROCEEDING. A complaint commencing an adversary proceeding is filed with the bankruptcy court clerk. Pleadings shall be prepared in the manner required by Local Bankruptcy Rule 9004-3. The court requires:

(1) the original and two (2) copies of Form B 104, *ADVERSARY PROCEEDING COVER SHEET,* and the complaint; and

(2) the original and two (2) copies of the completed Local Form CSD 3007, *SUMMONS IN AN ADVERSARY PROCEEDING.*

(b) ASSIGNMENT. Adversary proceedings shall be assigned to the bankruptcy judge assigned to the related Title 11 case.

(c) NOTICE OF RELATED CASE. Where counsel has reason to believe that a pending action or proceeding on file or about to be filed is related to another pending action or proceeding on file with the court, counsel shall promptly file and serve on all known parties to each related action or proceeding, a notice of related case, stating the title, number and filing date of each action or proceeding believed to be related, together with a brief statement of their relationship and the reasons why assignment to a single judge is likely to effect a saving of judicial effort and other economies. The clerk will promptly notify the assigned judges of such filing.

7003-2. JURY TRIAL.

If a complaint or answer contains a demand for a jury trial, the words "JURY DEMAND" shall also appear immediately following the title of the document. The words "JURY DEMAND" shall also be noted on the cover sheet required by Local Bankruptcy Rule 7003-1(a)(1). However, notation of the jury demand solely on the cover sheet shall not constitute a demand for jury trial under these rules.

RULE 7004. PROCESS ISSUANCE AND SERVICE

7004-1. SERVICE OF PROCESS.

(a) PRESENTATION OF SUMMONS FOR ISSUANCE.

(1) Local Form CSD 3007, *SUMMONS IN AN ADVERSARY PROCEEDING,* shall be prepared by the attorney, using forms supplied by the clerk, and presented concurrently with the filing of a complaint or petition commencing the action.

(2) If the statute of limitations applicable to a claim in the complaint runs before the summons can be prepared and issued, the complaint shall be accepted by the clerk for filing without a summons. The summons shall thereafter be presented for issuance within seven (7) days after the filing of the complaint.

(b) ALIAS SUMMONS. An alias summons must be issued if a summons is not timely served within the 14-day period provided in Fed. R. Bankr. P. 7004(f). The alias summons shall be prepared by counsel pursuant to Local Form CSD 3007, *SUMMONS IN AN ADVERSARY PROCEEDING,* with the word "ALIAS" typed above the word "SUMMONS" in the title and presented to the clerk along with a written request for the issuance of the alias summons. Service of an alias summons is governed by Fed. R. Bankr. P. 7004(e) as if it were an original summons.

RULE 7005. SERVICE OF PLEADINGS

7005-1. SERVICE OF PLEADINGS OTHER THAN PROCESS.

Service of an amended complaint, a counterclaim, a cross-claim, or a third-party complaint shall be made upon each new party to the litigation, whether or not multiple parties are represented by a single attorney. Service of all other pleadings authorized to be served under Fed. R. Bankr. P. 7005 shall be sufficient when served upon the attorney for a party, if the party is in fact represented by an attorney. Except as provided in this rule, where an attorney represents multiple parties, service of one (1) copy of a pleading shall constitute service of all parties represented by that attorney, unless the court otherwise orders.

[The Next Rule is 7012]

RULE 7012. ANSWER

7012-1. CONTENT.

Each statement of fact shall be made in numbered paragraphs which shall be limited, as far as practicable, to a statement of a single set of circumstances. Responsive pleadings shall contain numbered paragraphs, each of which corresponds to the paragraph to which it is directed.

[The Next Rule is 7016]

RULE 7016. PRE-TRIAL PROCEDURES

7016-1. APPLICABILITY OF RULE.

Pre-trial proceedings and setting of cases for trial shall be governed by Fed. R. Bankr. P. 7016 and this Rule, and by such orders as are issued pursuant thereto.

7016-2. EARLY CONFERENCE OF COUNSEL.

(a) TIME OF EARLY CONFERENCE. In all proceedings governed by Part VII of the Fed. R. Bankr. P., the parties shall comply with this Local Bankruptcy Rule, unless all defendants have defaulted. The plaintiff shall serve with the summons and complaint, a notice that compliance with this rule is required and a copy of Local Form CSD 3018, *CERTIFICATE OF COMPLIANCE WITH EARLY CONFERENCE OF COUNSEL.* The plaintiff shall file the proof of service of the notice together with the proof of service of the summons and complaint within the time provided by Local Bankruptcy Rule 9006-3. Counsel for the parties shall confer for the purposes set forth below. Such conference shall take place no later than thirty (30) days after the date all defendants have appeared or defaulted or forty-five (45) days from the date of the first appearance of any defendant, whichever occurs first. Where there are multiple defendants, plaintiff or its counsel shall take all reasonable steps to schedule the meeting or conference call so that counsel for all parties can attend. Where necessary, in multi-defendant cases and upon a showing of good cause, the court may grant an application for an extension of time within which to hold the early meeting.

(b) PURPOSE OF CONFERENCE. At the conference required by this Rule, the parties shall:

(1) DOCUMENTS. Exchange all documents and make all disclosures required by Fed. R. Bankr. P. 7026(a)(1) or fix a date to make such exchange.

(2) DISCOVERY. Develop a discovery plan using Exhibit A to Local Form 3018, *CERTIFICATE OF COMPLIANCE.*

(3) OTHER EVIDENCE. Exchange any other evidence then reasonably available to a party to obviate the filing of unnecessary discovery motions.

(4) LIST OF WITNESSES. Exchange a list of witnesses then known to have knowledge of the facts supporting the material allegations of the pleading filed by the party. The parties will then be under a continuing obligation to advise the opposing party of other witnesses as they may become known.

(5) SETTLEMENT. Discuss settlement possibilities, including the parties' willingness to go to mediation. If mediation agreed to, designate the first choice and alternate choice of mediator, using court-maintained mediator list or other mutually acceptable mediator. A list of mediators is available from the Office of the Clerk or on the court's website, *www.casb.uscourts.gov.*

(c) CERTIFICATE OF COMPLIANCE AND NOTICE OF HEARING FOR PRE-TRIAL STATUS CONFERENCE. No later than seven (7) days after the Early Conference of Counsel or Parties, a joint *CERTIFICATE OF COMPLIANCE*, Local Form CSD 3018, signed by all parties or counsel shall be filed by the counsel for the plaintiff together with Local Form CSD 3019, *NOTICE OF PRE-TRIAL STATUS CONFERENCE.* In advance of filing said *NOTICE OF PRE-TRIAL STATUS CONFERENCE*, it shall be the responsibility of the plaintiff or its counsel to obtain a hearing date for the pre-trial status conference form the courtroom deputy and serve said notice on all other parties.

7016-3. SETTING AND NOTICE.

After obtaining a hearing date from the courtroom deputy, plaintiff or counsel for the plaintiff shall give notice setting a pre-trial status conference on the calendar of the judge to whom the underlying bankruptcy case has been assigned.

7016-4. DISCUSSION OF MEDIATION ALTERNATIVES.

Prior to the pre-trial status conference, counsel shall confer with the client and discuss the mediation program, and shall ask the client for authorization to participate in the mediation program.

7016-5. STATUS CONFERENCE.

(a) Each party appearing at the status conference shall be represented by an attorney (or the party, if unrepresented) who is expected to conduct the trial on behalf of such party.

(b) Parties appearing at the status conference shall be prepared to discuss the following:

(1) state of discovery, including a description of completed discovery and a detailed schedule of all further discovery contemplated;

(2) a discovery cut-off date;

(3) a schedule of contemplated law and motion matters;

(4) prospects for settlement;

(5) whether the client has given authorization to participate in the mediation program as described in Local Bankruptcy Rule 7016-6;

(6) any other issues affecting the status or management of the case.

7016-6. MEDIATION PANEL PROCEDURES.

(a) LISTS OF MEDIATORS. The judges of the court shall establish and maintain two lists of qualified persons who agree to serve as mediators in contested matters and adversary proceedings pending before the court. One list shall contain the names of those mediators who are entitled to compensation as outlined below (Compensated Mediation Panel), and the other will contain those who will serve without compensation (Voluntary Mediation Panel).

(b) VOLUNTARY MEDIATION PANEL. To volunteer for this program, a person shall submit an application to the San Diego County Bar Association, which in turn shall submit the same to the clerk. The application shall set forth the qualifications described in subsection (1) or (2) and shall conform in format to Local Form CSD 4001, *APPLICATION TO JOIN VOLUNTARY MEDIATION PANEL.*

(1) ATTORNEY QUALIFICATIONS. In order to qualify for service on the Voluntary Mediation Panel, an attorney shall certify to the court that the attorney meets the following minimum qualifications:

(A) the attorney is an active member of the State Bar of California and is duly licensed to practice before the courts of the State of California and the Federal courts for the Southern District of California;

(B) the attorney has been admitted to practice in a state court for at least four (4) years; and

(C) the attorney has served as the attorney of record for at least three (3) bankruptcy cases from commencement through conclusion (i.e.; confirmation of a plan or discharge) or has served as the attorney of record for a party in interest for at least three (3) or more adversary proceedings or contested matters from commencement through completion (i.e.; judgment, order, or stipulated settlement); or has had other substantially equivalent bankruptcy experience.

(2) NON-ATTORNEY QUALIFICATIONS. In order to qualify for service on the Voluntary Mediation Panel, a non-attorney shall certify to the court that the following qualifications are met:

(A) the person is a member of the panel of trustees or examiners maintained by the Office of the United States Trustee; or

(B) the person is a Certified Public Accountant in the State of California; and

(C) in addition, the person complying with the requirements of subsection (A) or (B) above shall also demonstrate service to a bankruptcy estate in at least ten (10) asset estates as trustee, and/or in at least ten (10) cases as bankruptcy examiner or accountant for a trustee or debtor-in-possession from commencement through completion of such case; or has other substantially equivalent bankruptcy experience.

(c) COMPENSATED MEDIATION PANEL.

(1) To apply for this program, a person shall submit an application to the San Diego County Bar Association, which in turn shall submit the same to the clerk. The application shall set forth the qualifications described in subsection (A) and (B) below and shall conform in format to Local Form CSD 4000, *APPLICATION TO JOIN COMPENSATED*

MEDIATION PANEL. Effective September 8, 1997, mediators shall be entitled to join the Compensated Mediation Panel if they have completed twenty-five (25) hours of mediation training provided by the San Diego Mediation Center or an equivalent qualified training center consistent with the California Dispute Resolution Act (Title 16 California Code of Regulations, Sections 3615 through 3635, and Sections 465 through 467.7 of the California Business Professions Code). In addition, mediators seeking compensation must, within the calendar year preceding the year in which the mediation is conducted, satisfy one of the following:

(A) conduct two (2) bankruptcy mediations or six (6) hours of mediation from any source; or,

(B) attend a half-day refresher program provided by the San Diego Mediation Center or an equivalent qualified center consistent with the California Dispute Resolution Act.

(2) No later than December 15 of the year prior to the calendar year they will conduct compensated mediation, compensated mediators must submit to the Chief Judge of the Bankruptcy Court a renewal application for service on the Compensated Mediation Panel which certifies that they have satisfied the requirements set forth herein.

(d) LISTS OF ELIGIBLE MEDIATORS. Two lists of eligible mediators shall be submitted to the clerk once per calendar quarter by the San Diego County Bar Association.

(1) The lists to be submitted no later than March 15 shall be effective from April 1 through June 30.

(2) The lists to be submitted no later than June 15 shall be effective from July 1 through September 30.

(3) The lists to be submitted no later than September 15 shall be effective from October 1 through December 31.

(4) The lists to be submitted no later than December 15 shall be effective from January 1 through March 31 of the following year.

(e) ASSIGNMENT TO MEDIATION.

(1) A case may be assigned to mediation by order of the court at a status conference or other hearing. If a case is assigned to mediation, the parties attending the status conference shall be presented with the current lists of eligible mediators. If the parties cannot agree, the court shall appoint a mediator and alternates from the lists.

(2) Local Form CSD 4002, *ORDER APPOINTING MEDIATOR AND ASSIGNMENT TO MEDIATION,* shall be used to assign a matter to mediation. The original shall be retained in the court's file. The clerk will mail a copy to the mediator and to each party.

(f) MEDIATION PROCEDURE.

(1) TIME AND PLACE. The mediator shall fix the time and place for the mediation conference, and any adjourned session. The time and place selected shall be reasonably convenient for the parties, and the parties shall be given at least fourteen (14) days written notice of the initial conference. The conference shall be scheduled as soon as practicable but in no event more than forty-five (45) days after the mediator has been notified of the appointment. The mediator may, upon written stipulation of the parties filed with the court, grant one continuance of the conference, provided that the continuance granted does not extend the date of the conference to a date more than seventy-five (75) days after the mediator has been notified of the appointment.

(2) SUBMISSION OF COMPLETED CASE QUESTIONNAIRES. Each party shall provide the mediator with a completed case questionnaire in the format of Local Form CSD 4003, *CASE QUESTIONNAIRE IN CONNECTION WITH MEDIATION PROCEDURE.* The case questionnaire shall be served on the mediator and all other parties not less than seven (7) calendar days prior to the date noticed for the mediation conference as set forth in subsection (1) above.

(3) ATTENDANCE AND PREPARATION REQUIRED. The attorney who is primarily responsible for each party's case shall personally attend the mediation conference and any adjourned sessions of that conference. The attorney for each party shall come prepared to discuss the following in detail and in good faith:

(A) all liability issues;

(B) all damage issues; and

(C) the position of their client relative to settlement.

(4) MEDIATION COMPENSATION. A mediator who meets the requirements of paragraph (c) above is entitled to compensation at the rate of $200 per each half-day mediation session except, however, for the first half-day of the mediation session (3.5 hours) which shall be conducted free of charge. The mediation fee shall be borne equally by all parties attending the mediation. The $200 fee is to be paid at the beginning of each successive session. Unrepresented litigants are required to pay in cash or by cashiers check. Those parties represented by an attorney may pay with a check from the attorney's account.

(5) PARTIES TO BE AVAILABLE. All individual parties who reside within the County of San Diego shall personally attend the mediation conference unless excused by the mediator for cause. Parties, other than individuals, whose principal place of business is located in San Diego County, shall have a representative appear with authority to settle. Individuals and other parties who neither reside in San Diego County nor have their principal place of business located therein, shall be available for conference with their counsel to the mediator by telephone. The mediator shall decide when the parties are to be present in the conference room.

(6) FAILURE TO ATTEND. Willful or unexcused failure to attend the mediation conference shall be reported to the court by the mediator and may result in the imposition of sanctions by the court.

(7) PROCEEDINGS PRIVILEGED. All proceedings or writings of the mediation conference, including the case questionnaire, mediator's settlement recommendation, plus any statement made by any party, attorney or other participant, shall in all respects be privileged and not reported, recorded, placed in evidence, made known to the trial court or jury or construed for any purpose as an admission against interest. No party shall be bound by anything said or done at the conference unless a settlement is reached, in which event the agreement upon a settlement shall be reduced to writing and shall be binding upon all parties to that agreement. Federal Rule of Evidence 408 applies herein. A report of a failure to attend a mediation conference does not fall within this privilege.

(8) DUTY OF COUNSEL. The client shall be advised of the fact that the mediator is a qualified person and has volunteered to act as an impartial mediator, without compensation, in an attempt to help the parties reach an agreement and avoid the time, expense and uncertainty of trial. If the mediator makes any oral or written suggestions as to the advisability of a change in any party's position with respect to settlement, the attorney for that party shall promptly transmit that suggestion to the client.

(9) DUTY OF MEDIATOR. The mediator shall have the duty and authority to establish the time schedule for mediation activities, including a schedule for the parties to act upon the mediator's recommendation, having in mind that the purpose of this order is prompt dispute resolution. The mediator shall have no obligation to make any written comments or recommendations, but may have the discretion to provide a written settlement recommendation memorandum. No copy of any such memorandum shall be filed with the clerk or made available in whole or in part, directly or indirectly, either to the court and/or the jury.

(g) PROCEDURE UPON COMPLETION OF MEDIATION SESSION. Upon the conclusion of the first mediation session where all parties are in attendance, the following procedures shall be followed:

(1) If the parties have reached an agreement regarding the disposition of the proceeding, the parties shall designate a party to prepare a stipulation to dismiss, or enter a judgment on agreed terms, or continue the mediation session to a date convenient to all parties and the mediator. The party preparing the stipulation shall submit the stipulation, once fully executed by all parties, to the court for approval.

(2) The mediator shall prepare and file with the clerk, within fourteen (14) days, a Local Form CSD 4004, *MEDIATOR'S CERTIFICATE OF COMPLIANCE,* indicating whether a settlement was reached, and, if so, whether there was compliance with the settlement and mediation requirements of this rule.

7016-7. PREPARATION FOR FINAL PRE-TRIAL CONFERENCE.

(a) MEETINGS OF COUNSEL. The attorneys for the parties shall convene at a suitable time and place not later than fourteen (14) days in advance of the final pre-trial conference. The purpose of the meeting shall be to arrive at stipulations and reach agreements resulting in simplification of the triable issues. Counsel for the plaintiff shall have the duty of arranging for meetings of counsel and for preparation of the pre-trial order mandated by Local Bankruptcy Rule 7016-9.

(b) EXCHANGES BETWEEN COUNSEL. At the meeting, the following information shall be displayed and/or exchanged:

(1) exhibits other than those designed solely for purposes of impeachment or rebuttal; and

(2) lists of the names and addresses of witnesses, including experts, who will be called at trial (exclusive of witnesses whose testimony is to be used solely for purposes of impeachment or rebuttal).

(c) CONTENT OF EXHIBITS EXCHANGED. Each photograph, map, drawing and the like shall contain a legend on its face or reverse side. The legend shall state by date the matters of fact which the party offering the exhibit claims are fairly depicted.

(d) FAILURE TO DISPLAY AND/OR EXCHANGE EXHIBITS OR LISTS. Failure to display and/or exchange exhibits or lists to or with opposing counsel shall permit the court to decline admission of same into evidence.

7016-8. CONDUCT OF THE FINAL PRE-TRIAL CONFERENCE.

At the final pre-trial conference, the court shall consider and, where appropriate, rule upon:

(a) the pleadings, proposed amendments to the pleadings, papers and exhibits, stipulations, statements, memoranda and all other matters referred to in Fed. R. Bankr. P. 7016;

(b) all properly noticed motions and other proceedings then pending;

(c) the possibilities for settlement and other matters which may be presented concerning parties, process, pleading or proof, with a view to simplifying issues and bringing about a just, speedy and inexpensive determination; and

(d) future and additional pre-trial meetings where required and, upon termination of the final pre-trial conference, the date to be set for trial.

7016-9. PRE-TRIAL ORDER.

(a) RESPONSIBILITY OF PLAINTIFF'S COUNSEL. Plaintiff's counsel shall be responsible for preparing the pre-trial order and arranging the meetings of counsel attendant thereto. Plaintiff's counsel shall thereafter file the prepared pre-trial order with the clerk no later than seven (7) days prior to the final pre-trial conference.

(b) FORMAT. Attorneys for all parties appearing in the case shall approve the pre-trial order as to form and substance. The format of the order shall substantially conform to Local Form CSD 3021, *PRE-TRIAL ORDER*.

(c) ABANDONED ISSUES. Each party shall set forth a statement of any issues which have been abandoned.

(d) UNRESOLVED ISSUES OF FACT AND LAW. The parties shall agree upon a joint, and not separately listed, statement of issues of fact and law which remain to be litigated. Where there is disagreement as to whether a particular fact or point of law is in issue, that fact or point of law shall be deemed to be in issue and, therefore, to be litigated.

(e) EXHIBITS. Each party shall prepare a list of all exhibits such party expects to offer at the trial (other than those to be used for impeachment) with each exhibit sufficiently described for identification. The list shall substantially conform to Local Form CSD 3026, *LIST OF EXHIBITS SUBMITTED BY ATTORNEY.*

(f) OBJECTIONS TO EXHIBITS. All objections to the admissibility of any exhibits listed in paragraph (e), the applicable rule of evidence, and any case authority shall be set out with specificity and attached as an appendix to the pre-trial order.

(g) WITNESSES. The parties shall jointly prepare a list of the names and addresses of all prospective witnesses, except impeaching witnesses, and, in the case of expert witnesses, provide a brief narrative statement of the qualifications of such witnesses and the substance of the testimony which such witnesses are expected to give. Only witnesses so listed, and impeachment and rebuttal witnesses, shall be permitted to testify at the trial, except for good cause shown.

7016-10. TRIAL COUNSEL TO BE PRESENT.

Unless otherwise ordered by the court, counsel who will conduct the trial will appear at the final pre-trial conference.

7016-11. SANCTIONS; PRE-TRIAL.

Failure of counsel to appear before the court at pre-trial proceedings or to complete the necessary preparations for such proceedings may be deemed an abandonment or failure to prosecute or defend diligently, and judgment may be entered against the defaulting party with respect to a specific issue or the entire proceeding.

7016-12. PREPARATION FOR TRIAL.

Unless otherwise ordered, the parties shall complete the following activities not less than seven (7) calendar days prior to the commencement of trial:

(a) serve and file briefs on all significant disputed issues of law, including foreseeable procedural and evidentiary issues, setting forth concisely the party's position and supporting arguments and authorities;

(b) in jury cases, serve and file proposed voir dire questions, jury instructions, and forms of verdict;

(c) in proceedings tried without jury, and otherwise when so ordered, serve and file proposed findings of fact and conclusions of law;

(d) serve and file statements designating excerpts from depositions (specifying the witness and page and line references), from interrogatory answers and from responses to requests for admission to be offered at the trial for purposes other than impeachment or rebuttal; and

(e) exchange copies of all exhibits (other than for impeachment or rebuttal) and all schedules, summaries, diagrams and charts to be offered at trial. Each proposed exhibit shall be marked in the manner specified by Local Bankruptcy Rule 7016-9(e).

Upon request, the party offering the foregoing documents shall make the originals of the same available for inspection and copying.

7016-13. RETURN OF EXHIBITS

At the conclusion of the trial or hearing, every exhibit marked for identification or introduced in evidence shall be returned to the party who produced it unless otherwise ordered by the court. It shall be the responsibility of counsel to produce any and all exhibits as designated on appeal.

[The Next Rule is 7019]

RULE 7019. MOTION TO CHANGE VENUE IN ADVERSARY PROCEEDING

A motion to change venue under 28 U.S.C. § 1412 shall be filed with the bankruptcy court clerk. The motion shall be governed by Local Bankruptcy Rule 9014 and calendared for hearing before the bankruptcy court.

[The Next Rule is 7022]

RULE 7022. INTERPLEADER ACTIONS; DEPOSITS INTO INTEREST BEARING ACCOUNTS; DISBURSEMENTS

7022-1. DEPOSIT OF REGISTRY FUNDS; CONTENT OF ORDER.

Those parties seeking interpleader of certain funds shall personally serve a copy of the order on the clerk or chief deputy clerk. The order shall contain the following provisions:

"IT IS ORDERED, (pursuant to the attached stipulation signed by all parties named in the action,) that the clerk deposit the amount of $. . . . . in an automatically renewable (insert type of account or instrument as provided in the stipulation) in the name of the Clerk, United States Bankruptcy Court at (insert name of designated bank, savings and loan, brokerage house), said funds to remain invested pending further order of the court.

"IT IS FURTHER ORDERED that the clerk is directed to deduct from the income earned on the investment a fee, not exceeding that authorized by the Judicial Conference of the United States and set by the Director of the Administrative Office, whenever such income becomes available for deduction in the investment so held and without further order of the court.

"IT IS FURTHER ORDERED that counsel presenting this order shall personally serve a copy thereof on the clerk or the chief deputy clerk prior to making the deposit. Absent the aforesaid personal service, the clerk is hereby relieved of any personal liability relative to compliance with this order."

7022-2. DISBURSEMENTS OF REGISTRY FUND; CONTENT OF ORDER.

The clerk shall disburse funds on deposit in the registry of the court only pursuant to court order. The disbursement order shall contain a provision relieving the clerk from liability for loss of interest, if any, for early withdrawal of the funds. The order shall state the name and taxpayer identification number for each party who is to receive funds and the percentage of the balance and interest each is to receive. Funds shall be disbursed only after the time for appeal of the related judgment or order has expired, or upon approval by the court of a written stipulation by all parties.

[The Next Rule is 7026]

RULE 7026. DISCOVERY

7026-1. APPLICABILITY OF RULE.

Unless the court directs otherwise, all adversary proceedings and all contested matters under Fed. R. Bankr. P. 9014 to which the adversay proceeding rules apply, shall comply with Fed. R. Bankr. P. 7026 by following those procedures set forth in Local Bankruptcy Rule 7016-2. Failure to timely comply will be cause for issuance of a notice of dismissal.

7026-2. CONFERENCE REQUIRED.

The court shall entertain no motion pursuant to Fed. R. Bankr. P. 7026 through 7037 unless counsel shall have previously met and conferred by telephone or in person concerning all disputed discovery issues. Unless relieved by court order upon good cause shown or agreement of the parties, counsel for the non-moving party shall meet with counsel for the moving party within ten (10) days of service of a letter requesting such meeting and specifying the terms of the discovery order to be sought. If counsel for the moving party seeks to arrange such a conference and counsel for the non-moving party willfully refuses or fails to meet and confer, in the absence of a prior order excusing such a meeting for good cause, the judge may order the payment of reasonable expenses, including attorney's fees, pursuant to Fed. R. Bankr. P. 7037.

7026-3. CERTIFICATE OF COMPLIANCE.

At the time of filing any motion with respect to Fed. R. Bankr. P. 7026 through 7037, counsel for the moving party shall serve and file a certificate of compliance with this rule.

7026-4. PROTECTIVE ORDER.

Any person against whom a motion under Fed. R. Bankr. P. 7037(a), or Fed. R. Bankr. P. 9016(a)(2) is brought may, upon proper notice, request a hearing on a motion for a protective order under Fed. R. Bankr. P. 7026(c).

[The Next Rule is 7030]

RULE 7030. DEPOSITIONS

7030-1. APPLICABILITY OF RULE.

Except as specifically ordered by a bankruptcy judge, the following provisions of the Fed. R. Bankr. P. do not apply to actions in this court: Rules 7030(a)(2)(C) and 7031(a)(2)(C).

7030-2. ATTORNEYS DUTY TO STIPULATE.

Prior to giving notice, parties will make every reasonable effort to stipulate to the exact time and place for the commencement and resumption of all depositions. If an agreement cannot be reached, any party may apply by ex parte application to the court for an order fixing the time, place and/or other terms and conditions governing such a deposition and for any related order of relief.

7030-3. MATERIALS.

The deposing party shall furnish the officer designated to conduct the deposition with a copy of Fed. R. Bankr. P. 7028(c) and 7030(c).

7030-4. TRANSCRIPT COST.

The deposing party shall assume the cost of transcription unless, pursuant to the parties' agreement, the court orders a waiver of transcription or a different apportionment of cost.

7030-5. COURT COPY.

Whenever a deposition or any part thereof is to be read in court, counsel using the same shall furnish a copy to the court in addition to the original filed with the court.

7030-6. FILING.

Unless filing is ordered by the court on motion of a party or upon its own motion, depositions upon oral examination shall not be filed unless and until they are used in the proceeding.

[The Next Rule is 7033]

RULE 7033. INTERROGATORIES TO PARTIES

7033-1. APPLICABILITY OF RULE.

Except as specifically ordered by a bankruptcy judge, the requirement in Fed. R. Bankr. P. 7033(a) that interrogatories not be served prior to the time specified in Fed. R. Bankr. P. 7026(d) except by stipulation or leave of court, shall not apply to actions in this court.

7033-2. MOTION FOR LEAVE TO SERVE ADDITIONAL INTERROGATORIES.

Any motion for leave to serve additional party interrogatories shall be made pursuant to Local Bankruptcy Rule 9013-3(a).

7033-3. ANSWERS OR OBJECTIONS TO INTERROGATORIES.

Answers or objections to each interrogatory shall first identify and quote the interrogatory in full.

7033-4. FILING.

Interrogatories, related answers and objections shall not be filed with the court unless and until they are used in the proceedings or their filing is ordered by the court. The court may order filing on its own motion or upon the motion of a party.

RULE 7034. TIMING OF REQUESTS FOR PRODUCTION OF DOCUMENTS

7034-1. APPLICABILITY OF RULE.

Except as specifically ordered by a bankruptcy judge, the requirement in Fed. R. Bankr. P. 7034(b) that requests for production of documents or things or to examine land not be served prior to the time specified in Fed. R. Bankr. P. 7026(d) except by stipulation or leave of court, shall not apply to actions in this court.

[The Next Rule is 7036]

RULE 7036. REQUESTS FOR ADMISSION

7036-1. APPLICABILITY OF RULE.

Except as specifically ordered by a bankruptcy judge, the requirement in Fed. R. Bankr. P. 7036(a) that requests for admission not be served prior to the time specified in Fed. R. Bankr. P. 7026(d) except by stipulation or leave of the court, shall not apply to actions in this court.

7036-2. RESPONSES OR OBJECTIONS TO REQUESTS FOR ADMISSION.

Responses or objections to each request for admission shall first identify and quote the request for admission in full.

7036-3. FILING.

Requests for admission, related responses and objections shall not be filed with the court unless and until they are used in the proceedings or their filing is ordered by the court. The court may order filing on its own motion or upon the motion of a party.

[The Next Rule is 7040]

RULE 7040. ASSIGNMENT OF ADVERSARY PROCEEDING FOR JURY TRIAL

7040-1. PROCEDURE.

(a) APPLICABILITY. This rule shall govern conduct of jury trials, when appropriate.

(b) DEMAND FOR JURY TRIAL. Local Bankruptcy Rule 7003-2 governs the request for a jury trial.

7040-2. CONSENT TO JURY TRIAL.

(a) If the right to a jury trial applies, a timely demand has been filed under Fed. R. Civ. P. 38(b), and the bankruptcy judge has been specially designated to conduct the jury trial, the parties may consent to have a jury trial conducted by a bankruptcy judge under 28 U.S.C. § 157(e) by jointly or separately filing a statement no later than the first status conference.

(b) Fed. R. Civ. P. 38, 39, 47–51, and 81(c) insofar as it applies to jury trials, apply in cases and proceedings, except that a demand made under

Fed. R. Civ. P. 38(b) shall be filed in accordance with Fed. R. Bankr. P. 5005.

(c) Parties are deemed to have consented to the entry of a final order by the bankruptcy judge in a non-core proceeding.

7040-3. SIX-PERSON JURIES.

In all adversary proceedings in which a party is entitled to a jury trial, the jury shall consist of six (6) members and such alternates as the judge may determine.

7040-4. EXAMINATION OF JURORS.

Unless otherwise ordered, the examination of trial jurors shall be conducted by the judge. Counsel shall submit any questions which they desire to be propounded to the jurors in accordance with Local Bankruptcy Rule 7016-12(b).

7040-5. FILING, SERVICE AND FORM OF PROPOSED INSTRUCTIONS.

(a) Unless otherwise ordered, each party shall serve and file proposed jury instructions in accordance with Local Bankruptcy Rule 7016-12(b). At the discretion of the judge, additional requests for instructions may be received at any time prior to the commencement of closing argument to the jury.

(b) Each proposed instruction shall be concise and limited to one subject. The instruction shall set forth the identity of the party submitting it, be written out in full on a separate page, and set forth citations to the authorities supporting it. The instructions shall be consecutively numbered.

(c) Objections to proposed instructions may be filed with the court or made orally to the judge, as time permits. Such objections should normally be accompanied by citation to supporting authority. Prior to closing argument to the jury, the judge shall inform counsel of the instructions which will be given.

(d) If an instruction is submitted from a recognized book of instructions, it shall be from the latest edition thereof [so noticed at the bottom of the instruction]; and if modified in any way, deleted material shall be shown in parentheses and additions shall be underscored.

7040-6. ASSESSMENT OF JURY COSTS.

If for any reason attributable to counsel or parties, including settlement, the court is unable to commence a jury trial as scheduled where a panel of prospective jurors have reported for voir dire, the court may assess against counsel or parties responsible, all or part of the cost of the panel.

RULE 7041. DISMISSAL OF ADVERSARY PROCEEDING

7041-1. VOLUNTARY OR STIPULATED DISMISSALS.

If the stipulated or voluntary dismissal of an adversary proceeding removes a hearing from the court's calendar, the date and time of that hearing shall be inserted two (2) lines below the adversary number in the caption of the order.

7041-2. DISMISSAL FOR WANT OF PROSECUTION.

Actions or proceedings which have been pending in this court for more than three (3) months without any action having been taken during such period, may, after notice, be dismissed without prejudice unless otherwise ordered by the court.

7041-3. DISMISSAL OF RELATED TITLE 11 CASE.

(a) Whenever a Title 11 case is dismissed, any pending related adversary proceeding, in which a final judgment has not been entered, shall be dismissed without prejudice and without further order of the court.

(b) If the debtor files another petition for relief under Title 11 within ninety (90) days following entry of the order dismissing the prior case, any plaintiff, whose adversary proceeding was dismissed under this rule, may file an ex parte motion and proposed order to have the proceeding reopened and made applicable in the new case, as though the proceeding were originally filed therein.

7041-4. VOLUNTARY OR STIPULATED DISMISSAL OF OBJECTIONS TO DISCHARGE OF THE DEBTOR.

(a) PROCEDURE. A motion or stipulation for dismissal of a complaint which contains objections to the discharge under 11 U.S.C. § 727 may be approved only after notice to the United States Trustee and the trustee for the debtor, as provided in Fed. R. Bankr. P. 7041 and in accordance with Local Bankruptcy Rule 9013.

(b) CONTENT OF MOTION OR STIPULATION. The motion or stipulation shall contain: a statement signed and verified by both plaintiff and defendant that there has been no monetary settlement or other agreement made as consideration for dismissal of the § 727 claims for relief and that there has been no violation of 18 U.S.C. § 152.

(c) INTERVENTION BY THE UNITED STATES TRUSTEE OR TRUSTEE. If the United States Trustee or the trustee for the debtor desires to intervene as the plaintiff in an objection to discharge of a debtor, the United States Trustee and/or trustee shall file an objection to the proposed stipulation or motion and a cross-motion to intervene within the time provided by Local Bankruptcy Rule 9013-4.

[The Next Rule is 7054]

RULE 7054. FINDINGS OF FACT, CONCLUSIONS OF LAW, ORDERS AND JUDGMENTS

7054-1. APPLICABILITY OF RULE.

This rule is to be read in conjunction with Fed. R. Bankr. P. 7054 and 9021 and governs the preparation, submission and approval of findings of fact, conclusions of law, judgments, and orders.

7054-2. DUTY OF PREVAILING PARTY.

Unless the court directs otherwise, the prevailing party shall prepare and submit any judgments or orders and, if required, separate findings of fact and conclusions of law, in the manner provided in Local Bankruptcy Rule 7054-3. The pleadings shall also comply with Local Bankruptcy Rule 9004.

7054-3. PROCEDURES FOR SUBMISSION OF ORDERS AFTER HEARING.

(a) PROCEDURE BY CONSENT. The party preparing the order or judgment, and, if required, separate findings of fact and conclusions of law may submit the same to the opposing parties for their approval as to form and content. The opposing parties shall indicate their approval by promptly endorsing the lower-left corner of the signature page(s) and returning the original documents to the preparing party. The preparing party shall then submit the original documents to the court for signature and entry *without* having to comply with Local Bankruptcy Rule 7054-3(b). If approval is not obtained from the opposing parties, the preparing party shall then submit the original documents to the court in the manner set forth in Local Bankruptcy Rule 7054-3(b).

(b) PROCEDURE BY LODGMENT—CONTESTED ORDER OR JUDGMENT.

(1) NOTICE OF LODGMENT. The party preparing the order or judgment and, if required, separate findings of fact and conclusions of law shall file the same together with a notice of lodgment. The notice shall conform to Local Bankruptcy Rule 9004 and shall be accompanied by a proof of service on all opposing parties as provided in Fed. R. Bankr. P. 7005. The notice shall inform the opposing parties that any objections to the form and content of the proposed order or judgment must be filed and served within seven (7) days from the date of service of the originals. Assembly sequence for documents is as follows:

(A) the order or judgment and two (2) copies;

(B) findings of fact and conclusions of law, if any, and two (2) copies;

(C) an original notice of lodgment *with a copy* of the proposed order or judgment and, if required, separate findings of fact and conclusions of law attached as Exhibit "A" and "B", if applicable, followed by a proof of service, and two (2) copies; and

(D) an original Notice of Entry with the pre-addressed, postage-paid envelopes required by subsection (2) below.

(2) NAMES AND ADDRESSES OF OPPOSING PARTIES.

(A) The preparing party shall submit to the clerk, in addition to any proposed findings of fact, conclusions of law, and order or judgment, the original of Local Adversary Form CSD 3050, *NOTICE OF ENTRY OF JUDGMENT OR ORDER* or Local Case Form CSD 1190, *NOTICE OF ENTRY.* The Notice of Entry shall contain the names and addresses of opposing parties, their attorneys of record and, if the judgment or order affects property of the debtor or the estate, the names and addresses of the debtor, any trustee, their attorneys of record, the United States Trustee, and any co-owner of the property. The date of entry of the judgment or order shall remain blank.

(B) In addition to the Notice of Entry, the party shall also submit pre-addressed and postage-paid envelopes for each of the parties to receive notice of entry.

(3) OBJECTIONS TO LODGED DOCUMENTS. Any party who opposes the entry of the lodged order, judgment, or separate findings of fact and conclusions of law shall file an objection and an alternate order, judgment, or separate findings of fact and conclusions of law with the court. The alternate order, judgment, or separate findings of fact and conclusions of law shall be filed and served on the preparing party within seven (7) days from the date of service of the original notice of lodgment and shall conform to Local Bankruptcy Rule 9004. Notice of Lodgment of alternate order is not required. No further pleadings will be considered except upon leave of court.

7054-4. INTEREST ON JUDGMENT.

(a) RATE OF INTEREST. The legal rate of interest applied to a judgment or order shall be the rate provided by the United States Department of the Treasury pursuant to federal law and published by the Administrative Office of the United States courts in a rate table with a retrospective period of over ten (10) years.

(b) PUBLICATION OF INTEREST RATE. The clerk shall post notice of the current legal rate of interest in a public place and shall provide this information by telephone upon request at (619) 557-5620.

7054-5. COSTS.

(a) Costs will be taxed in conformity with the provisions of 28 U.S.C. §§ 1920 and 1923, Fed. R. Bankr. P. 7054 and Local Rule 54.1 of the United States District Court, except as otherwise provided in subsections (b) and (c) of this rule.

(b) Within fourteen (14) days after the entry of a judgment or order under which costs may be claimed, a party entitled to claim costs may request taxation of the costs itemized therein. The Bill of Costs shall be submitted using Local Form CSD 3066, *BILL OF COSTS.* The costs shall be separately and specifically itemized for each item of costs claimed.

(c) The prevailing party will give at least seven (7) days notice of the cost hearing to the party or parties against whom the costs are to be assessed. The hearing date and time may be obtained by calling the secretary to the Clerk.

(d) The procedure for the Bill of Costs and the items taxable as costs are set forth in Local Rule 54.1 of the United States District Court.

(1) Attorney fees may not be taxed as costs by the clerk.

(2) If attorney fees are claimed, a motion for allowance of fees must be made by the prevailing party in accordance with Local Bankruptcy Rule 9014.

RULE 7055. DEFAULT

7055-1. REQUIRED FORM FOR REQUEST TO ENTER

DEFAULT.

(a) A request to enter default under Fed. R. Bankr. P. 7055 shall conform substantially to Local Form CSD 3030, *REQUEST TO ENTER DEFAULT.*

(b) Unless previously filed, the request shall be accompanied by a separate verified affidavit in support thereof.

7055-2. FORM OF JUDGMENT.

A separate judgment, entitled "Judgment by Default", shall be prepared. The judgment shall state in simple and direct terms the judgment of the court and shall comply with Local Bankruptcy Rule 9004.

[The Next Rule is 7065]

RULE 7065. TEMPORARY RESTRAINING ORDER AND PRELIMINARY INJUNCTION

7065-1. REQUIREMENTS.

(a) Prior to submitting an application for a temporary restraining order or for a preliminary injunction, an adversary proceeding shall be filed seeking such relief as governed by Local Bankruptcy Rule 7003.

(b) An application for a temporary restraining order or for a preliminary injunction shall be made in a document separate from the complaint and shall be accompanied by:

(1) a separate memorandum of points and authorities in support of the application;

(2) a proposed temporary restraining order or preliminary injunction;

(3) a declaration or affidavit by the moving party or counsel for the moving party showing compliance with Fed. R. Bankr. P. 7065 regarding notice to opposing parties; and,

(4) a copy of the filed complaint.

[The Next Rule is 7069]

RULE 7069. ENFORCEMENT OF JUDGMENTS

7069-1. FORM.

Whenever a provisional remedy is sought or a judgment is enforced in accordance with state law as provided in Fed. R. Bankr. P. 7064 and 7069, the application and order shall conform substantially to Local Form CSD

3060, *APPLICATION FOR ORDER TO APPEAR FOR EXAMINATION AND ORDER THEREON.*

7069-2. DISCOVERY IN AID OF ENFORCEMENT OF JUDGMENTS.

As allowed by Fed. R. Bankr. P. 7069, except to the extent that a federal statute applies, a judgment creditor may obtain discovery from any person to aid in enforcing a judgment in the manner provided by Fed. R. Bankr. P. 7026 through 7037 or in the manner provided by state law. A judgment creditor may not use Fed. R. Bankr. P. 2004 to collect information to use to enforce a judgment.

7069-3. USE OF UNITED STATES MARSHAL.

The court encourages the use of state remedies and officers wherever appropriate to enforce judgments or obtain available remedies. The United States Marshal's Office is available to enforce federal judgments as necessary.

7069-4. REGISTRATION OF JUDGMENTS.

A judgment by a bankruptcy judge from any other district may be registered in the Southern District of California by filing with the bankruptcy clerk a certified copy of such judgment accompanied by Local Form CSD 3054, *CERTIFICATION OF JUDGMENT FOR REGISTRATION IN ANOTHER DISTRICT,* and by payment of the fee mandated by the Judicial Conference pursuant to 28 U.S.C. § 1930.

[The Next Rule is 9004]

RULE 9004. GENERAL REQUIREMENTS OF FORM

9004-1. APPLICABILITY OF RULE.

Fed. R. Bankr. P. 9004, read in conjunction with applicable Local Bankruptcy Rules, governs the preparation and filing of papers, except as otherwise required by the court. "Papers" as used in this rule include but are not limited to pleadings, documents, notices, exhibits and proofs of claim.

9004-2. ATTORNEY IDENTIFICATION AND SIGNATURE.

(a) STATE BAR MEMBERSHIP NUMBER. Attorneys presenting papers for filing shall insert their State Bar membership number immediately to the right of their name at the top of the title page. On proofs of claim, the number shall appear to the right of their name.

(b) RESPONSIBILITY OF LEAD ATTORNEY. For notice purposes, where there is more than one attorney of record, the attorney whose name first appears under the attorney identification section on the title page of a paper shall be known as the "lead attorney" and is the person upon whom the court will serve any notices and other papers. The lead attorney shall be responsible for promptly delivering copies of these notices and papers to any co-counsel.

9004-3. PAPERS PRESENTED TO THE COURT—FORM AND FORMAT.

(a) LEGIBILITY. All papers shall be typewritten or hand-printed or prepared by a photocopying or other duplicating process that will produce clear and permanent copies equally legible to printing, in black or dark blue ink. The typeface shall be no smaller than pica size, with not more than ten (10) typed characters per inch.

(b) SIGNATURES. All original papers shall be signed by the individual attorney for the party presenting them, or by the unrepresented party. The name of the person signing the paper shall be typed underneath the signature. Copies shall be conformed to the original.

(c) PAPER SIZE. The original of all papers shall be submitted on opaque, unglazed, white paper of standard quality not less than 13-pound weight. The paper shall be 8-1/2 by 11 inches with not more than twenty-eight (28) lines per page. Pre-printed forms provided by the clerk must be reproduced "heel-to-toe" so that they may be easily read without removal from the file; otherwise, only one side of the paper will be used. Papers shall be double-spaced except for the identification of counsel, title of the action, category headings, footnotes, quotations, exhibits and descriptions of real property. Quotations from cited cases or other authorities shall be clearly indented not less than five (5) spaces or more than twenty (20) spaces and may be single-spaced.

(d) TITLE PAGE. In the space commencing two (2) inches from the top and to the left of center-page, there shall be typed or printed single-spaced the following information:

(1) name of counsel and State Bar membership number presenting a paper, or if not represented by an attorney, the name of the party.

(2) office address, including the street address in addition to any post office box. If no office address, state residence address.

(3) Area code and telephone number of the party presenting the paper.

(4) Two (2) lines below the telephone number, the name and interest of the party on whose behalf the paper is presented shall be identified; in the instance of multi-party representation, reference may be made to the bottom of the signature page for including a complete list of co-counsel, including their State Bar membership numbers and addresses and telephone numbers, and parties represented.

(5) Two (2) lines below the last information required by subsection (4) herein, centered on the page, insert the name of the court, as follows:

UNITED STATES BANKRUPTCY COURT
Southern District of California

(e) CONTINUATION PAGES.

(1) When a proposed order, judgment, or findings of fact and conclusions of law contains more than the title page, the following information is required to be inserted at the lower-left corner of each continuation page:

(A) the name of the debtor or, for adversary proceedings, the name of the first plaintiff; and

(B) the case number and either the relief from stay number or the adversary proceeding number, if any; and

(C) the title of the order or judgment.

(2) If the signature page, at least three (3) lines of text shall continue from the previous page.

(3) Two (2) lines below the signature line at the left margin, insert information regarding the submitting attorney as follows:

"Signature by the attorney constitutes a certification under Fed. R. Bankr. P. 9011 that the relief provided by the order is the relief granted by the court.
Submitted by:
Firm name
By:____________________
Attorney for [party]"

(f) PAGINATION. All papers shall be numbered consecutively at the bottom of each page, including any attached exhibits.

(g) STIPULATIONS:

(1) shall conclude with the heading "ORDER"; and

(2) beneath the heading shall appear the words, "IT IS SO ORDERED"; and

(3) provide a line for the date and the signature of the bankruptcy judge, as provided in Local Bankruptcy Rule 9004-3(h).

(4) Any stipulation which extends time or provides for a continuance shall contain the reason for the change of date.

(h) SIGNATURE LINE FOR JUDGE. A signature line shall be provided with the words "Judge, United States Bankruptcy Court" typed beneath the line.

(i) EXHIBITS ATTACHED TO PAPERS. Exhibits shall not exceed 8-1/2 by 11 inches in size whenever practicable. Larger exhibits shall be folded in such a manner as not to exceed 8-1/2 by 11 inches. An exhibit smaller than 8-1/2 by 11 inches shall be attached to a 8-1/2 by 11 inch sheet.

(1) Unless the physical nature of the exhibit makes it impractical, an exhibit shall be securely fastened to the paper to which it relates. The exhibit shall be so attached that it will be easily read without detaching the exhibit from the paper.

(2) The exhibit number shall be placed immediately above or below the page number of each page of the exhibit. Exhibits shall be tabbed in sequential order.

(j) PAPERS TO BE PRE-PUNCHED. The original of all papers presented for filing or lodging shall be pre-punched with two normal-size holes (approximately 1/4" diameter), centered 2-3/4 inches apart, 1/2 to 5/8 inch from the top edge of the paper. All pages shall be firmly bound at the top left corner.

(k) SUBMITTING PAPERS FOR FILING. All papers submitted to the clerk for filing shall be flat and unfolded (except where necessary for presentation of exhibits). Blue backing sheets are prohibited.

(l) COPIES. Copies shall be marked "COPY" in the bottom margin on the face page and shall be conformed to the original in content, pagination, exhibits, additions, deletions, and interlineations. Conformed copies need not be executed.

(m) REQUIRED NUMBER OF COPIES. Unless otherwise prescribed by these rules, there shall be submitted:

(1) The original and two (2) copies of the pleadings that accompany an ex parte or emergency order.

(2) The original and one (1) copy of the order or judgment and any separate findings of fact and conclusions of law, if the consent procedure authorized by Local Bankruptcy Rule 7054-3(a) is used.

(3) The original and two (2) copies of the order or judgment and any separate findings of fact and conclusions of law and notice of lodgment, if the lodgment procedure authorized by Local Bankruptcy Rule 7054-3(b) is used.

(4) The original and two (2) copies of an objection to a lodged order, judgment, or separate findings of fact and conclusions of law as provided in Local Bankruptcy Rule 7054-3(b)(3).

(5) The original and two (2) copies of any notice of hearing required by Local Bankruptcy Rules 2002-3, 3015 and 9014-3 and related pleadings.

(6) The original and two (2) copies of any request for hearing required by Local Bankruptcy Rules 2002-2, 3007, 3013, 4001, 5010, and 9013 and related pleadings.

(7) The original and two (2) copies of any opposition, objection, reply memorandum or joinder required by Local Bankruptcy Rules 3015, 4001, 5011, 9006-1(d), 9013 and 9014 and related pleadings.

(8) The original and one (1) copy of all other pleadings.

(n) RETURN OF COURT CONFORMED COPY. The requested number of copies includes one to be file stamped by the clerk and returned to the party presenting the paper. If the copy is to be returned by messenger, a messenger slip shall be provided for that purpose. If the copy is to be returned by United States mail, a self-addressed, postage-paid envelope large enough to hold the copy shall be provided. When presenting ex parte motions and orders, two (2) messenger slips or envelopes shall be provided.

9004-4. CAPTION AND TITLE OF PAPERS FILED.

(a) REQUIRED CAPTION. In addition to the information generally required by Fed. R. Bankr. P. 1005 (for notices), 7010 (for adversary proceedings) and 9004(b) (for bankruptcy cases), the caption of each paper shall commence two (2) lines beneath the name of the court and set forth:

(1) the case number, followed by the initials of the currently assigned judge and chapter number, and, if the document is to be filed in the adversary proceeding, the adversary proceeding number;

(2) any relief from stay identification number, as required by Local Bankruptcy Rule 4001-1(b), inserted two (2) lines below the bankruptcy case (the designator "RS No." shall precede the number);

(3) a concise description of the nature of the paper (e.g., Notice of Motion for Summary Judgment, Complaint to Determine Dischargeability of Debt); and

(4) the date, time and name of the judge, if the paper (other than a notice of hearing) is to be considered at a future hearing. This information shall be inserted two (2) lines below the case number, adversary proceeding number, or "RS" number.

(b) RESPONSIBILITY OF ATTORNEY TO PROVIDE PROPER CASE NUMBER. The attorney presenting a paper for filing shall bear sole responsibility for ensuring that the case name, case number, adversary number, if any, and any required identification number for relief from stay matters match. The court may refuse to consider papers entered on the wrong docket or misfiled because of erroneous or omitted information provided by the attorney.

RULE 9006. TIME FOR MOTIONS AND OBJECTIONS; LENGTH OF BRIEFS; PROOF OF SERVICE

9006-1. TIME FOR MOTIONS AND OPPOSITION.

(a) SERVICE OF MOTION. In accordance with Fed. R. Bankr. P. 9006(d), Local Bankruptcy Rules 2002, 4001, 9013, and 9014 shall govern service of a written motion.

(b) NOTICE OF HEARING. In accordance with Fed. R. Bankr. P. 9006(d), Local Bankruptcy Rules 2002-3, 4001-3, and 9014 shall govern notice of hearing unless the hearing is deemed waived.

(c) OPPOSITION. In accordance with Fed. R. Bankr. P. 9006(d), Local Bankruptcy Rules 2002, 4001, 9013, and 9014 shall govern the time for filing any opposing affidavits and objections.

(d) JOINDERS. A joinder asserting additional grounds must be filed and served in the same period as required by these rules for the underlying motion or opposition.

(e) MOTION DAYS. When a hearing on a motion is required by Local

Bankruptcy Rules 2002-3 and 9014, the moving party shall obtain a date and time for the hearing from the courtroom deputy for the appropriate judge and give the notice required by that rule.

(f) EXTENDING AND SHORTENING TIME. Subject to the limitations of Fed. R. Bankr. P. 9006, a motion for an order extending or shortening time under the Fed. R. Bankr. P. or Local Bankruptcy Rules shall be submitted ex parte pursuant to Local Bankruptcy Rule 9013-6(a)(1)(F) and with a proposed order.

(g) INACCESSIBILITY OF THE COURT. The Clerk's Office is "inaccessible" within the meaning of Fed. R. Bankr. P. 9006 on any day when it is not available for both electronic filing of documents and paper filing of documents.

9006-2. LENGTH OF BRIEF IN SUPPORT OF OR IN OPPOSITION TO MOTION.

Briefs or memoranda in support of or in opposition to any pending motion shall not exceed twenty-five (25) pages, and reply memoranda shall not exceed ten (10) pages, without leave of a bankruptcy judge. Briefs and memoranda exceeding ten (10) pages in length shall have a table of contents and a table of authorities cited.

9006-3. PROOF OF SERVICE.

(a) Proof of service of all papers to be served, other than those for which the Fed. R. Bankr. P. prescribe a particular method, shall be promptly filed together with the original documents served with the clerk's office on the next business day following the date of service of the documents, and shall indicate the date and manner of service by attaching:

(1) written acknowledgment of service or the original served, by the attorney or authorized person receiving a copy thereof; or

(2) attorney's certificate or affidavit of the person who mailed or served the papers; or

(3) by any other court approved method.

(b) Delivery of pleadings by facsimile shall not constitute service for purposes of these rules unless by prior agreement of the parties or by court approval. The validity of the service is not affected by the failure to make the proof of service required.

(c) Forms approved for proof of service in the California State Courts, or Local Form CSD 3010, *PROOF OF SERVICE,* may be used for this purpose.

(d) Unless it would result in material prejudice to the rights of any party, the court may permit the proof of service to be amended at any time.

(e) No papers shall be filed with the clerk's office unless the service required by the Fed. R. Bankr. P. or these Local Bankruptcy Rules has been made.

[The Next Rule is 9009]

RULE 9009. LOCAL FORMS

9009-1. AVAILABILITY OF FORMS.

Appendix C contains copies of the forms routinely used by attorneys or that are referenced by these Local Bankruptcy Rules. Upon request and without cost, the clerk shall provide any local form used by this court. All forms shall be subsequently duplicated by the user as needed.

RULE 9010. APPEARANCE OF ATTORNEYS

9010-1. APPLICABILITY OF RULE.

Fed. R. Bankr. P. 9010 and Local District Court Rule 83.5 govern the appearance of attorneys in bankruptcy cases and adversary proceedings.

9010-2. APPLICATIONS FOR ADMISSION.

Applications for admission under Local District Court Rule 83.5(c)(1) shall be presented to the clerk of the United States District Court. The application shall be accompanied by the required fee. Checks should be made payable to "Clerk, United States District Court."

9010-3. PRO HAC VICE APPLICATION.

Pro hac vice applications under Local District Court Rule 83.5(c)(5) shall be presented to the clerk of the United States Bankruptcy Court. The application shall be accompanied by the required fee. Checks should be made payable to "Clerk, United States District Court."

9010-4. DUTY OF ATTORNEY TO KEEP MAILING ADDRESS AND TELEPHONE INFORMATION CURRENT.

Attorneys appearing in ongoing bankruptcy proceedings shall keep the court apprised of their current mailing address and telephone number. Any change of address must be submitted in writing; Local Form CSD 1546, *ATTORNEY CHANGE OF INFORMATION FORM,* may be used for this purpose. Merely noting such a change on a pleading submitted for filing shall not constitute compliance with this rule.

9010-5. SUBSTITUTION OF ATTORNEYS.

Substitution of attorneys is governed by Local Rule 83.5(j) of the United States District Court for the Southern District of California and, if applicable, Local Bankruptcy Rule 2014-1.

RULE 9011. SANCTIONS.

9011-1. TIME FOR FILING MOTION.

Any motion for sanctions pursuant to Fed. R. Bankr. P. 9011, plus all necessary supporting pleadings, shall be filed and served upon the adverse party's counsel, or, if none, the adverse party not later than thirty (30) days from the entry of the order or judgment and no earlier than the entry of an order directed to the pleading, petition or motion at issue. Local Bankruptcy Rules 9006 and 9014 govern the procedure for scheduling a hearing and the schedule for filing all other pleadings.

[The Next Rule is 9013]

RULE 9013. MOTIONS; FORMS AND SERVICE

9013-1. APPLICABILITY OF RULE.

This rule is to be read in conjunction with Fed. R. Bankr. P. 9013 and Local Bankruptcy Rules 2002 and 9014, and governs motion practice in the bankruptcy court for which notice to all creditors is not required by the Fed. R. Bankr. P.

Local Bankruptcy Rule 4001 governs the procedure for obtaining relief from automatic stay.

9013-2. CONTENT OF MOTIONS.

(a) GENERAL REQUIREMENTS. Except as provided in subsection (b), every motion:

(1) shall be accompanied by a memorandum of points and authorities; and,

(2) shall include affidavits or declarations of material facts, as appropriate, which are signed and verified in the manner provided by Fed. R. Bankr. P. 9011 and Local Bankruptcy Rule 9004-3(b), or appropriate requests for judicial notice.

(b) SPECIAL REQUIREMENTS. Unless otherwise ordered by the court:

(1) MOTION TO DISMISS CASE. A debtor's motion to dismiss a case shall set forth the terms of any arrangements or agreements with any entity regarding dismissal.

(2) MOTION FOR DISMISSAL OF COMPLAINTS OBJECTING TO DEBTOR'S DISCHARGE. A motion for the dismissal of an adversary complaint containing objections to the discharge of a debtor under 11 U.S.C. § 727(c) shall comply with Local Bankruptcy Rule 7041-4.

(3) MOTIONS TO AVOID LIENS UNDER 11 U.S.C. § 522(f). The debtor's motion to avoid a lien or other transfer of property under § 522(f) shall be accompanied by:

(A) a declaration of the debtor or other competent evidence of the fair market value of the property;

(B) the amount of the lien to be avoided;

(C) the value claimed exempt;

(D) the nature and amount of other liens against the property; and

(E) the statutory basis for the exemption. Lien avoidance motions on declared homesteaded property shall also be accompanied by a copy of the recorded homestead declaration.

(4) MOTION FOR EXEMPTION FROM CREDIT COUNSELING UNDER 11 U.S.C. § 109(h)(4). The motion shall contain information substantially conforming to Local Form CSD 1027, MOTION FOR EXEMPTION FROM CREDIT COUNSELING AND NOTICE OF OPPORTUNITY FOR HEARING.

(5) MOTION FOR ORDER CONFIRMING THAT AUTOMATIC STAY IS NOT IN EFFECT UNDER 11 U.S.C. § 362(c)(4)(A). The requesting party shall serve the request on the parties named in Local Bankruptcy Rule 4001-2(a)(1).

(6) CERTIFICATE OF CURE OF ENTIRE MONETARY DEFAULT UNDER 11 U.S.C. § 362(l). The certificate shall contain information substantially conforming to Local Form CSD 1033, CERTIFICATE OF CURE OF ENTIRE MONETARY DEFAULT PURSUANT TO 11 U.S.C. § 362(l) AND NOTICE OF OPPORTUNITY FOR HEARING.

(7) MOTION TO ACCESS FEDERAL INCOME TAX RETURNS UNDER 11 U.S.C. § 521(f). The moving party shall serve the motion on the debtor in addition to the parties required by Fed. R. Bankr. P. 9013.

9013-3. CONTENT OF NOTICE.

(a) NOTICE OF MOTION. The moving party shall serve affected parties in interest with a copy of the motion and a separate Notice of Motion which conforms to Local Form CSD 1182, *NOTICE OF MOTION FOR (DESCRIPTION OF ACTION).*

(b) OPPOSITION ANTICIPATED. Upon the affirmative representation of counsel for the movant that substantive opposition is reasonably anticipated, a hearing date may be obtained from the courtroom deputy and the movant may proceed pursuant to Local Bankruptcy Rule 9014.

9013-4. TIME FOR SERVICE OF OPPOSITION.

Except as otherwise provided by an order shortening time, each party opposing a motion shall serve that opposition and Local Form CSD 1184, *REQUEST AND NOTICE FOR HEARING,* not later than fourteen (14) days after service of the notice of motion, if personally served. If served by mail, opposing party shall have seventeen (17) days to serve such opposition as provided by Fed. R. Bankr. P. 9006(f). Objections to a motion filed under Local Bankruptcy Rule 9013-2 commence a contested matter governed by Local Bankruptcy Rule 9014-4(b).

9013-5. TIME FOR SERVICE OF REPLY.

Except as otherwise provided by an order shortening time, any reply memorandum must be filed and received by the adverse party the earlier of seven (7) days after service of the opposition or three (3) days prior to the date of the hearing. Service may be by facsimile upon prior agreement of the parties or upon court approval.

9013-6. HEARING ON MOTION.

(a) EX PARTE MOTIONS AND APPLICATIONS. An ex parte motion or application is one in which notice is not required to be given to any parties in interest or notice is limited to the United States Trustee or chapter 13 trustee, when required by the Fed. R. Bankr. P. or these local rules, and for which a hearing is not required. Unless otherwise directed by these rules or by the court, the ex parte motion or application shall be accompanied by an original order and required number of copies in conformance with Local Bankruptcy Rule 9004.

(1) MOTIONS AND APPLICATIONS NOT REQUIRING NOTICE. The following motions and applications may be made ex parte without notice unless otherwise required by the court:

(A) application for permission to pay filing fee in installments, as governed by Local Bankruptcy Rule 1006-2;

(B) motion for review of appointment of a creditors' committee organized before the date of the order for relief or for a special-interest committee, as governed by Fed. R. Bankr. P. 2007;

(C) motion for order fixing claims bar date in chapter 11 case, as governed by Local Bankruptcy Rule 3003;

(D) notice of removal of a proceeding from another court, as governed by Local Bankruptcy Rule 9027 and Fed. R. Bankr. P. 9027;

(E) motion to re-open an adversary proceeding, as governed by Local Bankruptcy Rule 7041-3(b);

(F) motion for order extending or shortening time, as governed by Local Bankruptcy Rule 9006;

(G) motion for order authorizing examination of an entity under Fed. R. Bankr. P. 2004;

(H) motion to file document or pleading under seal under Fed. R. Bankr. P. 9018;

(I) application for order to show cause regarding contempt under Fed. R. Bankr. P. 9020.

(J) certificate of exigent circumstances and motion for extension of time to file certificate of credit counseling under 11 U.S.C. § 109(h)(3); and

(K) motion for order directing United States Trustee to appoint a consumer privacy ombudsman under Local Bankruptcy Rule 6004-4(a).

(2) MOTIONS AND APPLICATIONS REQUIRING NOTICE TO UNITED STATES TRUSTEE AND OBTAINING A STATEMENT OF POSITION OF THE UNITED STATES TRUSTEE PRIOR TO FILING OF MOTION OR APPLICATION WITH THE COURT. Those motions and applications requiring service on the United States Trustee are enumerated in and governed by Local Bankruptcy Rule 9034-1.

(3) MOTIONS REQUIRING NOTICE TO CHAPTER 13 TRUSTEE. Those motions requiring service on the chapter 13 trustee are enumerated in and governed by Local Bankruptcy Rule 9034-2.

(b) EMERGENCY MOTIONS. Where a movant requires expedited treatment of a motion for which notice and a hearing is normally required, the motion must be made as an emergency motion in accordance with Local Bankruptcy Rule 9014-5.

9013-7. CONTENT OF ORDER OR REPORT ON NONCONTESTED MATTER.

After expiration of the last date for serving and filing objections, if no objections have been filed, the moving party shall submit to the court an appropriate order or, if applicable, the report required by Local Bankruptcy Rule 6004-3 or 6007-3. If an order is required, the order shall have attached thereto as Exhibit "A" a file-stamped copy of the notice of motion or notice of intended action and proof of service and shall set forth:

(a) the date the motion was filed with the clerk;

(b) a complete and concise statement of the relief to be granted;

(c) a statement that the moving party has received no pleadings in opposition thereto; and

(d) a full legal description and any street address for the property if the motion pertains to real property.

9013-8. SERVICE OF ORDER.

In all instances and upon receipt of the entered order, the party obtaining the relief shall mail a conformed copy of the entered order to the persons affected by the order and file proof of service with the court no later than the next business day following the date of service.

RULE 9014. CONTESTED AND EMERGENCY MOTIONS; OBJECTIONS AND HEARING

9014-1. APPLICABILITY OF RULE.

This Rule, read in conjunction with Fed. R. Bankr. P. 9014 and Local Bankruptcy Rule 9013, governs motion practice. Unless otherwise ordered by the court, the notice of hearing on motion procedure provided in this Rule shall apply to those motions for which notice and a hearing are required.

9014-2. CONTENT OF MOTION.

Unless otherwise provided by rule or order of court, all motions shall be in writing. Each motion filed and served shall be accompanied by:

(a) a statement of the relief sought and the reasons supporting the request;

(b) a memorandum of points and authorities upon which the movant is relying;

(c) affidavits or declarations of material facts, as appropriate, which are signed and verified in the manner provided by Fed. R. Bankr. P. 9011 and Local Bankruptcy Rule 9004-3(b), or appropriate requests for judicial notice; and

(d) authenticated copies of all other documentary evidence upon which the movant intends to rely.

9014-3. CONTENT OF NOTICE.

(a) HEARING DATE. Prior to giving notice of a hearing on a motion, the movant shall obtain a hearing date for the motion from the courtroom deputy.

(b) NOTICE OF HEARING. When notice to all creditors is required and the matter is governed by Local Bankruptcy Rule 9014, the moving party shall serve with the motion and supporting papers a separate notice which substantially conforms to Local Form CSD 1181, *NOTICE OF MOTION AND HEARING,* or Local Form CSD 1149, *NOTICE OF HEARING AND MOTION FOR APPROVAL OF DISCLOSURE STATEMENT, PLAN, OR MODIFIED PLAN,* and required by Local Bankruptcy Rule 2002-3(b).

(c) SERVICE. When notice to all creditors is not required by Fed. R. Bankr. P. 2002, the motion together with accompanying papers shall be served on the debtor, United States Trustee, the trustee, and other parties in interest. The notice shall conform to either Local Case Form CSD 1183 or Local Adversary Form 3015, *NOTICE OF MOTION AND HEARING,* as appropriate.

9014-4. TIME FOR SERVICE.

(a) TIME FOR SERVING MOTION. Any motion plus all necessary supporting pleadings, shall be served, when required by these rules or the Fed. R. Bankr. P., with the notice of motion as required Local Bankruptcy Rule 2002-1.

(b) TIME FOR SERVING OPPOSITION. Except as otherwise provided by an order shortening time, each party opposing a motion shall serve that opposition together with a memorandum of points and authorities on the movant's counsel, or, if none, the movant not later than fourteen (14) days after service of the notice of motion, if personally served. If served by mail, opposing party shall have seventeen (17) days to serve such opposition as provided by Fed. R. Bankr. P. 9006(f).

(c) TIME FOR SERVING OPPOSITION TO MOTION TO EXTEND AUTOMATIC STAY UNDER 11 U.S.C. § 362(C)(3)(B) AND MOTION FOR ORDER IMPOSING AUTOMATIC STAY UNDER 11 U.S.C. § 362(C)(4)(B). Except as otherwise provided by an order shortening time, each party opposing a motion to extend automatic stay under 11 U.S.C. § 362(c)(3)(B) or a motion to impose the automatic stay under 11 U.S.C. § 362(c)(4)(B) shall serve that opposition on the movant's counsel, or, if none, the movant not later than fourteen (14) days after service of the notice of motion, if personally served. If served by mail, opposing party shall have seventeen (17) days as provided by Fed. R. Bankr. P. 9006(f).

(d) TIME FOR SERVING OPPOSITION TO MOTION FOR APPROVAL OF DISCLOSURE STATEMENT AND MOTION FOR CONFIRMATION OF PLAN. Except as otherwise provided by an order shortening time, each party opposing a motion for approval of a disclosure statement or a motion for confirmation of a plan shall serve that opposition on the movant's counsel, or, if none, the movant not later than twenty-eight (28) days after service of the notice of motion, if personally served. If served by mail, opposing party shall have thirty-one (31) days as provided by Fed. R. Bankr. P. 9006(f).

(e) REPLY MEMORANDUM OF POINTS AND AUTHORITIES. Except as otherwise provided by an order shortening time, any reply memorandum must be filed and received by the adverse party the earlier of seven (7) days after service of the opposition or three (3) days prior to the date of the hearing. Service may be by facsimile upon prior agreement of the parties or upon court approval. No response to a reply is permitted without court order.

(f) FAILURE TO FILE OPPOSITION. Failure to timely file opposition to a motion by any party in interest including the United States Trustee and the chapter 13 trustee may be deemed by the court to be consent to the granting of the motion. Failure to timely file written opposition to a motion may also be deemed by the court to be a waiver of oral argument by the opposing party.

9014-5. EMERGENCY MOTIONS.

(a) When emergency relief is sought, the moving party shall personally serve written pleadings on parties or counsel for parties in interest including the United States Trustee or, if the parties or counsel are outside of the Southern District of California, then serve the pleadings by Express or Overnight Mail, and notify them telephonically of the movant's intention to seek emergency relief.

(b) A declaration must accompany any emergency motion, indicating what notice was given to parties in interest and whether any noticed party plans to oppose the relief requested.

(c) The emergency motion, declaration, and order for the relief requested should be filed in the clerk's office with a note that it be directed to the judge's law clerk. The word "Emergency" shall appear in the caption of all emergency motions and orders thereon.

(d) Any party in interest who opposes the emergency motion shall immediately notify the judge's law clerk of this position by telephone. No opposition shall be filed to the emergency motion unless the court otherwise directs.

(e) The court reserves discretion to grant or deny an emergency motion without further hearing. A denial without a hearing is not a disposition on the merits.

(f) The presentation to the court of unnecessary emergency motions, or the failure to comply fully with this Rule, may subject the offender to discipline, including the imposition of costs and attorney's fees. Such sanctions may be awarded regardless of the ultimate determination of the merits of the action when later heard as a fully noticed matter.

9014-6. ORDERS ON CONTESTED MATTERS.

Fed. R. Bankr. P. 7054 and Local Bankruptcy Rule 7054 govern the preparation of orders following hearing on a contested matter.

9014-7. NOTIFICATION OF COURTROOM DEPUTY OF MATTERS TO BE WITHDRAWN, SETTLED OR DISMISSED.

(a) REQUIRED NOTICE. For all matters or proceedings that have been calendared for hearing or conference, it is the duty of the attorney for the moving party to promptly advise the parties in interest and the judge's courtroom deputy by telephone of:

(1) matters or proceedings that have been settled by stipulation of the parties;

(2) matters or proceedings that have been or are being

dismissed; and

(3) submit for filing the proper pleading disposing of the matter within fourteen (14) days.

(b) SANCTIONS. Failure to comply with subsection (a) of this rule subjects the offender, at the discretion of the Court, to appropriate discipline, including the imposition of costs, attorney's fees, and court reporter costs as appropriate.

[The Next Rule is 9018]

RULE 9018. FILING OF SECRET, CONFIDENTIAL, SCANDALOUS, OR DEFAMATORY DOCUMENTS UNDER SEAL

9018-1. CONTENT OF MOTION AND ORDER.

A motion to file documents or pleadings containing secret, confidential, scandalous or defamatory matter under seal may be made ex parte pursuant to Local Bankruptcy Rule 9013-6(a)(1)(H). The ex parte motion shall be accompanied by an order which sets forth the term, if any, of the sealing as well as a general description, by title, of the documents or pleadings to be filed under seal. The order shall be placed in the court file for public inspection.

9018-2. FILING DOCUMENTS UNDER SEAL.

All documents or pleadings filed under seal shall contain the following legend to be contained on the face page of the document or pleading two (2) lines under the department listed for any hearing, or if no hearing has been scheduled, two (2) lines under the title of the document or pleading:

"THIS DOCUMENT IS FILED UNDER SEAL PURSUANT TO COURT ORDER."

9018-3. RETURN OF DOCUMENTS UNDER SEAL.

Documents filed under seal will be returned to the party submitting them upon entry of the final judgment or termination of the appeal, if any, unless otherwise ordered by the court.

RULE 9019. COMPROMISE AND SETTLEMENT OF CONTROVERSY

9019-1. NOTICE TO ALL CREDITORS.

Unless otherwise ordered by the court for cause shown, a stipulation, settlement, or compromise of a controversy may be approved by the court only after timely notice by the trustee or debtor-in-possession as provided by Local Bankruptcy Rules 2002-2(c) and 2002-4. The notice shall describe the nature of the controversy, the terms of the settlement and the financial impact upon the estate, if any. A copy of the notice and proof of service shall be attached as Exhibit "A" to any proposed order.

RULE 9020. CONTEMPT PROCEEDINGS

Unless otherwise ordered by the court, an application for an order to show cause regarding contempt shall be filed in accordance with Local Bankruptcy Rule 9013-6(a)(1)(I).

[The Next Rule is 9025]

RULE 9025. SECURITY AND BONDS; DEPOSIT AND APPROVAL

9025-1. DEPOSIT OF CASH SECURITY.

Whenever the security given pursuant to Fed. R. Bankr. P. 7067 or 9025 is in the form of cash, it shall be accompanied by a bond, signed by the principals, and by the order required by Local Bankruptcy Rule 7022. A copy of the order shall be personally served on the clerk or chief deputy clerk.

9025-2. SURETY BONDS.

An individual who executes a bond as a surety shall attach an affidavit which gives the individual's full name, occupation, residence and business addresses, and which demonstrates that the individual owns real or personal property within this district. After excluding property exempt from execution and deducting the individual's liabilities (including those which have arisen by virtue of giving suretyship on other bonds or undertakings), the real or personal property listed in the affidavit must be of a value no less than twice the amount of the bond. Individual surety bonds in excess of $1,000 shall be approved by a judge. Individual surety bonds of $1,000 or less, and all corporate surety bonds, shall be approved by the clerk. The bond shall have appended thereto the following statement:

"I hereby approve the foregoing bond.

Dated:

. . . .

Clerk [or Judge]"

9025-3. DISBURSEMENT OF FUNDS.

Local Bankruptcy Rule 7022 governs the disbursement of funds deposited with the court.

[The Next Rule is 9027]

RULE 9027. REMOVAL AND REMAND

9027-1. COMMENCEMENT OF A REMOVAL ACTION.

A notice of removal pursuant to Fed. R. Bankr. P. 9027 is filed with the bankruptcy court clerk. Pleadings shall be prepared in the manner required by Local Bankruptcy Rule 9004. The court requires:

(a) the original and two (2) copies of Form B 104, *ADVERSARY PROCEEDING COVER SHEET,* and the complaint;

(b) the original and two (2) copies of the notice of removal;

(c) three (3) copies of the additional process and pleadings required by Fed. R. Bankr. P. 9027(a)(1); and

(d) the original and two (2) copies of the completed Local Form CSD 3007, *SUMMONS IN AN ADVERSARY PROCEEDING.*

9027-2. JURY TRIAL.

If a removal action or answer contains a demand for a jury trial, the words "JURY DEMAND" shall also appear immediately following the title of the document. The words "JURY DEMAND" shall also be noted on the cover sheet required by Local Bankruptcy Rule 9027-1(a). However, notation of the jury demand solely on the cover sheet shall not constitute a demand for jury trial under these rules.

9027-3. REMAND.

A motion for remand under Fed. R. Bankr. P. 9027(d) shall be filed with the bankruptcy court clerk. The hearing on the motion shall be governed by Local Bankruptcy Rule 9014 and shall be calendared for hearing before a bankruptcy judge.

RULE 9028. CONCURRENT JURISDICTION

9028-1. CONCURRENT JURISDICTION.

Each of the bankruptcy judges appointed or assigned to hear cases in this district shall have concurrent district-wide jurisdiction to act in any and all cases and related adversary proceedings under the Bankruptcy Code or the Bankruptcy Act pending in the district.

9028-2. CONTINUING AUTHORITY.

The authority of a bankruptcy judge to whom a case has been referred shall not terminate upon conclusion of the case, but shall continue so long as the bankruptcy judge remains in office, unless the reference is expressly revoked.

[The Next Rule is 9034]

RULE 9034. TRANSMITTAL OF MOTIONS AND APPLICATIONS TO THE UNITED STATES TRUSTEE [OR CHAPTER 13 TRUSTEE] FOR STATEMENT OF POSITION

9034-1. MOTIONS AND APPLICATIONS REQUIRING A STATEMENT OF POSITION OF THE UNITED STATES TRUSTEE.

(a) In a chapter 7, 11, or 12 case, the statement of position of the United States Trustee shall be filed with the court along with the original and two (2) copies of the following motions or applications together with proof of service and the proposed order.

(1) Motions for extension of time for filing schedules and statements required by Fed. R. Bankr. P. 1007 and Local Bankruptcy Rule 1007 and enumerated in Local Bankruptcy Rule 1007-2(a).

(2) Applications to employ attorneys or other professionals including appraisers, auctioneers, agents, and brokers by a debtor-in-possession or trustee required by Local Bankruptcy rules 2014 and 6005.

(3) Applications for interim compensation of debtors and insiders required by Local Bankruptcy Rule 4002-2.

(4) Applications for entry of final decree on consummation of a chapter 11 plan and governed by Fed. R. Bankr. P. 3022.

(b) To obtain the statement of position of the United States Trustee, the moving party or applicant shall serve the motion or application, proposed order, and proof of service, together with a self-addressed stamped envelope, on the United States Trustee. The United States Trustee shall review the motion and proposed order and, no later than five (5) business days from the date of service, if personally served, and eight (8) business days from the date of service, if served by mail, serve upon the moving party or applicant a statement of position, if any, with respect to the motion. Upon the receipt of the statement of position, the moving party or applicant may proceed to file the papers with the court. In the event the statement of position is not timely served by the United States Trustee, the moving party or applicant may proceed to file the papers with the court accompanied by a declaration regarding the attempt to obtain the statement of position of the United States Trustee.

9034-2. MOTIONS REQUIRING A STATEMENT OF POSITION OF THE CHAPTER 13 TRUSTEE.

(a) In a chapter 13 case, the statement of position of the chapter 13 trustee shall be filed with the court along with the original and two (2) copies of the following motions together with proof of service and the proposed order.

(1) Motions for extension of time for filing schedules and statements required by Fed. R. Bankr. P. 1007 and Local Bankruptcy Rule 1007.

(2) Motions for extension of time for filing chapter 13 plan, as governed by Local Bankruptcy Rule 3015-3.

(3) Motions to sell real or personal property of the debtor, as governed by Fed. R. Bankr. P. 6004.

(b) To obtain the statement of position of the chapter 13 trustee, the moving party shall submit the motion, along with the proposed order, and a proof of service, to the trustee for review. The trustee shall stamp the back of the motion and proposed order with the date received and, no later than five (5) business days of receipt, file the motion, proposed order and proof of service, along with the trustee's statement of position with the court. If requested by the moving party, the trustee shall receive-stamp a copy of the motion and return it to the moving party when submitted or in a self-addressed stamped envelope provided by the moving party. In the event the statement of position is not timely filed by the trustee, the moving party or applicant may proceed to file the papers with the court accompanied by a declaration regarding the attempt to obtain the statement of position of the chapter 13 trustee.

[APPENDIX A TO LOCAL RULES]

[Schedule of Fees, January 1, 1998]

SCHEDULE OF FEES AND SPECIAL CHARGES COLLECTIBLE BY THE CLERK OF THE BANKRUPTCY COURT [28 U.S.C. § 1930]

[APPENDIX B TO LOCAL RULES]

[DISTRICT COURT LOCAL RULES: CROSS-REFERENCE TABLE]

LOCAL RULES OF THE UNITED STATES BANKRUPTCY COURT FOR THE SOUTHERN DISTRICT OF CALIFORNIA

CROSS-REFERENCE TABLE

District Court Local Rule		Bankruptcy Court Local Rule
1.1(a)	Modified by	1001-1
1.1(b)	Modified by	1001-2(b)
1.1(c)	Modified by	1001-2(a)
1.1(d)		Applies
1.1(e)	Modified by	1001-4
1.2(a)		Not Applicable
1.2(b)		Not Applicable
3.1	Modified by	7003-1(a), 9027-1(a)
3.2		Not Applicable
4.1(a)		Applies
4.1(b)	Modified by	7041-2
4.1(c)		Applies
4.1(d)	Modified by	7004-1(a), 7005-1
4.5	Modified by	Appendix A
5.1(a)	Modified by	9004-3(a)
5.1(b)	Modified by	9004-3(l)
5.1(c)		Not Applicable
5.1(d)	Modified by	1007-2(a), 9004-3(j)
5.1(e)	Modified by	9004-3(i)
5.1(f)		Not Applicable
5.1(g)	Modified by	7003-1
5.1(h)		Applies
5.1(i)(1)	Modified by	9004-3(m)
5.1(i)(2)		Not Applicable
5.1(i)(3)		Applies
5.1(i)(4)	Modified by	9004-3(n)
5.1(i)(5)	Modified by	9004-3(m)(8)
5.1(j)(1)	Modified by	9004-3(d)(1) to (4)
5.1(j)(2)	Modified by	9004-3(d)(5)

District Court Local Rule		Bankruptcy Court Local Rule
5.1(j)(3)	Modified by	7003-2, 9004-4, 9027-2
5.1(j)(4)	Modified by	7041-1, 9004-3(b), 9004-4(a)(4)
5.1(k)	Modified by	7012
5.1(l)		Applies
5.2	Modified by	9006-3
5.3	Modified by	5005
5.3(a)(1)	Modified by	5005-1(a)
5.3(a)(2)	Modified by	5005-1(b)
5.3(a)(3)	Modified by	5005-1(c)
5.3(b)	Modified by	5005-2
5.3(c)	Modified by	5005-3
5.3(d)	Modified by	5005-4
5.3(e)	Modified by	5005-5
7.1(a)		Applies
7.1(b)	Modified by	9006-1(e)
7.1(c)	Modified by	9006-1
7.1(d)(1)		Applies
7.1(d)(2)		Not Applicable
7.1(d)(3)		Not Applicable
7.1(e)(1)	Modified by	2002-1(b), 9006-1(e), 9013-3, 9014-3, 9014-4(a)
7.1(e)(2)	Modified by	9013-4, 9014-4(b)
7.1(e)(3)	Modified by	9013-5, 9014-4(d)
7.1(e)(4)		Not Applicable
7.1(e)(5)		Not Applicable
7.1(e)(6)	Modified by	9006-1(f)
7.1(e)(7)		Not Applicable
7.1(e)(8)		Not Applicable
7.1(f)(1)	Modified by	9013-2, 9014-2
7.1(f)(2)(a)	Modified by	9013-2, 9014-2
7.1(f)(2)(b)		Applies
7.1(f)(3)(a)		Applies
7.1(f)(3)(b)		Applies
7.1(f)(3)(c)	Modified by	9014-4(e)
7.1(g)(1)	Modified by	9014-7

District Court Local Rule		Bankruptcy Court Local Rule
7.1(g)(2)	Modified by	9014-7
7.1(g)(3)		Not Applicable
7.1(h)	Modified by	9006-2
7.1(i)(1)		Applies
7.1(i)(2)		Not Applicable
7.1(j)	Modified by	9006-1(d)
7.2(a)		Applies
7.2(b)	Modified by	9004-3(g)
7.2(c)	Modified by	9004-3(g)
8.2		Not Applicable
9.2		Not Applicable
11.1		Not Applicable
12.1	Modified by	9006-1(f)
15.1		Applies
16.1(a)(1)		Applies
16.1(a)(2)		Not Applicable
16.1(b)		Applies
16.1(c)		Not Applicable
16.1(d)	Modified by	7016-5
16.1(e)		Not Applicable
16.1(f)(1)	Modified by	7016-3
16.1(f)(2)		Not Applicable
16.1(f)(3)(a)		Not Applicable
16.1(f)(3)(b)	Modified by	7016-9(c)
16.1(f)(3)(c)	Modified by	7016-9(e)
16.1(f)(3)(d)	Modified by	7016-9(g)
16.1(f)(4)		Not Applicable
16.1(f)(5)(a)	Modified by	7016-7(a)
16.1(f)(5)(b)	Modified by	7016-7(b)
16.1(f)(5)(c)	Modified by	7016-7(c)
16.1(f)(5)(d)	Modified by	7016-7(d)
16.1(f)(6)(a)	Modified by	7016-8(a)
16.1(f)(6)(b)	Modified by	7016-8(b)
16.1(f)(6)(c)	Modified by	7016-8(c)
16.1(f)(6)(d)	Modified by	7016-8(d)
16.1(f)(6)(e)		Not Applicable
16.1(f)(7)(a)	Modified by	7016-9(a)
16.1(f)(7)(b)	Modified by	7016-9(a)

District Court Local Rule		Bankruptcy Court Local Rule
16.1(f)(7)(c)	Modified by	7016-9(b)
16.1(f)(7)(d)	Modified by	7016-9(d)
16.1(f)(8)	Modified by	7016-10
16.1(f)(9)	Modified by	7016-11
16.1(f)(10)(a)	Modified by	7016-12(a)
16.1(f)(10)(b)(1)	Modified by	7016-12(b)
16.1(f)(10)(b)(2)	Modified by	7016-12(c)
16.1(f)(10)(c)	Modified by	7016-12(d)
16.1(f)(10)(d)	Modified by	7016-12(e)
16.2		Not Applicable
16.3		Not Applicable
16.4	Modified by	7040-6
16.5(a) to (g)		Not Applicable
16.5(h)	Modified by	7016-6(e)
16.5(i)	Modified by	7016-6(a)
16.5(j)		Not Applicable
16.5(k)	Modified by	7016-2(a)
16.5(l)(1)		Not Applicable
16.5(l)(2)	Modified by	7041-2
16.5(l)(3)	Modified by	9006-1(f)
16.5(l)(4)	Modified by	7041-2, 7055
16.5(l)(5)		Not Applicable
16.5(l)(6)		Not Applicable
16.5(l)(7) to (11)		Not Applicable
16.6		Not Applicable
17.1(a)		Applies
17.1(b)		Applies
17.1(c)		Applies
23.1		Not Applicable
24.1		Not Applicable
26.1(a)	Modified by	7026-2
26.1(b)	Modified by	7026-3
26.1(c)	Modified by	7026-4
26.1(d)		Not Applicable
26.1(e)		Not Applicable
26.1(f)	Modified by	7026-1
28.1(a)		Not Applicable
28.1(b)(1)		Not Applicable

District Court Local Rule		Bankruptcy Court Local Rule
28.1(b)(2)		Applies
30.1(a)	Modified by	7030-4
30.1(b)	Modified by	7030-5
30.1(c)	Modified by	7030-6
30.1(d)	Modified by	7030-1
33.1(a)	Modified by	7033-2
33.1(b)	Modified by	7033-3
33.1(c)	Modified by	7033-4
33.1(d)	Modified by	7033-1
34.1	Modified by	7034
36.1(a)		Not Applicable
36.1(b)	Modified by	7036-2
36.1(c)	Modified by	7036-3
36.1(d)	Modified by	7036-1
38.1	Modified by	7003-2, 9027-2
40.1(a)		Applies
40.1(b)		Applies
40.1(c)		Applies
40.1(d)	Modified by	1015-2(c)
40.1(e)	Modified by	1015-2(a), 7003-1(c)
40.1(f)	Modified by	1015-2(b), 7003-1(c)
40.1(g)	Modified by	1015-2(c), 7003-1(c)
40.1(h)	Modified by	7003-1(b)
40.1(i)		Applies
41.1(a)	Modified by	7041-2
41.1(b)		Applies
47.1	Modified by	7040-4
48.1	Modified by	7040-3
51.1(a)	Modified by	7040-5(a)
51.1(b)	Modified by	7040-5(b)
51.1(c)	Modified by	7040-5(c)
51.1(d)	Modified by	7040-5(d)
52.1(a)(1)	Modified by	7054-4
52.1(a)(2)		Applies
52.1(a)(3)		Not Applicable
52.1(b)(1)	Modified by	7054-2
52.1(b)(2)		Applies
52.1(b)(3)		Applies

District Court Local Rule		Bankruptcy Court Local Rule
53.1		Not Applicable
54.1(a)	Modified by	7054-5(a)
54.1(b)	Modified by	7054-5(d)
54.1(c) to (j)		Applies
55.1	Modified by	7055
65.1(a) to (c)	Modified by	7065
65.1.2(a)		Applies
65.1.2(b)		Applies
65.1.2(c)		Applies
65.1.2(d)		Applies
65.1.2(e)	Modified by	9025-2
65.1.2(f)		Applies
65.1.2(g)		Applies
65.1.2(h)		Applies
66.1		Not Applicable
67.1(a)	Modified by	7022-2, 9025-3
67.1(b)		Applies
67.1(c)	Modified by	7022-1
67.1(d)(1)		Applies
67.1(d)(2)	Modified by	7022-1
72.1		Not Applicable
72.2		Not Applicable
73		Not Applicable
74		Not Applicable
77.1		Not Applicable
77.2		Applies
77.4		Applies
77.6		Applies
79.1	Modified by	7016-13
79.2(a)		Applies
79.2(b)	Modified by	9018-3
83.1(a)		Applies
83.1(b)		Applies
83.2		Applies
83.3		Applies by Reference in 9010-1
83.3(a)		Applies
83.3(b)		Applies

District Court Local Rule		Bankruptcy Court Local Rule
83.3(c)(1)		Applies by Reference in 9010-2
83.3(c)(2)		Applies
83.3(c)(3)		Applies
83.3(c)(4)		Not Applicable
83.3(c)(5)		Applies by Reference in 9010-3
83.3(c)(6)		Applies
83.3(d)		Applies
83.3(e)		Applies
83.3(f)	Modified by	9004-2
83.3(g) to (j)		Applies
83.4		Applies
83.5		Applies
83.6		Applies
83.7(a)	Modified	6004.2-(b)
83.7(b)		Applies
83.7(c)		Applies
83.7(d)		Not Applicable
83.8		Not Applicable
83.9		Applies
83.10	Modified by	7040
83.11(a)	Modified by	1002-1(b)
83.11(b)		Applies
HC.1		Not Applicable
HC.2		Not Applicable
HC.3		Not Applicable
A.1		Not Applicable
B.1		Not Applicable
C.1		Not Applicable
E.1		Not Applicable
F.1		Not Applicable
Criminal Rules 1.1 thru 58.2		Not Applicable

[APPENDIX C TO LOCAL RULES]

[REQUIRED FORMS CROSS-REFERENCE TABLE]

FORMS REQUIRED BY THE LOCAL RULES OF THE UNITED STATES BANKRUPTCY COURT FOR THE SOUTHERN DISTRICT OF CALIFORNIA

Number	Title	Reference
B 1	VOLUNTARY PETITION	LBR 1007-2(a)
B 104	ADVERSARY PROCEEDING COVER SHEET	LBR 7003-1(a)(1) LBR 9027-1(a)
CSD 1003	NOTICE OF RELATED CASES	LBR 1015-2
CSD 1004	DECLARATION RE: FILING OF PETITION, SCHEDULES & STATEMENTS	LBR 1007-2(a)(13)
CSD 1006	APPLICATION TO PAY FILING FEES IN INSTALLMENTS	LBR 1006-2 LBR 1007-2(a)(1)
CSD 1007	SPECIAL REQUIREMENTS FOR MAILING ADDRESSES	LBR 1007-1
CSD 1009	DISCLOSURE OF COMPENSATION OF ATTORNEY FOR DEBTOR	FRBP 2016(b)
CSD 1010	REQUEST FOR WAIVER OF DISKETTE REQUIREMENT	LBR 1007-2(a)(13)
CSD 1050	SUBPOENA FOR RULE 2004 EXAMINATION	LBR 2004-1(b)
CSD 1051	SUBPOENA IN A CASE UNDER THE BANKRUPTCY CODE	FRBP 9016
CSD 1099	BALANCE OF SCHEDULES AND/OR CHAPTER 13 PLAN	
CSD 1100	AMENDMENT	LBR 1009-2
CSD 1101	NOTICE TO CREDITORS OF THE ABOVE-NAMED DEBTOR ADDED BY AMENDMENT	LBR 1009-2
CSD 1105	ORDER CONVERTING CASE UNDER CHAPTER 7 TO CASE UNDER CHAPTER 11	LBR 1017-2(a)(1)
CSD 1106	ORDER CONVERTING CASE UNDER CHAPTER 7 TO CASE UNDER CHAPTER 12	LBR 1017-2(a)(1)

Number	Title	Reference
CSD 1107	ORDER CONVERTING CASE UNDER CHAPTER 7 TO CASE UNDER CHAPTER 13	LBR 1017-2(a)(1)
CSD 1108	ORDER CONVERTING CASE UNDER CHAPTER 11 TO CASE UNDER CHAPTER 7	LBR 1017-2(a)(1)
CSD 1109	ORDER CONVERTING CASE UNDER CHAPTER 11 TO CASE UNDER CHAPTER 12	LBR 1017-2(a)(1)
CSD 1119	SUMMONS TO DEBTOR IN INVOLUNTARY CASE	FRBP 1004 FRBP 1010
CSD 1129	NOTICE OF CONVERSION OF CASE UNDER CHAPTER 13 TO A CASE UNDER CHAPTER 7 BY DEBTOR	LBR 1017-2(b)(2)
CSD 1143	FEE APPLICATION SUMMARY (EXHIBIT "A")	LBR 2016-2(b)
CSD 1144	ORDER APPROVING (INTERIM) (FINAL) APPLICATION OF (APPLICANT) FOR COMPENSATION AND REIMBURSEMENT OF EXPENSES	LBR 2016-4
CSD 1148	REQUEST FOR SPECIAL CHARGES BY CHAPTER 11 PLAN PROPONENT	LBR 3020-1
CSD 1149	NOTICE OF HEARING AND MOTION FOR APPROVAL OF DISCLOSURE STATEMENT, PLAN, OR MODIFIED PLAN	LBR 2002-3(b)(2) LBR 3015-7(b) LBR 9014-3(b)
CSD 1151	SUMMARY OF BALLOTING ON CHAPTER 11 PLAN DATED	LBR 3018-2
CSD 1170	NOTICE OF MODIFIED CHAPTER 13 PLAN ***PRIOR*** TO CONFIRMATION	LBR 3015-7(a) LBR 3015-8(b)(1)
CSD 1172	OBJECTION TO CONFIRMATION OF CHAPTER 13 PLAN (See CSD 1173 for Notice)	LBR 3015-4
CSD 1173	NOTICE OF HEARING ON OBJECTION TO CONFIRMATION OF CHAPTER 13 PLAN	LBR 3015-8(b)(1)
CSD 1174	REQUEST BY DEBTOR FOR DISMISSAL OF CHAPTER 13 AND ORDER	LBR 1017-2(b)(1)

Number	Title	Reference
CSD 1176	ORDER DISMISSING CHAPTER 13 CASE ON REQUEST OF DEBTOR	LBR 1017-2(b)(1)
CSD 1180	NOTICE OF INTENDED ACTION AND OPPORTUNITY FOR HEARING (for notice to all creditors)	LBR 2002-2(c)
CSD 1181	NOTICE OF HEARING AND MOTION (ALL CREDITORS)-EXHIBIT A	LBR 2002-3(b)(1) LBR 9014-3(b)
CSD 1182	NOTICE OF MOTION FOR (DESCRIPTION OF ACTION) (for notice to less than all creditors)	LBR 5010-1 LBR 9013-3(a)
CSD 1183	NOTICE OF MOTION AND HEARING (for notice to less than all creditors)	LBR 9014-3(c)
CSD 1184	REQUEST AND NOTICE OF HEARING	LBR 2002-2(d) LBR 9013-4
CSD 1185	NOTICE OF FILING OF A MOTION FOR RELIEF FROM AUTOMATIC STAY	LBR 4001-2(c) LBR 4001-8
CSD 1186	REQUEST FOR HEARING ON MOTION FOR RELIEF FROM AUTOMATIC STAY AND NOTICE OF HEARING	LBR 4001-3
CSD 1190	NOTICE OF ENTRY (CASE)	LBR 7054-3(b)(2)
CSD 1229	REAFFIRMATION AGREEMENT (See CSD 1231 for Notice)	LBR 4008
CSD 1230	INSTRUCTIONS TO UNREPRESENTED DEBTORS REGARDING THE REAFFIRMATION OF A DEBT [See CSD 1231 for Notice]	LBR 4008-1
CSD 1231	NOTICE OF HEARING ON AGREEMENT TO REAFFIRM A DEBT	LBR 4008
CSD 1490	ORDER REOPENING ESTATE	LBR 5010-2
CSD 1514	GUIDELINES FOR THE SUBSTANTIVE CONSOLIDATION OR JOINT ADMINISTRATION OF RELATED DEBTOR ENTITIES	FRBP 1015
CSD 1546	ATTORNEY CHANGE OF INFORMATION FORM	LBR 9010-4
CSD 2015	OBJECTION TO CLAIM AND NOTICE THEREOF	LBR 3007-2(a)

Number	Title	Reference
CSD 2018	REPORT OF ABANDONMENT OF REAL PROPERTY	LBR 6007-3(a)(2)
CSD 2024	REPORT OF SALE	LBR 6004-3(a)(1)
CSD 2044	APPLICATION TO EMPLOY AUCTIONEER	LBR 6005-1(a)
CSD 2045	ORDER APPOINTING AUCTIONEER	LBR 6005-1(a)
CSD 3007	SUMMONS IN AN ADVERSARY PROCEEDING	LBR 7003-1(a)(2) LBR 7004-1 LBR 9027-1(d)
CSD 3008	THIRD-PARTY SUMMONS IN AN ADVERSARY PROCEEDING	FRBP 7014
CSD 3009	SUBPOENA IN AN ADVERSARY PROCEEDING	FRBP 9016
CSD 3010	PROOF OF SERVICE (ADVERSARY)	LBR 9006-3(c)
CSD 3015	NOTICE OF MOTION AND HEARING (ADVERSARY)	LBR 9014-3(c)
CSD 3018	CERTIFICATE OF COMPLIANCE WITH EARLY CONFERENCE OF COUNSEL [LOCAL BANKRUPTCY RULE 7016-2]	LBR 7016-2(c)
CSD 3019	NOTICE OF PRE-TRIAL STATUS CONFERENCE	LBR 7016-2(c)
CSD 3021	PRE-TRIAL ORDER	LBR 7016-9(b)
CSD 3026	LIST OF EXHIBITS SUBMITTED BY ATTORNEY	LBR 7016-9(e)
CSD 3029	JUDGMENT BY DEFAULT (See CSD 3030 for Request to Enter Default)	FRBP 7055 LBR 7055-1
CSD 3030	REQUEST TO ENTER DEFAULT	LBR 7055-1(a)
CSD 3050	NOTICE OF ENTRY OF JUDGMENT OR ORDER	LBR 7054-3(b)(2)
CSD 3054	CERTIFICATION OF JUDGMENT FOR REGISTRATION IN ANOTHER DISTRICT	LBR 7069-4
CSD 3060	APPLICATION FOR ORDER TO APPEAR FOR EXAMINATION AND ORDER THEREON	LBR 7069-1
CSD 3066	BILL OF COSTS	LBR 7054-5(b)

Number	Title	Reference
CSD 4000	APPLICATION TO JOIN COMPENSATED MEDIATION PANEL	LBR 7016-6(c)
CSD 4001	APPLICATION TO JOIN MEDIATION PANEL	LBR 7016-6(a)
CSD 4002	ORDER APPOINTING MEDIATOR AND ASSIGNMENT TO MEDIATION	LBR 7016-6(e)(2)
CSD 4003	CASE QUESTIONNAIRE IN CONNECTION WITH MEDIATION PROCEDURE	LBR 7016-6(f)(2)
CSD 4004	MEDIATOR'S CERTIFICATE OF COMPLIANCE	LBR 7016-6(g)(2)

APPENDIX D

APPENDIX D1
LOCAL RULES OF THE UNITED STATES BANKRUPTCY COURT
FOR THE SOUTHERN DISTRICT OF CALIFORNIA
GUIDELINES FOR FIRST DAY MOTIONS

1. The court recognizes that certain matters must be addressed immediately after the commencement of a chapter 11 case in. order to ensure the least possible disruption. to the debtor's ongoing business operations and thereby enhance the chances for success in chapter 11. Matters that typically require expedited consideration include, without limitation, requests to pay prepetition payroll, to honor customer deposits and obligations, to authorize maintenance of existing bank accounts and cash management systems, and to determine adequate assurance for utility companies. When expedited relief is sought by the debtor-in-possession at the outset of the case in the form of motions ("First Day Motions"), the debtor-in-possession shall serve written pleadings on parties or counsel for parties in interest, including the United States Trustee, any committee of creditors or equity security holders established prior or subsequent to the chapter 11 filing or, if none, the twenty largest unsecured creditors and any secured creditor whose collateral includes cash collateral or whose lien(s) might be affected by the relief sought.

2. When made in advance of the chapter 11 filing, service of the moving papers may be by Express or Overnight Mail. When made after the chapter 11 filing, service shall be made by facsimile, personal service or other electronic means (by consent) provided, however, that Express or Overnight

Mail may be used where a party is unable to notify by facsimile, personal service or other electronic means (by consent).

3. The First Day Motion, declaration, and order for the relief requested should be filed in the clerk's office with a note that it be directed to the judge's law clerk. The words "First Day Motion" shall appear in the caption of all emergency motions and orders thereon.

4. The debtor-in-possession shall advise the judge's law clerk and the United States Trustee by telephone of the filing of any First Day Motion(s).

5. First Day Motions with respect to the use of cash collateral and/or post-petition financing shall comply with Fed. R. Bankr. P. 4001(b) or (c).

6. Authorization for payment of insiders of the debtor may be obtained pursuant to First Day Motions. Any such motion shall state the nature and extent of the duties to be performed by the person to be compensated and the business justification for the amount of the compensation proposed and shall be limited in duration to sixty (60) days. A personal financial declaration wit the information required by Local Bankruptcy Rule 4002-2(b)(2-4) is required if the insider applicant has a 20% or greater ownership interest in the debtor or is a sole member of the Board of Directors.

7. The court reserves discretion to grant or deny a First Day Motion without further hearing. A denial. without a hearing is not a disposition on the merits.

8. Any party in interest who opposes a First Day Motion shall immediately notify the judge's law clerk of its position by telephone. No opposition shall be filed to a First Day Motion unless the court otherwise directs.

9. Within two (2) business days after the entry of any First Day Order, the debtor-in-possession shall serve a conformed copy of the order on any committee of creditors or equity security holders established prior or subsequent to the chapter 11 filing or, if none, the twenty largest unsecured creditors and any secured creditor whose collateral includes cash collateral or whose lien(s) might be affected by the relief sought, on the United States Trustee and on such other entities as the court may direct. A proof of service shall, be filed with the court no later than the next business day following the date of service.

10. Any party in interest may file a motion to modify any First Day Order under this rule, other than any order entered pursuant to 11 U.S.C. §§ 363 and 364 with respect to the use of cash collateral and/or approval of post-petition financing, within thirty (30) days of the entry of such order, unless otherwise ordered by the court. Any such motion for modification. shall be given expedited consideration by the court. In any such motion for modification, the debtor-in-possession shall have the burden of proof with respect to the propriety of the relief granted in the original First Day Order.

APPENDIX D2
LOCAL RULES OF THE UNITED STATES BANKRUPTCY COURT FOR THE SOUTHERN DISTRICT OF CALIFORNIA GUIDELINES FOR MOTIONS TO USE CASH COLLATERAL OR TO OBTAIN CREDIT

This court is often requested to rule on requests by debtors (and sometimes chapter 11 trustees) for authority to use cash collateral or obtain credit. In an effort to provide guidance to debtors and secured creditors, the court has adopted the following guidelines. As a preliminary matter, all financing motions should be by motion pursuant to Fed. R. Bankr. P. 2002, 4001, and 9014 and Local Bankruptcy Rule 9014 and should provide a summary of the essential terms of the proposed use of cash collateral and/or financing (e.g., the maximum borrowing available on a final basis, the interim borrowing limit, borrowing conditions, points or other costs, interest rate, maturity, events of default, use of funds limitations, and protections afforded under 11 U.S.C. §§ 363 and 364). The debtor should be prepared to present a budget at the interim hearing on such cash collateral usage and/or financing that would support the need for such interim funding. The budget should cover the period for which cash collateral use is sought.

In addition, the court will typically NOT authorize (particularly in interim orders) use of cash collateral and/or financing agreements that contain any one or more of the following:

1. Provisions that grant cross-collateralization protection (other than replacement liens) to the prepetition secured creditor (i.e., clauses that secure prepetition debt by post-petition assets in which the secured creditor would not otherwise have a security interest by virtue of its prepetition security agreement or applicable law).

2. Provisions or findings of fact that bind the estate or all parties in interest with respect to the validity, perfection or amount of the secured creditor's prepetition lien or debt or the waiver of claims against the secured creditors without first giving parties in interest at least seventy-five (75) days from the entry of the interim order and the official committee of unsecured creditors, if formed, no less than sixty (60) days notice from the later of the date of its formation or the date of its retention of counsel to investigate such matters, unless otherwise directed by the court.

3. Provisions that seek to waive rights under 11 U.S.C. § 506(c)).

4. Provisions that grant immediately to the prepetition secured creditor liens on the debtor's claims and causes of action arising under 11 U.S.C. §§ 544, 545, 547, 548, and 549.

5. Provisions that "roll over" prepetition debt of the prepetition secured creditor to post-petition debt.

6. Provisions which provide carveouts for administrative expenses that do not treat all professionals equally or on a pro rata basis.

7. Provisions in any agreement for use of cash collateral, financing or conditioning the automatic stay that in effect operate to divest the debtor-in-possession of any discretion. in the formulation of a plan or administration of the estate or limit access to the court to seek any relief under other applicable provisions of law. Such provisions include, without limitation, agreements with respect to the treatment of claims.

If a party believes that compelling circumstances justify a departure from these guidelines, the motion must: (a) recite whether the proposed form of order and/or underlying cash. collateral stipulation or loan agreement contains any provision of the type indicated above, (b) identify the location of any such provision in the proposed form of interim order, cash collateral stipulation and/or loan agreement, and (c) justify for the inclusion of such provision. In particular, the motion shall, in checklist fashion set forth below, identify departures from the guidelines:

Description of Provision	Page No.	Line No. (If Applicable)
☐ Cross-collateralization clauses		
☐ Provisions or findings of fact that bind the estate or all parties in interest with respect to the validity, perfection or amount of the secured party's lien or debt		
☐ Provisions that seek to waive rights under 11 U.S.C. § 506(c)		
☐ Provisions that grant immediately to the prepetition secured creditor liens on the debtor's claims and causes of action arising under 11 U.S.C. §§ 544, 545, 547, 548, and 549		

- ☐ Provisions that "roll over" prepetition debt of the prepetition secured creditor to postpetition debt
- ☐ Provisions which provide carveouts for administrative expenses that do not treat all professionals equally or on a pro rata basis
- ☐ Provisions that operate, as a practical matter, to divest the debtor-in-possession of any discretion in the formulation of a plan or administration of the estate or limit access to the court to seek any relief under other applicable provisions of law

If the above-described checklist is not submitted, counsel for the proponent of the cash collateral or relief from stay stipulation, must certify that no such provisions are contained in the agreement submitted for approval.

APPENDIX D3
LOCAL RULES OF THE UNITED STATES BANKRUPTCY COURT FOR THE SOUTHERN DISTRICT OF CALIFORNIA GUIDELINES FOR THE SALE OF SUBSTANTIALLY ALL ASSETS UNDER § 363 WITHIN 60 DAYS OF THE FILING OF THE PETITION

1. DECLARATION OF COUNSEL FOR DEBTOR-IN-POSSESSION.

In connection with any hearing to approve the sale of substantially all assets within sixty (60) days of the filing of the petition, the request for the special setting of a hearing or the sale motion itself when regularly noticed, should comply with Local Bankruptcy Rules 2002 and 6004 unless otherwise ordered by the court and be supported by a separate declaration by counsel for the debtor-in-possession covering the following points:

A. Retention of Counsel. The date counsel was retained by the debtor, the approximate number of hours of professional time expended prepetition, compensation paid to counsel prepetition including source of payment and the approximate amount of accrued but unpaid compensation.

B. Communications with Creditors, A description of any written communications of the debtor with creditors during the prepetition reorganization process. Copies of letters should be attached. If letters contain confidential information, counsel may apply to the court to submit such documents under seal pursuant to Local Bankruptcy Rules 9018-1 and 9018-2.

C. Communications with Shareholders or Partners. A description, of any written. communications with shareholders or partners of a partnership during the prepetition reorganization process. Copies of letters should be attached. If letters contain confidential information, counsel may apply to the court to submit such documents under seal pursuant to Local Bankruptcy Rules 9018-1 and 9018-2.

D. Creditors' Committee. If a creditors' committee existed prepetition, indicate the date and manner in which the committee was formed.

E. Counsel for Committee. If the prepetition creditors' committee retained counsel, indicate the date counsel was engaged and the selection process.

F. Sale Contingencies. Statement of all contingencies to the sale agreement together with a copy of the agreement.

G. Creditor Contact List. If no committee has been formed, a list of contact persons together with fax and phone numbers for each of the largest 20 unsecured creditors.

H. Administrative Debts. Assuming the sale is approved, an. estimate of administrative debts to be incurred prior to closing and the source of payment for such debts.

I. Proceeds of Sale. An estimate of the gross proceeds anticipated from the sale together with an estimate of the net proceeds coming to the estate with an explanation of the items making up the difference.

J. Debt Structure of Debtor. A brief description of the debtor's debt structure including the amount of the debtor's secured debt, priority claims and general unsecured claims.

K. Disposition of Proceeds. A statement setting forth, to the best of declarant's knowledge, the likely distribution of proceeds to secured claimants, administrative claimants, priority claimants and general unsecured creditors.

2. DECLARATION OF RESPONSIBLE INDIVIDUAL FOR DEBTOR-IN-POSSESSION.

Counsel's declaration referred to in paragraph 1 above should be accompanied by a declaration from the responsible individual covering the following matters:

A. Alternatives to Sale. A description of the efforts, if any, to pursue other alternatives such as financing, capital infusion, etc., including the period of time involved and the results achieved.

B. Marketing of Assets. A description of the manner in which the assets were marketed for sale including the period of time involved and the results achieved.

C. Decision to Sell. The date on which the debtor agreed to sell the assets.

D. Asset Valuation. Disclosure of the debtor's prior valuations, within the last year, of the assets to be sold, if any (i.e., book value, appraisals, financial statements, etc.).

F. Tax Consequences of the Sale. A statement by a qualified person describing the tax consequences of the proposed sale.

F. Relationship of Buyer. A statement identifying the buyer and setting forth, to the best of declarant's knowledge, all of the buyer's (including its officers, directors and shareholders) connections with the debtor, creditors, any other party in interest, their respective attorneys, accountants, the United States Trustee or any person employed in the office of the United States Trustee.

G. Post Sale Relationship with Debtor. A statement setting forth, to the best of declarant's knowledge, any relationship or connection the debtor (including its officers, directors, shareholders, and employees) will have with the buyer after the consummation of the sale, assuming it is approved.

H. Relationship with Secured Creditors. If the sale involves the payment of all or a portion of secured debt(s), a statement of all connections between. debtor's officers, directors, employees or other insiders and each secured creditor involved (for example, release of insider's guaranty).

I. Insider Compensation. Disclosure of current compensation received by officers, directors, key employees or other insiders pending approval of the sale. Declaration shall include the dates the orders approving compensation were entered, the terms of the orders, and whether the current compensation differs from the approved terms.

3. DECLARATION OF COUNSEL FOR CREDITORS' COMMITTEE.

Any counsel who has represented a prepetition creditors' committee should submit a declaration covering the following points:

A. Retention of counsel. Same as paragraph l.A above.

B. Communications with Creditors. Same as paragraph 1.8 above.

C. Communications with Shareholders or Partners. Same as paragraph l.C above.

D. Involvement in Sale. A description of the committee's and counsel's involvement in the negotiation of the sale.

4. HEARING AND NOTICE REGARDING BID PROCEDURES MOTIONS AND SALE MOTIONS.

Generally, the sale of substantially all assets must proceed in two steps as follows:

A. Sale Procedures Motions. In all assets sales where a debtor-in-possession seeks to set a procedure for overbids, including credit bidding, other than as provided in paragraph S below or to pay damages to a prospective purchaser as defined in paragraph 9 below, a motion to approve sale procedures must be filed and hearing held before notice of the sale is given.

B. Notice of Sale. All notices of sale given to creditors and other parties in interest must contain the information required by paragraphs 1.H through 1.K and paragraphs 2.A through 2.1-1 above, in addition to any other orders made as a result of a Sale Procedures Motion. Unless the court orders otherwise, all sales will be governed by these guidelines, including auctions or presentation of competing bids.

5. GOOD FAITH FINDING.

There must be an evidentiary basis for a finding of good faith under § 363(m). Evidence can be presented in the form of a declaration from the prospective purchaser.

6. COMPETING BIDS.

Unless the court orders otherwise, competing bids may be presented at the time of the hearing.

7. FINANCIAL ABILITY TO CLOSE.

Unless the court orders otherwise, any competing bidder must be prepared to demonstrate to the satisfaction of the court its ability to consummate the transaction if it is the successful bidder.

8. OVERBIDS.

Unless the court orders otherwise, each overbid must be at least 5% more than the amount of the original offer. The amount of the original offer is determined without regard to any commission or payment to a broker or agent.

9. DAMAGES PAYABLE TO PROSPECTIVE PURCHASER.

Whether denominated liquidated damages, breakup fee, topping fee or other designation, no damages of any kind are payable to a prospective purchaser or its agents absent approval of the court. If a provision for damages is contained in the original purchase agreement, the provision should provide that it must be approved separately from the agreement itself as part of the Sale Procedure Motion.

A request for the approval of a damage provision shall be supported by, in addition to any other required papers, a declaration from counsel for the debtor-in-possession setting forth the precise conditions under which damages would be payable and the factual basis on which the seller determined the provision was reasonable. Counsel for the proposed buyer may, but is not required to, submit a similar declaration.

APPENDIX D4
LOCAL RULES OF THE UNITED STATES BANKRUPTCY COURT FOR THE SOUTHERN DISTRICT OF CALIFORNIA GUIDELINES FOR PREPACKAGED CHAPTER 11 CASES

1. GOALS.

The purpose of this guideline is to establish a uniform approach for commencing and administering "prepackaged chapter 11 cases" in the United States Bankruptcy Court for the Southern District of California. Specifically, this guideline defines a "prepackaged chapter 11 case" and attempts to provide bankruptcy practitioners with help in dealing with practical matters which either are not addressed at all by statute or rules or are addressed indirectly in a piecemeal fashion. by statutes, general rules, and/or local rules that were not enacted specifically with prepackaged chapter 11 cases in mind. Although each case is different, many issues are common to all prepackaged cases. Judicial economy, as well as procedural predictability for debtors and creditors, will. be enhanced by promulgation of uniform guidelines to deal with these common issues. The guidelines are advisory only; the court retains the power to depart from them.

2. DEFINITION OF PREPACKAGED CHAPTER 11 CASE.

For purposes of these guidelines, a "prepackaged chapter 11 case" is one in which the debtor negotiates terms of a plan and solicits acceptances thereof prior to filing the petition. In these circumstances, the debtor shall file a motion scheduling a confirmation hearing for the prepackaged plan ("Prepackaged Scheduling Motion") as set forth below.

3. CRITERIA FOR PREPACKAGED CHAPTER 11 CASE; CONTENTS OF PREPACKAGED SCHEDULING MOTION.

A. Content of Prepackaged Scheduling Motion. The Prepackaged Scheduling Motion shall:

(1) represent that (a) the solicitation of votes to accept or reject the debtor's plan. required for confirmation of that plan was completed prior to commencement of the debtor's chapter 11 case, and that no additional solicitation of votes on that plan is contemplated by the debtor, or (b) the solicitation, of all votes to accept or reject the debtor's plan required for confirmation of that plan has been deemed adequate by the court pursuant to paragraph 3.C.(2) below such that no additional solicitation will be required;

(2) represent that the requisite acceptances of such plan have been obtained from each class of claims or interests as to which solicitation is required except as provided in paragraph 3.A.(3) below; and

(3) with respect to any class of interests that has not accepted the plan, whether or not it is deemed not to have' accepted the plan under § 1126(g), represent that the debtor is requesting confirmation under § 1129(b); and

(4) request entry of an order scheduling the hearing (a) on confirmation of the plan and (b) to determine whether the debtor has satisfied the requirements of either 11 U.S.C. § 1126 (b)(l) or 11 U.S.C. § 1126(b)(2), for a date that is not more than ninety (90) days following the petition date.

(5) The motion shall be supported by a declaration and have attached (a) a summary of the votes accepting or rejecting the debtor's plan; and (b) copies of any

solicitation used to solicit those votes.

B. Confirmation Pursuant to 11 U.S.C. § 1129(b)(2)(c). A chapter 11 case may constitute a "prepackaged chapter 11 case" for purposes of these guidelines notwithstanding the fact that the debtor proposes to confirm the plan pursuant to 11 U.S.C. § 1129(b)(2)(c) as to a class of interests.

C. Filing of Petition After Solicitation has Commenced but Before Expiration of Voting Deadline. Unless the court orders otherwise, if a chapter 11 case is commenced by or against the debtor, or if a chapter 7 case is commenced against the debtor and converted to a chapter 11 case by the debtor pursuant to 11 U.S.C. § 706(a), after the debtor has transmitted all solicitation materials to holders of claims and interests whose vote is sought but before the deadline for casting acceptances or rejections of the debtor's plan (the "Voting Deadline"),

(1) the debtor and other parties in interest shall be permitted to accept but not solicit ballots until the Voting Deadline; and

(2) after notice and a hearing the court shall determine the effect of any and all such votes.

D. Applicability of Guidelines to Cases Involving Cramdown of Classes of Claims and "Prepackaged Chapter 11 Cases." The court may, upon request of the debtor or other party in interest in an appropriate case, apply some or all of these guidelines to

(1) cases in which the debtor has satisfied the requirements of paragraph 3.A.(1) above but intends to seek confirmation of the plan pursuant to 11 U.S.C. § 1129(b) as to a class of claims (a) which is deemed not to have accepted the plan under 11 U.S.C. § 1126(g); (b) which is receiving or retaining property under or pursuant to the plan but whose members' votes were not solicited prepetition and whose rejection of the plan has been assumed by the debtor for purposes of confirming the plan; or (c) which is receiving or retaining property under or pursuant to the plan and which voted prepetition to reject the plan, as long as no class junior to such rejecting class is receiving or retaining any property under or pursuant to the plan; and

(2) "partial prepackaged chapter 11 cases"—i.e.; cases in

which acceptances of the debtor's plan were solicited prior to the commencement of the case from some, but not all, classes of claims or interests whose solicitation, is required to confirm the debtor's plan.

4. PREFILING NOTIFICATION TO THE UNITED STATES TRUSTEE AND THE CLERK OF COURT.

A. Notice of Proposed Filing to the United States Trustee. At least five (5) business days prior to the anticipated filing date of the prepackaged chapter 11 case, the debtor should (1) notify the United States Trustee of the Debtor's intention to file a prepackaged chapter 11 case and (2) supply the United States Trustee with one (1) copy of the debtor's plan and disclosure statement (or other solicitation document).

B. Notice of Proposed "First Day Orders" to the United States Trustee. If possible, drafts of all motions pursuant to which the debtor seeks entry of orders on or shortly after the filing of the petition ("First Day Motion"), with the proposed orders attached as exhibits, should be furnished to the United States Trustee at least two (2) business days in advance of the filing of the petition or as soon as practicable after the filing of an involuntary petition.

C. Notice of Proposed Filing to the Clerk of Court. At least two (2) business days prior to the anticipated filing of the prepackaged chapter 11 case, counsel should contact the Clerk of Court to discuss the anticipated filing, the amount of the debtor's assets, number and type of creditors, procedures for handling public inquiries (i.e., the names, addresses and telephone numbers of the persons to whom such inquiries should be directed), procedures for handling claims and proofs of claim or interest. The Clerk of Court will not assign the case to or discuss the case with a judge until the petition is filed.

5. FILING OF PREPACKAGED CHAPTER 11 CASE.

As soon as practicable following filing of a prepackaged chapter 11 case, the debtor shall furnish to the judge assigned to the case a copy of the plan, the disclosure statement (or other solicitation document), a summary of balloting as required by Local Bankruptcy Rule 3018, First Day Motions, and any other filed motion. To the extent that documents filed by the debtor at or following the commencement of the debtors chapter 11 case differ in substance from the versions supplied to the United States Trustee under paragraphs 4.A and 4.B above, the debtor shall furnish to the United States Trustee one (1) copy of any such documents that have been modified, preferably black lined to show changes.

APPENDIX D5
LOCAL RULES OF THE UNITED STATES BANKRUPTCY COURT FOR THE SOUTHERN DISTRICT OF CALIFORNIA GUIDELINES FOR ESTABLISHING INTERIM COMPENSATION PROCEDURES FOR PROFESSIONALS

The Bankruptcy Code (11 U.S.C. § 331) limits the frequency with which professionals employed under 11 U.S.C. § 327 or § 1103 may apply for compensation for services rendered and reimbursement for expenses to once every 120 days after the date of the order for relief unless the court otherwise permits.

These guidelines are intended to assist professionals in obtaining orders setting forth procedures for interim compensation provided that professionals satisfy the requirements of Knudsen Corp v. U.S. Trustee, 84 BR. 668 (9th Cir. BA.P. 1988).

1. NOTICE.

Notice of a hearing on a motion to approve interim compensation procedures should be given to the United States Trustee, all creditors and equity holders, the debtor, and. parties requesting special. notice in accordance with Local Bankruptcy Rule 2002-3.

2. CONTENT OF MOTION.

The motion to approve interim compensation procedures should describe in detail the proposed procedures.

3. GUIDELINES.

The court will generally approve interim procedures which:

A. Provide for the monthly payment of fees and reimbursement of expenses (subject to the other guidelines set forth herein).

B. Require service of copies of the invoices for which fees and costs are requested on the debtor, the United States Trustee, all official committees (or, if none appointed, the 20 largest unsecured creditors), and parties requesting special notice.

C. Provide those served in paragraph 3.B with an opportunity to object within ten (10) days after the service of the invoices by notifying the applicant in writing and setting forth the specific grounds for the objection;

D. Provide the applicant with the option to either request a hearing on the objection or hold back the amount of fees and/or expenses that are the subject of the objection until the hearing on the application for interim compensation.

E. Provide for an award of 80% of the fees requested with a hold-back of 20% of such fees and for an award of 100% of expenses; provided that the 20% hold-back of fees may include any fees to which an objection was raised.

F. Require that an application for an interim award of compensation and expenses, in compliance with applicable federal and local bankruptcy rules and the Guidelines of the Office of the United States Trustee for the Southern District of California, be filed with the court and noticed for hearing in accordance with Local Bankruptcy Rule 2002-3 approximately once every 120 days.

G. State that neither the United States Trustee nor any party in interest shall be barred from raising objections to any charge or expense in any professional fee application filed with the court on the ground that no objection was raised with respect to the invoice.

H. Provide that if the applicant fails to comply with the 120-day fee application procedure set forth in paragraph 3.F, said applicant shall not be entitled to continue to utilize the interim, fee compensation procedure previously approved.

Administrative Procedures and Guidelines for Electronic Filing Effective March 1, 2010

Section 1: The Electronic Filing System

a. Authorization for Electronic Filing

General Order No. 162-A, as amended on November 30, 2009, of the U.S. Bankruptcy Court for the Southern District of California ("Court") requires all attorneys admitted to the bar of this Court (including those admitted pro hac vice), panel and standing trustees, professionals and examiners to file documents (Defined in Section 3 below) as Registered Users in the Court's Case Management/

Electronic Case Files System ("CM/ECF"). Those who file fewer than ten (10) documents or other papers within a calendar year are exempt from this requirement. Filers who meet the criteria as set forth above, but who experience exigent circumstances that preclude their effective/efficient use of CM/ECF, may petition the Court for relief from participation as a Registered User. The Court will address these petitions/requests on a case-by-case basis.

All attorneys admitted to the bar of this Court (including those admitted pro hac vice), panel and standing trustees, professionals and examiners, are eligible for full access to CM/ECF. Eligibility of attorneys to participate in CM/ECF is governed by Local Bankruptcy Rule 9010.

Creditor representatives are eligible for limited access at the discretion of the Clerk of the Court ("Clerk") and as the Court deems appropriate.

b. Scope of Electronic Filing

All documents filed with the Court shall be filed through CM/ECF, except as otherwise provided for in these Court's Administrative Procedures and Guidelines for Electronic Filing, Local Form CSD 1800, ("Administrative Procedures") which shall be promulgated and revised hereafter as specified by the Clerk.

c. The Official Record

The official court record is the electronic file maintained on the Court's servers. This includes documents filed by electronic means as well as documents filed in paper form and then scanned into the CM/ECF system.

Electronic transmission of a document to CM/ECF consistent with the Administrative Procedures, together with the transmission of a Notice of Electronic Filing from the Court, constitutes filing of the document for all purposes of the Federal Rules of Bankruptcy Procedure and the Local Rules of this Court, and constitutes entry of the document on the docket kept by the Clerk under Fed. R. Bankr. P. 5003.

d. System Availability, Assistance and Technical Specifications

CM/ECF is designed to provide service 24 hours a day, 7 days a week. The Clerk's Office has established a Systems Help Desk (619-557-7415) to respond to questions regarding the CM/ECF system. The Systems Help Desk is staffed business days from 9:00 a.m. to 4:00 p.m. If you have case specific questions, call 619-557-

5620 or directly to the case administrator. The Clerk's Office phone list can be obtained on the Court's website (www.casb.uscourts.gov) go to Bulletin Board> Court Phone List.

Current technical specifications for CM/ECF can be found at the Court's official website. Specifications may change periodically. Registered Users may refer to the website for the most current requirements.

e. Registration and Training

Registration shall be in a form prescribed by the Clerk. Anyone eligible for a CM/ECF password must complete the online registration form and the training on the Court's website. A Training Help Line (619-557-7535) has been established to answer questions regarding registration and training for CM/ECF.

Eligible users who successfully complete the training shall receive a login and password. This login and password shall be e-mailed directly to the Registered User by the Clerk's Office.

f. Logins and Passwords

A full access password to participate in the electronic retrieval and filing of documents may be issued to the following:

- Each attorney admitted to practice in this Court,
- Panel and standing trustees,
- Professionals and examiners.

A limited access password may be obtained by creditor representatives to participate in the CM/ECF system. This limited access allows the filing of (a) creditor request for notice and/or notice of appearances; (b) proofs of claim; (c) withdrawals or transfers of claim; (d) reaffirmation agreements; and (e) request to restrict public access to proofs of claim.

No Registered User shall knowingly permit, cause to permit, utilize or cause another to utilize the CM/ECF password unless such person is an authorized agent.

Any Registered User may withdraw from participation in CM/ECF by providing the Clerk of Court, Chief Deputy Clerk or systems department with notice of such withdrawal. Such notice must be in writing. Upon receipt, the Clerk's Office shall immediately cancel the Registered User's password and will delete the Registered User's email address from any applicable electronic service list.

g. Fees

For filings that require a fee, payment shall be made online using an authorized credit card. The requisite fee must be paid within 24 hours or the Registered User shall be locked out of CM/ECF until the fee is paid.

Section 2: Electronic Filing and Service of Documents

a. Filing

Unless otherwise expressly provided in these Administrative Procedures or where exceptional circumstances preventing a Registered User from filing electronically, all documents required to be filed with the Court by a Registered User in connection with a case, must be electronically filed. All documents must be filed as a Portable Document Format (PDF) file.

Electronic filing must be completed before midnight Pacific Standard Time in order to be considered timely filed that day. Detailed procedures may be found in the Attorney/Trustee Manual available on the Court's website.

The person electronically filing a document will be responsible for designating a title for the document. To the extent possible, all documents filed electronically shall be titled using one of the Docket Events from the Document Event Directory in the Attorney/Trustee Manual located on the Court's website.

Emergency motions, supporting documents and objections shall be filed electronically as provided in these Administrative Procedures. The party filing the motion shall immediately advise the judge's law clerk of the filing by phone.

b. Signatures

The Registered User login and password serve as the user's signature on all electronic documents filed with the Court. The login and password also serve as a signature for purposes of Fed. R. Bankr. P. 9011 of the Federal Rules of Bankruptcy Procedure, the Local Rules of this Court, and any other purpose for which a signature is required in connection with proceedings before the Court.

Each document filed electronically must include a signature block in compliance with LBR 9004-3(b). The name of the attorney or party filing the document must be preceded by an "/s/" and typed in the space where the signature would otherwise appear, or appear as a scanned image. The correct format for an electronic signature is as follows:

/s/ Adam Attorney

The Declaration RE: Electronic Filing, Local Form CSD 1801, shall be filed electronically providing the original debtor(s) signature(s) in a scanned format.

Documents requiring signatures of more than one party must be electronically filed either by:

- Scanning and submitting the document containing all necessary signatures,
- Representing the consent of the other parties on the document by use of an "/s/"; i.e., "/s/ Jane Doe",
- Identifying on the document the parties whose signatures are required and by the submission of a notice of endorsement by the other parties no later than three business days after filing, or
- In any other manner approved by the Court.

c. Retention

A document that is electronically filed, and which requires an original signature other than that of the Registered User, must be maintained in paper form by the Registered User until five (5) years after the case is closed or the adversary proceeding was terminated. The Registered User must provide original papers for review upon request.

d. Service and Notice

By accepting a System login and password from the Court, a Registered User consents, in lieu of any right to receive notice by first-class mail, including notices issued pursuant to Fed. R. Bankr. P. 2002(a) (except 2002(a)(1)) and 9022, to the receipt of notice by electronic means from the Court.

By accepting a CM/ECF login and password from the Court, a Registered User consents, in lieu of any right to service of any document by personal service or by first-class mail from interested parties, to accept service from such parties by electronic means through the transmission facilities of the Court, excepting the service of process of a summons and complaint in an adversary proceeding under Fed. R. Bankr. P. 7004 and the service of a subpoena under Fed. R. Bankr. P. 9016.

A certificate of service, where required by these rules, must be included with documents filed electronically, indicating that service was accomplished through the Notice of Electronic Filing for parties and counsel who are participants in CM/ECF and indicating how service was accomplished on any party or counsel who is not a participant in the CM/ECF system.

Each Registered User of the System is responsible for assuring that their e-mail address is accurate, that the account is monitored regularly, and that e-mail notices are opened in a timely manner. Detailed procedures for System email account maintenance may be found in the Attorney/Trustee Manual available on the Court's website.

e. Orders

Electronically submitted orders may not be combined with the application or motion into one document. The application or motion must be entered on the docket prior to uploading the order electronically and the resulting Docket Entry No. must be noted on the order template. Orders uploaded through CM/ECF will be entered on the case docket at the time of signature.

Electronic orders shall be uploaded using the Orders Upload option in CM/ECF and formatted as provided in LBR 9004-5. Stipulated, emergency, ex parte, non-contested, and lodged orders may be uploaded electronically as outlined below.

The first page of any electronically uploaded order must substantially conform with the appropriate order template (CSD 1001A-C, CSD 1159 A-C, or CSD 3000A-C) maintained by the Court for standard orders, orders shortening time and lodged orders. The signature line must be fixed at 4.5 inches from the left edge of the paper and 3 inches from the bottom edge of the paper. Signature approving orders will be affixed electronically on the signature line. Deviations from the required format are not permitted. Notification of defects in an order will be provided by e-mail.

Exhibits required by LBR 4001-5 and 9013-7 may be referenced according to the specific Docket Entry No. assigned to the document at the time of its entry.

When electronically lodging an order after hearing, compliance with LBR 7054-3(b)(a)(D) requiring the Notice of Entry and envelopes is waived.

f. Sequence of Pleadings

An initiating document must be docketed separately. Examples of an initiating document include a motion, application, plan, objection to claim, notice of appeal, amendment, balance of schedules, and fee.

Separate PDF files of any supporting document(s) should be browsed and attached to the initiating document. Examples of supporting documents include memorandums of points and authorities and declarations.

Most subsequent documents filed (i.e. oppositions, Request and Notice of Hearing (CSD 1175, 1184 or 1186), and replies, etc.) must be referred/related during the filing process to the initiating documents. Any supporting document(s) for these filings should be browsed and attached to the subsequent document.

g. Exceptions to Electronic Filing

Documents which are filed by paper rather than electronically shall be served in the manner provided for in, and on those parties entitled to notice in accordance with, the Federal Rules of Bankruptcy Procedure and Local Bankruptcy Rules except as otherwise provided by order of the Court.

Documents to be filed under seal shall be filed by paper. A motion and order to file document(s) under seal shall be filed electronically. No document filed under seal shall be submitted until after the order granting the motion has been entered. The document(s) to be filed under seal shall contain the following caption "THIS DOCUMENT IS FILED UNDER SEAL PURSUANT TO COURT ORDER" and be placed in a large sealed envelope. A copy of the order shall be attached to the envelope and delivered to the Clerk's Office.

h. Privacy

Unless otherwise ordered by the Court, parties must refrain from including, or must partially redact where inclusion is necessary, the following personal identifiers from all documents filed with the Court, including exhibits thereto:

- Social Security numbers. If an individual's Social Security number must be provided, only the last four (4) digits of that number should be used.
- Names of minor children. If the name of a minor child must be provided, only the initials of that child should be used.
- Dates of birth. If an individual's date of birth must be provided, only the year should be used.
- Financial account numbers. If financial account numbers must be provided, only the last four digits of these numbers should be used.

The responsibility for redacting personal identifiers rests solely with the parties. The Clerk's Office will not review documents for compliance with this rule.

i. Document Exhibits

Registered Users must submit in electronic form all documents referenced as exhibits or attachments, unless the Court permits otherwise. Only excerpts of the referenced documents that are directly germane to the matter under consideration by the Court are to be submitted.

Excerpted material must be clearly and prominently identified as such. Registered Users who submit excerpts under these Administrative Procedures do so without prejudice to their right to timely submit additional excerpts or the complete documents that they believe are directly germane. The Court may require parties to submit additional excerpts or the complete document. Evidentiary and trial exhibits must be provided directly to the appropriate courtroom deputy and not submitted to the Clerk's Office.

Exhibits are to be numbered sequentially at the top and bottom of the first page and attached to the document they support. If an exhibit separator page is used, it must identify the succeeding exhibit at the top and bottom of the separator page. Exhibit files should be no larger than megabytes or 100 pages.

Each document containing exhibits shall have, as a cover page to the exhibits, a list indicating the name and page number of each of the succeeding exhibits.

The Registered User is required to verify the legibility of the scanned exhibits prior to electronically submitting them to the Court. Parties should scan documents in black and white, unless color is a critical feature of the information.

j. Hyperlinks

In order to preserve the integrity of the Court record, attorneys wishing to insert hyperlinks in filings shall continue to use the traditional citation method for the cited authority, in addition to the hyperlink. The Judiciary's policy on hyperlinks is that a hyperlink contained in a filing is no more than a convenient mechanism for accessing material cited in the document. A hyperlink reference is extraneous to any filed document and is not part of the Court's record.

The Court accepts no responsibility for, and does not endorse, any product, organization, or content at any hyperlinked site, or at any site to which that site may be linked. The Court accepts no responsibility for the availability or functionality of any hyperlink.

k. Correcting Filing or Docket Errors

Once a document is submitted and becomes part of the case docket, corrections to the docket may be made only by the Clerk's Office. The System will not permit the filing party to make changes to a filing once the transaction has been accepted.

The filing party must contact the Clerk's Office as soon as an error has been discovered and provide the case number and document number. If appropriate, the Clerk's Office will make a docket entry indicating the document was filed in error. The filing party will be advised if the document needs to be re-filed.

If the Clerk's Office discovers filing or docketing errors, the filer will be advised of what further action, if any, is required to address the error. However, if the error is minor, the Clerk's Office may correct the error, with or without notifying the parties.

In the event that it appears a document has been filed in the wrong case, the Clerk's Office will docket an entry indicating this possible error and notify the filing party. If it is confirmed as an error, the party will be directed to re-file the document in the correct case. The Clerk's Office will not delete any documents filed by a party unless ordered by the Court.

l. Public Access to the System

Any person or organization other than Registered Users must register with PACER and receive a login and password in order to access Court records online. Information regarding PACER may be found on the Court's Internet website at casb.uscourts.gov.

The public will have electronic access to the docket and documents filed in CM/ECF at the Clerk's Office, for viewing during regular business hours, Monday through Friday.

Copies and certified copies of electronically filed documents may be purchased at the Office of the Clerk, 325 West "F" Street., San Diego, California 92101-6991. The fee for copying and certification will be in accordance with 28 U.S.C. 1930.

m. Technical Failures

A Registered User whose filing is made untimely as the result of a technical failure may seek appropriate relief from the Court.

Section 3: Definitions

CASE MANAGEMENT/ELECTRONIC CASE FILES SYSTEM (CM/ECF) is the Internet-based system for filing documents and maintaining Court case files in the United States Bankruptcy Court for the Southern District of California.

DOCUMENTS include pleadings, motions, exhibits, declarations, affidavits, memoranda, papers, orders, notices, and any other filing by or with the Court.

ELECTRONIC FILING is submitting a document directly from the Registered User's computer in "Portable Document Format" (.pdf), using CM/ECF to file that document with the Court.

INITIATING DOCUMENTS include petitions, motions, applications, plans, objections to claim, notices of appeal, reopens, amendments, balance of schedules, and fees.

NOTICE OF ELECTRONIC FILING (NEF) is a notice automatically generated by CM/ECF at the time a document is filed with the Court. The notice sets forth the date and time of filing, the name of the attorney and/or party filing the document, the type of document, the text of the docket entry, the name of the party and/or attorney receiving the notice, and an electronic link (hyperlink) to the filed document which allows recipients to retrieve the document automatically.

PACER (Public Access to Court Electronic Records) is an automated system that allows a subscriber to view, print and download Court case file information over the Internet for a fee.

PORTABLE DOCUMENT FORMAT (PDF or.pdf) is a proprietary file format developed by Adobe Systems, Inc. A document file created with a word processor, or a paper document which has been scanned, must be converted to Portable Document Format to be electronically filed with the Court. Electronic documents can be converted to pdf directly from the original software application (e.g., Microsoft Word® or Corel WordPerfect®, petition software). Documents which exist only in paper form must be scanned into.pdf format for electronic filing.

REGISTERED USER is an individual who has been issued a login and password by the Court to electronically file documents.

SUBSEQUENT DOCUMENTS include oppositions, Requests and Notices of Hearing (CSD 1175, 1184 or 1186), and replies. These documents must refer to the initiating documents with any supporting document(s) as attachments.

TEXT files (.txt) are used for submitting debtors' information for opening a bankruptcy case. Text files are also the format used for creating the creditor's matrix.

UPLOADED DOCUMENTS such as Orders and Trustee Reports, are not be filed on the case docket until reviewed.

GENERAL ORDER 162 In re Provisions For Electronic Case Filing

Federal Rule of Civil Procedure 83 and Federal Rule of Bankruptcy Procedure 5005(a)(2), 9011, 9029, and Local Bankruptcy Rule 9004, authorize this court to establish practices and procedures for the filing, signing, and verification of pleadings and papers by electronic means; and

A proposal for *Administrative Procedures for Filing, Signing and Verifying Pleadings and Papers by Electronic Means* (Local Form CSD 1800) and an *Electronic Filing Participant Guide* (collectively, the "Electronic Filing Procedures") having been reviewed by the court;

IT IS ORDERED that:

1. The *Administrative Procedures for Filing, Signing and Verifying Pleadings and Papers by Electronic Means* and the *Electronic Filing Participant Guide* establishing administrative procedures for signing, filing, and verifying documents by electronic means in this court, including the procedure for registration of attorneys and for distribution of passwords to permit electronic filing and notice of pleadings and other papers (collectively the "Electronic Filing Procedures") are hereby approved by the court.

2. The electronic filing of a petition, pleading, motion or other paper by an attorney who is a registered participant in the Electronic Filing System shall constitute the signature of that attorney under Fed. R. Bankr. P. 9011 and Local Bankruptcy Rule 9004-3(b). The signature of the debtor(s) authorizing the electronic filing of the bankruptcy case shall be accomplished by filing an executed *DECLARATION RE: ELECTRONIC FILING, Local Form CSD 1801,* within 15 days of the electronic filing of the petition.

3. No attorney shall knowingly permit or cause to permit his/her password to be utilized by anyone other than an authorized employee of his/her law firm.

4. No person shall knowingly utilize or cause another person to utilize the password of a registered attorney unless such person is an authorized employee of the law firm.

5. The electronic filing of a pleading or other paper in accordance with the Electronic Filing Procedures shall constitute entry of that pleading or other paper on the docket kept by the clerk under Fed. R. Bankr. P. 5003.

6. The Office of the Clerk shall enter all orders, decrees, judgments, and proceedings of the court in accordance with the Electronic Filing Procedures, which shall constitute entry of the order, decree, judgment, or proceeding on the docket kept by the clerk under Fed. R. Bankr. P. 9021.

7. a. Whenever a pleading or other paper is filed electronically in accordance with the Electronic Filing Procedures, the Office of the Clerk shall serve the filing party with a "Notice of Electronic Filing" by electronic means at the time of docketing.

b. The filing party shall serve the pleading or other paper upon all persons entitled to notice or service in accordance with the applicable rules, or, if service by first class mail is permitted under the rules, the filing party may make service in accordance with sub-paragraph (c) below.

c. If the recipient of notice or service is a registered participant in the Electronic Filing System, service by electronic means of the Notice of Electronic Filing shall be the equivalent of service of the pleadings or other paper by first class mail, postage prepaid.

8. Participation in the Electronic Filing System by receipt of a password from the Court, shall constitute a request for service and notice electronically pursuant to Fed. R. Bankr. P. 9036. Participants in the Electronic Filing System, by receiving a password from the court, agree to receive notice and service by electronic means.

9. The original of this order shall be filed both in accordance with the Electronic Filing Procedures and conventionally with the Clerk of the Court.

10. Until further order, the provisions of this order shall apply only to chapter 7 cases (including adversary proceedings and contested matters in chapter 7 cases) filed on or after the effective date of this order. Amendments to this order may be entered from time to time in keeping with the needs of the court.

11. This order shall be in effect retroactively to March 25, 1998.

Filed: June 17, 1998

General Order No. 169 ADOPTION OF INTERIM BANKRUPTCY RULES

On April 20, 2005 the Bankruptcy Abuse Prevention and Consumer Protection Act of 2005 (the Act) was enacted into law and most provisions of the Act are effective on October 17, 2005.

The Advisory Committee on Bankruptcy Rules has prepared Interim Rules designed to implement the substantive and procedural changes mandated by the Act. The Committee on Rules of Practice and Procedure of the Judicial Conference of the United States has approved these Interim Rules to provide uniform procedures for implementing the Act. The general effective date of the Act has not provided sufficient time to promulgate rules after the appropriate public notice and an opportunity for comment.

NOW THEREFORE, pursuant to 28 U.S.C. § 2071, Fed. R. Civil P. 83 and Fed. R. Bankr. P. 9029, the attached Interim Rules are adopted in their entirety without change by this Court to be effective October 17, 2005 to conform to the Act. For cases and proceedings not governed by the Act, the Federal Rules of Bankruptcy Procedure and the Local Rules of this Court, other than the Interim Rules, shall apply. The Interim Rules shall remain in effect until further order of the court.

Dated: October 14, 2005

GENERAL ORDER 173 GUIDELINES REGARDING CHAPTER 13 ATTORNEY FEES

The United States Bankruptcy Court has adopted these guidelines regarding Chapter 13 attorney fees and compensation. The United States Bankruptcy Court generally will not require detailed applications in chapter 13 cases where the attorney meets the requirements set forth in Section I and complies with the Fee Schedule in Section II.

I. REQUIREMENTS:

A. Counsel shall file with the Court and serve on the Chapter 13 Trustee an executed copy of the "Rights and Responsibilities of Chapter 13 Debtors and Their Attorneys" within 15 days after the order for relief or within 15 days of retention. (These forms are available in the Office of the Chapter 13 Trustees and the United States Bankruptcy Court Website at www.casb.uscourts.gov).

B. Counsel shall ensure that there is a properly executed 2016(b) Statement filed with the Court and served on the Chapter 13 Trustee and the United States Trustee for the Southern District of California.

In all cases where counsel seeks "initial fees" pursuant to the United States Bankruptcy Court Guidelines regarding Chapter 13 Attorney Fees, counsel shall include in the 2016(b) Statement all the services described in the Rights and Responsibilities of Chapter 13 Debtors and their Attorney.

C. Counsel shall keep time records. Time entries should be kept contemporaneously with the services rendered in time periods of tenths of an hour for each case in the event there is an examination of fees for any reason. Should counsel fail to have accurate and contemporaneous time records, fees may be subject to objection in their entirety.

D. If counsel elects not to seek fees pursuant to this Guideline, counsel shall file a fee application in compliance with Rules 2002 and 2016 of the Federal Rules of Bankruptcy Procedure and Local Bankruptcy Rules 2002 and 2016.

E. The Notice for the Section § 341(a) Meeting of Creditors shall provide notice pursuant to Federal Rule of Bankruptcy Procedure 2002 of the "initial fees" requested.

II. FEE SCHEDULE:

A. Initial Fees:

Pursuant to In re Eliapo, 468 F.3d 592 (9th Cir. 2006), the judges of the U. S. Bankruptcy Court will generally not require fee applications for the following described services provided that the fees charged do not exceed the following amounts:

1. Chapter 13 Consumer Cases $3,300

To earn the "initial fees" in a consumer case, an attorney shall:

a. Meet with the debtor to review the debtor's assets, liabilities, income and expenses.

b. Analyze the debtor's financial situation, and render advice to the debtor in determining whether to file a petition in bankruptcy.

c. Counsel the debtor regarding the advisability of

filing either a Chapter 7 or Chapter 13 case, discuss both procedures with the debtor, and answer the debtor's questions.

d. Explain to the debtor how the attorney's fees and trustee's fees are paid.

e. Explain what payments will be made directly by the debtor and what payments will be made through the debtor's chapter 13 plan, with particular attention to mortgage and vehicle loan payments, as well as any other claims with accrued interest.

f. Explain to the debtor how, when, and where to make the chapter 13 plan payments.

g. Explain to the debtor that the first plan payment must be made to the Trustee within 30 days of the date the plan is filed.

h. Advise the debtor of the requirement to attend the § 341(a) Meeting of Creditors, and instruct the debtor as to the date, time and place of the meeting.

i. Advise the debtor of the necessity of maintaining liability, collision and comprehensive insurance on vehicles securing loans or leases.

j. Timely prepare, file and serve the debtor's petition, plan, schedules, statement of financial affairs, and any necessary amendments thereto, which may be required.

k. Provide an executed copy of the Rights and Responsibilities of Chapter 13 Debtors and their Attorneys and a copy of the Court's Guidelines regarding Chapter 13 Attorney Fees to the debtor.

l. Appear and represent the debtor at the § 341(a) Meeting of Creditors, the confirmation hearing, and any adjourned hearing thereof.

m. Respond to the objections to plan confirmation, and where necessary, prepare, file and serve an amended plan.

n. Provide Certification of Eligibility for Discharge pursuant to Local Bankruptcy Rule 4004-1.

o. Provide such other legal services as are necessary for the administration of the case before the Bankruptcy Court, which include, but are not limited to, a continuing obligation to assist the debtor by returning telephone calls, answering questions and reviewing and sending correspondence.

2. Chapter 13 Business Cases $4,000

To earn the "initial fees" in a business case, an attorney shall:

a. Provide all of the services as described above for consumer cases.

b. Prepare a Questionnaire for Chapter 13 Business Owners.

c. Provide documents and information requested by the Chapter 13 Trustee and the Court, including, but not limited to, an itemized list of all business assets and a profit and loss statement for each of the three months prior to the filing.

d. Attend on-site inspections of business at the Chapter 13 Trustee's request.

e. Assist the Debtor in performing duties pursuant to 11 U.S.C. § 1304.

B. Additional Fees

1. Additional services may be required, but are not included in the United States Bankruptcy Court's parameters for the "initial fees". If necessary and when appropriate, the attorney, at the debtor's request and only with the debtor's cooperation, shall provide the following services for "additional fees":

a. Prepare, file and serve necessary modifications to the plan post-confirmation, which may include suspending, lowering or increasing plan payments.

b. Prepare, file and serve necessary motions to buy, sell or refinance real property and authorize use of cash collateral or assume executory contracts or unexpired leases.

c. Object to improper or invalid claims.

d. Represent the debtor in motions for relief from stay.

e. Prepare, file and serve necessary motions to avoid liens on real or personal property.

f. Prepare, file and serve necessary oppositions to motions for dismissal of case.

g. Provide such other legal services as are necessary for the administration of the case before the Bankruptcy Court, which include but are not limited to, presenting appropriate legal pleadings and making appropriate court appearances.

2. Should additional services be provided and "additional fees" requested, the attorney shall:

a. Provide proper notice in accordance with Federal Rule of Bankruptcy Procedure 2002.

b. Advise the debtor of all "additional fees" requested and file a declaration with the court stating that counsel has so advised the debtor of the fees requested and the debtor has no objection to the requested fees.

3. The United States Bankruptcy Court's parameters for "additional fees," including all court appearances required to pursue described actions to which the Court will not generally object, are:

a. Modified Plan (Post-Confirmation)

$600 for fees and expenses for services rendered post-confirmation for preparing, filing, noticing, and attending hearings in regard to a debtor's modified plan under section 1329 of the Bankruptcy Code (including the preparation of amended income and expenses statements and providing proof of income). (These fees should be less for modification due to clerical error or other administrative issues.)

b. Opposition to Motions for Relief from Stay

$450 (Personal property) for fees and expenses of all services rendered in opposition $575 (Real property) to motions to modify or vacate the automatic stay.

c. Obtaining Orders re: Sale or Refinance of Real Property

$500 (By stipulation or for fees and expenses of all services rendered for obtaining noticed hearing) an order authorizing the sale or refinancing of real estate.

d. Objections to Claim

$250 (Uncontested objections for fees and expenses of all without hearing) services rendered for preparing, $350(Contested objections filing, and noticing objections with a hearing) to a claim.

(Fees shall not exceed 50% of the amount the trustee would have otherwise paid)

e. Oppositions to Dismissal/Motions to Avoid Lien/ Other Routine Pleadings

$450 for fees and expenses of all services rendered for preparing, filing, noticing, and attending hearings in opposition to a motion to dismiss the case, for motions to avoid lien and other routine pleadings.

f. Motions to Impose/Extend Automatic Stay

$350 (Unopposed) for fees and expenses of all services rendered for preparing, $500 (Opposed) filing, noticing and attending hearings in regard to a motion to impose/ extend automatic stay.

g. Novel and Complex Motions and Oppositions to Motions

These types of motions and oppositions may be billed at hourly rates and counsel shall file a fee application in compliance with Rules of 2002 and 2016 of the Federal Rules of Bankruptcy Procedure and Local Bankruptcy Rules 2002 and 2016.

These amounts should not be considered as recommendations by the United States Bankruptcy Court as to the reasonableness of an attorney fee in a given case.

Effective Date: January 14, 2008

CSD 1001a

Order

(Rev. 11/15/04)

CSD 1001a
Name, Address, Telephone Number & I.D. No.

UNITED STATES BANKRUPTCY COURT
SOUTHERN DISTRICT OF CALIFORNIA

In re

Debtor.

ORDER ON

____

____

__________, IT IS ORDERED THAT the relief sought as set forth on the continuation pages attached and numbered two (2) through__________ with exhibits, if any, for a total of __________ pages, is granted. Motion/Application Docket Entry No. __________

//

//

//

//

//

//

DATED: __________

____

Judge, United States Bankruptcy Court

Signature by the attorney constitutes a certification under Fed. R. of Bankr. P. 9011 that the relief in the order is the relief granted by the court.

Submitted by:
(Firm name)
By: __________
Attorney for ☐ Movant ☐ Respondent

CSD 1001b

Order Shortening Time for Hearing

(Rev. 11/15/04)

CSD 1001b

Name, Address, Telephone Number & I.D. No.

UNITED STATES BANKRUPTCY COURT

SOUTHERN DISTRICT OF CALIFORNIA

In re

Debtor.

ORDER SHORTENING TIME FOR HEARING ON

IT IS ORDERED THAT the relief sought as set forth on the continuation pages attached and numbered two (2) through ____________with exhibits, if any, for a total of ____________pages, is granted. Motion/Application Docket Entry No. ____________

//

//

//

//

//

//

DATED: ____________

____

Judge, United States Bankruptcy Court

Signature by the attorney constitutes a certification under Fed. R. of Bankr. P. 9011 that the relief in the order is the relief granted by the court.

Submitted by: ____________

(Firm name)

By: ____________

Attorney for: ☐ Movant ☐ Respondent

Upon review of the ex parte application for order shortening time for notice of hearing on the____________and for good cause appearing therefore,

IT IS ORDERED that this Court will conduct a hearing on the Motion, and any opposition, thereto on at _______.m. in Department No. ___________, Room___________of the United States Bankruptcy Court, Southern District of California, 325 West F Street, San Diego, California 92101-6991.

IT IS FURTHER ORDERED that the Notice of Motion and Motion must be filed and served no later than __________. Service will be deemed complete when delivered

- ☐ personally, or
- ☐ by electronic method, or
- ☐ by first class or overnight mail, or
- ☐ as provided for in the application for order shortening time.

IT IS FURTHER ORDERED that all opposition, if any, to the Motion must be filed and served no later than __________.

IT IS FURTHER ORDERED that a reply, if any, to the opposition to the Motion must be filed and served no later than ___________.

CSD 1001c

Order On

(Rev. 11/15/04)

CSD 1001c
Name, Address, Telephone Number & I.D. No.

UNITED STATES BANKRUPTCY COURT
SOUTHERN DISTRICT OF CALIFORNIA

In re

Debtor.

ORDER ON

IT IS ORDERED THAT the relief sought as set forth on the continuation pages attached and numbered two (2) through ___________with exhibits, if any, for a total of ___________ pages, is granted. Notice of Lodgment Docket Entry No. ___________

//

//

//

//

//

//

DATED: ___________

____

Judge, United States Bankruptcy Court

Signature by the attorney constitutes a certification under Fed. R. of Bankr. P. 9011 that the relief in the order is the relief granted by the court.

Submitted by:

____

(Firm name)

By: ___________

Attorney for ☐ Movant ☐ Respondent

SDCAL-129 S.D. CALIFORNIA

CSD 1001d

Facts and Conclusions of Law

(Rev. 11/15/04)

CSD 1001d
Name, Address, Telephone Number & I.D. No.

UNITED STATES BANKRUPTCY COURT
SOUTHERN DISTRICT OF CALIFORNIA

In re Debtor.	

FACTS AND CONCLUSIONS OF LAW RE:

The matter having been tried to the court on regular notice and after consideration of all properly admitted evidence, as well as argument thereon, the court makes the following findings of fact and conclusions of law as set forth on the continuation pages attached numbered two (2) through ________. Motion Docket Entry No. ________

//

//

//

//

//

DATED: ____________

____

Judge, United States Bankruptcy Court

Signature by the attorney constitutes a certification under Fed. R. of Bankr. P. 9011 that the relief in the order is the relief granted by the court.

Submitted by:

____
(Firm name)

By: ____________

Attorney for ☐ Movant ☐ Respondent

CSD 1001e

Findings of Fact and Conclusions of Law
(Rev. 11/15/04)

CSD 1001E [11/15/04]
Name, Address, Telephone No. & I.D. No.

UNITED STATES BANKRUPTCY COURT
SOUTHERN DISTRICT OF CALIFORNIA

325 West "F" Street, San Diego, California 92101-6991

LODGED

In Re Debtor.	BANKRUPTCY NO. Date of Hearing: Time of Hearing: Name of Judge:

FINDINGS OF FACT AND CONCLUSIONS OF LAW RE:

The matter having been tried to the court on regular notice and after consideration of all properly admitted evidence, as well as argument thereon, the court makes the following findings of fact and conclusions of law as set forth on the continuation pages attached numbered two (2) through ___________.

Notice of Lodgment Docket Entry No. ___________

//

//

//

//

//

DATED: ___________

____

Judge, United States Bankruptcy Court

Signature by the attorney constitutes a certification under Fed. R. of Bankr. P. 9011 that the relief in the order is the relief granted by the court.

Submitted by:

____

(Firm name)

By: ________________

Attorney for ☐ Movant ☐ Respondent

CSD 1003

Notice of Related Cases
(Rev. 01/12/07)

NOTICE OF RELATED CASE

TO THE CLERK OF COURT:

You are hereby advised that the above-entitled case is related to the case indicated below. The related case is or was pending within the past three (3) years. In accordance with Local Bankruptcy Rule 1015-2(c), the above-entitled case is to be assigned or reassigned to the judge to whom the prior case was assigned unless otherwise directed by the court. If the related cases are being filed simultaneously, they are to be assigned to one judge.

RELATED
CASE:________
CASE NO.:________ DATE FILED:________

Neither case is a chapter 13 and the relationship is based upon the fact that (*check all appropriate boxes*):

☐ the debtors in both cases are the same entity;

☐ the debtors in both cases are spouses or former spouses;

☐ the debtors in both cases are partners;

☐ the debtor in one case is a general partner of the debtor in the other case;

☐ the debtor in one case is an "affiliate," as that term is defined at 11 U.S.C. § 101(2), of the debtor in the other case;

☐ the debtors are corporations and have one or more common shareholder which owns twenty percent (20%) or more of each corporation;

☐ the debtors are partnerships and have one or more common general partner;

☐ the debtor in one case has, or within 180 days of the commencement of either of the related cases had, an interest in property that as or is included in the property of the other estate under 11 U.S.C. § 541(a); or

☐ the cases are otherwise so related as to warrant being treated as related to promote efficient administration of the estates.

Dated:

Attorney for Debtor

CSD 1007

Special Requirements For Mailing Addresses

(Rev. 05/15/03)

UNITED STATES BANKRUPTCY COURT

Southern District of California

TO THE DEBTOR(S) AND THE ATTORNEY FOR DEBTOR(S), IF ANY:

Effective SEPTEMBER 1, 2000, the debtor shall prepare and submit to the Court, at the time a voluntary petition under any chapter is filed, a mailing matrix on computer diskette which complies with the computerized noticing guidelines contained herein. Failure to do so will cause the petition to be rejected. This mailing matrix is required in addition to the various schedules required by Federal Rule of Bankruptcy Procedure 1007.

In order to ensure that the creditor matrix you file can be properly processed by the computer system currently used by the Court, we ask that you observe the following guidelines. Your cooperation is essential in helping us make improvements in our existing system and to better serve you—the public.

1.0 REQUEST FOR WAIVER OF CREDITOR MATRIX DISKETTE

If financial constraints and/or the inability to access the equipment necessary to produce a computer diskette would cause an undue hardship on the debtor, a scannable creditor matrix must be submitted accompanied by a completed Request for Waiver of Diskette Requirement, (CSD 1010). Compliance with these requirements are required.

2.0 DEBTOR'S OBLIGATION TO ASSURE ACCURACY

It shall be the responsibility of the debtor, the debtor's attorney, or such other person as the Court may order to ensure that the schedules, creditor matrix, equity holders matrix, and computer-readable data are complete and correct. The Clerk's office shall not be required to compare the names and addresses shown on the creditor matrix or diskette with those on the Petition, Schedules of Debts and Equity Security Holders. The Clerk's office may use either the schedules, the mailing lists or the computer-readable data for noticing creditors.

3.0 REQUIREMENTS FOR CREDITOR(S) MATRIX WHEN PETITION, STATEMENTS AND SCHEDULES ARE SUBMITTED ON PAPER

(A) Filing Requirements-A creditor matrix on a **diskette** is required whenever the following occurs:

(1) A new petition is filed.

(2) A case is converted on or after SEPTEMBER 1, 2000.

(3) Balance of schedules or an amendment to a case is filed on or after SEPTEMBER 1, 2000, which adds, deletes or changes creditor address information on the debtor's Schedule of Debts and/or Schedule of Equity Security Holders.

(B) Converted Cases

(1) When converting a Chapter 13 case filed before SEPTEMBER 1, 2000, to another chapter, ALL creditors must be listed on the creditor matrix at the time the conversion is filed.

(2) For Chapter 7, 11, or 12 cases converted to another chapter on or after SEPTEMBER 1, 2000, only post-petition creditors need be listed on the creditor matrix. The creditor matrix must be filed with the post-petition schedule of debts and/or schedule of equity security holders. If there are no post-petition creditors, a declaration so stating is required.

(C) Balance of Schedules or Amendment to Schedule of Debts and/or Schedule of Equity Security Holders. The creditor matrix is a document separate from the amended schedules and may not be used to substitute for any portion of the schedules. IT MUST BE SUBMITTED WITH THE AMENDMENT OR BALANCE OF SCHEDULES.

4.0 ADDRESSES FOR FEDERAL AND STATE AGENCIES [All Chapters]

(A) Mailing Addresses—Certain federal and state agencies specify particular addresses to which notice of bankruptcy proceedings should be directed. The Clerk maintains a Roster of State and Federal Agencies, (CSD 1271), and shall make the Roster available to the Bar and the public to enable compliance with the provisions of Federal Rule of Bankruptcy Procedure 2002(j).

When listing an indebtedness to a federal or state agency not included on the Roster, the debtor and the debtor's attorney shall use such address as will effect proper notice to the agency.

(B) United States Attorney—When listing an indebtedness to the United States for other than taxes, the debtor shall include both the United States Attorney and the federal agency through which the debtor became indebted. The name and address of the United States Attorney must include, in parentheses, the name of the federal agency. For example:

United States Attorney for the S. Dist. of CA
(For Department of Education)
940 Front Street, Room 5152
San Diego, CA 92101-8800

5.0 FORMAT FOR CREDITOR(S) MATRIX DISKETTE

(A) General Requirement—The debtor shall provide the Court with a computer-generated diskette containing the names and addresses of all creditors and equity security holders.

(B) Content—The computer diskette shall contain the name and complete mailing address of each entity listed as a creditor by the debtor.

(1) If the debtor is a partnership, the name and address of each general and limited partner shall be added to the computer diskette.

(2) If the debtor is a corporation, the name and address of the chief executive officer or other officer who will appear for the debtor shall be added to the computer diskette.

(C) Diskette Specifications

(1) Use a 3.5" disk only formatted for use on an IBM or compatible PC.

(2) One ASCII format file per disk (save as ASCII(DOS)TXT)).

(3) One case per file.

(4) File must be named with the debtor's last name (i.e.; johnson.txt, smith.txt, etc.) and may be shortened if necessary.

(5) Left justification required.

(6) The information must be four (4) lines or less per creditor.

(7) Each line may contain no more than 40 characters. No leading spaces.

(8) Each creditor must be separated by at least one blank line.

Example: jackson.txt

Line 1: Maria Careless
Line 2: 25 North Aria Blvd.
Line 3: Grecian, NY 80062
Line 4:
Line 5: Charles Prince Productions
Line 6: 3 Diana Court
Line 7: Balmoral, MD 12960
Line 8:
Line 9: Last Bank of San Diego
Line 10: Attn: Collections Dept.
Line 11: 12345 E. Main St.
Line 12: San Diego, CA 92101-1010

(9) ZIP code must be on the last line. Nine-digit ZIP codes should be typed with a hyphen separating the two groups of digits. Do NOT type "attention" lines or account numbers on the last line. If needed, this information must be placed on the second line of the name/address. Account numbers may not exceed 15 characters. (The ZIP code must be at the end of the same line as the city and state in order for the U.S. Postal ZIP code sorting equipment to find it.)

(10) Be sure to type the number "1" (one) rather than the lower case letter "l" (L) when using numerics.

6.0 FORMAT FOR SCANNABLE CREDITOR(S) MATRIX

(A) Matrix Format Requirements—All matrices must comply with the following:

(1) Lists must be typed in one of the following standard typefaces or print styles:

* Courier 10 pitch
* Prestige Elite
* Letter Gothic

(2) Lists shall be typed in a single column centered on the page rather than in two or three columns. See Attachment #2.

Addresses must be in a single column because the OCR scans the material automatically from left to right, line by line. If, for example, a list contains three columns and the first column has an address with three lines and the second column has a address with four lines, the optical character reader will see the blank line after the first address and not read any further. Thus, it is important to have single column addresses that will be read automatically and completely.

(3) Lists must be typed so that no letter is closer than 1.5" from any edge of the paper.

(4) Each name/address must consist of no more than four (4) total lines, with at least three (3) blank lines between each of the name/address blocks. ZIP codes must be located on the same line as city and state.

(5) All states must be two-letter abbreviations. Example: correct = CA; wrong = California, Calif.

(6) Each line must be 30 characters or less in length.

(7) All creditors are to be alphabetized. Do not duplicate names and addresses. Entities with more than one (1) address may be listed as many times as necessary to assure proper notice.

(8) DO NOT include the following entities since they will be retrieved automatically by the computer for noticing:

* Debtor
* Joint Debtor
* Attorney for the Debtor(s)

(B) Avoiding Problems

Although the Court is using sophisticated equipment and software to ensure accuracy in creditor list reading, certain problems may still occur. By following these guidelines, you will avoid delays or additional effort in mailing notices.

The following problems can result in your lists being improperly read by the optical scanner, requiring you to resubmit your creditor list in an acceptable form. See Attachment #3.

(1) Extra marks on the list—such as letterhead, dates, debtor name, coffee stains, handwritten marks.

(2) Non-standard paper such as onion skin, half-sized paper, or colored (i.e., yellow, blue, etc.) paper.

(3) Poor quality type caused by submitting a photocopy or a

carbon copy, using an exhausted typewriter, or using a typewriter with a fabric ribbon. Many times, they produce letters which are too fuzzy to be properly scanned.

(4) Unreadable type faces or print types such as proportionally-spaced fonts, dot-matrix printing, or exotic fonts (such as Olde English or Script). Use only Courier 10, Prestige Elite or Letter Gothic.

(5) Misaligned lists caused by removing the paper from the typewriter before completing the list, or inserting the paper into the typewriter crooked.

(6) Incorrect typewriter settings will cause unreadable lists. Make certain that your typewriter is set for 10 pitch if you are using a 10-pitch type style.

(7) Stray marks should be avoided. Do not type lines, debtor name, page numbers, or anything else on the front of a creditor list. Any identifying marks you choose to add can be typed on the back of the list.

(8) Upper case only (all capital letters) should be avoided. Type in upper and lower case as you would on a letter.

(9) ZIP code must be on the last line. Nine-digit ZIP codes should be typed with a hyphen separating the two groups of digits. Do NOT type "attention" lines or account numbers on the last line. If needed, this information must be placed on the second line of the name/address. Account numbers may not exceed 15 characters. (The ZIP code must be at the end of the same line as the city and state in order for the U.S. Postal ZIP code sorting equipment to find it.)

(10) Be sure to type the number "1" (one) rather than the lower case letter "l" (L) when using numerics.

UNITED STATES BANKRUPTCY COURT
Southern District of California

CHECK LIST FOR CREDITOR MATRIX DISKETTE

If using a third party software package (i.e.; Best Case Solutions, Specialty, E-Z Filing for Windows, Top Form):

1. Save the creditors to a diskette. Name the file: *creditor.txt*
2. Close your program and open your word processing package.

3. Open the *creditor.txt* file and check the following:

   Single column
   One blank line between each creditor
   Second line of each creditor must be either a street address number or a P.O. box with the periods (i.e.; 200 South Main Street or P.O. Box 241)
   Last line of each creditor must be in the format City, State (two-letter abbreviation) ZIP (i.e.; Alexandria, VA 22314)
   No account numbers may be included in creditor information

4. Chose "Save As" function in your word processing software. In earlier versions of WordPerfect, this is known as "Text In/Out." In most software packages, there will be a box that will indicate the format of the document (i.e.; Word 5.0 format, WordPerfect 5.1). This box is usually right underneath where you enter in the name of the file. The format for all diskettes should be one of the following (depending upon your software): ASCII DOS Text, Plan DOS Text, Text Only. These are the only formats which will be accepted. When you have selected the correct format, save the file.

If you are not using third party software:

1. Open your word processing software and enter in the creditor information making sure that there is:

   One column of information only
   One blank line between each creditor
   Second line of each creditor must be either a street address number or a P.O. box with the periods (i.e.; 200 South Main Street or P.O. Box 241)
   Last line of each creditor must be in the format City, State (two-letter abbreviation) ZIP (i.e.; Alexandria, VA 22314)
   No account numbers may be included in creditor information

2. Choose "Save As" function in your word processing software. In earlier versions of WordPerfect, this is known as "Text In/Out." In most software packages, there will be a box that will indicate the format of the document (i.e.; Word 5.0 format, WordPerfect 5.1). This box is usually right underneath where you enter in the name of the file. The format for all diskettes should be one of the following (depending upon your software): ASCII DOS Text, Plan DOS Text, Text Only. These are the only formats which will be accepted. When you have selected the correct format, save the file.

SAMPLE CREDITOR LIST USING "Courier 10 cpi"

R. U. Alldere, Esq.
2 Rushin Court
San Diego, CA 92189

Maria Careless
25 North Aria Blvd.
Grecian, NY 80062

Charles Prince Productions
3 Diana Court
Balmoral, MD 12960

First City Nat'l Bank of Beaumont
P.O. Box 3391
Beaumont, TX 77704

General Nuisance Elimination
P.O. Box 1230
Baltimore, MD 20984

Kelley Appliances
Attn: Parts Division
462 9th Avenue, North
Seattle, WA 98109

Attachment 3 to CSD 1007

ERRORS TO AVOID IN PREPARING CREDITOR LISTS

ERRORS TO AVOID IN PREPARING CREDITOR LISTS

Debtor: Allnet Svcs. **PAGE TITLES** ⇑⇑⇑ If you want to type title or other identification on lists type it on the back - never on the front.	Stephen R. Miller III Coal Building 1092 17th Street, NW Carlsbad, CA 92001	⇑⇑⇑ **TOO CLOSE TO EDGE** You must keep all typing at least 1.5" from any edge; top, bottom, or side.
ALL UPPER CASE ⇒⇒⇒ Use upper and lower case (capitals and small letters) as if you were typing a letter.	MULTI-TRONICS ANIMATIONS 3837 STRONG WAY NORTH SUITE 10 BALTIMORE, MD 20938 OR 1C7-D CASTLE BUILDING NORTH PARKWAY BLVD. HOUSTON, TX. 10938	**TOO LONG** A name/address block must be 4 lines of 30 characters each or less. ⇓ ⇓ ⇓
		FABRIC RIBBON Use an office-quality film ribbon to insure proper scanning. ⇐⇐⇐
BOLD TYPE ⇒⇒⇒ Do not use a boldface setting on your typewriter or word processor.	**Arctic Expeditions** **Incorporated** **536 East 48th Ave.** **Anchorage, AK 99505**	
WRONG FONT ⇒⇒⇒ You may use Courier 10, Prestige Elite or Letter Gothic. No other font is acceptable.	*Gow Fire Protection, Inc.* *459 North 98th Street* *Hoquiam, WA 98550* *ATTN: Steve Jamison*	**ATTENTION LINE** If you must type an attention line or account number for a creditor, put it on the second line of the address, not at the end. ⇐⇐⇐
WRONG PITCH ⇒⇒⇒ If you use a 10-pitch font, make sure typewriter is set to 10 pitch.	Larry Miller, Jr. Landover Food & Bev. Suite 12B Burg, MD 24309 5182	**DIGIT ZIP CODE** Separate the two groups of digits with a dash, not a space. ⇐⇐⇐
HANDWRITING ⇒⇒⇒ Handwriting is not scannable and will interfere with the reading of the rest of list.	Sundown Corporation P.O. Box 123 Cityville, CA	**STRAY MARKS** No lines, symbols, letterhead, or other non-address data should appear on creditor list. ⇓⇓⇓

****

PAGE NUMBER ⇒⇒⇒ Do not number pages or type anything but creditors on list.	- 3 -	

CSD 1010

Request for Waiver of Diskette Requirement
(Rev. 05/15/03)

REQUEST FOR WAIVER OF DISKETTE REQUIREMENT

The ☐ Debtor(s) ☐ Attorney for Debtor(s) ☐ Non-Attorney Petition Preparer hereby request that the Court waive the requirement of submission of the petition, schedules and statements, and the mailing matrix on a computer diskette as required by Local Bankruptcy Rule 1007-1. Due to financial constraints and the inability to access a computer to prepare this petition and comply with this requirement, the petitioner requests acceptance of the petition, schedules, statements, and matrix submitted in the hard-copy scannable format. I understand that I may be asked to prepare a list of creditors on a computer located at the court.

The undersigned understands that, should the Court obtain information which indicates that the criteria set forth in this request does not exist, compliance with Local Bankruptcy Rule 1007-1 shall be made within forty-eight (48) hours of the filing of the petition.

Dated: ____________________

Signed: ____________________

(Applicant)

____

(Joint Applicant)

CSD 1021

Order on Debtor's Application for Waiver of the Chapter 7 Filing Fee

(4/9/06)

ORDER ON DEBTOR'S APPLICATION FOR WAIVER OF THE CHAPTER 7 FILING FEE

Upon consideration of the debtor's application, the court orders that the application be:

☐ GRANTED. This order is subject to being vacated at a later time if developments in the administration of the bankruptcy case demonstrate that the waiver is unwarranted.

☐ DENIED.

IT IS FURTHER ORDERED THAT the debtor shall pay the fee in not more than two installment payments according to the following terms:

a) Within 10 days of entry of this order, pay to the Clerk $149.50 and

b) Not more than 30 days from entry of this order, pay to the Clerk the balance of $149.50.

Until the filing fee is paid in full, the debtor will not make any additional payment or transfer any additional property to an attorney or any other person for services in connection with this case. IF THE DEBTOR FAILS TO TIMELY PAY THE FILING FEE IN FULL OR TIMELY MAKE INSTALLMENT PAYMENTS, THE COURT MAY DISMISS THE DEBTOR'S CHAPTER 7 CASE.

DATED:

Judge, United States Bankruptcy Court

Signature by the attorney constitutes a certification under Fed. R. of Bankr. P. 9011 that the relief in the order is the relief granted by the court.

Submitted by:____________

(Firm name)

By:____________

Attorney for Movant

CSD 1027
Notice of Motion for Exemption and Opportunity for Hearing
(Rev. 8/14/06)

NOTICE OF MOTION FOR EXEMPTION AND OPPORTUNITY FOR HEARING RE:

☐ **CREDIT COUNSELING**

☐ **COMPLETION OF INSTRUCTIONAL COURSE CONCERNING PERSONAL FINANCIAL MANAGEMENT**

The undersigned debtor(s) certify that no credit counseling and/or personal financial management course is required and request exemption from the requirement because:

☐ I am incapacitated or disabled, as defined in 11 U.S.C. § 109(h)(4); or

☐ I am on active military duty in a military combat zone.

If you object to this Motion,

1. **YOU ARE REQUIRED** to obtain a hearing date and time from the appropriate Courtroom Deputy for the judge assigned to this bankruptcy case. Determine which deputy to call by looking at the Bankruptcy Case No. in the above caption of this notice. If the case number is followed by the letter:

— M —	call (619) 557-6019	— DEPARTMENT ONE (Room 218)
— A —	call (619) 557-6594	— DEPARTMENT TWO (Room 118)
— H —	call (619) 557-6018	— DEPARTMENT THREE (Room 129)
— B —	call (619) 557-5157	— DEPARTMENT FOUR (Room 328)

2. **WITHIN FOURTEEN (14)** [1] **DAYS FROM THE DATE OF SERVICE THIS NOTICE**, you are further required to serve a copy of your DECLARATION IN OPPOSITION and separate REQUEST AND NOTICE OF HEARING [Local Form CSD 1184[2]] upon the debtor, counsel for the debtor (if any), and the Chapter 7 trustee, together with any opposing papers. The opposing

---

[1] If you were served electronically or by mail, you have three (3) additional days to take the above-stated actions.

[2] You may obtain Local Form CSD 1184 from the office of the Clerk of the U.S. Bankruptcy Court.

declaration shall be signed and verified in the manner prescribed by Federal Rule of Bankruptcy Procedure 9011, and the declaration shall:

a. identify the interest of the opposing party; and

b. state, with particularity, the grounds for the opposition.

3. **YOU MUST** file the original Declaration and Request and Notice of Hearing with proof of service with the Clerk of the U.S. Bankruptcy Court at 325 West "F" Street, San Diego, California 92101-6991, no later than the next business day following the date of service.

IF YOU FAIL TO SERVE YOUR "DECLARATION IN OPPOSITION" and "REQUEST AND NOTICE FOR HEARING" within the 14-day[1] period, NO HEARING WILL TAKE PLACE, you shall lose your opportunity for a hearing and an order may be entered.

DATED: ____________________ ____________________
Debtor Joint Debtor

CERTIFICATE OF SERVICE

I, the undersigned whose address appears below, certify:

That I am, and at all times hereinafter mentioned was, more than 18 years of age;

That on ____________day of ____________, I served a true copy of the within NOTICE OF MOTION FOR EXEMPTION AND OPPORTUNITY FOR HEARING RE: CREDIT COUNSELING OR COMPLETION OF INSTRUCTIONAL COURSE CONCERNING PERSONAL FINANCIAL MANAGEMENT by [describe here mode of service]

on the following persons [set forth name and address of each person served] and/or as checked below:

[ ] Chapter 7 Trustee:

[ ] UNITED STATES TRUSTEE
Department of Justice
402 West Broadway, Suite 600
San Diego, CA 92101

I certify under penalty of perjury that the foregoing is true and correct.

Executed on ____________

(Date) (Typed Name and Signature)

(Address)
(City, State, ZIP Code)

CSD 1028

Order on Motion or Exemption

(8/14/06)

ORDER ON MOTION FOR EXEMPTION RE:

☐ CREDIT COUNSELING

☐ COMPLETION OF INSTRUCTIONAL COURSE CONCERNING PERSONAL FINANCIAL MANAGMENT

On consideration of the Debtor's Motion for Exemption from Credit Counseling and/or Completion of Instructional Course Concerning Personal Financial Management (Doc. #   ), the Court finds that the Debtor qualifies for an exemption under 11 U.S.C. § 109(h)(4), and for good cause showing therefor,

IT IS HEREBY ORDERED THAT the Debtor's Motion is granted.

//

//

//

//

DATED:

Judge, United States Bankruptcy Court

Signature by the attorney constitutes a certification under Fed. R. of Bankr. P. 9011 that the relief in the order is the relief granted by the court.

Submitted by:

____

(Firm name)

By:__________________________

Attorney for Movant

No. CSD 1050

Subpoena for Rule 2004 Examination

CSD 1050 [01/31/07]
Name, Address, Telephone No. & I.D. No.

UNITED STATES BANKRUPTCY COURT
SOUTHERN DISTRICT OF CALIFORNIA

325 West "F" Street, San Diego, California 92101-6991

In Re

Debtor. BANKRUPTCY NO.

SUBPOENA FOR RULE 2004 EXAMINATION

TO:

☐ YOU ARE COMMANDED to appear and testify at an examination under Rule 2004, Fed. R. Bankr. P., at the place, date, and time specified below. A copy of the court order authorizing the examination is attached.

PLACE OF TESTIMONY	DATE AND TIME

☐ YOU ARE COMMANDED to produce and permit inspection and copying of the following documents or objects at the place, date, and time specified below (list documents or objects):

PLACE	DATE AND TIME
ISSUING OFFICER SIGNATURE AND TITLE	DATE

ISSUING OFFICER'S NAME, ADDRESS
AND PHONE NUMBER

*If the bankruptcy case is pending in a district other than the district in which the subpoena is issued, state the district under the case number.

PROOF OF SERVICE

SERVED	DATE	PLACE
SERVED ON (PRINT NAME)		MANNER OF SERVICE
SERVED BY (PRINT NAME)		TITLE

DECLARATION OF SERVER

I declare under penalty of perjury under the laws of the United States of America that the foregoing information contained in the Proof of Service is true and correct.

Executed on

(Date)

(Typed Name and Signature of Server)

(Address)

(City, State, ZIP Code)

Rule 45, Fed. R.Civ. P., Parts (c) & (d) made applicable in cases under the Bankruptcy Code by Rule 9016, Fed. R.Bankr. P.

(c) PROTECTION OF PERSONS SUBJECT TO SUBPOENAS.

(1) A party or an attorney responsible for the issuance and service of a subpoena shall take reasonable steps to avoid imposing undue burden or expense on a person subject to that subpoena. The court on behalf of which the subpoena was issued shall enforce this duty and impose upon the party or attorney in breach of this duty an appropriate sanction, which may include, but is not limited to, lost earnings and a reasonable attorney's fee.

(2) (A) A person commanded to produce and permit inspection and copying of designated books, papers, documents or tangible things, or inspection of premises need not appear in person at the place of production or inspection unless commanded to appear for deposition, hearing or trial.

(B) Subject to paragraph (d)(2) of this rule, a person commanded to produce and permit inspection and copying may, within 14 days after service of the subpoena or before the time specified for compliance if such time is less than 14 days after service, serve upon the party or attorney designated in the subpoena written objection to inspection or copying of any or all of the designated materials or of the premises. If objection is made, the party serving the subpoena shall not be entitled to inspect and copy the materials or inspect the premises except pursuant to an order or the court by which the subpoena was issued. If objection has been made, the party serving the subpoena may, upon notice to the person commanded to produce, move at any time for an order to compel the production. Such an order to compel production shall protect any person who is not a party or an officer of a party from significant expense resulting from the inspection and copying commanded.

(3) (A) On timely motion, the court by which a subpoena was issued shall quash or modify the subpoena if it

(i) fails to allow reasonable time for compliance;

(ii) requires a person who is not a party or an officer of a party to travel more than 100 miles from the place where that person resides, is employed or regularly transacts business in person, except that, subject to the provisions of clause (c)(3)(B)(iii) of this rule, such a person may in order to attend trial be commanded to travel from any such place within the state in which the trial is held, or

(iii) requires disclosure of privileged or other protected matter and no exception or waiver applies, or

(iv) subjects a person to undue burden.

(B) If a subpoena

(i) requires the disclosure of a trade secret or other confidential research, development, or commercial information, or

(ii) requires disclosure of an unretained expert's opinion or information not describing specific events or occurrences in dispute and resulting from the expert's study made not at the request of any party, or

(iii) requires a person who is not a party or an officer of a party to incur substantial expense to travel more than 100 miles to attend trial, the court may, to protect a person subject to or affected by the subpoena, quash or modify the subpoena or, if the party in whose behalf the subpoena is issued shows a substantial need for the testimony or material that cannot be otherwise met without undue hardship and assures that the person to whom the subpoena is addressed will be reasonably compensated, the court may order appearance or production only upon specified conditions.

(d) DUTIES IN RESPONDING TO SUBPOENA.

(1) A person responding to a subpoena to produce documents shall produce them as they are kept in the usual course of business or shall organize and label them to correspond with the categories in the demand.

(2) When information subject to a subpoena is withheld on a claim that it is privileged or subject to protection as trial preparation materials, the claim shall be made expressly and shall be supported by a description of the nature of the documents, communications, or things not produced that is sufficient to enable the demanding party to contest the claim.

SDCAL-153 S.D. CALIFORNIA

CSD 1051

Subpoena in a Case Under the Bankruptcy Code
(Rev. 01/31/07)

SUBPOENA IN A CASE UNDER THE BANKRUPTCY CODE

TO:

☐ YOU ARE COMMANDED to appear in the United States Bankruptcy Court at the place, date, and time specified below to testify in the above case.

PLACE OF TESTIMONY	COURTROOM
	DATE AND TIME

☐ YOU ARE COMMANDED to appear at the place, date, and time specified below to testify at the taking of a deposition in the above case.

PLACE	DATE AND TIME

☐ YOU ARE COMMANDED to produce and permit inspection and copying of the following documents or objects at the place, date, and time specified below (list documents or objects):

PLACE	DATE AND TIME

☐ YOU ARE COMMANDED to permit inspection of the following premises at the date and time specified below.

PREMISES	DATE AND TIME

Any organization not a party to this proceeding that is subpoenaed for the taking of a deposition shall designate one or more officers, directors, or managing agents, or other persons who consent to testify on its behalf, and may set forth, for each person designated, the matters on which the person will testify. Fed.R.Civ.P. 30(b)(6) made applicable in bankruptcy cases and proceedings by Rules 1018, 7030, and 9014, Fed.R.Bankr.P.

ISSUING OFFICER SIGNATURE AND TITLE	DATE
ISSUING OFFICER'S NAME, ADDRESS AND PHONE NUMBER	

*If the bankruptcy case is pending in a district other than the district in which the subpoena is issued, state the district under the case number.

PROOF OF SERVICE

SERVED	DATE	PLACE
SERVED ON (PRINT NAME)		MANNER OF SERVICE
SERVED BY (PRINT NAME)		TITLE

DECLARATION OF SERVER

I declare under penalty of perjury under the laws of the United States of America that the foregoing information contained in the Proof of Service is true and correct.

Executed on
(Date)

(Typed Name and Signature of Server)

(Address)

(City, State, ZIP Code)

(c) PROTECTION OF PERSONS SUBJECT TO SUBPOENAS.

(1) A party or an attorney responsible for the issuance and service of a subpoena shall take reasonable steps to avoid imposing undue burden or expense on a person subject to that subpoena. The court on behalf of which the subpoena was issued shall enforce this duty and impose upon the party or attorney in breach of this duty an appropriate sanction, which may include, but is not limited to, lost earnings and a reasonable attorney's fee.

(2) (A) A person commanded to produce and permit inspection and copying of designated books, papers, documents or tangible things, or inspection of premises need not appear in person at the place of production or inspection unless commanded to appear for deposition, hearing or trial.

(B) Subject to paragraph (d)(2) of this rule, a person commanded to produce and permit inspection and copying may, within 14 days after service of the subpoena or before the time specified for compliance if such time is less than 14 days after service, serve upon the party or attorney designated in the subpoena written objection to inspection or copying of any or all of the designated materials or of the premises. If objection is made, the party serving the subpoena shall not be entitled to inspect and copy the materials or inspect the premises except pursuant to an order of the court by which the subpoena was issued. If objection has been made, the party serving the subpoena may, upon notice to the person commanded to produce, move at any time for an order to compel the production. Such an order to compel production shall protect any person who is not a party or an officer of a party from significant expense resulting from the inspection and copying commanded.

(3) (A) On timely motion, the court by which a subpoena was issued shall quash or modify the subpoena if it

(i) fails to allow reasonable time for compliance;

(ii) requires a person who is not a party or an officer of a party to travel to a place more than 100 miles from the place where that person resides, is employed or regularly transacts business in person, except that, subject to the provisions of clause (c)(3)(B)(iii) of this rule, such a person may in order to attend trial be commanded to travel from any such place within the state in which the trial is held, or

(iii) requires disclosure of privileged or other protected matter and no exception or waiver applies, or

(iv) subjects a person to undue burden.

(B) If a subpoena

(i) requires the disclosure of a trade secret or other confidential research, development, or commercial information, or

(ii) requires disclosure of an unretained expert's opinion or information not describing specific events or occurrences in dispute and resulting from the expert's study made not at the request of any party, or

(iii) requires a person who is not a party or an officer of a party to incur substantial expense to travel more than 100 miles to attend trial, the court may, to protect a person subject to or affected by the subpoena, quash or modify the subpoena or, if the party in whose behalf the subpoena is issued shows a substantial need for the testimony or material that cannot be otherwise met without undue hardship and assures that the person to whom the subpoena is addressed will be reasonably compensated, the court may order appearance or production only upon specified conditions.

(d) DUTIES IN RESPONDING TO SUBPOENA.

(1) A person responding to a subpoena to produce documents shall produce them as they are kept in the usual course of business or shall organize and label them to correspond with the categories in the demand.

(2) When information subject to a subpoena is withheld on a claim that it is privileged or subject to protection as trial preparation materials, the claim shall be made expressly and shall be supported by a description of the nature of the documents, communications, or things not produced that is sufficient to enable the demanding party to contest the claim.

CSD 1105

Order Converting Case Under Chapter 7 to Case Under Chapter 11

CSD 1105 [08/22/03]
Name, Address, Telephone No. & I.D. No.

UNITED STATES BANKRUPTCY COURT
SOUTHERN DISTRICT OF CALIFORNIA

325 West "F" Street, San Diego, California 92101-6991

In Re

Debtor.

BANKRUPTCY NO.

ORDER CONVERTING CASE UNDER CHAPTER 7 TO CASE UNDER CHAPTER 11

IT IS ORDERED THAT the relief sought as set forth on the continuation pages attached and numbered two (2) through ___________with exhibits, if any, for a total of ___________ pages, is granted. Motion Docket Entry No. ___________.

//
//
//
//
//
//

DATED:

____
Judge, United States Bankruptcy Court

Signature by the attorney constitutes a certification under Fed. R. of Bankr. P. 9011 that the relief in the order is the relief granted by the court.

Submitted by:

____
(Firm name)

By: _______________________
Attorney for Movant

☐ The debtor has filed a motion in accordance with 11 U.S.C. § 706(a), seeking to convert this case to a case under chapter 11 of the Bankruptcy Code (title 11 of the United States Code). The court finds that the case has not been previously converted under 11 U.S.C. § 1112, § 1208, or § 1307, and that the debtor is entitled to be a debtor under chapter 11.

☐ A party in interest has filed a motion in accordance with 11 U.S.C. § 706(b) seeking to convert the case to a case under chapter 11 of the Bankruptcy Code (title 11 of the United States Code). The court finds, after notice and a hearing, that the motion should be granted.

IT IS ORDERED THAT:

1. This chapter 7 case is converted to a case under chapter 11.
2. The debtor within 15 days of the date of this order shall file a list of the debtor's equity security holders of each class, showing the number and kind of interests registered in the name of each holder and the last known name and address or place of business of each holder, as required by Federal Rule of Bankruptcy Procedure 1007(a)(3).
3. The debtor within 15 days of the date of this order shall file the statements and schedules required by Federal Rule of Bankruptcy Procedure 1007(b), if such documents have not already been filed.
4. The debtor within 2 days of the date of this order shall file a list of the names, addresses, and amount of claims of the creditors that hold the 20 largest unsecured claims as required by Federal Rule of Bankruptcy Procedure 1007(d).
5. The chapter 7 trustee shall:
    a. forthwith turn over to the debtor in possession, or chapter 11 trustee if one has been appointed, all records and property of the estate under his custody and control; and
    b. within 30 days of the date of this order, file and transmit to the United States Trustee an accounting of all receipts and distributions made, together with a report on administration of the case, as required by 11 U.S.C.§ 704(9).
6. The moving party immediately shall pay any additional filing fee.
7. [Other provisions as needed]

CSD 1106

Order Converting Case Under Chapter 7 to Case Under Chapter 12

CSD 1106 [08/21/03]
Name, Address, Telephone No. & I.D. No.

UNITED STATES BANKRUPTCY COURT
SOUTHERN DISTRICT OF CALIFORNIA
325 West "F" Street, San Diego, California 92101-6991

In Re

Debtor.

BANKRUPTCY NO.

ORDER CONVERTING CASE UNDER CHAPTER 7 TO CASE UNDER CHAPTER 12

IT IS ORDERED THAT the relief sought as set forth on the continuation pages attached and numbered two (2) through __________with exhibits, if any, for a total of __________ pages, is granted. Motion Docket Entry No. __________.

//
//
//
//
//
//

DATED:

____
Judge, United States Bankruptcy Court

Signature by the attorney constitutes a certification under Fed. R. of Bankr. P. 9011 that the relief in the order is the relief granted by the court.

Submitted by:
____
(Firm name)
By: ____________________
Attorney for Movant

The debtor has filed a motion, in accordance with 11 U.S.C. § 706(a), seeking to convert this case to a case under chapter 12 of the Bankruptcy Code. The court has considered the record, and finds that the case has not been converted previously under 11 U.S.C. § 1112, § 1208 or § 1307.

IT IS ORDERED THAT:

1. This chapter 7 case is converted to a chapter 12 case.
2. The chapter 7 trustee within 30 days of the date of this order shall file and transmit to the United States Trustee:
   a. an account of all receipts and disbursements made in the chapter 7 case, and
   b. a report on the administration of the case pursuant to 11 U.S.C. § 704(9).
3. The chapter 7 trustee forthwith shall turn over to the chapter 12 trustee all records and property of the estate remaining in the chapter 7 trustee's custody and control.
4. The chapter 7 trustee or any other party entitled to compensation for services rendered in the chapter 7 case may within 30 days of the date of this order file an application for compensation and reimbursement of expenses.
5. The debtor within 15 days from the date of this order shall file:
   a. a list of the debtor's equity security holders of each class, showing the number and kind of interests registered in the name of each holder and the last known name and address or place of business of each holder, as required by Federal Rule of Bankruptcy Procedure 1007(a)(3), if the debtor is a corporation; and
   b. a chapter 12 Statement of Financial Affairs.
6. The debtor within 15 days of the date of this order shall file the statements and schedules required by Federal Rule of Bankruptcy Procedure 1007(b), if such documents have not already been filed.
7. The debtor immediately shall pay any additional filing fee.
8. The debtor within 90 days from the date of this order shall file a chapter 12 plan.
9. [Other provisions as needed]

CSD 1107

Order Converting Case Under Chapter 7 to Case Under Chapter 13

CSD 1107 [08/22/03]
Name, Address, Telephone No. & I.D. No.

UNITED STATES BANKRUPTCY COURT
SOUTHERN DISTRICT OF CALIFORNIA

325 West "F" Street, San Diego, California 92101-6991

In Re

Debtor.

BANKRUPTCY NO.

ORDER CONVERTING CASE UNDER CHAPTER 7 TO CASE UNDER CHAPTER 13

IT IS ORDERED THAT the relief sought as set forth on the continuation pages attached and numbered two (2) through ____________ with exhibits, if any, for a total of ____________ pages, is granted. Motion Docket Entry No. ____________.

//

//

//

//

//

//

DATED:

____
Judge, United States Bankruptcy Court

Signature by the attorney constitutes a certification under Fed. R. of Bankr. P. 9011 that the relief in the order is the relief granted by the court.

Submitted by:

____
(Firm name)

By: ____________________
Attorney for Movant

The debtor has filed a motion, in accordance with 11 U.S.C. § 706(a), seeking to convert this case to a case under chapter 13 of the Bankruptcy Code. The court has considered the record, and finds that the case has not been converted previously under 11 U.S.C. § 1112, § 1208 or § 1307.

IT IS ORDERED THAT:

1. This chapter 7 case is converted to a case under chapter 13.
2. The chapter 7 trustee within 30 days of the date of this order shall file and transmit to the United States Trustee:
    a. an account of all receipts and disbursements made in the chapter 7 case, and
    b. a report on the administration of the case pursuant to 11 U.S.C. § 704(9).
3. The trustee forthwith shall turnover to the debtor all records and property of the estate remaining in the trustee's custody and control.
4. The trustee or any other party entitled to compensation may within 30 days of the date of this order file an application for compensation and reimbursement of expenses.
5. The debtor within 15 days from the date of this order shall file the statements and schedules required by Federal Rule of Bankruptcy Procedure 1007(b), if such documents have not already been filed.
6. The debtor within 15 days from the date of this order shall file a chapter 13 plan.
7. [Other provisions as needed]

CSD 1108

Order Converting Case Under Chapter 11 to Case Under Chapter 7

CSD 1108 [08/22/03]
Name, Address, Telephone No. & I.D. No.

UNITED STATES BANKRUPTCY COURT
SOUTHERN DISTRICT OF CALIFORNIA

325 West "F" Street, San Diego, California 92101-6991

In Re

Debtor.

BANKRUPTCY NO.

ORDER CONVERTING CASE UNDER CHAPTER 11 TO CASE UNDER CHAPTER 7

IT IS ORDERED THAT the relief sought as set forth on the continuation pages attached and numbered two (2) through __________with exhibits, if any, for a total of __________ pages, is granted. Motion Docket Entry No. __________.

//
//
//
//
//
//

DATED:

____
Judge, United States Bankruptcy Court

Signature by the attorney constitutes a certification under Fed. R. of Bankr. P. 9011 that the relief in the order is the relief granted by the court.

Submitted by:

____
(Firm name)

By: ____________________
Attorney for Movant

☐ The debtor in possession has filed a motion in accordance with 11 U.S.C. § 1112(a), seeking to convert this case to a case under chapter 7 of the Bankruptcy Code (title 11 of the United States Code). The court finds that the case is not an involuntary case originally commenced under chapter 11, and that the case has not been converted to a case under chapter 11 on other than the debtor's request.

☐ A party in interest other than the debtor has filed a motion in accordance with 11 U.S.C. § 1112(b) seeking to convert the case to a case under chapter 7 of the Bankruptcy Code (title 11 of the United States Code). The court finds, after notice and a hearing, that the motion should be granted.

IT IS ORDERED THAT:

1. This chapter 11 case is converted to a case under chapter 7.
2. The debtor in possession or the chapter 11 trustee shall:
    a. forthwith turn over to the chapter 7 trustee all records and property of the estate under its custody or control as required by Federal Rule of Bankruptcy Procedure 1019(4);
    b. within 15 days of the date of this order, file a schedule of all unpaid debts incurred after the commencement of the chapter 11 case including the name and address of each creditor, as required by Federal Rule of Bankruptcy Procedure 1019(5)(A); and
    c. within 30 days of the date of this order, file and transmit to the United States Trustee a final report and account, as required by Federal Rule of Bankruptcy Procedure 1019(5)(B).
3. The debtor within 15 days of the date of this order shall file the statements and schedules required by Federal Rules of Bankruptcy Procedure 1019(1)(A) & 1007(b), if such documents have not already been filed.
4. The debtor within 30 days of the date of this order shall if the case is converted after the confirmation of a plan, file:
    a. a schedule of all property not listed in the final report and account of the debtor in possession or chapter 11 trustee which was acquired after the commencement of the chapter 11 case but before the entry of this conversion order;
    b. a schedule of executory contracts and unexpired leases entered into or assumed after the commencement of the chapter 11 case but before the entry of this conversion order; and

c. a schedule of unpaid debts not listed in the final report and account of the debtor in possession or chapter 11 trustee which were incurred after the commencement of the chapter 11 case but before the entry of this conversion order, as required by Federal Rule of Bankruptcy Procedure 1019(5); and

d. a statement of intention with respect to retention or surrender of property securing consumer debts, as required by 11 U.S.C. § 521(2)(A) and Federal Rule of Bankruptcy Procedure 1019(1)(B), and conforming to Official Form B8.

5. [Other provisions as needed]

CSD 1109

Order Converting Case Under Chapter 11 to Case Under Chapter 12

CSD 1109 [08/22/03]
Name, Address, Telephone No. & I.D. No.

UNITED STATES BANKRUPTCY COURT
SOUTHERN DISTRICT OF CALIFORNIA

325 West "F" Street, San Diego, California 92101-6991

In Re

Debtor.

BANKRUPTCY NO.

ORDER CONVERTING CASE UNDER CHAPTER 11 TO CASE UNDER CHAPTER 12

IT IS ORDERED THAT the relief sought as set forth on the continuation pages attached and numbered two (2) through ___________with exhibits, if any, for a total of ___________ pages, is granted. Motion Docket Entry No. ___________.

//
//
//
//
//
//

DATED:

____
Judge, United States Bankruptcy Court

Signature by the attorney constitutes a certification under Fed. R. of Bankr. P. 9011 that the relief in the order is the relief granted by the court.

Submitted by:

____
(Firm name)

By: _______________________
Attorney for Movant

The debtor in possession has filed a motion in accordance with 11 U.S.C. § 1112(d), seeking to convert this case to a case under chapter 12 of the Bankruptcy Code (title 11 of the United States Code). The court finds that the case has not been discharged under § 1141(d) and such conversion is equitable.

IT IS ORDERED THAT:

1. This chapter 11 case is converted to a case under chapter 12.
2. The debtor in possession or the chapter 11 trustee shall:
   a. forthwith turn over to the chapter 12 trustee all records and property of the estate under its custody and control: and
   b. within 30 days of the date of this order, file and transmit to the United States Trustee an accounting of all receipts and distributions made, together with a schedule of all unpaid debts incurred after the commencement of the chapter 11 case.
3. The debtor within 15 days of the date of this order shall file:
   a. the statements and schedules required by Federal Rule of Bankruptcy Procedure 1007(b), if such documents have not already been filed;
   b. a list of the debtor's equity security holders of each class, showing the number and kind of interests registered in the name of each holder and the last known name and address or place of business of each holder, as required by Federal Rule of Bankruptcy Procedure 1007(a)(3) if such list has not already been filed; and
   c. the chapter 12 Statement.
4. The debtor within 30 days of the date of this order shall if the case is converted after the confirmation of a plan, file:
   a. a schedule of all property not listed in the final report and account of the debtor in possession or chapter 11 trustee which was acquired after the commencement of the chapter 11 case but before the entry of this conversion order;
   b. a schedule of executory contracts entered into or assumed after the commencement of the chapter 11 case but before the entry of this conversion order; and
   c. a schedule of unpaid debts not listed in the final report and account of the debtor in possession or chapter 11 trustee which were incurred after the commencement of the chapter

11 case but before the entry of this conversion order, as required by Federal Rule of Bankruptcy Procedure 1019(5).

5. [Other provisions as needed]

SUMMONS TO DEBTOR IN INVOLUNTARY CASE

A petition under Title 11, United States Code, was filed against you on in this Bankruptcy Court, requesting an order for relief under Chapter ___________ of the Bankruptcy Code (Title 11 of the United States Code).

YOU ARE SUMMONED and required to submit to the Clerk of the Bankruptcy Court a motion or answer to the petition within 20 days after the service of this summons. A copy of the petition is attached.

Address of Clerk
Clerk, United States Bankruptcy Court
Southern District of California
325 West "F" Street
San Diego, California 92101-6991
At the same time, you must also serve a copy of the motion or answer on petitioner's attorney.

____

Name and Address of Petitioner's Attorney

If you make a motion, your time to answer is governed by Federal Rule of Bankruptcy Procedure 1011(c).

IF YOU FAIL TO RESPOND TO THIS SUMMONS, THE ORDER FOR RELIEF WILL BE ENTERED.

Barry K. Lander, Clerk

Dated: ___________

By: ___________, Deputy Clerk

PROOF OF SERVICE

I, ___________, certify that I am, and at all times during the service of process was, not less than 18 years of age and not a party to the matter concerning which service of process was made.

I further certify that the service of this summons and a copy of the complaint was made by:

[date]

[ ] Mail Service—Regular, first class United States mail, postage fully pre-paid, addressed to:

[ ] Personal Service—By leaving the documents with the following defendants(s) or an officer or agent of the defendant(s) at:

[ ] Residence Service—By leaving the documents with the following adult at:

[ ] Publication—The defendant was served as follows: [describe briefly]

[ ] State Law—The defendant was served pursuant to the laws of the State of __________, as follows: [describe briefly]

Under penalty of perjury, I declare that the foregoing is true and correct.

____________________ [Date] __________ [Signature]

____

Print Name

____

Business Address

____

City, State, Zip Code

CSD 1129

Notice of Coversion of Case Under Chapter 13 to a Case Under Chapter by Debtor

(Rev. 1/12/07)

NOTICE OF CONVERSION OF CASE UNDER CHAPTER 13 TO A CASE UNDER CHAPTER 7 BY DEBTOR

Pursuant to 11 U.S.C. § 1307(a) and Federal Rule of Bankruptcy Procedure 1017(d), the above-named Debtor(s) converts this Chapter 13 case to a case under Chapter 7 of the Bankruptcy Code (title 11 of the United States Code); and further states that

1. The Debtor(s) has filed concurrently with this notice the schedules and statements listed in Federal Rule of Bankruptcy Procedure 1007(b)(1) and a separate schedule listing the names and addresses of any creditors who are entitled to assert claims against the Debtor(s) or the estate under Federal Rule of Bankruptcy Procedure 1019(5) and 11 U.S.C. § 348(d) as required by Bankruptcy Local Rule 1017-2(b)(3)(B). The undersigned Debtor(s) further declare under penalty of perjury that the information provided in the schedules, statements, and creditor diskette, if any, is true and correct.

2. The Debtor(s) will file within 30 days of the date of filing of this notice if the case is converted after the confirmation of a plan:

   a. a schedule of all property not listed in the final report and account of the Chapter 13 Trustee which was acquired after the commencement of the Chapter 13 case but before the entry of this conversion order;

   b. a schedule of executory contracts entered into or assumed after the commencement of the Chapter 13 case but before the date of filing of this notice; and

   c. a statement of intention with respect to retention or surrender of property securing consumer debt, as required by 11 U.S.C.§ 521(2)(A), and Federal Rule of Bankruptcy Procedure 1019(1)(B), and conforming to Official Form 8.

DATED:

Attorney for Debtor(s)Debtor

Joint Debtor

REQUIRED FEES:

Conversion fee:	$25.00
Division of case fee*:	$235.00

---

* Due only in those instances when one debtor elects to continue under the provisions of a Chapter 13 while the other debtor converts to a Chapter 7.

CSD 1140

Notice of Objection to Debtor's Claim of Exemptions and Opportunity for Hearing

(Rev. 10/17/05)

NOTICE OF OBJECTIONS TO DEBTOR'S CLAIM OF EXEMPTIONS AND OPPORTUNITY FOR HEARING

TO THE ABOVE-NAMED DEBTOR AND ATTORNEY OF RECORD, IF ANY:

I, ___________, hereby declare that I am:

[ ] a creditor holding a claim against your estate,

[ ] the trustee appointed to administer your estate, or [ ] the United States Trustee, and that I hereby object to your claim of exemption (Schedule C) filed on ___________, with specific reference to the following described property of this estate:

You are required to attach and serve declarations supporting your objections in accordance with Local Bankruptcy Rule 9013-2(a)(2).

If you object to the proposed action:

1. **YOU ARE REQUIRED** to obtain a hearing date and time from the appropriate Courtroom Deputy for the judge assigned to your bankruptcy case. ***If a Chapter 7, 11, or 12 case***, determine which deputy to call by looking at the Bankruptcy Case No. in the caption on Page 1 of this notice. If the case number is followed by the letter:

— M —	call (619) 557-6019	—	DEPARTMENT ONE (Room 218)
— A —	call (619) 557-6594	—	DEPARTMENT TWO (Room 118)
— H —	call (619) 557-6018	—	DEPARTMENT THREE (Room 129)
— B —	call (619) 557-5157	—	DEPARTMENT FOUR (Room 328)

For ALL Chapter 13 cases, call (619) 557-5955.

2. **WITHIN TWENTY-EIGHT (28)[3] DAYS FROM THE DATE OF SERVICE OF THIS MOTION**, you are further required to serve a copy of your DECLARATION IN OPPOSITION TO MOTION and separate REQUEST AND NOTICE OF HEARING [Local Form CSD 1184[4]] upon the undersigned moving party, together with any opposing papers. The opposing declaration shall be signed and verified in the manner prescribed by Federal Rule of Bankruptcy Procedure 9011, and the declaration shall:
   a. identify the interest of the opposing party; and
   b. state, with particularity, the grounds for the opposition.
3. **YOU MUST** file the original and one copy of the Declaration and Request and Notice of Hearing with proof of service with the Clerk of the U.S. Bankruptcy Court at 325 West "F" Street, San Diego, California 92101-6991, no later than the next business day following the date of service.

IF YOU FAIL TO SERVE YOUR "DECLARATION IN OPPOSITION TO INTENDED ACTION" AND "REQUEST AND NOTICE OF HEARING" within the 28-day[2] period provided by this notice, NO HEARING SHALL TAKE PLACE, you shall lose your opportunity for hearing, and the objecting party may proceed to take the intended action.

DATED:

[ ] Trustee [ ] Creditor [ ] U.S. Trustee

CERTIFICATE OF SERVICE

I, the undersigned whose address appears below, certify:

That I am, and at all time hereinafter mentioned was, more than 18 years of age;

---

[3] If you were served electronically or by mail, you have three (3) additional days to take the above-stated actions.

[4] You may obtain Local Form CSD 1184 from the office of the Clerk of the U.S. Bankruptcy Court.

That on____________day of ____________, I served a true copy of the within NOTICE OF OBJECTIONS TO DEBTOR'S CLAIM OF EXEMPTIONS AND OPPORTUNITY FOR HEARING, together with the following pleadings [describe any other papers]:

by [describe here mode of service]:

on the following persons [set forth name and address of each person served] and/or as checked below:

[ ] For Chpt. 7, 11, & 12 cases: UNITED STATES TRUSTEE Department of Justice 402 West Broadway, Suite 600 San Diego, CA 92101	[ ] For ODD numbered Chapter 13 cases: THOMAS H. BILLINGSLEA, JR., TRUSTEE 530 "B" Street, Suite. 1500 San Diego, CA 92101	[ ] For EVEN numbered Chapter 13 cases: DAVID L. SKELTON, TRUSTEE 525 "B" Street, Suite 1430 San Diego, CA 92101-4507

[ ] Attorney for Debtor (or Debtor):

I certify under penalty of perjury that the foregoing is true and correct.

Executed on ________________________

(Date) (Typed Name and Signature)

(Address)
(City, State, ZIP Code)

No. CSD 1143

Fee Application Summary

CSD 1143 [04/28/96]

UNITED STATES BANKRUPTCY COURT
SOUTHERN DISTRICT OF CALIFORNIA

DEBTOR: .... DATE PETITION
CASE NO.: .... FILED: ....

FEE APPLICATION SUMMARY

APPLICANT: .... , REPRESENTING ....
ORDER APPROVING EMPLOYMENT: ....
....

CATEGORIES [1] INTERIM PERIOD
.... TO ......
....

	HOURS	AMOUNT REQUESTED
....		
....		
....		
....		
....		
....		
....		
....		
....		
....		
....		
TOTALS		
....		

NOTE: Attach all fee application summaries for prior interim hearings.

EXHIBIT "A" Page. . . . . . of . . . . . .

REPRINTED FROM THE U.S. TRUSTEE'S *GUIDELINES FOR REVIEWING APPLICATIONS FOR COMPENSATION AND REIMBURSEMENT OF EXPENSES DATED 1/30/96*

Here is a list of suggested project categories for use in most bankruptcy cases. Only one category should be used for a given activity. Professionals

---

[1] See categories suggested in UNITED STATES TRUSTEE GUIDELINES FOR REVIEWING APPLICATIONS FOR COMPENSATION AND REIMBURSEMENT OF EXPENSES.

should make their best effort to be consistent in their use of categories, whether within a particular firm or by different firms working on the same case. It would be appropriate for all professionals to discuss the categories in advance and agree generally on how activities will be categorized. The application may contain additional categories as the case requires. They are generally more applicable to attorneys in chapter 7 and chapter 11, but may be used by all professionals as appropriate.

ASSET ANALYSIS & RECOVERY: Identification and review of potential assets including causes of action and non-litigation recoveries.

ASSET DISPOSITION: Sales, leases (§ 365 matters), abandonment and related transaction work.

BUSINESS OPERATIONS: Issues related to debtor-in-possession operating in chapter 11 such as employee, vendor, tenant issues and other similar problems.

CASE ADMINISTRATION: Coordination and compliance activities, including preparation of statement of financial affairs; schedules; list of contracts; United States Trustee interim statements and operating reports; contacts with the United States Trustee; general creditor inquiries.

CLAIMS ADMINISTRATION & OBJECTIONS: Specific claim inquiries; bar date motions; analysis, objections and allowance of claims.

EMPLOYEE BENEFITS/PENSIONS: Review issues such as severance, retention, 401K coverage and continuance of pension plan.

FEE/EMPLOYMENT APPLICATIONS: Preparations of employment and fee applications for self or others; motions to establish interim procedures.

FEE/EMPLOYMENT OBJECTIONS: Review of and objections to the employment and fee applications of others.

FINANCING: Matters under §§ 361, 363 and 364 including cash collateral and secured claims; loan document analysis.

LITIGATION: There should be a separate category established for each matter (e.g., XYZ Litigation).

MEETING OF CREDITORS: Preparing for and attending the conference of creditors, the § 341(a) meeting and other creditors' committee meetings.

PLAN & DISCLOSURE STATEMENT: Formulation, presentation and confirmation; compliance with the plan confirmation order, related orders and rules; disbursement and case closing activities, except those related to the allowance and objections to allowance of claims.

RELIEF FROM STAY PROCEEDINGS: Matters relating to termination or continuation of automatic stay under § 362.

The following categories are generally more applicable to accountants and financial advisors, but may be used by all professionals as appropriate.

ACCOUNTING/AUDITING: Activities related to maintaining and auditing books of account, preparation of financial statements and account analysis.

BUSINESS ANALYSIS: Preparation and review of company business plan; development and review of strategies; preparation and review of cash flow forecasts and feasibility studies.

CORPORATE FINANCE: Review financial aspects of potential mergers, acquisitions and disposition of company or subsidiaries.

DATA ANALYSIS: Management information systems review, installation and analysis, construction, maintenance and reporting of significant case financial data, lease rejection, claims, etc.

LITIGATION CONSULTING: Providing consulting and expert witness services relating to various bankruptcy matters such as insolvency, feasibility, avoiding actions; forensic accounting, etc.

RECONSTRUCTION ACCOUNTING: Reconstructing books and records from past transactions and bringing accounting current.

TAX ISSUES: Analysis of tax issues and preparation of state and federal tax returns.

VALUATION: Appraise or review of appraisals of assets.

CSD 1144

Order Approving (Interim) (Final) Application of____________for Compensation and Reimbursement of Expenses

CSD 1144 [08/22/03]
Name, Address, Telephone No. & I.D. No.

UNITED STATES BANKRUPTCY COURT
SOUTHERN DISTRICT OF CALIFORNIA

325 West "F" Street, San Diego, California 92101-6991

In Re Debtor.	BANKRUPTCY NO. Date of Hearing: Time of Hearing: Name of Judge:

ORDER APPROVING (INTERIM) (FINAL) APPLICATION OF ____________FOR COMPENSATION AND REIMBURSEMENT OF EXPENSES

IT IS ORDERED THAT the relief sought as set forth on the continuation pages attached and numbered two (2) through ____________with exhibits, if any, for a total of ____________ pages, is granted.

//
//
//
//
//
//

DATED:

____
Judge, United States Bankruptcy Court

Signature by the attorney constitutes a certification under Fed. R. of Bankr. P. 9011 that the relief in the order is the relief granted by the court.

Submitted by:

____
(Firm name)

By: ________________________
Attorney for Movant

The (interim) (final) application for allowance of compensation and reimbursement of expenses of the party or parties named below came on regularly for hearing on the above date and time, the Honorable____________United States Bankruptcy Judge, presiding.

It appearing that proper notice was given and the Court having considered the application and papers filed in support thereof, and for good cause appearing therefor,

IT IS HEREBY ORDERED as follows:

1. The following interim fees and expenses for the period beginning____________and ending____________are allowed and authorized for immediate payment to applicant.

Applicant:
(Include state bar number, if any, and type of professional)

	Amount Requested	Allowed	Authorized for Payment
Fees:	$	$	$
Costs:	$	$	$
	________	________	________
	________	________	________
Totals:	$ 0.00	$ 0.00	$ 0.00

2. The following interim fees and expenses were previously allowed but not authorized for payment and are now allowed and authorized for immediate payment to applicant.

Applicant:
(Include state bar number, if any, and type of professional)

	Authorized for Payment
Fees:	$
Costs:	$
	________ ________
Totals:	$ 0.00

3. The following final fees and expenses are allowed and authorized for immediate payment to applicant.

Applicant:
(Include state bar number, if any, and type of professional)

	Allowed and Authorized for Payment
Fees:	$

Costs: $ ____________________

____

Totals: $

The trustee is authorized to pay ____________, without the need of an additional notice, hearing or court order, the actual amount accrued not to exceed $____________. ___ for compensation and costs of any miscellaneous work performed in connection with closing this case, subject to the trustee's review and approval of the additional fees and costs.

Payment of all fees and expenses will be made at the discretion of the trustee, if one has been appointed.

All fees and costs allowed by this order may be subject to disgorgement.

No. CSD 1148

Request for Special Charges by Chapter 11 Plan Proponent

CSD 1148 [03/13/98]

UNITED STATES BANKRUPTCY COURT
SOUTHERN DISTRICT OF CALIFORNIA
325 West "F" Street, San Diego, California 92101-6991

REQUEST FOR SPECIAL CHARGES BY CHAPTER 11 PLAN PROPONENT

PART I — To be completed by the (Attorney for) Plan Proponent and submitted not less than 21 days prior to plan confirmation hearing pursuant to Local Bankruptcy Rule 3020-1.

DATED:

TO: Case Administrator

FROM: ______________________, (Attorney for) Plan Proponent

CASE NAME: ______________________ Case No.: __________

(If this case has been consolidated with any other case, list case names and numbers below. Continue on reverse side if necessary.)

Confirmation Hearing set for: __________

PART II — To be completed by Case Administrator.

	AMOUNT DUE
Excess Notices (no. of copies x 50¢ if noticed prior to 1/1/98)	$
Deferred Adv. Pro. Filing Fees ($120 each filed prior to 12/18/96)	$
Deferred Adv. Pro. Filing Fees ($150 each filed on or after 12/18/96)	$
BALANCE DUE:	$

ATTORNEY FOR PLAN PROPONENT:

- Please return this form with your *ORDER CONFIRMING CHAPTER 11 PLAN* and a check made payable to the Clerk, U. S. Bankruptcy Court. If previously paid, please provide a copy of your receipt.
- **FAILURE TO SUBMIT THE FUNDS (OR RECEIPT COPY) MAY RESULT IN THE ORDER BEING RETURNED TO YOU UNSIGNED.**

DATED: Barry K. Lander, Clerk

By: ______________________, Deputy Clerk

cc: Courtroom Deputy

CSD 1149

Notice of Hearing and Motion for Approval of
(Rev. 10/17/05)

NOTICE OF HEARING AND MOTION FOR APPROVAL OF

☐ CHAPTER 11 DISCLOSURE STATEMENT ☐ CHAPTER 11 PLAN OF RE-ORGANIZATION

☐ CHAPTER 11 MODIFIED PLAN ☐ CHAPTER 13 MODIFIED PLAN

TO THE DEBTOR, ALL CREDITORS AND OTHER PARTIES IN INTEREST:

YOU ARE HEREBY NOTIFIED that on ___________, at ___________.m., in Department ___________, Room ___________, of the Jacob Weinberger United States Courthouse, located at 325 West "F" Street, San Diego, California 92101-6991, there will be a hearing regarding the Motion of ___________, for [check the appropriate box]:

[ ] Approval of disclosure statement in chapter 11 case;

[ ] Approval of plan of reorganization in chapter 11 case;

[ ] Modification of a chapter 11 plan prior to confirmation; or

[ ] Modification of a chapter 13 plan after confirmation.

If not required to be attached, a set of the moving papers will be provided, upon request, by the undersigned or may be inspected at the office of the Clerk.

Any opposition or other response to the motion must be served upon the undersigned and the original and one copy of such papers with proof of service must be filed with the Clerk of the U.S. Bankruptcy Court at 325 West "F" St., San Diego, California 92101-6991, NOT LATER THAN TWENTY-FIVE (25)[1] DAYS FROM THE DATE OF SERVICE.

DATED:

CERTIFICATE OF SERVICE

I, the undersigned whose address appears below, certify:

That I am, and at all times hereinafter mentioned was, more than 18 years of age;

That on ___________day of ___________, I served a true copy of the within NOTICE OF HEARING AND MOTION FOR APPROVAL by [describe here mode of service]

on the following persons [set forth name and address of each person served] and/or as checked below:

[ ] Attorney for Debtor (if required):

[ ] For Chpt. 7, 11, & 12 cases:
UNITED STATES TRUSTEE
Department of Justice
402 West Broadway, Suite 600
San Diego, CA 92101

[ ]For ODD numbered Chapter 13 cases:
THOMAS H. BILLINGSLEA, JR., TRUSTEE
530 "B" Street, Suite. 1500
San Diego, CA 92101

[ ] For EVEN numbered Chapter 13 cases:
DAVID L. SKELTON, TRUSTEE
525 "B" Street, Suite 1430
San Diego, CA 92101-4507

I certify under penalty of perjury that the foregoing is true and correct.

Executed on ______________________

(Date) (Typed Name and Signature)
(Address)
(City, State, ZIP Code)

No. CSD 1151

Summary of Balloting on Chapter 11 Plan

CSD 1151 [04/28/96]
Name, Address, Telephone No. & I.D. No.

. . . .

UNITED STATES BANKRUPTCY COURT
SOUTHERN DISTRICT OF CALIFORNIA

325 West "F" Street, San Diego, California 92101-6991

In Re

Debtor. BANKRUPTCY NO.

. . . .

SUMMARY OF BALLOTING ON CHAPTER 11 PLAN DATED . . . .[1]

Number			Amount
. . . . . .	CLASS. . . . . . Proofs of CLAIM filed in the total sum of		$ . . . .
. . . . . .	Scheduled Creditors who have not filed claims		$ . . . .
. . . . . .	CONSENTS filed in the total sum of		$ . . . .
. . . . . .	REJECTIONS filed in the total sum of		$ . . . .
. . . . . .		**TOTAL** sum of all debts in this class	$ . . . .
. . . . . .	CLASS . . . . Proofs of CLAIM filed in the total sum of		$ . . . .
. . . . . .	Scheduled Creditors who have not filed claims		$ . . . .

[1] It is the duty of the proponent of the plan to prepare this form in accordance with Local Bankruptcy Rule 3018, and to file it with the Clerk not later than seven (7) business days prior to the date fixed for hearing on confirmation of the plan. Ballots must reflect claims docket number to the extent available.

Refer also to Local Bankruptcy Rule 3020 regarding duty of proponent of the plan to prepare and file an estimate of deposit to be made upon confirmation of plan.

. . . . . .	CONSENTS filed in the total sum of		$ . . . .
. . . . . .	REJECTIONS filed in the total sum of		$ . . . .
. . . . . .		**TOTAL** sum of all debts in this class	$ . . . .
. . . . . .	CLASS. . . . . . . Proofs of CLAIM filed in the total sum of		$ . . . .
. . . . . .	Scheduled Creditors who have not filed claims		$ . . . .
. . . . . .	CONSENTS filed in the total sum of		$ . . . .
. . . . . .	REJECTIONS filed in the total sum of		$ . . . .
. . . . . .		**TOTAL** sum of all debts in this class	$ . . . .
. . . . . .	CLASS . . . . Proofs of CLAIM filed in the total sum of		$ . . . .
. . . . . .	Scheduled Creditors who have not filed claims		$ . . . .
. . . . . .	CONSENTS filed in the total sum of		$ . . . .
. . . . . .	REJECTIONS filed in the total sum of		$ . . . .
. . . . . .		**TOTAL** sum of all debts in this class	$ . . . .

CLASSIFICATION OF CLAIMS AS USED HEREIN:

CLASS . . . . = ...

CLASS . . . . = ...

CLASS . . . . = ...

CLASS . . . . = ...

CSD 1156

Final Decree

(Rev. 11/15/04)

CSD 1156 [11/15/04]
Name, Address, Telephone No. & I.D. No.

UNITED STATES BANKRUPTCY COURT
SOUTHERN DISTRICT OF CALIFORNIA

325 West "F" Street, San Diego, California 92101-6991

In Re

Debtor.

BANKRUPTCY NO.

FINAL DECREE

The estate of the above named debtor has been fully administered.

The deposit required by the plan has been distributed.

IT IS ORDERED THAT:

____

(name of trustee)

is discharged as trustee of the estate of the above-named debtor and the bond is cancelled;

the chapter case of the above named debtor is closed; and

[other provisions as needed]

DATED: ______________________________

Judge, United States Bankruptcy Court

Signature by the attorney constitutes a certification under Fed. R. of Bankr. P. 9011 that the relief in the order is the relief granted by the court.

Submitted by:

____

(Firm name)

By:

Attorney for Movant

CSD 1158

Notice of Motion and Opportunity for Hearing on Opposition to Motion

(Rev. 05/08/06)

NOTICE OF MOTION AND OPPORTUNITY FOR HEARING ON OPPOSITION TO MOTION TO

☐ **EXTEND THE AUTOMATIC STAY** ☐ **IMPOSE THE AUTOMATIC STAY**

YOU ARE HEREBY NOTIFIED that ___________, has filed a Motion for

[ ] an order extending the automatic stay under 11 U.S.C. § 362(c)(3)(B);

[ ] an order imposing the automatic stay under 11 U.S.C. § 362(c)(4)(B)

Accompanying this Notice are the Motion and Declaration(s) in Support of the Motion.

If you oppose the Motion, you must serve upon the undersigned and file with the Clerk of Court the original and one copy of such papers, together with the proof of service, at 325 West "F" St., San Diego, California 92101-6991, **NOT LATER THAN TEN (10)[1] DAYS FROM THE DATE OF SERVICE.**

A hearing will be held on ___________, at ___________.m., in Department ___________, Room ___________, on your opposition to this Motion. **IF YOU FAIL TO FILE AND SERVE WRITTEN OPPOSITION TO THIS MOTION WITHIN THE TIME INDICATED, THE MOVANT SHALL IMMEDIATELY SUBMIT AN ORDER GRANTING THE MOTION AND VACATING THE HEARING.**

DATED:

[Attorney for] Moving Party

CERTIFICATE OF SERVICE

I, the undersigned whose address appears below, certify:

That I am, and at all times hereinafter mentioned was, more than 18 years of age;

That on ___________day of ___________, I served a true copy of the within NOTICE OF MOTION AND OPPORTUNITY FOR HEARING ON OPPOSITION by [describe here mode of service]

on the following persons [set forth name and address of each person served] and/or as checked below:

[ ] Attorney for Debtor (if required):

[ ] For Chpt. 7, 11, & 12 cases:
UNITED STATES TRUSTEE
Department of Justice
402 West Broadway, Suite 600
San Diego, CA 92101

[ ] For ODD numbered Chapter 13 cases:
THOMAS H. BILLINGSLEA, JR., TRUSTEE
530 "B" Street, Suite. 1500
San Diego, CA 92101

[ ] For EVEN numbered Chapter 13 cases:
DAVID L. SKELTON, TRUSTEE
525 "B" Street, Suite 1430
San Diego, CA 92101-4507

I certify under penalty of perjury that the foregoing is true and correct.

Executed on ______________________________

(Date) (Typed Name and Signature)
(Address)
(City, State, ZIP Code)

CSD 1159A

Order On
(Rev. 11/15/04)

CSD 1159A [11/15/04]
Name, Address, Telephone No. & I.D. No.

UNITED STATES BANKRUPTCY COURT
SOUTHERN DISTRICT OF CALIFORNIA

325 West "F" Street, San Diego, California 92101-6991

In Re Debtor. Movant(s) Respondent(s)	BANKRUPTCY NO. RS NO. Date of Hearing: Time of Hearing: Name of Judge:

ORDER ON

IT IS ORDERED THAT the relief sought as set forth on the continuation pages attached and numbered two (2) through ____________with exhibits, if any, for a total of ____________ pages, is granted. Motion/Application Docket Entry No. ____________

//

//

//

//

DATED: ____

Judge, United States Bankruptcy Court

Signature by the attorney constitutes a certification under Fed. R. of Bankr. P. 9011 that the relief in the order is the relief granted by the court.

Submitted by:

____

(Firm name)

By:

Attorney for ☐ Movant ☐ Respondent

CSD 1159B

Order Shortening Time for Hearing On
(Rev. 11/15/04)

CSD 1159B [11/15/04]
Name, Address, Telephone No. & I.D. No.

UNITED STATES BANKRUPTCY COURT
SOUTHERN DISTRICT OF CALIFORNIA

325 West "F" Street, San Diego, California 92101-6991

In Re	
Debtor.	BANKRUPTCY NO.
Movant(s)	RS NO.
Respondent(s)	

ORDER SHORTENING TIME FOR HEARING ON

IT IS ORDERED THAT the relief sought as set forth on the continuation pages attached and numbered two (2) through ___________with exhibits, if any, for a total of ___________ pages, is granted. Motion/Application Docket Entry No. ___________

//

//

//

//

DATED: ___________________________________

Judge, United States Bankruptcy Court

Signature by the attorney constitutes a certification under Fed. R. of Bankr. P. 9011 that the relief in the order is the relief granted by the court.

Submitted by:

____

(Firm name)

By:

Attorney for ☐ Movant ☐ Respondent

Upon review of the ex parte application for order shortening time for notice of hearing on the and for good cause appearing therefore,

IT IS ORDERED that this Court will conduct a hearing on the Motion, and any opposition, thereto on ____________at _______.m. in Department No. ____________, Room ____________of the United States Bankruptcy Court, Southern District of California, 325 West F Street, San Diego, California 92101-6991.

IT IS FURTHER ORDERED that the Notice of Motion and Motion must be filed and served no later than ___________. Service will be deemed complete when delivered

personally, or
by electronic method, or
by first class or overnight mail, or
as provided for in the application for order shortening time.

IT IS FURTHER ORDERED that all opposition, if any, to the Motion must be filed and served no later than ____________________ .

IT IS FURTHER ORDERED that a reply, if any, to the opposition to the Motion must be filed and served no later than ____________________.

CSD 1159C

Order On

(Rev. 11/15/04)

CSD 1159C [11/15/04]
Name, Address, Telephone No. & I.D. No.

UNITED STATES BANKRUPTCY COURT
SOUTHERN DISTRICT OF CALIFORNIA

325 West "F" Street, San Diego, California 92101-6991

LODGED

In Re	BANKRUPTCY NO.
	RS NO.
Debtor.	Date of Hearing:
Movant(s)	Time of Hearing:
Respondent(s)	Name of Judge:

ORDER ON

IT IS ORDERED THAT the relief sought as set forth on the continuation pages attached and numbered two (2) through ___________with exhibits, if any, for a total of ___________pages, is granted. Notice of Lodgment Docket Entry No. ___________

//

//

//

//

DATED: ____________________________________

Judge, United States Bankruptcy Court

Signature by the attorney constitutes a certification under Fed. R. of Bankr. P. 9011 that the relief in the order is the relief granted by the court.

Submitted by:
(Firm name)
By:

Attorney for ☐ Movant ☐ Respondent

CSD 1159D

Findings of Fact and Conclusions of Law
(Rev. 11/15/04)

CSD 1159D [11/15/04]
Name, Address, Telephone No. & I.D. No.

UNITED STATES BANKRUPTCY COURT
SOUTHERN DISTRICT OF CALIFORNIA

325 West "F" Street, San Diego,
California 92101-6991

In Re	BANKRUPTCY NO.
	RS NO.
Debtor.	Date of Hearing:
Movant(s)	Time of Hearing:
Respondent(s)	Name of Judge:

FINDINGS OF FACT AND CONCLUSIONS OF LAW RE:

The matter having been tried to the court on regular notice and after consideration of all properly admitted evidence, as well as argument thereon, the court makes the following findings of fact and conclusions of law as set forth on the continuation pages attached numbered two (2) through ____________. Motion Docket Entry No. ____________

//

//

//

//

DATED: ______________________________

Judge, United States Bankruptcy Court

Signature by the attorney constitutes a certification under Fed. R. of Bankr. P. 9011 that the relief in the order is the relief granted by the court.

Submitted by:

____

(Firm name)

By:
Attorney for ☐ Movant ☐ Respondent

CSD 1159E

Findings of Fact and Conclusions of Law

(Rev. 11/15/04)

CSD 1159E [11/15/04]
Name, Address, Telephone No. & I.D. No.

UNITED STATES BANKRUPTCY COURT
SOUTHERN DISTRICT OF CALIFORNIA

325 West "F" Street, San Diego,
California 92101-6991

LODGED

In Re	BANKRUPTCY NO.
	RS NO.
Debtor.	Date of Hearing:
Movant(s)	Time of Hearing:
Respondent(s)	Name of Judge:

FINDINGS OF FACT AND CONCLUSIONS OF LAW RE:

The matter having been tried to the court on regular notice and after consideration of all properly admitted evidence, as well as argument thereon, the court makes the following findings of fact and conclusions of law as set forth on the continuation pages attached numbered two (2) through ____________of Lodgment Docket Entry No. ____________

//

//

//

//

DATED: ____________________________________

Judge, United States Bankruptcy Court

Signature by the attorney constitutes a certification under Fed. R. of Bankr. P. 9011 that the relief in the order is the relief granted by the court.

Submitted by:

____
(Firm name)
By:
Attorney for ☐ Movant ☐ Respondent

CSD 1160

Motion for Relief From Automatic Stay
(Rev. 05/15/03)

MOTION FOR RELIEF FROM AUTOMATIC STAY
☐ REAL PROPERTY ☐ PERSONAL PROPERTY

Movant in the above-captioned matter moves this Court for an Order granting relief from the automatic stay on the grounds set forth below.

1. A Petition under Chapter ☐ 7 ☐ 11 ☐ 12 ☐ 13 was filed on ____________.

2. Procedural Status:

   a. [ ] Name of Trustee Appointed *(if any)*:

   b. [ ] Name of Attorney of Record for Trustee *(if any)*:

   c. [ ] (Optional) Prior Filing Information: Debtor has previously filed a Bankruptcy Petition on: ____________. If applicable, the prior case was dismissed on: ____________.

   d. [ ] *(If Chapter 13 case)*: Chapter 13 Plan was confirmed on ____________or a confirmation hearing is set for ____________.

Movant alleges the following in support of its Motion:

1. The following real property is the subject of this Motion:

   a. Street address of the property including county and state:

   b. Type of real property (e.g., single family residence, apartment building, commercial, industrial, condominium, unimproved):

   c. Legal description of property is attached as Exhibit A.

   d. If a chapter 11 or 13 case and if non-payment of any post-petition payment is a ground for relief, attach the accounting required by Local Bankruptcy Rule 4001-2(a)(4) as Exhibit B.

   e. *Fair market value of property as set forth in the Debtor's schedules: $____________

   f. *Nature of Debtor's interest in the property:

2. [ ] The following personal property is the subject of this Motion *(describe property)*:

a. Fair market value of property as set forth in the Debtor's schedules: $____________.

b. Nature of Debtor's interest in the property:

3. *Fair market value of property according to Movant: $____________.

4. *Nature of Movant's interest in the property:

5.	*Status of Movant's loan:			
	a.	Balance owing on date of Order for Relief:		$ . . . .
	b.	Amount of monthly payment:		$ . . . .
	c.	Date of last payment:		. . . .
	d.	If real property,		
		(1)	Date of default:	. . . .
		(2)	Notice of Default recorded on:	. . . .
		(3)	Notice of Sale published on:	. . . .
		(4)	Foreclosure sale currently scheduled for:	. . . .
	e.	If personal property,		
		(1)	Pre-petition default: $. . . . . No. of months:	. . . .
		(2)	Post-petition default: $. . . . . No. of months:	. . . .
6.	*(If Chapter 13 Case, state the following:)*			
	a.	Date of post-petition default:		. . . .
	b.	Amount of post-petition default:		$ . . . .

7. Encumbrances:

   a. Voluntary encumbrances on the property listed in the Schedules or otherwise known to Movant:

   ....

   ....

Lender Name	Principal Balance	(IF KNOWN) Pre-Petition Arrearages Total Amount—# of Months	Post-Petition Arrearages Total Amount —# of Months
1st:			
2nd:			
3rd:			
4th:			
Totals for all Liens:	$	$	$

   b. Involuntary encumbrances of record (e.g., tax, mechanic's, judgment and other liens, lis pendens) as listed in schedules or otherwise known to Movant:
   ☐ See attached page, if necessary.

8. Relief from the automatic stay should be granted because:

   a. [ ] Movant's interest in the property described above is not adequately protected.

   b. [ ] Debtor has no equity in the ☐ real property ☐ personal property described above and such property is not necessary to an effective reorganization.

   c. [ ] The property is "single asset real estate", as defined in 11 U.S.C. § 101(51B), and 90 days (or ____________days as ordered by this court) have passed since entry of the order for relief in this case, and

      (1) the Debtor/Trustee has not filed a plan of reorganiza-

tion that has a reasonable possibility of being confirmed within a reasonable time; and

(2) the Debtor/Trustee has

(A) [ ] not commenced monthly payments to each creditor whose claim is secured by the property (other than a claim secured by a judgment lien or by an unmatured statutory lien), or

(B) [ ] commenced payments, but such payments are less than an amount equal to interest at a current fair market rate on the value of each creditors' interest in the property.

d. [ ] *Other cause exists as follows *(specify)*:
[ ] See attached page.

When required, Movant has filed separate Declarations pursuant to Local Bankruptcy Rule 4001-2(a)(5) and (6).

Movant attaches the following:

a. [ ] Other relevant evidence:

b. [ ] (Optional) Memorandum of points and authorities upon which the moving party will rely.

WHEREFORE, Movant prays that this Court issue an Order granting the following:

[ ] Relief as requested.

[ ] Other:

Dated: ______________________

______________________ [Attorney for] Movant

CSD 1162

Order on Noncontested Motion for Relief From Automatic Stay
(Rev. 08/22/03)

ORDER ON NONCONTESTED MOTION FOR RELIEF FROM AUTOMATIC STAY

☐ REAL PROPERTY ☐ PERSONAL PROPERTY

IT IS ORDERED THAT the relief sought as set forth on the continuation pages attached and numbered two (2) through ____________with exhibits, if any, for a total of ____________pages, is granted. Motion Docket Entry No. ____________

//

//

//

//

DATED: ____________

____

Judge, United States Bankruptcy Court

Signature by the attorney constitutes a certification under Fed. R. of Bankr. P. 9011 that the relief in the order is the relief granted by the court.

Submitted by:

____

(Firm name)

By: ________________________

Attorney for Movant

The Motion of ____________, ("Movant"), for relief from the automatic stay having been filed with the above-entitled court on ____________, and

The Notice of Filing of a Motion for Relief from Automatic Stay (a file-stamped copy of which is attached hereto as Exhibit A OR Notice Docket Entry No. ____________, if filed electronically), the Motion, and accompanying Declarations having been served upon the parties named below on ____________, and

[ ] Debtor *(Name)*:

[ ] Debtor's Attorney *(Name)*:

[ ] Trustee *(Name)*:

[ ] United States Trustee (in Chapter 11 & 12 cases), and

[ ] Others, if any *(Name)*:

No objection or Request for Hearing having been filed by or on behalf of the Debtor, IT IS HEREBY ORDERED as follows:

The automatic stay pursuant to 11 U.S.C. Section 362 is hereby terminated for all purposes as to Movant in connection with the estate's and the debtor's interest in

1. [ ] The following real property:

   a. [ ] Street address of the property including county and state:

   b. [ ] Legal description is ☐ attached as Exhibit B or ☐ described below:

2. [ ] The following personal property as described ☐ below or ☐ in Exhibit B attached:

IT IS FURTHER ORDERED that *(Optional)*:

CSD 1163

Motion for Relief from Automatic Stay (Unlawful Detainer)
(Rev. 05/15/03)

MOTION FOR RELIEF FROM AUTOMATIC STAY (UNLAWFUL DETAINER)

Movant in the above-captioned matter moves this Court for an Order granting relief from the automatic stay on the grounds set forth below.

1. A Petition under Chapter ☐ 7 ☐ 11 ☐ 12 ☐ 13 was filed on ___________.

2. Procedural Status:

   a. [ ] Name of Trustee Appointed *(if any)*:

   b. [ ] Name of Attorney of Record for Trustee *(if any)*:

   c. [ ] *(Optional)* Prior Filing Information: Debtor has previously filed a Bankruptcy Petition on: ___________. If applicable, the prior case was dismissed on: ___________.

   d. [ ] *(If Chapter 13 case)*: Chapter 13 Plan was confirmed on or a confirmation hearing is set for ___________.

Movant alleges the following in support of its Motion:

1. Debtor occupies the premises commonly known as *(specify street address)*:

2. Debtor occupies the premises:

   [ ] on a month-to-month tenancy

   [ ] on a hold-over tenancy

   [ ] on a tenancy at will

   [ ] pursuant to a lease in default

   [ ] after a foreclosure sale

   [ ] pursuant to a terminated lease

3. Debtor has failed to pay the monthly rent of $___________since ___________.

4. Procedural status in State Court *(fill in all applicable data for completed steps)*:

   a. [ ] On ___________, Movant served a Notice to Pay Rent

or Quit on the Debtor(s).

b. [ ] On ___________, Movant filed a Complaint for Unlawful Detainer in State Court.

c. [ ] Trial was held on ___________.

d. [ ] A Judgment was entered on said Complaint by the State Court on ___________

When required, Movant has filed separate Declarations pursuant to Local Bankruptcy Rule 4001-2(a)(5).

Movant attaches the following:

1. [ ] Copy of the State Court Unlawful Detainer Judgment.
2. [ ] Other relevant evidence:
3. [ ] *(Optional)* Memorandum of points and authorities upon which the moving party will rely.

WHEREFORE, Movant prays that this Court issue an Order granting the following:

[ ] Relief as requested.

[ ] Other:

Dated: ___________

______________________ [Attorney for] Movant

CSD 1165

Order on Noncontested Motion for Relief From Automatic Stay (Unlawful Detainer)

(Rev. 08/22/03)

ORDER ON NONCONTESTED MOTION FOR RELIEF FROM AUTOMATIC STAY (UNLAWFUL DETAINER)

IT IS ORDERED THAT the relief sought as set forth on the continuation pages attached and numbered two (2) through ___________with exhibits, if any, for a total of ___________ pages, is granted. Motion Docket Entry No. ___________.

//
//
//
//

DATED: ___________

____
Judge, United States Bankruptcy Court

Signature by the attorney constitutes a certification under Fed. R. of Bankr. P. 9011 that the relief in the order is the relief granted by the court.

Submitted by:

____
(Firm name)
By: ___________
Attorney for Movant

The Motion of ___________, ("Movant"), for relief from the automatic stay having been filed with the above-entitled court on ___________, and The Notice of Filing of a Motion for Relief from Automatic Stay (a file-stamped copy of which is attached hereto as Exhibit A OR Notice Docket Entry No. ___________, if filed electronically), the Motion, and accompanying Declarations having been served upon the parties named below on ___________, and

[ ] Debtor *(Name)*:

[ ] Debtor's Attorney *(Name)*:

[ ] Trustee *(Name)*:

[ ] United States Trustee (in Chapter 11 & 12 cases), and

[ ] Others, if any *(Name)*:

No objection or Request for Hearing having been filed by or on behalf of the Debtor, IT IS HEREBY ORDERED that:

a. The automatic stay pursuant to 11 U.S.C. Section 362 is hereby terminated as to the estate's or the debtor's interest in the following property and is legally described ☐ in Exhibit B attached, or ☐ described below (specify street address). If pertaining to a foreclosure, the full legal description in addition to the street address is required.

b. The Movant may proceed with any and all legal remedies available to recover possession of the above-described real property. Said remedies include, but are not limited to, the conclusion of unlawful detainer in State Court, without further restraint of this Court.

IT IS FURTHER ORDERED that *(Optional)*:

CSD 1170

Notice of Modified Chapter 13 Plan Prior to Confirmation

(Rev. 10/1/05)

NOTICE OF MODIFIED CHAPTER 13 PLAN PRIOR TO CONFIRMATION

TO:

YOU ARE HEREBY NOTIFIED that the attached Modified Chapter 13 Plan of the above-named Debtor(s) dated has been filed with the Court under the provisions of 11 U.S.C. § 1323 whereupon the Plan as modified became the Plan of the Debtor(s) and will be considered at the

[ ] § 341(a) Meeting of Creditors[5] or

[ ] Confirmation Hearing now set for ____________, at ____________.m., in Department No.____________, Room ____________, of the Jacob Weinberger United States Courthouse, located at 325 West "F" Street, San Diego, California 92101-6991.

YOU ARE FURTHER NOTIFIED that 11 U.S.C. § 1323(c) provides that: *"Any holder of a secured claim that has accepted or rejected the plan is deemed to have accepted or rejected, as the case may be, the plan as modified, unless the modification provides for a change in the rights of such holder from what such rights were under the plan before modification, and such holder changes such holder's previous acceptance or rejection."*

Any opposition or other response to the Modified Chapter 13 Plan must be served upon the undersigned, the debtor, and the Chapter 13 trustee, and the original and one copy of such papers with proof of service must be filed with the Clerk of the United States Bankruptcy Court at 325 West "F" Street, San Diego, California 92101-6991.

DATED: ____

[Attorney for] Debtor

CERTIFICATE OF SERVICE

I, the undersigned whose address appears below, certify:

That I am, and at all time hereinafter mentioned was, more than 18 years of age;

[5] § 341(a) Meeting set for ____________at ____________.m., at ____________

That on ____________day of ____________, I served a true copy of the within NOTICE OF MODIFIED CHAPTER 13 PLAN PRIOR TO CONFIRMATION by [describe here mode of service]:

on the following persons [set forth name and address of each person served] and/or as checked below:

[ ] For ODD numbered Chapter 13 cases:
THOMAS H. BILLINGSLEA, JR., TRUSTEE
530 "B" Street, Suite 1500
San Diego, CA 92101

[ ] For EVEN numbered Chapter 13 cases:
DAVID L. SKELTON, TRUSTEE
525 "B" Street, Suite 1430
San Diego, CA 92101-4507

I certify under penalty of perjury that the foregoing is true and correct.

Executed on ________________________
(Date) (Typed Name and Signature)
(Address)
(City, State, ZIP Code)

CSD 1172

Objection to Confirmation of Chapter 13 Plan
(Rev. 10/17/05)

OBJECTION TO CONFIRMATION OF CHAPTER 13 PLAN

TO THE DEBTOR, THE DEBTOR'S ATTORNEY AND THE CHAPTER 13 TRUSTEE:

☐ Thomas H. Billingslea, Jr., Chapter 13 Trustee

☐ David L. Skelton, Chapter 13 Trustee,

☐ (Insert Name and Complete Mailing Address of Objecting Party)

____________, a creditor in this case,

hereby objects to the Confirmation of the Chapter 13 Plan. The basis for the objection is stated below. (NOTE TO OBJECTING PARTY: YOUR STATEMENT OF OBJECTION MUST BE AS SPECIFIC AS POSSIBLE. CHECK ONLY THOSE SECTIONS WHICH ARE APPLICABLE TO YOUR OBJECTION AND PROVIDE AN EXPLANATION OF YOUR OBJECTION WHERE REQUESTED):

1. ☐ The Plan discriminates unfairly against the class(es) of unsecured claims because

   ____________. [§ 1322(b)(1)]

2. ☐ The Plan modifies the rights of a creditor whose claim is secured only by a security interest in real property that is the debtor's principal residence by providing that

   ____________. [§ 1322(b)(2)]

3. ☐ The Plan fails to provide for the curing of a default and maintenance payments on a secured or unsecured claim on which final payment is due after the proposed final payment under the Plan. [§ 1322(b)(5)]

4. ☐ The Chapter 13 Plan is not proposed in good faith because

   ____________. [§ 1325(a)(3)]

5. ☐ The debtor is distributing less to the allowed unsecured creditors than they would receive under a Chapter 7 liquidation. [§ 1325(a)(4)]

6. ☐ Objecting creditor has an allowed secured claim and objects because

☐ I have not accepted the Plan. [§ 1325(a)(5)(A)], OR

☐ the Plan fails to provide for a retention of lien securing my claim and the value of the property to be distributed to me is less than the allowed amount of my claim. ____________[§ 1325(a)(5)(B)]

Amount of Claim $____________

Value of Property $____________, OR

☐ the debtor has failed to surrender to me the property securing my claim. [§ 1325(a)(5)(C)]

7. ☐ The debtor has no ability to make the payments proposed by the Plan because

[§ 1325(a)(6)]

8. ☐ The debtor has failed to apply all projected disposable income to Plan payments for a period of not less than three years. [§ 1325(b)(1)(B)]

9. ☐ The debtor has failed to begin making payments prescribed in the Plan within thirty (30) days of the filing of the Plan. [§ 1326(a)(1)]

10. ☐ Other [cite applicable Code section or case authority]:

I have unsuccessfully attempted to resolve our objections at the § 341 Meeting.

I hereby certify under penalty of perjury that I have this date mailed a true copy of this Objection to Plan to the attorney for the debtor (or the debtor) and to the assigned Chapter 13 trustee as indicated below at the following addresses:

Attorney for Debtor (or Debtor:	Chapter 13 Trustee (select one):	
	For ODD numbered Chpt. 13 cases: THOMAS H. BILLINGS-LEA, JR., TRUSTEE 530 "B" Street, Suite 1500 San Diego, CA 92101	For EVEN numbered Chpt. 13 cases: DAVID L. SKELTON, TRUSTEE 525 "B" Street, Suite 1430 San Diego, CA 92101-4507

DATED:(Signature of (Attorney for) Moving Party)

(Please Type or Print Name)
(Address)
(City, State, ZIP)
(______________)
(Daytime Phone Number)

SDCAL-213 S.D. CALIFORNIA

CSD 1173

Notice of Hearing on Objection to Confirmation of Chapter 13 Plan
(Rev. 10/17/05)

NOTICE OF HEARING ON OBJECTION TO CONFIRMATION OF CHAPTER 13 PLAN

TO:

YOU ARE HEREBY NOTIFIED that on ____________, at ____________.m., in Department No. ____________, Room ____________, of the Jacob Weinberger United States Courthouse, located at 325 West "F" Street, San Diego, California 92101-6991, there will be a hearing regarding the attached Objection to Confirmation of the Debtor's Chapter 13 Plan filed by ____________________________________ .

(*Insert Name of Objecting Party*)

Any reply or other response to this objection must be served upon the undersigned and the original and one copy of such papers with proof of service must be filed with the Clerk of the U.S. Bankruptcy Court at 325 West "F" Street, San Diego, California 92101-6991, THE EARLIER OF SEVEN (7) DAYS FROM DATE OF SERVICE OR THREE (3) COURT DAYS PRIOR TO THE HEARING.

DATED:

[Attorney for] Objecting Party

THIS NOTICE MUST BE ACCOMPANIED BY YOUR WRITTEN OBJECTION TO THE CHAPTER 13 PLAN PURSUANT TO LOCAL BANKRUPTCY RULE 3015-4

CERTIFICATE OF SERVICE

I, the undersigned whose address appears below, certify:

That I am, and at all times hereinafter mentioned was, more than 18 years of age;

That on ____________day of ____________, I served a true copy of the within NOTICE OF HEARING ON OBJECTION TO CONFIRMATION OF CHAPTER 13 PLAN by [describe here mode of service]

on the following persons [set forth name and address of each person served] and/or as checked below:

[ ] For ODD numbered Chapter 13 cases:
THOMAS H. BILLINGSLEA, JR., TRUSTEE
530 "B" Street, Suite 1500
San Diego, CA 92101

[ ] For EVEN numbered Chapter 13 cases:
DAVID L. SKELTON, TRUSTEE
525 "B" Street, Suite 1430
San Diego, CA 92101-4507

[ ] Attorney for Debtor (or Debtor):

I certify under penalty of perjury that the foregoing is true and correct.

Executed on

(Date) (Typed Name and Signature)
(Address)
(City, State, ZIP Code)

CSD 1174

Request By Debtor for Dismissal of Chapter 13

(Rev. 09/15/06)

REQUEST BY DEBTOR FOR DISMISSAL OF CHAPTER 13

To the Honorable Judges of the United States Bankruptcy Court:

The undersigned debtor hereby requests that the pending Chapter 13 case be dismissed without prejudice. In support of said request, debtor hereby represents:

[ ] This Case first commenced by the filing of a voluntary Chapter 13.

[ ] Debtor is unaware of any pending motion by a creditor or the Chapter 13 Trustee for conversion of the pending Chapter 13 case to a case under Chapter 7 or Chapter 11 of Title 11, United States Code.

[ ] If checked, this case was filed by the filing of a joint petition and only one of the debtors is seeking dismissal of this case as it may apply to him or her, namely: ___________.

Wherefore, Debtor(s) prays that the Chapter 13 case herein be dismissed without prejudice.

I further certify under penalty of perjury that on ___________day of ___________, a true copy of this Request was served on the trustee indicated below:

☐ THOMAS H. BILLINGSLEA, JR., TRUSTEE, 530 "B" Street, Suite 1500, San Diego, CA 92101 (For ODD numbered Chapter 13 cases)

☐ DAVID L. SKELTON, TRUSTEE, 525 "B" Street, Suite 1430, San Diego, CA 92101-4507 (For EVEN numbered Chapter 13 cases)

Dated:

Joint Debtor

Debtor

Attorney for the Debtor

CSD 1175

Request and Notice of Hearing Regarding Chapter 13 Trustee's Notice of Intent to Dismiss Case

(Rev. 10/17/05)

REQUEST AND NOTICE OF HEARING REGARDING CHAPTER 13 TRUSTEE'S NOTICE OF INTENT TO DISMISS CASE

TO: [ ] THOMAS H. BILLINGSLEA, JR., Chapter 13 Trustee for ODD numbered cases

[ ] DAVID L. SKELTON, Chapter 13 Trustee for EVEN numbered cases

YOU ARE NOTIFIED that ___________, the debtor(s), hereby object to the Notice of Intent to Dismiss the Chapter 13 Case and request a hearing pursuant to the Notice of Intent.

Your Notice fixed ___________[6] as the last date for serving and filing this Request and Notice of Hearing and the accompanying Declaration of the debtor[7] stating specific grounds for objection.

You are further notified that a hearing will be held in Dept. No. ___________, Room ___________, of the Jacob Weinberger United States Courthouse, located at 325 West "F" Street, San Diego, California 92101-6991, on ___________, at ___________.m., or as soon thereafter as it can be hearing.

DATED:

[Attorney for] Debtor(s)

CERTIFICATE OF SERVICE

I, the undersigned whose address appears below, certify:

That I am, and at all time hereinafter mentioned was, more than 18 years of age;

---

[6] **IMPORTANT NOTICE:** Prior to this date, YOU MUST FILE the original and one copy of this Request and Notice of Hearing, together with your Declaration in Opposition and Proof of Service with the Clerk of the Bankruptcy Court at the address shown above, and serve a copy of the papers on the trustee. You may obtain a hearing date and time from the Court by calling the number specified in the Notice of Intent.

[7] **NOTE:** This form merely provides notice of the hearing and places it on the Court's calendar. You must also file supporting declaration of the debtor as required by Local Bankruptcy Rule 9014.

That on ___________ day of ___________, I served a true copy of the within REQUEST AND NOTICE OF HEARING REGARDING CHAPTER 13 TRUSTEE'S NOTICE OF INTENT TO DISMISS CASE by [describe here mode of service]:

on the following persons [set forth name and address of each person served] and/or as checked below:

[ ] For ODD numbered Chapter 13 cases:
THOMAS H. BILLINGSLEA, JR., TRUSTEE
530 "B" Street, Suite 1500
San Diego, CA 92101

[ ] For EVEN numbered Chapter 13 cases:
DAVID L. SKELTON, TRUSTEE
525 "B" Street, Suite 1430
San Diego, CA 92101-4507

[ ] Attorney for Debtor (or Debtor):

I certify under penalty of perjury that the foregoing is true and correct.

Executed on ______________________

(Date) (Typed Name and Signature)
(Address)
(City, State, ZIP Code)

CSD 1176

Order Dismissing Chapter 13 Case on Request by Debtor

CSD 1176 [08/22/03]
Name, Address, Telephone No. & I.D. No.

UNITED STATES BANKRUPTCY COURT
SOUTHERN DISTRICT OF CALIFORNIA
325 West "F" Street, San Diego, California 92101-6991

In Re Debtor.	BANKRUPTCY NO.

ORDER DISMISSING CHAPTER 13 CASE ON REQUEST BY DEBTOR

Upon consideration of the Debtor's Request for Dismissal of the above referenced Chapter 13 Case, Docket Entry No. ___________, it is ordered that:

This case be and the same is hereby dismissed and all automatic stays and any injunctions obtained by the debtor in any proceeding related to this case are hereby terminated and the provisions of 11 U.S.C. § 349 are herewith effective. The Chapter 13 Trustee is hereby directed to file a final report and account of his administration.//

//

//

DATED:

____
Judge, United States Bankruptcy Court

Signature by the attorney constitutes a certification under Fed. R. of Bankr. P. 9011 that the relief in the order is the relief granted by the court.

Submitted by:

____
(Firm name)

By: ______________________
Attorney for Movant

No. CSD 1180

Notice of Intended Action and Opportunity for Hearing

CSD 1180 [11/15/04]

Name, Address, Telephone No. & I.D. No.

. . . .

UNITED STATES BANKRUPTCY COURT

SOUTHERN DISTRICT OF CALIFORNIA

325 West "F" Street, San Diego, California 92101-6991

In Re

Tax I.D.#

Social Security #: xxx-xx-

Debtor

. . . .

BANKRUPTCY NO.

NOTICE OF INTENDED ACTION AND OPPORTUNITY FOR HEARING

TO THE DEBTOR, ALL CREDITORS AND OTHER PARTIES IN INTEREST:

YOU ARE HEREBY NOTIFIED that ____________, (select one:) [ ] the Trustee [ ] United States Trustee [ ] Debtor-in-Possession [ ] Creditor, herein, proposes to:

[ ] Use, sell or lease the following property not in the ordinary course of business [include information as required by Federal Rule of Bankruptcy Procedure 2002(c)(1)]; or

[ ] Abandon the following property [description of property to be abandoned]; or

[ ] Compromise or settle the following controversy [description of controversy to be settled and financial impact on estate as required by Local Bankruptcy Rule 9019]; or

[ ] Seek allowance of compensation or remuneration to debtor as follows [specify the nature]; or

[ ] Other [specify the nature of the matter]:

If you object to the proposed action:

1. **YOU ARE REQUIRED** to obtain a hearing date and time from the appropriate Courtroom Deputy for the judge assigned to your bankruptcy case. *If a Chapter 7, 11, or 12 case*, determine which deputy to call by looking at the Bankruptcy Case No. in the caption on Page 1 of this notice. If the case number is followed by the letter:

- M - call (619) 557-6019 - DEPARTMENT ONE (Room 218)
- A - call (619) 557-6594 - DEPARTMENT TWO (Room 118)
- H - call (619) 557-6018 - DEPARTMENT THREE (Room 129)
- B - call (619) 557-5157 - DEPARTMENT FOUR (Room 328)

For ALL Chapter 13 cases, call (619) 557-5955.

2. **WITHIN TWENTY-EIGHT (28) [1] DAYS FROM THE DATE OF SERVICE OF THIS MOTION**, you are further required to serve a copy of your DECLARATION IN OPPOSITION TO MOTION and separate REQUEST AND NOTICE OF HEARING [Local Form CSD 1184[2]] upon the undersigned moving party, together with any opposing papers. The opposing declaration shall be signed and verified in the manner prescribed by Federal Rule of Bankruptcy Procedure 9011, and the declaration shall:

   a. identify the interest of the opposing party; and

   b. state, with particularity, the grounds for the opposition.

3. **YOU MUST** file the original and one copy of the Declaration and Request and Notice of Hearing with proof of service with the Clerk of the U.S. Bankruptcy Court at 325 West "F" Street, San Diego, California 92101-6991, no later than the next business day following the date of service.

IF YOU FAIL TO SERVE YOUR "DECLARATION IN OPPOSITION TO INTENDED ACTION" AND "REQUEST AND NOTICE OF HEARING" within the 28-day[1] period provided by this notice, NO HEARING

---

[1] If you were served electronically or by mail, you have three (3) additional days to take the above-stated actions.

[2] You may obtain Local Form CSD 1184 from the office of the Clerk of the U.S. Bankruptcy Court.

SHALL TAKE PLACE, you shall lose your opportunity for hearing, and the moving party may proceed to take the intended action.

DATE OF SERVICE:

[U.S. TRUSTEE] [TRUSTEE] [DEBTOR-IN-POSSESSION]
[Attorney for Moving Party]

CSD 1181

Notice of Hearing and Motion

(Rev. 10/17/05)

NOTICE OF HEARING AND MOTION

TO THE DEBTOR, ALL CREDITORS AND OTHER PARTIES IN INTEREST:

YOU ARE HEREBY NOTIFIED that on ____________, at ____________.m., in Department ____________, Room ____________, of the Jacob Weinberger United States Courthouse, located at 325 West "F" Street, San Diego, California 92101-6991, there will be a hearing regarding the Motion of ____________, for [check the appropriate box]:

[ ] Dismissal of a chapter 7, 11 or 12 case;

[ ] Conversion of a chapter 7, 11 or 12 case by a party other than the debtor;

[ ] Allowance of [interim] [final] compensation or reimbursement of expenses of professionals as provided in Exhibit "A" [information required by Federal Rule of Bankruptcy Procedure 2002(c)(2)];

[ ] Appointment of a trustee in a chapter 11 case; or

[ ] Other [specify the nature of the matter]:

If not required to be attached, a set of the moving papers will be provided, upon request, by the undersigned or may be inspected at the office of the Clerk.

Any opposition or other response to the motion must be served upon the undersigned and the original and one copy of such papers with proof of service must be filed with the Clerk of the U.S. Bankruptcy Court at 325 West "F" St., San Diego, California 92101-6991, NOT LATER THAN FOURTEEN (14)[1] DAYS FROM THE DATE OF SERVICE.

DATED:

[Attorney for] Moving Party

CERTIFICATE OF SERVICE

I, the undersigned whose address appears below, certify:

That I am, and at all times hereinafter mentioned was, more than 18 years of age;

That on ____________day of ____________, I served a true copy of the within NOTICE OF MOTION AND HEARING by [describe here mode of service]

on the following persons [set forth name and address of each person served] and/or as checked below:

[ ] Attorney for Debtor (if required):

[ ] For Chpt. 7, 11, & 12 cases:
UNITED STATES TRUSTEE
Department of Justice
402 West Broadway, Suite 600
San Diego, CA 92101

[ ] For ODD numbered Chapter 13 cases:
THOMAS H. BILLINGSLEA, JR., TRUSTEE
530 "B" Street, Suite. 1500
San Diego, CA 92101

[ ] For EVEN numbered Chapter 13 cases:
DAVID L. SKELTON, TRUSTEE
525 "B" Street, Suite 1430
San Diego, CA 92101-4507

I certify under penalty of perjury that the foregoing is true and correct.

Executed on ________________________

(Date) (Typed Name and Signature)
(Address)
(City, State, ZIP Code)

CSD 1181A

Exhibit A to CSD 1181

(05/15/03)

APPLICANT ____________, REPRESENTING [Name & Title]

	FEES REQUESTED	FEES ALLOWED	FEES AUTHORIZED FOR PAYMENT	FEES HELD BACK	FEES DISALLOWED[2]	COSTS REQUESTED	COSTS AWARDED
1ST INTERIM to							
2ND INTERIM to							
3RD INTERIM to							
4TH INTERIM to							
TOTALS:							

[2] Please provide an explanation for this disallowance.

APPLICANT ____________, REPRESENTING [Name & Title]

	FEES RE-QUESTED	FEES AL-LOWED	FEES AUTHO-RIZED FOR PAY-MENT	FEES HELD BACK	FEES DISAL-LOWED[3]	COSTS RE-QUESTED	COSTS AWARDED
1ST IN-TERIM to							
2ND IN-TERIM to							
3RD IN-TERIM to							
4TH IN-TERIM to							
TOTALS:							

[3] Please provide an explanation for this disallowance.

CSD 1182

Notice of Motion
(Rev. 10/17/05)

NOTICE OF MOTION FOR ______

TO:

You are herewith served with the attached Motion by __________for:

and any accompanying declarations.

If you object to the Court granting the relief requested in the Motion:

1. **YOU ARE REQUIRED** to obtain a hearing date and time from the appropriate Courtroom Deputy for the judge assigned to this bankruptcy case. *If a Chapter 7, 11, or 12 case*, determine which deputy to call by looking at the Bankruptcy Case No. in the above caption of this notice. If the case number is followed by the letter:

— M — call (619) 557-6019 — DEPARTMENT ONE (Room 218)
— A — call (619) 557-6594 — DEPARTMENT TWO (Room 118)
— H — call (619) 557-6018 — DEPARTMENT THREE (Room 129)
— B — call (619) 557-5157 — DEPARTMENT FOUR (Room 328)

For ALL Chapter 13 cases, call (619) 557-5955.

2. **WITHIN FOURTEEN (14)[8] DAYS FROM THE DATE OF SERVICE OF THE MOTION**, you are further required to serve a copy of your DECLARATION IN OPPOSITION TO MOTION and separate REQUEST AND NOTICE OF HEARING [Local Form CSD 1184[9]] upon the undersigned moving party, together with any opposing papers. The opposing declaration shall be signed and verified in the manner prescribed by Federal Rule of Bankruptcy Procedure 9011, and the declaration shall:

a. identify the interest of the opposing party; and

b. state, with particularity, the grounds for the opposition.

3. **YOU MUST** file the original and one copy of the Declaration and Request and Notice of Hearing with proof of service with the Clerk of the U.S. Bankruptcy Court at 325 West "F" Street, San Diego, California

---

[8] If you were served electronically or by mail, you have three (3) additional days to take the above-stated actions.

[9] You may obtain Local Form CSD 1184 from the office of the Clerk of the U.S. Bankruptcy Court.

92101-6991, no later than the next business day following the date of service.

IF YOU FAIL TO SERVE YOUR "DECLARATION IN OPPOSITION TO INTENDED ACTION" AND "REQUEST AND NOTICE OF HEARING" within the 14-day[1] period provided by this notice, NO HEARING SHALL TAKE PLACE, you shall lose your opportunity for hearing, and the debtor or trustee may proceed to take the intended action.

DATED:

Attorney for Moving Party

CERTIFICATE OF SERVICE

I, the undersigned whose address appears below, certify:

That I am, and at all times hereinafter mentioned was, more than 18 years of age;

That on ____________day of ____________, I served a true copy of the within NOTICE OF MOTION by [describe here mode of service]

on the following persons [set forth name and address of each person served] and/or as checked below:

[ ] Attorney for Debtor (if required):

[ ] For Chpt. 7, 11, & 12 cases:
UNITED STATES TRUSTEE
Department of Justice
402 West Broadway, Suite 600
San Diego, CA 92101

[ ] For ODD numbered Chapter 13 cases:
THOMAS H. BILLINGSLEA, JR., TRUSTEE
530 "B" Street, Suite. 1500
San Diego, CA 92101

[ ] For EVEN numbered Chapter 13 cases:
DAVID L. SKELTON, TRUSTEE
525 "B" Street, Suite 1430
San Diego, CA 92101-4507

I certify under penalty of perjury that the foregoing is true and correct.

Executed on ________________________

(Date) ________________________

(Typed Name and Signature)

(Address)

(City, State, ZIP Code)

CSD 1183

Notice of Hearing and Motion
(Rev. 10/17/05)

NOTICE OF HEARING AND MOTION

TO:

YOU ARE HEREBY NOTIFIED that on ____________, at ____________.m., in Department No.____________, Room ____________the Jacob Weinberger United States Courthouse, located at 325 West "F" Street, San Diego, California 92101-6991, there will be a hearing regarding the motion of ____________, for

Any opposition or other response to this motion must be served upon the undersigned and the original and one copy of such papers with proof of service must be filed with the Clerk of the U.S. Bankruptcy Court at 325 West "F" Street, San Diego, California 92101-6991, NOT LATER THAN FOURTEEN (14) [1] DAYS FROM THE DATE OF SERVICE.

DATED:

[Attorney for] Moving Party

CERTIFICATE OF SERVICE

I, the undersigned whose address appears below, certify:

That I am, and at all times hereinafter mentioned was, more than 18 years of age;

That on ____________day of ____________, I served a true copy of the within NOTICE OF MOTION AND HEARING by [describe here mode of service]

on the following persons [set forth name and address of each person served] and/or as checked below:

[ ] Attorney for Debtor (if required):

---

[1] If you were served electronically or by mail, you have three (3) additional days to take the above-stated actions.

[ ] For Chpt. 7, 11, & 12 cases: UNITED STATES TRUSTEE Department of Justice 402 West Broadway, Suite 600 San Diego, CA 92101	[ ] For ODD numbered Chapter 13 cases: THOMAS H. BILLINGSLEA, JR., TRUSTEE 530 "B" Street, Suite. 1500 San Diego, CA 92101	[ ] For EVEN numbered Chapter 13 cases: DAVID L. SKELTON, TRUSTEE 525 "B" Street, Suite 1430 San Diego, CA 92101-4507

I certify under penalty of perjury that the foregoing is true and correct.

Executed on ______________________

(Date) (Typed Name and Signature)
(Address)
(City, State, ZIP Code)

CSD 1184

Request and Notice of Hearing
(Rev. 10/17/05)

REQUEST AND NOTICE OF HEARING[11]

TO:
RE: MOTION FILED ON BEHALF OF [insert name of moving party]
____

YOU ARE NOTIFIED that ____________,
the undersigned party in interest, hereby objects to your Motion [or Notice of Intent] and requests a hearing pursuant to your Notice of Motion [or Intent] to take the following action [insert description from Notice]:

Your Notice fixed ____________[12] as the last date for serving and filing this Request and Notice of Hearing and the accompanying Declaration[13] in Opposition to Motion [Notice of Intent]. The Opposing Party is [check one]:

[ ] Debtor [ ] United States Trustee [ ] Trustee
[ ] Creditor [ ] Other (specify):____________

You are further notified that a hearing will be held in Department ____________, Room ____________, of the Jacob Weinberger United States Courthouse, located at 325 West "F" Street, San Diego, California 92101-6991, on____________at ____________.m., or as soon thereafter as it can be held.

DATED: ____________

[Attorney for] Opposing Party

CERTIFICATE OF SERVICE

I, the undersigned whose address appears below, certify:

---

[11] DO NOT USE THIS FORM FOR REQUESTING A HEARING ON MOTION FOR RELIEF FROM STAY. USE LOCAL FORM CSD 1186 INSTEAD.

[12] IMPORTANT NOTICE: Prior to this date, YOU MUST FILE the original and one copy of the within Request and Notice of Hearing together with your Declaration in Opposition with Proof of Service with the Clerk of the Bankruptcy Court at the address shown above, and serve a copy of the papers on the moving party. You may obtain a hearing date and time from the Court by calling the number specified in the Notice of Motion [or Intent].

[13] NOTE: The within form merely notices the hearing and places it on the Court's calendar. Additional declarations, points and authorities, etc., may be necessary, since the Court expects full compliance with Local Bankruptcy Rule 9014-4(b).

That I am, and at all times hereinafter mentioned was, more than 18 years of age;

That on____________day of ___________, I served a true copy of the within REQUEST AND NOTICE OF HEARING and the following pleadings [describe]

by [describe here mode of service]

on the following persons [set forth name and address of each person served] and/or as checked below:

[ ] Attorney for Moving Party: [ ] Attorney for Debtor (if required):

[ ] For Chpt. 7, 11, & 12 cases:	[ ] For ODD numbered Chapter 13 cases:	[ ] For EVEN numbered Chapter 13 cases:
UNITED STATES TRUSTEE Department of Justice 402 West Broadway, Suite 600 San Diego, CA 92101	THOMAS H. BILLINGSLEA, JR., TRUSTEE 530 "B" Street, Suite. 1500 San Diego, CA 92101	DAVID L. SKELTON, TRUSTEE 525 "B" Street, Suite 1430 San Diego, CA 92101-4507

I certify under penalty of perjury that the foregoing is true and correct.

Executed on ______________________

(Date)

(Typed Name and Signature)

(Address)

(City, State, ZIP Code)

CSD 1185

Notice of Filing of a Motion for Relief from Automatic Stay

(Rev. 10/17/05)

NOTICE OF FILING OF A MOTION FOR RELIEF FROM AUTOMATIC STAY

TO THE ABOVE NAMED RESPONDENT(S)[1]:

YOU ARE HEREBY NOTIFIED that a Motion for Relief from the Automatic Stay provided by § 362 of the Bankruptcy Code has been filed. If you object to the Court granting relief from the automatic stay as requested in the Motion, **YOU MUST, WITHIN 11[2] DAYS FOLLOWING THE DATE OF SERVICE OF THIS NOTICE OF MOTION ON YOU**:

1. Obtain a hearing date and time from the appropriate Courtroom Deputy for the judge assigned to this bankruptcy case. ***If a Chapter 7, 11, or 12 case***, determine which deputy to call by looking at the Bankruptcy Case No. in the above caption of this notice. If the case number contains the letter:

— M — call (619) 557-6019 — DEPARTMENT ONE (Room 218)
— A — call (619) 557-6594 — DEPARTMENT TWO (Room 118)
— H — call (619) 557-6018 — DEPARTMENT THREE (Room 129)
— B — call (619) 557-5157 — DEPARTMENT FOUR (Room 328)

For ALL Chapter 13 cases, call (619) 557-5955.

2. File with the Clerk of the Bankruptcy Court, at the address shown above, the original and one copy of:
   (a) an "OPPOSITION TO MOTION"[2] (for real or personal property, use Form CSD 1161 of this Court);
   (b) a "DECLARATION IN OPPOSITION TO THE MOTION"[2]; and
   (c) a separate "REQUEST AND NOTICE OF HEARING ON MOTION," using Form CSD 1186 of this Court (this form may be obtained from the Office of the Clerk);
3. Serve a copy of these documents on the [Attorney for the] Moving Party named in the upper left hand corner.
4. Serve a copy of these documents on each of the additional parties as required by Local Bankruptcy Rule 4001-3.

IF YOU FAIL TO FILE WITH THE CLERK AND SERVE ON THE MOVING PARTY YOUR REQUEST FOR HEARING AND THE DECLARATION IN OPPOSITION TO MOTION WITHIN THE 11-DAY[2] PERIOD PROVIDED BY THIS MOTION, THE COURT MAY GRANT THE MOVING PARTY RELIEF FROM THE AUTOMATIC STAY WITHOUT FURTHER NOTICE TO YOU OR A HEARING.

Dated:

[Attorney for] Moving Party

1. **ALL PLEADINGS RELATED TO THIS PARTICULAR RS ACTION MUST CONTAIN THE ABOVE CAPTION.**

2. **INSTRUCTIONS TO RESPONDENT**: If you file a "Declaration in Opposition to the Motion," it must be signed by the respondent under oath; and

   (1) identify the interest of the respondent in the property;

   (2) state with particularity the grounds for the opposition;

   (3) if respondent is the debtor or the trustee, state the provable value of the property specified in the Motion and the amount of equity which would be realized by the debtor after deduction of all encumbrances; and

   (4) contain a statement as to competence of the declarant and the foundation for any opinion therein.

3. **INSTRUCTIONS TO MOVING PARTY**: Local Bankruptcy Rule 4001-2 provides that:

   "(a) A motion for stay relief . . . shall:

   "(1) name, as respondents, the debtor, the trustee, and other entities entitled to receive notice of default or notice of sale under applicable non-bankruptcy law governing foreclosure of real or personal property which is the subject of the motion, or the agents for such parties;

   "(2) state with particularity the relief or order sought, and the grounds for such relief or order;

   "(3) state the status of any pending foreclosure or repossession;

"(4) if the basis of the motion is lack of equity or adequate protection, and value is relevant, state by declaration the provable value of the subject property and the amount of any known encumbrances. The declaration shall also contain a statement as to the competency of the declarant and the foundation for any opinion therein; and

"(5) if the motion is brought for cause, state by declaration or other verified pleading the specific facts that constitute such cause.

"(b) Failure to set forth the information required by this rule may be grounds for denial of the relief requested.

"(c) The moving party shall serve the motion, together with Local Form CSD 1185, NOTICE OF FILING OF A MOTION FOR RELIEF FROM AUTOMATIC STAY, on the parties named in Local Bankruptcy Rule 4001-2(a)(1) above. In a chapter 11 or 12 case, a copy of the motion shall also be served on the United States Trustee."

**** MOTIONS FILED AFTER THE CASE IS CLOSED ARE NOT ENTITLED TO A REFUND OF FEES**

[The below Certification of Service must accompany the Notice of Motion printed on the reverse and any motion for entry of a default order pursuant to Local Bankruptcy Rule 4001-5.]

CERTIFICATE OF SERVICE

I, the undersigned whose address appears below, certify:

That I am, and at all times hereinafter mentioned was, more than 18 years of age;

That on__________ [DATE OF SERVICE[3]], I served a true copy of the within NOTICE OF FILING OF A MOTION FOR RELIEF FROM AUTOMATIC STAY, together with a copy of the Motion for Relief from Stay and [describe any other papers]:

by [describe mode of service]:

on the following persons [set forth name and address of each person served] and/or as checked below:

[ ] Attorney for Debtor (or Debtor), if required:

[ ] For Chpt. 7, 11, & 12 cases: UNITED STATES TRUSTEE Department of Justice 402 West Broadway, Suite 600 San Diego, CA 92101	[ ] For ODD numbered Chapter 13 cases: THOMAS H. BILLINGSLEA, JR., TRUSTEE 530 "B" Street, Suite. 1500 San Diego, CA 92101	[ ] For EVEN numbered Chapter 13 cases: DAVID L. SKELTON, TRUSTEE 525 "B" Street, Suite 1430 San Diego, CA 92101-4507

I certify under penalty of perjury that the foregoing is true and correct.

Executed on ____________________

(Date) (Typed Name and Signature)

(Address)

(City, State, ZIP Code)

CSD 1190

Notice of Entry
(Rev. 10/17/05)

NOTICE OF ENTRY

TO THE PARTIES IN INTEREST NAMED BELOW:

You are hereby notified that on ____________, this Court entered in the docket for the above-entitled case the following Judgment [or Order], to wit:

I hereby certify that a copy of this notice was mailed to the parties of interest on this date: [check as appropriate]

[ ] UNITED STATES TRUSTEE, Department of Justice, 402 West Broadway, Suite 600, San Diego, CA 92101

[ ] THOMAS H. BILLINGSLEA, JR., TRUSTEE, 530 "B" Street, Suite 1500, San Diego, CA 92101 (For ODD numbered Chapter 13 cases)

[ ] DAVID L. SKELTON, TRUSTEE, 525 "B" Street, Suite 1430, San Diego, CA 92101-4507 (For EVEN numbered Chapter 13 cases)

[ ] Chapter 7 Trustee:

and in addition: [Attach additional pages, if necessary]

CSD 1226

Reaffirmation Agreement
(For cases filed on or after 10/17/05)
(Rev. 08/04/06)

REAFFIRMATION AGREEMENT

[Check this box if] Creditor is a Credit Union as defined in § 19(b)(1)(a)(iv) of the Federal Reserve Act.

PART A: DISCLOSURE STATEMENT, INSTRUCTIONS AND NOTICE TO DEBTOR

3. DISCLOSURE STATEMENT

Before Agreeing to Reaffirm a Debt, Review These Important Disclosures:

SUMMARY OF REAFFIRMATION AGREEMENT

This Summary is made pursuant to the requirements of the Bankruptcy Code.

AMOUNT REAFFIRMED

a.	The amount of debt you have agreed to reaffirm:	$
b.	All fees and costs accrued as of the date of this disclosure statement, related to the amount of debt shown in a., above:	$
c.	The total amount you have agreed to reaffirm (Debt and fees and costs) (Add lines a. and b.):	$

Your credit agreement may obligate you to pay additional amounts which may come due after the date of this disclosure. Consult your credit agreement.

ANNUAL PERCENTAGE RATE

[The annual percentage rate can be disclosed in different ways, depending on the type of debt.]

a. If the debt is an extension of "credit" under an "open end credit plan," as those terms are defined in § 103 of the Truth in Lending Act, such as a credit card, the creditor may disclose the annual percentage rate shown in (i) below or, to the extent this rate is not readily available or not applicable, the simple interest rate showing in (ii) below, or both.

(i) The Annual Percentage Rate disclosed, or that would have been disclosed, to the debtor in the most recent periodic statement prior to entering into the reaffirmation agreement described in Part B below or, if no such periodic statement was given to the debtor during the prior six months, the annual percentage rate as it would have been so disclosed at the time of the disclosure statement: ___________%.

—And/Or—

(ii) The simple interest rate applicable to the amount reaffirmed as of the date this disclosure statement is given to the debtor: ___________%. If different simple interest rates apply to different balances included in the amount reaffirmed, the amount of each balance and the rate applicable to it are:

$___________@ ___________%;

$___________@ ___________%;

$___________@ ___________%.

b. If the debt is an extension of credit other than under an open end credit plan, the creditor may disclose the annual percentage rate showing in (i) below, or, to the extent this rate is not readily available or not applicable, the simple interest rate showing in (ii) below, or both.

(i) The Annual Percentage Rate under § 128(a)(4) of the Truth in Lending Act, as disclosed to the debtor in the most recent disclosure statement given to the debtor prior to entering into the reaffirmation agreement with respect to the debt or, if no such disclosure statement was given to the debtor, the annual percentage rate as it would have been so disclosed: ___________%.

—And/Or—

(ii) The simple interest rate applicable to the amount reaffirmed as of the date this disclosure statement is given to the debtor: ___________%. If different simple interest rates apply to different balances included in the amount reaffirmed, the amount of each balance and the rate applicable to it are:

$___________@ ___________%;

$___________@ ___________%;

$___________@ ___________%.

c. If the underlying debt transaction was disclosed as a variable rate transaction on the most recent disclosure given under the Truth in Lending Act:

The interest rate on your loan may be a variable interest rate which changes from time to time, so that the annual percentage rate disclosed here may be higher or lower.

d. If the reaffirmed debt is secured by a security interest or lien, which has not been waived or determined to be void by a final order of the court, the following items or types of items of the debtor's goods or property remain subject to such security interest or lien in connection with the debt or debts being reaffirmed in the reaffirmation agreement described in Part B.

Item or Type of Item	Original Purchase Price or Original Amount of Loan

Optional—At the election of the creditor, a repayment schedule using one or a combination of the following may be provided:

Repayment Schedule:

Your first payment in the amount of $__________is due on__________(date), but the future payment amount may be different. Consult your reaffirmation agreement or credit agreement, as applicable.

—Or—

Your payment schedule will be: (number) payments in the amount of $__________each, payable (monthly, annually, weekly, etc.) on the (day) of each__________(week, month, etc.), unless altered later by mutual agreement in writing.

—Or—

A reasonably specific description of the debtor's repayment obligations to the extent known by the creditor or creditor's representative.

2. INSTRUCTIONS AND NOTICE TO DEBTOR

Reaffirming a debt is a serious financial decision. The law requires you to take certain steps to make sure the decision is in your best interest. If these steps are not completed, the reaffirmation agreement is not effective, even though you have signed it.

1. Read the disclosures in this Part A carefully. Consider the decision to reaffirm carefully. Then, if you want to reaffirm, sign the reaffirma-

tion agreement in Part B (or you may use a separate agreement you and your creditor agree on).

2. Complete and sign Part D and be sure you can afford to make the payments you are agreeing to make and have received a copy of the disclosure statement and a completed and signed reaffirmation agreement.

3. If you were represented by an attorney during the negotiation of your reaffirmation agreement, the attorney must have signed the certification in Part C.

4. If you were not represented by an attorney during the negotiation of your reaffirmation agreement, you must complete, sign and serve Local Form CSD 1231, *NOTICE OF HEARING AND MOTION ON AGREEMENT TO REAFFIRM A DEBT.*

5. The original of this disclosure must be filed with the court by you or your creditor. If a separate reaffirmation agreement (other than the one in Part B) has been signed, it must be attached.

6. If the creditor is not a Credit Union and you were represented by an attorney during the negotiation of your reaffirmation agreement, your reaffirmation agreement becomes effective upon filing with the court unless the reaffirmation is presumed to be an undue hardship as explained in Part D. If the creditor is a Credit Union and you were represented by an attorney during the negotiation of your reaffirmation agreement, your reaffirmation agreement becomes effective upon filing with the court.

7. If you were not represented by an attorney during the negotiation of your reaffirmation agreement, it will not be effective unless the court approves it. You must notice the creditor, your attorney (if any), the chapter 7 trustee, and the U.S. Trustee of a hearing on your reaffirmation agreement. You must attend this hearing in bankruptcy court where the judge will review your reaffirmation agreement. The bankruptcy court must approve your reaffirmation agreement as consistent with your best interests, except that no court approval is required if your reaffirmation agreement is for a consumer debt secured by a mortgage, deed of trust, security deed, or other lien on your real property, like your home.

YOUR RIGHT TO RESCIND (CANCEL) YOUR REAFFIRMATION AGREEMENT

You may rescind (cancel) your reaffirmation agreement at any time before the bankruptcy court enters a discharge order, or before the expiration of the 60-day period that begins on the date your reaffirmation agreement is filed with the court, whichever occurs later. To rescind (cancel) your reaffirmation agreement, you must notify the creditor that your reaffirmation agreement is rescinded (or canceled).

Frequently Asked Questions:

What are your obligations if you reaffirm the debt? A reaffirmed debt remains your personal legal obligation. It is not discharged in your bankruptcy case. That means that if you default on your reaffirmed debt after your bankruptcy case is over, your creditor may be able to take your property or your wages. Otherwise, your obligations will be determined by the reaffirmation agreement which may have changed the terms of the original agreement. For example, if you are reaffirming an open end credit agreement, the creditor may be permitted by that agreement or applicable law to change the terms of that agreement in the future under certain conditions.

Are you required to enter into a reaffirmation agreement by any law? No, you are not required to reaffirm a debt by any law. Only agree to reaffirm a debt if it is in your best interest. Be sure you can afford the payments you agree to make.

What if your creditor has a security interest or lien? Your bankruptcy discharge does not eliminate any lien on your property. A "lien" is often referred to as a security interest, deed of trust, mortgage or security deed. Even if you do not reaffirm and your personal liability on the debt is discharged, because of the lien your creditor may still have the right to take the security property if you do not pay the debt or default on it. If the lien is on an item of personal property that is exempt under your State's law or that the trustee has abandoned, you may be able to redeem the item rather than reaffirm the debt. To redeem, you make a single payment to the creditor equal to the current value of the security property, as agreed by the parties or determined by the court.

NOTE: When this disclosure refers to what a creditor "may" do, it does not use the word "may" to give the creditor specific permission. The word "may" is used to tell you what might occur if the law permits the creditor to take the action. If you have questions about your reaffirming a debt or what the law requires, consult with the attorney who helped you negotiate this agreement reaffirming a debt. if you don't have an attorney helping you, the judge will explain the effect of your reaffirming a debt when the hearing on the reaffirmation agreement is held.

PART B: REAFFIRMATION AGREEMENT

I (we) agree to reaffirm the debts arising under the credit agreement described below.

1. Brief description of credit agreement:

2. Description of any changes to the credit agreement made as part of this reaffirmation agreement:

SIGNATURE(S):

Borrower:

____

(Print Name)________________________

(Print Name)

Co-borrower, if also reaffirming these debts:________________________

(Signature)________________________

(Signature)

Date: _______________ Date: _______________

Accepted by creditor:

____

(Print Name of Creditor)(Creditor's mailing address)

____

(Signature)

Print Name:________________________

Date of creditor acceptance: _______________

PART C: CERTIFICATION BY DEBTOR'S ATTORNEY (IF ANY)

[Check each applicable box.]

☐ I hereby certify that (1) this agreement represents a fully informed and voluntary agreement by the debtor; (2) this agreement does not impose an undue hardship on the debtor or any dependent of the debtor; and (3) I have fully advised the debtor of the legal effect and consequences of this agreement and any default under this agreement.

☐ *[If applicable and the creditor is not a Credit Union.]* A presumption of undue hardship has been established with respect to this agreement. In my opinion, however, the debtor is able to make the required payment.

Printed Name of Debtor's Attorney: ________________________

Signature of Debtor's Attorney:________________________

Date: _______________

PART D: DEBTOR'S STATEMENT IN SUPPORT OF REAFFIRMATION AGREEMENT

1. I believe this reaffirmation agreement will not impose an undue hardship on my dependents or me. I can afford to make the payments on the reaffirmed debt because my monthly income (take home pay plus any other income received) is $____________, and my actual current monthly expenses including monthly payments on post-bankruptcy debt and other reaffirmation agreements total $____________, leaving $____________to make the required payments on this reaffirmed debt. I understand that if my income less my monthly expenses does not leave enough to make the payments, this reaffirmation agreement is presumed to be an undue hardship on me and must be reviewed by the court. However, this presumption may be overcome if I explain to the satisfaction of the court how I can afford to make the payments here:

2. *Either:* I received a copy of the Reaffirmation Disclosure Statement in Part A and a completed and signed reaffirmation agreement.

—Or—

[If the creditor is a Credit Union and the debtor is represented by an attorney] I believe this reaffirmation agreement is in my financial interest. I can afford to make the payments on the reaffirmed debt. I received a copy of the Reaffirmation Disclosure Statement in Part A and a completed and signed reaffirmation agreement.

Signed: ________________________
(Debtor)

____
(Joint Debtor, if any)

Date: ____________

CSD 1229

Reaffirmation Agreement
(For cases filed on or before 10/16/05)
(Rev. 01/13/06)

REAFFIRMATION AGREEMENT

Creditor's Name and Address:

Instructions: 1) Attach a copy of all court judgments, security agreements, and evidence of their perfection.
2) Obtain creditor's signature on page 3.
3) File all the documents by mailing them or delivering them to the Clerk of the Bankruptcy Court.

NOTICE TO DEBTOR:

This agreement gives up the protection of your bankruptcy discharge for this debt.

As a result of this agreement, the creditor may be able to take your property or wages if you do not pay the agreed amounts. The creditor may also act to collect the debt in other ways.

You may rescind (cancel) this agreement at any time before the bankruptcy court enters a discharge order or within 60 days after this agreement is filed with the court, whichever is later, by notifying the creditor that the agreement is canceled.

You are not required to enter into this agreement by any law. It is not required by the Bankruptcy Code, by any other law, or by any contract (except another reaffirmation agreement made in accordance with Bankruptcy Code § 524(c)).

You are allowed to pay this debt without signing this agreement. However, if you do not sign this agreement and are later unwilling or unable to pay the full amount, the creditor will not be able to collect it from you. The creditor also will not be allowed to take your property to pay the debt unless the creditor has a lien on that property.

If the creditor has a lien on your personal property, you may have a right to redeem the property and eliminate the lien by making a single payment to the creditor equal to the current value of the property, as agreed by the parties or determined by the court.

This agreement is not valid or binding unless it is filed with the clerk of the bankruptcy court. If you were not represented by an attorney

during the negotiation of this reaffirmation agreement, the agreement cannot be enforced by the creditor unless 1) you have attended a reaffirmation hearing in the bankruptcy court, and 2) the agreement has been approved by the bankruptcy court. (Court approval is not required if this is a consumer debt secured by a mortgage or other lien on your real estate.)

REAFFIRMATION AGREEMENT

The debtor and creditor named above agree to reaffirm the debt described in this agreement as follows.

THE DEBT

Total Amount of Debt when Case was Filed		$
Total Amount of Debt Reaffirmed		$
	Above total includes the following:	
	Interest Accrued to Date of Agreement	$
	Attorney Fees	$
	Late Fees	$
	Other Expenses or Costs Relating to the Collection of this Debt (Describe)	$
Annual Percentage Rate (APR)		%
Amount of Monthly Payment		$
Date Payments Start		
Total Number of Payments to be made		
Total of Payments if paid according to schedule		$
Date any Lien is to be Released if paid according to schedule		$

The debtor agrees that any and all remedies available to the creditor under the security agreement remain available.

All additional Terms Agreed to by the Parties (if any):

Payments on this debt [were][were not] in default on the date on which this bankruptcy case was filed.

This agreement differs from the original agreement with the creditors as follows:

CREDITOR'S STATEMENT CONCERNING AGREEMENT AND SECURITY/COLLATERAL (IF ANY)

Description of Collateral. If applicable, list manufacturer, year and model.
____

Value $
Basis or Source for Valuation
Current Location and Use of Collateral
Expected Future Use of Collateral

Check Applicable Boxes:

☐ Any lien described herein is valid and perfected.

☐ This agreement is part of a settlement of a dispute regarding the dischargeability of this debt under Section 523 of the Bankruptcy Code (11 U.S.C. § 523) or any other dispute. The nature of dispute is .

DEBTOR'S STATEMENT OF EFFECT OF AGREEMENT ON DEBTOR'S FINANCES

My Monthly Income (take home pay plus any other income received) is $____________.

My currently monthly expenses total $____________not including any payment due under this agreement or any debt to be discharged in this bankruptcy case.

I believe this agreement [will][will not] impose an undue hardship on me or my dependents.

DEBTOR'S STATEMENT CONCERNING DECISION TO REAFFIRM

I agreed to reaffirm this debt because .

I believe this agreement is in my best interest because .

I [consider][did not consider] redeeming the collateral under Section 722 of the Bankruptcy code (11 U.S.C. § 722). I chose not to redeem because __________.

I [was][was not] represented by an attorney during negotiations on this agreement.

CERTIFICATION OF ATTACHMENTS

Any documents which created and perfected the security interest or lien [are][are not] attached. [*If documents are not attached*: The documents which created and perfected the security interest or lien are not attached because ____.]

SIGNATURES

(Signature of Debtor) (Date)(Name of Creditor)

(Signature of Joint Debtor) (Date)(Signature of Creditor Representative) (Date)

CERTIFICATION BY DEBTOR'S ATTORNEY (IF ANY)

I hereby certify that 1) this agreement represents a fully informed and voluntary agreement by the debtor(s); 2) this agreement does not impose a hardship on the debtor or any dependent of the debtor; and 3) I have fully advised the debtor of the legal effect and consequences of this agreement and any default under this agreement.

Date ____________

(Signature of Debtor's Attorney, if any)

No. CSD 1230

[Debt Reaffirmation Instructions For Pro Se Debtors]

CSD 1230 [01/13/06]

INSTRUCTIONS TO UNREPRESENTED DEBTORS REGARDING THE REAFFIRMATION OF A DEBT

These instructions are intended only for debtors who represent themselves. Debtors who are represented by an attorney should consult with their attorney if they intend to reaffirm a debt.

The reaffirmation of a debt means that you promise to pay the creditor under the terms of a new agreement, despite the fact that the debt might be discharged in your bankruptcy as permitted by 11 U.S.C. § 727. You may decide to reaffirm a debt that may be discharged in your bankruptcy. **YOU ARE UNDER NO OBLIGATION TO REAFFIRM ANY DEBT.**

The Court will approve a reaffirmation agreement only if:

• the agreement has been made in writing before you receive your discharge in bankruptcy *and*

• the Court finds that the agreement is in your best interest and does not impose an undue hardship on you and your family.

The deadline for a hearing on a reaffirmation of a debt is ***prior* to the expiration of the date for your creditors to object to your discharge.** That date is in the NOTICE OF MEETING OF CREDITORS previously mailed to you.

If you reaffirm a debt but fail to notice and attend the hearing, **THE ENTRY OF YOUR DISCHARGE MAY BE DELAYED**.

To reaffirm a debt, complete the following steps:

1. *Immediately* obtain a hearing date and time for the hearing on the reaffirmation agreement. You can do this by contacting the courtroom deputy for the judge assigned to your bankruptcy case. To determine which deputy to call, you must look at your bankruptcy case number. If the number ends in:

(a) —JM —call (619) 557-6019 —DEPARTMENT ONE (Room 218)
(b) —LA —call (619) 557-6594 —DEPARTMENT TWO (Room 118)
(c) —JH —call (619) 557-6018 —DEPARTMENT THREE (Room 129)
(d) —PB —call (619) 557-5157 —DEPARTMENT FOUR (Room 328)

The deputy will give you a hearing date, time, and department number.

2. Obtain an agreement in writing from the creditor whose debt you are reaffirming. You may use a form provided by the creditor or the court's form. For cases filed on or **before** 10/16/2005, use REAFFIRMATION AGREEMENT (CSD 1229). For cases filed on or **after** 10/17/2005, use REAFFIRMATION AGREEMENT (CSD 1226).

3. Complete the accompanying NOTICE OF HEARING ON AGREEMENT TO REAFFIRM A DEBT (CSD 1231):

- Enter your name, address, and bankruptcy case number in the top sections.
- Type or print the name and complete address of the creditor whose debt you are reaffirming in the creditor section.
- Type or print the name and address of your trustee in trustee section. Your trustee's name and address appears on your NOTICE OF MEETING OF CREDITORS.
- Enter the hearing date, time, department number and room number.
- Sign and date the NOTICE OF HEARING. If both husband and wife are reaffirming the debt, both debtors' signatures are required.
- Attach the reaffirmation agreement signed by you and the creditor.

If you have more than one reaffirmation agreement, a separate notice and agreement must be filed for each creditor.

4. **Twenty-eight (28) days before the hearing**, you must mail a **copy** of the NOTICE OF HEARING and AGREEMENT to:

- the creditor whose debt you are reaffirming,
- your trustee, and
- the United States Trustee,

AND

you must file the original and one copy of the NOTICE OF HEARING and AGREEMENT with the court.

5. You *must* attend the reaffirmation hearing. **If you do not attend the hearing, entry of your discharge may be delayed.** Your agreement is not effective unless approved by the court.

Court personnel are prohibited from giving you legal advice. 28 U.S.C. § 955. If you have any questions concerning these procedures, you should consult an attorney.

No. CSD 1231

Notice of Hearing on Agreement to Reaffirm a Debt

CSD 1231 [01/27/06]
Name, Address, Telephone No. & I.D. No.

....

UNITED STATES BANKRUPTCY COURT
SOUTHERN DISTRICT OF CALIFORNIA

325 West "F" Street, San Diego, California 92101-6991

In Re Debtor.	BANKRUPTCY NO.

NOTICE OF HEARING ON AGREEMENT TO REAFFIRM A DEBT

TO	CREDITOR:	.... (Name and Address of Creditor)
	TRUSTEE:	.... (Name and Address of Chapter 7 Trustee)
	UNITED STATES TRUSTEE:	402 West Broadway, Suite 600, San Diego, California 92101

The undersigned debtor(s) affirm the following to be true and correct: I believe this reaffirmation agreement is in my best interest based on the income and expenses I have disclosed in my Statement in Support of the reaffirmation agreement, and because *(provide any additional relevant reasons the court should consider)*:

I ask the court for an order approving this reaffirmation agreement.

PLEASE TAKE NOTICE that the debtor in the above-entitled case has calendared a hearing for approval of the accompanying Reaffirmation Agreement pertaining to the debt of the creditor named above.

HEARING DATE: ....
HEARING TIME: ....

The hearing will be held in **Department No** ......, **Room** ......, of the Jacob Weinberger United States

Courthouse, located at 325 West "F" Street, San Diego, California 92101-6991.

I herby declare under penalty of perjury that on this date a copy of this Notice and the accompanying Reaffirmation Agreement were mailed to the above named person(s).

DATED: ....

(Signature of Debtor)

____

Signature of Joint Debtor, if any

CSD 1490

Order Reopening the Estate

(Rev. 08/22/03)

ORDER REOPENING THE ESTATE

IT IS ORDERED THAT the relief sought as set forth on the continuation pages attached and numbered two (2) through ____________with exhibits, if any, for a total of ____________ pages, is granted. Motion Docket Entry No. ____________.

//

//

//

//

//

//

DATED: ____________

____

Judge, United States Bankruptcy Court

Signature by the attorney constitutes a certification under Fed. R. of Bankr. P. 9011 that the relief in the order is the relief granted by the court.

Submitted by:

____

(Firm name)

By: ____________________________

Attorney for Movant

Upon the Motion of ____________;

IT IS ORDERED that the estate of the above-named debtor be, and it is hereby reopened pursuant to Federal Rule of Bankruptcy Procedure 5010 for the purpose of

and for such other action as may be deemed necessary.

No. CSD 1514

Guidelines for the Substantive Consolidation or Joint Administration of Related Debtor Entities

CSD 1514 [04/28/96]

GUIDELINES FOR THE SUBSTANTIVE CONSOLIDATION OR JOINT ADMINISTRATION OF RELATED DEBTOR ENTITIES

TO: ATTORNEY FOR MOVANT

The following guidelines have been developed to assist you in achieving the cost-saving measures you desire.

1) In the **JOINT ADMINISTRATION** of related debtor entities, the assets and liabilities are not merged. It is done as a matter of convenience, a cost saving device. It does not affect creditors' rights. A single docket sheet is used but separate claims registers are maintained.

An order for joint administration *must* identify the following:

- Specify the lead case by name and number.
- Specify a single caption listing all debtors and their respective case numbers to be used on all pleadings, motions, operating reports and other papers served or filed in the cases. Include a completed title page as an exhibit. [See sample printed on reverse side.]
- Specify that a combined service list will be used for the cases.
- Specify that combined notices will be sent to the creditors of the estates.
- Specify that multiple claims registers will be maintained.
- Specify that any deviation from these procedures will be by order of the court.

2) With the **SUBSTANTIVE CONSOLIDATION** of related debtor entities, all assets and liabilities of the debtor entities are merged into a unitary debtor estate, to which all holders of allowed claims are required to look for distribution. It affects substantive rights of the parties and may impair the rights of certain creditors. A single docket sheet and a single claims register are maintained.

An order to substantive consolidation *must* identify the following:

- Specify the lead case by name and number.
- Specify a single caption listing all debtors and their respective case

numbers to be used on all pleadings, motions, operating reports and other papers served or filed in the cases. Include a completed title page as an exhibit. [See sample printed on reverse side.]

- Specify that a combined service list will be used for the cases.
- Specify that combined notices will be sent to the creditors of the estates.
- Specify that a single claims register will be maintained.
- Specify that any deviation from these procedures will be by order of the court.

SHOULD THE ORDER NOT COMPLY WITH THESE GUIDELINES, IT IS SUBJECT TO BEING RETURNED FOR CORRECTION.

Name of Counsel, State Bar No.
Firm Name, if any
Street Address
Post Office Box, if any
Area Code and Phone No.

Representation of Party in Interest

UNITED STATES BANKRUPTCY COURT
SOUTHERN DISTRICT OF CALIFORNIA

In re: LEAD CASE NAME, Debtor. ___ MEMBER CASE NAME 1, Member Case No. 1 MEMBER CASE NAME 2, Member Case No. 2 MEMBER CASE NAME 3, Member Case No. 3 MEMBER CASE NAME 4, Member Case No. 4 Debtors.	Bankruptcy No.: LEAD CASE NO. *Indicate:* (Jointly Administered) *or* (Substantively Consolidated) TITLE OF ORDER OR DOCUMENT

No. CSD 1546

Attorney Change of Information Form

CSD 1546 [01/01/02]

UNITED STATES BANKRUPTCY COURT
SOUTHERN DISTRICT OF CALIFORNIA

325 West "F" Street, San Diego, California 92101-6991

ATTORNEY CHANGE OF INFORMATION FORM

To the Clerk of the United States Bankruptcy Court,

The undersigned attorney represents to the Court the following change of information:

☐ new mailing address ☐ new street address
☐ change in firm association [1] ☐ new telephone number
☐ new e-mail address

Updated Information

Name of Attorney: . . . .
State Bar ID No.: . . . .
Firm Name: . . . .
Street Address: . . . .
Mailing Address: . . . .
City: . . . .
State: . . . . Zip Code
Phone No.: . . . .
E-Mail Address

Dated:
. . . .
(Signature of Attorney)

---

[1] Substitution of Attorney required—see District Court Local Rule 83.5(j).

1800

Administrative Procedures for Filing, Signing and Verifying Pleadings and Papers by Electronic Means
(Rev. 11/15/04)

UNITED STATES BANKRUPTCY COURT
Southern District of California

ADMINISTRATIVE PROCEDURES FOR FILING, SIGNING AND VERIFYING PLEADINGS AND PAPERS BY ELECTRONIC MEANS

I. REGISTRATION FOR THE ELECTRONIC FILING SYSTEM

A. PASSWORDS. Each attorney admitted to practice in this court shall be entitled to one Electronic Filing System ("System") password to permit the attorney to participate in the electronic retrieval and filing of pleadings and other papers in accordance with the System. Registration for a password is governed by Paragraph I.B.

B. REGISTRATION.

1. An attorney may complete the pre-class training online on the Court's Internet site at *www.casb.uscourts.gov* in *Front Counter*.

2. Each attorney who successfully completes the Electronic Case Files training shall receive a login and password. This login and password shall be e-mailed directly to the attorney by the Court's Systems Department.

3. Once certified in the system, an attorney/participant may withdraw from participation in the System by providing the Clerk of Court, Chief Deputy Clerk or Systems Department with notice of such withdrawal. Such notice must be in writing. Upon receipt, the Office of the Clerk will immediately cancel the attorney/participant's password and will delete the attorney/participant from any applicable electronic service list.

II. ELECTRONIC FILING AND SERVICE OF DOCUMENTS

A. FILING.

1. Except as expressly provided in Paragraph III.A below

and in exceptional circumstances which prevent an attorney/participant from filing electronically, all petitions, motions, pleadings, memoranda of law, or other documents required to be filed with the court in connection with a case assigned to the System shall be electronically filed on the System. Notwithstanding the foregoing, parties and attorneys who are not participants in the System are not required to electronically file pleadings and other papers in a case assigned to the System.

2. All documents which form part of a pleading and which are being filed at the same time and by the same party may be electronically filed together under one docket number; e.g., the motion and an attached supporting affidavit, with the exception of a memorandum of law. A memorandum of law shall be filed separately and shown as a related document to the motion.

3. Emergency motions, supporting pleadings and objections shall be filed electronically as provided in these *Administrative Procedures*. The party filing the motion shall advise the judge's law clerk of the filing by phone.

B. SERVICE.

1. Whenever a pleading or other paper is filed electronically in accordance with the Electronic Filing Procedures, the Office of the Clerk shall serve the filing party with a "Notice of Electronic Filing" by electronic means at the time of docketing.

2. The filing party shall serve the pleading or other paper upon all person entitled to notice or service in accordance with the applicable rules, or, if service by first class mail is permitted under the rules, the filing party may make service in accordance with Paragraph II.B.3 below.

3. If the recipient of notice or service is a registered participant in the Electronic Filing System, service of the Notice of Electronic Filing by electronic means shall be the equivalent of service of the pleading or other paper by first class mail, postage prepaid.

C. SIGNATURES; STATEMENT OF SOCIAL SECURITY NUMBER; AFFIDAVITS OF SERVICE.

1. Petitions, lists, schedules and statements requiring the signature of the debtor(s) shall be filed electronically with an originally executed DECLARATION RE: ELECTRONIC FILING, Local Form CSD 1801, and STATEMENT OF SOCIAL SECURITY NUMBER, Official Bankruptcy Form B21, filed with the court within 15 days of the electronic filing of the petition.

2. Amendments, pleadings, affidavits, and other documents which must contain original signatures or which require verification under Fed. R. Bankr. P. 1008 or an unsworn declaration as provided in 28 U.S.C. § 1746, shall be filed electronically. The original signed document shall be maintained by the attorney of record or the party originating the document for a period not less than the maximum allowable time to complete the appellate process. Upon request, the original document must be provided to other parties or the court for review. The pleading or other document electronically filed shall indicate a signature; e.g., "/s/ Jane Doe."

D. FEES PAYABLE TO THE CLERK. For filings that require a fee, payment shall be made online using one of the specified credit cards.

E. ORDERS. Stipulated, emergency, and non-contested orders may be submitted electronically as outlined below.

1. Electronically submitted orders must comply with all Local Bankruptcy Rules.

2. Electronically submitted orders may not be combined with the application or motion into one document. The application or motion must be entered on the docket prior to submitting the order electronically and the resulting *Docket Entry No.* must be noted on the order template.

3. The first page of any electronically submitted order must substantially conform with the order templates (CSD 1001A-C, CSD 1159A-C, and CSD 3000A-C) or findings of fact and conclusions of law template (CSD

1001D-E, CSD 1159D-E, and CSD 3000D-E) maintained by the Court. The signature line must be fixed at 4.5 inches from the left edge of the paper and 3 inches from the bottom edge of the paper. Signatures approving orders will be affixed electronically providing for little tolerance in this area. Orders which do not comply will be returned as defective.

4. Exhibits required by Local Bankruptcy Rules 4001-5 and 9013-7 may be referenced according to the specific *Docket Entry No.* assigned to the document at the time of it's entry.

5. All orders must be in a PDF format at the time of submission.

6. When electronically lodging an order after hearing, compliance with Local Bankruptcy Rule 7054-3(b)(a)(D) requiring the Notice of Entry and envelopes is waived.

7. Notification of defects in an order will be provided by *REPLY* e-mail.

8. Once entered, a conformed copy of the order may be obtained by accessing the System.

F. TITLE OF DOCKET ENTRIES. The person electronically filing a pleading or other document will be responsible for designating a title for the document by using one of the categories contained in the *Document Type Directory*.

III. CONVENTIONAL FILING OF DOCUMENTS

A. CONVENTIONAL FILINGS. The following documents shall be filed conventionally and not electronically unless specifically authorized by the court:

1. Documents to be Filed under Seal. A motion to file document(s) under seal shall be filed electronically; however, the actual document(s) to be filed under seal shall be filed conventionally. A paper copy of the order shall be attached to the document(s) under seal and be delivered to the Office of the Clerk.

2. Exhibits. Exhibits, including but not limited to leases, notes, and the like, which are not available in electronic

form, shall be filed conventionally with a copy of the Notice of Electronic Filing to indicate the referenced document. Wherever possible, however, such documents, or the relevant portions thereof, should be electronically imaged (i.e., "scanned") and filed using the Portable Document Format (PDF).

B. SERVICE OF CONVENTIONAL OR 3.5 INCH FLOPPY DISK FILINGS. Pleadings or other documents which are filed conventionally or on a 3.5 inch floppy disk rather than electronically shall be served in the manner provided for in, and on those parties entitled to notice in accordance with, the Federal Rules of Bankruptcy Procedure and Local Bankruptcy Rules except as otherwise provided by order of the court.

IV. PUBLIC ACCESS TO THE SYSTEM DOCKET

A. INTERNET ACCESS WITHOUT A PASSWORD. Any person or organization other than those referred to in Paragraph I.B must register with PACER and receive a login and password in order to access court records online. Information regarding PACER may be found on the Court's Internet site at *www.casb.uscourts.gov* in *File Room.*

B. PUBLIC ACCESS AT THE COURT. The public will have electronic access to the electronic docket and documents filed in the System at the Office of the Clerk, for viewing during regular business hours, Monday through Friday.

C. CONVENTIONAL COPIES AND CERTIFIED COPIES. Conventional copies and certified copies of the electronically filed documents may be purchased at the Office of the Clerk, 325 West "F" Street., San Diego, California 92101-6991. The fee for copying and certification will be in accordance with 28 U.S.C. § 1930.

No. CSD 2010
(Rev. 04/04/05)

U.S. Trustee's Notice of Hearing and Motion

UNITED STATES TRUSTEE'S NOTICE OF HEARING AND MOTION

TO THE DEBTOR, ALL CREDITORS AND OTHER PARTIES IN INTEREST:

YOU ARE HEREBY NOTIFIED that on, at.m., in Department ____________, Room, of the Jacob Weinberger United States Courthouse, located at 325 West "F" Street, San Diego, California 92101-6991, there will be a hearing regarding the Motion of the United States Trustee for [check the appropriate box]:

[ ] Dismissal of a chapter 7, 11 or 12 case;
[ ] Conversion of a chapter 7, 11 or 12 case
[ ] Other [specify the nature of the matter]:

If not required to be attached, a set of the moving papers will be provided, upon request, by the undersigned or may be inspected at the office of the Clerk.

Any opposition or other response to the motion must be served upon the undersigned and the original and one copy of such papers with proof of service must be filed with the Clerk of the U.S. Bankruptcy Court at 325 West "F" St., San Diego, California 92101-6991, NOT LATER THAN FOURTEEN (14) DAYS FROM THE DATE OF SERVICE.

DATED:

____
Attorney for the United States Trustee

CSD 2015

Objection to Claim and Notice Thereof
(Rev. 10/17/05)

REAFFIRMATION AGREEMENT

Creditor's Name and Address:

Instructions: 1) Attach a copy of all court judgments, security agreements, and evidence of their perfection.
2) Obtain creditor's signature on page 3.
3) File all the documents by mailing them or delivering them to the Clerk of the Bankruptcy Court.

NOTICE TO DEBTOR:

This agreement gives up the protection of your bankruptcy discharge for this debt.

As a result of this agreement, the creditor may be able to take your property or wages if you do not pay the agreed amounts. The creditor may also act to collect the debt in other ways.

You may rescind (cancel) this agreement at any time before the bankruptcy court enters a discharge order or within 60 days after this agreement is filed with the court, whichever is later, by notifying the creditor that the agreement is canceled.

You are not required to enter into this agreement by any law. It is not required by the Bankruptcy Code, by any other law, or by any contract (except another reaffirmation agreement made in accordance with Bankruptcy Code § 524(c)).

You are allowed to pay this debt without signing this agreement. However, if you do not sign this agreement and are later unwilling or unable to pay the full amount, the creditor will not be able to collect it from you. The creditor also will not be allowed to take your property to pay the debt unless the creditor has a lien on that property.

If the creditor has a lien on your personal property, you may have a right to redeem the property and eliminate the lien by making a single payment to the creditor equal to the current value of the property, as agreed by the parties or determined by the court.

This agreement is not valid or binding unless it is filed with the clerk of the bankruptcy court. If you were not represented by an attorney during the negotiation of this reaffirmation agreement, the agreement cannot be enforced by the creditor unless 1) you have attended a

reaffirmation hearing in the bankruptcy court, and 2) the agreement has been approved by the bankruptcy court. (Court approval is not required if this is a consumer debt secured by a mortgage or other lien on your real estate.)

REAFFIRMATION AGREEMENT

The debtor and creditor named above agree to reaffirm the debt described in this agreement as follows.

THE DEBT

Total Amount of Debt when Case was Filed	$
Total Amount of Debt Reaffirmed	$
Above total includes the following:	
Interest Accrued to Date of Agreement	$
Attorney Fees	$
Late Fees	$
Other Expenses or Costs Relating to the Collection of this Debt (Describe)	$
Annual Percentage Rate (APR)	%
Amount of Monthly Payment	$
Date Payments Start	
Total Number of Payments to be made	
Total of Payments if paid according to schedule	$
Date any Lien is to be Released if paid according to schedule	$

The debtor agrees that any and all remedies available to the creditor under the security agreement remain available.

All additional Terms Agreed to by the Parties (if any):

Payments on this debt [were] [were not] in default on the date on which this bankruptcy case was filed.

This agreement differs from the original agreement with the creditors as follows:

CREDITOR'S STATEMENT CONCERNING AGREEMENT AND SECURITY/COLLATERAL (IF ANY)

Description of Collateral. If applicable, list manufacturer, year and model.

____

Value $
Basis or Source for Valuation
Current Location and Use of Collateral
Expected Future Use of Collateral

Check Applicable Boxes:

☐ Any lien described herein is valid and perfected.

☐ This agreement is part of a settlement of a dispute regarding the dischargeability of this debt under Section 523 of the Bankruptcy Code (11 U.S.C. § 523) or any other dispute. The nature of dispute is ____________.

DEBTOR'S STATEMENT OF EFFECT OF AGREEMENT ON DEBTOR'S FINANCES

My Monthly Income (take home pay plus any other income received) is $____________.

My currently monthly expenses total $____________ not including any payment due under this agreement or any debt to be discharged in this bankruptcy case.

I believe this agreement [will][will not] impose an undue hardship on me or my dependents.

DEBTOR'S STATEMENT CONCERNING DECISION TO REAFFIRM

I agreed to reaffirm this debt because ____________.

I believe this agreement is in my best interest because ____________.

I [consider][did not consider] redeeming the collateral under Section 722 of the Bankruptcy code (11 U.S.C. § 722). I chose not to redeem because ____________.

I [was][was not] represented by an attorney during negotiations on this agreement.

CERTIFICATION OF ATTACHMENTS

Any documents which created and perfected the security interest or lien [are][are not] attached. [*If documents are not attached*: The documents which created and perfected the security interest or lien are not attached because ____ .]

SIGNATURES

____

(Signature of Debtor) (Date)(Name of Creditor)

____

(Signature of Joint Debtor) (Date)(Signature of Creditor Representative) (Date)

CERTIFICATION BY DEBTOR'S ATTORNEY (IF ANY)

I hereby certify that 1) this agreement represents a fully informed and voluntary agreement by the debtor(s); 2) this agreement does not impose a hardship on the debtor or any dependent of the debtor; and 3) I have fully advised the debtor of the legal effect and consequences of this agreement and any default under this agreement.

Date ____________

(Signature of Debtor's Attorney, if any)

No. CSD 2018

Report of Abandonment of Real Property

CSD 2018 [03/26/99]
Name, Address, Telephone No. & I.D. No.

UNITED STATES BANKRUPTCY COURT
SOUTHERN DISTRICT OF CALIFORNIA
325 West "F" Street, San Diego, California 92101-6991

In re . . . . Debtor.	BANKRUPTCY NO.

REPORT OF ABANDONMENT OF REAL PROPERTY

Pursuant to Bankruptcy Local Rule 6007, the undersigned Trustee hereby reports and represents that:

1. On . . . . , due notice of the Trustee's intent to abandon the property described herein was mailed to the debtor, the debtor's attorney and such other parties as required by Local Bankruptcy Rule 6007.

2. The time for filing a request for hearing has expired without an objection or request for hearing having been received by the undersigned.

3. The Trustee hereby abandons and forever disclaims any further interest in and to the following described real property of the debtor herein, to wit: (Provide full legal description and street address—use continuation sheet if necessary.)

4. The right of possession of the abandoned property is hereby relinquished to the debtor, to be assumed at no cost to the undersigned. Said abandonment is subject to and without prejudice to any rights of any entity holding a valid lien against the property or of any right of redemption that may be exercised by the debtor under 11 U.S.C. § 722.

I hereby declare under penalty of perjury that the foregoing statements are true to the best of my knowledge and belief.

DATED:

. . . .
Signature of Trustee

CERTIFICATE OF SERVICE

I, the undersigned whose address appears below, certify:

That I am, and at all times hereinafter mentioned was, more than 18 years of age;

That on. . . . . . day of . . . ., ..., I served a true copy of the within REPORT OF ABANDONMENT OF REAL PROPERTY by [describe here mode of service]

on the following persons [set forth name and address of each person served]:

UNITED STATES TRUSTEE
Department of Justice
402 West Broadway, Suite 600
San Diego, CA 92101

I certify under penalty of perjury that the foregoing is true and correct.

Executed on . . . .
(Date) (Typed Name and Signature)

. . . .
(Address)

. . . .
(City, State, ZIP Code)

No. CSD 2024

Report of Sale

CSD 2024 [04/28/96]
Name, Address, Telephone No. & I.D. No.

. . . .

UNITED STATES BANKRUPTCY COURT
SOUTHERN DISTRICT OF CALIFORNIA

325 West "F" Street, San Diego, California 92101-6991

In Re

debtor.

BANKRUPTCY NO.

REPORT OF SALE

Pursuant to Local Bankruptcy Rule 6004, the undersigned Trustee hereby reports and represents that:

1. On . . . . , due notice of the Trustee's intent to sell the property described herein was mailed to the debtor, the debtor's attorney and all creditors as required by Local Bankruptcy Rules 2002 and 6004.

2. The time for filing a request for hearing has expired without an objection or request for hearing having been received by the undersigned.

3. A description of the property sold, name of the purchaser(s), and the terms of sale are set forth in Exhibit "A" printed on Page 2.

4. If applicable, the following entities held a valid security interest in all or part of the property sold and were paid the stated sums in satisfaction thereof:

Name and Address	Property	Amount Paid

5. The purchase price has been paid in full and all property delivered to the purchaser.

I hereby declare under penalty of perjury that the within and attached statements are true to the best of my knowledge and belief.

DATED:

. . . .
Trustee in Bankruptcy

Exhibit "A"

. . . . DEBTOR, CASE NO. . . . .

Type of Sale: [1]

☐ Private Sale. Describe methods used to obtain best possible price:[2]

Description of Property Sold	Name and Address of Purchaser(s)	Sales Price per Item or Lot

Offers or bids received but not accepted from the following entities:

Name	Value of Offer

☐ Public Auction. Auction conducted by . . . .

Report of Auctioneer attached containing:[3]

List of the names of bidders and assigned bidding numbers, if any; and

— Description of items sold, purchase price, and name or bidder number for purchaser for each item or lot sold; plus

— A cover page containing a summation of the gross sales, and a statement of the commission and expenses applied for or retained by the auctioneer.

A statement that there was at the time of employment, and continued to be during the period of employment, a disinterested person as required under 11 U.S.C. § 327, or, if so, the nature thereof.

Auctioneer's Report Reviewed and Approved:

DATED:

Signed: . . . . , Trustee

INSTRUCTIONS

[1] Indicate method of sale, whether by sealed bids, negotiations, or otherwise.

[2] Describe advertising, telephone or other forms of solicitation for offers, negotiations and any other methods used to consummate sale.

[3] Auctioneer's report is to be signed under penalty of perjury, to contain all of the information here set forth, and to be reviewed and approved by trustee.

No. CSD 2044

Application to Employ Auctioneer

CSD 2044 [04/28/96]
Name, Address, Telephone No. & I.D. No.

. . . .

UNITED STATES BANKRUPTCY COURT
SOUTHERN DISTRICT OF CALIFORNIA

325 West "F" Street, San Diego, California 92101-6991

In Re Debtor.	BANKRUPTCY NO.

APPLICATION TO EMPLOY AUCTIONEER

The undersigned respectfully represents that:

1. Your applicant is the duly appointed and qualified Trustee of the estate of the above-named debtor.

2. Your applicant wishes to employ the following named person as Auctioneer in this case: [Name and Address]

3. It is necessary to employ an auctioneer because:

4. The property to be sold consists of [general description]:

5. The estimated proceeds from this auction will be $. . . . .

6. The proposed Auctioneer is competent and equipped to perform the auctioneering services required by the estate.

7. In addition to conducting the auction, the proposed Auctioneer will also perform the following services:

8. The Auctioneer has agreed to perform services for $. . . . . [or. . . . . . percent of gross sales], as commission, which amount is reasonable compensation for such services, plus expenses not to exceed the following amount [itemize]:

9. The attached is the verified statement required of the proposed Auctioneer under Local Bankruptcy Rule 6005-1.

10. The employment of an Auctioneer to sell the property is in the best interests of the estate and all the creditors.

WHEREFORE, your applicant prays for authorization to employ the Auctioneer named above in

2 as Auctioneer; that compensation be fixed and expenses be authorized in the amounts shown above in

8; and for such other and further relief as the Court may deem proper.

Dated: . . . . , Trustee

CSD 2045

Order Appointing Auctioneer

CSD 2045 [08/22/03]
Name, Address, Telephone No. & I.D. No.

UNITED STATES BANKRUPTCY COURT
SOUTHERN DISTRICT OF CALIFORNIA

325 West "F" Street, San Diego, California 92101-6991

In Re

Debtor.

BANKRUPTCY NO.

ORDER APPOINTING AUCTIONEER

IT IS ORDERED THAT the relief sought as set forth on the continuation pages attached and numbered two (2) through ___________with exhibits, if any, for a total of ___________ pages, is granted. Application Docket Entry No. ___________.

//
//
//
//
//
//

DATED:

____
Judge, United States Bankruptcy Court

Signature by the attorney constitutes a certification under Fed. R. of Bankr. P. 9011 that the relief in the order is the relief granted by the court.

Submitted by:

____
Trustee

Upon the Application of the Trustee in Bankruptcy for the estate of the above-named debtor, praying for authority to employ an Auctioneer, and to fix the compensation and expenses of the Auctioneer, and it appearing that no notice of a hearing on the application should be given, and no adverse interest having been represented, and sufficient reason appearing therefor,

IT IS ORDERED that:

1. The Trustee is authorized to employ_____________as Auctioneer for the Trustee.

2. The compensation of said Auctioneer is fixed at $_____________, and that expenses are authorized in an amount not to exceed $_____________.

3. Payment to the Auctioneer of the compensation and reimbursement of the expenses herein authorized shall be made only after compliance by the Auctioneer with Local Bankruptcy Rule 6005 and notice to creditors as required by Local Bankruptcy Rules 2002 and 6005-4.

4. The Trustee shall serve a copy of this order on the Auctioneer.

No. CSD 3007

Summons in an Adversary Proceeding

CSD 3007 [04/28/96]

UNITED STATES BANKRUPTCY COURT
Southern District of California

In re

Debtor
Plaintiff

v.

Defendant

Bankruptcy Case No.

Adversary Proceeding No.

SUMMONS IN AN ADVERSARY PROCEEDING

YOU ARE SUMMONED and required to submit a motion or answer to the complaint which is attached to this summons to the Clerk of the Bankruptcy Court within 30 days from the date of issuance of this summons, except that the United States and its offices and agencies shall submit a motion or answer to the complaint within 35 days of issuance.

Address of Clerk
Clerk, United States Bankruptcy Court
Southern District of California 325 West "F" Street
San Diego, California 92101-6991

At the same time, you must also serve a copy of the motion or answer upon the plaintiff's attorney.

Name and Address of Plaintiff's Attorney

If you make a motion, your time to answer is governed by Federal Rule of Bankruptcy Procedure 7012.

IF YOU FAIL TO RESPOND TO THIS SUMMONS, YOUR FAILURE WILL BE DEEMED TO BE YOUR CONSENT TO ENTRY OF A JUDGMENT BY THE BANKRUPTCY COURT AND JUDGMENT BY DEFAULT MAY BE TAKEN AGAINST YOU FOR THE RELIEF DEMANDED IN THE COMPLAINT.

. . . . Clerk
Dated

By: . . . .
Deputy Clerk

PROOF OF SERVICE

I, ... , certify that I am, and at all times during the service of process was, not less than 18 years of age and not a party to the matter concerning which service of process was made.

I further certify that this summons and a copy of the complaint was made. . . . . [date] by:

☐ Mail Service - Regular, first class United States mail, postage fully pre-paid, addressed to:

☐ Personal Service - By leaving the documents with the following defendant(s) or an officer or agent of the defendant(s) at:

☐ Residence Service - By leaving the documents with the following adult at:

☐ Publication - The defendant was served as follows: [describe briefly]

☐ State Law - The defendant was served pursuant to the laws of the State of . . . . , as follows: [describe briefly]

Under penalty of perjury, I declare that foregoing is true and correct.

. . . .
[Date] [Signature]

. . . .
Print Name

. . . .
Business Address

. . . .
City State ZIP

No. CSD 3008

Third Party Summons in an Adversary Proceeding

CSD 3008 [04/28/96]

UNITED STATES BANKRUPTCY COURT
Southern District of California

In re

Debtor
Plaintiff

v.

Defendant
Third-Party Defendant

Bankruptcy Case No.

Adversary Proceeding No.

THIRD PARTY SUMMONS IN AN ADVERSARY PROCEEDING

YOU ARE SUMMONED and required to submit a motion or answer to the complaint which is attached to this summons to the Clerk of the Bankruptcy Court within 30 days from the date of issuance of this summons, except that the United States and it offices and agencies shall submit a motion or answer to the complaint within 35 days of issuance.

Address of Clerk

Clerk, United States Bankruptcy Court
325 West "F" Street
San Diego, California 92101-6991

At the same time, you must also serve a copy of the motion or answer upon the plaintiff's attorney.

Name and Address of Plaintiff's Attorney

At the same time, you must also serve a copy of the motion or answer upon the defendant and third-party plaintiff's attorney.

Name and Address of Attorney

If you make a motion, your time to answer is governed by Federal Rule of Bankruptcy Procedure 7012. If you are also being served with a copy of the complaint of the plaintiff, you have the option of not answering the plaintiff's complaint unless this is an admiralty or maritime case subject to the provisions of Federal Rules of Civil Procedure 9(h) and 14(c), in which case you are required to submit a motion or an answer to both the plaintiff's complaint and the third-party complaint, and to serve a copy of your motion or answer upon the appropriate parties.

IF YOU FAIL TO RESPOND TO THIS SUMMONS, YOUR FAILURE WILL BE DEEMED TO BE YOUR CONSENT TO ENTRY OF A JUDGMENT BY THE BANKRUPTCY COURT AND JUDGMENT BY DEFAULT MAY BE TAKEN AGAINST YOU FOR THE RELIEF DEMANDED IN THE COMPLAINT.

Dated:
. . . ., Clerk
By: . . . ., Deputy Clerk

PROOF OF SERVICE

I, ..., certify that I am, and at all times during the service of process was, not less than 18 years of age and not a party to the matter concerning which service of process was made.

I further certify that this summons and a copy of the complaint was made. . . . . [date] by:

☐ Mail Service - Regular, first class United States mail, postage fully pre-paid, addressed to:

☐ Personal Service - By leaving the documents with the following defendant(s) or an officer or agent of the defendant(s) at:

☐ Residence Service - By leaving the documents with the following adult at:

☐ Publication - The defendant was served as follows: [describe briefly]

☐ State Law - The defendant was served pursuant to the laws of the State of . . . ., as follows: [describe briefly]

Under penalty of perjury, I declare that the foregoing is true and correct.

. . . .
[Date]

. . . .
[Signature]

. . . .
Print name

. . . .
Business Address

. . . .
City State ZIP

No. CSD 3009

Subpoena in an Adversary Proceeding

CSD 3009 [1/31/07]
Name, Address, Telephone No. & I.D. No.

UNITED STATES BANKRUPTCY COURT
SOUTHERN DISTRICT OF CALIFORNIA

325 West "F" Street, San Diego, California 92101-6991

In re . . . .
Debtor.
. . . .
Plaintiff(s)
. . . . BANKRUPTCY NO.
v.
. . . .
Defendant(s)

SUBPOENA IN AN ADVERSARY PROCEEDING

TO:

☐ YOU ARE COMMANDED to appear in the United States Bankruptcy Court at the place, date, and time specified below to testify in the above adversary proceeding.

PLACE OF TESTIMONY	COURTROOM
	DATE AND TIME

☐ YOU ARE COMMANDED to appear at the place, date, and time specified below to testify at the taking of a deposition in the above adversary proceeding.

PLACE OF DEPOSITION	DATE AND TIME

☐ YOU ARE COMMANDED to produce and permit inspection and copying of the following documents or objects at the place, date, and time specified below (list documents or objects):

PLACE OF DEPOSITION	DATE AND TIME

☐ YOU ARE COMMANDED to permit inspection of the following premises at the date and time specified below.

PREMISES	DATE AND TIME

Any organization not a party to this adversary proceeding that is subpoenaed for the taking of a deposition shall designate one or more officers, directors, or managing agents, or other persons who consent to testify on its behalf, and may set forth, for each person designated, the matters on which the person will testify. Fed.R.Civ.P. 30(b)(6) made applicable in adversary proceedings by Rules 7030, Fed.R.Bankr.P.

ISSUING OFFICER SIGNATURE AND TITLE (INDICATE IF ATTORNEY FOR PLAINTIFF OR DEFENDANT)	DATE
ISSUING OFFICER'S NAME, ADDRESS AND PHONE NUMBER	

*If the bankruptcy case or the adversary proceeding is pending in a district other than the district in which the subpoena is issued, state the district under the case number or adversary proceeding number.

PROOF OF SERVICE

SERVED	DATE	PLACE
SERVED ON (PRINT NAME)		MANNER OF SERVICE
SERVED BY (PRINT NAME)		TITLE

DECLARATION OF SERVER

I declare under penalty of perjury under the laws of the United States of America that the foregoing information contained in the Proof of Service is true and correct.

Executed on (Date)

(Typed Name and Signature of Server)

(Address)

(City, State, ZIP Code)

(c) PROTECTION OF PERSONS SUBJECT TO SUBPOENAS.

(1) A party or an attorney responsible for the issuance and service of a subpoena shall take reasonable steps to avoid imposing undue burden or expense on a person subject to that subpoena. The court on behalf of which the subpoena was issued shall enforce this duty and impose upon the party or attorney in breach of this duty an appropriate sanction, which may include, but is not limited to, lost earnings and a reasonable attorneys fee.

(2) (A) A person commanded to produce and permit inspection and copying of designated books, papers, documents or tangible things, or inspection of premises need not appear in person at the place of production or inspection unless commanded to appear for deposition, hearing or trial.

(B) Subject to paragraph (d)(2) of this rule, a person commanded to produce and permit inspection and copying may, within 14 days after service of the subpoena or before the time specified for compliance if such time is less than 14 days after service, serve upon the party or attorney designated in the subpoena written objection to inspection or copying of any or all of the designated materials or of the premises. If objection is made, the party serving the subpoena shall not be entitled to inspect and copy the materials or inspect the premises except pursuant to an order or the court by which the subpoena was issued. If objection has been made, the party serving the subpoena may, upon notice to the person commanded to produce, move at any time for an order to compel the production. Such an order to compel production shall protect any person who is not a party or an officer of a party from significant expense resulting from the inspection and copying commanded.

(3) (A) On timely motion, the court by which a subpoena was issued shall quash or modify the subpoena if it

(i) fails to allow reasonable time for compliance;

(ii) requires a person who is not a party or an officer of a party to travel more than 100 miles from the place where that person resides, is employed or regularly transacts business in person, except that, subject to the provisions of clause (c)(3)(B)(iii) of this rule, such a person may in order to attend trial be commanded to travel from any such place within the state in which the trial is held, or

(iii) requires disclosure of privileged or other protected matter and no exception or waiver applies, or

(iv) subjects a person to undue burden.

(B) If a subpoena

(i) requires the disclosure of a trade secret or other confidential research, development, or commercial information, or

(ii) requires disclosure of an unretained expert's opinion or information not describing specific events or occurrences in dispute and resulting from the expert's study made not at the request of any party, or

(iii) requires a person who is not a party or an officer of a party to incur substantial expense to travel more than 100 miles to attend trial, the court may, to protect a person subject to or affected by the subpoena, quash or modify the subpoena or, if the party in whose behalf the subpoena is issued shows a substantial need for the testimony or material that cannot be otherwise met without undue hardship and assures that the person to whom the subpoena is addressed will be reasonably compensated, the court may order appearance or production only upon specified conditions.

(d) DUTIES IN RESPONDING TO SUBPOENA.

(1) A person responding to a subpoena to produce documents shall produce them as they are kept in the usual course of business or shall organize and label them to correspond with the categories in the demand.

(2) When information subject to a subpoena is withheld on a claim that it is privileged or subject to protection as trial preparation materials, the claim shall be made expressly and shall be supported by a description of the nature of the documents, communications, or things not produced that is sufficient to enable the demanding party to contest the claim.

CSD 3009

No. CSD 3010

Proof of Service (Adversary)

CSD 3010 [04/28/96]
Name, Address, Telephone No. & I.D. No.

. . . .

UNITED STATES BANKRUPTCY COURT
SOUTHERN DISTRICT OF CALIFORNIA

325 West "F" Street, San Diego, California 92101-6991

In Re
Debtor.
. . . .
Plaintiff(s)
. . . .
v.
Defendants(s)
. . . .

BANKRUPTCY NO.
ADVERSARY NO.

PROOF OF SERVICE

I, ... , certify that I am, and at all times during the service of process was, not less than 18 years of age and not a party to the matter concerning which service of process was made. I further certify that I served a copy of the following documents [describe each document served]:

on . . . . by:
[date]

☐ Mail Service—Regular, first class United States mail, postage fully pre-paid, addressed to:

☐ Personal Service—By leaving the documents with the following named person(s) or an officer or agent of the person(s) at:

☐ Residence Service—By leaving the documents with the following adult at:

Under penalty of perjury, I declare that the foregoing is true and correct.

. . . .

[Date] [Signature]

. . . .
Print Name

. . . .
Business Address

. . . .
City, State, ZIP

No. CSD 3015

Notice of Motion and Hearing

CSD 3015 [01/01/02]
Name, Address, Telephone No. & I.D. No.

. . . .

UNITED STATES BANKRUPTCY COURT
SOUTHERN DISTRICT OF CALIFORNIA
325 West "F" Street, San Diego, California 92101-6991

In Re

Debtor.

. . . .

Plaintiff(s)

. . . .

v.

. . . .

Defendants(s)

BANKRUPTCY NO.

ADVERSARY NO.

NOTICE OF MOTION AND HEARING

TO:

YOU ARE HEREBY NOTIFIED that on . . . ., at . . . . .m., in Department . . . ., Room . . . ., of the Jacob Weinberger United States Courthouse, located at 325 West "F" Street, San Diego, California 92101-6991 there will be a hearing regarding the motion of . . . ., for

Any opposition or other response to this motion must be served upon the undersigned and the original and one copy of such papers with proof of service must be filed with the Clerk of the U.S. Bankruptcy Court at 325 West "F" Street, San Diego, California 92101-6991, NOT LATER THAN FOURTEEN (14) [1] DAYS FROM THE DATE OF SERVICE.

DATED:

________________________ [Attorney for] Moving Party

CERTIFICATE OF SERVICE

I, the undersigned whose address appears below, certify:

[1] If you were served electronically or by mail, you have three (3) additional days to take the above-stated actions.

That I am, and at all times hereinafter mentioned was, more than 18 years of age;

That on . . . . . . day of . . . . , ... , I served a true copy of the within NOTICE OF MOTION AND HEARING by [describe here mode of service]

on the following persons [set forth name and address of each person served] and as checked below:

[ ] Attorney for Debtor (if required):

I certify under penalty of perjury that the foregoing is true and correct.

Executed on . . . .

(Date) (Typed Name and Signature)

. . . .

(Address)

. . . .

(City, State, ZIP Code)

CSD 3018

Certificate of Compliance With Early Conference of Counsel

(05/15/03)

CERTIFICATE OF COMPLIANCE WITH EARLY CONFERENCE OF COUNSEL [LOCAL BANKRUPTCY RULE 7016-2]

TO THE HONORABLE UNITED STATES BANKRUPTCY JUDGE:

The parties submit the following CERTIFICATE OF COMPLIANCE WITH EARLY CONFERENCE OF COUNSEL requirements in accordance with Local Bankruptcy Rule 7016-2(c):

A. PLEADINGS/SERVICE:

1. Have all parties been served? ☐ Yes ☐ No
2. Have all parties filed and served answers to the complaint, counter-complaints, etc.? ☐ Yes ☐ No

B. DISCOVERY PLAN:

(1) Fed. R. Bankr. P. 7026 and Local Bankruptcy Rule 7016-2 require the parties to meet within thirty (30) days after all defendants have appeared or, in cases having multiple defendants, within forty-five (45) days after the first defendant appears. The parties to this case met on.

(2) The parties have agreed to make the disclosures required by Fed. R. Bankr. P. 7026(a)(1) by.

(3) **(Check one)**

A. The parties have agreed on the discovery plan attached as Exhibit A. ☐

or

B. The parties cannot agree on a discovery plan and scheduling order. The attached Exhibit A sets forth the parties' disagreements and reasons for each party's position. ☐

C. SETTLEMENT OR MEDIATION:

(1) What is the status of settlement efforts?

(2) Has this dispute been formally mediated? If so, when?

(3) Has mediation been discussed with your client? (See Local Bankruptcy Rule 7016-4.)

Plaintiff ☐ Yes ☐ No

Defendant ☐ Yes ☐ No

(4) The parties desire to go to voluntary, non-binding mediation. (See Local Bankruptcy Rule 7016-6.) They have reviewed the list of mediators on the court's website (**www.casb.uscourts.gov**) or obtained the list from the court and have selected the following persons subject to availability as first, second, and third choices for mediator:

First Choice:
Second Choice:
Third Choice:

Parties are requested to notify the courtroom deputy of their preferences at the time a pre-trial status conference date is obtained.

D. READINESS FOR TRIAL:

(1) When will you be ready for trial in this case?

Plaintiff Defendant

(2) If your answer to the above is more than five (5) months after the summons issued in this case, give reasons for further delay.

Plaintiff Defendant

(3) When do you expect to complete your discovery efforts?

Plaintiff Defendant

(4) What additional discovery do you require to prepare for trial?

Plaintiff Defendant

E. TRIAL TIME:

(1) What is your estimate of the time required to present your side of the case at trial (including rebuttal stage, if applicable)?

Plaintiff ______ Defendant ______

(2) How many witnesses do you intend to call at trial (including opposing parties)?

Plaintiff ______ Defendant ______

(3) Are any of the witnesses considered expert witnesses (Fed. R. Evid. 702)? If so, the parties agree to identify their expert witnesses by ______.
(See Fed. R. Bankr. P. 7026(a)(2)(C))

(4) How many exhibits do you anticipate using at trial?

Plaintiff ______ Defendant ______

(5) Are any special accommodations required for witnesses (e.g., assisted listening devices, etc.)? Check one:

☐ No ☐Yes—Please specify:

(6) Is any special equipment required for presentation of evidence? Check one:

☐ No ☐Yes—Please specify:

F. ADDITIONAL COMMENTS/RECOMMENDATIONS RE TRIAL: *(Use additional page if necessary.)*

Dated: ______ Dated: ______

______
Firm Name

______
Firm Name

By: ______
Name:
Attorney for: ______

By: ______
Name:
Attorney for: ______

Local Bankruptcy Rule 7016-2(c) requires this form to be filed no later than five (5) days after early conference of counsel together with the *NOTICE OF PRE-TRIAL STATUS CONFERENCE* (Local Form CSD 3019).

EXHIBIT A

1) **DISCOVERY PLAN**. The parties jointly propose to the court the

following discovery plan: [Use separate paragraphs or subparagraphs as necessary if parties disagree.]

Discovery will be needed on the following subjects: (brief description of subjects on which discovery will be needed)

All discovery commenced in time to be completed by ___________. [Discovery on (issue for early discovery) to be completed by ___________.]

Maximum of___________interrogatories by each party to any other part. [Responses due___________days after service.]

Maximum of___________requests for admission by each party to any other party. [Responses due___________days after service.]

Maximum of___________depositions by plaintiff(s) and___________by defendant(s).

Each deposition [other than of ___________] limited to maximum of___________hours unless extended by agreement of parties.

Reports from retained experts under Fed. R. Bank. P. 7026(a)(2) due:

a) from plaintiff(s) by ___________

b) from defendant(s) by ___________

Supplementations under Fed. R. Bank. P. 7026(e) due (time(s) or interval(s)).

2) **OTHER ITEMS**. [Use separate paragraphs or subparagraphs as necessary if parties disagree.]

Plaintiff(s) should be allowed until___________to join additional parties and until___________to amend the pleadings.

Defendant(s) should be allowed until___________to join additional parties and until___________to amend the pleadings.

All potentially dispositive motions should be filed by ___________.

Final lists of witnesses and exhibits under Fed. R. Bank. P. 7026(a)(3) should be due

a) from plaintiff(s) by ___________

b) from defendant(s) by ___________

Parties should have___________days after service of final lists of witnesses and exhibits to list objections under Fed. R. Bank. P. 7026(a)(3).

[Other matters.]

CSD 3021

Pre-trial Order

CSD 3021 [08/21/00]
Name, Address, Telephone No. & I.D. No.

UNITED STATES BANKRUPTCY COURT
SOUTHERN DISTRICT OF CALIFORNIA

325 West "F" Street, San Diego, California 92101-6991

In Re Debtor. Plaintiff(s) v. Defendants(s)*[sic]*	BANKRUPTCY NO. ADVERSARY NO. Date of Hearing: Time of Hearing: Name of Judge:

PRE-TRIAL ORDER

IT IS ORDERED THAT the relief sought as set forth on the continuation pages attached and numbered two (2) through ___________ with exhibits, if any, for a total of ___________ pages, is granted.

//
//
//
//

DATED:

____
Judge, United States Bankruptcy Court

Signature by the attorney constitutes a certification under Fed. R. of Bankr. P.9011 that the relief in the order is the relief granted by the court.

Submitted by:

____
(Firm name)

By: _______________________
Attorney for Movant

Following pre-trial proceedings pursuant to Fed. R. of Bankr. P.7016 and Local Bankruptcy Rule 7016,

IT IS ORDERED:

1. This is an action for: *[state nature of action, designate the parties and list the pleadings which raise the issues]*

2. Federal jurisdiction and venue are invoked upon the ground: *[list a concise statement of the facts and statutory basis requisite to confer federal jurisdiction and venue, including whether the matter is a core or non-core proceeding]*

3. The following facts are admitted and require no proof: *[list each admitted fact, including jurisdictional facts]*

4. The reservations as to the facts cited in paragraph 3 above are as follows: *[set forth any objection reserved by any party as to the admissibility in evidence of any admitted fact, and if desired by any party, limiting the effect of any issue of fact as provided by Federal Rule of Bankruptcy Procedure 7036]*

5. The following facts, though not admitted, are not to be contested at the trial by evidence to the contrary: *[list each]*

6. The following issues of fact, and no others, remain to be litigated during the trial: *[specify each; a mere general statement will not suffice]*

7. The exhibits to be offered at the trial, together with a statement of all admissions by, and all issues between, the parties with respect thereto, are as follows: *[list all documents and things intended to be offered at the trial by each party, other than those to be used for impeachment, in the sequence proposed to be offered, with a description of each sufficient for identification. Also include a statement of all admissions by and all issues between any of the parties as to the genuineness thereof, the due execution thereof, and the truth of relevant matters of fact set forth therein or in any legend affixed thereto, together with a statement of any objections reserved as to the admissibility in evidence thereof]*

8. A list of witnesses to be called by plaintiff and defendant is attached as Exhibit ____________.

9. The following issues of law, and no others, remain to be litigated upon the trial: *[set forth a concise statement of each]*

10. The foregoing admissions having been made by the parties, and the parties having specified the foregoing issues of fact and law remaining to be litigated, the order shall supplement the pleadings and govern the course of the trial of this cause, unless modified to prevent manifest injustice.

11. This case shall be tried by [jury] [the Court without a jury].

12. Time estimated for trial is ___________days.

APPROVED AS TO FORM AND CONTENT:

____

Attorney for Plaintiff

____

Attorney for Defendant

No. CSD 3026

List of Exhibits Submitted by Attorney

CSD 3026 [01/01/02]
Name, Address, Telephone No. & I.D. No.

. . . .

UNITED STATES BANKRUPTCY COURT
SOUTHERN DISTRICT OF CALIFORNIA

325 West "F" Street, San Diego, California 92101-6991M

In Re
Debtor.
. . . .
Plaintiff(s)
. . . .
v.
Defendants(s)
. . . .

BANKRUPTCY NO.
ADVERSARY NO.

LIST OF EXHIBITS SUBMITTED BY:

. . . . , Attorney for
[ ] Plaintiff(s) [ ] Defendant(s) [ ] Other:. . . . .

PLEASE COMPLY WITH INSTRUCTIONS ON REVERSE WHEN COMPLETING THIS FORM

EXHIBIT NUMBER	DATE SUB-MITTED	DATE ADMIT-TED	DATE RE-FUSED	DESCRIPTION
. . . .	. . . .	. . . .	. . . .	. . . .

EXHIBIT NUMBER	DATE SUB-MITTED	DATE ADMIT-TED	LEGAL GROUND FOR OBJEC-TION	DESCRIP-TION
. . . .	. . . .	. . . .	. . . .	. . . .

EXHIBITS ARE TO BE SUBMITTED TO THE COURT AT THE TIME OF TRIAL. THEY ARE NOT [TO] BE FILED WITH THE OFFICE OF THE CLERK.

GROUNDS FOR OBJECTION

1. No Objection: Admissibility Stipulated
2. Irrelevant
3. Hearsay
4. Best Evidence
5. Inadmissible Opinion
6. Insufficient Foundation (Relevancy, Personal Knowledge, Authenticity)
7. Unduly Time Consuming, Prejudicial, Confusing or Misleading
8. Other (Specify)

INSTRUCTIONS

1. Counsel for the plaintiff shall have the duty of arranging meetings of counsel prior to the first date fixed for trial or pre-trial.

2. In advance of the first date fixed for trial or pre-trial, the attorney for the parties shall meet together at a convenient time and place for the purpose of arriving at stipulations and agreements, all for the purpose of simplifying the issues to be tried. At this conference between counsel, all exhibits other than those to be used for impeachment shall be exchanged and examined and counsel shall also exchange a list of the name and addresses of witnesses to be called at the trial, including expert witnesses; each photograph, map, drawing and the like shall bear, upon the reverse side thereof, a concise legend stating the relevant matters of fact as to what is claimed to be fairly depicted thereby, and as of what date. Each attorney shall also then make known to opposing counsel his contention regarding the applicable facts and law. Exhibits are not to be filed with the Office of the Clerk.

FAILURE TO DISPLAY EXHIBITS TO OPPOSING COUNSEL AS REQUIRED BY LOCAL RULE SHALL AUTHORIZE THE COURT TO REFUSE TO ADMIT THE SAME INTO EVIDENCE

3. The form contained on the reverse side hereon, List of Exhibits, shall be completed prior to trial. The original shall be presented to the Bankruptcy Judge at the time of trial and copies shall be furnished to each opposing counsel.

4. Exhibits presented by the plaintiff shall be numbered in numerical sequence commencing with the number 1.

5. Exhibits presented by defendants shall be numbered in alphabetical sequence as follow: A-Z, AA-ZZ, AAA-ZZZ, etc. When more than one defendant, the numbering sequence should be further broken down by sub-numbers: exhibits for defendant number one would be A-1, B-1, C-1; for defendant number two A-2, B-2, C-2, and so forth.

. . . .

EXHIBIT NUMBER	DATE SUB-MITTED	DATE ADMIT-TED	LEGAL GROUND FOR OBJEC-TION	DESCRIPTION

. . . .

GROUNDS FOR OBJECTION

1. No Objection: Admissibility Stipulated
2. Irrelevant
3. Hearsay
4. Best Evidence
5. Inadmissible Opinion
6. Insufficient Foundation (Relevancy, Personal Knowledge, Authenticity)
7. Unduly Time Consuming, Prejudicial, Confusing or Misleading
8. Other (Specify)

CSD 3029

Judgment by Default

CSD 3029 [2/11/04]
Name, Addressee, Telephone No. & I.D. No.

UNITED STATES BANKRUPTCY COURT
SOUTHERN DISTRICT CF CALIFORNIA

325 West "F" Street, San Diego, California 92101-6991

In Re

Debtor.

____

Plaintiff(s)

v.

Defendants(s) [*sic*]

BANKRUPTCY NO.
ADVERSARY NO.

JUDGMENT BY DEFAULT

IT IS ORDERED THAT the relief sought as set forth on the continuation pages attached and numbered two (2) through ____________with exhibits, if any, for a total of ____________ pages, is granted. Request for Default Docket Entry No. ____________

//

//

//

//

DATED:

____

Judge, United States Bankruptcy Court

Signature by the attorney constitutes a certification under Fed. R. of Bankr. P. 9011 that the relief in the order is the relief granted by the court.

Submitted by:

____

(Firm name)

By: ______________________________

Attorney for Movant

Default was entered against defendant,____________on ____________. Therefore, on motion of the plaintiff, judgment is entered against that defendant in favor of the plaintiff as follows.

IT IS ORDERED THAT:

CSD 3030

Request to Enter Default
(Rev. 05/15/03)

REQUEST TO ENTER DEFAULT

TO THE APPLICANT: The following statements must be true in order to enter the default. Please verify by checking applicable boxes:

[ ] Service of Summons and Complaint was made at the defendant's dwelling house, usual place of abode or the place where the defendant regularly conducts business pursuant to FRBP 7004(b).

[ ] Service of Summons and Complaint was made on attorney for debtor, if any, pursuant to FRBP 7004(b)(9).

[ ] Service of Summons and Complaint on defendant was made within 10 days of issuance of the summons pursuant to FRBP 7004(e).

[ ] Proof of Service of the Summons and Complaint has been filed with the court pursuant to LBR 9006-3.

[ ] Neither a motion nor an answer to the complaint was filed by the defendant named above within 30 days of issuance of the summons pursuant to FRBP 7012. The United States, its offices and agencies, have 35 days to file a motion or answer.

[ ] The defendant is an individual and is not entitled to benefits of military status. The Declaration of Non-Military Status has been completed on page 2 of this Request.

[ ] The declaration or affidavit in support of this Request is filed concurrently as required by LBR 7055-1(b).

TO THE CLERK: Please enter the default in the above-entitled complaint of the following-named Defendant(s) ONLY.

(If additional space is need, attach an exhibit listing all Defendants for which a default is requested)

Check the applicable box:

[ ] A judgment by default is submitted herewith.

[ ] There are multiple defendants. Judgment by default will be included in the final judgment.

DATED: ____________

____

Signature of (Attorney for) Plaintiff

DECLARATION OF MAILING

[Complete if default is requested AFTER defendant entered appearance (F.R.Civ.P 55(b)(2).]

On ____________, a copy of this Request to Enter Default was mailed (by first-class mail or airmail, postage prepaid) to the defendant, if the debtor, and attorney for each defendant against whom the default is requested, at the last known address of each, addressed as follows:

The address of the following defendant and defendant's attorney of record is unknown to plaintiff and plaintiff's attorney:

I certify (or declare) under penalty of perjury that the foregoing is true and correct, and that this declaration is executed on ____________, at ____________, ____________.

____

(Type or Print Name)

____

(Signature of Declarant)

MEMORANDUM OF COSTS

Costs and disbursements are listed as follows:

a. Clerk's Filing Fee . . . . $
b. Process Server's Fees . . . . $
c. . . . . $
d. . . . . $
TOTAL . . . . $

I am (the attorney or agent for):____________, the party who claims these costs. To the best of my knowledge and belief the foregoing items of cost are correct and have been necessarily incurred in this action.

I certify (or declare) under penalty of perjury that the foregoing is true and correct, and that this declaration is executed on ____________, at ____________.

____

(Type or Print Name)

____
(Signature of Declarant)

DECLARATION OF NON-MILITARY STATUS

[Not required if the defendant is a partnership, corporation or trustee in bankruptcy.]

Defendant (Name): ____________, is not in the military service or in the military service of the United States as defined in Section 101 of the Soldiers' and Sailors' Relief Act of 1940, as amended, and not entitled to the benefits of the Act.

I certify (or declare) under penalty of perjury that the foregoing is true and correct, and that this declaration is executed on __________, at ____________.

____
(Type or Print Name)

____
(Signature of Declarant)

CSD 3050

Notice of Entry of Judgment (Rev. 10/17/05)

NOTICE OF ENTRY OF JUDGMENT OR ORDER

TO THE PARTIES IN INTEREST NAMED BELOW:

You are hereby notified that on ____________this Court entered in the docket for the above-entitled case the following Judgment [or Order] to wit:

I hereby certify that on this date a copy of this notice was mailed to the following parties in interest: [check as appropriate]

[ ] UNITED STATES TRUSTEE, Department of Justice, 402 West Broadway, Suite 600, San Diego, CA 92101

[ ] THOMAS H. BILLINGSLEA, JR., 530 "B" Street, Suite 1500, San Diego, CA 92112

(For ODD numbered Chapter 13 cases)

[ ] DAVID L. SKELTON, 600 "B" Street, Suite 2000, San Diego, CA 92101-4507

(For EVEN numbered Chapter 13 cases)

[ ] Chapter 7 Trustee:
and in addition: [Continue on reverse, if necessary]

DATED:____________ Barry K. Lander, Clerk

By: ________________________, Deputy Clerk

No. CSD 3054

Certification of Judgment for Registration in Another District

CSD 3054 [03/26/99]
Name, Address, Telephone No. & I.D. No.

. . . .

UNITED STATES BANKRUPTCY COURT
SOUTHERN DISTRICT OF CALIFORNIA
325 West "F" Street, San Diego, California 92101-6991

In Re
Debtor.
. . . .
Plaintiff(s)
. . . .
v.
Defendants(s)
. . . .

BANKRUPTCY NO.
ADVERSARY NO.

CERTIFICATION OF JUDGMENT FOR REGISTRATION IN ANOTHER DISTRICT

I, Clerk of the Bankruptcy Court of this District, do certify that the attached judgment is a true and correct COPY of the original judgment entered in the above entitled proceeding on . . . . , as it appears of record in my office, and that:

[ ] No notice of appeal from this judgment has been filed, and no motion of the kind set forth in Federal Rule of Civil Procedure 60, as made applicable by Federal Rule of Bankruptcy Procedure 9024, has been filed.

[ ] No notice of appeal from this judgment has been filed, and any motions of the kind set forth in Federal Rule of Civil Procedure 60, as made applicable by Federal Rule of Bankruptcy Procedure 9024, have been disposed of, the latest order disposing of such a motion having been entered on . . . .

[ ] An appeal was taken from this judgment, and the judgment was affirmed by mandate of the [ ] United States Court of Appeals [ ] United States District Court [ ] Bankruptcy Appellate Panel issued on . . . .

[ ] An appeal was taken from this judgment, and the appeal was dismissed by order entered on . . . .

DATED:
Barry K. Lander, Clerk
By: . . . . , Deputy Clerk

SDCAL-305 S.D. CALIFORNIA

No. CSD 3060

Application for Order to Appear for Examination and Order Thereon

CSD 3060 [04/28/96]
Name, Address, Telephone No. & I.D. No.

. . . .

UNITED STATES BANKRUPTCY COURT
SOUTHERN DISTRICT OF CALIFORNIA
325 West "F" Street, San Diego, California 92101-6991

In Re Debtor. . . . . Plaintiff(s) . . . . v. Defendants(s)	BANKRUPTCY NO. ADVERSARY NO.

APPLICATION FOR ORDER TO APPEAR FOR EXAMINATION AND ORDER THEREON

1. [ ] Judgment creditor [ ] Assignee of record [ ] Plaintiff who has a right to attach order applies for an order requiring *(name):* . . . . to appear and furnish information to aid in enforcement of the money judgment or to answer concerning property or debt.

2. The person to be examined is [ ] the judgment debtor [ ] a third person (1) who has possession or control of property belonging to the judgment debtor or the defendant or (2) who owes the judgment debtor or the defendant more than $250. An affidavit supporting this application under CCP § 491.110 or § 708.120 is attached.

3. The person to be examined resides or has a place of business in this county or within 150 miles of the place of examination.

4. [ ] This court is not the court in which the money judgment is entered or *(attachment only)* the court that issued the writ of attachment. An affidavit supporting an application under CCP § 491.150 or § 708.160 is attached.

5. [ ] The judgment debtor has been examined within the past 120 days. An affidavit showing good cause for another examination is attached.

I declare under penalty of perjury under the laws of the State of California that the foregoing is true and correct.

Dated:

________________________ [Attorney for] Moving Party

ORDER

1. TO *(name):*
2. YOU ARE ORDERED TO APPEAR personally at the place, date, and time specified below to
   a. [ ] furnish information to aid in enforcement of a money judgment against you,
   b. [ ] answer concerning property of the judgment debtor in your possession or control or concerning a debt you owe the judgment debtor, or
   c. [ ] answer concerning property of the defendant in your possession or control or concerning a debt you owe the defendant that is subject to attachment.

. . . .

PLACE DATE AND TIME

. . . .

3. This order may be served by a sheriff, marshal, constable, registered process server, or the following specially appointed person *(name):*

Dated:

. . . .

Judge, United States Bankruptcy Court

THIS ORDER MUST BE SERVED NOT LESS THAN 10 DAYS PRIOR TO THE DATE SET FOR EXAMINATION.

. . . .

APPEARANCE OF JUDGMENT DEBTOR (ENFORCEMENT OF JUDGMENT)

NOTICE TO JUDGMENT DEBTOR: If you fail to appear at the time and

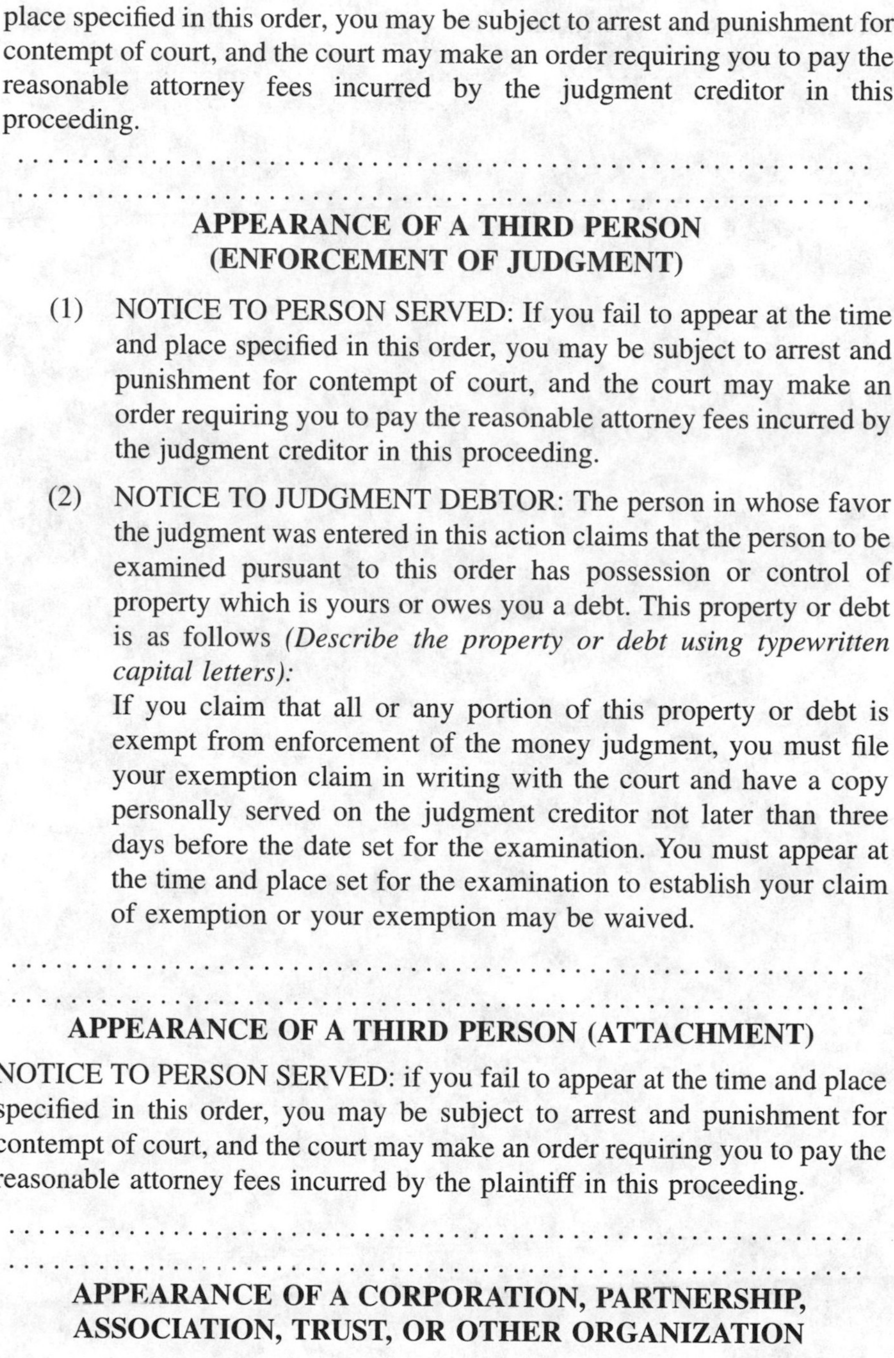

place specified in this order, you may be subject to arrest and punishment for contempt of court, and the court may make an order requiring you to pay the reasonable attorney fees incurred by the judgment creditor in this proceeding.

. . . .

. . . .

APPEARANCE OF A THIRD PERSON (ENFORCEMENT OF JUDGMENT)

(1) NOTICE TO PERSON SERVED: If you fail to appear at the time and place specified in this order, you may be subject to arrest and punishment for contempt of court, and the court may make an order requiring you to pay the reasonable attorney fees incurred by the judgment creditor in this proceeding.

(2) NOTICE TO JUDGMENT DEBTOR: The person in whose favor the judgment was entered in this action claims that the person to be examined pursuant to this order has possession or control of property which is yours or owes you a debt. This property or debt is as follows *(Describe the property or debt using typewritten capital letters):*

If you claim that all or any portion of this property or debt is exempt from enforcement of the money judgment, you must file your exemption claim in writing with the court and have a copy personally served on the judgment creditor not later than three days before the date set for the examination. You must appear at the time and place set for the examination to establish your claim of exemption or your exemption may be waived.

. . . .

. . . .

APPEARANCE OF A THIRD PERSON (ATTACHMENT)

NOTICE TO PERSON SERVED: if you fail to appear at the time and place specified in this order, you may be subject to arrest and punishment for contempt of court, and the court may make an order requiring you to pay the reasonable attorney fees incurred by the plaintiff in this proceeding.

. . . .

. . . .

APPEARANCE OF A CORPORATION, PARTNERSHIP, ASSOCIATION, TRUST, OR OTHER ORGANIZATION

It is your duty to designate one or more of the following to appear and be examined: officers, directors, managing agents, or other persons who are familiar with your property and debts.

. . . .

. . . .

SDCAL-309 S.D. CALIFORNIA

No. CSD 3066

Bill of Costs

CSD 3066 [03/26/99]
Name, Address, Telephone No. & I.D. No.

. . . .

UNITED STATES BANKRUPTCY COURT
SOUTHERN DISTRICT OF CALIFORNIA

325 West "F" Street, San Diego, California 92101-6991

In Re Debtor. . . . . Plaintiff(s) . . . . v. Defendants(s)	BANKRUPTCY NO. ADVERSARY NO. DATE: TIME:

BILL OF COSTS

Notice is given that the following Bill of Costs will be presented to the Clerk of the Bankruptcy Court on the date and at the time stated above in *Room 234* of the Jacob Weinberger U.S. Courthouse, 325 West "F" Street, San Diego, California.

Judgment was entered in the above entitled action on . . . . against:

The clerk of the bankruptcy court is requested to tax the following as costs:

Fees of the clerk	$ . . . . . .
Fees for service of summons and complaint	$ . . . . . .
Fees of the court reporter for any and all part of the transcript necessarily obtained for use in the case	$ . . . . . .
Fees and disbursements for printing	$ . . . . . .
Fees for witnesses (itemized on reverse)	$ . . . . . .
Fees for exemplifications and copies of papers necessarily obtained for use in this case	$ . . . . . .
Docket fees under 28 U.S.C. § 1923	$ . . . . . .

Costs incident to taking of depositions . . . . $ . . . . . .
Costs as shown on Mandate of appellate court . . . . $ . . . . . .
Other costs [Please itemize] $ . . . . . .
TOTAL $ . . . . . .

DECLARATION

I, attorney for . . . . , declare under penalties of perjury that the foregoing costs are correct and were necessarily incurred in this action, that the services for which fees have been charged were actually and necessarily performed, and that a copy of this Bill of Costs was mailed this day with postage fully prepaid to *(insert Name and Address of Judgment Debtor):*

DATED:

____________________ [Attorney for] Moving Party

COSTS ARE TAXED IN THE FOLLOWING AMOUNT AND INCLUDED IN THE JUDGMENT: $. . . . .

DATED:

. . . . , Clerk

. . . .

WITNESS FEES
(computation, cf. 28 U.S.C. 1821 for statutory fees)

NAME AND RESIDENCE	ATTENDANCE		SUBSISTENCE		MILEAGE		TOTAL COST EACH WITNESS
	DAYS	TOTAL COSTS	DAYS	TOTAL COSTS	MILES	TOTAL COSTS	
						TOTAL	

NOTICE

Section 1924, Title 28, U.S. Code provides:

"Before any bill of costs is taxed, the party claiming any item of cost or disbursement shall attach thereto an affidavit, made by himself or by his duly authorized attorney or agent having knowledge of the facts, that such item is correct and has been necessarily incurred in the case and that the services for which fees have been charged were actually and necessarily performed."

Section 1920 of Title 28 reads in part as follows:

"A bill of costs shall be filed in the case and, upon allowance, included in the judgment or decree."

The Federal Rules of Bankruptcy Procedure contain the following provisions:

FRBP 7054(b)

"COSTS. The court may allow to the prevailing party except when a statute of the United States or these rules otherwise provides. Costs against the United States, its officers and agencies shall be imposed only to the extent permitted by law. Costs may be taxed by the clerk on one day's notice; on motion served within five days thereafter, the action of the clerk may be reviewed by the court."

FRBP 9006(f)

"ADDITIONAL TIME AFTER SERVICE BY MAIL. When there is a right or requirement to do some act or undertake some proceedings within a prescribed period after service of a notice or other paper and the notice or paper other than process is served by mail, three days shall be added to the prescribed period."

Federal Rule of Civil Procedure 58 reads in part:

"Entry of the judgment shall not be delayed . . . in order to tax costs."

District Court Local Rule 54.1 governs costs in this district. CSD 3066

No. CSD 4000

Application to Join Compensated Mediation Panel

CSD 4000 [09/08/97]

UNITED STATES BANKRUPTCY COURT
Southern District of California

APPLICATION TO JOIN COMPENSATED MEDIATION PANEL

Name: . . . . Phone Number: . . . .
Address: . . . .

Applicant has completed 25 hours of mediation training at the San Diego Mediation Center or at . . . . , which is a training center qualified under Title 16 California Dispute Resolution Act, Section 3615–3635 and Sections 465–467.7 of the California Business and Professions Code. The training was completed on . . . .

During the preceding calendar year, applicant has

1) conducted two (2) bankruptcy mediations or six (6) hours of mediation for another source. Please describe mediation by case name or other identifying information:

OR

2) attended a half-day refresher program provided by the San Diego Mediation Center or an equivalent qualified center consistent with the California Dispute Resolution Act. The refresher program was held on . . . .

[ ] [Optional] Biographical information is set forth on Exhibit A.

[ ] [If an attorney] Applicant's California State Bar Number is: . . . .

Applicant understands that a yearly renewal application must be filed with the Chief Judge of the Bankruptcy Court no later than December 15 of the year prior to the calendar year in which compensated mediation will be conducted.

I hereby certify that the undersigned meets the qualifications for membership to the Compensated Mediation Panel and that the foregoing is true and correct.

Dated: . . . .
(Signature)

SDCAL-313 S.D. CALIFORNIA

FORWARD TO:

SAN DIEGO COUNTY BAR ASSOCIATION
Attn: Study Section
1434 Fifth Avenue
San Diego, California 92101

[Exhibit to CSD 4000]

CSD 4000 [09/08/97]—**EXHIBIT**

UNITED STATES BANKRUPTCY COURT
Southern District of California

MEDIATOR BIOGRAPHICAL INFORMATION

Name: .... Phone Number: ....
Address: .... Fax Number: ....
Education (list institutions, degrees, dates):
Mediation training (list name of trainer and number of hours):
Types of disputes handled and subject matter specialties (check all applicable categories):

[ ] General
[ ] Bankruptcy/Business/Commercial
[ ] Community/Neighborhood
[ ] Construction
[ ] Employment/Labor Relations
[ ] Environmental
[ ] Governmental/Public Agency
[ ] Family/Dissolution
[ ] Personal Injury
[ ] Property/Real Estate
[ ] Other:

Experience—How long have you been providing this service?

List relevant organizations, panels, or programs in which you are a member (e.g.; Superior Court Arbitration, American Arbitration Association, Center for Public Resources, etc.):

No. CSD 4001

Application to Join Voluntary Mediation Panel

CSD 4001 [09/08/97]

UNITED STATES BANKRUPTCY COURT
Southern District of California

APPLICATION TO JOIN VOLUNTARY MEDIATION PANEL

Name: . . . . Phone Number: . . . .
Address: . . . .

[ ] Applicant is an attorney. California State Bar Number:. . . . .

Are you a member of the United States District Court for the Southern District of California?

[ ] Yes-Date of Admission: . . . . [ ] No

List three bankruptcy matters in which you have either:

a. served as attorney of record from commencement to confirmation or discharge; or,

b. served as attorney of record for a party in interest in three or more adversary proceedings or contested matters from commencement through completion (i.e., judgment, order or stipulation).

Case Title	Case Number	Dates
1.		
2.		
3.		

[ ] Applicant is not an attorney. Applicant is [ ] a member of the panel of trustees or examiners maintained by the Office of the United States Trustee or [ ] a Certified Public Accountant in the State of California.

List ten bankruptcy matters in which you have demonstrated service as either:

a. a trustee in an asset bankruptcy estate; or

b. a bankruptcy examiner or accountant for a trustee or debtor-in-possession from commencement through completition [sic] of such case; or

c. or other substantially equivalent service.

Case Title Case Number Dates

1.
2.
3.
4.
5.
6.
7.
8.
9.
10.

I hereby certify that the undersigned meets the qualifications for membership to the Voluntary Mediation Panel and that the foregoing is true and correct.

Dated: ....

(Signature)

FORWARD TO:

SAN DIEGO COUNTY BAR ASSOCIATION
Attn: Study Section
1434 Fifth Avenue
San Diego, California 92101

No. CSD 4002

Order Appointing Mediator and Assignment to Mediation

CSD 4002 [04/28/96]

. . . .

UNITED STATES BANKRUPTCY COURT
SOUTHERN DISTRICT OF CALIFORNIA
325 West "F" Street, San Diego, California 92101-6991

In Re

Debtor.

. . . .

Plaintiff(s)

. . . .

v.

Defendants(s)

. . . .

BANKRUPTCY NO.

ADVERSARY NO.

ORDER APPOINTING MEDIATOR AND ASSIGNMENT TO MEDIATION

The above-captioned matter is hereby assigned to the following mediator or, if such mediator is unable to serve, to the alternate (insert Name, Address, & Telephone No.):

MEDIATOR: **ALTERNATE MEDIATOR:**

The matter concerns:

☐ Dischargeability ☐ Objection to Claim
☐ Lien Avoidance ☐ Other:

The Attorneys for the parties are (insert Name, Address, & Telephone No.):

The parties are ordered to comply with the provisions of Local Bankruptcy Rule 7016-6, including submission of the case questionnaire to the mediator seven (7) days before the mediation conference.

DATED:

. . . .
Judge, United States Bankruptcy Court

CERTIFICATE OF MAILING

I hereby certify that on this date a copy of the within order was mailed to all parties listed by name and address on this order.

DATED:
Clerk
By: . . . . , Deputy Clerk

SDCAL-319 S.D. CALIFORNIA

No. CSD 4004

Mediator's Certificate of Compliance

CSD 4004 [04/28/96]
Name, Address, Telephone No. & I.D. No.

. . . .

UNITED STATES BANKRUPTCY COURT
SOUTHERN DISTRICT OF CALIFORNIA

325 West "F" Street, San Diego, California 92101-6991

In Re Debtor. . . . . Plaintiff(s) . . . . v. Defendants(s)	BANKRUPTCY NO. ADVERSARY NO.

MEDIATOR'S CERTIFICATE OF COMPLIANCE

I, ... , the Court appointed Mediator, declare:

1. Date of Mediation: . . . .

Continued Date:

(If applicable) . . . .

2. The Rules governing mediation have . . . . . . have not . . . . . . been complied with.

3. A settlement of this matter has . . . . . . has not . . . . . . been reached.

4. If settlement has been reached, ... , (plaintiff) (defendant), shall prepare the stipulation for settlement.

Dated: . . . .

(Mediator)

FOR COURT USE ONLY (Case Management Section):

cc: Courtroom Deputy

CSD 4025

Documents Required for Processing an Application for Unclaimed Funds

CSD 4025 [01/06/00]

UNITED STATES BANKRUPTCY COURT
SOUTHERN DISTRICT OF CALIFORNIA

325 West F Street, San Diego, California 92101-6991

DOCUMENTS REQUIRED FOR PROCESSING AN APPLICATION FOR UNCLAIMED FUNDS

In order to timely process your application for funds you may be entitled to, the Court requires the original and two (2) copies of the documents listed below. In addition, a self-addressed stamped envelope must be submitted.

IF CLAIMANT IS ASSISTED BY A FUNDS LOCATOR, you must submit all of the following:

- ☐ Completed *APPLICATION FOR RETURN OF TENDERED FUNDS,* (CSD 4014)
- ☐ Completed *PROOF OF RIGHT TO PAYMENT OF DIVIDEND FROM UNCLAIMED FUNDS,* (CSD 4026)
- ☐ Completed Limited Power of Attorney form (attach to *APPLICATION*)

IF CLAIMANT REPRESENTS A CORPORATION, you must submit all of the following:

- ☐ Completed *APPLICATION FOR RETURN OF TENDERED FUNDS,* (CSD 4014)
- ☐ Completed *PROOF OF RIGHT TO PAYMENT OF DIVIDEND FROM UNCLAIMED FUNDS* (CSD 4026)
- ☐ Copy of Certificate/Article of Incorporation (attach to *PROOF OF RIGHT* form;)

OR

Certificate/Articles of Merger or Successor Corporation (attach to *PROOF OF RIGHT* form)

IF CLAIMANT IS AN INDIVIDUAL, you must submit all of the following:

☐ Completed *APPLICATION FOR RETURN OF TENDERED FUNDS*, (CSD 4014)

☐ Completed *PROOF OF RIGHT TO PAYMENT OF DIVIDEND FROM UNCLAIMED FUNDS*, (CSD 4026)

☐ Photocopy of current driver's license (attach to *PROOF OF RIGHT* form). If you do not have a current driver's license, other identification containing a photograph and current address is required.

☐ If claimant was the debtor, a photocopy of your Social Security card with number (attach to *PROOF OF RIGHT* form).

BARRY K. LANDER
Clerk of Court

CHAPTER 13 PLAN (CAS)

UNITED STATES BANKRUPTCY COURT
SOUTHERN DISTRICT OF CALIFORNIA

Chapter 13 Plan (Recommended Form)

In Re: Case Number: ____________________

☐ Original Plan
☐ Amended Plan

CREDITORS: YOU SHOULD READ THIS PLAN CAREFULLY AND DISCUSS IT WITH YOUR ATTORNEY. CONFIRMATION OF THIS PLAN BY THE BANKRUPTCY COURT MAY MODIFY YOUR RIGHTS IN SEVERAL WAYS INCLUDING PROVIDING FOR PAYMENT OF LESS THAN THE FULL AMOUNT OF YOUR CLAIM, SETTING THE VALUE OF THE COLLATERAL SECURING YOUR CLAIM, AND SETTING THE INTEREST RATE ON YOUR CLAIM.

1. **Plan Payments.** There shall be paid to the Chapter 13 Trustee the amount of____________________ each month by debtor(s), or any entity from whom debtor(s) receive income, in such installments as agreed upon with the Trustee, for payment of all existing debts of debtor(s) pursuant to this Plan, except as the Court may otherwise order. Payments from debtor(s) shall begin within 30 days of filing the petition or conversion order. Debtor(s) submit all future income to the supervision and control of the Trustee during this case and agree to pay sufficient funds to the Trustee on or before five years from commencement of this case to fully complete this Plan.

2. **Pre-confirmation Adequate Protection Payments.** If direct payments to creditors pursuant to §1326(a) are made, debtor will immediately provide trustee evidence of the payments including the creditor name and address and the amount and date of each payment. Trustee is under no obligation to adjust filed and allowed claims unless there is a court order or specific written direction from the claimant.

3. **Administrative Claims.** Trustee will pay allowed administrative claims and expenses in full pursuant to §1326(b) as set forth below unless the holder of such claim has agreed to a different treatment of its claim:

(A). Trustees Fees: The Chapter 13 Trustee shall receive a fee at the time of each disbursement, the percentage of which is set by the United States Trustee.

(B). Debtor's Attorney Fees: Debtor's attorney shall be paid after creditors listed in paragraph 7 except as checked below:

_____ Attorney fees to be paid in full prior to other claims. (Do not check this option if lease payments/adequate protection payments are necessary).

_____ Attorney fees to be paid at the rate of $_______________ per month prior to other claims. (If no amount is filled in attorney will be paid after creditors listed in paragraph 7).

(C). Except as ordered by the court, other §1326(b) claims will be paid in installments as set by the trustee in advance of other claims. All other claims entitled to priority and post petition claims allowed by law shall be paid in full by deferred payments in such priority and installments as the trustee in his discretion deems appropriate, unless this plan specifically provides otherwise.

4. **Specified Leases, Personal Property (Trustee to pay).** Debtor(s) elect to assume the existing lease of personal property with the below named creditors:

(A). REGULAR LEASE PAYMENTS: After payments provided in prior paragraphs, trustee shall make distribution to named lease creditors in the installment specified from funds available for distribution monthly until claim is paid in the amount allowed. Any option to purchase or any payments under a carry-over provision shall be paid by debtor(s) directly.

(B). ARREARS LEASE PAYMENTS: After the regular monthly lease payment above, trustee shall pay any lease arrears to named lease creditors in the installment specified from funds available monthly until claim is paid in the amount allowed.

Name of Creditor	Regular Monthly Payment Installment	Estimated Arrears	Arrears Installment
____________________	_______________	__________	__________
____________________	_______________	__________	__________

Case Number: ____________________

5. **Specified Secured Claims, Personal Property.** After payments provided for by prior paragraphs, Trustee shall make payment to creditors (their agents and assigns) named in this paragraph whose claims are allowed secured solely by personal property. Each named creditor shall be paid in installments from funds available for distribution monthly, non-cumulative, as indicated until claim is paid in amount allowed secured plus interest at seven percent (7%) per annum unless a different percentage is specified below. The balance of the claim shall be treated as unsecured. **Upon confirmation, creditor will be deemed to accept the classification, valuation and interest rate set forth and payment pursuant to this provision will be binding, even if creditor is not subject to §506 valuation, unless creditor timely objects and the court orders otherwise.**

Name of Creditor	Allowed Secured Value	Installment	(Optional) % Interest
____________	________	________	________
____________	________	________	________
____________	________	________	________

6. **Specified Secured Claims, personal Property (§506 valuation not applicable) (purchase money security interest in vehicles purchased for personal use within 910 days of filing the petition or other secured debt within one year of filing the petition).** Creditors named in this paragraph shall be paid in the same priority as creditors listed in paragraph 5 above but in full for allowed claims secured solely by personal property for which §506 valuation is not applicable. Each named creditor shall be paid in installments from funds available for distribution monthly, non-cumulative, as indicated until claim is paid in amount allowed plus interest at seven percent (7%) per annum unless a different percentage is specified below. **Upon confirmation, the interest rate set forth will be binding unless creditor timely objects and the court orders otherwise.**

Name of Creditor	Estimated Claim	Installment	(Optional) % Interest
____________	________	________	________
____________	________	________	________
____________	________	________	________

7. **Domestic Support Obligations**. After payments provided for in prior paragraphs, allowed claims for a domestic support obligation as defined by §507(a)(1), shall be paid, as to amounts due and payable at the commencement of the case, in full 100% to those creditors named below in installments from funds available for distribution monthly, non-cumulative, as indicated until claim is paid in amount allowed without interest unless an optional interest percentage is specified below. Holders of claims for domestic support obligations, other than creditors specifically named will be paid as indicated in paragraph 3 of this plan. Post-petition support shall be paid by the debtor directly to support creditors as such payments become due and payable.

Name of Creditor	Estimated Arrears	Installment	(Optional) % Interest
____________	________	________	________
____________	________	________	________

Assigned Domestic Support Obligations not to be paid in full. If debtor's projected disposable income for a period of five years will be applied to make payments under the plan, debtor may provide for less than full payment to assigned Domestic Support Obligations (DSOs) defined in §507(a)(1)(B). Although the unpaid DSOs remain nondischargable, after creditors provided for in prior paragraphs, debtor proposes to pay the below named assigned DSO creditors on their filed and allowed claims in installments from funds available for distribution monthly, non-cumulative, as indicated until the equivalent of 60 months of projected disposable income has been paid into the plan for distribution to creditors. If there are any remaining funds after payment to other creditors pursuant to the plan, those funds may be paid to any creditor in this paragraph whose claim is not paid in full.

Name of Creditor	Estimated Claim	Installment
____________	________	________

Case Number: ____________________

8. **Secured Co-debtor claims**. After payments provided for by prior paragraphs, creditors (their agents and assigns) named in this paragraph who have allowed claims secured by personal property with a co-debtor liable thereon, shall be paid by the trustee 100% of the claim as allowed plus interest at the contract rate (if clearly specified in the claim) in installments as indicated. Installments are to be paid from funds available for distribution monthly non-cumulative. If no contract rate of interest is clearly specified in the claim, pay the interest rate specified below or if none specified, pay 12% A. P. R. interest.

Name of Creditor	Installment	(Optional) % Interest
____________________	__________	__________

9. **Real Estate or Mobile Homes (Trustee to pay arrears only).** Notwithstanding any other provision of this plan, during this case and following completion of this case, debtors shall make the usual and regular payments (including any balloon payments) called for by any security agreements supporting non-voidable liens against debtor's real estate or mobile home, directly to lien holders in a current manner. However, arrears to named lien holders (their agents and assigns) shall be paid in installments by Trustee from funds available for distribution monthly, non-cumulative, and except for creditors paid pursuant to prior paragraphs of this plan, shall be paid in advance of periodic distribution to other creditors. Each named creditor shall be paid in installments indicated until arrears claim is paid in amount allowed plus interest at seven percent (7%) per annum, unless a different percentage is specified below.

Provisions of this paragraph shall operate to cure any default of any real estate or mobile home security agreement notwithstanding that by the terms thereof, or by the laws or processes of a governmental unit, the time for redemption or reinstatement has expired. If there exist creditors not dealt with by this plan holding statutory or other liens against debtor's real estate or mobile home and the obligation is fully due, for reasons other than the exercise of power of acceleration for failure to make installment payments, unless the Court orders otherwise, debtor(s) will pay said claim directly to said creditor in full on or before six months time following the date of confirmation of this Plan. Unless otherwise specifically provided for elsewhere in the plan, secured tax claims shall be paid as though secured only by personal property even if also secured by real property.

Name of Creditor	Estimated Arrears	Installment	(Optional) % Interest
____________________	__________	__________	__________
____________________	__________	__________	__________
____________________	__________	__________	__________

10. **Real Estate or Mobile Home (Trustee to pay entire claim).** Notwithstanding any other provisions of this plan, the below named creditors (their agents and assigns) who have security agreements supporting non-voidable liens against debtor's real estate or mobile home or are cross-collateralized shall be paid in installments by Trustee from funds available for distribution monthly, non-cumulative, and except for creditors paid pursuant to prior paragraphs of this plan shall be paid on their allowed claims in advance of periodic distribution to other creditors. Each named creditor shall be paid in installments as indicated until the allowed secured claim is paid 100% plus interest at seven percent (7%) per annum, unless a different percentage is specified below.

Name of Creditor	Estimated Claim	Installment	(Optional) % Interest
____________________	__________	__________	__________
____________________	__________	__________	__________

Case Number: ____________________

11. **Other secured personal property creditors and lease creditors.** After payments provided for in prior paragraphs, Trustee shall pay holders of other claims allowed secured solely by personal property. Any creditor holding a lease on personal property in debtor's possession with a filed and allowed claim, unless specifically dealt with elsewhere in this plan, shall be treated as a secured creditor herein. All claims pursuant to this paragraph shall be paid pro-rata with other such creditors to the amount allowed plus interest at seven percent (7%) per annum unless a different percentage is specified below and in advance of distribution to general unsecured creditors:

(Optional) % interest: ______________

12. **Unsecured co-debtor claims.** After payments provided for by prior paragraphs, creditors (their agents and assigns) named in this paragraph who have allowed unsecured claims with a co-debtor liable thereon, shall be paid by the trustee 100% of the claim as allowed plus interest at the contract rate (if clearly specified in the claim) in installments as indicated. Installments are to be paid from funds available for distribution monthly non-cumulative. If no contract rate of interest is clearly specified in the claim, pay the interest rate specified below or if none specified, pay 12% A.P.R. interest.

Name of Creditor	Installment	(Optional) % Interest
____________________	__________	__________
____________________	__________	__________

13. **Non-priority Unsecured Claims.** After dividends to all other creditors pursuant to the plan, trustee may pay dividends pro-rata to claims allowed unsecured. Unsecured non-priority creditors will receive:

__________**% or a pro-rata share of $**__________________, **whichever is greater**. (The dollar amount is the greater of (1) the non-exempt assets or (2) the applicable commitment period of 36 or 60 months multiplied by debtor's projected disposable income). If both the percentage and dollar amount are left blank, trustee is to pay 100% to unsecured creditors. If the percentage is left blank, trustee will pay the dollar amount to unsecured creditors. If the percentage is filled in at less than 100% and the dollar amount is left blank, trustee is authorized to increase the percentage if necessary to comply with the required applicable commitment calculation.

14. **Special Unsecured Claims**. Notwithstanding any other provision of the plan, creditors named in this paragraph shall be paid as an unsecured claim but in full 100% of the claim amount allowed [Debtors represent compliance with section §1322(b)(1)].

Name of Creditor	Optional interest rate
__________________________	__________________________

15. **Exclusion of creditor.** Notwithstanding any other provision of the plan, debtor(s) elect to assume the existing lease or contract with creditors in this paragraph. These named creditors shall not be dealt with or provided for by this plan. All pre-petition and post-petition payments due to listed creditors, including defaults, shall be disallowed as claims for payment herein, unless agreed upon by the Trustee with notice and an opportunity to object by Debtor.

Name of Creditor	Collateral
__________________________	__________________________
__________________________	__________________________

Case Number: ____________________

16. **Rejection of Claim, Return of Collateral**. Debtor(s) elect not to assume the lease or contract with creditors (their agents and assigns) named in this paragraph and shall surrender to such creditor the collateral subject to creditor's lien or lease in full satisfaction of any secured claim arising from the transaction creating creditor's interest in said property.

Name of Creditor	Collateral
____________________	____________________
____________________	____________________

17. **Post-Petition Claims**. Claims allowed for post-petition debts incurred by debtor(s) may be paid in full 100% of the claim in such order and on such terms as the Trustee, in his sole discretion, may determine. Trustee or any adversely affected party in interest may file to dismiss case if debtor(s) incur post-petition debts without the written consent of Trustee and debtor(s) fail to make sufficient payments to keep such obligations current.

18. **General Provisions**. Post-Petition earnings while this case is pending shall remain property of the estate and shall not vest in the debtor notwithstanding §1327. Any remaining funds held by the Trustee after dismissal or conversion of a confirmed case may be distributed to creditors pursuant to these Plan provisions. Pursuant to §1322(b)(3), Trustee shall have the power to waive, in writing and on such conditions as the Trustee may impose, any default in debtor's payment to Trustee under this Plan. Any tax refunds or other funds sent to the debtor(s) in care of the Trustee during this case may be deposited to debtor(s) account and disbursed to creditors pursuant to the plan.

Special Note: This plan is intended as an exact copy of the Chapter 13 (recommended form) plan revised 9/05, except as to any added paragraphs after paragraph 18 above. The trustee shall be held harmless from any changes in this plan from the recommended plan dated 9/05.

Plan Dated: ____________________ Debtor: ____________________
(DATE IS MANDATORY)

Joint Debtor: ____________________

SDCAL-327 S.D. CALIFORNIA

AMENDMENT COVER PAGE (CASA 1100)

CSD 1100 [09/26/06]
Name, Address, Telephone No. & I.D. No.

UNITED STATES BANKRUPTCY COURT
SOUTHERN DISTRICT OF CALIFORNIA
325 West "F" Street, San Diego, California 92101-6991

In Re

BANKRUPTCY NO.

Debtor.

AMENDMENT

Presented herewith are the original and one conformed copy of the following [Check one or more boxes as appropriate]:

[ ] Petition
[ ] Exhibit A to Voluntary Petition
[ ] Exhibit C to Voluntary Petition
[ ] Exhibit D - Individual Statement of Compliance with Credit Counseling
[ ] Summary of Schedules
[ ] Statistical Summary of Certain Liabilities and Related Data
[ ] Schedule A & B - Schedule of Real or Personal Property
[ ] Schedule C - Schedule of Property Claimed Exempt
[ ] Schedule D, E, or F, and/or Matrix, and/or list of Creditors or Equity Holders - REQUIRES COMPLIANCE WITH LOCAL RULE 1009
  [ ] Adding or deleting creditors (diskette required), changing amounts owed or classification of debt - $26.00 fee required. See instructions on reverse side.
  [ ] Correcting or deleting other information. See instructions on reverse side.
[ ] Schedule G - Schedule of Executory Contracts & Expired Leases
[ ] Schedule H - Schedule of Co-Debtor
[ ] Schedule I - Current Income of Individual Debtor(s)
[ ] Schedule J - Current Expenditure of Individual Debtor(s)
[ ] Statement of Financial Affairs
[ ] Statement of Current Monthly Income and Means Test Calculation (Form B22A)
[ ] Statement of Current Monthly Income (Form B22B)
[ ] Statement of Current Monthly Income and Calculation of Commitment Period and Disposable Income (Form B22C)

Dated: Signature ______________________
Attorney for Debtor

DECLARATION OF DEBTOR

I [We] ______________________ and ______________________, the undersigned debtor(s), hereby declare under penalty of perjury that the information set forth in the amendment attached hereto, consisting of________ pages, and on the creditor matrix diskette, if any, is true and correct to the best of my [our] information and belief.

Dated: ______________________ ______________________
Debtor Joint Debtor

CSD 1100 **REFER TO INSTRUCTIONS ON REVERSE SIDE**

CSD 1100 (Page 2) [09/26/06]

INSTRUCTIONS

A. Each amended page is to be in the same form as the original but is to contain ONLY THE INFORMATION TO BE CHANGED OR ADDED. Pages from the original document which are not affected by the change are not to be attached.

1. Before each entry, specify the purpose of the amendment by inserting:
   a. "ADDED," if the information was missing from the previous document filed; or
   b. "CORRECTED," if the information modifies previously listed information; or
   c. "DELETED," if previously listed information is to be removed.
2. At the bottom of each page, insert the word "AMENDED."
3. Attach all pages to the cover page and, *if a Chapter 7, 11, or 12 case*, serve a copy on the United States Trustee, trustee (if any) and/or the members of a creditors' committee. *If a Chapter 13 case*, serve a copy on the trustee; DO NOT serve a copy on the United States Trustee.

B. Comply with Local Bankruptcy Rule 1009 when adding or correcting the names and/or addresses of creditors (diskette required when Amendment submitted on paper) or if altering the status or amount of a claim.

AMENDMENTS THAT FAIL TO FOLLOW THESE INSTRUCTIONS MAY BE REFUSED
**** AMENDMENTS FILED AFTER THE CASE IS CLOSED ARE NOT ENTITLED TO A REFUND OF FEES ****

CERTIFICATE OF SERVICE

I, the undersigned whose address appears below, certify:

That I am, and at all times hereinafter mentioned was, more than 18 years of age;

That on ____ day of ____________________, I served a true copy of the within AMENDMENT by [describe here mode of service]

on the following persons [set forth name and address of each person served] and/or as checked below:

[ ] Chpt. 7 Trustee:

[ ] For Chpt. 7, 11, & 12 cases:
UNITED STATES TRUSTEE
Department of Justice
402 West Broadway, Suite 600
San Diego, CA 92101

[ ] For ODD numbered Chapter 13 cases:
THOMAS H. BILLINGSLEA, JR., TRUSTEE
530 "B" Street, Suite. 1500
San Diego, CA 92101

[ ] For EVEN numbered Chapter 13 cases:
DAVID L. SKELTON, TRUSTEE
525 "B" Street, Suite 1430
San Diego, CA 92101-4507

I certify under penalty of perjury that the foregoing is true and correct.

Executed on ________________ (Date)

______________________________ (Typed Name and Signature)

______________________________ (Address)

______________________________ (City, State, ZIP Code)

SDCAL-329 S.D. CALIFORNIA

APPLICATION FOR CONFIRMATION OF PLAN (CAS)

CSD 1006 [04/09/06]
Name, Address, Telephone No. & I.D. No.

UNITED STATES BANKRUPTCY COURT
SOUTHERN DISTRICT OF CALIFORNIA
325 West "F" Street, San Diego, California 92101-6991

In Re

BANKRUPTCY NO.

Debtor.

APPLICATION TO PAY FILING FEES IN INSTALLMENTS

In accordance with Federal Rule of Bankruptcy Procedure 1006, application is made for permission to pay half the filing fee at the time the petition is filed with the balance of the fee in not more than one installment due within 30 days of the date my petition is filed (check one):

[ ] Chapter 7 payment of $149.50 [ ] Chapter 13 payment of $137.00
[ ] Chapter 11 payment of $519.50 [ ] Chapter 12 payment of $119.50

I certify that I am unable to pay the filing fee except in installments.

Until the filing fee is paid in full, I will not make any additional payment or transfer any additional property to an attorney or any other person for services in connection with this case.

I understand that entry of my discharge [or confirmation of any plan] will be delayed until the filing fee is paid in full or, if not paid, that my case will be dismissed without further notice.

Dated:

Signed:____________________________
Signature of Debtor

Signed:____________________________
Signature of Joint Debtor (if any)

Dated:

____
Attorney for Debtor(s)

If this document is prepared by a NON-ATTORNEY BANKRUPTCY PETITION PREPARER, the certification printed on page 2 must be completed

Form of payment: Please do not mail cash. Money orders or certified checks only; personal checks of the debtor will not be accepted.

CSD 1006 (Page 2) [04/09/06]

DECLARATION AND SIGNATURE OF NON-ATTORNEY BANKRUPTCY PETITION PREPARER
(See 11 U.S.C. § 110)

I declare under penalty of perjury that: (1) I am a bankruptcy petition preparer as defined in 11 U.S.C. § 110; (2) I prepared this document for compensation and have provided the debtor with a copy of this document and the notices and information required under 11 U.S.C. §§ 110(b), 110(h), and 342(b); (3) if rules or guidelines have been promulgated pursuant to 11 U.S.C. § 110(h) setting a maximum fee for services chargeable by bankruptcy petition preparers, I have given the debtor notice of the maximum amount before preparing any document for filing for a debtor or accepting any fee from the debtor, as required under that section; and (4) I will not accept any additional money or any other property from the debtor before the filing fee is paid in full.

______________________________ ______________________________
Printed or Typed Name and Title, if any, of Bankruptcy Petition Preparer
Social Security No. (Required by 11 U.S.C. § 110)

If the bankruptcy petition preparer is not an individual, state the name, title (if any), address, and social security number of the officer, principal, responsible person, or partner who signs the document.

____

____
Address

X ______________________________
Signature of Bankruptcy Petition Preparer

____
Date

Names and Social Security numbers of all other individuals who prepared or assisted in preparing this document, unless the bankruptcy petition preparer is not an individual:

If more than one person prepared this document, attach additional signed sheets conforming to the appropriate Official Form for each person.

A bankruptcy petition preparer's failure to comply with the provisions of title 11 and the Federal Rules of Bankruptcy Procedure may result in fines or imprisonment or both. 11 U.S.C. § 110; 18 U.S.C. § 156.

SDCAL-331 S.D. CALIFORNIA

APPLICATION TO PAY FILING FEES IN INSTALLMENTS (CASA 1006)

CSD 1006 [04/09/06]
Name, Address, Telephone No. & I.D. No.

UNITED STATES BANKRUPTCY COURT
SOUTHERN DISTRICT OF CALIFORNIA
325 West "F" Street, San Diego, California 92101-6991

In Re

BANKRUPTCY NO.

Debtor.

APPLICATION TO PAY FILING FEES IN INSTALLMENTS

In accordance with Federal Rule of Bankruptcy Procedure 1006, application is made for permission to pay half the filing fee at the time the petition is filed with the balance of the fee in not more than one installment due within 30 days of the date my petition is filed (check one):

[ ] Chapter 7 payment of $149.50
[ ] Chapter 11 payment of $519.50
[ ] Chapter 13 payment of $137.00
[ ] Chapter 12 payment of $119.50

I certify that I am unable to pay the filing fee except in installments.

Until the filing fee is paid in full, I will not make any additional payment or transfer any additional property to an attorney or any other person for services in connection with this case.

I understand that entry of my discharge [or confirmation of any plan] will be delayed until the filing fee is paid in full or, if not paid, that my case will be dismissed without further notice.

Dated:

Signed:______________________________
Signature of Debtor

Signed:______________________________
Signature of Joint Debtor (if any)

Dated:

____
Attorney for Debtor(s)

If this document is prepared by a NON-ATTORNEY BANKRUPTCY PETITION PREPARER, the certification printed on page 2 must be completed

Form of payment: Please do not mail cash. Money orders or certified checks only; personal checks of the debtor will not be accepted.

CSD 1006 (Page 2) [04/09/06]

DECLARATION AND SIGNATURE OF NON-ATTORNEY BANKRUPTCY PETITION PREPARER
(See 11 U.S.C. § 110)

I declare under penalty of perjury that: (1) I am a bankruptcy petition preparer as defined in 11 U.S.C. § 110; (2) I prepared this document for compensation and have provided the debtor with a copy of this document and the notices and information required under 11 U.S.C. §§ 110(b), 110(h), and 342(b); (3) if rules or guidelines have been promulgated pursuant to 11 U.S.C. § 110(h) setting a maximum fee for services chargeable by bankruptcy petition preparers, I have given the debtor notice of the maximum amount before preparing any document for filing for a debtor or accepting any fee from the debtor, as required under that section; and (4) I will not accept any additional money or any other property from the debtor before the filing fee is paid in full.

Printed or Typed Name and Title, if any, of Bankruptcy Petition Preparer

Social Security No. (Required by 11 U.S.C. § 110)

If the bankruptcy petition preparer is not an individual, state the name, title (if any), address, and social security number of the officer, principal, responsible person, or partner who signs the document.

Address

X

Signature of Bankruptcy Petition Preparer

Date

Names and Social Security numbers of all other individuals who prepared or assisted in preparing this document, unless the bankruptcy petition preparer is not an individual:

If more than one person prepared this document, attach additional signed sheets conforming to the appropriate Official Form for each person.

A bankruptcy petition preparer's failure to comply with the provisions of title 11 and the Federal Rules of Bankruptcy Procedure may result in fines or imprisonment or both. 11 U.S.C. § 110; 18 U.S.C. § 156.

SDCAL-333 S.D. CALIFORNIA

BALANCE OF SCHEDULES AND/OR CHAPTER 13 PLAN (CASA 1099)

CSD 1099 [09/26/06]
Name, Address, Telephone No. & I.D. No.

UNITED STATES BANKRUPTCY COURT
SOUTHERN DISTRICT OF CALIFORNIA
325 West "F" Street, San Diego, California 92101-6991

In Re

BANKRUPTCY NO.

Debtor.

BALANCE OF SCHEDULES, STATEMENTS, AND/OR CHAPTER 13 PLAN

Presented herewith are the original with the number of copies required by Local Bankruptcy Rule 1007-2(b) of the following [Check one or more boxes as appropriate]:

[ ] Summary of Schedules
[ ] Statistical Summary of Certain Liabilities and Related Data
[ ] Schedule A - Schedule of Real Property
[ ] Schedule B - Schedule of Personal Property
[ ] Schedule C - Schedule of Property Claimed Exempt
[ ] Schedule D - Creditors Holding Secured Claims
[ ] Schedule E - Creditors Holding Unsecured Priority Claims
[ ] Schedule F - Creditors Holding Unsecured Nonpriority Claims
[ ] Schedule G - Schedule of Executory Contracts & Unexpired Leases
[ ] Schedule H - Schedule of Co-Debtor
[ ] Schedule I - Current Income of Individual Debtor(s)
[ ] Schedule J - Current Expenditures of Individual Debtor(s)
[ ] Statement of Financial Affairs
[ ] Statement of Current Monthly Income and Means Test Calculation (Form B22A)
[ ] Statement of Current Monthly Income (Form B22B)
[ ] Statement of Current Monthly Income and Calculation of Commitment Period and Disposable Income (Form B22C)
[ ] Chapter 13 Plan

IF ADDITIONAL CREDITORS ARE ADDED AT THIS TIME, THE FOLLOWING ARE REQUIRED:

1. Computer diskette containing only the added names and addresses (when the Balance of Schedules are filed on paper).
2. Local Form CSD 1101, *NOTICE TO CREDITORS OF THE ABOVE-NAMED DEBTOR ADDED BY AMENDMENT OR BALANCE OF SCHEDULES*, as required by Local Bankruptcy Rule 1007-4. See instructions on reverse side.

Dated: Signed: ______________________________
Attorney for Debtor

I [We] __________________ and __________________, the undersigned debtor(s), hereby declare under penalty of perjury that the information set forth in the balance of schedules and/or chapter 13 attached hereto, consisting of ______ pages, and on the creditor matrix diskette, if any, is true and correct to the best of my [our] information and belief.

Dated: sdafasdf

______________________________ Debtor

______________________________ Joint Debtor

CSD 1099 (Page 2) [09/26/06]

INSTRUCTIONS

1. Local Form CSD 1101, *NOTICE TO CREDITORS OF THE ABOVE-NAMED DEBTOR ADDED BY AMENDMENT OR BALANCE OF SCHEDULES*, may be used to notify any added entity. When applicable, copies of the following notices shall accompany the notice: Order for and Notice of Section 341(a) Meeting, Discharge of Debtor, Notice of Order Confirming Plan, and Proof of Claim.

2. If not filed previously and this is an ECF case, the *DECLARATION RE: ELECTRONIC FILING OF PETITION, SCHEDULES & STATEMENTS* (Local Form CSD 1801) must be filed in accordance with General Order #162.

CERTIFICATE OF SERVICE

I, the undersigned whose address appears below, certify:

That I am, and at all times hereinafter mentioned was, more than 18 years of age;

That on ____ day of ______________________, I served a true copy of the within BALANCE OF SCHEDULES AND/OR CHAPTER 13 PLAN by [describe here mode of service]

on the following persons [set forth name and address of person served]:

[ ] For Chpt. 7, 11, & 12 cases:

UNITED STATES TRUSTEE
Department of Justice
402 West Broadway, Suite 600
San Diego, CA 92101

[ ] For ODD numbered Chapter 13 cases:

THOMAS H. BILLINGSLEA, JR., TRUSTEE
530 "B" Street, Suite. 1500
San Diego, CA 92101

[ ] For EVEN numbered Chapter 13 cases:

DAVID L. SKELTON, TRUSTEE
525 "B" Street, Suite 1430
San Diego, CA 92101-4507

[ ] Chpt. 7 Trustee, if any:

[ ] If Chpt. 11, each member of any committee appointed:

I certify under penalty of perjury that the foregoing is true and correct.

Executed on __________
(Date)

____
(Typed Name and Signature)

____
(Address)

____
(City, State, ZIP Code)

DISCLOSURE OF COMPENSATION OF ATTORNEY FOR DEBTOR (CAS) (CASA 1009)

CSD 1009 [04/28/96]
Name, Address, Telephone No. & I.D. No.

UNITED STATES BANKRUPTCY COURT
SOUTHERN DISTRICT OF CALIFORNIA
325 West "F" Street, San Diego, California 92101-6991

In Re

BANKRUPTCY NO.

Debtor.

DISCLOSURE OF COMPENSATION OF ATTORNEY FOR DEBTOR

1. Pursuant to 11 U.S.C. § 329(a) and Federal Rule of Bankruptcy Procedure 2016(b), I certify that I am the attorney for the above-named debtor(s) and that compensation paid to me within one year before the filing of the petition in bankruptcy, or agreed to be paid to me, for services rendered or to be rendered on behalf of the debtor(s) in contemplation of or in connection with the bankruptcy case is as follows:

   For legal services, I have agreed to accept .... $________________

   Prior to the filing of this statement I have received .... $________________

   Balance Due .... $________________

2. The source of the compensation paid to me was:

   ☐ Debtor ☐ Other (specify)

3. The source of compensation to be paid to me is:

   ☐ Debtor ☐ Other (specify)

4. ☐ I have not agreed to share the above-disclosed compensation with any other person unless they are members and associates of my law firm.

   ☐ I have agreed to share the above-disclosed compensation with a person or persons who are not members or associates of my law firm. A copy of the agreement, together with a list of the names of the people sharing in the compensation, is attached.

5. In return for the above-disclosed fee, I have agreed to render legal service for all aspects of the bankruptcy case, including:

   a. Analysis of the debtor's financial situation, and rendering advice to the debtor in determining whether to file a petition in bankruptcy;

   b. Preparation and filing of any petition, schedules, statement of affairs and plan which may be required;

   c. Representation of the debtor at the meeting of creditors and confirmation hearing, and any adjourned hearings thereof;

 [Continued on Page 2]

CSD 1009 (Page 2) [04/28/96]

d. Representation of the debtor in adversary proceedings and other contested bankruptcy matters;

e. [Other provisions as needed]

6. By agreement with the debtor(s), the above-disclosed fee does not include the following services:

CERTIFICATION

I certify that the foregoing is a complete statement of any agreement or arrangement for payment to me for representation of the debtor(s) in this bankruptcy proceeding.

DATED:

____

(Typed Name and Signature)

____

(Name of Law Firm)

SDCAL-337 S.D. CALIFORNIA

CERTIFICATE OF EXIGENT CIRCUMSTANCES AND REQUEST FOR EXTENSION OF TIME TO FILE CERTIFICATE OF CREDIT COUNSELING (DEBTOR) (CASA 1025)

CSD 1025 [09/15/06]
Name, Address, Telephone No. & I.D. No.

UNITED STATES BANKRUPTCY COURT
SOUTHERN DISTRICT OF CALIFORNIA
325 West F Street, San Diego, California 92101-6991

In Re

Debtor.

BANKRUPTCY NO.

CERTIFICATE OF EXIGENT CIRCUMSTANCES AND
MOTION FOR EXTENSION OF TIME TO FILE
CERTIFICATE OF CREDIT COUNSELING
PURSUANT TO 11 U.S.C. § 109(h)(3)

The undersigned debtor(s) declare under penalty of perjury that the following exigent circumstances exist which have prevented me from obtaining budget and credit counseling within the 180-day period prior to the filing of my bankruptcy petition.

Those circumstances include (*provide a detailed explanation in the space provided below)*

I further declare that I requested credit counseling services from:

____

an approved nonprofit budget and credit counseling agency,

on ______________________, but was unable to obtain the services during the 5-day period following my request.
(*date*)

I understand that this initial counseling does not replace or waive the necessity to complete a course concerning personal financial management. I understand that I must file a Certification of Completion of Instructional Course Concerning Personal Financial Management (Official Form 23) no later than forty-five (45) days from (1) the first date set for the first meeting of creditors under § 341 in order to receive a chapter 7 discharge or (2) if a chapter 13 debtor, no later than the last payment made as required by my chapter 13 plan or the filing of a motion for entry of a discharge under § 1328(b) in my chapter 13 case.

I request that I be granted an extension of thirty (30) days from the date of the filing of my petition within which to complete the credit counseling, obtain and file a Certificate of Credit Counseling issued by a United States Trustee approved nonprofit budget and credit counseling agency.

DATED:

______________________ ______________________
Debtor Joint Debtor

CSD 1025 **SUBMIT WITH ORDER ON MOTION FOR EXTENSION OF TIME (CSD 1026)**

DECLARATION RE: FILING OF PETITION, SCHEDULES, & STATEMENTS ON DISKETTE (CASA 1004)

CSD 1004 [10/17/05]
Name, Address, Telephone No. & I.D. No.

UNITED STATES BANKRUPTCY COURT
SOUTHERN DISTRICT OF CALIFORNIA
325 West "F" Street, San Diego, California 92101-6991

In Re

Debtor.

BANKRUPTCY NO.

DECLARATION RE: FILING OF PETITION, SCHEDULES, & STATEMENTS ON DISKETTE

The undersigned debtor(s), ***declare under penalty of perjury*** that information provided in this petition, statements, and schedules as marked below is true and correct.

PART I - Select one:

☐ COMPLETE PETITION including all Schedules, Statements, and List of Creditors

☐ PETITION and List of Creditors filed with the following Schedules and Statements. (Remainder to be filed within 15 days.)

CHECK ITEMS BEING FILED WITH PETITION

	Schedule A		Schedule D		Schedule G		Schedule J			Chapter 13 Plan, if any
	Schedule B		Schedule E		Schedule H		Summary of Schedules			Attorney Fee Disclosure, if any
	Schedule C		Schedule F		Schedule I		Statement of Financial Affairs			Statement of Intention, if any
	Statement of Current Monthly Income & Means Test Calculation (Individual Chapter 7 debtors only)				Statement of Current Monthly Income (Individual Chapter 11 debtors only)					Statement of Current Monthly Income & Calculation of Commitment Period & Disposable Income (Chapter 13)

PART II - Select one:

☐ [If petitioner is an individual whose debts are primarily consumer debts and has chosen to file under chapter 7] I am aware that I may proceed under chapter 7, 11, 12 or 13 of 11 United States Code, understand the relief available under each such chapter, and choose to proceed under chapter 7. I request relief in accordance with the chapter specified in this petition.

☐ [If petitioner is a corporation or partnership] I declare under penalty of perjury that the information provided in this petition is true and correct, and that I have been authorized to file this petition on behalf of the debtor. The debtor requests relief in accordance with the chapter specified in this petition.

Dated: Signed:____________________ ____________________
(Debtor) (Joint Debtor)

Dated: ____________________
Attorney for Debtor

Certification & Signature of Non-Attorney Petition Preparer

I declare under penalty of perjury that: (1) I am a bankruptcy petition preparer as defined in 11 U.S.C. § 110; (2) I prepared this document for compensation and have provided the debtor with a copy of this document and the notices and information required under 11 U.S.C. § 110(b), 110(h), and 342(b); and (3) if rules or guidelines have been promulgated pursuant to 11 U.S.C. § 110(h) setting a maximum fee for services chargeable by bankruptcy petition preparers, I have given the debtor notice of the maximum amount before preparing any document for filing for a debtor or accepting any fee from the debtor, as required in that section.

Printed Name of Bankruptcy Petition Preparer Social Security Number (Required by 11 U.S.C. §110(c).)

Address____________________
Names and Social Security numbers of all other individuals who prepared or assisted in preparing this document:

If more than one person prepared this document, attach additional sheets conforming to the appropriate official form for each person.

X ____________________
Signature of Bankruptcy Petition Preparer Date

A bankruptcy petition preparer's failure to comply with the provisions of title 11 and the Federal Rules of Bankruptcy Procedure may result in fines or imprisonment or both. 11 U.S.C. § 110; 18 U.S.C. § 156.

CSD 1004

SDCAL-339 S.D. CALIFORNIA

OPPOSITION TO MOTION FOR RELIEF FROM AUTOMATIC STAY (CASA 1161)

CSD 1161 [05/15/03]
Name, Address, Telephone No. & I.D. No.

UNITED STATES BANKRUPTCY COURT
SOUTHERN DISTRICT OF CALIFORNIA
325 West "F" Street, San Diego, California 92101-6991

In Re Debtor.	BANKRUPTCY NO.
Moving Party	RS NO.
Respondent(s)	Hearing Date: Hearing Time:

OPPOSITION TO MOTION FOR RELIEF FROM AUTOMATIC STAY
☐ **REAL PROPERTY** ☐ **PERSONAL PROPERTY**

Respondent in the above-captioned matter moves this Court for an Order denying relief from the automatic stay on the grounds set forth below.

1. A Petition under Chapter ☐ 7 ☐ 11 ☐ 12 ☐ 13 was filed on ______________.

2. Procedural Status:
   a. ☐ Name of Trustee Appointed *(if any)*:

   b. ☐ Name of Attorney of Record for Trustee *(if any)*:

   c. ☐ *Prior Filing Information:
   Debtor has previously filed a Bankruptcy Petition on:________________.
   If applicable, the prior case was dismissed on: ________________.

   d. ☐ *(If Chapter 13 case)*: Chapter 13 Plan was confirmed on ________________ or a confirmation hearing is set for ______________.

3. *Number of unsecured creditors _______. Amount of unsecured debt $________________.

4. *Last operating report filed:________________

5. *Disclosure statement: Filed? (yes/no)________. Approved? (yes/no) ________________.
   If yes, date of plan confirmation hearing:________________

---

*Only required if respondent is the debtor.

CSD 1161

CSD 1161 (Page 2) [05/15/03]

Respondent alleges the following in opposition to the Motion:

1. ☐ The following real property is the subject of this Motion:
   a. Street address of the property including county and state:
      asdfasdfasdf
   b. Type of real property (e.g., single family residence, apartment building, commercial, industrial, condominium, unimproved):
      adsfasdfasf
   c. Legal description of property is attached as Exhibit A.
   d. **Fair market value of property: $______________.
   e. **Nature of Respondent's interest in the property:

2. ☐ The following personal property is the subject of this Motion *(describe property)*:
   dsfasdfasdf
   a. **Fair market value of property: $______________.
   b. **Nature of Respondent's interest in the property:

3. Status of Movant's loan:
   a. Balance owing on date of Order for Relief: $______________
   b. Amount of monthly payment: $______________
   c. Date of last payment: ______________
   d. If real property,
      (1) Date of default: ______________
      (2) Notice of Default recorded on: ______________
      (3) Notice of Sale published on: ______________
      (4) Foreclosure sale currently scheduled for: ______________
   e. If personal property,
      (1) Pre-petition default: $______________ No. of months:______________
      (2) Post-petition default: $______________ No. of months:______________

4. *(If Chapter 13 Case, state the following:)*
   a. Date of post-petition default: asdfasdfasdf
   b. Amount of post-petition default: $______________

5. Encumbrances:
   a. Voluntary encumbrances on the property:

Lender Name	Principal Balance	Pre-Petition Arrearages Total Amount - # of Months		Post-Petition Arrearages Total Amount - # of Months	
1st:					
2nd:					
3rd:					
4th:					
Totals for all Liens:	$ 0.00	$ 0.00		$ 0.00	

**Separately filed Declaration required by Local Bankruptcy Rule 4001-4.

CSD 1161

b. Involuntary encumbrances of record (e.g., tax, mechanic's, judgment and other liens, lis pendens):
☐ See attached page, if necessary.

6. Relief from the automatic stay should not be granted because:

a. ☐ Movant's interest in the property described above is adequately protected.

b. ☐ Debtor has equity in the property described above and such property is necessary to an effective reorganization.

c. ☐ The property is not "single asset real estate", as defined in 11 U.S.C. § 101(51B).

d. ☐ The property is "single asset real estate", as defined in 11 U.S.C. § 101(51B), and less than 90 days (or ______ days ordered by this court) have passed since entry of the order for relief in this case, or

(1) the Debtor/Trustee has filed a plan of reorganization that has a reasonable possibility of being confirmed within a reasonable time; or

(2) the Debtor/Trustee has commenced monthly payments to each creditor whose claim is secured by the property (other than a claim secured by a judgment lien or by an unmatured statutory lien) which payments are equal to interest at a current fair market rate on the value of each creditors' interest in the property.

e. ☐ Other *(specifiy)*: ☐ See attached page.

When required, Respondent has filed a separate Declaration pursuant to Local Bankruptcy Rules 4001-4.

Respondent attaches the following:

1. ☐ Other relevant evidence:

2. ☐ *(Optional)* Memorandum of points and authorities upon which the responding party will rely.

WHEREFORE, Respondent prays that this Court issue an Order denying relief from the automatic stay.

Dated:

____

[Attorney for] Respondent

ORDER ON MOTION FOR EXTENSION OF TIME DUE TO EXIGENT CIRCUMSTANCES (CASA 1026)

CSD 1026 [04/03/06]
Name, Address, Telephone No. & I.D. No.

UNITED STATES BANKRUPTCY COURT
SOUTHERN DISTRICT OF CALIFORNIA
325 West "F" Street, San Diego, California 92101-6991

In Re

BANKRUPTCY NO.

Debtor.

ORDER ON MOTION FOR EXTENSION OF TIME DUE TO EXIGENT CIRCUMSTANCES

On consideration of the Debtor's Certificate of Exigent Circumstances and Motion for Extension of Time (Doc. #_______), the Court finds that such circumstances exist to justify extending the time within which the Debtor must comply with 11 U.S.C. § 109(h)(3), and for good cause showing therefor,

IT IS HEREBY ORDERED THAT the time within which the Debtor must file a Certificate of Credit Counseling is extended for a period not to exceed thirty (30) days from the date the petition was filed.

//

//

//

//

//

DATED:

____
Judge, United States Bankruptcy Court

Signature by the attorney constitutes a certification under Fed. R. of Bankr. P. 9011 that the relief in the order is the relief granted by the court.

Submitted by:

____
(Firm name)

By:____________________________________
Attorney for Movant

SDCAL-343 S.D. CALIFORNIA

POST-CONFIRMATION ORDER MODIFYING CHAPTER 13 PLAN (CAS)

Attorney for Debtor(s)

United States Bankruptcy Court
Southern District of California

In Re:

Debtor(s)

Bankruptcy No:

Hearing Date:

Hearing Time:

Hearing Dept:

POST-CONFIRMATION ORDER MODIFYING CHAPTER 13 PLAN

Chapter 13 Plan Modification Dated: ____________.

The confirmed Chapter 13 Plan dated ____________, shall be modified as follows:

- ☐ Plan payment Debtor pays to the Trustee is increased to $__________.
- ☐ The dividend paid to unsecured creditors in Plan Paragraph 10 is increased to ______%.
- ☐ The allowed secured claim of ____________ in Plan Paragraph ____ shall be paid ________ % annual percentage rate of interest.
- ☐ The filed and allowed unsecured claims shall be paid ________% annual percentage rate of interest.
- ☐

Except as hereinabove amended, the above referenced Plan shall remain in full force and effect. This amendment is not effective unless signed by the Chapter 13 Trustee/Trustee's Attorney.

Acknowledged and Agreed:

X________________________ Dated: __________
Debtor(s) or Debtor(s) Attorney
(By signing, attorney represents he/she is authorized to sign on behalf of client.)

X________________________ Dated:
Chapter 13 Trustee/Trustee's Attorney

It is so ordered:

X________________________ Dated: __________
Judge, U.S. Bankruptcy Court

I hereby certify that a Court filed copy of this modification was mailed this date to the Debtor(s) named above, the attorney of record and the Trustee at their respective addresses of record.

By: ____________________ Barry K. Lander Dated: __________
Deputy Clerk

PRE-CONFIRMATION MODIFICATION TO CHAPTER 13 PLAN (CAS)

Attorney for Debtor(s)

United States Bankruptcy Court
Southern District of California

In Re:	**Bankruptcy No:**
	Hearing Date:
	Hearing Time:
Debtor(s)	**Hearing Dept:**

PRE-CONFIRMATION MODIFICATION TO CHAPTER 13 PLAN

Chapter 13 Plan Modification Dated: ______________.

The Chapter 13 Plan dated ______________, shall be modified as follows:

- ☐ Plan payment Debtor pays to the Trustee is increased to $______________.
- ☐ The dividend paid to unsecured creditors is increased to ________%.
- ☐ The allowed secured claim of ______________________ in Plan Paragraph ______ shall be paid ________ % annual percentage rate of interest.
- ☐ The filed and allowed unsecured claims shall be paid ________% annual percentage rate of interest.
- ☐ [ ]
- ☐ [ ]

Except as hereinabove amended, the above referenced Plan shall remain in full force and effect. This amendment is not effective unless signed by the Chapter 13 Trustee/Trustee's Attorney.

Acknowledged and Agreed:

X______________________________ Dated: ____________
Debtor(s) or Debtor(s) Attorney
(By signing, attorney represents he she is authorized to sign on behalf of client)

X______________________________ Dated: ____________
Chapter 13 Trustee/Trustee's Attorney

SDCAL-345 S.D. CALIFORNIA

REQUEST FOR HEARING ON MOTION FOR RELIEF FROM AUTOMATIC STAY AND NOTICE OF HEARING (CAS)

CSD 1186 [10/17/05]
Name, Address, Telephone No. & I.D. No.

UNITED STATES BANKRUPTCY COURT SOUTHERN DISTRICT OF CALIFORNIA 325 West "F" Street, San Diego, California 92101-6991	
In Re Debtor.	BANKRUPTCY NO.
Moving Party	RS NO.
Respondent(s)	Hearing Date: Hearing Time:

REQUEST FOR HEARING ON MOTION FOR RELIEF FROM AUTOMATIC STAY AND NOTICE OF HEARING

TO:[1]

YOU ARE NOTIFIED that ____, a party in interest, objects to the above-entitled Motion for Relief from Automatic Stay. Respondent is [check one]:

[ ] Debtor [ ] United States Trustee [ ] Trustee

[ ] Creditor [ ] Other (specify): ____________________________

According to the Moving Party's Notice of Filing a Motion for Relief from Automatic Stay, the last date for filing and serving this Request is ____________________.[2]

YOU ARE FURTHER NOTIFIED that a hearing will be held to consider and act upon the Motion in Dept. No.____, Room ____, Jacob Weinberger United States Courthouse, 325 West "F" Street, San Diego, California 92101-6991, on ____________________, at ________.m.

DATED: ____________________

____
(Typed Name and Signature)

____
(Address)

____
(City, State, ZIP Code)
[ ] Attorney for Respondent
[ ] Respondent

[1]Local Bankruptcy Rule 4001-3, printed on the reverse, governs service of this Notice.
[2]Date is calculated as the 11th day after the day of service of the Notice of Motion, as indicated in the Certification of Service that accompanies that Notice. If you were served electronically or by mail, the date is calculated as the 14th day after the day of service.

ALL PLEADINGS RELATED TO THIS PARTICULAR RS ACTION MUST CONTAIN THE ABOVE CAPTION

[Continued on Page 2]

CSD 1186 (Page 2) [10/17/05]

LOCAL BANKRUPTCY RULE 4001-3

"(a) Objections to a motion for relief from stay, together with Local Form CSD 1186, REQUEST FOR HEARING ON MOTION FOR RELIEF FROM AUTOMATIC STAY AND NOTICE OF HEARING, shall be served upon the movant, named respondents and the United States Trustee within eleven (11) days from the date of service of the motion for relief from stay and notice. The original and two (2) copies of the pleadings shall be filed with the clerk within the same 11-day period. If the objection relates to real or personal property, the objection shall substantially conform to Local Form CSD 1161, OPPOSITION TO MOTION FOR RELIEF FROM AUTOMATIC STATY (REAL PROPERTY OR PERSONAL PROPERTY).

"(b) Prior to serving the objection, it shall be the duty of the objecting party to obtain from the court a date and time for a hearing on the objections. Such information shall be listed on Local Form CSD 1186, REQUEST FOR HEARING ON MOTION FOR RELIEF FROM AUTOMATIC STAY AND NOTICE OF HEARING, and in the caption of the objection."

CERTIFICATE OF SERVICE

I, the undersigned whose address appears below, certify:

That I am, and at all times hereinafter mentioned was, more than 18 years of age;

That on _____ day of ______________________, I served a true copy of the within REQUEST FOR HEARING ON MOTION FOR RELIEF FROM AUTOMATIC STAY AND NOTICE OF HEARING, together with a copy of the accompanying DECLARATION IN OPPOSITION TO MOTION FOR RELIEF FROM STAY and [describe any other papers]

by [describe here mode of service]:

on the following persons [set forth name and address of each person served] and/or as checked below:

[ ] Attorney for Moving Party:

[ ] Attorney for Debtor (if required):

[ ] For Chpt. 7, 11, & 12 cases:
UNITED STATES TRUSTEE
Department of Justice
402 West Broadway, Suite 600
San Diego, CA 92101

[ ] For ODD numbered Chapter 13 cases:
THOMAS H. BILLINGSLEA, JR., TRUSTEE
530 "B" Street, Suite. 1500
San Diego, CA 92101

[ ] For EVEN numbered Chapter 13 cases:
DAVID L. SKELTON, TRUSTEE
525 "B" Street, Suite 1430
San Diego, CA 92101-4507

I certify under penalty of perjury that the foregoing is true and correct.

Executed on ______________
(Date)

____
(Typed Name and Signature)

____
(Address)

____
(City, State, ZIP Code)

SDCAL-347 S.D. CALIFORNIA

RIGHTS AND RESPONSIBILITIES OF CHAPTER 13 DEBTORS AND ATTORNEYS (BUSINESS CASE)

Name, Address, Telephone No. & I.D. No.	
UNITED STATES BANKRUPTCY COURT SOUTHERN DISTRICT OF CALIFORNIA 325 West "F" Street, San Diego, California 92101-6991	
In Re Tax I.D. / S.S. #: Debtor.	BANKRUPTCY NO.

UNITED STATES BANKRUPTCY COURT SOUTHERN DISTRICT OF CALIFORNIA RIGHTS AND RESPONSIBILITIES OF CHAPTER 13 DEBTORS AND THEIR ATTORNEY (Business Case)

It is important for debtors who file a bankruptcy case under Chapter 13 to understand their rights and responsibilities. It is also important that the debtors know what their attorney's responsibilities are, and understand the importance of communicating with their attorney to make the case successful. Debtors should also know that they may expect certain services to be performed by their attorney. It is also important for debtors to know the costs of attorneys' fees through the life of a plan. To assure that debtors and their attorney understand their rights and responsibilities in the bankruptcy process, the following rights and responsibilities provided by the United States Bankruptcy Court are hereby agreed to by the debtors and their attorney. (Nothing in this agreement should be construed to excuse an attorney from any ethical duties or responsibilities under Federal Rule of Bankruptcy Procedure 9011.)

UNLESS THE COURT ORDERS OTHERWISE,

The debtor shall:

1. Provide accurate financial information.
2. Provide information in a timely manner.
3. Cooperate and communicate with the attorney.
4. Discuss with the attorney the debtor's objectives in filing the case.
5. Keep the trustee and attorney informed of the debtor's address and telephone number.
6. Inform the attorney of any wage garnishments or attachments of assets which occur or continue after the filing of the case.
7. Contact the attorney promptly if the debtor loses his/her job or has other financial problems.
8. Let the attorney know immediately if the debtor is sued before or during the case.
9. Inform the attorney if any tax refunds the debtor is entitled to are seized or not returned to the debtor by the IRS or Franchise Tax Board.
10. Contact the attorney before buying, refinancing, or selling real property or before entering

into any long-term loan agreements to find out what approvals are required.

11. Pay any filing fees and filing expenses that may be incurred directly to the attorney.
12. Pay appropriate attorney's fees commensurate with this agreement and the United States Bankruptcy Court's Guideline regarding Chapter 13 Attorney Fees. If a court order is entered regarding attorney's fees, fees should be paid in accordance with the court's order.

To receive $3,300, which is within the United States Bankruptcy Court's parameters for "initial fees," the attorney shall:

1. Meet with the debtor to review the debtor's assets, liabilities, income and expenses.
2. Analyze the debtor's financial situation, and render advice to the debtor in determining whether to file a petition in bankruptcy.
3. Counsel the debtor regarding the advisability of filing either a Chapter 7 or Chapter 13 case, discuss both procedures with the debtor, and answer the debtor's questions.
4. Explain to the debtor how the attorney's fees and trustee's fees are paid.
5. Explain what payments will be made directly by the debtor and what payments will be made through the debtor's chapter 13 plan, with particular attention to mortgage and vehicle loan payments, as well as any other claims with accrued interest.
6. Explain to the debtor how, when, and where to make the chapter 13 plan payments.
7. Explain to the debtor that the first plan payment must be made to the Trustee within 30 days of the date the plan is filed.
8. Advise the debtor of the requirement to attend the § 341(a) Meeting of Creditors, and instruct the debtor as to the date, time and place of the meeting.
9. Advise the debtor of the necessity of maintaining liability, collision and comprehensive insurance on vehicles securing loans or leases.
10. Timely prepare, file and serve the debtor's petition, plan, schedules, statement of financial affairs, and any necessary amendments thereto, which may be required.
11. Prepare a Questionnaire for Chapter 13 Business Owners.
12. Provide documents and information requested by the Chapter 13 Trustee and the Court, including, but not limited to, an itemized list of all business assets and a profit and loss statement for each of the three months prior to the filing.
13. Attend on-site inspections of business at the Chapter 13 Trustee's request.
14. Provide an executed copy of the Rights and Responsibilities of Chapter 13 Debtors and their Attorneys and a copy of the Court's Guidelines regarding Chapter 13 Attorney Fees to the debtor.
15. Appear and represent the debtor at the § 341(a) Meeting of Creditors and the confirmation hearing, and any adjourned hearing thereof.
16. Respond to the objections to plan confirmation, and where necessary, prepare, file and serve an amended plan.
17. Assist the Debtor in performing duties pursuant to 11 U.S.C. § 1304, including but not limited to, the filing of periodic operating reports.
18. Provide such other legal services as are necessary for the administration of the case before the Bankruptcy Court, which include, but are not limited to, a continuing obligation to assist the debtor by returning telephone calls, answering questions and reviewing and sending correspondence.

Additional services may be required, but are not included in the "initial fees" of $3,300. If necessary and when appropriate, the attorney, at the debtor's request and only with the debtor's cooperation, shall provide the following services for "additional fees" described below:

1. Prepare, file and serve necessary modifications to the plan post-confirmation, which may include suspending, lowering or increasing plan payments.

2. Prepare, file and serve necessary motions to buy, sell or refinance real property and authorize use of cash collateral or assume executory contracts or unexpired leases.
3. Object to improper or invalid claims.
4. Represent the debtor in motions for relief from stay.
5. Prepare, file and serve necessary motions to avoid liens on real or personal property.
6. Prepare, file and serve necessary oppositions to motions for dismissal of case.
7. Provide such other legal services as are necessary for the administration of the case before the Bankruptcy Court, which include but are not limited to, presenting appropriate legal pleadings and making appropriate court appearances.

Should additional services be provided and "additional fees" requested, the attorney shall:

1. Provide proper notice in accordance with Federal Rule of Bankruptcy Procedure 2002.
2. Advise the debtor of all "additional fees" requested and file a declaration with the court stating that counsel has so advised the debtor of the fees requested and the debtor has no objection to the requested fees.

The "Guidelines Regarding Chapter 13 Attorney Fees" provide for "additional fees" within the United States Bankruptcy Court's parameters in the following amounts and include all court appearances required to pursue described actions:

Modified Plan (Post-Confirmation) **$550**

for fees and expenses for services rendered post-confirmation for preparing, filing, noticing, and attending hearings in regard to a debtor's modified plan under section 1329 of the Bankruptcy Code (including the preparation of amended income and expenses statements and providing proof of income). (These fees should be less for modification due to clerical error or other administrative issues.)

Opposition to Motions for Relief from Stay

$450 (Personal property)	for fees and expenses of all
$575 (Real property)	services rendered in opposition to motions to modify or vacate the automatic stay.

Obtaining Orders re: Sale or Refinance of Real Property

$425 (By stipulation)	for fees and expenses of all
$450 (By noticed hearing)	services rendered for obtaining an order authorizing the sale or refinancing of real estate.

Objections to Claim

$250 (Uncontested objections without hearing)	for fees and expenses of all services rendered for preparing,
$350 (Contested objections with a hearing)	filing, and noticing objections to a claim. (Fees shall not exceed 50% of the amount the trustee would have otherwise paid)

Oppositions to Dismissal/Motions to Avoid Lien/Other Routine

Pleadings **$425**

for fees and expenses of all services rendered for preparing, filing, noticing, and attending hearings in opposition to a motion to dismiss the case, for motions to avoid lien and other routine pleadings.

Motions to Impose/Extend Automatic Stay **$575**

for fees and expenses of all services rendered for preparing, filing, noticing and attending hearings in regard to a motion to impose/extend automatic stay.

Novel and Complex Motions and Oppositions to Motions

These types of motions and oppositions may be billed at hourly rates and counsel shall file a fee application in compliance with Rules of 2002 and 2016 of the Federal Rules of Bankruptcy Procedure and Local Bankruptcy Rules 2002 and 2016.

Initial fee charged in this case is $______________

All post-filing fees shall be paid through the plan, unless the court orders otherwise. The attorney may not receive fees directly from the debtor other than the initial retainer, unless the court orders otherwise. All "additional fees," as described above, may only be paid upon court authorization after compliance with the "Guidelines Regarding Chapter 13 Attorney Fees". The attorney may seek fees above the additional fees provided a fee application is noticed, filed and approved by the court.

If the debtor disputes the legal services provided or the fees charged by the attorney, the debtor may file an objection with the court and set the matter for hearing. The attorney may move to withdraw or the debtor may discharge the attorney at any time.

Dated: ______________________________
Debtor

Dated: ______________________________
Debtor

Dated: ______________________________
Attorney for Debtor(s)

RIGHTS AND RESPONSIBILITIES OF CHAPTER 13 DEBTORS AND ATTORNEYS (CONSUMER CASE)

Name, Address, Telephone No. & I.D. No.	
UNITED STATES BANKRUPTCY COURT SOUTHERN DISTRICT OF CALIFORNIA 325 West "F" Street, San Diego, California 92101-6991	
In Re Tax I.D. / S.S. #: Debtor.	BANKRUPTCY NO.

UNITED STATES BANKRUPTCY COURT
SOUTHERN DISTRICT OF CALIFORNIA
RIGHTS AND RESPONSIBILITIES OF CHAPTER 13 DEBTORS AND THEIR ATTORNEY
(Consumer Case)

It is important for debtors who file a bankruptcy case under Chapter 13 to understand their rights and responsibilities. It is also important that the debtors know what their attorney's responsibilities are, and understand the importance of communicating with their attorney to make the case successful. Debtors should also know that they may expect certain services to be performed by their attorney. It is also important for debtors to know the costs of attorneys' fees through the life of a plan. To assure that debtors and their attorney understand their rights and responsibilities in the bankruptcy process, the following rights and responsibilities provided by the United States Bankruptcy Court are hereby agreed to by the debtors and their attorney. (Nothing in this agreement should be construed to excuse an attorney from any ethical duties or responsibilities under Federal Rule of Bankruptcy Procedure 9011.)

UNLESS THE COURT ORDERS OTHERWISE,

The debtor shall:

1. Provide accurate financial information.
2. Provide information in a timely manner.
3. Cooperate and communicate with the attorney.
4. Discuss with the attorney the debtor's objectives in filing the case.
5. Keep the trustee and attorney informed of the debtor's address and telephone number.
6. Inform the attorney of any wage garnishments or attachments of assets which occur or continue after the filing of the case.
7. Contact the attorney promptly if the debtor loses his/her job or has other financial problems.
8. Let the attorney know immediately if the debtor is sued before or during the case.
9. Inform the attorney if any tax refunds the debtor is entitled to are seized or not returned to the debtor by the IRS or Franchise Tax Board.
10. Contact the attorney before buying, refinancing, or selling real property or before entering

into any long-term loan agreements to find out what approvals are required.

11. Pay any filing fees and filing expenses that may be incurred directly to the attorney.
12. Pay appropriate attorney's fees commensurate with this agreement and the United States Bankruptcy Court Guidelines regarding Chapter 13 Attorney Fees. If a court order is entered regarding attorney's fees, fees should be paid in accordance with the court's order.

To receive $2,800, which is within the United States Bankruptcy Court's parameters for "initial fees," the attorney shall:

1. Meet with the debtor to review the debtor's assets, liabilities, income and expenses.
2. Analyze the debtor's financial situation, and render advice to the debtor in determining whether to file a petition in bankruptcy.
3. Counsel the debtor regarding the advisability of filing either a Chapter 7 or Chapter 13 case, discuss both procedures with the debtor, and answer the debtor's questions.
4. Explain to the debtor how the attorney's fees and trustee's fees are paid.
5. Explain what payments will be made directly by the debtor and what payments will be made through the debtor's chapter 13 plan, with particular attention to mortgage and vehicle loan payments, as well as any other claims with accrued interest.
6. Explain to the debtor how, when, and where to make the chapter 13 plan payments.
7. Explain to the debtor that the first plan payment must be made to the Trustee within 30 days of the date the plan is filed.
8. Advise the debtor of the requirement to attend the § 341(a) Meeting of Creditors, and instruct the debtor as to the date, time and place of the meeting.
9. Advise the debtor of the necessity of maintaining liability, collision and comprehensive insurance on vehicles securing loans or leases.
10. Timely prepare, file and serve the debtor's petition, plan, schedules, statement of financial affairs, and any necessary amendments thereto, which may be required.
11. Provide an executed copy of the Rights and Responsibilities of Chapter 13 Debtors and their Attorneys and a copy of the Court's Guidelines regarding Chapter 13 Attorney Fees to the debtor.
12. Appear and represent the debtor at the § 341(a) Meeting of Creditors, the confirmation hearing, and any adjourned hearing thereof.
13. Respond to the objections to plan confirmation, and where necessary, prepare, file and serve an amended plan.
14. Provide such other legal services as are necessary for the administration of the case before the Bankruptcy Court, which include, but are not limited to, a continuing obligation to assist the debtor by returning telephone calls, answering questions and reviewing and sending correspondence.

Additional services may be required, but are not included in the "initial fees" of $2,800. If necessary and when appropriate, the attorney, at the debtor's request and only with the debtor's cooperation, shall provide the following services for "additional fees" described below:

1. Prepare, file and serve necessary modifications to the plan post-confirmation, which may include suspending, lowering or increasing plan payments.
2. Prepare, file and serve necessary motions to buy, sell or refinance real property and authorize use of cash collateral or assume executory contracts or unexpired leases.
3. Object to improper or invalid claims.
4. Represent the debtor in motions for relief from stay.
5. Prepare, file and serve necessary motions to avoid liens on real or personal property.
6. Prepare, file and serve necessary oppositions to motions for dismissal of case.
7. Provide such other legal services as are necessary for the administration of the case before

the Bankruptcy Court, which include but are not limited to, presenting appropriate legal pleadings and making appropriate court appearances.

Should additional services be provided and "additional fees" requested, the attorney shall:

1. Provide proper notice in accordance with Federal Rule of Bankruptcy Procedure 2002.
2. Advise the debtor of all "additional fees" requested and file a declaration with the court stating that counsel has so advised the debtor of the fees requested and the debtor has no objection to the requested fees.

The "Guidelines Regarding Chapter 13 Attorney Fees" provide for "additional fees" within the United States Bankruptcy Court's parameters for "additional fees" in the following amounts and include all court appearances required to pursue described actions:

Modified Plan (Post-Confirmation) **$550**

for fees and expenses for services rendered post-confirmation for preparing, filing, noticing, and attending hearings in regard to a debtor's modified plan under section 1329 of the Bankruptcy Code (including the preparation of amended income and expenses statements and providing proof of income). (These fees should be less for modification due to clerical error or other administrative issues.)

Opposition to Motions for Relief from Stay

$450 (Personal property)
$575 (Real property)
for fees and expenses of all services rendered in opposition to motions to modify or vacate the automatic stay.

Obtaining Orders re: Sale or Refinance of Real Property

$425 (By stipulation)
$450 (By noticed hearing)
for fees and expenses of all services rendered for obtaining an order authorizing the sale or refinancing of real estate.

Objections to Claim

$250 (Uncontested objections without hearing)
$350 (Contested objections with a hearing)
for fees and expenses of all services rendered for preparing, filing, and noticing objections to a claim. (Fees shall not exceed 50% of the amount the trustee would have otherwise paid)

Oppositions to Dismissal/Motions to Avoid Lien/Other Routine Pleadings **$425**

for fees and expenses of all services rendered for preparing, filing, noticing, and attending hearings in opposition to a motion to dismiss the case, for motions to avoid lien and other routine pleadings.

Motions to Impose/Extend Automatic Stay **$575**

for fees and expenses of all services rendered for preparing, filing, noticing and attending hearings in regard to a motion to impose/extend automatic stay.

Novel and Complex Motions and Oppositions to Motions

These types of motions and oppositions may be billed at hourly rates and counsel shall file a fee application in compliance with Rules of 2002 and 2016 of the Federal Rules of Bankruptcy Procedure and Local Bankruptcy Rules 2002 and 2016.

Initial fee charged in this case is $________________

All post-filing fees shall be paid through the plan, unless the court orders otherwise. The attorney may not receive fees directly from the debtor other than the initial retainer, unless the court orders otherwise. All "additional fees," as described above, may only be paid upon court authorization after compliance with the "Guidelines Regarding Chapter 13 Attorney Fees". The attorney may seek fees above the additional fees provided a fee application is noticed, filed and approved by the court.

If the debtor disputes the legal services provided or the fees charged by the attorney, the debtor may file an objection with the court and set the matter for hearing. The attorney may move to withdraw or the debtor may discharge the attorney at any time.

Dated: ______________________________
Debtor

Dated: ______________________________
Debtor

Dated: ______________________________
Attorney for Debtor(s)

SDCAL-355 S.D. CALIFORNIA

VERIFICATION OF CREDITOR MATRIX (CALIFORNIA SOUTH)

CSD 1008 [08/21/00]

Name, Address, Telephone No. & I.D. No.

Phone: Fax:
I. D. No.

UNITED STATES BANKRUPTCY COURT
SOUTHERN DISTRICT OF CALIFORNIA
325 West "F" Street, San Diego, California 92101-6991

In Re:

Debtor.

VERIFICATION OF CREDITOR MATRIX

PART I (check and complete one):

[ ] New petition filed Creditor diskette required. TOTAL NO. OF CREDITORS: ____________

[ ] Conversion filed on ______________________________________ . *See instructions on reverse side.*

[ ] Former Chapter 13 converting. Creditor diskette required. TOTAL NO. OF CREDITORS: ____________

[ ] Post-petition creditors added. Scannable matrix required.

[ ] There are no post-petition creditors. No matrix required.

[ ] Amendment or Balance of Schedules filed concurrently with this original scannable matrix affecting Schedule of Debts and/or Schedule of Equity Security Holders. *See instructions on reverse side.*

[ ] Names and addresses are being ADDED.

[ ] Names and addresses are being DELETED.

[ ] Names and addresses are being CORRECTED.

PART II (check one):

[ ] The above-named Debtor(s) hereby verifies that the list of creditors is true and correct to the best of my (our) knowledge.

[ ] The above-named Debtor(s) hereby verifies that there are no post-petition creditors affected by the filing of the conversion of this case and that the filing of a matrix is not required.

Dated: ____________________

____
Debtor

REFER TO INSTRUCTIONS ON REVERSE SIDE

CSD 1008 (Page 2) [08/21/00]

INSTRUCTIONS

1) Full compliance with Special Requirements for Mailing Addresses (CSD 1007) is required.

2) A creditors matrix with Verification is required whenever the following occurs:

   a) A new petition is filed. Diskette required.

   b) A case is converted on or after SEPTEMBER 1, 2000. (See paragraph 4b concerning post-petition creditors.)

   c) An amendment to a case on or after SEPTEMBER 1, 2000, which adds, deletes or changes creditor address information on the debtor's Schedule of Debts and/or Schedule of Equity Security Holders. Scannable matrix format required.

3) The scannable matrix must be originally typed or printed. It may not be a copy.

4) CONVERSIONS:

   a) When converting a Chapter 13 case filed before SEPTEMBER 1, 2000, to another chapter, ALL creditors must be listed on the mailing matrix at the time of filing and accompanied by a Verification. Diskette required.

   b) For Chapter 7, 11, or 12 cases converted on or after SEPTEMBER 1, 2000, only post-petition creditors need be listed on the mailing matrix. The matrix and Verification must be filed with the post-petition schedule of debts and/or schedule of equity security holders. If there are no post-petition creditors, only the verification form is required. Scannable matrix format required.

5) AMENDMENTS AND BALANCE OF SCHEDULES:

   a) Scannable matrix format required.

   b) The matrix with Verification is a document separate from the amended schedules and may not be used to substitute for any portion of the schedules. IT MUST BE SUBMITTED WITH THE AMENDMENT/BALANCE OF SCHEDULES.

   c) Prepare a separate page for each type of change required: ADDED, DELETED, or CORRECTED. On the **REVERSE** side of each matrix page, indicate which category that particular page belongs in. Creditors falling in the same category should be placed on the same page in alphabetical order.

6) Please refer to CSD 1007 for additional information on how to avoid matrix-related problems.

CSD 1008

OPERATING AND REPORTING REQUIREMENTS FOR CHAPTER 11 CASES

Section 586(a)(3) of Title 28 of the United States Code provides for the supervision of the administration of Chapter 11 cases by the United States Trustee. Pursuant to that Section, the United States Trustee for Region 15 has promulgated the following requirements. Timely compliance with each of the following requirements is essential and required by United States Bankruptcy Code ("U.S.C.") Section 1107(a), Federal Rule of Bankruptcy Procedure ("Fed.R.Bankr.P.") 2015.

A. MEETINGS AND CONFERENCES

1. INITIAL DEBTOR CONFERENCES

The United States Trustee may require the debtor and its counsel to meet with a member of the staff of the United States Trustee at an initial debtor conference, which is generally held seven to ten calendar days after the filing of a voluntary petition. The purpose of the conference is to discuss the debtor's particular financial situation, its operating framework under Chapter 11, and the requirements of the United States Trustee. The debtor and debtor's attorney will be notified by mail if such a conference is set.

2. MEETING OF CREDITORS

A meeting of creditors will be held by the United States Trustee within 20 to 40 days after the filing of a voluntary petition. The debtor and debtor's attorney are required to appear, and in the case of a joint petition, both debtors must appear. All creditors and other parties in interest are notified of the meeting by the Clerk of the Bankruptcy Court. The debtor(s) will be examined under oath by the representative of the United States Trustee, creditors, and other parties in interest in attendance pursuant to 11 U.S.C. §§ 341 and 343, and Fed.R.Bankr.P. Rule 2003(b).

B. BOOKS, RECORDS, AND ACCOUNTS

1. BOOKS AND RECORDS

The books and records of the debtor must be closed out as of the date of the filing of the petition, and new books and records opened immediately thereafter, covering the post-petition period of the debtor-in-possession.

2. BANK ACCOUNTS

All pre-petition bank accounts and other deposits of which the debtor has possession, custody, control, ownership, use, or access must be closed upon the filing of the petition, and three new debtor-in-possession accounts opened: the general, payroll, and tax accounts. If the debtor possesses cash collateral, additional accounts must be established and maintained in accordance with 11 U.S.C. § 363(c)(4). The debtor may not use cash collateral without the consent of the secured creditor or an order of the bankruptcy court. See, 11 U.S.C. § 363(c)(2).

All funds received or held by the debtor-in-possession must be deposited into an account with a financial institution designated by the United States Trustee as an authorized depository. A copy of the list of authorized depositories for the Southern District of California may be obtained from the office of the United States Trustee.

The new bank signature cards for the bank accounts of the debtor-in-possession must clearly indicate that the debtor is a "chapter 11 debtor-in-possession." All checks shall be sequentially numbered, with the case name, case number, the words "Debtor-in-Possession", and type of account (general, payroll, tax, or cash collateral) imprinted on the face of each check, in substantially the following form:

ABC Produce Supply Debtor-in-Possession, 92-XXXXX GENERAL ACCOUNT 5555 Market Street San Diego, CA 92100 Pay to the Order of ______________________________ ______________________________ 00XXX-XXX-00-XXXXX 000XXX-XX00	No. 00001 _____________________, 20_______ $_______________ _______________ Dollars _____________________

3. BUSINESS CREDIT CARD ACCOUNTS

The debtor-in-possession shall close all business credit card accounts immediately. Copies of the closing statement for each such account must be attached to the monthly operating report when received.

C. REPORTS AND REQUIRED DOCUMENTS

1. EVIDENCE OF INSURANCE COVERAGE

The debtor-in-possession, within seven calendar days after the date of the filing of the petition, must provide the United States Trustee with certificates of insurance or other verified documents showing that each policy of insurance required for the estate is in full force and effect. Each policy must disclose the type and extent of coverage, effective dates, names of the insurance carrier and broker, and the agent's name, address and telephone number. The debtor-in-possession is responsible for including the address of the United States Trustee and the Bankruptcy case number as an additional interest holder, and on the cancellation notice. Additionally, the debtor-in-possession is required to provide a copy of either a renewal or new policy of insurance prior to the time that any existing policy or coverage is to expire.

Generally, the following types of insurance are required:

a. General Comprehensive/Public Liability;

b. Casualty coverage (tangible assets capable of loss by fire, weather, theft, vandalism, etc.);

c. Workers' Compensation;

d. Vehicle;

e. Product Liability.

2. PROJECTED OPERATING STATEMENT

The debtor-in-possession, within seven calendar days after the filing of the petition, is required to submit to the United States Trustee a Projected Operating Statement for the first ninety days of operations under Chapter 11. The statement must be submitted in the form of a profit and loss statement which includes an itemized list of income and expenses.

3. MONTHLY OPERATING REPORT

In accordance with 28 U.S.C. § 586(a)(3)(D), and 11 U.S.C. § 1106(a)(1), the debtor-in-possession shall file an original of the monthly Operating Report with the Clerk of the Bankruptcy Court no later than twenty calendar days after the close of each month. A copy of each Operating Report shall be served on the United States Trustee. The debtor-in-possession is required to attach copies of the monthly bank statements, bank reconciliations, and federal payroll tax deposit receipts, if applicable, to the Operating Reports. The monthly Operating Report should conform to the form attached.

4. RECENT INCOME TAX RETURNS

The debtor-in-possession, within 30 days of the filing of the petition, shall provide to the United States Trustee copies of its state and federal income tax returns filed for the two years prior to the filing of the petition.

5. REAL PROPERTY QUESTIONNAIRE

The debtor, within seven calendar days after the filing of the petition, shall submit to the United States Trustee, a Real Property Questionnaire for each parcel of real property owned or leased by the debtor. A Real Property Questionnaire form is attached.

6. PHYSICAL INVENTORY

The debtor, within thirty calendar days after the filing of the petition, is required to submit to the United States Trustee a physical inventory as of the date of the petition which provides an itemized cost value of the inventory held by the estate.

7. POST-CONFIRMATION REPORTS

The United States Trustee requires quarterly reports after confirmation of a plan of reorganization until the court grants a final decree. In accordance with 28 U.S.C. § 586(a)(3)(D) and 11 U.S.C. § 1106(a)(1), the reorganized debtor shall file an original quarterly Post-Confirmation Report with the clerk of the bankruptcy court no later than twenty calendar days after the close of each calendar quarter. A copy of each Post-Confirmation Report shall be served on the United States Trustee. The reorganized debtor should be prepared to substantiate anything reported on the Post-Confirmation Report to the United States Trustee. Requested substantiation could include, but is not limited to, such items as disbursement registers or bank statements. A Post-Confirmation Report is attached for your use.

8. REPORTS IN CASES CONVERTED TO CHAPTER 7

Should the case convert to a chapter 7, the debtor or chapter 11 trustee must comply with Fed.R.Bankr.P. 1019(1), (4), and (5) and LBR 1019-1. All records and property must be turned over to the chapter 7 trustee. Property of the estate must be secured and preserved.

The debtor or chapter 11 trustee must also file a final report and account with the Court, with a copy served on the United States Trustee and the chapter 7 trustee assigned to the case. The final report and account should include a verified schedule of all property of the estate as of the date of conversion. This schedule of assets must be filed within 5 days after entry of the order converting the case to chapter 7. Additionally, a schedule of unpaid debts incurred after commencement of the superseded case including the name and address of each creditor must be filed and served within 15 days after the entry of the order converting the case. A final report and account form is attached for your use.

9. SERVICE OF DOCUMENTS ON THE U.S. TRUSTEE

The debtor must serve the United States Trustee with a copy of all documents submitted to or filed with the Bankruptcy Court and all matters served on parties in interest pursuant to the Bankruptcy Rules. See, Fed.R.Bankr.P. 9034. See also, United States Trustee Attorney Guideline Number 1. The United States Trustee accepts service of documents at 402 West Broadway, Suite 600, San Diego CA 92101-8511.

DO NOT serve the United States Trustee with documents filed in adversary proceedings, other than the initial Complaint and the initial Answer, unless requested to do so in writing by the office of the United States Trustee. DO NOT serve pleadings or documents by facsimile machine unless requested to do so by the office of the United States Trustee. Transmission of copies by facsimile does not constitute service of process under the Bankruptcy Local Rule ("LBR") 9006-3.

D. UNITED STATES TRUSTEE QUARTERLY FEES

Debtors are required to pay quarterly fees in all pending chapter 11 cases pursuant to 28 U.S.C. § 1930(a) and Fed.R.Bankr.P. 2015(a)(5). Fees must be paid to the United States Trustee each calendar quarter based upon the dollar amount of disbursements made during that quarter. Fees for the first quarter are calculated from the date of the filing of the petition to the end of the calendar quarter. Fees for the last quarter are calculated from the beginning of that quarter to the date of the entry of the order closing, converting, or dismissing the case.

TOTAL QUARTERLY DISBURSEMENTS	QUARTERLY FEE
$0 to 14, 999.99	$325 [1]
15,000.00 to 74,999.99	650
75,000.00 to 149,999.99	975
150,000.00 to 224,999.99	1,625
225,000.00 to 299,999.99	1,950
300,000.00 to 999,999.99	4,875
1,000,000.00 to 1,999,999.99	6,500
2,000,000.00 to 2,999,999.99	9,750
3,000,000.00 to 4,999,999.99	10,400
5,000,000.00 to 14,999,999.99	13,000
15,000,000.00 to 29,999,999.99	20,000
30,000,000.00 or more	30,000

A minimum fee of $325 is due each quarter even if no disbursements are made during that quarter, and even if the case was pending during that quarter for only one day.

The United States Trustee Program began assessing interest on unpaid Chapter 11 quarterly fee balances on October 1, 2007. The assessment is retroactive to the date the case was originally filed. The interest rate, as determined by the Treasury Department, is based upon the effective rate when your account became past due. The interest will be waived and need

[1] The amount of the Quarterly Fees changed on January 1, 2008. For the amounts imposed for calendar quarters before October 1, 1996, contact the Office of the United States Trustee for a copy of the prior fee schedule.

not be paid if the total principal amount due is received within thirty (30) days of the date of the first interest assessment notice.

The amount of fees owed must be substantiated through the filing of Operating Reports. The maximum fee of $30,000 per quarter may be imposed in cases where substantiation of the fee amount cannot be determined due to the debtor's failure to file timely Operating Reports.

A plan of reorganization must provide for the payment of quarterly fees until the case is either closed by the court, dismissed by the court or converted to another chapter.

Quarterly fees are billed by direct mail to the debtor-in-possession, and payments should be mailed to:

U.S. Trustee Payment Center
Post Office Box 70937
Charlotte, NC 28272-0937

If any check for the payment of quarterly fees is dishonored, then all future quarterly fee payments must be made by cashier's check, certified funds, or money order. Failure to pay the quarterly fee is cause for conversion or dismissal of the chapter 11 case pursuant to 11 U.S.C. § 1112(b)(10).

E. GENERAL RESTRICTIONS

1. POST-PETITION TAXES, WAGES, AND EXPENSES OF ADMINISTRATION

The debtor-in-possession must remain current with all expenses of administration during the pendency of the chapter 11 case. The debtor-in-possession, as a fiduciary, must withhold, collect, and deposit all taxes owed to the Internal Revenue Service and state and local taxing authorities. These taxes include, but are not limited to, federal and state withholding, employee's portion of F.I.C.A., federal and state unemployment insurance, transient occupancy taxes, and sales and use taxes. All administrative priority wages, employee related payments and other expenses of administration must be paid as they become due.

2. OBTAINING CREDIT

11 U.S.C. § 364(b) provides that the debtor-in-possession may not obtain credit nor incur unsecured debt other than in the ordinary course of business without prior court approval. Section 364(c) also requires court approval before the obtaining of credit or the incurring of debt with priority over certain administrative expenses. Section 364(c) requires

court approval before obtaining credit or incurring debt that is secured by a lien on property of the estate. The debtor-in-possession should also consult with its attorney before extending credit or lending funds to third parties. The debtor-in-possession shall serve the United States Trustee with a copy of any such application filed with the court.

3. USE, SALE, OR LEASE OF PROPERTY OF THE ESTATE

11 U.S.C. § 363(b) requires a debtor to obtain prior court approval for the use, sale, or lease of property of the estate when such use, sale, or lease is not in the ordinary course of business of the debtor. The debtor shall serve the United States Trustee with copies of any such application filed with the court.

4. EMPLOYMENT OF ATTORNEYS AND OTHER PROFESSIONALS

A debtor-in-possession may employ an attorney, accountant, or other professional only upon authorization by the court. No payments may be made to such attorneys, accountants, or other professionals after the filing of the petition without prior court authorization after notice to all creditors and the opportunity for a hearing. See, 11 U.S.C. §§ 327 through 331 and Fed.R.Bankr.P. 2014, 2016, and 2017.

5. COMPENSATION OF PRINCIPALS, PARTNERS, OFFICERS, OR DIRECTORS OF THE DEBTOR

No compensation or other remuneration shall be paid by the debtor to any officer, director, or shareholder of a corporation, to any partners of a debtor partnership or to an individual debtor without first complying with the provisions of Bankruptcy Local Rule 4002-2.

6. PAYMENT OF PRE-PETITION DEBT

There are specific prohibitions and restrictions against payment of certain debts incurred prior to the filing of the petition without court authorization. The debtor is cautioned to consult with its attorney regarding any payment of pre-petition debts.

7. CHANGE OF ADDRESS OR TELEPHONE NUMBER

The debtor must notify the United States Trustee, in writing within forty-eight (48) hours, of any change of address or telephone number of the debtor and debtor's attorney. The debtor must also file with the Clerk of the Bankruptcy Court a change of address form.

F. MODIFICATIONS

The United States Trustee may, at any time, amend or modify the requirements of a particular chapter 11 case. Additional requirements may include the submission of audited and unaudited financial statements, state and federal payroll or income tax returns, state sales tax returns (with all schedules and attachments), copies of trust agreements or conveyances, and examination of the debtor's books, records, and bank statements. Any request to amend or modify these requirements must be submitted in writing, and no such amendments or modifications are valid unless and until they are approved by the office of the United States Trustee in writing.

Dated: March 1, 2008

TIMETABLE AND CHECKLIST

I. Contemporaneous With Filing of Petition

A. Bankruptcy Petition Cover Sheet.

B. Petition with required Exhibits (See, Local Bankruptcy Rule 1007-3(3)).

II. Immediately After Filing of Petition

A. Close all pre-petition bank accounts, books, and records and all business credit card accounts.

B. Open new debtor-in-possession books and records, and debtor-in-possession bank accounts (General, Tax, and Payroll accounts).

C. Conduct physical inventory.

D. Amend all insurance policies to include the United States Trustee as an additional interest holder and to include bankruptcy case number.

III. Within Seven Days After Filing of Petition

A. Provide evidence of appropriate insurance coverage to the United States Trustee.

B. Provide proof of the opening of new debtor-in-possession bank accounts by providing copies of the signature cards to the United States Trustee.

C. Submit Real Property Questionnaire for each parcel of real estate in which the debtor has an interest to the United States Trustee.

D. Submit Projected Operating Statement to the United States Trustee.

E. Submit copies of the Debtor's state and federal income tax returns for the last two years to the United States Trustee.

IV. A. File Schedules of Assets and Liabilities and Statement of Financial Affairs if not filed with the Petition and Exhibits.

B. Attend Initial Debtor Conference (if scheduled).

V. Within Thirty Days After Filing of Petition

A. Submit Physical Inventory to the United States Trustee.

B. File and Serve Applications to Employ Professionals or Other Professionals (See, United States Trustee Attorney Guideline Number 2).

VI. During the Chapter 11 Case.

A. Submit timely payments of United States Trustee Quarterly Fees each quarter.

B. File and serve Operating Reports for each month within twenty calendar days of the end of the month.

C. Submit renewals or new policies of insurance for property of the estate prior to the expiration of existing policies.

D. Serve the United States Trustee with copies of all documents filed with the Court.

E. File Disclosure Statement and Plan of Reorganization within 120 days of the filing of the Petition.

SDCAL-367 S.D. CALIFORNIA

UNITED STATES DEPARTMENT OF JUSTICE
OFFICE OF THE UNITED STATES TRUSTEE
SOUTHERN DISTRICT OF CALIFORNIA

In re: Debtor(s).	CHAPTER 11 CASE NO. ______________ DEBTOR-IN-POSSESSION REAL PROPERTY QUESTIONNAIRE

OWNED PROPERTY

SUBMIT THIS QUESTIONNAIRE TO THE OFFICE OF THE UNITED STATES TRUSTEE ONLY. DO NOT FILE WITH THE BANKRUPTCY COURT.

The debtor-in-possession is required to complete a Real Property Questionnaire for each parcel of real property in which the debtor held a legal or equitable interest at the time of the filing of the petition. This includes, but is not limited to, property held under ownership, leasehold, land sale, or open escrow. A continuation sheet should be attached for each question where additional space is needed.

A. General Property Information

1. Address of property including county and state in which it is located:

____

____

2. Type of real property (i.e., single family residence, condominium, apartment building, office building, commercial, industrial, unimproved):

____

____

3. Description of property (i.e., number of units or offices, square footage, amenities, and present condition):

____

____

4. Define the debtor's interest in thc rcal property:

__________ Ownership (i.e., fee ownership).

__________ Land Sale.

__________ Other—Explain: ______________________

5. Does the property presently conform to all local, state, and federal requirements, such as health, building, safety, earthquake, fire, or other regulations?

____________ Yes.

____________ No.

Explain: ____

B. Income and Management of the Property

1. Is any income being generated from rental or use of the property by third parties?

____________ Yes. Present gross monthly income: $____________

____________ No.

2. If the property is being used or occupied by a third party, provide the name of that party, explain the relationship, if any, to the debtor-in-possession and explain the terms of any agreement with that party.

____

____

3. Is there any person or entity managing the property?

____________ No.

____________ Yes. Provide the name, address, and telephone number of the managing person/entity and attach a copy of the management agreement.

____

____

____

____

4. Is the manager (or principals of the management company) in any way related to or affiliated with the debtor?

____________ No.

____________ Yes. Provide complete information regarding the relationship or affiliation.

____

____

5. Has a real estate broker or agent been employed by the debtor for this property?

____________ No.

____________ Yes. Provide the name and address of the broker or agent and the date on which the broker or agent was employed.

____

____

C. Ownership Items

1. Is the debtor the titleholder to the property?

____________ Yes.

____________ No. Explain. ________________________

2. Provide the percentage interest and type of ownership (i.e., fee simple, tenants in common, joint tenancy, etc.) held in the property by the debtor.

____________ ____________%
Type of Ownership

3. Date of acquisition of the property: ____________________
Total purchase price of the property: ____________________
4. Present fair market value: $____________________
Source and basis of the fair market value: ________________

____

____

5. Voluntary encumbrances recorded against the property (e.g., mortgages/ trust deeds, stipulated judgments):

	Name of Lender	Outstanding Principal Amount	Installment Payments/ Frequency	Number of Delinquent Payments
1st		$	$	
2nd		$	$	
3rd		$	$	
4th		$	$	
5th		$	$	

6. If any pre-petition debt service payments remained unpaid as a result of a dispute, were such payments escrowed into a separate trust account: Yes ____________/No ____________

If yes, please provide the name of the depository, branch, account number, and amount of funds on hand.

____

____

____

7. Involuntary encumbrances recorded against the property (i.e., tax, mechanics, judgment, lis pendens, and other liens). State the type of lien, amount, and date recorded:

____

____

____

8. Itemize all the monthly expenses related to the property, <u>excluding</u> debt service (attach a separate listing, if necessary):

____

____

____

I, ________________________ (Name and title), declare under penalty of perjury that I have fully read and understood the foregoing debtor-in-possession Real Property Questionnaire and that the information contained herein is true and correct to the best of my knowledge.

Date: ______________________________
Principal for Debtor-In-Possession

UNITED STATES DEPARTMENT OF JUSTICE
OFFICE OF THE UNITED STATES TRUSTEE
SOUTHERN DISTRICT OF CALIFORNIA

In Re: Debtor(s).	CHAPTER 11 CASE NO. __________ DEBTOR-IN-POSSESSION REAL PROPERTY QUESTIONNAIRE

LEASED PROPERTY

SUBMIT THIS QUESTIONNAIRE TO THE OFFICE OF THE UNITED STATES TRUSTEE ONLY. <u>DO NOT FILE WITH THE BANKRUPTCY COURT</u>.

The debtor-in-possession is required to complete a Real Property Questionnaire for each parcel of real property in which the debtor held a legal or equitable interest at the time of the filing of the petition. This includes, but is not limited to, property held under ownership, leasehold, land sale, or open escrow. A continuation sheet should be attached for each question where additional space is needed.

A. General Property Information

1. Address of property including county and state in which it is located:

____

____

2. Type of real property (i.e., single family residence, condominium, apartment building, office building, commercial, industrial, unimproved):

____

3. Description of property (i.e., number of units or offices, square footage, amenities, and present condition):

____

____

4. Does the property presently conform to all local, state, and federal requirements, such as health, building, safety, earthquake, fire or other regulations?

____________ Yes

____________ No. Explain: ____________

B. Property Leased by the Debtor-in-Possession

1. What is the name, address and telephone number of the lessor?

____

____

2. Does the lessor own the property?

____________ Yes.

____________ No. Provide the name, address, and telephone number of the owner.

____

____

3. Does a written lease exist between the Debtor-in-Possession and the lessor?

__________ Yes. Please attach a copy of the lease.

__________ No. Please explain the terms of the lease.

____

____

____

4. Lease payment amount: $__________

Per: __________ Month/ __________ Quarter/ __________ Year/ __________ Other: __________

5. Number and amount of unpaid pre-petition lease payments:

Number: __________/ Amount: $__________

6. If any pre-petition lease payments remained unpaid as a result of a dispute, were such payments escrowed into a separate trust account?

__________ No.

__________ Yes. Please provide the name of the escrow holder, account number, and amount of funds on hand:

____

____

____

____

I, ____________________ (Name and title), declare under penalty of perjury that I have fully read and understood the foregoing Real Property Questionnaire and that the information provided herein is true and correct to the best of my knowledge.

Date: ____________________

Principal for Debtor-In-Possession

STANDING PANEL OF BANKRUPTCY TRUSTEES STANDING ADMINISTRATION GUIDELINES

I. Debtor's Representation and Attendance at Meeting of Creditors

A. Attendance at Section 341 Meeting:

Debtors must attend the initial Section 341 Meeting and, unless excused by the United States Trustee, any continued Section 341 Meeting. Panel Trustees do not have the authority to excuse the debtor from attending his or her Section 341 Meeting.

B. Identification:

At the § 341(a) Meeting, pursuant to 11 USC 521(h)(1) and (2), each individual debtor must present original government issued photo identification and confirmation of the full social security number. Any document used must be an original except that a copy of a W-2 Form, an IRS Form 1099, or a recent payroll advice may be accepted to confirm debtor's social security number. Acceptable forms of picture identification (ID) include; driver's license, U.S. government ID, state ID, passport (and current U.S. visa, if not a U.S. citizen), military ID, resident alien card, and identity card issued by a national government authority (if authorized by the United States Trustee). Acceptable forms of proof of social security number include: social security card, medical insurance card, pay advice, W-2 Form, IRS Form 1099, and Social Security Administration (SSA) Statement.

C. Alternative Meetings:

Debtor's attorney or the debtor in pro per must independently contact the United States Trustee (619-557-5013) for consideration of alternative procedures, i.e., telephonic, etc. Debtor's attorney must be physically present at the time of the alternative procedure for appearance for conducting the Creditors Meeting, with a completed Questionnaire authenticated and executed by the debtor.

II. Supporting Documentation

Certain supporting documentation is required in each case to allow the Trustee to fulfill his or her fiduciary duty and due diligence in investigating the financial affairs of the debtor pursuant to 11 USC § 704. The preferred method of delivery is the E-DOCS method. The debtor, and/or the debtor's attorney, must provide, in addition to debtor's duties as set forth in 11 USC § 521:

1. Proof of Income

a) Copies of pay stubs for the 60 days prior to filing. If debtor(s) do not have current pay stubs they should be brought to the Section 341(a) Meeting; and

b) If a summary of debtor's income for the six (6) month period prior to case filing was not submitted as an exhibit to Schedule B-22, completion of the Form attached as Exhibit "A" or alternatively "A-1" showing six (6) months computations prepared for means test, including signature by attorney certifying review of those representations by debtors.

c) Self-employed. Completion of a Profit and Loss Statement showing gross income and gross expenses for the six (6) months prior to case filing, with specificity, as to expenses to enable the Trustee to fully analyze the business operations of the debtor.

2. Value of Vehicles:

Written documentation as to the basis for valuation of motor vehicles. In this regard a Statement of Value can be easily obtained via the Internet at www.kbb.com or www.nadaguides.com and is the preferred form of valuation. If valuation is not available from these services, documentation upon which debtor based his or her representation of value. An estimation purely based on debtor's opinion is unacceptable.

3. Vehicles:

a) Copy of current vehicle registration or copy of certificate of title (please note: registration renewal notices are not acceptable unless that notice shows the lien holder);

b) Written proof of payoff balance for liens on vehicles, i.e., statements, credit report, etc;

c) Copy of Security Agreement associated with sale of vehicle if registered in a state other than California that does not denote liens on registration;

d) Copy of Declarations page of insurance for each vehicle which sets forth the period of coverage and extent of coverage. The Insurance Card is insufficient. In order to protect the estate from liability and preserve assets for the estate, uninsured vehicles are not to be operated by debtors or others until either:

(i) Coverage for liability and property damage is placed with the estate being added as an additional insured;

(ii) Debtor's exemption is effective pursuant to FRBP 4003; or

(iii) Effective abandonment by the trustee pursuant to 11 USC § 554.

4. Value of Real Property:

Written documentation as to the basis for valuation of real property. Comparable reports are acceptable only if reasonable ranges of values are presented with identifiable comparable properties.

5. Real Property:

a) Copy of first 1-2 pages only of Deed of Trust showing identity of lender and including recording stamp;

b) Copy of Grant Deed showing how title is held by debtor, and legal description;

c) Written proof of payoff balance for all loans in form of most recent Statements or other documentation from the lenders;

d) If property acquired or refinanced within one (1) year of filing, a copy of closing statement;

e) If noninstitutional lender, copies of documents demonstrating the actual loan advance by creditor to debtor;

f) Copy of Declaration page of insurance setting forth the period of coverage and extent of coverage. If the property is uninsured a Statement of such from the debtor.

6. Personal Property Liens—Financing Statements:

a) Copies of UCC-1/Security Agreements documenting filing with the Secretary of State;

b) Copies of documents demonstrating the actual loan advance for noninstitutional creditors; and

c) Written proof of payoff balance

7. Trust Documents:

Copies of any Trust instrument including exhibits and amendments in which the debtor has an interest of any type, i.e., beneficiary, trustee, or trustor, upon request of Trustee.

8. Depository Statements:

a) Copies of depository statements covering the date of the filing of the bankruptcy case are to be brought to the Section 341(a) Meeting for delivery to the Trustee.

9. Tax Returns:

a) Complete copy of most recent tax year federal IRS return including all Statements and Schedules, or return transcript (please note: worksheets provided to accountants do not need to be provided).

b) If no return has been filed within three (3) years then a declaration from debtor(s) must be provided to that effect.

10. Expenses in Excess of IRS or Means Test Standards:

To be brought to the Section 341(a) Meeting. Copies of receipts and other documentation, including the calculations demonstrating how the debtor arrived at his/her estimate of expenses, to support increased expenses claimed by debtor for examination by the Trustee.

11. Health Care Cases:

Notify the trustee immediately upon filing of the bankruptcy case of the existence of patients in the case to facilitate the orderly administration of the case. All documents submitted must include a cover page indicating the case number, date and time of the Section 341 Meeting. A sample Supporting Documentation Cover Sheet is attached as Exhibit "B." All relevant documents are to be received by the Trustee within fifteen (15) days of the filing of the case. Failure to timely provide such required supporting documents may result in continuance of the Creditor Meeting without the debtor(s) being examined until all documents are presented.

III. Disclosure of Amount of Debt

In addition to a Trustee's obvious duty to liquidate non-exempt assets for the benefit of creditors and to evaluate the Means Test Form B-22, Trustees also examine a debtor's ability to pay debts pursuant to 11 USC § 707(b), i.e. totality of circumstances. It is impossible for the Trustee to analyze these issues when debtor schedules "unknown" for an obligation. It is incumbent upon debtors to estimate all claims so that such an analysis can be conducted. In this analysis, debtors should not overstate the claims, i.e., a repossession or foreclosure should reflect the deficiency not the debt before repossession or foreclosure; and the actual pay off, not the eventual payments plus interest. Cases that do not provide such information may be continued so that accurate information is available to the Trustee.

IV. Claim of Exemption

CCP 703.140(a)(2) requires a married debtor filing without the spouse to elect the exemptions under CCP 704 et seq., unless the non-filing spouse executes a written waiver. A sample Wavier form is attached as Exhibit "C." The Waiver is to be filed with the court. A conformed copy is to be provided to the Trustee.

V. Questionnaires to be Completed and Delivered at Creditors Meeting

A Questionnaire has been developed for individual debtors (Exhibit "D" hereto) and Partnership/Corporate debtors (Exhibit "E" hereto) to address certain inquiries that the Trustees believe will facilitate the examination of debtors. Debtors must personally execute (fill out) the appropriate Questionnaire and deliver such to the Trustee at the Creditors Meeting.

VI. Unincorporated Self-Employed, Professionals, and Business Cases

If a debtor is operating a business or profession and there is no liability insurance covering the operation of the business or profession it is necessary for the business or profession to be suspended until liability insurance is placed in effect, with evidence of such to the Trustee. The Trustee must be notified of any such business or profession immediately.

At a minimum, the Trustee is to be informed in writing within 24 hours of filing of the following:

1. The status and fair market value of all assets of the estate including secured, lessor or exemption claims, that are to be utilized in the business or profession operations;

2. Evidence of current property and/or liability insurance coverage in connection with the operation of the business if non-exempt property of the estate is to be utilized in operations;

3. Evidence of current Workers Compensation insurance in connection with the operation of business, if applicable;

4. Evidence of current Errors and Omissions insurance coverage, if applicable;

5. Evidence of a reserve tax account to address employee/employer taxes; and

6. The existence of any environmental, law enforcement or federal or state regulatory issues that affect the business of profession.

Business operations utilizing property of the estate are not to be conducted post-petition under any circumstances prior to abandonment, or allowance of exemption of property of the estate utilized in the business or profession, without the written concurrent of the Trustee, or Order of the United States Bankruptcy Court.

VII. Corporate Cases

All business operations are to be terminated on the filing of the case. The Trustee is to be informed in writing within 24 hours of filing the case, of the following:

1. The identity and location of all remaining assets of the debtor corporation;

2. Contact information and/or keys for access to business locations, and all storage locations, as well as all security codes and computer access passwords;

3. Contact information for landlord(s) and secured creditors, if applicable;

4. The need for immediate action of the Trustee to preserve assets of the estate; and

5. The existence of any environmental, law enforcement or federal or state regulatory issues that affect the business of profession;

In order for the Trustee to conclude a corporate and/or partnership debtor's 11 USC § 341(a) Meeting certain documents may be required for examination, and should be made available to the Trustee if requested:

1. Minute Book

2. Shareholder Register

3. Complete Tax returns for past two years

4. Income and Expense and Balance Sheet, Reports for past 1 year

5. Bank Statements and canceled checks for past 1 year

6. Copies of last two inventories, if applicable

7. Documentation of Intellectual property, i.e., patents, trademarks, copyrights, royalties, etc., if applicable; and

8. Accounts Receivables, with all documents associated therewith. The above documents should be available for the Trustee if requested

9. UCC-1, or other evidence of liens.

10. Cash Receipts and Disbursements Journal for prior year.

Exhibit "A"

CURRENT MONTHLY INCOME DETAILS FOR THE DEBTOR

Income for the Period ______________________________ to ______________________________

Gross wages, salary, tips, bonuses, overtime, commissions

Source of Information: ______________________________

Income by Month; Date $ Sum

6 Months Ago: ______________________________

5 Months Ago: ______________________________

4 Months Ago: ______________________________

3 Months Ago: ______________________________

2 Months Ago: ______________________________

Last Month: ______________________________

Average per month: ______________________________

Deductions:

Source of Information: ______________________________

6 Months Ago: ______________________________

5 Months Ago: ______________________________

4 Months Ago: ______________________________

3 Months Ago: ______________________________

2 Months Ago: ______________________________

Last Month: ______________________________

Average per month: ______________________________

Average net income per month: ______________________________

Date: ______________

____

Debtor

____

Co-Debtor

ATTORNEY CERTIFICATE

I have reviewed the documentation of the debtor upon which the representations of the debtor are made in this Statement.

Date:____________

____

Attorney for Debtor (Printed/Signed)

Exhibit "A-1"

CURRENT MONTHLY INCOME DETAILS FOR THE DEBTOR

Employer:____

Year to Date gross as of ____________: $____________

Year to Date gross as of ____________: $____________

Total Gross during period $____________/____________months (or other period)

Average Monthly Gross $____________

Year to Date expenses as of ____________: $____________

Year to Date expenses as of ____________: $____________

Total expenses during period $____________/____________months (or other period)

Average Monthly Expenses $____________

Note: If more than one employer during six month period prior to filing of bankruptcy case, provide additional form for each employer.

ATTORNEY CERTIFICATE

I have reviewed the documentation of the debtor upon which the representations of the debtor are made in this Statement.

Date:____________

____

Attorney for Debtor (Printed/Signed)

Exhibit "B"

Supporting Documentation Cover Sheet

In Re:____________Case Number____________341(a):____________

Deficiencies:

[__________] 1. Income Verification (i.e., pay stubs or Profit & Loss Statement)

[__________] 2. Valuation of motor vehicles

[__________] 3. Pay off documentation motor vehicles (i.e., balance due)

[__________] 4. Vehicle registration

[__________] 5. Valuation of real property

[__________] 6. Pay off Documentation Real Property (i.e., balance due)

[__________] 7. Trust Deeds on real property

[__________] 8. Grant Deed on real property

[__________] 9. Closing Statement on real property

[__________] 10. Loan advances documentation (i.e., evidence of disbursement)

[__________] 11. UCC-1 (recorded) and evidence of payoff balance

[__________] 12. Tax Return

[__________] 13. CCP 703.140(a) Waiver.

[__________] 14. Declaration Page—Vehicle Insurance (*Not* Insurance Card)

[__________] 15. Declaration Page—Real Property Insurance

Exhibit "C"

MUTUAL WAIVER OF RIGHT TO CLAIM STATE EXEMPTIONS, OTHER THAN
THOSE PROVIDED IN CALIFORNIA CODE OF CIVIL PROCEDURE SECTION
703.140(b), DURING PENDENCY OF BANKRUPTCY CASE
(California Code of Civil Procedure § 703.140(a)(2))

1. IDENTIFICATION OF PARTIES. This mutual waiver, is made by __________ and __________, husband and wife.

2. PURPOSE OF THIS WAIVER. This waiver is made to satisfy the requirement set forth in California Code of Civil Procedure § 703.140(a)(2) regarding the election of exemptions pursuant to § 703.140(b) by married debtors who file an individual Bankruptcy petition.

3. LEGAL RIGHTS WAIVED. California Code of Civil Procedure § 703.140(a)(2) provides:

IF A PETITION IS FILED INDIVIDUALLY, AND NOT JOINTLY, FOR A

HUSBAND OR A WIFE, THE EXEMPTIONS PROVIDED BY THIS CHAPTER OTHER THAN THE PROVISIONS SUBDIVISION (b) ARE APPLICABLE, EXCEPT THAT, IF BOTH HUSBAND AND WIFE EFFECTIVELY WAIVE IN WRITING THE RIGHT TO CLAIM, DURING THE PERIOD THE CASE COMMENCED BY FILING THE PETITION IS PENDING, THE EXEMPTIONS PROVIDED BY THE APPLICABLE EXEMPTION PROVISIONS OF THIS CHAPTER, OTHER THAN SUBDIVISION (b), IN ANY CASE COMMENCED BY FILING A PETITION FOR EITHER OF THEM UNDER TITLE 11 OF THE UNITED STATES CODE, THEN THEY MAY ELECT INSTEAD TO USE THE APPLICABLE EXEMPTIONS SET FORTH IN SUBDIVISION (b).

4. RIGHT TO HAVE INDEPENDENT COUNSEL REVIEW WAIVER. Both parties acknowledge that they have been informed of their right to consult an attorney regarding the effect of this waiver on them.

5. MUTUAL WAIVER. Both parties, by executing this agreement below, hereby waive their right to claim any state exemptions, other than those provided in California Code of Civil Procedure § 703.140(b), during the pendency of the Chapter 7 Bankruptcy of ___________, filed in the U.S. Bankruptcy Court for the Southern District of California. The foregoing is agreed to by:

Dated: ____________________ ________________________
wife

Dated: ____________________ ________________________
husband

Exhibit "D"

341(a) Meeting of Creditors Questionnaire

Name: ________________________ Case No: ________________________

INTRODUCTION AND INSTRUCTIONS

YOU HAVE A DUTY TO COOPERATE: As part of your Bankruptcy, the Trustee must examine and investigate your financial affairs and related information. Under the law, it is your duty to fully cooperate with and assist the Trustee in this investigation. These are standard questions that each debtor must answer. You may receive further requests for additional documents from the Trustee.

The Trustee may conduct further investigation as needed. You are obligated to provide this additional information and documents as well.

YOUR ANSWERS MUST BE TRUE, COMPLETE AND ACCURATE: It is important that all your answers to the questions are true, complete and accurate. If you have made any mistakes in your bankruptcy documents, it is absolutely essential that you inform your Trustee by correcting those mistakes NOW. Failure to do so may result in severe consequences. IT IS A FEDERAL CRIME TO INTENTIONALLY GIVE FALSE OR MISLEADING INFORMATION AND TESTIMONY TO YOUR BANKRUPTCY TRUSTEE.

ALL YOUR PROPERTY IS NOW THE PROPERTY OF THE ESTATE UNTIL YOUR CASE IS CLOSED BY THE COURT, ANY CLAIM OF EXEMPTION PURSUANT TO FRBP 4003 BECOMES EFFECTIVE OR THE STATUTORY TIME FOR AN ABANDONMENT NOTICE FROM THE TRUSTEE TO BECOME EFFECTIVE YOU CANNOT SELL, REFINANCE, OR OTHERWISE ENCUMBER ANY OF YOUR PROPERTY.

IF YOU HAVE QUESTIONS: If you have any questions or require further information, you should consult with your attorney or other legal source as the trustee cannot give you legal advice.

Please respond to the following questions. You should discuss your response with your attorney for any clarification:

1. I am represented by counsel and have reviewed my Petition, Schedules and Statement of Financial Affairs and they were explained to me by that counsel before I signed them.

Yes ___ No ___, or

I am representing myself and have reviewed and understand them.

Yes ___ No ___

2. Do you understand you are required to disclose to the Trustee all pre-bankruptcy rights to money or property even if you won't receive it until after filing bankruptcy (example, money from lawsuits, unpaid commissions, earned by unpaid bonuses, accounts receivable) and to not do so could result in denial of your discharge of debts and civil, as well as criminal penalties?

Yes ___ No ___

3. Do you understand that "property" means anything you own or have a present, future or contingent interest, not just real estate?

Yes ___ No ___

4. Do you understand that you are to report to the Court and Trustee, by formal written Amendment filed with the Court, any rights to an inheritance, property settlement agreement, or life insurance proceeds that occur within 180 days of the date your case was filed?

Yes ___ No ___

5. If currently married, have you disclosed all property and asset interests of your spouse even if you are now separated?

Yes ___ No ___

6. Are you entitled to receive a death benefit under a will or insurance policy? Answer "yes" only if that person has died.

Yes ___ No ___

7. Are you the beneficiary, trustee or trustor of a trust?

Yes ___ No ___

8. Within four years prior the filing of your bankruptcy have you made any payments, or transferred any property to any person or entity other than for regular monthly contract payments?

Yes ___ No ___

9. Do you have, or have you had in the past four years, any interests in any corporations, partnerships, LP's and/or LLC's?

Yes ___ No ___

10. Do you now or have you had in the past one year any interests in offshore accounts, i.e., accounts outside the borders of the United States?

Yes ___ No ___

11. Are you seeking recovery in any current lawsuits, or do you have a belief you have grounds to file a lawsuit or counter suit, (whether you desire to do so or not.) SEEKING DAMAGES?

Yes ___ No ___

12. Does anyone and or any entity owe you any money ?

Yes ___ No ___

13. Please identify any of your creditor claims in Schedules D, E and/or F that are disputed except for those that are already identified as disputed in you schedules?

____

14. Have you listed accurate claim amounts in your Schedule D, E or F to the best of your knowledge?

Yes ___ No ___

15. Please read the following:

III

Disclosure of When Debtor Incurred Debt

Schedules D, E & F require the debtor to provide "date claim was incurred." This information is necessary for Trustee to evaluate certain issues pursuant to 18 USC § 3057(a) and 11 USC § 727. The required information is not the initial date a credit account was established.

The Trustees' interpretation of the term "date claim was incurred" is the period between which the "amounts claimed" were estimated to be actually incurred. This will require Counsel, or debtors in Pro Per, to adequately perform their research duties under BAPCA, to provide the period of time that the current claim was incurred.

Does the information in your Schedule D, E and F, accurately estimate the dates of creditor's claims disclosed in those schedules?

Yes ___ No ___

16. Are you obligated to pay child support or spousal support pursuant to a Court Order, property settlement agreement or determination by a governmental unit?

Yes ___ No ___

17. If your response was "yes" to question 16, please provide:

Name of claimant: ___________

Address of claimant: ___________

Telephone number of claimant: ___________

18. Do you understand the Trustee is relying on your responses in this questionnaire, as well as all other documents and statements you are making to administer this case?

Yes ___ No ___

19. Have you continually resided in the State of California for the two years prior to the filing of your case?

Yes ___ No ___

20. As of the date you filed your bankruptcy were you or are you entitled to

an income tax refund for any current or prior years including amendments to filed returns?

Yes ___ No ___

21. If your response to question 20 was "yes," approximately how much was, or is, your Federal and State refund?

Federal ____________

State ____________

Approximate Date Received (if applicable) ____________

22. Have you made any balance transfers with credit cards or credit line accounts within 90 days of the filing of your bankruptcy petition?

Yes ___ No ___

23. [Real Property]—When did you buy your real estate and how much did you pay for it?

Purchase Price ____________ When ____________

Address ______________________________

Purchase Price ____________ When ____________

Address ______________________________

24. [Real Property]—Please identify the approximate costs of any improvements you have made to the property since your bought it.

____

____

____

25. [Real Property]—Did you refinance your property at any time since your purchase?

Yes ___ No ___ N/A ___

26. [Real Property]—Did you receive any money from any refinance of your property within the last 1 year?

Yes ___ No ___ N/A ___

27. [Real Property]—Has a foreclosure been started on any of your properties?

Yes ___ No ___ N/A ___

28. Have you ever tendered a claim to an insurance company which has been denied?

Yes ___ No ___

I DECLARE UNDER PENALTY OF PERJURY THAT THE STATEMENTS MADE HEREIN ARE TRUE AND CORRECT.

Dated: ______________________ ______________________
Debtor

Dated: ______________________ ______________________
Co-Debtor

Attorney of Record Statement

I have discussed with the debtor(s) the content of this Questionnaire, reviewing each question and debtor(s) response thereto, and have responded to questions the debtor(s) may have had to any Question herein.

Dated: ______________________ ______________________
Attorney for Debtor(s)

Printed: ______________________

Revised 09/09/08

Exhibit "E"

CORPORATE OR PARTNERSHIP DEBTOR QUESTIONNAIRE AND DOCUMENT REQUIREMENTS

THIS FORM MUST BE COMPLETED, SIGNED AND RETURNED TO THE TRUSTEE AT THE TIME OF YOUR EXAMINATION

Name:

Briefly describe the nature of the debtor's business:

____

1. Have the bankruptcy schedules in this case been reviewed and explained to you by counsel?

Yes ___ No ___

2. Are the bankruptcy petition and schedules in this case complete, true and accurate?

Yes ___ No ___

3. Has the business entity made any payments to corporate officials, investors or shareholders, or partners; family members of corporate officials,

investors or shareholder, or partners; on a prebankruptcy debt within one year of filing for bankruptcy?

Yes ___ No ___

4. Has the business entity made any payments to creditors in excess of $5,000.00 cumulative on a prebankruptcy debt within three months of filing for bankruptcy?

Yes ___ No ___

5. Has the business entity transferred any money or anything of value to another entity or person within four years of filing for bankruptcy outside the ordinary course of business?

Yes ___ No ___

6. Is the business entity seeking recovery in any current lawsuits, or is there a belief grounds exists to file a lawsuit or counter suit SEEKING DAMAGES?

Yes ___ No ___

7. Does the business entity have any claims against any insurance company for any losses or damages to any personal or real property?

Yes ___ No ___

8. Were any loans made by the business entity to any individual persons or entities?

Yes ___ No ___

9. Is the business entity entitled to any tax refunds or loss carry-backs?

Yes ___ No ___

10. When was business started and when did it stop operations:

Start:____________Stop:____________

11. Were any vehicles utilized in the business entities operations?

Yes ___ No ___

12. Does the business entity have any rights or interest in intellectual property?

Yes ___ No ___

13. Have any records of the business entity been destroyed?

Yes ___ No ___

14. Are there any known environmental and/or contamination issues or problems arising out of or relating to this business entity?

Yes ___ No ___

I DECLARE UNDER PENALTY OF PERJURY THAT THE STATEMENTS MADE HEREIN ARE TRUE AND CORRECT.

Dated: ______________ ________________________________

Debtor

RULES OF THE UNITED STATES BANKRUPTCY APPELLATE PANEL OF THE NINTH CIRCUIT

PREAMBLE

These rules of the United States Bankruptcy Appellate Panel of the Ninth Circuit are promulgated under the authority of Federal Rule of Bankruptcy Procedure 8018. Adopted, as Revised: February 24, 2000.

RULE 8001(a)-1 NOTICE OF APPEAL

Order Being Appealed. The appellant shall attach to the notice of appeal filed in bankruptcy court a copy of the entered judgment, order or decree from which the appeal was taken. The clerk of the bankruptcy court shall forward these items to the BAP Clerk. If the notice of appeal is filed before entry of the order being appealed, it is appellant's duty to forward to the BAP Clerk a copy of the judgment or order immediately upon entry.

RULE 8001(e)-1 ELECTION TO TRANSFER APPEAL TO DISTRICT COURT

(a) Transfer. The Panel may transfer an appeal to the district court to further the interests of justice, such as when a timely statement of election has been filed in a related appeal, or for any other reason the Panel deems appropriate.

(b) Election Procedure When Motion for Leave to Appeal is Pending. If appellant moves for leave to appeal pursuant to FRBP 8003, and fails to file a separate notice of appeal concurrently with filing the motion for leave, the motion for leave shall be treated as if it were a notice of appeal for purposes of calculating the time period for filing an election.

RULE 8006-1 TRANSCRIPTS

The excerpts of the record shall include the transcripts necessary for adequate review in light of the standard of review to be applied to the issues before the Panel. The Panel is required to consider only those portions of the transcript included in the excerpts of the record. Parties shall consult local bankruptcy rules with regard to the proper procedure for ordering transcripts or for indicating that transcripts are not necessary.

Explanatory Note:

This rule addresses two problems. The first occurs when appellants challenge the oral tentative rulings, and/or the oral findings of fact and conclusions of law of the bankruptcy court, and do not include sufficient transcripts in the excerpts of the record to allow the Panel to properly review the bankruptcy court's decision. If findings of fact and conclusions of law were made orally on the record, a transcript of those findings is mandatory. In re McCarthy, 230 B.R. 414, 416 (9th Cir. BAP 1999).

The second problem arises when an appellant challenges a factual finding. In order to review a factual finding for clear error, the record should usually include the entire transcript and all other relevant evidence considered by the bankruptcy court. See In re Friedman, 126 B.R. 63, 68 (9th Cir. BAP 1991) (failure to provide an adequate record may be grounds for affirmance); In re Burkhart, 84 B.R. 658 (9th Cir. BAP 1988).

RULE 8007(b)-1 DOCKETING APPEAL AND APPELLATE RECORD

As soon as the statement of issues, designation of record, and any transcripts that have been designated are filed with bankruptcy court, the clerk of the bankruptcy court shall transmit to the BAP Clerk a certificate that the record is complete. The BAP Clerk shall forthwith notify the parties of the date the certificate is filed at the BAP, and this date shall constitute the date of entry of the appeal on the docket for purposes of FRBP 8009. The record shall be retained by the clerk of the bankruptcy court. The BAP Clerk may request a copy of the record from the clerk of the bankruptcy court.

RULE 8008(a)-1 COMMUNICATIONS

All communications to the BAP shall be addressed to the Clerk of the United States Bankruptcy Appellate Panel of the Ninth Circuit, Richard H. Chambers Court of Appeals Building, 125 South Grand Avenue, Pasadena, California 91105.

RULE 8008(a)-3 FAX FILING

The BAP does not accept for filing documents transmitted by telephone facsimile machine ("fax"), except in emergency circumstances. Permission of the BAP Clerk, prior to the transmittal of the document, is always required.

Any document transmitted to the BAP by fax must be served on all other parties by fax or hand delivery, unless another form of service is authorized by the BAP Clerk, and the method of service shall be expressly stated on the proof of service. Within three days after the fax transmittal, the filing party shall file a signed original and the necessary copies with the BAP.

RULE 8009(a)-1 BRIEFS; NUMBER OF COPIES; EXTENSIONS OF TIME

(a) Number. A party filing briefs shall file an original and four (4) copies with covers, bound separately from the excerpts of the record. At the direction of the BAP the parties may be required to provide additional copies.

(b) Motion for Extension of Time for Filing Brief.

(1) Requirements. A motion for extension of time to file a brief shall be filed within the time limit prescribed by these rules for the filing of such brief and shall be accompanied by a proof of service. The motion shall be supported by a declaration stating:

(A) When the brief was initially due;

(B) How many extensions of time, if any, have been granted;

(C) Reasons why this extension is necessary;

(D) The specific amount of time requested; and

(E) The position of the opponent(s) with respect to the motion or why the moving party has been unable to obtain a statement of such position(s).

(2) BAP Clerk Authority. The BAP Clerk is authorized to grant extensions of time under the direction and guidelines of the Panel.

(3) Consequences. Appellant's failure to file a brief timely may result in the dismissal of the appeal. A brief received after the due date will not be accepted for filing unless it is accompanied by a motion for an extension of time and the motion is granted. The Panel has no obligation to consider a late brief. Sanctions may be imposed, such as the waiver of oral argument, monetary sanctions or dismissal.

RULE 8009(b)-1 APPENDIX (EXCERPTS OF THE RECORD)

(a) Number and Form. A party filing excerpts of the record shall file an original and four (4) copies bound separately from the briefs.

(1) Each copy shall be reproduced on white paper by any duplicating process capable of producing a clearly legible image.

(2) Each copy shall be bound with a white cover.

(3) The cover of the excerpts shall contain the caption information specified by 9th Cir. BAP Rule 8010(a)-1(a)(2).

(b) Organization of Appendix.

(1) Documents in the appendix shall be divided by tabs.

(2) The pages of the excerpts shall be continuously paginated.

(3) The appendix shall contain a complete table of contents listing the documents and identifying both the tab and page number where each document is located. If the appendix has more than one volume, the table of contents shall also identify the volume in which each document is located.

Explanatory Note:

The Panel generally limits its review to an examination of the excerpts of the record as provided by the parties. The Panel is not obligated to examine portions of the record not included in the excerpts. See In re Kritt, 190 B.R. 382, 386-87 (9th Cir. BAP 1995); In re Anderson, 69 B.R. 105, 109 (9th Cir. BAP 1986).

The parties are further referred to FRBP 8010 (a)(1)(D) and (a)(2) which address the related problem created by appellants who do not make explicit references to the parts of the record that support their factual allegations and arguments. Opposing parties and the court are not obliged to search the entire record unaided for error. See Dela Rosa v. Scottsdale Memorial Health Systems, Inc., 136 F.3d 1241 (9th Cir. 1998); Syncom Capital Corp. v. Wade, 924 F.2d 167, 169 (9th Cir. 1991); FRAP Rule 10(b)(2).

RULE 8010(a)-1 FORM OF BRIEFS AND CERTIFICATION REQUIREMENTS

(a) Form.

Briefs shall be produced by a standard typographic printing process that produces a clear black image on white paper, 8½ inches by 11 inches, with one-inch margins, in at least 14 point proportional type, or 10.5 point monospaced type, double-spaced, on opaque, unglazed paper.

(1) BRIEF COVER COLORS:

Appellant's opening brief:	BLUE
Appellee's opening brief:	RED
Appellant's reply brief:	GREY

(2) COVER INFORMATION: Name of court

Case numbers (BAP, bankruptcy court case, and if applicable, adversary

numbers)
Name of Debtor
Names of appellant(s) and appellee(s)
Title of document
Name, address, telephone number, and bar number of counsel filing document

(b) Certification as to Interested Parties. To enable the judges of a Panel to evaluate possible disqualification or recusal, all parties, other than governmental parties, shall attach to the inside back cover of their initial briefs, a list of all persons, associations of persons, firms, partnerships and corporations that have an interest in the outcome of the case. The certification should be in substantially the following form:

Certification Required by BAP Rule 8010(a)-1(b)

[BAP NUMBER, DEBTOR'S NAME]

The undersigned certifies that the following parties have an interest in the outcome of this appeal. These representations are made to enable judges of the Panel to evaluate possible disqualification or recusal [list the names of all such parties and identify their connection and interest]:

____
Signed

____
Dated

(c) Certification of Related Cases. The appellant shall attach to the inside back cover of each copy of the opening brief a statement of all known related cases and appeals before the United States Court of Appeals, the United States District Court, or the BAP. A related case is defined as one which involves substantially the same litigants, substantially the same factual pattern or legal issues, or arises from a case previously heard by the Panel. The certification should be in substantially the following form:

Certification Required by BAP Rule 8010(a)-1(c)

[BAP NUMBER, DEBTOR'S NAME]

The undersigned certifies that the following are known related cases and appeals [list the case name, court and status of all related cases and appeals]:

____
Signed

____

Dated

Explanatory Note:

Failure to comply with the Briefing Rules may result in striking the brief and dismissing the appeal, N/S Corp. v. Liberty Mutual Ins. Co., 127 F.3d 1145 (9th Cir. 1997), or imposing sanctions, In re MacIntyre, 181 B.R. 420, 422 (9th Cir. BAP 1995), aff'd, 77 F.3d 489 (9th Cir. 1996).

Briefs and excerpts of the record shall be securely fastened by any appropriate means.

RULE 8010(c)-1 LENGTH OF BRIEFS

Except with leave of the Panel, appellant's and appellee's initial briefs shall not exceed thirty (30) pages, and reply briefs shall not exceed twenty (20) pages, exclusive of pages containing the table of contents, tables of citations and any addendum containing statutes, rules, regulations or similar materials.

Explanatory Note:

Motions for leave to exceed page limitations are rarely granted. Motions should be filed well in advance of the due date for the brief.

RULE 8011(d)-1 EMERGENCY MOTIONS

(a) Form and Number. An emergency motion must have a cover page bearing the legend "Emergency Motion" in large, bold type. The motion must be filed with the BAP Clerk in an original and three copies.

(b) Contents. The motion and supporting declaration(s) must set forth the facts showing the existence and nature of the alleged immediate and irreparable harm.

(c) Appendix. The emergency motion must be accompanied by an appendix containing:

(1) A conformed copy of the notice of appeal, and

(2) A copy of the entered judgment, order or decree from which the appeal was taken;

(3) If the emergency motion concerns a stay pending appeal, the appendix must also contain:

(i) a conformed copy of the court's order denying or granting the stay and any explanation by the court of its ruling, or a declaration explaining why such a copy is unavailable; and

(ii) copies of all papers regarding the stay filed in bankruptcy court.

(d) Service. The motion and appendix must be accompanied by a proof of service showing service on all parties.

Explanatory Note:

When the emergency motion concerns a stay pending appeal, the parties are directed to In re Wymer, 5 B.R. 802, 805-07 (9th Cir. BAP 1980), for standards in granting a stay pending appeal.

RULE 8011(e)-1 DELEGATION OF AUTHORITY TO ACT ON MOTIONS

The BAP judges may delegate to the BAP Clerk authority to act on motions that are subject to disposition by a single judge pursuant to FRBP 8011(e), upon the condition that the order entered on the motion does not dispose of the appeal or resolve a motion for stay pending appeal. The order disposing of the motion is subject, to reconsideration by a judge if a written request for judicial review is received within fourteen (14) days of the entry of the order.

RULE 8012-1 ORAL ARGUMENT

The BAP Clerk will provide notice of the time and place of argument. Once the hearing date is scheduled, a motion for continuance will be granted only under exceptional circumstances.

The Panel may determine that oral argument is not needed either *sua sponte* or on motion for submission of the appeal on the briefs. If the Panel determines that oral argument is not needed, it will issue an order to that effect.

RULE 8012-2 EN BANC HEARING AND DETERMINATION OF APPEALS

(a) En Banc Hearing and Disposition Authorized; Not Favored. The Panel may hear and dispose of an appeal by sitting en banc as authorized in this rule. An en banc hearing or decision of an appeal is not favored and ordinarily will not be ordered unless it appears that it is necessary to secure or maintain uniformity of the Panel's decisions including, without limitation, when there is a challenge to an existing precedent of the Panel.

(b) Procedure for a Party to Request an En Banc Hearing.

(1) Motion. A party may request that the Panel hear and decide an appeal en banc. The request must be made by motion filed with the Clerk and served upon the other parties to the appeal (including any party appearing amicus curiae). Such motion should be filed and served not later than the date set for the filing of that party's opening brief. If made, the motion must be accompanied by a brief setting forth the reasons why an en banc hearing and decision of an appeal is appropriate under the standard set forth in subsection (a).

(2) Response. Any other party to the appeal (including any party appearing amicus curiae) may file and serve a response to the motion and brief not later than fourteen (14) days after the motion is filed. No reply brief is authorized.

(3) Page Limit. The motion or response, together with the brief in support thereof, must not exceed a combined total of 15 pages.

(c) Procedure for the Panel Initially Assigned to Appeal to Request an En Banc Hearing. Two or more of the judges assigned to hear and decide the merits of an appeal, including any pro tem judge, may request that the Panel should hear and decide an appeal en banc. The request should be made prior to the disposition of the appeal.

(d) Procedure for Determining Whether Appeal Should Be Heard En Banc.

(1) Vote of the Panel. If a timely request for an en banc hearing and decision is made under either subsection (b) or (c), the Clerk will promptly poll the regular members of the Panel eligible to participate in the disposition of that appeal.

(2) Affirmative Vote; Minimum Number of Judges Who Must Participate. The appeal will be heard (or, as appropriate, reheard) and decided en banc if:

(a) at least five regular members of the Panel are eligible to participate, and do participate, in the vote; or, if less than five members of the Panel are eligible to participate in the en banc call, the Chief Judge of the Ninth Circuit, after consultation with the Presiding Judge, shall designate such pro tem judges as may be necessary to bring the number of the judges considering the en banc call to five, and all five judges vote; and

(b) a majority of the judges polled vote in favor of the request.

(3) Negative Vote. If a timely request for an en banc hearing and decision is made under subsection (b) or (c), and no affirmative vote as required by paragraph (2) is obtained within fourteen (14) days of the initial polling, the matter will not be heard en banc.

(e) Procedure After Request and Vote.

(1) Constituting the En Banc Panel. If the Panel votes to hear and decide a matter en banc, the en banc panel shall consist of all members of the Panel eligible to participate in the appeal's disposition, but in no event may an en banc panel consist of fewer than five judges. If fewer than five members of the Panel are eligible to participate in the en banc hearing, the Chief Judge of the Ninth Circuit, after consultation with the Presiding Judge, shall designate such pro tem judges as may be necessary to bring the membership of the en banc panel to five.

(2) Order Regarding Vote; Procedure Thereafter. The Presiding Judge of the Panel shall promptly cause an order to be entered that is consistent with the results of any vote taken in accordance with subsection (d), and with the actions required by subsection (e). Thereafter, the Clerk, in consultation with the Presiding Judge, will take such actions as are necessary or appropriate to carry out such order.

RULE 8013-1 DISPOSITION OF APPEAL

(a) Disposition. The Panel will dispose of all appeals by entry of an Opinion, Memorandum or Order.

(b) Designation.

(1) Opinion. A disposition of an appeal may be designated as an Opinion if it:

(A) Establishes, alters, modifies or clarifies a rule of law;

(B) Calls attention to a rule of law which appears to have been generally overlooked;

(C) Criticizes existing law; or

(D) Involves a legal or factual issue of unique interest or substantial public importance.

(2) Memorandum or Order. A disposition of an appeal not designated as an Opinion will be designated as either a Memorandum or an Order.

(3) Manner of Designation. A disposition shall be designated an Opinion if:

(A) two of the three judges assigned to hear and dispose of the appeal, including the author of the disposition, agree that the disposition shall be designated an Opinion at the time such disposition is filed with the Clerk, or within 28 days thereof; or

(B) an interested party, or any member of the Panel, requests, in writing, that a Memorandum or Order be redesignated as an Opinion, and that it be published. The request must be received no later than 28 days after the filing of the Memorandum or Order and must state concisely the reasons for publication. The judges assigned to hear and dispose of the appeal shall vote on whether to change the initial designation and, if two of the three judges assigned to hear and dispose of the appeal, including the author of the disposition, agree that the disposition shall be designated an Opinion.

(c) Citation and Effect.

(1) Opinions. Opinions shall be published. They shall bind the Panel as precedent unless they are modified or reversed in an Opinion issued by the Panel sitting en banc, or unless they no longer are precedent due to changes in the law, whether by act of Congress or by decision of the Ninth Circuit Court of Appeals or the Supreme Court.

(2) Memoranda and Orders. Except as provided in subsection (d), Memoranda and Orders will not be published, shall have no precedential value, and may not be cited except when relevant under the doctrine of law of the case, or under rules of claim or issue preclusion.

(d) Publication.

(1) Opinions. If the disposition is to be published, the BAP Clerk will release a copy to recognized channels for dissemination to the public.

(2) Orders. An Order may be designated for publication if so designated by the process provided in subsection (b)(3), with the following changes:

(i) only two judges, one of whom is the author of the Order, need to agree as to publication; and

(ii) the Order shall be treated as if it were a disposition of the appeal for all other purposes of applying that subsection. When so published, the Order may be used for any purpose for which an Opinion may be used. Upon designation as published, the BAP Clerk will release a copy to recognized channels for dissemination to the public.

RULE 8014-1 COSTS

Costs under FRBP 8014 are taxed by filing a bill of costs with the clerk of the bankruptcy court.

RULE 8018(b)-1 SILENCE OF LOCAL RULES

In cases where Part VIII of the Federal Rules of Bankruptcy Procedure and these rules are silent as to a particular matter of practice, a Panel may apply the Rules of the United States Court of Appeals for the Ninth Circuit and the Federal Rules of Appellate Procedure.

RULE 8018-2 CITATION TO RULES

These rules shall be cited as:
"9th Cir. BAP R. ____________"

RULE 8070-1 DISMISSAL FOR FAILURE TO PROSECUTE

When an appellant fails to file an opening brief timely, or otherwise fails to comply with rules or orders regarding processing the appeal, the BAP Clerk, after notice, may enter an order dismissing the appeal. The order dismissing the appeal is subject to reconsideration by the Panel if a written request for judicial review is received within fourteen (14) days of the entry of the order.

RULE 9001-1 DEFINITIONS

(a) The words "BAP Clerk" as used in these rules mean the Clerk of the United States Bankruptcy Appellate Panel of the Ninth Circuit.

(b) The word "Judge" as used in these rules, unless otherwise designated, means a member of the United States Bankruptcy Appellate Panel of the Ninth Circuit.

(c) The word "Panel" as used in these rules means a panel of the judges of the United States Bankruptcy Appellate Panel of the Ninth Circuit.

(d) The acronym "BAP" as used in these rules means United States Bankruptcy Appellate Panel of the Ninth Circuit.

(e) The acronym "FRBP" as used in these rules means Federal Rules of Bankruptcy Procedure.

(f) The acronym "FRAP" as used in these rules means Federal Rules of Appellate Procedure.

RULE 9010-1 ATTORNEYS—DUTIES, WITHDRAWAL, SUBSTITUTION

(a) Duties. Counsel must ensure that the appeal is perfected on behalf of the represented party in a manner and within the times prescribed in these rules and must prosecute the appeal with diligence. Counsel must provide counsel's name, bar number, address, and telephone number on all documents filed with the BAP. Changes in address of counsel or client must be reported to the BAP Clerk in writing.

(b) Admission. Any attorney admitted to practice before a District Court of the Ninth Circuit or the Court of Appeals for the Ninth Circuit and who is in good standing before such court shall be deemed admitted to practice before the BAP. An attorney not so admitted may apply to the BAP for permission to appear in a particular appeal.

(c) Withdrawal and Substitution. No attorney who has appeared in an appeal before the BAP may withdraw without either:

(1) Filing and Serving a Notice of Substitution of Attorney. The notice shall contain substitute counsel's name, bar number, address, telephone number and signature; or

(2) Obtaining an order of the BAP allowing the attorney to withdraw. The BAP may grant such an order if an attorney files and serves on opposing counsel and the attorney's client a motion to withdraw as counsel. Any motion to withdraw shall include the client's current address and telephone number.

(d) Notice of Appearance. Immediately upon undertaking the representation, any attorney who represents a party in an appeal, and who is not identified in either the notice of appeal or a notice of substitution of attorney, shall file and serve a notice of appearance containing counsel's name, bar number, address, and telephone number.

RULE 9010-2 PRO SE PARTIES

Parties unrepresented by counsel and appearing before the Panel are considered to be "pro se parties" representing themselves. Only individuals are permitted to appear pro se. Pro se parties must ensure their appeal is perfected in a manner and within the time limits prescribed in these rules and must prosecute the appeal with diligence. Changes in address must be reported to the BAP Clerk in writing.

Explanatory Note:

See In re Rainbow Magazine, Inc., 77 F.3d 278 (9th Cir. 1996); In re Eisen, 14 F.3d 469, 471 (9th Cir. 1994). Corporations, partnerships and associations are not permitted to appear in federal court except through a licensed attorney. Rowland v. California Men's Colony, 506 U.S. 194 (1993); In re America West Airlines, Inc., 40 F.3d 1058 (9th Cir. 1994).

AMENDED ORDER CONTINUING THE BANKRUPTCY APPELLATE PANEL OF THE NINTH CIRCUIT

1. Continuing the Bankruptcy Appellate Panel Service.

(a) Pursuant to 28 U.S.C. § 158(b)(1) as amended by the Bankruptcy

Reform Act of 1994, the judicial council hereby reaffirms and continues a bankruptcy appellate panel service which shall provide panels to hear and determine appeals from judgments, orders and decrees entered by bankruptcy judges from districts within the Ninth Circuit.

(b) Panels of the bankruptcy appellate panel service may hear and determine appeals originating from districts that have authorized such appeals to be decided by the bankruptcy appellate panel service pursuant to 28 U.S.C. § 158(b)(6).

(c) All appeals originating from those districts shall be referred to bankruptcy appellate panels unless a party elects to have the appeal heard by the district court in the time and manner and form set forth in 28 U.S.C. § 158(c)(1) and in paragraph 3 below.

(d) Bankruptcy appellate panels may hear and determine appeals from final judgments, orders and decrees entered by bankruptcy judges and, with leave of bankruptcy appellate panels, appeals from interlocutory orders and decrees entered by bankruptcy judges.

(e) Bankruptcy appellate panels may hear and determine appeals from final judgments, orders, and decrees entered after the district court from which the appeal originates has issued an order referring bankruptcy cases and proceedings to bankruptcy judges pursuant to 28 U.S.C. § 157(a).

2. Immediate Reference to Bankruptcy Appellate Panels. Upon filing of the notice of appeal, all appeals are immediately referred to the bankruptcy appellate panel service.

3. Election to District Court-Separate Written Statement Required. A party desiring to transfer the hearing of an appeal from the bankruptcy appellate panel service to the district court pursuant to 28 U.S.C. § 158(c)(1) shall timely file a separate written statement of election expressly stating that the party elects to have the appeal transferred from the bankruptcy appellate panel service to the district court.

(a) Appellant: If the appellant wishes to make such an election, appellant must file a separate written statement of election with the clerk of the bankruptcy court at the time of filing the notice of appeal. Appellant shall submit the same number of copies of the statement of election as copies of the notice of appeal. See Bankruptcy Rule 8001(a). When such an election is made, the clerk of the bankruptcy court shall forthwith transfer the case to the district court. The clerk of the bankruptcy court shall give notice to all parties and the clerk of the bankruptcy appellate panels of the transfer at the same time and in the same manner as set forth for serving notice of the appeal in Bankruptcy Rule 8004.

(b) All Other Parties: In all appeals where appellant does not file an election, the clerk of the bankruptcy court shall forthwith transmit a copy of the notice of appeal to the clerk of the bankruptcy appellate panels. If any other party wishes to have the appeal heard by the district court, that party must, within thirty (30) days after service of the notice of appeal, file with the clerk of the bankruptcy appellate panels a written statement of election to transfer the appeal to the district court. Upon receipt of a timely statement of election filed under this section, the clerk of the bankruptcy appellate panels shall forthwith transfer the appeal to the appropriate district court and shall give notice of the transfer to the parties and the clerk of the bankruptcy court. Any question as to the timeliness of an election shall be referred by the clerk of the bankruptcy appellate panels to a bankruptcy appellate panel motions panel for determination.

4. MOTIONS DURING ELECTION PERIOD [. ***sic*****]** All motions relating to an appeal shall be filed with the bankruptcy appellate panel service unless the case has been transferred to a district court. The bankruptcy appellate panels may not dismiss or render a final disposition of an appeal within thirty (30) days from the date of service of the notice of appeal, but may otherwise fully consider and dispose of all motions.

5. PANELS [. ***sic*****]** Each appeal shall be heard and determined by a panel of three judges from among those appointed pursuant to paragraph 6, provided however that a bankruptcy judge shall not participate in an appeal originating in a district for which the judge is appointed or designated under 28 U.S.C. § 152.

6. MEMBERSHIP OF BANKRUPTCY APPELLATE PANELS [. ***sic*****]** The bankruptcy appellate panel shall consist of seven members serving seven-year terms (subject to reappointment to one additional three-year term). The judicial council shall periodically examine the caseload of the bankruptcy appellate panel service to assess whether the number of bankruptcy judges serving should change. Appointment of regular and pro tem bankruptcy judges to service on the bankruptcy appellate panel shall be governed by regulations promulgated by the Judicial Council.

(a) When a three-judge panel cannot be formed from the judges designated under subparagraph (a) to hear a case because judges have recused themselves, are disqualified from hearing the case because it arises from their district, or are otherwise unable to participate, the Chief

Judge of the Ninth Circuit may designate one or more other bankruptcy judge(s) from the circuit to hear the case.

(b) In order to provide assistance with the caseload or calendar relief, or otherwise to assist the judges serving, or to afford other bankruptcy judges with the opportunity to serve on the bankruptcy appellate panels, the Chief Judge of the Ninth Circuit may designate from time to time one or more other bankruptcy judge(s) from the circuit to participate in one or more panel sittings.

7. CHIEF JUDGE [. ***sic*****]** The members of the bankruptcy appellate panel service by majority vote shall select one of their number to serve as chief judge.

8. RULES OF PROCEDURE.

(a) Practice before the bankruptcy appellate panels shall be governed by Part VIII of the Federal Rules of Bankruptcy Procedure, except as provided in this order or by rule of the bankruptcy appellate panel service adopted under subparagraph (b).

(b) The bankruptcy appellate panel service may establish rules governing practice and procedure before bankruptcy appellate panels not inconsistent with the Federal Rules of Bankruptcy Procedure. Such rules shall be submitted to, and approved by, the Judicial Council of the Ninth Circuit.

9. PLACES OF HOLDING COURT. Bankruptcy appellate panels may conduct hearings at such times and places within the Ninth Circuit as it determines to be appropriate.

10. CLERK AND OTHER EMPLOYEES.

(a) Clerk's Office. The members of the bankruptcy appellate panel service shall select and hire the clerk of the bankruptcy appellate panel. The clerk of the bankruptcy appellate panel may select and hire staff attorneys and other necessary staff. The chief judge shall have appointment authority for the clerk, staff attorneys and other necessary staff. The members of the bankruptcy appellate panel shall determine the location of the principal office of the clerk.

(b) Law Clerks. Each judge on the bankruptcy appellate panel service shall have appointment authority to hire an additional law clerk.

11. EFFECTIVE DATE [. ***sic*****]** This Order shall be effective as to all appeals originating in those bankruptcy cases that are filed after the effective date of this Order. For all appeals originating in those bankruptcy cases that were filed before October 22, 1994, the Judicial Council's prior Amended Order, as revised October 15, 1992, shall apply. This Order, insofar as just and practicable, shall apply to all appeals originating in those bankruptcy cases that were filed after the effective date of the Bankruptcy Reform Act of 1994, October 22, 1994, but before the date of this Order.

IT IS SO ORDERED.

DATE: April 28, 1995; amended May 9, 2002.

MANUAL FOR LITIGANTS

Winter 2008

This summary is the cumulative work of many current and former BAP judges, law clerks and staff dedicated to the common pursuit of providing up-to-date materials to the public and bar.

While they have been updated numerous times, these materials were first prepared and released on March 15, 1985, by the Hon. Sidney C. Volinn, who served as a BAP Judge and Bankruptcy Judge from the Western District of Washington.

The analysis contained herein is summary in nature, is not intended as legal advice, and is no substitute for legal research. It is the responsibility of attorneys and litigants to review and comply with applicable laws and rules governing appellate practice and procedure.

I. INTRODUCTION

These materials are designed to assist counsel involved in a bankruptcy appeal before the BAP.

Appellate rules are found in Part VIII of the Federal Rules of Bankruptcy Procedure (FRBP), Rule 8001 et seq. http://www.access.gpo.gov/uscode/title11a/11a_1_.html

Local rules of either the district court or the BAP also apply. Revised local rules for practice before the BAP were adopted by the Ninth Circuit Judicial Council on February 24, 2000, and may be found on the BAP website at http://pacer.bap09.uscourts.gov/rules/baprules.pdf

Where national and local rules are silent or where they so specify, the Federal Rules of Appellate Procedure (FRAP), the Federal Rules of Civil Procedure (FRCP), the Federal Rules of Evidence (FRE) or the Ninth Circuit Rules (Circuit Rules) may apply. See 9th Cir. BAP R. 8018(b)-1.

II. JURISDICTION OF THE BAP

Under the Bankruptcy Code, the district court has always had the jurisdiction to review decisions of a bankruptcy court. 28 U.S.C. § 158(a). However, a circuit may establish a BAP, 28 U.S.C. § 158(b), and the Ninth Circuit has had BAP since the effective date of the Bankruptcy Code, October 1, 1979. The Bankruptcy Reform Act of 1978, which became effective on October 1, 1979, authorized the creation of the BAP.

Following the decision of Northern Pipeline Constr. Co. v Marathon Pipe Line Co., 458 U.S. 50 (1982) (holding that the Act unconstitutionally conferred the essential attributes of judicial power on non-Article III bankruptcy judges), and passage of the Bankruptcy Amendments and Federal Judgeship Act of 1984, the Ninth Circuit re-established the BAP by Order of the Judicial Council, in 1985. That order was most recently amended as of May 9, 2002, and is set forth at the end of these materials.

Specific issues of appellate jurisdiction are discussed in sections V and VII.C, below.

III. INTRODUCTION TO THE BAP

Seven bankruptcy judges are authorized by the Ninth Circuit Judicial Council to serve on the BAP. Each appeal is heard by a panel of three judges. No bankruptcy judge may hear an appeal originating from his or her district. 28 U.S.C. § 158(b)(5).

The BAP judges are all active bankruptcy court judges from districts within the ninth circuit. All maintain a regular trial docket in their home districts. Currently there are six members of the BAP; the seventh position is being intentionally left vacant to reflect the BAP's reduced filing numbers and to allow opportunities for pro tem judge participation. The current members of the BAP are:

Hon. Christopher M. Klein (E.D. Cal.), Chief Judge

Hon. Dennis Montali (N.D. Cal.)

Hon. Jim D. Pappas (D. Idaho)

Hon. Randall L. Dunn (D. Oregon)

Hon. Meredith A. Jury (C.D. Cal.)

Hon. Bruce A. Markell (D. Nevada)

BAP judges are appointed by the Circuit for a seven-year term. At the end of that term, they may seek reappointment for an additional three years. Each BAP judge has an additional law clerk. Some judges utilize both clerks on BAP matters and on their regular "home court" assignments while others segregate the duties of their clerks.

The BAP also routinely utilizes pro tem judges in order to give appellate experience to other bankruptcy judges within the Ninth Circuit. Pro tem judges sit for one-day merits calendar assignments and have equal votes with the regular BAP judges. Normally, they only participate on motions in appeals where they have been assigned to hear the merits. The contribution of the pro tem judges allows the BAP to set more calendars and hear more cases than it could otherwise. Collectively, the pro tem judges perform the work equivalent to an additional BAP judge.

The BAP hears cases nine months out of the year, with the three-judge panels traveling to various venues in the Ninth Circuit. The Panel does not normally hold hearings during April, August and December.

The BAP utilizes both teleconferencing and video conferencing, and continues to explore the use of new technology to facilitate more convenient hearings for counsel and litigants. Video conference equipment in both the Pasadena and San Francisco courtrooms allows litigants to appear in scheduled cases via live video from bankruptcy courthouses throughout the Ninth Circuit.

The BAP is staffed by its Clerk, two staff attorneys, and other personnel who maintain the files and dockets and otherwise run the business of the court.

Address: Bankruptcy Appellate Panel, Court of Appeals Building, 125 South Grand Avenue, Pasadena, CA 91105

Telephone: Appeals from Central District of California (626) 229-7220; appeals from all other districts (626) 229-7225.

Filing Hours: Monday—Friday, 8:30 a.m. to 5:00 p.m.

Web Sites: 1) http://pacer.bap09.uscourts.gov/ 2) www.ce9.uscourts.gov/bap

IV. PRACTICE BEFORE THE BAP

To practice before the BAP, an attorney must be admitted and in good standing to practice before the Ninth Circuit Court of Appeals, or before a district court within the Ninth Circuit. An attorney not so admitted may request permission to appear in a specific case by motion to the BAP. 9th Cir. BAP R. 9010-1.

V. STARTING THE APPEAL PROCESS

A. Time and Method for Filing a Notice of Appeal

A notice of appeal must be filed with the bankruptcy court within 10 calendar days of entry of the judgment, order, or decree appealed from. FRBP 8001(a), 8002, and 9006(a). If a timely notice of appeal is filed, any other party may file a notice of appeal (often a cross-appeal) within 10 days of the date on which the first notice of appeal was filed. Id. The appellant must attach to the notice of appeal a copy of the entered judgment, order or decree from which the appeal was taken, if available. 9th Cir. BAP R. 8001(a)-1. The timely filing of a notice of appeal is "mandatory and jurisdictional." Browder v. Director, Dep't of Corrections, 434 U.S. 257, 264 (1978); see also Slimick v. Silva (In re Slimick), 928 F.2d 304, 306 (9th Cir. 1990).

Discretionary extensions may be granted by the bankruptcy court, with some exceptions, upon written motion. Any extension granted may not exceed the latter of: (1) 20 days from the expiration of the time for filing a notice of appeal, or (2) 10 days from the entry of the extension order.

If the motion is filed not later than 20 days after the expiration of the original 10-day period, an extension may be granted upon a showing of excusable neglect. See Pincay v. Andrews 389 F.3d 853 (9th Cir. 2004)(en banc)(mistake by attorney in delegating task of determining appeal deadline to non-lawyer, who misinterpreted the unambiguous deadline, can be considered excusable neglect at the trial court's discretion). Once the appeal period has expired, it cannot be resurrected. The BAP may not extend the time requirements of FRBP 8002. See FRBP 8019 and 9006(b)(3).

B. Tolling Motions

The time for filing an appeal is tolled if, within 10 days of entry of the judgment, order or decree, a party files a motion

(1) to amend or make additional findings of fact under FRBP 7052,

(2) to alter or amend the judgment under FRBP 9023,

(3) for a new trial under FRBP 9023, or

(4) for relief under FRBP 9024, then the 10 days for filing an appeal runs from the entry of the order disposing of the last such motion outstanding. FRBP 8002(b).

The BAP considers a motion for reconsideration filed within 10 days to be a motion to "alter or amend the judgment" within the meaning of FRBP 8002(b). Bentley v. Bank of Coronado (In re Crystal Sands Props.), 84 B.R. 665 (9th Cir. BAP 1988). See generally 16A Wright & Miller, Federal Practice & Procedure, § 3950.4.

C. Premature Notice of Appeal

A premature notice of appeal (a notice of appeal filed after the announcement of a decision but before entry of the judgment or order) is treated as filed after such entry and on the day thereof. FRBP 8002(a).

If the notice of appeal is filed before entry of the order being appealed, the appellant must forward to the BAP Clerk a copy of the judgment or order immediately upon entry. 9th Cir. BAP R. 8001(a)-1.

A notice of appeal also is premature if an unresolved tolling motion is pending (see § V.B above).

D. Appeal Fees and In Forma Pauperis Motions

A filing and docketing fee of $255 is required and should be made payable to the "Clerk of Court." The fee should be paid to the bankruptcy court at the same time the notice of appeal is filed.

Under Perroton v. Gray (In re Perroton), 958 F.2d 889 (9th Cir. 1992) and Determan v. Sandoval (In re Sandoval), 186 B.R. 490, 496 (9th Cir. BAP 1995), the BAP has no authority to grant in forma pauperis motions under 28 U.S.C. § 1915(a) because bankruptcy courts are not "court[s] of the United States" as defined in 28 U.S.C. § 451.

E. Election to the District Court (Opt-Out)

The appeal from the bankruptcy court automatically goes to the BAP unless a party timely elects to have the appeal heard by the district court. 28 U.S.C. § 158(b)(1).

A party might choose to have an appeal heard by the district court if other litigation or related appeals are already pending in the district court, or if there is adverse BAP authority on the party's issue.

1. The objection to having the appeal heard by the BAP must be made as a "Statement of Election" in a separate writing. FRBP 8001(e); Arkansas Teachers Ret. Sys. v. Official Inv. Pool Participants Comm. (In re County of Orange), 183 B.R. 593 (9th Cir. BAP 1995) (election must be in a separate document, filed separately from the notice of appeal). Amended Order Continuing Bankruptcy Appellate Panel of the Ninth Circuit (Amended May 9, 2002).

2. Deadline for Appellant's Statement of Election. In Ioane v. Collins (In re Ioane), 227 B.R. 181, 183 (9th Cir. BAP 1998), the BAP held that the statutory deadline for an appellant's election is the time the notice of appeal is filed (rather than the date that the order is entered), even if the notice of appeal is filed prematurely.

If the appellant moves for leave to appeal but fails to concurrently file a separate notice of appeal, the motion for leave shall be treated as if it were a notice of appeal for purposes of calculating the time period for filing an election. 9th Cir. BAP R. 8001(e)-1(b).

3. "Any other party" (e.g., the appellee) must make the election not later than 30 days after service of notice of the appeal. 28 U.S.C. § 158(c)(1). In HBI, Inc. v. Sessions Payroll Mgm't, Inc. (In re Mackey), 232 B.R. 784 (9th Cir. BAP 1999), the BAP held that the 30-day deadline begins to run on the date of the court's mailing, not the date that the order being appealed is entered, and that the 3-day extension provided for by FRBP 9006(f) applies when service is performed by mail.

Caution: While the BAP has not yet published a decision on point, it is likely that parties receiving notice by e-mail would not enjoy the 3-day extension under FRBP 9006(f).

4. The BAP Panel "may transfer an appeal to the district court to further the interests of justice, such as when a timely statement of election has been filed in a related appeal, or for any other reason the Panel deems appropriate." 9th Cir. BAP R. 8001(e)-1.

F. Petition to Appeal Directly to Court of Appeals

1. Where the underlying bankruptcy case was filed on or after October 17, 2005, the parties may petition to appeal directly to the Court of Appeals. Bankruptcy Abuse Prevention and Consumer Protection Act ("BAPCPA") § 1501.

The petition generally is brought before the Court of Appeals in the same manner as petitions for leave to appeal under 28 U.S.C. § 1292(b). See BAPCPA § 1233(b) (making FRAP 5 § permissive appeals applicable to direct bankruptcy appeals). A timely, effective notice of appeal from a bankruptcy court order or judgment is a prerequisite. Interim Rule 8001(f)(1).

2. Before the parties file their direct appeal petitions with the Circuit Clerk, they generally must first obtain a certification from either the bankruptcy court, the district court or the BAP, as contemplated in 28 U.S.C. § 158(d)(2)(B).

3. A request for certification must be filed in and determined by:

i. the bankruptcy court, until a Certificate of Readiness has been received and filed by the BAP or district court, or a motion for leave to appeal has been granted (whichever occurs first); or

ii. the BAP, after: (a) the BAP receives and files a Certificate of Readiness; or (b) the BAP grants leave to appeal; or

iii. (if an election has been timely filed) the district court, after: (a) the district court receives and files a Certificate of Readiness; or (b) the district court grants leave to appeal.

See 28 U.S.C. § 158(d)(2); BAPCPA § 1233(b)(2); Interim Rule 8001(f)(2)-(3) (defining which court has authority to rule on a direct appeal request).

4. The court in which the certification request is properly filed must serve the request on all parties to the appeal. Interim Rule 8001(f)(3)(B).

5. If all of the parties to the appeal unanimously agree that a direct appeal is appropriate, then the parties may self-certify their appeal. 28 U.S.C. § 158(d)(2)(A). The parties' self certification must be filed in the appropriate court. Interim Rule 8001(f)(2)(B). While there is a sixty-day time limit for certification requests made pursuant to 28 U.S.C. § 158(d)(2)(B) (see 28 U.S.C. § 158(d)(2)(E)), there is no express time limit specified in BAPCPA for self-certifications, or for a court certification made on the court's own motion.

6. Once a certification is entered on the court's docket, the parties have only 10 days to file their petition to appeal to the Court of Appeals with the Clerk of the Court of Appeals. BAPCPA § 1233(b)(4)(A) (not codified—see footnote 7, supra).

7. Absent an order to the contrary, neither the issuance of a certification nor the Circuit's granting of a petition suspends prosecution of an appeal before the BAP or the district court. 28 U.S.C. § 158(d)(2)(D). If the Circuit grants the direct appeal petition, the BAP might either stay or dismiss the corresponding BAP appeal.

G. Final Orders vs. Interlocutory Orders

In general, the BAP has jurisdiction to hear bankruptcy appeals from final judgments, orders, and decrees. See 28 U.S.C. § 158. In addition, the BAP has jurisdiction to hear appeals from two types of interlocutory orders:

(1) Orders under 11 U.S.C. § 1121(d) increasing or reducing exclusivity time periods, 28 U.S.C. § 158(a)(2), Official Committee of Unsecured Creditors v. Henry Mayo Newhall Memorial Hospital (In re

Henry Mayo Newhall Memorial Hospital), 282 B.R. 444 (9th Cir. BAP 2002); and

(2) Interlocutory orders as to which the BAP grants a motion for leave to appeal, 28 U.S.C. § 158(a)(3). See also Official Comm. of Unsecured Creditors v. Credit Lyonnais Bank Nederland, N.V. (In re NSB Film Corp.), 167 B.R. 176, 180 (9th Cir. BAP 1994). See generally 16A Wright & Miller, Federal Practice & Procedure § 3950.2. The BAP lacks jurisdiction to hear appeals from interlocutory orders (except § 1121(d) orders) unless and until the BAP grants leave to appeal.

1. Definition of Finality

The standard for determining finality in the bankruptcy context is more flexible than in other areas. NSB Film Corp., 167 B.R. at 180. In contrast to an ordinary civil case where "a complete act of adjudication ends the litigation on the merits and leaves nothing for the court to do but execute the judgment," a bankruptcy order is final if it "end[s] any interim disputes from which appeal would lie." Slimick, 928 F.2d at 307 n.1 (internal quotation marks and citations omitted).

An order can be appealed under the "flexible finality" doctrine if it "1) resolves and seriously affects substantive rights and 2) finally determines the discrete issue to which it is addressed." Elliott v. Four Seasons Props., Inc. (In re Frontier Props., Inc.), 979 F.2d 1358 (9th Cir., CCA 1992).

For a recent discussion of pragmatic finality in bankruptcy, Saxman v. Educ. Credit Mgt. BJR Corp (In re Saxman), 325 F.3d 1168 (9th Cir. CCA 2003) (and the dissent). But see Belli v. Temkin (In re Belli), 12 268 B.R. 851 (9th Cir. BAP 2001) (holding that, for purposes of jurisdiction over bankruptcy appeals under 28 U.S.C. § 158(a)(1), finality in adversary proceedings does not differ from finality in ordinary federal civil actions under 28 U.S.C. § 1291, and thus FRCP 54(b) applies.).

Examples of orders held to be final include orders:

• Granting or denying relief from stay, In re Conejo Enters., Inc., 96 F.3d 346, 351 (9th Cir. 1996);

• Regarding adequate protection, Kamai v. Long Beach Mortgage Co. (In re Kamai), 316 B.R. 544, 547-48 (9th Cir. BAP 2004);

• Confirming a chapter 11 debtor's reorganization plan, Pizza of

Hawaii, Inc. v. Shakey's, Inc. (In re Pizza of Hawaii, Inc.), 761 F.2d 1374 (9th Cir. 1985);

• Allowing or disallowing an exemption, In re Jones, 768 F.2d 923 (7th Cir. 1985);

• Substantively consolidating bankruptcy cases, Alexander v. Compton (In re Bonham), 229 F.3d 750 (9th Cir. 2000);

• Approving a final application for compensation of professional, Circle K Corp. v. Houlihan, Lokey, Howard & Zukin, Inc., (In re Circle K Corp.), 279 F.3d 669 (9th Cir. 2002);

• For sale of property to good-faith purchasers, In re Southwest Products, Inc., 144 B.R. 100 (9th Cir. BAP 1992), but see In re M Capital Corp. 290 B.R. 743 (9th Cir. BAP 2003); Thomas v. Namba (In re Thomas, 287 B.R. 782 (9th Cir. BAP 2002); and

• Dismissing an action, even without prejudice. De Tie v. Orange County, 152 F.3d 1109 (9th Cir. 1998).

Examples of orders held to be interlocutory include orders:

• Denying a motion to dismiss a bankruptcy case or adversary proceeding, Dunkley v. Rega Props., Ltd. (In re Rega Props., Ltd.), 894 F.2d 1136 (9th Cir. 1990); Morrison-Knudsen Co., Inc. v. CHG Int'l, Inc., 811 F.2d 1209, 1214 (9th Cir. 1987); Ditter v. Greenberg (In re Ditter), 205 B.R. 213 (9th Cir. BAP 1996);

• Granting a trustee's motion to employ a professional pursuant to 11 U.S.C. § 327, Sec. Pac. Bank Wash. v. Steinberg (In re Westwood Shake & Shingle, Inc.), 971 F.2d 387 (9th Cir. 1992);

• Denying a motion for summary judgment, Comsource Independent Foodservice Cos., Inc. v. Union Pacific R.R. Co., 102 F.3d 438, 441-42 (9th Cir. 1996);

• Granting partial summary judgment without the certification required by FRCP 54(b), Belli v. Temkim (In re Belli), 268 B.R. 851 (9th Cir. BAP 2001); a partial summary judgment certified without sufficient findings is arguably interlocutory. Janus v. Marco Crane & Rigging Co. (In re JWJ Contracting Co., Inc.), 287 B.R. 501, 506 n.7 (9th Cir. BAP 2002), aff'd, 371 F.3d 1079 (9th Cir. 2004);

• Imposing monetary sanctions against an attorney, Cunningham v. Hamilton County, Ohio, 527 U.S. 198 (1999); Cato v. Fresno City, 220 F.3d 1073, 1074 (9th Cir. 2000). But see Knupfer v. Lindblade (In re Dyer), 322 F.3d 1178, 1187 (9th Cir. 2003) (exercising jurisdiction over sanctions issue because immediate review might obviate the need for further fact finding on remand and because court was compelled to immediately review nonsanctions issues, thus avoiding piecemeal litigation); Golant v. Levy (In re Golant), 239 F.3d 931, 935 (7th Cir. 2001) ("we were unable to uncover any cases discussing how Cunningham might alter the long-held view that sanctions which completely eliminate the possibility of a decision on the merits—such as a default judgment or dismissal—are 'final' for the purpose of appeal."); Reorganized Solomat Enters., Inc. v. Ibar (In re Solomat Partners, L.P.), 231 B.R. 149, 151 (2d Cir. BAP 1999) (holding that denial of civil contempt motions was final and appealable);

• Granting a motion to reopen a bankruptcy case, Wilborn v. Gallagher (In re Wilborn), 205 B.R. 202 (9th Cir. BAP 1996); and

• Dismissing a complaint with leave to amend. WMX Technologies, Inc. v. Miller, 104 F.3d 1133 (9th Cir. 1997).

2. Separate Document Rule

FRBP 9021 requires that the order/judgment appealed must be entered on a separate document.

FRBP 9021, making applicable FRCP 58; Corrigan v. Bargala, 140 F.3d 815, 817 (9th Cir. 1998); United States v. Schimmels (In re Schimmels), 85 F.3d 416, 420-21 (9th Cir. 1996). The separate document rule applies in both contested matters and adversary proceedings, and any order that does not comply with the rule may be held to be not final. See Garland v. Estate of Maloney (In re Garland), 295 B.R. 347, 353 (9th Cir. BAP 2003). FRCP 58, as amended in 2002, now deems orders final after 150 days even if not set forth as separate judgments. See id. at 351.

Application of the separate document rule may be waived. See Sallie Mae Servicing, LP v. Williams (In re Williams), 287 B.R. 787, 791 n. 10 (9th Cir. BAP 2002); Boggan v. Hoff Ford, Inc. (In re Boggan), 251 B.R. 95, 98 n.2 (9th Cir. BAP 2000).

3. Minute Entries/Minute Orders

A minute entry is a final order if it states that it is an order, was mailed to counsel, is signed by the clerk who prepared it, and is entered on the docket sheet. Kuan v. Lund (In re Lund), 202 B.R. 127, 130 (9th Cir. BAP 1996). To be a final order, a minute entry also must include "dispositive language sufficient to put the losing party on notice that his entire action—and not just a particular motion or proceeding within the action—is over and that his next step is to appeal." Brown v. Wilshire Credit Corp. (In re Brown), 484 F.3d 1116, 1121 (9th Cir. 2007).

4. Leave to Appeal

To appeal an interlocutory order, one must file a notice of appeal along with a motion for leave to appeal. FRBP 8001(b). Although filed in the bankruptcy court, the leave motion is to the Panel. The Panel is the court that grants or denies leave. The motion for leave to appeal must contain:

(1) A statement of facts necessary to an understanding of the questions to be presented by the appeal;

(2) A statement of the questions to be presented;

(3) A statement of the reasons why the appeal should be heard; and

(4) A copy of the judgment, order, or decree complained of and any opinion or memorandum relating to that order or judgment. FRBP 8003(a).

Note: Depending upon the nature of the interlocutory order, the appellant can also seek certification from the bankruptcy judge under FRCP 54(b), made applicable by FRBP 7054 and 9021 (through FRCP 58).

If the bankruptcy court makes an "express determination that there is no just reason for delay" in entry of a final judgment on a distinct claim or cause of action, the court can then make an "express direction" for the entry of final judgment on that claim, and the matter is then final as to that claim for purposes of appeal.

An order that purports to be a final order on fewer than all causes of action or parties will not be considered final absent such express determination and direction.

i. Standard for Granting Leave to Appeal

Leave to appeal is usually limited to situations that would avoid wasteful litigation, involve a controlling question of law as to which there is substantial ground for difference of opinion, and would materially advance the ultimate termination of the litigation. Roderick v. Levy (In re Roderick Timber Co.), 185 B.R. 601, 604 (9th Cir. BAP

1995); In re Travers 202 B.R. 624, 626 (9th Cir. BAP 1996).

The BAP's decision to deny leave to appeal is an exercise of discretion and generally is not open to review by the Silver Sage Partners, Ltd. v. City of Desert Hot Springs (In re City of Desert Hot Springs), 339 F.3d 782, 787-88 (9th Cir. CCA 2003). See also Baldwin v. Redwood City, 540 F.2d 1360, 1364 (9th Cir. 1976) (holding that the appellant could not pursue an interlocutory appeal because it was untimely, but that interlocutory order would merge into the final judgment and could be challenged upon timely appeal from the final judgment).

VI. DESIGNATION OF THE RECORD

A. Perfection of the Appeal

Within 10 days after filing the notice of appeal, the appellant must file with the clerk of the bankruptcy court and serve on the appellee a designation of items to be included in the record ("DOR") on appeal and must file and serve a Statement of Issues on Appeal ("SOI"). FRBP 8001 & 8006. For appeals pending before the BAP, a DOR is not a copy of every item to be included in the record. It is a list of the items that make up the record, usually identified by docket number and filing date, as well as a description of the item (e.g. "plaintiff's opposition to motion for fees," "declaration in support of motion to dismiss"). Within 10 days of service of the appellant's DOR and SOI, the appellee may file a designation of additional items to be included in the record. FRBP 8006.

The Panel need not consider items not included in the DOR. See id. Items that were not before the bankruptcy court generally will not be allowed unless they pertain to mootness that arose after the order on appeal. See Graves v. Myrvang (In re Myrvang), 232 F.3d 1116, 1119 (9th Cir. 2000); Kirshner v. Uniden Corp. of America, 842 F.2d 1074, 1077 (9th Cir. 1988). The BAP may take judicial notice of the bankruptcy court docket or of matters relevant to the appeal. FRE 201(c) & (f); O'Rourke v. Seabord Surety Co. (In re E.R. Fegert, Inc.), 887 F.2d 955, 957-58 (9th Cir. 1989); United States ex rel. Robinson Rancheria Citizens Council v. Borneo, Inc., 971 F.2d 244, 248 (9th Cir. 1992).

If the appellee has cross appealed, it may file an SOI to be presented on cross appeal and a DOR. Rule 8006. Otherwise, appellees do not file an SOI, even if they disagree with the appellant's framing of the issues. Any such conflict should be addressed in the appellee's brief.

The DOR shall identify all transcripts necessary for adequate review in light of the standard of review to be applied to the issues before the Panel.

See 9th Cir. BAP R. 8006-1. Sallie Mae Servicing, L.P. v. Williams (In re Williams), 287 B.R. 787, 792 (9th Cir. BAP 2002). If the DOR includes a transcript, the party designating the transcript must immediately deliver to the court reporter and file with the bankruptcy court clerk a written request for the transcript and make arrangements for payment. FRBP 8006.

If a tentative ruling is necessary to an understanding of the final ruling, it must be included in the DOR and in the excerpts of record. Welther v. Donell (In re Oakmore Ranch Mgmt.), 337 B.R. 222, 226 (9th Cir. BAP 2006); Gertsch v. Johnson & Johnson Fin. Corp. (In re Gertsch), 237 B.R. 160, 169 (9th Cir. BAP 1999).

The appellant shall serve and file excerpts of the record as an appendix when the opening brief is filed. FRBP 8009(b). See Section VIII.A.9., infra.

B. Completion of the Record

When the reporter completes the transcript, the reporter files it with the clerk of the bankruptcy court. FRBP 8007(a). The reporter is supposed to complete the transcript within 30 days, but may ask the clerk for an extension. Id.

When the record is complete, the clerk of the bankruptcy court transmits a Certificate of Readiness to Transmit Record to the clerk of the BAP. See FRBP 8007(b); 9th Cir. BAP R. 8007(b)-1. After reviewing the appeal for jurisdiction, the BAP clerk will issue a briefing schedule.

C. Consequences of Incomplete Record

The burden of presenting a proper record to the appellate court is on the appellant. Williams, 287 B.R. at 791; Kritt v. Kritt (In re Kritt), 190 B.R. 382, 387 (9th Cir. BAP 1995). Unless the record before the appellate court affirmatively shows the matters on which appellant relies for relief, the appellant may not argue those matters on appeal. 10 L. King Collier on Bankruptcy ¶ 8006.03[1] (15th ed. rev. 2006); Everett v. Perez (In re Perez), 30 F.3d 1209, 1217 n.12 (9th Cir. 1994).

The failure to provide an adequate record may result in dismissal of the appeal or a waiver of issues dependent upon the record. McCarthy v. Prince (In re McCarthy), 230 B.R. 414, 416-17 (9th Cir. BAP 1999). When an appellant challenges a factual finding, the failure to provide an adequate record may be grounds for affirmance. Friedman v. Sheila Plotsky Brokers, Inc. (In re Friedman), 126 B.R. 63, 68 (9th Cir. BAP 1991). But see Ehrenberg v. Cal. State Univ., Fullerton Found. (In re

Beachport Entm't), 396 F.3d 1083, 1088 (9th Cir. 2005) (holding that it was inappropriate to dismiss an appeal for an inadequate record where omitted items were minimal and where the Panel neither considered alternative sanctions nor gave the appellant advance warning and an opportunity to cure the procedural defect).

The appellee must police the record, and take steps to assure that it is sufficiently complete to defend the bankruptcy court's ruling. Kyle v. Dye (In re Kyle), 317 B.R. 390, 394 (9th Cir. BAP 2004).

VII. MOTIONS

A. An aspect of appellate practice that is familiar to appellate lawyers, but not necessarily to trial lawyers and trial judges, is the sheer number of motions filed in appellate cases. The BAP receives approximately 40 to 50 motions a month. The BAP judges rotate sitting on monthly "motions panels." These panels consist of one to three judges who decide the motions in a collegial manner. Motions that are not case dispositive (e.g., extension of time to file briefs) may be decided by one or two judges, or by the BAP Clerk, based on delegated authority.

Typically, the progress of a motion is:

1. The motion is filed with the BAP. FRBP 8011(a).

The motion must state with particularity the grounds for bringing the motion and set forth the relief sought. Declarations and supporting materials must be attached. Id.

On a substantive motion, the opposing party has seven days after service to file an opposition. Id.

Motions for procedural orders may be acted upon at any time without an opportunity to respond. FRBP 8011(b).

2. The motion is immediately reviewed and summarized by a staff attorney. The staff attorney prepares a written analysis and recommendation, and prepares a proposed form of order.

3. The motion, any responses or replies, and the staff attorney's workup are transmitted to the motions panel judges by e-mail or overnight delivery.

4. Motions panel judges immediately review the paperwork, and communicate their votes and modifications of the proposed order to one another and to the staff attorney. Motions are decided without a hearing unless the court orders otherwise. FRBP 8011(c).

5. Once a decision has been voted upon by each of the panel judges and certified by the assigned lead judge, the Clerk will issue the order on behalf of the Panel and distribute it to the parties.

Occasionally, the panel judges will differ, which results in a dissent or a separate concurrence on the motion.

Motions are handled expeditiously so that oral argument times are not delayed. Orders disposing of motions are rarely published except where an important point of law has been resolved (e.g., T.C. Invs. v. Joseph (In re M Capital Corp.), 290 B.R. 743, 747 (9th Cir. BAP 2003) (burden of proof on party asserting good faith seeking protection of 11 U.S.C. § 363(m) to prove good faith with evidence); Ho v. Dai Hwa Electronics (In re Ho), 265 B.R. 603, 604-05 (9th Cir. BAP 2001) (bankruptcy court retains jurisdiction to rule on motion for stay pending appeal after notice of appeal has been filed).

6. Rulings by a motions panel are not binding on the merits panel. Wiersma v. O.H. Kruse Grain & Milling (In re Wiersma), 324 B.R. 92, 104 n. 12 (9th Cir. BAP 2005).

B. Motion for Stay Pending Appeal

Requests for a stay pending appeal normally should be presented to the bankruptcy judge first. FRBP 8005. The bankruptcy court retains jurisdiction to rule on a motion for stay pending appeal after a notice of appeal has been filed. Ho, supra.

Parties may file a motion for stay pending appeal directly with the appellate court only if an explanation is given why relief was not first sought from the bankruptcy court. FRBP 8005.

The movant has the burden of showing that the bankruptcy court abused its discretion in not granting a stay. 9th Cir. BAP R. 8011(d)-1 (explanatory note) (citing Wymer v. Wymer (In re Wymer), 5 B.R. 802, 805-07 (9th Cir. BAP 1980)). A stay pending appeal is in the nature of a preliminary injunction and must satisfy four elements: (1) appellant is likely to succeed on the merits; (2) appellant will suffer irreparable injury if no stay is granted; (3) no substantial harm will come to appellee as a result of a stay; and (4) the stay will not harm the public interest. Wymer, 5 B.R. at 806.

The bankruptcy court may require the posting of a bond as a condition of granting a stay pending appeal. FRBP 8005. If an appeal is from a money judgment in bankruptcy, the supersedeas stay is available as a matter of right. The court has discretion in determining the sufficiency of the bond and the adequacy of the surety. FRBP 7062(d); Farmer v. Crocker Nat'l Bank (In re Swift Aire Lines, Inc.), 21 B.R. 12, 13-14 (9th Cir. BAP 1982).

C. Motions to Dismiss for Lack of Jurisdiction

Appellants occasionally appeal an issue that the BAP does not have jurisdiction to consider for various reasons, including the appellants lack standing, the notice of appeal was untimely, or the appeal has become moot. Although jurisdictional issues may be raised by the court sua sponte, see Vylene Enters., Inc. v. Naugles, Inc. (In re Vylene Enters., Inc.), 968 F.2d 887, 889 (9th Cir. 1992), it generally makes sense for an appellee to file a motion to dismiss the appeal as early as possible to save the cost of briefing in a case that will ultimately be dismissed. Thus, it is important to recognize the following concepts of finality, standing and mootness in a bankruptcy context.

1. Untimeliness and Lack of Finality

Appeals can be either too early or too late (§§ V.A—V.F, above). Both defects can be the basis for a motion to dismiss for lack of jurisdiction.

2. Lack of Standing

Standing is a jurisdictional issue that is open to review at all stages of the litigation. See National Org. For Women, Inc. v. Scheidler, 510 U.S. 249, 255 (1994). Questions of standing are reviewed de novo. See Barrus v. Sylvania, 55 F.3d 468, 469 (9th Cir. 1995). Because standing is a jurisdictional requirement, the BAP must dismiss an appeal when no standing exists.

Neither the Bankruptcy Code nor Title 28 lays out the requisites for appellate standing. See 1

Collier on Bankruptcy ¶ 5.06. The Court of Appeals and the BAP follow the "person aggrieved" standard for standing in bankruptcy appeals. See Fondiller v. Robertson (In re Fondiller), 707 F.2d 441, 442-43 (9th Cir. 1983) (only parties that are pecuniarily affected by a bankruptcy court order or judgment have standing to appeal). Accord, Darby v. Zimmerman (In re Popp), 323 B.R. 260, 265 (9th Cir. BAP 2005).

Normally, only a bankruptcy trustee or a debtor-in-possession has standing on appeal to pursue or defend the rights of the bankruptcy estate. A chapter 7 debtor usually lacks standing on appeal unless: (1) the debtor is pursuing or defending his or her own personal rights (as opposed to those of the bankruptcy estate). See Fondiller, 707 F.2d at 442 (stating that, "a hopelessly insolvent debtor does not have standing to appeal orders affecting the size of the estate."); or (2) the bankruptcy estate might be a surplus estate. A debtor has standing to challenge a bankruptcy court's order if a surplus estate is likely. Duckor Spradling & Metzger v. Baum Trust (In re P.R.T.C., Inc.), 177 F.3d 774, 778 n.2 (9th Cir. 1999).

The United States Trustee ("UST") has statutory standing conferred by 11 U.S.C. § 307 to appeal and to intervene in an appeal. Stanley v. McCormack, Barstow, Sheppard, Wayte & Carruth (In re Donovan Corp.), 215 F.3d 929, 930 (9th Cir. 2000).

Beyond appellate standing, there are several other standing doctrines that may be grounds for a motion to dismiss the appeal. See Culver, LLC v. Chiu (In re Chiu), 266 B.R. 743, 748-52 (9th Cir. BAP 2001); In re Godon, Inc., 275 B.R. 555, 563-66 (Bankr. E.D. Cal. 2002).

3. Mootness

In addition to the constitutional mootness implicit in the Article III "case" or "controversy" requirement, two lines of bankruptcy mootness cases have developed in the Court of Appeals. One line focuses on the court's ability to fashion meaningful relief. See Baker & Drake, Inc. v. Public Service Commission of Nevada (In re Baker & Drake, Inc.), 35 F.3d 1348, 1351-52 (9th Cir, 1994); Ederel Sport, Inc. v. Gotcha Int'l L.P. (In re Gotcha Int'l L.P.), 311 B.R. 250, 253-55 (9th Cir. BAP 2004).

The other applies when an order authorizes the sale of property, and implements 11 U.S.C. § 363(m) premised on the particular need for finality of such orders. Onouli-Kona Land Co. v. Estate of Richards (In re Onouli-Kona Land Co.), 846 F.2d 1170, 1172 (9th Cir. 1988) ("Bankruptcy's mootness rule 'developed from the general rule that occurrence of events which prevent an appellate court from rendering effective relief renders an appeal moot, and the particular need for finality in orders regarding sales in bankruptcy.' "); Arnold & Baker Farms v. United States (In re Arnold & Baker Farms), 85 F.3d 1415, 1419-20 (9th Cir. 1996), cert. denied, 519 U.S. 1054, 117 S. Ct. 681 (1997); Vista Del Mar Assocs., Inc. v. West Coast Land Fund (In re Vista Del Mar Assocs.), 181 B.R. 422, 424-25 (9th Cir. BAP 1995).

Note, however, that this mootness rule operates only when a purchaser bought an asset in good faith. See T.C. Invs. v. Joseph (In re M Capital Corp.), 290 B.R. 743, 746 (9th Cir. BAP 2003) (emphasizing the need to establish an evidentiary record with necessary findings of fact and conclusions of law on the good faith issue).

Examples of Mootness

The following are common examples of mootness in the bankruptcy context:

• When funds have been disbursed to non-parties or when the failure to obtain a stay causes "such a comprehensive change of circumstances as to make it inequitable to consider the merits of the appeal." Beatty v. Traub (In re Beatty), 162 B.R. 853, 856 (9th Cir. BAP 1994); see also Ederel Sport, Inc. v. Gotcha Int'l. L.P. (In re Gotcha Int'l. L.P.), 311 B.R. 250, 253-55 (9th Cir. BAP 2004);

• Where a chapter 11 plan has "been so far implemented that it [would be] impossible to fashion effective relief for all concerned" and where reversal of the order confirming the plan "would do nothing other than create an unmanageable, uncontrollable situation for the Bankruptcy Court." Trone v. Roberts Farms, Inc. (In re Roberts Farms, Inc.), 652 F.2d 793, 797 (9th Cir. 1981); but cf, Varela v. Dynamic Brokers, Inc. (In re Dynamic Brokers, Inc.) 293 B.R. 489 (9th Cir. BAP 2003) (concluding that chapter 11 plan was not so far consummated, or so exceedingly complex, as to render it impossible to fashion meaningful relief);

• Where real property central to the appeal has been foreclosed upon without leaving appellant statutory rights of redemption, see Onouli-Kona Land Co., 846 F.2d at 1172-73;

• Sales of real property, Comty. Thrift & Loan v. Suchy (In re Suchy), 786 F.2d 900, 902 (9th Cir. 1985);

• Orders involving § 363(m), which approve a sale or lease of property, Paulman v. Gateway Venture Partners III, L.P. (In re Filtercorp., Inc.), 163 F.3d 570, 576 (9th Cir. 1998); but see Thomas v. Namba (In re Thomas), 287 B.R. 782, 786 (9th Cir. BAP 2002) (remanding for factual determination of good faith purchaser); and

D. Emergency Motions

1. If the motion requests immediate action in order to avoid irreparable harm, the term "EMERGENCY" should appear in the title. FRBP 8011(d). Include a cover page bearing the label "Emergency Motion" in large, bold type. 9th Cir. BAP R. 8011(d)-1(a). An original and three copies of both the motion and the appendix, containing the items specified by 9th Cir. BAP R. 8011(d)-1(c), must be filed with the

BAP Clerk.

2. Always attach a declaration stating the nature of the emergency. FRBP 8011(d); 9th Cir. BAP R. 8011(d)-1(b). The motion should also state whether all grounds in support of the motion were submitted to the bankruptcy judge, and if not, why the motion should not be remanded to the bankruptcy judge for reconsideration. FRBP 8011(d).

3. Notify opposing counsel and state in a declaration when and how counsel was notified; there is a specific duty on the movant to "make every practicable effort to notify opposing counsel in time for counsel to respond to the motion." FRBP 8011(d). The motion papers must be accompanied by a proof of service showing service on all parties. 9th Cir. BAP R. 8011(d)-1(d).

4. Include an appendix that contains a conformed copy of the notice of appeal and the entered judgment, order or decree from which the appeal was taken. 9th Cir. BAP R. 8011(d)-1(b).

5. If the emergency motion concerns a stay pending appeal, the appendix must contain: (1) A conformed copy of the bankruptcy court's order denying or granting the stay and an explanation by the court of its ruling, or a declaration explaining why such a copy is unavailable; and (2) Copies of all papers regarding the stay filed in the bankruptcy court. 9th Cir. BAP R. 8011(d)-1(c).

E. Writ of Mandamus

Although it denied a petition for a writ of mandamus on the merits in Salter v. Bankruptcy Court (In re Salter), 279 B.R. 278 (9th Cir. BAP 2002), the BAP in this case of first impression concluded that it did have the power to issue such a writ because the BAP is a court "established by Act of Congress" which is authorized by the All Writs Act to issue writs of mandamus.

VIII. BRIEFING THE ISSUES

A. Filing and Formatting

1. After the BAP clerk receives a Certificate of Record from the bankruptcy clerk, a briefing schedule is issued. The appellant's opening brief and excerpts of record shall be served and filed within 15 days. FRBP 8009(a)(1). Briefs are deemed filed on the day of mailing. FRBP 8008(a).

2. The appellee's responsive brief shall be served and filed within 15 days after service of the appellant's opening brief. If the appellee has filed a cross-appeal, the brief shall contain the issues and argument pertinent to the cross-appeal, denominated as such, and the response to the appellant's brief. FRBP 8009(a)(2); 9006(f) (three additional days allowed when service is performed by mail.)

3. Reply Briefs. If the appellant elects to file a reply brief, it must be served and filed within 10 days after service of the appellee's brief. If the appellee has cross-appealed, he or she may file and serve a reply brief to the response of the appellant, addressing the issues presented in the cross-appeal, within 10 days after service of the reply brief. FRBP 8009(a)(3); 9006(f) (three additional days allowed when service is performed by mail).

4. Contents of Briefs. Briefs shall conform to FRBP 8010 and 9th Cir. BAP R. 8010(a)-1. The appellant's brief shall contain under appropriate headings:

(1) A table of contents, table of cases, statutes and other authorities, with references to the pages of the brief where they are cited;

(2) A statement of the basis of appellate jurisdiction;

(3) A statement of the issues presented and the applicable standard of review;

(4) A statement of the case;

(5) A statement of facts with appropriate references to the record;

(6) An argument; and

(7) A short conclusion stating the precise relief sought. FRBP 8010(a)(1).

The appellee's brief shall conform to the same requirements established for the appellant's opening brief except that a statement of the basis of appellate jurisdiction, issues, or the case need not be made. FRBP 8010(a)(2).

5. Certificates. Appellant's opening brief must include certifications of (1) interested parties, and (2) related cases. Appellee's responsive brief must also include a certification of interested parties. 9th Cir. BAP R. 8010(a)-1.

6. Formatting of Briefs. The BAP requires briefs to be produced by a standard typographic printing process with one-inch margins and at least 14 point proportional type or 10.5 point monospaced type, double-spaced, on opaque, unglazed paper. 9th Cir. BAP R. 8010(a)-1.

The BAP Rules also require specific information on the cover, designated cover colors for the opening, responsive and reply briefs, and require the parties to attach certifications of interested parties and related cases to the covers. Id.

7. Length of Briefs. Except with leave of the Panel, the appellant's and appellee's initial briefs shall not exceed 30 pages and reply briefs shall not exceed 20 pages, exclusive of pages containing table of contents, tables of citations and addendums. 9th Cir. BAP R. 8010(c)-1. A motion for leave to file an oversize brief should be filed well in advance of the deadline for filing the brief. The party requesting the oversize brief should explain the need for going over the page limit (for example, if there are consolidated appeals or multiple issues).

8. Reference to Excerpts of Record (Appendix). The briefs must make specific references to the relevant portions of the record. FRBP 8010(a)(1)(D); see Dela Rosa v. Scottsdale Mem'l Health Sys., Inc., 136 F.3d 1241 (9th Cir. 1998); Mitchel v. General Elec. Co., 689 F.2d 877, 878-79 (9th Cir. 1982).

Opposing parties and the court are not obliged to search the entire record, unaided, for error.

Mitchel, 689 F.2d at 879.

An affirmance may be premised on the failure of appellant to provide an adequate record. Ashley v. Church (In re Ashley), 903 F.2d 599, 605-06 (9th Cir. 1990), abrogation on other grounds recognized by In re Denbleyker, 251 B.R. 891, 896 (Bankr. D. Colo. 2000).

An appellate court may dismiss an appeal for failure to provide adequate citations of the record to permit review. See Mitchel, 689 F.2d at 879; see also N/S Corp. v. Liberty Mut. Ins. Co., 127 F.3d 1145, 1146 (9th Cir. 1997) ("By and large, we have been tolerant of minor breaches of one rule or another. Perhaps we are too tolerant sometimes. But there are times when our patience runs out. Then we strike an appellant's briefs and dismiss the appeal."); Perez, 30 F.3d at 1217 n.12 ("[T]he parties must comply with our rules sufficiently to enable us (and the BAP) to examine those materials that bear on their arguments.").

The BAP's imposition of sanctions for noncompliance with non-jurisdictional procedural requirements is reviewed by the Court of Appeals under an abuse of discretion standard. Morrissey v. Stuteville

(In re Morrissey) 349 F.3d 1187, 1190 (9th Cir. 2003) (appropriate sanctions may include summary affirmance of the bankruptcy court's decision). But see Ehrenberg v. Cal. State Univ., Fullerton Found. (In re Beachport Entm't) 396 F.3d 1083, 1088 (9th Cir. 2005) (BAP abused its discretion by dismissing appeal based on deficient excerpts of the record, where it did not consider alternative sanctions and where the record before the BAP was sufficient to decide the merits of the appeal).

9. Appendix to Brief (Excerpts of the Record). Appellant must serve and file with appellant's brief "excerpts of the record" as an Appendix in all BAP appeals. FRBP 8009(b).

Caveat: The requirement of an Appendix is separate and distinct from the requirement of preparing the record per FRBP 8006-8007. Each BAP judge reviewing the appeal receives a copy of the Appendix to Brief, not a copy of the record and not a copy of an appendix to an appellate motion.

i. Contents. The Appendix must include copies of the following:

(a) complaint and answer or other equivalent pleadings;

(b) any pretrial order;

(c) judgment, order, or decree from which the appeal is taken;

(d) any other orders relevant to the appeal;

(e) the opinion, findings of fact, or conclusions of law filed or delivered orally by the court and citations of the opinion if published;

(f) any motion or response on which the court rendered decision;

(g) the notice of appeal;

(h) the relevant entries of the bankruptcy docket; and

(i) the transcript or pertinent portion thereof. FRBP 8009(b).

ii. The appellee may also serve and file an Appendix that contains additional materials omitted by appellant. Id.

iii. Form.

The BAP has prescribed additional form requirements for the Appendix. Among other things, the BAP requires that the Appendix be bound separately with white covers, be continuously paginated, have a table of contents, and have documents divided by tabs. 9th Cir. BAP R. 8009(b)-1.

iv. Defective Appendix.

The BAP is not obligated to examine portions of the record that are not included in the Appendix, Kritt, 190 B.R. at 386-87; accord, Bank of Honolulu v. Anderson (In re Anderson), 69 B.R. 105, 109 (9th Cir. BAP 1986); cf. Ashley, 903 F.2d at 31 605-06 (incomplete transcript in bankruptcy appeal to District Court), although it may do so, and take judicial notice when appropriate. O'Rourke v. Seaboard Surety Co. (In re E.R. Fegert, Inc.), 887 F.2d 955, 957-58 (9th Cir. 1989); In re Bankruptcy Petition Preparers Who Are Not Certified Pursuant to Requirements of the Arizona Supreme Court, 307 B.R. 134, 138 n.5 (9th Cir. BAP 2004).

v. Remedies for a Defective Appendix.

The BAP sometimes exercises its discretion to take judicial notice of items from the bankruptcy court record, as reflected in the bankruptcy court docket. See e.g. Atwood v. Chase Manhattan Mortgage Co. (In re Atwood), 293 B.R. 227, 233, n.9 (9th Cir. BAP 2003).

Further, appeal dismissal based on a deficient Appendix may be inappropriate if the BAP has before it "everything needed in order to address the merits of the appeal." See Ehrenberg v. Cal. State Univ., Fullerton Found. (In re Beachport Entm't), 396 F.3d 1083, 1088 (9th Cir. 2005).

B. Standard of Review

The appellant's opening brief must state the appropriate standard of review for the appeal. FRBP 8010(a)(1). Both sides should be familiar with the standard under which the appellate courts will review each issue. Findings of fact are reviewed for clear error, FRBP 8013, and legal issues are generally reviewed de novo, which means that the appellate court looks at the entire record before the bankruptcy court and gives no deference to the bankruptcy judge's legal conclusions. Mixed questions of law and fact are reviewed de novo. Murray v. Bammer (In re Bammer), 131 F.3d 788, 792 (9th Cir. BAP 1997).

The abuse of discretion standard of review applies to many types of bankruptcy court orders. A bankruptcy court necessarily abuses its discretion if it bases its decision on an erroneous view of the law or clearly erroneous factual findings. Cooter & Gell v. Hartmarx Corp., 496 U.S. 384, 405 (1990). Before reversal is proper under the abuse of discretion standard, the Panel must be definitely and firmly convinced that the bankruptcy court committed a clear error of judgment.

Alonso v. Summerville (In re Summerville), 361 B.R. 133, 139 (9th Cir. BAP 2007).

The Panel does not reverse for harmless error, i.e., an error not affecting substantial rights of the parties, and may affirm for any reason supported by the record. 28 U.S.C. § 2111; FRCP 61, incorporated by FRBP 9005; Dittman v. California, 191 F.3d 1020, 1027 n.3 (9th Cir. 1999); Polo Bldg. Group v. Rakita (In re Shubov), 253 B.R. 540, 547 (9th Cir. BAP 2000).

C. Service

Copies of all papers filed by any party (and not required by the rules to be served by the clerk of the BAP) shall, at or before the time of filing, be served by the party or a person acting for the party on all other parties to the appeal. Service on a party represented by counsel shall be made on counsel. FRBP 8008(b).

D. Motions for Extension of Time

1. Procedure.

If a party seeks to file a brief but is unable to do so within the time prescribed by the BAP's scheduling order, the party may move for an extension of time for filing a brief. 9th Cir. BAP R. 8009(a)-1. Requests for extensions should be limited to 30 days, and 15 days is preferable. A motion for an extension of time for filing a brief shall be made within the time limit prescribed by the BAP Rules for the filing of such brief and shall be accompanied by a proof of service.

2. Contents.

The motion shall be supported by a declaration stating the time when the brief is due, how many extensions of time, if any, have been granted, when the brief was first due, and whether any previous requests have been denied or denied in part. The motion shall also state the reasons why such an extension is necessary and the amount of time requested. Finally, the motion shall state the position of the opponent(s) in respect to the motion or state why the moving party has been unable to obtain a statement of such position(s). Id.

3. No Automatic Extensions.

The BAP has no obligation to consider a late brief and may impose sanctions such as waiver of oral argument, monetary sanctions, or dismissal. 9th Cir. BAP R. 8009(a)-1(3).

E. Issues on Appeal

1. Generally, appellate courts do not consider arguments "that are not 'properly raise[d]' in the trial courts." O'Rourke v. Seaboard Sur. Co. (In re E.R. Fegert, Inc.), 887 F.2d 955, 957 (9th Cir. 1989). Concrete Equip.

Co., Inc. v. Fox (In re Vigil Bros. Constr., Inc.), 193 B.R. 513, 520 (9th Cir. BAP 1996)

2. The Court of Appeals recognizes three narrow, discretionary exceptions to the general rule:

(1) to prevent a miscarriage of justice or to preserve the integrity of the judicial process;

(2) when a change in law raises a new issue while an appeal is pending; and

(3) when the issue is purely one of law. Jovanovich v. United States, 813 F.2d 1035, 1037 (9th Cir. 1987), citing Bolker v. Commissioner of Internal Revenue, 760 F.2d 1039, 1042 (9th Cir. 1985).

3. In addition, the BAP must consider matters affecting its jurisdiction sua sponte even if not briefed by the parties. See Vylene Enters., Inc. v. Naugles, Inc. (In re Vylene Enters., Inc.), 968 F.2d 887, 889 (9th Cir. 1992), citing Pizza of Hawaii, 761 F.2d at 1377.

4. FRBP 8010(a)(1)(C) requires appellant to file a statement of issues to be decided. The Panel may nevertheless consider an issue not so listed if the issue is purely one of law and there is no prejudice. Huerta-Guevara v. Ashcroft, 321 F.3d 883, 886 (9th Cir. 2003).

5. An appellate court generally will not consider an issue raised by an appellant for the first time in a reply brief. See United States v. Montoya, 45 F.3d 1286, 1300 (9th Cir. 1995) (issues not raised and argued in the opening brief are deemed waived); Law Offices of Neil Vincent Wake v. Sedona Inst. (In re Sedona Inst.), 220 B.R. 74, 76 (9th Cir. BAP 1998). However, an issue raised by an appellant for the first time in a reply brief is not waived if the appellee has briefed the issue. See United States v. Bohn, 956 F.2d 208, 209 (9th Cir. 1992) ("Although we ordinarily decline to consider arguments raised for the first time in a reply brief, we may consider them if . . . appellee raised the issue in its brief.").

F. Developments while Appeal Pending

1. Duty of Attorneys.

Attorneys have a "continuing duty to inform the Court of any development which may conceivably affect the outcome' of the litigation." Board of License Comm'rs v. Pastore, 469 U.S. 238, 240 (1985) (quoting Fusari v. Steinberg, 419 U.S. 379, 391 (1975)). See also Arizonans for Official English v. Arizona, 520 U.S. 43, 68 n.23 (1997) ("It is the duty of counsel to bring to the federal tribunal's attention, 'without delay,' facts that may raise a question of mootness.")

2. Procedures for Informing the BAP.

Although counsel has a duty to inform the court of a change in law or facts that may affect the appeal, neither FRBP nor BAP Rules address the manner for doing so. It is likely that a party may simply provide a case citation with a short explanation (and serve it on all parties to the appeal) why the new ruling, development, or statute substantively affects the appeal. In addition, the BAP has sometimes permitted an appellant to supplement the appellate record. See Plaintiff's Class Claimants in New Jersey Actions v. Elsinore Corp. (In re Elsinore Corp.), 228 B.R. 731, 733 n.1 (9th Cir. BAP 1998) (appellants permitted to supplement appellate record with a district court decision decided after the notice of appeal was filed because it was helpful in clarifying appellants' claims against the debtor). But see Morgan v. Safeway Stores, Inc., 884 F.2d 1211, 1213 (9th Cir. 1989) (denying motion to supplement record with "newly discovered evidence" that was not shown to be in fact newly discovered and was neither probative, nor added to the record).

3. Once the appeal is set for oral argument, it is particularly important to advise the BAP if the parties have settled or are in the process of settling. If settlement requires approval of the bankruptcy court, any motion for continuance should be supported by a declaration regarding the status of the settlement discussions and indicating whether a hearing on approval has been set before the bankruptcy court.

G. Amicus Curiae Briefs

1. The BAP accepts amicus briefs on occasion. E.g., In re Bankruptcy Petition Preparers Who Are Not Certified Pursuant to Requirements of the Arizona Supreme Court, 307 B.R. 134, 139 (9th Cir. BAP 2004); Rancho Bernardo Ltd. P'ship v. First Alliance Corp. (In re First Alliance Corp.), 140 B.R. 531, 532 (9th Cir. BAP 1992); Canadian Commercial Bank v. Hotel Hollywood (In re Hotel Hollywood), 95 B.R. 130 (9th Cir. BAP 1988); Industrial Indem. Co. v. Seattle-First Nat'l Bank (In re North Side Lumber Co.), 83 B.R. 735, 737 (9th Cir. BAP 1987), aff'd, 865 F.2d 264 (9th Cir. 1988).

2. Since there is no mention of amicus curiae in the BAP Rules or in Part VIII of FRBP, the BAP looks to FRAP 29 and 9th Cir. R. 29-1 for the appropriate procedure. 9th Cir. BAP R. 8018(b)-1 ("Silence of Local Rules"). Under FRAP 29, an amicus brief may only be filed if accompanied by the written consent of all parties, or by leave of court granted on motion or at the request of the court (except that consent or leave shall not be required when the brief is presented by the United States or an officer or agency thereof, or by a State, Territory or Commonwealth). FRAP 29.

3. The 9th Circuit forbids reply briefs to amicus briefs, disfavors multiple amicus briefs raising the same points in support of one party, and encourages those who merely wish to join in arguments asserted in another brief to file and serve a short letter so stating in lieu of a brief. Circuit Rule 29-1 (Advisory Committee Note).

IX. ORAL ARGUMENT

A. Scheduling

Oral argument is scheduled in nearly all fully-briefed cases. The BAP clerk typically sets oral argument to occur 30-45 days after the briefs are filed. By separate pleading or letter at the time they file their opening briefs, counsel should notify the BAP Clerk of known scheduling conflicts occurring during the third week of upcoming months, when BAP arguments are likely to be scheduled. The calendar page of the BAP website, www.ce9.uscourts.gov/bap, identifies the dates that the BAP's judges have set aside for argument each year. If counsel knows or suspects that they will be unavailable on one of the listed dates, they should file as soon as practicable a notice of unavailability, as indicated above.

Once a case has been set for oral argument, continuances are rarely granted. The BAP Clerk will work with the parties to resolve scheduling conflicts and other matters concerning argument. Prior to contacting the Clerk, the movant should contact opposing counsel so that the position of both sides may be conveyed.

B. Submission Without Argument

Counsel usually have the option of electing to submit their case on their briefs without attending oral argument. In that event, unless the Panel dispenses with oral argument entirely, opposing counsel may appear and argue without opposition. Counsel choosing not to present oral argument must notify the clerk and opposing counsel of that election as soon as practicable.

Upon party request or on the Panel's own motion, the Panel may determine that oral argument is not necessary and order the appeal submitted on the briefs without argument. FRBP 8012. Before submitting the appeal without argument, the Panel will give the parties an opportunity to file a statement explaining why oral argument should be held. Id.

C. Location of Hearing

The BAP Clerk provides notice of the time and place of argument. The BAP can sit at any location in the Ninth Circuit. When economical and feasible, the appeal will be set for hearing in the location at which the appeal arose. Counsel who desire and agree to a different location should inform the BAP Clerk in writing at the earliest possible date and not later than the time the appellee's brief is filed. Once scheduled, continuances are granted only under exceptional circumstances. 9th Cir. BAP R. 8012-1.

D. Video and Telephone Conference Hearings

The BAP permits counsel to request permission to appear and argue via video or telephone conference. Additionally, the BAP may set an appeal for oral argument by video or telephone conference in the interest of expeditious scheduling of oral argument. In such instances, counsel normally has the option of appearing from the remote location or traveling to the site at which the Panel is sitting.

E. BAP Panel Preparation

The three Panel judges review the briefs and the Appendices to Brief before oral argument. Additionally, the "lead" judge (for purposes of writing the final disposition) prepares a bench memorandum that is circulated to the other Panel members. The judges usually discuss each case prior to oral argument to expound upon the issues and survey tentative positions of each judge.

F. Effective Oral Argument

1. Oral argument is typically limited to fifteen minutes per side. Parties aligned on the same side typically are asked to split their fifteen minutes. Appellants usually reserve five of their fifteen minutes for rebuttal. Appellees usually are not allowed to reserve time for rebuttal.

2. Counsel should not attempt to address every fact and argument in the briefs; the BAP judges thoroughly review the briefs and the excerpts of record before oral argument. Rather, counsel should summarize the arguments and directly answer the judges' questions in order to clarify factual or legal issues or to address any concerns.

3. At oral argument, counsel should not make the mistake of disregarding or sidestepping a judge's question. Counsel's response may be the pivotal point in a judge's vote. Given the limited amount of time available, counsel should make every effort to satisfy the judges' concerns before moving on to the remainder of the argument.

4. Good appellate advocates are not wedded to their scripts. Counsel should be familiar with every aspect of the case, including the arguments of opposing counsel, pertinent facts, legal issues, controlling or persuasive case law, and the current procedural posture of the bankruptcy case. Counsel should also be prepared to elaborate on legal or factual issues that may not have been emphasized in their briefs, to explore a narrow legal issue, and to discuss the ramifications of a published decision. Fewer than fifteen minutes is certainly acceptable if there are no questions.

G. New Matters or Matters Outside of the Briefs

Generally, an appellate court will not consider matters that are not specifically and distinctly argued in the appellant's opening brief. See United States v. Ullah, 976 F.2d 509, 514 (9th Cir. 1992); see also Martinez v. Ylst, 951 F.2d 1153, 1156-57 (9th Cir. 1991) (issue raised in reply brief would not be considered, particularly since the appellant's failure to properly brief the issue "clearly misled the appellee"); Sedona Inst., 220 B.R. at 76.

X. SANCTIONS

Sanctions for frivolous appeals, in the form of just damages and single or double costs, are awarded only upon a separately-filed motion or after notice from the BAP and reasonable opportunity to respond. FRBP 8020. This Rule is strictly enforced, Tanzi v. Comerica Bank-California (In re Tanzi), 297 B.R. 607, 613 (9th Cir. BAP 2003). The panel usually ignores requests for sanctions made in the briefs.

XI. DECISIONS

A. After Oral Argument

The judges confer immediately after the hearing to come to a tentative decision. The judge assigned to write the disposition then circulates a draft for formal votes. Once all comments have been considered by the lead judge, and any concurrences or dissents have been prepared, the lead judge transmits the disposition to the BAP Clerk, who files it on behalf of the Panel and serves the parties. Most BAP appeals are decided within ten months of filing of the notice of appeal.

B. Opinions and Memoranda

An "opinion" is a written, reasoned disposition of the case that is intended for publication. See 9th Cir. BAP R. 8013-1. A "memorandum" is a written, reasoned disposition of a case that is not intended for publication. Both memoranda and opinions may be cited, see FRAP 32.1, but unpublished memoranda do not have any precedential value. In 2006, about 20 percent of final BAP decisions were published.

C. Publication

The criteria used by the Panel for determining whether to publish a decision as an opinion are: does it (1) establish, alter, modify, or clarify a rule of law; (2) call attention to a rule of law which appears to have been generally overlooked; (3) criticize existing law; or (4) involve a legal or factual issue of unique interest or substantial public importance. 9th Cir. BAP R. 8013-1(a).

D. Request for Publication

A request by a party for publication of any unpublished disposition may be made by letter addressed to the BAP clerk, stating concisely the reasons for publication. Such a request must be received by the clerk no later than 30 days after the filing of the memorandum. 9th Cir. BAP R. 8013-1(d).

E. Mandate

The mandate returns jurisdiction over the matter to the bankruptcy court. The BAP mandate is a certified copy of the Panel's judgment or final order that is sent to the bankruptcy court. It is issued in accordance with the time frame set forth in FRAP 41. Copies are not usually sent to the parties.

F. Motions for Rehearing—FRBP 8015

FRBP 8015 requires motions for rehearing to be filed within ten days after entry of the judgment of the BAP. The Rule does not set forth standards for granting rehearing, so the Panel looks to FRAP 40, a similar provision, for guidance. Kosmala v. Imhof (In re Hessco Indust., Inc.), 295 B.R. 372, 375 (9th Cir. BAP 2003). Under FRAP 40, a party seeking rehearing must "state with particularity each point of law or fact that the petitioner believes the court has overlooked or misapprehended and must argue in support of the petition." Petitions for rehearing are designed to ensure that the appellate court properly considered all relevant information in rendering its decision, and are not a means by which to reargue a party's case. Id.

If a timely motion for rehearing has been filed, the time for appeal to the Court of Appeals begins to run from the entry of an order disposing of the motion for rehearing. See also FRAP 4(a)(4). Motions for rehearing will delay issuance of the appellate court's mandate until seven days after the order is entered. FRAP 41.

G. Appeals to the Court of Appeals from Decisions of the BAP—FRAP 6

A notice of appeal to the Court of Appeals must be filed within 30 days after the entry of a final judgment/order of the BAP (60 days if the United States or an officer or agency thereof is one of the parties.) FRAP 4(a)(1) and FRAP 6.

The notice of appeal is filed with the clerk of the BAP. A filing fee of $455 is required and should be made payable to the "Clerk of Court." A timely motion for rehearing under FRBP 8015 tolls the time for filing the notice of appeal. See FRAP 4(a) and FRAP 6.

Unlike the district court and the BAP, the Court of Appeals does not ordinarily have jurisdiction to hear interlocutory appeals. See 28 U.S.C. § 158(d); Silver Sage Partners, Ltd. v. City of Desert Hot Springs (In re City of Desert Hot Springs), 339 F.3d 782, 787-88 (9th Cir. 2003). The order on appeal must be a final order of both the bankruptcy court and the district court or BAP. Alexander v. Compton (In re Bonham), 229 F.3d 750, 761 (9th Cir. 2000). However, if the underlying bankruptcy case was filed on or after October 17, 2005, a party might be able to obviate the need for a final order by petitioning for a direct appeal to the Court of Appeals. See 28 U.S.C. § 158(d)(2)(A); Interim Rule 8003(d). (For a discussion of direct appeals, see section V.E, supra.)

Note: Although remand orders are generally interlocutory, in certain circumstances they may be considered final. See Virtual Vision, Inc. v. Praegitzer Indus., Inc. (In re Virtual Vision, Inc.), 124 F.3d 1140, 1143 (9th Cir. 1997); Vylene Enters., Inc. v. Naugles, Inc. (In re Vylene Enters., Inc.), 968 F.2d 887, 890 (9th Cir. 1992). See also Scovis v. Henrichsen (In re Scovis), 249 F.3d 975 (9th Cir. 2001).

Requests for stay pending appeal to the Court of Appeals are presented first to the BAP, in the same fashion as BAP appeal stay requests are initially made to the bankruptcy court. FRAP 8(a)(1)(A) (made applicable by FRAP 6(b)(1)(C)).

XII. BAP DECISIONS AS PRECEDENT

A. The Court of Appeals has not determined whether BAP decisions are binding in the "circuit as a whole." Zimmer v. PSB Lending Corp. (In re Zimmer), 313 F.3d 1220, 1225 n. 3 (9th Cir. 2002) (noting that the binding nature of BAP decisions is still an open issue in the Ninth Circuit); Bank of Maui v. Estate Analysis, Inc., 904 F.2d 470, 472 (9th Cir. 1990) (BAP decisions cannot bind district courts, but declining to decide the authoritative effect of a BAP decision).

B. The BAP has held that its decisions bind all bankruptcy courts in the Ninth Circuit. In re Windmill Farms, Inc., 70 B.R. 618, 622 (9th Cir. BAP 1987), rev'd on other grounds, 841 F.2d 1467 (9th Cir. 1988). However, some bankruptcy courts have ruled that BAP decisions do not bind them. Compare CASC Corp. v. Milner (In re Locke), 180 B.R. 245, 254 (Bankr. C.D. Cal. 1995) (BAP decisions not binding on bankruptcy courts), with Life Ins. Co. of Va. v. Barakat (In re Barakat), 173 B.R. 672, 676-80 (Bankr. C.D. Cal. 1994) (BAP decisions binding on bankruptcy courts), aff'd on other grounds, 99 F.3d 1520 (9th Cir. 1996).

C. The BAP, for itself, regards the precedents established in prior published BAP opinions as binding on itself, absent changes in statute or controlling Court of Appeals or Supreme Court precedent. Palm v. Klapperman (In re Cady), 266 B.R. 172, 181 n.8 (9th Cir. BAP 2001), aff'd, 315 F.3d 1121 (9th Cir. 2003); Salomon N.A. v. Knupfer (In re Wind N' Wave), 328 B.R. 176, 181 (9th Cir. BAP 2005). Unpublished memoranda generally are not binding on subsequent panels. See 9th Cir. BAP R. 8013-1(c).

D. The BAP has no procedure for en banc review of its 3-judge Panel decisions. Ball v. Payco-General Am. Credits, Inc. (In re Ball), 185 B.R. 595, 597 (9th Cir. BAP 1995). But see Saddleback Valley Cmty. Church v. El Toro Materials Co., Inc. (In re El Toro Materials Co., Inc.), 2007 WL 2822019 n.7 (9th Cir. October 1, 2007) (suggesting that the interests of judicial efficiency would be served if the BAP were to institute en banc procedures in select cases).

E. As a practical matter, experience teaches that well-reasoned BAP opinions are commonly regarded as persuasive by the Court of Appeals, and by district courts and bankruptcy courts within the Ninth Circuit, regardless of whether they are formally binding.

XIII. INFORMATION AND STATISTICS

The BAP has historically handled between 50-60% of the total number of Ninth Circuit bankruptcy appeals under 28 U.S.C. § 158(a), with an "opt-out" rate of between 40% and 50%.

Between one third and one half of all BAP appeals go through the entire process of briefing, oral argument, and decision on the merits. Of the appeals that completed that process for the twelve months ending June 30, 2007, the median time from commencement of the appeal to final disposition was 9.8 months. The median time from submission to final disposition was about 45 days. 163 appeals were disposed of on the merits and the reversal rate was about 20%.

During this same twelve-month period, 177 bankruptcy appeals were filed at the Court of Appeals for second-level appellate review: 86 from decisions of the Bankruptcy Appellate Panel and 91 from decisions of the district courts. Thus, of the 392 appeals closed by the Bankruptcy Appellate Panel during this time period, 78% were fully resolved, with only about 22% seeking second-level review.

The BAP's websites (http://pacer.bap09.uscourts.gov/ and www.ce9.uscourts.gov/bap) include recently-published opinions, unpublished memoranda, the BAP's rules, oral argument calendars and other information for litigants.

XIV. CONCLUSION

This guide is merely an introduction to the sometimes arcane world of bankruptcy appeals. It is a procedural road map that should be of assistance, but is no substitute for preparation and familiarity with the FRBP and the BAP Rules.

One of the main advantages of the BAP is that the Panel judges are seasoned bankruptcy judges who are experts in bankruptcy law. Additionally, the Panel is dedicated to producing the predictability that is a by-product of a uniform body of law based on carefully-reasoned decisions, rendered as promptly as possible.

APPENDIX I Do's and Don'ts for an Effective Appeal

DO:

1. Know what relief you want (and why).

2. Know your audience. BAP judges generally possess a level of expertise in bankruptcy matters superior to that of most district court judges and their law clerks.

3. Understand the role of the appellate court. While its dominant role is to assess whether the trial court reached the correct result, the appellate court is also concerned with the overall impact of its ruling on the general body of bankruptcy law.

4. Clarify the standard of review and frame arguments around that standard.

5. Simplify the story. Write with punch—short, crisp, essential facts.

6. Organize your brief with short headings, rather than long sentence headings.

7. Paraphrase quotes whenever possible. Long block quotes are soporific.

8. Focus your appellant's argument on areas where the judge's ruling is most susceptible to being reversed.

9. Provide an adequate record, and know what is in it. Follow the rules with respect to organizing, paginating and tabbing the record (appendix), so that the judges and law clerks can find pertinent excerpts quickly.

10. Use a conversational tone rather than a formally structured oral argument. This helps facilitate the transitions that are inevitable when interrupted with questions from the Panel. Feel free to take less than your allotted time. Expect the most questions to be asked of the party with the weakest position, and expect numerous questions about facts and procedure.

11. Be honest and direct in answering the Panel members' questions. Acknowledge the weaknesses of your case. Use policy arguments sparingly, if at all.

12. Listen to the questions being asked of your opponent and be ready to fill in the blanks on matters of concern to the Panel.

DON'T:

1. Use many words when a few will do.

2. Make convoluted arguments.

3. Make grammatical or typographical errors.

4. Write in a disorganized and unintelligible manner.

5. Attack the trial judge or opposing counsel.

6. Use block quotes extensively.

7. Plagiarize/fail to attribute quoted sources

8. Overuse policy arguments or § 105.

9. Avoid direct answers to the judges' questions.

10. Deflect the question and distract the judge if it is not the question you wanted to hear.

11. Cut off the judge's question in mid-sentence.

12. Be ignorant of the record or mischaracterize the record.

13. Blame your unfamiliarity with the record on the fact that you did not handle the case at the trial level. (The "SODDI" excuse—"some other dude did it").

APPENDIX II Potential Traps for the Unwary

1. 10-day appeal period. This refers to calendar days, not court days. FRBP 9006(a). The period begins from entry of the judgment or order to be appealed, not notice. Failure to receive notice or failure of the clerk to serve notice of the entry of the order will not excuse an untimely notice of appeal. It is the appealing party's responsibility to monitor the docket for entry of the order.

2. A motion to dismiss an appeal as untimely that is made before the time to request an extension has expired under FRBP 8002(c) alerts your opponent how to save the appeal.

3. An appeal from an untimely tolling motion under FRBP 8002(b) only raises the issue of the appropriateness of the order resolving the tolling motion, not the underlying order. Obtaining reversal of a denial of reconsideration is usually much harder than reversing the initial decision. File a timely appeal or move to extend the time to appeal if your tolling motion is not timely filed.

4. An Appellant's Statement of Election to have the appeal heard by the district court must be filed at the same time as the Notice of Appeal, in a separate document, not attached to or incorporated in the body of the Notice of Appeal.

5. If the order on appeal is not final, appellant must obtain FRCP 54(b) certification from the trial court (applicable via FRBP 7054) or move the BAP for leave to appeal.

6. Obtain a stay pending appeal, if necessary, to avoid mootness. Motions for stay ordinarily will not be considered unless they are first made to the bankruptcy court or the movant explains why the stay wasn't obtained from the bankruptcy court. FRBP 8005. "I didn't think the bankruptcy judge would grant my stay" is not usually a sufficient explanation. The BAP typically denies without prejudice stay requests where the movant does not bring the motion before the bankruptcy court in the first instance. If time is of the essence, make sure that your stay motion is made before the correct court. At the beginning of your request for stay directed to the bankruptcy court, you may wish to cite Ho v. Dai Hwa Electronics (In re Ho), 265 B.R. 603 (9th Cir. BAP 2001), to show that the bankruptcy court retains jurisdiction to rule on a motion for stay pending appeal, even after a notice of appeal has been filed.

7. Understand the standard of review and what hurdles need to be overcome to obtain a reversal.

8. Separate judgment rule. Be aware that a separate judgment is usually required. Your appeal may be delayed until a separate judgment is entered.

9. Support your brief with your excerpts of the record. Do not expect that the Panel will look at any supporting documents filed with intermediate motions. The excerpts of the record need to stand alone as support for your position. The excerpts may only contain items that are part of the record on appeal. FRBP 8006. Make sure your excerpts include the items listed in FRBP 8009(b); each item is clearly tabbed; pages are consecutively numbered.

10. Arguments not made both before the bankruptcy court and in the opening brief may be considered waived. In re Bankruptcy Petition Preparers, 307 B.R. 134, 141 (9th Cir. BAP 2004).

11. Failing to participate in a BAP appeal may preclude an appeal to the In re Lam, 192 F.3d 1309, 1311 (9th Cir. 1999); and arguments not made to the BAP, absent exceptional circumstances, are waived on appeal to the circuit. In re Burnett, 435 F.3d 971, 976 (9th Cir. 2006).

12. Court of Appeals jurisdiction may differ from BAP or district court jurisdiction. The Court of Appeals generally has jurisdiction over final orders only. A district court or BAP decision on an interlocutory appeal is not reviewable by the Circuit until the matter becomes final at the bankruptcy court level, unless the Court of Appeals grants a direct appeal petition.

13. Motions for reconsideration or rehearing must be made within 10 days after the BAP has rendered its decision. FRBP 8015. A timely motion for reconsideration or rehearing tolls the time to appeal to the Circuit. An untimely motion does not. The time to appeal to the Circuit is normally 30 days from the entry of the BAP decision; if the United States is a party, the time is 60 days. FRAP 4 and 6.

14. Requests for stay pending appeal to the Circuit are made to the BAP, the same way BAP appeal stay requests are initially made to the bankruptcy court. FRAP 8(a)(1)(A) (made applicable by FRAP 6(b)(1)(C)).

15. Requests for sanctions must be made in a separately-filed motion. FRAP 8020.

16. Appellees: supplement an inadequate record sparingly, as you may be inadvertently helping the appellant. File a motion to dismiss for inadequate record instead. See generally Kyle v. Dye (In re Kyle), 317 B.R. 390, 394 (9th Cir. BAP 2004).

APPENDIX III NEW BANKRUPTCY APPEAL FILINGS FOR THE TWELVE MONTH PERIOD ENDING JUNE 30, 2007

[Omitted]

APPENDIX IV RULES GOVERNING POST-TRIAL MOTIONS DETERMINED BY BANKRUPTCY JUDGE

[Omitted]

APPENDIX V AMENDED ORDER CONTINUING THE BANKRUPTCY APPELLATE PANEL OF THE NINTH CIRCUIT JUDICIAL COUNCIL OF THE NINTH CIRCUIT AMENDED ORDER CONTINUING THE BANKRUPTCY APPELLATE PANEL OF THE NINTH CIRCUIT

1. Continuing the Bankruptcy Appellate Panel Service.

(a) Pursuant to 28 U.S.C. § 158(b)(1) as amended by the Bankruptcy Reform Act of 1994, the judicial council hereby reaffirms and continues a bankruptcy appellate panel service which shall provide panels to hear and determine appeals from judgments, orders and decrees entered by bankruptcy judges from districts within the Ninth Circuit.

(b) Panels of the bankruptcy appellate panel service may hear and determine appeals originating from districts that have authorized such appeals to be decided by the bankruptcy appellate panel service pursuant to 28 U.S.C. § 158(b)(6).

(c) All appeals originating from those districts shall be referred to bankruptcy appellate panels unless a party elects to have the appeal heard by the district court in the time and manner and form set forth in 28 U.S.C. § 158(c)(1) and in paragraph 3 below.

(d) Bankruptcy appellate panels may hear and determine appeals from final judgments, orders and decrees entered by bankruptcy judges and, with leave of bankruptcy appellate panels, appeals from interlocutory orders and decrees entered by bankruptcy judges.

(e) Bankruptcy appellate panels may hear and determine appeals from final judgments, orders, and decrees entered after the district court from which the appeal originates has issued an order referring bankruptcy cases and proceedings to bankruptcy judges pursuant to 28 U.S.C. § 157(a).

2. Immediate Reference to Bankruptcy Appellate Panels.

Upon filing of the notice of appeal, all appeals are immediately referred to the bankruptcy appellate panel service.

3. Election to District Court-Separate Written Statement Required.

A party desiring to transfer the hearing of an appeal from the bankruptcy appellate panel service to the district court pursuant to 28 U.S.C. § 158(c)(1) shall timely file a separate written statement of election expressly stating that the party elects to have the appeal transferred from the bankruptcy appellate panel service to the district court.

(a) Appellant:

If the appellant wishes to make such an election, appellant must file a separate written statement of election with the clerk of the bankruptcy court at the time of filing the notice of appeal. Appellant shall submit the same number of copies of the statement of election as copies of the notice of appeal. See Bankruptcy Rule 8001(a). When such an election is made, the clerk of the bankruptcy court shall forthwith transfer the case to the district court. The clerk of the bankruptcy court shall give notice to all parties and the clerk of the bankruptcy appellate panels of the transfer at the same time and in the same manner as set forth for serving notice of the appeal in Bankruptcy Rule 8004.

(b) All Other Parties:

In all appeals where appellant does not file an election, the clerk of the bankruptcy court shall forthwith transmit a copy of the notice of appeal to the clerk of the bankruptcy appellate panels. If any other party wishes to have the appeal heard by the district court, that party must, within thirty (30) days after service of the notice of appeal, file with the clerk of the bankruptcy appellate panels a written statement of election to transfer the appeal to the district court. Upon receipt of a timely statement of election filed under this section, the clerk of the bankruptcy appellate panels shall forthwith transfer the appeal to the appropriate district court and shall give notice of the transfer to the parties and the clerk of the bankruptcy court. Any question as to the timeliness of an election shall be referred by the clerk of the bankruptcy appellate panels to a bankruptcy appellate panel motions panel for determination.

4. MOTIONS DURING ELECTION PERIOD

All motions relating to an appeal shall be filed with the bankruptcy appellate panel service unless the case has been transferred to a district court. The bankruptcy appellate panels may not dismiss or render a final disposition of an appeal within thirty (30) days from the date of service of the notice of appeal, but may otherwise fully consider and dispose of all motions.

5. PANELS

Each appeal shall be heard and determined by a panel of three judges from among those appointed pursuant to paragraph 6, provided however that a bankruptcy judge shall not participate in an appeal originating in a district for which the judge is appointed or designated under 28 U.S.C. § 152.

6. MEMBERSHIP OF BANKRUPTCY APPELLATE PANELS

The bankruptcy appellate panel shall consist of seven members serving seven-year terms (subject to reappointment to one additional three-year term). The judicial council shall periodically examine the caseload of the bankruptcy appellate panel service to assess whether the number of bankruptcy judges serving should change. Appointment of regular and pro tem bankruptcy judges to service on the bankruptcy appellate panel shall be governed by regulations promulgated by the Judicial Council.

(a) When a three-judge panel cannot be formed from the judges designated under subparagraph (a) to hear a case because judges have recused themselves, are disqualified from hearing the case because it arises from their district, or are otherwise unable to participate, the Chief Judge of the Ninth Circuit may designate one or more other bankruptcy judge(s) from the circuit to hear the case.

(b) In order to provide assistance with the caseload or calendar relief, or otherwise to assist the judges serving, or to afford other bankruptcy judges with the opportunity to serve on the bankruptcy appellate panels, the Chief Judge of the Ninth Circuit may designate from time to time one or more other bankruptcy judge(s) from the circuit to participate in one or more panel sittings.

7. CHIEF JUDGE

The members of the bankruptcy appellate panel service by majority vote shall select one of their number to serve as chief judge.

8. RULES OF PROCEDURE

(a) Practice before the bankruptcy appellate panels shall be governed by Part VIII of the Federal Rules of Bankruptcy Procedure, except as provided in this order or by rule of the bankruptcy appellate panel service adopted under subparagraph (b).

(b) The bankruptcy appellate panel service may establish rules governing practice and procedure before bankruptcy appellate panels not inconsistent with the Federal Rules of Bankruptcy Procedure. Such rules shall be submitted to, and approved by, the Judicial Council of the Ninth Circuit.

9. PLACES OF HOLDING COURT

Bankruptcy appellate panels may conduct hearings at such times and places within the Ninth Circuit as it determines to be appropriate.

10. CLERK AND OTHER EMPLOYEES

(a) Clerk's Office. The members of the bankruptcy appellate panel service shall select and hire the clerk of the bankruptcy appellate panel. The clerk of the bankruptcy appellate panel may select and hire staff attorneys and other necessary staff. The chief judge shall have appointment authority for the clerk, staff attorneys and other necessary staff. The members of the bankruptcy appellate panel shall determine the location of the principal office of the clerk.

(b) Law Clerks. Each judge on the bankruptcy appellate panel service shall have appointment authority to hire an additional law clerk.

11. EFFECTIVE DATE

This Order shall be effective as to all appeals originating in those bankruptcy cases that are filed after the effective date of this Order. For all appeals originating in those bankruptcy cases that were filed before October 22, 1994, the Judicial Council's prior Amended Order, as revised October 15, 1992, shall apply. This Order, insofar as just and practicable, shall apply to all appeals originating in those bankruptcy cases that were filed after the effective date of the Bankruptcy Reform Act of 1994, October 22, 1994, but before the date of this Order.

IT IS SO ORDERED.

DATE: April 28, 1995; amended May 9, 2002.